The Law of
TORTS

First edition 1957
Second edition 1961
second impression 1963
Third edition 1965
second impression 1967
third impression 1969
Fourth edition 1971
second impression 1972
third impression 1973
Fifth edition 1977
second impression 1981
Sixth edition 1983
Seventh edition 1987
second impression 1989
third impression 1990
Eighth edition 1992

CANADA AND U.S.A.

The Carswell Company Ltd
Agincourt, Ontario

HONG KONG

Bloomsbury Books Ltd

MALAYSIA

Malayan Law Journal Pte Ltd
Kuala Lumpur

SINGAPORE

Malayan Law Journal Pte Ltd

UNITED KINGDOM

Sweet & Maxwell Ltd
London

U.S.A.

Wm W. Gaunt & Sons, Inc.
Holmes Beach, Florida

The Law of
TORTS

by

JOHN G. FLEMING
D.C.L., Hon. LL.D.
Turner Professor of Law, Emeritus
University of California, Berkeley;
Formerly Dean and Robert Garran Professor of Law,
Australian National University

EIGHTH EDITION

THE LAW BOOK COMPANY LIMITED
1992

Published in Sydney by

The Law Book Company Limited
44-50 Waterloo Road, North Ryde, N.S.W.
490 Bourke Street, Melbourne, Victoria
40 Queen Street, Brisbane, Queensland
81 St George's Terrace, Perth, W.A.

National Library of Australia
Cataloguing-in-Publication entry

Fleming, John G. (John Gunther).
The law of torts.

8th ed.
Bibliography.
Includes index.
ISBN 0 455 21141 8.
ISBN 0 455 21142 6 (pbk.).

1. Torts. 2. Torts—Australia. I. Title.

346.03

Designed and edited by Tricia Hogan

Typeset in Times Roman, 10 on 11 point, by Mercier Typesetters Pty Ltd, Granville, N.S.W.
Printed by Macarthur Press Pty Ltd, Parramatta, N.S.W.

PREFACE

Every quinquennium between editions of this book seems to carry its own distinctive imprint. The last, to which the current, the eighth, edition bears witness, was marked by retrenchment, compelled by a strained economy and inspired by the pervasive message of Thatcherism. Thus the spreading legislation in Australia imposing monetary limits on damages or limiting recourse to tort recovery for work injuries and motor vehicle accidents, followed by New Zealand's substantial curbs on the cover of the Accident Compensation scheme. The judicial record in England has similarly been marked by retreat, not only in the prominent field of economic loss, but also in such varied contexts as nervous shock, causation (loss of chance, creating a mere risk) and others. Australian and other Commonwealth courts have been less programmatic. Moreover, some legislation, completed or in the offing, bears a different face. Strict products liability has become the law of Europe under the directive of the EEC, waiting to be adopted also in Australia. Also under way at last is a pending large scale reform of defamation in order to bring some measure of uniformity for the Australian media industry.

No wonder then that all these and many other changes have required a great deal of rewriting and updating, rather more than usual even in this ever-volatile area of law. Thus despite some savings resulting from the rationalisation of occupiers' liability in *Zaluzna*, the present edition is 40 pages longer than the last, the first substantial increase since the beginning in 1957. No less than 450 new cases also reflect the momentum of change and growing complexity of the subject. Besides the primary focus on Australia, English, Canadian and New Zealand developments have been kept up-to-date, for the benefit of the wider readership the book has come to serve.

This edition is based on materials available to me at mid-year 1992.

JOHN G. FLEMING

Berkeley, California
August 1992

TABLE OF CONTENTS

Chapter

MISCELLANEOUS

TABLE OF CASES

TABLE OF STATUTES

IMPERIAL

5 Rich. II 1381
  cl. 8: 90

UNITED KINGDOM

Administration of Justice Act 1969
  s. 20: 401

Administration of Justice Act 1970
  s. 40: 32

Administration of Justice Act 1982: 237, 665
  s. 2: 660, 661
  s. 3(3): 670
  s. 4: 666, 674
  s. 6: 226

Administration of Justice (Miscellaneous Provisions) Act 1933
  s. 6: 619

Airports Authority Act 1965
  s. 15: 47

Animals Act 1971: 353, 356, 358, 363, 365
  s. 2: 358
  s. 4: 356
  s. 4(2): 355
  s. 5: 89, 363
  s. 5(2): 363
  s. 6: 358
  s. 6(3)(a): 362
  s. 6(5): 363

Animals Act 1972: 363
  s. 10: 362

Apportionment of Damages Amendment Act 1971: 662

Bill of Lading Act 1855
  s. 1: 181

Carriage by Railway Act 1972: 332

Carriage of Goods by Sea Act 1971: 295

Children and Young Persons Act 1933
  s. 55: 683

Civil Aviation Act 1982
  s. 76(1): 47
  s. 76(2): 331
  s. 77: 47

Civil Evidence Act 1968
  s. 10: 130
  s. 11: 35
  s. 13: 556

Civil Liabilities (Contribution) Act 1978
  s. 1: 261
  s. 1(3): 263
  s. 1(4): 262
  s. 2(3): 262

Civil Liability (Contribution) Act 1978
  s. 3: 258

Civil Procedure Act 1883: 676

Common Law Procedure Act 1854: 74

Congenital Injuries (Civil Liability) Act 1976
  s. 1: 168
  s. 1(2)(a): 167
  s. 1(7): 168
  s. 4(5): 169

Consumer Credit Act 1974
  s. 158: 608

Consumer Protection Act 1961: 484
  s. 2: 487, 500
  s. 3: 132

Consumer Protection Act 1987: 497
  s. 1(2): 500
  s. 2(4): 500
  s. 3(1): 498
  s. 3(2): 499
  s. 3(2)(a): 500
  s. 3(2)(b): 500
  s. 4(1)(d): 500
  s. 4(e): 499
  s. 5: 501
  s. 5(2): 496
  s. 5(5): 502
  s. 5(6): 502
  s. 6: 283
  s. 6(4): 500
  s. 6(6): 502

Consumer Safety Act 1978
  s. 6: 125

Contempt of Court Act 1981
  s. 10: 570

Copyright Act 1956
  s. 43: 526

Copyright Act 1988
  s. 77: 717

Courts and Legal Services Act 1990
  s. 58: 625

Crimes Act 1967: 100

Criminal Justice Act 1988: 36
  s. 109: 37
  Pt VI: 35

AUSTRALIA

Commonwealth

Australian Capital Territory

New South Wales

Northern Territory

Queensland

South Australia

Tasmania

Victoria

Western Australia

CANADA

FRANCE

EIRE

NEW ZEALAND

SCOTLAND

SOUTH AFRICA

UNITED STATES

ABBREVIATIONS AND BIBLIOGRAPHY

A.C.T.R.	Australian Capital Territory Reports
A.L.J.	Australian Law Journal
A.L.J.R.	Australian Law Journal Reports
A.L.R.	Australian Law Reports
A.L.R.C.	Australian Law Reform Commission
A.L.R. 2d	Amercian Law Reports Annotated, Second Series
Annual L. Rev.	Annual Law Review of the University of Western Australia
Arg. L.R.	Argus Law Reports
Atiyah, *Accidents*	Accidents, Compensation and the Law (3rd ed., 1980)
Atiyah, *Vicarious Liability*	Vicarious Liability in the Law of Torts (1967)
A.T.R.	Australian Torts Reports
Blackstone	Commentaries on the Laws of England (1765-1769)
Bohlen, Studies	Studies in the Law of Torts (1926)
C.C.L.T.	Canadian Cases on the Law of Torts
C.L.R.	Commonwealth Law Reports
Cam. L.J.	Cambridge Law Journal
Can. B. Rev.	Canadian Bar Review
Cane	Tort Law and Economic Interests (1991)
Clerk & Lindsell	Law of Torts (16th ed., 1989)
Col. L. Rev.	Columbia Law Review
Cooper-Stephenson & Saunders	Personal Injury Damages in Canada (1981)
D.L.R.	Dominion Law Reports (Canada)
Faulks	Committee on Defamation (Cmd 5909), 1975
Fifoot	History and Sources of the Common Law (1949)
F.L.R.	Federal Law Reports (Australia)
F.R.D.	Federal Rules Decisions (U.S.A.)
Gatley	Gatley on Libel and Slander (8th ed., 1981)
Goff & Jones	Law of Restitution (3rd ed., 1986)
Goodhart, *Essays*	Essays in Jurisprudence and the Common Law (1931)
Harper, James & Gray	Law of Torts (2nd ed., 1986)
Hart & Honoré, Causation	Causation in the Law (2nd ed., 1985)
Holdsworth	History of English Law (14 vols)
Ind. L.J.	Industrial Law Journal
Int. Encycl. Comp. L.	International Encyclopedia of Comparative Law (1971-)
I.R.	Irish Reports
Jurid. Rev.	Judicial Review
K.I.R.	Knight's Industrial Reports
Knox	Reports of the Supreme Court of New South Wales (1877)
L.G.R.A.	Local Government Reports of Australia
L.Q.R.	Law Quarterly Review
Legge	Reports of Supreme Court of New South Wales (1825-1862)
Linden	Canadian Tort Law (4th ed., 1988)
Luntz	Assessment of damages for personal Injury and Death (2nd ed., 1983)

McGregor	McGregor on Damages (14th ed., 1980)
Mod. L. Rev.	Modern Law Review
Morris, *Torts*	Morris on Torts, by Clarence Morris (2nd ed., 1980)
N.I.	Northern Ireland Reports
N.S.W.	New South Wales
Nw. U.L. Rev.	Northwestern University Law Review
N.Z.L.J.	New Zealand Law Journal
N.Z.L.R.	New Zealand Law Reports
North, *Animals*	Modern Law of Animals (1972)
North, *Occupiers' Liability*	Occupiers' Liability (1971)
O.R.	Ontario Reports
Osg. H.L.J.	Osgoode Hall Law Journal
O.W.N.	Ontario Weekly Notes
Pearson	Royal Commission on Civil Liability and Compensation for Personal Injury (1978)
Pollock	Law of Torts (15th ed., 1952, by P. A. Landon)
Prosser & Keeton	Handbook of the Law of Torts (5th ed., 1984)
Qld	Queensland
Qd R.	Queensland Reports
Q.S.R.	State Reports, Queensland
Q.W.N.	Queensland Weekly Notes
Res Jud.	Res Judicatae, Journal of Law Students' Society of Victoria
Rest. 2nd	Restatment of the Law of Torts, Second (A.L.I., 1965-1979)
R.P.C.	Reports of Patent Cases
S.A.S.R.	South Australian State Reports
S. Afr. L.R.	South African Law Reports
S.C.	Session Cases (Scotland)
S.C.R.	Supreme Court Reports, Canada
S.C.R. (N.S.W.)	Supreme Court Reports, New South Wales
S.R. (N.S.W.)	State Reports, New South Wales
Salmond & Heuston	Law of Torts (19th ed., 1987)
Sol. Jo.	Solicitor's Journal
S.L.T.	Scot Law Times
Stone, *Province and Function*	Province and Function of Law (1946)
Street	Law of Torts (5th ed., 1972)
Street, *Damages*	Principles of the Law of Damages (1962)
Tas. S.R.	Tasmanian State Reports
Todd	The Law of Torts in New Zealand (1991)
Treitel	Law of Contract (6th ed., 1983)
Trinidade & Cane	Law of Torts in Australia (1985)
Vic.	Victoria
V.L.R.	Victorian Law Reports
V.R.	Victorian Reports (1957-)
W.A.	Western Australia
W.A.L.R.	Western Australia Law Reports
W.N.	Weekly Notes (England)
W.N. (N.S.W.)	Weekly Notes (New South Wales)
W.W. & a'B.	Wyatt, Webb and a'Beckett (Victorian Reports, 1864-1869)
W.W.R.	Western Weekly Reports (Canada)
Weir	A Casebook on Tort (7th ed., 1992)
Williams, *Animals*	Liability of Animals (1939)

Williams, *Joint Torts*	Joint Torts and Contributory Negligence (1951)
Winfield & Jolowicz	On Torts (12th ed., 1984)
Winfield, *Essays*	Select Legal Essays (1952)
Winfield, *Abuse*	Present Law of Abuse of Legal Procedure (1921)
Yale L.J.	Yale Law Journal

1

INTRODUCTION

1. WHAT IS A TORT?

At the commencement of a book, it is customary to give some indication of its subject matter and scope. "Tort" derives from the Latin tortus, meaning twisted or crooked, and early found its way, via the French, into the English language as a general synonym for "wrong". Later the word disappeared from common usage, but retained its hold on the law and ultimately acquired its current technical meaning.[1] In very general terms, a tort is an injury other than a breach of contract, which the law will redress with damages. But this definition is far from informative nor even strictly accurate in view of other remedies, like self-help and equitable relief by injunction, which are sometimes available against a tort, actual or threatened.

Perhaps the most profitable method of delimiting the field of tort liability is to describe it in terms of the policies which have brought it into existence and contrast these with the policies underlying other forms of liability.[2] Broadly speaking, the entire field of liability may be divided according to its purposes into criminal, tortious, contractual and restitutionary. Each of these is distinguishable by the nature of the conduct or its consequences and the purpose for which legal remedies are given.

The laws of tort and crime, despite their common origin in revenge and deterrence,[3] long ago parted company and assumed distinctly separate functions. A crime is an offence against the State, as representative of the public, which will vindicate its interests by punishing the offender. A criminal prosecution is not concerned with repairing an injury that may have been done to an individual, but with exacting a penalty in order to protect society as a whole. Tort liability, on the other hand, exists primarily to compensate the victim by compelling the wrongdoer to pay for the damage done. True, some traces of its older link with punishment and crime have survived to the present day, most prominently[4] exemplary damages

1. See Winfield, *Province of the Law of Tort* (1931) ch. 2. For a comparative survey of the province of tort the reader is confidently referred to Tunc, XI Int. Encycl. Comp. L. ch. 1.
2. This approach is suggested by Seavey, in his review of Winfield's *Province*, 45 Harv. L. Rev. 209 (1932). But there are no airtight compartments as the very history of English law demonstrates: *assumpsit* (contract) arose from *case* (tort), and restitution (quasi-contract) from assumpsit. The interdependence is Hadden's theme, *Contract, Tort and Crime*, 87 L.Q.R. 240 (1971).
3. Roman and Germanic (including Anglo-Saxon) law have had a remarkably similar evolution: see Girard, *Manuel Elem. Droit Romain* (8th ed. 1929) 418ff.; *Holdsworth* ii, 43-54.
4. Another used to be the common law rule that tort claims did not survive the death of either party: see below, p. 676.

to punish and deter contumelious and outrageous wrongdoing.[5] Yet the principal concern of the law of torts nowadays is with casualties of accidents, that is, of unintended harm. In this wider field, the law is concerned chiefly with distributing losses which are an inevitable by-product of modern living, and, in allocating the risk, makes less and less allowance to ideas of punishment, admonition and deterrence.

The law of contract exists, at least in its most immediate reach, for the purpose of vindicating a single interest, that of having promises of others performed.[6] This it does either by specifically compelling the promisor to perform or by awarding the promisee damages to put him in as good a position as if the promise had been kept. Thus while contract law as a rule assures the promisee the benefit of the bargain, tort law has the different function of primarily compensating injuries or losses.[7] Moreover, by comparison the interests vindicated by the law of torts are much more numerous. They may be interests in personal security, reputation or dignity, as in actions for assault, personal injuries and defamation. They may be interests in property, as in actions for trespass and conversion; or interests in unimpaired relations with others, as in causing injury or death to relatives. Hence the field covered by the law of torts is much broader, and certainly more diverse, than that of contract.

According to another distinction, tort duties are said to be "primarily fixed by law", in contrast to contractual obligations which can arise only from voluntary agreement.[8] Certainly, in classical theory, the function of contract is to promote voluntary allocation of risks (typically, but not exclusively, commercial risks) in a self-regulating society, while tort law allocates risks collectively in accordance with community values by the fiat of court or legislature. But this distinction, though still fundamentally sound, has become somewhat blurred as the area of self-regulation by contract is being progressively narrowed by regulatory legislation and judicial policing for fairness inspired by collectivist and egalitarian ideals.[9] Besides, contractual terms (where not expressly spelled out) are "implied" (imposed) by law and usually identical with tort duties arising from one party's "undertaking" to act for another, as in the case of professional and other services.[10]

The third field of legal liability calling for demarcation from tort, restitution, serves the idea that justice requires the restitution of unintended benefits so as to prevent unjustified enrichment. Common illustrations are the return of money paid under mistake or the recovery of a bribe[11] or profit (rather than loss) from misappropriation.[12] Unlike the law of contract, it has nothing to do with promises and, unlike tort, with losses.

5. See below, p. 241.
6. For a compact review of contract theories see Coote, *The Essence of Contract*, 1 J. Contract L. 91 (1988).
7. The difference is well illustrated by contrasting damages for misrepresentation (tort) and breach of warranty (contract): see below, p. 637.
8. *Winfield & Jolowicz* 5. On the commonality of notions in tort and contract see Cane, *The Basis of Tortious Liability*, in *Essays for Atiyah* 351 (1991).
9. See Atiyah, *Rise and Fall of Freedom of Contract* (1979); Collins, *The Law of Contract* (1986).
10. See below, p. 186.
11. See Needham, *Recovering the Profits of Bribery*, 95 L.Q.R. 536 (1979).
12. See Birks, *Introduction to the Law of Restitution* (1985); *Goff & Jones* ch. 32.

To summarise, criminal liability is distinguished from tort by the fact that its object is to punish, not to compensate; contractual liability by reason of the different interests protected and the fact that risks are allocated primarily voluntarily rather than collectively; and restitution because it is concerned with the restitution of benefits, not compensation for losses.

2. WHAT INTERESTS ARE PROTECTED?

The law of torts, then, is concerned with the allocation of losses incident to man's activities in modern society. "Arising out of the various and ever-increasing clashes of the activities of persons living in a common society, carrying on business in competition with fellow members of that society, owning property which may in any of a thousand ways affect the person or property of others—in short, doing all the things that constitute modern living—there must of necessity be losses, or injuries of many kinds sustained as a result of the activities of others. The purpose of the law of torts is to adjust these losses and afford compensation for injuries sustained by one person as the result of the conduct of another".[13] Clearly, however, the law could not attempt to compensate all losses. Such an aim would not only be over-ambitious, but might conflict with basic notions of social policy. Society has no interest in the mere shifting of loss between individuals for its own sake. The loss, by hypothesis, has already occurred, and whatever benefit might be derived from repairing the fortunes of one person is exactly offset by the harm caused through taking that amount away from another. The economic assets of the community are not increased and expense is incurred in the process of reallocation.[14] True, security and stability are generally accepted as worthwhile social objects, but there is no inherent reason for preferring the security and stability of plaintiffs to those of defendants. Hence, a shifting of loss is justified only when there exists special reason for requiring the defendant to bear it rather than the plaintiff on whom it happens to have fallen.[15]

The task confronting the law of torts is, therefore, how best to allocate these losses, in the interest of the public good. For the solution of this problem, no simple and all-embracing formula can be offered, because the concrete fact problems are manifold and often complex. To start with, much may depend on the kind of harm for which reparation is sought. Early law, as we might expect, was, in the main, content with affording protection against bodily injury and physical damage to a person's tangible property. Somewhat later, it offered a remedy for injury to reputation from libel or slander; and now in our more highly sophisticated culture, demands are being made for legal protection against less palpable injuries, like indignity or emotional distress. Obviously, different considerations are called into play when dealing with such diverse injuries. It is one thing to require compensation for a brutal assault fracturing the victim's skull, but

13. Wright, *Introduction to the Law of Torts*, 8 Cam. L.J. 238 (1942).
14. See Holmes, *Common Law* (1881) 96.
15. Ibid. at 50.

quite another for mere fright or distress at the sight of a street accident. The possibility of opening the door too widely to faked claims, suspicions concerning the reliability of medical evidence and so forth may militate against a remedy for mental disturbance, while little hesitation would obviously be felt in allowing compensation for a broken arm in a road collision.

Viewed from a slightly different angle, the law has to differentiate between the various kinds of interests for which individuals may claim protection against injury by others. Elementary in all legal systems is the protection afforded to personal security and tangible property. But the desire for security, especially in modern times, is more pretentious. People wish to be safeguarded not only against physical aggression, but also against detrimental consequences to their pocket-book. Hence the demand for a remedy against deceit, unfair competition, and interference with profitable relations they maintain with business associates or employees. The desire for unimpaired domestic relations may warrant protection against alienation of affections and compensation for loss of a breadwinner. Individual feelings of modesty, personal integrity and self-respect might call for legal support against invasions of privacy and other humiliating practices. In each of these instances, the human interest involved has a different weight in the scale of social values, and for this a discriminating analysis must perforce make allowance.[16]

The second variable element in tort problems is the nature of the defendant's conduct. No classification is fraught with greater significance, in point of the policies involved, than that between intentional and accidental harm. Deliberate injury to others is almost invariably devoid of social utility and, excepting situations where on supervening grounds of policy a special privilege is recognised, as in cases of self-defence or necessity, a defendant who intentionally invades another's interests of personality or reputation, or meddles with another's things and, in many situations, with the pecuniary interests of another, is held responsible for the harm he thereby causes.[17] In comparison, protection against unintended harm is more modest, because greater weight is given to the countervailing interest of the defendant in freedom of action. Accidental harm may have been caused either negligently or without any fault at all. In the former case, the element of "fault" or "blameworthiness" will most often supply a reason for tilting the balance against the actor, but this is by no means universally so. Much depends on the nature of the plaintiff's interest that has been violated. A duty not to expose others to unreasonable risks is most generally recognised with reference to physical harm to persons or tangible things. More reservations have been evident in regard to purely financial loss and to non-external injury like mental distress. Finally, there is the vexing problem of whether, and in what circumstances, to admit strict liability for unintended and non-negligent harm ("no-fault" liability), in view of the widespread fear that this would impose an undue burden and tend to discourage enterprise.

16. The most profitable discussion on these lines is still found in Pound's pioneering article, *Interests of Personality*, 28 Harv. L. Rev. 343 at 445 (1915). Comparative: Lipstein, *Protected Interests in the Law of Torts*, [1963] Cam. L.J. 85.
17. See Seavey, *Principles of Torts*, 56 Harv. L. Rev. 72 at 84 (1942).

3. TORT OR TORTS?

The question may well be put at this point whether there is some broad unifying principle underlying tortious liability or merely a random collection of miscellaneous wrongs which have little or no relation to each other, except perhaps for a vague notion that avoidable harm should be compensated.[18] Some writers, notably Sir John Salmond, have taken the view that there is no such thing as a law of *tort*, but merely a large group of unconnected wrongs, each with its own name, and that a plaintiff seeking recovery must find a pigeonhole in which to fit the defendant's conduct and the harm he has suffered before the courts will afford a remedy: "Just as the criminal law consists of a body of rules establishing specific offences, so the law of torts consists of a body of rules establishing specific injuries. Neither in the one case nor in the other is there any general principle of liability. Whether I am prosecuted for an alleged offence, or sued for an alleged tort, it is for my adversary to prove that the case falls within some specific and established rule of liability, and not for me to defend myself by proving that it is within some specific and established rule of justification or excuse."[19]

This approach is open to at least two objections. First, in so far as it suggests that the burden of proof is on the plaintiff to establish that the facts proved by him will, as a matter of law, result in liability, it is plainly wrong because there is no onus of proof in matters of law. In other words, there is no presumption that the law is in anybody's favour, whether he be defendant or plaintiff.[20] Secondly, tortious liability is constantly expanding and there is ample evidence that a plaintiff's claim is not necessarily prejudiced because he is unable to find a specific label for the wrong of which he complains. New and innominate torts have been constantly emerging in the long course of our history and the courts have shown no inclination at any stage to disclaim their creative functions, if considerations of policy pointed to the need for recognising a new cause of action. The most obvious illustration is the ever-expanding concept of tortious negligence, saliently revealed in the recent admission of liability for negligent misrepresentation and for purely pecuniary loss (1964).[21] Others are the rule of strict liability for certain abnormally dangerous activities (1868),[22] and the torts of intimidation (1964),[23] interference with contractual relations (1881),[24] and intentional infliction of mental disturbance (1897).[25]

At the other extreme is the bold attempt to reduce the entire law of torts to a single unifying principle, that the infliction of all harm is tortious unless

18. See Williams, *Foundation of Tortious Liability*, 7 Cam. L.J. 111 (1939); Rudden, *Torticles*, 617 Tulane Civ. L. Forum 105 (1991-2).
19. *Salmond & Heuston* 14.
20. Williams, 7 Cam. L.J. 111 at 112 (1939).
21. *Hedley Byrne v. Heller* [1964] A.C. 465. Each new "duty of care" creates in effect a new tort. See below, ch. 8.
22. *Rylands v. Fletcher* (1868) L.R. 3 H.L. 330. See below, ch. 16.
23. *Rookes v. Barnard* [1964] A.C. 1129.
24. *Bowen v. Hall* (1881) 6 Q.B.D. 333. See below, ch. 30.
25. *Wilkinson v. Downton* [1897] 2 Q.B. 57. See below, p. 32.

it can be "justified".[26] Taken literally, this formulation at once invites the criticism that it does not square with the conditions of actionability of several torts, such as malicious prosecution, where proof of absence of justification is an indispensable part of the *plaintiff's* case, in contrast to some others, like libel, which cast the burden of exculpation on the defendant. Besides, such statements are really question begging, because they avoid facing the crucial problem of what the law will recognise as "justification". Any comprehensive survey of the field of tort liability must yield the disappointing conclusion that the countless situations in which loss is held uncompensable defy explanation by reference to any systematic index of "exceptions" or "defences". This is not to say that the law of civil wrongs consists of "nothing but shreds and patches",[27] but rather points to the futility of seeking to impose a spurious unity upon a very complex congeries of problems. As already pointed out, the adjudication of tort claims calls for a constant adjustment of competing interests. Opposed to the plaintiff's demand for protection against injury is invariably the defendant's countervailing interest not to be impeded in the pursuit of his own wants and desires. Hence the administration of the law involves a weighing of these conflicting interests on the scales of social value, with a view to promoting a balance that will minimise friction and be most conducive to the public good. But since the forms, which clashes between individuals take, are protean and the social importance attached to different human wants varies from one to the next and in relation to each other, it must become obvious why a resolution of these conflicts in concrete situations cannot be achieved on the basis of any single formula.

4. POLICIES OF TORT LIABILITY

The history of the law of torts has hinged on the tension between two basic interests of individuals—the interest in security and the interest in freedom of action. The first demands that one who has been hurt should be compensated by the injurer regardless of the latter's motivation and purpose; the second that the injurer should at best be held responsible only when his activity was intentionally wrongful or indicated an undue lack of consideration for others. The former is content with imposing liability for faultless causation; the latter insists on "fault" or "culpability".

Individual responsibility

Primitive law, preoccupied with preserving the peace and providing a substitute for private vengeance, looked to causation rather than fault: "not so much to the intent of the actor as the loss and damage of the party

26. Winfield, *Province of the Law of Tort* (1931) ch. 3 (somewhat modified in later editions). See also his *Foundation of Liability in Tort*, 27 Col. L. Rev. 1 (1927), reprinted in Winfield, *Essays* ch. 1.
27. The phrase is Pollock's, speaking of Salmond's theory, 47 L.Q.R. at 589 (1931).

suffering."[28] Even so, notions of fault were not wholly excluded.[29] For one thing, the apparent indifference of early law to the wrongdoer's state of mind may have been based on its inability or unwillingness to conceive the unintentional infliction of harm rather than a lack of concern with such intention: experience suggested that immediate harmful contact (trespass) was mostly the result of hostile aggression.[30] For another, the myth has long been exposed that early English law ever adhered to an unqualified principle that man acted at his peril and became responsible for all resulting harm.[31] Moreover, the limited causes of action then recognised stamped the overall system as one of no liability rather than pervasive liability without fault.[32] Gradually, however, the law began to pay greater heed to exculpatory considerations and, partially under the influence of the Church, tilted towards moral culpability as the proper basis for tort. This subjectivation of the test of civil liability necessarily tended to benefit the injurer and curtail protection for the injured. During the 19th century, the "moral advance" of tort law vastly accelerated. With the blessings of the moral philosophy of individualism (Kant) and the economic postulate of laissez faire, the courts attached increasing importance to freedom of action and ultimately yielded to the general dogma of "no liability without fault". This movement coincided with, and was undoubtedly influenced by, the demands of the Industrial Revolution.[33] It was felt to be in the better interest of an advancing economy to subordinate the security of individuals, who happened to become casualties of the new machine age, rather than fetter enterprise with the cost of "inevitable" accidents. Liability for faultless causation was feared to impede progress because it gave the individual no opportunity for avoiding liability by being careful and thus confronted him with the dilemma of either giving up his projected activity or incurring the cost of any resulting injury.[34] Fault alone was deemed to justify a shifting of loss, because the function of tort remedies was seen as primarily admonitory or deterrent.[35] An award against a tortfeasor served as a punishment for him and a warning to others; it was, in a sense, an

28. *Lambert & Olliot v. Bessey* (1681) T. Raym. 421 at 422; 83 E.R. 220. See MacCormack, *Revenge and Compensation in Early Law*, 21 Am. J. Comp. L. 69 (1973).
29. There has been some difference of opinion among legal historians as to whether the progression has been from liability based on actual intent or moral fault to a gradual acceptance of external standards, as Holmes suggested in his famous work on *Common Law* (1881) ch. 1, or the reverse, which is the more generally accepted view today: see *Holdsworth* iii, 375-377; viii, 446-459; Wigmore, *Responsibility for Tortious Acts: Its History*, 7 Harv. L. Rev. 315 at 383, 441 (1894); Ames, *Law and Morals*, 22 Harv. L. Rev. 97 (1908). But note the more cautious survey by *Fifoot* ch. 9.
30. Ehrenzweig, *Psychoanalysis of Negligence*, 47 Nw. U.L. Rev. 855 (1953). Typically, the claim was by a passive victim against an active defendant. Change came with collisions between moving actors.
31. Winfield, *Myth of Absolute Liability*, 42 L.Q.R. 37 (1926).
32. See below, p. 135.
33. On the interlock of philosophical and economic postulates see Woodward, *Reality and Social Reform: Transition from Laissez-Faire to Welfare State*, 72 Yale L.J. 286 (1962); Atiyah, *Rise and Fall of Freedom of Contract* (1979).
34. "The true explanation of the reference of liability to a moral standard . . . is not that it is for the purpose of improving men's hearts, but that it is to give a man a fair chance to avoid doing the harm before he is held responsible" (Holmes, *Common Law* (1881) 144).
35. Both Austin, *Jurisprudence* (2nd ed. 1970) Lecture XX, and Salmond, *Jurisprudence* (1937) 538 believed that the object of tort liability was penal, not compensatory.

adjunct to the criminal law designed to induce anti-social and inconsiderate persons to conform to the standards of reasonable conduct prescribed by law. The significance attached to the element of deterrence operated, of course, on the assumption that an adverse judgment would be paid out of the defendant's own pocket. Personal fortunes were regarded as the sole source of compensation, making the deterrent lash both real and inescapable.

Today, we are in the process of revising this approach. Morality will, of course, continue to dominate intentional injuries, and tort law (whatever its prospects of survival elsewhere) appears to have an assured future in this regard. However, in the core area of tort—accidents—our viewpoint has been changing drastically. It is being increasingly realised that human failures in a machine age exact a large and fairly regular toll of life, limb and property, which is not significantly reducible by standards of conduct that can be prescribed and enforced through the operation of tort law.[36] Accident prevention is more effectively promoted through the pressure exerted by penal sanctions attached to safety regulations and such extra-legal measures as road safety campaigns, insurance premiums based on the insured's safety record, improvements in the quality of roads and motor vehicles and of production processes in industry.[37] But despite all these controls, accidents and injuries remain. Some no doubt are attributable to negligence in the conventional sense, that is, to unreasonable risks, but others to "unavoidable" accidents. Either may fairly be ascribed, not just to the immediate participants, but to the activity or enterprise itself with which they are connected. The progress of society is linked to the maintenance and continuance of industrial operations and fast methods of transport, and must therefore suffer the harms associated with them. The question is simply, who is to pay for them, the hapless victim who may be unable to pin conventional fault on any particular individual or those who benefit from the accident producing activity? If rules of law can be devised that will require each industry or those engaging in a particular activity, like drivers of motor cars, to bear collectively the burden of its own operating costs, public policy may be better served than under a legal system that is content to leave the compensation of casualties to a "forensic lottery"[38] based on outdated and unrealistic notions of fault and excessively expensive to operate.

Loss spreading

This approach suggests that a proper function of tort law should be not simply a redirection of losses from the victim to the wrongdoer as the allocation of risks and losses according to broader utilitarian goals, a shift corresponding to the philosophies of corrective and distributive justice.[39]

36. Adverse publicity of managerial failures through tort litigation is the theme of Linden, *Tort Law as Ombudsman*, 51 Can. B. Rev. 155 (1973).
37. See Klein & Waller, *Causation, Culpability and Deterrence in Highway Crashes*, Auto. Ins. & Compensation Study, D.O.T. (1970).
38. Ison, *Forensic Lottery* (1967).
39. Corrective justice, as a moral Kantian postulate, still enjoys rigorous defence among tort theorists like Weinrit, *Tort Law* (1991); Fletcher, *Fairness and Utility in Tort*, 85 Harv. L. Rev. 537 (1972); Stoljar, *Accidents, Costs and Legal Responsibility*, 36 Mod. L. Rev. 233 (1973). See Englard, *The Basis of Tort Liability: Moral Responsibility and Social Utility in Tort Law*, 10 Tel Aviv Stud. in Law 89 (1990).

As already emphasised, no social value attaches to the mere shifting of loss so long as its effect is merely to impoverish one individual for the benefit of another. In order to warrant such a result, the law had to find a compelling reason for subordinating the defendant's interests to the plaintiff's, and inevitably focused attention on the culpability of the individual participants in the accident. On the other hand, if a certain type of loss is looked upon as the more or less inevitable by-product of a desirable but dangerous activity, it may well be just to distribute its costs among all who benefit from that activity, although it would be unfair to impose it upon each or any one of those individuals who happened to be the faultless instruments causing it. Such a basis for administering losses has been variously described as "collectivisation of losses" or "loss distribution". It leads to the selection of defendants, not necessarily because they happen to be morally blameworthy, but because they represent a conduit for "internalising" the accident cost to the risk-creating activity and distributing it among its beneficiaries through higher prices and/or liability insurance.

Sometimes this approach would point to the victim as the better loss bearer, viz. when he can better calculate and control the risk. This would be true of many business losses, as when a factory is idled by an interruption of power supply,[40] and of property losses which are more economically absorbed by first party (for example, fire) insurance than third party (liability) insurance.[41] More often, however, it points to the injurer. A good illustration is workers' compensation. Towards the close of the last century, it had become obvious that the judicial policy of protecting industry from the impact of accident losses suffered by its workers no longer corresponded either with the growing sense of social responsibility or the needs of the economy. It was increasingly felt that, instead of the worker subsidising the growth of industrial development at the cost of his life or health, industry itself should bear the cost of its accidents by writing it off as an overhead charge of its operations and ultimately distributing it among its consumers. In response to this change in attitude, the first system of social insurance was inaugurated, entitling the casualties of accidents in the course of employment to compensation regardless of negligence in the conventional sense. Liability for compensation was placed on the employer who, in turn, had to cover himself against the risk by compulsory insurance.

Liability insurance

A potent influence on the growing trend towards loss distribution is the modern prevalence of liability insurance.[42] Insurance has the effect that an

40. *Spartan Steel v. Martin* [1973] Q.B. 27. But Lord Denning's reasoning had no appeal for Stephen J. in *Caltex Oil v. The Willemstad* (1976) 136 C.L.R. 529 at 580-581.
41. E.g. *Photo Production v. Securicor* [1980] A.C. 827 at 851. First party insurance can be tailored to the needs of particular insureds, thus refining the risk pool (e.g. cheaper cars. Why should they subsidise expensive ones?). Moral hazards can be guarded against by deductibles. Generally Priest, *The Current Insurance Crisis and Modern Tort Law*, 96 Yale L.J. 1521 (1987).
42. See Atiyah, *Accidents* ch. 10; Smith, *Miscegenetic Union of Liability Insurance and the Tort Process*, 54 Cornell L. Rev. 645 (1969); James, *Accident Liability Reconsidered: The Impact of Liability Insurance*, 57 Yale L.J. 549 (1948); Braybrooke, *Impact of Liability Insurance*, 3 U. Tas. L. Rev. 53 (1968); Cane, *Justice and Justifications for Tort Liability*, 2 Oxf. J. Leg. Stud. 30 (1982).

adverse judgment no longer merely shifts a loss from one individual to another, but tends to distribute it among all policy holders carrying insurance on this type of risk.[43] The person cited as defendant is, in reality, only a nominal party to the litigation, a mere "conduit through whom this process of distribution starts to flow".

The fact that, through this device of indemnity insurance, some of the benefits of a regime of "collectivisation of losses" are already being attained under our traditional rules of tort law, suggests several observations. In the first place, insurance creates a moral hazard by removing an incentive to be careful and thus weakens tort liability's goal of deterrence. This is especially true of flat-rated insurance, such as motor insurance in Australia.[44] But the argument that liability insurance is incompatible with tort law and therefore void was soon abandoned in the light of its beneficial compensatory function. Morever, the assumed deterrent value of tort damages can be overrated especially in relation to activities like driving if the instinct of self-preservation, police enforcement and the prospect of increased insurance premiums are not themselves sufficient.[45]

Secondly, the traditional concern that liability might overtax the capacity of a particular class of defendants is apt to be weakened or dispelled by knowledge that the judgment will not be borne singlehandedly by the one defendant. This has in turn resulted in a steady erosion of the traditional control devices, a vast expansion of the scope of liability, and substantially stricter liability especially in areas where insurance is mandatory as in the case of motoring and work accidents. This pervasive trend runs like a golden thread throughout this book.

Thirdly, while in theory insurance follows liability, in experience insurance often paves the way to liability. In short, it is a "hidden persuader".[46] A special technique is to "channel" liability exclusively to one from among several potential targets, so as to obviate the wasteful need of multiple (pyramiding) insurance. This may be achieved by contract, as when a head contractor agrees to indemnify all subcontractors for accidents on a building project, or by legislation imposing, for example, exclusive "liability" for nuclear accidents (like fissionable material in transit) on reactor operators.[47]

43. It therefore completely changes the emphasis of Holmes' observation that "civil liability, *in its immediate working*, is simply a redistribution of an existing loss between two individuals" (*Common Law* (1881) 50).

44. Experience related premiums may create incentives for care when tort liability would not, for drivers without additional resources. See generally Schwartz, *The Ethics and Economics of Tort Liability Insurance*, 75 Cornell L. Rev. 313 (1990).

45. Discounting deterrence of tort law is common among advocates of no-fault: e.g. Harris, *Evaluating the Goals of Personal Injury Law: Some Empirical Evidence*, in *Essays for Atiyah* 289 (1991).

46. But now increasingly brought into the open in judicial opinions, not only in the U.S.: e.g. *Lamb v. Camden L.B.C.* [1981] Q.B. 625 at 637; *Robertson v. Swincer* (1989) A.T.R. 80-271 at 68,880; *Takaro Properties v. Rowling* [1978] 2 N.Z.L.R. 318 at 323; Denning, *The Discipline of the Law* 280 (1979). Lord Simmons still expressed the old-fashioned, formalistic view in *Davie v. New Merton Mills* [1959] A.C. 604 at 627; *Lister v. Romford Ice Co.* [1957] A.C. 555 at 572.

47. *Nuclear Installations Act* 1965 (U.K.) s. 12 (i)(b); *Price Anderson Act* 1956-1966 (U.S.) (umbrella insurance). For vicarious liability of employers see below, ch. 19. A remarkable

Fourthly, perhaps the most important aspect of this symbiotic relationship is that without liability insurance the tort system would long ago have collapsed under the weight of the demands put on it and been replaced by an alternative, and perhaps more efficient, system of accident compensation.

Economic theory

The shift towards dissociating compensation from individual culpability, discussed in the preceding sections, has lent impetus to frankly instrumentalist goals advanced chiefly by legal economists. Their primary objective being the reduction of accidents as a means of reducing their cost, they view tort liability's function as seeking to influence human conduct ex ante (before accident) rather than as correcting ex post a disturbed equilibrium. Primary reduction of accidents can be promoted by "specific deterrence", that is, by collective action such as safety measures enforced by fines and other penalties, or by "general deterrence" through the operation of the market.[48] By "internalising", that is allocating, the cost of accidents to the activity that caused it, the price of its products will reflect the cost of its accidents and affect their competitive attraction to consumers, hopefully either stimulating remedial managerial response or a reduction of consumer demand. In either event, internalisation of accident costs is indispensable to the efficient allocation of resources. By the same token, "externalising" the cost of accidents, that is, exempting an industry from bearing it, will be inefficient, as when the cost of pollution is borne by the public rather than the culprit enterprise whose products will appear cheaper than they should be and thus in greater demand and producing more harm.

From this point of view, strict liability seems preferable to negligence in that the latter would allow non-negligent but accident causing activities to escape.[49] Loss distribution and deep pocket liability also reduce the social cost of accidents on the theory of the diminishing marginal utility of money. This recognises the importance of compensation, which the first, the accident reduction, goal would trivialise.

Another economic approach, however, defends the negligence basis as best suited to promote (but only) cost-justified precautions.[50] It would be inefficient to aim at the prevention of all accidents, in particular accidents whose cost of prevention would exceed its benefits.[51]

Economic and other instrumentalist theories find more resonance among policy makers than on the Bench where litigation between injurer and

47. *Continued*
instance of judicial channelling is *Goldberg v. Kollsman Instruments* 191 N.E. 2d 81 (N.Y. 1963) (manufacturer of aircraft, not of defective altimeter, liable).

48. See especially Calabresi, *The Cost of Accidents* (1970). Interest in the economic implications of legal rules was stimulated by Coase, *The Problem of Social Cost*, 3 J. Law & Econ. 1 (1960); pioneered by Mataja in Austria in late 19th century: see Englard, 10 Int'l Rev. L. & Econ. 173 (1990).

49. To resolve the problem of "What causes what?", Calabresi suggests resort to the cheapest cost avoider.

50. This economic calculus was seen implicit in Judge Learned Hand's famous formula of negligence (see below, p. 119).

51. Posner, *Law and Economics* (3rd ed. 1986).

injured is naturally seen more in interpersonal terms. Besides, their emphasis on self-interested pre-accident behaviour assumes responsive actors, more likely to be found among industrial managers than car drivers, workers and others engaged in humdrum activities.[52]

Crisis of contemporary law

The impact of the contextual developments described has been unsettling to contemporary tort law. Earlier adjustments to changing social and economic perceptions, like the 19th century credo in liability without fault, did not impugn the traditional view of tort law as concerned only with interpersonal equities. By contrast, the notion of looking beyond the immediate participants and including more wide-ranging social and economic policies of how to allocate given losses may seem to move tort law from the familiar function of "commutative" to that of "distributive" justice. The dialectic between compensation and deterrence, the conventional twin aims of tort law, is being played out on a larger canvas. Policy has of course always influenced the direction of law, but the new policy dimension may appear to be more germane to the legislative than the judicial function.[53] Yet as already suggested, the change in perspective is in large part dictated by inescapable external developments, to ignore which would be deliberately short-sighted and self-defeating.

A second, even more serious, crisis looms from the very challenge of tort law as a suitable method of compensating accident victims in the modern welfare state. This challenge represents a logical extension of the contemporary movement from individualism to collectivism as the basic philosophy of compensation.

Compensation plans

The tort system has incurred mounting criticism from many quarters.[54] Its inefficiency as a system of accident compensation is most marked in the limited and capricious class of its beneficiaries and its high operating costs. As to the first, the tort system discriminates between different victims not according to their deserts but according to the culpability of the defendant. This causes unfairly unequal treatment in several ways: between victims of the same injury, for example cancer, one of whom can but another cannot point to a legally responsible cause; between one who succeeds and another who fails to carry his burden of proof against a defendant; and between those who can and who cannot collect from responsible defendants. In the upshot, only a small proportion of the disabled are adequately compensated

52. Critical: Englard, *System Builders*, 9 J. Leg. Stud. 27 (1980) and *Law and Economics in American Tort Cases*, 41 U. Tor. L.J. 359 (1991); Steiner, *Economics, Morality and the Law of Torts*, 26 U. Tor. L.J. 227 (1976); Atiyah, *Accidents* ch. 24.
53. See the misgivings by Stephens J. in *Caltex Oil v. The Willemstad* (1976) 136 C.L.R. 529 at 567.
54. Not only from scholars, e.g. Ison, *Forensic Lottery* (1967), but now also from prominent judges, e.g. the Woodhouse Report, *Compensation for Personal Injury in New Zealand* 1967 and *Pearson* Report 1 §246-263. Generally: Fleming, *Is There a Future for Tort*? 58 A.L.J. 131 (1984); Sugarman, *Doing Away with Personal Injury Law* (1989).

by damages.[55] Secondly, the system is inordinately expensive, with little more than half the insurance premium reaching the victim.[56] These high transaction costs are inherent in the system itself, the primary cause being the adversary relation between claimant and the compensation source. Both liability and damages require investigation by expensive professionals and are frequently contested. The system is geared to individualised processing and does not favour economies of scale.

While some reformers have advocated extensions of strict liability in order to increase the range of protection, for example to all defective products, others have turned their back on the tort system in favour of the alternative model of "compensation plans". Specialised plans for particular kinds of accidents, starting with workers' compensation nearly a century ago, have proliferated since, in response as a rule to varying but pressing inadequacies of the tort system in specific areas such as motor vehicle accidents,[57] victims of violent crimes,[58] and medical treatment,[58a] drug and vaccine injuries[59] and others.[60] Common features are standardised benefits, often limited to material loss, usually flowing directly to the victim (first party) rather than through a defendant (third party insurance), and bureaucratic instead of judicial administration. But while the political appeal of these plans lies in meeting a specific need without commitment to a basic reform of the tort system, by the same token most of them are open to the objection of unfairly favouring one class of victims to the exclusion of others very similarly placed, for example, victims of cancer from drugs but not from other causes; research volunteers but not other public champions; victims of motor traffic but not of aircraft.[61]

Critics view these special plans, not as potentially evolving into a more comprehensive system of compensation, but as diverting resources from a fundamental reform of completely replacing the tort system here and now with a comprehensive compensation plan for all accidents or, better still, for illness as well.[62] This would largely eliminate "horizontal inequities"

55. *Pearson* chs 3, 4: 3 mill. injuries annually in U.K. (720,000 at work; 290,000 on road); of ¼ mill. tort *claims* 85-90% are successful, but only 6.5% of all *injuries* receive tort compensation. Similarly, Harris, *Compensation and Support for Illness and Injury* (1984) ch. 2.
56. *Pearson* §83 estimated operating costs at 85% of the value of tort compensation payments. Litigation costs alone: $4,000 to $7,000 a day for each party in Vic. Sup. Ct.; *Age*, 1 Feb. 1990. By comparison, the administrative cost of the N.Z. accident scheme is under 8%.
57. See below, p. 400.
58. See below, p. 35.
58a. See Sappideen, *Look Before You Leap: Reform of Medical Malpractice Liability*, 13 Syd. L. Rev. 523 (1991).
59. Either a special fund or exceptional strict liability for drugs exists in Sweden, West Germany and Japan. See Fleming, *Drug Injury Compensation Plans*, 30 Am. J. Comp. L. 297 (1982). Vaccine: *Vaccine Damage Payments Act* 1979 (U.K.).
60. E.g. participants in organised sports (*Sporting Injuries Insurance Act* 1978 (N.S.W.)); miners suffering black-lung (British National Coal Board Scheme 1974; *Pearson* §790); medical research volunteers: *Pearson* §1340.
61. See e.g. the criticism of *Pearson* by Dworkin in *Accident Compensation after Pearson* (1979) ch. V; Ogus, Corfield & Harris, *Pearson: Principled Reform or Political Compromise*, 7 Indust. L.J. 143 (1978); Ison, *Politics of Reform*, 27 U. Tor. L.J. 385 (1977); Stapleton, *Disease and the Compensation Debate* (1986).
62. See esp. Harris, *Compensation and Support for Illness and Injury* (1984).

between different categories of the disabled and divert the savings from the steep transaction costs of the tort system to a vastly extended class of beneficiaries. It also appeals to the fear that our existing system is outrunning its financial capacity to cope with mass disasters in the nuclear, aviation and pharmaceutical fields. For funding, the same sources can be tapped as under present liability insurance and some deterrence can be built in through individualised rating.[63] Following the famous Woodhouse Report, this model has been actually operating in New Zealand since 1974. An even more ambitious project, covering not only accidents but also congenital disability and sickness, was also once close to adoption in Australia.[64]

A less radical strategy of reform, long favoured in Scandinavia[65] and embraced by the British Pearson Commission (1978),[66] is to reduce the incentive for tort claims by increasing the comparative attraction of social insurance benefits. Since the Second World War social security has assumed a large role in providing income replacement and medical services for disability, and in several countries like Great Britain has already become the "senior partner"[67] to torts in compensating victims of accident. The object of eroding the tort system can therefore be promoted by steadily increasing the benefits of social insurance and/or reducing the attractiveness of tort damages, for example by limiting awards for non-pecuniary loss.[68] But until tort law has thus withered away, it will remain a segment of the contemporary patchwork of compensation sources with all the attendant problems of self-identity and interrelation.[69]

5. SYNOPSIS

No particular arrangement of the vast and complex material which passes under the name of torts has found universal favour. There are many possible approaches, each with its own appeal and disadvantages. Thus, from a theoretical point of view, we might well have adopted a classification according to the nature of the interest for which the plaintiff is claiming legal protection. But this would have ill-fitted with the developing open-ended concept of negligence (with its emphasis on the injurer's conduct) or with the traditional emphasis of our law upon duties rather than their corresponding rights.[70] Indeed, its very name implies a concern with "wrongs", a pathological condition in the legal system representing not law

63. See Trebilcock, *Incentive Issues in the Design of "No-Fault" Compensation*, 39 U. Tor. L.J. 19 (1989).
64. See below, p. 407.
65. See *Accident Compensation: The Swedish Alternative*, 34 Am. J. Comp. L. 613 (1986).
66. See Fleming, *Pearson Report: Its Strategy*, 42 Mod. L. Rev. 249 (1979); Marsh, *Pearson Report*, 95 L.Q.R. 513 (1979).
67. *Pearson* §1732. Social Security: £421 mill. annually; torts: £202 mill. (I, 13). No similar figures are available for Australia. A concise survey of Australian social welfare is contained in *Pearson* III ch. 9.
68. Ibid. at §389 (excluding first three months).
69. Critically analysed from an economist's point of view by Rea, *Disability Insurance and Public Policy* (Ontario Economic Council, 1981).
70. Primarily the legacy of Austin's jurisprudence. Exceptional are the anomalous property torts like trespass and conversion, based on proprietary rights.

but disregard of law. A related arrangement might look to the nature of the injury for which reparation is sought. Thus, the suggestion has been made to divide torts into physical harms, harms of appropriation and harms to relational interests.[71] This scheme, however, is also open to the objection that it would cut too much across traditional arrangements and terminology inherited from the vicissitudes of historical evolution. Our substantive law has sprung from the procedural background of the forms of action which continue to haunt us from their grave.[72]

This book follows the classification first suggested by Holmes[73] and adopted by the American *Restatement of Torts.*[74] It commences with examining in turn the three bases, upon one of which every case of liability has to rest. These are (1) an intent to interfere with the plaintiff's interests, (2) negligence, and (3) strict liability or liability without "fault". This familiar conduct-based classification reflects the conventional view of tort law in its primarily corrective function of interpersonal wrongs.[75] In the second half of the book, particular fields of liability have been selected for separate treatment, partly because their inherent importance warrants extended discussion, partly because this enables the grouping together of problems which are related by reason of the particular interest that has been invaded rather than because there is any uniform basis of liability in the abovementioned sense. This applies for example to nuisance, the responsibility of occupiers of land, liability for defective products, defamation and so forth.

71. Green, *Judge and Jury* (1930) ch. 1.
72. See Maitland, *Forms of Action at Common Law* (2nd ed. 1962) 2.
73. *Theory of Torts*, 7 Am. L. Rev. 652 (1873) which long preceded the first English generalised treatment of torts, similarly organised, by Pollock (1887), itself dedicated to Holmes. See White, *Intellectual Origins of Torts in America*, 86 Yale L.J. 671 (1977).
74. Originally published in 1934 by the American Law Institute, it was superseded by *Rest.* 2nd in 1965-1977.
75. Arguing, inter alia, for merging the first into the second category is Cane, *Justice and Justification of Tort Liability*, 2 Oxf. J. Leg. St. 30 (1982).

2

TRESPASS AND INTENTIONAL INTERFERENCE WITH THE PERSON

1. TRESPASS AND CASE

Like other primitive legal systems, the early common law was replete with formalism. Substantive law was "secreted in the interstices of procedure",[1] and the writ system in particular was dominant among the forces that moulded the growth of our law of torts. All litigation commenced with the issue of a writ indicating the nature of the plaintiff's claim in a conventional form. The plaintiff's success or failure depended on whether a form of action was available to cover the facts of his case. Thus, a *cause* of action recognised by law implied the existence of an appropriate *form* of action, that is, a specific writ setting out that cause in a particular form. Without a writ there was no remedy, and it was through the expansion of the writs that the scope of legal protection was correspondingly enlarged.

The principal writs which the developed common law offered against tortious misconduct were two[2]—trespass and case.[3] Trespass emerged in the 13th century as a remedy for obvious forcible wrongs, involving breach of the peace. If the defendant did not appear, he would be outlawed, and if convicted was liable to fine[4] and imprisonment, besides being mulcted in damages in favour of the injured plaintiff. It was only at a later stage that this close association between the law of crime and tort disappeared, though not before the semi-criminal character of the action of trespass had become firmly rooted.[5]

Trespass became the remedy for all forcible, direct and immediate injury, whether to the person, land or goods of the plaintiff; in short, against conduct most likely to cause breach of the peace by provoking retaliation. The action on the case was developed rather later as a remedy for injuries that did not fit the pejorative pleading of trespass. In such situations, a writ might issue setting out the allegation of damage and the particular circumstances in which it had been suffered. The various writs settled in this manner, and constantly expanding the area of legal control, came in time to be regarded as collectively constituting a new form of action, called *case*. By the late 18th century,[6] the discrimen between trespass and case became

1. Maine, *Early Law and Custom* (1861) 389.
2. Detinue and replevin which vindicated proprietary rights were not purely delictual remedies. They were later superseded by trover, an action on the case: see below, p. 55.
3. See Milsom, *Historical Foundations of the Common Law* (2nd ed. 1981) ch. 11; *Fifoot* ch. 3; Kiralfy, *Action on the Case* (1951).
4. The fine was abolished by statute in 1694.
5. Throughout its existence, the writ alleged that the trespass had been committed vi et armis and contra suam pacem, though this became a mere formality at a very early stage.
6. Largely attributable to Blackstone.

whether the injury was the direct result of the defendant's force[7] or was due merely to an omission or an act not immediately but only consequentially injurious to the plaintiff's interests. It was a primitive distinction based on the nature of the causal sequence connecting the defendant's conduct with the plaintiff's harm. To illustrate: if Simpkins threw a log over his fence into the road, hitting Jenkins, the action was trespass. But if Watkins later stumbled over it, the action was case.[8]

The principal substantive consequences flowing from the distinction between wrongs redressable by trespass and case were twofold. Trespass[9] was actionable per se, that is, without proof of actual damage, whereas generally[10] damage was of the gist of case. The explanation for this disparity is probably to be found in the fact that wrongs of direct forcible injury were so likely to arouse violent resentment in primitive times that it was expedient to provide a remedy in the interest of public security, even though the outraged victim did not or could not prove material damage; whereas the very fact of material injury was the catalyst which induced the courts to furnish redress by an action on the case in situations not covered by the limited scope of trespass. The second difference between the two forms of action was that trespassory harm was prima facie wrongful and it was for the defendant to raise any issue of justification or excuse, such as self-defence or unavoidable necessity. In contrast, the action on the case required proof by the plaintiff of either wrongful intent or negligence on the part of the defendant.

The trend of yet later development was to associate actions on the case with negligent harm and trespass with intentional wrongs. This shift of emphasis was gradual. In the first place, as the critical distinction between immediate and consequential was being refined, it came rather close in practice to that between wilful and inadvertent injuries. Losing control over a vehicle, the usual cause of a "consequential" collision, was classified as neglect properly vindicated by an action on the case;[11] while hardly anything short of wilfully ramming into the plaintiff[12] would be deemed so "direct" as to require a count in trespass. Eventually, it even became permissible to sue either in trespass or case if the injury, though immediate, was not wilful.[13] Plaintiffs thereafter preferred to sue in case for all negligent injuries, even when the cause of action could have qualified as a "residuary form" of trespass, in order to avail themselves of the procedural advantages of case and to avoid the risk of losing if they eventually failed

7. This included cases where the act set in motion an unbroken series of continuing consequences, the last of which ultimately caused the injury, as in the celebrated *Squib Case: Scott v. Shepherd* (1773) 2 W. Bl. 892; 96 E.R. 525. See also *Hillier v. Leitch* [1936] S.A.S.R. 490.
8. *Hutchins v. Maughan* [1947] V.L.R. 131; *Hillier v. Leitch* [1936] S.A.S.R. 490 at 495.
9. This includes quasi-trespasses, i.e., direct infringements of incorporeal property rights such as the right to vote at parliamentary elections. Such wrongs closely resemble trespass, but were redressible in case because the injury could not be accounted forcible. They had, however, all the attributes of trespass: see *Ashby v. White* (1703) 2 Ld Raym. 938; 92 E.R. 126; *Nicholls v. Ely Beet Sugar Factory* [1936] Ch. 343; *Constantine v. Imperial Hotels* [1944] K.B. 693.
10. There are some exceptions, e.g. slander actionable per se: see below, p. 548.
11. *Gibbons v. Pepper* (1695) 1 Ld Raym. 38; 91 E.R. 922.
12. As in *Savignac v. Roome* (1794) 6 T.R. 125; 101 E.R. 470.
13. *Williams v. Holland* (1833) 10 Bing. 112; 131 E.R. 848. But if the injury was wilful and immediate, trespass alone would lie; but if it was consequential, case alone.

to establish direct and forcible injury.[14] By contrast, over the centuries the more common types of trespass to the person developed into the nominate torts of assault, battery and false imprisonment which are exclusively associated with direct and intentional aggression. When, in addition, the earlier identification of trespass with strict liability yielded to the modern view that trespass, like case, was not actionable in the absence of negligence or intent,[15] it becomes intelligible why today we have come to think of trespass as an (almost) exclusively intentional wrong.[16]

In England, the forms of action were finally abolished by the *Judicature Act* 1873, culminating in fundamental changes in the forms of pleading and procedure. Instead of pleading his cause of action, that is, the legal result of the facts of his case, as heretofore, the plaintiff now merely pleads the facts and argues at the trial whether these facts disclose a cause of action. The purpose of this reform, since adopted everywhere else in the common law,[17] was not only to simplify and modernise procedure but, in burying the ancient forms of action, to emancipate substantive law from the distorting effect they had exerted on developing doctrine. After a slow adjustment to the new regime over a century's operation, we are finally discarding the last doctrinal vestiges of the long obsolete procedural past, and are able to resolve questions like the standard of liability or the appropriate period of limitation[18] by reference to functionally oriented modern criteria, like the distinction between intended and accidental injuries, rather than the fine-spun and cabalistic learning about trespass and case.

2. TRESPASS AND NEGLIGENCE

For injuries to the person or property which were the immediate and direct result of the defendant's force and for which an action of trespass would lie, the early common law imposed a rather strict responsibility. Though perhaps never absolute because a few defences like unavoidable necessity and self-defence gained very early recognition,[19] it was not apparently contingent on wrongful intent or negligence. Even a faultless trespassory

14. See Goodhart & Winfield, *Trespass and Negligence*, 49 L.Q.R. 359 (1933). The procedural difficulties prior to 1833 facing a plaintiff injured in a collision on land or water, especially those involving joinder of several counts, are vividly explained by Pritchard, *Rule in Williams v. Holland* [1964] Cam. L.J. 234.
15. See below, pp. 18-24.
16. See below, n. 40.
17. In Australia, N.S.W., the last stronghold, surrendered only in 1970.
18. Most jurisdictions now have one common period for all personal injuries. The widely followed English formula (since 1954, now 1980) prescribing three years for all personal injuries caused by "negligence, nuisance or breach of duty" (six years for other torts) has been expansively construed to include even claims for trespass, intentional (*Long v. Hepworth* [1968] 1 W.L.R. 1299) as well as negligent: *Letang v. Cooper* [1965] 1 Q.B. 232 (C.A.); *Kruber v. Grzesiak* [1963] V.R. 621. N.S.W. (1969), Vic. (1983), Qld (1974), S.A. (1956), Tas. (1974), N.T. (1981), A.C.T. (six). W.A. applies a six-year period for negligence and a four-year period for trespass to the person: no plaintiff would wish to rely on the latter, and the defendant cannot compel him, if the claim alleges negligent (not intentional) injury: *Williams v. Milotin* (1957) 97 C.L.R. 465; see below, n. 40. Thus the problem has disappeared.
19. Winfield, *Myth of Absolute Liability*, 42 L.Q.R. 37 (1926). Milsom (*Historical Foundations of the Common Law* (2nd ed. 1981) ch. 11) contends that juries were also free to consider fault under the "general issue" though unlikely to take an indulgent view.

contact was actionable, unless the defendant could show that the accident was inevitable—"judged utterly without his fault; as if a man by force take my hand and strike you".[20] On the other hand, if the harm was merely "consequential", the plaintiff was obliged to sue in case and therewith to submit some item of fault in lieu of the missing element of trespass. This committed the law to a dual standard of responsibility for accidental (unintended) harm, dependent on the fortuitous nature of the causal sequence between the actor's conduct and the resulting injury. He would act at his peril on the chance that it turned out to be trespass, but otherwise go quit in the absence of fault or social inadequacy.[21]

This capricious allocation of civil liability did not long survive the advent of industrialisation and its attendant manifestations of rapidly increasing urbanisation and denser as well as faster transport. The immense conglomeration of individuals on the roads and in factories would have made it intolerable to persist with liability for the consequences of purely accidental contact. "No liability without fault" reflected the necessities of a rapidly expanding society based on private enterprise. It postulated that the risk of unavoidable harm should be borne by the accident victim himself as the price of participating in the larger benefits accruing to society as a whole from private initiative and exertion, provided the particular activity did not create an unreasonable hazard by prevailing community standards. In consequence, the old regime of strict liability for all trespass came to be substantially modified in the second half of the last century in favour of the modern principle that no one can ordinarily complain of personal injury unless it be caused by the defendant's intentional aggression or negligent default.

Road accidents

The first break occurred in connection with ordinary running-down actions. In the third quarter of the 19th century, the view emerged that regardless of his form of action, a plaintiff could no longer recover in the absence of negligence when he or his chattels on the highway, or his property adjacent thereto, had been unintentionally damaged as the result of the defendant's conduct on the highway.[22] Any scruples were dispelled by the immense prestige of its sponsors, Lords Blackburn[23] and Bramwell.[24] At first it was fashionable to disguise the change by explaining the modern rule as an application of the principle of voluntary assumption of risk, that is, that those who go on the highway, or have their property adjacent thereto, subject themselves to the risk of unavoidable accidents.[25] But this formulation savours of fiction, since it is not open to a plaintiff, like a baby in a pram, to insist that he did not in fact assume

20. *Weaver v. Ward* (1616) Hob. 134; 80 E.R. 284. *Leame v. Bray* (1803) 3 East 593; 102 E.R. 724. This could also be explained as non-causal, like *Platt v. Nutt* (1988) 12 N.S.W.L.R. 231 (plaintiff responsible for harmful contact).
21. Leaving aside such cases as nuisance, fire, etc.
22. The evolution is traced by Goodhart & Winfield, *Trespass and Negligence*, 49 L.Q.R. 359 (1933).
23. *Fletcher v. Rylands* (1866) L.R. 1 Ex. 265 at 286; *River Wear Comm. v. Adamson* (1877) 2 App. Cas. 743 at 767.
24. *Holmes v. Mather* (1875) L.R. 10 Ex. 261.
25. *Fletcher v. Rylands* (1866) L.R. 1 Ex. 265 at 286-287.

such a risk. Indeed, in the course of time it has become almost uniformly accepted that the trespass theory in these cases is now obsolete: a plaintiff must henceforth also assume the burden of proving the defendant's neligence[26] and can invoke the (longer) period of limitation for negligence actions.[27]

In retrospect, the wisdom of discarding strict liability for highway accidents seems less obvious today since the advent of the motor car than it was in the days of more tranquil traffic a century ago. Indeed, the "devil wagon" seems at first sight to have turned the legal no less than the lay mind to the analogy of wild beasts,[28] but this imagery was eventually not pursued.[29] Subsequent experience, however, far surpassing the wildest fears, has seriously challenged the claim of fault liability as an adequate solution. Truly, if the highway created the negligence law of the 19th century, the highway of the 20th has doomed it to eventual oblivion. No-fault plans have been adopted or recommended most everywhere, and even where the negligence rule has formally survived, the fault requirement has become greatly diluted under the collective influence of compulsory insurance.[30]

Other trespasses

Once the idea of negligence had crept into the sphere of highway trespass, it was perhaps inevitable that it should also encroach upon other forms of trespass to the person. In this residuary field, however, the adjustment was more gradual and is not definitively settled even yet.

We have seen that every voluntary trespassory contact used to expose the actor to prima facie liability even "though it happen accidentally or by misfortune".[31] The plea of "not guilty" in trespass, unlike case, encompassed no more than a denial that the defendant had done an act amounting to the trespass charged, and such defences as contributory negligence or inevitable accident had to be specially pleaded.[32] According to one view, moreover, inevitable accident meant not simply lack of negligence, but some occurrence over which the defendant had no control and the effect of which he could not have avoided by the *greatest* care and skill.[33] Yet in 1890, in *Stanley v. Powell*,[34] Denman J. braved the

26. *Gayler & Pope v. Davies* [1924] 2 K.B. 75; *Venning v. Chin* (1974) 10 S.A.S.R. 299 (F.C.).
27. E.g., *Williams v. Milotin* (1957) 97 C.L.R. 465; *Eisener v. Maxwell* [1951] 3 D.L.R. 345. This problem has now been largely eliminated by modern statutes: see above, n. 18.
28. *Walton v. Vanguard Motor Bus* (1908) 25 T.L.R. 13 (bus liable to skid in wet weather held to be a public nuisance); *Hutchins v. Maunder* (1920) 37 T.L.R. 72 (car with defective steering entails strict liability, analogous to "wild beast"). See Spencer, *Motor Cars and the Rule in Rylands v. Fletcher* [1983] Cam. L.J. 65.
29. See *Phillips v. Britannia Hygienic Laundry* [1923] 1 K.B. 539 at 550-555.
30. See below, p. 398.
31. *Leame v. Bray* (1803) 3 East 593 at 600; 102 E.R. 724 at 727 per Grose J.
32. *Cotterill v. Starkey* (1839) 8 C. & P. 691; 173 E.R. 676. This, at any rate, was settled in the first half of the 19th century, though previous authority seems to have been the other way: see *Fowler v. Lanning* [1959] 1 Q.B. 426 at 434.
33. This view, encountered primarily in maritime cases, found its most authoritative exponent in Lord Esher M.R. in *The Schwan* [1892] P. 419 at 429, but was by no means unanimous (see e.g. Fry L.J. at 432-433).
34. [1891] 1 Q.B. 86.

traditionalists by holding that no action for unintended personal injury lay in the absence of fault. During a shoot the defendant had accidentally wounded a beater when a pellet, aimed at pheasants, unexpectedly ricocheted off a tree. It was held that, once the jury had negatived the allegation of negligence, the plaintiff could not recover whether he framed his cause of action in trespass or in case. Despite its somewhat scanty historical support, the decision has been accepted as an accurate statement of the modern position.[35] Its underlying rationale was succinctly explained by Holmes: "The public generally profits by individual activity. As action cannot be avoided, and tends to the public good, there is obviously no policy in throwing the hazard of what is at once desirable and inevitable upon the actor."[36] Not by coincidence, the same conclusion had been reached independently in America, though almost half a century earlier, when in the celebrated dogfight case of *Brown v. Kendall*[37] Shaw C.J. of Massachusetts decided that, in the absence of negligence, the owner of one of two quarrelling dogs was not liable to the owner of the other for accidentally putting out his eye while raising a stick in order to separate the animals.

But despite this advance, the weight of British professional opinion still clung to the notion that, even if strict liability had been exorcised from trespass, the defendant continued to labour under the disadvantage of carrying the onus of *disproving* negligence—not because he had perchance engaged in an extra-hazardous venture but simply because the harm had fortuitously resulted from a "direct" hit. Such an anachronism could be ascribed only to a misguided desire to preserve a semblance of doctrinal continuity by forcing the modern principle of negligence into the old pattern of "inevitable accident", even if it had to be accepted that no more than *ordinary* care was now required to meet the standard set by law. Fortunately for the rational development of thc law, Diplock J. in 1959 finally laid to rest the last ghost of the long buried forms of action by boldly refusing to accept defunct pleading rules[38] as a guide to the modern burden of proof, and decided that the onus of establishing negligence in all personal injury actions lay with the plaintiff, whether the action be framed in trespass or negligence and whether the accident occurred on the highway or

35. *Fowler v. Lanning* [1959] 1 Q.B. 426; *N.C.B. v. Evans* [1951] 2 K.B. 861; *Beals v. Hayward* [1960] N.Z.L.R. 131; *Walmsley v. Humenick* [1954] 2 D.L.R. 232; *Blacker v. Waters* (1928) 28 S.R. (N.S.W.) 406.

36. *Common Law* (1881) 95; ch. 3 contains an excellent discussion of this topic. It is doubly unfortunate that the enunciation of this principle in England should have been linked to *Stanley v. Powell*: first, because it is arguable that the plaintiff should have lost his action in any event by reason of his voluntary assumption of risk, and, secondly, because the insistence on fault in connection with a shooting accident made no allowance for a principle of strict liability for ultra-hazardous activities (see below, ch. 16): to this day, discharging firearms while hunting is not subject to strict liability: e.g. *Dahlberg v. Naydiuk* (1969) 10 D.L.R. (3d) 319.

37. 60 Mass. 292 (1850). The American development is traced by Gregory, *Trespass to Negligence to Absolute Liability*, 37 Va. L. Rev. 359 (1951): Roberts, *Negligence: Blackstone to Shaw to?* 50 Corn. L.Q. 191 (1965).

38. "Inevitable accident" had come to be a specially pleaded defence: see above, n. 32. It is one thing to require a party to plead a particular issue to protect the other from unfair surprise, but quite another to impose upon him the burden of proof. The latter turns on wholly different considerations like access to evidence, notions of probability, etc.: see below, p. 313.

elsewhere.[39] For unintended injury, direct or indirect, a claim must now meet all the requirements of the modern tort of negligence.[40]

But while this development seems now to be regarded as fairly settled in England,[41] it has not (yet) been uniformly accepted as definitive in Australia[42] or Canada.[43] This reluctance finds its explanation less in a policy tilt towards stricter liability than in a misplaced cult of historicism. Later we shall have occasion to dwell at length on the modern trend towards strict(er) liability, both within and without the conventional sphere of negligence. But that trend is based on a rationale more responsive to the contemporary scene than the casuistic and primitive distinction between trespass and case.

Infants and lunatics

Related to the preceding inquiry is the question whether lunatics and infants, to whom fault in the conventional sense cannot be attributed, are yet to be held responsible for acts of aggression amounting to trespass.[44] So long as trespass was regarded as a tort of strict liability, there was no inclination to make allowance for the fact that the defendant was incapable of forming a culpable intent because of extreme youth or mental deficiency. As Lord Kenyon said in 1799, "if an infant commit an assault, or utter slander, God forbid that he should not be answerable for it in a Court of Justice."[45] Likewise, as long ago as 1616 it was affirmed that "if a lunatick hurt a man, he should be answerable in trespass,"[46] because the civil action, unlike the criminal law, looked to the damage of the victim and not the intent of the injurer.[47] Divergent views have been expressed on whether this severity of the earlier law should now be modified in conformity with the change in theory regarding liability for trespass.[48] It

39. *Fowler v. Lanning* [1959] 1 Q.B. 426. Many cases of "direct" injury may, of course, warrant a strong inference of negligence so as to invoke res ipsa loquitur: see below, p. 315.
40. *Letang v. Cooper* [1965] 1 Q.B. 232 (C.A.). According to Lord Denning (and Danckwerts L.J.), trespass for unintended injury is now defunct; according to Diplock L.J., trespass may still be a permissible label for a cause of action that must, however, meet all the requirements of tortious negligence, including duty and damage. *Williams v. Milotin* (1957) 97 C.L.R. 465 reveals a more old-fashioned view, but preceded the reorientation in England and elsewhere.
41. See above, nn. 39, 40, but in the absence of a H.L. confirmation, doubts remain in some minds, e.g., *Salmond & Heuston* 135.
42. Not followed: *McHale v. Watson* (1964) 111 C.L.R. 384 per Windeyer J.; *Venning v. Chin* (1974) 10 S.A.S.R. 299 (F.C.). Followed: *Platt v. Nutt* (1988) 12 N.S.W.L.R. 231 (Kirby P.); *Beals v. Hayward* [1960] N.Z.L.R. 131; and see *Hackshaw v. Shaw* (1984) 155 C.L.R. 614 at 619. See Heffey & Glasbeek, 5 Melb. U.L. Rev. 158 (1966); Trindade, 20 I.C.L.Q. 706 (1971).
43. See *Linden* 249 who approves of this pro-plaintiff bias; Atrens, *Studies in Canadian Tort Law* (1968) 395-397 who does not.
44. See Todd, *Liability of Lunatics*, 26 A.L.J. 299 (1952); Bohlen, *Studies* ch. 11; Alexander & Szasz, *Mental Illness as an Excuse to Civil Wrongs*, 43 Notre Dame L. 24 (1967).
45. *Jennings v. Rundall* (1799) 8 T.R. 335 at 337; 101 E.R. 1419 at 1420; *O'Brien v. McNamee* [1953] Ir. R. 86 (arson).
46. *Weaver v. Ward* (1616) Hob. 134; 80 E.R. 284.
47. See Serj. Manning's note in *Borradaile v. Hunter* (1843) 5 Man. & G. 639 at 669; 134 E.R. 715 at 728.
48. There seems to be a consensus, however, that intellectual incapacity remains irrelevant for remaining heads of strict liability, except perhaps where knowledge of the exceptional risk (e.g. scienter) is required.

seems to be generally admitted that in cases where liability depends on some specific state of mind, infancy or lunacy will be a good defence if the defendant was incapable of forming the specific intent required. For instance, in actions for malicious prosecution or libel on a privileged occasion, the mental disability of the defendant may go to show that the necessary element of malice was absent. Beyond this, however, authority is divided.

With respect to lunatics, some courts would have us perpetuate the older lore of making no allowance whatever for insanity, even if the actor was quite incapable of understanding what he was doing,[49] while at least one has gone to the opposite extreme of endowing a lunatic with the same immunity in civil as in criminal proceedings and therefore excusing him, if he either did not understand the nature and quality of his act *or* did not know that what he was doing was wrong.[50] A middle course, which has enlisted the largest modern support,[51] would hold a lunatic liable who knew what he was doing, even if he did not understand that he was doing wrong. Conceding that intent or negligence are today essential to liability for trespass, the court found that the defendant's mind "directed the blows he struck" and thus entertained the requisite intent. This test is quite consistent with the general logic of intentional torts: if the best of motives or even reasonable mistake do not ordinarily excuse,[52] why should incapacity to form a reasonable judgment (as distinct from incapacity to understand the nature of his acts)? This conclusion is shared by the better reasoned American cases,[53] and has the merit of neither giving undue scope to the defence of insanity nor departing from the modern basis of liability for trespass which, as we have seen, requires intentional or negligent conduct by the actor.[54] More questionable, however, was the award of general damages.[55] If the decisive factor against taking an indulgent view of subnormal individuals is the paramount policy of compensating the injured, there is less justification for awarding damages beyond what is sufficient to repair their actual physical or material loss.

The same approach appears to govern also the liability of infants. The child must at least be old enough to understand the nature of his action: thus a three-year-old who had dragged another baby from its pram was excused because he was thought incapable of forming the requisite intent for battery.[56] On the other hand, a five-year-old who had actually intended to slash his playmate with a razor was not excused on account

49. *Donaghy v. Brennan* (1900) 19 N.Z.L.R. 289; *Stanley v. Hayes* (1904) 8 O.L.R. 81 (where defendant *did* know what he was doing).
50. *White v. Pile* (1951) 68 W.N. (N.S.W.) 176.
51. *Morriss v. Marsden* [1952] 1 All E.R. 925; *Beals v. Hayward* [1960] N.Z.L.R. 131; *Whaley v. Cartusiano* (1990) 68 D.L.R. (4th) 58 (Ont. C.A.).
52. See below, p. 78.
53. E.g. *McGuire v. Almy* 8 N.E. 2d 760 (Mass. 1937).
54. Hence, if the defendant is so insane as to lack all mental control over his actions, he should be excused because his conduct, like that of a sleepwalker, must be regarded as involuntary and beyond legal sanction.
55. In *Morriss v. Marsden* [1952] 1 All E.R. 925 the plaintiff was awarded £5,500 general damages, in addition to special damages for actual injury; contra: *Donaghy v. Brennan* (1900) 19 N.Z.L.R. 289 at 291; *Phillips v. Soloway* (1956) 6 D.L.R. (2d) 570 at 580.
56. *Tillander v. Gosselin* (1966) 60 D.L.R. (2d) 18. See also *Walmsley v. Humenick* [1954] 2 D.L.R. 232 (no intent to hit playmate with arrow).

merely of his failure to appreciate its seriousness.[57] Although this result, as previously pointed out, is consistent with the internal logic of intentional torts, it entails the incongruity that an infant, too young for negligence because incapable of appreciating the risk, may well be old enough for a more heinous "intentional" wrong although equally innocent of moral culpability.

3. BATTERY AND ASSAULT

Of the various forms of trespass to the person the most common is the tort known as battery, which is committed by intentionally bringing about a harmful or offensive contact with the person of another. The action, therefore, serves the dual purpose of affording protection to the individual not only against bodily harm but also against any interference with his person which is offensive to a reasonable sense of honour and dignity. The insult in being touched without consent has been traditionally regarded as sufficient, even though the contact is only trivial and not attended with actual physical harm. "The least touching of another in anger is a battery,"[58] and so is such offensive and insulting behaviour as spitting in another man's face,[59] cutting his hair[60] or kissing a woman. The element of personal indignity is given additional recognition by awarding aggravated or even exemplary damages to compensate for any outrage to the plaintiff's feelings.[61] The plaintiff need not even have been conscious of the contact at the time it occurred, as when a woman is abused while asleep or under an anaesthetic. The affront is as serious to her when she discovers it after the event as if she had been conscious of it at the time.[62]

Harmful physical contact may result not only from hostile[63] behaviour, but also from such as sexual intercourse by one knowingly infected with AIDS or a venereal disease.[64] Nor is it necessary that there be an actual and immediate physical contact with the person of the plaintiff; it is sufficient to pour water over him, to pull a chair from under him so that he is thrown on the ground,[65] to fire a pistol so close to his face as to burn him,[66] or to seize something from his hand.[67] The defendant must,

57. *Hart v. A.-G. for Tasmania and Pascoe* (unreported, Tas., *S.M.H.*, 30 May 1979); likewise *Garratt v. Dailey* 279 P. 2d 1091 (Wash. 1955). Parental liability, however, would sound in negligence: see below, p. 682.
58. *Cole v. Turner* (1704) 6 Mod. 149; 87 E.R. 907 per Holt C.J.
59. *R. v. Cotesworth* (1704) 6 Mod. 172; 87 E.R. 928.
60. *Forde v. Skinner* (1830) 4 C. & P. 239; 172 E.R. 687.
61. *Lamb v. Cotogno* (1987) 164 C.L.R. 1 (exemplary: $5,000). For the distinction between aggravated and exemplary damages: see below, pp. 241-243. In N.Z. exemplary damages survived the accident compensation system: *Donselaar v. Donselaar* [1982] 2 N.Z.L.R. 97.
62. *Rest. 2d* §18, comment *d.*
63. See below, n. 69.
64. See below, p. 80.
65. *Hopper v. Reeve* (1817) 7 Taunt. 698 at 700; 129 E.R. 278. Or to strike a horse whereby it throws its rider: *Dodwell v. Burford* (1669) 1 Mod. 22; 86 E.R. 703.
66. *R. v. Hamilton* (1891) 12 L.R. (N.S.W.) 111. The Criminal Codes of Qld (s. 245) and W.A. (s. 222) define "force" as including the application of "heat, light, electrical force, gas, odour or any other substance or thing whatever if applied in such a degree as to cause injury or personal discomfort". This definition is probably also an accurate statement of the common law.
67. *Green v. Goddard* (1704) 2 Salk. 641; 91 E.R. 540.

however, have done some positive and affirmative act; mere inaction such as a passive obstruction of the plaintiff's passage[68] does not constitute a battery, though it may amount to some other tort like nuisance.

The contact must be offensive outside the accepted usages of daily life.[69] Hence it is not ordinarily actionable to tap another on the shoulder to attract his attention[70] (at least in the absence of any sign that it would be resented) or to brush against someone in a narrow passage or crowd.[71] It is otherwise if such conduct is committed in a hostile manner, as where the defendant forces his way in a "rude and inordinate fashion".[72]

Battery is an intentional wrong:[73] the offensive contact must have been desired (purposive) or known to be substantially certain to result.[74] On the other hand, it is not necessary that the actor intended to inflict bodily harm, since we have seen that the legal injury is complete without it. Indeed it may be sufficient that he intended only to frighten but in a manner fraught with serious risk of bodily contact or harm.[75] Nor is liability confined to foreseeable consequences, as is liability for negligence:[76] deliberate aggression should be deterred by carrying the risk of even accidental injury in the affray.[77]

Assault

Assault consists in intentionally[78] creating in another person an apprehension of imminent harmful or offensive contact. If the threat is actually carried out, the whole incident is properly described as an "assault and battery". Usually both offences occur in rapid succession, and in common parlance the word "assault" is frequently used as including a battery.[79] But the one offence may be committed without the other. A battery may be inflicted on a victim who does not expect it and therefore

68. *Innes v. Wylie* (1844) 1 C. & K. 257; 174 E.R. 800.
69. *Wilson v. Pringle* [1987] Q.B. 237 (C.A.) (speaks, ineptly, of "hostile": rejected in *T. v. T.* [1988] Fam. 52). Cf. *Criminal Code* 1924 (Tas.) s. 182(3): "An act which is reasonably necessary for the common intercourse of life if done only for the purpose of such intercourse, and which is not disproportionate to the occasion, does not constitute an assault."
70. See *Collins v. Wilcock* [1984] 1 W.L.R. 1172, distinguishing detention with force.
71. *Cole v. Turner* (1704) 6 Mod. 149; 87 E.R. 907; *Campbell v. Samuels* (1980) 23 S.A.S.R. 389.
72. Ibid.
73. The traditionalist may insist that there can be a "negligent battery", but modern usage relegates it to the province of negligence and reserves "battery" for intentional wrongs: e.g., *Gorely v. Codd* [1967] 1 W.L.R. 19.
74. The first may be called "actual" intent, the second "oblique" (Bentham). See the definition of intent in *Rest. 2d* §8A, applied in *Garratt v. Dailey* 279 P. 2d 1091 (Wash. 1955). *R. v. Venna* [1976] Q.B. 421 held "reckless" sufficient for crime.
75. Cf. *Gray v. Barr* [1971] 2 Q.B. 554 (not an "accident"); *Co-op. v. Saindon* [1976] 1 S.C.R. 735 ("with intent to bring about the loss").
76. See below, ch. 9.
77. *Bettel v. Yim* (1978) 88 D.L.R. (3d) 543; *Allan v. New Mt Sinai Hospital* (1980) 28 O.R. (2d) 356; *Wilson v. Pringle* [1987] Q.B. 237 (assumed); *Wilkinson v. Downton* [1897] 2 Q.B. 57 at 59 (see below, p. 32). So long as it is direct, as held in *Harnett v. Bond* [1925] A.C. 669. Cf. Williams, 77 L.Q.R. 200 at 202 (1961). Trespass to land: see below, p. 40.
78. *Hall v. Fonceca* [1983] W.A.R. 309 (F.C.). While recklessness may be enough, mere negligence is not: *McPherson v. Brown* (1975) 12 S.A.S.R. 184.
79. Such indiscriminate use is found even in criminal statutes: *Crimes Act* 1900 (N.S.W.) ss 493-500; *Crimes Act* 1958 (Vic.) ss 37-43; *Criminal Code* 1899 (Qld) s. 245; *Criminal Code* 1913 (W.A.) s. 222.

cannot complain of assault, as where he is struck from behind without warning.[80] Conversely, there may be an assault without a battery if the threat to inflict unlawful force is not in fact carried out.

The tort is exceptional inasmuch as mere emotional disturbance unaccompanied by external injury is not otherwise actionable, whether because of its triviality or for fear of inviting spurious claims. Long ago, however, it was felt that assault warranted legal redress, partly as an aid to punishing offenders who had attempted to commit the crime of battery, partly because it minimised the temptation to retaliate.

Since the gist of assault lies in the *apprehension* of impending contact, the effect on the victim's mind created by the threat is the crux, not whether the defendant actually had the intention or the means to follow it up. The intent required for the tort of assault is the desire to arouse apprehension of physical contact, not necessarily to inflict actual harm. Hence it is actionable to point a pistol for the mere purpose of frightening.[81] It is sufficient if the threat would have aroused an expectation of physical aggression in the mind of a reasonable person not afflicted with exaggerated fears or peculiar and abnormal timidity.[82] But the plaintiff need not have been actually frightened: apprehension is not the same as fear, and one too courageous to be intimidated is nonetheless entitled to redress.[83] There must, however, be an apparent ability to carry out the threat immediately,[84] not like lunging at someone who is obviously out of range, unless his victim had reasonable grounds for fearing that he could and would do so.[85] Thus it is an assault to point a pistol at another in such a way as to make him believe that he is about to be shot even if, unknown to him, the pistol is unloaded.[86]

It is sometimes categorically asserted that some bodily movement is essential to assault: that neither passive inaction nor mere words, however offensive, are sufficient.[87] But this is true only to the extent of restating the overriding requirement that the victim must have apprehended imminent physical contact.[88] For there is neither reason nor authority that the command of a motionless highwayman "Stand and Deliver" would not

80. *Gambriell v. Caparelli* (1974) 54 D.L.R. (3d) 661 at 664.
81. *R. v. Hamilton* (1891) 12 L.R. (N.S.W.) 111 at 114.
82. Unless, perhaps, the victim's peculiar sensitivity was known to the defendant: cf. *Bunyan v. Jordan* (1937) 57 C.L.R. 1: see below, p. 33.
83. *Brady v. Schatzel* [1911] Q.S.R. 206 at 208. Parke B.'s stress on "fear" in *R. v. St George* (1840) 9 C. & P. 483; 173 E.R. 921 (see also *R. v. MacNamara* [1954] V.L.R. 137) must be understood as referring merely to apprehension of imminent contact.
84. Note the definition of assault in the Criminal Codes of Qld (s. 245) and W.A. (s. 222): "A person who, by any bodily act or gesture, attempts or threatens to apply force of any kind to the person of another without his consent, under such circumstances that the person making the attempt or threat has *actually or apparently* a present ability to effect his purpose." Cf. *Criminal Code* (Tas.) s. 182.
85. *Stephens v. Myers* (1830) 4 C. & P. 349; 172 E.R. 735 (defendant intercepted at last moment).
86. *Brady v. Schatzel* [1911] Q.S.R. 206; *McClelland v. Symons* [1951] V.L.R. 157 at 163-164.
87. E.g. the definition cited in note 84 (above) and the explicit provision in the *Criminal Code* (Tas.) s. 182(2) that words alone cannot constitute an assault.
88. Alarming words, not threatening immediate physical aggression, may, however, be actionable for the discrete tort of intentional infliction of emotional distress: see below, p. 31. See Handford, *Threatening or Insulting Words*, 54 Can. B. Rev. 563 (1976).

qualify.[89] Words may also give colour to an act that might otherwise be found to be inoffensive, as where a man follows up an immoral suggestion to a woman by menacingly advancing towards her.[90] Conversely, they may unmake an assault by dispelling the impression of imminent danger, as when the defendant laid his hand on his sword but remarked "If it were not assize-time, I would not take such language from you".[91]

Battery and assault are crimes as well as torts.[92] Civil proceedings and criminal prosecutions are ordinarily cumulative, but some Australian legislation[93] has followed the English example[94] of enacting that summary proceedings before a magistrate for assault, whether they result in a conviction or acquittal, shall be a bar to further civil proceedings for the same cause.[95] But most of these States also empower magistrates upon conviction to direct that a sum be paid to the person aggrieved by way of compensation for the injury or loss.[96]

4. FALSE IMPRISONMENT

The action for false imprisonment protects the interest in freedom from physical restraint and coercion[97] against the wrong of intentionally and without lawful justification subjecting another to a total restraint of movement by either actively causing his confinement or preventing him from exercising his privilege of leaving the place in which he is. As its name seems to imply, the action was probably at first designed to furnish redress against wrongful[98] incarceration in the colloquial sense, but has long outgrown these primitive beginnings.[99] It is now regarded as a sufficient deprivation of freedom if the driver of a car proceeds at such a speed as to

89. See *Barton v. Armstrong* [1969] 2 N.S.W.R. 451 at 455 (even threats over telephone).
90. *Fogden v. Wade* [1945] N.Z.L.R. 724.
91. *Turberville v. Savage* (1669) 1 Mod. 3; 86 E.R. 684. If the threat is immediate ("I will wring your neck unless you get out of here" (*Read v. Coker* (1853) 13 C.B. 850; 138 E.R. 1437); *Police v. Greaves* [1964] N.Z.L.R. 295 (C.A.)), it is not dispelled by being conditional, if the offered alternative is obedience to a command which he is not privileged to enforce by the threatened action (cf. *Rest. 2d* §30): it is therefore as actionable to threaten "Your money or your life" as "*My* money or your life".
92. Still, the standard of proof in civil proceedings is only the civil standard of probability, not the criminal standard of proof beyond all reasonable doubt: see *Rejfek v. McElroy* (1965) 112 C.L.R. 517; *McClelland v. Symons* [1951] V.L.R. 157.
93. *Crimes Act* 1900 (N.S.W.) s. 49; *Criminal Code* 1899 (Qld) s. 345; *Criminal Law Consolidation Act* 1935 (S.A.) s. 46. Mostly repealed in Canada: 3 C.C.L.T. 153, 366 (1977-1978).
94. *Offences against the Person Act* 1861 s. 45.
95. But not against his employer or other joint tortfeasor: *Dyer v. Munday* [1895] 1 Q.B. 742; *Olma v. Zaia* [1958] S.R. (N.S.W.) 299.
96. N.S.W. (s. 554: not exceeding $600; s. 437: $4,000 (any court after conviction for any crime)); S.A. ("as shall appear just"); Tas. (up to $1,000 for *any* crime, on application by prosecutor and with written consent of the victim. Judgment either way becomes res judicata: *Criminal Code* s. 425A); cf. *Police Offences Amendment Act (No. 2)* 1952 (N.Z.) s. 6 (fine payable to victim, but not a bar to civil claim). Also see below, pp. 35-38.
97. Herbert Spencer's "freedom of motion and locomotion".
98. False is to be understood in the sense of wrongful.
99. Mere restraint in a public street was held to constitute imprisonment as early as 1348. The action is not available for wrongful treatment of prisoners: *R. v. Deputy Governor of Parkhurst Prison, ex p. Hague* [1992] 1 A.C. 58.

prevent a passenger from alighting,[100] if a person is cast adrift in a boat,[101] or submission to the control of another is procured by threat of force or assertion of legal authority, as when a store detective or (even more) a policeman without actually laying hands on the plaintiff or formally arresting him gives him to understand that he must submit or else be compelled.[102]

The retraint must, of course, occur against the plaintiff's will, so that voluntary compliance with a police request to come along and clear himself does not necessarily amount to imprisonment.[103] On the other hand, excessive zeal or brusqueness entails a risk that obedience by the plaintiff in order to avoid public humiliation will be treated as an involuntary submission to an implied threat of force.[104] For appealing as may be the plight of stores and supermarkets in wishing to deal more effectively with the increasing menace of shoplifting, the law has not seen fit to condone any further encroachments on the liberty of the individual beyond those well recognised situations where arrest, with or without the aid of the police, has been traditionally considered justified. Better that such losses be counted part of the cost of doing business than that they be minimised at the expense of individual freedom.

The older notion of confinement, however, has been retained in that the restraint must be total. A partial obstruction of the freedom to go whither one pleases does not constitute imprisonment, though it might support an action on the case.[105] Hence, it is not actionable as trespass to obstruct the plaintiff's passage in one direction only[106] or to prevent his leaving a confined area through a particular exit if escape by another route is feasible and known to him.[107] But the available means of escape must be reasonable without risk of injury or serious inconvenience, like jumping into the water to escape from a ship.[108]

Although false imprisonment is a species of trespass, it need not involve the use of actual force or direct physical contact. Provided there is a constraint upon a person's will,[109] so great as to induce him to submit, there may be an arrest without imposition of hands. Thus, for this species

100. *Burton v. Davies* [1953] Q.S.R. 26.
101. *R. v. Macquarie* (1875) 13 S.C.R. (N.S.W.) 264.
102. *Watson v. Marshall* (1971) 124 C.L.R. 621; *Symes v. Mahon* [1922] S.A.S.R. 447. A fortiori, if a man is shown a warrant and yields to the implied threat that force will be used if he does not comply: *Grainger v. Hill* (1838) 4 Bing. N.C. 212; 132 E.R. 769.
103. *Alderson v. Booth* [1969] 2 Q.B. 216. Likewise, a summons by telephone to call at the police: *Ferguson v. Jensen* (1920) 53 D.L.R. 616.
104. *Myer Stores v. Soo* [1991] 2 V.R. 597 (aggravated damages); *Chaytor v. London Assoc.* (1961) 30 D.L.R. (2d) 527.
105. *Bird v. Jones* (1845) 7 Q.B. 742 at 752; 115 E.R. 668; *Williams v. Hursey* (1959) 103 C.L.R. 30 at 78. Such action, however, would require proof of actual damage, whereas false imprisonment being trespass is actionable per se.
106. *Bird v. Jones* (1845) 7 Q.B. 742; 115 E.R. 668.
107. *Balmain New Ferry Co. v. Robertson* (1906) 4 C.L.R. 379 at 387.
108. *R. v. Macquarie* (1875) 13 S.C.R. (N.S.W.) 264; *Rest. 2d* §36, comment *a.* But note *Wright v. Wilson* (1699) 1 Ld Raym. 739; 91 E.R. 1394 (defendant not liable although means of escape would involve trespass on another's land).
109. The threat may be against the plaintiff himself or against some other person or even valuable property: *R. v. Garrett* (1988) 50 S.A.S.R. 392 (F.C.).

of trespass, words (such as "I arrest you") are sufficient.[110] But though in this respect the emphasis seems to be rather upon the impression created in the victim's mind, resembling the apprehension of contact in assault, the contrary view has prevailed that one need not be conscious of the restraint at the time:[111] "a person can be imprisoned while he is asleep, while he is unconscious or while he is a lunatic. So a man might in fact be imprisoned by having the key of a door turned against him so that he is imprisoned in a room in fact although he does not know that the key has been turned."[112] This seems to be the sounder view because his humiliation is not lessened by only hearing about it afterwards or others having observed his predicament. False imprisonment trenches not only on a person's liberty but also on his dignity and reputation, and this is reflected in the calculation of damages.[113]

Usually the restraint upon the plaintiff is imposed by positive action, but it may equally well consist in breach of a duty to release him from confinement, as by failing to discharge a prisoner at the termination of his sentence.[114] Ordinarily, no doubt, an occupier of premises need not exert himself in order to enable others to leave; but if I have induced someone to put himself in a place which it is impossible for him to leave without my assistance, by words or other conduct which gives him reason to believe that I will give it when it is needed, my refusal to do so will constitute imprisonment.[115] In such cases, his right to claim release is usually determined, in the absence of unforeseen circumstances, by the contract or licence under which he submitted to the restriction upon his liberty, and a refusal to free him at some other time or in some other way than that contemplated is not actionable. Thus, a worker who descends a mine shaft for the purpose of working a shift cannot, after refusing to undertake the task assigned to him, claim the right to be hauled to the surface before the normal time;[116] a factory worker who enters with notice that there is no exit during working hours cannot complain if he is not allowed to depart earlier;[117] and a train passenger is not entitled, merely because the train has been stopped by signal, to call for the compartment doors to be opened to let him out before arrival at his destination.[118] In *Balmain New Ferry Co. v. Robertson*[119] the plaintiff entered the company's wharf at Sydney, intending to cross the harbour to Balmain. Near the turnstiles was posted

110. *Greenwood v. Ryan* (1846) 1 Legge 275 at 278. Aliter, if the plaintiff does not submit, because "mere words will not constitute an arrest" (*Russen v. Lucas* (1824) 1 C. & P. 153; 171 E.R. 1147).
111. *Murray v. Ministry of Defence* [1988] 1 W.L.R. 692; *Rest. 2d* §42 compromised ("unless the person physically restrained knows of the confinement or is harmed by it").
112. *Meering v. Graham-White Aviation Co.* (1919) 122 L.T. 44 at 53 per Atkin L.J.
113. *Walter v. Alltools Ltd* (1944) 171 L.T. 371; *Hook v. Cunard S.S. Co.* [1953] 1 W.L.R. 682. Apart from such "aggravated" damages (e.g. $2,000 in *McIntosh v. Webster* (1980) 30 A.C.T.R. 19), "exemplary" damages may also be awarded: e.g. *Bahner v. Marwest Hotel* (1969) 6 D.L.R. (3d) 322.
114. *Withers v. Henley* (1614) Cro. Jac. 379; 79 E.R. 324; and see *Morriss v. Winter* [1930] 1 K.B. 243.
115. *Rest. 2d* §45. Likewise, having unintentionally confined another, I fall under a duty after discovering his plight to secure his release.
116. *Herd v. Weardale Steel Co.* [1915] A.C. 67.
117. *Burns v. Johnston* [1916] 2 I.R. 444, affd [1917] 2 I.R. 137.
118. *Balmain New Ferry Co. v. Robertson* (1906) 4 C.L.R. 379 at 388-390.
119. (1906) 4 C.L.R. 379.

a notice that any person passing through in either direction would be charged a penny whether he had travelled by ferry or not. On getting inside, the plaintiff changed his mind when discovering the next steamer would not depart for 20 minutes, and sought to leave the wharf. He was, however, refused exit except on payment of a further penny, and his attempt to climb the turnstile was for a short time resisted by the defendant's servants. The High Court held that this did not constitute false imprisonment because the plaintiff was aware, and therefore bound by, the terms on which he had gained admittance. In the Privy Council,[120] Lord Loreburn in dismissing the appeal suggested that it was immaterial whether the notice had been brought to his knowledge because the notice itself was immaterial, and that the defendants were entitled to impose any reasonable condition before allowing him to pass the turnstile. As against this, however, it is well established that, in the absence of statutory authority, one cannot imprison another without due process of law in order to enforce a civil claim,[121] and it seems preferable to rest the decision on the ground that the plaintiff was bound by the condition as to exit because he had knowingly submitted to it on entering the quay.[122]

False imprisonment, a trespass, does not lie unless the defendant directly and *intentionally* caused the plaintiff's bodily restraint. If done negligently, like carelessly locking someone inside a library or freezer, the plaintiff must prove actual injury.[123]

Malicious prosecution distinguished

False imprisonment arising from an improper arrest of a suspect bears a resemblance to the tort of malicious prosecution, which consists in maliciously and without reasonable and probable cause instituting a groundless criminal prosecution.[124] The distinction between them lies in whether the restraint on the plaintiff's liberty is directly imposed by the defendant himself, acting either personally or by his agent, or whether there is interposed the exercise of an independent discretion.[125] A person who brings about an arrest by merely setting in motion the formal process of law, as by making a complaint before a justice of the peace[126] or applying for a warrant,[127] is not liable for false imprisonment, because courts of

120. [1910] A.C. 295.
121. *Balmain New Ferry Co. v. Robertson* (1906) 4 C.L.R. 379 at 388; and Amos, 44 L.Q.R. 464 (1928). Tan criticises both *Herd* and *Robertson* (44 Mod. L. Rev. 166 (1981)), contending that revocation of consent must be accommodated unless highly inconvenient.
122. This interpretation was placed on the decision by Lord Haldane in *Herd v. Weardale Steel Co.* [1915] A.C. 67 at 72. Besides, there being another reasonable exit (via the ferry), it could not be imprisonment.
123. *Rest. 2d* §35, comment *h* and illustration. Cf. *Sayers v. Harlow U.D.C.* [1958] 1 W.L.R. 623. While the insult would not be actionable, agony over prolonged loss of freedom may conceivably qualify, as it has for negligent certification into mental asylum; see Heffey, *Negligent Infliction of Imprisonment*, 14 Melb. U.L. Rev. 53 (1983). The German C.C. specifically lists liberty as a protected interest against negligence.
124. See below, ch. 27.
125. See *Myer Stores v. Soo* [1991] 2 V.R. 597. Hence the remedy for false imprisonment is trespass, for malicious prosecution an action on the case.
126. *Brown v. Chapman* (1848) 6 C.B. 365; 136 E.R. 1292.
127. *Leake v. Sutherland* (1868) 2 S.A.L.R. 158.

justice are not agents of the prosecutor and their acts are not imputable to him.[128] He is liable, if at all, only for the misuse of legal process by procuring an arrest for an improper purpose for which the appropriate remedy is an action for *malicious* prosecution. This rule provides a valuable protection against liability for mere error in the course of legal proceedings.

Hence, if the plaintiff has been wrongfully arrested without warrant and is then taken before a stipendiary who remands him in custody, the proper remedy for the initial arrest is false imprisonment, but there is no liability for the period of confinement subsequent to the remand unless it be for malicious prosecution.[129] Where the unlawful arrest has been procured with the aid of the police, the prosecutor's liability depends on whether the detention was carried out at his own direction or was the result of an independent decision by the police. Merely giving information[130] or signing the charge-sheet[131] does not expose the complainant to an action for false imprisonment, if the police act on their own initiative in making an arrest. On the other hand, if he does not content himself with proffering information, but actually directs the officer to make an arrest, he thereby makes the constable his ministerial agent and incurs responsibility as if it were his own act.[132] Although these principles are well understood, their application to particular fact situations often gives rise to difficulty, and some of the decisions are not easy to reconcile.[133] The balance between safeguarding the liberty of the individual and the competing policy of not discouraging complaints of crime is a delicate one which is easily tilted by giving an extended scope to the action for false imprisonment. Nevertheless, the courts have not consistently heeded the admonition of Pollock C.B. that "in the absence of mala fides we ought not to be too critical in our examination of the facts to see if something is not done without which the charge against the suspected person would not have been proceeded with".[134]

5. EMOTIONAL DISTRESS

Although the action for assault gave early recognition to the claim for protection against emotional injury, it remained rooted to the idea that the defendant must have committed an act in the nature of an attempted battery, and was not extended beyond threats intended to arouse apprehension of imminent physical contact. Not until modern times did the courts take the further step of interceding against other forms of reprehensible conduct inducing severe emotional distress, words no less than actual physical aggression.

128. This is so even though the court exceeds its authority: see above, nn. 126, 127.
129. *Diamond v. Minter* [1941] 1 K.B. 656 at 663.
130. *Grinham v. Willey* (1859) 4 H. & N. 496; 157 E.R. 934; *Ryan v. Simpson* (1872) 6 S.A.L.R. 38.
131. *Sewell v. National Telephone* [1907] 1 K.B. 557; but contrast *Clubb v. Wimpey & Co.* [1936] 1 All E.R. 69.
132. *Dickenson v. Waters* (1931) 31 S.R. (N.S.W.) 593.
133. The question is one for the jury, and particularly N.S.W. appellate courts used to show great reluctance to set aside verdicts for the plaintiff: see *Dickenson v. Waters* above.
134. *Grinham v. Willey* (1859) 4 H. & N. 496 at 499; 157 E.R. 934 at 935.

In 1896, Wright J. in *Wilkinson v. Downton*[135] first laid down the principle that if a person wilfully does an act "calculated" to cause harm to another and thereby infringe his legal right to personal safety, and in consequence causes physical harm including mental distress, a cause of action arises in the absence of lawful justification. This pronouncement occurred long before liability for *negligent* infliction of mental distress was permitted at all, let alone on conditions of parity with external injury.[136] The greater readiness to permit recovery in the present circumstances must be attributed not so much to the availability of more satisfactory proof of the injury and of its causal connection as to the absence of a legitimate competing interest on the part of the defendant. Liability for mere negligence raises concern over unduly burdening legitimate human activity, but intended harm is clearly anti-social and warrants reproof.

Cases will be rare where nervous shock involving physical injury was fully intended. More frequently, the defendant's aim would have been merely to frighten, terrify or alarm his victim. But this is quite sufficient, provided his conduct was of a kind reasonably capable of terrifying a normal person, or was known or ought to have been known to the defendant to be likely to terrify the plaintiff for reasons special to him.[137] Such conduct could be described as reckless.[138] On this basis, recovery was allowed in *Wilkinson v. Downton*[139] where a practical joker falsely informed a woman that her husband had been severely injured in an accident; also where private detectives, masquerading as military policemen, addressed pernicious threats to a foreigner in war-time Britain, accusing her of association with spies in order to frighten her into handing over certain letters.[140] In the former case it was said: "It is difficult to imagine that such a statement, made suddenly and with apparent seriousness, could fail to produce grave effects under the circumstances upon any but an exceptionally indifferent person, and therefore an intention to produce that effect must be imputed, and it is no answer in law to say that more harm was done than was anticipated, for that is commonly the case with all wrongs."[141] Harassing or terrorising debtors or tenants ("Rachmanism") could meet this test.[142]

This stringent approach, often expressed in the aphorism that a person is presumed to intend the natural consequences of his act, reflects the less exacting standard applied (at least in practice) to issues of causation against intentional wrongdoers. Here the strong moral disapproval of the

135. [1897] 2 Q.B. 57. See Handford, 16 U.W.A.L. Rev. 31 (1985); Trindade, 6 Oxf. J. Leg. Stud. 219 (1986).
136. See below, pp. 159ff.
137. *Bunyan v. Jordan* (1936) 36 S.R. (N.S.W.) 350 at 353; *Timmermans v. Buelow* (1984) 38 C.C.L.T. 136.
138. *Co-op. v. Saindon* [1976] 1 S.C.R. 735 at 738 per Laskin C.J. Reckless = consciously indifferent to obvious risks. However, originally "calculated" may well have been a synonym for "intended" rather than "tended". Motive is clearly immaterial: *Bunyan v. Jordan* (1937) 57 C.L.R. 1 (mere exhibitionism). *Rest. 2d* §46 postulates recklessness.
139. [1897] 2 Q.B. 57.
140. *Janvier v. Sweeney* [1919] 2 K.B. 316.
141. [1897] 2 Q.B. 57 at 59.
142. But statutes like the *Administration of Justice Act* 1970 (Eng.) s. 40 ("calculated to subject . . . alarm, distress or humiliation"); *Protection from Eviction Act* 1977 (Eng.) s. 1 do not create a civil remedy: *McCall v. Abelesz* [1976] Q.B. 585 at 594. Cf. *Drane v. Evangelou* [1978] 2 All E.R. 437 (exemplary damages for trespass).

defendant's anti-social conduct dispenses with the safeguards considered necessary for hedging the liability of less reprehensible misconduct, like mere carelessness.[143]

Sometimes the aggressor's act is directed at one person but another suffers the shock, as when the defendant shoots down a man in his wife's presence. "Calculated" to cause harm has not been narrowly interpreted here either. Seemingly, that shock to the plaintiff was foreseeable is at least as sufficient here as when the defendant was merely negligent. Indeed, the range of foreseeability might well be larger in comparison, both because an intentional aggressor would necessarily have directed his mind to his act and because he deserves less leniency. At any rate, persons closely connected with the victim or witnessing the attack are entitled to redress.[144]

Wilkinson v. Downton pioneered liability not only for nervous shock but also for speech. Liability for negligent misrepresentation inducing reliance had just been rejected,[145] and liability for merely negligent words causing shock had to wait long for future acceptance.[146] The new principle has been applied to acts no less than words calculated to cause shock or other physical harm, such for example as physical attack,[147] firing a gun,[148] or committing suicide.[149]

Several stringently enforced safeguards have been designed to discourage spurious claims and set a limit beyond which the law is not at present prepared to intercede against uncivilised conduct. "Liability cannot be extended to every trivial indignity. There is no occasion to intervene with balm for wounded feelings in every case where a flood of billingsgate is loosened in an argument over a back fence. . . . There is liability [only] for conduct exceeding all bounds usually tolerated by society, of a nature which is especially calculated to cause and does cause mental damage of a very serious kind."[150] Two control devices in particular deserve attention. In the first place, there must be proof that the alleged misconduct was reasonably likely to cause terror in a normal person, unless indeed the defendant was actually aware of his victim's peculiar susceptibility to emotional shock. Australian courts, especially, have postulated a high degree of robustness in the average citizen's reaction to the vicissitudes of life, and have consistently refused "to expose all forms of human behaviour to the arbitrary and unfettered discretion of a jury, so long as some person is ready to swear that the behaviour caused him injurious fright".[151] By way of example, the view has been taken that firing a revolver, after a threat

143. See Malone, *Ruminations on Cause-in-Fact*, 9 Stan. L. Rev. 60 (1956); Note, 14 Stan. L. Rev. 362 (1962).
144. *Battista v. Cooper* (1976) 14 S.A.S.R. 225; *Purdy v. Woznesensky* [1937] 2 W.W.R. 116; *Bielitski v. Obadiak* (1922) 65 D.L.R. 627 (spread rumour that son hanged himself); cf. *Fagan v. Crimes Compensation Tribunal* (1982) 150 C.L.R. 666 at 681.
145. See below, p. 633.
146. See below, p. 173. Most probably, the claim in *Wilkinson* would today succeed on that basis.
147. *Bunyan v. Jordan* (1937) 57 C.L.R. 1.
148. *Battista v. Cooper* (1976) 14 S.A.S.R. 225 (murder of husband).
149. *A. v. B.'s Trustees* (1906) 13 S.L.T. 830; *Blakeley v. Shortal's E.* 20 N.W. 2d 28 (Iowa 1945).
150. *Prosser & Keeton* 59-60. *Rest 2d* §46: "extreme and outrageous conduct".
151. *Bunyan v. Jordan* (1936) 36 S.R. (N.S.W.) 350 at 355.

to shoot somebody, could not be regarded as likely to have serious effect on a normal young female who heard the explosion.[152]

A second safeguard against extravagant claims is that the plaintiff's emotional distress must have been accompanied by objective and substantially harmful physical or psychopathological consequences, such as actual illness. Mere anguish or fright will not do. This means, in effect, that our courts, while at last admitting that injury to mental health is capable of causing recognisable physical injury, are not yet prepared to protect emotional tranquility as such, except in the anomalous case of assault. In the United States, the view is gaining ground that the enormity of the outrage itself may sometimes carry conviction that there has in fact been a severe emotional shock, neither feigned nor trivial, so as to dispense with proof of physical injury as a guarantee of the genuineness of the plaintiff's claim.[153]

Other intentional injuries

The principle enunicated in *Wilkinson v. Downton* has implications well beyond its immediate relevance to nervous shock. Its wider significance lies in the fact that it finally committed our law to the comprehensive proposition that, in the absence of a privilege, all intentional infliction of *bodily* harm is actionable regardless of the means employed to procure it, be it by direct physical aggression, injurious words or by setting in motion a force which directly or indirectly accomplishes the desired result. It thus offers both a unifying principle enveloping the whole area of liability for intentional physical injury and supplements the conventional trespass wrongs of assault, battery and false imprisonment.

A few random examples must suffice to illustrate its scope. Suppose a defendant, falsely and with intent to harm, shouts "Fire!" to the sufferer of a heart disease; removes essential medicines from the victim of an incapacitating illness; blocks a road for the purpose of delaying a patient on his way to hospital; or sets out for him poisoned drink[154] or adulterated food. In all these instances, one or other of the essential ingredients of trespass may be lacking, but liability for the resulting injury will ensue because it had been intentionally procured.

But this unifying principle never extended to other than physical injury; unlike the United States, we shrank from a "prima facie" tort encompassing economic loss because of the difficulty of developing a corresponding theory of justification.[155] Thus confined to physical injury, is there any point in distinguishing intentional from negligent torts, seeing that in the above cited instances liability could have been based on fault, embracing both negligent and intentional conduct?[156]

152. *Bunyan v. Jordan* (1937) 57 C.L.R. 1, affg 36 S.R. (N.S.W.) 350. See also *Chester v. Waverley Corp.* (1939) 62 C.L.R. 1. Contrast *Stevenson v. Basham* [1922] N.Z.L.R. 225 where fright and miscarriage were treated as a not abnormal consequence of a landlord's threat to "burn the house down" if the plaintiff did not leave by next morning.
153. Prosser, *Insult and Outrage*, 44 Cal. L. Rev. 40 (1956). See now *Rest 2d* §46. Cf. Handford, *Threatening or Insulting Words*, 54 Can. B. Rev. 563 (1976).
154. As in *Smith v. Selwyn* [1914] 3 K.B. 98 (seduction after administering drug in brandy).
155. See below, p. 699.
156. Thus Atiyah, 7 Oxf. J. Leg. Stud. at 284.

The category of intentional torts is admittedly a modern generalisation[157] but, stemming from the old forms of trespass, they retain certain characteristics. The principal one is their prima facie liability, that is, the burden of proving any one of the recognised defences is on the defendant. Other features purport to further enhance the deterrent effect of liability: (1) contributory negligence is not a defence reducing damages;[158] (2) there is authority for extending liability to unintended consequences even if not foreseeable;[159] (3) in most jurisdictions exemplary or punitive damages may be awarded;[160] and (4) insurance against liability for intended harm is not available.[161]

6. VICTIMS OF CRIME

Intentional torts to the person are, as a rule, also crimes. Primitive systems of law are apt to distinguish less clearly than we do between criminal and civil process, with punishment often taking the form of a money payment to the victim or his family.[162] However, in later legal development, punishments (even fines) came to be recognised as a debt solely due to society, and claims to compensation by the victim are relegated to independent civil proceedings.[163] Restitution of property is sometimes ordered by criminal courts, but its purpose is not so much to compensate the victim as to promote the offender's rehabilitation.[164] Also, unlike in many civil law countries, the victim could not join a civil claim to the criminal prosecution, though increasingly convicts may be ordered, as part of the criminal sanction, to compensate him for personal injuries or loss.[165] An additional, but now obsolete, obstacle used to be the rule that civil proceedings were suspended until a *felony* had first been prosecuted.[166]

157. Recall that fault was not an original ingredient of trespass, and that trespass to the person came to be identified with intentional injury only in modern law: see above, p. 17.
158. See below, p. 281.
159. See below, p. 40.
160. See below, p. 241.
161. Coverage is either excluded (not an "accident" or "injury intentionally caused") or would be against public policy: *Gray v. Barr* [1971] 2 Q.B. 554; *Co-op. v. Saindon* [1976] 1 S.C.R. 735. This misses the mark by hurting victims more than criminals: Fleming, 34 Mod. L. Rev. 176 (1971).
162. E.g. the *wer* and *bot* compositions of Anglo-Saxon law: Pollock & Maitland, *History of English Law* (1968) vol. 1, 47-48.
163. So strict was the segregation that criminal conviction, far from making the issue of guilt res judicata, was not even admissible in evidence: *Hollington v. Hewthorn* [1943] 1 K.B. 587; contra: *Jorgensen v. News Media* [1969] N.Z.L.R. 961 (C.A.). This rule has lately been abrogated in many jurisdictions: *Evidence Act* of N.S.W. (s. 23); Qld (s. 79(3)), S.A. (s. 34a), Tas. (s. 76); *Civil Evidence Act* 1968 (Eng.) s. 11. Cf. *Hunter v. Police* [1980] Q.B. 283 (issue estoppel?).
164. E.g. *Crimes Act* 1958 (Vic.) s. 546.
165. Some modern statutes have enlarged judicial power to award compensation e.g. *Criminal Justice Act* 1988 (Eng.), Pt VI (not applicable to motor accidents); *Victims Compensation Act* 1987 (N.S.W.); *Invasion of Privacy Act* (Qld) s. 48A(8); *Criminal Justice Act* 1985 (N.Z.) s. 28. Comparative: Schafer, *Restitution to Victims of Crime* (1960); Stoll, XI Int. Encycl. Comp. L. ch. 8 §49-62; Jolowicz, ibid. ch. 13 §5-40; Scott, *Victims Offenders and Restitution*, 56 A.L.J. 156 (1982).
166. This rule, originally meant to ensure the Crown's long obsolete right to forfeit a felon's chattels and to encourage prosecution, has been superseded by the court's discretion to

In any event, criminal defendants are usually without means,[167] and only in recent years has there been any sentiment for the state to undertake financial provision for their victims.[168] Such schemes for the compensation of victims of crime have remained essentially humanitarian in motive and disclaimed any responsibility, moral or legal, on the part of the state for the occurrence of the crime or for failing to prevent it.[169] Hence the benefits are mostly expressed to be ex gratia rather than as of right. The popular acclaim for the enactment of these schemes must be ascribed to politicisation of the issue of criminal violence rather than to any more policy-oriented justification for conferring preferential treatment to this class of accident victims.[170]

The various schemes differ both in structure and scope.[171] In Britain,[172] New South Wales, Victoria, Western Australia and the Northern Territory[173] claims are made to a compensation board or tribunal, whose decisions are virtually final. The other model[174] built on an existing provision empowering a court to order a convicted offender to pay a sum, as compensation to a victim sustaining loss or injury by reason of a felony or misdemeanour. Upon such an order being made, the victim may now apply and receive out of Consolidated Revenue the difference between the amount so awarded and any sums he received or is entitled to receive from other sources. The advantage of this procedure is that the criminal court will be already fully apprised of the facts of the case, but this is overshadowed by the long time lag before any assistance is received. This delay, moreover, contrasts most unfavourably and inexcusably with the comparatively prompt processing of direct applications for grants in cases where the crime remains unsolved.

166. *Continued*
stay where civil proceedings would interfere with a fair criminal trial: *Halabi v. Westpac* (1989) 17 N.S.W.L.R. 26 (C.A.); *Supreme Court Act* 1958 (Vic.) s. 63B; *Criminal Code Act* 1924 (Tas.) s. 9; *Crimes Act* 1908 (N.Z.) s. 405; *Criminal Law Act* 1967 (Eng.) s. 1; *Criminal Code* (Can.) 2.13. U.S.: *Prosser & Keeton* 8.

167. A rare case was *W. v. Meah* [1986] 1 All E.R. 935 where victim recovered £10,250 from rapist after award of £3,600 from Crim. Inj. Bd. Also *Stubbins v. Webb* [1991] 3 W.L.R. 383 (sexual abuse); *B. v. B.* (1991) 7 C.C.L.T. (2d) 105 (incest).

168. Inspired by Margery Fry, the penal reform crusader, in *The Observer*, 7 July 1957.

169. Cf. below, p. 158 (no duty of police protection even for threatened victim). Besides, as an argument for legislation, some responsibility can also be imputed to the state for impairing the efficacy of civil redress by incarcerating him and thus depriving him of the means for making restitution. The case for and against special benefits is succinctly put in Note, 33 U. Chi. L. Rev. 531 (1966).

170. Miers, *Responses to Victimisation* (1978) ch. 2. The N.Z. scheme, pioneer in the field (1963), was absorbed in 1974 in the comprehensive Accident Compensation scheme: see below, p. 405.

171. Burns, *Criminal Injuries Compensation* (1980); Chapell, *Providing for the Victims of Crime: Political Placebos or Progressive Programs?* 4 Adel. L. Rev. 294 (1972). Comparative: Miller, 20 C.I.L.S.A. 47 (1987).

172. *Criminal Justice Act* 1988, continuing a more informal scheme since 1964. See Miers, *Compensation for Criminal Injuries* (1990); Greer, *Criminal Injuries Compensation* (1991).

173. *Victims Compensation Act* 1987 (N.S.W.); *Criminal Injuries Compensation Act* 1983 (Vic.); *Criminal Injuries Compensation Act* 1982 (W.A.); *Crimes (Victims Assistance) Act* 1989 (N.T.).

174. The *Criminal Injuries Compensation Act* of S.A. (now 1977-1978), W.A. (1982), Tas. (1976), A.C.T. (1983); also the *Criminal Code Amendment Act* 1968 (Qld).

Is compensation limited to only certain crimes and injuries? Victoria originally went no farther than to draw within the scope of workers' compensation persons who had suffered injury in the course of assisting the police or crime prevention, a category deserving commendation for their public spirit in addition to sympathy for their injuries.[175] The British scheme covers only victims of violent crimes,[176] but all current Australian schemes now cover a broader range of crime victims, viz. anyone suffering "physical or mental injury, including pregnancy, mental or nervous shock" as a result of "any offence". Not only the immediate victim of the crime but also relatives, like children of a murdered mother, qualify even if not eyewitnesses, the test being purely causal and independent of tort notions of foreseeability.[177] Property offences are excluded, most probably because insurance is widely held to protect household belongings against theft.[178]

There is considerable diversity in the nature and amount of compensation. Awards under the British scheme mirror essentially common law damages: they may include expenses, loss of earnings and even pain and suffering, but nothing of any exemplary or punitive nature.[179] The Australian statutes impose varying maxima, ranging from $2,000 to $50,000 (N.S.W.); however, a consensus has emerged that the award is essentially compensatory and that the statutory limit represents a ceiling only rather than the top of a graduated scale.[180] In contrast to workers' compensation and most other compensation schemes, pain and suffering is usually included, and for good reason.[181] But as a rule, any contributory behaviour by the victim or his being a member of the offender's household may either reduce or preclude an award.[182] These benefits, modest to paltry, combine with the bureaucratic machinery and lack of popular awareness to prevent most of the Australian schemes from making more than a token contribution to the financial needs of crime victims. In effectiveness, they bear no comparison with the funds for compensating

175. *Police Assistance Compensation Act* 1968 (Vic.). Ontario had a somewhat similar beginning, since 1971 overtaken by a much more ambitious scheme.

176. Defined in s. 109 of *Criminal Justice Act* 1988.

177. *Fagan v. Crimes Compensation Tribunal* (1982) 150 C.L.R. 666.

178. A singular exception is the notorious Irish legislation which compensates for malicious property damage (originally perpetrated by rebellious peasantry). See Miers, *Paying for Malicious Injury Claims*, 5 Ir. Jur. 50 (1970). A forerunner, long since abolished in Britain but still surviving here and there in the U.S.A., is the local liability for riot damage, intended to encourage timely preventative measures (see 68 Col. L. Rev. 57 (1968)).

179. Earnings exceeding twice the industrial average are excluded. In 1984-1985 some 15,000 awards cost £35 mill. A suggested tariff for non-pecuniary injuries: [1982] 3 C.L. 39a. See Atiyah, *Accidents* ch. 13.

180. See Westling, *Some Aspects of the Judicial Determination of Compensation Payable to Victims of Crime*, 48 A.L.J. 428 (1974).

181. Burns, *Recovery for Pain and Suffering under Criminal Injuries Compensation*, 29 U.N.B. L.J. 47 (1980) criticises the exclusion under several Canadian and most American schemes.

182. In England and Victoria the last-mentioned category is entirely disqualified; elsewhere the court seems to have a discretion merely to reduce the award (*Re Poore* (1973) 6 S.A.S.R. 308 at 311, 313). In *Re Hondros* [1973] W.A.R. 1 an adulterer caught in flagrante delicto recovered nothing. Police, who used to account for about 20% of beneficiaries in the U.K., are now virtually disqualified.

victims of uninsured motorists, no doubt because the cost must here be borne by general revenue instead of being conveniently passed on to the motoring public.

The compensation schemes do not replace tort liability.[183] But damages, if worth pursuing at all, are reduced by the award.[184]

183. Though this has found a receptive ear where the defendant is not the criminal but someone else responsible for his acts: *Lamb v. Camden L.B.C.* [1981] Q.B. 625 at 636 per Lord Denning; and see *Leeds C.C. v. W. Yorkshire* [1983] 1 A.C. 29 at 40.
184. *Moignard v. Marriott* [1977] W.A.R. 83. Most statutes entitle the state to reimbursement from the offender.

3

INTENTIONAL INVASION OF LAND

1. TRESPASS

From earliest times the common law protected the possessory rights of landlords against unauthorised entry by an action of trespass, known as quare clausum fregit. The remedy was not, as its name might suggest, confined to intrusions upon enclosed lands because, says Blackstone, "every man's land is in the eye of the law inclosed and set apart from his neighbour's."[1]

In the course of its history, this action of trespass came to be used for a number of different purposes which have left their mark on its conditions of liability. In origin, trespass was a remedy for forcible breach of the King's peace, aimed against acts of intentional aggression. This early association with the maintenance of public order explains why the action lies only for interference with an occupier's *actual* possession. Its proprietary aspect became more dominant when it was later used for the purpose of settling boundary disputes, quieting title and preventing the acquisition of easements by prescriptive user.[2] These latter functions account for the rule that the plaintiff is not required to prove material loss,[3] and that a mistaken belief by the defendant that the land was his affords no excuse.[4] The temptation for the occupier to resort to violence in defence of his boundary and privacy was not lessened by the absence of pecuniary loss, while in less serious cases nominal damages were justified to vindicate his rights against adverse claims. Likewise, if mistake as to title had been admitted as a defence, trespass would have been a less suitable remedy for settling claims to disputed land.

In addition, the action of trespass also came to serve the wholly distinct function of an ordinary tort remedy for material damage sustained by an occupier as the direct result of another's activity involving an entry, whether personal or by means of animate[5] or inanimate objects. Such cases call for a different appraisal. In particular, those aspects of strict liability which are meaningful in relation to its earlier-mentioned functions are here opposed by the modern policy of confining liability to intended and negligent harm.

Basis of liability

The old strict liability associated with the early action of trespass is therefore no longer a safe guide for allocating responsibility in modern law.

1. 3 Comm. 209; *Wuta-Ofei v. Danquah* [1961] 1 W.L.R. 1238.
2. The last-mentioned function is noted in *Lemmon v. Webb* [1894] 3 Ch. 1 at 24.
3. *Ashby v. White* (1703) 2 Ld Raym. 938 at 955; 92 E.R. 126 at 137; *Embrey v. Owen* (1851) 6 Ex. 353 at 368; 155 E.R. 579 at 585.
4. *Basely v. Clarkson* (1681) 3 Lev. 37; 83 E.R. 565.
5. Cattle-trespass.

The contemporary trend, already noted in connection with trespass to the person,[6] is to deny recovery for harm caused without fault unless resulting from an ultra-hazardous activity. Hence, consideration of the defendant's conduct—intentional, negligent or faultless—can no longer be safely avoided by simply tagging the problem as trespass.

Intentional invasions are actionable whether resulting in harm or not. Neither the intruder's motive is material nor the fact that his entry actually benefited the occupier.[7] The requisite intent is present if the defendant desires to make an entry, although unaware that he is thereby interfering with another's rights. Thus, it makes no difference whether the intruder knows his entry to be unauthorised or honestly and reasonably believes the land to be his. It may, however, affect the quantum of damages. A deliberate trespass is no trifling matter,[8] but in cases of mistake where no perceptible damage is done, only nominal damages are awarded, yet the verdict against the defendant is justified in order to defeat his adverse claim to the land. If, on the other hand, actual damage has occurred, as when A believing B's land to be his cuts a stand of timber or works a seam of coal, the award no more than compensates the plaintiff for the loss he has suffered as the result of the unauthorised entry.[9] Viewed realistically, therefore, trespass as a remedy against dispossession is a tort of strict liability, vindicating a proprietary interest rather than a tort obligation.[10]

Moreover, according to the traditional view, an intentional trespasser is strictly liable for all damage, "directly and immediately"[11] caused by his presence on the land, even if it resulted from conduct that would not otherwise have incurred liability; for example if he were to collide with the occupier in the dark, though without the least fault.[12] But now that trespass to land has, it seems, become a tort based on fault (intentional or negligent), should liability not also be limited to foreseeable consequences?[13] At any rate, where the trespass merely provided the occasion rather than increased the risk of the damage, a defendant was excused when his car parked without permission (and therefore trespassing) unexpectedly caught fire and did unforeseeable damage to the garage.[14]

Accidental injury

Accidental trespassory *harm*, however, must today meet the modern conditions of liability for unintended injury stemming from the competing action on the case.

6. See above, pp. 18-24.
7. *Rest. 2d* §163, comment *d*; in the *Case of Thorns* (1466) Y.B. 6 Ed IV, 7, pl. 18 the defendant was held liable for entering the plaintiff's land to retrieve cuttings accidentally dropped by him.
8. *Plenty v. Dillon* (1991) 171 C.L.R. 635 at 654.
9. *Gilchrist v. Logan* [1927] St. R. Qd 185.
10. *Cane* 28-29 (intentional being merely a synonym for voluntary).
11. This is also the discrimen between trespass and case.
12. *Wormald v. Cole* [1954] 1 Q.B. 614 at 625; *Turner v. Thorne* (1959) 21 D.L.R. (2d) 29; *Rest. 2d* §162.
13. See *The Wagon Mound (No. 2)* [1967] 1 A.C. 617, below, pp. 208ff.; Williams, *The Wagon Mound*, 77 L.Q.R. 202 at 204 (1961). Consequential damage was foreseeable in *Hogan v. Wright* [1963] Tas. S.R. 44; *Svingos v. Deacon* (1971) 2 S.A.S.R. 126.
14. *Mayfair v. Pears* [1987] 1 N.Z.L.R. 459 (C.A.). Cf. below, p. 356 (cattle-trespass).

All vestiges of the older strict liability were progressively discarded as it came to be established that claims for unintended injury, whether formulated in trespass or case, had to conform to the conditions of liability postulated by the latter form of action. Proof of negligence became essential: first, in cases of highway accidents causing damage to adjacent property (such as a car veering off the road[15] or a bull disporting himself into a china shop[16]); and eventually, as the development in the analogous cases of personal injury[17] and damage to chattels[18] bears out, in all residuary situations which would formerly have fallen within the purview of trespass to land. Strict liability is thus exorcised except where the injury resulted—not, as once upon a time, directly rather than consequentially from *whatever* the defendant happened to be doing—but from extra-hazardous activities alone, such as blasting within the principle of *Rylands v. Fletcher*.[19]

Defendant's conduct

There must be physical entry upon the possessor's territory. Mere interference with his amenities, such as emitting noxious fumes or noise, may amount to nuisance but not trespass.[20] Indeed, some forms of annoyance, however objectionable, may not be actionable torts at all, like cutting off a tenant's gas or electricity.[21] Moreover, to be actionable as trespass, the defendant's conduct must have consisted of a voluntary *and* affirmative act. If A has a seizure and falls[22] or is pushed against his will by B upon the plaintiff's land,[23] A is not liable, though B may be. Cutting down a tree so that it falls on neighbouring land is trespassory harm; failing to remove a decayed branch before it falls will at best support an action on the case, being mere non-feasance.[24] This corresponds with the traditional reluctance of the common law to demand duties of affirmative action.[25]

Trespass may be committed not only by an entry in person, but equally by propelling an object or a third person onto the plaintiff's land. Indeed, most cases of trespass involving actual damage deal with situations where there has been no personal entry but the defendant has initiated a force

15. *Mayfair v. Pears* [1987] 1 N.Z.L.R. 459 (C.A.). Cf. below, p. 354 (cattle-trespass).
16. *A.N.A. v. Phillips* [1953] S.A.S.R. 278; *Nickells v. Melbourne Corp.* (1938) 59 C.L.R. 219. This goes back to Lord Blackburn's dicta in *Fletcher v. Rylands* (1866) L.R. 1 Ex. 265 at 286 and *River Wear Comm. v. Adamson* (1877) 2 App. Cas. 743 at 767.
17. *Tillett v. Ward* (1882) 10 Q.B.D. 17.
18. See below, p. 53. But just as in the case of personal injury it remains clouded on whom the burden of proof lies: *Bell Canada v. Bannermount* (1973) 35 D.L.R. (3d) 367 (Ont. C.A.) still left it on the defendant.
19. See below, ch. 16.
20. (1868) L.R. 3 H.L. 330. See below, ch. 15. This is the view taken by *Rest. 2d* §166 and accords with the famous *Nitro-Glycerine Case* 15 Wall. 524 (1872) which had the approval of *Pollock*, 99ff. The surviving strict liability for cattle-trespass, modified only by the highway rule (see below, p. 354), is based on wholly different considerations: it originated in the requirements of a predominantly agricultural society and is based on the notion of control of a dangerous agency.
21. See below.
22. *Perera v. Vandiyar* [1953] 1 W.L.R. 672 ("no tort of eviction").
23. *Public Transport Comm. v. Perry* (1977) 137 C.L.R. 107.
24. *Smith v. Stone* (1647) Style 65; 82 E.R. 533; cf. *Braithwaite v. S. Durham Steel* [1958] 1 W.L.R. 986 (inadvertent).
25. See *Star v. Rookesby* (1711) 1 Salk. 335; 91 E.R. 295.

which directly causes rubbish, stones or other projectiles to be cast on or over another's property.[26] Here again, the old distinction between direct and indirect invasion looms large. The discharge of water may be trespass or case according to whether it is immediately poured upon or only ultimately flows onto the plaintiff's property, as by being first discharged on somebody else's land and later carried down to the plaintiff's.[27] In many American blasting cases it has been held that damage from flying rocks is trespass, but from vibration or concussion at most nuisance.[28] This proposition, which has been castigated as a marriage of legal technicality with scientific ignorance,[29] is nonetheless commendable because any encroachment of trespass on the traditional province of nuisance would lead to undesirable restrictions on user of land.[30]

Trespass may be committed not only by an initial unprivileged entry, but also by failing to leave the possesor's land after a *licence* to enter has terminated or the purpose for which the privilege was given has been accomplished. Thus a lodger or theatre patron becomes a trespasser if he misbehaves and then does not heed a request to get out.[31] Not so, however, a person lawfully in *possession* of land who omits or refuses to give it up at the termination of his interest: a lessee, for example, who holds over may be liable in an action of ejectment, but not in trespass.[32]

Authority to enter the land may have been limited to a particular purpose. Entry for a different purpose would then become trespassory, as when a neighbour entered for the purpose of stealing instead of looking after the house in the owner's absence,[33] or when TV people invaded with cameras rolling.[34] Even a subsequent abuse of privilege by one who enters under authority of law may convert that entry into a trespass ab initio, under a somewhat archaic doctrine justifiable at best as a constitutional safeguard against abuse of governmental authority.[35]

If a structure or other object is placed on another's land, not only the initial intrusion but also failure to remove it constitute an actionable wrong. There is a "continuing trespass" as long as the object remains; and on account of it both a subsequent transferee of the land may sue[36] and a purchaser of the offending chattel or structure be liable,[37] because the

26. E.g. *Rigby v. Chief Constable* [1985] 1 W.L.R. 1242 (gas canister fired by police).
27. *Nicholls v. Ely Beet Sugar Factory* [1931] 2 Ch. 84 at 86-87; *Fletcher v. Rylands* (1865) 3 H. & C. 774 at 792; 159 E.R. 737 at 744.
28. See Gregory, *Trespass to Negligence to Absolute Liability*, 37 Va. L. Rev. 359 (1951).
29. Smith, *Liability for Substantial Physical Damage to Land by Blasting*, 33 Harv. L. Rev. 542, 667 (1920); *Prosser & Keeton* 553.
30. Nuisance, unlike trespass, makes allowance for reasonable use. Again, abnormal sensitivity of the plaintiff's user of land is a defence in nuisance, but not in trespass: see below, p. 421.
31. *Wood v. Leadbitter* (1845) 13 M. & W. 838; 153 E.R. 351; *Cowell v. Rosehill Racecourse* (1937) 56 C.L.R. 605; *Duffield v. Police* [1971] N.Z.L.R. 378.
32. *Hey v. Moorehouse* (1839) 6 Bing. N.C. 52; 133 E.R. 20. Unless the landlord first regained possession: *Haniotis v. Dimitriou* [1983] 1 V.R. 498.
33. See *Barker v. R.* (1983) 153 C.L.R. 338.
34. *Lincoln Hunt v. Willesee* (1986) 4 N.S.W.L.R. 457.
35. The doctrine, now obsolete in the U.S. (*Rest. 2d* §214 (2)), was described by Lord Denning as "a by-product of the old forms of action. Now that they are buried, it can be interred with their bones." (*Chic Fashions v. Jones* [1968] 2 Q.B. 299 at 313).
36. *Hudson v. Nicholson* (1839) 5 M. & W. 437; 151 E.R. 185.
37. *Rest. 2d* §161, comment *f*; *Prosser & Keeton* 83.

wrong gives rise to actions de die in diem until the condition is abated. Likewise, if the chattel was initially placed on the land with the possessor's consent, termination of the licence creates a duty to remove it; and it seems that, according to modern authority,[38] a continuing trespass is committed by failure to do so within a reasonable time. In all these cases, the plaintiff may maintain successive actions, but, in each, damages are assessed only as accrued up to the date of the action. This solution has the advantage to the injured party that the statute of limitations does not run from the initial trespass, but entails the inconvenience of forcing him to institute repeated actions for continuing loss.[39]

The doctrine of "continuing trespass" applies only to omissions to remove something brought on the land and wrongfully left there; not where a defendant fails to restore the land to the same condition in which he found it, as where he digs a pit in his neighbour's garden and fails to fill it up. Here the plaintiff can only treat the initial entry as trespass and must content himself with one action in which damages are recoverable for both past and future loss.[40]

Plaintiff's title

The action of trespass vindicates only violations of actual possession, and is not concerned with protecting the interests of persons out of possession at the time of the intrusion. Thus, a purchaser cannot sue for a trespass occurring before title passed[41] nor a landlord during the subsistence of a lease.[42] By the same token, the mere use of land without exclusive possession is insufficient.[43] Thus, a plaintiff who had a concession from a canal company to the exclusive right of keeping pleasure-boats for hire, being a mere licence, failed against a stranger who interfered with his monopoly. On the other hand, the grantee of a legal or equitable[44] interest in land in the nature of an easement or profit à prendre, like a fishery[45] or right to cut timber,[46] can sue in trespass for direct interference[47] by strangers.

38. *Konskier v. Goodman* [1928] 1 K.B. 421; *Rest. 2d* §160; contra: Goodhart, 55 L.Q.R. at 124 (1955). The criticism ignores the analogous situation in the case of *persons* entering by licence.
39. For the court's power alternatively to sanction the wrong in futuro, subject to compensation, see below, p. 445.
40. *Clegg v. Deardon* (1848) 12 Q.B. 576; 116 E.R. 986. But if the neighbour actually falls into the pit, he may apparently sue on a trespass theory: see *Kopka v. Bell Telephone Co.* 91 A. 2d 232 (Pa. 1952).
41. *Townsview v. Sun Constructions* (1974) 56 D.L.R. (3d) 330. But for a true owner seeking possession, actual entry is not required, and the burden is on the defendant to confess and avoid: *Portland Managements v. Harte* [1977] Q.B. 306.
42. But he may recover for injury to his reversionary interest on proof of permanent injury to the land: *Rodrigues v. Ufton* (1894) 20 V.L.R. 539; *Loxton v. Waterhouse* (1891) 7 W.N. (N.S.W.) 98.
43. *Hill v. Tupper* (1863) 2 H. & C. 121; 159 E.R. 51; *Moreland Timber Co. v. Reid* [1946] V.L.R. 237 at 249-250; contra, *Vaughan v. Benalla S.* (1891) 17 V.L.R. 129 (not cited in *Reid's* case); *Nuttall v. Bracewell* (1866) L.R. 2 Ex. 1 at 11, allowing a claim for actual damage.
44. This seems to have been assumed without argument in *Mason v. Clarke* [1955] A.C. 778; contra: *Moreland Timber Co. v. Reid* [1946] V.L.R. 237.
45. *Nicholls v. Ely Beet Sugar Factory* [1931] 2 Ch. 84; *Fitzgerald v. Firbank* [1897] 2 Ch. 96.
46. See *Moreland Timber Co. v. Reid* [1946] V.L.R. 237.
47. And in nuisance for indirect invasion.

Possession of land may be in a person who has no legal title to it and is himself in wrongful occupation as regards another. A disseisor is nonetheless a possessor although, as between himself and the rightful owner, he has no *right* to possession until his adverse possession has ripened into ownership by lapse of time. But, just as legal title to land without possession does not support an action of trespass against third parties, so possession without legal title thereto is sufficient. Hence, a defendant in an action of trespass cannot set up the right of the true owner in order to justify his infringement of the plaintiff's de facto possession: he cannot plead the so-called jus tertii, that is, assert that another has a better right to possession than the plaintiff, unless he committed the entry by his authority.[48] The reason is that it is more conducive to the maintenance of order to protect de facto and even wrongful possession against disturbance by all and sundry than to deny legal aid to a disseisor merely because of the flaw in his title.

He who has a right to immediate possession is deemed, on entry, to have been in possession ever since his right to entry accrued, and may sue for any act of trespass committed since that time.[49] This fiction, known as the doctrine of *trespass by relation*, partially corrects the balance which the older law tilted so heavily in favour of actual possession to the prejudice of bare title. Thus, a disseisee has his remedy after re-entry against anyone who intruded on his land during the period of his dispossession, just as a tenant has for any trespass committed between the granting of the lease and his entry.[50]

Trespass beneath and above the surface

The interest in exclusive possession of land is not confined to the surface; it extends both below and above, but the boundaries of the claim to possession of vertical strata are not as yet precisely defined. Ordinarily, entry underneath the surface at any depth is trespass, unless possession of the surface has been severed from that of the subsoil, as by a grant of mining rights. Thus, it is actionable to tunnel into adjoining land for the purpose of exploiting a coal seam[51] or to slant-drill into a neighbouring oil zone.[52] But it is questionable whether the surface owner is protected with respect to claims over subterranean areas which he is unable to subject to his dominion. The old sophistry, that the owner of the surface is the owner

48. *Graham v. Peat* (1801) 1 East 244; 102 E.R. 95; *Nicholls v. Ely Beet Sugar Factory* [1931] 2 Ch. 84; *Mt Bischoff Tin Mining Co. v. Mt Bischoff Extended Tin Mining Co.* (1913) 15 C.L.R. 549; *Hansard v. Tame* [1957] N.Z.L.R. 542.
49. *Ocean Accident Co. v. Ilford Gas Co.* [1905] 2 K.B. 493; *Ebbels v. Rewell* [1908] V.L.R. 261; *Wynne v. Green* (1901) 1 S.R. (N.S.W.) 40.
50. In States like N.S.W. and Victoria where the doctrine of interesse termini has been abolished, it is probably no longer necessary to rely on the principle of trespass by relation in such a case, because a lease now takes effect from the commencement of the term without actual entry.
51. E.g. *Bulli Coal Mining Co. v. Osborne* [1899] A.C. 351.
52. See Note, 27 Cal. L. Rev. 192 (1939). Unauthorised drilling must be distinguished from draining a neighbouring zone with a drill kept within the lateral confines of the surface occupied by the defendant—a practice permitted in the U.S.: 5 A.L.R. 421 (1920).

of everything from zenith to nadir, is correct in its application to mining rights, but has been rarely tested with respect to claims to an area he cannot use but which may be of benefit to others. The problem arose in a Kentucky case[53] where the defendant owned land with the entrance to a cave which he developed into a tourist attraction. The cave at some point passed 350 feet below the surface of the land owned by the plaintiff, who claimed an account of receipts. This he was granted, but over a strong dissent expressing the more commendable view that the surface owner owns only those substances upon, above or under it which he can subject to his control: "No man can bring up from the depth of the earth the Stygian darkness and make it serve his purposes, unless he has the entrance to it."[54]

The extent of ownership and possession of superincumbent airspace has become a topic of considerable controversy since the advent of flying. Much play has been made of the maxim "cuius est solum ejus est utque ad coelum" ("he who owns the surface owns up to the sky"), but this "fanciful phrase"[55] of dubious ancestry[56] has never been accepted in its literal meaning of conferring unlimited rights into the infinity of space over land. The cases in which it has been invoked establish no wider proposition than that the air above the surface is subject to dominion in so far as the use of space is necessary for the proper enjoyment of the surface.[57] Thus, building restrictions apart, the owner has the right to erect structures to any height[58] and for any purpose.[59] Most of the case law has been concerned with competing claims by adjacent occupiers with respect to overhanging parts of buildings and branches of trees. Here, the weight of authority clearly favours the view that direct invasion by artificial projections, like a swinging crane,[60] advertising signs,[61] electric cables,[62] or the overlap of a wall,[63] constitutes trespass[64] actionable per se and, in suitable cases, warranting a mandatory injunction to compel removal. In contrast, protruding branches, even of artificially-planted trees, are treated as

53. *Edwards v. Sims* 24 S.W. 2d 619 (Ky 1929).
54. The judgment by Logan J. is a fine piece of literature. *Prosser & Keeton* 82 has called the majority opinion "dog-in-the-manger law". The "effective control" theory was adopted in *Boehringer v. Montalto* 254 N.Y.S. 276 (1931) (sewer commission permitted to maintain sewer 150 ft below surface).
55. *Wandsworth Bd of Works v. United Telephone Co.* (1884) 13 Q.B.D. 904 at 915 per Brett M.R.
56. Its origin is traced by Bouvé, *Private Ownership of Airspace*, 1 Air L. Rev. 232 (1930); Hackley, *Trespassers in the Sky*, 21 Minn. L. Rev. 773 (1937).
57. *Bernstein v. Skyviews* [1978] Q.B. 479; Tebbutt, 52 A.L.J. 160 (1978).
58. *Corbett v. Hill* (1870) L.R. 9 Eq. 671; *Atlantic Aviation v. N.S. Light & Power* (1965) 55 D.L.R. (2d) 554.
59. *Victoria Park Racing Co. v. Taylor* (1937) 58 C.L.R. 479.
60. *Anchor Brewhouse Developments v. Berkeley House* [1987] 2 E.G.L.R. 173 (injunction without suspension); *Graham v. Morris* [1974] Qd R. 1.
61. *Kelsen v. Imperial Tobacco* [1957] 2 Q.B. 334.
62. *Barker v. Adelaide C.* [1900] S.A.L.R. 29; *Wandsworth Bd of Works v. United Telephone Co.* (1884) 13 Q.B.D. 904; Irvine, 37 C.C.L.T. 99 (1986).
63. *Williamson v. Friend* (1901) 1 S.R. (N.S.W.) (Eq.) 23 at 27; *Lawlor v. Johnston* [1905] V.L.R. 714 (ventilation pipe). Aliter, if a fence encroaches due to action of the weather: *Mann v. Saulnier* (1959) 19 D.L.R. (2d) 130 (comment, 23 Mod. L. Rev. 188 (1960)).
64. Contra: *Pickering v. Rudd* (1815) 4 Camp. 219; 171 E.R. 70 (board): semble *Fay v. Prentice* (1845) 1 C.B. 828; 135 E.R. 769 (cornice).

consequential, not direct, encroachments for which the remedy is in nuisance,[65] requiring proof of damage or actual inconvenience except in support of the privilege to abate by cutting back the offending branch.[66]

As regards transient incursions, authority is quite inconclusive. Some support for a theory of unlimited ownership over airspace has been claimed from *Ellis v. Loftus Iron Co.*[67] where a horse on one side of a fence having bit and kicked a mare on the other, recovery was allowed without a showing of negligence on the ground that the intrusion into space over the plaintiff's land constituted trespass. But this decision affords scant guidance for momentary and harmless intrusions into airspace beyond the reach of the surface owner. More pertinent is a group of decisions dealing with the firing of guns across adjacent land. Lord Ellenborough once suggested a distinction between a shot striking the soil and firing in vacuo without touching anything: the former being trespass, while the latter was not actionable unless as nuisance.[68] But in a later case,[69] holding a defendant liable for shooting a cat perched on an adjacent shed, the court regarded all entry into airspace as trespassory, at any rate at that particular height, though admitting the difficulty of "how far the rights of a landowner ad coelum will have to be reduced to permit the free use of" aircraft.

Aircraft

Flying has become so important that it is idle to speculate whether courts might not inhibit it by an extravagant application of the ad coelum maxim. The question is rather how to adjust, with the least friction, the conflict between the competing claims of aircraft operators to reasonable scope for their activities and of landowners to unimpeded enjoyment of their property. The only modern case to have considered the problem[70] held that an owner's rights in airspace above his land were restricted to such height as was necessary for the ordinary enjoyment of the land and structures thereon, but that above that height he had no greater rights than any other members of the public. Thus he could not object to overflights even when these had the purpose, not of "innocent passage" analogous to the public's right of using the highway, but to take aerial photographs of his property. However, flights which interfere with the use and enjoyment of the land beneath, for example by polluting the air, causing excessive

65. *Lemmon v. Webb* [1894] 3 Ch. 1; [1895] A.C. 1; *Davey v. Harrow Corp.* [1958] 1 Q.B. 60; contra, *Simpson v. Weber* (1925) 41 T.L.R. 302 at 304 (Virginia creeper treated as trespass). See below, p. 416.
66. *Lemmon v. Webb* [1894] 3 Ch. 1; and see *Fencing Act* 1908 (N.Z.) s. 26A.
67. (1874) L.R. 10 C.P. 10.
68. *Pickering v. Rudd* (1815) 4 Camp. 219; 171 E.R. 70; followed in *Clifton v. Bury* (1887) 4 T.L.R. 8 where, however, the firing of bullets at 75 ft was held to be an unreasonable interference with the enjoyment of land and thus a nuisance, as in *Evans v. Finn* (1904) 4 S.R. (N.S.W.) 297. See also *Big Point Club v. Lozon* [1943] 4 D.L.R. 136.
69. *Davies v. Bennison* (1927) 22 Tas. L.R. 52. Cf. *Bridges v. Forest Protection* (1976) 72 D.L.R. (3d) 335 at 361 (aerial spray causing direct damage may be trespass).
70. *Bernstein v. Skyviews* [1978] Q.B. 479; accord: *Rest. 2d* §159(2) and the *Uniform Aeronautics Act*, adopted in over 20 States in the U.S.

noise or vibrations,[71] or harassing the occupier by persistent surveillance, may constitute actionable nuisance.[72]

Legislation occasionally reinforces this position. Following a British statute,[73] several Australian States[74] and New Zealand[75] have enacted that "no action shall lie in respect of trespass or nuisance, by reason only of the flight of an aircraft over any property at a height above the ground which, having regard to wind, weather, and all the circumstances of the case is reasonable, or the ordinary incidents of such flight, so long as the provisions of the Air Navigation Regulations are duly complied with." This statute has also been construed expansively to include flights for whatever purpose, even aerial photography.[76] It is balanced however by imposing strict liability (irrespective of fault) on the owner of aircraft for all "material loss or damage" to person or property while in flight, taking off or landing.[77] This covers sonic booms and other damaging vibrations[78] as well as aircraft crashes.

Damages and injunction

For actual damage to the land or its structures by the trespass, the plaintiff is entitled to compensation on the same principles as for negligence.[78a] Otherwise, the basic measure of damages is the use value of the land, regardless of whether and how the owner would otherwise have exploited it.[79] In this "user principle" the action reveals its primarily proprietary focus, beyond the owner's purely economic interests, besides preventing the defendant's unjust enrichment. For intrusions by police or judicial officers substantial damages are in order to vindicate the plaintiff's civil rights and society's interest in law and order.[80] For inadvertent and evanescent trespasses, only nominal damages would be appropriate; while

71. There is no Australian legislation on aircraft noise. Exposed to liability are not only aircraft operators but also the Commonwealth as owner and operator of practically all airports. But according to the prevailing view, there is no constitutional requirement to compensate on just terms (Const. s. 51(31)) for diminution in the value of adjacent land due to aircraft noise at aerodromes any more than for a prohibition or limitation on the use of such land imposed by a regulation, like reg. 92 of the *Air Navigation Regulations*. In the U.S., "taking" has been more liberally interpreted: *U.S. v. Causby* 328 U.S. 256 (1946); *Griggs v. Allegheny County* 369 U.S. 84 (1962). In Britain and N.Z. (Civil Aviation Acts of 1982 s. 77, and of 1964 s. 23) compliance with regulations confers immunity for nuisance "by reason only of the noise and vibrations caused by aircraft *on* an aerodrome" (see McNair, *Law of Air* (3rd ed. 1964) 123-125; [1968] N.Z.L.J. 372-373). This does not apply to aircraft *in flight*; also the *Airports Authority Act* 1965 (U.K.) s. 15 conferred a power to make grants towards the cost of soundproofing dwellings.
72. A case argued solely on the basis of negligence was *Nova Mink v. T.C.A.* [1951] 2 D.L.R. 241 (noise damage to mink farm).
73. *Civil Aviation Act* (U.K.) 1982 s. 76(1).
74. The Damage by Aircraft Acts: N.S.W. 1952 s. 2; W.A. 1964 s. 4; Tas. 1963 s. 3; and *Wrongs Act* 1958 (Vic.) s. 30.
75. *Civil Aviation Act* 1964 s. 23.
76. *Bernstein v. Skyviews* [1978] Q.B. 479.
77. See below, p. 331.
78. *Steel-Maitland v. B.A.* 1981 S.L.T. 110.
78a. E.g. *Hansen v. Gloucester Developments* [1992] 1 Qd R. 14 (unimproved land). See below, p. 250.
79. *Swordheath Properties v. Tabet* [1979] 1 W.L.R. 285 (C.A.).
80. *Plenty v. Dillon* (1991) 171 C.L.R. 635.

wilful and contumacious conduct may warrant aggravated damages for any affront and indignity to the plaintiff or exemplary damages to punish him.[81]

Consequential damages, if not too remote, are also recoverable, as where trespassers left a gate open, through which cows entered and damaged the plaintiff's olive trees[82] or where diseased cattle infected the plaintiff's herd.[83]

An injunction may be the most effective remedy to stop actual or merely threatened[84] intrusion. Against continuing trespass injunction will ordinarily issue as a matter of course, whether or not damages would adequately compensate for actual damage done.[85] Equally where no such damage has occurred, as in the case of a crane violating the plaintiff's airspace. But in a controversial ruling, the court suspended the injunction until the construction work had been completed, thereby in effect granting the plaintiff a compulsory licence.[86] Only in exceptional circumstances will an injunction be denied, as where the plaintiff waited until a house built in violation of a use restriction was almost completed.[87]

It should be noted that the choice between injunction and damages implicates who will set the price in case the plaintiff is prepared to negotiate. By granting an injunction the court will leave negotiation to the parties; by denying it and granting damages in lieu it will set the price itself. The latter would be economically efficient and justifiable only in order to prevent the owner from unfairly exploiting his bargaining position.[88]

2. EJECTMENT

We have seen that the action of trespass is available only to those in possession at the time of the unauthorised entry. The claim to recovery of land by persons out of, but with an immediate right to, possession is alone enforced by the action of ejectment, or action for the recovery of possession of land as it is called today. Ejectment was a form of the action of trespass, originally designed to protect the tenant for a term of years. At first, only damages could be recovered, but by the end of the 14th century it had become a remedy for the specific recovery of the term itself.[89] Because of its procedural advantages over the ancient real actions, and with the aid of elaborate fictions, it rapidly developed into an action for the trial of title to freehold as well as leasehold interests, and eventually superseded all other remedies as a means of recovering possession from occupiers with an

81. *XL Petroleum v. Caltex Oil* (1985) 155 C.L.R. 148; *Pollack v. Volpato* [1973] 1 N.S.W.L.R. 653 (C.A.).
82. *Svingos v. Deacon* (1971) 2 S.A.S.R. 126; *Hogan v. Wright* [1963] Tas. S.R. 44.
83. *Anderson v. Buckton* (1719) 1 Stra. 192; 93 E.R. 467 (cattle-trespass).
84. To avoid irreparable harm: see *Lincoln Hunt v. Willesee* (1986) 4 N.S.W.L.R. 457.
85. *Patel v. W. H. Smith* [1987] 1 W.L.R. 853 (C.A.).
86. *Woollerton v. Costain* [1970] 1 W.L.R. 411. Should not damages have been granted in lieu of injunction?
87. *Bracewell v. Appleby* [1975] Ch. 408 (instead: willing grantor/grantee price).
88. Or where "transaction costs" impede bargaining. See below; *Cane* 58-59.
89. *Holdsworth* iii 214-217.

inferior title.[90] Thus, an offspring of trespass came to serve the function of determining questions of ownership.

Title

It is incumbent on the plaintiff to establish a right to immediate possession, and he "must recover upon the strength of his own title, and not by the weakness of the defendant's".[91] All the same, the common law continued to adhere to the principle, developed in relation to the real actions, that the nature of the right asserted in ejectment is merely the plaintiff's better right to possession rather than abstract ownership or an absolute right good against the world. Thus, our modern law, like the medieval, recognises only relatively good or relatively bad rights to possession. This conclusion was not reached without some hesitation, and for a time it seems to have been thought that a plaintiff must prove possession for at least 20 years, that is, a possessory title for a period which, under the current statute of limitations, barred the right of entry of all claimants.[92] It is now settled, however, that the plaintiff need not remove every possibility of title in another person and that possession anterior to that of the defendant's for any period may be sufficient to make a prima facie case.[93]

The claimant in an action of ejectment fails if it appears that the right to possession is in some third party. In other words, the presumption that possession is prima facie evidence of title, is rebutted if either the defendant can negative the plaintiff's title by proving that it is in some third party or if it is disclosed in the plaintiff's own case that he has no right to the land.[94] To this rule, that the so-called jus tertii is a good defence, there are two exceptions: it cannot be pleaded by one who is a trespasser vis-à-vis the plaintiff, since otherwise an intruder would be in a better position in ejectment than in an action of trespass.[95] It is deemed impolitic to permit a trespasser, by the very act of wrongful entry, immediately and without acquiescence, to give himself what the law understands by possession against the person he ejects, and to drive him to produce his title.[96]

90. *Holdsworth* vii 4-23.
91. *Martin d. Tregonwell v. Strachan* (1743) 5 T.R. 107n; 101 E.R. 61 per Lee C.J.; *Roe d. Haldane v. Harvey* (1769) 4 Burr. 2484 at 2487; 98 E.R. 302 at 304 per Mansfield C.J.
92. See authorities cited by *Holdsworth* vii 62-63.
93. *Perry v. Clissold* [1907] A.C. 73; (1906) 4 C.L.R. 374; *Allen v. Roughley* (1955) 94 C.L.R. 98; *N.R.M.A. Ins. v. B. & B. Shipping Co.* (1947) 47 S.R. (N.S.W.) 273; *Oxford Meat Co. v. McDonald* (1963) 80 W.N. (N.S.W.) 681. The contrary view, espoused by *Holdsworth*, is not supported by the authorities.
94. *Doe d. Carter v. Barnard* (1849) 13 Q.B. 945; 116 E.R. 1524; *Wood v. Eisen* (1947) 48 S.R. (N.S.W.) 5 at 13. There is a dictum to the contrary in *Asher v. Whitlock* (1865) L.R. 1 Q.B. 1 at 6; but neither in that case nor in *Perry v. Clissold* [1907] A.C. 73 was, or could, jus tertii have been raised as a defence: see *N.R.M.A. Ins. v. B. & B. Shipping Co.* (1947) 47 S.R. (N.S.W.) 273 at 279 and the discussion by Wiren, 41 L.Q.R. 139 (1925); Hargreaves, 56 L.Q.R. 376; Holdsworth, 56 L.Q.R. 479 (1940) and *Holdsworth* vii 62ff.
95. *Davison v. Gent* (1857) 1 H. & N. 744; 156 E.R. 1400.
96. Where the plaintiff has desisted from attempts at reinstating himself, leaving the other in undisturbed occupation for a time, it is for the jury to decide whether the defendant has gained possession as distinguished from the mere lawless intrusion of a trespasser: *Hawdon v. Khan* (1920) 20 S.R. (N.S.W.) 703.

Secondly, one who has acquired possession through another cannot, in an action of ejectment brought by that other or anyone claiming through him, allege that the title is defective,[97] though he may show that it has since expired or been parted with.[98] A common illustration of this principle of estoppel is found in cases of landlord and tenant.[99]

Mesne profits

As long as ejectment was an action of trespass available only to lessees, a plaintiff could recover not only the land but also consequential damages. But concomitant with its extension to freeholders, damages for dispossession became nominal, and a separate action of trespass for mesne profits was created to permit recovery for loss suffered in consequence of the ouster.[100] This action is based on the doctrine of "trespass by relation" which we have already encountered.[101] For, though it is not trespass to continue in possession of land in the absence of an initially wrongful intrusion, as when a tenant holds over without consent, yet upon re-entry the plaintiff is deemed to have been in possession ever since the accrual of his right of entry and may sue in trespass for all acts done upon the land during the period of his dispossession. But as a corollary, it is necessary for the plaintiff to have re-entered the land before suing for mesne profits.[102] To this requirement an exception has long been allowed wherever entry is impossible because the plaintiff's title to possession has since terminated.[103] Moreover, by statute[104] a claim for mesne profits may now be coupled with proceedings for ejectment and, if the plaintiff elects to do so rather than to sue separately, prior re-entry is no longer required. In that event, ejectment may once again be regarded not only as a proprietary action for the recovery of land, but also as a tort remedy for consequential loss.[105]

Damages are not confined to the rent of the premises, but include other loss resulting from the dispossession, like interest on a sum offered as a premium by a prospective tenant[106] or loss of custom caused by the defendant shutting up an inn.[107] Apparently, no set-off is allowed for the

97. *Dalton v. Fitzgerald* [1897] 2 Ch. 86; *Smith v. Smythe* (1890) 11 L.R. (N.S.W.) 295. *Asher v. Whitlock* (1865) L.R. 1 Q.B. 1 has been explained on this ground: Radcliffe & Miles, *Cases* (1904) 282.
98. *Claridge v. MacKenzie* (1842) 4 Man. & G. 143; 134 E.R. 59.
99. *Dudley v. Brown* (1888) 14 V.L.R. 655; *Cavenough v. Buckridge* (1868) 8 S.C.R. (N.S.W.) 90.
100. *Holdsworth* vii 15.
101. See above, p. 43.
102. *Minister of State v. R.T. Co. Pty Ltd* (1962) 107 C.L.R. 1.
103. 2 Rolle Abr. 550 (k).
104. *Landlord and Tenant Act* 1899 (N.S.W.) s. 12 (landlord and tenant only); Vic.: R.S.C., O. 18, r. 2; Qld: R.S.C., O. 4, r. 2; O.15, r. 9; S.A.: R.S.C., O. 18, r. 2; W.A.: R.S.C., O. 18, r. 2; Tas.: R.S.C., O. 20, r. 2; A.C.T.: R.S.C., O. 22, r. 2; N.Z.: *Code of Civil Procedures*, r. 101; and see *Dunlop v. Macedo* (1891) 8 T.L.R. 43.
105. *Nilan v. Nilan* (1951) 68 W.N. (N.S.W.) 271 at 272.
106. *Lee v. Blakeney* (1887) 8 L.R. (N.S.W.) 141.
107. *Dunn v. Large* (1783) 3 Doug. 335; 99 E.R. 683. Where a landlord forfeits a lease for breach of tenant's covenant, mesne profits other than rent are assessable from the date of the writ, not the breach: *Elliott v. Boynton* [1924] 1 Ch. 236; criticised by Denning, *Re-entry for Forfeiture*, 43 L.Q.R. 53 (1932).

value of improvements made by a defendant, even if he acted under a misapprehension that the land was his[108] except when the plaintiff had stood by and countenanced his acts.[109]

108. *Tai Te Whetu v. Scandlyn* [1952] N.Z.L.R. 30.
109. *Cawdor v. Lewis* (1835) 1 Y. & C. Ex. 427; 160 E.R. 174.

4

INTENTIONAL INTERFERENCE WITH CHATTELS

1. TRESPASS

Corresponding to the protection granted to landholders, the common law provided an action of trespass for direct interference with possessory rights in chattels. The earliest cases to attract attention involved total destruction or asportation, and for these wrongs a special writ, known as trespass de bonis asportatis, was created. Much later, it came to be extended to cases of mere damage.[1] But the popularity of trover, an action on the case which emerged during the 15th century, led to a gradual encroachment on the preserve of trespass, until eventually it was but rarely used as a remedy for interference with chattels. Trespass retained some vitality, however, because the two actions never wholly overlapped. Trover was not available for acts of intermeddling which merely affected the physical condition of chattels without involving substantial destruction or a denial of title, and in this field, curiously the last to be occupied by trespass, the older action retained its monopoly.

Any unprivileged interference with a chattel in the possession of another is a trespass, provided the injury is sufficiently direct and immediate to have qualified under the old procedure for a writ of trespass rather than case. It may be committed by an act which brings the defendant into contact with the chattel, as by destroying, damaging[2] or merely using[3] goods, beating[4] or killing[5] animals, or removing an article from one place to another.[6] The contact need not be personal, but may have been brought about by propelling an object against it, as by throwing a stone or driving a vehicle against the plaintiff's. In some cases, not even actual contact is required because chasing cattle has been traditionally treated as trespass;[7] yet, while the throwing of poisoned baits *to* dogs may be trespass, the *laying* of baits will only support an action on the case.[8]

Basis of liability

Trespass to chattels is primarily a wrong of *intentional* interference, now that inadvertent damage has long ago become the exclusive concern of

1. Ames, *History of Trover*, 11 Harv. L. Rev. 277 at 285-286 (1898).
2. *Fouldes v. Willoughby* (1841) 8 M. & W. 540 at 549; 151 E.R. 1153 at 1156.
3. *Penfolds Wines v. Elliott* (1946) 74 C.L.R. 204 at 214-215 (e.g. driving a car, riding a horse or filling a bottle).
4. *Slater v. Swann* (1730) 2 Stra. 872; 93 E.R. 906.
5. *Sheldrick v. Abery* (1793) 1 Esp. 55; 170 E.R. 278.
6. *Kirk v. Gregory* (1876) 1 Ex. D. 55; *G. W. K. v. Dunlop Rubber* (1926) 42 T.L.R. 376 (taking tyre from a car on exhibition and replacing it with another).
7. *Farmer v. Hunt* (1610) 1 Brownl. 220; 123 E.R. 766.
8. *Hutchins v. Maugham* [1947] V.L.R. 131.

negligence. The requisite intent, however, does not necessarily presuppose moral fault. It is present whenever the act deliberately uses or otherwise interferes with a chattel, without so much as an inkling that this happens to be violating somebody else's possessory rights.[9] Thus, as in trespass to land, a mistake of law or fact which leads him to believe that the chattel is his or that the owner has consented to his dealing with it, does not defeat liability.[10]

For unintended trespassory contacts there is no liability in modern law in the absence of negligence, as when contractors damaged an unsuspected underground cable.[11] Moreover, it may now be stated with some confidence that the old *defence* of "inevitable accident" has at last been superseded by placing the burden of proving negligence on the plaintiff, whether the action be framed in trespass or negligence and regardless of whether the accident occurred on the highway or elsewhere.[12]

But it is still moot whether the action lies without proof of actual damage, as for harmlessly touching the fender of a car or a painting in an art gallery. The analogy of trespass to the person and to land would seem to favour liability,[13] but it is open to serious question whether the peculiar sanctity with which the early law regarded land and the well founded policy of protecting the individual against offensive contacts furnish convincing reasons for vindicating a mere dignitary interest in relation to chattels. Such meagre authority as there is points the other way.[14] A modern New Zealand decision denied recovery for casual and unintended harmless contacts and inclined to the same conclusion for intentional interference.[15] Likewise, the prevailing American doctrine repudiates liability unless there is damage, however slight, like asportation which deprives the possessor of the use of the chattel.[16]

Plaintiff's title

The action of trespass is solely concerned with protecting actual possession. An owner out of possession cannot maintain it,[17] though we shall see that if entitled to immediate possession, he might well have a cause of action for conversion.

Few exceptions are admitted to this basic proposition. Aside from the special position of trustees,[18] personal representatives[19] and perhaps owners of a franchise (like the right to take a wreck[20]), the most notable is that apparently allowed in favour of one with a mere right to possession whose servant,[21] agent or bailee at will had actual possession at the time of

9. *Rest. 2d* §218 comment *a*.
10. *Colwill v. Reeves* (1811) 2 Camp. 575; 170 E.R. 1257; *Wilson v. New Brighton Panelbeaters* [1989] 1 N.Z.L.R. 74.
11. *N.C.B. v. Evans* [1951] 2 K.B. 861.
12. *Fowler v. Lanning* [1959] 1 Q.B. 426 (semble); see above, p. 21.
13. *Leitch & Co. v. Leydon* [1931] A.C. 90 at 106; *Pollock* 264-265.
14. *Slater v. Swann* (1730) 3 Stra. 872; 93 E.R. 906; *Everitt v. Martin* [1953] N.Z.L.R. 298.
15. *Everitt v. Martin* [1953] N.Z.L.R. 298.
16. *Rest. 2d* §218, comment *f*.
17. *Penfolds Wines v. Elliott* (1946) 74 C.L.R. 204 at 224-225, 242.
18. *Baker v. Furlong* [1891] 2 Ch. 172 (trust chattels held by beneficiary).
19. *Tharpe v. Stallwood* (1843) 5 Man. & G. 760; 134 E.R. 766 (titles relates back to death).
20. *Bailiffs of Dunwich v. Sterry* (1831) 1 B. & Ad. 831 at 842; 109 E.R. 995 at 999.
21. See also below, p. 66.

the wrong. This concession, difficult to harmonise with the general theory of trespass, can only be explained as a survival from a time when trover was still insufficiently developed to provide a needed remedy in these circumstances.[22]

Possession of chattels, as of land, is protected against interference by others, even though it is not supported by title and is wrongful vis-à-vis a third party, since any other rule would be "an invitation to all the world to scramble for . . . possession".[23] A mere stranger cannot be heard to say that one whose possession he has violated was not entitled to possess: he cannot set up the jus tertii to excuse his trespass,[24] unless he acted by authority of the true owner.[25]

Measure of damages

A plaintiff who has been actually deprived of goods in his possession is entitled to recover their full value[26] as in an action for conversion: the judgment, in effect, forces a compulsory purchase upon the wrongdoer. But in case of mere damage, falling short of complete destruction, the proper measure of damages is the actual loss suffered in consequence of the trespass, as for example any diminution in value of the chattel.

2. CONVERSION

Conversion may be defined as an intentional exercise of control over a chattel[27] which so seriously interferes with the right of another to control it that the intermeddler may justly be required to pay its full value.[28] Characteristic of this tort is that the ordinary measure of damages is the full value of the chattel.[29] In truth, the action is proprietary in substance, only tortious in form.[30] As has been perceptively observed, the action in effect forces an involuntary purchase on the converter; it permits the plaintiff to

22. It is in any event confined to actions against strangers and does not entitle a bailor to sue the bailee in trespass for an unauthorised use of the chattel: *Penfolds Wines v. Elliott* (1946) 74 C.L.R. 204 at 226-228; Pollock & Wright, *Possession* (1888) 145-147.
23. *Webb v. Fox* (1797) 7 T.R. 391 at 397; 101 E.R. 1037 at 1040 per Kenyon C.J. Aliter, *Torts (Interference with Goods) Act* 1977 (Eng.) s. 8.
24. *Woadson v. Nawton* (1727) 2 Stra. 777; 93 E.R. 842. This rule applies alike whether the plaintiff sues in trespass or trover: see below, p. 66.
25. *Blades v. Higgs* (1861) 10 C.B. (N.S.) 713; 142 E.R. 634.
26. Except against a defendant who has himself a limited interest in them, when he must be content (as in conversion: below, p. 71) with an amount proportioned to his interest: *Brierly v. Kendall* (1852) 17 Q.B. 937.
27. Although choses in action cannot be "converted", intangible rights represented by documents are in fact protected by including their value in assessing the worth of the converted instrument: *Lloyd's Bank v. Chartered Bank* [1929] 1 K.B. 40 at 55-56; *Arrow Transfer v. Royal Bank* (1971) 19 D.L.R. (3d) 420 (cheque); *Bavins v. L. & S. W. Bank* [1900] 1 Q.B. 270 (debt); *Watson v. McLean* (1858) E.B. & E. 75; 120 E.R. 435 (life policy); *M'Leod v. M'Ghie* (1841) 2 Man. & G. 326; 133 E.R. 771 (guarantee). Conversion will also lie for fixtures, timber and minerals upon severance from the freehold.
28. Cf. *Rest. 2d* §222A.
29. See below, p. 69.
30. For want of a vindicatory action, English law early had to employ a tort remedy as substitute.

say to him: "You have bought yourself something."[30a] This in turn provides the clue for determining whether a tortious intermeddling is serious enough to justify the drastic sanction of compelling the wrongdoer to buy the plaintiff out.

Trover

The tort of conversion is of more recent growth than trespass and owes its development to the action of *trover*. A brief digression into legal history will help to understand certain features of the modern law relating to the protection of possessory rights over chattels, for which it would be difficult to account without reference to the old forms of action which "in their life were powers of evil and even in death have not wholly ceased from troubling".[31] There are three ways in which one might deprive another of his property: by wrongfully taking it, detaining it, or disposing of it. In the first, the defendant gains possession by wrongful appropriation, in the second he acquires possession rightfully but retains it wrongfully, and in the third he neither takes nor retains it wrongfully but so disposes of the chattel that it is lost to the owner, as for example by destruction or sale. Corresponding to these modes of dispossession, the common law provided three actions: trespass for the first, detinue for the second and trover for the third.

Trover emerged in the second half of the 15th century as an action on the case in which the plaintiff alleged that he was possessed of certain goods and casually lost them, and that the defendant found and converted them to his own use. Since the allegations of loss and finding were untraversable, that is, could not be denied, the issue was simply whether the plaintiff's right to possession had been infringed by an act of "conversion". For procedural and other reasons, trover became so popular that it soon challenged and ultimately almost superseded detinue.[32] True, detention was not conversion in its original sense because, "just as man cannot both eat his cake and have it, so he cannot convert another's goods to his own use and at the same time detain them."[33] But it came to be accepted at an early date that refusal to deliver after demand was evidence of conversion, and this remains a distinctive feature of modern law. The two actions, however, never completely overlapped because detinue alone lay where a bailee was unable to return the chattel because of sheer passive carelessness, as by allowing it to be lost; while, conversely, we shall encounter many forms of conversion other than detention.

Emboldened by its first victory, trover next encroached upon the province of trespass and eventually became the almost universal remedy whenever a plaintiff had been deprived of his goods, whether by wrongful taking, detention or disposal. Indeed, at one stage the view gained vogue that any asportation could be treated as conversion, though later it was

30a. See *Qualifying as Plaintiff in an Action for Conversion*, 49 Harv. L. Rev. 1084 (1936); Warren, *Trover and Conversion* (1936); Prosser, *Nature of Conversion*, 42 Corn. L.Q. 168 (1957).

31. Salmond, *Observations on Trover and Conversion*, 21 L.Q.R. 43 at 47 (1905). For a detailed historical account, see also *Fifoot* ch. 6; *Holdsworth* vii 402-447; Ames, *History of Trover*, 11 Harv. L. Rev. 277 at 374 (1898).

32. See Simpson, *Action on the Case for Conversion*, 75 L.Q.R. 364 (1959).

33. *Salmond* (13th ed.) 259.

admitted that trivial interferences with possession not involving a denial of the plaintiff's title, such as scratching the fender of his car or knocking his cap off his head, do not warrant the drastic sanction of compelling the defendant to pay the full value of the article.[34] Such conduct still falls within the exclusive preserve of trespass.

In England, the old actions have now been replaced by a comprehensive action for "wrongful interference with goods" but without greatly affecting the substantive law.[35]

Defendant's conduct: Intent

Conversion can result only from an intentional act, not from negligent loss or destruction. The required intent is to interfere or deal with the goods by exercising dominion over them on one's own behalf or of someone other than the plaintiff. But it is not necessary that the defendant should have been minded to commit a wrong, because he may be liable for acting in ignorance or under an innocent mistake.[36] An agent who buys or sells stolen goods in good faith on behalf of a client is no less liable because unaware of the true owner's rights.[37] This constitutes the most effective safeguard against rogues profiting from their dishonesty, as it encourages utmost circumspection by the business community: "it requires brokers at their peril to buy from the right person, not merely to have some perfectly good reason for having bought from the wrong person."[38]

Again, as the hoary maxim has it, a man is presumed to intend the natural and probable consequences of his intentional act.[39] If he deals with another's property in a manner fraught with serious risk of loss, he will not be heard to contend that, far from desiring it, he had hoped against hope that it would not materialise. Thus when a smuggler borrowed a car to transport contraband watches and, being caught, the car was confiscated, he was held for its conversion on the footing that he had intentionally pursued a course of conduct calculated to entail its forfeiture.[40]

On the other hand, no conversion is committed by mere passive negligence: there must be a positive act of misfeasance. Mere detention of goods is no conversion,[41] although continued neglect to hand them back may be evidence of wilful refusal to return them and be construed as an active denial of the owner's title. Again, one who leaves his car in a parking lot cannot complain of conversion if the attendant carelessly allows a thief

34. *Fouldes v. Willoughby* (1841) 8 M. & W. 540 at 549; 151 E.R. 1153 at 1156.
35. *Torts (Interference with Goods) Act* 1977. In substance, the new tort has become the successor of conversion, detinue being abolished except for a bailee's inability to redeliver because of loss or destruction of the chattel. Critical: Palmer, *Abolition of Detinue*, 1981 Convey. 62.
36. E.g. *Rendell v. Assoc. Finance* [1957] V.R. 604; *Blenheim River Bd v. British Pavements* [1940] N.Z.L.R. 564.
37. *Hollins v. Fowler* (1875) L.R. 7 H.L. 757.
38. Warren, *Trover and Conversion* (1936) 86, 95.
39. The High Court's censure, in *Parker v. R.* (1963) 111 C.L.R. 610 at 632, was only apropos its application to criminal cases.
40. *Moorgate Mercantile Co. v. Finch* [1962] 1 Q.B. 701.
41. *Spackman v. Foster* (1883) 11 Q.B.D. 99.

to drive it away,[42] although there may be a sufficient "dealing" if the attendant drives the car to the gate or hands over the ignition key. Likewise, a carrier who negligently loses his client's goods is not guilty of conversion, unlike one who mistakenly delivers them to the wrong person.[43]

Taking possession

Anyone who, without lawful justification, takes a chattel out of another's possession with intent to exercise dominion over it, commits conversion no less than trespass. The tort is complete without prior demand for the return of the goods.[44] Nor is it necessary that the defendant should have intended to acquire full ownership: taking a car for the purpose of acquiring a lien on it[45] or just using it temporarily for a joyride[46] is sufficient.

But, as already pointed out, not every trespass is conversion. Trover never lay for merely removing a chattel from one place to another without any intent to assume possession of it or dispute the owner's title. The classical illustration is *Fouldes v. Willoughby*[47] where the plaintiff, after embarking his horses on a ferry, got involved in a dispute with the boatman. The latter requested him to get off and remove his horses, but when the passenger refused to comply, he put them ashore himself. The plaintiff again declined to leave the boat and was then carried across the river. It was held that the defendant, by merely turning out the horses, had not committed a conversion: the wrong was not so serious as to make it proper to require him to pay the full value. His possession was for a short time only, no damage was done to the horses and, far from disputing the owner's title, his conduct throughout emphasised that he did not want any part of them. On the other hand, had the horses been destroyed, lost or substantially injured, he would surely have been treated as a converter.[48] The controlling factor therefore seems to be, not necessarily the defendant's act viewed in isolation, but whether it has *resulted in a substantial interference* with the owner's rights so serious as to warrant a forced sale. Hence, a particular type of intermeddling is probably not, under any and all circumstances, necessarily a conversion. What may be decisive are such additional factors as the extent and duration of the interference, the harm done to the chattel and, not least, the defendant's intent.[49] If A takes B's hat from a clubroom rack, mistaking it for his own, and immediately

42. But a duty care, entailing liability for negligence, will devolve if the garaging qualified as a bailment, i.e. possession was transferred (as evidenced, e.g., by handing over the ignition key or by making "redelivery" of the car conditional on production of a ticket: *Sydney C.C. v. West* (1965) 114 C.L.R. 481; *Shorters Parking Station v. Johnson* [1963] N.Z.L.R. 135; *Heffron v. Imperial Parking* (1974) 46 D.L.R. (3d) 642 (Ont. C.A.). Otherwise there may be no liability whatever: *Tinsley v. Dudley* [1951] 2 K.B. 18.
43. *Joule Ltd v. Poole* (1924) 24 S.R. (N.S.W.) 387.
44. *Bruen v. Roe* (1665) 1 Sid. 264; 82 E.R. 1095.
45. *Tear v. Freebody* (1858) 4 C.B. (N.S.) 228; 140 E.R. 1071.
46. At any rate when the car is wrecked: *Schemmel v. Pomeroy* (1989) 50 S.A.S.R. 450; *Aitken v. Richardson* [1967] N.Z.L.R. 65.
47. (1841) 8 M. & W. 540; 151 E.R. 1153.
48. See ibid. at 548-549; 1156. The horses were in fact lost as the result of subsequent events, but the sole issue for decision was the correctness of the jury instruction that the mere act of removal was conversion.
49. Prosser, *Nature of Conversion*, 42 Corn. L.Q. 168 (1957).

returns it, this is too trifling to constitute conversion. However, if he keeps it for a long period[50] or it is lost even without his fault, he will probably be treated as a converter. So, if A removes B's car, his liability will depend on whether he intended to steal it or merely wanted parking space for himself; and in the latter case, whether he moved it only a little distance or locked it up in an unknown garage without informing the owner.[51]

Withholding possession: Detinue

Merely being in possession of another's goods without his authority is not a tort. If lawfully acquired, detention alone does not become a wrong in the absence of some manifestation of intent to keep them adversely or in defiance of his rights.[52] A bailee who merely holds over may be liable for breach of contract, but neither for conversion nor detinue. The finder of a chattel, not knowing the true owner, commits no wrong by simply keeping it for safe custody.[53]

To establish that the detention had become adverse and in defiance of his rights, the claimant must prove that he demanded return of the chattel and that the defendant refused to comply, as when a railway depot refused to deliver up the plaintiff's goods because it feared union retaliation.[54] but such refusal must be categorical; if qualified for a reasonable and legitimate purpose, without expressing or implying an assertion of dominion inconsistent with the plaintiff's rights, it amounts to neither detinue nor conversion.[55] One does not always act unreasonably in refusing to deliver up property immediately on demand but may inquire first into the rights of the claimant.[56] Moreover, a mere omission to reply to a letter of demand cannot of itself be construed as a refusal;[57] and it seems clear that, save by contract, the defendant cannot ordinarily be expected to do more than simply permit the owner to come and get the goods.[58]

The reason for insisting on a prior demand is to ensure that one who came into possession innocently be first informed of the defect in his title and have the opportunity to deliver the property to the true owner. There is some support for dispensing with this requirement when the defendant, with full information on the plaintiff's claim, categorically refutes it in his

50. Cf. *384238 Ontario v. R.* (1983) 8 D.L.R (4th) 676 (seizing goods for three days not a "dealing").
51. In *Wellington C. v. Singh* [1971] N.Z.L.R. 1025 wrongfully impounding a car (subsequently stolen) until all expenses were paid was held to be conversion. Also *Wilson v. New Brighton Panelbeaters* [1989] 1 N.Z.L.R. 74.
52. *Spackman v. Foster* (1883) 11 Q.B.D. 99.
53. *Hollins v. Fowler* (1875) L.R. 7 H.L. 757 at 766. Aliter, if he knows who the owner is and does not return it: *Johnstone v. Kaine* (1928) 23 Tas. L.R. 43 at 58.
54. *Howard Perry v. British Rlys* [1980] 1 W.L.R. 1375 (conversion).
55. But mere negligent delay puts the goods at bailee's peril: *Mitchell v. Ealing B.C.* [1979] Q.B. 1.
56. *Clayton v. Le Roy* [1911] 2 K.B. 1031; *McCurdy v. P.M.G.* [1959] N.Z.L.R. 553. It is doubtful whether a servant who holds goods for his master becomes a converter by refusing a stranger's request for delivery. Is it not better policy to encourage servants to obey their masters? Would he even be allowed to interplead? See Warren, *Trover and Conversion* (1936) 48-49.
57. *Nelson v. Nelson* [1923] Q.S.R. 37.
58. *Capital Finance v. Bray* [1964] 1 W.L.R. 323.

defence and thereby shows that a prior demand would in any event have been refused.[59]

No demand is necessary if conversion can be established in some other way, for example where possession was unlawfully acquired[60] or the defendant has wrongfully disposed of the goods. Herein lies an important distinction between trover and detinue: refusal is of the gist of detinue,[61] but only one of many possible forms of conversion. That this difference may still be occasionally exploited today is illustrated by the established rule that, when a bailee has converted goods, the bailor may still demand their return and sue in detinue upon the bailee's failure to deliver, even when his remedy for the prior conversion is already statute barred:[62] the bailee's duty to deliver is not accelerated by his precedent default and can be pursued by making demand,[63] even though his inability to comply be due to a prior act of conversion which is no longer actionable.

Another important difference between the two actions springs from the rule that for detinue it is immaterial whether the bailee's inability to redeliver was due to a prior intentional act of wrongful disposition or to mere negligence resulting in the loss or destruction of the goods.[64] In contrast, a bailee does not become a converter on demand when the goods are no longer in his possession. If he damaged[65] or lost[66] them through negligence, he cannot be sued in trover at all, because liability is predicated solely on intentional acts of misfeasance; while if he had wilfully disposed of them as by delivery to a stranger, he is liable in conversion for that act, but not for his later failure to comply with the demand for their return.

Transferring possession

The classical mode of conversion consists in unauthorised transfer or disposal of the goods, whether by sale and delivery,[67] pledge,[68] or mistaken delivery to the wrong person.[69] As already intimated, it is not even an answer to have acted under authority from someone who had himself no right to dispose of them, so that a sale and delivery by an agent or auctioneer constitutes conversion as against the true owner, although

59. *Baud Corp. v. Brook* (1973) 40 D.L.R. (3d) 418; Note, 53 Can. B. Rev. 121 (1975).
60. *Brown v. Mackenzie* (1871) 10 S.C.R. (N.S.W.) 302 (defendant gained possession by claiming the goods as his and plaintiff complied under protest).
61. It is a condition precedent for this action that there be a demand and refusal before issue of the writ.
62. *Goulding v. Victorian Rly* (1932) 48 C.L.R. 157; *Abrahams v. Comm. Rlys* [1958] S.R. (N.S.W.) 134; *Wilkinson v. Verity* (1871) L.R. 6 C.P. 206; and see *Brown v. Fazal Deen* (1962) 108 C.L.R 391. The position is reversed by modern statutes of limitation which date the period from the first of successive conversions: e.g. *Limitation Act*: (N.S.W.) s. 21; (Vic.) s. 6; (Tas.) s. 6; (A.C.T.) s. 18; (N.T.) s. 19; (Eng.) s. 3.
63. *Jones v. Dowle* (1841) 9 M. & W. 19; 152 E.R. 9; *Reeve v. Palmer* (1858) 5 C.B. (N.S.) 84.
64. Ibid.; and see *Thomas v. High* [1960] S.R. (N.S.W.) 401 at 407.
65. *Rushworth v. Taylor* (1842) 3 Q.B. 699; 114 E.R. 674.
66. *Williams v. Gesse* (1837) 3 Bing. (N.C.) 849; 132 E.R. 637.
67. *Glass v. Hollander* (1935) 35 S.R. (N.S.W.) 304.
68. *Singer Co. v. Clark* (1879) 5 Ex D. 37.
69. *Youl v. Harbottle* (1791) 1 Peake 49; 170 E.R. 81; *Helson v. McKenzies* [1950] N.Z.L.R. 878. Cf. *Goulding v. Victorian Rly* (1932) 48 C.L.R. 157; *Tozer Kemsley v. Collier's Transport* (1956) 94 C.L.R. 384.

made in the honest belief that his principal had title to the goods. Property rights are protected at the expense of an innocent mistake.

A bare sale or other attempted disposition without delivery is not ordinarily actionable, because it affects neither possession nor title.[70] It will, however, amount to conversion once consummated by transfer of possession to the buyer[71] or if it occurs in those exceptional circumstances when a person in possession of goods without title can so dispose of them by sale, pledge or otherwise as to confer a good title on an innocent transferee in the interest of commercial convenience, because its effect will be to deprive the true owner of his title.[72]

As a general rule, both transferor and transferee are joint wrongdoers, since the giving and taking are but different facets of the same unlawful disposition. This means that even a bona fide purchaser becomes a converter as soon as he takes delivery, without any prior demand and refusal,[73] save in those exceptional situations when a good title vests in him under the commercial law, like Factors Acts.[74] The law has dealt more leniently, however, with innocent pledgees whose mere acceptance of goods by way of security is not deemed sufficiently unequivocal to constitute conversion.[75]

Again, although misdelivery is ordinarily treated as conversion, this is considered too harsh for one who deals with goods he did not ask for, in a reasonable manner and solely with the aim of restoring them to the true owner, especially if the latter was himself responsible for investing him with the power of thus disposing of them. An involuntary bailee at least, that is one who comes into possession of a chattel against his wish, though now responsible for due care in its custody,[76] may acquit himself by delivering it to one whom he reasonably believes to be entitled to possession or to his apparently trustworthy agent. In the leading case, by an ingenious fraud, a rogue instructed X to supply a quantity of coats to Y and then sent a telegram to Y in X's name informing him that the goods had been dispatched in error and that he would send a van to collect them. Relying on the instruction, Y handed the goods over to an accomplice of the swindler and both absconded with the loot. Y was acquitted of conversion once the jury found that he had acted reasonably and without

70. *Lancashire Wagon Co. v. Fitzhugh* (1861) 6 H. & N. 502; 158 E.R. 206.
71. Contrast *Hollins v. Fowler* (1875) L.R. 7 H.L. 757 with *Public Trustee v. Jones* (1925) 25 S.R. (N.S.W.) 526.
72. *Consolidated Co. v. Curtis* [1892] 1 Q.B. 495 at 498.
73. *Wilkinson v. King* (1809) 2 Camp. 335; 170 E.R. 1175; *Hilbery v. Hatton* (1864) 2 H. & C. 822; 159 E.R. 341; *Rest. 2d* §229. The English Law Reform Commission (Report 12, 1966) rejected apportionment between owner and acquirer.
74. The purchaser's immunity is also reflected on his bona fide agent (*Hollins v. Fowler* (1875) L.R. 7 H.L. 757 at 764) but not apparently on the bona fide agent of the tortious seller: *Delaney v. Wallis* (1884) 14 L.R. Ir. 31. American authority, in the last respect, is to the contrary: *Prosser & Keeton* 98, note 90; *Rest.* §233(4).
75. *Spackman v. Foster* (1883) 11 Q.B.D. 99. Reversed by *Torts (Interference with Goods) Act* 1977 (Eng.) s. 11(2).
76. Semble, *Elvin & Powell v. Plummer Roddis* (1934) 50 T.L.R. 158; Palmer, *Bailment* (2nd ed. 1991) ch. 12. Modern statutes restrict liability of recipients of unsolicited goods to wilful and unlawful loss or damage: *Trade Practices Act* 1974 (Cth) s. 65 and concurrent State legislation: Palmer 766-772.

negligence.[77] Despite an older decision to the contrary,[78] the same conclusion seems proper where the defendant, without being actually in possession, endorses a delivery warrant for goods he did not order, in favour of one whom he reasonably believes to be authorised by the consignor; for surely, it would make little sense to draw a distinction according to whether the defendant is technically a bailee or not.

The law has also shrunk from extending the onerous liability for unauthorised dispositions by an innocent agent to simple ministerial dealings. Thus, a bailee who is holding over does not become liable for merely giving temporary custody to his servant or agent,[79] since he does not thereby alter his position in relation to the goods: no wrong is done, unless he purports to give to a stranger, along with possession, some right over the chattel itself. Similarly, an agent who thus innocently holds the goods on behalf of an apparent owner escapes liability, unless he proceeds to deal with them in a manner inconsistent with the true owner's title. The line of demarcation defies precise formulation, but seems to be drawn according to whether the dealing involves so serious an assumption of control that it deserves to be treated as an involuntary purchase. If the agent actually negotiates a transaction for his prinicpal, he actively imperils the true owner's title, by "setting the goods afloat on a sea of persons".[80] In contrast, a warehouseman with whom goods have been deposited is excused for merely keeping and restoring them to the depositor.[81] Redelivery does not amount to conversion because, though involving a transfer of possession, its purpose is not to affect any rights in the goods, but merely to restore them to the bailor. But a bailee with notice of an adverse claim redelivers at his peril; his proper course is to interplead and thus safely disengage himself from the dispute.[82]

The position is less certain when the agent delivers, at the principal's order, to some third person. Even then he is probably excused, at any rate if unaware that his delivery is pursuant to a sale or other disposition purporting to affect the title rather than merely possession of the goods. Thus a carrier who delivers goods to a consignee is not responsible, although the transaction constitutes a conversion on the part of the consignor.[83] Where however the carrier, warehouseman or other agent has actual knowledge that his delivery is pursuant to a transaction affecting title of the property, authority is unclear. If the agent negotiates the transaction he is liable,[84] but otherwise it might well be thought that the conflict between safeguarding property rights and ensuring reasonable mobility in commercial dealings is best resolved by excusing an agent who merely

77. *Elvin & Powell v. Plummer Roddis*; and see *James v. Oxley* (1939) 61 C.L.R. 433 at 447.
78. *Hiort v. Bott* (1874) L.R. 9 Ex. 86 (persuasively criticised by Burnett, *Conversion by Involuntary Bailee*, 76 L.Q.R. 364 (1960) who advances the alternative suggestion of at least reducing the plaintiff's damages on account of contributory negligence).
79. *Canot v. Hughes* (1836) 2 Bing. N.C. 448; 132 E.R. 176.
80. *Cochrane v. Rymill* (1879) 40 L.T. 744; *Consolidated Co. v. Curtis* [1892] 1 Q.B. 495; *Johnston v. Henderson* (1896) 28 O.R. 25 (auctioneer selling); *Hollins v. Fowler* (1875) L.R. 7 H.L. 757 (agent purchasing).
81. *Hollins v. Fowler* (1875) L.R. 7 H.L. 757 at 767; *Union Credit Bank v. Mersey Bd* [1899] 2 Q.B. 205 at 215-216; and see *Rest. 2d* §230-231.
82. *Winter v. Bancks* (1901) 84 L.T. 504.
83. *Greenway v. Fisher* (1824) 1 C. & P. 190; 108 E.R. 786; *Re Samuel* [1945] Ch. 408.
84. *Willis v. British Car Auctions* [1978] 1 W.L.R. 438 (C.A.).

redelivers to his bailor or to his order, provided he has no knowledge of any adverse claim.

Destruction, damage and user

Intentionally destroying[85] or consuming[86] another's chattel or so altering its physical condition as to change its identity[87] is treated as conversion. Thus, grinding wheat into flour, making grapes into wine, transforming marble into a statue change the identity of the original substance to an extent that will justify treating the defendant as a converter.[88] On the other hand, lesser damage would not warrant an enforced sale,[89] nor should it be forgotten that the casualty must in any event have been intended and not the result of mere carelessness: one who negligently wrecks a car he has hired or borrowed may be answerable to its owner for breach of contract or negligence, but not for conversion.[90]

Mere (unauthorised) use of a chattel, even without resulting damage, has often in the past been flatly treated as conversion,[91] but lately a more differentiated approach seems to be gaining ground. Clearly, if the misuse is serious, as where it involves an obvious defiance of the owner's rights, the drastic sanction of conversion is appropriate. Thus, a milkman would be liable in trover for using another's bottles in delivering milk to his customers, because subjecting them to the risk of breakage and loss in the way of his trade amounts to a sufficiently serious intermeddling, probably regardless of whether he knows that the bottles do not belong to him.[92] In contrast, a casual and harmless use, without any assertion of title, seems now to be regarded as too trivial to warrant a compulsory sale.[93] Thus, the

85. *Richardson v. Atkinson* (1723) 1 Stra. 576; 93 E.R. 710 (diluting liquor with water); *M'Leod v. M'Ghie* (1841) 2 Man & G. 326; 133 E.R. 771 (mutilating guarantee); *Penfolds Wines v. Elliott* (1946) 74 C.L.R. 204 at 229 (cutting seals from a deed).
86. *Philpott v. Kelley* (1835) 3 Ad. & E. 106; 111 E.R. 353.
87. *Keyworth v. Hill* (1820) 3 B. & Ald. 685; 106 E.R. 811. This type of "conversion" (change of identity) may have been the starting point of the action, with "conversion" only later becoming a synonym for "misappropriation" (Simpson, 75 L.Q.R. 364 (1959)).
88. The related question which so much taxed Roman lawyers, as to who owned the new creation (specificatio), presents little difficulty in our modern law. Ownership of the material remains unchanged by its alteration, but is relinquished upon the claimant receiving its value in satisfaction. Whether he may insist on specific restitution is discussed below, p. 74.
89. *Simmons v. Lillystone* (1853) 8 Ex. 431; 155 E.R. 1417. For mere damage there had been an action on the case since the late 14th century, preceding the action for conversion by 100 years.
90. *Rest. 2d* §226, comment g; and see *Rushworth v. Taylor* (1842) 3 Q.B. 699; 114 E.R. 674. The distinction may be important because he will be liable only for the *damage* actually done, not the full value of the chattel (as in conversion).
91. *Petre v. Heneage* (1701) 12 Mod. 519; 88 E.R. 1491; *Poulton v. Wilson* (1858) 1 F. & F. 403; 175 E.R. 782; *Craig v. Marsh* (1935) 35 S.R. (N.S.W.) 323.
92. *Model Dairy v. White* (1935) 41 A.L.R. 432; *Milk Bottles Recovery v. Camillo* [1948] V.L.R. 344.
93. *Penfolds Wines v. Elliott* (1946) 74 C.L.R. 204, 229; *McKenna v. Excavations Ltd* [1957] S.R. (N.S.W.) 515 at 517 (even though there was some damage), where defendants were not authorised to use the chattel at all. So also, in bailments for use, a use contrary to agreed terms does not necessarily constitute conversion, unless the departure is so serious as to amount to a denial of the bailor's title, e.g. a sale or pledge. Yet violation of the terms of the bailment exposes the bailee to strict liability for any damage to the chattel. Thus, a carrier who deviates from the agreed route is held to guarantee absolutely the

milkman's customers would not be liable for receiving and returning the bottles, if unaware of any adverse claim,[94] nor should unauthorised use by an innocent agent or servant of the possessor or by one who borrows the chattel from him qualify as conversion, as when I lend Jones' car to Brown without authority and Brown uses it thinking it is mine.[95]

This question was canvassed, though not actually settled,[96] in *Penfolds Wines v. Elliott*.[97] The plaintiffs made wine and sold it in bottles on which were embossed the words "This bottle is the property of Penfolds Wines Ltd". Their sales invoice prohibited the use of bottles for any purpose other than for retailing, consuming or using the plaintiff's products. The defendant, a hotelkeeper, was in the habit of selling bulk wine to customers who provided bottles in which to carry it away. His brother brought him several of the plaintiff's bottles which he accordingly filled with his own wine. The brother was undoubtedly guilty of conversion, because the transfer of possession of the bottles for this purpose was prohibited and determined the bailment; while equally clearly the defendant committed no wrong by merely receiving the bottles without any intention of exercising permanent or temporary dominion over them. Did it make any difference that he also used them for the purpose of his own trade? Dixon and Starke JJ. thought not, because no intention could be imputed to the defendant of asserting any title to the bottles; there was no user on the footing that he was owner or that the plaintiffs had no title: "In point of policy, there is no reason why the law should make it a civil wrong to put a chattel to some temporary and harmless use at the request and for the benefit of a person possessed of the chattel."[98] In contrast, Latham C.J.[99] and McTiernan J.[100] took the view that the use of the bottles for the purpose of the defendant's trade amounted to a dealing, under a claim of right, which was inconsistent with the dominion of the true owner. Williams J.[101] doubted whether it would have been conversion, had the bottles not carried the inscription, but regarded the endorsement on them as sufficient to impute to the defendant a knowledge of the plaintiff's title, with the result that the use could not be excused as an act done in bona fide ignorance of the plaintiff's rights.

93. *Continued*
safety of the goods: *Davis v. Garrett* (1830) 6 Bing. 716; 130 E.R. 1456; *Lilley v. Doubleday* (1881) 7 Q.B.D. 510; *McKenna v. Excavations Ltd* [1957] S.R. (N.S.W.) 515 at 518.
94. Ibid.
95. Cf. *Rest. 2d* §227. Related is the position of an innocent agent who has been directed by his employer to change the identity of plaintiff's goods. In *Philpott v. Kelley* (1835) 3 Ad. & E. 106 at 114; 111 E.R. 352 at 356 there is a dictum against liability, but Blackburn J. in *Hollins v. Fowler* (1875) L.R. 7 H.L. 757 at 768 declined to commit himself.
96. The majority was constituted by Dixon, Starke and McTiernan JJ., of whom the first two held that there was no tort of any kind. McTiernan J. agreed with the dissenters, Latham C.J. and Williams J., that conversion had been committed, but sided with the majority in refusing an injunction on the ground that the plaintiff should be left to damages. The difficulty of extracting a ratio decidendi is discussed by Paton & Sawer, 63 L.Q.R. 461 at 469-470 (1956).
97. (1946) 74 C.L.R. 204.
98. Ibid. at 231. Query, if there had been damage.
99. Ibid. at 218-219.
100. Ibid. at 234-235.
101. Ibid. at 243.

Asserting ownership

The gist of conversion is interference with the title or possession of chattels. A bare assertion of ownership, unaccompanied by circumstances which make it a "dealing" with the goods, is not, according to the better view, sufficient to constitute conversion.[102] We have already seen that a mere sale, without delivery of possession, does not make the defendant a converter unless it takes place in those exceptional situations where a non-owner can confer title on the purchaser and thereby extinguish the owner's title.[103] Yet very little more is required to complete the tort. "Constructive" delivery is sufficient, as where the goods are already in possession of the purchaser[104] or where the defendant, although never in actual possession, causes a bailee to deliver them directly to him.[105] In the first case, there is a change in the character of the possession,[106] and in the second a "dealing" resulting directly in a transfer of it.

An unequivocal[107] assertion of ownership by anyone in actual possession probably also qualifies as conversion. In *Oakley v. Lyster*,[108] the plaintiff leased a plot of land to store some hard core pending disposal. The defendant acquired the freehold and thereafter, in addition to removing some of the material, also informed the plaintiff that he would be treated as a trespasser if he removed any of it. This was held to be conversion, because in the circumstances the defendant could be regarded as in possession of the material and exercising control over it in derogation of the plaintiff's rights. The decision is no authority that a bare claim to ownership, unaccompanied by some degree of control over the subject matter, is sufficiently serious to be treated as conversion,[109] since here the defendant had not merely denied the owner's right to the material, but had also backed up his assertion by using some of it himself and by stopping the owner and his purchaser from removing it.

Plaintiff's title

The plaintiff in an action for conversion must have been either in actual possession or entitled to immediate possession of the goods[110] when they were converted.[111] This emphasis on possession, rather than ownership, is

102. Confirmed by *Torts (Interference with Goods) Act* 1977 (Eng.) s. 11(3).
103. See above, p. 60.
104. *Van Oppen v. Tredegars* (1921) 37 T.L.R. 504.
105. *Motor Dealers v. Overland* (1931) 31 S.R. (N.S.W.) 516; *Douglas Valley Finance v. Hughes* [1969] 1 Q.B. 738. See also *Foster v. Franklin* [1924] V.L.R. 269.
106. This distinguishes *Australia Assurance v. Coroneo* (1938) 38 S.R. (N.S.W.) 700 where the unauthorised letting did not effect any change in the character of the *immediate* possession of the goods.
107. The claim must be unqualified: *England v. Cowley* (1873) L.R. 8 Ex. 126.
108. [1931] 1 K.B. 148.
109. *Australia Assurance v. Coroneo* (1938) 38 S.R. (N.S.W.) 700; *Short v. City Bank* (1912) 15 C.L.R. 148 at 158.
110. In the latter case, he must also show, in addition, a "proprietary right" in the goods, at any rate to support a claim in detinue. A bare contractual right to delivery will not apparently support a tort action: *Jarvis v. Williams* [1955] 1 W.L.R. 71.
111. It is doubtful if an *equitable* mortgagee, not in actual possession, has sufficient title: *White v. Elder, Smith* [1934] S.A.S.R. 56 at 61. But an equitable owner in possession under a trust may sue at common law without even joining the trustee: *Healey v. Healey* [1915] 1 K.B. 938.

a legacy from an earlier time when wealth was primarily associated with tangibles and the law was preoccupied with repressing physical violence, combined with the persistent influence on legal thinking of the forms of action which developed out of these conditions. This explains the seeming paradox that a possessor without title, such as a finder,[112] a bailee,[113] a sheriff who has seized goods,[114] and perhaps even a thief,[115] may recover their full value; whereas an owner who has neither possession nor a right to immediate possession, like a lienor or bailor during an unexpired term,[116] cannot compel the wrongdoer to buy him out.[117] So great is the emphasis on protecting possession that even an owner may be guilty of conversion, as by dispossessing his bailee during the subsistence of a bailment not determinable at will.[118]

But although a reversionary owner cannot sue in trover,[119] he has an action on the case for such damage as he may sustain from being deprived of the benefit of his reversionary interest. Thus, he may sue if the chattel has been destroyed or permanently damaged[120] or so disposed of that a valid title thereto has become vested in a third party, as by sale in market overt. But he cannot complain if the chattel has merely been wrongfully taken or detained from its temporary possessor, because it is wholly speculative whether his own reversionary interest will be impaired thereby.[121]

Sometimes, however, the owner's right to immediate possession is remitted by the very act of conversion so as to entitle him to sue in trover. Thus, where goods have been placed in the hands of a bailee for a limited

112. *Armory v. Delamirie* (1722) 1 Stra. 505; 93 E.R. 664.
113. *Nicolls v. Bastard* (1835) 2 Cr.M. & R. 659; 150 E.R. 279.
114. *Wilbraham v. Snow* (1669) 2 Saund. 47a; 85 E.R. 624.
115. There is no actual decision to this effect, but it has been repeatedly asserted by text-writers (except *Prosser & Keeton* 103). In *Buckley v. Gross* (1863) 3 B. & S. 566; 122 E.R. 213 it was assumed to be irrelevant in what manner the plaintiff's possession was acquired; and in *Bird v. Fort Frances* [1949] 2 D.L.R. 791 where the question is fully discussed, a plaintiff who had found money whilst trespassing was allowed to recover it from the police, the occupier having made no claim.
116. *Gordon v. Harper* (1796) 7 T.R. 9; 101 E.R. 828; *Wertheim v. Cheel* (1885) 11 V.L.R. 107. See the forceful criticism by Warren, *Qualifying as a Plaintiff in an Action for a Conversion*, 49 Harv. L. Rev. 1084 at 1100 ff. (1936).
117. *Lord v. Price* (1874) L.R. 9 Ex. 54 (purchaser of goods in hands of seller subject to vendor's lien); *Standard Electronics v. Stenner* [1960] N.S.W.R. 447 (lienee); *Short v. City Bank* (1912) 15 C.L.R. 148; *Kahler v. Midland Bank* [1950] A.C. 24. A fortiori, a hire-purchaser whose goods were repossessed and wrongfully sold during the statutory waiting period: *Harris v. Lombard* [1974] 2 N.Z.L.R. 161; *Carr v. Broderick* [1942] 2 K.B. 275 (but repossessor is liable for breach of statutory duty).
118. *City Motors v. S. Aerial Service* (1961) 106 C.L.R. 477 (detinue); *Roberts v. Wyatt* (1810) 2 Taunt. 268; 127 E.R. 1080; *Howe v. Teefy* (1927) 27 S.R. (N.S.W.) 301.
119. I.e., he can recover neither the value of the chattel nor the value of his interest therein.
120. *Mears v. L. & S. W. Rly* (1862) 11 C.B. (N.S.) 850; 142 E.R. 1029; *Dee Trading Co. v. Baldwin* [1938] V.L.R. 173; *Drive-Yourself v. Burnside* [1959] S.R. (N.S.W.) 390. Though these were negligence actions, the same principle would apply to conversion. In so far as *Dee* holds the value of a hire-purchase company's interest to be more than the outstanding equity it is incompatible with *Wickham Holdings v. Brooke Motors* [1967] 1 W.L.R. 295 (C.A.). See also Fleming, *Tort Liability for Damage to Hire Purchase Goods*, 32 A.L.J. 267 (1958). A trustee may sue, but will hold the proceeds in trust for the beneficiary: *Buchanan v. Oliver Plumb Co.* (1959) 18 D.L.R. (2d) 575 (vendor-purchaser).
121. *Tancred v. Allgood* (1859) 4 H. & N. 438; 157 E.R. 910.

purpose and he deals with them in a manner inconsistent with the terms of the bailment, as by selling them, the right to possession revests in the owner who can forthwith sue the bailee for conversion.[122] A common example occurs on the fraudulent sale of a car by a hire-purchaser, with the result that the finance company can claim the outstanding balance from the subpurchaser.[123]

In "simple" bailments, that is those determinable at will, like a loan of one's car to a friend, either the bailor or bailee may sue:[124] the latter, because he is in actual possession; and the former, because he can at any moment exercise his right to immediate possession. Thus when a brewer sent certain casks of porter to a customer on condition that they be returned when emptied and empty casks were subsequently seized in execution for the publican's debts, the brewer was held entitled to sue the sheriff for conversion because, having the right to demand the return of the casks as soon as they were emptied, the right to immediate possession had reverted to him at the time of seizure and the publican had become a mere bailee at will.[125]

A servant who has mere custody of goods on behalf of his master is not treated as being in possession: the master has not only the right to possession but "constructively" the possession itself.[126] The origin of this anomalous rule is somewhat obscure, but it is possibly a survival from a time when servants were slaves and their inability to possess was an incident of their servile status.[127] Yet a servant may become a bailee and sue for trespass or conversion, if an intent can be inferred to invest him with exclusive possession, as when the plaintiff was employed at weekly wages to navigate a ship and himself engaged and paid an assistant.[128] So too, where goods are handed to a servant for delivery to his master, he has possession of them until he has done some act which transfers them to his employer; for example, a shop assistant has possession of money paid to him by a customer until he puts it into the cash register.[129]

Jus tertii

Possession, even without title, is protected against wrongful appropriation, whether the plaintiff chooses to sue in trespass or conversion. A possessor of goods has a good title as against every stranger, and one who takes them from him cannot defend himself by showing that the true title lies in some third person: he cannot, in the technical idiom,

122. *Milk Bottles Recovery v. Camillo* [1948] V.L.R. 344; *Penfolds Wines v. Elliott* (1946) C.L.R. 204 at 214, 217-218, 241-242.
123. *Citicorp. v. Stillwell Ford* (1979) 21 S.A.S.R. 142; *North General Wagon Co. v. Graham* [1950] 2 K.B. 7 (C.A.); *Moorgate Mercantile Co. v. Finch* [1962] 1 Q.B. 701 (misuse resulting in forfeiture).
124. *Rooth v. Wilson* (1817) 1 B. & Ald. 59; 106 E.R. 22; *Nicolls v. Bastard* (1835) 2 Cr. M. & R. 659; 150 E.R. 279; *Sandeman v. Robinson* (1877) Knox 382 (detinue).
125. *Manders v. Williams* (1849) 4 Ex. 339; 154 E.R. 1242.
126. See *Richard v. Nowlan* (1959) 19 D.L.R. (2d) 229.
127. Holmes, *Common Law* (1881) 227-228; but cf. Pollock & Wright, *Possession* (1888) 58-59.
128. *Moore v. Robinson* (1831) 2 B. & Ald. 817; 109 E.R. 1346; but see *The Jupiter (No. 3)* [1927] P. 122 at 131.
129. *Winfield & Jolowicz* 488.

plead the jus tertii.[130] This principle, derived from the medieval axiom that possession is as good as title against all but the true owner, vindicates the actual possessor's right to *retain* possession by discouraging seizure committed in the hope of finding a flaw in the possessor's title. It is subject to two exceptions where a jus tertii (a third party's superior right) may be pleaded.[131] First, where the true owner has authorised or ratified the act of the defendant; and secondly, where a bailee, under the true owner's authority, is defending an action brought against him by his bailor or where he has been evicted under the owner's title paramount.[132] Perhaps this may be generalised to cover every case, not limited to bailees, where a third party has intervened to claim title.[133]

"Possessory title" confers a right to *obtain* immediate possession against later possessors. A defendant may dispute the plaintiff's possessory title, for example, by showing that the latter transferred or lost it by operation of law. May he also plead the jus tertii, that is to say, that, though the plaintiff has a possessory title, the true title is in somebody else? According to a widely prevailing view, identified with Holdsworth,[134] a person not dispossessed but with an immediate right to possession must, in modern law, prove an absolute title in himself and be ready to defeat a plea of just tertii. Two exceptions had to be allowed: first, a finder (as we shall see presently) has been held to prevail against a possessor notwithstanding a jus tertii;[135] second, a bailee is ordinarily estopped, in an action brought against him by his bailor, from denying the latter's title,[136] although he may of course defend on some other ground, such as that the period of hire has not yet run out and that the bailor therefore had no right to immediate possession.[137] A bailee is permitted to set up a superior title against his bailor only when he defends the action on behalf of and by authority of the true owner or when he has already, on demand from the true owner, surrendered possession to him.[138] Allowing the plea of jus tertii in other cases is motivated by a reluctance to expose a generally innocent defendant to double liability, once at the suit of the plaintiff, once at the suit of the true owner.[139]

130. (1721) 2 Stra. 505; 93 E.R. 664.
131. As is, a fortiori, a plaintiff with a mere right to possession.
132. See *Wilson v. Lombank* [1963] 1 W.L.R. 1294.
133. *Salmond* 108-109.
134. *Holdsworth* vii, 424-431, based on his reading of *Leake v. Loveday* (1842) 4 Man. & G. 972. Followed in *H. Berry v. Rushton* [1937] Q.S.R. 109 at 118-121. Cf. the same view concerning title in ejectment (see above, p. 49).
135. *Armory v. Delamirie* (see below, p. 68) where the finder had temporarily yielded possession to the defendant.
136. He is precluded from showing not only that the bailor had no title at the date of the bailment, but also that the title has since terminated: *Rogers v. Lambert* [1891] 1 Q.B. 318; *Re Savoy E.* [1948] Ch. 622.
137. See e.g. *Henry Berry v. Rushton* [1937] Q.S.R. 109.
138. This defence was first allowed where the goods had been taken by the owner vi et armis contra voluntatem the bailee, being later extended to all cases where a lawful demand is made by the true owner (but not by one with a mere contractual right to possession: *Elkin v. Specialised T.V.* [1961] S.R. (N.S.W.) 165) against which the bailee has no defence: see *Edwards v. Amos* (1945) 62 W.N. (N.S.W.) 204.
139. Payment or surrender of the chattel does not discharge him from additional liability to the true owner: *Wilson v. Lombank* [1963] 1 W.L.R. 1294.

Another view, however, would confine the jus tertii to instances where the third party has actually intervened.[140] It is defended, apart from its historical roots, on the ground that double liability cannot in any event be avoided where the true owner is unknown at the time of the plaintiff's claim so that a jus tertii cannot be established, and that the policy of returning the chattel to its true owner would be furthered by it. Better still is the English reform which allows the defence of jus tertii in all actions for wrongful interference with goods, but requires the plaintiff to identify other claimants and authorises the court to deprive any third party who fails to appear of his right of action against the defendant.[141]

Finder

The finder of a chattel ordinarily acquires a good title against all but the rightful owner. In the ancient case of *Armory v. Delamirie*,[142] a chimney sweep's boy found a jewel and handed it for appraisal to a goldsmith who, under the pretence of weighing it, extracted the stone from its setting and offered 1½d. for it. When the boy rejected the offer, the jeweller refused to return the stone. He was held liable in trover, because the boy had acquired a possessory title which was not impaired by temporarily entrusting custody to the defendant.[143]

If the chattel is found on somebody else's property, it has been a much controverted question whether the occupier has a better right than the finder.[144] It is sometimes argued that this would aid its return to the true owner because he would trace it there, but it could as well have the opposite effect of inducing finders to conceal their trove. In two situations the finder clearly acquires no rights. First, where he finds as servant or agent of the occupier, he takes possession not for himself but for his employer.[145] Secondly, where he is a trespasser,[146] perhaps even when he takes possession with a dishonest intent of concealing his find rather than taking steps to discover the true owner as by handing it over for temporary custody to, or at least notifying, the occupier or the police.[147]

140. Forcibly put by Baker, 16 Q.L.J. 46 (1990). See also Atiyah and Jolly, 18 Mod. L. Rev. 97 and 371 (1955).
141. *Torts (Interference with Goods) Act* 1977 ss. 7, 8.
142. (1721) 2 Stra. 505; 93 E.R. 664.
143. See also *Bird v. Fort Frances* [1949] 2 D.L.R. 791 at 799-800. But the finder must have asserted an independent possession of his own prior to handing it over. Thus when a boatswain found some contraband coins on a ship and immediately handed them to the master, he could not reclaim them from the customs authorities to whom they had been turned over: *Willey v. Synan* (1937) 57 C.L.R. 200 at 212-213, 216-217.
144. See Goodhart, *Three Cases on Possession*, 3 Cam L.J. 195 (1928); Marshall, *Problem of Finding*, 2 Cur. Leg. Prob. 68 (1949); Harris, *Oxford Essays in Jurisprudence* (1961) 80-98; Tay, *Possession and the Modern Law of Finding*, 4 Syd. L. Rev. 383 (1964).
145. This was not the ratio announced by Lord Russell in *Sharman* but has been so interpreted in later cases: *Heddle v. Bank of Hamilton* (1912) 5 D.L.R. 11 (bank porter picking up money whilst sweeping up); *Willey v. Synan* (1937) 57 C.L.R. 200 at 216 ff. (boatswain finding contraband on ship); *Grafstein v. Holme* (1958) 12 D.L.R. (2d) 727; *London Corp. v. Appleyard* [1963] 1 W.L.R. 982. Aliter, *Byrne v. Hoare* [1965] Qd R. 135 (F.C.) when employer is not the occupier.
146. See *Hibbert v. McKiernan* [1948] 2 K.B. 142 (trespasser on golf links finding balls). But if the occupier makes no claim, even a wrongful finder acquires possession protected against appropriation by others to avoid a "free for all" (*Bird v. Fort Frances* [1949] 2 D.L.R. 791).
147. *Parker v. British Airways* [1982] Q.B. 1004 at 1017 ("very limited rights").

In other situations, the occupier's claim seems to depend on whether he had manifested an intention to exercise control over the area and anything upon or in it (whether or not he was actually aware of the presence of the chattel). Such an intent is presumed with respect to things *attached to* or *in* the occupier's building or land, like an historic boat embedded in the soil,[148] a ring found in a pool being cleaned,[149] or a cache of banknotes under the foundations of a house under renovation.[150] If the thing is found *on* the land, it is a question of fact whether the occupier had manifested an intent to control and thereby gained prior possession. The nature of the place is obviously relevant. On one side is the private home, on the other such places as the floor of a shop[151] or of an airport lounge even with restricted admission.[152]

Measure of damages

A plaintiff who has been deprived of his chattel is ordinarily entitled to its full[152a] value.[152b] Thus in a controversial decision where gravel had been removed from the plaintiff's land, the measure of damages was held to be its market value rather than a royalty the defendant might have paid if it had invoked its statutory powers. Crediting the plaintiff with the cost of severance and removal gave him a windfall but was thought justified to prevent the defendant gaining an advantage from his own wrong.[153] In Australia, though not in England, exemplary damages may also be proper.[154]

In periods of fluctuating prices, some importance attaches to the question whether the value of the property should be calculated as at the date of the wrong or of judgment or some intermediate period.[155] The answer once seemed to hinge on whether the plaintiff laid his claim in detinue or conversion. For, the conventional rule in trover was to take the value

148. *Elwes v. Briggs Gas Co.* (1886) 33 Ch. D. 562; *Webb v. Ireland* [1988] I.R. 201 (antique hoard).
149. *S. Staffordshire Water Co. v. Sharman* [1896] 2 Q.B. 44.
150. *Ranger v. Giffin* (1968) 87 W.N. (Pt 1) N.S.W. 531.
151. *Bridges v. Hawkesworth* (1851) 21 L.J. Q.B. 75.
152. *Parker v. British Airways* [1982] Q.B. 1004 (C.A.).
152a. Ordinarily the market value, it may be the cost of replacement: *Hall v. Barclay* [1937] 3 All E.R. 620. In case of doubt, it is assumed to be the highest possible value (*Armory v. Delamirie* (1721) 1 Stra. 505; 93 E.R. 664), unless there is evidence and description of the converted property: *Ley v. Lewis* [1952] V.L.R. 119.
152b. In the case of converted documents, like cheques, guarantees, or insurance policies, their value includes the intangible rights represented by them: *Morison v. London Bank* [1914] 3 K.B. 356 at 365; *Bavins v. L. & S.W. Bank* [1900] 1 Q.B. 270; *Rest. 2d* §242.
153. *Bilambil-Terranora v. Tweed S.C.* [1980] 1 N.S.W.L.R. 465 (C.A.); cf. *Livingstone v. Rawyards Coal* (1880) 5 App. Cas. 25.
154. E.g. *Healing v. Inglis Electrix* (1968) 121 C.L.R. 584 ($3,500 for seizing goods worth $10,000); *Egan v. State Transport* (1982) 31 S.A.S.R. 481 ($25,000 out of a total damages award of $570,000). This might prove an incentive to civil sanctions against shoplifting and other petty theft.
155. See *Cane* 46-49. If the defendant sold the goods, the plaintiff may alternatively "waive the tort" and claim the proceeds in a restitutionary action for money had and received. This may well be more or less than the value assessed in a tort action, besides occasionally offering procedural and other advantages: see *United Australia v. Barclay's Bank* [1941] A.C. 1; *Suttons Motors v. Campbell* [1956] S.R. (N.S.W.) 304; *Thomas v. High* [1960] S.R. (N.S.W.) 401; *Goff & Jones* ch. 32.

prevailing at the time of wrong,[156] whereas in detinue it was that of judgment in view of the procedural nicety that the judicial order has always been cast in the alternative for recovery either of the goods or their value, and the latter was therefore not unreasonably thought to be that *then* prevailing.[157]

But there is now authority for a more flexible solution, less dependent on the choice of pleading and better adjusted to the parties' real deserts. A distinction must be drawn between fluctuations in "real" value and mere nominal increases due to inflation. As regards the latter, the plaintiff in conversion no less than detinue should be entitled to the value expressed in the money prevailing at the date of judgment. This alone will put him in the same position as if the conversion had not been committed, without in any way mulcting the defendant in extra costs.[158] A plaintiff's duty to mitigate becomes relevant only in cases of real increase of costs, for example due to scarcity. So also where the converted property consists in an item of fluctuating value like shares, the plaintiff may not ordinarily claim any rise in market value after he became aware or ought to have become aware of the conversion or some reasonable time in which to bring suit, lest he gamble at the defendant's expense.[159] On the other hand, a broker who fraudulently sold a client's shares but later repurchased them for less was held liable for their difference in value between sale and redelivery: it was evidently thought better to deprive him of an improper gain than to keep the client to his net loss.[160]

A converter is entitled to credit for improvements to the chattel,[161] if only because value is assessed as of the date of conversion.[162] Nor does it therefore seem to matter whether the improver acted in good faith or was the original converter rather than an innocent purchaser from him.[163] Similar allowance must be made by a plaintiff seeking restitution from an improver.[164]

In addition to the value of the chattel, the plaintiff is also entitled to compensation for any special damage which the law does not regard as too remote. Thus, a racehorse owner recovered for loss of the chance of racing it[165] and an artist for lost profits during the wrongful detention of his work kit.[166] Conversion of a profit-making machine, like a dredger

156. *Mercer v. Jones* (1813) 3 Camp. 477; 170 E.R. 1452; *Reid v. Fairbanks* (1853) 13 C.B. 692 at 728; 138 E.R. 1371 at 1386.
157. *Rosenthal v. Alderton* [1946] K.B. 374; *General & Finance Co. v. Cooks Cars* [1963] 1 W.L.R. 644; *Ley v. Lewis* [1952] V.R. 119.
158. *Egan v. State Transport* (1982) 31 S.A.S.R. 481. Less persuasive is to allow the later value as consequential damages added to the earlier value at the conversion date.
159. *Asamera Oil v. Sea Oil* [1979] 1 S.C.R. 633, adopting the "N.Y. rule" (annot. 31 A.L.R. 3d 1286 (1970)). In *Sachs v. Miklos* [1948] 2 K.B. 23 the same formula was wrongly applied to an inflation case.
160. *Solloway v. McLaughlin* [1938] A.C. 247 (P.C.).
161. *Greenwood v. Bennett* [1973] Q.B. 195 (C.A.) (cost of repairing damaged car).
162. But *Greenwood v. Bennett* [1973] Q.B. 195 (C.A.) assumed the same result where the improver committed a subsequent conversion by selling the repaired car. Criticised by Matthews [1981] Cam. L.J. 340.
163. *Nash v. Barnes* [1922] N.Z.L.R. 303. The *Torts (Interference with Goods) Act* 1977 (Eng.) s. 6 helps only improvers acting in mistaken but honest belief as to title.
164. Below, p. 74.
165. *Howe v. Teefy* (1927) 27 S.R. (N.S.W.) 301.
166. *Brilawsky v. Robertson* (1916) 10 Q.J.P.R. 113.

employed on work in a harbour, entitles its owner to compensation for loss in his business prior to getting a replacement;[167] just as use of a chattel which is normally let out on hire, entails liability for the full market rate of hire that the owner might otherwise have received; he need not show that he suffered an actual loss in that the equipment would have been rented out: he is entitled to remuneration as the price of permission to use it.[168] On the other hand, the resale price under a subcontract, concluded by the owner with a third party several months before the conversion, cannot be taken into account unless the defendant had notice.[169]

Now that general damages have come to be allowed for negligent damage to chattels,[170] a case can be made for applying the same principle to conversion. Distress over loss of a stamp album has been held compensable.[171]

Limited interests

A possessor or person with a right to possession whose chattel has been converted by a stranger is entitled to recover its full value, even though he is not the owner. As we have seen, modern law has retained the medieval axiom that possession is title against a wrongdoer:[172] damages are merely a substitute for such possession and must therefore be the equivalent of the chattel and amount to its full value.

The traditional solicitude for mere possessory rights did not stop at permitting full recovery to persons in possession under a claim of title, but has gradually been extended to all possessors, whether they assert ownership for themselves or not. In the leading case of *The Winkfield*,[173] earlier doubts were set at rest by holding that a bailee may collect full damages regardless even of the fact that he is not liable over to the bailor. The action arose out of a collision between two vessels caused by the defendant's negligent navigation. The Postmaster-General claimed for the mails lost in the accident and, although not accountable to the senders, was permitted to recover their full value on the ground that "as between bailee and stranger possession gives title—that is, not a limited interest, but absolute and complete ownership, and he is entitled to receive back a complete equivalent for the whole loss."[174] This principle is of general application, to actions for negligence no less than conversion.[175]

167. Semble, *Liesbosch (Dredger) v. The Edison* [1933] A.C. 449; *Mizza v. McKay-Massey Harris* (1935) 37 W.A.L.R. 87; *Venables v. West* (1903) 3 S.R. (N.S.W.) 54.
168. *Strand Electric v. Brisford E.* [1952] 2 Q.B. 246; and see *Mrs Eaton's v. Thomasen* [1973] 2 N.Z.L.R. 686 (loss of profit on converted stock in trade). But a finance company is ordinarily entitled only to interest on its value: *British Wagon Co. v. Shortt* [1961] I.R. 164. See Sharpe & Waddams, *Damages for Loss of Opportunity to Bargain*, 2 Oxf. J. Leg. St. 290 (1982).
169. *The Arpad* [1934] P. 189. (C.A.); *Heskell v. Continental Express* [1950] 1 All E.R. 1033; and see Goodhart, *Two Cases on Damages*, 2 U. Tor. L.J. 1 (1937). Resale price may however be evidence of market value: *France v. Gaudet* (1871) L.R. 6 Q.B. 199.
170. Below, p. 253.
171. *Graham v. Voight* (1989) 89 A.C.T.R. 11.
172. Above, p. 66.
173. [1902] P. 42.
174. Ibid. at 60 per Collins M.R.
175. *Swire v. Leach* (1865) 18 C.B. (N.S.) 479; 144 E.R. 531; *Glenwood Lumber Co. v. Phillips* [1904] A.C. 405; *Thorne v. MacGregor* (1973) 35 D.L.R. (3d) 687. The same

As between bailor and bailee, the latter is obliged to account for any excess of what he has recovered beyond his own interest, and this helps to "soothe a mind disconcerted by the notion that a person who is not himself the complete owner should be entitled to receive back the full value of the chattel converted or destroyed."[176] More controversial is the rule that the wrongdoer, having once paid full damages to the bailee, is free from any further claim by the bailor, satisfaction made to either of them constituting a bar against the others.[177] This may seriously prejudice the owner who has no safeguards against a bailee mishandling the litigation or accepting a disadvantageous settlement. Nor does it necessarily follow that, because a bailor has sufficient confidence in the bailee to entrust his property to him for custody, he should also abide in the latter's control over the proceeds.[178] If the bailee goes bankrupt or absconds with the money, the owner's position is hapless, since his proprietary right to the goods has been lost by judgment and for it substituted a mere personal claim against the bailee who may be financially irresponsible.[179] This difficulty could be overcome by permitting a bailee to recover the full value only with the express or implied consent of the bailor, besides giving the latter an opportunity to be joined as co-plaintiff.[180] English legislation has, more generally, sought to minimise a converter's exposure to double liability and to compel an accounting by one entitled to damages beyond his own interest in the goods to other interested parties, such as a finder or bailee to the true owner.[181]

But a converter who has himself a continuing interest in the chattel is liable only for the value of the other's limited interest. This tends to avoid unjust enrichment for the plaintiff and excessive liability for the defendant. Thus an unpaid vendor who wrongfully disposes of the goods instead of delivering them to the purchaser is entitled to deduct the price for which the purchaser is no longer liable;[182] a finance company wrongfully seizing its car from the hire-purchaser is accountable only for its present market value less the amount of unpaid instalments;[183] nor can a pledgee[184] or

175. *Continued*
principle applies to pledgees: *The Jag Shakti* [1986] A.C. 337 (P.C.). Its application to hire purchase is discussed by Fleming, 32 A.L.J. 267 (1958).

176. *The Winkfield* [1902] P. 42 at 60; *Tomlinson v. Hepburn* [1966] A.C. 451 at 467-468, 480.

177. *The Winkfield* [1902] P. 42 at 61; *Nicolls v. Bastard* (1835) 2 Cr. M. & R. 659 at 660; 150 E.R. 279 at 280 (but cf. *Courtenay v. Knutson* (1957) 26 D.L.R. (2d) 768 where bailee recovered for loss of use after defendant had settled with the bailor for the value of the chattel). As already noted, the rule is otherwise where satisfaction has been made to a mere possessor such as a disseisor or finder: *Attenborough v. L. & St K. Docks* (1878) 3 C.P.D. 450 at 454.

178. Aliter Lord Porter, *Morrison S.S. Co. v. Greystoke Castle* [1947] A.C. 265 at 293.

179. See the criticism by Warren, *Qualifying as Plaintiff in Conversion*, 49 Harv. L. Rev. 1084 (1936); Clerk, *Title to Chattels by Possession*, 7 L.Q.R. 224 (1891).

180. This suggestion is not inconsistent with *The Winkfield* where consent by the owners of the mail could be reasonably inferred.

181. *Torts (Interference with Goods) Act* 1977 s. 7.

182. *Chinery v. Viall* (1860) 5 H. & N. 288; 157 E.R. 1192 (aliter, if purchaser is not relieved from price: *Healing v. Inglis Electrix* (1968) 121 C.L.R. 584; Sutton, *Damages for Conversion of Goods Sold*, 43 A.L.J. 95 (1969)); *Butler v. Egg Bd* (1966) 114 C.L.R. 185; *Johnson v. Stear* (1863) 15 C.B. (N.S.) 330; 143 E.R. 812 (pledgee).

183. *City Motors v. S. Aerial Service* (1961) 106 C.L.R. 477.

184. *Maynegrain v. Compafina* [1982] 2 N.S.W.L.R. 141 (C.A., revd on other grounds).

hire-purchase company[185] claim more than the amount of its outstanding debt at the time of judgment, not the resale value of the article at the time of its conversion.

Return of chattel

According to the traditional view, conversion empowers the plaintiff to enforce a sale and recover the value of the chattel. But though it is conceded that damages may be reduced by returning the goods,[186] can the plaintiff be forced to take them back against his will? In detinue, tender has always been a good plea, because the action is primarily for recovery of the goods themselves rather than its equivalent in damages.[187] In trover, however, the plaintiff was not originally bound to accept a return,[188] and it is of course up to him in the first instance to select the remedy he prefers.

After some hesitation, the courts eventually assumed a discretionary power, on application by the defendant, to order that restoration be accepted with nominal damages, and costs,[189] but they will only so intervene to stay proceedings which they regard as an abuse of process. When the application is made promptly it has the merit of an offer to restore the plaintiff's property without putting him to the expense and risk of litigation and serves the desirable object of encouraging litigants to compose their differences.[190] But this is equally a reason for refusing it after verdict, because it is not in the public interest to encourage litigation by granting the same indulgence to a defendant who has taken the chance of a verdict in his favour.

Very exceptionally, even after judgment, a defendant may be relieved from the damages awarded against him; for example where, as in conversion of title deeds, the chattels are assessed at a sum which bears no relation to their value in the defendant's hands.[191] But if the verdict represents the value of the goods to anyone who wants them, a defendant who has been recalcitrant up to the point of judgment, has forfeited his claim to sympathy.[192] In no circumstances, will a plaintiff be forced to

185. *Wickham Holdings v. Brooke House Motors* [1967] 1 W.L.R. 295 (C.A.) (even against an assignee in breach of the agreement: see Peden, 44 A.L.J. 65 (1970)); *W. Credits v. Dragan Motors* [1973] W.A.R. 184 (F.C.). But it cannot recover *more* than its value: *Chubb v. Crilley* [1983] 1 W.L.R. 599. For negligence claims see above, n. 120.
186. *Solloway v. McLaughlin* [1938] A.C. 247; *Aitken Agencies v. Richardson* [1967] N.Z.L.R. 65; *Brandeis v. W. Transport* [1981] Q.B. 864 (nominal). For conversion, plaintiff is entitled to difference in meantime value; aliter for mere detainer: *B.B.N.B. v. Eda* [1990] 1 W.L.R. 409 (P.C.).
187. *Crossfield v. Such* (1852) 8 Ex. 159; 155 E.R. 1301.
188. *Olivant v. Berino* (1743) 1 Wils. K.B. 23; 95 E.R. 471.
189. *Fisher v. Prince* (1762) 3 Burr. 1363; 97 E.R. 876; *Tucker v. Wright* (1826) 3 Bing. 601; 130 E.R. 645.
190. Another form of pressure is that a plaintiff who refuses to accept redelivery but fails in his claim for substantial damages, may be made to pay costs notwithstanding an award of nominal damages: *Hiort v. L.N.W. Rly* (1879) 4 Ex. D. 188 at 195.
191. *Coombe v. Sansom* (1822) 1 D. & Ry. (K.B.) 201; *Plevin v. Henshall* (1833) 10 Bing. 24; 131 E.R. 814.
192. *Bernstein v. Adelaide Corp.* [1932] S.A.S.R. 320; *Huddart Parker v. McGowan* [1919] N.Z.L.R. 705. See the full discussion by Culshaw, *Redelivery of Converted Property*, 6 A.L.J. 329 (1933).

accept a return of the property, unless it can be restored in the same condition as when it was taken.[193]

Specific restitution

A claimant bent on recovering his chattel would always sue in detinue where judgment was in the alternative for return of the property or payment of its assessed value.[194] But because the common law left the defendant an unabridged option with which one to comply, the owner had in effect no *right* to specific restitution, though he might resort to Chancery for a discretionary order of redelivery in case damages were not an adequate remedy.[195]

In train with the procedural reforms of the 19th century,[196] the common law courts were also empowered to order return of the chattel detained without giving the defendant an option to pay its value. This remedy, however, is still discretionary and not a matter of right. It will not be granted, for example in case of unreasonable delay[197] or if the chattel is an ordinary article of commerce and of no special value generally or to the plaintiff.[198] Again, in case the defendant added to its value, an unconditional order for redelivery would be the more unfair as, in assessing damages, he would be entitled to credit for it;[199] hence if anxious for its return in specie, the plaintiff must be prepared to make a fair allowance for the improvements.[200] In certain cases of this sort, an order would be refused altogether. For instance, if a defendant misappropriated a car and fitted it with new tyres, it would not be incompatible with justice to order specific restitution subject to an allowance for the expenditure incurred; but if he converted a slab of marble and made a statue out of it, *he* would have a better claim to its possession than the owner of the raw material who should be left to his claim for damages. In these situations, the court will be guided by the relative values of the interest of the rival claimants.[201]

From medieval times has also come down to us a summary process, known as *replevin*, by which one out of whose possession goods have been taken may obtain their return until the right to the goods can be determined by a court of law. Replevin arose out of the need of a turbulent society to discourage resort to self-help and, although for a long time primarily used in disputes about distress between landlord and tenant, it was gradually

193. *Fisher v. Prince* (1762) 3 Burr. 1363; 97 E.R. 876; *Moon v. Raphael* (1835) 2 Bing. N.C. 310 at 314; 132 E.R. 122 at 123.
194. Coupled with damages for detention up to redelivery: *General & Finance v. Cooks Cars* [1963] 1 W.L.R. 644; *Toronto Corp. v. Roman* (1962) 37 D.L.R. (2d) 16 (affd 41 D.L.R. (2d) 290).
195. *Pusey v. Pusey* (1684) 1 Vern. 273; 23 E.R. 465; aliter, if damages were adequate: *Dowling v. Betjemann* (1862) 2 J. & H. 544; 70 E.R. 1175.
196. Originally introduced in England by the *Common Law Procedure Act* 1854. E.g. *Supreme Court Act* (N.S.W.) 1970 s. 93.
197. *Baud v. Brook* (1973) 40 D.L.R. (3d) 418.
198. See *Howard Perry v. British Rlys* [1980] 1 W.L.R. 1375.
199. See above, p. 70.
200. *Greenwood v. Bennett* [1973] Q.B. 195 (C.A.); *McKeown v. Cavalier Yachts* (1988) 13 N.S.W.L.R. 303; *Torts (Interference with Goods) Act* 1977 (Eng.) s. 6.
201. On the question of accession see *McKeown*; *Rendell v. Assoc. Finance* [1957] V.L.R. 604; *Thomas v. Robinson* [1977] 1 N.Z.L.R. 385.

expanded to cover all wrongful dispossessions.[202] Indeed, if the plaintiff wanted return of his chattel in specie, replevin was a more appropriate remedy than either trespass or trover. Restoration of the property is, of course, only provisional, pending determination of title. The procedure is for the claimant to apply to the court officer for a warrant for restitution, on security of a bond or deposit of money that he will prosecute an action for replevin and return the goods if he should lose. But should he succeed, he may not only keep his property but also recover for any special damage, such as expenses of the replevin bond and compensation for annoyance or injury to his credit and reputation in trade.[203] Replevin is still exercised mainly in cases of distress, whether for rent, damage feasant or otherwise, though it is theoretically available for all kinds of taking amounting to trespass.[204]

As repeatedly pointed out, judgment against the defendant in trover is equivalent to an involuntary sale to the converter.[205] But the plaintiff is not actually divested of his title until judgment for the value of the chattel has been satisfied.[206] Until paid, he may exercise all his rights as owner, like seizing the chattel or suing anyone else for other acts of misappropriation, whether committed before or after the conversion complained of in his first action.[207] But he cannot have double recovery so that, once he receives its value from one defendant, he loses his right to enforce a second judgment against another.[208]

202. *Holdsworth* iii 283-287.
203. *Smith v. Enwright* (1893) 69 L.T. 724; but note *Dixon v. Calcraft* [1892] 1 Q.B. 458 at 464, 466.
204. But not otherwise *Mennie v. Blake* (1856) 6 E. & B. 842; 119 E.R. 1078.
205. *Purcell v. Thomas* [1904] Q.S.R. 189. Cf. *Franklin v. Giddins* [1978] Qd R. 72 at 78.
206. *Ex parte Drake* (1877) 5 Ch. D. 866 at 870; *McKay v. Stanwix* (1897) 1 N. & S. 54 (Tas.); *Torts (Interference with Goods) Act* 1977 (Eng.) s. 5.
207. *Ellis v. Stenning* [1932] 2 Ch. 81.
208. Cf. *King v. Bulli Coal Co.* (1877) Knox 389 (owner who has recovered full value of vessel negligently sunk by defendant cannot maintain trover, if defendant raises it for salvage).

5

DEFENCES TO INTENTIONAL TORTS

One who has intentionally invaded another's interests so that ordinarily liability would ensue may yet be excused because his conduct is privileged in the particular circumstances. As the early common law attached liability to trespass on mere proof of direct causation, it became necessary, after the later admission of exculpatory considerations, for the defendant to "justify" or "excuse" his conduct by specially pleading and proving the circumstances which negatived its actionable quality. Thus "justification" became an affirmative defence. "Privilege" is the modern and more convenient term to describe those considerations which confer immunity on conduct that would otherwise be actionable. It signifies that the defendant may claim a wider range of action than is ordinarily permitted, for the purpose of protecting some interest of his own or that of a third person or of the public, which is of such social importance as to justify even the intentional infliction of injury on another.[1] The admission of a privilege involves a value judgment that the interest advanced by the defendant's conduct, as compared with that which is necessarily or probably invaded by it, is rated so highly that the defendant should not be deterred from it, and that—moreover—resistance to it should be discouraged by imposing liability on one who does not submit to its exercise.

Similar considerations are given weight in negligence cases in determining whether the defendant's conduct was reasonable. Negligence, as we shall see, is actionable only if it involves an *unreasonable* risk of harm, and this depends, in general terms, on weighing the utility of the defendant's conduct against the harm it is likely to cause.[2] In that context, however, the conclusion that the act is likely to do more good than harm is not expressed by saying that it is "privileged", but by holding that it is not negligent. The difference in approach is due to the fact that the law of intentional wrongs developed principally within the frame of the old action for trespass, with its notion of prima facie causal liability, while the law of negligence emerged through the action on the case where fault was from the start a necessary element of liability.

1. MISTAKE

Although the strict liability of the early law of trespass has today given way to fault, defendants continue, as a general rule, to be held responsible for unavoidable mistakes. The distinction between accident and mistake calls for explanation. "Intention", "negligence" and "accident" have reference to the consequences produced by conduct and not to the conduct itself,

1. *Rest. 2d* §10.
2. See below, ch. 7.

because otherwise almost all torts would be intentional in the sense that the actor's bodily activity was intended.[3] An intentional tort, properly so-called, is one in which the wrongdoer either desires to bring about a result which is an injury to another,[4] or believes that the result is substantially certain to follow from what he does.[5] A negligent tort is one where the defendant, as a reasonable person, should have foreseen that his conduct involved a foreseeable risk, though falling short of substantial certainty that such a result would ensue. Inevitable accident, finally, refers to cases where the particular consequence was neither intended nor so probable as to make it negligent. By contrast, in cases of mistake, the consequence is often intended and the error consists in thinking that such a result does not constitute an invasion of another's legally protected interests.[6] To illustrate: one who cuts down a tree in the vicinity of his boundary in such a manner that it will in all probability fall on his own ground, commits but an accidental trespass, if it crashes onto a neighbour's land. The unauthorised entry, which is the injurious effect of the person's activity, was neither intended nor reasonably to be anticipated, and he is consequently absolved now that such an accidental trespass is no longer actionable. On the other hand, if the person had thought that he owned all the land on which the tree would possibly fall and intentionally cut it so that it would come down on land which turns out to be a neighbour's, he has committed an intentional trespass under mistake. The actual result which has come to pass was intended under the erroneous notion that it would not violate another's rights.[7]

Such a mistake, even if one which a reasonable person might have made, is not as a general rule admitted as an excuse to civil liability.[8] A trespasser who honestly believes that he is the owner or has the owner's authority or merely mistakes the boundary is nonetheless guilty of unlawful entry.[9] One who misappropriates another's property (as by taking coal from the plaintiff's seam or taking the plaintiff's sheep and driving it off to market) does not escape responsibility because he believes that the property is his own. An auctioneer who sells and delivers goods on behalf of a client in the honest but false belief that he has title, is nevertheless liable to the true owner for conversion.[10]

At first blush, the inadmissibility of the plea of unavoidable mistake seems difficult to reconcile with the policy of exonerating defendants for accidental harm, since the actor is as blameless in the one case as in the other. The different treatment accorded to inevitable accident and unavoidable mistake could be superficially explained on the ground that,

3. Holmes, *Common Law* (1881) 91.
4. But he need not desire to cause injury in the sense of interfering with another's legal rights.
5. See above, p. 25.
6. Some mistakes negative intent as when, digging a trench, I pierce the plaintiff's pipeline not knowing it was there (*N.C.B. v. Evans* [1915] 2 K.B. 861); or when I fire a gun in his direction, erroneously believing that it contains only a blank cartridge: *Beals v. Hayward* [1960] N.Z.L.R. 131 at 143.
7. Whittier, *Mistake in the Law of Torts*, 15 Harv. L. Rev. 335 at 337 (1902).
8. It is otherwise in criminal liability: e.g. Criminal Codes of Qld and W.A., s. 24; Williams, *Criminal Law* (2nd ed. 1983) §6.8.
9. *Baseley v. Clarkson* (1681) 3 Lev. 37; 83 E.R. 565.
10. *Hollins v. Fowler* (1875) L.R. 7 H.L. 757.

whereas the courts had irreversibly committed themselves at an early stage on the latter question, they found little authority standing in the way of transforming trespass into a remedy requiring proof of intentional or negligent wrongdoing. More significant, however, is the fact that the mistake usually relates to title and that tort actions have traditionally been used for the purpose of vindicating property rights. The rule works no injustice where a mere technical trespass to land or chattels has been committed, because only nominal damages would be awarded and the action will have served the function of quieting title. Again, where the defendant has misappropriated another's goods, he is rightly held for their value, because there is no reason for allowing the defendant to be unjustly enriched at the expense of the true owner. But the rule is harsher in its application to a defendant who, bona fide and without negligence, had bought the goods from another, for he is now compelled to account for them once more to the true owner. The dilemma of who of two innocent parties is to suffer is here resolved in favour of the owner except in those situations where, in the interest of commercial expediency, an innocent purchaser acquires a good title and escapes the penalties of conversion. It must also be borne in mind that the defendant may, in turn, have recourse against his own seller, although undoubtedly all too often the latter will turn out to be a man of straw.

Less easy to justify are decisions which reject the defence of unavoidable mistake where the error does not relate to title and the defendant has derived no benefit corresponding to the plaintiff's loss, as when a farmer shot another's dog under the impression that it was a wolf.[11] This situation does not differ markedly, as regards the policies involved, from the case where firing on a wolf he accidentally hits a dog, and would accordingly be absolved.[12] Most cases of this type of mistake are concerned with the exercise of a privilege. In some of them the defendant is held liable, in a few he is excused. Mistake does not aid: where an officer with a valid warrant arrests the wrong person[13] or a private individual arrests for a felony when none has been committed[14] or a person erroneously believes the plaintiff to be a lunatic proper to be imprisoned,[15] where a sheriff levies execution on the wrong goods,[16] or a hitchhiker accepts a lift from a driver whose employer had specifically prohibited it.[17] On the other hand, mistake excuses: where a police officer erroneously thinks that a felony has been committed and arrests one whom he reasonably believes to be the offender,[18] or when the officer seizes goods under a reasonable belief that they were stolen;[19] and it may be that a person who honestly though mistakenly believes himself to be attacked is privileged to defend himself.[20]

11. *Ranson v. Kitner* (1888) 31 Ill. App. 241.
12. *Stanley v. Powell* [1891] 1 Q.B. 86.
13. *Shadgett v. Clipson* (1807) 8 East 328; 103 E.R. 368. But criminal liability is negated in Qld (*Criminal Code* s. 252), W.A. (s. 299), Tas. (s. 24), and N.Z. (*Crimes Act* 1961 s. 30).
14. *Samuel v. Payne* (1780) 1 Doug. 359; 99 E.R. 230.
15. *Fletcher v. Fletcher* (1859) 28 L.J.Q.B. 134.
16. *Glasspoole v. Young* (1829) 9 B. & C. 696; 109 E.R. 259.
17. *Conway v. George Wimpey* [1951] 2 K.B. 266 at 273.
18. *Beckwith v. Philby* (1827) 6 B. & C. 635; 108 E.R. 585.
19. *Chic Fashions v. Jones* [1968] 2 Q.B. 299 (C.A.): goods not covered by search warrant.
20. This, at least, is the prevailing American doctrine: *Prosser & Keeton* 111.

While there is therefore a strong tendency to reject the plea of unavoidable mistake, it is not universal. In each situation, the boundaries of the privilege are marked out in the light of the special reasons of policy or expediency bearing on the particular case. As regards wrongful arrest, the common law has traditionally espoused the role of guardian of civil liberty, and in general takes the view that unlawful infringements are best discouraged by throwing the risk of an innocent mistake on him who interferes with the freedom of others. But while private citizens are not encouraged to take the law into their own hands, police officers are under a duty to act for the protection of the public against crime and are therefore treated with greater leniency. Similarly, it has been suggested[21] that a mistake is privileged when it appears necessary to act quickly in protection of a right, as to the existence of which the defendant is not mistaken: for example, when the defendant believes that he is being attacked and acts in self-defence.

2. CONSENT

The pronounced individualism of the common law is reflected in the axiom that no wrong is done to one who consents—volenti non fit injuria.[22] The courts have traditionally adhered to John Stuart Mill's postulate that ordinarily it is not the law's function to save a man from himself rather than leave him free to act as he pleases. Actually, strictly speaking, consent is not a privilege at all, because lack of it is of the very gist of assault and battery, false imprisonment, and trespass to land or goods. "An assault must be an act done against the will of the party assaulted; and therefore, it cannot be said that a party has been assaulted by his own permission."[23] But consent should now be a matter of defence, with the burden of proof on the defendant.[24]

Consent may be given expressly, as when a patient authorises a surgeon to perform an operation, but it may just as well be implied: actions often speak louder than words. Holding up one's bare arm to a doctor at a vaccination point is as clear an assent as if it were expressed in words.[25] Similarly, acquiesence by a landowner in the use by the public of a shortcut across his property permits the inference of an implied licence and prevents the landowner from treating such intruders as trespassers until he has made it clear that further entry is prohibited.[26] Participants in games or sports involving a likelihood of bodily contact, such as wrestling or boxing, consent to all the risks ordinarily incidental, though not to undue violence

21. *Prosser & Keeton* 111.
22. This maxim reaches back to Bracton: *Winfield & Jolowicz* 700. Consent, as a defence to claims for intended harm, in particular trespass to land or goods, is often referred to, according to the old form of plea, as "leave and licence".
23. *Christopherson v. Bare* (1848) 11 Q.B. 473 at 477.
24. *Sibley v. Milutinovic* (1990) A.T.R. 81-013 (A.C.T.). Contra: Blay, 61 A.L.J. 25 (1987).
25. *O'Brien v. Cunard S.S. Co.* 28 N.E. 266 (Mas. 1891) "Words or conduct which are reasonably understood by another to be intended as consent constitute apparent consent and are as effective as consent in fact" (*Rest. 2d* §892(2)). This rule was relevant in *Schweizer v. Central Hospital* (1974) 53 D.L.R. (3d) 494 (like *O'Brien*, involving a foreigner).
26. See below, p. 465.

or unfair play.[27] Even silence and inaction may in some circumstances be interpreted as an expression of willingness. Failure to resist or protest indicates consent if a reasonable person who is aware of the consequences and capable of protest or resistance would voice his objection. A girl who is silent to an amorous proposal cannot afterwards capriciously complain of assault.[28]

Reality of consent

Consent must be genuine. Clearly it is not if obtained by (threat of) force or given under the influence of drugs, as when a patient retracted an earlier "no" to a spinal injection while already under heavy sedation.[29] More insiduous pressures, however, have been disregarded, such as being a prisoner consenting to an injection[30] or the economic duress which prompted a Victorian housemaid to submit, under sobs and protests, to a medical examination ordered by her mistress in order to ascertain if she was pregnant.[31]

Some misapprehensions also vitiate consent. Deceit as to the real nature of the defendant's conduct clearly does, as when it was held to be rape for a choir master to seduce a naive young pupil under the pretence that this would improve her voice.[32] Not so, however, a deceit relating to a wholly collateral matter which operates merely as an inducement. Thus, a woman who lives with her paramour under a false promise that he would marry her, cannot maintain that every act of intercourse is a battery;[33] nor may a hotelkeeper treat as trespassers a couple who falsely registered themselves as man and wife.[34] The remedy, if any, in these cases must be an action for deceit.

More debatable is an intermediate group of situations where the plaintiff is aware of the real nature of the proposed contact but not of its harmful or offensive quality, and the defendant conceals it with knowledge that disclosure would have induced the other to withhold consent.[35] In an old case[36] a mistress sued her lover for infecting her with venereal disease, but lost her claim (based on assault), partly on the ground that there was no legally enforceable duty of disclosure, partly because it was tainted by the meretricious nature of her relationship. However debatable the latter proposition,[37] the former is open to the most serious doubt. It rests

27. *Wright v. McLean* (1956) 7 D.L.R. (2d) 253; *Reid v. Mitchell* (1885) 12 R. 1129. Duty of care: see below, p. 117.
28. Aliter, if no reasonable person would interpret silence as consent, as when the plaintiff stands his ground after being told that he would be punched on the nose.
29. *Beausoleil v. Communauté* (1964) 53 D.L.R. (2d) 65.
30. *Freeman v. Home Office (No. 2)* [1984] Q.B. 524 (C.A.).
31. *Latter v. Braddell* (1880) 50 L.J.Q.B. 448. Aliter, in modern cases of "power dependency" (*Norberg v. Wynrib* (1992 S.C. Can.) (sex between drug addict and physician)).
32. *R. v. Williams* [1923] 1 K.B. 340; *R. v. Harms* [1944] 2 D.L.R. 61.
33. *Hegarty v. Shine* (1878) 4 L.R. Ir. 288 at 294.
34. *McGrath v. Marshall* (1898) 14 W.N. (N.S.W.) 106.
35. *Rest. 2d* §55 imposes liability.
36. *Hegarty v. Shine* (1878) 4 L.R. Ir. 288.
37. Once emancipated from Victorian morality, is it not sounder policy to discourage conduct like the seducer's rather than penalise the seduced for her easy virtue? But in *Lasher v. Kleinberg* 164 Cal. Rptr 618 (1980) a man cross-claimed in a paternity suit against the mother for misrepresenting that she was using a contraceptive. It was held that this would encourage unwarranted invasion of privacy.

exclusively on decisions which hold that it is not a criminal assault for a husband knowingly to infect his wife, because the mistake relates not to the nature of the connection but merely to its consequences.[38] But the policy favouring acquittal in criminal cases[39] has little weight in civil and should not be decisive in the present context.[40] An assent to bodily contact under a mistake as to its harmful or offensive character ought not to be treated as a genuine consent, if the mistake is known and concealed by the defendant. Thus an action for battery ought to be available to one who permits another to touch him with a piece of metal which, unknown to him but known to the actor, is heavily charged with electricity;[41] or to a woman who consents to intercourse with a man who inveigled her into a bigamous marriage without disclosing that he already had a wife,[42] or to a naive girl who submits to indecent liberties by a physician in the belief that this is a necessary part of the treatment.[43] Such mischief is best deterred by permitting recovery.

How much must a doctor tell a patient about a proposed treatment? Misapprehension about its basic nature would negative the patient's consent,[44] not so however misapprehension about mere consequential risks. The physician's duty to inform the patient about the latter so as to enable him to make a rational choice is measured by the physician's duty of care, breach of which may amount to negligence, but not battery.[45] Consent does not have to be "informed" to be "real". The reason for this distinction lies less in doctrinal finesse[46] than in the perceived need for a more elastic and doctor-friendly standard. Besides, one is loath to equate a healing physician to a violent ruffian.[47]

Minors can give an effective consent if endowed with the intellectual and emotional capacity to comprehend the nature and consequences of

38. *R. v. Clarence* (1888) 22 Q.B.D. 23. Accord: *Papadimitropoulos v. R.* (1957) 98 C.L.R. 249 (no "rape" when woman consented to intercourse under belief, fraudulently induced by the man, that she was married to him; no mistake as to identity of man and character of what he was doing).
39. See Hooper, *Fraud in Assault and Rape*, 3 U.B.C. L.Rev. 117 (1968).
40. There is at least a duty to inform, sounding in negligence or fraud: see below, p. 109. See Keown, *The Ashes of AIDS and the Phoenix of Informed Consent*, 52 Mod. L. Rev. 790 (1989).
41. *Rest. 2d* §55.
42. In *Garnaut v. Rowse* (1941) 43 W.A.L.R. 29 and *Graham v. Saville* [1945] 2 D.L.R. 489 recovery was permitted in actions for deceit, but in *Smythe v. Reardon* [1949] Q.S.R. 74 the court followed the conventional view that damages in deceit are not at large and dismissed the claim, though suggesting that the plaintiff might have succeeded in an action for assault. The restricted scope of deceit emphasises the need for a remedy in trespass whenever there is an offensive interference unaccompanied by material injury. Anyway, deceit does not lie unless the marriage is invalid: *Said v. Said* (1986) 33 D.L.R. (4th) 382 (mere personal characteristics of groom).
43. *Rest 2d* §55, ill. 3, 4; based on *De May v. Roberts* 9 N.W. 146 (Mich. 1881) (its counterpart: *Bolduc v. R.* [1967] S.C.R. 677).
44. *Halushka v. Univ. Sask.* (1965) 53 D.L.R. 2d 436 (experiment volunteer); *R. v. Flattery* (1877) 2 Q.B.D. 410 (sexual intercourse under pretence of surgical operation). Here the plaintiff's burden of proof is lighter than in negligence: e.g., he need not prove that he would not have consented, that the disclosure was required, nor is expert testimony needed.
45. See below, p. 109.
46. Such as that the misapprehension relates to risk, not certainty, of injury.
47. Battery also lacks causation as a safety valve (see below) nor does it cover (non-invasive) advice.

whatever is proposed (for example, medical treatment or sexual intercourse), without requiring parental consent.[48] For children who are too young, parents can give the necessary consent at any rate to procedures which are in the (best) interest of the child, perhaps even to any procedure to which a "reasonable parent"[49] would consent.

Consent to criminal acts

There is surprisingly little guidance on whether the plaintiff's consent bars a civil action for an assault which is also a crime. The criminal law in many cases refuses to recognise the consent of the injured party as a defence to a prosecution, for the good reason that the interests of the state cannot be waived by a private individual. A public affray is nonetheless a breach of the peace although the participants mutually consented to fight it out. But "considerations affect prosecutions not applicable to civil actions. In the former, we are concerned with public interests and consequently public policy; in the latter, with the reciprocal rights and liabilities of individuals. Mutual consent to a prize fight might prevent the pugilists having a remedy inter se, but would not make it less a breach of the peace, or exonerate those engaged from punishment."[50]

Nor would it be a deterrent against breaches of the peace to permit the participants in an illegal fight to sue each other, as has occasionally been asserted. For, if fear of liability is assumed to be a deterrent, the hope of recovering damages, if one gets the worst of an affray, could be as great an incentive. Thus one who deliberately started the fight can be met with the defence, not of provocation, but of volenti non fit injuria (consent) and ex turpi causa non oritur actio (illegality).[51]

Likewise, with regard to criminal statutes fixing the age of consent to intercourse, it would seem pessimi exempli to allow a girl an action for assault because, unless she was genuinely too young to understand the enormity of her conduct, a favourable judgment would offer her a cash reward for abandoning her virtue.[52]

Exceeding consent

Consent is no defence, unless it is given to the precise conduct in question, or at least to acts of a substantially similar nature.[53] One who

48. *Gillick v. W. Norfolk A.H.A.* [1986] A.C. 112 (contraception); *Johnson v. Wellesley Hospital* (1970) 17 D.L.R. (3d) 139; *M.M. v. K.K.* (1987) 39 C.C.L.T. 81 (sex); *Minor (Property and Contracts) Act* 1970 (N.S.W.) s. 49; *Criminal Code* (Tas.) s. 51; *Guardianship Act* 1968 (N.Z.) s. 25 (over 16); *Family Law Reform Act* 1969 (Eng.) (over 16). See Skegg, *Consent to Medical Procedures on Minors*, 36 Mod. L. Rev. 370 (1973).
49. *S. v. McC.; W. v. W.* [1972] A.C. 24 at 57 per Lord Hodson. Parental consent appears to be sufficient, at least if the child is too young to be consulted, for therapeutic as well as forensic (e.g. blood test to determine paternity) purposes. See also *Re L.* [1968] P. 119 at 132.
50. *Hegarty v. Shine* (1878) 4 L.R. Ir. 288 at 294 per Ball C.
51. *Murphy v. Cullane* [1977] Q.B. 98 (C.A.); *Wade v. Martin* [1955] 3 D.L.R. 635 (unless defendant has used excessive or unnecessary force or a weapon, as in *Lane v. Holloway* [1968] 1 Q.B. 379 (C.A.)); *Rest. 2d* §60.
52. *J.L.N. v. A.M.L.* [1989] 1 W.W.R. 438; aliter in case of foster father: *M. v. K.* (1989) 61 D.L.R. (4th) 392 (C.A.).
53. *Rest. 2d* §§53, 54.

challenges another to a fist fight does not sanction an attack with a knife;[54] boxers and wrestlers agree to violent bodily contact typical of the sport, but not to deliberate foul play.[55] Nor is a surgeon, charged with a particular operation, justified to depart from instructions and perform a different one;[56] the only occasion which would justify his proceeding without prior authority is when it is "necessary to save the life or preserve the health of the patient".[57] In other words, here the balance between preservation of life and self-determination is found in authorising medical procedure only when it would be unreasonable, not just inconvenient, to postpone until consent could be sought.[58] Justification for this is found not in fictitiously imputing to the patient a consent he has obviously not given, but in the humanitarian duty of the medical profession. Thus a doctor is privileged to amputate the gangrenous foot of an emergency patient who requires immediate surgery and is either unconscious or a child too young to give a valid consent and whose parents cannot be reached in time.[59] But, without statutory authority,[60] an intervention, even to save life, against the declared wishes of a mentally competent adult or guardian of a minor is not permitted. The individual's right to self-determination prevails over the sanctity of life.[61]

In the case of the mentally ill, with permanent inability to consent, statutes usually prescribe procedures for authorising therapeutic interventions, or authority is vested in the court as guardian or parens patriae. Non-therapeutic treatments are highly controversial. Sterilisation has been justified where "there are no two views of what was in the best interest of the patient's health."[62] But at least prior judicial authorisation would seem preferable,[63] and even then for so drastic and irreversible a

54. *Lune v. Holloway* [1968] 1 Q.B. 379 (C.A.).

55. *Pallante v. Stadiums (No. 1)* [1976] V.R. 331 (boxing); *McNamara v. Duncan* (1971) 26 A.L.R. 584 (football); *Agar v. Canning* (1965) 54 W.W.R. 302 (hockey).

56. *Parmley v. Parmley* [1945] S.C.R. 635; *Schweizer v. Central Hospital* (1974) 53 D.L.R. (3d) 494. It is now customary for surgeons to demand from their patients a general authorisation for any treatment deemed appropriate.

57. *Marshall v. Curry* [1933] 3 D.L.R. 260. The privilege, commonly referred to as "necessity", is not confined to medical aid but applies also where, e.g., one restrains a mentally disordered person or would-be suicide: *Crimes Act* 1961 (N.Z.) s. 41; *Rest. 2d* §62.

58. Explicitly recognised in *Criminal Code* (Tas.) s. 51; cf. Qld (s. 282) and W.A. (s. 259). See Skegg, *A Justification for Medical Procedures Performed Without Consent*, 90 L.Q.R. 512 (1977). A doctor may also apparently claim remuneration in quasi-contract for services rendered pursuant to his privilege, by analogy to necessaries supplied to a lunatic: *Matheson v. Smiley* [1932] 2 D.L.R. 787.

59. See Skegg, *Capacity of Minors to Consent to Medical Treatment* [1969] N.Z. Recent L. 295, analysing special N.Z. legislation on blood transfusion and other therapy. The proper common law criterion is whether the minor is "too young to exercise a reasonable discretion in the matter" (*Criminal Code* (Tas.) s. 51).

60. As under the *Human Tissue Act* 1982 (Vic.) s. 24.

61. *Malette v. Shulman* (1990) 67 D.L.R. (4th) 321 (C.A.): Jehovah's Witness's pre-accident declaration. So the dying may opt against life being artificially prolonged. See *Medical Treatment Act* 1988 (Vic.); *Giesen* §36.

62. *T. v. T.* [1988] Fam. 52; critical: 51 Mod. L. Rev. 634; 53 Mod. L. Rev. 91 (1990).

63. As in the case of wardship jurisdiction: *Re B (A Minor)* [1988] A.C. 199; *Re F (Mental Patient)* [1990] 2 A.C. 1. A minor can be made ward of the court, but in England (unlike Australia) the parens patriae jurisdiction was abolished.

procedure, motivated by general social advantage rather than the patient's immediate welfare, the issue would best be left to legislative judgment.[64]

3. SELF-DEFENCE

Since "nature prompts a man who is struck to resist",[65] it has been recognised since early days that he may ward off his assailant by means necessary for his own protection.[66] The privilege arises from reasonable apprehension of physical aggression.[67] It is not necessary that the person threatened should wait until he is actually struck, so that if one raises his hand against you within reachable distance you may strike to prevent him. Mere provocation, however, not menacing to physical security is not counted at common law as a defence in civil proceedings,[68] though it may mitigate aggravated and exemplary damages[69] or qualify by statute (as in Queensland and perhaps Western Australia[70]); thus it would not excuse an irate husband for setting upon his wife's lover after surprising him in flagrante delicto.[71] Nor does the privilege sanction blows struck in revenge rather than self-defence, for example once the assailant is disabled and all danger past.[72]

The force used must not exceed what reasonably appears to be necessary to beat off the attack.[73] This is a question of fact and depends on such variable factors as the degree of violence offered, the nature of the weapons used by the assailant or the assailant's previous conduct and reputation for violence.[74] A simple assault cannot be justifiably resisted with firearms or

64. *Re Eve* [1987] 2 S.C.R. 1.
65. *Anon.* (1836) 2 Lewin 48; 168 E.R. 1075 per Parke B.
66. *Chapelyn de Greyes Inne v.* —— (1400) Y.B. 2 H. IV, pl. 40. Unlike in criminal law, the burden of proof rests on the defence: *R. v. Lobell* [1957] 1 Q.B. 547.
67. Whether such aggression is actually intended or not: *Rest. 2d* §63, comment *i*; aliter under the Codes: see *Hall v. Fonceca* [1983] W.A.R. 309. Belief must be reasonable, as in criminal law (*Zecevic v. D.P.P.* (1987) 162 C.L.R. 645; contra: *Beckford v. R.* [1988] A.C. 130 (P.C.)).
68. *McClelland v. Symons* [1951] V.L.R. 157 at 163; *Lowry v. Barlow* [1921] N.Z.L.R. 316; *Evans v. Bradburn* (1915) 25 D.L.R. 511. U.S.: 35 A.L.R. 4th 947 (1985).
69. But not general damages for pain and suffering and loss of amenities: *Fontin v. Katapodis* (1962) 108 C.L.R. 177; *Lane v. Holloway* [1968] 1 Q.B. 379, modified in *Murphy v. Culhane* [1977] Q.B. 94 (only when plaintiff's misconduct trivial); *Hoebergen v. Koppens* [1974] 2 N.Z.L.R. 597; *Landry v. Patterson* (1979) 93 D.L.R. (3d) 345. Criticised by Blay, 4 Q. U.T.L.J. 151 (1988).
70. Respectively s. 269 and s. 246 of the *Criminal Code*: any provocation "likely to deprive an ordinary person of the power of self-control and to induce him to assault the person by whom the act or insult is done or offered". The Code esp. refers only to "criminal action for assault", but the analogy has been regarded as sufficient to warrant its application to civil proceedings: *White v. Connolly* [1927] Q.S.R. 75; *Grehan v. Kann* [1948] Q.W.N. 40 criticised by Regan, 16 U.Q.L.J. 117 (1990).
71. As happened in *White v. Connolly* [1927] Q.S.R. 75.
72. *McClelland v. Symons* [1951] V.L.R. 157 at 162-163; *R. v. Driscoll* (1841) 1 C. & M. 214; 174 E.R. 477; and see *Packett v. R.* (1937) 58 C.L.R. 190.
73. Authority is split as to who carries the burden of proof on the issue of excessive force: *McClelland v. Symons* [1951] V.L.R. 157 and *Green v. Costello* [1961] N.Z.L.R. 1010 place it on the plaintiff, but *Mann v. Balaban* [1970] S.C.R. 74 and *Pearce v. Hallett* [1969] S.A.S.R. 423 on the defendant.
74. See *Wackett v. Calder* (1965) 51 D.L.R. (2d) 598; *R. v. Keith* [1934] Q.S.R. 155.

other deadly weapons;[75] far less does a mere raising of fists and an oral threat warrant the pointing of a loaded rifle with menace to discharge it.[76] But when attacked with such extreme violence that his very life is in danger, a person is privileged to inflict grievous bodily harm or even kill, provided the person believes on reasonable grounds that he cannot preserve himself by lesser means.[77] Nor is it any longer imperatively required that the person attacked must avail himself of all safe means of retreat before applying lethal force; today, this is merely one element in judging the reasonableness of conduct.[78]

If, acting in self-defence, the defendant misses his aim and hits a stranger, he is excused in the absence of negligence, the injury being ascribed to "inevitable accident".[79] But should he intentionally injure an innocent bystander, as by deliberately running him down in order to escape from a pursuer, the case is one of "necessity"; and it has been suggested that, while there might be no liability for the purely technical tort, he should be required to make good any actual damage.[80]

A defendant who is liable because he has used excessive force may, of course, have a counter-claim against the plaintiff for the initial attack and thus scale down the latter's recovery. This may leave both parties to bear the loss, and tends to deter the fault of either one.

Defence of others

Concomitant to the feudal obligation of mutual aid and protection between lord and liege, medieval law recognised a master's privilege to defend members of his household, that is, his family and servants, against personal attack.[81] Likewise, servants were justified in coming to the defence of their master,[82] and ultimately the same privilege was admitted as between other members of the same family.[83] Today our heightened social solidarity calls for a right to protect any fellow citizen against an aggressor.[84] In this respect, the Queensland and Western Australian Codes do not seem to go beyond the common law in providing that "in any case in which it is lawful for any person to use force of any degree for the purpose of defending himself against an assault, it is lawful for any other person acting in good faith in his aid to use a like degree of force for the

75. *Cook v. Beal* (1699) 1 Ld Raym. 176; 91 E.R. 1014.
76. *McClelland v. Symons* [1951] V.L.R. 157.
77. See Criminal Codes of Qld (ss 271, 272), W.A. (ss 248, 249), Tas. (ss 46, 47). These sections apply to civil proceedings: ss 6, 5 and 9(1) of the respective Criminal Code Acts.
78. *R. v. Howe* (1958) 100 C.L.R. 448; *Fontin v. Katapodis* (1962) 108 C.L.R. 177.
79. This is clear since *Stanley v. Powell* [1891] 1 Q.B. 86, but was apparently recognised as early as 1773: see *Scott v. Shepherd* (1773) 2 W. Bl. 892 at 900; 96 E.R. 525 at 529.
80. *Prosser & Keeton* 129. Cf. *Cordas v. Peerless Transport* 27 N.Y.S. 2d 198 (1941) (driver menaced by bandit jumped from moving taxi which careered into pedestrian, but held not negligent).
81. *Seaman v. Cuppledick* (c. 1610) Owen 150; 74 E.R. 966.
82. *Barfoot v. Reynolds* (1734) 2 Stra. 953; 93 E.R. 963.
83. *Leward v. Basely* (1695) 1 Ld Raym. 62; 91 E.R. 937.
84. *Pearce v. Hallett* [1969] S.A.S.R. 423; *Rest. 2d* §76. Support is usually derived also from the privilege to prevent a felony or breach of the peace, recognised at common law (see *Goss v. Nicholas* [1960] Tas. S.R. 133; *R. v. Duffy* [1967] 1 Q.B. 63) and reinforced by the Criminal Codes of Qld (s. 260) and W.A. (s. 237); *Criminal Law Act* 1967 (Eng.) s. 3 (public right to use force in the prevention of crime).

purpose of defending such first mentioned person."[85] As in the case of self-defence, so urgent is the call for instant action that allowance should be made for any reasonable mistake by the intervener in thinking that his action was necessary to ward off an attack and that the force used was reasonably proportioned to the exigency.[86]

4. DEFENCE OF PROPERTY

Property may be defended against intrusion or dispossession on principles closely akin to self-defence against personal aggression. The privilege is recognised no less for the protection of movables than of land, for it is law as old as the time of Henry VII that a man may justify an assault to prevent abduction of his dog.[87]

None but a possessor may exercise this privilege. Hence, while peaceable possession without title is sufficient against a wrongdoer,[88] the mere use of property without possession, such as presence thereon under a licence, will not justify force to exclude others.[89] At common law, therefore, the privilege is available in the same circumstances as the right of action for trespass and, since we shall see hereafter that the owner (or, more precisely, the person with the right to possession) has a privilege of forcible entry on land held by an adverse possessor,[90] it follows that the latter has no privilege to defend his possession against the owner, but only against persons with no better title than his own. This has been modified in Queensland, Western Australia and Tasmania, where it is lawful for a person in peaceable possession, *under a claim of right*, to defend his interest even against the person entitled to possession.[91]

The amount of force that one may use to exclude or expel a trespasser varies with the nature of the intrusion and the resistance encountered. Ordinarily, no force at all is justified, until he has first been requested to leave and given a reasonable opportunity to comply.[92] But when a trespass is committed with actual force, counterforce may be applied forthwith, since the intruder's conduct makes it clear that a formal request to desist would be futile.[93] If the intrusion threatens no harm to the physical

85. Respectively, s. 273 and s. 250. The *Criminal Code* (Tas.) s. 49 (and the *Crimes Act* 1961 (N.Z.) s. 51) speaks only of "defence of his own person or of the person of anyone under his protection", but authority for the defence of strangers is found in the preservation of *common law* "justification or excuse" (*Criminal Code Act* s. 8): *Goss v. Nicholas* [1960] Tas. S.R. 133.
86. *R. v. Fennell* [1971] 1 Q.B. 428 at 431; *Gambriell v. Caparelli* (1974) 54 D.L.R. (3d) 661.
87. *Norton v. Hoare* (1913) 17 C.L.R. 310 at 321-322 and authorities there cited.
88. Remember that a possessor without title can bring trespass for intrusion committed by anyone but the person with a right to possession: see above, p. 43. The privilege is codified in the Criminal Codes of Qld (ss 274, 277), W.A. (ss 251, 254) and Tas. (ss 41, 43).
89. *Dean v. Hogg* (1834) 10 Bing. 345; 131 E.R. 937; *Holmes v. Bagge* (1833) 1 E. & B. 782; 118 E.R. 629; *Roberts v. Tayler* (1845) 1 C.B. 117; 135 E.R. 481.
90. See below, p. 90.
91. The Criminal Codes of Qld (ss 275, 278; applied to civil proceedings in *Lotz v. Bullock* [1912] Q.S.R. 36); W.A. (ss 252, 255); Tas. (ss 42, 44).
92. *Polkinhorn v. Wright* (1845) 8 Q.B. 197; 115 E.R. 849; *Long v. Rawlins* (1874) 4 Q.S.C.R. 86.
93. *Polkinhorn v. Wright* (1845) 8 Q.B. 197 at 206; 115 E.R. 849 at 853.

condition of the property or the security of the possessor, the latter is privileged to use only the mildest of force—such as was expressed in the old form of pleading "mollitur manus imposuit". This clearly excludes any force calculated to cause grievous bodily harm, such as firing a shotgun even if only for the purpose of disabling a getaway car rather than hitting the thief.[94] But the requirement of "gentleness" need not be taken too literally: the occupier may lead, carry, pull or push but must not use deliberately damaging force.[95] However, if the trespasser assaults the occupier in the course of eviction, he is privileged to act in self-defence and, if threatened with serious bodily harm, may even retaliate with force intended or likely to endanger life or limb. Moreover, any burglar or forcible intruder may be resisted at the outset with appropriate force; but it has become doubtful whether deadly force is any longer justifiable to resist eviction, even from one's home, if there is no reasonable ground for believing one's own life to be threatened.[96]

Where greater force than necessary or reasonable has been used to exclude or expel the intruder, he is entitled to compensation for the excess of violence. This may include an award for affront to his dignity, as when a plaintiff, after being removed from a meeting, was jammed in the door for a considerable time.[97] Sometimes, indeed, the privilege must yield altogether to the superior claim of the trespasser's bodily security. Not being justified to maim or kill, the possessor cannot expel the trespasser, if to do so would expose him to serious physical harm. Thus a tramp may not be thrown from a fast moving train,[98] or an intoxicated patron ejected from a bar when he is incapable of coping with the traffic outside.[99]

Defence against animals

In defence of property threatened with damage or destruction by marauding animals, the owner may adopt such measures as are necessary and reasonable to avert the danger and, in the last resort, may even shoot to kill. In order to justify this extreme expedient, the owner must prove that his property was in real or imminent danger and that there were either no other practical means open to him for stopping or preventing a renewal of

94. *Hackshaw v. Shaw* (1984) 155 C.L.R. 614 (negligent).
95. *Cullen v. Rice* (1981) 120 D.L.R. (3d) 641 denied liability for mere negligence and required at least wilful or reckless or inhumane conduct: cf. below, p. 466. Under the Codes of Qld (ss 274, 275, 277, 278) and W.A. (ss 251, 252, 254, 255) the force must not be such as to cause "bodily harm". In Tas. (ss 41-44) the force must not be "intended and not likely to cause death or grievous bodily harm". In no event may it exceed what is "reasonably necessary in order to defend his possession of the property" (see *Greenbury v. Lyon* [1957] Q.S.R. 433).
96. Modern police force, speedy remedy for recovery of possession and the prevailing belief in precedence for sanctity of life over property render the few pronouncements of older vintage suspect: pace, McInerny J. in *Shaw v. Hackshaw* [1983] V.R. 65 at 100-101; revd (1984) 155 C.L.R. 614. This accords with the American view: *Rest. 2d* deleted original §87(2); also *Model Penal Code* §3.06. The Criminal Codes of Qld (s. 267), W.A. (s. 244) and Tas. (s. 40) allow "necessary force" to prevent forcible intrusion of dwelling house. There is no justification whatever for shooting *escaping* burglars: *Bigcharles v. Merkel* [1973] 1 W.W.R. 324.
97. *Kohan v. Stanbridge* (1916) 16 S.R. (N.S.W.) 576.
98. *Kline v. Central Pacific Rly* 37 Cal. 400 (1869).
99. *Menow v. Honsberger* [1974] S.C.R. 239; 38 D.L.R. (3d) 105.

the attack, or that the owner acted reasonably in regarding shooting as necessary for the protection of his crops or livestock.[100] Thus circumstances may allow a farmer to fire on dogs chasing his sheep[101] or attacking an aviary of breeding pheasants,[102] but he would not ordinarily be justified in shooting homing pigeons until he had first attempted to ward them off his crops by a scaring shot.[103] In no event is it permissible to kill a trespassing dog merely because it is playing with one's own.[104]

The common law has not gone beyond sanctioning measures against an existing or imminent attack: in particular it does not justify the killing of animals merely because they have done damage in the past. However, in view of the peculiar menace of dogs to livestock, much wider powers have been conferred on graziers, including the right to destroy dogs roaming at large or within enclosed paddocks.[105]

Short of destroying a trespassing animal, a landowner enjoys the privilege of impounding it, usually in addition to claiming for any damage it has done. This power, strictly regulated by statute,[106] has in practice largely superseded[107] the ancient common law remedy of *distress damage feasant*. However, the latter can be invoked not only against trespassing cattle but against any chattel, such as an unlawfully parked car, which encumbers the land and causes damage.[108] A merely technical trespass does not suffice and it is unclear whether the cost of removal would be recoverable (as in an action for trespass).[109] Nor may the privilege be exercised over animals or chattels in personal control or use of its possessor.[110] Where the circumstances permit the occupier to use this remedy, it would ordinarily be unreasonable for him to resort instead to destructive force in warding off the marauders.

Indirect methods of protection

Rather than act personally, occupiers may prefer defence by means of barriers, mechanical devices or animals. But such methods are incapable of making discriminations as to the precise amount of force such as are

100. *Cresswell v. Sirl* [1948] 1 K.B. 241; *Workman v. Cowper* [1961] 2 Q.B. 143 (privilege not confined to owner).
101. Ibid.; *Goodway v. Becher* [1951] 2 All E.R. 349. See also Prentice, *Marauding Cats*, 32 A.L.J. 372 (1960).
102. *Miles v. Hutchings* [1903] 2 K.B. 714.
103. *Hamps v. Darby* [1948] 2 K.B. 311.
104. *Barnard v. Evans* [1925] 2 K.B. 794.
105. N.S.W.: *Dog and Goat Act* 1898 ss 12(2), 20, and see *Jolliffe v. Dean* (1954) 54 S.R. (N.S.W.) 157; Vic.: *Dog Act* 1970 s. 24; Qld: *Animal Protection Act* 1925 ss 4(3), 7(1)(c); S.A.: *Dog Control Act* 1979 s. 36; W.A.: *Dog Act* 1903 ss 22, 22a, 23a; Tas.: *Law of Animals Act* 1962 ss 11-14; N.Z.: *Dogs Registration Act* 1955 ss 22-28. These statutes are far from uniform.
106. E.g. *Impounding Act* 1898 (N.S.W.); *Local Government Act* 1918 (Pt 18).
107. Abolished by *Animals Act* 1977 (N.S.W.) s. 5; *Civil Liabilities (Animals) Act* 1984 (A.C.T.).
108. *Ambergate Rly v. Midland Rly* (1853) E. & B. 793; 118 E.R. 964 (railway engine); *Forhan v. Hallett* (1959) 19 D.L.R. (2d) 756 (car); *Wormer v. Biggs* (1845) 2 C. & K. 31; 175 E.R. 13; *Forhan v. Hallet* (1959) 19 D.L.R. (2d) 756.
109. See Bickley, *Trespassing Vehicles* [1984] N.Z.L.J. 81.
110. *Jamieson's Tow & Salvage v. Murray* [1984] 2 N.Z.L.R. 144.

expected from the occupier, were he present, and of first warning the trespasser before taking action. Strict adherence to the caution that "one may not do indirectly what is unlawful to do directly"[111] would inhibit all such means of defence, because the possessor would run the risk that the injury inflicted might be in excess of what would otherwise be proper. A compromise has accordingly been adopted, which is usually expressed in the distinction between devices that are and that are not likely to cause death or serious bodily injury, the latter alone being lawful.[112] Thus, it is a statutory offence to set spring guns, man traps and other engines calculated to destroy human life or to inflict grievous bodily harm, except by night and in a dwelling house for its protection;[113] and even at common law a trespasser hurt in this way has been allowed to recover,[114] unless he was actually aware of the presence of guns.[115] On the other hand, it is permissible to put up barbed wire or set broken glass and spikes on a wall, because their utility far outweighs the chance that a harmless trespasser may occasionally suffer slightly excessive injury.

As an alternative test, it has been suggested that an occupier is free to set up "deterrent" dangers intended to keep intruders out, but not "retributive" dangers whose purpose is primarily to inflict injury.[116] Objects, such as spiked railings or barbed wire, can only be used deterrently, since in day time they carry their own warning unless concealed and at night the notoriety of their customary use supplies the place of knowledge which trespassers by day obtain by observation. On the other hand, the setting of retributive dangers which are not obvious but concealed, exposes an occupier to liability unless the harm caused is no more than he would have been privileged to inflict personally and directly. Spring guns cannot be used deterrently and their use is improper, unless the occupier could justify "personally firing the shot".[117]

Trespassers have received short shrift for dog bites and other injuries by animals. An occupier is entitled to employ a guard dog on the premises to keep intruders out—apparently even without a specific warning sign, at any rate if the place is locked or marked "keep out".[118]

111. *Addie v. Dumbreck* [1929] A.C. 358 at 376.
112. Bohlen & Burns, *Privilege to Protect Property by Dangerous Barriers and Mechanical Devices*, 35 Yale L.J. 525 (1926); *Rest. 2d* §85.
113. *Crimes Act* 1900 (N.S.W.) s. 49; *Crimes Act* 1958 (Vic.) s. 32; *Criminal Law Consolidation Act* 1935 (S.A.) s. 34; Criminal Codes of Qld (s. 327); W.A. (s. 305); Tas. (s. 179); *Crimes Act* 1908 (N.Z.) s. 205.
114. *Bird v. Holbrook* (1828) 4 Bing. 628; 130 E.R. 911 where Best C.J. regarded the statute creating the criminal offence as declaratory of the common law, except in so far as it prohibited the setting of guns even with notice. Note, however, the doubt expressed in *Jordin v. Crump* (1841) 8 M. & W. 782 at 789; 151 E.R. 1256 at 1259.
115. *Ilott v. Wilkes* (1820) 3 B. & Ald. 304; 106 E.R. 674; see Evatt, 53 Harv. L. Rev. 1145 at 1148-52 (1936).
116. Hart, *Injuries to Trespassers*, 47 L.Q.R. 92 at 101-105 (1931).
117. *Addie v. Dumbreck* (1929) A.C. 358 at 376; *Rest. 2d* §85, comment *a*. On this view, *Ilott v. Wilkes* was wrongly decided: Palmer, *Iowa Spring Gun Case*, 56 Iowa L. Rev. 1219 (1971).
118. *Trethowan v. Capron* [1961] V.R. 460; *Cummings v. Granger* [1977] Q.B. 397 (*Animals Act* 1971 s. 5: "reasonable"). Also see below, p. 363.

5. FORCIBLE ENTRY

The early common law allowed one who had been disseised of his land to repossess himself by force, provided he did so within four days. Later, this time span was greatly extended until the privilege was found to have become incompatible with the due maintenance of order. In consequence, a series of Statutes of Forcible Entry[119] were passed, commencing in the latter half of the 14th century, which made entry vi et armis even by one wrongfully dispossessed[120] an indictable offence. This legislation was received into Australia and is in force in all jurisdictions.[121]

An entry is regarded as forcible when it is effected by breaking outer doors or windows[122] or is accompanied by personal violence or threats.[123] But apparently no offence is committed, if the purpose was not to assume or resume possession of the premises but merely to remove some chattel.[124]

The precise effect of the statute upon the civil rights of an owner was for long unsettled. Clearly, the owner was not liable in trespass for entering his own premises because, though indictable for breaking the peace, the owner had infringed no "right" of the plaintiff and inflicted no injury for which the latter was entitled to compensation, provided no greater force than necessary was applied to eject the plaintiff.[125] But a line of decisions starting in 1840[126] held that, while the owner was privileged to use force in gaining possession of his land, he could not justify independent wrongful acts committed in the course of forcible entry, like personal violence against the occupier or removing the occupier's chattels, even if they were necessary to accomplish the purpose of expelling him. The practical effect was that "an occupier having no colour of right on whom an entry was made under the true title could manufacture a cause of action for assault by a show of merely passive or symbolic resistance."[127] Behind this new judicial approach was probably the feeling that the system of legal administration had become confident enough to discourage self-help and compel recourse

119. The most important is the Act of 1381, 5 Rich. II c. 8. Replaced by *Criminal Law Act* 1977 (U.K.) s. 6.
120. But there is an undefined interval before the intruder has gained possession sufficient to prohibit his forcible ejection: *McPhail v. Persons Unknown* [1973] Ch. 447 at 456 (controversially extended by Lord Denning until the owner has acquiesced).
121. N.S.W.: see *R. v. Waugh* (1934) 52 W.N. (N.S.W.) 20; *Crimes Act* 1958 (Vic.) s. 207; *Criminal Code* (S.A.) s. 70; *Criminal Law Consolidation Act* 1935 (S.A.) s. 543; Criminal Codes of Qld (s. 70), W.A. (s. 69), Tas. (s. 79); *Crimes Act* 1961 (N.Z.) s. 91.
122. Comm. Dig., Forcible Entry, A. 2; but apparently not by lifting off the roof of a house: *Jones v. Foley* [1891] 1 Q.B. 730.
123. Hawkins, P.C. i, 501; *Edwick v. Hawkes* (1881) 18 Ch. D. 199 at 211-212.
124. *R. v. Waugh* (1934) 52 W.N. (N.S.W.) 20, preferring *R. v. Pike* (1898) 2 Can. Crim. Cas. 314 to *R. v. Bullock* (1924) 88 J.P. 335.
125. *Pollen v. Brewer* (1859) 7 C.B. (N.S.) 371; *Clifton Securities v. Huntley* [1948] 2 All E.R. 283 (cutting off utilities, barricading access). This goes back to the Y.B.: *Holdsworth* iii, 280. The privilege is not lost because the owner has invoked legal process up to a certain point, e.g. by recovering judgment in an action of ejectment, provided this does not cause the other to change his position in reliance on the owner's call on the law: *Aglionby v. Cohen* [1955] 1 Q.B. 558.
126. *Newton v. Harland* (1840) 1 Man. & G. 644; 133 E.R. 490; *Beddall v. Maitland* (1881) 17 Ch. D. 174.
127. *Pollock* 292.

to the judicial process. The trend was, however, reversed in 1920 when in *Hemmings v. Stoke Poges Golf Club*[128] the English Court of Appeal denied to a tenant, who had been evicted after holding over, an action for assault and for damage caused by removing his goods from the premises, thereby obliterating the distinction between (privileged) entry and any (unprivileged) collateral wrong. In view of the modern facilities for summary proceedings in which an owner can recover possession by legal process with little delay and cost, this change of the law has not passed without criticism.

The common law privilege of forcible entry has been abridged in Queensland, Western Australia and Tasmania, whose Criminal Codes[129] make it lawful for a person in peaceable possession of land, structure or a vessel, *under a claim of right*, to use such force as is necessary to defend his possession even against one who is entitled by law to the possession of such property.[130] This privilege of the possessor appears necessarily to rule out any conflicting privilege by the owner to repossess himself by force in such circumstances.[131]

Besides, modern tenants' protection Acts have also abridged a landlord's right of eviction. In many jurisdictions, a landlord must apply to a tribunal for an order to terminate a residential tenancy; even peaceful repossession being prohibited.[132] Otherwise, a landlord who peacefully re-enters upon termination of the tenancy may remove the lessee's goods, upon giving reasonable notice, so long, it has been said, as any damage or loss is not wholly disproportionate to the injury averted.[133]

6. RECAPTURE OF CHATTELS

One dispossessed of a chattel may in some circumstances invoke the privilege of recapturing it instead of resorting to judicial process. The survival of this mode of self-redress must be attributed largely to certain inadequacies of the traditional legal machinery, foremost among which used to be the common law's inability to compel specific restitution.[134] Besides, failure promptly to regain control of a chattel may result in its complete loss because it may become untraceable or its owner's title extinguished by a subsequent transfer to an innocent holder.[135] The scope of the privilege has widened steadily since medieval times with increasing confidence in the ability of law to regulate extra-judicial redress;[136] but

128. [1920] 1 K.B. 720.
129. Respectively, ss 278, 255 and 42.
130. Provided he does not do bodily harm to such person. (In Tas.: provided such force is not intended and is not likely to cause death or grievous bodily harm.)
131. It is also noteworthy that, in the case of land, the Codes do not confer a privilege of entry corresponding to that of the owner of movables who may take them from a person in possession holding with a claim of right. (Qld: s. 276; W.A.: s. 253; Tas.: s. 45).
132. E.g. *Residential Tenancies Act* (N.S.W. 1987, s. 53); (Vic. 1980, s. 149), (S.A. 1978, s. 61).
133. *Haniotis v. Dimitriou* [1983] 1 V.R. 498 at 502.
134. See above, p. 74.
135. E.g. by sale in market overt.
136. The history is traced by Branston, *Forcible Recaption of Chattels*, 28 L.Q.R. 262 (1918).

this trend, which reached its zenith during the last century, is likely to be reversed rather than followed today. Still, owing to the dearth of modern authority and some conflict among the older decisions, the present position cannot be stated in all respects with a high degree of confidence.[137]

There is no doubt about the privilege of retaking a chattel from one who has appropriated it by trespass, including the use of whatever force is reasonably necessary to wrest control from him.[138] Originally, force was justified only for a recapture proceeding immediately or on fresh pursuit, when the owner could be regarded as defending his original possession rather than trying to regain what had been definitely lost. Lapse of some time, however, no longer seems to defeat the owner's right of forcible recaption,[139] except perhaps after a considerable interval during which the owner has given up all intention of self-help.[140]

According to the better opinion, force is not justified unless the plaintiff's adverse possession was wrongful from its inception. Against a bailee, for example, the owner must resort to law, at any rate if repossession cannot be accomplished peacefully.[141] There is some authority, however, for a wider privilege, based on the view that "the plaintiff's wrongful detention against the request of the defendant would be the same violation of the right of property as the taking of the chattels out of the actual possession of the owner."[142] Yet this dictum really begs the question, because it assumes that the privilege inheres in all persons with an immediate right to possession, thereby ignoring the distinction between violation of actual possession and a mere right to possession, which determines whether the conduct amounts to trespass or conversion. It is contrary to the early common law[143] and even went beyond the facts of the case whence it originated. There a dealer bought some rabbits from a poacher who had unlawfully killed them on the defendant's land. When he called for them at the station, the defendant's servants made demand and, upon his refusal to give them up, used force to retake them. Although it was held that the defendant had a good defence to an action for assault, it must be remembered that there had been an original wrongful taking by the poacher; and a more recent Canadian decision refused to extend the holding to a case where the initial possession of the plaintiff, as distinct from the subsequent detention, was not wrongful but due to the act of the defendant himself.[144] In Queensland, Western Australia and Tasmania, however, it is lawful for any person entitled by law to the possession of movable property to take it from an adverse possessor who does not hold it under a claim of

137. See English Law Reform Committee (Report 18, 1971) 39-42.

138. *R. v. Mitton* (1827) 3 C. & P. 31; 172 E.R. 309. The Criminal Codes of Qld (s. 274) and W.A. (s. 251) forbid bodily harm; Tas. (s. 43) force which is intended or likely to cause death or grievous bodily harm.

139. See *Blades v. Higgs* (1861) 10 C.B. (N.S.) 713; 142 E.R. 634.

140. *Rest. 2d* §103 requires the owner to act "promptly after his dispossession or after his timely discovery thereof".

141. *Rest. 2d* §108. As pointed out in *Devoe v. Long* [1951] 1 D.L.R. 203 at 218, the contrary propositions accepted in *De Lambert v. Ongley* [1924] N.Z.L.R. 430 is not supported by authority.

142. *Blades v. Higgs* (1861) 10 C.B. (N.S.) 713 at 720.

143. *Pollock* 293.

144. *Devoe v. Long* [1951] 1 D.L.R. 203.

right, and to use such force to overcome resistance as is necessary to obtain possession, provided he does not inflict bodily harm.[145]

No force is justified until there has first been a demand to yield up possession peaceably,[146] unless perhaps such a request would be futile or dangerous.[147] Moreover, the owner may not use more violence than is reasonably necessary for recapture; if excessive, the other is justified in repelling it.[148] On the other hand, unlawful resistance to a reasonable mode of recapture may be countered by stronger force and, if the owner is threatened with serious bodily harm, he may exercise his privilege of self-defence and, if necessary, even adopt means calculated to maim or kill.

Entry on land

Closely allied is the privilege of entering another's land to regain a lost chattel. It is not disputed that where the land is that of the wrongdoer[149] or of a third party who knew of, or assented to, his wrong,[150] the person dispossessed may enter and even use force, but no more than reasonably necessary for the purpose.

If the chattel has come upon the land by accident, as where fruit falls or a tree is blown across the boundary[151] and the claimant was not himself actively responsible for its being there,[152] he is privileged to enter, though almost certainly not to use force. Entry is apparently also permitted to retake goods that have been carried upon the occupier's land by a felon[153]—a privilege which appears to have originated in a desire to promote the pursuit of felons whose conviction was once of pecuniary advantage to the Crown. But if to be perpetuated at all, it might as well also be applied now to misdemeanours, so as for example to permit recapture of a car "borrowed" for a joyride and later abandoned in someone else's yard.[154]

In no other circumstances, however, would a privilege of entry be warranted today. Particularly there is none for retaking goods, the original possession of which was lawfully acquired by the occupier,[155] apparently even if he refuses to hand them back on demand, like a bailee on

145. The Criminal Codes, ss 276, 253 and 45 respectively. In Tas.: "provided such force is not intended and is not likely to cause death or grievous bodily harm."
146. *Blades v. Higgs* (1861) 10 C.B. (N.S.) 713; 142 E.R. 634.
147. *Rest. 2d* §104.
148. *R. v. Mitton* (1827) 3 C. & P. 31; 172 E.R. 309.
149. *Patrick v. Colerick* (1838) 3 M. & W. 483; 150 E.R. 1235; *Cox v. Bath* (1893) 14 L.R. (N.S.W.) 263.
150. *Huet v. Lawrence* [1948] Q.S.R. 168 (occupier actively assisted to defeat plaintiff's rights).
151. *Anthony v. Haney* (1832) 8 Bing. 186 at 192; 131 E.R. 372 at 374.
152. *Ibid.*; *Case of Thorns* (1466) Y.B. 6 Ed. IV, 7, pl. 18; *Read v. Smith* (1836) 2 N.B.R. 288 (Can.).
153. *Blackstone* iii, 5; *Anthony v. Haney* (1832) 8 Bing. 186 at 192; 131 E.R. 372 at 374.
154. Instead of extending the privilege, the assimilation of felonies to misdemeanours in England by the *Criminal Law Act* 1967 may have abolished it altogether.
155. E.g. a bona fide purchaser (*Murray v. M'Neill* (1885) 1 W.N. (N.S.W.) 136) or because the goods were on the premises when he took possession (*Zimmler v. Manning* (1863) 2 S.C.R. (N.S.W.) 235) or because the plaintiff himself either forgetfully left them there (*Devoe v. Long* [1951] 1 D.L.R. 203) or his animals have escaped there: *Kearry v. Pattinson* [1939] 1 K.B. 471 at 481.

termination of the hire or an instalment buyer after default.[156] Though his recalcitrance amounts to conversion,[157] law and order are best served by compelling the claimant to vindicate his rights by legal process rather than by condoning self-help.

7. NECESSITY

In some circumstances, a person is privileged to infringe the interests of another for the purpose of preventing harm either to his own interests or those of third parties if the harm he intends is not out of proportion to that he seeks to avoid. This defence, known as "necessity", involves more obviously than any of the preceding a hard choice between competing values and a sacrifice of one to the other.[158] It differs from self-defence, in that it justifies action adverse to the interests of someone who is not in any way responsible for creating the threat to the actor; and from inevitable accident, because injury to the innocent party is an intended or at least highly probable consequence. Its basis has been described as "a mixture of charity, the maintenance of public good and self-protection",[159] appealing either to compassion or utility.[160]

Public champion

The immunity of a public champion has been recognised from early times. Thus it was said by Coke that "for the commonwealth, a man shall suffer damage; as for saving a city or town, a house shall be plucked down if the next be on fire . . . and a thing for the commonwealth every man may do without being liable to an action."[161] Here the privilege is complete in the sense that it both justifies the infliction of injury and also exempts the actor from being required to make compensation.[162] Not only is it felt to be unfair to make the actor pay out of his own pocket for the whole of the damage done by an intervention from which he obtained none, or only a negligible part,[163] of the benefit; but also the owner of the house that is pulled down to prevent the spread of a conflagration is a better risk bearer

156. Hire-purchase legislation in Australia and England uniformly invalidates any *contractual* provision purporting to confer such a privilege: e.g., *Hire-Purchase Act* of N.S.W. (1960, s. 36(1)(g)); Vic. (1959, s. 28(g)); Eng. (1964, s. 34). Strictly speaking, this leaves open the position otherwise. See Turner, *Repossession under the Australian "uniform" Hire Purchase Legislation*, 7 Syd. L. Rev. 1 at 14-26 (1973).
157. Courts have in any event displayed extreme reluctance to infer conversion from an occupier's mere refusal to hand back a chattel left on his land by someone else: *British Lamp Co. v. Empire, Mile End* (1913) 29 T.L.R. 386.
158. "The language of necessity disguises the selection of values that is really involved" (Williams, *Defence of Necessity*, 6 Cur. Leg. Prob. 216 at 224 (1953)). The defence is also recognised in criminal law: Williams, *Criminal Law* (2nd ed. 1983) ch. 26; *R. v. Loughnan* [1981] V.R. 443.
159. *Winfield & Jolowicz* 722.
160. This duality has its counterpart in the distinction between excuse and justification in criminal law theory.
161. *Saltpetre's Case* (1606) 12 Co. Rep. 12 at 13; 77 E.R. 1294. It has been questioned whether nowadays the privilege is not confined to fire brigades: *Burmah Oil v. Lord Advocate* [1965] A.C. 75 at 165.
162. *Rest. 2d* §§196, 262.
163. See *Mouse's Case* (1609) 12 Co. Rep. 63; 77 E.R. 1341.

than the fire fighter. Property owners are usually insured and can better calculate the amount of cover they need than the fire brigade or municipal authority. Moreover, if the latter were held responsible, the ultimate loss would fall on the rate payers, who are approximately the same people who pay fire insurance premiums.[164] It is significant that uniform legislation throughout Australia not only authorises fire brigades to destroy houses for the purpose of extinguishing or preventing the spread of fire, thereby placing their immunity beyond doubt, but also enacts that any damage thus caused shall be deemed to be damage by fire within the meaning of any fire insurance policy covering the property.[165] This is a clear expression of policy as to the most efficient method of distributing losses of this kind.

Even in situations where there is less likelihood of the plaintiff's property being insured, it would be unfair to require the public champion to make good the loss, at any rate when he is in no position to distribute it among those for whose benefit the sacrifice was exacted. Thus there is no liability for the value of cargo jettisoned in order to save the lives of passengers in a storm on a *river*[166]—as distinct from *at sea* where the maritime principle of "general average" assures the more equitable solution of the vessel and cargo contributing rateably towards indemnifying the plaintiff, thereby spreading the cost fairly among all those who benefit from the sacrifice instead of its being borne wholly either by the altruistic plaintiff or by whoever first took the initiative on behalf of others. If private property is sacrificed in the public interest by a public agent, democratic values might well suggest that the cost be borne by the community. This principle is widely recognised in the statutory, if not constitutional, obligation to provide fair compensation for property taken for public purposes under powers of eminent domain.[167] In other situations, however, the common law has not been forthcoming.[168]

Private interests

An intentional invasion of another's legally protected interests may even be privileged if done solely for the purpose of protecting a private interest of one's own. Provided the means taken to avert the threatened harm are reasonably necessary, in the sense that they are acts which in all the circumstances a reasonable man would do to meet a real and imminent

164. Hall & Wigmore, *Compensation for Property Destroyed to Stop the Spread of Conflagration* 1 Ill. L. Rev. 501 (1907).
165. *Fire Brigades Act* 1909 (N.S.W.) ss 29, 32; *Metropolitan Fire Brigade Act* 1958 (Vic.) ss 33, 54; *Fire Brigade Act* 1920 (Qld) Sched. Pt III ss 24, 33; *Fire Brigade Act* 1936 (S.A.) ss 45, 71; *Fire Brigade Act* 1942 (W.A.) ss 34, 64; *Fire Brigade Act* 1945 (Tas.) ss 33, 56; *Fire Brigade Ordinance* 1957 (A.C.T.) s. 9; *Fire Services Act* 1949 (N.Z.) ss 45-46. Many of these statutes confer immunity for all bona fide performance of duty, as does the *Police Regulations Act* 1899 (N.S.W.) s. 26A on police. This seems to cover even negligence. See *Vincent v. Fire Comm.* [1977] 1 N.S.W.L.R. 15; Churches, *"Bona Fide" Police Torts*, 6 U. Tas. L. Rev. 294 (1980).
166. *Mouse's Case* (1609) 12 Co. Rep. 63; 77 E.R. 1341.
167. See also *Burmah Oil v. Lord Advocate* [1965] A.C. 75 (comment, 79 Harv. L. Rev. 614; 28 Mod. L. Rev. 574 (1965)), requiring compensation for destruction of private British property by military abroad. The decision was shamelessly nullified by *War Damage Act* 1965.
168. Cf. *Rigby v. Chief Constable* [1985] 1 W.L.R. 1242 (police smoking out criminal); *Lapierre v. A.-G.* [1985] 1 S.C.R. 241 (Que.).

peril,[169] society's concern in the preservation of human and material resources tips the scales in favour of the privilege. If the emergency is sufficiently great and the good it is intended to do is not disproportionate to the harm likely to result, one may trespass upon the land of another to save himself or his property,[170] discharge oil on another's beach to ease his ship off a sandbank,[171] tow away a vessel to save his wharf,[172] or set alight a strip of heather to prevent a fire reaching his valuable aviary.[173] More doubtful is whether this utilitarian orientation could ever justify personal injury. What little authority there is seems to deny such a privilege, at any rate if it would involve serious bodily harm or death.[174] It could be, however, that one who is threatened with very serious injury may subject an innocent stranger to slight harm, disproportionately smaller than any from which the person is himself trying to escape.[175]

At all events, only an urgent situation of imminent peril can ever raise the defence, lest necessity become simply a mask for anarchy. Thus it is that not even the hungry are excused for stealing bread or the homeless for sheltering on someone else's property.[176] In this respect, the defence of necessity has its counterpart in the very limited duty of assisting the needy: our law generally disfavours coerced benevolence.[177] Nor is the defence available when the need to act was brought about by the actor's own negligence.[178]

But if the privilege is recognised, resistance to its exercise becomes unlawful and entails liability for resulting harm.[179] In *Ploof v. Putnam*,[180] the plaintiff's sloop was overtaken by a violent squall. To save it, he moored it to the defendant's dock, but the latter cast it adrift with the result

169. Justification depends on the state of things as they appear at the time of the interference, not *after* the event: *Cope v. Sharpe (No. 2)* [1912] 1 K.B. 496.
170. *Sherrin v. Haggerty* [1953] O.W.N. 962 at 964. Analogous is the privilege of passing across private land in order to overcome an obstruction of the highway: *Dwyer v. Staunton* [1947] 4 D.L.R. 393; aliter, if the right of way is private: *Taylor v. Whitehead* (1781) 2 Doug. 745; 99 E.R. 475.
171. Cf. *Esso v. Southport Corp.* [1956] A.C. 218: see below, n. 184.
172. *Beckingham v. P.J. & M. Co.* [1957] S.R. (N.S.W.) 403.
173. *Cope v. Sharpe (No. 2)* [1912] 1 K.B. 496. For defence against flood waters see below, p. 431.
174. Criminal law has traditionally responded by executive clemency rather than recognising a legal defence: Williams, *Criminal Law*, ch. 17. But see the new approach of *Perka v. R.* [1984] 2 S.C.R. 232. The only civil case is *Laidlaw v. Sage* 52 N.E. 679 (N.Y. 1899) where it was assumed that one is liable who, being about to be shot by a gunman, deliberately seizes a bystander as a shield (evidence failed to establish seizure). In contrast, no liability was held to attach to instinctive action for self-preservation, as where one about to fall grasped another for support: *Filippone v. Reisenburger* 119 N.Y.S. 632 (1909). Note also that, in negligence cases, where a person is faced with the choice between endangering himself or another, the second alternative is not necessarily "unreasonable": see below, p. 117.
175. See *Rest. 2d* §73, *caveat.* If the harm is threatened by the plaintiff himself, even though he be legally innocent as in the case of a child, self-help is conceivably privileged to the same extent as in the case of self-defence against intentional or negligent aggression.
176. *Southwark L.B.C. v. Williams* [1971] Ch. 734 (C.A.).
177. See below, p. 147.
178. *Rigby v. Chief Constable* [1985] 1 W.L.R. 1242 at 1253.
179. In Hohfeldian terminology, the actor's is not just a privilege but a *right*, because the other is under a *duty* to submit to its exercise.
180. 81 Vt 471, 71 Atl. 188 (1908).

that the boat was driven ashore and the passengers injured. The defendant was held liable for the damage.

There remains the question whether a person who has lawfully exercised the privilege of necessity is required to make compensation for any actual damage he has caused thereby. As long ago as 1832,[181] Tindal C.J. contemplated this possibility in a dictum which was later invoked in the leading American case of *Vincent v. Lake Erie Transportation Co.*,[182] where it was held that a shipowner who kept his vessel moored to a dock during a storm was liable for the actual damage done by the buffeting because, though "the situation was one in which the ordinary rules regulating property rights were suspended by force beyond human control", the defendant had preserved his ship at the expense of the dock and was responsible as to the extent of the injury. The decision recognises what has been called an "incomplete" privilege,[183] that is one which justifies a technical interference with the plaintiff's property and enjoins the latter from resisting it, but does not relieve the invader from liability to pay for any actual damage done. Although our case law does not preclude a similar solution,[184] it has usually been tacitly assumed that, because an act is lawful in the sense that it may not be opposed, it cannot subject the actor to liability. This approach has the superficial attraction of symmetry, but makes no allowance for the competing principle of restitution for benefits gained at another's expense.[185] Society has an interest in saving human life and property from destruction, but its only concern with the cost of salvage is that it should be allocated justly: is it not fairer that it be borne by him who derived the benefit from sacrificing the other's property?

The converse situation occurs where the defendant acted for the purpose of protecting the plaintiff's own health or property: here, instead of subordinating the plaintiff's interests to his own, the defendant actually sought to advance them. Examples are force-feeding a prisoner on hunger strike,[186] restraining a dangerous lunatic,[187] performing an emergency operation on an unconscious patient,[188] perhaps even efforts by volunteers to salvage property on occasions of urgent necessity, such as removing

181. *Anthony v. Haney* (1832) Bing. 186 at 193; 131 E.R. 372 at 374.
182. 109 Minn. 456, 124 N.W. 221 (1910); *Rest. 2d* §§197, 263; German *Civil Code* §904; Limpens, XI Int. L. Encycl. Comp. L. ch. 2 §175.
183. Bohlen, *Incomplete Privilege*, 39 Harv. L. Rev. 307 (1926).
184. *Munn v. "Sir J. Crosbie"* [1967] 1 Ex. C.R. 94 on virtually identical facts is to the contrary. *Esso v. Southport Corp.* [1956] A.C. 218; [1954] 2 Q.B. 182; [1953] 3 W.L.R. 773 (discharged of oil to save ship) did not yield a clear ruling on this point, as it seems to have been assumed throughout that the defendant was at most guilty of negligent, not intentional, harm, i.e., the case was treated as if there had been only a risk, not substantial certainty, of harm. *Burmah Oil v. Lord Advocate* [1975] A.C. 75 recognised that the lawfulness of an act does not preclude a duty to compensate.
185. *Rest. of Restitution* §122. See D. Friedmann, *Restitution of Benefits*, 80 Col. L. Rev. 504 at 540-546 (1980). In principle it is closely akin to strict liability, where pursuit of a lawful activity is also made conditional on compensation for ensuing injury: see below, p. 329.
186. *Leigh v. Gladstone* (1909) 26 T.L.R. 139; *Re Children's Aid Society* (1981) 128 D.L.R. (3d) 751 (suicide).
187. *Scott v. Wakem* (1862) 3 F. & F. 328; 176 E.R. 147; *Watson v. Marshall* (1971) 124 C.L.R. 621.
188. See above, p. 83.

furniture in danger from flood or halting a runaway car.[189] In such an event, the actor is excused even if, in the excitement of the moment, he embarks on a course which in retrospect turns out to have been mistaken.[190] But these instances in which a privilege has been recognised are rare. Our law does not favour thrusting unrequested benefits on others. Far from recognising claims to recompense such efforts,[191] it is reluctant even to condone "officious intermeddling". It certainly would require very special circumstances to justify interfering with another's property, once its owner had been informed of the peril but elected to do nothing about it.[192]

So long as strict liability dominated trespass, duress was not recognised as an excuse, and even the threat of death by armed bandits did not excuse a man for accompanying them into the plaintiff's house and thus making an unlawful entry.[193] Actual physical compulsion, however, was a defence, as "if a man take my hand by force and strike you",[194] because there never was liability for involuntary conduct. Since modern law no longer attaches liability for a trespass in the absence of fault, it is perhaps an open question whether duress would not today be admitted as a defence in civil proceedings under the same conditions as in criminal law.[195]

8. DISCIPLINE

The early common law invested the husband and father, as head of the household, with broad disciplinary powers over members of his family. His duty of protection conferred on him a corresponding privilege to maintain order and obedience by the use of summary force and restraint. Thus he might administer moderate chastisement to his wife, though it seems to have been understood that he ought not to employ a stick thicker than his thumb. This privilege of correction, as Blackstone tells us,[196] began to be doubted "in the politer reign of Charles the Second" and became obsolete with the general improvement in the social and legal condition of married women. Today, a husband may no longer use force against his wife, even to restrain her from leaving his company[197] or compel submission to his caresses,[198] but the legal sanction is primarily for the criminal and matrimonial courts rather than a tort action for damages.[199]

189. *Proudman v. Allen* [1954] S.A.S.R. 336.
190. Ibid. Provided, of course he exercises such care as could reasonably be expected of him in the circumstances: *Beckingham v. P.J. & M. Co.* [1957] S.R. (N.S.W.) 403; *Kirk v. Gregory* (1876) 1 Ex. D. 55.
191. *Falcke v. Scottish Imperial Ins.* (1886) 34 Ch. D. 234 at 248; Rose, *Restitution for the Rescuer*, 9 Oxf. J.L. St. 167 (1989); *Rest. of Restitution* §117; Note, 74 Cal. L. Rev. 85 (1986); see above, n. 58. A salient exception is the maritime doctrine of salvage; see *The Goring* [1988] A.C. 831.
192. *Sherrin v. Haggerty* [1953] O.W.N. 962.
193. *Gilbert v. Stone* (1647) Aleyn 35; 82 E.R. 902.
194. *Weaver v. Ward* (1616) Hob. 134; 80 E.R. 284; *Smith v. Stone* (1647) Style 65; 82 E.R. 533.
195. See Criminal Codes of Qld (s. 31(4)); W.A. (s. 31(4)); Tas. (s. 20); N.Z. (s. 24); and generally Walters, *Murder under Duress*, 8 Leg. St. 61 (1988).
196. 1 Comm. 444-445.
197. *R. v. Jackson* [1891] 1 Q.B. 671.
198. *R. v. Miller* [1954] 2 Q.B. 282.
199. See below, p. 680.

The parents' privilege of meting out reasonable punishment to their children, whether by confinement or chastisement, has survived to the present day,[200] despite occasional challenge by sophisticated educational reformers. The authority of disciplining minors belongs to a parent or anyone standing in his place, but its exercise is rarely, if ever, called in question in civil proceedings, although there appears to be no legal obstacle to a tort action for the use of excessive force.[201] The more effective safeguard against abuse is the threat of criminal proceedings on the initiative of social organisations[202] or the Crown.

More frequent, however, are actions for assault against teachers. The authority of teachers to correct their pupils used to be explained, on Blackstone's theory, as resting on a delegation of parental authority, but this has become threadbare since the advent of compulsory schooling, and it is doubtful if the privilege can be abridged by a parent's refusal to assent to its exercise.[203] It is therefore more realistic and proper to ascribe the privilege to the necessity of maintaining order in and about the school, as an independent attribute of the teacher.[204] The existence of internal school regulations forbidding corporal punishment does not, according to the better opinion, deprive a teacher of his defence if the correction is otherwise reasonable, at any rate so far as public schools are concerned;[205] and in serious matters affecting the safety of the children the teacher may even override the authority of a particular parent.[206] The teacher is privileged to inflict corporal punishment, provided it is moderate, reasonable and not dictated by bad motives,[207] and has a defence not only to claims for assault, but also other interferences with dignitary interests, like keeping a child after class to learn over a lesson or exposing the child to the derision of his mates by making him stand in a corner or placing a dunce's cap on his head.[208] Nor is the teacher's authority of correction confined to offences committed on the school premises; it extends also to misconduct outside school hours which have a reasonable connection with scholastic discipline, such as smoking in a public street in defiance of an express prohibition.[209] A serious deterrent against excessive force is the right of the school authority, if held vicariously liable, to seek an indemnity from the offending teacher.[210]

200. See Criminal Codes of Qld (s. 280), W.A. (s. 257) and Tas. (s. 50).
201. See below, p. 681.
202. E.g. the R.S.P.C.C.
203. Note the hesitation in *Mansell v. Griffin* [1908] 1 K.B. 947, and that was more than 70 years ago!
204. *Hansen v. Cole* (1890) 9 N.Z.L.R. 272; *Ramsay v. Larsen* (1964) 111 C.L.R. 16 (passim); *Murdock v. Richards* [1954] 1 D.L.R. 766 at 769.
205. *King v. Nichols* (1939) 33 Q.J.P. 171; and see *Mansell v. Griffin* [1908] 1 K.B. 947.
206. *Craig v. Frost* (1936) 30 Q.J.P. 140 (galloping on horseback from and to school); *Rest. 2d* §153.
207. *Mansell v. Griffin* [1908] 1 K.B. 947; *Byrne v. Hebden* [1913] Q.S.R. 233; *Hansen v. Cole* (1890) 9 N.Z.L.R. 272; *Murdock v. Richards* [1954] 1 D.L.R. 766.
208. *Mansell v. Griffin* [1908] 1 K.B. 160 at 167.
209. *R. v. Newport Justices* [1929] 2 K.B. 416.
210. *Ryan v. Fildes* [1938] 3 All E.R. 517. The old notion that an employer is not liable for discretionary acts of a school teacher (see *Hole v. Williams* (1910) 10 S.R. (N.S.W.) 638) is now exploded.

Somewhat akin to military discipline exercised by officers over their subordinates,[211] is the authority vested in any person in command of a vessel on a voyage or aircraft in flight to use, for the purpose of maintaining order and discipline on board, such force both against crew and passengers as he reasonably believes to be necessary.[212] Whilst the captain need not wait for an actual mutiny, there must at least be some act reasonably calculated to interfere with the safety of the ship or the prosecution of the voyage. Hence the captain will be liable for putting a passenger in irons for merely calling him the landlord of a floating hotel[213] or for confining a steward to his room in order to placate a passenger rather than because he believes in the charge of misconduct levelled against him.[214] Ordinarily, an inquiry should precede punishment and the accused be given an opportunity of being heard in his own defence.[215]

9. LEGAL AUTHORITY

For purposes of criminal law enforcement the police as well as private citizens have the right, perhaps still even the duty, to make arrests and thereby interfere with the rights of others in circumstances specified by the common law and statute. It is of course preferable to obtain first a warrant and thereby gain the protection of judicial authority,[216] but the need for timely prevention of crime or stopping the criminal's escape justifies speedier action. The common law confined such authority to treason, felonies and breaches of the peace, but statutes have variously extended it to some misdemeanours.[217] Because criminal law enforcement had to rely primarily on the private citizen until well into the 19th century, his common law powers of arrest were almost as extensive as those of peace officers, but modern legislation has generally tended to increase police powers disproportionately.[218] Today, the conditions for arrest without warrant vary significantly in detail from one State to another, on which the interested reader should consult specialised works.[219]

211. See *Groves v. Commonwealth* (1982) 150 C.L.R. 113 on crown liability for exercise of military discipline and immunity for soldier's obedience to orders.
212. See Criminal Codes of Qld (s. 281) and W.A. (s. 258).
213. *King v. Franklin* (1858) 1 F. & F. 360; 175 E.R. 764.
214. *Hook v. Cunard Steamship Co.* [1953] 1 W.L.R. 682.
215. *The Agincourt* (1824) 1 Hagg. 271; 166 E.R. 96.
216. E.g. *Police Regulations Act* 1899 (N.S.W.) s. 26; *Police Regulation Act* 1958 (Vic.) s. 124; Criminal Codes of Qld (s. 251), W.A. (s. 228) and Tas. (s. 23) (defence to civil proceedings?); *Police Force Act* 1947 (N.Z.) s. 38. Judges both of superior and inferior courts enjoy absolute immunity when acting judicially in the bona fide exercise of their office: *Sirros v. Moore* [1975] Q.B. 118 (C.A.); Aronson & Whitmore, *Public Torts and Contracts* (1982) 138-153.
217. Some modern legislation, like the *Crimes Act* 1967 (Eng.), has replaced that distinction by a new category of "arrestable offences".
218. E.g. *Crimes Act* 1914 (Cth) s. 8A; *Criminal Law Act* 1900 (N.S.W.) s. 352; *Crimes Act* 1958 (Vic.) ss 235, 457-463; *Criminal Code* (Qld) ss 5, 546ff.; *Police Act* 1936 (S.A.) Pt VII; *Criminal Law Consolidation Act* 1935 ss 271-272; *Criminal Code* (W.A.) ss 5, 564ff.; *Criminal Code* (Tas.) s. 27; (A.C.T.) *McIntosh v. Webster* (1980) 30 A.C.T.R. 19; *Crimes Act* 1967 (N.Z.) s. 32ff.
219. E.g. Harding, "Law of Arrest in Australia", in *Australian Criminal Justice System* (1972) 333.

6

NEGLIGENCE: INTRODUCTION

Accident losses are today, for most significant purposes, governed by the concept of negligence. Yet as an independent basis of tort liability, negligence liability is of very recent origin.[1] The early common law was almost exclusively preoccupied with the intentional wrongdoer, and gave little attention to inadvertent harm. Even later, the formalism of the writ system precluded fruitful speculation concerning theories of culpability, since the entrenched causes of action were rigidly defined by reference to the nature of the plaintiff's injury rather than the quality of the defendant's conduct. It was of little moment whether trespassory harm or nuisance was occasioned by intentional or negligent misconduct, so long as the primitive requirements of causation were satisfied and the loss was of a kind for which the law was prepared to grant redress in accordance with the prevailing standards of a socially and economically primitive community.

What slender notion there was about negligence, developed in connection with the amorphous action on the case, but until the 19th century this yielded little more than "a bundle of frayed ends".[2] The earliest illustrations of what is now known as tortious negligence are found in the liability of those who professed a "common calling", like artificers, innkeepers, carriers, surgeons and attorneys. Holding themselves out to the public as competent to pursue their profession, they were required to conform to the standard of reasonable skill and proficiency. Most of the early cases were concerned with positive acts of misfeasance and, apart from a very limited number of situations more akin to contract than tort, liability for mere omission made little headway down to the end of the 18th century.

In the first quarter of the 19th century, these hitherto disconnected threads of embryonic liability for neglect began to combine into a discernible principle of wider application, from which gradually emerged the modern concept of negligence as a separate basis of tort liability. Its rise broadly coincided with the Industrial Revolution and was undoubtedly stimulated by the advent of machinery, urbanisation and the faster traffic along turnpike and railway. Untold new sources of risk and losses made their appearance and confronted the law with problems it was unable to solve by recourse to its inherited, archaic tort remedies. At this crucial stage of social and economic transformation, the courts responded to the call for a new pattern of loss adjustment by fastening on the concept of negligence. The axiom "no liability without fault" was quickly raised to a dogmatic postulate of justice, because it was best calculated to serve the interests of

1. Winfield, *History of Negligence*, 42 L.Q.R. 184 (1926); *Fifoot* ch. 8.
2. Ibid. at 185. Pritchard (*Trespass, Case*, [1964] Cam. L.J. 234; *Scott v. Shepherd and the Emergence of the Tort of Negligence*, Selden Soc. lecture (1976)) argues for a date, at least a century earlier.

expanding industry and the entrepreneurial class, in relieving them from the hampering burden of strict liability and conducing to that freedom of individual will and enterprise which was at the forefront of contemporary aspirations. Borne by these forces, the negligence concept in little more than a century completely transformed the basis of tort liability. The measure of its success is attested by the fact that negligence litigation today overwhelmingly occupies the attention of the courts, and has proved so pervasive as to transform even the erstwhile strict liability of trespass.[3] Helped by, and in turn assisting, the disintegration of the old forms of action, negligence became a unifying force of vast dimension.

Negligence however also contained a counterbalancing potential for expanding liability in lateral directions: it came to include omissions (duties to act) and other more complex causal relations than those ever envisaged by the action of trespass.[4] Paradoxically, the fault concept itself, in origin contemplating only interpersonal justice, eventually opened itself to a consideration also of social needs, distributive justice and stricter liability. This transformation has been rapidly gaining pace since the individualistic fault dogma began to yield to the mid-20th century quest for social security, and the function of the law of torts came to be seen less in its admonitory potential than in ensuring compensation of accident victims and distributing the cost among those who can best bear it. The resulting stresses stem on the one hand from this lack of consensus as to the purposes of tort law and, on the other, from a growing frustration over its inadequacy in coping with the problem of accident compensation in a welfare state. This crisis will be observed throughout the ensuing discussion.

Elements of cause of action

Although it may be historically correct that the parent of negligence as an independent basis of liability was negligence as a mode of committing certain torts, like nuisance or trespass, it is important to grasp at the outset that negligence is not a state of mind, but conduct that falls below the standard regarded as normal or desirable in a given community. The subjective notion of personal "fault" has long been discarded in favour of the stricter, impersonal standard of how a reasonable person should have acted in the circumstances. In this manner, while retaining a *verbal* link with the moral criterion of fault, the admonitory function of the principle has been largely overshadowed for the sake of compensating accident victims, regardless of the "wrongdoer's" subjective blameworthiness.[5]

Despite widespread current usage, it is misleading to speak of *a* tort of negligence.[6] Negligence is a basis of liability rather than a single nominate tort. Some interests are protected against negligent interference, others are not. However welfare minded, we are still far from exacting tort compensation for *every* kind of harm caused to *anyone* by conduct fraught with risk of *some* injury. Negligence is a matter of risk, that is of

3. See above, p. 21.
4. See Kretzmer, *Transformation of Tort Liability in 19th Century*, 4 Oxf. J.L. Stud. 46 (1984).
5. See below, ch. 7.
6. Wright, 11 U. Tor. L.J. 84 at 87-88 (1955).

recognisable danger of harm. This immediately raises the question "Risk to whom?" and "Risk of what?".

For the purpose of dealing with these questions, the courts have evolved a number of artificial concepts, like "duty of care" and "remoteness of damage", which are concerned with the basic problems of what harms are included within the scope of the unreasonable risk created by the defendant, and what interest the law deems worthy of protection against negligent interference in consonance with current notions of policy. Since the definition of tortious negligence does not furnish any clue to its conditions of actionability beyond a mere reference to the nature of the defendant's conduct, these ancillary mechanisms assume a vital importance in delimiting the scope of legal protection against inadvertent harm. A basic problem in negligence is, therefore, that of limitation of liability, and no less than four "control" or "hedging" devices are employed with this single purpose in view: "duty of care", "remoteness of damage", "contributory negligence" and "voluntary assumption of risk".[7] We shall have occasion to see that the courts have not committed themselves categorically to any particular analysis of negligence cases, so that these various formulae, in particular the first two, are often used interchangeably in the formulation of judicial opinions. The resulting flexibility in analysis, though a source of difficulty to the beginner, has the functional advantage of leaving ample scope for experimentation and growth—vital assets in a branch of law which sets a high premium on progessive "social engineering".

The elements of the cause of action for negligence may, therefore, be itemised as follows:[8]

1. A duty, recognised by law, requiring conformity to a certain standard of conduct for the protection of others against unreasonable risks. This is commonly known as the "duty issue".

2. Failure to conform to the required standard of care or, briefly, breach of that duty. This element usually passes under the name of "negligence".

3. Material injury resulting to the interests of the plaintiff. Since the modern action for negligence traces its descent from the old form of action on the case, damage is of the gist of liability. Merely exposing someone to danger is not an actionable wrong if the hazard is averted in time. Nor is there any question here of vindicating mere dignitary interests or compensating fright or apprehension in the absence of ascertainable physical injury, such as traumatic shock.

4. A reasonably proximate connection between the defendant's conduct and the resulting injury, usually referred to as the question of "remoteness of damage" or "proximate cause".

5. The absence of any conduct by the injured party prejudicial to his recovering in full for the loss he has suffered. This involves a consideration of two specific defences, contributory negligence and voluntary assumption of risk.

7. See Fleming, *Duty and Remoteness: The Control Devices in Liability for Negligence*, 31 Can. B. Rev. 471 (1953).
8. See *Rest. 2d* §281.

In view of the functional similarity between the "duty" and "remoteness" issues, and their link with the last mentioned defences as devices for delimiting liability, it is thought more convenient to start first with an examination of the standard of care or what conduct amounts to negligence.

7

STANDARD OF CARE

Negligence is conduct falling below the standard demanded for the protection of others against unreasonable risk of harm.[1] This standard of conduct is ordinarily measured by what the reasonable person of ordinary prudence would do in the circumstances. The behaviour of individuals is so incalculable in its variety, and the possible combination of circumstances giving rise to a negligence issue so infinite, that it has been found undesirable, if not impossible, to formulate precise rules of conduct for all conceivable situations. In order to ensure a high degree of individualisation in the handling of negligence cases, the law has adopted an abstract formula, that of the "reasonable man", and has left to the jury, or to a judge in their stead, the task of concretising and applying that standard in individual cases. Only in a few situations has it been deemed advisable, on grounds of weightier competing policies, to crystallise the required standard into more definite and uniform legal rules. One such departure, we shall see,[2] used to be the precise formulation of standards of care to which an occupier must conform for the safety of persons coming on his land—due, it would seem, to the conviction prevalent during the last century that the general formula of reasonable care would have invested the jury[3] with greater latitude than was fair in the interest of landholders. Again in other situations the legislature may have prescribed a definite standard of conduct, for example to fence circular saws or not to overtake a stationary tram. If the case falls under such a crystallised rule, the evaluative process is taken out of the hands of the jury, because any departure from the legislative standard is conclusively deemed to be negligence as a matter of law.[4]

The general standard of conduct required by law is a necessary complement of the legal concept of "duty". There is not only the question "Did the defendant owe a duty to be careful?" but also "What precisely was required of him to discharge it?" Indeed, it is not uncommon to encounter formulations of the standard of care in terms of "duty", as when it is asserted that a motorist is under a duty to keep a proper lookout or give a turn signal. But this method of expression is best avoided. In the first place, the duty issue is already sufficiently complex without fragmenting it further to cover an endless series of details of conduct. "Duty" is more appropriately reserved for the problem of whether the relation between the parties (like manufacturer and consumer or occupier and trespasser) warrants the imposition upon one of an obligation of care for the benefit of the other, and it is more convenient to deal with individual conduct in

1. *Rest. 2d* §282.
2. See below, ch. 22.
3. Green, *Judge and Jury* (1930) 128-130.
4. See below, pp. 124-134.

terms of the legal standard of what is required to meet that obligation.[5] Secondly, it is apt to obscure the division of functions between judge and jury.[6] It is for the court to determine the existence of a duty relationship and to lay down in general terms the standard of care by which to measure the defendant's conduct; it is for the jury to translate the general into a particular standard suitable for the case in hand and to decide whether that standard has been attained. Thus if at issue is the supervision of school children during the midday break, a court would ordinarily be content with instructing the jury that the duty of the school is that of a "reasonably careful parent", without in any way attempting to prescribe in detail appropriate rules of discipline.[7]

1. THE REASONABLE MAN

The "reasonable man of ordinary prudence" is the central figure in the formula traditionally employed in passing the negligence issue for adjudication to the jury. Disqualified from passing judgment himself on the *particular* defendant in the litigation, the judge is obliged, in formulating his instruction to the jury, to convert the problem of conduct into an abstraction sufficiently intelligible to guide them as to the legal considerations which they ought to apply in assessing the quality of this defendant's conduct. In order to objectify the law's abstractions, like "care", "reasonableness" or "foreseeability", the "man of ordinary prudence"—the man on the Clapham omnibus or the Bondi tram—was invented[8] as a model of the standard to which all are required to conform. He is the embodiment of all the qualities we demand of the good citizen: and if not exactly a model of perfection,[9] yet altogether a rather better man than probably any single one of us happens,[10] or perhaps even aspires,[11] to be.

On the whole, the law has chosen external, objective standards of conduct.[12] This means that individuals are often held guilty of legal fault

5. Morison & Fleming, *Duty of Care and Standard of Care*, 1 Syd. L. Rev. 69 (1953). But *Smith v. Littlewoods* [1987] A.C. 241 illustrates the tenuousness of the distinction.
6. Where trial is by a judge alone, as nowadays in most jurisdictions (see below, p. 312) he discharges the functions of a jury and in that role will direct himself as he would a jury. His conclusion on the facts is not a rule of law of precedential impost any more than would be a jury's.
7. *Ricketts v. Erith B.C.* [1943] 2 All E.R. 629.
8. Its progenitor was Tindal C.J. in *Vaughan v. Menlove* (1837) 3 Bing. N.C. 468 at 475; 132 E.R. 490 at 493; and note the classical formulation of "negligence" by Alderson B. in *Blyth v. Birmingham Waterworks Co.* (1856) 11 Ex. 781 at 784; 156 E.R. 1047 at 1049.
9. The link with community standards is stressed by Greer L.J.'s description of him as " 'the man in the street' or 'the man in the Clapham omnibus', or, as I recently read in an American author, 'the man who takes the magazines at home, and in the evening pushes the lawn mower in his shirt sleeves' " (*Hall v. Brooklands Club* [1933] 1 K.B. 205 at 224).
10. Thus it is a misdirection to tell the jury to put themselves in the defendant's shoes and consider what they would have done in his place: *Arland v. Taylor* [1955] 3 D.L.R. 358.
11. Cf. "this excellent but odious character" (*Fardell v. Potts* (Is there a reasonable woman?) in Herbert's *Uncommon Law* (1935) 4).
12. "Instead, therefore, of saying that the liability for negligence should be co-extensive with the judgment of each individual, which would be as variable as the length of the foot of each individual, we ought rather to adhere to the rule which requires in all cases a regard to caution such as a man of ordinary prudence would observe" (*Vaughan v. Menlove*

for failing to live up to a standard which as a matter of fact they cannot meet. Moral blameworthiness and legal default do not invariably coincide.[13] In the first place, legal control stops short of inquiry into the internal phenomena of conscience. Because of administrative limitations, the law can only work within the sphere of external manifestations of conduct.[14] Secondly, legal standards are standards of general application. When men live in society, a certain average of conduct, a sacrifice of individual peculiarities going beyond a certain point, is necessary for the general welfare.[15] If the standard were relaxed for defendants who cannot attain the normal, the burden of accident losses resulting from the extra hazards created by society's dangerous group of accident-prone[16] would be thrown on the innocent victims of substandard behaviour.

But although the legal "standard of foresight of the reasonable man . . . eliminates the personal equation and is independent of the idiosyncrasies of the particular person whose conduct is in question",[17] it is probably inevitable that in actual practice subjective factors are not wholly ignored by the jury.[18] The difference lies between law in "black letter" and law in operation, between jural postulates and jury judgments.[19] Moreover, negligence consists in failure to do what the reasonable man would have done "under the same or similar circumstances", and the latitude of that expression in effect makes some allowance not only for external facts, but also for many of the personal characteristics of the actor himself.

Moral qualities and knowledge

The objective community ideal alone determines whether the defendant's conduct attained the point of proper balance between self-interest and altruism. The individual's moral notions and qualities, like courage, self-control and willpower, are irrelevant, be they higher or lower. "Some persons are by nature unduly timorous and imagine every path beset with lions; others, of more robust temperament, fail to foresee or nonchalantly disregard even the most obvious dangers. The reasonable man is presumed to be free from overapprehension and from overconfidence."[20]

12. *Continued*
(1837) 3 Bing. N.C. 468 at 475; 132 E.R. 490 at 493). The question of whether negligence is objective or subjective is discussed by Parsons, *Negligence and Contributory Negligence*, 1 Melb. U.L. Rev. 163 (1957); Seavey, *Negligence—Subjective or Objective*?, 41 Harv. L. Rev. 1 (1927); Edgerton, *Negligence, Inadvertence and Indifference*, 39 Harv. L. Rev. 849 (1926); Green, *Judge and Jury* (1930) ch. 5; 2 *Harper, James & Gray* ch. 16.
13. Honoré, *Responsibility and Luck*, 104 L.Q.R. 530 (1988) attempted a reconciliation in terms of outcome-responsibility.
14. Holmes, *Common Law* (1881) 110.
15. Ibid. at 108. "The notion of a duty tailored to the actor, rather than to the act which he elects to perform, has no place in the law of tort" (*Wilsher v. Essex H.A.* [1987] Q.B. 730 at 750 per Mustill L.J.).
16. A high incidence of accidents must be laid at the door of the accident-prone, but while accident-proneness is often due to a personality defect, it seldom points to anything like moral fault: see James & Dickinson, *Accident Proneness and Accident Law*, 63 Harv. L. Rev. 769 (1950).
17. *Glasgow Corp. v. Muir* [1943] A.C. 448 at 457 per Lord Macmillan.
18. This will occur more frequently in judging a *plaintiff's* conduct (for contributory negligence) than a defendant's. Thus, its effect will generally be to enlarge rather than curtail liability: see below, p. 285.
19. Green, *Judge and Jury* (1930) 178.
20. *Glasgow Corp. v. Muir* [1943] A.C. 448 at 457 per Lord Macmillan.

Closely allied is the quality of being able to perceive and appreciate what risks are involved in a particular activity. Perception of risk is the correlation of past experience with the specific facts in a situation, which depends to a large extent on knowledge as the basis for judging the harmful potentialities of contemplated conduct. The defendant is credited with such perception of the surrounding circumstances and such knowledge of other pertinent matters as a reasonable man with the actor's own superior perception and knowledge, if any, would possess.[21] Thus an individual's substandard experience or knowledge is not generally considered an excuse[22] save in the exceptional case of children,[23] but if the defendant has more extensive knowledge, the propriety of his judgment as to the risk involved is determined by what a man with such knowledge would regard as probable. An employer, therefore, with greater than average experience of a particular risk may have to respond with more than average precautions;[24] while a father who permits his child to go to school despite symptoms which a competent doctor would diagnose as scarlet fever, will be judged by whether he is a layman or a medic.[25] Again, what was excusable ignorance yesterday, may become negligence today.[26] "Once warned, twice shy" epitomises the normal reaction of reasonably intelligent human beings and becomes the standard whereby to judge the individual's conduct in the light of his own previous experience.[27] Moreover, as life in our industrial and urban communities becomes increasingly complex, so the field of expectable knowledge is continuously pushed outwards, in step with scientific advances and the general expansion of the frontiers of human knowledge. For example, the advisability of using seat belts in cars has changed considerably over the last ten years or so.[28]

Skill

Skill is that special competence which is not part of the ordinary equipment of the reasonable man but the result of aptitude developed by special training and experience.[29] Those who undertake work calling for special skill must not only exercise reasonable care but measure up to the standard of proficiency that can be expected from such professionals. Thus a ship's officer will be held to the knowledge and experience in matters maritime typical of *his* calling rather than of a layman,[30] manufacturers must pursue thorough research into scientific literature in order to ascertain and give warning of the hazards of little known products.[31]

21. *Rest. 2d* §289.
22. Should this be invoked also against the odd individual whose past has not enabled him to share in otherwise common knowledge? *Geier v. Kujawa* [1970] 1 Ll. Rep. 364 excused a German girl for not using a seat belt because she had not seen one before.
23. See below, p. 285.
24. *Stokes v. G.K.N.* [1968] 1 W.L.R. 1776. Also expected to be familiar with the current literature on the relevant industrial risks: *Cartwright v. Sankey* (1973) 14 K.I.R. 349; *Smith v. Inglis* (1978) 83 D.L.R. (3d) 215 at 231 (expert).
25. *Rest. 2d* §289, ill. 12.
26. E.g. the risk of AIDS in blood transfusions was unknown in 1983 but not later: *Dwan v. Farquhar* [1988] Qd R. 234.
27. See *Bolton v. Stone* [1951] A.C. 850 at 863.
28. See below, p. 280.
29. *Rest. 2d* §299A, comment *a*.
30. *The Wagon Mound (No. 2)* [1963] 1 Ll. Rep. 402 at 409; [1963] S.R. (N.S.W.) 948 at 955.
31. *Vacwell Engineering v. B.D.H. Chemicals* [1971] 1 Q.B. 88.

Physicians—informed consent

The problem is most acute in the case of physicians because of rising public expectations in their proficiency and greater claims consciousness in recent years. A physician will be adjudged by the standard of the average practitioner of the class to which he belongs or holds himself out to belong:[32] a higher level of skill will be demanded from a specialist than a general practitioner, but both acquit themselves by conforming to practices accepted as proper by a responsible section of their profession, and cannot be made liable merely because there is a body of opinion which takes a contrary view—the "Bolam test".[33] There used to be a trend, especially in England, to dilute the standard further by explaining away "mere errors of clincial judgment". This benevolent attitude was no doubt motivated by the well founded need to distinguish between bad decisions and decisions that turn out badly; also by the fear of otherwise encouraging "defensive medicine" as in America. But the antithesis has now been condemned: failure to measure up to the appropriate standard of skill in *any* respect amounts to negligence.[34] Australian and Canadian courts, on the other hand, do not seem to recognise professional practice as necessarily having the last word; otherwise the profession could set a deficient standard by subordinating the patient's to its own interest. Rather, here as elsewhere, the ultimate test is that of reasonable care.[35]

The preceding standard applies not only to the physician's duty of diagnosis and treatment but also to his duty of disclosing to the patient the risks of any proposed treatment or indeed non-therapeutic advice, for example relating to abortion or birth control.[36] Failure to disclose such "collateral risks" is treated as negligence rather than battery (which is reserved for lack of consent to the therapy itself)—a distinction harking back to the archaic heritage of trespass and case, with unfavourable consequences to plaintiffs. American and Canadian cases speak of the patient's right to "informed consent" and tend to measure the physician's duty by a prudent patient's legitimate expectations rather than by a professional medical judgment.[37] Australian courts have been leaning the

32. For country practitioners see *Challand v. Bell* (1959) 18 D.L.R. (2d) 150; for chiropractors, *Penner v. Theobald* (1962) 35 D.L.R. (2d) 700.

33. *Bolam v Friern Hospital* [1957] 1 W.L.R. 582 (criticised 21 Mod. L. Rev. 259 (1958)); *Maynard v. W. Midlands H.A.* [1984] 1 W.L.R. 634 (H.L.); *Ostrowski v. Lotto* (1970) 15 D.L.R. (3d) 402 (Ont. C.A.); *E. v. Austr. Red Cross* (1991) 105 A.L.R. 53 (AIDS). See also below, p. 121 (expert testimony).

34. See *Whitehouse v. Jordan* [1981] 1 W.L.R. 246 (H.L.). The dramatic rise in medical malpractice claims in the U.S. and Canada has not been equalled in the U.K. and Australia, but claims have at least doubled in the last 15 years (*Pearson* §1318, 1326: 500 claims p.a. against 85,000 doctors, some payment for 30-40%). On the other hand, it has been easier to procure highly reputable expert testimony on behalf of plaintiffs.

35. *F. v. R.* (1983) 33 S.A.S.R. 189; *Rogers v. Whitaker* (1991) 23 N.S.W.L.R. 600 (C.A.); A.L.R.C. 50 (Informed Decisions about Medical Procedures); Can.: *Reibl v. Hughes* [1980] 2 S.C.R. 880. See *Cassidy, Malpractice—Medical Negligence in Australia*, 66 A.L.J. 67 (1992).

36. *Gold v. Haringey H.A.* [1988] 1 Q.B. 481 (C.A.). In *Thake v. Maurice* [1986] Q.B. 644 (C.A.) plaintiff succeeded in absence of evidence of medical practice not to warn.

37. *Reibl v. Hughes* [1980] 2 S.C.R. 880; *Cobbs v. Grant* (Cal. 1972) 502 P. 2d 1 at 11 ("the patient's right of self-decision is the measure of the physician's duty to reveal"). Advocated by Robertson, *Informed Consent*, 97 L.Q.R. 102 (1981). Germany: Shaw, 35 I.C.L.Q. 864 (1986).

same way.[38] The English approach, however, as anchored in the House of Lords decision in *Sidaway*,[39] has remained more conservative, preferring here also the standard of responsible professional practice, on the ground that the issue relates not to the patient's claim to self-determination but to the doctor's duty, and that the judgment of what it demands in the interest of the patient calls for professional expertise. In short, the "reasonable doctor" rather than the "reasonable patient" sets the standard. In practice, information is required only of "material" or "substantial", not "remote" risks;[40] and in some cases none at all where disclosure would pose a serious threat of psychological or physical detriment to the patient ("therapeutic privilege"[41]). Matters to be considered, it has been said,[42] include the nature of the matter to be disclosed, the nature of the treatment and health of the patient, and the general surrounding circumstances, but the paramount consideration should be that a person is entitled to make his own decisions about his life. As a concession, the professional standard would not be absolutely conclusive; it might be unreasonable, for example "if the profession, by an excess of paternalism, denies their patients a real choice. In a word, the law will not permit the medical profession to play God."[43] Also, a patient would ordinarily be entitled to a frank answer to specific questions:[44] at least the inquisitive patient has a right to know.

Sidaway, a decision of a divided House of Lords, was both muddied and, even as qualified, seemed unduly pusillanimous in denying independent protection to a "patient's right of choice", though it may reflect the prevailing attitude of most patients to "follow doctors' orders".[45] What justifies some concern, however, is idiosyncratic patients and self-serving testimony on the issue of causation. (For unlike battery, negligence requires proof, not only of resulting injury but that the patient would otherwise not have consented and been injured.[46]) This could make "informed consent" a surrogate for in effect imposing strict liability for unsuccessful treatment. If the "right of choice" had been recognised as a dignitary interest protected, like battery, by symbolic damages, the link with physical injury and causation would have been avoided.

38. *F. v. R.* (1983) 33 S.A.S.R. 189; *Ellis v. Wallsend Hosp.* (1989) 17 N.S.W.L.R 553. Three Australian law reform commissions have recommended the formulation by the National Health and Medical Research Council of guidelines for the provision of information to patients, which legislation would require to be considered in legal proceedings: A.L.R.C. 50 (1989).
39. *Sidaway v. Bethlem Hospital* [1985] A.C. 871. *F. v. R.* anticipated Lord Scarman's more patient-oriented approach of requiring disclosure of all matters which might influence a reasonable patient.
40. As in *F. v. R.* (1983) 33 S.A.S.R. 189 (1 in 100). Surely this should be related to the nature of the risk.
41. This established exception in American Law was rejected in *Myer Estate v. Rogers* (1991) 6 C.C.L.T. (2d) 102.
42. *F. v. R.* (1983) 33 S.A.S.R. 189 at 192 (King C.J.).
43. *Sidaway v. Bethlem Hospital* [1984] Q.B. 493 at 513.
44. Ibid. at 659, 661, 664; *Smith v. Auckland Hospital* [1965] N.Z.L.R. 191.
45. Manderson, *Following Doctors' Orders: Informed Consent in Australia*, 62 A.L.J. 430 (1988). Why should "consent" be decisive only in touching battery cases, while "informed consent" is submerged in professional competence? See Kennedy, 47 Mod. L. Rev. 454 (1984).
46. Patients frequently fail to mount this cause hurdle. But Australian courts have preferred a subjective test to that of the reasonable patient: *Ellis v. Wallsend Hosp.* (1989) 17 N.S.W.L.R. 553 (C.A.); contra, *Reibl v. Hughes* [1980] 2 S.C.R. 880. See *Giesen* §26.

Beginners

At the other end of the spectrum of skill are beginners. While it is necessary to encourage them, it is equally evident that they cause more than their proportionate share of accidents. The paramount social need for compensating accident victims, however, clearly outweighs all competing considerations, and the beginner is, therefore, held to the standard of those who are reasonably skilled and proficient in that particular calling or activity. This is all the more obvious when, as in the case of driving, the law has evinced its concern for public safety by licensing only those who have passed a test of competency.[47] A further safeguard to the public is provided by the duty resting on employers to supervise an inexperienced employee and guide him in the learning process. That duty, however, does not modify the employee's responsibility,[48] though the employer's share of responsibility for an accident cannot, as between himself and the employee, be thrust wholly on the latter. As was said in one such case, "it would be in the highest degree unjust that the hospital board, by getting inexperienced doctors to perform their duties for them, without adequate supervision, should be able to throw all responsibility on those doctors as if they were fully experienced practitioners".[49]

In cases where the parties have entered into a voluntary relationship with each other, public policy is not ordinarily opposed to one party agreeing to accept, with full knowledge, a substandard skill from the other. This result might be explained in alternative ways: "If a man accepts a lift from a car driver whom he knows to have lost a limb or an eye or to be deaf, he cannot complain if he does not exhibit the skill and competence of a driver who suffers from no defect. It is perhaps not often of much practical importance whether the passenger is regarded as voluntarily assuming the risks which are involved and so absolving the car driver from a standard of duty to which otherwise he would be subject, or the passenger is considered primarily to be entitled only to that standard of duty or of care which arises from the relation that he has established, namely a passenger in a car driven by a defective driver."[50] The latter rationale gained acceptance in Australia as a result of a series of drunk driver cases,[51] but has been repudiated by the English Court of Appeal.[52] In allowing a claim against a learner driver by her own instructor friend, the court turned down the idea of varying standards as too complex in practice and invoked the same standard of full competence as it would have done in favour of any outsider.[53]

47. Cf. *McCrone v. Riding* [1938] 1 All E.R. 157.
48. *Wilsher v. Essex A.H.A.* [1987] Q.B. 730 (C.A.) (junior member of surgical team).
49. *Jones v. Manchester Corp.* [1952] 2 Q.B. 852 at 871 per Denning L.J., where 80% of reponsibility was attributed to the hospital and 20% to the doctor.
50. *Ins. Comm. v. Joyce* (1948) 77 C.L.R. 39 at 56 per Dixon J.
51. See below, p. 304. See also Kidner, *The Variable Standard of Care, Contributory Negligence and Volenti*, 11 Leg. St. 1 (1991).
52. *Nettleship v. Weston* [1971] 2 Q.B. 691.
53. Voluntary assumption of risk had been ruled out because of the plaintiff's anxiety to ascertain that he was covered by the defendant's insurance; and the court was evidently concerned that this result should not be sidestepped via a lower standard of care.

Need for experts

Related is the question in what circumstances the reasonable man must enlist the skill of an expert. Clearly this depends on prevailing community standards.[54] Many tasks, like medical treatment or engineering, so obviously call for the professional touch as to make the answer seem self-evident. On the other hand, the awesome progress of technological knowledge in our time has not only widened the gulf between amateur and expert, but also entailed a constantly rising expectation regarding the level of competence for performing a multitude of tasks that only yesterday were regarded as quite commonplace and within anybody's grasp. On the whole, so far the law has dealt rather leniently with the "little man", conscious both of his financial handicap as regards employing experts and his lack of liability insurance. Thus in matters like maintenance of household appliances[55] and simple repairs in the home,[56] the reasonable man may still rest content with his own humble skills. But for tasks demanding expert skill, especially those impinging immanently on public safety, even the layman will be judged by the standard of the expert, as when interfering with telephone lines[57] or even in regard to the maintenance of big trees adjacent to the highway by large estate managements or the National Trust, who combine greater financial resources with greater social responsibility.[58]

Physical, intellectual and emotional characteristics

The subjective standard has made most headway in relation to physical attributes, most probably because they can be more easily verified than any alleged deficiency in temperament or judgment. Thus the physically handicapped is judged by the standard of what can be expected from a reasonably prudent person suffering from his disability.[59] But though allowance is due for his lessened faculty, he may have to take correspondingly greater precautions in other respects to compensate for it: a blind man is not required to see, but may have to use his other senses more sharply than one who can.[60] A compromise has here to be struck between allowing the handicapped a reasonable degree of freedom in participating in the ordinary activites of life and safeguarding the general public against the peculiar risks created by that section of the community. Thus, a reasonable blind person would refrain from driving a car, but may venture unattended into the street even at the risk of thereby occasionally impeding

54. Or, in consensual relations, on the understanding between the parties.
55. *Watson v. George* (1953) 89 C.L.R. 409 (gas heater).
56. *Wells v. Cooper* [1958] 2 Q.B. 265 (door knob). But work on stairs for tenants?: *Lyons v. Nicholls* [1958] N.Z.L.R. 409.
57. *Papatonakis v. Telecom* (1985) 156 C.L.R. 7.
58. *Quinn v. Scott* [1965] 1 W.L.R. 1004; *Caminer v. N. Investment Trust* [1951] A.C. 88: cf. "it does end by making the standard of the expert the test of liability" (per Lord Radcliffe) with "Would a reasonable and careful owner without expert knowledge but accustomed to dealing with his trees and having a countryman's knowledge about them think it necessary to call in an expert?" (per Lord Reid).
59. *S.A. Ambulance v. Wahlheim* (1948) 77 C.L.R. 215 (driver with defective hearing absolved from contributory negligence for failing to hear ambulance siren).
60. *Henderson v. P.T.C.* (1981) 56 A.L.J.R. 1 (defective peripheral vision requires extra effort to look sideways).

traffic. Also, drivers are generally excused for losing control as the result of a sudden collapse[61] or other involuntary conduct,[62] though it is questionable whether such refinements of morality are any longer relevant to our modern regime of compulsory insurance. For this reason alone, courts should not be overfastidious about concluding that previous symptoms ought to have put the driver on guard.[63]

As far as mental and emotional characteristics are concerned, the objective test prevails, and the individual is required to conform to the intelligence and stability of the standard person.[64] "The law takes no account of the infinite varieties of temperament, intellect and education which makes the internal character of a given act so different in different men."[65] Significantly, therefore, no allowance is made for the factors most responsible for accident-proneness.[66]

Age and lunacy

In the case of children, the law has made considerable concessions to the subjective standard. Most of the decisions have been concerned with contributory negligence, where there is greater temptation to take an indulgent view and give added weight to exculpatory considerations;[67] but there is no doubt that a child, whether as plaintiff or defendant, is only expected to conform to the standard appropriate for normal children of similar age and experience.[68] This governs alike the child's capacity to perceive the risk as well as his sense of judgment and behaviour. Thus it was held not negligent for a boy of eight to be striking matches in a barn,[69] for a five-year-old to be shooting with arrows[70] or even a 12-year-old throwing a metal dart in the course of a game.[71] Some safeguard to the public is afforded by the obligation of parents and school authorities to observe reasonable care in the supervision of children under their control.[72] Moreover, a minor who engages in dangerous adult activities,

61. *Robinson v. Glover* [1952] N.Z.L.R. 669; *Waugh v. Allan* 1964 S.C. (H.L.) 162; *Slattery v. Haley* [1923] 3 D.L.R. 156; *Kay v. Mills* (1961) 28 D.L.R. (2d) 554 (driver suddenly overcome by sleep). But though a tramway company may have to provide technical safeguards against such a happening (*Mercer v. Comm. Road Transport* (1936) 56 C.L.R. 580), an employer is not generally under a duty to have his drivers medically examined: *Ryan v. Youngs* [1938] 1 All E.R. 522.
62. E.g. spasms during epileptic fit or whilst attacked by bees (see *Hill v. Baxter* [1958] 1 Q.B. 277 at 286; *Scholz v. Standish* [1961] S.A.S.R. 123), but "automatism is confined to *complete* unawareness" (*Roberts v. Ramsbottom* [1980] 1 W.L.R. 823; criticised 96 L.Q.R. 503).
63. E.g. *Gordon v. Wallace* (1973) 42 D.L.R. (3d) 342 (heart); *Boomer v. Penn* (1965) 52 D.L.R. (2d) 673 (diabetic).
64. *Baxter v. Woolcombers* [1963] C.L.Y. 2320 (low intelligence).
65. Holmes, *Common Law* (1881) 108.
66. See James & Dickinson, *Accident Proneness and Accident Law*, 63 Harv. L. Rev. 769 (1950), referring to studies reinforced by *Medical Aspects of Fitness to Drive* (London, 1971).
67. See below, p. 285.
68. *McHale v. Watson* (1966) 115 C.L.R. 199.
69. *Yorkton Agricultural Assoc. v. Morley* (1967) 66 D.L.R. (2d) 37.
70. *Walmsley v. Humenick* [1954] 2 D.L.R. 232.
71. *McHale v. Watson* (1966) 115 C.L.R. 199.
72. See below, p. 683.

such as driving a car or handling industrial equipment, must conform to the standard of the reasonably prudent adult;[73] his position being analogous to that of beginners who, as we have seen, are held to the objective standard.

There is some authority for similar discrimination in case of the aged and infirm. Some allowance for their lack of mobility has been made when charged with contributory negligence as pedestrians,[74] but as drivers they must conform to the ordinary standard of competence.[75]

The position of lunatics remains controversial. Some courts have been prepared to excuse defendants whose insanity was so extreme as to preclude them from appreciating their duty to take care, on the ground that negligence presupposes an ability for rational choice.[76] An intermediate view insists that they must at least be capable of foreseeing harm.[77] But the weight of authority regards it as unfairly prejudicial to accident victims if any allowance were made for a defendant's mental abnormality.[78] Although this conclusion may seem incompatible with the lingering practice to excuse loss of consciousness by "normal" defendants,[79] it is a welcome recognition of the fact that considerations of moral fault are out of place, especially in relation to traffic accidents where personal liability has been displaced by insurance.[80]

2. APPLICATION OF THE STANDARD

What are the considerations to which the reasonable man will defer in guiding his conduct? Negligence, it will be recalled, consists in conduct involving an *unreasonable* risk of harm. Almost any activity is fraught with some degree of danger but, if the remotest chance of mishap were sufficient to attract the stigma of negligence, most human action would be inhibited. Inevitably, therefore, one is only required to guard against those risks which society recognises as sufficiently great to demand precaution. The risk must be unreasonable before he can be expected to subordinate his own interests to those of others. Whether the act or omission in question is one which a reasonable person would recognise as posing an unreasonable risk must be determined by balancing the magnitude of the risk, in the light of the likelihood of an accident happening and the possible seriousness of its

73. See e.g. *Tucker v. Tucker* [1956] S.A.S.R. 297 (16-year-old driver); *McErlean v. Sarel* (1987) 42 D.L.R. (4th) 577 (Ont. C.A.); *Rest. 2d* §283A, comment *c*. This is the more desirable because there is here an opportunity for loss distribution through insurance.
74. *Daly v. Liverpool Corp.* [1939] 2 All E.R. 142: contributory negligence.
75. *Roberts v. Ramsbottom* [1980] 1 All E.R. 7 at 15.
76. *Slattery v. Haley* [1923] 3 D.L.R. 156 at 160; *Buckley v. Smith Transport* [1946] 4 D.L.R. 721.
77. *A.-G. of Canada v. Connolly* (1989) 64 D.L.R. (4th) 84.
78. *Adamson v. Motor Vehicle Trust* (1957) 58 W.A.L.R. 56; *Wenden v. Trikla* (1991) 8 C.C.L.T. (2d) 138; *Rest. 2d* §283B.
79. Above notes 61-62.
80. Pedrick, *Lunatic Driver*, 31 A.L.J. 354 (1957). Perhaps for the same reason, American courts overwhelmingly make allowance for mental impairment of *plaintiffs*: 91 A.L.R. 2d 393 (1963); cf. below, p. 285.

consequences, against the difficulty, expense or any other disadvantage of desisting from the venture or taking a particular precaution.[81]

Magnitude of risk

The gravity, frequency and imminence[82] of the recognisable risk are among the most important factors in the balance. Conduct cannot be treated as negligent unless there is more than a mere theoretical chance that it will miscarry *and* thereby subject others to harm. There must be a recognisable risk of *injury* sufficient to cause a reasonable man to pause. Hence it is not necessarily negligent to play cricket in the vicinity of a populated area merely because there is a chance of an occasional six: at all events one would have to consider the likelihood of its actually hitting a member of the public.[83] Similarly, the odd chance that an ordinary, well constructed bus might skid on a greasy road in wet weather does not make it unreasonable to put it into service: the risk is too small to pronounce this and all other buses for that reason as unfit for street traffic.[84]

Commonly it is said that the risk must be "foreseeable". But how foreseeable? Clearly, the chance of injury need not attain comparative *probability*; the test of "more probable than not" we use to establish that a certain event has happened in the past,[85] not whether it is fraught with danger in the future. In fact, the test has become so "undemanding"[86] that the injury need not even be "likely".[87] All that is required is that the risk be "real" in the sense that a reasonable person would not "brush it aside as far-fetched"or fanciful.[88] The hazard in overtaking another vehicle below the crest of a hill or near a curve is no less unreasonable because only a few cars a day travel the stretch and the chance of meeting an oncoming vehicle is therefore statistically negligible.[89] Even if the risk is small, it must not be neglected unless there is some valid reason for doing so.[90]

Moreover, risk is a relative thing: it may be greater to one individual than to another. Hence the same act or omission may be negligent to the first,

81. *Morris v. W. Hartlepool Navigation Co.* [1956] A.C. 552 at 574; *Wyong S.C. v. Shirt* (1980) 146 C.L.R. 40 at 47-48; *Rest. 2d* §291; Terry, *Negligence*, 29 Harv. L. Rev. 40 (1915).
82. *Mercer v. Comm. Road Transport* (1936) 56 C.L.R. 580 at 601.
83. *Bolton v. Stone* [1951] A.C. 850, where it was held that the possibility of such occurrence involved a risk so small that a reasonable man would feel justified to disregard it. The decision is explained in *The Wagon Mound (No. 2)* [1967] 1 A.C. 617 at 642 and may be contrasted with *Miller v. Jackson* [1977] Q.B. 966. Cf. *Swinley v. Stephenson* (1962) 79 W.N. (N.S.W.) 750; *Hilder v. Assoc. Cement Manufacturers* [1961] 1 W.L.R. 1434; *Close v. Steel Co.* [1962] A.C. 367.
84. *Wing v. L.G.O. Co.* [1909] 2 K.B. 652 (C.A.).
85. See below, p. 317.
86. Glass J.A. in *Shirt v. Wyong S.* [1978] 1 N.S.W.L.R. 631 at 641.
87. " 'Likelihood' means something less than probability but more than a remote foreseeability" (*Sheen v. Fields* (1984) 51 A.L.R. 345 at 348).
88. *The Wagon Mound (No. 2)* [1967] 1 A.C. 617 at 643 per Lord Reid; *Wyong S.C. v. Shirt* (1980) 146 C.L.R. 40.
89. See *Schiller v. Mulgrave S.* (1972) 129 C.L.R. 116 where the chance of a dead tree falling at the precise time a (rare) visitor passed along the wilderness trail was very small, but not small enough to dispense with the need for inspection and maintenance.
90. *The Wagon Mound (No. 2)* at 642.

but not to the second; for example more in the way of warning against live wires is required to a layman than to a skilled electrician.[91]

Not only the greater risk of injury, but also the risk of greater injury is a relative factor. Hence if A and B, engaged on the same work, run precisely the same risk of an accident happening but the results of it will be more serious to A than B, precautions adequate in the case of B may not be adequate in the case of A. Thus a one-eyed worker who is exposed to the danger of flying metal splinters is entitled to exceptional safeguards from his employer, because an accident to only one eye might reduce him to total blindness.[92]

Except in matters of common knowledge, evidence must be given as to the degree of the particular risk in order to measure it against the steps that might eliminate or reduce it.[93]

Utility of conduct

The gravity of the risk created by the defendant must be weighed against the utility of his conduct. The question is whether "the game is worth the candle".[94] If all vehicles travelled at only 10 kilometres an hour there would be fewer accidents, but life would be intolerably slowed down: the additional safety would be procured at too high a price in terms of general convenience.[95] By the same token it is sometimes permissible to take a "calculated risk", as a doctor might in undertaking a risky operation or in prescribing a radical drug to alleviate a condition so serious that it is worth running the risk of harmful side effects.[96]

Rescuers are treated with exceptional leniency.[97] A fire brigade or ambulance may proceed at a speed and take some traffic risks that would be unjustifiable for a Sunday driver,[98] though it must still conform to the standard of care proper for one bent on such an errand or urgency.[99] Nor may a policeman, in discharging his duty to apprehend felons, ignore entirely the safety of innocent persons, though he is apparently justified to

91. *Sydney C.C. v. Dell'Oro* (1974) 132 C.L.R. 97. But there is no absolute rule that an expert tradesman must look to his own safety as regards known risks involved in his daily work: *Bus v. Sydney C.C.* (1989) 167 C.L.R. 78.
92. *Paris v. Stepney B.C.* [1951] A.C. 367.
93. *Maloney v. Comm. Rlys* (1978) 52 A.L.J.R. 292 (open train door). But exact odds on incurring the risk are rarely available, as they were in *Davis v. Wyeth Laboratories* 399 F. 2d 121 (9 Cir. 1968) (polio vaccine); *Helling v. Carey* 519 P. 2d 981 (Wash. 1974) (glaucoma).
94. *Rest. 2d* §291, comment *a*.
95. *Daborn v. Bath Tramways* [1946] 2 All E.R. 333 at 336; *Mercer v. Comm. Road Transport* (1936) 56 C.L.R. 580 at 589.
96. E.g. *Male v. Hopmans* (1967) 64 D.L.R. (2d) 105 (but must he not inform the patient and leave the choice to *him*?).
97. See below, p. 170. Salvors: *The St Blane* [1974] 1 Ll. Rep. 557 at 560.
98. Emergency vehicles are specifically exempt from ordinary speed limits: *Motor Traffic Act* 1909 (N.S.W.) s. 4A(7); *Transport Act* 1949 (N.Z.) s. 37. Speeding police: *Gaynor v. Allen* [1959] 2 Q.B. 403; *Johnstone v. Woolmer* (1977) 16 A.C.T.R. 6. The fleeing felon may be liable anyway: 51 A.L.R. 3d 1226 (1973).
99. See *Fire Comm. v. Ardouin* (1961) 109 C.L.R. 105; *S.A. Ambulance v. Wahlheim* (1948) 77 C.L.R. 215 at 219-220; *Blight v. Warman* [1964] S.A.S.R. 163; *Brown's Bread v. Saunders* (1959) 22 D.L.R. (2d) 766; *Watt v. Herts C.C.* [1954] 1 W.L.R. 835 at 838. Far from being absolved from maintaining an efficient lookout, the driver should compensate for his extra speed by increased vigilance.

resort to measures, even the use of firearms, which involve some risk of injury to bystanders but are no more than reasonably necessary to effect his purpose.[100] So also some allowance must be made to competitors in races and games for the "excitement of the sport".[101]

The conduct claimed to be negligent may have value to the actor or to someone else; it may be impelled by selfishness or altruism. In either case, the law will assess its value against the risk of harm. Thus, it is not necessarily negligent to dash into the path of a runaway horse[102] or swerve from the road,[103] in order to save a child at the risk of injury to oneself or others.[104] Nor would it probably be culpable to run over the child if the sole alternative were driving over a precipice with the prospect of certain death.[105] In these situations the value of the actor's conduct is sufficiently great to prevent the risk of harm threatened to others from being regarded as unreasonable.

Of course, just as the utility of the defendant's activity deserves credit, so its disutility will be counted against him. An idle, pointless or unlawful act fraught with the slightest risk may be unreasonable when the same act prompted by a laudable purpose would be excused. Thus there is a world of difference between throwing a burning object into the street below just for the fun of it or in order to save a house on fire.[106]

Burden of eliminating risk

Finally, allowance is due to the cost and inconvenience of precautions or alternatives that might eliminate or minimise the danger.[107] "One must balance the risk against the measures necessary to eliminate the risk."[108] The classical example is our traditional tolerance of level railway crossings, the cost of providing under- or overpasses being viewed as excessive in the light of much cheaper, alternative warning devices. So while it may be reasonable to expect a supermarket to keep a frequent watch for garbage in the aisles, particularly around vegetable bins,[109] it would be altogether

100. *Priestman v. Colangelo* [1959] S.C.R. 615; *Beim v. Goyer* [1965] S.C.R. 638; *Marshall v. Osmond* [1982] Q.B. 857, affd [1983] Q.B. 1034 (criminal injured). Cf. *Farrell v. M.O.D.* [1980] 1 All E.R. 172 (H.L.; security forces in N.I.). A lower standard due to the criminal? See *Marshall v. Osmond* [1983] Q.B. 1034 (C.A.).
101. *Wilks v. Cheltenham Cycle Club* [1971] 1 W.L.R. 668 (C.A.) ("foolhardy"); *Johnston v. Frazer* (1990) 21 N.S.W.L.R. 89 (C.A.) rejecting the "reckless disregard of spectators" standard of *Wooldridge v. Sumner* [1963] 2 Q.B. 43 (C.A.). Aliter if the fault did not occur in the "excitement of the sport" (e.g. brake misalignment in *Harrison v. Vincent* [1982] R.T.R. 8) or was caused by a sportsman in a non-competitive exercise, as in *Cleghorn v. Oldham* (1927) 43 T.L.R. 465 (golfer, not in course of play, swinging club); *Quire v. Coates* [1964] S.A.S.R. 294 (fox shoot by truck).
102. *Haynes v Harwood* [1935] 1 K.B. 146 (contributory negligence).
103. Cf. *Carmarthenshire C.C. v. Lewis* [1955] A.C. 549: see below, p. 173.
104. *O'Hara v. Central S.M.T. Co.* 1941 S.C. 363 (passengers); *Symeonakis v. Symeonakis* (1990) A.T.R. 81-034 (dog).
105. See *Thurmond v. Pepper* 119 S.W. 2d 900 (Tex. 1938). Cf. *Romney Marsh v. Trinity House* (1870) L.R. 5 Ex 204 (saving valuables in ship at expense of sea wall).
106. *The Wagon Mound (No. 2)* [1967] 1 A.C. 617 at 642.
107. *Bressington v. Comm. Rlys* (1947) 75 C.L.R. 339 at 348; *Hicks v. B.T.C.* [1958] 1 W.L.R. 493 at 505.
108. *Watt v. Herts C.C.* [1954] 1 W.L.R. 835 at 838 per Denning L.J.
109. See below, p. 455.

too burdensome for telephone companies to inspect regularly its untold number of cement boxes on street level in the suburbs.[110]

The actual resources available to the defendant are not, of course, relevant in mitigation; as a reasonable person he must bring adequate resources to his enterprise commensurate to the risk entailed.[110a] Again, if the only precaution available to eliminate one risk would involve the creation of another, it may not be unreasonable to run the first, at any rate if the activity in question is so important that the actor could not be expected to abandon it altogether. In *Mercer v. Commissioner for Road Transport*,[111] a collision occurred as the result of a tram driver collapsing at the controls and the tram continuing on its way despite all efforts by the conductors to apply hand brakes. It was urged that the transport authority had acted unreasonably in failing to guard against a driver's collapse by installing a device for automatically cutting off the motor, but counterevidence showed that the equipment of a so-called "dead man's handle" would subject the driver to undue strain and create other dangers, such as sudden halts with a corresponding risk of collisions from the rear. The task of weighing these risks, one against the other, was essentially a function for the jury, and their reluctant verdict for the plaintiff was upheld.

In some cases it might be asking too much of a defendant to desist from a given activity permanently, though not to postpone it temporarily so as to avoid unnecessary injury to others. Thus spraying insecticide should be postponed while neighbouring bees are feeding on flowering crops[112] and noisy road building during the whelping season of adjacent mink.[113]

Just as the burden of any particular safety precaution militates against the plaintiff, so its relative ease does against the defendant. Contrast a mere warning that could have been uttered on the spot or affixed to a label or sign post from an elaborate redesign of industrial plant or highway complex. Also, in so far as the cost factor is raised, it may lose weight if the cost need not be absorbed by the defendant personally but can (and even should) be passed on to the beneficiaries of his enterprise.

Cost/benefit analysis

The negligence concept, with its complex balance just described, has a decidedly utilitarian flavour. Indeed, it has been forcibly argued that the negligence matrix reflects norms of economic efficiency, tending to maximise wealth and minimise costs, by encouraging cost-justified accident prevention while discouraging excessive investment in safety. If the loss

110. *Rickards v. Telecom* [1983] 3 N.S.W.L.R. 155 (concrete telephone "pit"). But the risk may be so great that one must abandon an activity if unable to devise adequate safeguards: *Christmas v. General Cleaning Contractors* [1952] 1 K.B. 141 at 149; *Bolton v. Stone* [1951] A.C. 850 at 867. Contrast *Daborn v. Bath Tramways* [1946] 2 All E.R. 333 (left-hand drive ambulance during war).

110a. *PQ v. Austr. Red Cross* [1992] 1 V.R. 19. See 108 L.Q.R. 8.

111. (1936) 56 C.L.R. 580. See also *Parkinson v. Liverpool Corp.* [1950] 1 All E.R. 367; *Sutherland v. Glasgow Corp.* 1949 S.C. 563 (driver's duty to consider the safety of his passengers when pulling up sharply to avoid running over a dog).

112. *Tutton v. Walter* [1986] Q.B. 61.

113. See below, p. 425.

caused by a given activity to the actor and his victim is greater than its benefit, the activity should be (and is) discouraged by being labelled negligent and requiring the actor to compensate the victim; if the balance is the other way, the actor may go ahead scot-free.[114]

But negligence cannot be reduced to a purely economic equation.[115] True, economic factors are given weight, especially regarding the value of the defendant's activity and the cost of eliminating the risk. In a few situations, allowance for the defendant's limited financial resources has been expressly sanctioned.[116] But in general, judicial opinions do not make much of the cost factor, and for good reasons. For one thing, our legal tradition in torts has strong roots in an individualistic morality with its focus primarily on interpersonal equity rather than broader social policy. The infusion of economic criteria like insurability, loss distribution and efficient resource allocation has so far remained largely unsystematic, interstitial and controversial. Secondly, the calculus of negligence includes some important non-economic values, like health and life, freedom and privacy, which defy comparison with competing economic values. Negligence is not just a matter of calculating the point at which the cost of injury to victims (that is the damages payable) exceeds that of providing safety precautions. In particular, avoiding harm is commonly considered more important than promoting increased public welfare.[117] In short, the reasonable man is by no means a caricature cold blooded, calculating Economic Man. Lastly, courts remain sceptical of their ability, let alone that of juries, to pursue economic analyses; especially as precise data are rarely available, particularly in personal injury cases, to quantify the relevant factors.[118]

Common practice

Since the standard of care is determined by reference to community valuations, considerable evidentiary weight attaches to whether or not the defendant's conduct conformed to standard practices accepted as normal and general by other members of the community in similar circumstances.[119] This has both a negative and positive side.

114. See Posner, *A Theory of Negligence*, 1 J. Leg. Stud. 29 (1972) and *Economic Analysis of Law* (2nd ed. 1977) ch. 6. See Englard, *Law and Economics in American Tort Cases: A Critical Assessment of the Theory's Impact on Courts*, 41 U. Tor. L.J. 359 (1990). Impetus was given to such an equation by Judge L. Hand's famous algebraic formula in *U.S. v. Carroll Towing* 159 F. 2d 169 at 173 (1947): if the probability be called P, the injury L and the burden B, liability depends on whether $B > PL$.
115. See Calabresi, *The Costs of Accidents* (1970).
116. Liability for natural conditions (see below, p. 431) and to trespassers: see below, p. 468. Should it favour public authorities as suggested by *Cekan v. Haines* (1990) 22 N.S.W.L.R. 296 (C.A.)? Discussed 108 L.Q.R. 9 (1992).
117. "It is widely felt that it is unfair to require a few individuals to suffer significant specialised harms in order to produce widespread benefits, even if the total benefit exceeds the total harm" (Regan, *Glosses on Dworkin*, 76 Mich. L. Rev. 1213 at 1232 (1978)).
118. For an example of property damage see *City of Richmond v. Scantelbury* [1991] 1 V.R. 638, discussed in 108 L.Q.R. 9 (1992).
119. *Paris v. Stepney B.C.* [1951] A.C. 367 at 382; *Kauffman v. T.T.C.* [1960] S.C.R. 251; *Vancouver Hospital v. MacDaniel* [1934] 4 D.L.R. 593 (P.C.); and see below, p. 509 (work accidents). See also Morris, *Custom and Negligence*, 42 Col. L. Rev. 1147 (1942); Linden, *Custom in Negligence Law*, 11 Can. B.J. 151 (1968).

Failure to adopt the general practice is often the strongest possible indication of want of care, because it suggests at once that the defendant did not do what others considered proper and that there is no problem of feasibility. Indeed, if failure to take a recognised precaution is followed by the very damage which that precaution was designed to prevent, the burden shifts to the defendant to justify himself.[120] But the presumption is not conclusive because it would otherwise close the door to new methods, stultifying progress.[121]

Conformity with general practice, on the other hand, usually dispels negligence. It tends to show what others in the same "business" considered sufficient, that the defendant could not have learnt how to avoid the accident by the example of others, that most probably no other practical precautions could have been taken, and that the impact of an adverse judgment (especially in cases involving industry or a profession) will be industry-wide and thus assume the function of a "test case". Finally, it underlines the need for caution against passing too cavalierly upon the conduct and decision of experts.

All the same, even a common practice may itself be condemned as negligent if fraught with obvious risks. "If it is unreasonable to do absolutely nothing to one's driveway in the face of clearly treacherous conditions, it matters little that one's neighbours also act unreasonably."[122] In the last analysis the standard of reasonable care is measured by what *ought* ordinarily to be done rather than what *is* ordinarily done. Were it otherwise, an entire industry would be free, by maintaining careless methods to save time, effort or money, to set its own uncontrolled standard with no incentive to devise new and more efficient safety precautions.[123] Accordingly, proper regard for the safety of others may require the adoption of some device only recently discovered,[124] mindful however of the truism that while an omission to adopt a safety device is not necessarily answered by the argument that such an accident had not happened before,[125] yet nothing is so easy as to be wise after the event.[126] Again, there may be special circumstances, as in the case of the one-eyed workman already noted, which demand *extra*ordinary precautions, so that the ordinary practice of employers will throw little light on the question of what special steps a prudent employer would have taken for the protection of this particular plaintiff.[127]

120. *Clark v. MacLennan* [1983] 1 All E.R. 416 (medical). But cf. *Brown v. Rolls Royce* [1960] 1 W.L.R. 210 (H.L.) (industrial).
121. *Hunter v. Hanley* 1955 S.C. 200 at 206 (medical).
122. *Waldrick v. Malcolm* [1991] 2 S.C.R. 456 at 473 (general practice of not sanding icy residential driveway).
123. *Rest. 2d* §295A, comment *k*.
124. *Mercer v. Comm. Road Transport* (1936) 56 C.L.R. 580 at 589; *Wise Bros v. Comm. Rlys* (1947) 75 C.L.R. 59 at 72.
125. *Fryer v. Salford Corp.* [1937] 1 All E.R. 617 at 620.
126. *Cornman v. E. Counties Rly* (1859) 4 H. & N. 781 at 786; 157 E.R. 1050 at 1052; *Baker v. Bethnal Green B.C.* [1944] 2 All E.R. 301 at 307; *MacKay v. Saskatoon* (1960) 26 D.L.R. (2d) 506. Hence safeguards taken after the accident are admissible in evidence only as probative that they would have been practicable, not that their absence was negligent: *Nelson v. Lysaght* (1975) 132 C.L.R. 201; *Theilemann v. Commonwealth* [1982] V.R. 713.
127. *Paris v. Stepney B.C.* [1951] A.C. 367.

Common practice plays a conspicuous role in medical negligence actions. Conscious at once of the layman's ignorance of medical science and apprehensive of the impact of jury bias on a peculiarly vulnerable profession, courts have resorted to the safeguard of insisting that negligence in diagnosis and treatment (including disclosure of risks[128]) cannot ordinarily be established without the aid of expert testimony or in the teeth of conformity with accepted medical practice.[129] However there is no categorical rule. Thus an accepted practice is open to censure by a jury (nor expert testimony required[130]) at any rate in matters not involving diagnostic or clinical skills, on which an ordinary person may presume to pass judgment sensibly, like failure to remove a sponge,[131] an explosion set off by an admixture of ether vapour and oxygen[132] or injury to a patient's body outside the area of treatment.[133]

Safety codes

Safety standards are increasingly formulated by expert professional or administrative bodies. They may be directed to such common activities as motoring (highway code) or to highly specialised matters like the location of high voltage cables or the design of machinery and equipment. If issued under legislative authority and purporting to be mandatory, such standards are, of course, binding and non-compliance, as we shall see, may be treated as negligence per se.[134] But even if of lesser authority (for example, issued by professional bodies), they have an important role in the determination of negligence, for they are usually highly persuasive evidence of expert opinion as to minimum safety requirements. Thus non-compliance is at least evidence of negligence; not compelling perhaps, but calling for a convincing explanation the more the standard in question is adhered to by everyone else.[135] In this manner, expert opinion and common practice combine in formulating the legal standard of requisite care.

Anticipation of negligent conduct

Ordinarily, we may assume that others will take reasonable care to look out for themselves. Traffic would be unduly slowed down if road users were not entitled to repose some confidence in the reasonable conduct of others, provided there is nothing to indicate that such trust would be misplaced. A motorist need not ordinarily adjust his speed against pedestrians

128. See above, p. 109.
129. The "Bolam principle" from *Bolam v. Friern Hospital* [1957] 1 W.L.R. 582; see above, p. 109. The doctor's own practice is of course irrelevant: *Chin Keow v. Government of Malaysia* [1967] 1 W.L.R. 813 (P.C.).
130. See below as to the propriety of invoking res ipsa loquitur.
131. *Anderson v. Chasney* [1949] 4 D.L.R. 71; affd [1950] 4 D.L.R. 223.
132. *Crits v. Sylvester* (1956) 1 D.L.R. (2d) 502; also *Penner v. Theobald* (1962) 35 D.L.R. (2d) 700; *Goode v. Nash* (1979) 21 S.A.S.R. 419.
133. In all other cases, American law treats conformity as conclusive: see McCoid, *Care Required of Medical Practitioners*, 12 Vand. L. Rev. 549 (1959). There is perhaps no such categorical rule under English law: at least conformity to a *local* standard is not conclusive: *Albrighton v. Royal Hospital* [1979] 2 N.S.W.L.R. 165.
134. See below, p. 124 (statutory standards).
135. Such e.g. is the English treatment of the *Highway Code*: see below, p. 129.

unexpectedly dashing into his path[136] or other drivers flouting the rules of the road. Not that he may drive at any speed he chooses so far as roads coming in on his left are concerned, or with complete indifference to the possibility of a car suddenly emerging from a side road as the result of accident, miscalculation, carelessness[137] or for any other reason.[138] The mere fact, however, that he sees another car approaching from a side street on his left does not make it imperative for him to stop, for he may assume that the other will advance only far enough to survey the traffic on his right. Again, it is not ordinarily unreasonable to suppose that other motorists are proceeding at proper speeds and, if one is in this way misled into underestimating the speed of an unreasonably fast car approaching an intersection, only the latter will be adjudged guilty of negligence.[139]

The difficulty often lies in prognosticating precisely when these assumptions become untenable. Liberty to act on an expectation of non-negligence in others ceases as soon as there are indications that they are, or are likely to be, acting imprudently. The ever-present possibility of negligent behaviour demands constant scrutiny in every direction whence danger may loom, and the greater the risk the more tentative must be the assumption that others will conduct themselves with reasonable care.[140] Thus a train driver need not slow down for a level crossing on the assumption that motorists will stay clear; but he must keep continuing watch for approaching traffic in order to slow down, if not to stop, as soon as it becomes apparent that a car is not giving way.[141]

There are many situations in which it becomes incumbent to take precautions against negligent, and occasionally even criminal misconduct of others. And, it has been observed, "the law has placed an increasing emphasis upon the relevance of the possibility of negligence or inadvertence on the part of the person to whom a duty of care is owed."[142] In some situations, the prospect that a third person will so act is the very hazard which makes it negligent not to adopt precautions against it, and here the only *real* problem is either as to the existence of a duty of care[143] or whether that duty has been adequately discharged. Typical are the many accidents caused by an unauthorised stranger, often a child, tampering with an unguarded bulldozer or scaffolding on a construction site or with railway trucks on a siding, and the question arises whether adequate precautions were taken to secure the object against such interference.[144] In another

136. *Jensen v. Hall* [1961] N.Z.L.R. 800.
137. *Sibley v. Kais* (1967) 118 C.L.R. 424; *Taylor v. Miller* [1969] V.R. 987 (upholding 50:50 verdict); *L.P.T.B. v. Upson* [1949] A.C. 155.
138. E.g. because, as in S.A. (*Road Traffic Act* 1934 s. 156(a)), the left-hand vehicle, being an ambulance, is exempted from the right-hand priority rule: *S.A. Ambulance v. Wahlheim* (1948) 77 C.L.R. 215.
139. *Trompp v. Liddle* (1941) 41 S.R. (N.S.W.) 108 at 109-110; *Tucker v. McCann* [1948] V.L.R. 222 at 228.
140. *Kiely v. Angliss* [1944] S.A.S.R. 87 at 90-91; *Lang v. London Transport* [1959] 1 W.L.R. 1168.
141. *Petropoulos v. Comm. Rlys* (1962) 80 W.N. (N.S.W.) 659; *Hale v. Victorian Rly* (1953) 87 C.L.R. 529.
142. *Bus v. Sydney C.C.* (1989) 167 C.L.R. 78 at 90 (two electricians working in same area).
143. E.g. *Northwestern Utilities v. London Guarantee* [1936] A.C. 108; *Stansbie v. Troman* [1948] 2 K.B. 48; see below, p. 151.
144. *McDowall v. Gt W. Rly* [1903] 2 K.B. 331; *Cuttress v. Scaffolding (G.B.)* [1953] 1 W.L.R. 1311; *Wright v. McCrea* [1965] 1 O.R. 300.

class of case, however, the defendant's conduct is negligent because of other risks which it entails, but the culpable intervention of a third party may still be sufficiently "on the cards" to come within the risk thereby created. The latter type of case does not raise any question as to the standard of care, but rather as to the extent of responsibility for an admitted breach of duty. Both deal with kindred, though not identical, aspects commonly associated with "remoteness of damage", and will be discussed in greater detail in that context.[145]

3. DEGREES OF NEGLIGENCE

In theory, the common law of torts adheres to a single standard of care and refuses to recognise different degrees of negligence. The controlling standard is that of the reasonable man adjusted to the individual circumstances of each case. This viewpoint stands in contrast to the criminal law which regards "negligent" and "reckless" driving as distinct offences, and to the law of bailment which, under the influence of Roman law analogies, has given some countenance to different kinds of negligence—ordinary, gross and slight.[146] A number of jurisdictions in Canada and the United States borrowed this idea and introduced it into the sphere of tort liability, for example by relieving the driver of a car from liability to gratuitous passengers except in the case of "gross" negligence or "wilful", "wanton" or "reckless" misconduct.[147] These "guest statutes" have no parallel in England or Australia.[148]

But although unfamiliar with different degrees of negligence, we do acknowledge different degrees of care. True, there is only one single standard of care, but it may demand greater or less precaution depending on the nature of the particular risk. A reasonable man need not show the same anxious care when handling a kilogram of butter as he would a kilogram of dynamite. In this sense, it is true to say that "the nature of the thing may very well call for different degrees of care."[149]

Moreover, a realistic view of the legal process would recognise the discrepancy, which is so marked in this context, between official theory as reflected in jury instructions and court opinions, on the one hand, and law in action on the other. In practice, there is a noticeable variance in the standard applied to different relations in accordance with current notions of social responsibility and other factors bearing on the allocation of risks. For example, the standard tends to special stringency ("negligence without

145. See below, p. 220.

146. Actually, there is but scant modern authority for the view that, in bailments solely for the benefit of the bailor, the bailee is liable only for gross negligence: *Houghland v. Low* [1962] 1 Q.B. 694 at 698; *Campbell v. Pickard* (1961) 30 D.L.R. (2d) 152. See Palmer, *Bailment* (1991) 598ff. Wright's 1927 thesis, *Gross Negligence*, 33 U. Tor. L.J. 184 (1983), subjects the term to trenchant historical analysis.

147. See *Prosser & Keeton* 285; *Linden* 574.

148. "Wilful misconduct" is exceptionally encountered in contract clauses: e.g. *Transport Comm. v. Neale* (1954) 92 C.L.R. 214; *Royal Victorian Aero Club v. Commonwealth* (1954) 92 C.L.R. 236.

149. *Donoghue v. Stevenson* [1932] A.C. 562 at 569 per Lord Atkin. See e.g. *Dahlberg v. Nayduik* (1969) 10 D.L.R. (3d) 319 (firearms); *Gilmour v. Simpson* 1958 S.C. 477 (blowlamp) and below, p. 490.

fault"[150]) in the case of defendants like motorists[151] and employers,[152] who offer a well recognised focus for loss distribution, particularly when insurance is either compulsory or widely held. This tilt against "deep pocket" defendants is particularly prevalent among juries. In contrast, a discernible pattern of leniency prevails in judging medical doctors whose professional reputation is peculiarly vulnerable to adverse verdicts.[153] Most noticeable of all is the dual standard in dealing with the respective issues of negligence and contributory negligence; because, here again, the factor of loss-bearing capacity and the policy of aiding loss distribution support alike a distinction which appeals to a widespread contemporary sense of fairness.[154]

4. STATUTORY STANDARDS

For some situations the appropriate standard of conduct is prescribed by the legislature instead of being left to the evaluative process of judge and jury. The complexity of modern life has spawned a myriad of governmental regulations, demanding observance of fixed and specific rules of conduct for the safety of industrial operations, building construction, road traffic and so forth. Unlike jury verdicts which pass judgment on a specific accident after it has happened and rarely have widespread effect on the future behaviour of (non-institutional) individuals, statutory standards tend to be widely promulgated among those they seek to influence and primarily aim at preventing accidents. Rarely do they address themselves to their possible effect on civil liability, being content with prescribing a minor criminal sanction, usually a fine, for disobedience whether or not it causes injury to anyone. Yet the absence of any expressed intention to provide a remedy in damages has not prevented the courts from treating non-compliance with the statutory rule as having a decided bearing on civil recovery. For whenever a penal statute lays down a standard of conduct for the purpose of preventing injury or loss, non-compliance is at least admissible as *evidence* of negligence (breach of the common law duty of care).[155] Indeed, not infrequently the unexcused violation of a safety statute is treated as negligence per se, that is, negligence as a matter of law. Non-observance of such duty is then "statutorily equivalent to negligence"[156] or, in short, "statutory negligence".

According to the received doctrine in England and Australia, the negligence per se rule rests on a supposed or "presumed" intention by the

150. See Ehrenzweig, *Negligence Without Fault* (1951).
151. See e.g. *Daly v. Liverpool Corp.* [1939] 2 All E.R. 142 ("very high standard of care"). But juries should not be so directed: *Russell v. Harris* [1960] N.Z.L.R. 902).
152. See below, ch. 23.
153. See above, p. 109.
154. See below, p. 285.
155. Laskin J. spoke of a statute "crystallising a fact situation" (*Menow v. Honsberger* [1974] S.C.R. 239 at 246) or being a "fortifying element in the recognition of a common law duty" (*Horsley v. MacLaren* [1972] S.C.R. 441 at 463). This "reinforcement" view was also invoked in *O'Rourke v. Schacht* [1976] 1 S.C.R. 53 (duty by police to report accidents): see below, p. 148.
156. *David v. Britannic Merthyr Coal Co.* [1909] 2 K.B. 146 at 164 per Fletcher Moulton L.J.

legislature to provide a civil remedy, so long as this can be "inferred" as a matter of construction, having regard to the scope, purview and structure of the provision. But, save in exceptional cases,[157] this is a barefaced fiction because, consonant with accepted canons of statutory interpretation, the legislature's silence on the question of civil liability rather points to the conclusion that it either did not have it in mind or deliberately omitted to provide for it. In reality, an intent to give or deny an action for damages to the person injured has more often than not been ascribed to the legislature as a result of presumptions or judicial policy rather than the meaning of the instrument.[158] But being based on the pretence that the civil claim is a creature of the statute, the cause of action—"breach of statutory duty"—is classified as distinct from any (often concurrent) claim for negligence (breach of a common law duty).[159]

More plausible is the prevailing American theory[160] which frankly disclaims that the civil action is in any true sense a creature of the statute, for the simple enough reason that the statute just does not contemplate, much less provide, a civil remedy. Any recovery of damages for injury due to its violation must, therefore, rest on common law principles. But though the penal statute does not create civil liability, the court may think it proper to *adopt* the legislative formulation of a specific standard in place of the unformulated standard of reasonable conduct, in much the same manner as when it rules peremptorily that certain acts or omissions constitute negligence as a matter of law. By accepting the legislative standard it rules in effect that the defendant's conduct fell below that of the reasonable man as the court conceives it. For once it has been officially determined that certain risks must be avoided by taking a prescribed precaution on pain of criminal penalties, non-compliance cannot be regarded as other than substandard in the absence of some cogent countervailing reason.

This approach permits adoption of the legislative standard even when the statute cannot apply proprio vigore, as when there is some technical defect in its promulgation[161] or when it would be beyond the legislative body's power to create a *civil* cause of action,[162] or perhaps even when there

157. E.g. specifically *Health and Safety at Work Act* 1974 (Eng.) s. 47 and *Consumer Safety Act* (Eng.) 1978 s. 6; *Consumer Protection Act* 1969 (N.S.W.) s. 38; or on the basis of a preamble (as in *Factories, Shops and Industries Act* 1962 of N.S.W.) or reference to a civil defence (as in *Mines and Quarries Act* 1954 (Eng.) s. 157, the *Mines Act* 1958 (Vic.) s. 411, the *Coal Mines Act* 1925 (N.Z.) s. 147 and *Mining Act* 1926 (N.Z.) s. 295). Sometimes the scope of authority conferred by the authorising statute affords a clue to whether regulations made pursuant to it were intended to confer a private remedy besides the penalty prescribed: *Henwood v. Municipal Tramways* (1938) 60 C.L.R. 438; *Gorris v. Scott* (1874) L.R. 9 Ex. 125; *Tucker v. McCann* [1948] V.L.R. 222 at 225. Cf. *A.I. & S. v. Ryan* (1957) 97 C.L.R. 89. The English Law Com. (No. 21) proposed enactment (foiled in 1980) of a presumption that, in the absence of an express provision to the contrary, breach of all statutory duties become actionable.

158. See *O'Connor v. Bray* (1937) 56 C.L.R. 464 at 474-478 per Dixon J.

159. See further below, p. 188. A plaintiff who relies on breach both of statutory and common law duty, should plead them as separate causes of action: Bullen & Leake's *Precedents of Pleading* (11th ed. 1959) 546; *Smith v. Wilkins* [1958] N.Z.L.R. 958 at 963; *Darling Isl. Stevedoring v. Long* (1957) 97 C.L.R. 36 (semble, not res judicata).

160. Seminal was Thayer's article, *Public Wrong and Private Action*, 27 Harv. L. Rev. 317 (1913).

161. *Clinkscales v. Carver* 136 P. 2d 777 (Cal. 1943).

162. *Wasney v. Jurazsky* [1933] 1 D.L.R. 616 (C.A.): *Criminal Code* of Canada enacted by *Dominion* legislature.

would have been a defence to criminal responsibility which would not be suitable for civil liability.[163]

The Supreme Court of Canada has recently sided with the American approach of integrating statutory breach within the framework of negligence rather than following its Anglo-Australian classification as a separate tort.[164] Perplexed by the fictitiousness of the legislative intent theorem, its arbitrary results and inflexible application, it preferred to treat breach of statutory duty henceforth merely as at best evidence of negligence.

Purpose of statute

The most disconcerting feature of the traditional judicial preoccupation with pursuing "the will o' the wisp of a non-existing legislative intention"[165] is that it tends to obscure, rather than elucidate, the controlling factors in deciding whether a particular penal statute should be held to fix conclusively a specific standard or merely furnish some evidence, like proof of custom, to assist a judge or jury in applying the unformulated standard of reasonable care. It is often said, for instance, that the mere fact that a statute aims to prevent certain kinds of harm is not a sufficient reason for affording a civil remedy, unless there is also evident, from a consideration of the purpose of the statute, an intention to confer a correlative private right in addition to the penal sanction. But when is this inference permissible, seeing that ex hypothesi the legislature refrained from declaring its intention? Various presumptions or modes of interpretation have been suggested, but none have succeeded in providing so much as a reasonably reliable working formula. Thus, it has often been tediously repeated that the crucial test is whether the duty created by the statute is owed primarily to the state and only incidentally to the individual, or vice versa.[166] But like most verbal tests concealing a value judgment based on policy or intuition, this formulation is at best question begging, if not actually misleading. It is equivalent to saying that because the duty is owed to everybody, it is owed to nobody.[167] As has been pointed out, "the duty may be of such paramount importance that it is owed to all the public. It would be strange if a less important duty, which is owed to a section of the public, may be enforced by an action, while a more important duty owed to the public at large cannot. The right of action does not depend on whether a statutory commandment or prohibition is pronounced for the benefit of the public or for the benefit of a class. It may be conferred on

163. Contrast *Harrison v. N.C.B.* [1950] 1 K.B. 466 at 676 (no) with *Potts v. Reid* [1943] A.C. 1 at 31 (yes). Also *Sovar v. Lane* (1967) 116 C.L.R. 397.

164. *R. v. Sask. Wheat Pool* [1983] 1 S.C.R. 205 (except possibly for "industrial penal statutes"). See *Linden* ch. 7.

165. *Harper, James & Gray* §17.6 n. 5. See generally Buckley, 100 L.Q.R. 204 (1984); Williams, 23 Mod. L. Rev. 233 (1960); Fricke, 76 L.Q.R. 240 (1960); Alexander, 42 Can. B. Rev. 243 (1964); Lowndes, 16 Minn. L. Rev. 361 (1932); Morris, 46 Harv. L. Rev. 453 (1933), 49 Col. L. Rev. 21 (1949). Traditionally expository: Stanton, *Breach of Statutory Duty in Tort* (1986).

166. *Read v. Croydon Corp.* [1938] 4 All E.R. 631 at 652.

167. This has not prevented an increasingly liberal attitude for private individuals (with special interest) to enforce such duties via public law remedies: e.g. *Ex parte Island Records* [1978] Ch. 122.

anyone who can bring himself within the benefit of the Act."[168] In the last resort, considerations of judicial policy alone are decisive, "without either the authority of any general rule of law or the application of any definite rule of construction".[169]

Most important, perhaps, among the latent premises which influence the judicial approach, is that a penal statute will more readily be accepted as a source of civil liability if it enacts a safety standard in a matter where the person upon whom the duty is laid is already, under the general law of negligence, bound to exercise reasonable care. In such a case, the effect of the provision is only to define specifically what must be done in performance of that general duty.[170] This explains the readiness with which industrial safety regulations have been treated as conclusively determining the standard of care owed by employers for the protection of their men.[171] Conversely, if the grant of a private right of action would involve recognition of an interest that is not otherwise protected by law against negligence, courts have evinced the strongest reluctance to extend the protection of penal statutes beyond the specific sanction actually provided. A striking example is the well known decision in *Atkinson v. Newcastle Waterworks*,[172] where a householder whose property had been gutted by fire vainly sought to establish a cause of action against a water supply company on the basis of its failure to comply with a statutory duty to maintain a specified pressure in its pipes. In this situation, it used to be thought unwise to shift the loss because the householder is clearly a better insurance carrier against fire risk, and this explains the refusal alike to recognise a common law duty of care[173] and to permit recourse to penal legislation. The same reasoning has been urged in support of the more general thesis that negligence per se cannot ordinarily apply to statutes directing the provision of a service or benefit, since the common law rarely exacts duties of affirmative action.[174] No less would it explain the entrenched policy against construing positive duties imposed on public authorities (for example to construct roads or sewers[175] or for fire brigades "by all possible means to extinguish the fire"[176]) as intended for the benefit of citizens as individuals, though here the primary reason is undoubtedly an unwillingness to impede the exercise of administrative functions and a fear of unduly taxing limited budgets.[177]

168. *Phillips v. Britannia Laundry* [1923] 2 K.B. 832 at 841-842 per Atkin L.J.; *Whittaker v. Rozelle Wood Products* (1936) 36 S.R (N.S.W.) 204 at 208.
169. *O'Connor v. Bray* (1937) 56 C.L.R. 464 at 478 per Dixon J., whose judgment is particularly noteworthy for its singular scepticism concerning the conventional judicial make-believe.
170. Ibid. at 478.
171. See below, p. 510.
172. (1877) 2 Ex. D. 441; contra: *MacEachern v. Pukekohe Borough* [1965] N.Z.L.R. 330; *Dawson v. Bingley U.D.C.* [1911] 2 K.B. 149.
173. *Moch Co. v. Rensellaer Water Co.*, 159 N.E. 896 (1928); contra: *Laurentide Motels v. Beauport* [1989] 1 S.C.R. 705 (Que.).
174. Thayer, 27 Harv. L. Rev. 317 at 329 (1913). Linden, *Tort Liability for Criminal Nonfeasance*, 44 Can. B. Rev. 25 (1966) argues against this policy.
175. *Pasmore v. Oswaldthwistle U.D.C.* [1898] A.C. 387 at 397 (against "policy and convenience"). See also below.
176. *Bennett & Wood v. Orange C.C.* (1967) 67 S.R. (N.S.W.) 426 (C.A.).
177. See below, pp. 155, 403.

Again, although far from consistently acknowledged, there is really no justification for invoking any criminal statute in support of an accident claim unless the statute prescribes a fixed *standard of conduct* as a substitute for that of the reasonably prudent man, which ordinarily guides the decision of judge and jury. It is only when the very object of the legislation is to put beyond controversy whether the particular precaution is one which ought to be taken, that the doctrine of statutory negligence has any legitimate place.[178] Thus it is easy enough, and quite proper, to infer an intention to create correlative private rights from the enactment of *specific* safety measures to be observed in the operaton of industrial equipment or the layout of premises.[179] On the other hand, to give the same effect to a statute which does not address itself to the observance of specific precautions, but merely utters an open-ended exhortation for "expeditious, safe and efficient performance"[180] or "merely enjoins the end but not the means" like prohibiting the driving[181] or selling[182] of a defective vehicle would make the offender an outright insurer and thereby impose a burden far in excess of the standard of reasonable care and the penalty enacted by the legislature. An intermediate solution in such a case would be to condition liability on failure to observe reasonable care.[183]

Subordinate legislation

For reasons of delicacy rarely, if ever, avowed, but in many a case probably the last straw, is the fact that the prescription is laid down by a municipal bylaw, local ordinance or some subordinate legislation rather than in an orginal parliamentary statute. Not that this invariably or conclusively counts against it, for at all events in the industrial field detailed safety regulations promulgated by expert agencies, like the relevant "Minister", have long become a familiar and accredited source of duties sounding in damages.[184] Some other bodies, however, even if technically invested with delegated power to make the regulation in question,[185] do

178. See *Lochgelly Iron Co. v. M'Mullan* [1934] A.C. 1 at 9.
179. Including even a categorical prohibition against employing youngsters for work with certain dangerous machines: *Baguley v. Babcock & Wilcox* [1962] S.R. (N.S.W.) 286. For factory legislation see also below, p. 510; for fire precautions *Solomons v. Gertzenstein* [1954] 2 Q.B. 243; *Wright v. T.I.L. Services* [1956] S.R. (N.S.W.) 413; for construction work (lateral support) *Anderson v. Mackellar C.C.* (1968) 69 S.R. (N.S.W.) 444 (C.A.).
180. *Smith v. Macquarie Stevedoring* (1965) 65 S.R. (N.S.W.) 32: statute regulating an industry rather than setting safety standards. The same distinction was held to define the validity of regulations under the *Scaffolding and Lifts Act* (N.S.W.) s. 22; *Jacob v. Utah Construction* (1966) 116 C.L.R. 200.
181. *Phillips v. Britannia Laundry* [1923] 2 K.B. 832; *Tan Chye Choo v. Chong* [1970] 1 W.L.R. 147 (P.C.); *Hopwell v. Baranyay* [1962] V.R. 311. With compulsory insurance, there is a strong case for legislation making the owner or driver absolutely responsible for the mechanical condition of his car (as e.g. under French and German law).
182. *Badham v. Lambs* [1946] K.B. 45. Cf. *R. v. Sask. Wheat Pool* [1983] 1 S.C.R. 205 (delivering infested grain).
183. Thus *Read v. Croydon Corp.* [1938] 4 All E.R. 631 at 650; *Hammond v. St Pancras Vestry* (1874) L.R. 9 C.P. 316 (defective sewer).
184. See *A.I. & S. v. Ryan* (1957) 97 C.L.R. 89.
185. E.g., regulations can be attacked on the ground that authority to prescribe "the manner of carrying out" certain work or "safeguards and measures" does not include the imposition of *absolute* duties of ensuring safety (e.g. "to protect securely every tunnel") rather than specific means for promoting it: *Utah Construction v. Pataky* [1966] A.C. 629 (P.C.) see also above, n. 157.

not apparently command sufficient judicial trust to be credited with implied power to affect civil rights, besides passing mere police regulations.[186] This more than anything else probably explains the consistent refusal to attach tort sanctions to municipal bylaws imposing on abutting occupiers a duty to maintain footpaths clear of snow and debris,[187] and many other instances in which ordinances of local authorities or administrative agencies have been similarly disdained.[188]

Traffic regulations

A potent factor which has militated against certain regulations being construed as a source of duties of absolute obligation is the feeling that the categorical legislative prescription would introduce too inflexible a yardstick for measuring civil liability. This apprehension has been most influential in relation to traffic regulations which rarely make specific allowance for justification or excuse so that, in the absence of a judicial dispensing power corresponding to the benevolent discretion of the police,[189] considerable hardship might result from inexorably subjecting purely technical offenders to civil liability. For example, failure to carry a rear light is no less a literal violation of the traffic code because the driver had no reason to know that it had suddenly gone out.[190] Moreover, compliance with these regulations, far from being exhaustive of what reasonable care demands,[191] may actually amount to negligence as when, in the paramount interest of safety, it may become imperative to steer into a prohibited highway lane in order to avoid certain collision with an oncoming vehicle or jaywalker.[192]

One way of avoiding this impasse is to predicate civil liability on wilful and negligent breaches alone or to admit the excuse of inevitable accident, mistake and necessity; another is to reject all rules of thumb in the particular context and leave to the trier of facts what weight to attach to the statutory prescription in the light of all attendant circumstances. The first solution has much support in American law,[193] but has never gained acceptance as a general proposition in British jurisdictions,[194] aside from Canada[195]—due, no doubt, to an entrenched reluctance to qualify a

186. Most strongly *Askin v. Knox* [1989] 1 N.Z.L.R. 248 (C.A.) (building regulation).
187. *Commerford v. School Comm.* [1950] 2 D.L.R. 207; *Hagen v. Goldfarb* (1961) 28 D.L.R. (2d) 746; De Graff, *Snow and Ice*, 21 Corn. L.Q. 436; *Prosser & Keeton* 223.
188. E.g. *Dennis v. Brownlee* [1963] S.R. (N.S.W.) 719 (highway regulations).
189. See Smart, *Criminal Responsibility for Failing to Do the Impossible*, 103 L.Q.R. 532 (1987).
190. See *Clarke v. Brims* [1947] K.B. 497; *West v. Lawson* 1949 S.C. 430 (not negligence per se); *Sterling T. Corp. v. Postma* [1965] S.C.R. 324 (negligence per se).
191. Conformity rarely qualifies as care per se, because only very exceptionally can a statutory regulation be construed as giving legislative approval to complying conduct: *Hirst v. Jessop* (1962) 79 W.N. (N.S.W.) 619; *Choat v. Cohn* [1948] S.A.S.R. 21 at 29-30; *Franklin v. Gramophone Co.* [1948] 1 K.B. 542 (C.A.); also *Hazelwood v. Webber* (1934) 52 C.L.R. 268; *Schiffner v. C.P.R.* [1951] 4 D.L.R. 172; *Wintle v. Bristol Tramways* (1917) 86 L.J. K.B. 240, 936.
192. *Wallace v. Bergius* 1915 S.C. 205 (not contributory negligence).
193. *Rest. 2d* §288A.
194. Except from Salmond J. in *Canning v. R.* [1924] N.Z.L.R. 118 at 123. But see below, n. 227.
195. *Sterling T. Corp. v. Postma* [1965] S.C.R. 324, later overtaken by *R. v. Sask. Wheat Pool* [1983] 1 S.C.R. 205 which made violations mere evidence of negligence. See above, n. 164.

legislative fiat. Instead, our courts have preferred the alternative expedient of inferring an absence of legislative intent to confer a private cause of action for violation of statutory prescriptions which it would be unwise to apply without some qualification. It is primarily for this reason that traffic regulations[196] may only be considered by the jury as prima facie evidence of negligence rather than negligence per se;[197] though in practice a violator will scarcely avoid an adverse verdict in the absence of convincing justification for his breach.[198] In New South Wales there is the additional reason that, if traffic violations qualified as breach of statutory duty, contributory negligence would disappear as a defence—a rather startling by-product of a statutory reform intended primarily to promote recovery for industrial accidents.[199]

Licences and certificates of competence

The decisive consideration for rejecting licensing requirements as a basis for tort liability is the difficulty of establishing causal relation between an accident and failure to comply with the statutory mandate. In actions for breach of statutory duty, no less than for common law negligence, it is incumbent on a claimant to prove on a balance of probabilites that his injury would not have happened but for the defendant's transgression. To satisfy this requirement, it is not sufficient merely that the defendant *happened* to be engaged in an unlawful activity, unless it also increased the risk of injury to the plaintiff.[200] Hence, driving a car without a rear light has no bearing on a head-on collision with a pedestrian;[201] nor has driving an unregistered vehicle, because there is no basis for saying that the accident would not have occurred if the licence had been procured; apart altogether from the primary purpose of the measure being to raise revenue rather than to aid road safety.[202]

More critical is the question of certificates designed to assure a minimum level of competence in a profession or an activity like driving a car or a crane. Some cases of this kind present no serious problem of causal

196. Even those relating to pedestrian crossings which so obviously contemplate a particular class of beneficiaries: *Abela v. Giew* (1965) 65 S.R. (N.S.W.) 485. Some English cases, especially *L.P.T.B. v. Upson* [1949] A.C. 155, convey a contrary bias.

197. *Tucker v. McCann* [1948] V.L.R. 222; *Dennis v. Brownlee* [1963] S.R. (N.S.W.) 719 (mechanically applied to all, even non-traffic, highway regulations); *Smith v. McIntyre* [1958] Tas. S.R. 36. The *Road Traffic Act* 1972 (U.K.) s. 37(5) expressly declares violation of the *Highway Code* to be evidence of negligence; moreover *Civil Evidence Act* 1968 (Eng.) s. 10 admits conviction as evidence in civil proceedings.

198. See *Mitchell v. Clancy* (1960) 107 C.L.R. 86 at 100-101; *Goodger v. Knapman* [1924] S.A.S.R. 347 at 352 ("as no justification was proved by the defendant . . . the negligence stands unanswered"). Failure to direct the jury on the relevance of traffic regulations constitutes reversible error: *Lane v. Norton* (1928) 28 S.R. (N.S.W.) 143.

199. *Statutory Duties (Contributory Negligence) Act* 1945. This was a reason stressed in *Abela v. Giew* (1965) 65 S.R. (N.S.W.) 485.

200. See below, pp. 195, 279.

201. Notwithstanding the false reasoning by Bankes L.J. in *Phillips v. Britannia Laundry* [1923] 2 K.B. 832 at 839-40.

202. *Roy Swail Ltd v. Reeves* (1956) 2 D.L.R. (2d) 326; *Nominal Defendant v. Haslbauer* (1967) 117 C.L.R. 448 (assumed without contest); also *Vancouver C. v. Burchill* [1932] S.C.R. 620 (chauffeur's licence, which had lapsed, was required for revenue and trade register, not safety).

relevancy, either because there is independent evidence of it, as when the accident was due to epilepsy, the very reason for the driver's disqualification;[203] or conversely because any hypothesis as to causality is disproved by the very nature of the accident, as when a disqualified motorcyclist was rear-ended while waiting at a stop light.[204] But many other cases, particularly those involving such simple activities as driving a car, do not admit so confident a conclusion for the plain reason that, just as a driving licence does not assure competence, neither is its mere lack probative of incompetence, still less of specific negligent acts, at least in relation to the particular accident. If the driver's negligence can be established independently, there is ordinarily no occasion for reinforcing his liability by reference to his breach of statute; but if it cannot, recourse to the statute would subject him to strict liability for any mishap, however innocent his own participation, and thus add a penalty beyond that provided by the legislature. Apprehensive about so drastic a sanction, Anglo-American courts have generally declined to treat lack of any licence as negligence per se[205] or even to condone its admission in evidence for fear of its highly prejudicial effect on juries.[206]

Similar objections have been raised against treating drunk driving as negligence per se. Only unsafe driving can cause an accident, not the driver's condition as such.[207] Yet, as in the case of the unlicensed driver, would it not be a better solution to reverse the onus of proof and require the defendant to show that the violation was not causal? This would give some weight to the prohibition but no more than consonant with the hypothesis that the accident would *most probably* have otherwise been avoided.[208]

A change of course may be discerned in an important decision which distinguished a statute prohibiting employment of an "unqualified operator" of a dangerous tool, qualification being defined by age, training and knowledge. Violation, it was held, created a presumption that the injury was caused by incompetence, rebuttable by proof only that the injury was due to some other cause, like defectiveness of the tool.[209]

Persons protected and risk covered

As a corollary of the legislative purpose doctrine, a plaintiff cannot found his claim on statutory violation unless he belongs to the particular class of individuals which, in the court's opinion, the statute was intended to protect. Factory legislation, for example, has in general been interpreted

203. As in *Balmer v. Hayes* 1950 S.C. 477, where nonetheless a demurrer was sustained.
204. *Matthews v. McCullock* [1973] 2 N.S.W.L.R. 331; also *Lomax v. Reed* [1952] S.A.S.R. 225 (vehicle safety certificate).
205. *Leask Timber v. Thorne* (1961) 106 C.L.R. 33 (crane driver); *Matthews v. McCullock* [1973] 2 N.S.W.L.R. 331 (motorcyclist); *Schlederer v. Ship Red Fin* [1979] 1 N.S.W.L.R. 258 (coxswain); *Brown v. Shyne* 151 N.E. 197 (N.Y. 1926) (quack judged by standard of licensed physician). See Becht & Miller, *Factual Causation* (1961) §16.
206. See *Edwards v. Weeks* [1930] V.L.R. 225 (contributory negligence).
207. *Stickel v. San Diego* 195 P. 2d 416 (Cal. 1948). Cf. *Watt v. Bretag* (1981) 27 S.A.S.R. 301 at 313.
208. Causation doubts are similarly resolved in res ipsa cases: see below, p. 322.
209. *Pfeiffer Pty Ltd v. Canny* (1981) 148 C.L.R. 218.

as designed for the safety of persons employed or working at the plant,[210] but not of customers[211] or firemen.[212] So, a duty imposed on railways to secure gates at level crossings was construed as intended for the benefit of highway travellers only and not an engine driver in a passing train.[213] The general disposition has been conservative, largely because courts have on the whole preferred to seek their answers in textual exegesis of the statutory instrument rather than in any more rewarding inquiry into the evident purpose of the legislation. This trend has resulted in such questionable conclusions as that a statutory mandate for the supply of unadulterated drinking water or milk enured for the benefit of a rate payer or purchaser alone, but not for members of his household or other consumers.[214]

Next, the logic of the legislative purpose doctrine also demands that the injury incurred must be of a kind which it is the object of the statute to prevent. In other words, only harm falling within the scope of the risk contemplated by the provision will subject the offender to liability in damages.[215] In the leading case of *Gorris v. Scott*,[216] a shipowner disregarded a statutory direction that all cattle be carried in pens of certain specifications. The plaintiff's sheep were washed overboard in rough weather, a loss that would clearly have been avoided if pens had been provided as required. But since the only mischief aimed at was the spreading of disease among crowded animals, not the perils of the sea, the action failed. Similarly, a plaintiff who was injured by an *explosion* of phosphorous rat poison in a restaurant vainly sought to rely on a statutory prohibition against setting out poison in a public place, because it was aimed solely at preventing the poisoning of human beings.[217]

There was a tendency to construe statutes as intended to afford protection against a narrowly restricted type of hazard only and not to extend it to related risks that could well have been anticipated as likely to

210. Including employees of contractors not engaged in work of the factory (*Massey-Harris-Ferguson v. Piper* [1956] 2 Q.B. 396; *Quilty v. Bellambi Coal* (1966) 67 S.R. (N.S.W.) 193) and even employees momentarily pursuing a private venture or frolic (*Westwood v. P.O.* [1974] A.C. 1; *Howell v. Caxton* [1971] N.Z.L.R. 1068: "employed" does not import a limitation (as under workmen's compensation) to cases "arising out of and in the course of employment"). The protected class is often defined by the statute or regulations made thereunder and varies accordingly: see the comprehensive review of English decisions in 22 Mod. L. Rev. 528 (1959).

211. *Daly v. Greybridge Co-op.* (1963) 99 Ir. L.T.R. 157; cf. *Mummery v. Irvings* (1956) 96 C.L.R. 99 at 108.

212. Firemen (even though "employed" there just as much as independent contractors) cannot expect safe premises when called in to fight a fire: *Flannigan v. British Dyewood* 1970 S.L.T. 285; *Goodman v. New Plymouth Fire Bd* [1958] N.Z.L.R. 767.

213. *Knapp v. Rly Executive* [1949] 2 All E.R. 508. But a railway fencing statute was rightly construed as intended for the safety, not only of passengers, but also humans (no less than animals) getting on the tracks: *Paulsen v. C.P.R.* (1963) 40 D.L.R. (2d) 761 (C.A.); cf. *Mitchell v. C.N.R.* [1975] 1 S.C.R. 592.

214. *Read v. Croydon Corp.* [1938] 4 All E.R. 631; *Square v. Model Farm Dairies* [1939] 2 K.B. 365. Aliter, *Consumer Protection Act* 1961 (U.K.) s. 3 imposing a duty in favour of a person "who may be affected by the contravention" (of a safety regulation relating to goods).

215. This rule is severely criticised by Lowndes, 16 Minn. L. Rev. 361 at 373ff. (1932), as due to the misconception that the civil action is created by the penal statute.

216. (1874) L.R. 9 Ex. 125.

217. *Larrimore v. Am. Ins.* 89 P. 2d 340 (Okla. 1939); see also *Whittaker v. Rozelle Wood Products* (1936) 36 S.R. (N.S.W.) 204; *Long v. Saorstat S.S. Co.* (1952) 93 Ir. L.T.R. 137.

follow their violation. A glaring example was to construe the requirement that dangerous machinery be "securely fenced" as intended to guard only against "keeping the worker out, not keeping the machine or its product in".[218] Lately, however, a more liberal attitude has prevailed in formulating the ambit of affected risks. For example, a statute directing that roofs in a mine be made secure was held to cover not only the obvious risk of a colliery worker being hit from above, but also a bogie in which he travelled becoming derailed by fallen debris.[219] A recent Australian case went so far as to hold that a statute prohibiting firearms being supplied to a minor extended to the risk of the latter allowing a companion to take possession of a gun and accidentally shoot himself.[220] Yet another court propounded the test, borrowed from common law rules of remoteness,[221] that, provided the injury was not totally different in kind from that which it was the object of the regulation to prevent, it was immaterial that it happened in a way not precisely contemplated.[222]

Statutory negligence and strict liability

If the court is satisfied to accept the legislative judgment as conclusively determining the standard of conduct appropriate to the occasion, it follows that any unexcused deviation is negligence per se. This dispenses with any recourse to the ordinary evaluative process for determining whether a defendant has measured up to the general standard of reasonable care, since it would be invidious for a jury to form an independent judgment in competition with the statutory prescription. In sum, "it is no longer left to the chance opinion of a jury to decide whether the precautions may properly be omitted. The legislature decides the question for them, and accordingly non-compliance with the provisions of the statute carries with it the same civil consequences that a verdict of negligence would do."[223]

The effect of the doctrine is, therefore, in the first instance, to promote fixed and predictable standards of negligence, in place of the "featureless generality"[224] of the jury verdict in each individual case. It thus aids accident prevention by telling people precisely how to behave before accidents happen. Moreover, it displaces the judgment of amateurs for that of experts and professionals in many matters on which the layman is increasingly less able to form a confident and dependable appraisal. Because the formulation of statutory standards is in large measure delegated to persons intimately acquainted with the details of industrial operations, the building industry and the problems of accident prevention, expert judgment is thus brought directly and decisively to bear on the judicial process.

218. *Close v. Steel Co.* [1962] A.C. 367; *Sparrow v. Fairey Aviation* [1964] A.C. 1019; *Mummery v. Irvings* (1956) 96 C.L.R. 99.
219. *Grant v. N.C.B.* [1956] A.C. 649.
220. *Pask v. Owen* [1987] 2 Qd R. 421 (F.C.). The court (mis)treated the issue as one of causation.
221. See below, p. 211. The legislative purpose doctrine under discussion serves, of course, the same purpose of delimiting liability that the so-called rules on "remoteness of damage" do in relation to non-statutory torts.
222. *Donaghey v. Boulton & Paul* [1968] A.C. 1 at 26 (Lord Reid).
223. *David v. Britannic Merthyr Coal Co.* [1909] 2 K.B. 146 at 164 per Fletcher Moulton L.J.
224. Holmes, *Common Law* (1881) 111.

Finally, most important of all perhaps is its tendency to promote, if not strict, at any rate stricter liability. For the duty to comply is one of "absolute obligation".[225] This means in the first instance that the defendant will not be heard to excuse his failure to adopt the prescribed safeguard by arguing that what he did was quite adequate or just as good. Moreover, except in so far as authorised by the statute itself, no specific excuses are allowed, such for example as that the specified fence became defective owing to some accident or the act of a trespasser over which the defendant had no control.[226] Nor for that matter is it an answer that he had exercised all reasonable care to obey the statutory mandate, if what is demanded is nothing short of actual compliance.[227] This stringent regime undoubtedly has the effect of visiting on some defendants what in the circumstances amounts to liability without any fault whatever. In the industrial sphere, this prospect has long become acceptable as a complement to workers' compensation,[228] but in other situations it probably accounts more than any other factor for the generally unenthusiastic attitude displayed, especially by British courts, towards the whole doctrine of statutory negligence.[229] In this respect, their inveterate practice of appealing to the oracle of a presumed legislative intent has served them well in hiding from public scrutiny not only their own unexpressed prejudices but also their startling lack of resourcefulness, compared with that of American courts, in so handling the doctrine that it may serve as a useful adjunct in negligence litigation without becoming tyrannical. At bottom, their failure to come to terms with it is primarily due to the fact that their frame of reference does not seem to admit of any media via between, on the one hand, the most literal application of the statutory mandate whose terms rarely make express allowance for unavoidable inability to conform or some other equally compelling excuse and, on the other hand, a refusal to ascribe any force to it at all other than, perhaps, as mere evidence of negligence.[230]

225. Lord Wright in *L.P.T.B. v. Upson* [1949] A.C. 155 at 168 inclined to the view that it belonged more properly to the category of strict liability. Whether the term "negligence" (in a statute, indemnity policy, etc.) includes breach of statutory duty depends entirely on the context: *Lochgelly Iron Co. v. M'Mullan* [1934] A.C. 1; *Murfin v. United Steel* [1957] 1 W.L.R. 104.

226. *Cooper v. Rly Executive* [1953] 1 W.L.R. 223 at 228.

227. Sporadically, a statutory duty unqualified on its face has been read down to demand no more than reasonable care to ensure the prescribed result, like supplying pure water (in *Read v. Croydon Corp.* [1938] 4 All E.R. 631) or the duty to cleanse sewers in *Hammond v. St Pancras Vestry* (1874) L.R. 9 C.P. 316 (where, in the doctrine's infancy, it was broadly announced that statutory duties be construed as duties of reasonable care rather than absolute obligation, unless the contrary was expressed in the plainest terms).

228. See below, p. 488.

229. There is some edge to Williams' bold observation: "When it concerns industrial welfare, such legislation results in absolute liability in tort. In all other cases it is ignored" (*Penal Legislation in the Law of Tort*, 23 Mod. L. Rev. 232 (1960)). For a few scattered exceptions see *Read v. Croydon Corp.* [1938] 4 All E.R. 631 (pure water); *Thomas v. British Rlys* [1976] Q.B. 912 (railway fencing); *Solomons v. Gertzenstein* [1954] 2 Q.B. 243 (fire escape); *Reffell v. Surrey C.C.* [1964] 1 W.L.R. 358 (safe school premises); *Pask v. Owen* [1987] 2 Qd R. 421 (entrusting gun).

230. Between treating a statutory norm as (1) merely relevant or (2) absolutely binding, lie (3) accepting it as prima facie evidence of negligence and (4) reversing the onus of proof. Res ipsa offers illustrations of (3) and (4): see below, p. 322. Canadian courts have on occasion required the defendant to prove "inevitable accident", and American law plays the whole gamut.

8

DUTY OF CARE

1. INTRODUCTION

Negligence does not entail liability unless the law exacts a "duty" in the circumstances to observe care.[1] "Duty" may therefore be defined as an obligation, recognised by law, to avoid conduct fraught with unreasonable risk of danger to others.

The duty concept made a tardy entrance into our legal system and did not attain prominence until the middle of the 19th century.[2] Traces of it are found in the conditions attaching under the old writ system to actionability for inadvertent harm. As we have seen, the action on the case for negligence emerged during the formative era of the common law in a limited number of situations where a defendant could be held responsible for loss caused by negligence which would not have been actionable by the writs of trespass or nuisance. Such a duty to take care was recognised where a person had assumed control of dangerous things or occupied a status demanding special professional skill, as in public callings. When negligence began to crystallise as an independent tort around the turn of the 19th century and became actionable in less formal situations, as where a man carelessly drove a carriagc or left a coal hole uncovered, "duty" ceased for a time to be the subject of critical attention, but reappeared with new vigour in the "contract-tort" catena of cases[3] and was irrevocably established as a constituent element of tortious negligence by 1882.[4]

The functional significance of the "duty" issue cannot be understood without recalling that the definition of tortious negligence fails to furnish any clue to its conditions of actionability beyond referring to the negligent nature of the defendant's conduct. One of the basic differences between negligence and nominate torts of the traditional pattern, like assault or defamation, lies in the fact that the scope of protection afforded by the action for negligence is, on its face, unlimited: not defined by reference either to a particular type of harm or a particular interest invaded. Yet to permit the imposition of liability for *any* loss suffered by *anyone* as the result of carelessness would have imposed too severe and indiscriminate a restriction on individual freedom of action by exposing the actor to the prospect of unpredictable liability. Hence, the basic problem in the "tort"

1. "A man is entitled to be as negligent as he pleases towards the whole world if he owes no duty to them" (*Le Lievre v. Gould* [1893] 1 Q.B. 491 at 497 per Lord Esher M.R.).
2. The classical historical account is by Winfield, *Duty in Tortious Negligence*, 34 Col. L. Rev. 41 (1934), reprinted in his *Essays* 70.
3. *Langridge v. Levy* (1837) 2 M. & W. 519; 150 E.R. 863; *Winterbottom v. Wright* (1842) 10 M. & W. 109; 152 E.R. 402; below, p. 482. Viewed in somewhat different perspective: Pritchard, *Scott v. Shepard and the Emergence of the Tort of Negligence* (Seldon Society lecture) (1976).
4. *Heaven v. Pender* (1883) 11 Q.B.D. 503 per Brett M.R.

of negligence is that of limitation of liability. One or more control devices were required to prevent the incidence of liability from getting out of hand. Among these, "duty of care" occupies today a paramount position.

It might have been more elegant to speak, as Civilians do,[5] of a plaintiff's protected rights rather than of a defendant's duty, especially when the focus is on the kind of injury the plaintiff has suffered, for example whether liability extends to purely economic loss or mere mental distress. The choice of nomenclature was due to historical accident and has no substantive implications.[6]

The question whether a duty exists in the particular situation involves a determination of law for the court, and has precedential force (unlike findings of negligence or "breach of duty"). It thus offers the procedural advantage of raising the issue as a preliminary question of law (or demurrer) or permitting the case to be withdrawn from a jury even if there is sufficient evidence for a finding of negligence against the defendant. It thus aids consistency in the common law and serves as a brake upon the proclivity of juries to indulge their compassion for accident victims without due regard for the wider implications of their findings in imposing undue burdens on particular activities.[7]

The duty concept has been reproached as otiose, "an unnecessary fifth wheel on the coach",[8] as just duplicating the function of "remoteness of damage". The latter, to be sure, could have sufficed for the task of marking the outer perimeter of liability, but the common law is by no means alone in relying on more than just one mechanism for that purpose.[9] Though fashions have shifted,[10] and no hard and fast line has ever been drawn, the prevailing pattern is to express in terms of "duty" judicial policies of a more or less generalised nature, for example whether the plaintiff's *kind* of injury (like pre-natal trauma or purely pecuniary loss) is compensable at all; leaving to "remoteness of damage" the evaluation of more contingent and idiosyncratic features of each particular case. Otherwise expressed, if the policy against recovery is quite categorical, too insistent to be confided every time to the chance arbitrament of each individual trial judge or jury's speculations about "risk" or "cause", the rule in question is nowadays generally formulated as one of "no duty". Beyond all else, however, this configuration was shaped by quirks of precedent (now only of historical interest)[11] and by elusive turns of fashion.[12]

5. Especially German. See Markesinis, *The German Law of Torts* ch. 2.
6. *Tate & Lyle v. G.L.C.* [1983] 2 A.C. 509 (H.L.) is a rare case where plaintiff's negligence claim was defeated specifically on the ground that he lacked a legally protected interest (to deep water access to his jetty).
7. The same goes for appellate control over trial judges as triers of fact.
8. Buckland, *Duty to Take Care*, 51 L.Q.R. 637 at 639 (1935) and *Some Reflections on Jurisprudence* 110 at 115 (1945), dominated by the absence of such a concept in Roman law. For a renewed criticism in light of recent H.L. judgments see Howarth, *Negligence after Murphy: Time to Rethink* [1991] Cam. L.J. 58.
9. For German and other parallels see Hart & Honoré, *Causation* ch. 17; Lawson, *Duty of Care: a Comparative Study*, 22 Tulane L. Rev. 111 (1947); Markesinis, *Not So Dissimilar Tort and Delict*, 93 L.Q.R. 78 (1977).
10. See Fleming, *Remoteness and Duty: Control Devices in Liability for Negligence*, 31 Can. B. Rev. 471 (1953).
11. See below, pp. 144, 208, 214.
12. The to-and-fro is well illustrated by the nervous shock cases: below, p. 161, with its apocalyptic end in Lord Denning's judgment in *King v. Phillips* [1953] 1 Q.B. 429. For a schematic allocation of these concepts see Smith, *Liability in Negligence* (1984).

Determinant of duty

No generalisation can solve the problem upon what basis the courts will hold that a duty of care exists. Everyone agrees that a duty must arise out of some "relation", some "proximity", between the parties, but what that relation is no one has ever succeeded in capturing in any precise formula.

The classical pronouncement of a general formula for "duty" is Lord Atkin's apodictic "neighbour test" in *Donoghue v. Stevenson*:[13]

> "There must be, and is, some general conception of relations giving rise to a duty of care, of which the particular cases found in the books are but instances. . . . The rule that you are to love your neighbour becomes in law you must not injure your neighbour; and the lawyer's question, Who is my neighbour? receives a restricted reply. You must take reasonable care to avoid acts or omissions which you can reasonably foresee would be likely to injure your neighbour. Who, then, in law, is my neighbour? The answer seems to be persons who are so closely and directly affected by my act that I ought reasonably to have them in contemplation as being so affected when I am directing my mind to the acts or omissions which are called in question."

Although this inspired[14] passage has become a sacrosanct preamble to any judicial disquisition on duty, it contains a noticeable ambiguity. Does it propound merely a test of foresight or, if it does make allowance for other factors, does that raise a tension between "principle" and "policy"?

Lord Wilberforce addressed these questions almost 50 years later in another famous generalisation:[15]

> "The position has now been reached that in order to establish that a duty of care arises in a particular situation, it is not necessary to bring the facts of that situation within those of previous situations in which a duty of care has been held to exist. Rather the question has to be approached in two stages. First one has to ask whether, as between the alleged wrongdoer and the person who has suffered damage there is a sufficient relationship of proximity or neighbourhood such that, in the reasonable contemplation of the former, carelessness on his part may be likely to cause damage to the latter, in which case a prima facie duty of care arises. Secondly, if the first question is answered affirmatively, it is necessary to consider whether there are any considerations which ought to negative, or to reduce or limit the scope of the duty or the class of person to whom it is owed or the damages to which a breach of it may give rise."

This prescription has been understood by some as a mandate for an expansive application of liability to all foreseeable harm, unless opposed by a specifically defined, peremptory legal policy, not simply a vacuous appeal to "opening floodgates".[16] That interpretation was the more plausible because of its context, the decision in *Anns v. Merton L.B.C.* which pushed

13. [1932] A.C. 562 at 580.
14. Rooted in Old and New Testament "neighbour" aphorisms.
15. *Anns v. Merton L.B.C.* [1978] A.C. 728 at 751-752; building on Lord Reid's formulation in *Dorset Y. C.* [1970] A.C. 1004 at 1027.
16. From *Anns* (1978) to *McLoughlin v. O'Brian* [1983] 1 A.C. 410 and *Junior Books v. Veitchi Co.* [1983] 1 A.C. 520 the H.L. identified proximity with foreseeability. The floodgates argument was disparaged in both latter cases.

the reach of negligence liability into several hitherto unchartered fields: see below.

A more conservative view, reacting strongly against some extreme decisions in the interval,[17] has refused to accept the prima facie identification of duty with foreseeability. For one thing, the phrases "proximity" and "closely and directly affected" were well understood signposts for qualifying the generality of the negligence (foresight) principle; for another, specific legal policies are obviously involved at both stages,[18] and not all courts were prepared to accept (as yet) that mere foreseeability of harm represented the "principle" which would only exceptionally yield to a specific opposing "policy". If the Wilberforce approach was to be understood as a mandate for judicial activism, boldly opening new areas of liability, it has since been repudiated by the House of Lords itself,[19] by the Privy Council[20] and by the High Court of Australia.[21] Rather, it has been said, the law proceeds "incrementally and by analogy with established categories".[22]

Lord Atkin's "proximity" has cast a baleful shadow over judicial ruminations on "duty". Borrowed from the context of causation, where "proximate cause" and its mirror image "remoteness" had long served to identify the problem of limiting responsibility for consequential damage, it became a convenient excuse for not disclosing any specific reasons behind a decision for or against a finding of "duty". This pervasive failure to give reasons, rather than postulating unsubstantiated conclusions, has its roots in the embarrassment with which the British conservative tradition has generally treated the role of policy in judicial decision making.[23] Many English judges continue to extol "proximity" as the "self-answering" lodestar,[24] though the term obviously lacks definition when intended to suggest that there is more to it than foreseeability.[25] A current formula,

17. "Since *Anns* put the floodgates on the jar, a fashionable plaintiff alleges negligence. The pleading assumes that we are all neighbours now, Pharisees and Samaritans alike, that foreseeability is a reflection of hindsight and that for every mischance in an accident-prone world someone must be liable in damages" (*C.B.S. Songs v. Amstrad* [1988] A.C. 1013 at 1059 (Lord Templeman)).
18. Reconciliation has been attempted by construing the Wilberforce formula as not denying a role for legal policy at the first stage of determining proximity, but emphasising that beyond it other considerations may narrow it further: *Jaensch v. Coffey* (1984) 155 C.L.R. 549 at 576 per Brennan J.
19. *Peabody Fund v. Parkinson* [1985] A.C. 210; *Leigh & Sillivan v. Aliakmon* [1986] A.C. 785.
20. *The Mineral Transporter* [1986] A.C. 1; *Yeun Kun Yeu v. A.-G. for Hong Kong* [1988] A.C. 175.
21. *Sutherland S.C. v. Heyman* (1985) 157 C.L.R. 424. The Supreme Court of Canada has not yet declared its hand (*B.D.C. v. Hofstrand* [1986] 1 S.C.R. 228), but the N.Z. Court of Appeal remains attached: *Takaro Properties v. Rowling* [1986] 1 N.Z.L.R. 22.
22. *Sutherland S.C. v. Heyman* (1985) 157 C.L.R. 424 at 481 (Brennan J.).
23. See Bell, *Policy Arguments in Judicial Decisions* (1983) esp. ch. III; Paterson, *The Law Lords* (1988). Dworkin's *Taking Rights Seriously* (1977) has a different target.
24. Less in Australia. Brennan J., a consistent critic, called it "a Delphic criterion" in *Hawkins v. Clayton* (1988) 164 C.L.R. 539 at 555; *Gala v. Preston* (1991) 172 C.L.R. 243 at 259ff., in contrast to the majority judgment which blatantly used; also McHugh J. in *Neighbourhood, Proximity and Reliance*, in Finn, *Essays in Tort* ch. 2. See also Keeler, *The Proximity of Past and Future*, 12 Adel. L. Rev. 93 (1989).
25. Deane J. in *Jaensch v. Coffey* (1984) 155 C.L.R. 549 at 584 (it may reflect "physical, circumstantial and causal" factors).

demanding "foreseeability, proximity and what is fair and reasonable",[26] is no more helpful. As Lord Oliver recently observed, "In the end, it has to be accepted that the concept of 'proximity' is an artificial one which depends more upon the Court's perception of what is the reasonable area for the imposition of liability than upon any logical process of analogical deduction."[26a] Indeed, one may well ask what purpose any generalisation about "duty" can hope to serve as a guide to reaching a *reasoned* judgment in the great variety of individual cases. It were better to abandon the effort altogether.

In the decision whether to recognise a duty in a given situation, many factors interplay: the hand of history, our ideas of morals and justice, the convenience of administering the rule and our social ideas as to where the loss should fall.[27] Hence, the incidence and extent of duties are liable to adjustment in the light of evolving community attitudes.[28] "The categories of negligence are never closed."[29] In 1842, Lord Abinger foresaw that "the most absurd and outrageous consequences, to which I can see no limit, would ensue", if it should ever be held that a party to a contract was under a duty to anyone but the promisee.[30] This standpoint, based on the fear of impeding industrial development, has long since given way to a policy of making negligent manufacturers, repairers and others shoulder the accident losses of ultimate consumers. Here, the advent of insurance[31] and a more realistic appreciation of the methods available for the distribution of losses has led to an enormous widening of the field of duty.

The decision in *Donoghue v. Stevenson*[32] where this reversal occurred in 1932 became a landmark far beyond its immediate application to products liability; for Lord Atkin's famous foresight test was intended and understood as a mandate for a more general expansive approach to duties, responsive to more demanding social responsibility in our time. A further impetus was given in 1964 by another House of Lords decision, *Hedley Byrne v. Heller*,[33] which opened the door to negligent economic loss, almost reaching into the borderland of contract. As a result of these judicial and some legislative reforms, the scope of liability for negligence has expanded beyond all recognition during this century, with "no duty" enclaves disappearing one after another. The recent conservative turn in England marks but a temporary halt to this advance of communitarian values.

On the other hand, public policy still militates in a variety of settings against the imposition of a duty, especially regarding claims for economic

26. *Peabody v. Parkinson* [1985] A.C. 210 at 240 (Lord Keith).
26a. *Alcock v. Chief Constable* [1991] 3 W.L.R. 1057 at 1115.
27. Green, *Judge and Jury* (1930) ch. 3. Symmons, *Duty of Care in Negligence: Recently Expressed Policy Elements*, 34 Mod. L. Rev. 394 at 528 (1971), extrapolates four factors: the administrative ("when will it all end?"), public interest, "social occasion" and legislative policy. Others would stress the economic factor of efficiency: see above, p. 118.
28. They are conditional both in time and place. That they may differ as between England and N.Z. was expressed in *South Pacific Ins. v. N.Z. Security* (1991) 3 N.Z.B.L.C. 102, 301.
29. *Donoghue v. Stevenson* [1932] A.C. 562 at 619 (Lord MacMillan).
30. *Winterbottom v. Wright* (1842) 10 M. & W. 109 at 114; 152 E.R. 402 at 404.
31. On the effect of insurance see M. Davies, *The End of the Affair: Duty of Care and Liability Insurance*, 9 Leg. St. 67 (1989).
32. [1932] A.C. 562; below ch. 23.
33. [1964] A.C. 465.

loss. For example, that the accident happened in the course of an illegal activity may make it invidious to determine the standard of care due from one participant to another.[34] No duty is exacted from regulatory agencies whose functions involve a broader public interest than concern for the protection of individual investors.[35] Judges cannot be made civilly liable in respect of exercising their jurisdiction.[36] At common law the Crown could not be sued for negligence or any other tort, and even today has waived its immunity only to the extent prescribed by the controlling statute.[37] Similar immunities attached to discretionary functions protect arbitrators against claims by disappointed litigants[38] and examiners against students.[39] Perhaps on somewhat related grounds, implicating national security, a duty of care has been denied regarding combat operations against the enemy causing civilian loss or injury.[40] In order to avoid relitigating old scores, barristers are not liable to their clients for negligence in the conduct of litigation;[41] nor are litigants to one another.[42] In these instances there are adequate safeguards against procedural impropriety and it is thought that the threat of liability could prejudice the proper discharge of these functions.

Among more general countervailing policies is the concern of not impinging on other areas of civil liability. For example, settled rules of tort liability conditioned on malice, like defamation on occasions of qualified privilege or malicious prosecution, would be undercut if a plaintiff could succeed on mere negligence.[43] Equally strong has been the resistance of late to supplement contractual arrangements with tort liability for economic loss, especially where the aggrieved party had the opportunity of protecting himself by contract but failed to do so.[44]

34. See below, p. 305.
35. *Yuen Kun Yeu v. A.-G. of Hong Kong* [1988] A.C. 175 (deposit taking companies); *Davis v. Radcliffe* [1990] 1 W.L.R. 821 (P.C.) (bank deposits). Other obstacles are that the loss is financial and that the duty postulates liability for the fault of others.
36. *Sirros v. Moore* [1975] Q.B. 118 (C.A.); *Nakla v. McCarthy* [1978] N.Z.L.R. 291 (C.A.): both false imprisonment. See Brasier, [1976] P.L. 397.
37. See below, p. 374. Another, now defunct, immunity was that between spouses: below, p. 680.
38. *Sutcliffe v. Thackrah* [1974] A.C. 727. See also *Calveley v. Chief Constable* [1989] Q.B. 136 (C.A.) (investigating officer to policemen under investigation).
39. *Thorne v. University of London* [1966] 2 Q.B. 237.
40. *Shaw, Savill v. Commonwealth* (1940) 66 C.L.R. 344 (esp. at 361); criticised by Hogg, *Liability of the Crown* (1972) 95. Compensation for war damage is usually available under special legislation. For peacetime accidents civilians and even members of the Armed Services may sue the Crown: *Groves v. Commonwealth* (1982) 150 C.L.R. 113; *Commonwealth v. Connell* (1986) 5 N.S.W.L.R. 218. Contra by statute in U.K., Can., U.S.: Ashton, 10 U. Qld L.J. 157 (1978). Duty to fellow policemen? See *Griffiths v. Haines* [1984] 3 N.S.W.L.R. 653 at 665.
41. *Rondel v. Worsley* [1969] 1 A.C. 191; *Giannarelli v. Wraith* (1988) 165 C.L.R. 543. A fortiori opposing counsel: *Love v. Robbins* (1990) 2 W.A.R. 510. See Roxburgh, 84 L.Q.R. 178 (1968); *Cane* 245-250 (critical). The immunity also applies to solicitors "in court".
42. *Business Computers v. Registrar* [1988] Ch. 229 (at arms length); *N.Z. Political League v. O'Brien* [1984] 1 N.Z.L.R. 84 (C.A.). Exceptional: *Al Kandari v. Brown* [1988] Q.B. 665.
43. *Bell-Booth Group v. A.-G.* [1989] 2 N.Z.L.R. 148; *Balfour v. A.-G.* [1991] 1 N.Z.L.R. 519; *South Pacific Ins. v. N.Z. Security* (1991) 3 N.Z.B.L.C. 102, 301. Contra: *Lawton v. BOC Transhield* [1987] 2 All E.R. 608.
44. See below, p. 185.

The Anns case: an illustration

An instructive introduction to the interplay of factors relevant to a decision on "duty" is offered by the very case of *Anns v. Merton L.B.C.*[45] which, as we have just seen, is at the centre of the larger question whether the issue is susceptible to what, if any, level of generalisation.

In *Anns* a block of flats had been constructed, allegedly on foundations shallower than those approved by the local authority on the basis of submitted plans. Years later when subsidence resulted in substantial damage to the structure, tenants under long leases claimed damages against (among others) the council for negligently omitting to inspect the foundations or failing to discover the defect. Did these claims disclose a cause of action that would justify a trial on the facts?

This situation differed in several significant respects from the run of the mill situation of a negligent motorist striking a pedestrian or colliding with another car. For one thing, the builder, not the council, had created the defect: the council had at most failed to protect the lessees from the builder's default. For another, was the council under any responsibility to the lessees to exercise its statutory powers of supervising building construction? Should such a governmental function be subject to scrutiny by courts instead of the political process? Lastly, the loss complained of did not consist of bodily injury nor of damage to *other* property, but of purely pecuniary detriment, viz. the cost of repair or the lessened value of the property. Put bluntly, was there any *accident* at all?

Each and all of these features offered an argument against liability. For though the council may have been negligent in the sense that it could have prevented the damage, it did not follow that its victims had a claim to damages. In fact, what made the decision in *Anns* a landmark was that the House of Lords brushed aside or ignored all these objections and thereby propelled tort law upon a more ambitious, if controversial, mission.

As regards the first of the above-mentioned problems, the law has been traditionally chary of postulating duties of affirmative action, that is, of protecting potential victims of someone else's wrongdoing. Often enough, however, the culprit (here the builder) lacks the financial means to pay the damages, being either un- or under-insured. One of the more notable features of modern tort law has been a creeping extension of liability to "deep pocket defendants" whose relation to the accident is much more remote and often consists merely in a pure omission to avert harm threatening from another source. The *Anns* decision, by converting the *power* to inspect into a duty, for the sake of protecting others from a risk created by someone else, almost insouciantly endorsed this tendency.[46]

Next, it is one thing for the law to prescribe how to drive a motor car or sink an oil well, but quite another to tell a governmental authority what powers to exercise for the sake of greater public safety. Traditionally, we have looked to the political, not the legal process to monitor the performance of public agencies and enforce public, not private accountability. The *Anns* court, considering this to be the cardinal issue of

45. [1978] A.C. 728.
46. See Smith & Burns, *Donoghue v. Stevenson—The Not So Golden Anniversary*, 46 Mod. L. Rev. 147 (1983).

the case, drew on the American distinction between decisions on a planning and an operational level. Once the council had decided to embark on and enforce inspection—a non-justiciable decision of the first order—it could be held amenable to legal responsibility in regard to the manner in which such an inspection was actually carried out.

Lastly, the principal function of tort law has customarily been seen in the compensation of physical injuries, whether to person or tangible property. Purely pecuniary losses occupied a lower order of priority. Besides, such claims sounding in tort were apt to conflict with established principles of contract law. For example, should there be tort liability henceforth for negligent breaches of contract, even to persons not "in privity"? In the *Anns* case, the damage being to the defective building itself, not to other property, the complaint was less that the structure was dangerous as that the lessees had "bought a lemon". If they could not claim from the builder (who might be protected by his contract with the developer), should they be free to pursue third parties, such as the council? These implications would haunt the future, but were in the instance obscured by treating the defect as damage to property rather than as purely pecuniary loss and by perhaps confining the decision to defects immanently threatening safety as distinct from defects merely lessening the value of the building.

This brief analysis had its object less in probing the merits of the actual decision in *Anns* than in illustrating the sometimes complex and many-layered nature of the duty issue and the consequential need for a high level of judicial craft. The following sections of this chapter seek to probe in greater detail the more typical "duty" problems.

2. SCOPE OF DUTY: THE UNFORESEEABLE PLAINTIFF

It is axiomatic that "English law does not recognise a duty in the air, so to speak; that is, a duty to undertake that no one shall suffer from one's carelessness."[47] To be liable for an injury he has caused, the defendant's carelessness must not only have been in breach of a duty to exercise care, but the duty must have been owed to the plaintiff. In other words, the latter cannot take advantage of the fact that the defendant happened to be committing a wrong to someone else; he must bottom his claim on violation of a right of his own. Duties are in many instances abridged by reason of the plaintiff's status or special relation to the defendant: as an occupier the defendant might be responsible to any lawful visitor who fell into an open hole in the dark, but not to a trespasser; as a drunk driver he might be liable to anyone hurt in a collision except his boon companion who incited him to daredevilry.

Even in the absence of such a special disqualification, the plaintiff may still fail because he was outside the foreseeable range of injury, however many others happened to be within it. Our law has become committed to limiting the range of liability to persons alone who were *foreseeably* imperilled, lest defendants be crushed by the burden of excessive liability for some quite trivial fault. Not that there is anything inexorable about this

47. *Bottomley v. Bannister* [1932] 1 K.B. 458 at 476 per Greer L.J.

proposition, for there is much also to the opposing view that, as between one whose negligence set the whole thing in motion and his wholly innocent victim, the equities favour the latter. That view indeed once enjoyed considerable vogue,[48] but was eventually cast aside, first in a celebrated judgment by Cardozo J. in New York, later by the House of Lords.

In *Palsgraf v. Long Island R.R.*[49] two train guards, assisting a passenger, carelessly knocked a small parcel from his arms which, despite its innocent appearance, contained fireworks. An explosion occurred when the parcel fell beneath a moving train, causing scales some distance away to topple on the plaintiff. Although the jury found that the guards had been negligent, the verdict in favour of the plaintiff was set aside on the ground that, though they may have been in breach of duty to the embarking passenger because of foreseeable damage at least to his parcel, this was of no avail to Helen Palsgraf who was beyond the range of foreseeable peril:

> "If no hazard was apparent to the eye of ordinary vigilance, an act innocent and harmless, at least to outward seeming with reference toward her, did not take to itself the quality of a tort because it happened to be a wrong, though apparently not one involving the risk of bodily insecurity, with reference to someone else. . . . A wrong to another cannot be the basis of the plaintiff's claim and even less a wrong to a mere property interest. . . . The risk reasonably to be perceived defines the duty to be obeyed and risk imports relation. . . . The victim does not sue derivatively or by right of subrogation to vindicate an interest invaded in the person of another. . . . He sues for breach of duty owing to himself."

The dissent[50] reasoned substantially in accordance with the supposedly then prevailing English view:

> "Everyone owes to the world at large a duty of refraining from those acts which unreasonably threaten the safety of others. . . . When there is an unreasonable act and some right that may be affected there is negligence. . . . It is a wrong not only to those who happen to be within the radius of danger but to all who might have been there—a wrong to the public at large. . . . Harm to someone being the natural result of the act, not only that one alone, but all those in fact injured may complain."

The *Palsgraf* rationale did not pass unheeded, and after first being invoked by the High Court of Australia to defeat two successive claims for nervous shock,[51] was finally canonised in the not dissimilar case of *Bourhill v. Young.*[52] A speeding motorcyclist crashed into a car and was killed a short distance after passing a stationary tram from which the plaintiff, a pregnant fishwife, had just alighted. Though suffering a miscarriage, allegedly as the result of hearing the impact and afterwards

48. See *Re Polemis* [1921] 3 K.B. 560 (unforeseeable damage to foreseeable plaintiff: below, p. 207); *Smith v. L. & S.W. Rly* (1870) L.R. 6 C.P. 14 (unforeseeable plaintiff).
49. (1928) 162 N.E. 99; 59 A.L.R. 1253. See Prosser, *Palsgraf Revisited*, 52 Mich. L. Rev. 1 (1952); Green, *Judge and Jury* (1930) ch. 8.
50. Per Andrews J.
51. *Bunyan v. Jordan* (1937) 57 C.L.R. 1 and *Chester v. Waverley Corp.* (1939) 62 C.L.R. 1, where Evatt J. called it a "truism" (at 33).
52. [1943] A.C. 92.

seeing a pool of blood, her claim was dismissed on the ground that, being herself in a position of apparent safety, she was not a foreseeable casualty and could not invoke the defendant's breach of duty to the motorist with whom he collided. As Lord Wright summed it up in language unmistakably resonant of Cardozo J., "if the appellant has a cause of action it is because of a wrong to herself. She cannot build on a wrong to someone else. Her interest which was in her bodily security was of a different order from the interest of the owner of the car."[53]

In an action for negligence, therefore, it is now incumbent on a claimant to establish a breach of an independent duty to himself as a particular individual; proof of negligence to other users of the highway for example will not suffice.[54] And if this is true of cases like the preceding where some third party is actually injured, it applies all the more obviously when such a victim luckily remains hypothetical. Accordingly, a cyclist who suddenly darts into the path of a speeding car cannot enlist the argument that the driver should have slowed down in any event because of the presence of toddlers in the area.[55]

We shall later have occasion to see that this limitation of liability to "foreseeable plaintiffs" is nowadays matched by a similar limitation to "foreseeable damage".[56] That the first is expressed in terms of "duty", but the second in terms of "remoteness of damage", reflects only an inconsequential and largely accidental choice. Moreover, there has been a parallel tendency to take an expansive view of what is foreseeable. Thus in the present context, it is not required that the plaintiff be "foreseeable" as an identified individual; he need only belong to the *class* of persons within the foreseeable range of risk. This may well include among the potential victims of negligent driving: the real owner of a borrowed car mistakenly believed to belong to the borrower;[57] a doctor who comes to the aid of a person injured;[58] a pregnant woman and her baby who is subsequently born deformed;[59] perhaps, even a father donating a kidney to the victim.[60]

Separate interests

Should the doctrine of the "unforeseeable plaintiff" be extended to different interests of the same plaintiff? There used to be some support for

53. Ibid. at 108.
54. This principle is today applied with almost pedantic rigour, as in the instructive decisions on issue estoppel like *Edwards v. Joyce* [1954] V.L.R. 216 (liability to several passengers injured in same collision does not present identical issues) and *Jackson v. Goldsmith* (1950) 81 C.L.R. 446 (a finding that driver A was not in breach of duty to driver B does not preempt the question of his liability to B's passenger). In contrast to the prevailing Australian and N.Z. (*Craddock's Transport v. Stuart* [1970] N.Z.L.R. 499 (C.A.)) hostility, some English decisions have adopted a more "robust" and sensible view of "substantially identical issues" (e.g. *Wood v. Luscombe* [1966] 1 Q.B. 169). See Kelly, *Issue Estoppel and Negligence on the Highway*, 41 A.L.J. 12, 46 (1967) whose plea for modest change was rejected in *Ramsey v. Pigram* (1968) 118 C.L.R. 271. American law is infinitely more hospitable to issue estoppel, no longer insisting either on mutuality or even identity of parties: *Rest. Judgments 2d* §29.
55. *Jolly v. Hutch* [1960] W.A.R. 172. See also *Eva v. Reeves* [1938] 2 K.B. 393; *Moor v. Nolan* (1956) 94 Ir. L.T.R. 153.
56. See below, pp. 208ff.
57. *Awad v. Pillai* (C.A.), noted 46 Mod. L. Rev. 73 (1983).
58. *Chapman v. Hearse* (1961) 106 C.L.R. 112; below, p. 171.
59. *Watt v. Rama* [1972] V.R. 353; below, p. 168.
60. *Urbanski v. Patel* (1978) 84 D.L.R. (3d) 650.

the contrary "threshold tort" doctrine, whereby a plaintiff, once having established violation of a legally protected interest, could recover "parasitic damages" for other injury without having to establish its own credentials for protection.[61] Indeed, the more limited principle has survived that one who has suffered foreseeable physical injury can recover also for unforeseeable aggravation.[62]

On the other hand, without going so far as to fragment a plaintiff's interests into infinitely separable components, the more recent trend has been to demand that a plaintiff establish that each head of damage, had it stood alone, would have qualified under the "duty" rules, in particular the restrictive rules relating to nervous shock and economic loss. Thus, a passenger injured in a collision cannot recover for mental distress suffered as a result, not of contemporaneous perception, but of hearing afterwards about her husband's death.[63] Nor could she recover for losing her job as *his* secretary.[64]

Relational interests

Despite repeated reconsideration in recent years, our law remains opposed to claims by persons who suffer injury because of their relation to the primary accident victim. The duty, it is said, is bounded by a geographical circle and does not extend, for example, to the family circle of those immediately threatened or injured.[65] The rejection of derivative claims, already noted, thus includes also relational interests. While this rule once used to be explained on the ground of unforeseeability, it is now clear that it is precisely because of the high probability and frequency of such injury that the law regards the resulting burden to defendants as too onerous and therefore denies recovery as a matter of policy.

The principal impact of this exclusionary rule is on claims for consequential non-physical loss by relatives of the accident victim, such as distress over injury to a spouse or child[66] or for financial detriment by his family, business associates or creditors.[67] But the problem is occasionally also encountered in regard to bodily injury where admittedly the concern over burden is less and the nature of the injury more central to traditional tort protection. It defeated for example a wife's claim for sexual abuse at the hands of her husband who had undergone a personality change as the result of the accident.[68] The line drawn here does however reflect spatial and temporal factors, since nervous shock suffered by a wife who was a witness or co-victim of the accident[69] or an assault by a deranged husband

61. E.g. *Schneider v. Eisovitch* [1960] 2 Q.B. 430 (shock); *Seaway Hotels v. Grigg* (1960) 21 D.L.R. (2d) 264 (property damage/economic loss).
62. See below, p. 204.
63. See below, p. 163.
64. *Malcolm v. Broadhurst* [1970] 3 All E.R. 508. Also *Spartan Steel v. Martin* [1973] Q.B. 27 (property damage/economic loss).
65. *Kirkham v. Boughey* [1958] 2 Q.B. 338 at 341.
66. Below, pp. 159-173.
67. Below, pp. 177-185.
68. *Marx v. A.-G.* [1974] 1 N.Z.L.R. 164 (C.A.). But the husband might recover: *Meah v. McCreamer* [1985] 1 All E.R. 367; *Jones v. Jones* [1985] Q.B. 704 (C.A.).
69. See below. Also *Malcolm v. Broadhurst* [1970] 3 All E.R. 508 (where the wife was herself injured in the same accident and recovered for depression caused by husband's pathological bad temper).

on the very scene of the accident would not be excluded.[70] In other words, the injury is treated as consequential and disqualified only when the plaintiff's *sole* claim to being foreseeably affected by the tort is based on his (or her) relation to the primary victim.

3. DUTIES OF AFFIRMATIVE ACTION

Negligence is commonly defined to include both acts and omissions involving an unreasonable risk of harm, and for most purposes such generalisations provide an adequate working rule. In some respects, however, it is still important to advert to the distinction, deeply rooted in the common law and common sense causal notions, between misfeasance and non-feasance, between active misconduct working positive injury to others and passive inaction, failing merely to take positive steps to benefit others or to protect them from some impending harm.[71]

The early common law furnished redress only for injury wrought directly by affirmative misconduct, because its capacity for effective intervention was fully taxed by the Hobbesian commitment to suppress violations of the peace. Inaction was too remote a focus for imposing legal responsibility. Liability for failing to act entered the law at a later stage when there was present an assumpsit supported by consideration, and contract has to this day remained the foremost progenitor of duties of affirmative action. The reluctance to extend the reach of legal obligation beyond this point drew sustenance from the long fashionable philosophy of individualism, which was content to condone the indifference of the Priest and the Levite and to dismiss the solicitude of the Samaritan as an aspiration merely of private morality.[72] The laissez-faire approach of the common law restrained men from committing affirmative acts of injury, but shrank from converting the law into an agency for forcing them to help each other.[73] Obviously, it involves a more serious restraint on individual liberty to require a person to act than it is to place limits on his freedom to act. Besides, the plaintiff's loss is unequal in the two situations. In the case of commission, the defendant has positively made his position worse: he has *created* a risk; in the case of inaction, he has merely failed to benefit him by not interfering in his affairs.[74] Yet today, though far from defunct, the strength of these sentiments is steadily being sapped by an increasing sense of heightened social obligation and other communitarian tendencies in our midst. Accordingly, the legal doctrine which they once sustained is itself under retreat.

70. See below, p. 224.
71. See articles by Bohlen, *Studies* 291; McNiece & Thornton, 58 Yale L.J. 1272 (1949); Seavey, 64 Harv. L. Rev. 913 (1951); Weinrib, 90 Yale L.J. 247 (1980).
72. Cf. the distinction between "morality of aspirations" and "morality of duty" drawn by Fuller, *Morality of the Law* (rev. ed. 1969).
73. Other legal systems have been more insistent on duties of co-operation: *Charter of Human Rights and Freedoms* 1975 (Que.) ss 2, 49. Socialist codes place duties to prevent harm before duties to compensate harm.
74. As Bohlen put it in mathematical terms: In the first, the defendant has created a "minus quantity, a positive loss", in the second "there is loss only in the sense of an absence of a plus quantity" (Bohlen, *Studies* 295).

The borderline between active misconduct and passive inaction has never been easy to draw. What superficially looks like non-feasance is often, upon correct analysis, a case of misfeasance. A motorist's failure to brake in time to prevent a collision is not an example of supine inaction:[75] an omission is involved, but it is merely the element that makes his *active* conduct—driving—negligent. So, creating a situation of peril, however blamelessly,[76] generates a consequential duty to adopt precautions before it culminates in injury,[77] like warning approaching traffic after breaking down just before the crest of a hill or warning a purchaser after becoming aware of a defect in a product.[78] Nor is there any doubt that removing a casualty to a spot where his plight would pass unnoticed amounts to an interference which, by depriving him of the benefit of help from others, makes his condition actively worse:[79] in sum, the actor has "advanced to such a point as to have launched a force or instrument of harm", beyond "where inaction is at most a refusal to become an instrument for good".[80]

Duty to rescue

Only in situations of purest non-feasance, does our modern law continue to disclaim any *general* duty of care. Thus, where the plaintiff is endangered from a source quite unconnected with the defendant, the latter is not required to come to his assistance, although it is in his power to remove the peril with little effort ("easy rescue").[81] A doctor may flout his Hippocratic oath and deny aid to a stranger,[82] even in an emergency like a road accident; a good swimmer on the beach is free to ignore the call for help from someone in danger of drowning.[83] These remnants of excessive individualism are apt to evoke invidious comparison with affirmative duties of good neighbourliness in most countries outside the common law orbit.[84]

75. This was wrongly described as non-feasance in *Kelly v. Metropolitan Rly* [1895] 1 Q.B. 944.
76. A fortiori, if negligently: e.g. *Connolly v. Grenier* (1909) 42 S.C.R. 242.
77. *Johnson v. Rea* [1961] 1 W.L.R. 1400; *Oke v. Carra* (1963) 38 D.L.R. (2d) 188; 41 D.L.R. (2d) 53 at 61-62; *Rest. 2d* §321. Left undecided in *McKinnon v. Burtatowski* [1969] V.R. 899.
78. *Rivtow Marine v. Washington Iron Works* [1974] S.C.R. 1189 (non-negligent dealer no less than negligent manufacturer).
79. *Zelenko v. Gimbel Bros* 287 N.Y.S. 134 (1936).
80. *Moch Co. v. Rensselaer Water Co.* 159 N.E. 896 at 898 per Cardozo C.J. (N.Y. 1928).
81. Although he is the "cheaper cost-avoider", the law in this instance clearly abjures the economic standard of efficiency.
82. But may thereby render himself liable to professional discipline: e.g. *Medical Practitioners' Act* 1963 (N.S.W.) s. 27(2)(c). See Walker, *Rescue and the Common Law: England and Australia*, in *Good Samaritan and the Law* (1966) 141; Gray & Sharpe, *Doctors, Samaritans and the Accident Victim*, 11 Osg. L.J. 1 (1973).
83. *Gautret v. Egerton* (1867) L.R. 2 C.P. 371 at 375; *Quinn v. Hill* [1957] V.R. 439 at 446; *Dorset Y.C. v. Home Office* [1970] A.C. 1004 at 1027. But a person who exposes another to an unreasonable risk of injury thereby falls under a duty to a rescuer (see below, p. 170): the common law is prepared to support altruistic action, but stops short of compelling it.
84. *The Good Samaritan and the Law* (1966); Feldbrugge, 14 Am. J. Comp. L. 630 (1966); Markesinis, *Negligence, Nuisance and Affirmative Duties of Actions*, 105 L.Q.R. 104 (1989).

However, it remains an open question whether once embarked on rescue, one does not come under a duty to carry it through.[85] Some continue to believe that a Good Samaritan should not be liable unless he actually made the victim's condition worse, as by inflicting fresh injury on him or discouraging others by his own intervention from coming to his aid.[86] According to an intermediate view, a duty arises at least once he has taken charge of the situation, as by beginning to pull a drowning man out of the water; while the most liberal proponents would impose a duty to complete the rescue once he has so much as started on it. Thus, whatever the position of a hospital if it closed its doors to all comers, it incurred liability to a caller once the duty nurse passed on his complaint to the medical officer who negligently refused to attend him.[87] Other decisions, to be noted presently, have even imposed a duty of care upon gratuitous promisors as soon as they started on performance.[88]

There is, moreover, strong support for a duty of affirmative care, including aid and rescue, incidental to certain special relations, like that of employer and employee, captain (or driver) and passengers, occupier and his lawful visitors.[89] To all of these the law has long come to attach exceptional obligations of protective care, because of the peculiar vantage by one party to such a relation in preventing accidents and a corresponding dependence by the other on such help.[90] Once it has come to be held that this imported a duty for the former to safeguard the latter even from perils not of his own making,[91] it was but a short step to insist also on a duty to aid and rescue so long as the latter remained within his protective pale. In other cases also the defendant may, by reason of his position, have assumed a duty of affirmative action. Thus there is a fundamental difference between a lifesaver and the ordinary public regarding their duty to rescue a swimmer in peril;[92] also between the police and ordinary motorists as regards warning oncoming traffic of hazardous conditions.[93]

So also, a duty has been demanded from anyone who happened, however innocently, to be the cause of the plaintiff's plight, as when a pedestrian is

85. The question was raised but remained undecided in *Horsley v. MacLaren* [1972] S.C.R. 441 (below, p. 280), since a duty was found in the passenger relation. The Ont. C.A. majority favoured the first, the trial judge the third view. See Alexander, 22 U. Tor. L.J. 98 (1972).

86. In order to encourage rescue and first aid, "Good Samaritan" statutes in the U.S. exempt medics from liability for negligence. The *Police Act Amendment Act* (Qd) 1987 does the same for police.

87. *Barnett v. Chelsea Hospital* [1969] 1 Q.B. 428. And see *R. v. Taktak* (1988) 14 N.S.W.L.R. 226 (manslaughter).

88. See below, p. 149.

89. *Horsley v. MacLaren* [1972] S.C.R. 441 (social guest in a pleasure boat); *Robitaille v. Vancouver Club* (1981) 124 D.L.R. (3d) 228 (employee); *Rest. 2d* §314A and B. Since *Herrington* (below, p. 467) this should include a humanitarian duty to rescue even trespassers: *Pridgen v. Boston Housing* 308 N.E. 2d 467 (Mass. 1974).

90. See the defence of "distinctive duties" by Honoré, *Are Omissions Less Culpable?*, in *Atiyah Essays* 31.

91. Below chs 21 and 22 (occupiers), 24 (employers).

92. See Gruzman, *Liability of Search and Rescue Authorities for Negligence*, 65 A.L.J. 646 (1991).

93. *O'Rourke v. Schacht* [1976] 1 S.C.R. 53.

struck by a motorist who was in no way to blame for the accident.[94] Since a positive duty to take corrective action clearly devolves upon any actor though he has merely created a *risk* of harm (as for example to remove the carcase of an animal after colliding with it),[95] it would be incongruous to require less once his conduct had actually resulted in injuring the plaintiff. Even stronger is the case against a defendant who has placed the plaintiff in a situation which he is unable to handle, as when organisers of a highly dangerous competition failed to disqualify an obviously intoxicated participant.[96] In none of these instances would a legal duty of assistance be particularly arduous (often requiring only a single warning[97]) or burdened with serious administrative difficulties, as the person on whom it is to rest is clearly pinpointed, and a jury may well be entrusted with the decision whether the defendant entertained a reasonable belief in the existence of the danger and had the ability to remove it without undue risk to himself. Nor is it altogether idle to entertain the hope that the demands of elementary civilised conduct will yet be reinforced by legal sanctions, if nothing more onerous than a simple warning would suffice to safeguard a fellow-being from imminent peril to life and limb, like alerting a blind person or even a trespasser about to walk over a precipice.

Gratuitous undertakings: reliance

At the heart of the non-feasance rule is the adamant refusal to attach legal sanctions, whether sounding in contract or tort, to gratuitous undertakings to confer a benefit on the promisee: under common law a promise must be supported by consideration. Yet though the law will not heed his disappointment at losing the benefit of the promised performance, it does not disqualify him from complaining of genuine *tort* losses inflicted on him by the promisor. Thus if the latter actually starts on performance, he must observe reasonable care not to injure him in some way other than through mere failure to confer the benefit. To draw upon a classical example, one who promises to store another's cask of brandy without reward may freely renege on his undertaking even if it puts that other to extra expense in passing up another offer; yet he can be called to account for so carelessly handling the keg that it breaks open or for just exposing it to the risk of damage from intruders.[98] There has been no disposition to be over-scrupulous in what may thus qualify as misfeasance, for in effect once the promisor embarks on performance he is required to do so with care. Thus long ago, a vendor who voluntarily undertook to procure renewal of the fire policy but carelessly failed to ensure that it was properly endorsed in the name of the purchaser, was held liable for the loss the latter

94. *Rest. 2d* §322; *Racine v. C.N.R.* [1923] 2 D.L.R. 572 (semble, duty at least to continue assistance). Some American courts have found hit-and-run statutes (like *Motor Traffic Act* (N.S.W.) s. 8; *Road Traffic Act* 1988 (U.K.) s. 170) a welcome crutch for postulating such a duty.
95. See above, n. 77.
96. *Crocker v. Sundance Resorts* [1988] 1 S.C.R. 1186.
97. Contrast when warning would have to be given to an indeterminate class and the prospective loss would be pecuniary, as in *Johns v. Savings Bank* (1980) S.A.S.R. 224 (stolen bank cheques).
98. Contrast *Coggs v. Bernard* (1703) 2 Ld Raym. 909; 92 E.R. 107 with *Elsee v. Gatward* (1793) 5 T.R. 143; 101 E.R. 82.

sustained when the house burnt to the ground and the insurer refused to pay up.[99]

A closer question is whether a duty may spring from the fact that, though the promisor has not lifted a finger, the promisee has been lulled into a sense of dependence by abstaining from taking steps for his own protection.[100] The case for tort is strongest where reliance has resulted in physical injury rather than frustrated benefits.[101] Symptomatic was a conviction for manslaughter of an old woman's companion for failing to procure food and medical aid when her patient contracted gangrene in the leg and could no longer help herself. Lord Coleridge observed:

> "It would not be correct to say that every moral obligation involves a legal duty; but every legal duty is founded on a moral obligation. A legal common law duty is nothing else than the enforcing by law of that which is a moral obligation without legal enforcement. There can be no question in this case that it was the clear duty of the prisoner to impart . . . so much as was necessary to sustain life. . . . It was only through the instrumentality of the prisoner that the deceased could get the food. There was, therefore, a common law duty imposed upon the prisoner which she did not discharge."[102]

Even in the absence of such an intimate personal relationship, a duty may be found in justifiable reliance on a more general assumption of protective care. Thus railways have been repeatedly held responsible for level crossing accidents to persons who had relied on a practice of signals or closing gates at the approach of trains.[103] In such cases the defendant "ought to have contemplated that if a self-imposed duty is ordinarily performed, those who know of it will draw an inference if on a given occasion it is not performed".[104] A more intriguing technique was employed in another case[105] where a gratuitous passenger, assisting his host to change a wheel, was crushed by an oncoming vehicle whose driver had failed to notice the

99. *Wilkinson v. Coverdale* (1793) 1 Esp. 75; 170 E.R. 284; *Kostiuk v. Union Acceptance Corp.* (1967) 66 D.L.R. (2d) 430; *Fine's Flowers v. General Acceptance Assurance* (1977) 81 D.L.R. (3d) 139. An alternative stratagem has been to spell out a contractual relationship as in *Bennett v. Puna* [1956] N.Z.L.R. 629 and *Pilcher v. Leyland Motors* [1932] N.Z.L.R. 449. An affirmation that insurance *does* exist may be actionable as a negligent misrepresentation: *Mason v. Morrow's* [1977] 2 W.W.R. 738, noted 16 Alta L. Rev. 20.
100. Cf. *E. Suffolk Catchment Bd v. Kent* [1941] A.C. 74 at 107.
101. See *Rest. of Agency 2d* §354.
102. *R. v. Instan* [1893] 1 Q.B. 450 at 543-544. Criminal cases are reviewed in *R. v. Taktak* (1988) 14 N.S.W.L.R. 226 (C.A.); also Criminal Codes of Qld (ss 285, 324), W.A. (ss 262, 302), Tas. (ss 144, 177) and N.Z. (ss 151-153) which provide a sound analogue for civil damage actions: see *Jarvis v. A.-G.* [1957] Tas. S.R. 220 at 253-254.
103. *Mercer v. S.E. & C.R. Rly* [1922] 2 K.B. 549 (apparently classifying the pedestrian as "invitee"); *Smith v. S.E. Rly* [1896] 1 Q.B. 178 (discussed in *Fraser v. Victorian Rly* (1909) 8 C.L.R. 54). Also *Knight v. Sheffield Corp.* [1942] 2 All E.R. 411 (accustomed to warning light over hole in the street, he was "trapped through [it] being out"); *Thomas v. Elder Smith* (1982) 30 S.A.S.R. 592 (promise to open gate).
104. *Mercer v. S.E. & C.R. Rly* [1922] 2 K.B. 549 at 554 per Lush J. In short, the defendant must use reasonable care to see that reliance by the public upon his representation of safety is not converted into a trap. The situation, therefore, may well be regarded as involving misfeasance.
105. *Hehir v. Harvie* [1949] S.A.S.R. 77. See also *Smith v. Jago* (1975) 11 S.A.S.R. 286 (police responsible after placing driver under directions).

stationary car. He recovered from his host on the footing that the latter owed him a duty of care to prevent injury from the risks of traffic. On one view, the source of this affirmative obligation was to be found in an invitor-invitee relationship[106] between them as long as the plaintiff was engaged in carrying out a purpose to their mutual advantage. By assuming a position with the jack in front of the car with his back turned to the oncoming traffic, the plaintiff had relinquished his own protection in dependence upon the vigilance of the defendant. Alternatively, the case was one of misfeasance in that the defendant had placed his passengers in a position of peril by leaving the car on the wrong side of the road and was guilty of a "continuing breach of his duty of care" which, in conjunction with the other driver's negligence, contributed to the plaintiff's injury.

Reliance has made a strong appeal for recovery even of economic loss. For example, a solicitor was held liable to his client in tort, independently of any liability in contract, for failing to register an option, on the broad principle that "if someone possessed of a special skill undertakes, quite irrespective of contract, to apply that skill, a duty of care arises".[107] Then it did not matter whether the breach took the form of misfeasance or non-feasance, nor apparently whether it made the plaintiff's position worse or merely failed to confer a benefit on him.

Should it matter that the service is undertaken and its promised performance relied upon by someone other than its intended beneficiary? Solicitors have been held liable, though not uniformly, for failing to prepare a will in time, which would have benefited the intended legatee.[108] On the other hand, in the case of defectively built houses, later purchasers have not been able to invoke the reliance of their predecessors on inspections by the local authority.[109]

Duties to control others

Duties to control the conduct of third persons provide yet another illustration of obligations of affirmative action. Ordinarily, it is true, the law does not demand that one interfere with the activities of another for the purpose of preventing harm to him or strangers, but certain relations call for special assurances of safety in accordance with prevailing assumptions of social responsibility. Such a special relation may subsist either between the defendant and the injured person who is entitled to rely upon him for protection or between the defendant and the third party who is subject to the former's control.[110]

106. See below, p. 451.
107. *Midland Bank v. Hett* [1979] Ch. 384 at 411, invoking Lord Morris in *Hedley Byrne v. Heller* [1964] A.C. 465 at 502. As a result, the plaintiff could avail himself of the more favourable tort statute of limitations.
108. Cf. below, p. 184.
109. Semble, *Sutherland S.C. v. Heyman* (1985) 157 C.L.R. 424; *Murphy v. Brentwood D.C.* [1991] A.C. 398.
110. *Rest. 2d* §315; Harper & Kime, *Duty to Control the Conduct of Another*, 43 Yale L.J. 886 (1934). We are not here concerned with problems relating to the *extent* of an admitted duty of care, e.g. whether it extends to risks created by the intervention of others. *Vicarious* liability is also excluded from this discussion which deals only with *personal* duties.

Illustrative of the former are the conventional relations between occupier and visitor,[111] employer and employee,[112] innkeeper and guest, carrier and passenger. Thus a theatre, hotel or restaurant owes a responsibility to its patrons to safeguard them from molestation or other harmful misconduct by other guests and intruders.[113] So, anyone in charge of children, whether as parent[114] or teacher,[115] owes a duty to protect his charges from foreseeable dangers whatever their source. The Bondi beach authority has to watch for surfboard riders injuring swimmers between flags.[116] Even street ice cream vendors have been held responsible for the safety of children crossing the road: like latter-day pied pipers, they lure into peril (misfeasance) those incapable of protecting themselves.[117] Usually, the duty is to protect the plaintiff from dangers threatened by others, but it may also be to protect the plaintiff from injuring himself. Thus patrons must not be plied with liquor until they become incapable of coping with traffic on their way home.[118]

A relevant factor is that the defendant stands to gain an economic benefit from his relation with the plaintiff, especially stressed in the duty to patrons of entertainment.[118a] Conversely, its absence helps to explain why no general duty is owed to protect one's neighbours, for example against the risk of burglars intruding via one's own premises: to make them lockfast or burglar-proof would be too onerous and the neighbours can be expected to protect themselves.[119] Apparently one need not take precautions in general even against vandals creating a source of danger on one's land, which results in damage to neighbours, for example, by spreading fire or escaping water. Mere foreseeability is probably not enough; there must be specific knowledge of the risk of intrusion and vandalism.[120] More vigilance, however, is required over persons allowed on one's land in token of the control thereby assumed.[121]

Even less is there a duty owed by the police to any of a large class of potential victims of a criminal known to be at large, such as to all young

111. Below, ch. 22.
112. See *Chomentowski v. Red Garter* (1970) 92 W.N. (N.S.W.) 1070 (employer liable for attack on employee during deposit of cash in bank's night safe).
113. *Chordas v. Bryant* (1988) 92 F.L.R. 401.
114. In detail, below, p. 682.
115. *Barnes v. Hants C.C.* [1969] 1 W.L.R. 1563 (H.L.) (infant released too early from school). Analogous is a gaoler's duty to protect his prisoner against fellow-inmates (below, n. 137) or the risk of fire: see *Howard v. Jarvis* (1958) 98 C.L.R. 177. Cf. *Quinn v. Hill* [1957] V.R. 439; *Hall v. Whatmore* [1961] V.R. 225.
116. *Glasheen v. Waverley C.* (1990) A.T.R. 81-016.
117. *Teno v. Arnold* (1974) 55 D.L.R. (3d) 57, and many American cases there cited and collected in 84 A.L.R. 3d 826 (1980).
118. *Menow v. Honsberger* [1974] S.C.R. 239 (patron with known propensity for excessive drinking recovers 50%); see Silverberg, *Intoxicated Patron*, 20 McG. L.J. 491 (1974).
118a. See Menow; *Crocker v. Sundance Resorts* [1988] 1 S.C.R. 1186 (organisers of dangerous competition permitted intoxicated person to participate).
119. *Perl v. Camden L.B.C.* [1984] Q.B. 342 (C.A.). Also *Smith v. Scott* [1973] Ch. 314 (no duty to neighbours in selecting tenants).
120. *Smith v. Littlewoods* [1987] A.C. 241 (where varying standards were expressed: see Markesinis, *Negligence, Nuisance and Affirmative Duties of Action*, 105 L.Q.R. 104 (1989)).
121. Such responsibility sounds in nuisance as well as negligence: below, p. 430. Fire: below, p. 351.

women threatened by a multiple murderer or rapist in the area.[122] Unlike the case of an escaping prisoner, here the culprit is not under the control of the police; besides, unless perhaps the plaintiff is threatened as a specific individual,[123] the class of potential victims is too large. Moreover, courts are reluctant to investigate the efficiency of the police as distinct from specific acts: such inquiries would be too far-ranging, call into question the deployment of police resources and divert police manpower from more pressing tasks.[124]

Least compelling would be a duty to prevent others from causing financial loss, as in the case of public agencies regulating bank deposits and the like.[125] So an insurance underwriter, aware that a broker was defrauding clients, was under no obligation to inform them, not even though parties to an insurance contract owe each other reciprocal duties of utmost good faith.[126]

Alternatively an obligation to control another may arise by dint of a special relationship between the defendant and that person. But in the absence of a right to control, there is ordinarily no corresponding duty to exercise it for the protection of others. Thus an ordinary passenger bears no responsibility for his driver's operation of the car, even if he fails to draw his attention to a traffic risk of which he has become aware.[127] By contrast, a car owner instructing a learner driver assumes responsibility, to the latter no less than to the public, concomitant to his right of control.[128] But merely *relinquishing* control to another, for example by entrusting him with his car, will not be sufficient, unless he had reason to believe that the latter was incompetent[129] or bent on using it in a dangerous manner. In recent years, though, there has been a growing tendency to shoulder owners with increased responsibility for damage caused by their cars. If the owner was a passenger in his own vehicle at the time of the accident, liability has been justified by imputing to him a "right to control" the manner of driving.[130] Even against absent owners recourse is now frequently available to traffic victims, either on the basis of widespread statutory vicarious liability or an extended notion of agency whenever the driver was not solely engaged on purposes of his own.[131] This development is of course primarily attributable to the desire to tap the owner's insurance policy.

Probably, the most familiar illustration of a duty to control another arises from the relation of parent and child. Without going so far as to

122. *Hill v. Chief Constable* [1989] A.C. 53.
123. Cf. *Doe v. Metro Police* (1990) 5 C.C.L.T. (2d) 77 (triable issue where area circumscribed).
124. Cf. below, p. 158.
125. *Yuen Kun Yeu v. A.-G. of Hong Kong* [1988] A.C. 175; *Davis v. Radcliffe* [1990] 1 W.L.R. 821 (P.C.).
126. *Bank Keyser Ullmann v. Skandia Insurance* [1991] 2 A.C. 249.
127. *Rest. 2d* §315, comment *b*. But though not liable to third persons, he may prejudice his own recovery on account of contributory negligence.
128. *Preston v. Dowell* (1987) 45 S.A.S.R. 111. Also below, p. 304.
129. *Ontario Hospital Comm. v. Borsoski* (1974) 54 D.L.R. (3d) 339; *Harris v. Van Spijk* [1986] 1 N.Z.L.R. 275 (even incompetent recovers).
130. *Samson v. Aichison* [1912] A.C. 844; *Rest. 2d* §318. The duty may even be owed to the driver himself, especially if the latter is younger or less experienced: *Harper v. Adams* [1976] V.R. 44 (F.C.).
131. See below, p. 388.

attach vicarious liability, the common law insists that parents at least exercise reasonable care, commensurate with their peculiar ability to keep their offspring under discipline and supervise their activities for the sake of public safety.[132] Although most often charged with negligence for conniving at their children's mischief-making or possession of dangerous implements, parental responsibility may also be activated by far less sensational puerile hazards, like toddlers diving into traffic and causing drivers to imperil themselves in evasive manoeuvres.[133] Akin is the responsibility of schools to maintain reasonable supervision and discipline in the interest alike of the children's own safety[134] and that of fellow pupils[135] or the public.

Indeed, a duty to control devolves on anyone who takes charge even of an adult with known dangerous propensities, like the mental hospital that allowed a lunatic with a history of sexual crime to escape and commit an indecent assault.[136] Similarly, prison authorities must exercise care to protect not only fellow inmates from dangerous prisoners,[137] and outsiders from escapees,[138] but even to guard mentally depressed prisoners from suicide.[139] Though the establishment of such a system is an unreviewable governmental decision, it does not dispense with the requirement that within that system, due care be exercised in the interest of public safety.[140] The difficulty, however, remains how to define the extent of such liability. Is the duty owed only to nearby residents?[141] Or, only for crimes committed in the immediate aftermath of the escape? Although the risk may well persist until recapture, any more extensive responsibility is perceived as going too far.

Sufficient control has also been found over passengers and baggage allowed on aircraft[142] and over outpatients with dangerous tendencies.[143] Exceptionally in even less formal relationships: as when a recreation ground advertised a parachute descent and thereby attracted a crowd which trampled a neighbouring turnip field,[144] and when a radio station ran a

132. Below, p. 682.
133. *Carmarthenshire C.C. v. Lewis* [1955] A.C. 549.
134. *Commonwealth v. Introvigne* (1982) 150 C.L.R. 258; *H. v. Pennell* (1987) 46 S.A.S.R. 158 (F.C.). But no duty to provide accident insurance: *Van Oppen v. Bedford Trustees* [1990] 1 W.L.R. 235 (C.A.). See Heffey, 11 Monash U.L. Rev. 1 (1985).
135. *Geyer v. Downs* (1978) 52 A.L.J.R. 142; *Victoria v. Breyer* (1970) 44 A.L.J.R. 174; *Richards v. Victoria* [1969] V.R. 136 (F.C.); *Rich v. L.C.C.* [1953] 1 W.L.R. 895.
136. *Holgate v. Lancashire Hosp.* [1937] 4 All E.R. 19.
137. *L. v. Commonwealth* (1976) 10 A.L.R. 269 (N.T.); *Dixon v. W.A.* [1974] W.A.R. 65; *Ellis v. Home Office* [1953] 2 All E.R. 149. Whether a felon convicted of a non-capital offence can sue at common law is an open question: see *Dugan v. Mirror Newspaper* (1978) 142 C.L.R. 583; *Treason and Felonies Act* 1981 (N.T.).
138. *Dorset Y.C. v. Home Office* [1970] A.C. 1004 (open Borstal; at least where, as here, the theft of yacht was "glaringly obvious" or "highly foreseeable"); *Thorne v. W.A.* [1964] W.A.R. 147 (attack on wife unforeseeable).
139. *Kirkham v. Chief Constable* [1990] 2 Q.B. 283 (C.A.).
140. See below, p. 157.
141. Under a Home Office scheme, compensation for uninsured property is limited to property in the neighbourhood. In *Dorset* it was insured.
142. *Air India Flight Claimants v. Air India* (1987) 44 D.L.R. (4th) 317.
143. *Tarasoff v. U.C.* 551 P. 2d 334 (Cal. 1976) (psychotherapist). But must a doctor inform the partner of an AIDS patient? See O'Dair, [1990] Cur. L. Prob. 219.
144. *Perl v. Camden L.B.C.* [1984] Q.B. 342 at 356, citing *Scott's Trustees v. Moss* (1889) 17 R. 32; also *Fabbri v. Morris* [1947] 1 All E.R. 315 (nuisance).

contest which enticed teenagers into dangerous driving on freeways.[145] These cases are noteworthy both because the requisite control is created by the very act of negligence rather than being antecedent and because of the special causal relationship of "inducing" others (not previously identified) to inflict harm.[146]

Public powers: private duties

The distinction between misfeasance and non-feasance has also played a role in defining the responsibility of public authorities for harm caused to private individuals in exercising, or failing to exercise, statutory powers. While it had long been accepted that public authorities did not enjoy a blanket immunity for negligence in the performance of statutory powers,[147] a distinction was drawn between positive injury caused by an active exercise of their powers and a mere failure to exercise them at all or adequately in a manner that would have averted injury. An extreme illustration was *East Suffolk Catchment Board v. Kent*,[148] where the plaintiff's lands had been flooded by a bursting river and the defendants had undertaken to repair the dike, but carried it out so inefficiently that the land remained flooded unnecessarily long. Still they were excused because their statutory *power* did not create a legal *duty* to come to the plaintiff's assistance; they had merely failed to benefit the plaintiff, not made his condition worse, as by additional flooding.

This view was challenged in the great case of *Anns v. Merton L.B.C.*[149] which allowed a claim against a local authority for the cost of repairing dangerous foundations on the footing that it either failed properly to exercise its discretion under statutory powers to make an inspection or, having decided to inspect, had failed to exercise reasonable care to ensure that the foundations complied with its bylaws. True, the defendant was under no public duty, but the statutory power conferred on it for the health and safety of the public engendered a private duty, once having decided to exercise that power, to carry it out with due care. This seductive argument did not convince the High Court of Australia which failed to discern, without more, in a public power the source of a private duty of affirmative action. In a case much like *Anns*, the majority insisted that there had to be reliance by the complainant, if not on some specific assurance, at least *general* reliance on the defendant's continued exercise of its statutory powers by intended beneficiaries who would find it impracticable to protect themselves.[150] Not even the fact that the council had actually conducted an

145. *Weirum v. RKO* 539 P. 2d 36 (Cal. 1975).
146. On "facilitating" see *Paterson Zochonis v. Merfarken* [1986] 3 All E.R. 522 at 539-542 (Goff L.J.).
147. *Geddis v. Bann Reservoir* (1878) 3 App. Cas 430 at 455. If the authority has *created* a danger it is under affirmative duty to defuse it: e.g. *Fisher v. Ruislip U.D.C.* [1945] K.B. 584 (failure to light shelter); *Bird v. Pearce* [1979] R.T.R. 369 (failure to post warning sign); *Casley Smith v. Evans* (1989) A.T.R. 80-227 (failure to control fire on rubbish tip).
148. [1941] A.C. 74 (Lord Atkin notably dissented from the refusal to extend *Donoghue v. Stevenson* [1932] A.C. 562).
149. [1978] A.C. 728.
150. *Sutherland S.C. v. Heyman* (1985) 157 C.L.R. 424. Gibbs C.J. (and Wilson J.) followed *Anns* in finding a duty but no breach. Mason J. insisted on reliance. Brennan and Deane JJ. denied a duty for non-feasance.

inspection, though not of the defective foundations, converted the conduct from non-feasance to misfeasance.

Both kinds of reliance were present in a case where the plaintiff had complained over a period of six months to her city council about an adjoining burnt out cottage. The council, she was told, was pursuing the matter but it did no more than serve a demolition notice. It was held liable for a fire originating from the ruin to her house, either because she had been led to believe that something would be done (and thus desisted from pursuing other alternatives) or because there was a general reliance on councils remedying such situations by exercising their powers of demolition.[151]

The Canadian[152] and New Zealand[153] courts, on the other hand, followed the message of *Anns* without reservation. Eventually, however, the House of Lords overruled *Anns* on the ground that the scope of the duty, if any, did not include purely economic loss, no more in claims against a local authority than against the negligent building contractor.[154] The question whether a common law duty could be derived at all from the statutory setting at least for cases of actual physical damage was left open. From a policy point of view, it is arguable that the sacrifice of individual liberty, implicit in affirmative duties on private individuals, has no counterpart in the case of public authorities specifically entrusted with powers and resources for the sake of public health and safety. On the other hand, it raises the fear of discouraging beneficial programmes and adding to the cost of taxpayers.

Policy/operational activities

Beyond these private (tort) law aspects, the exercise of statutory powers by public authorities also raises a public law dimension: concern over the constitutional separation of powers.[155] It would be highly impolitic to allow legal challenges, in negligence actions, of decisions by public bodies involving a conscious choice in the allocation of scarce resources, or a deliberate balancing between claims of efficiency and thrift, or a decision how best to implement a discretionary power entrusted by statute. In short, "the government must be free to govern."[156] On the other hand, it is not invidious to subject to scrutiny the manner in which the policy thus determined is actually carried out, whether by commission or omission, by making the plaintiff's condition worse or merely failing to improve it. The

151. *Parramatta C.C. v. Lutz* (1988) 12 N.S.W.L.R. 283 (C.A.). But reliance must be reasonable: *Corren v. Greater Taree C.C.* (1992) A.T.R. 81-152 (C.A.).
152. *Kamloops v. Nielson* [1984] 2 S.C.R. 2.
153. *Johnson v. Mount Albert* [1979] 2 N.Z.L.R. 234 (C.A.).
154. *Murphy v. Brentwood D.C.* [1991] 1 A.C. 398; below, p. 474. See Brennan J., *Liability in Negligence of Public Authorities: The Divergent Views*, in *The Paisley Papers* 79 (1991).
155. See Baker, *Maladministration and the Law of Torts*, 10 Adel. L. Rev. 207 (1985); Craig, *Negligence in Exercise of Statutory Power*, 94 L.Q.R. 428 (1978); Cohen & Smith, *Entitlement and the Body Politic: Rethinking Negligence in Public Law*, 64 Can. B. Rev. 1 (1986).
156. *Just v. British Columbia* [1989] 2 S.C.R. 1228 at 1239 per Cory J.

suggested demarcation, borrowed from American public law,[157] is expressed as that between error on the "policy" and the "operational" level.[158]

From that point of view, the *Kent* case could only be justified on the ground that it involved an improper challenge to the board's decision not to invest more resources on repairing the dike, as distinct from any dilatory and careless manner of executing repairs.[159] Clearer guidance came from Lord Diplock in *Dorset Y.C. v. Home Office*[160] and Lord Wilberforce in *Anns v. Merton L.B.C.*[161] In the former, Borstal boys on a working party escaped and damaged a yacht. The Home Office, it was held, could be held responsible, on the assumption at least that the officers "acted outside any discretion delegated to them and disregarded their instructions as to the precautions which they should take to prevent the trainees from escaping".[162] For that would not have constituted an improper challenge to the department's decision of how to balance public safety against the public interest in the reform of young offenders. The *Anns* case, as already indicated, posed the problem of a local authority's responsibility for the failure of its inspectors to ensure construction of a building with foundations complying with its bylaws. The authority's decision of what type of inspections, if any, to authorise would be in the area of policy and immune from attack, at any rate so long as it gave proper consideration to that question. But once the guidelines were established, an inspector's careless failure to comply with them was operational negligence, for which the authority could be held liable without infringing its administrative discretion.[163] *Anns* has since been discredited, not for this conclusion but for its finding of a (necessarily antecedent) affirmative duty to protect subpurchasers of a defective building against purely economic loss.

The dividing line between policy decisions and implementing activities is not clear-cut; it can be "a matter of very fine distinctions".[164] It would be a mistake to treat every discretionary feature as falling into the policy area. After all, many a private actor's negligence consists in faulty judgment, subject to scrutiny in civil proceedings. As Mason J. observed, "a public authority is under no duty of care in relation to decisions which involve or are directed by financial, economic, social or political factors or

157. The "discretionary function" exception of the F.T.C.A., as interpreted in *Dalehite v. U.S.* 346 U.S. 15 (1953): "where the question is not negligence but social wisdom, not due care but political practicability, not reasonableness but economic expediency. Tort law simply furnishes an inadequate crucible for testing the merits of social, political or economic decisions" (*Blessing v. U.S.* 447 F. Supp. 1160 at 1170 (1978)). See Whitmore & Aronson, *Public Torts and Contracts* (1982) ch. 2.
158. *Anns v. Merton L.B.C.* [1978] A.C. 728 at 754 per Lord Wilberforce; *Kamloops v. Nielsen* [1984] 2 S.C.R. 2. A more cautious test, by Lord Reid at 1032, would require that "the person purporting to exercise his discretion has acted in abuse or excess of power."
159. *Barratt v. N. Vancouver* [1980] 2 S.C.R. 418 held frequency of inspecting roads to be a policy decision by municipality.
160. [1970] A.C. 1004.
161. [1978] A.C. 728.
162. Ibid. at 758 per Lord Wilberforce. Cf. Hamson, *Escaping Borstal Boys*, 27 Cam. L.J. 273 (1969). Also above, p. 153 (police protection).
163. See also *Just v. British Columbia* [1989] 2 S.C.R. 1228 (highway maintenance); *Laurentine Hotels v. Beauport* [1989] 1 S.C.R. 705 (maintenance of fire hydrants).
164. *Kamloops v. Nielsen* [1984] 2 S.C.R. 2 at 23.

constraints. . . . But it may be otherwise when the courts are called upon to apply a standard of care to action or inaction that is merely the product of administrative discretion, expert or professional opinion, technical standards or general standards of reasonableness.''[165]

The characterisation of the decision rests on the nature of the decision rather than on the level of authority of the decision-maker, although policy is usually the function of a higher level. ''Policy'' decisions initiate programmes and formulate general principles; details concerning the manner of implementing them belong to the operational sphere. The tendency has been to resolve close calls in favour of justiciability.

Thus in the leading Canadian case where the city council desisted from taking action on its inspector's report that the bylaws had been flouted. In the court's majority view, there was a sufficient operational element when the council had not, or not in good faith, considered the question of enforcing the bylaws, as distinct from reaching the same conclusion after proper deliberation.[166] In another expansive ruling, a New Zealand court held a government Minister liable for mistakenly refusing a licence on a ground that, to his knowledge, was impermissible. Even if that decision was made in good faith, at the highest level and on policy grounds, the Minister could not excuse himself for negligently applying ''extraneous policy considerations''.[167] The Privy Council, while allowing an appeal on a different ground (no negligence), intimated its concern over the effect of the decision in leading to bureaucratic delay (for which there can be no redress) for the sake merely of leading to recovery in a very rare case and then only for the consequences of a short delay before the Minister's decision could have been quashed.[168] In short, the existence of alternative means of challenging the decision of a public authority (by administrative procedure) strongly argues against tort, even though it might not provide the precise remedy desired by the claimant.[169] Additional factors militating against ''justiciability in negligence'' were: the extreme unlikelihood that an error of law of this kind could ever be categorised as negligent, the danger of ''overkill'' (cautious civil servants going to extremes in ensuring that legal advice is obtained, in turn leading to unnecessary delay)—and, of course, the fact that the claim was for purely financial loss.

Courts have been noticeably averse to scrutinising police decisions. To impose liability on police for failing to apprehend a criminal, to answer a call for protection by someone threatened with violence or to respond to a report of malfunctioning traffic lights might involve, it is feared, intrusion into matters of policy like diversion of scarce manpower to this in preference to other calls.[170]

165. *Sutherland S.C. v. Heyman* (1985) 157 C.L.R. 424 at 469.
166. *Kamloops v. Nielsen* [1984] 2 S.C.R. 2 (economic loss). Mason J. considered this relevant to mandamus but not to negligence.
167. *Takaro Properties v. Rowling* [1986] 1 N.Z.L.R. 22.
168. *Rowling v. Takaro Properties* [1988] A.C. 473 (P.C.).
169. Ibid. at 501-503. See also *Jones v. Department of Employment* [1989] Q.B. 1 (administrative appeal); *Hill v. Chief Constable* [1989] A.C. 53 (Criminal Injuries Compensation).
170. Respectively, *Hill v. Chief Constable* [1989] A.C. 53; *Riss v. New York* (1968) 240 N.E. 2d 860; *Clough v. Bussan* [1990] 1 All E.R. 431. Cf. *Jane Doe v. Metrop. Toronto* (1990) 72 D.L.R. (4th) 588.

The availability of administrative correction of the bureaucracy will generally militate against a common law remedy particularly for merely economic loss, such as a claim for payment of social welfare benefits[171] or for prompt processing of a development application.[172] Misfeasance apart, such decisions of a government department or officer are susceptible only in public law to judicial review or appeal. Injection of the common law process would be as officious as it is unnecessary.

4. INTERESTS PROTECTED: PERSONAL SECURITY

The law's protection against negligent interference with an individual's personal security is today subject to few limitations; thus bearing out our expectation that people must ordinarily conduct themselves with reasonable care to avoid causing physical injury to others within the foreseeable range of their activities.[173] But close as the law has thus come in identifying itself with the aspirations of Lord Atkin's aphorismic neighbour, in a few stubborn instances countervailing factors still give pause. Most prominent and instructive are those associated with claims for mental distress and pre-natal injury.

I. Nervous Shock

The pronounced caution which courts have evinced towards claims for injury to the nervous system is founded on two, far from negligible, considerations. First is the fear that to treat nervous shock on the same lines as external injuries from physical impact would open up "a wide field for imaginary claims".[174] There used to be, though now waning, scepticism in judical minds concerning the degree of reliance which can safely be placed on medical diagnosis both as to the existence of such trauma and its causal connection with the defendant's conduct.[175] Mental disturbance is more easily simulated than external injury, and exposure of counterfeit claims rendered difficult by the time lag between accident and trial. This apprehension goes far to explain why the courts soon modified their opposition to nervous shock as a head of "parasitic damages", ancillary to bodily injury from actual impact.[176] It also makes intelligible their categorical refusal to permit recovery for mental suffering, unaccompanied by objective and substantially harmful physical or psychopathological consequences: mere fright, anguish or grief[177] is deemed too trivial or

171. *Jones v. Department of Employment* [1989] Q.B. 1 (C.A.).
172. *Coshott v. Woollahra M.C.* (1988) 14 N.S.W.L.R. 675.
173. Cf. Lord Reid's dictum in *Dorset Y.C. v. Home Office* [1970] A.C. 1004 at 1027, that nowadays negligent injury should be actionable "unless there existed some justification or valid explanation for its exclusion".
174. *Victorian Rly v. Coultas* (1888) 13 App. Cas. 222 at 226.
175. Particularly useful from a medical point of view are Havard, *Reasonable Foresight of Nervous Shock*, 19 Mod. L.Rev. 478 (1956); Smith, *Relation of Emotions to Injury and Disease: Legal Liability for Psychic Stimuli*, 30 Va. L. Rev. 193 (1944). Generally: Heffey, 48 A.L.J. 196, 240 (1974); Trindade [1986] Cam. L.J. 476.
176. E.g. *Toronto Rly v. Toms* (1911) 44 S.C.R. 268. Cf. *Edmonds v. Armstrong Funeral Home* [1931] 1 D.L.R. 676 (unauthorised post-mortem on wife's body treated like trespass).
177. *De Franceschi v. Storrier* (1988) 85 A.C.T.R. 1; *Re Gollan* (1979) 21 S.A.S.R. 79; *Hinz v. Berry* [1970] 2 Q.B. 40 at 42.

easily faked unless it either accompanies some external injury[178] (when it will readily qualify as but another of the scrambled strands composing the conventional item of "pain and suffering") or constitutes a causal link with some later external injury, as when alarm impels the plaintiff to jump off a high platform.[179] Otherwise emotional shock must amount to "physical injury", or more precisely, it must have resulted in some organic damage, like miscarriage, coronary thrombosis or stroke, or in severe psychiatric injury like hysteria or anxiety neurosis.[180] "Shock" is hereafter used as a shorthand term for such injury resulting from shock.

The second factor militating against claims for nervous shock is the fear that an unduly onerous burden would be placed on human activity, if liability were indiscriminately imposed for failure to adjust one's conduct to the risk of inadvertently exposing others to shock, particularly when the victim was not apprehending injury to himself but to someone else. Foreseeability of physical trauma (impact) imports spatial and temporal limitations lacking in the case of psychic injury.

At first, the objection against all recovery for nervous shock unaccompanied by actual impact was assigned to the ground that the damage was "too remote", a consequence which "in the ordinary course of things would not flow from the negligence".[181] This explanation was scarcely convincing, because it could not really account for a categorical denial of recovery, regardless of the probabilities and risks involved in a particular situation.[182] A second string to the same bow was the crude view that trauma to the nervous system sustained through the eye or the ear without external impact could not, in the nature of things, qualify as "physical injury". Gradually, however, this assumption yielded to increasing pathological knowledge that there was no real scientific distinction between mental disturbance and bodily injury, and that psychic injury, in contrast perhaps to mere anguish, resulting from shock must be recognised as physical injury.[183]

Accordingly, the quite categorical rejection by the Privy Council in 1888 of the first claim for nervous shock[184] did not long prevail. As early as 1901 an English court sustained the claim of a barmaid who suffered a miscarriage from fear of personal injury to herself when the defendant's van hurtled into her husband's pub.[185] Ever since, the problem has been to define the outer limit of the liability once broached.[186]

Several limiting devices were tried. One approach was to insist on arbitrary limitations, such as that the shock must have resulted from fear

178. Even damage to property: see below, p. 253.
179. E.g. *Devine v. Colvilles* 1969 S.C. (H.L.) 67.
180. The distinction is that between primary and secondary responses to traumatic stimulus. The former are means for coping with such a stimulus (e.g. anger, fright), the latter reflect inability to do so and are invariably manifested by physical symptoms. *Molien v. Kaiser Hospital* 616 P. 2d 813 (Cal. 1980) was the first to abandon this requirement in favour of "serious mental injury", at least when the injury is "direct"(?).
181. *Victorian Rly v. Coultas* (1888) 13 App. Cas. 222.
182. As early as *Dulieu v. White* [1901] 2 K.B. 669 "remoteness" was discarded in favour of "duty" as a preferable way of expressing the relevant legal policy.
183. *Bourhill v. Young* [1943] A.C. 92 at 103.
184. *Victorian Rly v. Coultas* (1888) 13 App. Cas. 222.
185. *Dulieu v. White* [1901] 2 K.B. 669.
186. *Coultas* was expressly abrogated by statute in several Australian jurisdictions.

of injury to oneself[187] or at least to a near relative; or only from witnessing an accident with one's own unaided senses;[188] or that the plaintiff must have been within the zone of physical risk.[189] Inevitably, the increasing popularity of the "duty" analysis left its mark also in this context, bringing with it its familiar emphasis on foreseeability. For a time the older limitations continued to militate sub rosa against findings of foreseeability, for example, by dismissing a mother's shock on seeing her dead child recovered from a water-filled trench[190] or on witnessing from an upstairs window a toddler being run over in the street.[191] Today, however, subject to recognised limitations on policy grounds (below), liability purports to be predicated genuinely on whether the defendant created an unreasonable (foreseeable) risk of nervous shock to someone in the plaintiff's position.[192] The older tradition is now reflected only, if at all, in a rather more cautious judicial approach to foresight.[193]

Foreseeable shock

Several important questions however call for a closer anatomy of foreseeability, now that this requirement has assumed so critical a role also in the present context.

What must be foreseeable is physical or psychic injury from *shock*, not injury from impact. It used to be thought that if the plaintiff was actually struck, he could recover as "parasitic damages" for any shock, whether foreseeable or not. This reasoning was applied not only when the shock was actually caused by the bodily injury (post-traumatic shock),[194] but even to an unrelated shock as when the plaintiff, himself injured, and rendered unconscious, is afterwards told of the death of a relative in the same accident.[195] Now, however, the "threshold tort" doctrine is no longer available to him in these circumstances, and the question becomes whether such shock—standing alone—was foreseeable.

Now that the focus is on shock, not impact, negligent words no less than negligent acts may become actionable. A false death notice in a newspaper,[196] a false notification to a wife that her husband has been admitted to an asylum,[197] and the unauthorised disclosure of confidential information[198] are examples. Despite protestations that foreseeability is just a question of fact, it really remains a matter of policy how to define the foreseeable risk.[199] Thus while passengers have frequently recovered

187. Suggested by Kennedy L.J. in *Dulieu v. White* [1901] 2 K.B. 669 at 675.
188. *Hambrook v. Stokes* [1925] 1 K.B. 141 at 152 (C.A.).
189. Lords Thankerton, Russell and Macmillan in *Bourhill v. Young* [1943] A.C. 92.
190. *Chester v. Waverley Corp.* (1939) 62 C.L.R. 1.
191. See below, n. 215.
192. Settled by authoritative dictum in *The Wagon Mound (No. 1)* [1961] A.C. 388 at 426.
193. "Law, marching with medicine but in the rear and limping a little" (*Mt Isa Mines v. Pusey* (1970) 125 C.L.R. 383 at 395 per Windeyer J.).
194. E.g. *Moricz v. Grundel* [1963] S.A.S.R. 112 (pre-accident neurosis); *Enge v. Trerise* (1960) 26 D.L.R. (2d) 529.
195. *Schneider v. Eisovitch* [1960] 2 Q.B. 430 (wife) was the last prominent case to proceed on that view.
196. Notwithstanding *Guay v. Sun Publishing Co.* [1953] 2 S.C.R. 216.
197. *Barnes v. Commonwealth* (1937) S.R. (N.S.W.) 511.
198. *Furniss v. Fitchett* [1958] N.Z.L.R. 396.
199. See Lords Wilberforce and Edmund-Davies in *McLoughlin v. O'Brian* [1983] 1 A.C. 410.

for shock from physical fear for themselves or from reaction to their injuries, mental illness from feelings of guilt over allowing a friend to drive who himself became a quadriplegic as the result of the accident, has been excluded.[200] This for the reason that being a passenger and being herself injured was unrelated to her neurosis, so that the proper test was not whether some shock by a passenger, but rather whether shock from feelings of guilt, was foreseeable. On the other hand, the mere fact that acute schizophrenia was a quite exceptionally severe reaction to the sudden sight of a fellow worker in flames was held to be no obstacle, so long as some shock sufficiently substantial to qualify for redress actually was foreseeable.[201] Shock has even been held foreseeable on seeing one's home ablaze.[202]

But shock must have been foreseeable at least to a person of "normal fortitude".[203] This looks like a desirable safeguard against unduly interfering with otherwise tolerable conduct, like making a loud noise in traffic that could shock only a hypersensitive person.[204] On the other hand, normality in psychic tolerance is a standard both scientifically untenable and impracticable to apply. Is a pregnant woman abnormal? Many have recovered. And where are we to stop along the unmarked slope of psychic infirmity? Moreover, normality, as we shall see, is no longer the recognised standard even in cases of bodily handicaps, like blindness or allergy.[205] In practice here as elsewhere an "open", pragmatic test of foreseeability appears to prevail.[206] This means that mere statistical abnormality (however determined), including predisposition or aggravation because of parental failings,[207] does not necessarily prevent the shock from being foreseeable; also that in practice the standard is left to the trier of fact instead of being pre-empted by law. Moreover, if some form of compensable shock is foreseeable, an even "abnormal" aggravation is included.[208]

Relatives and bystanders

Claims for shock suffered as the result of witnessing an accident from a position of physical safety used to be defeated on the ground that one either had to fear for one's own safety[209] or one had to be within the zone of impact risk.[210] The first alternative derived some support from a reputable medical view that *lasting* damage to the nervous system can ordinarily result only from fear for oneself.[211] The second deliberately sought to limit the

200. *Rowe v. McCartney* [1976] 2 N.S.W.L.R. 72 (C.A.); *Klug v. Motor Insurance Board* (1991) A.T.R. 81-134; *Duwyn v. Kaprielian* (1978) 94 D.L.R. (3d) 424 (Ont. C.A.).
201. *Mt Isa Mines v. Pusey* (1970) 125 C.L.R. 383.
202. *Attia v. Brit. Gas* [1988] Q.B. 304 (C.A.). In *Davies v. Bennison* (1927) 22 Tas. L.R. 52 damages for trespass included shock from seeing a pet cat killed.
203. *Jaensch v. Coffey* (1984) 155 C.L.R. 549.
204. Like the pregnant fishwife in *Bourhill v. Young* [1943] A.C. 92. It was Lord Wright who, in that case (at 110), propounded the "normality" requirement.
205. See below, p. 165.
206. Esp. Windeyer J. in *Mt Isa Mines v. Pusey* (1970) 125 C.L.R. 383 at 405.
207. *Nader v. Urban Transit* (1985) 2 N.S.W.L.R. 501 (C.A.), doubting *McLaren v. Bradstreet* (1969) 113 S.J. 471 (C.A.).
208. An application of the "eggshell skull" rule: below, p. 205.
209. See above, n. 188.
210. See above, n. 189.
211. See Havard, 19 Mod. L. Rev. 478 (1956).

range of responsibility to primary accident victims, in tune with the traditional unconcern for secondary victims.[212]

Neither limitation has survived. The first received a severe jolt as early as 1925 when a mother recovered for a shock she sustained from fear for her own and her children's safety from a runaway lorry.[213] Later decisions, however, remained ambivalent. In *Bourhill v. Young*[214] the House of Lords dismissed the claim of a pregnant Musselburgh fishwife who suffered a miscarriage on hearing the noise of a collision and afterwards seeing some blood without herself being at all endangered. Some of the speeches proceeded simply on the view that the injury was not foreseeable, but others rested on the fact that she was outside the area of impact. In the next case, a court was content to conclude that shock by a mother, upon witnessing from an upstairs window her infant being crushed by a backing taxicab, was unforeseeable; evidently still giving hostage to the old limitations, albeit under the cloak of "foreseeability", a so-called question of fact.[215]

Recent decisions, however, have dispelled these lingering reservations and consistently supported recovery for shock at the sight of injury to a close relative not only by plaintiffs who were themselves victims of the same accident,[216] but also by those in a position of personal safety. Has foreseeability then become the only lodestar just as in all cases of external physical injury?

Now that the presence with the actual impact zone is no longer categorically required, must the plaintiff not at least have personally witnessed the accident or its immediate aftermath? Hearing or reading about it afterwards is not sufficient, not even simultaneously on radio[217] or even television, as did close relatives of spectators crushed in a football stadium disaster.[218] The T.V. broadcast did not show (nor under the code of ethics was it permitted to show) pictures of suffering of recognisable individuals and thus could not be equated with "the sight or hearing of the event or its immediate aftermath". It thus failed to satisfy the test of "proximity to the scene of the disaster in time and space", based on the perception that only the immediate and horrifying impact of the accident could result in foreseeable shock. Short of viewing the accident itself "with one's own unaided senses", coming upon the victim on the immediate aftermath appears now to qualify.[219] But there must have been a shock in

212. See above, p. 145.
213. *Hambrook v. Stokes* [1925] 1 K.B. 141 (C.A.). But "duty" was admitted in the pleadings.
214. [1943] A.C. 92.
215. *King v. Phillips* [1953] 1 Q.B. 429. The C.A. declined to interfere with the conclusion of the trial judge that the shock was unforeseeable because the driver had no reason to expect the mother to watch. Criticised by Goodhart, *Emotional Shock and the Unimaginative Taxicab Driver*, 69 L.Q.R. 347 (1953) and *Shock Cases and the Area of Risk*, 16 Mod. L. Rev. 14 (1953).
216. As in *Vana v. Tosta* [1968] S.C.R. 71.
217. *Rhodes v. C.N.R.* (1990) 5 C.C.L.T. (2d) 118 (B.C.C.A.).
218. *Alcock v. Chief Constable of South Yorkshire* [1991] 3 W.L.R. 1057 (H.L.).
219. As in *Jaensch v. Coffey* (1984) 155 C.L.R. 549; *McLaughlin v. O'Brian* [1983] 1 A.C. 410; *Alcock*, disapproving *Hevican v. Ruane* [1991] 3 All E.R. 65 and *Ravenscroft v. Rederiaktiebolaget* [1991] 3 All E.R. 73.

the sense of a sudden sensation rather than the accumulated effect of, say, nursing the accident victim.[220]

Another qualification concerns the relation between the plaintiff and the accident victim. Some decisions have allowed recovery to remoter relatives, like siblings, even to strangers, like the fellow employee who immediately saw a victim of a horrible explosion[221] and a volunteer rescue worker after a night amongst the carnage of a train disaster.[222] The House of Lords took a middle course between categorically excluding all but the closest relatives and leaving it entirely to the test of foreseeability.[222a] The class was not limited to any particular relationship, like that of husband and wife or parent and child, but was based on ties of love and affection, which can exist between remoter relatives and even in friendship and de facto relations. But such remoter relations required close scrutiny; even an unrelated bystander was not necessarily excluded "if the circumstances of a catastrophe occurring very close to him were particularly horrific".

Statutory reforms

Statutes in several Australian jurisdictions have expressly restricted damages for psychic injury in motor accident cases to persons present on the scene of the accident or to close relatives of the victim, and specifically excluded "normal emotional or cultural grief reaction".[223] Although not precisely defined, such injury, as also understood at common law, seems to require objectively verifiable symptoms of severe injury understandable to a lay trier of fact and exclude evanescent emotional distress which life prepares most of us to bear with fortitude in the face of the tragedies of life.

In the opposite direction, much earlier, New South Wales[224] and the two Territories,[225] in anticipation of the liberalisation yet to come, had removed several of the traditional limitations by statute:

> "The liability of any person in respect of injury caused . . . by an act, neglect or default by which any other person is killed, injured or put in peril, shall extend to include liability for injury arising wholly or in part from mental or nervous shock sustained by (a) a parent or the husband or wife of the person so killed, injured, or put in peril; or (b) any other member of the family of the person so killed, injured or put in peril within the sight or hearing of such member of the family."

In contrast to the common law, this dispenses with the need to establish an independent duty to the claimant who qualifies regardless of whether his

220. *Campbelltown C.C. v. Mackay* (1988) 15 N.S.W.L.R. 501 (C.A.); *Spence v. Percy* (1991) A.T.R. 81-116 (Qld F.C.); *Anderson v. Smith* (1990) 101 F.L.R. 34 (N.T.).
221. *Mount Isa Mines v. Pusey* (1970) 125 C.L.R. 383.
222. *Chadwick v. B.T.C.* [1967] 1 W.L.R. 912; *Bechard v. Haliburton Estate* (1991) 84 D.L.R. (4th) 668 (Ont. C.A.).
222a. *Alcock v. Chief Constable of South Yorkshire* [1991] 3 W.L.R. 1057.
223. *Motor Accidents Act* 1988 (N.S.W.) s. 77; *Wrongs Act* (S.A.) s. 35a. Also recommended in Tas. (1988).
224. *Law Reform (Miscellaneous Provisions) Act* 1944 s. 4(1). "Parent", "child" and "member of the family" are defined in s. 4(5). Section 4(1) is applicable only to actions in the Supreme Court: s. 4(4). If the plaintiff sues in the District Court, he must comply with the common law aided by s. 3 of the Act.
225. *Law Reform (Miscellaneous Provisions) Acts*: (A.C.T.), Pt VI; (N.T.) s. 25.

shock was foreseeable, including "distant shock" by a parent or spouse.[226] His claim is not even contingent on an existing liability to the initial victim. True (despite the statutory ellipsis), the defendant must have been in breach of duty to the latter, but it need not have been actionable. Hence, just as at common law, the shock victim is in no wise prejudiced by the fact that the relative was merely "put in peril" without sustaining actual injury, or that he was contributorily negligent or had for any other reason failed in an action against the defendant.[227]

Primary or secondary duty?

Though the plaintiff's shock in these cases is typically consequent on the defendant's having injured or imperilled someone else, his cause of action is not dependent on, or "secondary" to, the primary victim's. The defendant's liability arises from breach of a duty of care owed to the plaintiff directly, not derivatively, even if it is generally at once also a breach of duty to the other.[228] Thus it is no defence that the primary victim could not himself recover, be it because he suffered no injury or was contributorily negligent or he lost his claim for some other reason.[229] Indeed it would seem the defendant need not even be in breach of a duty to the primary victim, as when he imperilled himself.[230]

Duty to abnormal persons

The nervous shock cases raise with singular insistence, as already observed, the question whether a person's peculiar susceptibility to injury entitles him to special regard in the exercise of care from others. There used to be impressive support for the view[231] that conformity to an external and objective standard of normality was postulated for plaintiff and defendant alike, in the interest of one as much as the other: of the former, because his right of recovery would not be prejudiced by thc peculiar shortcomings, moral or physical, of anyone whose substandard conduct caused him injury; of the latter, because he should be entitled to regulate his conduct on assumptions of normality by those within the foreseeable range of his activities, as otherwise the burden on him and activity in general would be incalculable.

Eventually, however, this viewpoint yielded to the more open-minded foreseeability test. Normality is a biologically indefensible standard and tends to exclude too many deserving plaintiffs from legal protection. Instead, we have come to recognise that even those endowed with less psychic robustness than the model person[232] as well as the physically handicapped are entitled to consideration from those whose activities

226. E.g. *State Rail v. Sharp* [1981] 1 N.S.W.L.R. 240 (parent). But the statute should not be construed as precluding recovery to other persons on common law principles: *Rowe v. McCartney* [1975] 1 N.S.W.L.R. 544 at 549; *Wilks v. Haines* (1991) A.T.R. 81-078.
227. *Scala v. Mammolitti* (1965) 114 C.L.R. 153.
228. Cf. *Chester v. Waverley C.* (1939) 62 C.L.R. 1 at 44 where Evatt J. spoke ambiguously of primary and secondary duties.
229. *Scala v. Mammolitti* (1965) 114 C.L.R. 153 at 159.
230. Contra: *Klug v. Motor Bd* (1991) A.T.R. 81-134, reluctantly following dictum in *Jaensch v. Coffey* (1984) 155 C.L.R. 549 at 604; also *Alcock v. Chief Constable of South Yorkshire* [1991] 3 W.L.R. 1057 at 1120. Cf. rescue: see below, p. 171.
231. *Bourhill v. Young* [1943] A.C. 92 at 109-110 per Lord Wright.
232. See above, p. 112.

foreseeably create unreasonable hazards in their path, and that the burden which this might impose on the ordinary business of life is but a factor in deciding what reasonable care demands for their protection.[233] In the case of the blind, for example, it is relevant to consider how great was the chance of a blind person coming to harm and how difficult the precautions that might have been taken; always bearing in mind that we may assume the blind to proceed with extra caution and that nothing more elaborate would be called for than to alert them to the danger, for example by placing a warning guard around an excavation, rather than to furnish elaborate safety devices, padded lamp posts and city streets that are injury-proof. This compromise reconciles the need of the blind for reasonable locomotion with concern lest it unduly tax such common activities as street repairs, the maintenance of public utilities and so forth.

The same approach applies in the case of little children for whose heedlessness and propensity to get into mischief allowance is due from occupiers of land and those carrying on activities within their reach.[233a] Likewise, manufacturers of cosmetics and detergents cannot ignore allergies afflicting even a minority of potential users who are entitled to warning at least against dangers they could not reasonably have expected in the product and thus guarded against themselves.[234]

Finally, sometimes allowance may have to be made for foreseeable proclivity to harm of property. This is a special problem in Canada during the whelping season of mink which are prone to devour their young when frightened by noise. Accordingly, it has been held that, once apprised of the danger, reasonable care may demand that one adjust one's own activity to reduce or eliminate that risk, for example by desisting from low flying over a mink ranch[235] or by even temporarily suspending road construction in the vicinity.[236]

II. Pre-Natal Injuries

Some of the arguments impeding legal protection against mental shock have also cast their shadow over claims for pre-natal injuries. Again, for long the most formidable impediment to the recognition of such claims by the child was the prevailing scepticism (especially in the context of jury trial) regarding the reliability of pathological knowledge in establishing causal connection between the accident and foetal injury.[237] Until almost the middle of this century, Anglo-American courts evinced a consistent and unanimous opposition which has only now been dramatically reversed. Just as in the case of nervous shock, the difficulties of proof have ceased to be regarded as an adequate reason for a categorical denial of redress, however much they may emphasise the need for strict insistence on convincing

233. *Haley v. London Electricity Bd* [1965] A.C. 778 (blind). See ten Broek, *Right to Live: the Disabled in the Law of Torts*, 54 Cal. L. Rev. 841 (1966).

233a. See below, p. 457.

234. *Board v. Thomas Hedley* [1951] 2 All E.R. 431 at 432 (unless "altogether exceptional").

235. *Nova Mink Ltd v. T.C.A.* [1951] 2 D.L.R. 241.

236. *Grandel v. Mason* [1953] 1 S.C.R. 459; *MacGibbon v. Robinson* [1953] 2 D.L.R. 689; *Sullivan v. Hydro Electric Comm.* (1960) 23 D.L.R. (2d) 756 (mink); and below, p. 425.

237. Avoiding such an egregious error as in *Montreal Tramways v. Léveillé* [1933] 4 D.L.R. 337 (Que.) when club-feet, a congenital defect, were attributed to a traffic accident.

medical evidence. Indeed, it is our vastly increased knowledge and awareness of the widespread teratogenic hazards, especially from modern drugs (ethical and others), that have projected insistent demands for legal protection.[238]

Two theoretical difficulties had to be faced: one was that of foreseeability, the other than the foetus was not at the time of the accident a legal person. As regards the first, we have already noted that injury to the *specific* individual need not be foreseeable;[239] it is sufficient that a surgeon knew his patient to be pregnant;[240] even that one would have to expect a pregnant woman to be a passenger in a car and that a collision would cause injury to her as well as to the child she is carrying.[241] More problematical are pre-conception injuries.[242] It is one thing to find it foreseeable that a pediatrician's failure to diagnose syphilis in a woman during a previous pregnancy may transmit that disease to a later conceived child;[243] it is another to link a birth injury to a car accident three years before which caused a birth canal obstruction in the mother.[244]

The problem of legal personality can be overcome in two ways: first, if we postulate that the time when it must exist is that of the accident (that of birth not being sufficient), there is no reason, in the common law any more than in the civil,[245] for not deeming the unborn plaintiff to be a person entitled on birth to compensation for injury caused while en ventre sa mère.[246] This fiction has been accepted whenever it is necessary for the protection of the unborn child: in order to claim as a "child" under a will,[247] under the *Fatal Accidents Act*,[248] or workers' compensation.[249] Alternatively, if the relevant time is that of birth—the complaint being for having been *born* afflicted—the problem is no longer one of legal personality but how to formulate the duty relation. Obviously, a defendant's negligent act may occur well before the plaintiff's cause of action accrued, since the latter does not arise until the damage is suffcred. Indeed, as already mentioned, there is no reason why that act may not occur even before the plaintiff was conceived. Hence it is sufficient that the accident could foreseeably result in the plaintiff later being born in an injured condition. After that, it is merely a point of doctrinal eclecticism whether the result is explained by postulating a continuing duty (by

238. The most rewarding analysis of the problem's legal and medical aspects is the English Law Commission (No. 60 1974) and *Pearson* ch. 26; also Lovell & Griffith-Jones, "*The Sins of Their Fathers*", 90 L.Q.R. 531 (1974); Bennett, *Liability of Manufacturers of Thalidomide*, 39 A.L.J. 256 (1965).
239. See above, p. 144.
240. *B. v. Islington H.A.* [1991] 2 W.L.R. 501.
241. *Watt v. Rama* [1972] V.R. 353 at 360.
242. The latter are specifically recognised by the *Congenital Injuries (Civil Liability) Act* 1976 (Eng.) s. 1(2)(a).
243. *X v. Pal* (1991) 23 N.S.W.L.R. 26 (C.A.).
244. *Hegyes v. Unjian Enterprises* (1991) 286 Cal. Rptr. 85, not following *Renslow v. Mennonite Hosp.* 367 N.E. 1250 (1977) (transfusing incompatible blood).
245. *Pinchin v. Santam Ins.* 1963(2) S.Af. 254; *Montreal Tramways v. Léveillé* [1933] 4 D.L.R. 337 (Que.).
246. *Watt v. Rama* [1972] V.R. 353 at 377 per Gillard J.
247. *Villar v. Gilbey* [1907] A.C. 139.
248. See below, p. 665.
249. *Williams v. Ocean Coal* [1907] 2 K.B. 422 (C.A.).

projecting the relationship of duty into the future) or by relating the breach at birth to an act antecedent to the accrual of the cause of action.[250]

In the absence of an authoritative common law decision, doubts continued to nag until in 1972 the Supreme Court of Victoria, in *Watt v. Rama*,[251] endorsed the claim for a pre-natal injury resulting from an accident to the mother early in her pregnancy. In doing so, the court expressed a decided preference for the second of the above mentioned rationales. Its emphasis that the cause of action did not accrue until the plaintiff was born (alive), disposed at once of claims based on stillbirths[252] and of the requirement, sponsored by some American courts, that the foetus must at least have been viable at the time of the injury.[253] Indeed, the early stage of embryonic development is peculiarly vulnerable (from German measles to Thalidomide). In England the same position has been reached by statute.[254]

Aside from the infant's claim, the mother herself may recover for any distress over a resulting miscarriage[255] or the child being born deformed;[256] or perhaps just the fear of such an eventuality. If she happened also to sustain some somatic injury in the accident, her anguish would clearly qualify as "parasitic damages"; while cases of nervous shock without impact fall to be decided according to whether *she*, not the foetus was a foreseeable casualty.

More complex is the question whether a child should have a claim for pre-natal injury against a parent. A distinction is in order between the general duty to avoid injury which the defendant owes to all others and those peculiar to parenthood.[257] An instance of the former is the duty to drive carefully, which even the mother at the wheel owes to her foetus.[258] On the other hand, there is strong aversion against inquisition into alleged parental indiscretions during pregnancy, like excessive smoking, drinking or taking drugs.

250. *Watt v. Rama* [1972] V.R. 353 at 361.
251. [1972] V.R. 353 (F.C.). An appeal to the P.C. was eventually abandoned against the background of strong public indignation over the settlement offer by Distillers Ltd to the Thalidomide victims. The Thalidomide claims were originally compromised at 40%, discounted both for difficulties of proving negligence and legal doubts over pre-natal injury: see *S. v. Distillers* [1970] 1 W.L.R. 114; Bennett, 39 A.L.J. 265 (1965). *Watt v. Rama* has since been followed in *Duval v. Seguin* (1973) 40 D.L.R. (3d) 666 (Ont. C.A.).
252. This accords with the U.S. majority view and the *Congenital Disabilities (Civil Liability) Act* 1976 (Eng.) s. 1. It dispenses with the perplexities of assessing damages and presents no incompatibility with the modern law on voluntary abortion: no birth, no rights. Critical: Cane, *Injuries to Unborn Children*, 51 A.L.J. 704 (1977).
253. The viability requirement, linked to the foetus' capacity for independent existence (about the seventh month), is perhaps as much a response to doctrinal concern over the question of the plaintiff's legal personality as to anxiety over the reliability of medical testimony concerning earlier injuries. It provides the test for criminal liability under the *Infant Life (Preservation) Act* 1929 (Eng.).
254. *Congenital Disabilities (Civil Liability) Act* 1976 s. 1.
255. *Stevenson v. Basham* [1922] N.Z.L.R. 225 (£50 general damages).
256. *Dulieu v. White* [1901] 2 K.B. 669 (shock); *X v. Pal* (1991) 23 N.S.W.L.R. 26 (shock).
257. Cf. below, p. 681.
258. *Lynch v. Lynch* (1991) A.T.R. 81-142 (N.S.W.C.A.). The English Act of 1976 excludes *maternal* liability except for motor accidents (compulsory insurance!), but *Pearson* §1471-2 recommended immunity for both parents (except where compulsorily insured) and repeal of s. 1(7) which imputes parental negligence to the child's claim against third parties.

Unwanted birth

Negligent failures of contraception, voluntary sterilisation or abortion[259] or failures to diagnose genetic defects have raised the question of liability by physicians, pharmacists and even parents for an unwanted birth. Such claims have particular poignancy where the unwanted child was born, as feared, with congenital defects.[260] Even so, the critical distinction from the foregoing cases remains that here the defendant has not caused the infant's injury but merely failed to prevent its birth. To hold a physician responsible for possibly lifetime support of the child may well strike one as an altogether excessive and disproportionate sanction for his fault.

There appears to be a broad consensus against such claims by the infant himself ("wrongful life"), whether born healthy or impaired. Objection is made on the supposedly value-free ground that it is legally and logically impossible to assess damages on a comparison between non-existence and life even in a flawed condition. Yet such comparison is not required with respect to added (medical) expenses, which are moreover recognised in parental claims.[261] Also symbolic awards are regularly made for pain and suffering, even for loss of expectation of life. The real reason, one of policy, is that it is thought repugnant to our cultural ethos to complain about the circumstances of one's conception.[262] Otherwise one might envisage even claims by the child against his own parents for causing his birth under some prejudice, like illegitimacy,[263] poverty or a physical imperfection.[264]

Parental claims for "wrongful birth" or "conception" have met with more success, at least for the cost of the unwanted delivery, the stress of pregnancy, even impairment of marriage prospects. Decisions are divided over damages for the cost of rearing the child, including medical care for congenital defects. Against, it is argued that it is impossible to strike a balance between that and competing benefits like mutual love, and that it would be against public policy, having regard to the sanctity of human life and the child's feeling of rejection for being branded as unwanted.[265] The contrary view, which ultimately prevailed in England, is that while the joy of having the child extinguishes any claim for the time and trouble of rearing it, it does not mitigate actual expenditures of upbringing nor the pain and suffering of pregnancy (different interests), that such a claim even in the case of a healthy child is not opposed by public policy and that it is not unreasonable for a woman to decline an abortion.[266] This liberal

259. Assuming abortion to be lawful: *Rance v. Mid-Downs H.A.* [1991] 1 Q.B. 587.
260. See Teff, *Action for "Wrongful Life" in England and the U.S.*, 34 I.C.L.Q. 423 (1985); German Law: Stoll, 22 C.I.L.S.A. 206 (1989).
261. To argue that a notional set-off for benefits of life would be required but be incapable of evaluation and must *therefore* defeat the whole damage claim offends the rule that set-off is confined to like interests: see below, p. 228.
262. *McKay v. Essex H.A.* [1982] Q.B. 1166; *Bannerman v. Mills* (1991) A.T.R. 81-079; the English Act s. 4(5). U.S. agrees: 83 A.L.R. 3d 15 (1978); Capron, *Tort Liability and Genetic Counselling*, 79 Col. L. Rev. 619 (1979).
263. The claim was rejected in *Zepeda v. Zepeda* 190 N.E. 2d 849 (Ill. App. 1963).
264. E.g. that the father infected the mother and foetus with venereal disease.
265. *Udale v. Bloomsbury A.H.A.* [1983] 1 W.L.R. 1098 (healthy).
266. *Emeh v. Kensington A.H.A.* [1985] Q.B. 1012 (C.A.: including the extra cost of a child born with congenital abnormalities which were only statistically foreseeable); *Thake v. Maurice* [1986] Q.B. 644 (C.A.: healthy, £2,500); *F. v. R.* (1982) 29 S.A.S.R. 437

standpoint, though, is somewhat undermined in practice by reluctance to find physicians negligent for failing to inform patients of the risk of unsuccessful contraceptive procedures.[267] Damages should also be confined to injury which the procedure was designed to avoid. Thus no rearing expenses should be allowed where the purpose of the failed sterilisation was to spare the mother the dangers of childbirth or where the child, feared to be handicapped, is actually born healthy.[268]

III. Rescue

A remarkable change has overtaken the legal position of the rescuer; once the Cinderella of the law, he has since become its darling. It used to be that his claim for injury[269] in coming to the aid of someone imperilled by the defendant was defeated in short shrift on the ground that his "voluntary" intervention either severed the causal link with the defendant's negligence or showed that he voluntarily assumed the risk. These theories have all toppled like ninepins; indeed in its anxiety to support the rescuer, modern law has generally evinced little interest in the conventional requirements of "foreseeability" and "duty".[270]

In the memorable phrase by Cardozo J.,[271]

> "Danger invites rescue. The cry of distress is the summons to relief. The law does not ignore these reactions of the mind in tracing conduct to its consequences. . . . The risk of rescue, if only it be not wanton, is born of the occasion. The emergency begets the man. The wrongdoer may not have foreseen the coming of a deliverer. He is accountable as if he had."

The general tendency is thus to postulate that negligence in imperilling the person rescued is also negligence towards his rescuer. Is this, then, an exception to the general axiom that a plaintiff cannot claim derivatively as the vicarious beneficiary of a primary duty owed to someone else?[272]

Foreseeability has rarely been problematical. That rescue as such is unforeseeable has long ceased to be arguable, and rarely have the peculiar circumstances of a particular rescue been held so unforeseeable as to deny a remedy to the rescuer. One such instance involved the crash of a helicopter on its way to pick up an injured motorist in a remote area; but here it was not so much that the crash was unforeseeable as that it was unrelated to the

266. *Continued*
(healthy, $10,000); *Cherry v. Borsnan* (1991) 5 C.C.L.T. (2d) 243. See Symmons, *Policy Factors in Actions for Wrongful Birth*, 50 Mod. L. Rev. 307 (1987). American courts are divided on damages for rearing a healthy child.

267. E.g. *Gold v. Haringey H.A.* [1988] Q.B. 481, above, p. 110. See Grubb, *Conceiving—a New Cause of Action*, in *Medicine, Ethics and the Law* 121 (1988).

268. *Hartke v. McKelway* 707 F. 2d 1544 (1983); *Giesen* 248 (German law).

269. Besides personal injury, this should include the financial cost of rescue as expenses reasonably incurred in mitigation: cf. *N.Z. Forest Prod. v. O'Sullivan* [1974] 2 N.Z.L.R. 80 (fighting fire).

270. Tiley, *Rescue Principle*, 30 Mod. L. Rev. 25 (1967); Linden, *Rescuers and Good Samaritans*, 34 Mod. L. Rev. 241 (1971).

271. *Wagner v. Int. R.R.* 133 N.E. 437; 19 A.L.R. 1 (N.Y. 1921).

272. Sole judicial support comes from Evatt J.'s dissent in *Chester v. Waverley Corp.* (1939) 62 C.L.R. 1 at 36 ff.

peculiar risks of a rescue operation.[273] In any event, foreseeability must here be a very broad notion, in marked contrast especially to the nervous shock cases at the opposite end of the spectrum. The divergent judicial reaction to these two situations strikingly illustrates the fact that, far from foreseeability being the true or sole determinant of duty, weighty policy considerations militate, in the one case in favour, in the other against the plaintiff's claim to legal protection. Behind the ambivalence of the foreseeability formula lies the desire, on the one hand, to encourage altruistic action[274] and, on the other, a decided hesitation based on administrative grounds to permit recovery for mental distress.[275]

Emphasis on the independence of the duty to the rescuer typically comes to the fore when identification with the person imperilled would prejudice recovery. That the latter was perchance guilty of contributory negligence or altogether outside the pale of legal protection as a trespasser[276] has been dismissed as irrelevant. So also has the fact that the defendant imperilled himself rather than some third person.[277] Thus a careless motorist who was thrown into the roadway as the result of a collision had to bear his share of responsibility for the death of a doctor who came to his aid and was run over by another car.[278] This could not have been so, if the duty to the rescuer had depended on breach of a primary duty to someone else, because it is axiomatic that a person cannot owe a duty to himself. These various difficulties are therefore best overcome by basing the rescuer's cause of action on the defendant's negligence, not in its tendency to imperil the person rescued but in its tendency to induce the rescuer to encounter danger. Thus viewed, the duty to the rescuer is clearly independent rather than derivative, and it becomes immaterial that the person to be rescued and the defendant are one and the same.

So far has the law advanced that responsibility to a rescuer may be incurred not only by him whose negligence or other culpable conduct[279] created the original situation of peril, but even by another (negligent) rescuer. Thus in the celebrated *Ogopogo* case,[280] where a passenger fell from a pleasure yacht through his own fault but the owner's unsuccessful manoeuvres to rescue him prompted another passenger to jump after him,

273. *Maltman v. Sauer* 530 P. 2d 254 (Wash. 1975). *Crossley v. Rawlinson* [1982] 1 W.L.R. 369 may be explainable on the same ground, not so *Knightley v. Johns* [1982] 1 W.L.R. 349 (C.A.).

274. Reinforced by legislation exempting ambulance (N.S.W.) or medical personnel (Qld) for good faith efforts: *Ambulance Services Act* 1976 (N.S.W.) s. 26; *Voluntary Aid in Emergency Act* 1973 (Qld), following American model of Good Samaritan statutes.

275. In *Chadwick v. B.T.C.* [1967] 1 W.L.R. 912 a rescuer, stranger to the direct victims, recovered for nervous shock!

276. *Videan v. B.T.C.* [1963] 2 Q.B. 650 (C.A.).

277. *Chapman v. Hearse* [1961] S.A.S.R. 51, affd 106 C.L.R. 112; *Harrison v. British Rly* [1981] 3 All E.R. 679. The real problem here is not the technical problem of "duty" but the policy of whether to encourage unsolicited aid. Note that a non-negligent rescuee is not liable for the expense of even a successful rescue on principles of unjust enrichment: see above, p. 98.

278. *Chapman v. Hearse* [1961] S.A.S.R. 51, affd 106 C.L.R. 112.

279. Like the seller's breach of warranty in *Guarino v. Mine Safety Appliance Co.* 255 N.E. 2d 173, 44 A.L.R. 3d 467 (N.Y. 1969).

280. *Horsley v. MacLaren* [1972] S.C.R. 441; see Alexander, 22 U. Tor. L.J. 98 (1972). It should make no difference whether the defendant's rescue was in duty bound, as here, or absolutely voluntary.

the owner (if found negligent) would have been liable for the drowning of the second.

At one time the voluntariness of rescues used to pre-empt most of the debate, recovery then being persistently defeated on the twin grounds of voluntary assumption of risk and remoteness of damage. Of these the first is now refuted[281] because the duty, legal or moral, thrust upon the would-be rescuer to intercede excludes all real choice, whether he is a volunteer or a professional (such as a policeman or fireman[282]). Courage deserves no lesser reward because danger is deliberately faced. Nor is the rescuer debarred because it afterwards turns out that his attempt was doomed from the start, for example because the person to be rescued was already dead[283] or was never actually in danger at all: reasonable belief by the rescuer is enough. But to be a "rescuer", he must have acted in emergency; he might be a policeman stopping a runaway horse,[284] a station master snatching a toddler from in front of an oncoming train[285] or a passing doctor giving aid at the scene of an accident.[286] Even a father donating a kidney has been included.[287]

Much like voluntary assumption of risk, so the plea of contributory negligence has also fallen into disfavour. Today it stands no real chance of success unless the rescue attempt was utterly foolhardy.[288] Nor does the causal argument fare any better; once the voluntariness of the recuer's intervention was no longer deemed to render his injury too "remote", causation (just like "duty") ceased to be a general problem.[289]

The same approach governs rescue of property as of persons;[290] though to the extent that it is relevant to consider whether the risk encountered bears a reasonable relation to the value of the object rescued, due allowance should no doubt be made for the fact that we place a greater premium on the preservation of human life than worldly goods.[291]

281. *Haynes v. Harwood* [1935] 1 K.B. 146 (C.A.); *Baker v. Hopkins* [1959] 1 W.L.R. 966. The change of attitude was influenced by Goodhart's article, *Rescue and Voluntary Assumption of Risk*, 5 Cam. L.J. 192 (1934).
282. *Haynes v. Harwood* [1935] 1 K.B. 146 (C.A.); *Ogwo v. Taylor* [1988] A.C. 431, rejecting the American "fireman's rule" (below, p. 454).
283. *Wagner v. Int. R.R.* 133 N.E. 437 (N.Y. 1921); *Chester v. Waverley Corp.* (1939) 62 C.L.R. 1 at 38.
284. *Haynes v. Harwood* [1935] 1 K.B. 146.
285. *Videan v. B.T.C.* [1963] 2 Q.B. 650 (C.A.).
286. *Chapman v. Hearse* [1961] S.A.S.R. 51. Or a motorist running to phone for help: *Corothers v. Slobodian* (1975) 51 D.L.R. (3d) 1. *Crossley v. Rawlinson* [1982] 1 W.L.R. 369 is difficult to support.
287. *Urbanski v. Patel* (1978) 84 D.L.R. (3d) 650; also below, p. 218. A less laboured solution: below.
288. *Baker v. Hopkins* [1959] 1 W.L.R. 966; *Horsley v. MacLaren* [1972] S.C.R. 441; *Morgan v. Aylen* [1942] 1 All E.R. 489. Rescuers are not prudent; they are heroes. Cf. *Harrison v. British Rly* [1981] 3 All E.R. 679 at 686 (failing to avert original danger).
289. It continues, of course, to raise the specific problem whether the circumstances of the *particular* rescue were not too remote; e.g. the risk of a helicopter crashing because of a mechanical defect is not a risk enhanced by its rescue mission and thus outside the ambit of the special rescue risk: see above, n. 273.
290. *Hyett v. Gt W. Rly* [1947] 2 All E.R. 264; *Russell v. McCabe* [1961] N.Z.L.R. 385, affd [1962] N.Z.L.R. 392. It is not decisive whether the property belonged to the rescuer, the defendant or a third party.
291. Cf. *Malcolm v. Dickson* 1951 S.C. 542.

Akin to the rescuer is the altruist who would rather sacrifice himself than injure someone else, however innocently. Thus a motorist who took his chance in swerving into a tree rather than run over a toddler readily recovered from a school that had negligently allowed the infant to stray.[292]

5. NEGLIGENT WORDS

Liability for negligence in word has, in material respects, developed differently from liability for negligence in act.[293] First, it has been argued,[294] because even quite careful people take less trouble over what they say than what they do, especially when expressing opinions on social or informal occasions rather than in their business or professional capacity. Secondly, "words are more volatile than deeds, they travel fast and far afield, they are used without being expended"[295] in contrast, for instance, to negligently made articles whose capacity for mischief is usually exhausted in a single accident. Nor is their wider range of potential danger offset by the likely injury being less severe. Physical injury, let alone financial loss, caused by misrepresentation may be as extensive as that looming from defective products or dangerous enterprises. Indeed, arsenic labelled salt is fraught with greater peril than dynamite labelled dynamite.[296] Lastly, in case of careless words the victim's own decision to act upon them is typically interposed, while physical negligence usually causes the injury "directly"—a difference which lies in the realm of causation[297] and the plaintiff's co-operation in his own plight.

In this context, much concern has been attached to whether the claim is for physical injury (to person or tangible property) or for purely financial loss. Generalisations about negligence in word are mostly associated with claims for economic loss, and as this and the next section will show, it is the latter distinction rather than the former which has emerged as the more critical. Indeed, in many situations acts and words are so difficult to distinguish that the criterion would be unworkable.[298]

Economic loss

Pecuniary interests are relative latecomers to the law of torts. Early law saw its task primarily in vindicating the security of the person and his tangible property; and it was not until 1789 that a *general* obligation of honesty was first recognised and the action for deceit launched upon its principal function of protecting the pocket-book.[299] Almost two more

292. *Carmarthenshire C.C. v. Lewis* [1955] A.C. 549. But unlike German law (see 1968 VersR 209; Dawson, *Rewards for the Rescue of Human Life* in *Yntema Essays* (1961) 142) ours (but now rather dated) would not permit recovery from the person saved, unless he were himself negligent.
293. *Nocton v. Ashburton* [1914] A.C. 932 at 947.
294. *Hedley Byrne v. Heller* [1964] A.C. 465 at 482 per Lord Reid.
295. Ibid. at 534 per Lord Pearce.
296. E.g. *The Pass of Ballater* [1942] P. 112.
297. See Hart & Honoré, *Causation* 51 ("Interpersonal Transactions: Reasons and Causes").
298. E.g. did Decca's mistaken chart amount to misrepresentation in the *Caltex* case (1976) 136 C.L.R. 529 at 552? Also, most negligent certificates are based on negligent investigations.
299. *Pasley v. Freeman* (1779) 3 T.R. 51; 100 E.R. 450.

centuries were to elapse, and more than 30 years since Lord Atkin's classical canonisation of the neighbourly duty of care before English law was ready to lend even limited countenance to the recovery of tort damages for pecuniary loss caused by negligent, as distinct from fraudulent, misrepresentation. The courts were daunted by the prospect of a vast liability that was feared to descend on the frail shoulders of such as accountants, surveyors, bankers and lawyers whose daily job it is to offer guidance in financial transactions of frequently considerable dimensions. Such information is apt to be used by many persons other than the immediate client, but the cost of liability cannot be spread among them the way a manufacturer of goods can spead it over all his products. In consequence the burden of potential liability could be wholly disproportionate to the professional's fee. Plausibly, it was more economical to impose the risk of error on the user of the information rather than discourage the flow of valuable information.[300] Subsidiary reasons stem from the difficulty of verifying the extent of economic loss in complex commercial settings and the "moral hazard" of weakening the recipient's own caution.

Eventually, however, the great case of *Hedley Byrne v. Heller*[301] concluded in 1963 that a categorical denial of liability was not necessary in order to shield defendants against "liability indeterminate in amount, time and class".[302] For one thing, contracting parties can bargain over the risk and a disclaimer of responsibility would bind even third parties. For another, the responsibility could be limited with respect to the class both of potential defendants and plaintiffs: as will appear later in greater detail,[303] it is imposed only on those who assume responsibility for information or advice; indeed, according to a narrow view, only those whose business or profession it is, like auditors or doctors; and it is owed only to persons who, if not precisely identified, are at least known to be relying on it for guidance in a particular kind of transaction, such as a contemplated investment, mortgage or other credit deal.

Where a negligent misrepresentation misleads someone else to the plaintiff's detriment, the absence of reliance by the *plaintiff* would ordinarily preclude recovery.[304] For example, slander of goods and other injurious falsehoods concerning the plaintiff's business are actionable only if actually known to be false.[305]

Physical injury

Other factors come into play in considering claims for physical injury. For one thing, personal security has evoked a stronger protective response than any purely pecuniary interest; for another, we tend to be more alive to physical danger and accordingly trim our sails to such risks as much when speaking as when acting. Misrepresentations of safety are a common cause

300. See Bishop, *Negligent Misrepresentation through Economists' Eyes*, 96 L.Q.R. 360 (1980); Siciliano, *Negligent Accounting*, 86 Mich. L. Rev. 1929 (1988).
301. [1964] A.C. 465.
302. These oft-cited triple indeterminates stem from Cardozo J.'s opinion in *Ultrameres Corp. v. Touche* 174 N.E. 441 at 444; 74 A.L.R. 1139 (N.Y. 1931).
303. See below, p. 640.
304. Some deviant cases are noted below, p. 647.
305. Below, p. 711.

of personal injury and a familiar form of negligence which the law has long considered actionable, as in the case of dangerous premises and products concealing a trap or flaw beneath a misleading appearance of safety. Scant, if any, attention has been paid in these and other contexts to the fact that the gist of complaint against the defendant is that he created the risk by misrepresentation rather than by failing to inspect or actually digging the pitfall. Admittedly, often enough the misrepresentation consists, not in something he said, but in his failing to say anything at all (that is to warn); but this should matter no more than whether the communication was by gesture (like waving a motorist over a level crossing into the path of an approaching train)[306] or by means of the spoken or written word. Indeed, the distinction becomes even more evanescent whenever the negligent statement precipitates physical injury immediately (as when a wife suffered shock on being mistakenly informed by an official that her husband had been admitted to a lunatic asylum[307]) instead of merely inducing the plaintiff to rely on it for guidance in some venture upon which he embarks on his own volition, as in almost all cases of resultant pecuniary loss.

All this has meant that negligence in word was recognised as a source of liability for physical injury long before its more belated admission in cases of economic loss, and that the conditions for recovery are much more liberal in the first instance than in the second. Assumption of responsibility is no doubt the touchstone in the one as in the other, but it will be more readily found when someone ventures to speak on something that may impinge on another's safety in life and limb. Thus, though a duty of care against pecuniary loss will rarely be postulated outside professional and business communications, the range of occasions justifying reliance in face of physical risks is nowhere nearly so restricted. Obviously, a doctor must observe the same professional skill and care in relation to medical advice and prescription of drugs as to physical treatment like massage or surgery.[308] But no less may a duty devolve upon someone who takes it upon himself to give an assurance of safety without pretending to any professional skill. All that is needed is that he do so with an air of assurance inviting justifiable reliance, as for instance with respect to an area or structure under his control. Thus, a harbour master was held responsible for misinformation about the safety of a lock,[309] a lake authority for posting misleading depth signs,[310] a laboratory supplier for mislabelling a chemical,[311] and a chart maker for a misleading approach chart for an airport.[312]

The second difference between claims for economic and physical injury is that the range of protected persons is here far less restricted. Anyone in fact may qualify who, in consonance with the conventional criterion for physical injury, was likely to be harmed as the result of the defendant's

306. See *Dutton v. Bognor Regis* [1972] 1 Q.B. 373 at 410.
307. *Barnes v. Commonwealth* (1937) 37 S.R. (N.S.W.) 511.
308. *Banbury v. Bank of Montreal* [1918] A.C. 626 at 657, 689; *Everett v. Griffiths* [1920] 3 K.B. 163 (certifying lunatic).
309. *The Apollo* [1891] A.C. 499. Also *Robson v. Chrysler Corp.* (1962) 32 D.L.R. (2d) 49 (invitee instructed to step back).
310. *Shirt v. Wyong C.* [1978] 1 N.S.W.L.R. 631.
311. *Pease v. Sinclair Refining Co.* 104 F. 2d 183 (1939); *Kubach v. Hollands* [1937] 3 All E.R. 907.
312. *Brocklesby v. U.S.* 753 F. 2d 794 (1985).

negligent statement, no matter seemingly whether it be communicated to him directly or influence someone else to pursue a course of action perilous to him. Thus it does not appear necessary for the plaintiff to have been personally identified in advance as someone likely to place justifiable reliance on the communication for the purpose of a specific transaction, as this is understood in the context of pecuniary damage.[313] He may claim provided justifiable reliance would endanger someone in his position or class, like subsequent occupiers of a building carelessly certified as safe by a building inspector,[314] owners of a submarine cable mislocated on a navigational map[315] or perhaps sailors jeopardised by an incorrect weather forecast.[316]

Moreover, liability has been repeatedly imposed for physical harm resulting from a third party acting in reasonable reliance on misleading information and thereby imperilling the plaintiff. Thus the case of the architect who assured a demolition contractor that he could safely leave a wall standing which later collapsed on a workman,[317] and the distributor who supplied a dangerous hair dye to a barber with an assurance that it was harmless and who in turn applied it to a customer's head causing dermatitis.[318] More arresting still are several decisions against a representor who derived no semblance of pecuniary gain from the transaction—a circumstance to which the common law attaches more readily a duty of care, especially in this context where it is some guarantee that the advice would be taken seriously. In one of these, a truck driver gave a "ready to be overtaken" signal without regard for a pedestrian who was crossing in front of him and emerged in the path of the overtaking vehicle,[319] in another, one member of a party of motorcyclists, pretending to familiarity with the way, misled the rest unto some waste land where a pillion rider was thrown off.[320]

Finally, there is no reservation at all concerning *deliberate* misrepresentations fraught with unreasonable risk of physical injury, as when a practical joker in a cinema shouts "fire" in a manner calculated to cause a stampede[321] or blandly informs a guileless motorist that he has tested a frozen river and found it safe to cross. Such conduct, whether motivated by spite or foolishness, is so plainly outrageous as to merit the severest reproof. Undoubtedly, therefore, he will be held to answer at the very least for all foreseeable injury: in deceit to him to whom he made the intentional misrepresentation,[322] and in negligence to anyone else injured as the result of the former placing reasonable reliance upon it, like a passenger in the car driven over the insecure sheet of ice.[323]

313. See below, p. 647.
314. *Anns v. Merton L.B.C.* [1978] A.C. 728 (unaffected by subsequent reversal in *Murphy v. Brentwood D.C.* [1991] A.C. 398).
315. *Caltex Oil v. The Willemstad* (1976) 136 C.L.R. 529 (Decca Survey).
316. Millington, *Weather, Forecasting and the "Limitless Seas"*, 104 L.Q.R. 234 (1987).
317. *Clay v. Crump* [1964] 1 Q.B. 533; *Driver v. Willett* [1969] 1 All E.R. 665; *Voli v. Inglewood S.* (1963) 110 C.L.R. 74 (dangerous design).
318. *Watson v. Buckley* [1940] 1 All E.R. 174.
319. *Grange Motors v. Spencer* [1969] 1 W.L.R. 53 (C.A.).
320. *Sharp v. Avery* [1938] 4 All E.R. 85 (C.A.).
321. *Bunyan v. Jordan* (1936) 36 S.R. (N.S.W.) 350 at 358.
322. *Burrows v. Rhodes* [1899] 1 Q.B. 816.
323. See *Rest 2d* §310.

Relation to other torts

The existence of already established torts for certain types of harmful speech raises the question whether their sedulously fostered limitations can be bypassed by resort to the open-ended principle of negligence. One instance is the settled rule that slander of goods and other injurious falsehoods concerning the plaintiff's business are actionable only if actually known to be false.[324] Another concerns defamation which is hedged by various constraints (privileges) in the interest of free speech. Suppose then that a former employer without observing due care gives an untrue and defamatory character reference about an ex-employee or that a government agency declares a particular product marketed by the plaintiff ineffective. The "duty" in these cases has long been defined in specific ways, which would be subverted by introducing negligence into a field for which it was not designed and is not appropriate.[325]

6. ECONOMIC INTERESTS

Lord Atkin's ambitious generalisation about duty relations—bounded only by the horizon of foreseeability of injury—could hardly have envisaged risks other than personal injury or damage to tangible property. For, to take but one obvious example, it would clash with paramount policies of a free market economy if the prospect of economic loss to a competitor should impede one's commercial activities.[326] Indeed, claims for protecting purely economic interests against negligence, such as expectations of financial advantage or the integrity of the pocket-book, received short shrift until 1964 when *Hedley Byrne*[327] at last opened the door to financial loss caused by negligent misrepresentations, thus leapfrogging even liability for negligent *acts* and mandating a fresh start.

No consensus, however, has emerged after more than a quarter century's judicial grappling with the problem. Indeed, it has been and remains the most controversial area of torts—one which has been in the eye of the storm over the development of the "duty" concept itself.[328] Two polar views identify the controversy. On the one hand, to segregate economic from other losses is seen by some as an "impossible distinction";[329] to others it represents a fundamental demarcation between tort and contract, between tort's limited communitarian role and the residual individual's responsibility to look out for himself. To begin with, the first view, championed by Lords Denning and Wilberforce, was ascendant; it gained temporary dominance in the House of Lords[330] and remains (so far) the

324. See below, p. 711.
325. *Bell-Booth Group v. A.-G.* [1989] 3 N.Z.L.R. 148 (C.A.); *Balfour v. A.-G.* [1991] 1 N.Z.L.R. 519 (C.A.); contra: *Lawton v. BOC Transhield* [1987] 2 All E.R. 608, criticised 104 L.Q.R. 191 (1988).
326. See below, ch. 29.
327. See above, p. 174.
328. See above, pp. 139-140.
329. *Dutton v. Bognor Regis U.D.C.* [1972] 1 Q.B. 373 at 396 (Lord Denning). See Cooke, *An Impossible Distinction*, 107 L.Q.R. 46 (1991).
330. *Anns v. Merton L.B.C.* [1978] A.C. 728 (Lord Wilberforce); *Junior Books v. Veitchi Co.* [1983] 1 A.C. 520.

orthodoxy in many Commonwealth courts, particularly in Canada[331] and New Zealand.[332] Associated by its detractors with the false gospel of welfarism, it has more recently been emphatically repudiated by the current House of Lords in a series of decisions with the message of keeping the ambit of torts within its traditional bounds.[333] From this standpoint, *Hedley Byrne* remains the exception to a general immunity for negligent economic loss, even if the resulting distinction between words and acts, depending on the nature of the defendant's conduct rather than the kind of loss, looks unprincipled and puzzling.[334]

The High Court of Australia has not yet had occasion to take sides on this controversy. It purported to accept *Anns* before that authority fell, but without enthusiasm.[335]

The following discussion seeks to analyse the principal case groupings from a less dogmatic point of view.[336]

Consequential on physical loss

Economic losses associated with physical injury have caused least concern. There is the long established practice of allowing recovery not only for the cost of repairing physical damage to person or tangible property,[337] but also for "consequential" loss of earnings or profits resulting from such damage during rehabilitation or repair.[338] So, a mother who lost a child during delivery due to medical neglect recovered for the financial loss she would incur in undergoing another pregnancy to replace the child.[339] Nor does the law cavil at expenses incurred in mitigation of physical damage, like the cost of cleaning up debris on the highway[340] or hiring a temporary substitute for a damaged machine.[341] It would be but a short step to allow also for expenses incurred in avoiding or mitigating personal or property damage *threatened* by the defendant's negligence, such as the cost of salvaging goods from a carrier's truck damaged in a collision,[342] or fighting a fire heading towards one's home. In these instances, damages are relatively circumscribed and tied up with physical damage to person or property, core areas of tort protection.

The more controversial area lies beyond, concerning pecuniary loss *standing alone*. Yet it is not always self-evident whether a particular loss

331. *Kamloops v. Nielsen* [1984] 2 S.C.R. 2; *Norsk Pacific Steamship Co. v. C.N.R.* [1992] S.C.R. —
332. *Mount Albert v. Johnson* [1979] 2 N.Z.L.R. 234.
333. *Peabody v. Parkinson* [1985] A.C. 210; *Murphy v. Brentwood D.C.* [1991] A.C. 398.
334. See Stapleton, *Duty of Care and Economic Loss*, 107 L.Q.R. 249 (1991).
335. See *Sutherland S.C. v. Heyman* (1985) 157 C.L.R. 424. *Caltex Oil v. The Willemstad* (1976) 136 C.L.R. 529 has become difficult to reconcile with the new orientation.
336. See generally Cane, *Tort Law and Economic Interests* (1991); Feldthusen, *Economic Negligence* (2nd ed., 1989). Comparative: Lawson & Markesinis, *Tortious Liability* (1982) 80-93; Marshall, 24 I.C.L.Q. 748 (1975).
337. Property is clearly an economic value, and even in cases of personal injury *Baker v. Willoughby* [1970] A.C. 467 teaches that the claim in not for loss of the leg, but for its economic consequences.
338. E.g. *S.C.M. v. Whittall* [1971] 1 Q.B. 337: see below, p. 182.
339. *Kralj v. McGrath* [1986] 1 All E.R. 54.
340. *A.-G. v. Fatehi* [1984] 2 S.C.R. 536.
341. See below, pp. 251-252.
342. *Morrison S.S. Co. v. Greystoke Castle* [1947] A.C. 265 at 280.

should be classified as damage to property or purely economic.[343] Claims against a negligent builder for the cost of repairing defective foundations used to be treated as property damage (and recoverable in tort) until reversed on the principle that until personal injury or damage to *other* property actually occurred, the owner's claim was merely for the lessened value of the defective property, which lay in contract alone and required privity to support it.[344] To allow the claim in tort was thought to undermine the integrity of the division between tort and contract. Yet here, liability would be limited both in regard to person, the quondam owner, and in amount. Would not a more principled demarcation be between defects affecting safety and those merely lessening the value of the property?

Secondary losses: relational interests

The most ingrained opposition is against recovery for injury to relational interests. Generally, the law has considered itself fully extended by affording compensation only to persons immediately injured, such as the accident victim himself, without going to the length of compensating also third persons who, secondarily (par ricochet), incur expenses or lose their livelihood, support or expected benefits from their association with him. The reason for this is not so much that these claims are for pecuniary detriment as that the burden of compensating anyone besides the primary casualty is feared to be unduly oppressive because most accidents are bound to entail repercussions, great or small, upon all with whom he had family, business or other valuable relations.

A strong illustration is the categorical refusal to protect profitable contractual expectancies against negligent, as distinct from intentional,[345] damage. Thus a tug owner failed in his claim for losing the benefit of his towing contract when the defendant negligently sank his tow;[346] as did a contractor engaged in driving a tunnel against a water company for negligently letting water escape, which increased his cost of completing the lump sum contract.[347] Another example is the denial of recovery for payments under a contractual obligation voluntarily entered into with a third party. For example, a voluntary scheme under which tank owners agreed to pay compensation for pollution damage offered no basis for reimbursement from a negligent manufacturer of a defective coupling which had caused the spillage.[348] Nor has an insurance company an independent cause of action against a tortfeasor whose negligence brought about the loss insured against, for example personal injury or death under

343. Is birth of inferior calves due to mix-up of semen a physical or economic loss: *Port v. N.Z. Dairy Bd* [1982] 2 N.Z.L.R. 282? Or damages awarded against a rapist (in his claim for reimbursement against driver who caused his personality change: *Meah v. McCreamer (No. 2)* [1986] 1 All E.R. 943)?

344. *D. & F. Estates v. Church Comrs* [1989] A.C. 177. The principle applies a fortiori to defective products, where serial damage may be more extensive. Below, p. 474 (property); p. 495 (products).

345. A highly developed tort, discussed below ch. 30, section 2.

346. *Société Anonyme v. Bennetts* [1911] 1 K.B. 243. Aliter, if his tug had been sunk instead.

347. *Cattle v. Stockton Waterworks* (1875) L.R. 10 Q.B. 453.

348. *Esso v. Hall, Russell* [1989] A.C. 643. Aliter, if they had claimed as subrogees by assignment in name of those who had suffered the physical damage or if their obligation had been by force of law rather than contract.

an accident or life policy or damage to property under a fire policy.[349] Indeed, in this instance denial of recovery is reinforced by additional factors. In the first place, it is doubtful if the insurer can be said to have suffered injury in any real sense. For how can realisation of the risk insured against constitute a loss when that very risk was calculated into the premium? For that matter, how can the fact that one is called upon to perform a contractual obligation ever constitute an injury, let alone a tortious injury?[350] Secondly, to give an insurer an independent right of action would tend to defeat cardinal rules of subrogation, specifically the principle that such recourse is available only in case of indemnity policies (like liability or fire insurance) and not in case of personal injuries.[351] Last of all, recovery by life insurers would face the additional obstacle that at common law the death of a human being may not be complained of as an injury.[352]

The case against recovery becomes even stronger when the claimant has a non-vested expectancy, like employees who lost their job when their factory was burnt down[353] or the auctioneer who lost sales when the local cattle market had to be closed as a result of foot and mouth disease originating in an escape of virus from a research station,[354] or the distributor of merchandise who lost turnover when goods still in the possession of his regular supplier were damaged by the defendant.[355]

The only exception stems from the ancient action for loss of services, which was originally based on the anomalous notion that a master, husband or parent had a proprietary interest in the services of his servant, wife or child. The master's action is now generally regarded as anachronistic and barely surviving.[356] But within the family circle it has retained its vitality[357] and been reinforced by the statutory claim by close relatives of a person killed for loss of their dependency.[358] Other secondary losses, however, like a daughter's giving up a job to nurse the victim, are excluded.[359] Still, mitigating is the fact that the accident victim himself is often able to recover on his own account for some or all of the loss in question and so able to indemnify the benefactor. Thus gratuities may be repaid,[360] expenses

349. *Simpson v. Thomson* (1877) 3 App. Cas. 279.
350. This has also provided the reason for resisting recovery by an employer of disability pay, etc., furnished under contract to an injured employee: see below, p. 687.
351. In *Simpson v. Thomson* the marine insurer had no right of subrogation because the ship insured and the culpable ship belonged to one and the same owner.
352. See below, p. 663. Moreover, in so far as such a policy cannot be set off against the estate or dependants (see below, p. 673), the tortfeasor would be exposed to double liability.
353. *Adams v. S.P.* 23 Cal. Rptr. 216 (1975); *Stevenson v. E. Ohio Gas* 73 N.E. 2d 200 (1946). Partner: *Foodlands v. Mosscrop* [1985] W.A.R. 215.
354. *Weller v. Foot & Mouth Disease Research Institute* [1966] 1 Q.B. 569.
355. *French Knit Sales v. Gold* [1972] 2 N.S.W.L.R. 132 (C.A.). That the plaintiff and its supplier were associated companies made no more difference than that the plaintiff also happened to sustain actionable damage to its own goods. In the last respect, cf. *Spartan Steel v. Martin* [1973] Q.B. 27 (C.A.).
356. See below, p. 684. Otherwise claims for expenses incurred on behalf of an injured employee have been rejected as too remote: *R. v. C.P.R.* [1947] S.C.R. 185.
357. See below, p. 659 (injured wife), p. 660 (child).
358. See below, p. 665. Note that the dependants' claim can never exceed what the defendant would have had to pay the deceased had he survived.
359. *Pratt v. Pratt* [1975] V.R. 378 (F.C.); *Kirkham v. Boughey* [1958] 2 Q.B. 338.
360. See below, p. 245.

incurred by relatives may be refunded[361] and, as we have seen, insurance companies may enjoy certain rights of subrogation. To that extent, the general rule serves less to exclude than to channel claims so as to spare the defendant from more than one suit.

Non-proprietary interests

The older principle[362] has also been reaffirmed that only persons with a proprietary or possessory interest at the time of the accident can sue for loss arising from damage to property; loss based on mere contractual rights to such property being dismissed as "purely pecuniary" and irrecoverable in tort.[363] The generality of this proposition, redolent of archaic notions that left their mark on the law of conversion, detinue and trespass, is open to question. As originally applied to relational claims, such as those of the tug owner and the tunnel contractor previously mentioned, it is perfectly defensible for setting a limit to secondary losses, potentially indeterminate in number and amount.

In some other situations, also, it may merely underline the absence of any protected interest by the plaintiff. Such was the case where the faulty design of a jetty caused the silting of a river near the plaintiff's wharf. Their claim in negligence for the cost of dredging failed for want of any riparian or other right regarding the depth of the channel.[364]

Less compelling is its extension to situations of "transferred loss", that is where the loss, instead of being suffered by the owner or possessor, is suffered by the plaintiff by reason of an intervening transfer of risk. Such is the case where a time charterer seeks to recover for damage to the ship and for loss of use during repairs[365] or where goods are damaged during transit after the risk (but not the property) has passed to the buyer.[366] This result is difficult to justify by reference to the need for limiting "floodgate" losses, since to allow the claim would merely substitute one claimant for another without increasing the defendant's liability. The outcome is made tolerable only by the cumbersome device of allowing the owner to recover from the tortfeasor by virtue of his bare proprietary/possessory title and holding the proceeds for those who sustained the ultimate economic loss.[367]

Power blackout

Other illustrations of the principle limiting recovery to persons with a proprietary or possessory interest in a damaged chattel come from the

361. See below, p. 231, n. 53.
362. Enunciated in *Simpson v. Thomson* (1877) 3 App. Cas. 279 at 290.
363. *Leigh & Sillavan v. Aliakmon* [1986] A.C. 785. An inexplicably narrow view of "possessory" was taken in *Nacap v. Moffat Plant*, 1987 S.L.T. 221 (I.H.); a more realistic view in *Williams v. A.-G.* [1990] 1 N.Z.L.R. 646 (C.A.).
364. *Tate & Lyle v. G.L.C.* [1983] 2 A.C. 509. However, the claim for public nuisance (obstruction of navigable river) succeeded.
365. *The Mineral Transporter* [1986] A.C. 1 (P.C.); *Robins Dry Dock v. Flint* 275 U.S. 303 (1927); *East River S.S. v. Transamerica* (1986) 476 U.S. 858 (manufacturer).
366. *Leigh & Sillavan v. Aliakmon* [1986] A.C. 785. Aliter, if the property had passed: *Albacruz v. Albazero* [1977] A.C. 774 at 847 (negligence); *Bill of Lading Act* 1855 (U.K.) s. 1. Cf. *Latent Damage Act* 1986 (Eng.) s. 3.
367. *Obestain v. National Mineral Corp.* [1987] 1 Lloyd's Rep. 465; *Albacruz v. Albazero* at 845; *Anderson v. Deere* (1988) 15 N.S.W.L.R. 363 (C.A.).

problem of negligent damage to power cables supplying nearby businesses. Here an additional factor is the spectre of incalculable commercial losses. English cases eventually settled on a distinction between loss of profits from two different causes. In case of physical damage to the plant or material itself, as when molten metal solidified as the result of a power failure, the plaintiff might recover not only for the value of items damaged or destroyed but also for profit lost during the resulting shutdown.[368] The economic loss is here described as consequential on physical damage, and akin to loss of earnings resulting from personal injuries. On the other hand, loss of profit due solely to the interruption of power supply is classified as "purely economic" and irrecoverable.[369] Nor would it avail the plaintiff in that case that he also suffered some unrelated physical damage,[370] like the fish merchant who lost a tankful of live lobsters as the result of defective oxy-pumps and recovered the value of the lobsters, but not the lost profits on intended sales or the cost of the pumps.[371] English law does not recognise a "threshold tort" doctrine by which an unprotected interest could thus slip into the fold.

Opposition to recovery for lost production could rest on the reasoning that the plaintiff is better able to calculate such losses into his own cost structure and pass them on to his customers than the defendant who, be he businessman or private motorist, cannot foresee the amount of such losses (as distinct from the accident itself) and would have to protect himself through the far more costly and clumsy device of liability insurance.[372] Yet the distinction drawn in the preceding cases does not exclude all business losses and in any event seems rather fine spun and fortuitous.[373]

Specifically foreseeable plaintiffs

In what circumstances, then, will the courts relent from their continuing negative attitude to claims for negligent economic loss? No generalisation has as yet emerged, but several criteria have been identified which separately or in combination have at times passed the test of control. This may signify not so much a failure to achieve consensus as a recognition that no universal test may satisfy the peremptory need of controlling a potentially explosive source of liability.

The first of these criteria, borrowed from the law of negligent misrepresentation, would exceptionally allow recovery for economic, perhaps even secondary, loss to a claimant who was specifically, not just generally, foreseeable as likely (probable?) to suffer the loss in question.[374] The principal exemplar is the leading Australian case of *Caltex Oil*.[375]

368. *S.C.M. v. Whittall* [1971] 1 Q.B. 337 (C.A.).
369. *Spartan Steel v. Martin* [1973] Q.B. 27 (C.A.).
370. Ibid.
371. *Muirhead v. I.T.S.* [1986] Q.B. 507 (profits: ten times cost). Contra: *Seaway Hotels v. Gragg* (1960) 21 D.L.R. (2d) 264 (Ont. C.A.).
372. Cf. *Dunlop v. F.M.C.* 385 N.Y.S. 2d 971 at 975 (N.Y. 1976) ("a delay in the production of tyres which if not produced and sold today will be produced and sold tomorrow").
373. *Spartan Steel* was criticised in *Caltex Oil* (1976) 136 C.L.R. 529 at 568, 602 and not followed in *N.Z. Forest Products v. A.-G.* [1986] 1 N.Z.L.R. 14; *Mainguard v. Hilton Haulage* [1990] 1 N.Z.L.R. 360.
374. See above, p. 174.
375. *Caltex Oil v. The Willemstad* (1976) 136 C.L.R. 529; *Norsk Pacific Steamship Co. v. C.N.R.* [1992] S.C.R. — (collision with bridge used by only one railway).

A dredge negligently broke an underwater pipe owned by AOR, which carried petroleum across Botany Bay from its refinery to a Caltex terminal. Here, not only did AOR recover for the damage to its pipe and contents, but so did Caltex for the cost of alternatively transporting its products until the pipe was repaired.[376] The High Court stressed that liability was "controlled" both as regards claim and loss. The defendants knew of the risk to Caltex as a specific individual rather than as a general class, and the loss claimed was not of profits but of an expenditure necessarily incurred by someone who, to their knowledge, relied directly on the use of the pipe, which itself was within the scope of their duty of care. Indeed, in a sense AOR and Caltex were engaged in a common venture, and since the same loss would clearly have been recoverable by AOR, it was not really increasing the defendants' burden to allow it alternatively to Caltex.

But this decision has remained isolated. More frequently voiced is the converse proposition, categorically disqualifying plaintiffs who were merely members of a larger class of potential victims such as people affected by damage to a bridge,[377] fishermen (39) whose trawling grounds were disturbed;[378] or ordinary purchasers of defective products. All the more it defeated the claim against a courier for delay in delivering an envelope to a Land Office as a result of which the plaintiff lost a valuable contract.[379] Even to count the latter as specifically identified would have unrealistically stretched the concept, considering that the courier had no knowledge whatever that the rights of third parties could be affected.

Assumption of responsibility: reliance

Claims for direct, as distinct from secondary, economic loss offer a somewhat brighter prospect of success. Such, of course, was the seminal case of negligent misrepresentation in *Hedley Byrne*; its touchstone: a voluntarily assumed responsibility to a plaintiff known to rely on the accuracy of the information or advice for a particular purpose. Should the same narrow test be applied also to negligent *acts* (or omissions) causing economic loss?[380]

The double requirement of assumption of responsibility and reliance was clearly satisfied in the classical case of the public weigher who overestimated a load of beans with the result that the buyer overpaid the seller.[381] So also where the intending purchaser of a home relies in the ordinary course on a valuer engaged by the mortgage lender.[382]

376. Little attention has been paid in the cases to the type of damages recoverable for economic negligence. Where consequential to injury to person or property, recovery has included loss of profits: see below, p. 251. In *Caltex* (1976) 136 C.L.R. 529 at 577 Stephen J. contrasted the cost of alternative transport from "collateral commercial arrangements", but loss of profits were not claimed. As Cane points out (12 Melb. U.L. Rev. 408 (1980)), the distinction between lucrum cessans and damnum emergens is often fortuitous.

377. *Bethlehem Steel v. St Lawrence Seaway* (1977) 79 D.L.R. (3d) 522; *Re Kinsman (No. 2)* 388 F. 2d 821 (2d Cir. 1968). Contrast *Norsk Pacific Steamship Co. v. C.N.R.* [1992] S.C.R. —.

378. *Ball v. Cons. Rutile* (1990) A.T.R. 81-023. A fortiori, losses by others, as in *Louisiana v. M/V Testbank* 752 F. 2d 1019 (1985).

379. *B.D.C. v. Hofstrand* [1986] 1 S.C.R. 228.

380. Thus e.g. Smillie, *Negligence and Economic Loss*, 32 U. Tor. L.J. 231 (1982).

381. *Glanzer v. Shepard* 135 N.E. 275 (N.Y. 1922).

382. *Smith v. Bush* [1990] 1 A.C. 831.

The claim of a disappointed legatee against the testator's lawyer for negligently drawing the will satisfies the requirement of assumed responsibility but not of reliance. Here only the testator, not the legatee, relied, and *he* suffered no loss. Nor, for that matter, did the legatee suffer a "loss", only disappointment of an expected advantage, indeed one so precarious as a mere spes successionis. If most courts have eventually allowed the claim, it is because the defendant did assume responsibility, knew that (and by how much) it would directly and exclusively affect the plaintiff's pocket-book, and would not otherwise be subject to any sanction for his dereliction.[383] In any event, why should reliance be an indispensable element when causation of loss can be established independently as it clearly can in cases other than misrepresentation? Indeed, the plaintiff's position was stronger for not being able to avert the loss by making his own protective arrangements—a factor to which increasing attention is being paid in assessing the equity of claims for economic loss.[384]

Pseudo-contractual relations

Hedley Bryne has been interpreted as implicitly sanctioning concurrent tort liability for negligence in the performance of a contract between the parties, whether the resulting loss is purely economic or physical and whether it was caused by misrepresentation or other conduct.[385] The principle applies not only to professional but also to ordinary commercial contracts.[386] Several factors explain the readiness with which it has been accepted: contractual relationship is one of reliance and dependence, the obligations can be modified or excluded and any economic loss is more or less calculable. The result, if not the motivation, has been to give plaintiffs the benefit of more favourable rules of tort law, such as the terminus a quo for the statute of limitations or a more generous measure of damages.

More problematical is the extension to relationships "equivalent to contract", as was the case in *Hedley Byrne* itself.[387] Later it helped an intending home purchaser against a valuer engaged by the mortgage lender (but in reality paid by the borrower),[388] even a building owner against a designated supplier who was under contract (but only) with the main contractor.[389] In these and other cases tort liability helped to make up for the refusal of contract law to recognise contracts for the benefit of third

383. *Ross v. Caunters* [1980] Ch. 297; *Watts v. Public Trustee* [1980] W.A.R. 97; *Gartside v. Sheffield* [1983] N.Z.L.R. 37 (C.A.). Also *Hawkins v. Clayton* (1988) 164 C.L.R. 539 (duty on solicitor/custodian of will to inform executor). Contra: *Seale v. Perry* [1982] V.R. 193 (F.C.).

384. *Leigh & Sillavan v. Aliakmon* [1986] 1 A.C. 785 at 819. Stapleton (above, n. 334) has raised inadequacy of alternative protection to a necessary, albeit not sufficient, condition of tort recovery.

385. See below, p. 186.

386. E.g. *Esso v. Mardon* [1976] Q.B. 801 (C.A.; franchise).

387. [1964] A.C. 465 at 530.

388. *Smith v. Bush* [1990] 1 A.C. 831 ("akin to contract" at 796). Even when the report is not shown to purchaser. But liability could be disclaimed by a valid exclusion clause. Also *Ward v. McMaster* [1988] I.R. 388.

389. *Junior Books v. Veitchi* [1983] 1 A.C. 520 at 533 ("only just short of direct contractual relationship"). Now regarded as implicitly overruled.

parties.[389a] Quite the opposite has been the argument insistently voiced in recent cases, that failure to enter into a contractual relationship in the setting of a planned transaction is reason enough to deny the plaintiff a gap-filling tort duty. For example, on construction projects involving multiple parties, the structure of their contractual relationships may have been understood to exclude complementary obligations in tort: if the plaintiff had wanted a contractual commitment from the defendant, why did he not stipulate for it? In one such case the defendant subcontractor had actually entered into a contract with the building owner, though not dealing with liability for negligent damage;[390] in another the contract between the engineer and the owner specifically disclaimed personal liability by the engineer (who was sued by the contractor for negligent under-certification).[391] But even without these additional pointers, in other construction project cases attempts to jump across structured relationships with a view to recovering for purely economic loss dissociated from any structual damage have failed.[392]

Even in less structured contexts, the need for importing tort liability against a third party is largely defused by the availability of a remedy for the loss against a contractual partner. Thus an insured can contest an accusation of arson in an action against the insurer without resorting to tort against the investigator.[393] By contrast, the disappointed legatee could maintain an action against the negligent probate lawyer precisely because he would otherwise have been denied all redress.[394]

A second argument against liability in these triangular cases[395] revolves around the question whether an exemption clause in the subcontract would modify also a tort duty of the subcontractor, as it clearly would if his liability to the owner were recognised as contractual (to a third party beneficiary). This has generally been answered affirmatively on the ground either that the duty the sub otherwise owed was qualified by the terms of his contract or that it would not be "just and reasonable" to impose a tort duty.[396]

A plaintiff's ability to plan against the risk of economic loss by resort to contract (including self-insurance) could explain the denial of a tort remedy not only in the preceding situations of interlocking (network) relations, typical of construction projects, but conceivably also in other cases where such an opportunity was practically available.[397]

389a. See Markesinis, *An Expanding Tort Law—The Price of a Rigid Contract Law*, 103 L.Q.R. 354 (1987); Law Com., Consulting Paper No. 121 (Priority of Contract) (1991).

390. *Greater Nottingham Co-op. v. Cementation* [1989] Q.B. 71 (employer v. subcontractor).

391. *Pacific Associates v. Baxter* [1990] Q.B. 993 (C.A.).

392. *Simaan v. Pilkington* [1988] Q.B. 758 (C.A.) (contractor v. sub-subcontractor).

393. *South Pacific Ins. v. N.Z. Security* (1991) 3 N.Z.B.R.C. 102, 301.

394. See above, n. 383.

395. E.g. *Junior Books v. Veitchi* [1983] A.C. 520 at 546; *Leigh & Sillivan v. Aliakmon* [1986] A.C. 785 at 817 per Lord Brandon.

396. *Norwich City v. Harvey* [1989] 1 W.L.R. 828 (C.A.); *Muirhead v. I.T.S.* [1986] Q.B. 507 (C.A.). In *Southern Water v. Carey* [1985] 2 All E.R. 1077 the clause was in the head, not the sub, contract: here the basis is plaintiff's assumption of risk. See Markesinis, 106 L.Q.R. 556 (1990) who, like Beyleveld & Brownsword, 54 Mod. L. Rev. 48 (1991), argues for modification of the privity rule.

397. The importance of contractual elements is stressed by Blom, *Interface between Tort and Contract*, in *The Paisley Papers* 139 (1991). But this rationale is hardly conformable with *Hedley Byrne*, which answered to a different drummer.

7. CONCURRENT DUTIES IN TORT AND CONTRACT

"There is no tort more likely to co-exist with breach of contract than negligence. In a great number of instances a contractor fails in what he has promised because he has acted incompetently."[398] Similarly, tortious and contractual duties[399] are concurrently owed by an employer to an employee, a bailor to a bailee, a carrier to a passenger, an occupier to a paying visitor.[400] At one time it was thought that such a defendant was answerable only to the promisee in privity and then only in contract and not in tort. Both propositions are at last overturned: The first, when it was held in *Donoghue v. Stevenson* (1932) that a contract duty to A did not preclude a tort duty to B, so that a manufacturer could henceforth incur liability for negligent injury to an ultimate consumer.[401] The second proposition, that a contract duty to the plaintiff excluded a tort duty to him, remained more recalcitrant. It commands attention because, despite the disappearance of the old forms of action and their procedural quirks, important distinctions remain which call for a decision whether the plaintiff's cause of action is ex contractu or ex delicto.[402] It may affect contributory negligence,[403] contribution among defendants,[404] the period and terminus a quo of statutes of limitation,[405] remoteness[406] and kind of damages,[407] and other matters.[408]

There are two opposing views.[409] One holds that tort has no role to play where the parties' relationship is governed by a contract between them, whether their obligations are expressly defined therein or implied by law; in particular, that it would be unfair to impose on the promisor any harsher consequences of tort liability. In the opposing view, the plaintiff should be free to choose from among concurrent causes of action, for why should he forfeit his tort rights merely by entering into a formal contract unless he actually agreed to limit or exclude them?

398. Winfield, *Province of the Law of Tort* (1931) 3. And—only if he has acted incompetently. Ordinarily contracts for services call only for care: e.g. *Thake v. Maurice* [1986] Q.B. 644 (failed sterilisation); below, p. 501.
399. Although it is not uncommon to speak of concurrent tort and contract *duties*, there is really only one duty generating alternative remedies or causes of action.
400. See Swanton, *Convergence of Tort and Contract* 12 Syd. L. Rev. 40 (1989).
401. See below.
402. The typical lapse into Latin may itself be a sign of judicial discomfort in dealing with this problem: Poulton, *Tort or Contract*, 82 L.Q.R. 346 at 356 (1966).
403. See below, p. 281.
404. See below, p. 261.
405. *Midland Bank v. Hett* [1979] Ch. 384 and *McLaren v. Fletcher* [1973] 2 N.Z.L.R. 100 (C.A.) illustrate different results in tort and contract claims: in tort the cause of action does not accrue until damage or discovery, in contract, on breach.
406. *Koufos v. Czarnikow* [1969] 1 A.C. 350 at 413, 422. Contract damages must have been "contemplated" by the parties, tort damages need only be "foreseeable" in the sense defined below, pp. 208ff. But see *Parsons v. Uttley Ingham* [1978] Q.B. 791 at 806-807.
407. E.g. damages for mental distress are recoverable only for breach of a contract to provide peace of mind, not even for wrongful dismissal: *Vivian v. Coca-Cola* [1984] 2 N.Z.L.R. 289; *Bliss v. S.E. Thames H.A.* [1985] I.R.L.R. 308. See Bridge, 62 Can. B. Rev. 323 (1984). Expectation damages are recoverable in contract, but only reliance damages in tort: see below, p. 637.
408. See Guest, *Tort and Contract*, 3 U. Mal. L. Rev. 191 (1961); Holyoak, *Tort and Contract after Junior Books*, 99 L.Q.R. 591 (1983).
409. Dividing also civil law countries: Weir, XI Int. Encycl. Comp. L. ch. 12 §24-29.

During the heyday of the forms of action, the plaintiff appears to have been free to choose whichever suited him best, but thereafter the view gained ground that only one claim, either tortious or contractual, could arise out of a particular set of facts, depending on the "substance", "gist" or "gravamen" of the claim. For example, physical damage resulting from misfeance was treated as a tort, as when a cleaner's negligence caused a chandelier to fall;[410] whereas economic losses were invariably associated with contract. This distinction was apt to subject doctors, dentists, carriers and other bailees to tort, but solicitors, accountants and stockbrokers to contract. Another distinction retained the ancient tort liability of the older professions and "common callings", but denied it to newcomers in the information business like solicitors, engineers and architects.

The last ten years have seen a decisive return to the "concurrent" approach[411] stimulated by the breakthrough in *Hedley Byrne*, which opened up a new field of tort liability for negligent information causing economic harm and thus vastly increased the situations in which a contractual undertaking was the source of the defendant's duty of reasonable care in performance.[412] If the plaintiff would have had a cause of action in tort had the work been performed gratuitously, the existence of a contract should not deprive him of that remedy. For it would be odd if a paying client were to be worse off than a non-paying one or some third party like the client's wife.

Accordingly, in cases of concurrent liability, the plaintiff (regardless of his pleading) may claim the benefit of such more favourable tort rules as damages for inconvenience and distress,[413] exemplary damages,[414] rules of remoteness,[415] contribution,[416] and the statute of limitations.[417] By the same token, he can no longer defeat a plea of contributory negligence "merely because of the ancient habiliments into which counsel may have managed to put the action".[418]

The plaintiff is relegated exclusively to his contractual claim only when he must rely on a specific provision in the contract,[419] as distinct from any duty of reasonable care implicit in the particular relationship. Nor can he escape any provision in the contract excluding or limiting liability for acts

410. *Jackson v. Mayfair Cleaners* [1952] 1 All E.R. 215; *Parsons v. Uttley Ingham* [1978] Q.B. 791 at 802 (Denning M.R.). This enjoys continuing support in the U.S.: Prosser, *Select Topics on Torts* ch. 7 (1954).
411. Starting with *Midland Bank v. Hett* [1979] Ch. 384 (solicitor); *Esso v. Mardon* [1976] Q.B. 801 (C.A.: landlord); *Central Trust v. Rafuse* [1986] 2 S.C.R. 147; semble, *Day v. Mead* [1987] 2 N.Z.L.R. 443; *Mouat v. Clark Boyce* [1992] 2 N.Z.L.R. 559 (C.A.).
412. For the tort-contract issue in precontractual representations: see below, p. 643.
413. *Brickhill v. Cooke* [1984] 3 N.S.W.L.R. 396 at 400-401 (C.A.); *Perry v. Phillips* [1982] 1 W.L.R. 1297 at 1302-3 (C.A.).
414. *Drane v. Evangelou* [1978] 1 W.L.R. 455 (C.A.) (pleaded as breach of right to quiet enjoyment).
415. *Brickhill v. Cooke* [1984] 3 N.S.W.L.R. 396.
416. *MacPherson v. Prunty* [1983] 1 V.R. 573 (F.C.).
417. *Moore v. Ferrier* [1988] 1 W.L.R. 267 (C.A.); *Central & E. Trust v. Rafuse* [1986] 2 S.C.R. 147 (solicitors).
418. *Queensbridge Motors v. Edwards* [1964] Tas. S.R. 93 at 97 per Crisp J. Below, p. 282.
419. As in *Jarvis v. Moy* [1936] 1 K.B. 399 (stockbroker flouting specific instructions). Or where the defendant merely failed to confer a benefit on the plaintiff, as distinct from making his position worse: *Midland Bank v. Hett* [1979] Ch. 384 suggests that this distinction is not always heeded.

performed thereunder, however he formulates his claim.[420] This priority of contract over tort applies not only to exclusion clauses and the like, but also precludes the imposition of a tort duty to deal with an aspect of the relation not expressly covered by the contract: unless a contractual term to the same effect can be implied, no tort duty can fill the gap.[421]

8. STATUTORY DUTIES

Duties may be prescribed by statute no less than by the common law. Difficulties arise where such a statute is in terms only directory or merely attaches a penal sanction, such as a fine, without specifically addressing the question of damages. Our law has been opposed to any general principle that would attach civil liability to the mere fact that the injury resulted from the commission of an illegal act.[422] There must be some more specific reason for conferring a private cause of action on anyone suffering injury.

As previously explained, according to the prevailing English view such reason must be found in a presumed statutory intent, difficult though it may be to discover in the absence of any statutory say-so. In practice such an intent is more readily attributed to statutes which prescribe specific rules of conduct for greater safety in industry and other situations where the common law already demands observance of reasonable care. Thereby the statutory prescription crystallises the appropriate standard and violation can be described as "statutory negligence". It was from this point of view that the question was previously discussed in the context of standards of care.[423]

Much more rarely has tort liability been ascribed to statutes which impose duties in situations where the common law does not require it. To give a penal statute such an effect would not just crystallise an accepted obligation of care but recognise a novel, "statutory duty". To do so, it has been argued, is improper because it would create new rights under colour of a statute which has stopped short of authorising them. Such, for example, would be the effect of statutes imposing an affirmative duty to provide public services like supplying gas[424] or water pressure for fire hydrants[425] or directing the payment of social welfare benefits,[426] where an additional reason for denying a civil remedy could be found in the judicial policy against interfering with discretionary functions of public bodies.[427] We have already seen that these and other concerns militate against the imposition of statutory duties even in more traditional areas. Prominent is

420. *Elder Dempster v. Paterson* [1924] A.C. 522 at 548; *Tai Hing v. Liu Chong Hing Bank* [1986] A.C. 80 at 107; *Central & E. Trust v. Rafuse* [1986] 2 S.C.R. 147 at 206.

421. *Greater Nottingham Co-op. v. Cementation* [1989] Q.B. 71; *Bank of Nova Scotia v. Hellenic Association* [1990] 1 Q.B. 818 at 900-903; *Canadian Pacific Hotels v. Bank of Montreal* [1987] 1 S.C.R. 711.

422. *Lonrho v. Shell* [1982] A.C. 173; below, p. 700. For opposing views, especially France, see *Intern. Encycl. Comp. L.* XI ch. 2, 74-77.

423. See above, pp. 124ff.

424. *Clegg, Parkinson v. Earby Gas Co.* [1896] 1 Q.B. 592. Contra: *Pease v. Eltham B.* [1962] N.Z.L.R. 437.

425. *Atkinson v. Newcastle Waterworks* (1877) 2 Ex. D. 441.

426. See *Jones v. Department of Employment* [1989] Q.B. 1 (C.A.).

427. See above, p. 156.

the unwillingness to do so in the case of open-ended (though safety related) prohibitions, such as against selling defective vehicles or contaminated grain, because it would replace fault with warranty liability.[428]

In a few cases, though, civil liability has been attached to violation of statutes in circumstances in which no common law duty of care had been recognised. Here, then, the effect of the statute was not merely to crystallise the standard of care, but also to establish an antecedent duty. This has been defended as a desirable exercise, in appropriate circumstances, of the plenary power of common law courts to develop the law in accordance with their view of public policy.[429] An example was the famous decision of the English Court of Appeal to hold a car owner liable for injury caused by someone he had allowed to drive without insurance cover in violation of statute.[430] In another, it allowed a claim against a local authority for failing to provide accommodation to a homeless person.[431] And in a third, a municipality was held liable for supplying polluted water, though the court reduced the duty to the exercise of all reasonable care.[432]

These decisions are all controversial on their factual merits; they also lack any guide as to why a duty was there recognised in contrast to other, very similar or even more deserving, cases where it was not.[433] This injects an element of arbitrariness.

Defences

Defences specified for criminal prosecutions under the statute are not necessarily applicable to civil actions. Excuse from criminal liability does not lessen the duty, which alone is the "given" for the purpose of civil liability. Thus where an industrial safety statute provided as a defence that the employer "took all precautions necessary to avoid the risk of injury to any person", it was held to be nonetheless a contravention entitling the injured worker to recover damages.[434]

Beyond that, contributory negligence provides a defence, nowadays by reducing damages in proportion to the claimant's share of responsibility.[435] In relation to employment accidents, though, the principal area for breach of statutory duty, the standard of care demanded from workers is greatly attenuated so as not to defuse the effect of the employer's statutory duty.[436] The defence of voluntary assumption of risk is altogether excluded in that context as it would violate public policy to permit workers to contract out of the statute's protection.[437]

A different theory

Some 19th century equity cases proceeded on a principle that an injunction could be claimed by a person who suffered damage to a property

428. E.g. *R. v. Saskatchewan Wheat Pool* [1983] 1 S.C.R. 205.
429. Buckley, *Liability in Tort for Breach of Statutory Duty*, 100 L.Q.R. 204 (1984).
430. *Monk v. Warby* [1935] 1 K.B. 75.
431. *Thornton v. Kirklees B.C.* [1979] Q.B. 626.
432. *Read v. Croydon Corp.* [1938] 4 All E.R. 631; above, p. 132.
433. Cf. e.g. *Phillips v. Britannia Laundry* [1923] 1 K.B. 539; *Clegg, Parkinson v. Earby Gas Co.* [1896] 1 Q.B. 592.
434. *Sovar v. Lane* (1967) 116 C.L.R. 397; *Potts v. Reid* [1943] A.C. 1 at 11.
435. See below, p. 275.
436. See below, p. 510.
437. *Wheeler v. New Merton Bd Mills* [1933] 2 K.B. 669 (C.A.).

interest of his by a crime. This was invoked against a bootleg recording of a live musical performance, prohibited by a fine.[438] In the famous case of *Lonrho v. Shell*,[439] however, the House of Lords repudiated the broader notion that anyone who suffered "special damage" as the result of a crime was entitled to recover; the earlier cases dealt "not with public rights created by statute but with public rights existing at common law", particularly claims for public nuisance on the highway.[440]

In a subsequent bootleg case the recording company also failed on the conventional ground that the statute was not intended to create a private cause of action, although the statutory purpose was undeniably to protect performers.[441] No reason was given other than the discredited one that a criminal penalty had been provided.

438. *Ex parte Island Records* [1978] Ch. 122 (C.A.).
439. [1982] A.C. 173 at 185.
440. See below, p. 700.
441. *R.C.A. Corp. v. Pollard* [1983] Ch. 135.

9

DAMAGE

1. DAMAGE DEFINED

Actual damage or injury[1] is a necessary element of tort liability for negligence. Unlike assault and battery or defamation, where violation of a mere dignitary interest like personal integrity or reputation is deemed sufficiently heinous to warrant redress, negligence is not actionable unless and until it results in damage to the plaintiff.

What qualifies as actionable damage is a question of policy largely defined by the "duty" rules considered in the preceding chapter.[2] The reason is that the concept is relative, dependent on the circumstances of the occasion. For example, while physical injury from external trauma is categorically included, liability for mental distress is more hedged, depending on whether it results from an external injury or mere mental processes, whether it is merely evanescent, whether the plaintiff was in the impact zone and so forth.[3] Similarly, economic loss is no longer absolutely foreclosed but has become actionable under controlled conditions.[4]

For merely threatened harm, an injunction but no claim for damages will lie.[5] Persons exposed to radiation or toxic chemicals must await the onset of injury if any, and even damages for cancerphobia or the cost of medical surveillance appear foreclosed.[6] In other words, merely creating a *risk* of injury is not actionable; injury must have become actual.[7] This may inhibit speculative claims but rather discredits the pretence that tort law seeks to discourage accident-prone behaviour.[8]

Since damage is an essential element of liability, no cause of action accrues *until* damage has occurred. The statute of limitation therefore begins to run from the time not of the culpable conduct but its injurious consequences. This may make it more attractive to sue in tort rather than contract (where the cause of action accrues on breach and nominal damages are recoverable even in the absence of actual loss). Thus the purchaser of a defective product injured many years after buying it may by then have lost

1. Common lawyers generally use "injury" as synonymous with "damage". Only rarely is it used in the wider sense of *any* violation of a legal right, including injuria absque damno, as in trespass to the person.
2. By contrast, French lawyers treat this question comprehensively under "dommage".
3. See above, pp. 159ff.
4. See above, pp. 177ff.
5. E.g. *Van Win v. Eleventh Mirontron* [1986] V.R. 484 (claim struck out).
6. Such damages are increasingly allowed in American toxic tort litigation: e.g. *Woodrow Sterling v. Velsicol*, 855 F. 2d 1188 (1988); 83 Nw. U.L. Rev. 512 (1989).
7. See *Wilsher v. Essex A.H.A.* [1988] A.C. 1074; below, p. 199.
8. Hence Calabresi's advocacy of ex ante probability as a better deterrent: *Concerning Cause and the Law of Torts*, 43 U. Chi. L. Rev. 69 (1975).

his cause of action against the seller for breach of warranty, but could still be in time to sue him or the manufacturer for negligence.[9] This advantage has become more available as a result of two developments already noted, viz. the plaintiff's option to sue in tort for negligent performance of an obligation undertaken by contract[10] and the extension of negligence liability for economic loss.[11]

But what precisely qualifies as damage in cases of bodily injury or property damage, and when does it occur so as to start the limitation period running? According to the English rule, disabling symptoms need not have appeared nor injurious consequences become discoverable; "the secret onset" of the disease or some physical change in property is sufficient. For example, asbestosis often remains undiagnosed for many years after exposure, yet the injury is deemed to occur as soon as a lesion would have been discoverable by x-ray.[12] Similarly, a complaint against the designers of a chimney was statute barred because time ran not from discovery of the first substantial cracks but their earlier formation.[13] The selection of this occurrence not only lacks scientific basis but is also difficult to apply. It does postpone claims after an exposure until threatened injury has become actual and thereby defeats speculation about possible future damage;[14] it also affords the plaintiff some extra time in cases of latent injury. On the other hand, the victim may lose his cause of action before becoming aware of it. In order to avoid this inequity, the English rule was subsequently reversed by statute with respect to property damage;[15] nor was it followed in Canada[16] or New Zealand.[17] In case of personal injury[18] modern statutes either authorise courts to extend the period when it is "just and reasonable"[19] or postpone its running until the plaintiff has the means of knowing that his (personal) injuries are significant and attributable to the defendant.[20]

2. CAUSATION

I. The Problem

Not only must there be damage (injury); it must have been *caused* by the defendant's fault. Causation has plagued courts and scholars more than any

9. See *Watson v. Winget* 1960 S.C. (H.L.) 92 (despite "within three years of the act, neglect or default").
10. See above, p. 187.
11. See above, p. 177.
12. *Cartledge v. Jopling* [1963] A.C. 758. Cf. *Footner v. B.H. Smelters* (1983) 33 S.A.S.R. 58 (mesothelioma latent much longer than asbestosis).
13. *Pirelli v. Faber* [1983] 2 A.C. 1. Criticised: Todd, *A Defence of the "Discoverability" Test*, 10 N.Z.U.L. Rev. 311 (1983); Stapleton, *The Gist of Negligence I*, 104 L.Q.R. 213 (1988).
14. See above.
15. *Latent Damage Act* 1986, subject to a "long stop" of 15 years from breach. Also *Limitation Act* 1985 (A.C.T.), s. 40. See Mullany, *Reform of Law of Latent Damage*, 54 Mod. L. Rev. 216, 349 (1991).
16. *Kamloops v. Nielsen* [1984] 2 S.C.R. 2; *Central & Eastern Trust v. Rafuse* [1986] 2 S.C.R. 147.
17. *Askin v. Knox* [1989] 1 N.Z.L.R. 248 (C.A.).
18. The following statutes except S.A. and N.T. apply only to personal injury.
19. Limitation Acts of Vic. (1983), S.A. (1975) and Tas. (1974); A.C.T. (1985); N.T. (1981) "thinks fit"; Eng. (1980) "equitable".
20. *Limitation Act* 1980 (Eng.) ss 11, 14.

other topic in the law of torts.[21] Some of the perplexity that has been experienced is due to the undifferentiated use of the word "cause", accompanied by such adjectives as "legal", "proximate" or "remote", in dealing with two rather distinct inquiries. The first involves the "factual" question whether the relation between the defendant's breach of duty and the plaintiff's injury is one of cause and effect in accordance with "scientific" or "objective" notions of physical sequence. If such a causal relation does not exist, that puts an end to the plaintiff's case: to impose liability for loss to which the defendant's conduct has not *in fact* contributed would be incompatible with the principle of individual responsibility on which the law of torts has been traditionally based.

The second problem involves the question whether, or to what extent, the defendant should have to answer for the consequences which his misconduct has actually helped to produce. As a matter of practical politics, some limitation must be placed upon legal responsibility, because the consequences of an act theoretically stretch into infinity. There must be a reasonable connection between the harm threatened and the harm done. This inquiry, unlike the first, presents a much larger area of choice in which legal policy and accepted value judgments must be the final arbiter of what balance to strike between the claim to full reparation for the loss suffered by an innocent victim of another's culpable conduct and the excessive burden that would be imposed on human activity if a wrongdoer were held to answer for all consequences of his default.

II. Cause-in-Fact

The first task, then, in attributing legal responsibility for a particular injury is to ascertain whether the defendant's culpable conduct was a causally relevant factor. Every event or occurrence is the result of many conditions that are jointly sufficient to produce it. This complex set of conditions includes all antecedents, active or passive, creative or receptive, that were factors actually involved in producing the consequence. In particular, it embraces both "causes" and what are commonly called mere causal "conditions"; for that distinction, whatever its value in the context of the later inquiry into "proximate" cause, does not correspond to any functional difference as regards the de facto relation between antecedents and their consequents. A fire ignited in a wastepaper basket is, in this sense, caused not only by the dropping of a lighted match, but also by the presence of combustible material and oxygen, a failure of the cleaner to empty the basket and so forth. Fortunately, in legal inquiries it does not matter if we are unable to identify all, or even most, of the individual elements which constitute the complex set of conditions jointly sufficient to produce a given consequence. The reason is that we are usually interested only to investigate whether one, two or perhaps three specific conditions (for example

21. See generally the grand monograph by Hart & Honoré, *Causation in the Law* (2nd ed. 1985). Comparative: Honoré, XI Int. Encycl. Comp. L. ch. 7 (Causation and Remoteness of Damage).

identified acts or omissions by the defendant or other participants in the accident) were causally relevant.

Whether a particular condition qualifies as a causally relevant factor will depend on whether it was *necessary* to complete a set of conditions jointly *sufficient* to account for the given ocurrence.[22] Hence the traditional preoccupation with "necessary" condition or "causa sine qua non" as the touchstone of causality.

The "but for" test

The so-called "but for" test enjoys almost universal acceptance as a key for ascertaining causal relation in the above-mentioned sense.[23] It is at once relatively simple to apply and, allowing for certain complications, to be noted later, theoretically satisfactory.[24] The formula postulates that the defendant's fault *is* a cause of the plaintiff's harm if such harm would not have occurred without (but for) it. Thus a bather would not have drowned if a lifeguard had been present;[25] the customer would not have fallen down the stairs if there had been a handrail; nor would he have suffered the brain haemorrhage if he had not received a blow on the forehead.[26] Conversely, it is *not* a cause if the harm would have happened just the same, fault or no fault. A doctor's delay in attending a patient is causally irrelevant if the latter was in any event doomed,[27] as is an omission to warn if the person endangered was in no position to heed it.[28]

The objection is sometimes raised that the question is not what might have happened, but what did happen.[29] But the hypothetical test is really indispensable, since direct perception cannot solve at all causality of omissions (non-events) and, anyway, causation is based on inference from experience of how things *generally* happen. Such causal generalisations rest on the belief that a cause is necessary for the occurrence of a consequence, that "but for" it the consequence would not have happened. It is reinforced by the basic notion of torts that injury could have been avoided by acting differently.

The hypothetical inquiry of what would otherwise have happened is linked to the tortious aspect of the defendant's conduct, not his conduct in general. What we are interested in is whether his negligence rather than his

22. This test is based on the concept of causation by the philosopers David Hume and John Stuart Mill, and systematically elaborated for legal purposes by Hart & Honoré, *Causation in the Law* (2nd ed. 1985). See esp. Wright, *Causation in Tort Law*, 73 Cal. L. Rev. 1735 (1985).
23. With doubtful reservations from some members of the High Court: see *March v. Stramore* (1991) 171 C.L.R. 506.
24. In addition to the preceding see Becht & Miller, *Factual Causation* (1961); *Cooper-Stephenson & Saunders* ch. 12; Williams, *Causation in the Law* [1961] Cam. L.J. 62.
25. *Haft v. Lone Palm Hotel* 478 P. 2d 465 (Cal. 1970).
26. *Hole v. Hocking* [1962] S.A.S.R. 128; cf. *Blackstock v. Foster* [1958] S.R. (N.S.W.) 341.
27. *Hotson v. East Berks A.H.A.* [1987] A.C. 750.
28. *Davis v. Bunn* (1936) 56 C.L.R. 246. Other examples: *I.C.I.A.N.Z. v. Murphy* (1973) 47 A.L.J.R. 122; *Tichener v. B.R.B.* [1983] 1 W.L.R. 1427; *Hopewell v. Baranyay* [1962] V.R. 311; *Knight v. Laurie* [1961] W.A.R. 174. Statutory violation: see below, n. 36.
29. E.g. Thode, *Indefensible Use of the Hypothetical Case to Determine Cause in Fact*, 46 Tex. L. Rev. 423 (1968).

general conduct was the cause.[30] Suppose the defendant hands a loaded gun to a child who drops it on his foot.[31] What makes the conduct negligent is that the gun was loaded, but that was not the cause of the injury which would have happened just the same if the gun had been unloaded. Again, suppose the defendant leaves a poisonous substance around, which is later moved close to a flame and explodes. The defendant's negligence is not causal because the explosion would have happened just the same if the substance had not been poisonous. The fact that in either case the injury would have been avoided if the defendant had not handed the gun to the child or left the poison around, does not make it a consequence of the defendant's *negligence*.[32]

This principle finds frequent illustration also where the defendant's fault consists in violation of a statutory duty. Suppose that a motorist exceeding the speed limit hits a toddler who dashes suddenly into the road. The question to be asked is whether the collision would have been avoided if he had proceeded at the maximum allowable speed. Or suppose that a decayed tree falls on a speeding car. The question is—would the accident have been avoided if, when passing the tree, the car had been driving more slowly.[33] In all these instances, denial of causality saves the defendant from liability for merely being engaged in unlawful conduct, unless the accident was caused by whatever made his conduct negligent, that is, by diminished control. An alternative, non-causal, explanation is to say that these accidents did not fall within the risk which it was the purpose of the rule to obviate.[34]

The hypothetical "what if" inquiry, whether compliance with the law by the defendant would have averted the harm, not infrequently fails to elicit a confident answer, being a matter of inference rather than capable of direct proof.[35] It is compounded by the fact that the standard of proof, which ordinarily rests on the plaintiff, is the balance of probability (more probable than not). The onus of proof might well have been pushed on defendants once their negligence has been established, and in case of breach of statutory duty this solution was briefly favoured but later dismissed.[36] Even less did reducing awards proportionally to the degree of (less than 51 per cent) causal probability gain support.[37] Forensic reality, however, may help, for whatever the technical allocation and standard of proof, the resolution of causal uncertainty is apt to be influenced by the strength of disapproval of the defendant's fault. It militates most strongly against intentional wrongdoers[38] and such reprehensible carelessness as driving without working brakes or failure to protect employees against obvious

30. See esp. Becht & Miller, *Factual Causation* (1961) §2.2, calling for a "parallel series" by changing the actor's actual conduct just enough to make it conform to the law.
31. *Rest 2d* §281; ill. 2.
32. For application of the same principle to strict liability see below, p. 329.
33. But speeding might make a difference if the tree falls in front of the car, as in *Quinn v. Scott* [1965] 1 W.L.R. 1004.
34. See below, p. 215.
35. E.g. *Barnes v. Hay* (1988) 12 N.S.W.L.R. 337 at 350-356; *Alexander v. Cambridge Credit* (1987) 9 N.S.W.L.R. 310.
36. *Bonnington v. Wardlaw* [1956] A.C. 613. See below, p. 199.
37. See below, p. 226 (loss of chance).
38. See above.

risks,[39] tapering down to such comparatively "weak" violations as medical misjudgments.[40]

Alternative sufficient causes

In some cases, which have been found most perplexing, more than one set of sufficient conditions can account for a single injury. Here the simplified "but for" test must make way for the complete causal inquiry, previously formulated, whether the particular condition (the defendant's negligence) was a necessary element of a set of antecedent actual conditions that was sufficient for the occurrence of the consequence (the injury).[41]

Most frequent is the case where another factor, itself sufficient, combined with or duplicated the effect of the defendant's act to jointly produce the injury, as when two persons simultaneously approach a leaking gas pipe with lighted candles or several fires merge and destroy a house.[42] Here the proxy "but for" test could lead to the conclusion, affronting common sense, that neither was the cause because the same injury would have ocurred without one or the other. If both factors were culpable, it would be idiotic for the victim to be denied redress while each defendant was endlessly shifting the blame to the other; moreover, it would be whimsical if a fully sufficient cause did not qualify when a less than sufficient cause does. This absurdity is avoided by affirming that each actor was a cause because his conduct was necessary for a set of sufficient antecedent conditions. The co-existence of two such conditions does not negate the causality of either.

The same test confirms that, in a case of pollution from several sources, all can be regarded as causal, even if none was necessary nor independently sufficient for the injury. Suppose that five units of pollution were necessary and sufficient and that each of seven defendants discharged one unit. Although each defendant's unit was neither necessary nor sufficient, it was necessary for the sufficiency of *a* set of conditions that included *any* four others.[43]

In a second type of case the effects of one factor are pre-empted by another. A kills B, but had he not done so C would have killed him; a negligent explosion razes a house doomed to destruction by an impending earthquake. In both cases, the first factor was necessary to complete a set of sufficient *actual* conditions which pre-empted the second: the first was causal, the second not. Policy considerations may, however, affect the measure of damages.

Thus in a celebrated American case a boy fell from a bridge to almost certain death on the rocks below but was instead electrocuted on the defendant's negligently suspended wires. Without denying the causality of

39. E.g. *McGee v. N.C.B.*, below, p. 199.
40. E.g. *Wilsher v. Essex A.H.A.* [1988] A.C. 1074; below, p. 199. See Malone, *Ruminations on Cause-in-Fact*, 9 Stan. L. Rev. 60 (1958).
41. See Wright, 73 Cal. L. Rev. 1735 at 1788-1803 (1985) (reviewing the abundant literature and suggesting the following solution).
42. *Anderson v. Minn. Rly* 179 N.W. 45 (Minn. 1908) (fires); *Corey v. Havener* 65 N.E. 69 (Mass. 1902) (motorcyclists frightening horse); *Barker v. Permanent* [1983] 2 Qd R. 561 (exposure to two chemicals).
43. *Crossley v. Lightowler* (1867) 2 Ch. D. 478.

that negligence, the court discounted the award to the value of his limited life expectancy at that moment.[44] The same principle was applied in a later English case[45] when a man with varicose veins contracted an ulcer as a result of a tortious graze which required an operation to strip them. His award for loss of earnings during convalescence was substantially reduced because of the probability that he would have had to undergo a similar operation in a few years' time. These decisions do not really go far beyond the familiar principle in personal injury and fatal accident cases of making allowance for the fact that the particular victim's life span happened to be shorter than normal because of some fatal disease, much in the same way as account is taken of advanced age or, in the case of property, its dilapidation.[46] The only difference is that in these latter situations the value-reducing factor had already taken its toll, whereas in the first two it was still in prospect, though already in operation and fairly imminent when the defendant caused the harm.[47]

Supervening causes

Additional complexities arise in cases of successive and causally unrelated injuries,[48] as when the plaintiff is first injured by A and later by B in such a way that the second injury would have sufficed to cause the damage inflicted by the first, for example when his earning capacity is first reduced by 50 per cent and later destroyed completely. It is common ground that events subsequent to an accident but before trial may not be ignored in their bearing on damage assessment;[49] hence the effect of B's injury calls for consideration. There are three possibilities: (1) to limit A's liability to the period before B's intervention on the ground that thereafter the loss was "obliterated" or "overwhelmed" by B. However, if B were only responsible for the additional 50 per cent on the familiar principle that a tortfeasor takes his victim as he finds him—in this case, already 50 per cent disabled—it would entail the shocking result that the plaintiff was worse off than if he had not been tortiously injured by A at all. This dilemma, however, could be overcome by making B liable for the total subsequent loss on the theory that his tort deprived the plaintiff of his remedy against A.[50] (2) The second alternative is to continue holding A responsible for the first 50 per cent and B only for the extra. (3) A third solution would impose

44. *Dillon v. Twin State Gas* 163 Atl. 111 (N.H. 1932). See Peaslee, *Multiple Causation and Damage*, 47 Harv. L. Rev. 1127 (1934); Williams, *Causation in the Law* [1961] Can. L.J. 62 at 75-79. Criticised by Carpenter, *Concurrent Causation*, 83 U. Pa. L. Rev. 941 (1935).
45. *Cutler v. Vauxhall Motors* [1971] 1 Q.B. 418 (C.A.); *Smith v. Cawdle Fen Comm.* [1938] 4 All E.R. 64 at 71; *Zumeris v. Testa* [1972] V.R. 839 (F.C.).
46. E.g. *Watts v. Rake* (1960) 108 C.L.R. 158; *Muio v. MacGillivray* [1962] Qd R. 554 and *Hole v. Hocking* [1962] S.A.S.R. 128 (pre-accident disease); *Performance Cars v. Abraham* [1962] 1 Q.B. 33 (dented Rolls Royce).
47. In contrast to the school example of the passenger who missed the Titanic because of the cabdriver's negligence. See also the pre-existing disposition cases, below, n. 100.
48. Aggravation of injury by a later event, tortious or non-tortious, which would not have occurred but for the first may raise an issue of remoteness but not of causation: below, pp. 204ff.
49. See below, p. 228.
50. Thus the C.A. in *Baker v. Willoughby* [1970] A.C. 467; adopted by *Griffiths v. Commonwealth* (1983) 50 A.C.T.R. 7. Lord Pearson (at 496-497) considered such loss too remote.

joint and several liability on both A and B for the continuing injury just as if their contributions had been simultaneous instead of successive.[51]

In the controversial case of *Baker v. Willoughby*, the English Court of Appeal espoused the first, but the House of Lords the second solution.[52] In 1964 the plaintiff suffered a severe permanent injury to his leg as a result of the defendant's negligent driving; in 1967 he was shot in the same leg in a hold-up, when his leg had to be amputated. The House decided that the defendant's responsibility did not cease after the amputation but remained a concurrent cause of the plaintiff's loss, in effect adopting solution (2). But how could this be reconciled with the established practice of diminishing damages in the light of later vicissitudes like a widow's remarriage? The difference lay in distinguishing between a later injury or event which either reduces the existing disability or shortens its period and one that leaves the original disability undiminished. To say that the amputation relieved the plaintiff of his stiff leg lost sight of the fact that his claim was for reduced earning capacity which had not been obliterated, but rather increased, by the amputation; only future pain due to expected further degeneration of the leg might have been brought to an end.

A similar solution has been applied to property damage. For example, when a ship suffers two successive collisions, each rendering her unseaworthy, and repairs are carried out simultaneously, the first must bear the cost of the delay and cannot take advantage of the delay which repair of the second would have necessitated.[53] Where a car had its fender dented but before the repair could be carried out was damaged in the same spot by the defendant, the latter escaped responsibility for the cost of respraying because he caused in this respect no additional loss:[54] the defendant had to take his victim as he found him, for better or worse.

The House of Lords later disavowed its concurrent-cause approach in *Baker v. Willoughby* and preferred to explain the decision as justified at best by the perceived inequity of letting the victim fall between two tortfeasors.[55] It had no bearing on a supervening cause of "innocent" origin, as in *Jobling v. Associated Dairies*[56] where the plaintiff first sustained a back injury in an industrial accident and was later found suffering from an unconnected condition which proved totally disabling. To ignore the later event would have been incompatible with the established

51. Favoured by *Cooper-Stephenson & Saunders*, 662-672 and obviously the most favourable solution for plaintiffs, being proof against either defendant's insolvency.
52. [1970] A.C. 467. See McGregor, 33 Mod. L. Rev. 378 (1970); Wagner, *Successive Causes*, 10 Osg. H.L.J. 369 (1972). Accord: *Nicholson v. Walker* (1979) 21 S.A.S.R. 481; *Hicks v. Cooper* (1973) 41 D.L.R. (3d) 454 (Ont. C.A.).
53. *The Haversham Grange* [1905] P. 307 (C.A.); *Sunrise Co. v. The "Lake Winnipeg"* (1991) 77 D.L.R. (4th) 701 (S.C.C.). (The dissent opted for the more equitable third solution: sharing for the period after the second collision). See *McGregor* §§1015-19.
54. *Performance Cars v. Abraham* [1962] 1 Q.B. 33. Also *Taylor v. Auto Trade* [1972] N.Z.L.R. 102 (successive subsidences while property in different hands).
55. The distinction was followed in *Nominal Defendant v. Pollard* (unreported, N.S.W. C.A., 29 May 1982). Would it apply also if the second tortfeasor were uninsured or untraceable? Should the plaintiff carry the burden of proving that the second cause was tortious? In any event, how can the distinction be justified in terms of causation? See criticism in *Nilon v. Bezzina* [1988] Qd R. 420. For a justification see Rosenthal, 41 U. Tor. L.J. 600 (1991).
56. [1982] A.C. 794. See Kidd, 56 A.L.J. 389 (1982).

principle of discounting vicissitudes for non-compensable events: here the vicissitude of a developing disease had indeed become a fact.[57] Moreover, it would have involved a distinction between pre-existing and subsequent conditions, since (as we have seen) the first are now taken into discount. Such a distinction is difficult to justify both theoretically and because it is impracticable in view of the difficulties of definition and proof.[58]

Burden of proof

In some instances it will be difficult to segregate the effect of alternative causes, concurrent or successive. If one is innocent and the other guilty, it would be tempting to require the guilty defendant to carry the burden of proving for what damage he is not responsible. This solution, however, is no longer open to English courts. In one case of concurrent causes[59] the plaintiff contracted pneumoconiosis from inhalation of dust from two sources at work, one innocent in the sense that his employer was not negligent with respect to it, the other guilty. The court upheld a judgment for the plaintiff, though not on the ground that the defendant had failed to prove that the guilty dust had caused the disease. Rather it concluded from the evidence that the guilty dust had made a material contribution to the disease and that this was sufficient to sustain the award. In other words, the two causes were cumulative rather than alternative.

The same principle was applied to successive causes, when the plaintiff contracted dermatitis which might have been caused by brick dust adhering to his sweaty skin during work (for which his employer was not negligent) or from negligently failing to provide washing facilities so that he had to cycle home with his face still caked with dust. Lord Wilberforce seemed willing to shift the burden of proof to the defendant whose negligence had created a mere *risk of the injury*,[60] but as later interpreted, the plaintiff's recovery could only be sustained because, both risks being of the same kind (dust), it could be inferred that the two causes operated cumulatively in causing the dermatitis.[61] Although in these cases the defendant had not caused the whole of the damage, the all-or-nothing principle entitled him to recover the full amount of his loss rather than merely one reduced by the probable contribution of the other cause.[62]

On the other hand, where the only choice is between two alternative causes, one guilty, the other innocent, the plaintiff will fail unless he can prove on a balance of probabilities that the defendant's negligence created not merely a risk of injury, but the injury itself. This was impossible when it remained unclear whether a baby's blindness had been caused by its

57. See Borrowdale, *Vicissitudes in Anglo-Australian Perspective*, 32 I.C.L.Q. 651 (1983). The supervening injury need not be proven "more probable than not"; the chance, if substantial, will be discounted: *Malec v. Hutton* (1990) 169 C.L.R. 638, below, p. 227.
58. E.g. it would be quite arbitrary to date the condition only from the time it was first discovered, as the trial judge did in *Jobling v. Assoc. Dairies* [1982] A.C. 794.
59. *Bonnington Castings v. Wardlaw* [1956] A.C. 613. Contrast *Wintle v. Conaust* [1989] V.R. 951 (F.C.) where only one exposure from among several could have triggered the disease.
60. *McGhee v. N.C.B.* [1973] 1 W.L.R. 1 at 6 (H.L.).
61. *Wilsher v. Essex A.H.A.* [1988] A.C. 1074 at 1086-90.
62. *Cf. Hotson v. East Berks. H.A.* [1987] A.C. 750: see below, p. 227.

premature birth or by the doctor's excessive administration of oxygen.[63] Should the same apply where both of two alternative causes are negligent?[64] Canadian and American decisions have cast the burden on each to exculpate himself if he can, as when two hunters fired simultaneously but quite independently in the same direction and the plaintiff was hit by a single pellet.[65] Revulsion against letting an innocent victim of undoubted negligence fall between two guilty tortfeasors has, as already noted,[66] also led to the conclusion that a negligent actor is not absolved by a later negligent (as distinct from an innocent) act which could have caused the same injury.

III. Concurring Causes

The law does not excuse a defendant from liability for a consequence merely because other causal factors for which he is not responsible were also necessary to produce it. As we have seen, every event is the result of a complex set of (jointly sufficient) conditions, and if a defendant were allowed to escape because his conduct, unaided by other factors, would not alone have produced the harm, no plaintiff would ever be compensated. Liability is not necessarily precluded even by the presence of contributory causes which involve the wrongdoing of others. If two negligent drivers collide and injure a pedestrian, one is as accountable as the other. Indeed, responsibility may ensue even for loss caused by thc acts of two or more parties each of which, standing alone, would not be wrongful at all. If, for example, several defendants create a noise,[67] cause an obstruction[68] or pollute a stream[69] so as to amount in the aggregate to a nuisance, they are all separately liable,[70] notwithstanding that they were acting independently of each other and the act of each would have been harmless by itself.

Usually the interaction of several, though independent, wrongful acts produces a single indivisible result. They may have been simultaneous, as when two cars collide injuring a passenger; or successive as where one car is dangerously parked and another piles into it. The resulting harm (to which both contributed) being indivisible, each will be answerable for all the

63. *Wilsher v. Essex A.H.A.* [1988] A.C. 1074. *Farrell v. Snell* [1990] 2 S.C.R. 311 avoided the result by relaxing the burden of proof.
64. In *Fitzgerald v. Lane* [1987] Q.B. 781 the C.A. shifted the burden of proof on a view of *McGhee* since repudiated in *Wilsher*. The Lords evidently viewed the case as one of cumulative causation.
65. *Cook v. Lewis* [1951] S.C.R. 830; *Woodward v. Begbie* (1961) 31 D.L.R. (2d) 22; *Summers v. Tice* 199 P. 2d 1 (Cal. 1948); 5 A.L.R. 2d 91; *Civil Liabilities Act* 1961 (Eire) s. 11(3); *Rest 2d* §433 B. A fortiori, where both were insured by the same fund: Tunc, 1963 Rev. trim. dr. civ. 555. Should contributory negligence disqualify the plaintiff (*Lange v. Bennett* (1963) 41 D.L.R. (2d) 691) instead of merely reducing his recovery? Probabilistic causation was taken to extremes in *Sindell v. Abbott Labs* 607 P. 2d 924 (Cal. 1980). See Fleming, *Probabilistic Causation in Tort Law*, 68 Can. B. Rev. 661 (1989).
66. See above, p. 198.
67. *Lambton v. Mellish* [1894] 3 Ch. 163.
68. *Thorpe v. Brumfitt* (1873) L.R. 8 Ch. App. 650.
69. *Duke of Buccleuch v. Cowan* (1866) 5 Macph. 214; *Pride of Derby v. British Celanese* [1952] 1 All E.R. 1326.
70. At least if each was aware of what the other was doing and his contribution was more than just negligible (de minimis). See also *Rookes v. Barnard* [1963] 1 Q.B. 623 at 633.

damage (in solidum[71]), though the plaintiff is of course not entitled to more than a single satisfaction of his claim.[72] If one of them makes good the loss, he may today have recourse against the other for contribution in an amount which the court deems just and equitable, having regard to his share of responsibility for the damage.[73] But such eventual contribution among the tortfeasors is an internal matter between themselves, which in no way impairs the plaintiff's claim to full compensation from each.[74]

The effect of several causes may be cumulative in the sense that each independently contributed a share to the aggregate damage. If it is impossible to segregate their effect, each is liable for the whole damage. Thus when a worker suffered pneumoconiosis from inhalation of dust from two sources for only one of which the employer was responsible, he nevertheless recovered for the whole of his injury.[75] Nor does it matter in such a case that the causes were successive rather than concurrent, as when the plaintiff suffered injury to his spine in two separate accidents but their respective contributions could not be segregated.[76] That the defendant is held for the whole damage, though having contributed to only part, can be explained more easily on pragmatic than causal grounds, seeing that the plaintiff might go empty-handed if compelled to prove the precise amount allocatable to each cause.

Apportionable damage

By contrast, where each of several defendants causes only part of the total damage and it is practically feasible to split up the aggregate of loss and attribute identifiable parts to each of them, liability will ordinarily be confined to that portion for which each is separately responsible. Thus if a victim's leg is first injured in one accident and as the result of a later accident has to be amputated, the first defendant is liable only for the original injury, the second only for the additional loss.[77]

Again, some elements of the injury may be separable, but not all: for example, where several identifiable fractures sustained in a chain collision lead to psychosomatic complications, or separate publications of a libel in

71. Hence known also as the principle of solidary liability.
72. See below, p. 258.
73. See below, pp. 259ff.
74. *Speirs v. Caledonian Collieries* [1957] S.R. N.S.W. 483; *Andrews v. Lake* [1961] V.R. 458; *Parkland v. Stetar* [1975] 2 S.C.R. 884. The course taken in *Pride of Derby v. British Celanese* [1952] 1 All E.R. 1326 of apportioning the loss against each defendant is unwarranted because it may unfairly prejudice a plaintiff if one of them is insolvent. (Aliter, if plaintiff is also contributorily negligent: see below, p. 275.) The only recognised exception exists in actions by the owner of cargo or property on board a *delinquent* vessel involved in a maritime collision (but not in actions for personal injury or death or for property damage to or on an innocent vessel): see Williams *Joint Torts* §8.
75. *Bonnington Castings v. Wardlaw* [1956] A.C. 613.
76. *Nilon v. Bezzina* [1988] Qd R. 420 (F.C.).
77. See *Baker v. Willoughby* [1970] A.C. 467 (above, n. 52); *Berns v. Campbell* (1974) 59 D.L.R. (3d) 44 (overlapping injuries). The first may exceptionally incur responsibility for the second accident as well, e.g. by negligently leaving the victim exposed to the risk of being struck again before being removed to safety (*Evans v. Parberry* (1969) 92 W.N. (N.S.W.) 146) or by causing an injury which is aggravated by negligent medical care: see below, p. 221.

different journals with a distinct reading public combine in causing the plaintiff anguish and humiliation.[78]

Apportionment is, of course, equally proper where a separable part of the damage is attributable to an innocent rather than a culpable cause. Thus, a motorist who faultlessly knocks down a pedestrian but thereafter fails to apply his brakes promptly, will be answerable only for those injuries due to his subsequent failure to stop in time.[79] If an embankment improperly diverts floodwater upon neighbouring land, the defendant is not liable for so much of the damage as would have been caused by some of the water reaching it in any event.[80] Finally, apportionment may be possible even between a plaintiff and defendant, as when the former's own carelessness contributed to some, but not all, of his injuries.[81]

Whether injury is susceptible to apportionment seems to depend on pragmatic rather than purely theoretical considerations. For example, the tendency has been to apportion in cases of nuisance where the harm, though intermingled, is yet capable of division on a rational basis.[82] Thus each defendant was held responsible only for an apportioned amount corresponding to his share in the damage: where a river was polluted by effluent from three separate sources,[83] land flooded due to the obstruction of a stream by two weirs,[84] a herd savaged in successive raids by different dogs[85] or crops trampled by trespassing cattle belonging to several owners.[86] In a case of hearing loss over two periods, the earlier innocent, the court preferred a rough quantification of the guilty share rather than hold the defendant liable for the whole injury.[87] Since the legislative introduction of contribution among tortfeasors,[88] these decisions are less compelling.

3. PROXIMATE CAUSE

That the defendant's negligence has been established as a causal factor of the injury does not necessarily suffice for legal liability. All systems of compensation, however ambitious, have their limits in respect of the class of beneficiaries and the type of relevant losses (no less than the monetary size of awards), in view of the practical need to draw a line somewhere so that the cost will not crush those who have to foot the bill. If this is true

78. *Dingle v. Associated Newspapers* [1961] 2 Q.B. 162 at 189-190.
79. *Middleton v. Melbourne Tramway* (1913) 16 C.L.R. 572; *Thompson v. Smiths Shiprepairers* [1984] Q.B. 405.
80. *Workman v. Gt N. Rly* (1863) 32 L.J.Q.B. 279; *Tate & Lyle v. G.L.C.* [1983] 2 A.C. 509; *Re Armstrong* [1952] V.L.R. 187.
81. See below, p. 280.
82. This accords with American authority: *Rest 2d* §433A, comment *d*.
83. *Pride of Derby v. British Celanese* [1952] 1 All E.R. 1326, though based on unsupportable reasoning. But where pollution from three sources killed two cows, Scots law not surprisingly declined to apportion: *Fleming v. Gemmill* 1908 S.C. 340. *Michie v. National Steel* 495 F. 2d 213 (1974) applied liability in solidum against three polluters.
84. *Bank View Mill v. Nelson Corp.* [1942] 2 All E.R. 477 at 483.
85. *Piper v. Winnifrith* (1917) 34 T.L.R. 108. Unless the dogs acted jointly: *Arneil v. Paterson* [1931] A.C. 560; *Lankshear v. Fair* [1930] N.Z.L.R. 347.
86. *Allen v. Popika* [1946] 3 D.L.R. 783.
87. *Gray v. Smiths Shiprepairers* [1984] Q.B. 405.
88. See below, p. 260.

even of such comprehensive social security schemes as workers' compensation[89] and social welfare,[90] moderation is the more imperative for any system of compensation like the common law, which purports to place liability on individuals rather than on society as a whole, lest they be saddled with more than a fair share of the social cost of accidents. Liability for negligence, in particular, has been traditionally geared to the individualistic concept of fault, and the limitations on legal responsibility inevitably reflect a policy of keeping a rough correlation between what made the defendant's conduct culpable and what consequences he shall be answerable for. Yet as insurance and loss distribution are attaining greater prominence in the allocation of risk, the fault criterion is bound to diminish in appeal not only on the question of when to attach liability, but also for how much. Correspondingly, limitations on recovery come to assume a more functional orientation, having regard to the kind of losses that are normally incident to the enterprise in question and that could be more economically absorbed by it than by someone else.[91]

In the last resort, the practical task of drawing the line where recovery should cease is one which defies precise verbal definition in fixed rules. The defendant's default must be accounted a "proximate" cause of the harm, the consequence must not be "remote". And what is meant by "proximate" is "that because of convenience, of public policy, or a rough sense of justice, the law arbitrarily declines to trace a series of events beyond a certain point. This is not logic. It is practical politics."[92] Many have been the earnest attempts to reduce the solution of this problem to a system of formal rules, to some monistic formula, or even to a non-legal referent, like "common sense notions of attributing causal responsibility".[93] But none have proved at all adequate to the task. In essence, the question is whether, and if so how far, to push liability in excess of fault. This raises a major policy choice between two countervailing pulls.

On the one hand, strict adherence to the foreseeability limitation might deprive an innocent victim of recovery for damage caused by an admitted wrongdoer and thus impede effective distribution of the loss; while on the other hand, its abandonment could involve a person in wide and serious liability wholly disproportionate to his accidental lapse. Corresponding to these viewpoints are two formulas which have been respectively championed as *the* universal solvent for all and every problem of

89. See *Hogan v. Bentinck Collieries* [1949] 1 All E.R. 588. The (original) requirement that the accident arose "*out of* and in the course of employment" was designed to restrict coverage to accidents due to risks peculiar to the employment. N.Z. accident compensation scheme: below, p. 405.
90. See *Minister of Pensions v. Chennell* [1947] K.B. 250.
91. See Ehrenzweig, *Negligence without Fault* (1951); James & Perry, *Legal Cause*, 60 Yale L.J. 761 (1951); Calabresi, *Concerning Cause*, 43 U. Chi. L. Rev. 69 (1975) (cause analysed in terms of compensation and deterrence goals). In the case of private insurance, a countervailing factor is the greater need for calculability of risks: see Clarke, *Insurance: The Proximate Cause in English Law* [1981] Cam. L.J. 284.
92. *Palsgraf v. Long Island R.R.* 248 N.Y. 339 at 352 per Andrews J. (1928). Cf. Lord Wright: "The law must abstract some consequences as relevant, not perhaps on the grounds of pure logic but simply for practical reasons" (*Liesbosch v. The Edison* [1933] A.C. 449 at 460).
93. This is the burden of Hart & Honoré, *Causation*, centring on normality and voluntariness. Critical reviews by Stapleton, 8 Oxf. J. Leg. St. 111 (1988); by social psychologist Lloyd-Bostock, 42 Mod. L. Rev. 143 (1979).

"remoteness". The one, now generally associated with *The Wagon Mound*,[94] is that the risk which determines the existence of negligence in the first instance also delimits recovery for it, and that the same considerations which characterise the conduct as wrongful define also the scope of liability for its consequences.[95] The other, identified with *Re Polemis*,[96] is that what the defendant might or should have foreseen is important in determining whether he was at fault at all, but is not decisive as to the extent of the consequences for which, once negligent, he will be liable.[97] The courts have in fact vacillated between these two positions, not only in the sense that both have enjoyed periods of ascendancy, but that neither ever gained complete dominance without some concession to the other. If this ambivalence has left its mark even on the face of declared doctrine, it is reflected in yet larger measure in the actual pattern of decisions which suggest that the outward boundary of liability lies somewhere in the middle ground between the restricted scope of the original risk and the extravagant lengths to which a theory of unabridged causal responsibility might lead.

I. Direct Consequence Test

Tortfeasor takes his victim as he finds him

Liability beyond foreseeable consequences has exerted its strongest and quite consistent appeal for the stock problem of unexpectedly aggravated personal injuries. For none is so well accepted as the familiar legal saw that "a tortfeasor must take his victim as he finds him."[98] True, a plaintiff's abnormal susceptibility to injury may have an important bearing on whether the defendant's conduct was negligent towards him, because ordinarily no more is demanded in the way of care than precaution against the risk of what might injure normal individuals.[99] But once a breach of duty to him has been found because *some* of his injury should have been foreseen, responsibility embraces any aggravation due to a latent physical

94. [1961] A.C. 388.
95. This theory's most prominent champions have been Pollock (*Liability for Consequences*, 38 L.Q.R. 165 (1922)) and Goodhart (*Unforeseeable Consequences of a Negligent Act*, 39 Yale L.J. 449 (1930) and *Essays* ch. 7; *Imaginary Necktie and the Rule in Re Polemis*, 68 L.Q.R. 514 (1952); *Liability and Compensation*, 76 L.Q.R. 567 (1960)) in England, Justice Cardozo (in the *Palsgraf* case) and Seavey (*Mr Justice Cardozo and the Law of Torts*, 52 Harv. L. Rev. 372 (1939)) in America. It goes back to the formula of limiting liability to the "natural and probable" consequences of the defendant's act, enunciated by Pollock C.B. in *Rigby v. Hewitt* (1850) 5 Ex. 240 at 243; 155 E.R. 103 at 104 and *Greenland v. Chaplin* (1850) 5 Ex. 243 at 248; 155 E.R. 104 at 106 which held unchallenged sway until Lord Sumners' pronouncement in *Weld-Blundell v. Stephens* [1920] A.C. 956 at 984.
96. [1921] 3 K.B. 568.
97. This theory stems from dicta in *Smith v. L. & S.W. Rly* (1971) L.R. 6 C.P. 14 at 20, 21, and *Weld-Blundell v. Stephens* [1920] A.C. 956 at 984. It has been defended both by counsel who lost and who won *Re Polemis*: the former, Lord Wright (14 Mod. L. Rev. 393 (1951)), the latter, Lord Porter: 5 Cam. L.J. 176 (1934).
98. The locus classicus is Kennedy J.'s judgment in *Dulieu v. White* [1901] 2 K.B. 669 at 679; also Lord Wright in *Bourhill v. Young* [1943] A.C. 92 at 109.
99. See above, p. 165.

condition, however abnormal.[100] Thus even the most sanguine supporters of the fault theory accept it as perfectly fair that a *tortfeasor* be held to the risk of his victim happening to be afflicted with an "eggshell skull", a weak heart,[101] or some rare blood disease like haemophilia.[102] Nor does it make any difference whether the injury is just more severe than expected or actually entails wholly unexpected sequelae. Thus when a burn was the reasonably foreseeable type of injury, responsibility extended also to a fatal cancer which developed from an unusual pre-malignant condition of the victim;[103] similarly, when a minor laceration calling for an anti-tetanus injection led to encephalitis because of the plaintiff's rare allergy to the vaccine[104] or when, as a result of medical negligence, a blood transfusion was required which was infected with AIDS.

Indeed, as with an eggshell skull, so with an eggshell personality: for example a predisposed neurosis that flares up after the accident,[105] perhaps even one that ends in suicide.[106] Yet nervous shock is treated as an injury "different in kind",[107] as is a heart attack from worry over business losses[108] or exceptional economic losses[109] which must all be specifically foreseeable (at least) to qualify for recovery.[110] These entirely arbitrary distinctions, on top of the fortuity that the plaintiff must first have suffered, if only a scratch, underline the haphazardness of the basic rule.

Closely related is the principle that if the initial trauma was foreseeable, it matters nothing that the extent was aggravated beyond all reasonable

100. The apparent harshness of this solution (for defendants) is somewhat mitigated by allowing for the victim's "reduced value" owing to the disease: see above, p. 197. Thus if the defendant precipitated a fatal coronary occlusion in a sufferer of arterial sclerosis, he cannot avoid liability for the death, but damages would be assessed on the basis of the deceased's abnormally brief life expectancy: *Wilson v. Peisley* (1975) 50 A.L.J.R. 207; *Smith v. Leech Brain* [1962] 2 Q.B. 405; also *Zumeris v. Testa* [1972] V.R. 839 (F.C.); *Donjerkovic v. Adelaide Industries* (1980) 24 S.A.S.R 347. Such injury need not be "more probable than not"; the chance if substantial will be discounted: *Malec v. Hutton* (1990) below, p. 227.
101. *Love v. Port of London* [1959] 2 Ll. Rep. 541; also *Watts v. Rake* (1960) 108 C.L.R. 158 (quiescent spondylitis); *Sayers v. Perrin (No. 3)* [1966] Qd R. 89 (polio).
102. *Bishop v. Arts & Letters Club* (1978) 83 D.L.R. (3d) 107.
103. *Smith v. Leech Brain* [1962] 2 Q.B. 405; *Warren v. Scrutton's* [1962] 1 Ll. Rep. 497. Generally Linden, *Down with Foreseeability!* 47 Can. B. Rev. 545 (1969); Rowe, *Demise of the Thin Skull Rule?* 40 Mod. L. Rev. 377 (1977).
104. *Robinson v. P.O.* [1974] 1 W.L.R. 1176 (C.A.).
105. *Hoffmueller v. Commonwealth* (1981) 54 F.L.R. 48 (C.A.); *Nader v. Urban Transit* (1985) 2 N.S.W.L.R. 501 (C.A.) (neurosis caused by subsequent parental response); *Malcolm v. Broadhurst* [1970] 3 All E.R. 508 (exacerbated by co-injured spouse). "Compensation neurosis" (see 35 A.L.J. 206 (1961); 22 Med. Sci. Law 143 (1982)) is likewise compensable, depending on causation, not foreseeability: *James v. Woodall* [1969] 1 W.L.R. 903 (C.A.), but plaintiff must press his claim promptly to minimise its effect: *Marziale v. Hathazi* (1975) 13 S.A.S.R 150.
106. *Cotic v. Gray* (1981) 124 D.L.R. (3d) 641.
107. See above, p. 162.
108. *Connery v. Government of Manitoba* (1970) 15 D.L.R. (3d) 303 at 314.
109. *Malcolm v. Broadhurst* [1970] 3 All E.R. 508 ("A tortfeasor does not take his victims as he finds them in relation to their economic infirmities" (loss of part-time wages the wife earned as secretary to her now permanently disabled husband)). Cf. *Liesbosch v. The Edison* [1933] A.C. 449: see below, p. 226.
110. In doctrinal terms, these are issues of duty (more narrowly protected interests), not remoteness.

prevision by some physiological change due, for example, to subsequent sepsis. Thus where an unknown virus had infected a wound in the hand, causing irreversible brain damage;[111] or where a tetanus virus had entered the wound and flared up 18 months later when a bone graft was made on the injured leg.[112] The better view is that all that needs to be foreseeable in these cases is the open wound; in no event more than the risk of a subsequent infection, never mind its precise nature or development.[113] The more liberal of these alternatives seems preferable because it saves all inquiry, almost as formidable for physicians as for laymen, into the foreseeability of physiological processes or compartmentalised bodily risks.[114] Human bodies are too fragile and life too precarious to permit a defendant nicely to calculate how much injury he might inflict. Besides the great administrative advantage of this easy to apply formula, its fairness is enhanced by the fact that, while plaintiffs are rarely insured against personal injury, a defendant's liability policy would furnish blanket cover for "all personal injury or death" caused by him.

Often compared with the egg-skull gent is the "shabby millionaire"[115] who personifies the principle that a tortfeasor cannot invoke the plea that he had no reason to expect his victim to be so expensive. Thus a negligent motorist must be prepared to indemnify a pedestrian he has knocked down for loss of his unexpectedly high earning capacity as a senior executive or fashionable surgeon though he looked as if he was a tramp. This rule is of course distinguishable from the former in being concerned with responsibility, not for unexpected consequences but for the unexpectable cost of expected consequences. In terms of conventional analysis, it is a rule of compensation rather than remoteness of damage, of merely calculating in dollars and cents the cost of an injury that falls within the accepted range of the tortfeasor's responsibility. It also differs in terms of policy. Starkly individualistic, it sharply contrasts with the pattern of social security systems which tend to limit disability benefits to average earnings or at least to impose an absolute ceiling, with the corollary that persons of exceptionally high earnings must make their own arrangements for any excess rather than burden and distort the compensation fund. Inasmuch as that risk is better calculable in advance by the would-be victim, the problem of excessive earnings therefore appears in a rather different light from that of excessive injuries. Hence one might expect that the existing tort rule of unlimited compensation will become an early victim of the current egalitarian trend.[116]

111. *Stephenson v. Waite Tileman* [1973] 1 N.Z.L.R. 152 (C.A.).
112. *Beavis v. Apthorpe* (1962) 80 W.N. (N.S.W.) 852; also *Burden v. Watson* 1961 S.L.T. (N.) 67 (coronary thrombosis resulting from shock of collision).
113. See above, n. 103.
114. That the *precise* physical injury need not be foreseeable is also illustrated by the general aversion against fragmenting injury to health: if e.g. cold and chilblains are foreseeable consequences of exposure to exceptional cold, the fact that frostbite was unforeseeable is irrelevant: *Bradford v. Robinson Rentals* [1967] 1 W.L.R. 337.
115. *The Arpad* [1934] P. 189 at 202 per Scrutton L.J.
116. This process has already gone far in Norway and Denmark: Selmer, *Limitation of Damages According to the Circumstances of the "Average Citizen"*, 5 Scand. Stud. L. 131 (1961).

Property damage

The established rule of dealing with the foregoing problems of personal injury applies equally to property damage. If one were to rear-end another car, it would be no more of an excuse that it turned out to be a Rolls Royce rather than a minicar, or that the damage unexpectedly went beyond a few dents and caused structural distortion of the chassis. Perhaps it should not matter even that, among the debris in the boot, there was a precious cargo of Venetian crystal rather than groceries.[117] But the dividing line would apparently be crossed if there had been explosives or isotopes and the explosion or released radiation had damaged the car beyond repair, not to mention more extensive destruction in the vicinity. For would this not be damage of a different kind rather than extent? Damage by unforeseeable explosion or radiation rather than foreseeable impact?

The problem was raised in the great case of *Re Polemis*[118] where a careless stevedore dropped a plank into the hold of a ship in which petrol had been stored. On hitting the bottom it struck a spark which ignited petrol vapour and eventually caused the total destruction of the vessel. The defendants were held responsible for the whole of this damage despite the finding of fact (which was unreviewable though taxing credulity) that the stevedore had no reason to anticipate any fire risk. But this decision was based on reasoning which has since been overruled—viz. that, once a defendant's conduct is characterised as negligent because fraught with risk of *some* foreseeable damage (to the plaintiff), the extent of his liability fell to be determined, not by what damage was foreseeable, but whether it was the "direct consequence" of the culpable act. Yet though we have now returned to the formula of limiting liability to the foreseeable kind of damage, this reversal has not entirely disposed of the possibility that the disapproval of *Re Polemis* struck only at the supporting reasoning, not the decision itself. From one point of view, the vaporous hold was akin to some pre-existing quiescent disease triggered off by the defendant's intervention and therefore within the purview of the rule that he must take his victim—whether man, beast or boat—as he found him. Still, the better opinion probably is that, since the line between these competing principles must be drawn somewhere, this was really a case of damage unexpectedly different not only in extent but also in kind: damage by unforeseeable explosion and fire in contrast to foreseeable structual damage to the plank and perhaps some cargo.

Ominous as the *Polemis* formula—liability for all direct consequences—might at first sound, it was rarely taken to extravagant lengths,[119] hardly even in the original case once allowance is made for the strong likelihood that the court distrusted the arbitrator's finding that the fire was unforeseeable. In practice, save in a few isolated instances, the *Polemis* formula was reserved for cases where the harm fell broadly within the

117. But might it not be contributory negligence to carry such vulnerable cargo? Boberg, *Uncommon Cause* in *Fiat Justitia* (1983) 145.

118. [1921] 3 K.B. 560 (C.A.).

119. The most extreme were *Pigney v. Pointers Transport* [1957] 1 W.L.R. 1121 (suicide) and *Patten v. Silberschein* [1936] 3 W.W.R. 169 (subsequent robbery of disabled casualty), considering that these injuries could not have been consummated without somebody else's (abnormal) intervention and were yet held "direct".

hazard that made the defendant's conduct negligent but where, because the stage was set for it, its *extent* exceeded the bounds of reasonable foresight. Even then, it was subject to the overriding requirement, evolved largely as a counterweight, that only a "foreseeable plaintiff" was entitled to redress, because only to him, as will be recalled, would a "duty" of care be owed.[120] Thus unless at least *some* injury to *him* was foreseeable, he would not be entitled to claim for any injury, still less for all direct injury.

All this hardly adds up to anything like the image of an oppressive regime of liability. In truth, whatever its original potential, the *Polemis* rule had long become tamed to the point that, when *The Wagon Mound*[121] eventually dislodged it in 1961, it was with the comment that this would actually have little practical effect on the operation of the law. The ultimate apotheosis of the foresight test was thus more in the nature of a sacerdotal rite than a harbinger of drastic change.

II. Foresight Test

What then are the credentials of the foresight test which, after so brief an interlude of 30 years, once again demonstrated its superior appeal? Foremost among the claims made for it is that it alone is consistent with the basic philosophy of negligence. Foreseeability is of course inseparable from any system based on fault. Negligence postulates actual or imputed appreciation of the risk of injury to others; and accordingly no one is held to account for the consequences, however injurious, of his conduct unless he was, or at all events should have been, aware that it was fraught with risk of at least *some* harm to *somebody*. But granted that this condition is satisfied and that the responsible conduct can therefore be branded as negligent and unlawful, are we committed to the corollary that responsibility shall not extend beyond the injury to be foreseen?

Attempts have not been wanting to invest this postulate with the accolade of a logical imperative. The argument runs: Because the legal quality of conduct cannot be determined in isolation from its consequences and an act can only be negligent with respect to a given consequence, it is *illogical* to hold a defendant responsible for *negligence* with respect to any consequence which was unforeseeable and which reasonable care therefore did not require him to avoid.[122]

But in truth, the premise does not compel the conclusion. It may be thought *politic* that the reason for creating liability should also delimit it; but it is just as tenable, and certainly as logical, to insist that there are good reasons within the framework of fault for holding a proven wrongdoer liable for injury he has caused even if some of it went beyond all ken. "The judgment lies in the realm of values and what you choose depends on what you want."[123]

Even the much vaunted claim[124] that foreseeability is the more attractive for subsuming the two questions of culpability and extent of liability to one

120. *Bourhill v. Young* [1943] A.C. 92; see above, pp. 142ff.
121. [1961] A.C. 388.
122. As Goodhart consistently maintained in writings cited above, n. 95.
123. Gregory, *Proximate Cause in Negligence—A Retreat from Rationalisation*, 6 U. Chi. L. Rev. 36 at 47 (1938).
124. E.g. *The Wagon Mound (No. 1)* [1961] A.C. 388 at 423.

and the same test, fails to stand up to closer scrutiny. In practice at least, it seems far easier for an event to qualify as a foreseeable consequence of negligent conduct than for conduct to be held initially negligent because of risks that are foreseeable.[125] Again, frequently an act is branded as negligent only because of the *aggregate* of risks it poses; but although any one of these risks in isolation might therefore not have been enough to turn the scales, to suppose that it would not have been deemed sufficiently foreseeable to pass the test of remoteness would be quite unrealistic. Especially in cases of so-called "ulterior" injury, recovery has often been countenanced as foreseeable although it could not have figured intelligently among the reasons for condemning the defendant of negligence. A typical example is that of the negligent driver who is thrown into the roadway after a collision and receives assistance from a passer-by when the latter is struck by another motorist. Repeatedly, the first has been held liable to the Samaritan on the ground that the second accident was "a consequence of the same general character that was reasonably foreseeable as not unlikely to follow a collision on a dark wet night upon a busy highway".[126] Yet could one realistically suppose that it would have entered into the calculations of the reasonable man as a reason for driving carefully to start with? Besides, if the prospect of the first collision would have been sufficient, to ask him whether he would have been deterred by the second is to put a question he cannot answer.[127]

The purely doctrinal arguments in favour of the foresight test are therefore less than compelling. But this is not to say that it may not be commendable on less pretentious grounds. Perhaps most insistent is the widespread conviction that it would "not seem consonant with current ideas of justice and morality that for an act of negligence, however slight or venial, which results in some trivial foreseeable damage the actor should be liable for all consequences however unforeseeable and however grave, so long as they can be said to be 'direct' ".[128] The argument postulates in effect, if not an exact, at all events a rough correlation between a person's fault and the extent of his liability. Yet in terms of kerbstone morality, there is at least as much to be said in favour of the innocent plaintiff as the hapless defendant, for the harshness of burdening the actor with potentially far reaching liability is surely matched by the injustice of denying his victim redress and letting the loss lie where it happened to fall. And at a different level of discourse, the social value of shifting the loss, especially when the defendant is in a favoured position for distributing it, would seem to outweigh by far any conceivable social good that might come from relieving tortfeasors. Indeed in this respect, the policy orientation of *The Wagon Mound*—pro-defendant in sentiment and imbued with a purely individualistic notion of tort responsibility—is rather at odds with general trends of contemporary tort law.[129]

125. One reason for this is that the calculus of balancing the odds against the burden of eliminating the risk seems quite inappropriate for the issue of remoteness. Another, that there is less compunction about a defendant once shown to have violated plaintiff's rights. Generally: Kidner, 9 Leg. Stud. 1 (1989).
126. *Chapman v. Hearse* (1961) 106 C.L.R. 112 at 120; *Dwyer v. Southern* [1961] S.R. (N.S.W.) 896; *Connolly v. S. Ireland Asphalt* [1977] I.R. 99.
127. Hart & Honoré, *Causation* 264.
128. *The Wagon Mound (No. 1)* [1961] A.C. 388 at 422.
129. Rumour has it that the P.C. was split 3:2: *Foresight Saga* 3 (Haldane Society 1962).

No doubt for that very reason, the decision's edge has been severely blunted by subsequent interpretation. In the first place, the competing principle that "a tortfeasor takes his victim as he finds him" survives to ensure that, in the crucial area of personal injuries where the defendant's loss bearing capacity is typically much the greater, the foresight test will play only a subordinate role.[130] Secondly, judicial approval has been given to so expansive a view of foreseeability that the test has for all practical purposes lost much of its limiting bite.

How foreseeable?

The Wagon Mound (No. 1)[131] established the requirement that the injury must be foreseeable; *The Wagon Mound (No. 2)*[132] probed how foreseeable it must be.

The defendant-charterer of the vessel *Wagon Mound* negligently spilled a quantity of oil while bunkering at the Caltex wharf, in Mort Bay, Sydney Harbour. The slick flowed over to Sheerlegs Wharf, Balmain where ships were undergoing repairs. Owing to its high flash point, the oil was not considered a fire hazard; yet catch fire it did (in all likelihood because molten metal from oxy welding dropped into the water and ignited some floating waste material) and caused extensive damage to the docks and ships. Based on the finding of the trial judge that, on the evidence, the defendant neither knew nor could reasonably be expected to know that the oil was capable of ignition, the Privy Council dismissed the claim of the dock owners. Not only did injury have to be foreseeable, but it had to be the "particular" injury for which the claim was raised. Fouling the dock was no doubt foreseeable, but that was wholly different in kind from damage by fire and therefore irrelevant. In so holding, it became necessary to overrule *Re Polemis*[133] where, it will be recalled, judgment had gone for the plaintiffs although the gutting of the tanker had been just as unforeseeable and different in kind from the suface damage that could have been foreseen from the fall of the ill-fated plank.

The *Wagon Mound* charterer, however, fared less well in a subsequent action by the owner of one of the damaged ships. This time, on somewhat different evidence, the trial court found that the officers of the *Wagon Mound* had reason to regard furnace oil as very difficult, though not impossible to ignite; the possibility, however, being one that would occur only rarely and in very exceptional circumstances. Once the risk was at all foreseeable, how great had to be the odds on it? The spectrum of probability is wide, ranging—so far as our crude, conventional terminology can reflect the calibration—from "fantastically remote" through

130. See above, p. 204.
131. *Overseas Tankships (U.K.) v. Morts Dock & Engineering Co.* [1961] A.C. 388 (P.C.). See Dias [1962] Cam. L.J. 178; Fleming, 39 Can. B. Rev. 489 (1961); Green, 61 Col. L. Rev. 1401 (1961); Jackson, 39 A.L.J. 3 (1965); Morison, 34 A.L.J. 317 (1961); Payne, 25 Mod. L. Rev. 1 (1963); Smith, 2 U.B.C.L. Rev. 159 (1965); Williams, 77 L.Q.R. 179 (1961).
132. *Overseas Tankships (U.K.) v. Miller S.S. Co.* [1967] 1 A.C. 617 (P.C.).
133. See above, n. 188. In neither case, without at any rate detailed analysis of insurance rating experience, was one of the parties identifiable as a better loss absorber. The precise issue in *Re Polemis* was actually whether the charterer could avail himself of an exemption in the charterparty for "loss or damage from fire on board".

"possible" to "not unlikely", "likely", "probable" and "substantially certain". According to the Privy Council, it was sufficient that it was a "real risk, one which would occur to the mind of a reasonable man in the defendant's position and which he would not brush aside as far-fetched".[134] Thus the *Wagon Mound* was liable for the fire damage, whether it was viewed as a "foreseeable" consequence of the original act of negligent bunkering or of the later failure to do anything about the spillage.

An equally expansive view has prevailed as regards the kind of injury that must have been foreseeable.

Difference in kind

According to the official formulation, foreseeability is required of the "particular" injury that occurred,[135] yet neither of the precise *manner* in which it came about nor of its *extent*. What is the scope of these modifiers?

The first came to be considered by the House of Lords in *Hughes v. Lord Advocate*[136] where a post office maintenance gang left an open manhole near the road edge, with a tent over it and surrounded by four kerosene warning lamps, and took off for a tea break. During their brief absence, two boys came upon the scene and took a lamp into the tent to explore. One of them tripped over the lamp which fell into the manhole, an explosion followed and he was thrown all the way down where he suffered severe burns. The foreseeable risk was that spilled kerosene might catch alight and burn; what actually happened was that quite unpredictably it exploded because vapours were formed by the heat of the lamp and set off by the flame. A majority of the Court of Session in Scotland felt constrained by *The Wagon Mound* to dismiss the claim because, although the boy was admittedly injured by burning kerosene and it was immaterial that his injuries were much more severe than could have been anticipated, yet the accident could not be meaningfully described without reference to the unforeseeable explosion, which was therefore not just "an unpredictable incident in the kind of chain of events which might have been foreseen, but an essential event outside it".[137] The House of Lords, however, unanimously allowed the appeal, rejecting as altogether too fine the suggested distinction between burning and exploding; the accident was but a variant of the foreseeable, clearly within the risk created by the negligence, expecially having regard to the fact that its cause was a known source of danger (the lamp), even if it behaved in an unpredictable way. Moreover, the accident could well be explained without referring to the explosion: the injuries, foreseeable as well as actual, were the result of burning by contact with paraffin and a naked flame, the difference between ignition of liquid paraffin and paraffin vapour being much too trivial to convert the resulting injuries into two different kinds of accident.

134. [1967] 1 A.C. 617 at 643 "however unlikely it may be, unless it can be brushed aside as far-fetched" (*Koufos v. Czarnikow* [1969] 1 A.C. 350 at 422).
135. Lord Simonds' favourite phrase in *The Wagon Mound (No. 1)*.
136. [1963] A.C. 837.
137. 1961 S.C. 310 at 333 per Lord Sorn. Accord: *Republic of France v. U.S.* 290 F. 2d 395 (5 Cir. 1961), [1961] 1 Ll. Rep. 504 (ammonium nitrate known to be combustible but not explosive).

So with reference to the *extent* of injury. If an explosion was foreseeable, the fact that its magnitude exceeded all reasonable expectation makes no difference.[138] Similarly, recovery would be unduly narrowed if bodily[139] or psychiatric[140] injuries were compartmentalised and foreseeability demanded for the precise trauma that occurred.[141]

The tendency is thus to define the risk, or rather harm within the scope of the risk, somewhat broadly—insisting on foreseeability not so much of the "particular" injury as of "harm of a like *general* character"[142]—and paying heed neither to the extent nor the precise manner of its occurrence. The question, "must we see shapes clearly defined or may we see in a glass darkly?"[143] is thus, generally speaking, resolved in the latter sense. A striking admonition that one must not concentrate too much on any particular incident, but rather on the whole happening, comes from a modern case where a worker operating a winch was negligently hit by a falling object. Seeing him stagger back, a fellow employee sought to turn off the winch but in doing so let go of a rope which held a load under tension, with the result that the rope pulled away and caused him to lose a leg. It was held that a jury could conclude that this was "in a general sense a happening of a kind that could be foreseen as possibly occurring if a worker was suddenly disturbed by the fall of an object".[144] By focusing (with hindsight) on each link in a chain of events one after another, it is easy to fall into the error of concluding that, because each link made the next foreseeable, the last was therefore also the foreseeable consequence of the first. This effect is well illustrated by a case which argued that entrusting to an inexpert the job of repairing a wheel bearing made it foreseeable that the wheel might come off, that the axle bouncing on the road would strike sparks, that the sparks on a hot Australian summer day would ignite the grass verge and eventually burn down a building 12 kilometres away.[145] To credit the defendant with such foresight overstretched that notion unduly.

Where the sequence of events was actually freakish, quite abnormal or (what often amounts to the same thing) wholly different from anything within the purview of the rule of conduct which the defendant violated, the disposition has been to deny recovery, even though the harm itself, looked at in isolation, was just what one could have expected. Thus if a contractor were to leave an unguarded excavation on the footpath, he would be liable to anyone who broke his leg by stumbling into it or even being jostled; not

138. *Vacwell Engineering v. B.D.H. Chemicals* [1971] 1 Q.B. 88.
139. E.g. *Richards v. State of Victoria* [1969] V.R. 136 (F.C.).
140. E.g. *Nader v. Urban Transit* (1985) 2 N.S.W.L.R. 501 (C.A.). If no bodily harm but only shock is suffered, the latter must be foreseeable: above, p. 161.
141. The same policy is evident in discarding foreseeability for (1) aggravation and (2) peculiar susceptibility: see above, p. 204.
142. This is the most widely used American jury instruction. Cf. *Rest. 2d* §435. The synonymous phrase "consequence of the same general character" was used in *Chapman v. Hearse* (1961) 106 C.L.R. 112 at 120; "an event of the same 'kind' 'class' or 'type' " in *Siwek v. Lambourn* [1964] V.R. 337; "property in some form or another" in *Heeney v. Best* (1978) 94 D.L.R. (3d) 451 (baby chicks asphyxiated after power pole knocked down). "Class of injuries" (accidents?) is the key for Coval, Smith & Rush, 61 Can. B. Rev. 559 (1983).
143. *Harvey v. Singer Manufacturing Co.* 1960 S.C. 155 at 165 per Lord Thomson.
144. *Castellan v. Electrical Power* (1967) 69 S.R. (N.S.W.) 159 at 170 (C.A.).
145. *Haileybury College v. Emanuelli* [1983] V.R. 323.

however if he were pushed by his enemy out of spite.[146] In cases such as this, therefore, the ambit of the risk does not include the strikingly abnormal manner in which the foreseeable harm of a broken leg actually came about.

The manner of describing the risk to be perceived when comparing it with the harm that occurred plays an important role, if not in influencing the decision-making process, at least as a technique with some potential for subtle manipulation in justifying decisions and giving them the deceptive appearance of inevitability.[147] The more specific the description of the expectable hazard, the less likely that it will correspond with what actually happened. If the only apparent risk of a fan without guard to a repairman is that his necktie might get caught, should it be liberally defined to include any personal injury through contact with the revolving blades (in case his fingers got stubbed in some unexplained manner) or even a chill from the draught set up by them?[148] Where an asbestos cover had slipped into a cauldron of extremely hot cyanide but, instead of splashing somebody as might have been foreseen, underwent a chemical change and caused an unexpected eruption of the liquid, it was held to be "unrealistic to describe the accident as a variant of the perils from splashing": the apparent risk was limited to the cover being immersed, not disintegrating and causing an eruption.[149] On the other hand, when a fire in a building under construction set alight insulating material, believed to be fire resistant, but which instead unexpectedly erupted in tremendous smoke and asphyxiated a worker a good distance away, his death was still held to be "fire-caused" and thus a foreseeable consequence.[150] Clearly it is a matter of judgment where to draw the line, and in problematical cases this will depend largely on what outcome the court wishes to reach. Overriding, perhaps, is the guiding principle that the hazard should not be defined with over-much particularity, lest the unique features inherent in every case disqualify the injury from falling within the description of the apprehended risk.[151] Nor should it be defined too broadly, lest a defendant be held liable for all resulting harm of which his default was a cause-in-fact.[152]

Finally, even the rule that the extent of the harm, as distinct from its kind, need not be foreseeable is not without all qualification. Its most important "stopper" is of course the now familiar requirement that at least

146. See below, p. 222.
147. See Jackson, *A Kind of Damage*, 39 A.L.J. 3 (1965); Fridman & Williams, *Atomic Theory of Negligence*, 45 A.L.J. 117 (1971).
148. See *Thurogood v. Van den Berghs* [1951] 2 K.B. 537; discussed by Goodhart, *Imaginary Necktie*, 68 L.Q.R. 514 (1952). The chill is clearly a risk in no way *increased* by the absence of a guard.
149. *Doughty v. Turner Manufacturing Co.* [1964] 1 Q.B. 518; criticised by Dworkin, 27 Mod. L. Rev. 344 (1964).
150. *Cuckow v. Polyster Products* (1970) 19 F.L.R. 122. Similarly *McKenzie's T. v. Edinburgh* 1979 S.L.T. (Sh. Ct) 60 (risk of fire includes explosion).
151. Modern examples of included risks: *Versic v. Conners* (1969) 90 W.N. (Pt 1) (N.S.W.) 33 (pinned under truck, drowned from banked-up rainwater); *Malleys v. Rogers* (1955) 55 S.R. (N.S.W.) 390 (falling bar, instead of hitting deceased, made him stumble backwards and sustain concussion); *Harrison v. S. Clifton Mining* [1963] S.R. (N.S.W.) 689 (faulty fuel governor distracted tractor driver, causing him head injuries); *Hayward v. Georges* [1966] V.R. 202 (thump on her back caused plaintiff unexpectedly to twist sharply and fall off a stool).
152. See *Rowe v. McCartney* [1976] 2 N.S.W.L.R. 72.

some injury to the *plaintiff* must have been foreseeable. Merely because there existed a recognisable risk of the particular kind of harm to *someone else* will no longer support a claim by a plaintiff himself beyond the area of apparent danger. In short, he cannot "build on a wrong to someone else".[153] It matters nothing that this rule is couched in the terminology of duty rather than remoteness, as both concepts serve precisely the same function of marking the outer boundaries of recovery.[154] That foreseeability of the plaintiff is not handled in any narrower fashion than foreseeability of harm generally is shown by the fact that, even if it is insisted that he be within the area of potential peril, he need not be a particular individual whom the defendant had reason to expect there at the time. Thus, when an overloaded truck failed to clear a bridge and a box fell on a boy who was about to climb aboard, it was held to be no answer that his presence as a potential passenger could not have been anticipated: the likelihood was sufficient that someone close behind the lorry might get hurt, whatever his reason for being there.[155] Nor is there any apparent taste for refinements concerning the precise character of the foreseeable casualty, for it has been consistently held that a motorist who runs over a nondescript object takes his chance that it turns out to be, not just more valuable than he thought, but actually a human being rather than a bundle of rags.[156]

On the other hand, the "unforeseeable plaintiff" may well serve as a useful brake on any extravagant application of the principle that the extent of the foreseeable harm is irrelevant. The need for such a corrective is particularly keen in fire cases, not only because of the ease with which fire can get out of hand, but even more because the destruction it wreaks is usually covered by the plaintiff's fire insurance which offers by far the most economical method of absorbing such losses.[157] In this manner it is possible to cut off liability at whatever point along its path is thought proper by simply declaring any damage beyond it to have been

153. See above, p. 144. In practice this "area" test has played a significant role only in nervous shock cases: see above, p. 161.
154. The preference for "duty" in this instance was in any event dictated by purely ephemeral considerations of precedent, i.e. to circumvent the *Polemis* rule. It would, of course, be perfectly feasible to subsume *all* aspects of proximity either to the "duty" category (as advocated by Leon Green, e.g. 61 Col. L. Rev. 1401 (1961)) or to "remoteness of damage" (as appears to have been the English practice until the "duty" limitation was discovered in the 1930s). At one time, indeed, this led to the suggestion of refining "duty" according to the several "interests" of a person, such as his bodily security, property and the like, and demanding foreseeable infringement of any one of them specifically as a condition of recovery for breach of a duty to such an interest (see the quotations from Cardozo J. and Lord Wright, above, p. 143). Though no different in *effect* from dismissing as too "remote" any "particular" damage that was unforeseeable, this refinement of duty has been widely deprecated both for adding needlessly to the doctrinal complexity and encouraging too limited recovery: Goodhart, *Essays* 149; *Prosser & Keeton* 289-290, *Azzopardi v. Bois* [1968] V.R. 183 (issue estoppel); contra: Machin, *Duty and Interest*, 17 Mod. L. Rev. 405 (1954).
155. *Farrugia v. Gt W. Rly* [1947] 2 All E.R. 565.
156. *Law v. Visser* [1961] Q.R. 46; *Edwards v. Litster* [1960] S.A.S.R. 173.
157. A graphic illustration is the New York "fire rule" (*Ryan v. N.Y. Central Rly* 35 N.Y 210 (1866)) which limits liability arbitrarily to the first building burned down, but by statute does not apply to forest fires. Much the same justification underlies the not uncommon statutory limit on the liability of railways for fire, e.g. $20,000 in N.S.W.: *Government Railways Act* 1912 s. 145.

unforeseeable.[158] True, such a line can apparently only be drawn as between different owners and not different "properties" which happen to be in the same hands,[159] but that is a negligible drawback from a practical standpoint, however aggravating to the theoretical purist.

Scope of risk

Risk being the central notion of legal negligence, an alternative and increasingly favoured formulation is to inquire whether the consequences may fairly be regarded as within the risk created by that negligence.[160] Though from one point of view just a generalised version of the foresight test, it has the advantage of not being committed to any of the potentially misleading implications of the "foresight" criterion and of focusing attention on certain aspects of the problem which might otherwise go by default. Thus, allowance can more frankly be made to such other pertinent factors as the purpose of the legal rule violated by the defendant, analogies drawn from accepted patterns of past decisions, general community notions regarding the allocation of "blame" as well as supervening considerations of judicial policy bearing on accident prevention, loss distribution and insurance.

Most helpful of all is that the "ambit of the risk" approach directs attention to the purpose behind the rule flouted by the defendant as a clue to the kind of consequences that (not only would, but) should have been avoided.[161] This is, of course, strongly reminiscent of the "legislative purpose" doctrine that has, as we have seen,[162] traditionally delimited liability for breach of *statutory* duties to the kind of risk which it was the purpose of the statutory rule to prevent. But though focusing on substantially the same criterion, that doctrine has been conventionally handled in too narrow a fashion to provide an exact model for breach of common law duties or to reflect fairly the course of modern decisions. Accordingly, while recognising the close conceptual link between them, "scope of the risk" as used in the present context is a more embracing notion, one which would not, for example, disqualify a consequence merely because the *primary* or *principal* purpose was to guard against another hazard; for categorically to confine liability to such injury alone the precise risk of which made the defendant negligent would be to exclude "ulterior"

158. But in *Edwards v. Blue Mts C.C.* (1961) 78 W.N. (N.S.W.) 864 where 188 buildings were destroyed by a bush fire emanating from a municipal rubbish tip, the court was not apparently sensitive to these considerations in allowing the plaintiff recovery for his home about a mile away. One of the oldest controversial fire cases is *Smith v. L. & S.W. Rly* (1870) L.R. 6 C.P. 14, where a majority of the Exchequer Chamber declared themselves in favour of liability for the unforeseeable spread of fire to the plaintiff's cottage from dry clippings belonging to the defendants even across a field apparently owned by a third party. The foreseeability test would allow sufficient latitude (as borne out by the jury verdict) for the same result *if* such were desired.
159. Cf. *Jeffrey v. Copeland Flour Mills* [1923] 4 D.L.R. 1140 where A caused a subsidence exerting a pull on adjoining buildings which, unknown to him, were joined by tie-rods with the result that they all collapsed like a row of dominoes. B recovered not only for the first but also for the second which he happened to own. The overruling of *Re Polemis* should not affect this result.
160. E.g. Denning L.J. in *Roe v. M.O.H.* [1954] 2 Q.B. 66 at 85.
161. See Honoré, XI Int. Encycl. Comp. L. ch. 7, 60-62 for an appraisal of this theory ("purpose of the norm") from a comparative viewpoint.
162. See above, p. 131.

harm, like injury aggravated by negligent medical treatment or to a rescuer, which precedent has long sanctioned as compensable.

In some cases the "scope of risk" approach is merely another way of expressing the causal principle, already encountered,[163] that the injury must have resulted from the *negligent* element of the defendant's conduct. Suppose once more that, while speeding, a car is hit by a falling tree or that, on his way to hospital after the accident, the injured passenger is hit by a falling tile. The specious argument that the speeding was causally relevant because the victim would not otherwise have reached the scene of the accident when he did, is most effectively met by pointing out that the purpose of the speed rule is to guard against the risks flowing from lessened control over the vehicle, not to ensure that a driver reaches a given spot at any particular time. So, if an adult entrusts a loaded gun to a boy of ten who clumsily dropped it on the plaintiff's toe, the reason for dismissing the claim can be founded either on the absence of causal relation between the defendant's negligence and the injury (the same would have occurred if the gun had been unloaded) or on the fact that the purpose of the rule against handing firearms to youngsters is to protect the public against their discharge and that the plaintiff's injury was consequently outside the "ambit of the protected risks".

III. Intervening Causes

For the sake of convenient analysis of cause problems, it has been a long-standing judicial technique to isolate certain intervening forces which, in combination with the defendant's default, precipitate or aggravate the plaintiff's injury. The question then arises whether the original wrongdoer is to be held for loss contributed to by the external force or whether, in the favoured legal vernacular, it "snapped the chain of causation".

An intervening force is one which actively operates in producing the harm *after* the actor's negligent act or omission has been committed.[164] It involves a somewhat artificial distinction between later events that act on a situation already created by the defendant and conditions existing at the time of the wrongdoer's conduct which are—so to speak—part of the stage set for his activity. Thus, a determinist would regard as illusory the distinction between an already existing blood disease in an accident victim which unexpectedly aggravates his injury[165] and blood poisoning set off by an unsterilised scalpel used in treating him after the accident,[166] because in his eyes the stage in either case was irrevocably set long before the occurrence of these events.[167] More important perhaps is the fact that all too obviously there is a rather arbitrary element in the judicial practice of isolating certain co-operating causes and treating them as "independent" supervening forces, while disregarding others as inoperative to interrupt the "direct" sequence between the wrongdoer's default and the ultimate consequences. For example, the usual assumption that physiological disturbances from a wound are part of the defendant's direct force rests

163. See above, pp. 194-195.
164. *Rest. 2d* §441.
165. See above, p. 204.
166. See below, p. 221.
167. James & Perry, *Legal Cause*, 60 Yale L.J. 761 at 792 (1951).

simply upon a refusal or inability to analyse these physiological processes.[168] If then, for the practical purpose of analysing a case, courts refuse to go beyond a certain point in looking for new active forces, it is the more important to recognise that this evaluation lends a certain measure of imprecision and unpredictability to decisions.

Another verbalism that has plagued the solution of these problems is the addiction, now happily waning, to metaphors culled from mechanics,[169] like "snapping the chain of causation", "active and passive forces" that are either still "in motion" or have happily "come to rest", "conduit pipes" and "transmission gears" and similar images that spell the illusion of scientific and objective reasoning, but are in reality only a screen behind which judges have all too often in the past retreated to avoid the irksome task of articulating their real motivation. No less is true of the fancied division of antecedent factors into "conditions" (which merely make possible the harm) and real "causes" (which attract liability). Far from serving as an aid in reaching decisions, this is at best a restatement of the original problem in a different set of words, unless a meaningful index is provided for determining just what is a "cause" and what is a mere "condition".[170]

Non-culpable intervention

Nowadays it is no longer open to serious question that the operation of an intervening force will not ordinarily clear a defendant from further responsibility, if it can fairly be considered a not abnormal incident of the risk created by him—if, as sometimes expressed, it is "part of the ordinary course of things". Nor is there room any longer for any categorical distinction in this regard between forces of nature, like rain or ice,[171] and human action even when consciously controlled.[172]

Least difficult are instances of just normal and reasonable response to the stimulus of the hazard engendered by the defendant's negligence. Typical human reactions, such as fear of impending injury to oneself[173] or the desire to avert harm or escape an inconvenience,[174] are sufficiently within the realm of foreseeability to make the defendant answerable for injury sustained owing to the plaintiff or someone else responding to them in a

168. McLaughlin, *Proximate Cause*, 39 Harv. L. Rev. 149 at 165 (1925).
169. A fascination for the 19th century mind.
170. The provision of such an index in terms of abnormality and "voluntary" human action, which they contend reflect common sense and policy-neutral notions of causality, is the theme of Hart & Honoré's *Causation*. "Minimalists" like the present writer confine the province of cause to cause-in-fact and view proximate cause or remoteness as policy determined.
171. See *Comm. Rlys v. Stewart* (1936) 56 C.L.R. 520 (rainfall); *Manchester Corp. v. Markland* [1936] A.C. 360 (ice).
172. *The Oropesa* [1943] P. 32 at 37.
173. E.g. *Colvilles v. Devine* [1969] 1 W.L.R. 475 (H.L. (Sc.)); *Malleys v. Rogers* (1955) 55 S.R. (N.S.W.) 390.
174. E.g. *Caterson v. Comm. Rlys* (1973) 128 C.L.R. 99 (train prematurely pulling out of station; passenger jumps rather than be carried 60 miles); *Sayers v. Harlow U.D.C.* [1958] 1 W.L.R. 623 (climbing out of lavatory without inside doorhandle); *Abbott v. Kasza* (1976) 71 D.L.R. (3d) 581 (backing truck angled across highway).

more or less normal manner.[175] A time honoured illustration is the famous *Squib Case*[176] where a wag threw a lighted firework into a market whence it was tossed from one stall to another in order to save the wares until it eventually exploded in the plaintiff's face. Yet it was held that *trespass* lay because "all that was done subsequent to the original throwing was a continuation of the first force and first act and continued until the squib was spent by bursting." Indeed it makes no difference that in the light of calm contemplation or hindsight, it would have been better to leave well alone: a passenger who jumps from a vehicle out of control[177] or a bystander who starts running for safety[178] may nonetheless recover for his broken bones, though he would almost certainly have remained unscathed had he remained still.

By the same token, as already noted,[179] a reasonable endeavour to avert a peril with which a third person or his property is threatened is now also readily blamed on the defendant. "The risk of rescue, if only it be not wanton, is born of the occasion. The emergency begets the man."[180] In cases such as these where the plaintiff's conduct is especially meritorious, the law has sympathetically stretched foreseeability to a transparent fiction. A recent extreme example was to hold it foreseeable that a father would donate a kidney to a daughter whose own—surprisingly sole—kidney had been mistakenly removed in lieu of a cyst.[181] Here his moral compulsion dispelled even the traditional arguments that he had voluntarily incurred the loss and, unlike ordinary rescuers, acted after due deliberation.

Maritime collisions also frequently call for the application of this "emergency principle". If one vessel, owing to the negligent navigation of another, is placed "under the heavy hand of the casualty", the reasonable conduct of the captain in seeking to save further loss is not regarded as absolving the defendant from responsibility for harm sustained as a result of measures taken in the emergency. "What those in charge of the injured ship do to save it may be mistaken, but if they do whatever they do reasonably, although unsuccessfully, their mistaken judgment may be a natural consequence for which the offending ship is responsible."[182] Such, for example, was the case where the damaged vessel, owing to its loss of navigation equipment, was ultimately grounded and became a total casualty in an endeavour to reach a port of safety,[183] or where the captain ordered some of the crew into a lifeboat in order to solicit the help of the other ship and the boat capsized.[184]

175. If the risk taken by the plaintiff is excessive, it is a matter of degree whether it should bar his recovery altogether on the theory that the damage is too remote, or be regarded merely as contributory negligence so as to reduce the award: see *Sayers v. Harlow U.D.C.* [1958] 1 W.L.R. 623.
176. *Scott v. Shepherd* (1773) 2 W. Bl. 892; 96 E.R. 525. Cf. *Bradford v. Kanellos* [1974] S.C.R. 409 (out of line with current trend).
177. *Jones v. Boyce* (1816) 1 Stark. 493; 171 E.R. 540.
178. *Parry v. Yates* [1963] W.A.R. 42.
179. See above, p. 170.
180. *Wagner v. International R.R.* 232 N.Y. 176 at 180 (1921) per Cardozo J.
181. *Urbanski v. Patel* (1978) 84 D.L.R. (3d) 650.
182. *The Metagama* (1927) 138 L.T. 369 at 370 per Lord Haldane.
183. *City of Lincoln* (1889) 15 P.D. 15; also *The Guildford* [1956] P. 364. Contrast *The Fritz Thyssen* [1968] P. 255 (unreasonable refusal to accept aid).
184. *The Oropesa* [1943] P. 32.

The long stream of "children cases" proceeds upon the analogous principle that those who should anticipate the presence of children within the scope of hazard of their own activities are not relieved from liability for injury caused by them in pursuit of their natural instincts of meddlesome curiosity, lack of judgment, or even propensity for mischief.[185] Hence precautions may be necessary to guard against juveniles tampering with unsecured cover plates on public footpaths,[186] climbing on parked vehicles in the street[187] or even breaking open a steel safe for detonators in a quarry.[188] To put something highly inflammable like petrol into the hands of a small boy is to subject him to temptation and the risk of injury, for which liability cannot be avoided even by pleading that the boy had resorted to deceit in order to overcome the defendant's scruples.[189] Nor is it an answer that the child committed a trespass on private grounds if prudence would have suggested precautions against such a possibility.[190]

Again, a defendant who wrongfully impedes the exercise of another's rights or privileges cannot treat as a supervening cause the other's reasonable efforts to remove the impediment[191] or to exercise the right or privilege notwithstanding.[192] Thus a painter who unlawfully left a ladder standing on the footpath after his day's work was held responsible when some passer-by moved it out of the way but placed it so insecurely that it fell on the plaintiff.[193] Evidence of a more realistic acceptance of changing social mores is also that abandonment of a disabled or disfigured spouse is no longer dismissed as abnormal.[194]

On the other hand, legal responsibility ceases with the occurrence of an event quite outside the range of ordinary experience. Man must guard against normal phenomena of nature, not against unusual ones, such as unprecedented frosts which cause water mains to burst despite all ordinary precautions.[195] He is responsible for the normal behaviour of animals

185. *Glasgow Corp. v. Taylor* [1922] 1 A.C. 44 at 67; *Thompson v. Bankstown Corp.* (1953) 87 C.L.R. 619 at 631.
186. *Wells v. Metropolitan Water Bd* [1937] 4 All E.R. 639; also *Pearson v. Lambeth B.C.* [1950] 2 K.B. 353 (grille at public toilet exit); *Coates v. Rawtenstall Corp.* [1937] 3 All E.R. 602 (playground chute).
187. *Lynch v. Nurdin* (1841) 1 Q.B. 29; *Haynes v. Harwood* [1935] 1 K.B. 146. See also *Culkin v. McFie* [1939] 3 All E.R. 613 (passing truck loaded with leaking sugar bags) and the loaded gun cases: *Dixon v. Bell* (1816) 5 M. & S. 198; 105 E.R. 1023; *Sullivan v. Creed* [1904] 2 I.R. 317. Contrast *Donovan v. Union Cartage Co.* [1933] 2 K.B. 71 (recovery denied to child falling from *unhorsed* van left unattended in the street); *Prince v. Gregory* [1959] 1 W.L.R. 177 (householder cannot be expected to foresee that lime mortar left in the street pending use might be put to mischievous use by children).
188. *McCarthy v. Wellington City* [1966] N.Z.L.R. 481; *Holian v. United Grain* (1980) 112 D.L.R. (3d) 611.
189. *Yachuk v. Oliver Blais* [1949] A.C. 386.
190. *Davis v. St Mary's Demolition* [1954] 1 W.L.R. 592 (unsafe wall on demolition site); *Wylie v. Lilley* 1961 S.L.T. (N.) 33 (detonators).
191. *Clark v. Chambers* (1878) 3 Q.B.D. 327 (negligent intervening act).
192. *Clayards v. Dethick* (1848) 12 Q.B. 439 (see below, p. 283); *Rest. 2d* §446.
193. *Cunningham v. McGrath Bros* (1963) 99 Ir.L.T.Rep. 183; *Clark v. Chambers* (1878) 3 Q.B.D. 327.
194. *Jones v. Jones* [1985] Q.B. 704 (C.A.); *Hird v. Gibson* [1974] Qd R. 14 (F.C.).
195. *Blyth v. Birmingham Waterworks* (1856) 11 Ex. 781; 156 E.R. 1047. Is it a foreseeable consequence of a negligent failure to close a paddock gate that sheep will stray and be devoured by bears which were not usually in the neighbourhood? See *Gilman v. Noyes* (1876) 57 N.H. 627 (held to be question for jury).

under his control, but not for their unpredictable actions. A milkman who leaves his pony for a long while unattended in the street ought to foresee that it might become restive and paw a passer-by,[196] but the owner of a bullock, in the absence of knowledge of its vicious propensity, is not responsible if the beast, having escaped from his control, viciously attacks a cyclist.[197]

Also, liability does not reach into infinity in time. Thus a later accident due to the victim's vulnerable condition may well be within the risk of the original accident,[198] but there comes a time when convalescence is over and the victim must stand on his own feet.[199]

Last wrongdoer

Only within comparatively recent times has it come to be allowed that a negligent, even an intentional or criminal, intervention by a stranger may fall within the risk and responsibility engendered by the defendant's original negligence. For long, the arbitrary principle prevailed that if, after the defendant's default, there intervened the culpable act of a third person, the "last human wrongdoer" was alone answerable for the plaintiff's injury. That rule may have been partly due to the naive idea that the law fulfilled its function so long as it offered *one* legally responsible defendant to the plaintiff and that it was superfluous to offer more, and partly to the common law refusal to allow contribution among tortfeasors which encouraged the traditional preoccupation with finding a *sole* responsible cause.

Instead, should we now confide the issue to the slippery criterion of reasonable foreseeability? According to one view, intervening human action must have been "very likely" or "the very kind of thing likely to happen" in order to justify saddling someone else with responsibility for it;[200] according to another, one must approach the problem of what was foreseeable "with particular care" in view of the unpredictability of human behaviour ("people are constantly doing stupid or criminal acts");[201] according to yet other counsels, "a robust and sensible approach", "instinctive feeling"[202] or, finally, "policy"[203] alone will guide towards the correct result.

196. *Aldham v. United Dairies* [1940] 1 K.B. 507: see below, p. 364.
197. *Lathall v. Joyce* [1939] 3 All E.R. 854.
198. Like refracture during convalescence, as in *Jacques v. Mathews* [1961] S.A.S.R. 205 (12 months later); *Wieland v. Cryil Lord* [1969] 3 All E.R. 1006; aliter, if due to unreasonable act of convalescent (*M'Kew v. Holland* 1970 S.C. (H.L.) 20), which in extreme cases (but was this really one?) might bar recovery completely ("unforeseeable").
199. In cases of longer time lapse and more questionable causal relation, an alternative solution has been to make an allowance for the plaintiff's increased vulnerability rather than the actual loss sustained in the second mishap: *Neal v. Watson* (1960) 34 A.L.J.R. 364 (pneumonia 17 months later); *Edwards v. Pelvay* [1961] S.A.S.R. 171 (refracture 18 months later). Not followed: *Powell v. Guttman* (1978) 89 D.L.R. (3d) 180.
200. *Home Office v. Dorset Y.C.* [1970] A.C. 1004 at 1030 per Lord Reid. Interpreted as referring only to the intervention of the later tortfeasor, not the likelihood of his negligence: *Thorpe Nominees v. Henderson & Lahey* [1988] 2 Qd R. 216 (F.C.).
201. *Lamb v. Camden L.B.C.* [1981] Q.B. 625 at 642 per Oliver L.J.
202. Ibid. at 647 per Watkins L.J.
203. Ibid. at 639 per Lord Denning.

Generally speaking, it may be true that the intervention of third parties behaving in a substandard fashion, let alone bent on mischief, is less readily expectable, but this bears on the question of foreseeability rather than causation and, in any event, does not admit of generalisation. The strongest case for liability is presented by cases where the defendant's conduct is negligent precisely because it unreasonably increases the risk of negligent harm by a third party. For it would be incongruous to treat as too remote, a harm which the defendant was duty bound to avoid. Examples include leaving a loaded gun about,[204] entrusting a car to an incompetent driver,[205] serving excessive alcohol to a motorist,[206] a landlord's failure to secure locks against a rapist,[207] perhaps even leaving an unlocked car (especially with an ignition key) in the street with the result that it is either turned loose by trouble makers[208] or stolen by a careless driver.[209] Others involve conduct provoking dangerous behaviour, such as a radio station running a contest which enticed teenagers into dangerous driving[210] or a speeding motorist trying to shake off a pursuing police car.

But even in situations where the defendant's conduct is negligent primarily because of some different risk, it may well encompass responsibility also for the additional risk of negligence by others. Thus a defendant whose negligence causes a highway collision may become liable for additional damage due to another motorist negligently piling into the wreckage[211] or a physician's negligent treatment of the victim.[212] Nor is modern law inclined to give any greater weight to the excuse that the intervener's negligence consisted in a culpable *omission*; for experience suggests as even more likely that someone may fall down on his job in *not* doing his duty. Thus, it has long ceased to be an excuse for a negligent manufacturer that a distributor failed in his duty of inspecting the article, save perhaps when there was reason for him to rely on its being properly done.[213] Likewise, responsibility for a slipshod job can no longer be conveniently shifted by a contractor or repairer to his customer merely because the latter "accepted the job",[214] or some other intermediary, like a subcontractor[215] or certificating authority,[216] failed in its duty to detect the flaw.

204. See above, p. 216.
205. See above, p. 153.
206. *Vesely v. Sager* 486 P. 2d 151 (Cal. 1971).
207. *Q. v. Minto* (1985) 15 D.L.R. (4d) 581.
208. *Martin v. Stanborough* (1924) 41 T.L.R. 1 (C.A.); *Bohdal v. Streets* [1984] Tas. R. 82 (not in private grounds).
209. But policy may militate against it: *Spagnolo v. Margesson's* (1983) 145 D.L.R. (3d) 381 (at least for accident six days later). American law is divided: Peck, *Auto Theft* [1969] Wis. L. Rev. 909; *Prosser & Keeton* 313-314. *Hayman v. L.C.C.* (1981) C.L.Y. §137 found liability.
210. *Weirum v. RKO*: above, n. 145.
211. *Chapman v. Hearse* (1961) 106 C.L.R. 112 (rescuer). If the second motorist is himself injured, he may recover a share apportioned to his contributory negligence: *March v. Stramare* (1991) 171 C.L.R. 506; *Rouse v. Squires* [1973] Q.B. 889 (C.A.).
212. *Mahony v. Kruschich* (1985) 59 A.L.J.R. 504; *Price v. Milawski* (1977) 82 D.L.R. (3d) 130 (successive negligence by several doctors); *Duwyn v. Kaprielian* (1978) 94 D.L.R. (3d) 427 at 441. Cf. *R. v. Cheshire* [1991] 1 W.L.R. 844 (C.A.).
213. Below, p. 488.
214. Below, p. 474.
215. *Clay v. Crump* [1964] 1 Q.B. 533 (C.A.); *Power v. Bedford Motor* [1959] I.R. 391.
216. *Voli v. Inglewood S.* (1963) 110 C.L.R. 74; *Maindonald v. M. Aero Club* [1935] N.Z.L.R. 371.

If the intervening negligence is that of the plaintiff himself, rather than a third person's, the last human wrongdoer doctrine was for long given pride of place in the defence of contributory negligence and its refinement, the "last opportunity" rule.[217] But apportionment legislation has spoilt the taste for throwing all the blame on one or the other party alone on outmoded causal reasoning.

Deliberate harm

Even mischievous acts by third parties if within the foreseeable risk created by the defendant's negligence do not excuse, as when a boy threw a stone at an unattended horse and made it bolt[218] or an unruly crowd overturned a corroded gate at a football stadium and knocked down a bystander.[219]

More problematical are situations where the intervener's deliberate act was not just fraught with risk of injury to the plaintiff but actually intended to bring it about. Here the isolation test at one time invariably exonerated the original wrongdoer. As forcibly expressed by Lord Sumner in *Weld-Blundell v. Stephens*, "In general . . ., even though A is in fault, he is not responsible for injury to C which B, a stranger to him, deliberately chooses to do. Though A may have given the occasion for B's mischievous activity, B then becomes a new and independent cause."[220] Undoubtedly, this viewpoint is deeply rooted in our sense of fairness, reflecting the individualistic outlook of our culture and expressing what has been claimed to be no less than a common sense notion concerning causal relationship.[221] A contractor who leaves an open pit in a road is not accountable to a sheriff who is deliberately thrown into it by an escaping prisoner;[222] a farmer who leaves his loaded gun around may have to answer for mischief by meddlesome children, but not for an adult purposely firing it at his enemy;[223] a carrier who carelessly deposits some highly flammable material in a factory yard is not responsible for an explosion set off by an arsonist, as distinct from a passing typist who carelessly flings away her cigarette or even touches the material deliberately, though without fully appreciating the danger.[224] But this conclusion is attributable, not so much to any peculiar "causal potency" of deliberate human action, as to the fact that the wilful wrongdoing of others cannot ordinarily be accounted a normal risk of the dangerous situation created by the defendant.

In an increasing range of situations, however, the law is now prepared, if still somewhat hesitantly,[225] to exact liability for negligently providing an opportunity for wrongdoers to cause deliberate harm. Easiest are those

217. Cf. *Grant v. Sun Shipping Co.* [1948] A.C. 549 at 563; below, ch. 12.
218. *Haynes v. Harwood* [1935] 1 K.B. 146.
219. *Hosie v. Arbroath Club* 1978 S.L.T. 122.
220. [1920] A.C. 956 at 986 (a libel case: below, p. 552).
221. Hart & Honoré, *Causation* ch. 3.
222. *Alexander v. Town of New Castle* 17 N.E. 200 (Ind. 1888).
223. See *Dixon v. Bell* (1816) 5 M. & S. 198; 105 E.R. 1023; *Hughes v. Hughes* (1862) 1 S.C.R. (N.S.W.) 208.
224. *Philco Radio v. Spurling* [1949] 2 All E.R. 882.
225. Revealing was Lord Reid's dictum in *Dorset Y.C. v. Home Office* [1970] A.C. 1004 at 1039 that the intervention must have been "very likely", not just "a mere foreseeable possibility". Since spurned in *Lamb v. Camden L.B.C.* [1981] 2 Q.B. 625.

where the defendant is duty bound to guard against that very eventuality; where, in other words, the risk of such intervention is *the*, or at least *a*, reason for calling him negligent.[226] Such was the case of the painter who, being left alone in a house, absented himself for two hours without locking the door. In holding him liable for the loss of jewellery stolen during his absence, the court emphasised that "the very act of negligence itself consisted in the failure to take reasonable care to guard against the very thing that in fact happened."[227] On the same principle, the manufacturer of a defective alarm system may incur liability for a burglary loss,[228] a mental hospital or prison for damage by an escapee,[229] or a restaurateur for requiring his headwaiter to deposit the evening's takings in a night safe of a bank without protecting him against robbery.[230] Yet there is certainly no *general* duty to protect others against theft, vandalism or the like.[231] True, a carrier or other bailee for reward is responsible to the owner for care in guarding against theft of goods in his custody,[232] so that a service garage would be responsible for leaving a customer's car unattended in public with the ignition key in the switch, with the result that it is stolen and subsequently wrecked.[233] But no similar obligation, sounding in tort or implied contract, devolves on employers for the security of their employees' possessions in cloakrooms,[234] or on hotelkeepers for the safety of vehicles left by patrons in adjoining carparks.[235]

Reluctance to extend responsibility to the deliberate wrongdoing of others is obviously most pronounced where such an eventuality was not the risk contemplated by the rule violated by the defendant, for example when the plaintiff's unattended car is vandalised during his absence in hospital after a collision,[236] or a railway company negligently allows a carriage to be over-crowded, thereby facilitating pickpocketing.[237] In neither

226. Cf. *Rest. 2d* §§448-449.

227. *Stansbie v. Troman* [1948] 2 K.B. 48 at 52; also *Marshall v. Caledonia Rly* (1899) 1 R. 1060. In *Liberty National Life Ins. v. Weldon* 100 So. 2d 696 (Ala. 1958) an insurance company was held liable for the death of a person whose life it assured in favour of the murderer, absent an insurable interest. Is that rule directed against gambling or murder, or both?

228. *Reg. Glass v. Rivers* (1968) 120 C.L.R. 516; *Dove v. Banham's Locks* [1983] 1 W.L.R. 1436; *McNeil v. Village Locksmith* (1981) 129 D.L.R. (3d) 543; U.S.: 37 A.L.R. 4th 47 (1985).

229. *Holgate v. Lancashire Mental Hospital* [1937] 4 All E.R. 19; *Dorset Y.C. v. Home Office* [1970] A.C. 1004 (theft of yacht by Borstal boys).

230. *Chomentowski v. Red Garter Restaurant* (1970) 92 W.N. (N.S.W.) 1070; 45 A.L.J.R. 713 (H.C.). Also *Barnes v. Hay* (1988) 12 N.S.W.L.R. 337 (solicitor liable for his client, whose lease had lapsed, being harrassed by landlord).

231. *Smith v. Littlewoods* [1987] A.C. 241; see above, p. 152.

232. *Lee Cooper v. Jeakins* [1967] 2 Q.B. 1. For theft by his own servant entrusted with custody, the bailor is vicariously liable: *Morris v. Martin* [1966] 1 Q.B. 716 (C.A.); see below, p. 381.

233. *Forbes v. Aberdeen Motors* 1965 S.L.T. 333.

234. *Deyong v. Shenburn* [1946] K.B. 227; *Edwards v. W. Hertfordshire Hospital* [1957] 1 W.L.R. 415.

235. *Tinsley v. Dudley* [1951] 2 K.B. 18. But licensees for reward (like boarders or hotel guests), unlike tenants, are entitled to a duty of care from their "landlord" in safeguarding property in their rooms against theft: *Appah v. Parncliffe Investments* [1964] 1 W.L.R. 1064 (C.A.).

236. *Lamb v. Camden L.B.C.* [1981] Q.B. 625 at 642; *Duce v. Rourke* (1951) 1 W.W.R. (N.S.) 305.

237. *Cobb v. Gt Western Rly* [1894] A.C. 419.

situation, could it be said that the rule of conduct violated by the defendant was aimed against theft, and courts have generally declined to postulate a supplementary duty to guard against such an eventuality as a normal accompaniment of other hazards, at least in the absence of special knowledge by the defendant that it was specially likely to occur. This tendency becomes even more manifest the farther the deliberate injury is spatially and temporally removed from the defendant's tort. Thus when a broken sewer caused damage to an adjoining house so that it had to be evacuated, subsequent vandalising by squatters over the next three years was held to be the responsibility of the owners and their agents rather than the culpable contractor's.[238]

Equally problematical are situations where the accident victim himself intentionally aggravates his injuries, as when he is given to drink or drugs to alleviate his pain[239] or commits suicide.[240] Here recovery has generally been allowed if the train of events was foreseeable and at least viewed as involuntary. But where the victim inflicts intentional injury on a third party, such as rape following a personality change caused by the accident, it is thought to go too far to hold the tortfeasor liable for the result of a rational and voluntary decision to engage in criminal activity. The law cannot at once punish and reward such conduct. It must therefore defeat claims for loss of earnings during imprisonment,[241] all the more for indemnification for damages awarded to the rape victim against the plaintiff.[242]

238. *Lamb v. Camden L.B.C.* [1981] Q.B. 625 (C.A.). Clearly, defendant was negligent, not because of the risk of vandalising, but of water damage. Lord Denning thought such loss was best absorbed by the owner's property insurance. Cf. *Ward v. Cannock C.* [1986] Ch. 546 and "duty" cases discussed above, pp. 151-155.

239. *Havenaar v. Havenaar* [1982] 1 N.S.W.L.R. 626 (C.A.) (alcohol); *Yates v. Jones* (1990) A.T.R. 81-009 (N.S.W.C.A.) (heroin).

240. *Haber v. Walker* [1963] V.R. 339; *Murdoch v. British Israel Foundation* [1942] N.Z.L.R. 600; *Pigney v. Pointer's Transport* [1957] 1 W.L.R. 1121. A hospital or mental institution charged with the duty to guard its patients from harming themselves is liable regardless of any pretence of the suicide's mental derangement because it is the very risk which makes its conduct negligent: *Pallister v. Waikato Hospital* [1975] 2 N.Z.L.R. 725 at 736, 741-748 (C.A.); comment thereon: Coote, *Suicide and the Claim of Dependants* [1976] N.Z.L.J. 54. An epileptic's jump from a window during an involuntary spasm is an a fortiori case: *Lepine v Univ. Hospital* (1964) 50 D.L.R. (2d) 255; (1965) 53 W.W.R. 513. Also *Kirkham v. Chief Constable* [1990] 2 Q.B. 283 (C.A.); *Funk v. Clap* (1986) 68 D.L.R. (4th) 229 (prisoners).

241. *State Rail v. Wiegold* (1991) A.T.R. 81-148 (N.S.W.C.A.), disapproving *Meah v. McCreamer* [1985] 1 All E.R. 367.

242. *Meah v. McCreamer* [1986] 1 All E.R. 943. Cf. *Marx v. A.-G.* [1974] 1 N.Z.L.R. 164 (C.A.) (no duty to battered wife).

10

DAMAGES

1. PERSONAL INJURY

Once a particular injury qualifies as the proximate result of the defendant's tort for which he is responsible in accordance with the foregoing principles, the question remains how it is to be compensated. Suppose the plaintiff has lost his leg in the accident. For which of the resulting disadvantages to him—some pecuniary (like loss of earnings), others non-pecuniary (like pain)—can he claim damages, and how are they measured in dollars and cents?[1]

Lump sums

The only form of compensation known to the common law is a lump sum award,[2] in contrast for example to the German system of quarterly pensions (based on the theory of equivalence for losses incurred from day to day) and our own modern social welfare benefits including workers' compensation.

As a corollary, the plaintiff must sue "once and for all" his loss: past, present and future.[3] Neither may he split his cause of action by suing separately for different heads of damage[4] nor can a subsequent action be brought either to increase or decrease the award in case the loss turns out to be greater or less than expected at the time of the trial.[5] A speculative guess is always required at the time of the award concerning all future contingencies, ranging from the developing health picture of the victim (including his earlier death)[6] to the possible remarriage of his widow in case of fatal accidents.[7] Since this can be resolved only by estimating the

1. The leading Australian work is *Luntz*. Canada: *Cooper-Stephenson & Saunders*; Waddams; England: *McGregor*; Kemp & Kemp, *Quantum of Damages* (4th rev. ed. 1982); Ogus, *Law of Damages* (1973); Street, *Principles of the Law of Damages* (1961). Comparative: McGregor, XI Int. Encycl. Comp. L. ch. 9 (Personal Injury and Death).
2. *Fournier v. C.N.R.* [1927] A.C. 167 (P.C.).
3. *Fitter v. Veal* (1701) 12 Mod. 542; 88 E.R. 1506.
4. But what does that mean in the context? In Canada (*Cahoon v. Franks* [1967] S.C.R. 455) and most of the U.S. (James & Hazard, *Civil Procedure* §11.11) he can sue only once for the same accident. But in England and Australia, he can split personal injury and property damage: *Brunsden v. Humphrey* (1884) 14 Q.B.D. 141; *Marlborough Harbour v. Charter Travel* (1990) 18 N.S.W.L.R. 223 (C.A.); defended by Luntz, 32 Mod. L. Rev. 119 (1969); assailed by Gerber, 44 A.L.J. 119 (1970). But though the causes of action are different, the issues of fault may be identical and support issue estoppel: *Bollen v. Hickson* [1981] Qd R. 249 (F.C.).
5. Last minute reopening: *Doherty v. Liverpool Hospital* (1991) 22 N.S.W.L.R. 284 (C.A.); *Gamser v. Nominal Defendant* (1977) 136 C.L.R. 145; *Mulholland v. Mitchell* [1971] A.C. 666.
6. E.g. *Jones v. Griffith* [1969] 1 W.L.R. 795 (epilepsy); *McWilliams v. McWilliams* (1967) 87 W.N. (Pt 1) (N.S.W.) 6 (premature death).
7. See below, p. 670.

value of the chance (on a hunch or, at best, statistical evidence), it is bound to result either in a windfall or in a denial of adequate redress to the plaintiff.

A "wait and see" solution would be preferable. One way is to empower the court, as was done in England,[8] in cases where there is a chance of subsequent serious deterioration, to award damages initially on the assumption that this would *not* occur but award further damages if it does. Another is to award periodical payments from the start subject to future variation, as in some Continental countries.[9] This has long been the model under workers' compensation, and has been authorised for motor vehicles in New South Wales.[10] A less drastic solution is to defer the final award of a lump sum pending substantial uncertainties, with periodic payments in the interim. This reform has been adopted in South Australia[11] and recommended in England.[12] But opposition to any general mandatory scheme of variable periodical payments remains strong.[13] Insurance companies prefer finality and foresee enormous costs in establishing reserves, let alone in indexing benefits against inflation. The purchase of indexed annuities, however, would meet most objections, a device which is in fact being increasingly used in voluntary, so-called structured settlements.[14]

Standard of proof—loss of chance

Proof of past events, which either happened or did not happen, such as the defendant's alleged negligence or the plaintiff's loss, must at least attain a "balance of probability"; but if it does, the fact is then treated as a certainty. This "all or nothing" approach does not, however, apply to the assessment of future damages, in deference to the inescapable fact that the future itself is uncertain. Instead, the law is here content to value the mere chance of injury provided it is a realistic possibility, not merest speculation.[15] Under a system of periodical payments, one can avoid speculation as to the future and await the actual turn of events, but the common law system of "once and for all" lump sum awards requires a here and now assessment of "vicissitudes". Thus, such possibilities as the future onset of arthritis or epilepsy,[16] or of possible mitigating events like the

8. *Administration of Justice Act* 1982 s. 6.
9. Fleming, *Damages: Capital or Rent* 19 U. Tor. L.J. 295 (1969). This can only be done legislatively: *Lim v. Camden H.A.* [1980] A.C. 174 at 183; *Watkins v. Olafson* [1989] 2 S.C.R. 750. Recommended in Tas. (Report no. 52, 1988).
10. *Motor Accidents Act* 1988 s. 81 (for future economic loss other than loss of earning capacity). To be extended to other tort claims by the Personal Injury Damages Bill 1991. *Pearson* ch. 14 recommended, by majority, variable and indexed periodicals for death or serious and lasting injury. In the U.S. many States now permit or require periodicals against health care providers. On this and the *Uniform Act* see Elligett, 46 Ins. C.J. 130 (1979).
11. *Supreme Court Act* s. 30(b). E.g. *Walker v. Tugend* (1981) 28 S.A.S.R. 194.
12. *Pearson* §§574-611.
13. See Veitch, *Cosmetic Reform: Periodic Payments & Structured Settlements*, 7 U. Tas. L. Rev. 136 (1982); Rea, *Lump Sum versus Periodical Damage Awards*, 10 J. Leg. Stud. 131 (1981) who stresses the "moral hazard".
14. See Lewis, 15 J.L. & Soc. 392 (1988); Weir, *Structured Settlements* (1983). Such annuities are tax exempt in Britain and the U.S.
15. *Davies v. Taylor* [1974] A.C. 207 at 212, 220 (Lord Reid: "substantial" rather than "speculative"; Lord Simon: "substantial" rather than "fanciful or remote possibility").
16. *Callaghan v. Lynch* [1962] N.S.W.R. 871 (F.C.); *Jones v. Griffith* [1969] 1 W.L.R. 795 (C.A.); *Schrump v. Koot* (1977) 82 D.L.R. (3d) 553 (Ont. C.A.).

chances of successful surgery[17] or that the disability would have been suffered in any event in the future,[18] will be discounted by either increasing or reducing the award by a percentage corresponding to its "simple" probability. It is more equitable to discount the damages than either to deny damages altogether or award them in full.

This principle of proportioned recovery has not, however, been applied to causal indeterminacy as distinct from quantification of damages. Suppose a doctor's delay diminished the patient's chances of survival from 40 to 20 per cent. As the claimant cannot prove the defendant's causal responsibility for the death on a balance of probabilities (51 per cent), can he formulate his claim as one, not for the physical injury, but for loss of a chance of avoiding it? In *Hotson*[19] the plaintiff injured his hip in a fall. He claimed that his resulting disability was due to negligent delay in diagnosing his condition. On the basis that he would otherwise have had a 25 per cent chance of recovery, he was awarded damages discounted by 75 per cent, but the House of Lords dismissed his claim altogether. Once the judge had found that more probably than not (75 per cent) the disability was irreversible, that conclusion, it was said, definitively negatived causal responsibility for the injury (lame hip) and could not be sidestepped by arguing that the defendant's negligence deprived the plaintiff of a 25 per cent chance of recovery. Thus the chance of a timely operation being successful would have to exceed 50 per cent; yet however much greater the chance above 50 per cent, he could presumably recover 100 per cent.

In view of the uncertainties of medical diagnosis, this approach is apt to blunt the sanction against negligent medical treatment. It under-deters the guilty but overcompensates plaintiffs who succeed in mounting the 50 per cent hurdle. As against this, the court may have feared that recognition of a cause of action for loss of a chance of avoiding physical injury would encourage speculative claims not only where the chance was less than probable, but all the more before such injury had actually occurred.

In some situations, however, loss of chance has been held compensable, as where a solicitor fails to commence proceedings in time and thereby deprives his client of a chance to win[20] or where personal injury deprives the victim of a chance of winning a competition.[21] These exceptions can perhaps be explained on the ground that the chance has remained suspended, whereas in the medical case the loss actually occurred and the loss of chance argument is invoked to overcome proof of what was its cause.[22]

17. See below, p. 253 (mitigation).
18. *Mallec v. Hutton* (1990) 169 C.L.R. 638 (proof of what might or might not have happened; reconcilable with *Hotson*?: 69 Can. B. Rev. 136 (1991).
19. *Hotson v. East Berks A.H.A.* [1987] A.C. 750; *Laferrière v. Lawson* [1991] 1 S.C.R. 541 (Que.). See Stapleton, *The Gist of Negligence—II*, 104 L.Q.R. 389 (1988); Fleming, *Probabilistic Causation in Tort Law*, 68 Can. B. Rev. 661 (1989).
20. *Johnson v. Perez* (1988) 166 C.L.R. 351; *Nikolaou v. Papasavas* (1988) 166 C.L.R. 394. Now tort: see above, p. 187. Also *Takaro Properties v. Rowland* [1976] N.Z.L.R. 22.
21. *Mulvaine v. Joseph* 112 Sol. J. 927 (1968); also *Howe v. Teefy* (1927) 27 S.R. (N.S.W.) 301 (conversion of racehorse).
22. See *Cane* 148-154 and the discussion of French authorities in *Laferrière v. Lawson*. Another explanation, by Coote, 62 A.L.J. 761 (1988), allows recovery where the duty is to avoid purely economic loss.

Indemnity principle

The overriding purpose of our law of damages is to compensate the injured, not to punish the injurer.[23] "Punitive" or "exemplary" damages, over and above compensatory, are allowed (if at all) only against defendants guilty of contumelious disregard of plaintiffs' rights, as in cases of deliberate libel or wanton physical attack.[24]

Even in assessing compensatory damages, the law seeks at most to indemnify the victim for the loss he has suffered, not to mulct the tortfeasor for the injury he has caused. Hence the plaintiff must give credit for savings which minimised particular loss items (for example what he would have spent on food if he had not been in hospital)[25] or for any reduction in the anticipated extent of the injury due to subsequent events[26] (like a widow's remarriage,[27] the victim's death[28] or a later accident[29]).

Finally, allowance may have to be made for benefits which offset losses. But to warrant a set-off, the gain must be fairly closely linked to the loss, not "collateral" or "res inter alios acta":[30] for example, where loss of profits due to inability to replace equipment was mitigated by a later opportunity to purchase a replacement at a lower cost,[31] or where the extra cost of replacing an old tractor with a new one was reduced by reselling it after a short while when it was no longer needed.[32] Those transactions were "part of a continuous dealing with the situation in which the plaintiff found himself"[33] as the result of the accident; in contrast to independent or disconnected events, for example, where neighbouring land damaged by the blow-out of an oilwell increased in value due to the discovery of oil[34] or where a surgeon left a swab in a patient albeit the operation saved his life.[35] The distinction is well illustrated by the case of a physician who failed to warn a patient that her sterilisation was not foolproof. In consequence she did not recognise that she was pregnant until an abortion was no longer practicable. Her damages for the trouble of her pregnancy and childbirth were reduced by not having to undergo an abortion. Even more fine-tuned was the holding that, while the joy of

23. The indemnitory (or compensatory) principle of tort damages was reacclaimed in *B.T.C. v. Gourley* [1956] A.C. 185 (loss of earnings after-tax: see below, p. 234).
24. See below.
25. Preferably by deducting the "domestic element" from cost of medical care: *Lim v. Camden H.A.* [1980] A.C. 174 at 191. In "lost years" cases (see below) the more speculative criterion of what the deceased would have spent on himself must perforce be used: ibid.
26. See above.
27. See below.
28. *Zeppos v. Pridue* (1967) 86 W.N. (Pt 1) (N.S.W.) 270 (C.A.); *McCann v. Sheppard* [1973] 1 W.L.R. 540 (C.A.); *Pratt v. Beaman* [1930] S.C.R. 284.
29. See above, p. 198. Even supervening events between trial and appeal may be admitted: see *Mulholland v. Mitchell* [1971] A.C. 666; *Perry v. Phillips* [1982] 1 W.L.R. 1297 (C.A.); *Warr v. Santos* [1973] 1 N.S.W.L.R. 432.
30. See *Rest. 2d.* §920.
31. *Bellingham v. Dhillon* [1973] Q.B. 304; dist. *Hussey v. Eels* [1990] 2 Q.B. 227 (C.A.).
32. *Hoad v. Scone Motors* [1977] 1 N.S.W.L.R. 88 (C.A.); see below, p. 251.
33. 12 Halsbury (4th ed.) 481.
34. *Green v. General Petroleum* (1928) 205 Cal. 328 at 336.
35. *Male v. Hopmans* (1967) 64 D.L.R. (2d) 105 at 116-117 (benefit not the "direct result" of the injury).

having the baby set off the trouble and care of looking after it (both non-economic items), it did not reduce the cost of its upbringing and medical care.[36]

The indemnity ideal has not, however, been pursued with absolute rigour. For example, the plaintiff need not bring into account many benefits accruing to him from outside sources as the result of the accident and may, to that extent, end up being overcompensated. But the problem of collateral benefits is complex and will be discussed in a separate section.[37] In some instances, also, the law has been prepared to compensate a plaintiff beyond his particular needs, for example by awarding heavy damages for loss of the amenities of life to an insentient (living death).[38] But against these "excesses" must be balanced the fact that the plaintiff's indemnity is rarely complete because of the adverse biases in calculating his loss (as we shall see) and the fact that he usually has to bear some of his own legal expenses.[39] A tragic feature which belies the indemnitory ideal is that the more serious and permanent the injury, the less adequate will be the compensation in practice.

Special and general damages

In personal injury actions, damages are conventionally divided into special and general. The distinction reflects a pleading rule which has changed over time.[40] Originally "general damage" referred to loss which was presumed to be the natural and probable consequence of the tort and therefore did not have to be pleaded. Only if the claim was unusual was notice required. Today, however, "specials" refers to all items of damage capable of (more or less) precise quantification, comprising medical and other expenses as well as lost earnings up to the date of trial.[41] Although natural and probable, the defendant is entitled to notice because they are quantifiable and help him to evaluate the claim. "General damages", on the other hand, comprise all non-pecuniary losses, past and future, as well as future earnings (earning capacity). The overriding modern pleading rule, however, is that a defendant is entitled to notice of any unusual circumstances affecting even the assessment of general damages.[42]

So far as special damages are concerned, the avowed aim is to put the victim in the same financial position he would have been in had the accident not happened. This is often expressed by saying that he is entitled to restitutio in integrum. With respect to general damages, however, the plaintiff receives compensation, not restitution.[43] If he has lost an eye or an arm, money can never restore what he has lost; the most it can do is to help him bear the loss with least discomfort, indignity and expense and perhaps console him a little, so far as public policy will permit money to

36. *Thake v. Maurice* [1986] Q.B. 644; see above, p. 169.
37. See below, pp. 243ff.
38. See below, p. 238.
39. Party-and-party costs awarded to successful plaintiffs rarely meet their actual expenses. In the U.S. where they have to give up one third to one half of the award to their own lawyer, pro-plaintiff rules (pre-tax earnings, award not taxable, collateral source rule) are usually justified on this ground: see Fleming, *The American Tort Process* ch. 6.
40. See Jolowicz, [1960] Cam. L.J. 214; *Luntz* 56-63; *McGregor* 16-19.
41. *Paff v. Speed* (1961) 105 C.L.R. 549 at 558-559; *Sticca v. Jouvelet* [1988] V.R. 899 (F.C.). In N.S.W. known as "out of pocket".
42. *Domsalla v. Barr* [1969] 1 W.L.R. 630 (C.A.) (plaintiff's plan to set up his own business).
43. *B.T.C. v. Gourley* [1956] A.C. 185 at 208, 212.

be a salve. The defendant must not be punished but can no longer hope to short-change his victim by pleading ruinous consequences for himself, his insurance company or the public (through increased premiums).[44]

Cutting across this formal division between special and general damages, and of peculiar importance in personal injury cases, are the twin categories of pecuniary and non-pecuniary losses.[45]

I. Pecuniary Loss

Pecuniary loss consists either in expenditures necessitated by the accident or in diminution of earning capacity; the first due to increased needs; the second due to lost gains.[46] Both are usually more susceptible to precise calculation than non-pecuniary injury and subject to relatively well defined rules.

Although the cause of action in tort arises at the time of injury, damages are assessed in values prevailing at the verdict, thereby in fairness to the plaintiff taking into account any fall in the value of money since the accident.[47] While interest is nowadays generally allowed as from the earlier date,[48] its purpose is not to mitigate inflation but to compensate the plaintiff for being kept out of money and to discourage delay by the defendant.

The principal item under the first head concerns hospital, medical and nursing expenses, past and future.[49] These are recoverable if reasonably necessary.[50] Under an older view they could be claimed only if they were legally or at least morally incurred by the victim, not if he received them free[51] as is often the case when a spouse or other relative cares for him and perhaps gives up a paying job to do so. Rather than permit the latter to claim in his own right, modern decisions however permit the victim himself to recover the value of such nursing and domestic services, the test being his need, not expenses incurred.[52] This solution provides an indirect means

44. *Lim v. Camden H.A.* [1980] A.C. 174 at 187.
45. Although the verdict results in a global sum, each item must stand on its own: *Lai Wee v. Singapore Bus* [1984] A.C. 729 (P.C.).
46. Damnum emergens, lucrum cessans.
47. *Phillips v. Ward* [1956] 1 W.L.R. 471 at 474; *Johnson v. Perez* (1988) 166 C.L.R. 351 passim.
48. See below, n. 55.
49. Awards for future care are discountable at the same rate as awards for future loss of earnings: *Todorovic v. Waller* (1981) 150 C.L.R. 402; see below, n. 69.
50. Australian courts are less forthcoming than Canadian regarding the standard of medical care: cf. *Sharman v. Evans* (1977) 138 C.L.R. 563 with *Andrews v. Grand* [1978] 2 S.C.R. 229 on future home versus institutional care for quadriplegics. Deductible is the "domestic element" in order to preclude overlap in the award for lost earnings: *Lim v. Camden H.A.* [1980] A.C. 174 at 191.
51. E.g. *Blundell v. Musgrave* (1956) 96 C.L.R. 73 (where it was held however that the plaintiff had promised to pay the public hospital). While the tortfeasor may not benefit from gifts of cash (see below, p. 245), he would, inconsistently, benefit from gifts of services.
52. *Griffiths v. Kerkemeyer* (1977) 139 C.L.R. 161; *Donnelly v. Joyce* [1974] Q.B. 454 (C.A.); *Thornton v. School Bd* [1978] 2 S.C.R. 267 at 285 (in trust); *Administration of Justice Act* 1982 (Sc.) s. 8. Even if rendered by defendant under compulsory insurance: *Lynch v. Lynch* (1991) A.T.R. 81-142. The claim was abolished in Tas. (*Common Law (Miscellaneous Actions) Act* 1986 s. 5) and limited in N.S.W. (*Motor Accidents Act* 1988 s. 72), Vic. (*Transport Accident Act* 1986 s. 174) and S.A. (*Wrongs Act Amendment Act*

for reimbursing the donor[53] and accords with a compelling sense of fairness where the benefaction stems from a non-public source.[54]

The second head of recovery—lost earnings—is now split into two segments. Earnings between accident and trial, being "special damages", are assessed with the aid of hindsight in the light of actual developments, including increased rates of pay. They must be itemised and may carry interest.[55]

Although future loss is commonly spoken of (especially in England) as lost earnings, the official view in Australia is that the plaintiff is entitled to damages not for loss of future earnings, but for the present impairment of his *capacity* to earn in the future.[56] But this distinction has been of little practical consequence.[57] On the one hand, it is true, the idea may be to provide the victim not so much with a fund for future periodical income, equivalent to his prospective earnings, as with a capital sum with which he may do as he pleases. This may explain why the award is not taxable as income;[58] perhaps even why the award should not be increased as such for future inflation.[59] On the other hand, it did not dissuade the High Court from assessing the loss on the basis of post-tax earnings;[60] and damages

52. *Continued*
1986). In N.S.W. awards are deliberately kept low by excluding "support commonly expected amongst family members" and injecting a discretionary element: *Kovac v. Kovac* [1982] 1 N.S.W.L.R. 656; Graycar, 14 Syd. L. Rev. 86 (1992); see below, p. 235, n. 92. (Not accepted by the Federal Court in *Hodges v. Frost* (1984) 53 A.L.R. 373.) Contrary to *Masinovic v. Motor Vehicle Trust* (1988) 42 S.A.S.R. 161, *Settree v. Roberts* [1982] 1 N.S.W.L.R. 649 disallowed interest unless remunerated. Reimbursement for hospital visits by relations can also rest on this theory or on the ground that they assist the patient's recovery and thus mitigate the loss: *Wilson v. McLeay* (1961) 106 C.L.R. 523.

53. But the plaintiff is not a trustee for the donor nor to be put under other judicial compulsion to refund: *Griffiths v. Kerkemeyer* (1977) 139 C.L.R. 161 at 176, 193. The provider has no independent standing to sue, except by statute in Ont. (below) or a husband's claim for loss of consortium (over which the injured wife should have precedence: *Hodges v. Frost* (1984) 53 A.L.R. 373 at 389).

54. Dicta suggest that a defendant is not bound to pay the cost of services provided free by a public institution: *Griffith* at 394, 413; *Cunningham v. Harrison* [1973] Q.B. 942 at 952.

55. *Thompson v. Faraonio* [1979] 1 W.L.R. 1157; 24 A.L.R. 1 (P.C.); *Wheeler v. Page* (1982) 31 S.A.S.R. 1 (4%); *Cookson v. Knowles* [1979] A.C. 556 (short-term investment rate). Economic loss being assessed by value prevailing when incurred, commercial rate is applicable to take account both of inflation and the cost of being kept out of money; but as a rough-cut for only half the period. Authorisation of such interest, designed to discourage dilatory tactics by insurers, varies in detail (e.g. in England and Victoria starting from commencement of action rather than injury). In N.S.W. interest is only exceptionally allowed in motor cases: *Motor Accident Act* 1988 s. 73.

56. *O'Brien v. McKean* (1968) 118 C.L.R. 540. This theorem applies even to earnings prior to trial, which are conventionally treated as "specials". In England, though, "loss of earning *capacity*" is a term commonly reserved for plaintiffs who have not suffered a current loss of remuneration but might do so in the future: *Moeliker v. Reyrolle* [1977] 1 W.L.R. 132.

57. See Atiyah, *Loss of Earnings or Earning Capacity*, 45 A.L.J. 228 (1971); *Luntz* ch. 5. *Pearson* §338 agreed with the English Law Commission in regarding the distinction as "unreal".

58. *Tinkler v. F.C.T.* (1979) 29 A.L.R. 663 at 667; *Andrews v. Grand* [1978] 2 S.C.R. 229 at 259.

59. *O'Brien v. McKean* (1968) 118 C.L.R. 540; *Taylor v. O'Connor* [1971] A.C. 115. But see below, n. 66 (discount factor). Comparative: Fleming, *Impact of Inflation on Tort Compensation*, 26 Am. J. Comp. L. 51 (1978).

60. Only Barwick C.J., a great champion of the "capacity" theory, invoked it in dissent in *Cullen v. Trappell* (1980) 146 C.L.R. 1.

for the underemployed[61] and housewives[62] are generally assessed on the basis of what they *would*, rather than *could*, have earned. In any event, what counts is the plaintiff's loss, not his needs. Thus the fact that he will be institutionalised for life and die without dependants,[63] or that he has non-earned income[64] will not reduce the award.

Moreover, the loss is generally calculated by computing an amount equal in value to the expected stream of earnings for the remainder of the relevant period (in case of permanent disability, until retirement). For this purpose it would of course be a mistake to pick the sum which, invested, would yield an income equal to the lost earnings, since it would leave the plaintiff at the end of the period with the capital sum. Instead, it must be the sum which, together with interest thereon, will yield the required replacement income and be exhausted at the end.[65] In accounting parlance, the sum of future earnings must be reduced to present value. For example, the present value of receiving $10,000 for 20 years, assuming interest of 5 per cent, is $124,600.[66] In an inflation-free economy, the appropriate discount factor would be the yield of the best and safest investments, that is, government securities, typically well below the market rate because of their reduced risk.

But under inflationary conditions, the interest rate contains an inflation factor to compensate for the falling value of money in addition to its "real" cost. Discounting by the inflated rate would have to be compensated by also taking into account any future inflationary rise of earnings. That, however, is more speculative, especially over longer periods, than using instead an inflation-free discount factor (the "real interest rate")[67] for unadjusted earnings determined as of the time of judgment. The latter method has the added advantage of dispensing with the necessity of expert testimony at every trial. It has therefore achieved the widest following.[68] The

61. The first-mentioned criterion was adopted in *Forsberg v. Maslin* [1968] S.A.S.R. 432, the second in *Tzouvelis v. Victorian Rlys* [1968] V.R. 112 at 136. *Mann v. Elbourn* (1974) 8 S.A.S.R. 298 (F.C.) favoured the intermediate position of adding to the loss of the plaintiff's earning capacity he would have exercised an allowance for the loss of the chance to exploit his residual capacity. Cf. *McMahon v. Ins. Office* (1984) 26 N.T.R. 5 (compensation scheme).
62. See below, p. 235.
63. *Lim v. Camden H.A.* [1980] A.C. 174 (rejecting the fatal accident model).
64. *Phillips v. L. & S.W. Rly* (1879) 5 C.P.D. 280 (no means test).
65. A plaintiff directly disabled from attending to his affairs is also entitled to allowance for fund management: *Treonne v. Shaheen* (1988) 12 N.S.W.L.R. 522 (C.A.).
66. See Prevett, *Actuarial Assessment of Damages*, 35 Mod. L. Rev. 140, 257 (1972). An annuity table, like that in 33 A.L.J. 28 (1959), computing the present value of various weekly payments, may be handed to the jury with suitable explanation: *Maronet v. Christie* [1964] V.R. 806 (F.C.); *Luntz* ch. 6; *Lai Wee v. Singapore Bus* [1984] A.C. 729 (comparing English use of "multipliers"). Beyond such purely arithmetical aid, actuarial evidence relating to life expectancy according to sex, occupation, etc., or contingencies of death or remarriage are also occasionally used in Australia, though cautiously: Wickens, *Actuarial Assistance in Assessing Damages*, 48 A.L.J. 286 (1974).
67. The real interest rate fluctuates greatly over shorter periods, but over longer periods in the past has been between 1% and 3%.
68. U.S.: *Jones & Laughlin v. Pfeifer* 462 U.S. 523 (1983) (generally 1-3%); Canada: *Arnold v. Teno* [1978] 2 S.C.R. 287 (7%); criticised Rea, *Inflation, Taxation and Damage Assessment*, 58 Can. R. Rev. 280 (1980); *Lewis v. Todd* [1980] 2 S.C.R. 694 (4¼% minus 2% productivity factor). English courts cling to the traditional 4-5% based multipliers: *Pritchard v. Cobden* [1988] Fam. 22 (C.A.).

Australian High Court has prescribed a uniform rate of 3 per cent;[69] most Australian States have adopted a statutory rate.[70]

Further adjustments may be in order to take into account the plaintiff's future prospects, good and bad. These may relate to his developing physical condition, including life expectancy, or to his career. As regards the latter, difficulties increase the younger the plaintiff's age: for example, promotion in the case of young employees, let alone the prospects of a young child.[71] There used to be a tendency to over-assess adverse contingencies, like unemployment and sickness. Nowadays, however, a discount for such eventualities is only rarely justified:[72] "There is no sound basis for supposing that there is always a preponderance of bad luck over good luck."[73]

If the victim's life expectancy has been reduced, the basis of calculating his loss of earning capacity is his pre-, not his post-accident life expectancy.[74] If he recovers in his lifetime, his dependants would be barred from any later claim of their own for his accelerated death;[75] thus damages for his "lost years" not only compensate a real loss of his own but alone offer a chance of compensation to his surviving family. This still leaves a marked discrepancy between claims finalised before and after his death: before, he recovers for his own future loss and he can dispose of the award as he likes; after, only dependants can claim and for their own loss.[76]

Tax

Lump sum awards for personal injury are income tax free, even to the extent that they seek to compensate for loss of earnings.[77] There are

69. *Todorovic v. Waller* (1981) 150 C.L.R. 402 (this includes the tax component on the notional investment income and future changes in wage rates and prices). See Davis, 56 A.L.J. 168 (1982); Sieper, 17 Melb. U.L. Rev. 614 (economic analysis).
70. *Motor Accidents Act* 1988 (N.S.W.) s. 71 (5%); *Transport Accident Act* 1986 (Vic.) s. 173 (6%); *Common Law Practice Act* 1981 (Qld) (5%); *Wrongs Act Amendment Act* 1986 (S.A.) (5% for motor accidents); *Acts Amendment (Actions for Damages) Act* 1986 (W.A.) (6%); *Acts Amendment (Miscellaneous Actions) Act* 1986 (Tas.) s. 4 (7% or Order).
71. See *D'Ambrosio v. De Souza* (1985) 60 A.C.T.R. 18; *Beasley v. Marshall* (1986) 40 S.A.S.R. 544; *Taylor v. Bristol Omnibus Co.* [1975] 1 W.L.R. 1054 at 1059 (father's position as starting point); *Hughes v. McKeown* [1985] 1 W.L.R. 963 (girl's marriage prospects ignored).
72. *Faulkner v. Keffalinos* (1970) 45 A.L.J.R. 80. In no event are arbitrary deductions at a stated percentage justifiable today: *Bresatz v. Przibilla* (1962) 108 C.L.R. 541; *Teubner v. Humble* (1963) 108 C.L.R. 491 at 508-509; *Andrews v. Grand* [1978] 2 S.C.R. 229 (where, however, 20% was deducted). According to actuarial calculations, a reduction of no more than 2-3% is justified (Traversi, *Actuaries and the Courts*, 29 A.L.J. 557 (1956)), which would be balanced by the chance of earning beyond 65 (the usual cut-off point): *Tzouvelis v. Victorian Rlys* [1968] V.R. 112 at 136.
73. *Cullen v. Trappell* (1980) 146 C.L.R. 1 at 33 per Aickin J.
74. *Skelton v. Collins* (1966) 115 C.L.R. 94; *Andrews v. Grand* [1978] 2 S.C.R. 229 at 252; *Pickett v. British Rail* [1980] A.C. 136. Deducted are his living expenses, including his share of joint expenditures such as housing and car: *Harris v. Empress Motors* [1984] 1 W.L.R. 212 (C.A.); *Sharman v. Evans* (1977) 138 C.L.R. 563.
75. See below, p. 666.
76. See below, p. 677. But see *Croke v. Wiseman* [1982] 1 W.L.R. 71 (denying damages for lost years to a young man without dependants).
77. Australia: *Atlas Tiles v. Briers* (1978) 144 C.L.R. 202; *Finance Act* 1965 (U.K.) s. 27(8).

several reasons: first is the view that what is being compensated is loss not of earnings but of earning capacity, a capital asset. Secondly, in the absence of provision for spreading the tax over the relevant number of years, it would be unfair, indeed punitive, to apply the income tax (or even capital gains tax) rate to the total damages when awarded.[78] Thirdly, it would be repugnant to public morality for the tax collector to demand his cut out of the meagre compensation received by victims of misfortune.[79] It is as well to recognise, however, that the taxpayer thus makes a substantial contribution to the cost of accident compensation.

More divisive has been the question of whether the proper base for assessing damages should be the plaintiff's pre- or post-tax earnings. England adopted the latter rule,[80] and so did Australia after reconsideration;[81] Canada followed the predominant American practice of assessing gross earnings.[82] In favour of the English rule it is argued that the plaintiff must prove a real (not just a technical) loss, and that to ignore the tax component under modern conditions of high taxation, usually deducted at source, would confer on him a windfall. But an "open-handed rather than a close-fisted approach" should be adopted,[83] and as a counterweight, allowance must be made for tax payable on the notional income of the award.[84] Opponents contend that on a conceptualistic level, it is difficult to justify a distinction between ignoring "collateral benefits" like pensions[85] and the incidence of tax: neither the notion of remoteness nor of necessary expenditure could provide a guide. It was therefore better to view also this problem as depending on "justice, reasonableness and public policy."[86] Paramount was the difficulty of estimating the plaintiff's *future* tax liability which could vary both with changing tax rates and his own tax planning, as well as increasing the award by the tax on the notional interest earned—apt to convert these calculations into a computer program. Worst of all, the benefit the legislature (by not taxing the award) intended for the victim was being usurped by the tortfeasor.[87]

78. The award could be taxed on the basis of the present value of the future tax on the gross income: Yoran, *Tax Aspects in Tort Compensation*, 22 Isr. L. Rev. 37 (1987). An alternative division into capital and income is proposed by Bishop & Kay, 104 L.Q. Rev. 211 (1987).
79. This argument has most force in the U.S. because of the contingent fee: Fleming, *Tort Process* 211-214.
80. *B.T.C. v. Gourley* [1956] A.C. 185 (personal injuries); *Lewis v. Daily Telegraph* [1964] A.C. 234 (libel).
81. *Cullen v. Trappell* (1980) 146 C.L.R. 1 (banco). Anticipated by *Wrongs Act* 1979 (Vic.) s. 28A; *Common Law Practice Act* 1978 (Qld) s. 4.
82. *R. v. Jennings* [1966] S.C.R. 532. A new direction may have been given to the American practice by the adoption of post-tax income for F.E.L.A. actions in *Norfolk & W. Rly v. Liepelt* 444 U.S. 490 (1980).
83. *Cullen v. Trappell* (1980) 146 C.L.R. 1.
84. *Taylor v. O'Connor* [1971] A.C. 115; *Watkins v. Olafson* [1989] 2 S.C.R. 750 (future care). In Australia merged in the 3% discount rate: *Todorovic v. Waller* (1981) 150 C.L.R. 402, thereby side-stepping a division over whether notional or actual investment returns (and capital gains) should be considered.
85. See below, p. 247.
86. *Parry v. Cleaver* [1970] A.C. 1 at 13 per Lord Reid; see below, p. 244.
87. Moreover, the tortfeasor if self-insured will often claim tax exemption for the damages awarded against him: cf. *Strong v. Woodifield* [1906] A.C. 448. Generally: Bishop & Kay, *Taxation of Damages*, 104 L.Q.R. 211 (1987). An acceptable formula could be found: e.g. to tax damages as ordinary income in the years in which it would have been earned (minority recommendation of the Law Reform Commission (No. 7, 1958)).

Housewives

In the past, economic loss resulting from injury to a housewife was conceived as one to be primarily claimed by the husband's action for loss of her services. This archaism is gradually yielding to the recognition of her own right to assert impairment of her housekeeping capacity, accompanied either by the complete abolition of the husband's action or by its contraction to non-pecuniary injury.[88] The preferable basis of her claim is the cost of replacement services[89] rather than the psychological loss of satisfaction in rendering services for others[90] (which would yield less) or what she might have been able to earn outside the home (yielding more if she had skills that she preferred not to exercise).[91] A niggling hesitation, so far confined to New South Wales, is to disregard replacement services when rendered "in the ordinary course of family life and obligation".[92]

Critique

Although the courts have in the more recent past engaged in an intense review of the damage rules, the result has not repaid these efforts. Pragmatism and compromise once again proved stronger than adherence to agreed principles.[93] Instead of becoming simpler, the rules have increased in complexity, more suitable for computers than the rules of thumb characteristic of the traditional common law. Complex calculations are required on the often unrealistic assumption that the plaintiff will invest his award in an annuity. Moreover, in cases of longer-lasting incapacity, the combination of variables like the discount rate, tax rates and contingencies tend to defeat the aims of predictability and uniformity so devoutly pursued especially by English courts.[94]

II. Non-Pecuniary Loss

Non-pecuniary loss poses an entirely different problem: Money may compensate for loss of earnings and other pecuniary loss, but can neither undo nor offer an equivalent for pain and distress. The most damages can furnish is solace, by providing the victim with the means of distraction and substitute activities.[95] Not all the gold in the Bank of England can make good excruciating pain, loss of sight or limb or cosmetic injuries,[96] but it may finance holidays, recreation and extra comforts. However imperfect,

88. See below, p. 658.
89. *Hodges v. Frost* (1983) 53 A.L.R. 373 (Fed. C.A.); *Franco v. Wolfe* (1974) 52 D.L.R. (3d) 355 (Ont. C.A.). Also "housekeeping allowance" under Tas. no-fault statute.
90. As proposed in *Burnicle v. Cutelli* [1982] 2 N.S.W.L.R. 26 (C.A.); *Maiward v. Doyle* [1983] W.A.R. 210.
91. See Graycar, *Compensation for Loss of Capacity to Work in the Home*, 10 Syd. L. Rev. 528 (1985); Riseley, *Sex, Housework and the Law*, 7 Adel. L. Rev. 121 (1981). A.L.R.C. recommended valuation based on gross median weekly but *Law Reform (Miscellaneous Provisions) Act* (A.C.T.) s. 23 prescribed discretionary guides.
92. *Kovac v. Kovac* [1982] 1 N.S.W.L.R. 656; *Law Reform (Miscellaneous Provisions) Act* (A.C.T.) s. 33. Implicit is the larger question of whether the *Kerkemeyer* principle (see above, n. 52) applies at all to services rendered for others.
93. See McLachlan, *What Price Disability?* 59 Can. B. Rev. 1 (1981).
94. For a striking illustration see *Paul v. Rendell* (1981) 55 A.L.J.R. 371 (P.C.).
95. E.g. *Skelton v. Collins* (1966) 115 C.L.R. 94 at 131 per Windeyer J.; *Andrews v. Grand* [1978] 2 S.C.R. 229 at 262 per Dickson J.
96. *Ralevski v. Dimovski* (1986) 7 N.S.W.L.R. 487 (same for men as for women).

the overriding purpose remains compensation, not retribution or punishment[97] as in some other legal systems.[98] All the same, more than half the total amount paid out under the present tort system is apparently attributable to non-pecuniary loss, and to a particularly high proportion of small payments (in settlements).[99] The Pearson Commission recently recommended against awards for the first three months after the injury with a view to discouraging tort claims for minor or transient injuries.[100] But at common law for every personal injury, however transitory, a plaintiff is entitled to damages.

In the absence of any logical process for assessing such damages, courts are inevitably driven to a conventional scale or tariff acceptable to the prevailing sense of what is fair and equitable. It is to this aspect that such common (but troubling) admonitions are addressed, as that "compensation should aim to be fair rather than full or perfect."[101] The resulting trend to more or less standardised awards ("flexible judicial tariffs")[102] is reinforced by the great value our law attaches to predictability, which promotes settlements and satisfies a sense of justice demanding equal treatment for equal cases. Uniformity is maintained by appellate control over awards[103] and, especially in England, by displacing juries entirely from assessing damages[104] in favour of judges whose professionalism ensures adherence to prevailing judicially-imposed norms.[105]

In contrast to the practice in England and many other Commonwealth jurisdictions, the High Court of Australia has opposed citation to prior awards in similar cases on the ground that no one case is like another and that "the judgment of a court awarding damages is not to be overborne by what other minds have judged right and proper for other situations."[106] Its concession, however, that "a judge will be aware of and give weight to current general ideas of fairness and moderation" undermined that premise, there being no rational basis for such information other than a comparison with other awards. Most courts, perplexed by this discordant

97. Punishment would not only be impermissible, but will also be frustrated because in most instances the award would be paid out of insurance premiums, not the defendant's own pocket: *Prather v. Hamel* (1976) 66 D.L.R. (3d) 109 at 127.
98. See Stoll, *Penal Purposes of the Law of Tort*, 18 Am. J. Comp. L. 3 (1970).
99. *Pearson* §382. In S.A. 44%.
100. §388. The strong Western cultural attachment to non-pecuniary damages is underlined by the remarkable resistance of most Socialist countries to the Soviet rejection: McGregor, XI Int. Encycl. Comp. L. ch. 9 §§36-38.
101. E.g. *Warren v. King* [1964] 1 W.L.R. 1, passim (C.A.). Censured by Edmund Davies L.J. in *Fowler v. Grace*, *The Times*, 20 Feb. 1970.
102. *Pickett v. British Rail* [1980] A.C. 136 at 168 per Lord Scarman.
103. Appellate courts have often more reason, but less authority, to interfere with awards by juries than by judges. A favoured formula is whether the award is so small or large as to shock the appellate tribunal as being out of all proportion: *Thatcher v. Charles* (1961) 104 C.L.R. 57; *Precision Plastics v. Demir* (1975) 132 C.L.R. 362 (juries); *Bratovich v. Mitchell* [1968] V.R. 556 (judge).
104. The English C.A. firmly opposed discretionary allowance of a jury even when the injury is very unusual: *H. v. Ministry of Defence* [1991] 2 W.L.R. 1192 (unconsented penectomy); *Ward v. James* [1966] 1 Q.B. 273. For jury trial see below, pp. 308ff.
105. English awards are regularly reported in *Current Law* and may be cited to a judge, but not a jury: *Waldon v. War Office* [1956] 1 W.L.R. 51; see below, p. 311. In Australia: *Planet Fisheries v. La Rosa* (1968) 119 C.L.R. 118 interdicted citation even on appeal. Criticised: *Moran v. McMahon* [1985] 3 N.S.W.L.R. 700 at 724.
106. *Planet Fisheries v. La Rosa* (1968) 119 C.L.R. 118 at 124.

advice, in practice inform themselves of "overall comparability",[107] aided by several publications specifically serving this purpose.[108]

The award, even in cases of long-lasting disability, is treated as for a present loss, and therefore not notionally spread over the whole (future) period and discountable.[109] And it is assessed in monetary values prevailing at the time of assessment.[110]

Objective or subjective?

As a matter of practice, non-pecuniary loss is broken down into several elements. First is actual pain and suffering, an entirely subjective sensation of conscious distress.[111] Next is an element, variously referred to as loss of "faculty", of "capacity" or "amenities", the inability to enjoy the normal activities and functions of life consequent, for example, upon loss of a limb. The tariffs previously referred to usually include both of these elements under categories like "paraplegia", "quadriplegia", "eyesight", etc.

Certain cases, however, have called for closer analysis of the element known as loss of faculty. When the victim has either died more or less instantaneously or suffered a "living death" (permanent unconsciousness), is the loss of his ability to enjoy life measured "objectively" or in terms only of his capacity to sense that loss, that is, "subjectively"? With respect to "loss of expectation of life", belatedly recognised in the mid-1930s, the courts adopted the first alternative.[112] Their enthusiasm, however, quickly waned, and the claim was first peremptorily frozen to a purely nominal sum,[113] and later abolished either outright (as in England[114]) or at least as a claim transmissible on death (as in Australia and Canada[115]).

This interlude has inspired no less than three different responses to the wider problem of "loss of amenity". One was to say that the test was "conceptual" and "objective", independent of the victim's actual sense of loss and calling for a substantial award, symbolic of the injury, although he never appreciated his loss at all, as when rendered permanently unconscious. This approach avoids speculation about that most elusive

107. *Hirsch v. Bennett* [1969] S.A.S.R. 493 at 498; *Moran v. McMahon* (1985) 3 N.S.W.L.R. 700.
108. *CCH Australian Tort Reporter*; *Australian Legal Monthly Digest*.
109. Nor, therefore, may the award be increased for tax on income from any notional investment, as in the case of pecuniary loss. By statute prejudgment interest is allowable, but only 4%: *MBP (S.A.) v. Gogic* (1991) 171 C.L.R. 657; *Wright v. British Rlys* [1983] 2 A.C. 773 (2%). Not under *Motor Vehicle (Third Party) Insurance Act* 1942 (N.S.W.) s. 35D; *Supreme Court Act* 1935 (W.A.) s. 32 (since 1986).
110. Inflation thus being taken care of, the rate of interest should be less than the commercial rate, as recognised in Qld and S.A., but not in N.S.W. in deference to a misleading dictum in *Cullen v. Trappell* (1980) 146 C.L.R. 1 at 21 (*Bryce v. Tapalis* (1989) A.T.R. 21,302-4). In N.S.W., Vic. and S.A. no interest whatever is allowed under motor vehicle legislation; in W.A. in all actions: *Supreme Court Act* 1935 s. 32(2).
111. But the plaintiff's tender age does not justify substantial reduction: *Del Ponte v. Del Ponte* (1987) 11 N.S.W.L.R. 498 (C.A.).
112. *Rose v. Ford* [1937] A.C. 826; *Morgan v. Scoulding* [1938] 1 K.B. 786.
113. *Benham v. Gambling* [1941] A.C. 157 (£500); *Sharman v. Evans* (1977) 138 C.L.R. 563 at 584 ($2,000) currently under $10,000 (A.T.R. 21,1243). Canadian practice is much more generous, following the personalised approach: *Cooper-Stephenson & Saunders* 364-367. After death: see below, p. 677.
114. *Administration of Justice Act* 1982.
115. See below, p. 677.

experience, an individual's sense of happiness,[116] it promotes standardisation, and generally leads to much larger awards. It eventually prevailed in England,[117] though not without vigorous dissent.[118]

The opposing viewpoint was to dismiss the analogy of "loss of expectation of life" altogether as an obviously lamentable aberration,[119] and to insist that all non-pecuniary loss, not only actual pain and suffering, was predicated on "subjective" sensation. To say, as we are wont to do, that compensation is due for loss of an eye or a leg obscures the fact that the real injury consists in the loss of its profitable and pleasurable use. Hence without awareness there can be no loss of the latter kind. This conclusion, however, was too extreme for practical politics. But it strongly influenced the compromise, now adopted in Australia, that "loss of faculty" consists of an amalgam of objective and subjective elements: what the plaintiff has actually lost and what he feels about it. On the model of "loss of expectation of life", the loss itself is compensable, but at a much more modest level than when accompanied by full appreciation. On this basis, the High Court approved an award of no more than $3,000 in 1966 for a comatose plaintiff in comparison with ten times and more in comparable English cases.[120] Here as elsewhere, one must also suppress any wish to punish the defendant: this would not only be impermissible, but would also be frustrated because in most instances the award would be paid out of insurance premiums, not the defendant's own pocket.[121]

In contrast to the preceding approaches which seek to place a value on what the plaintiff has lost, either objectively or subjectively, an alternative, "functional" approach focuses instead on ways money could ameliorate the plaintiff's distress by providing substitute satisfactions.[122] The mentally afflicted plaintiff, for example, would be assessed in the light, not of his appreciation of the loss, but of his capacity to enjoy any benefit of compensation.[123] While this comes closer to the compensatory purpose of damages and discourages extravagant awards, it has all the disadvantages of the subjective approach: personalised awards, with resultant lack of uniformity, rather than tariffs; a "premium on protestations of

116. "It would be lamentable if the trial of a personal injury claim put a premium on protestations of misery and a long face was the only safe passport to a large award" (Lord Pearce in *West v. Shephard* [1964] A.C. 326 at 369).
117. *West v. Shephard* [1964] A.C. 326 (£17,500 to 41-year old woman rendered virtually insensate); *Lim v. Camden H.A.* [1980] A.C. 174 at 188 (£20,000). But though "objective", the loss is affected by the importance to the victim of the particular faculty lost: a cripple would suffer less from loss of a leg than an athlete; also the relevant period is the victim's post-accident life expectancy: *Andrews v. Freeborough* [1967] 1 Q.B. 1 (C.A.) (£2,000 for eight-year old who never regained consciousness and died within one year). U.S.: *Macdougald v. Garber* 73 N.Y. 2d 246 (1989), rejecting "hedonic damages" for loss of enjoyment of life.
118. E.g. Lords Reid and Devlin in *West v. Shephard* [1964] A.C. 326. Also *Pearson* §389.
119. Repentance was, after all, carried as far in *Benham v. Gambling* [1941] A.C. 157 as precedent permitted.
120. *Skelton v. Collins* (1966) 115 C.L.R. 94. But limited consciousness of plight still justifies quite substantial awards: *Lindsley v. Hawkins* [1973] 2 N.S.W.L.R. 581 ($30,000).
121. *Prather v. Hamel* (1976) 66 D.L.R. (3d) 109 at 127.
122. See Ogus, *Damages for Lost Amenities: For a Foot, a Feeling or a Function*? 35 Mod. L. Rev. 1 (1972).
123. This was the reason why *Pearson* §389 disapproved the claim of a *completely* insensate plaintiff. Aliter, a very young child or mentally afflicted victim with no sense of loss but some capacity to benefit. Comparative: Stolker, 39 I.C.L.Q. 82 (1990).

misery";[124] and disincentive to rehabilitation. It has nonetheless gained verbal acceptance from the Supreme Court of Canada[125] and from some judges both in England[126] and Australia.[127]

New interests

Besides these more conventional items of non-pecuniary loss, more novel types of injury have also come to be recognised, such specifically as loss of enjoyment of sex[128] or a holiday,[129] depression unconnected with any physical or mental injury,[130] even the effect of imprisonment for crimes resulting from a personality change.[131] This trend not only entails stealthy recognition of novel interests protected by the law of torts, but facilitates awards by treating these injuries as items of "pain and suffering" without apparently requiring that they be foreseeable. It thereby sets up a double standard for claimants who can establish a threshold tort like personal injury, and others who must establish independent credentials like "duty" and "foreseeability".[132]

III. Financial Limits

The common law knew nothing of arbitrary fixed ceilings ("caps") or thresholds (minima) for damages, instead tailoring awards to the specifics of the individual plaintiff. Only rarely have courts deviated from this principle, as when the English courts rather than abolishing damages for loss of expectation of life reduced them to a nominal sum[133] or when the Supreme Court of Canada limited awards for non-pecuniary injury to the 1978 equivalent of $100,000.[134]

The absence of any top limit has come under criticism from several quarters. One is directed against the very object of full earnings-related compensation under modern conditions of social welfare.[135] First, since the cost is ultimately borne either by insurance payers or the consumer public, it tends to be regressive in that the poorer have to pay a larger share to compensate the higher income earners. In contrast, benefits under social security or other compensation schemes are either "flat" or linked to average earnings.[136] Secondly, full compensation poses a "moral hazard"

124. See above, n. 116.
125. *Andrews v. Grand* [1978] 2 S.C.R. 229; *Lindal v. Lindal* [1981] 2 S.C.R. 629. *Knutson v. Farr* (1984) 12 D.L.R. (4th) 658 thought that this reversed *R. v. Jennings* [1966] S.C.R. 532, which allowed damages to an unconscious plaintiff.
126. Lord Denning was a consistent advocate of the "need" criterion: from *Fletcher v. Autocar* [1968] 2 Q.B. 322 at 336 to *Lim v. Camden H.A.* [1979] 1 Q.B. 196 at 216.
127. E.g. Windeyer J. in *Skelton v. Collins* (1966) 115 C.L.R. 94 at 131; *Teubner v. Humble* (1963) 108 C.L.R. 491 at 507.
128. *Hodges v. Harland & Wolff* [1965] 1 W.L.R. 523; *Cook v. Kier* [1970] 1 W.L.R. 556 (loss of taste or smell, and impotence).
129. *Ichard v. Frangoulis* [1977] 1 W.L.R. 556.
130. See below, p. 253.
131. *Meah v. McCreamer* [1985] 1 All E.R. 367.
132. See e.g. above.
133. *Benham v. Gambling* [1941] A.C. 157 (see above, n. 113).
134. *Andrews v. Grand & Toy Alberta* [1978] 2 S.C.R. 229 ($100,000 for quadriplegic; since adjusted for inflation (now about $200,000)).
135. See Luntz, *Damages for Personal Injury: Rhetoric, Reality and Reform from an Australian Perspective*, 38 Cur. Leg. Prob. 29 (1985).
136. *Pearson* §391 recommended limitation to five times average industrial earnings, §427 solatium to ½.

by discouraging rehabilitation. Would it not be more efficient and equitable, it is asked, to raise social security benefits to a level of average earnings, based on earnings-related contributions and remit excess earners to self-insurance?

Statutes in several jurisdictions have sought to combat the "insurance crisis" in the field of motor vehicle third party insurance[137] by restrictions on, mainly non-pecuniary, damages.[138] New South Wales, after a brief interval under a no-fault compensation scheme, restored common law damages but subject to severe limitations.[139] In the first instance, non-pecuniary damages are not allowed at all unless the claimant's ability to lead a normal life is significantly impaired. Beyond this threshold the maximum amount is $180,000 (indexed) for "a most extreme case", such as quadriplegia, the award in any particular case being in proportion thereto.[140] Further reductions of $15,000 are required for awards of less than $55,000. The model was an earlier South Australian statute, by which non-pecuniary damages are reduced to a maximum of $60,000 on a scale of 0 to 60.[141]

Victoria adopted the alternative model of a cut-off of $200,000 (minimum $20,000) on non-pecuniary damages and of $450,000 (minimum $20,000) on pecuniary loss.[142] Unlike the New South Wales and South Australian reforms which were enacted to replace or avoid a no-fault scheme, the Victorian complements one.[143] Analogous limitations have also been placed on non-pecuniary damages for work injuries against employers.[144]

Another concern, increasingly faced in the United States, is the capacity of insurance and corporate defendants to shoulder catastrophic losses involving multiple victims which occur more frequently with growing technology (from jumbo jets[145] to Thalidomide[146]). One solution is to impose a maximum monetary limit on liability for any one disaster, as an international legislation on nuclear accidents[147] and products liability.[148] In

137. See Keeler, *The Crises of Liability Insurance*, 1 Ins. L.J. 182 (1988).
138. Following the model of American statutes on medical negligence claims in the "insurance crisis" of the mid-1970s. For a plea to extend such limitations nationally and to all tort actions, see Mullany, 17 U. Melb. L. Rev. 714 (1991).
139. *Motor Accidents Act* 1988 s. 79; *Dell v. Dalton* (1991) 23 N.S.W.L.R. 528 (C.A.). The Personal Injury Damages Bill 1991 would set similar limits for other torts.
140. See *Southgate v. Waterford* (1990) 21 N.S.W.L.R. 427 (C.A.).
141. *Wrongs Act* s. 35a, later extended to train accidents. See *Percario v. Kordysz* (1990) 54 S.A.S.R. 259 (F.C.).
142. *Transport Act* 1986 s. 93.
143. Little more than 1% of awards made in 1984-1985 would likely have qualified under the Act. See below, p. 404.
144. See below, p. 504.
145. See e.g. Johnson, *Last Nine Minutes* (1976) on the DC-10 Turkish Airline crash.
146. See Sunday Times team, *Suffer the Children: The Story of Thalidomide* (1979). Products liability policies typically set a limit on total liability for any one "occurrence" or "all occurrences of a series" (*all* Thalidomide births: *Distillers v. Ajax Ins.* (1974) 130 C.L.R. 1).
147. The *Nuclear Installations Act* 1965 (U.K.) limits the liability of nuclear operators to £5 mill., and the *Price-Anderson Act* 1957 (U.S.) to $560 mill. On the policy justifying such "subventions" see Green, *Nuclear Power: Risk, Liability and Indemnity*, 71 Mich. L. Rev. 479 (1973).
148. E.g. E.E.C. Directive (1985), see below, p. 501. Britain did not avail itself of this option.

the last resort, extraordinary intervention by government is required to settle peculiarly costly catastrophes.[149]

IV. Exemplary Damages

Unlike compensatory damages so far considered, "exemplary or punitive" damages focus not on injury to the plaintiff but on outrageous conduct of the defendant, so as to warrant an additional sum, by way of penalty, to express the public's indignation and need for deterrence. In the past, a clear distinction was rarely drawn between these and "aggravated damages" (to assuage the victim's lacerated feelings), so that it came more as a jolt to familiar notions than as portent of important practical change when the House of Lords in 1964, in *Rookes v. Barnard*,[150] dramatically renounced exemplary damages as incompatible with the essentially compensatory nature of civil liability, except when expressly authorised by statute or against oppressive, arbitrary and unconstitutional acts of government servants or to prevent a tortfeasor reaping a calculated profit from his wrong. But elsewhere, including Australia, New Zealand and Canada, exemplary damages survive as a mark of public censure against egregious misconduct.[151] The criminal law offers no really effective alternative in many situations, especially defamation. Thus exemplary damages provide an incentive for private initiative of law enforcement where compensatory damages would often not be sufficient. Where the defendant has made a profit from his wrong exceeding the plaintiff's injury, exemplary damages serve the cause of preventing unjust enrichment.[152] Nor does the existence of liability insurance preclude an award, precisely because the object is not only to punish but also to be symbolic of the public's indignation.[153]

Awards must, however, be kept within bounds, as American awards have not always been,[154] lest the conventional safeguards against excessive punishment are thrown to the winds.[155] The award should aim exclusively

149. This occurred in Britain and Germany over the Thalidomide disaster. See Fleming, *Mass Torts*, 1988 Denning L.J. 37. For the rich American experience with mass torts see Fleming, *The American Tort Process* ch. 7 (1988); *Claims Resolution Facilities and the Mass Settlement of Mass Torts*, 53 (Pt 4) Law & Contemp. Prob. (1990).

150. [1964] A.C. 1129. Category 1 is illustrated (perhaps) by the Copyright Act, category 2 by *Holden v. Chief Constable* [1987] 1 Q.B. 380, category 3 by *Cassell v. Broome* [1972] A.C. 1136.

151. *Australian Consolidated Press v. Uren* [1969] 1 A.C. 590, affg *Uren v. Fairfax* (1966) 117 C.L.R. 118. N.Z.: *Taylor v. Bere* [1982] 1 N.Z.L.R. 81, surviving the ACC; *Donselaar v. Donselaar* (see below, p. 407); Canada: *Vorvis v. I.C.B.C.* [1989] 1 S.C.R. 1085. N.S.W. has abolished them in motor accident and industrial injury claims: *Motor Accidents Act* 1988 s. 81A; *Workers Compensation Act* 1987 s. 151R; also *Defamation Act* 1974 s. 46.

152. In England exemplary damages are exceptionally allowed against a defendant whose purpose was to make a profit from his tort, not just to disgorge profit generally. Nor are exemplary damages limited by the amount of profits. On the restitutionary function of compensatory damages see *Cane* 321-326.

153. *Lamb v. Cotogno* (1987) 164 C.L.R. 1 (assault by motor vehicle). American law is divided: 4 *Harper, James & Gray* 529. Dubitante: *Dupont v. Agnew* [1987] Ll. Rep. 585. Against intended injury, however, insurance is void.

154. See Fleming, *The American Tort Process*, 214-224 (1988); *Pacific Mutual Ins. v. Haslip* (1991) 111 S. Ct. 1032 (compatibility with "due process").

155. *XL Petroleum v. Caltex* (1985) 155 C.L.R. 448 (should be "moderate": verdict of $400,000 reduced to $150,000 against large corporate defendant).

to punish the defendant, not to deter others;[156] and only to the extent that the sum for compensatory (including aggravated) damages is inadequate to punish. A prior criminal conviction or a very substantial award for aggravated damages would be sufficient punishment.[157] Also, it should focus on how the defendant's behaviour affected the particular plaintiff, not including its effect on others.[158] The defendant's wealth is a relevant factor to assure that the punitive sting is felt.[159] But the award does not have to be proportionate to compensatory damages, since it would trivialise exemplary damages in cases where the insult is not accompanied by substantial injury.

While frequently associated with malice, contumelious behaviour even short of actual malice is sufficient. But there must be intent to injure or at least recklessness in the sense not merely of aggravated negligence but of "conduct showing a conscious disregard of the plaintiff's rights".[160] Not that the plaintiff must necessarily have been targeted as an individual; it would be sufficient that the manufacturer of a defective product deliberately disregarded the safety of potential users. While more common in actions for defamation,[161] trespass or nuisance,[162] exemplary damages have also been awarded in actions for negligence, such as for products liability[163] or unsafe working conditions.[164] They are not, however, available for breach of contract, not even for wrongful dismissal.[165] The position with respect to vicarious liability is uncertain. In the United States there is a tendency to postulate some measure of complicity such as managerial involvement.[166]

Aggravated damages

Since 1964 it has become practice to segregate "aggravated damages", alike in jurisdictions which have and those which have not retained "exemplary" damages. In the latter the distinction has of course attained critical significance, although in practice it may be a matter "more of words than ideas".[167] For aggravated damages the defendant's misconduct is relevant only in so far as it affects the plaintiff's feelings. As it has been aptly put, "aggravated damages are given for conduct which shocks the *plaintiff*: exemplary damages for conduct which shocks the *jury*."[168]

156. *Vorvis v. I.C.B.C.* [1989] 1 S.C.R. 1085 at 1106; *Rookes v. Barnard* [1964] A.C. 1129 at 1227.
157. E.g. *Walker v. CFTO* (1987) 39 C.C.L.T. 121 (Ont. C.A.).
158. The very high awards in the U.S. are in part attributable to the deterrence rationale, in contrast to the purely retributive purpose recognised by our law.
159. *Rookes v. Barnard* at 1228.
160. *XL Petroleum v. Caltex* at 471 per Brennan J.
161. See below, p. 596.
162. E.g. *XL Petroleum v. Caltex* (trespassory property damage); *Commonwealth v. Murray* (1988) A.T.R. 80-207; *Guppys v. Brookling* (1984) 269 E.G. 942 (C.A.) (nuisance); *Weiss Forwarding v. Omnus* [1976] 1 S.C.R. 776 (business conspiracy).
163. *Vichek v. Koshel* (1988) 52 D.L.R. (4th) 371 (B.C.C.A.).
164. *Coloca v. B.P. Australia* (1992) A.T.R. 81-153 (Vic.).
165. *Vorvis v. I.C.B.C.* at 1085. American law also favours this limitation: *Foley v. Interactive Data Corp.* 765 P. 2d 373 (Cal. 1989).
166. See *Rest. 2d* §909.
167. Stone, *Double Count and Double Talk: The End of Exemplary Damages?*, 46 A.L.J. 311 (1972).
168. *Salmond* 592.

Because corporations have no feelings, aggravated (unlike exemplary) damages are inappropriate.

In *Rookes v. Barnard* aggravated damages served to reconcile the disavowal of exemplary damages with the past practice of awarding extra damages against atrocious misconduct by parading them as compensatory, not punitive. But this left unanswered why such damages for injury to feelings and dignity, if they are no more than compensatory, should be reserved only for victims of outrageous behaviour. Injury to pride and dignity are already recognised as items of general damages in some ordinary cases, for example in defamation;[169] while more generally they are disallowed for being too trivial or difficult to assess.[170] If outrageous conduct then makes the difference, their purpose must be to punish, unless perhaps such misconduct is viewed as making the injury less than trivial.[171] All this goes to underline the ambiguity of the concept of aggravated damages.

2. COLLATERAL BENEFITS

Nowadays most persons injured in an accident manage to draw on private or on some form of social insurance for meeting part or all of their losses. This raises the question of whether the tortfeasor should be allowed to reduce his own liability by benefits that have thus accrued to the plaintiff. It is but one facet of the wider concern over how to allocate accident losses as between the tortfeasor and other available sources of compensation.[172]

There are three possible solutions: the first is to let the injured person cumulate, that is, to keep the collateral benefit and recover damages in full; the second is to ensure eventual reimbursement to the collateral fund; the third would (per contra) apply the collateral benefit in relief of the tortfeasor's liability. The last of these is accomplished simply by setting off the benefit against tort damages with no possibility of further adjustment; the second, however, can be brought about in a number of different ways. The most obvious of these is to confer on the collateral fund a right of recoupment from the tortfeasor, such as a claim for indemnity (under workers' compensation) or a right of subrogation (under insurance). In order to spare the tortfeasor from double liability, he is necessarily entitled to set off this amount in reduction of tort damages. Alternatively, much the same result can be achieved by either leaving it to the injured person to reimburse his benefactor[173] or through the device of terminating the collateral benefit, as by stopping social security payments after a successful tort recovery. Implicit in either of the last-mentioned methods, however, is that tort damages remain unreduced.

169. See below, p. 595.
170. E.g. *Kralj v. McGrath* [1986] 1 All E.R. 54 (mother's loss of child in birth).
171. Ontario L.R.C., Report on Exemplary Damages 27-30 (1991), recommending merger in general damages regardless of excessive behaviour.
172. See 2 *Harper, James & Gray* §25.23; Fleming, *Collateral Source Rule and Loss Allocation*, 54 Cal. L. Rev. 1478 (1966). Comparative: Fleming, XI Int. Encycl. Comp. L. ch. 11 (Collateral Benefits).
173. E.g. holding benefits in pari materia in trust for the collateral source, as recommended by Ontario L.R.C. (1987).

All of these solutions have found a place in relation to one or other collateral benefit. The overall position is therefore exceedingly complex. At least three reasons account for this mosaic: first, the disparate nature of the various benefits; secondly, lack of consensus as to ultimate policy objectives; and thirdly, want of co-ordination in dealing with a problem that is three- rather than two-dimensional. The question of whether a particular benefit should be set off against damages is typically faced as an isolated issue involving only the tortfeasor and his victim. This has encouraged solutions by appeal to theories of "remoteness", "causation" and, more recently, to the purpose or intent of the benefit rather than by a more comprehensive analysis of where best to allocate the burden as between tortfeasor, victim *and* the collateral fund.

The same criticism may be levelled against viewing the question as a choice simply between the compensatory and punitive theory of damages. Quite apart from the fact that these labels might well be question begging or pejorative, it may be posing a false dilemma since the second of the above-mentioned solutions (that is, the tortfeasor reimbursing the collateral fund) offers at least one felicitous method of reconciling both theorems, by limiting the victim to a mere indemnity for his net loss while holding the tortfeasor to the full measure of the damage he has done. Disillusionment with the search for a comprehensive formula has lately prompted a more pragmatic appeal to "justice, reasonableness and public policy".[174] Each type of benefit requires individual treatment.

Private insurance

Beyond all question, the plaintiff's own private insurance is not available to the tortfeasor in relief of his liability.[175] In the case of indemnity policies, like collision or fire, this does not involve double recovery since the insurance company is subrogated to the rights of the insured against the tortfeasor to the extent of its payments.[176] In the case of accident and life policies, however, the insurer has no right of subrogation[177] nor, as already seen,[178] any independent claim against the tortfeasor. Hence the plaintiff may in this instance have cumulative recovery.[179] So far as life or endowment policies are concerned, this is perfectly unexceptionable in view of their heavy saving features, but applied to term or accident insurance, there is less weight in the argument[180] that it would be unfair for the tortfeasor to intercept the benefit of the policy without having paid the premiums. Once free of the notion that somehow the tortfeasor deserves punishment and should not escape his just due, there is really no reason why

174. *Parry v. Cleaver* [1970] A.C. 1 at 13 per Lord Reid.
175. *Bradburn v. Gt W. Rly* (1874) L.R. 10 Ex. 1 (accident policy). It is probably the same, if someone else—other than the defendant (see below, p. 249)—paid the premiums.
176. See below, p. 395.
177. See below, p. 396.
178. See above, p. 179.
179. Life assurance used to be deducted from fatal accident claims because of the narrow construction of *Lord Campbell's Act*, but amending legislation has almost everywhere reversed that position: see below, p. 673.
180. Another (rather technical) argument is that the contingency on which the fixed sum becomes payable under the policy is the accident and not the pecuniary loss, if any, by the assured such as would be relevant in assessing damages for loss of earnings: *Browning v. War Office* [1963] 1 Q.B. 750 at 769-770.

he should not take advantage of the fortuity that part or all of the injury has already been made good, even if as the result of the victim's own providence. Yet the practice is now firmly entrenched of allowing the plaintiff full recovery without any set-off for insurance proceeds, whatever the nature of the policy, probably for no other reason than a pervasive feeling that damages never fully compensate for the enormity of personal injuries. Moreover, so long as accident policies are fairly rare and usually low, multiple recovery can be more easily tolerated.[181]

Gifts

Neither need credit be given for any charitable aid received by the injured, whether in the form of cash[182] or services like free nursing.[183] The common if curt explanation is simply that the donor intended to bestow a benefit on the donee, not on the tortfeasor. Besides, there is usually no real equivalence between the two payments: philanthropy seeks to express the donor's sympathy or relieve the victim's general plight rather than specifically to replace his lost wages or pay his medical bills.

But while there is every reason against the tortfeasor diverting such gifts to his own benefit, cumulation by the donee is more difficult to justify. Would it not be more conformable to the indemnitory ideal, and probably to the donor's intentions, if the gift were returned to him in case of a successful tort recovery? Indeed, the rule against deduction may be justified precisely for enabling the donee to repay the gift, bearing in mind that the donor is usually a kin or friend, financially much weaker than the defendant or his insurer. However, in general, reimbursement has been left to extra-legal sanctions.[184]

Employment benefits

Workers' compensation, the oldest form of social security, has always been strictly anchored to the indemnitory principle. Accordingly, tort claims by an injured worker against third parties no less than against his own employer are reduced by compensation already received; coupled (in the former case) with a right of the employer (or his insurer) to be indemnified by the tortfeasor.[185]

A common feature of modern employment is the provision of "fringe benefits" such as disability pay, pensions and medical services in case of illness and accident. It was in this area that the great debate over collateral benefits came to be fought out amidst considerable fluctuations of doctrine, reflecting judicial perplexity and lack of direction. Starting from principled

181. Atiyah, *Collateral Benefits Again*, 32 Mod. L. Rev. 397 at 404-405 (1969).
182. *National Insurance v. Espagne* (1961) 105 C.L.R. 569 at 580, 597-598; *Deering v. Norton* (1970) 92 W.N. (N.S.W.) 437; *Browning v. War Office* [1963] 1 Q.B. 750 at 770; see below, p. 674 (fatal accidents). State relief of property damage: *Wollington v. S.E.C.* [1980] V.R. 91 (F.C.). The rule possibly applies even to compassionate bounty from employers (see below, n. 192).
183. See above, p. 230.
184. A few older cases directing repayments have been consistently disavowed in Australia. *Griffiths v. Kerkemeyer* (1977) 139 C.L.R. 161 at 174-176, 193. The donor himself has no direct claim against the tortfeasor: *The Amerika* [1917] A.C. 38; *Rawson v. Kasman* (1956) 3 D.L.R. (2d) 376 (Ont. C.A.).
185. See below, p. 522.

opposition to double recovery,[186] sentiment later swung sharply against set-off,[187] only to revert once more to the original starting point.[188]

The indemnitory ideal was never seriously compromised with respect to wages[189] and wage-alikes such as sick leave entitlement[190] and unemployment benefits,[191] on the ground that they diminish or extinguish the loss of earnings (or earning capacity) under that head. In other words, they are treated not as gains which might or might not be set off against an actual loss, but (like free medical services in Britain) as preventing a loss from ever arising. In adopting this view in *Graham v. Baker*, the High Court was not deterred by the argument either that, in Australia, the loss is predominantly considered to be for earning *capacity* rather than earnings, or that the right to disability pay was in effect earned by the plaintiff and thus analogous to insurance benefits.

It is still an open question whether set-off is required not only for payments which the employer was contractually bound to make, but also for those he made voluntarily.[192] Are gifts or wages the appropriate analogy? On the one hand, having regard to the extinction-of-loss rationale, why should it matter that the payment was received as a bounty rather than as of right? On the other hand, set-off might conceivably discourage benevolence, not only because the donee would not be able to repay his donor, but also because the donor has almost certainly no right to reimbursement from the tortfeasor. Also, if the employer advanced wages conditional on repayment in case of a successful recovery from the tortfeasor, set-off would leave the recipient worse off than if he had not received them at all.[193] All the more is set-off precluded if the promise to repay was unconditional, that is to say, was no more than a loan.[194]

186. The influence of *B.T.C. v. Gourley* [1956] A.C. 185 (see above, p. 234) was most evident in *Browning v. War Office* [1963] 1 Q.B. 750, the highwater mark of that theory. See McGregor, *Compensation versus Punishment*, 28 Mod. L. Rev. 629 (1965). The Australian attitude was much more non-committal.

187. In Australia starting with *National Insurance v. Espagne* (1961) 105 C.L.R. 569, in England with *Parry v. Cleaver* [1970] A.C. 1, in Canada with *Boarelli v. Flannigan* (1973) 36 D.L.R. (3d) 4 (Ont. C.A.). None went as far as the American "collateral source doctrine" which treats all collateral benefits as res inter alios acta: see *Fleming*, Process 206-11.

188. *Hussain v. New Taplow Paper Mills* [1988] 1 A.C. 514; *Hodgson v. Trapp* [1989] A.C. 807; *Ratych v. Bloomer* [1990] 1 S.C.R. 940.

189. *Graham v. Baker* (1961) 106 C.L.R. 340; *Parry v. Cleaver* [1970] A.C. 1; *Ratych v. Bloomer* [1990] 1 S.C.R. 940 (except where subrogation). So also holiday pay: *Bosch v. Liebe* [1976] V.R. 265 (F.C.); *North v. Thompson* [1971] W.A.R. 103 (F.C.).

190. *Graham v. Baker* (1961) 106 C.L.R. 340 at 351; *North v. Thompson* [1971] W.A.R. 103 (F.C.); *Dell v. Vermette* (1963) 42 D.L.R. (2d) 326.

191. *Westwood v. Secretary of State* [1985] A.C. 20; *Parsons v. B.N.M.* [1964] Q.B. 95 (C.A.).

192. *Hobbelen v. Nunn* [1965] Qd R. 105; *Koremans v. Sweeney* [1966] Q.W.N. 46 required set-off. Not so: *Volpato v. Zachory* [1971] S.A.S.R. 166; *Boarelli v. Flannigan* (1973) 36 D.L.R. (3d) 4 (Ont. C.A.); cf. *Cunningham v. Harrison* [1973] Q.B. 942 (pension). In assessing *future* loss of earnings, the prospect that the employer will, as of grace, retain the plaintiff despite his disability is a reducing factor: *Ivkovic v. A.I. & S.* [1963] S.R. (N.S.W.) 598 (C.A.); *Murphy v. Stone-Wallwork* [1969] 1 W.L.R. 1023 (H.L.) (passim).

193. *Juranovich v. McMahon* [1961] N.S.W.R. 190 (F.C.); *Volpato v. Zachory* [1971] S.A.S.R. 166; *Treloar v. Wickham* (1961) 105 C.L.R. 102 contains opposing views over the "*Blundell v. Musgrave*" point: see above, n. 51.

194. *Treloar v. Wickham* (1961) 105 C.L.R. 102.

The retreat from strict indemnity was most evident in dealing with pensions from private employment. These, it was held, need not be brought into account because they are "benefits conferred on the plaintiff not only independently of the existence in him of a right to redress against others but so that they may be enjoyed by him although he may enforce that right".[195] In the first place, pensions are again different in kind from earnings lost: they do not extinguish the loss since, unlike disability and unemployment pay, they are as a rule payable whether the plaintiff lost earnings or not.[196] Secondly, the distinct policy question of whether this gain should be set off against the loss received a negative answer, primarily on the ground that the plaintiff in effect earned these benefits as part of his employment and that they are therefore essentially analogous to insurance. A pension is therefore not deductible even where the tortfeasor was the plaintiff's employer.[197] Nor does it make any difference whether the pension is contributory or not, because in either event it is—realistically—earned by the plaintiff as part of his wages. When paid ex gratia, there is the added argument concerning donative intent.[198]

In the leading English case of *Parry v. Cleaver*[199] a policeman was prematurely retired as the result of his injuries. He was given a lower paying clerical job and became entitled to a disability pension for life, but lost the higher pension he would have received on retirement in 1975. The House of Lords held that he had to give credit for his clerical wages, but not for his pension until 1975; thereafter he could claim only the difference between his disability pension and the retirement pension he would have received, since both pensions stemmed from the same insurance scheme and were therefore a loss and gain of the same kind.[200]

The latest decisions evince a strong reaction to this line of reasoning. In particular, it is questioned how one can infer an intention, one way or the other, as to whether the benefit was intended to be enjoyed cumulatively. Also, the proper focus, it would seem, should be rather on the policy governing damages than on an elusive intent behind the collateral benefit. At any rate, while at pains to distinguish pensions from wage make-ups, the House of Lords recently held that a long-term sickness benefit proportioned to pre-accident wages required set-off. Though a fringe benefit and thus in a sense "earned" by the plaintiff, it was not, on any view of "justice, reasonableness and public policy", analogous to a victim's private

195. *National Insurance v. Espagne* (1961) 105 C.L.R. 569 at 573 per Dixon C.J. In Australia, the matter of employment pensions was first broached in *Paff v. Speed* (1961) 105 C.L.R. 549, decided passim in *Espagne* (a social security pension) and specifically in *Jones v. Gleeson* (1965) 39 A.L.J.R. 258; in England in *Parry v. Cleaver* [1970] A.C. 1 (where it was noted with satisfaction that this brought personal injuries in line with earlier statutory reform for fatal accidents: see below, p. 674; in Canada *Guy v. Trizec Eq.* [1979] 2 S.C.R. 756).

196. *Parry v. Cleaver* [1970] A.C. 1 at 21 per Lord Reid.

197. *Smoker v. London Fire Authority* [1991] 2 W.L.R. 1052 (H.L.).

198. *Cunningham v. Harrison* [1973] Q.B. 942 (C.A.).

199. [1970] A.C. 1. Contra: *Dippenaar v. Shields Ins.* 1979 (2) S.A. 904 (A.D.), adopting the dissenters' view that the pension was an integral part of the employment contract. Should it matter if it was not?

200. So in *Paff v. Speed* (1961) 105 C.L.R. 549 evidence of a policeman's disability pension was held admissible (quaere to what precise effect?) in relation to his claim for loss of retirement pension rights.

insurance. "It positively offends [one's] sense of justice that a plaintiff, who has certainly paid no insurance premiums as such, should receive full wages during a period of incapacity to work from two different sources, her employer and the tortfeasor. It would seem still more unjust and anomalous where, as here, the employer and the tortfeasor are one and the same."[201]

Even more difficult to condone than double recovery is double liability. Thus if the tortfeasor has to pay full damages to the victim, he must at least be spared from additional claims for reimbursement by the employer or pension fund. Such co-ordination, however, has not been deliberately promoted, though (as it happens) clashes will be rare. Restitutionary claims by an employer in quasi-contract have been ruled out on the challenging ground that the employer's payment did not save the tortfeasor any expense (even when his damages were correspondingly reduced!).[202] Even the employer's action for loss of services, in so far as available at all, does not seem to allow reimbursement for such payments.[203]

Social welfare

Even with regard to benefits from social security or other publicly funded welfare schemes, the courts for long fumbled. One might well have thought that social welfare being plainly based on a philosophy of need and paid out of public funds, there was no justification for allowing a claimant to recover in the aggregate from that source and the tortfeasor more than an indemnity for his net loss. Here the analogy of private insurance and private benevolence, the two exceptions, is quite unrealistic. Statutory benefits are met by the taxpayer, including such as the plaintiff and defendant. The benefits derive from public funds and are received not as "public benevolence" but as entitlement. Nor is it realistic to ask if it was the statutory intent to benefit the "wrongdoer", considering that the damages will in most cases come out of insurance funds, such as motor vehicle liability insurance to which all vehicle owners contribute.[204] Mindful of these considerations, the House of Lords eventually corrected earlier mistakes by insisting on set-off for statutory benefits under welfare legislation.[205] Statute finally cleared the deck by requiring the tortfeasor to repay the social security benefits directly to the Secretary of State,[206] thereby preventing the tortfeasor from gaining a windfall.

In Australia the High Court had been on a different tack, in tenacious pursuit of a statutory intent whether the benefits were "conferred on the plaintiff not only independently of the existence in him of a right of redress against others but so that they may be enjoyed by him although he may enforce that right". That there was a discretionary element in the grant of the benefit was interpreted as such a sign, as was the general hypothesis that it could not have been the statutory purpose to benefit the

201. *Hussain v. New Taplow Paper Mills* [1988] 1 A.C. 514 at 532. Even more forceful was Lord Bridge's speech in *Hodgson v. Trapp* [1989] A.C. 807 (see below, n. 204).
202. *Receiver of Metropolitan Police v. Croydon Corp.* [1957] 2 Q.B. 154 (C.A.).
203. See below, p. 687. But in case of pensions a clash would be possible.
204. *Hodgson v. Trapp* [1989] A.C. 807 at 823.
205. Ibid.
206. *Social Security Act* 1989 (U.K.) s. 22.

"wrongdoer".[207] In the result the plaintiff would keep both the benefit and the award, with the exception of unemployment benefit as a substitute for wages.[208] This outcome also had to be reversed by a statutory amendment which compels reduction or repayment of all social security benefits on receipt of any form of compensation for the injury.[209]

Benefits from tortfeasor

The case for crediting the tortfeasor for benefits with which he has himself furnished the plaintiff is perhaps strongest: here there is no room for the argument that it would subsidise the tortfeasor at someone else's expense; moreover, it encourages voluntary aid by those who are often in the best position to offer it to their victims when it is most needed.

Cash advances are an obvious example. Where the defendant is the plaintiff's employer, he may have provided and paid for disability benefits for the injured employee, often by a scheme of insurance. If these benefits are in the nature of sick pay, they are deductible.[210] On the other hand, an insurance for lump sums quantified without reference to damages suffered has been treated as an ex gratia payment, for which the defendant could claim no credit.[211]

3. PROPERTY DAMAGE

Property damage is for most purposes treated similarly to personal injury. In particular, no distinction is in general drawn between them in staking out the boundaries of legal protection against negligence under the perspectives of "duty" and "remoteness". Thus the traditional reservations concerning recovery for purely pecuniary losses[212] have not noticeably impinged on the protection against damage to tangible property, though both are concerned alike with economic values. Ordinarily, no doubt, the extent of tangible damage is apt to be relatively manageable,[213] and the situations entailing risk of property damage are generally identical with those posing personal danger, in contrast to purely pecuniary losses.

The ubiquity of first party insurance for property, especially of buildings and equipment against fire and of motor vehicles against collision, provides an argument that here the plaintiff is a better loss bearer than the defendant. This may furnish a clue to the less sympathetic treatment,

207. *National Ins. v. Espagne* (1961) 105 C.L.R. 569 at 573 (Dixon C.J.: pension for the blind involving a discretionary element, but should that matter?); *Redding v. Lee* (1983) 151 C.L.R. 117 (invalid pension; despite means test which is incompatible with its being intended as bounty, yet operates to relieve public funds if reduction of damages is *denied*); *Pacific v. Gill* [1973] S.C.R. 654 (Canada Pension Plan).
208. *Evans v. Muller* (1983) 151 C.L.R. 117 (4:3) (past benefits; for future see *Bertram v. Kapodistrias* [1984] V.R. 619).
209. *Social Security Act* 1991 s. 1166.
210. *Hussain v. New Taplow Paper Mills* [1988] 1 A.C. 514.
211. *McCamley v. Cammell Laird* [1990] 1 W.L.R. 963 (C.A.).
212. See above, p. 177.
213. It is precisely in the rare catastrophic fire cases that a retreat from the ordinary principles of liability has been noticeable. See below, n. 214.

sometimes discernible, of tort claims for fire losses[214] and to the argument for relegating all collision damage to motor vehicles[215] and strict products liability for property damage[216] to first party insurance.

Given that the accident calls for compensation,[217] how are the damages assessed?

Assessing the loss

In this respect, property damage presents relatively little controversy compared with personal injury. Whether the property be damaged or destroyed, the plaintiff is in the first instance entitled to restitution for the loss of its value to him.[218] Usually this loss—the differential in value before and after the accident—amounts to the cost of repair or replacement.[219] If not, may the plaintiff choose whichever is the larger?

To this there is no universal answer: each case depends on how the plaintiff can be restored to his previous position while doing everything reasonable to mitigate the cost to the defendant. What would a prudent owner who had himself to bear the loss, do in the circumstances?[220] If an ordinary car would be cheaper to replace with a similar model than to repair it, the plaintiff must be content with the former.[221] Not so, however, if the article were of unique or legitimately sentimental value, such as a vintage car or heirloom.[222]

The same goes for landed property. Despite a widespread impression favouring difference in value, there is in fact no categorical rule. That measure is undoubtedly proper where the owner had already decided to pull down the house in any event[223] or the cost of repair or replacement is out of all proportion, as when expensive engineering would be required to drain land inundated by the sea or whenever there is an available market for a

214. Quite explicit: Lord Denning in *Lamb v. Camden L.B.C.* [1981] Q.B. 625 at 638; *Ryan v. N.Y. Central Rly* 35 N.Y. 210 (1866).
215. In connection with compensation plans (see below, p. 400): e.g. in Michigan (1972, somewhat modified in 1979).
216. E.g. English Law Commission (Report 82, 1977) §120.
217. For title to sue, see above, p. 181.
218. In *Seale v. Perry* [1982] V.R. 193 at 204 Lush J. favoured valuation of property as of time of judgment where increase in value was due only to inflation. *Caltex v. Aquaheat* [1983] N.Z. Recent L. 120 refused to allow for inflation with respect to past expenditures on repairs, citing C.A. of Ontario and B.C. in 90 D.L.R. (3d) 13; 27 O.R. (2d) 363.
219. Exceptionally it may include also the amount, if any, by which the value of the repaired article has diminished by reason of being involved in the accident: *Payton v. Brooks* [1974] R.T.R. 169 (C.A.); *Bowen v. Paramount Builders* [1977] 1 N.Z.L.R. 394. Where the value has been increased by defendant prior to destruction, credit must be given: *Dean v. Thomas* [1981] Qd R. 62; see above, p. 70.
220. *Pomphrey v. Cuthbertson* 1951 S.C. 147 at 161 per Lord Jamieson.
221. *Darbyshire v. Warran* [1963] 1 W.L.R. 1067 (C.A.); *Jansen v. Dewhurst* [1969] V.R. 421; *Van der Wal v. Harris* [1961] W.A.R. 124. Fully stated, the question is whether the cost of a comparable car minus the salvage value of the old is less than the cost of repairs plus the use of a substitute in the interval. In contrast to the preceding cases, in *Bartlett v. Small* [1967] N.Z.L.R. 260 the second was the lesser. Cf. *Davidson v. Gilbert* [1986] 1 Qd R. 1 (owner recovered diminution in value exceeding cost of repair).
222. As in *O'Grady v. Westminster* [1962] 2 Ll. Rep. 238.
223. *Taylor v. Auto Trade* [1972] N.Z.L.R. 102; *Taylor v. Hepworths* [1977] 1 W.L.R. 659; *Waterloo v. Swenco Manufacturing* (1975) 58 D.L.R. (3d) 180. A similar rule applies to insurance claims: *Lucas v. N.Z. Ins.* [1983] V.R. 698.

similar property, as in the case of most urban dwellings.[224] So also where a surveyor's appraisal failed to reveal that a house to be purchased had rotten timbers, the point of reference was the lesser sales value, not the cost of repair.[225] On the other hand, a plaintiff may well be justified to insist on his right to repair or rebuild, as in the case of a home to which the owner has become specially attached,[226] or of a factory without any reasonable alternative for carrying on the business and retaining its labour force.[227]

If the plaintiff is entitled to replacement, it often happens that the old thing destroyed can only be replaced by one that is new. Must he then give credit for "betterment", that is, the extent to which the new one is more valuable either because of a greater life span or efficiency? This was negatived in a case where a gutted factory was replaced by another of equivalent capacity but more modern design, on the ground that to demand a set-off would be equivalent to forcing the plaintiff to invest in modernisation of his plant.[228] It is otherwise where the destroyed item (for example, a tractor) has only a very limited life and would later have had to be replaced anyway.[229]

Consequential loss

In case of damage or destruction of a profit-earning object, the plaintiff may claim either for loss of profits,[230] or for the cost of a substitute[231] pending repair or replacement. Thus when a dredger engaged on work for a harbour board was sunk, the owners recovered, in addition to the cost of a substitute, for the extra cost incurred by them (for example interest on investments, penalties, etc.) through the consequential delay in carrying out that contract.[232] Damages may even include the loss of a future charter to

224. *Public Trustee v. Hermann* (1968) W.N. (Pt 1) (N.S.W.) 442; *Jones v. Perth S.* [1971] W.A.R. 56 (trespass); *Moss v. Christchurch R.C.* [1925] 2 K.B. 750 (nuisance); *Munnelly v. Calcon* [1978] I.R. 387 (commercial).
225. *Philips v. Ward* [1956] 1 W.L.R. 471 (C.A.).
226. *Parramatta v. Lutz* (1988) 12 N.S.W.L.R. 293 (C.A.); *Evans v. Balog* [1976] 1 N.S.W.L.R. 36 (C.A.); *Ward v. Cannock D.C.* [1986] Ch. 546. Some older cases have taken a severer view.
227. *Harbutt's Plasticine v. Wayne's Tank* [1970] 1 Q.B. 447 (C.A.). The same criterion is applied to assessment of loss under fire insurance: Ivamy, *Fire and Motor Insurance* (1968) 166-167.
228. *Harbutt's Plasticine v. Wayne's Tank* [1970] 1 Q.B. 447 (C.A.); *Anthoness v. Bland S.* [1960] S.R. (N.S.W.) 659 (rare car); *James Street Hardware v. Spizziri* (1987) 43 C.C.L.T. 9.
229. *Hoad v. Scone Motors* [1977] 1 N.S.W.L.R. 88 (C.A.).
230. *Lonie v. Perugini* (1977) 18 S.A.S.R. 201 (until replacement trees found).
231. *Athabaska Airways v. Sask. Government Airways* (1957) 12 D.L.R. (2d) 187 allowed recovery of the latter though it exceeded the former.
232. *Liesbosch (Dredger) v. The Edison* [1933] A.C. 449. On the principle that a wrongdoer takes his victim as he finds him, he is chargeable even for exceptionally high profits which the plaintiff would actually have earned (at 464); contra: *The Naxos* [1972] 1 Ll. Rep. 149 (average rate). Also for outstanding hire purchase balance though in excess of car's value: *Millar v. Candy* (1980) 39 A.C.T.R. 74. Yet the extra cost of having to hire rather than buy a substitute, because of impecuniosity, was disallowed in *The Edison* as "extrinsic" and too remote—a ruling suspect since the demise of *Polemis* and not followed in modern cases like *A.-G. v. Geothermal Produce* [1987] 2 N.Z.L.R. 348 (C.A.) (nuisance); *Doyle v. Olby* [1969] 2 Q.B. 158 (deceit); *Bevan v. Blackhall (No. 2)* [1978] 2 N.Z.L.R. 97 at 119 (architect's negligence); *Freedhoff v. Pomalift* (1970) 13 D.L.R. (3d) 523 (impecuniosity caused by wrong); Phillips, 20 Osg. H.L.J. 18 (1982); Wexler, 66 Can. B. Rev. 129 (1987).

commence upon completion of the current voyage.[233] Also, extra delay due to a strike while the ship was in dock under repair has been held to be a risk within the defendant's responsibility.[234] As in the case of personal injury, the risk of future loss need not exceed 50 per cent: loss of a chance, provided it is substantial and not entirely speculative, is compensable, as when a racehorse is injured and loses its chance of winning prize money. A plaintiff is also entitled to reimbursement for any payment required by law (though not under a voluntary agreement) for consequential damage to third parties, as when a ship disabled by the defendant damaged an adjacent dock.[235] But as already noted[236] this sympathetic attitude towards commercial loss consequential on physical damage to one's property does not extend to claims for consequential loss suffered by third persons, as illustrated by the power cable cases.

Are lost profits assessed at the pre-tax (gross) or post-tax (net) rate? In the case of personal injuries, as we have seen,[237] the plaintiff in England and Australia is entitled only to net earnings because the award itself is not taxable. Since awards for lost profits are, however, taxable,[238] the majority view has been in favour of the gross rate.[239] A more exact, if more complicated, alternative is to assess the net loss but add a supplement for the tax liability of the award.[240]

Is the plaintiff entitled to damages for loss of use in case of damage to a non-profit earning object, like a pleasure craft or private car? He is clearly entitled to the reasonable cost of hiring a substitute during repairs if he actually hires one.[241] But what if he does not? The guiding principle, here as in the case of personal injury,[242] should be that his loss is not the expenditure incurred for a substitute, but his need for it. Thus he is entitled to substantial general damages for loss of use, usually calculated as the interest on the capital value of the damaged object at the time of the collision[243] or (where the plaintiff keeps a stand-by) the daily cost of maintaining it.[244]

233. *The Argentino* (1889) 14 App. Cas. 519. Provided only that charter was an ordinary engagement.
234. *H.M.S. London* [1914] P. 72.
235. *Esso Petroleum v. Hall Russell* [1989] A.C. 643.
236. See above, p. 178.
237. See above, p. 234.
238. *Income Tax Assessment Act* 1936 (Cth) s. 26(j).
239. *Williamson v. Comm. Rlys* [1960] S.R. (N.S.W.) 252 (C.A.); *Robert v. Collier's* [1959] V.R. 280; *Parsons v. B.N.M. Laboratories* [1964] Q.B. 95 (C.A.); *Bevan v. Blackhall (No. 2)* [1973] 2 N.Z.L.R. 45.
240. *Gill v. Australia Wheat Bd* [1980] 2 N.S.W.L.R. 795 (where plaintiff's tax rate in the year of receipt was exceptionally low and he would otherwise have been greatly overcompensated).
241. *Martindale v. Duncan* [1973] 1 W.L.R. 574 (C.A.); *Moore v. DER Ltd* [1971] 1 W.L.R. 1476 (see below, p. 254, n. 254); *Penman v. St John Toyota* (1972) 30 D.L.R. (3d) 88.
242. *Donnelly v. Joyce* [1974] Q.B. 454 (C.A.).
243. *Millar v. Candy* (1981) 38 A.L.R. 299. Also *Nauru L.G.C. v. N.Z. Seamen's Union* [1986] 1 N.Z.L.R. 466 (loss of non-profitable use).
244. *Admiralty Comm. v. S.S. Susquehanna* [1926] A.C. 655 at 662; *Birmingham Corp. v. Sowsbery* (1969) 113 Sol. J. 877 (bus). The use of a stand-by is no longer recognised as neutralising the loss, though the plaintiff would most probably have allowed for this expense in his general cost calculations. But should not the cost of hiring an outside substitute represent a ceiling?

When the damaged (or destroyed) object is insured, the owner would ordinarily in the first place claim from his insurance company rather than the tortfeasor. If he does so, the former will be subrogated pro tanto to the victim's tort claim against the latter; but the victim himself may still retain a beneficial claim of his own with respect to such consequential losses as the "deductible" or forfeiture of a "no-claim" bonus.[245]

Non-material injury

It used to be thought that damages for non-material injury were allowed only consequent on physical injury but not damage to property, such for example as grief over the death of a cat or distress and inconvenience over damage to one's home[246] or car. But there has lately been a change: damages for foreseeable worry and anxiety, or physical inconvenience are now being awarded in cases of negligently constructed homes,[247] even business premises,[248] and at least for intentional shooting of pets.[249] Equally in cases of purely economic loss, such as resulting from misrepresentation.[249a]

4. MITIGATION

After the accident every claimant has a "duty" to mitigate damages, in the sense of being denied compensation at the higher scale.[250] Though fully entitled to be as extravagant as he pleases in making good the loss, he must not do it at the expense of the defendant. Conversely, any additional loss or expense incurred in endeavouring by reasonable means to minimise the damage is recoverable by him as part of the compensation for the wrong.[251]

In case of personal injuries, the victim might have to submit to surgery or other disagreeable therapy[252] in order to alleviate his condition and, if he unreasonably refuses to do so, cannot unload upon the defendant the

245. *Patel v. L.T. Executive* [1981] R.T.R. 29 (C.A.); contra: *Millar v. Candy* (1981) 38 A.L.R. 299, based on wrong approach.
246. *Attia v. British Gas* [1988] Q.B. 304 (C.A.; not for grief short of psychiatric damage).
247. *Campbelltown v. MacKay* (1988) 15 N.S.W.L.R. 501 (C.A.; substantial damages); *Clarke v. Gisborne S.* [1984] V.R. 971 (but not "mere" inconvenience); *Perry v. Phillips* [1982] 1 W.L.R. 1297 (C.A.); *Gabolinscy v. Hamilton* [1975] 1 N.Z.L.R. 150; *Young v. Tomlinson* [1979] N.Z.L.R. 441 at 462 ("annoyance, frustration, discomfort and inconvenience").
248. *Carll v. Berry* [1981] 2 N.Z.L.R. 76.
249. *Davies v. Bennison* (1927) 22 Tas. L.R. 52; *Borza v. Banner* (1975) 60 D.L.R. (3d) 304 (aggravated damages); cf. *Newell v. C.P.A.* (1976) 74 D.L.R. (3d) 574 (breach of contract: loss of dog). U.S.: 8 A.L.R. 4th 1287 (1981).
249a. See below, p. 650.
250. Failure to mitigate does not (most probably) fall under apportionment (see below, pp. 271ff), except in Eire: *Civil Liability Act* 1961 s. 34(2). The distinction is between conduct before and after the accident, not between conduct contributing to the accident and merely to the injury.
251. *The Oropesa* [1943] P. 32; *N.Z. Forest Products v. O'Sullivan* [1974] 2 N.Z.L.R. 80; *A.-G. v. Crompton* (1976) 74 D.L.R. (3d) 345. Even if the effort is abortive or the ultimate cost is greater than if no steps had been taken: *Gardner v. R.* [1933] N.Z.L.R. 730.
252. E.g. *Clarke v. Damiani* (1973) 5 S.A.S.R. 427 at 432 (wearing eye patch to mitigate double vision).

consequences of his own stupidity or irrational scruples.[253] But while the standard is that of reasonableness, it is not too high in view of the fact that it was the defendant's wrong which put the plaintiff under the dilemma.[254] Should the test be sternly objective as enunciated in the older English cases, postulating a reasonable person of "manly character", or should it compassionately follow the analogy that a tortfeasor takes his victim as he finds him?[255] An acceptable compromise which has gained support in Australia asks whether "a reasonable person in the circumstances as they existed for the plaintiff" would have refused treatment, thereby making allowance for his difficulty of understanding, even for an anxiety neurosis caused by the accident itself.[256]

There is no peremptory rule that the plaintiff is not required to spend money or incur expense to mitigate damage. Thus he may have to undergo an operation or make repairs, besides being entitled to reimbursement for the cost, if he acts with reasonable prudence.[257] On the other hand, he is not ordinarily expected to risk money or lay out capital, nor is he obliged to do something he cannot afford.[258]

The burden is on the defendant to prove that the plaintiff's refusal to mitigate was unreasonable.[259] If discharged, the plaintiff is precluded from recovering any resulting loss, though not necessarily all loss following the refusal. Suppose the recommended surgery entailed only a 70 per cent chance of success. That contingency should be discounted just like any future loss;[260] for even if he had acted reasonably, he would have faced a 30 per cent risk of failure for which he is entitled to compensation.[261]

253. *Watts v. Rake* (1960) 108 C.L.R. 158 at 159; *McAuley v. London Transport Executive* [1957] 2 Ll. Rep. 500. U.S.: 62 A.L.R. 3d 9 at 70 (1975).
254. *Moore v. DER Ltd* [1971] 1 W.L.R. 1476 (C.A.).
255. Strictly speaking, that principle applies only to pre-accident infirmities (see above, p. 204); post-accident infirmities, including injury neurosis, fall under the test of reasonable foreseeability.
256. *Fazlic v. Milingimbi C.* (1982) 56 A.L.J.R. 211; *Selvanayagam v. Uni. W.I.* [1983] 1 W.L.R. 585 (P.C.); *Karabotsos v. Plastex* [1981] V.R. 675 (F.C.). But *Janiak v. Ippolito* [1985] 1 S.C.R. 146 postulates that a pre-existing psychological infirmity must have deprived him of his capacity to make a reasonable choice.
257. *Matters v. Baker & Fawcett* [1951] S.A.S.R. 91; *Hoad v. Scone Motors* [1977] 1 N.S.W.L.R. 88 at 100.
258. *Dodd Properties v. Canterbury C.C.* [1980] 1 W.L.R. 433 (C.A.); *Bevan v. Blackhall (No. 2)* [1978] 2 N.Z.L.R. 97 at 115-116. See Phillips, *Losses Flowing from Impecuniosity*, 20 Osg. H.L.J. 18 (1982).
259. *Janiak v. Ippolito* [1985] 1 S.C.R. 146; *Munce v. Vinidex* [1974] 2 N.S.W.L.R. 235 (C.A.). Contra: *Selvanayagam v. Uni. W.I.* [1983] 1 W.L.R. 585 (P.C.).
260. See above, p. 226.
261. *Janiak v. Ippolito* [1985] 1 S.C.R. 146; *Newell v. Lucas* (1964) 82 W.N. (N.S.W.) 265 (F.C.); *Plenty v. Argus* [1975] W.A.R. 155 (F.C.).

11

JOINT TORTFEASORS AND CONTRIBUTION

In the preceding chapter, the complicating factor of multiple tortfeasors figured prominently in problems of causation and remoteness. It remains to deal with two related aspects of concurrent liability.

1. JOINT AND CONCURRENT TORTS

For a number of purposes, the common law used to, and to a modified extent still does, attach some significance to the distinction between "joint" and "several" tortfeasors. The problem arises where one and the same injury is attributable to the tort of two or more wrongdoers. Such concurrent tortfeasors are regarded as "joint" when there is concurrence not only in the causal sequence leading to the single damage, but also in some common enterprise; they are "several" or "independent" when the concurrence is exclusively in the realm of causation.[1] The former are responsible for the same tort, the latter only for the same damage. In the first case, there is but one cause of action in contemplation of law; while in the second, there are as many separate causes of action as there are tortfeasors.

A tort is imputed to several persons as joint tortfeasors in three instances: agency,[2] vicarious liability,[3] and concerted action.[4] The first two will be considered later.[5] The critical element of the third is that those participating in the commission of the tort must have acted in furtherance of a common design. There must be "concerted action to a common end",[6] not mere parallel activity or "a coincidence of separate acts which by their conjoined effect cause damage".[7] Broadly speaking, this means a conspiracy with all participants acting in furtherance of the wrong, though it is probably not necessary that they should realise they are committing a tort.[8] All persons acting in pursuance of a common end, being thus identified with each other, are accordingly responsible for the entire result; and so it was laid down in 1612 that "all coming to do an unlawful act, and of one party, the act is the act of all of the same party being present."[9] Hence, where the plaintiff was set upon by three defendants, all were held

1. Williams, *Joint Torts* 1. This is the leading treatise.
2. E.g. *Palmer v. Blowers* (1987) 75 A.L.R. 509.
3. *The Koursk* [1924] P. 140 at 155; *Vancouver v. Rhodes* [1955] 1 D.L.R. 139 (release).
4. Another used to be the joint liability of husband and wife for the wife's torts.
5. See below, ch. 19.
6. *The Koursk* [1924] P. 140 at 156.
7. Ibid. at 159-160.
8. At least, if A and B jointly write and publish a libel, they are joint tortfeasors whether they knew it to be defamatory or not: see *Dougherty v. Chandler* (1946) 46 S.R. (N.S.W.) 370; Williams, *Joint Torts* 10.
9. *Heydon's Case*, 11 Co. Rep. 5a at 5b; 77 E.R. 1150 at 1151.

liable for the entire damage, although only one committed the battery, another the imprisonment, and the third stole the silver buttons.[10] While the requisite degree of participation has not been precisely defined in modern decisions, there is cogent support both in principle and ancient authority for the suggestion that it may well correspond with the description attached by the criminal law to principals in the first and second degree.[11] This would include, besides the actual perpetrator, anyone who "aids and abets", whether or not he actively intervenes. Knowingly assisting, encouraging or merely being present as a conspirator at the commission of the wrong would suffice.

Although conspiracy is mostly associated with intended harm, it can also occur, if more rarely, in the context of negligent torts: for example, manufacturers agreeing not to warn consumers of unreasonable risk associated with asbestos or cigarettes,[12] or two motorists agreeing to race each other[13] or stopping on an expressway to quarrel.[14] Its farthest reach was probably explored in a case[15] where a landlord procured a lodger's assistance in searching for a gas leak and, both approaching it negligently with a naked flame, an explosion was set off by the lodger. The landlord was held responsible on the ground, among others, that both had employed the same negligent means, acting in concert and pursuant to a common enterprise. Clearly, the joint undertaking to discover the leak was not an agreement to engage in a negligent activity; but the defendant's acquiescence, nay, the example he set in being the first to strike a match, coupled with his position of authority, was evidently the decisive factor in attracting joint liability. There is admittedly a twilight zone in which the agency concept can be stretched to convert many a joint enterprise into a vehicle for vicarious liability, but this expedient has been rarely exploited except in some sporadic cases involving motor cars, with the evident purpose of tapping available insurance.[16] Ordinarily, however, it is probably not enough, nor should it be, for fear of deterring neighbourly co-operation, that two persons are engaged merely in a joint pursuit that is not unlawful or inherently dangerous,[17] and neither having any reason to anticipate that the other would act negligently. Thus, where two friends go out hunting and one of them accidentally hits a stranger, they are not treated as joint tortfeasors so as to permit the negligence of one to be imputed to the other, even if they had agreed to divide the bag at the end of the shoot.[18]

10. *Smithson v. Garth* (1691) 3 Lev. 324; 83 E.R. 711; see also *Schumann v. Abbott* [1961] S.A.S.R. 149; *Johnston v. Burton* (1970) 16 D.L.R. (3d) 660.
11. Williams, *Joint Torts* 11.
12. *Rogers v. Reynolds Tobacco* 761 S.W. 2d 788 (Tex. 1988).
13. *McDonald v. Dalgleish* (1973) 35 D.L.R. (3d) 486.
14. *Mason v. Burke* (1968) 68 D.L.R. (2d) 19 at 23.
15. *Brooke v. Bool* [1928] 2 K.B. 578.
16. Primarily Canadian: *Copp v. Clancy* (1957) 16 D.L.R. (2d) 415 (towing disabled car); *Gramak v. O'Connor* (1973) 41 D.L.R. (3d) 14. Significantly, the American doctrine of "joint enterprise" is also primarily confined to motor cars; somewhat similar British cases are noted below, p. 385. Joint ownership of a car does not entail joint liability, unless one actually acts as agent or servant of the other: *Launchbury v. Morgans* [1973] A.C. 127 at 145.
17. Exceptional treatment of "inherently dangerous" ventures may find support, inter alia, in the liability for independent contractors (see below, p. 391) and the agency doctrine for car owners: see below, p. 386.
18. *Cook v. Lewis* [1951] S.C.R. 830; *Summers v. Tice* 199 P. 2d 1; 5 A.L.R. 2d 91 (Cal. 1948); *Willis v. Allen* [1923] S.A.S.R. 146.

To be contrasted with concerted action are independent acts of negligence accidentally resulting in one damage, as in the familiar situation of two cars colliding and causing injury either to a pedestrian or passenger.[19] Other illustrations are cases where access to a shop is obstructed by vans belonging to neighbouring occupiers[20] or a house subsides owing to the negligent excavation of one person, in conjunction with the negligence of a water company in failing to stop up its main.[21] Here, the only nexus between the defendants is that the damage would not have occurred without the negligence of both of them. This, however, is not sufficient to make them joint tortfeasors. They are admittedly both liable for the total damage,[22] but their liability is several, not joint, and therefore spares them from the peculiar consequences of joint liability.

Consequences of joint liability

The most important corollary of joint liability, as already explained, is that participation in a joint tort entails collective responsibility for the resulting harm, regardless of whose hand struck the actual blow. This will be of inestimable help to plaintiffs who might otherwise be unable to prove who had done it or, in case of multiple injuries, who had done which. By contrast, "several" tortfeasors may ordinarily take advantage of a plaintiff's inability to identify their individual contributions to an aggregate of theoretically divisible harms; though, as already noted,[23] the thrust of progressive decisions has tended to mitigate his plight once the defendants' negligence has been established. In this manner, the theory of joint liability has furnished a useful analogy in a closely related context where the policy choice as between an entirely innocent plaintiff and a proven wrongdoer is equally compelling.

Much more questionable is the occasional suggestion that joint tortfeasors are also disqualified from suing each other for injury resulting in the course of the joint enterprise.[24] This could be justified only to the extent that accomplices in a joint *criminal* enterprise are so debarred.[25]

Turning to the procedural consequences, the first is that the liability of joint tortfeasors is joint and several. This means that the person injured may, at his option, sue each of them separately for the whole amount of the loss or all of them jointly in the same action, though even in the latter case judgment obtained against all may be executed in full against any one of them.[26] Joinder, therefore, is permissive, not compulsory.[27] In contrast, "several" tortfeasors could not be joined at common law, so that the possibility of joining defendants in one action was for long the crucial test of joint liability. This it is no longer today, since procedural reforms freely

19. *The Koursk* [1924] P. 140 (merger); *Bridge v. Chadwick* (1950) 50 S.R. (N.S.W.) 230 at 233-234; *Dodsworth v. Holt* (1964) 44 D.L.R. (2d) 480 (release).
20. *Sadler v. Gt W. Rly* [1896] A.C. 450; contrasted in *Mendoza v. Mayor of Melbourne* (1897) 22 V.L.R. 611.
21. *Thompson v. L.C.C.* [1899] 1 Q.B. 840.
22. See above, pp. 200-201.
23. See above, p. 201.
24. E.g. *Mason v. Burke* (1968) 68 D.L.R. (2d) 19 at 23 (two drivers stopping on expressway to quarrel, injured by oncoming car).
25. See below, p. 305.
26. *Rich v. Pilkington* (1691) Carth. 171; 90 E.R. 704; *Mitchell v. Tarbutt* (1794) 5 T.R. 649.
27. Even in actions for conspiracy: *Mills v. Mills* (1631) Cro. Car. 239; 79 E.R. 809.

permit joinder of concurrent tortfeasors as co-defendants despite the causes of action against them being separate.[28]

At common law, a judgment against one joint tortfeasor, even if unsatisfied, barred all further action against the others.[29] The act of one being the act of all, it was considered that there was but one cause of action which "merged" in the judgment, despite liability being both joint *and* several. This rule was quite distinct from the truism that a claimant may not have more than full satisfaction for his injury and that therefore *satisfaction*, partial or complete, from one tortfeasor (whether pursuant to judgment or settlement) discharges pro tanto the liability of all others.[30] The last-mentioned rule applies, of course, to all concurrent tortfeasors alike, be they joint or several; the former, however, availed joint tortfeasors alone and had the more drastic effect of barring a second action, even if judgment in the first remained unsatisfied. This preposterous rule has at last been abrogated by statute.[31]

As a corollary of the "merger" doctrine, only one judgment for one sum of damages could be rendered against joint tortfeasors. But now that they can be sued separately, it is possible to award exemplary damages against one but not the others.[32] However, if multiple tortfeasors are sued jointly, their liability for compensatory damages will ordinarily be the same. Moreover, statute now provides that even if sued separately (whether as joint tortfeasors or otherwise), the sums recoverable under the judgments given in those actions shall not in the aggregate exceed the amount awarded in the first,[33] and the plaintiff shall not be entitled to costs in any of those actions other than the first, unless the court is of the opinion that there was a reasonable ground for bringing the action. This reform has the object of deterring verdict-shopping, for the sake both of reducing litigation and of avoiding the complication of inconsistent verdicts on claims for

28. This reform, inaugurated in England in 1896, has been adopted throughout Australia.
29. *Brinsmead v. Harrison* (1871) L.R. 7 C.P. 547; in contrast to "several" tortfeasors: *Sadler v. Cresco Fertilisers* [1939] V.L.R. 438; *United Australia v. Barclay's Bank* [1941] A.C. 1.
30. *Castellan v. Electric Power (No. 2)* (1967) 69 S.R. (N.S.W.) 159; *Kohnke v. Karger* [1951] 2 K.B. 670; *Sadler v. Cresco Fertilisers* [1939] V.L.R. 438; *Cassimjee v. Jarrett* (1975) 59 D.L.R. (3d) 174. Settlements often raise the tricky question whether they were in full or only partial satisfaction: e.g. *Carrigan v. Duncan* 1971 S.L.T. (Sh. Ct) 33.

    Whether satisfaction by a stranger discharges a tortfeasor depends on whether the payment purported to do so or merely to help P. In the latter case, it is treated like any other donation from an outside source and cannot be set off: *Dawson v. Sawatzky* [1946] 1 D.L.R. 476.
31. N.S.W.: *Law Reform (Miscellaneous Provisions) Act* 1946; Vic.: *Wrongs Act* 1958 s. 24AA; Qld: *Law Reform Act* 1952, Pt II; S.A.: *Wrongs Act* 1936 s. 25; W.A.: *Law Reform (Contributory Negligence and Tortfeasors' Contribution) Act* 1947 s. 7; Tas.: *Tortfeasors and Contributory Negligence Act* 1954 s. 3; A.C.T. and N.T.: *Law Reform (Miscellaneous Provisions) Acts* 1955 (s. 11) and 1956 (s. 12); N.Z.: *Law Reform Act* 1936 s. 17; *Civil Liability (Contribution) Act* 1978 (Eng.) s. 3. Whether the two were sued in the same action or separately: *Wah Tat Bank v. Chan* [1975] A.C. 507 (P.C.); *Bryanston Finance v. de Vries* [1975] Q.B. 703 (C.A.).
32. *XL Petroleum v. Caltex* (1985) 155 C.L.R. 448, rejecting *Cassell v. Broome* [1972] A.C. 1027 as per incuriam.
33. The Eng. (s. 3) and Vic. (s. 24AB) Acts only retained the cost sanction. In the U.S., the plaintiff is generally allowed to select the higher of two inconsistent judgments: see *Consequences of Proceeding Separately against Concurrent Tortfeasors*, 68 Harv. L. Rev. 697 at 700-702 (1955).

contribution between tortfeasors. A second action, while not prohibited, will only benefit a plaintiff when the defendant in the first action is judgment proof.

Release

As an assumed corollary of the "one cause of action" theory, it was early settled that the release of one joint tortfeasor, by deed or accord and satisfaction, discharges all.[34] This rule has not been abrogated expressly except in Tasmania;[35] but it may have been implicitly: by authorising successive actions, the unity of the common law action against all tortfeasors may have been severed in its entirety.[36] The effect of the rule was in any event pernicious, either discouraging settlements or ensnaring the unwary. It was all the more difficult to justify because the law has otherwise been most solicitous to encourage settlements with one or more multiple tortfeasors by only reducing the settlor's claim against the others pro tanto rather than in equal shares (pro rata)[37]—thus making no distinction between what is received in partial satisfaction under a settlement and under a judgment.[38] Presumably the nefarious rule would not have survived so long if the whole category of joint torts were not so narrow, and a convenient, if pettifogging, escape were not available to those with knowledge of legal niceties employing a "covenant not to sue" rather than a "release".[39] Regardless of the terminology employed, an *express* reservation has also long been recognised as saving it from being treated as a release. A more recent decision ascribed the same effect to a reservation *implied* from a clear intimation of the settlor's intent.[40]

2. CONTRIBUTION AMONG TORTFEASORS

The common law did not countenance contribution among tortfeasors. This was established in 1799 in *Merryweather v. Nixan*,[41] where one of two defendants who had been held jointly liable for conversion sought contribution of a moiety from the other after the whole of the judgment had been executed against him by the plaintiff. In a "somewhat meagre"[42] opinion, Lord Kenyon non-suited the claimant and, failing precedent, contented himself with a reference to the maxim "ex turpi causa non oritur actio". Despite its questionable rationale,[43] the rule came to be accepted

34. *Cutler v. McPhail* [1962] 2 Q.B. 292; *Palmer v. Blowers* (1987) 75 A.L.R. 509.
35. Section 3(3). Also *Civil Liabilities Act* 1961 (Eire) s. 17. Denning M.R. boldly treated it as now obsolete: *Bryanston Finance v. de Vries* [1975] Q.B. 703 at 723 (consent judgment).
36. See *XL Petroleum v. Caltex* (1985) 155 C.L.R. 448 at 459, 466.
37. See also below, p. 263.
38. See above, n. 30.
39. *Duck v. Mayeu* [1892] 2 Q.B. 511; *Apley Estates v. De Bernales* [1947] Ch. 217; *Vancouver v. Rhodes* [1955] 1 D.L.R. 139.
40. *Gardiner v. Moore* [1969] 1 Q.B. 55.
41. 8 T.R. 186.
42. *Palmer v. Wick* [1894] A.C. 318 at 324 per Lord Herschell.
43. Questionable at any rate beyond the context of plain crime, such as the notorious case of the highwayman in 1725 (*Everet v. Williams*, 9 L.Q.R. 197 (1893)) who had the effrontery to seek an accounting of spoils from his companion. Not only was the bill dismissed by the Exchequer, but both were hanged into the bargain.

as settled doctrine, and was later even extended to unintentional as well as to "several" tortfeasors.[44]

The most controversial aspect of the rule was, no doubt, the power it conferred on the plaintiff to determine the incidence of loss distribution between co-tortfeasors at his own whim, allowing him to throw the whole loss, if so minded, on one of them and completely exempt the other. This had the result in most cases of allocating the loss to him who, in the plaintiff's estimate, had the deeper pocket. For this reason, the rule against contribution has been defended as a welcome device for promoting loss distribution, inasmuch as a defendant who is best able to absorb the loss is prevented from obtaining partial or complete reimbursement from a co-defendant who may be uninsured or financially weak.[45]

On the other hand, a system which allows the entire loss to be shifted to that one of two admitted tortfeasors who is better able to pay might be thought to invite irresponsibility on the part of those members of the public who wish to enjoy the advantages of risky activity but eschew its responsibilities.[46] So long, therefore, as our system of tort liability remained linked to the notion of fault, it was difficult to resist the demand for contribution among tortfeasors in order to permit a "fair" distribution of the loss in accordance with their respective shares of responsibility—limited as this would be in practice anyway by the realities of their respective financial resources (including insurance). Contribution also has the incidental, though by no means negligible, attraction of lessening the temptation for manipulating causal concepts in order to protect defendants against a liability that would be disproportionate if it could not be shared.[47] Accordingly, statutory reform eventually adopted contribution.

Right to contribution

The model followed throughout Australasia[48] is the original English Act of 1935[49] which provided:

> "where damage is suffered by any person as a result of a tort (whether a crime or not), any tortfeasor liable in respect of that damage may recover contribution[50] from any other tortfeasor who is, or would if

44. Williams, *Joint Torts* §26. Australia: *Dall v. Blue Wren Taxi* [1926] V.L.R. 365.
45. James, *Contribution Among Joint Tortfeasors: A Pragmatic Criticism*, 54 Harv. L. Rev. 1156 (1941). The rule is also marginally more "efficient" because it deters accidents as well as does contribution but is administratively cheaper. See Landes & Posner, *Joint and Multiple Tortfeasors: An Economic Analysis*, 9 J. Leg. Stud. 517 (1980).
46. Gregory, *Contribution Among Joint Tortfeasors: A Defence*, 54 Harv. L. Rev. 1170 (1941).
47. See above, p. 220.
48. N.S.W.: *Law Reform (Miscellaneous Provisions) Act* 1946; Vic.: *Wrongs Act* 1958 s. 24; Qld: *Law Reform Act* 1952, Part II; S.A.: *Wrongs Act* 1936 s. 25; W.A.: *Law Reform (Contributory Negligence and Tortfeasors' Contribution) Act* 1947 s. 7; Tas.: *Tortfeasors Act* 1954 s. 3; A.C.T. and N.T.: *Law Reform (Miscellaneous Provisions) Act* Pt IV; N.Z.: *Law Reform Act* 1936 s. 17. In Canada, the same enactment is in force in Alberta, Manitoba, New Brunswick and Nova Scotia, but the other Provinces employ a somewhat different formula: see Cheifetz, *Apportionment of Fault in Tort* (1981). General survey: Kutner, 63 Can. B. Rev. 1 (1985).
49. *Law Reform (Married Women and Tortfeasors) Act* 1935 s. 6. A critical commentary is the classical text by Glanville Williams, *Joint Torts* (1951).
50. Contribution does not include costs of defending the plaintiff's claim, which remain discretionary: *Hanson v. Mathew Bros* (1991) 55 S.A.S.R. 183.

> sued have been, liable in respect of the same damage, whether as joint tortfeasor or otherwise; so, however, that no person shall be entitled to recover contribution from any person entitled to be indemnified by him in respect of the liability in respect of which the contribution is sought."

Despite its apparent simplicity, this provision has proved to be "a piece of law reform which seems itself to call somewhat urgently for reform".[51]

There must, first of all, be a common liability in tort. This excludes not only claims between contractors, but also between a tortfeasor and someone liable only for breach of contract, warranty or trust, as (formerly) in the common situation where P complains of defective workmanship against D1 (a contracting party) who in turn seeks to implicate D2, an architect or engineer (liable to P only in tort for negligence).[52] This troublesome restriction has since been removed in England and several other jurisdictions.[53]

The right to contribution belongs only to a tortfeasor "liable" in respect of the plaintiff's damage.[54] This has been interpreted to mean that, if D1 has actually been sued by P and held liable in judgment, D2 cannot contest a claim for contribution by reopening the issue of D1's liability. It is neither incumbent on D1 to prove that he was guilty of the alleged tort nor is it open to D2 to show that the claimant was not "answerable in law" despite the adverse judgment.[55]

The requirement that the claimant be "liable" in respect of the plaintiff's damage may be satisfied not only when he has been actually held liable but also when he has settled.[56] It is generally assumed, however, that he would have to prove that he was "liable" rather than merely that he settled in good faith.[57] This is apt to deter settlements in case of doubt as to liability,[58]

51. *Bitumen & Oil v. Government Transport* (1955) 92 C.L.R. 200 at 211.
52. *McLaren v. Fletcher* [1973] 2 N.Z.L.R. 100 at 117; *McConnell v. Lynch-Robinson* [1957] N.I. 70. The problem has lost some of its importance since D1 can now be sued in tort as well as contract: see *Macpherson v. Prunty* [1983] V.R. 573 (F.C.) (solicitors); see above, p. 187.
53. *Civil Liabilities (Contribution) Act* 1978 (Eng.) s. 1; Vic. (s. 23A) ("Any person liable in respect of any damage . . . whatever the legal basis of his liability, whether tort, breach of contract, breach of trust or otherwise"). Recommended in N.S.W. (1988).
54. Presumably, the right to *claim* does not arise until payment (cf. *M'Gillivray v. Hope* [1935] A.C. 1); but does it apply only to what he has paid in excess of his share of the common liability as under the American *Uniform Contribution Act* §1(b) and under contribution between co-trustees and co-guarantors: *Wolmershausen v. Gullick* [1893] 2 Ch. 514?
55. *Bitumen & Oil v. Government Transport* (1955) 92 C.L.R. 200. This is strictly by virtue of the statutory language, not issue estoppel as in cases where P sues both D1 and D2; for in the first, unlike the second case (*Rest.*, Judgments §106), D2 would not in any sense have been a party to the original proceedings. But though the judgment is conclusive as to both existence and amount of liability, a claim by D2 that it was excessive may perhaps be raised in deciding what is his "just and equitable" share: ibid. at 212-213.
56. *Stott v. W. Yorkshire Car Co.* [1971] 2 Q.B. 651 (C.A.); *Baylis v. Waugh* [1962] N.Z.L.R. 44; *Bitumen & Oil v. Government Transport* (1955) 92 C.L.R. 200 at 212. Hence time does not start running before (statute apart: see below, n. 68); *Van Win v. Eleventh Mirontron* [1984] V.R. 484.
57. *Stott v. W. Yorkshire Car Co.* [1971] 2 Q.B. 651 (passim); *Corry v. Clarke* [1967] N.I. 62 (consent judgment).
58. Why should D2 get off on proof that, even though *he* was liable, D1 was not? Indeed, D1 seems to have an even stronger claim for relief than if he were actually a tortfeasor, as held in *Rusch v. Korth* 86 N.W. 2d 464 (Wis. 1957); *Marschler v. Masser's Garage* (1956) 2 D.L.R. (2d) 484 (Ont. *Negligence Act*).

hence the desirable amendment to qualify bona fide settlements.[59] But as regards quantum, the settlement need only be reasonable rather than hit exactly the amount a court would have awarded.

Liability to contribution

Contribution may be claimed only from a tortfeasor "who is, or would if sued have been, liable in respect of the same damage". Thus he must either have been sued and held liable or be someone who, though not sued, would have been held liable for it if sued. The torts may have been committed simultaneously, as in the stock situation of two cars colliding, or at an interval, as when the original injury is aggravated by negligent medical treatment[60] or when a rescuer is hit by another negligent motorist.[61] What is at once necessary and sufficient is that both defendants be liable for the same damage.[62] "Liable" means "responsible in law", thus excluding anyone who has actually been *held* not liable to the injured party[63] or someone who, if sued, would have had a good defence against him.[64] A common illustration used to be a wife hurt in a collision by the combined negligence of her husband and another driver: the latter, liable to her in full, would be unable to make the husband share,[65] unless (as is now generally the case) marital immunity has been abrogated.[66]

But what about defences that become available to a tortfeasor only *after* the tort cause of action accrued, for example because the victim's claim has since become statute barred or released? The first contingency arose in *Wimpey v. B.O.A.C.*[67] when P sued both defendants but failed against D2, a public authority, because of a shorter period of limitation. This, it was finally held by the House of Lords, also defeated D1's claim for contribution on the narrow ground that D2, having been actually held *not liable* to P, was thus not a "tortfeasor who is, or would if sued have been,

59. *Civil Liabilities (Contribution) Act* 1978 (Eng.) s. 1(4); Vic.: ss. 23(B)(4), 24(2B); Tas.: s. 3(1)(d); *Civil Liabilities Act* 1961 (Eire) s. 22. In the first two, doubts may be factual.
60. *Mahony v. Kruschich* (1985) 156 C.L.R. 522.
61. *Chapman v. Hearse* (1961) 106 C.L.R. 112.
62. Not satisfied in *Dillingham v. Steel Mains* (1975) 132 C.L.R. 323 when the first employer was not liable for the second accident but at most for having made the plaintiff more vulnerable (?). If D2's liability is limited (e.g. because D2 is a railway or P was contributorily negligent vis-à-vis D2), he is still liable to D1 for his share of the *total* damage, but not exceeding the limit: *Unsworth v. Comm. Rlys* (1958) 101 C.L.R. 73; *Plant v. Calderwood* [1969] N.Z.L.R. 752; 1978 English Act s. 2(3).
63. *Wimpey v. B.O.A.C.* [1955] A.C. 169; *Parkland v. Stetar* [1975] 2 S.C.R. 884.
64. *Alex Kay v. Fife* (1966) 9 F.L.R. 246 (prior release); *Giffels v. East. Constructions* [1978] 2 S.C.R. 1346 (guarantee expired); *Dowling v. Brown* (1956) 94 Ir. L.T.R. 67 (common employment); *Sinkevitch v. C.P.R.* [1954] O.W.N. 21 (workers' compensation).
65. *Chant v. Read* [1939] 2 K.B. 346; *Macklin v. Young* [1933] S.C.R. 603.
66. See below, p. 680.
67. [1955] A.C. 169. It is thus irrelevant whether the judgment exonerating D2 was on the merits or on a technicality (as in *Walsh v. Curry* [1955] N.I. 112); aliter if the action against D2 was dismissed merely for want of prosecution (*Hart v. Hall* [1969] 1 Q.B. 405; *Canberra Formwork v. C. & C.* (1982) 41 A.C.T.R. 1) or was collusive: *Corvi v. Ellis* 1969 S.L.T. 350. But if P failed in his claim against D2 but succeeded against D1, the latter can appeal D2's acquittal so as to preserve his right of contribution: *Wright v. Commonwealth* [1958] V.R. 318; *Hanson v. Wearmouth Coal* [1939] 3 All E.R. 47. Rather inflexibly, however, the contrary has been held once D1 paid off P because D2's liability to P would thereby have been irretrievably discharged: *Castellan v. Electrical Power (No. 2)* (1967) 69 S.R. (N.S.W.) 159 (C.A.).

liable". However, in later cases the view prevailed that the statutory formula meant "liable at any time", so that D2 cannot escape contribution on the ground merely that P's claim against him would by then have become statute barred.[68]

Finally, can contribution be claimed from a tortfeasor who has settled with the victim? Suppose D2 settles for $2,000 and P later recovers a judgment against D1 for an extra $3,000 ($5,000 – $2,000) with a finding that he was half to blame. Apparently, D2 remains liable to contribute $500, being one who "would if sued have been liable" to P.[69] Because this frustrates most of the attraction of settling with P, the American *Uniform Contribution Act* (1955) expressly exempts a tortfeasor who settles in good faith. Any inequity to D1 could be corrected by reducing P's claim against him, not by the amount of the settlement but by D2's share of responsibility.[70]

Basis of apportionment

A general guide to the mode of apportionment is furnished by the statutory mandate that "the amount of the contribution recoverable from any person shall be such as may be found by the court[71] to be just and equitable having regard to the extent of that person's *responsibility* for the damage; and the court shall have power to exempt any person from liability to make contribution, or to direct that the contribution to be recovered from any person shall amount to a complete indemnity." In contrast to an earlier statutory pattern in America,[72] contribution is therefore not necessarily borne in equal (pro rata) shares.

The formula is, in effect, substantially the same as that for contributory negligence; it is accordingly applied in much the same way[73] except for the possible difference that here the issue is uncomplicated by the problem of

68. *Brambles Construction v. Helmers* (1966) 114 C.L.R. 213; *Harvey v. O'Dell* [1958] 2 Q.B. 78; *MacKenzie v. Vance* (1977) 74 D.L.R. (3d) 383. (This involved repudiation of Lord Reid's contrary view in *Wimpey*, adopted however in *Calderwood v. Nominal Defendant* [1970] N.Z.L.R. 296 (C.A.). The H.C. in *Brambles* was studiedly non-committal regarding *Wimpey*.) Cf. the English Act of 1978 s. 1(3) ("notwithstanding that [D2] has ceased to be liable since the time when the damage occurred") and the N.Z. Act ("if sued in time").

Contribution claims have, of course, their own period of limitation. In Victoria (besides certain other alternatives) and Tasmania there is a special 12 months period commencing after the writ of the original action has been served on D1; in N.S.W. (1969), S.A. (1972), A.C.T. (1985), N.T. (1981) and England a two-year period from the accrual of D1's right of action, i.e. when his liability was ascertained. In the absence of any such special provision, the period begins to run from the last-mentioned time, the action not being one in tort but sui generis (e.g. not abating on death: *Ronex v. Laing* [1983] Q.B. 398): *Harvey v. O'Dell* [1958] 2 Q.B. 78; *Nickels v. Parks* (1948) 49 S.R. (N.S.W.) 124; *Limitation Act* 1950 (N.Z.) s. 14 interpreted in *Moloney v. Mullan* [1963] N.Z.L.R. 865; *Steele v. Grey* [1972] N.Z.L.R. 498.

69. *Harper v. Gray* [1985] 1 W.L.R. 1196; *Wrongs Act* 1936 (S.A.) s. 25(1)(ca)(ii).

70. Thus the Tas. (s. 3(3)) and the *Uniform Comparative Fault Act* 1977 (U.S.). Recommended by Mallon, 6 Otago L. Rev. 499 (1987).

71. This excludes the jury (except in Vic.: "jury or court"): *Caledonian Collieries v. Fenwick* (1959) 76 W.N. (N.S.W.) 482; *Stevens v. Collinson* [1938] N.Z.L.R. 64.

72. But comparative contribution is now recommended by the *Uniform Comparative Fault Act* 1977.

73. See below, pp. 272ff.

withholding recovery from an injured party.[74] Hence, there may be a tendency to give greater weight to the element of individual culpability. Besides fault, the broad statutory criterion of "responsibility"[75] also invites consideration of such other factors as the greater risk potential (the "causal factor"[76]), perhaps even the greater loss-bearing capacity of one of the tortfeasors. Significantly, it has been held that due weight be given to the fact that one may have been under a "higher" duty than the other, like an employer compared with a mere licensor.[77] Courts are divided on whether a strictly liable defendant should be entitled to a complete indemnity from one who was found negligent.[78] Shifting the whole loss to the latter may seem justified by the fact that he was the only one at fault; on the other hand, "responsibility" is more inclusive than "fault" and deserves consideration of the policy underlying the exceptional risk which prompted the imposition of strict liability. Nor is there any specific prohibition against contribution among intentional tortfeasors; however, some such claims might conceivably still be defeated on grounds of overriding public policy.[79]

Trial judges do not make a practice of elaborate explanations for their apportionment, being usually content merely with the conclusion that it would be "just and equitable" to divide responsibility in the stated proportion. This conforms with the general admonition that apportionment should be "dealt with somewhat broadly and upon common sense principles".[80] What is thereby lost in precedential value is gained in discouraging appeals.[81]

If one of several tortfeasors is judgment proof, how is his share distributed among the others? In case of only two tortfeasors, the risk of insolvency by one is of course borne wholly by the other because liability is "entire" (in solidum), at any rate if the plaintiff was not himself contributorily negligent.[82] But among three or more tortfeasors, the share

74. *Dare v. Dobson* [1960] S.R. (N.S.W.) 474 at 476-477 argues against attaching issue estoppel to a previous apportionment on the other issue: see *Jackson v. Goldsmith* (1950) 81 C.L.R. 446; but some English courts have overcome these scruples: *Bell v. Holmes* [1956] 1 W.L.R. 1359; *Wood v. Luscombe* (1964) 235 L.T.J. 700.
75. Exceptionally, the W.A. statute contents itself simply with what is "just and equitable".
76. Early cases were divided, but the causal factor has since been endorsed in relation to contributory negligence: see below, p. 274.
77. *Braithwaite v. S. Durham Steel Co.* [1958] 1 W.L.R. 986 (6:4); but see *Sinclair v. Arnott* (1963) 64 S.R. (N.S.W.) 88 (employer:invitor—⅓:⅔); *Collen Bros v. Scaffolding* [1959] I.R. 245 (employer:contractor—0:100).
78. At least defendants liable for breach of *statutory* duty have not gone scot-free: *Daniel v. Rickett Cockerell* [1938] 2 K.B. 322; *Wilkinson v. Rea* [1941] 1 K.B. 688; *Jerred v. Dent* [1948] 2 All E.R. 104; *Dooley v. Cammell Laird* [1951] 1 Ll. Rep. 271; cf. *Safeway v. Nest-Kart* 579 P. 2d 441 (Cal. 1978) (products liability); aliter, *Sherras v. van der Maat* [1989] Qd R. 114; *Higgins v. Inglis* [1978] 1 N.S.W.L.R. 649 (dangerous bull). Two defendants held vicariously liable without individual fault will share equally: *Soblusky v. Egan* (1960) 103 C.L.R. 215 at 235; *Everett's Blinds v. Ballinger* [1965] N.Z.L.R. 266. Cf. contributory negligence: see below, p. 275.
79. The Act specifically guards itself against validating agreements that are unenforceable at common law.
80. *The Volute* [1922] 1 A.C. 129 at 144 per Viscount Birkenhead (contributory negligence).
81. For the reluctance of appellate courts to interfere see *Jennings v. Maumill* (1956) 30 A.L.J. 100, and cf. below p. 276 (contributory negligence).
82. Discussed below, p. 275.

of one insolvent should be distributed proportionately among the remainder.[83]

Indemnity

The common law's all-or-nothing ethos ruled out sharing (contribution) but not a complete shifting (indemnity) of the loss. An indemnity was (and is) allowed, generally speaking, whenever anyone, himself blameless, is held liable for someone else's tort. The most obvious illustration is vicarious liability;[84] others are where a servant or agent committed a tort in bona fide execution of orders[85] or where the claimant's complicity was procured by the other's fraud or misrepresentation.[86] It may also be based on contract (for example, a specific clause expressly indemnifying a party against liability for negligence[87]) or on implied warranty. Thus a retail seller of defective equipment may have to indemnify his purchaser for the latter's liability to his own employee for negligently failing to notice the defect.[88]

More controversial is the employer's right, contractual[89] or under the Contribution Act, to be indemnified by servants for whose default he has incurred vicarious liability. As reaffirmed by the House of Lords in *Lister v. Romford Ice Co.*,[90] it can be invoked not only against servants guilty of intentional and wanton misconduct,[91] but equally against the merely negligent. Nor, it was there held by a narrow majority, would that right be negatived by the common assumption on the part of employees that their employer would procure the necessary insurance to cover them against personal liability (at least for risks inherent in the nature of their

83. *Fisher v. C.H.T.* [1966] 2 Q.B. 475 (insolvency known prior to judgment). The *Civil Liabilities Act* 1961 (Eire) s. 28; *Apportionment Act* 1956 (S. Afr.) s. 2(11) and the *Uniform Comparative Fault Act* (U.S.) §2(d) provide for a supplementary judgment.
84. See *Lister v. Romford Ice Co.* [1975] A.C. 555 (car owners).
85. *Edwards v. Joyce* [1954] V.L.R. 216 at 220.
86. See *Burrows v. Rhodes* [1899] 1 Q.B. 816; *Parmley v. Parmley* [1945] S.C.R. 635. The W.A. statute (s. 7) alone enumerates the cases where a person is entitled to a complete indemnity: fraud, vicarious liability and the intriguing category of cases "where the act was not clearly illegal or tortious in itself and the person seeking indemnity had no knowledge when the tort was committed of the true legal character of the act". In *Jones v. Richards* [1955] 1 W.L.R. 444 the indemnitee was unknowingly in breach of statute.
87. Such indemnity clauses are construed like exclusion of liability clauses: see below, p. 293. Claims for indemnity and breach of contract are distinguished in *T.A.L. v. Vaughan* [1989] V.R. 545 (F.C.).
88. *Mowbray v. Merryweather* [1895] 2 Q.B. 640. But the warranty expires once the purchaser becomes aware of the defect: *Lambert v. Lewis* [1982] A.C. 225.
89. It is an implied term of the employment that the servant will not intentionally or negligently cause damage to his employer (e.g. *Behrendorff v. Soblusky* (1975) 98 C.L.R. 619; *Digby v. General Accident* [1943] A.C. 121) or involve him in vicarious liability. The employer's right to reimbursement is therefore contractual (at any rate as regards default in matters involving the special skill for which the employee was hired: *Harvey v. O'Dell* [1958] 2 Q.B. 78), though he would also be entitled to a complete indemnity under contribution legislation (ibid.). But if he himself bears some responsibility, he must suffer a reduction, as where a hospital permits an inexperienced doctor to act as anaesthetist without adequate supervision: *Jones v. Manchester Corp.* [1952] 2 Q.B. 852.
90. [1957] A.C. 555.
91. As in *Ryan v. Fildes* [1938] 3 All E.R. 517; *Finnegan v. Riley* [1939] 4 D.L.R. 434; *Davenport v. Comm. Rlys* (1953) 53 S.R. (N.S.W.) 552.

employment, like that of a lorry driver).[92] In the result, the employer's insurer was able to insist on being subrogated to the employer's right of indemnity against the negligent employee, contrary to the very desire of the insured himself.[93] This outcome was of course intolerable in the industrial context.[94] Employers themselves would not ordinarily dare or wish to assert such a right for fear of provoking union retaliation; and the English insurance industry was promptly persuaded officially to waive its future exercise under a government threat of otherwise abolishing it outright by legislation,[95] as it has now been in Australia.[96]

The preceding considerations have relevance only to employees, not to independent contractors. Carelessness by employees is now a recognised element of the *employer's* business risk; but independent contractors are expected to absorb the losses of their business themselves by pricing of their services and insurance, and the persons who commission the work become exceptionally liable only as guarantors. It follows that, as between themselves, the contractor is primarily liable and must therefore indemnify his principal.[97]

Procedure

The most satisfactory disposition in cases of concurrent liability is to litigate all connected claims in one proceeding.[98] As already noted, the plaintiff is today free to join all concurrent tortfeasors as co-defendants in a single action, whether they are jointly or only severally liable for the injury. The issue of contribution can then be litigated at the same time as the plaintiff's claim, in what are called third party proceedings. If the plaintiff chooses to proceed against only one of the tortfeasors, that one may give a third party notice to any other and thus join a claim for

92. Specifically, the majority of the H.L. rejected the contention that a term negativing indemnity should be implied into the contract of employment, on the ground that it was not necessary to do so in order to give it business efficacy (*The Moorcock* test).
93. But more recently, under Lord Denning's aegis, the C.A. refused to *imply* such a right of subrogation into an indemnity contract between an indemnitee and the tortfeasor's employer, on the ground that it would be both inequitable and contrary to understanding in an industrial setting: *Morris v. Ford Motor Co.* [1973] Q.B. 792.
94. Especially in Australia: *Rowell v. Alexander Mackie College* (1988) A.T.R. 80-183 (N.S.W.C.A.) where a majority, rejecting *Lister*, was prepared to imply a term for insurance, though not covering intoxication. Aliter, if the employee is himself insured, as in *Shortland C.C. v. G.I.O.* [1973] 2 N.S.W.L.R. 257.
95. The "gentlemen's agreement", in terms limited to accidents between co-employees, is discussed 22 Mod. L. Rev. 652 (1959) and in *Morris v. Ford Motor Co.* [1973] Q.B. 792 at 847.
96. *Insurance Contracts Act* 1984 (Cth) s. 66; *Employees Liability (Indemnification of Employers) Act* 1982 (N.S.W.), but held to preclude also tort claim under Contribution Act: *McGrath v. Fairfield C.* (1985) 156 C.L.R. 672; *Wrongs Act* (S.A.) s. 27c; *Law Reform (Miscellaneous Provisions) Act* (N.T.) s. 22A; Exceptions: serious and wilful misconduct. *Workers' Compensation Act* 1927 (Tas.) s. 34 requires insurance.
97. *Honeywill v. Larkin Bros* [1934] 1 K.B. 191. If the principal was not just vicariously, but personally, liable for his own negligence, his claim is not for indemnity but contribution: e.g. *Voli v. Inglewood S.* (1963) 110 C.L.R. 74; *Daniel v. Rickett Cockerell* [1938] 2 K.B. 322. If neither was negligent but both were strictly liable, the principal may have to indemnify: *Clearlite Holdings v. Auckland Corp.* [1976] 2 N.Z.L.R. 729 at 744.
98. *A.M.P. v. Dixon* [1982] V.R. 833; *Croston v. Vaughan* [1938] 1 K.B. 540 at 565; Williams, *Joint Torts* ch. 7.

contribution.[99] Admittedly, the latter does not thereby become a party to the action by the plaintiff[100] but, being interested in defeating his claim, may be given leave to defend it. The great advantage of this third party procedure is, of course, to get the third party bound by the decision between plaintiff and defendant,[101] to settle the issue between the defendant and the third party as soon as possible after the defendant's liability to the plaintiff has been adjudged, and to save the expenses involved in two separate actions.[102]

Less satisfactory is the position where P sues D1 alone, and D1 fails to join D2 as a third party. If judgment is given against him, D1 will be forced to bring separate proceedings against D2 in order to recover contribution. This involves a completely new trial of many of the issues already litigated. There is a good deal of merit in the suggestion that a defendant who wishes to claim contribution must serve a third party notice as soon as is reasonably possible or lose his right to recoupment altogether.[103] Unfortunately, the courts have taken a narrow view of the scope of issue estoppel and, despite facilities for joinder and third party procedure, there remain many situations in which substantially similar issues may have to be relitigated and, what is more, at the risk of inconsistent verdicts.[104]

99. N.S.W.: *Law Reform (Miscellaneous Provisions) Act* 1946 ss 2, 3; Vic. R.S.C., O. 16A; Qld: R.S.C., O. 17; S.A.; R.S.C., O. 16A; W.A., R.S.C., O. 16, Pt V; Tas.; R.S.C., O. 18, rr. 58-69; A.C.T., R.S.C., O. 20. But the court has a discretion in the matter and may order a separate hearing of the issues between the plaintiff and defendant on the one hand, and between the defendant and the third parties, on the other: *Standen v. Varley* [1956] 56 S.R. (N.S.W.) 346; *Bell v. Baker* [1953] Q.S.R. 303.

100. *Commonwealth v. Temple* (1949) 49 S.R. (N.S.W.) 373.

101. The English R.S.C., O. 16A, r. 8 empowers a judge to "give such directions as appear proper . . . as to the mode and extent in and to which the third party shall be bound or made liable by the decision or judgment in the action".

102. *Barclays Bank v. Tom* [1923] 1 K.B. 221 at 223.

103. Williams, *Joint Torts* 185-186. Thus the 1939 version of the American *Uniform Act* 1939 §7. The Ontario statute does not permit separate proceedings for contribution at all: *Cohen v. McCord* [1944] 4 D.L.R. 753.

104. In *Ramsay v. Pigram* (1968) 118 C.L.R. 271 the H.C. reaffirmed its hostility to issue estoppels, stemming from *Jackson v. Goldsmith* (1950) 81 C.L.R. 446. See above, p. 144, n. 74. A much more sympathetic approach is found in *Civil Liabilities Act* 1961 (Eire) s. 29.

12

CONTRIBUTORY NEGLIGENCE

Preceding chapters dealt with two of the major judicial techniques designed to contain liability for negligence: "duty" and "remoteness of damage". In addition, there exist two defences, properly so-called, which, unlike the former controls, must be specially pleaded[1] and proved[2] by the *defendant*. These are contributory negligence and voluntary assumption of risk by the person injured. In line with the general tendency to expand liability for negligence, these defences have been suffering a steady decline.

Contributory negligence is a plaintiff's failure to meet the standard of care to which he is required to conform for his own protection and which is a legally contributing cause, together with the defendant's default, in bringing about his injury.[3] The term "contributory negligence" is unfortunately not altogether free from ambiguity. In the first place, "negligence" is here used in a sense different from that which it bears in relation to a defendant's conduct. It does not necessarily connote conduct fraught with undue risk to *others*, but rather failure on the part of the person injured to take reasonable care of himself in his *own* interest. Often, no doubt, what a plaintiff has done or omitted to do is calculated to endanger not only himself but also others, as when a pedestrian steps off a kerb without looking; but that he may thereby also imperil a passing motorist is as superfluous for the present purpose as if he could not conceivably have hurt anyone but himself (for example by stumbling into an excavation).[4] Secondly, the term "contributory" might misleadingly suggest that the plaintiff's negligence, concurring with the defendant's, must have contributed to the *accident* in the sense of being instrumental in bringing it about. Actually, it means nothing more than his failure to avoid getting hurt[5] by the defendant, for example by riding in a car without fastening the seat belt[6] or with a driver known to be incompetent or intoxicated;[7] even failing to switch on a back-up power unit in case of an electricity outage.[8]

1. Even after apportionment: *Fookes v. Slaytor* [1978] 1 W.L.R. 1293 (C.A.); *Christie v. Bridgestone* (1983) 33 S.A.S.R. 377; *Brown v. Heathcote C.C. (No. 2)* [1982] 2 N.Z.L.R. 618.
2. Even after apportionment: *Hercules Mills v. K. & H.* [1955] V.L.R. 310.
3. *Rest. 2d* §463.
4. *Nance v. B.C. Electrical Rly* [1951] A.C. 601. Thus, even in a collision between two drivers, a prior judgment holding P guilty of contributory negligence does not create an issue estoppel as to his negligence when later sued by D, for non constat that it did not consist in lack of self-care only. Aliter, a judgment acquitting P of contributory negligence, for this would necessarily (semble) negative also any breach of duty owed to D: *Noall v. Middleton* [1961] V.R. 285; and see *Ramsay v. Pigram* (1968) 118 C.L.R. 271.
5. Note the reference to "damage" in the Apportionment Acts (see below, p. 272).
6. *Froom v. Butcher* [1976] Q.B. 286; *Motor Accidents Act* 1988 (N.S.W.) s. 74; see below, p. 280.
7. *Ins. Comm. v. Joyce* (1948) 77 C.L.R. 39; *Owens v. Brimmell* [1977] Q.B. 859; *Motor Vehicles Act* 1988 (N.S.W.) s. 74; see below, pp. 298ff. *Motor Vehicle Ins. v. Wilson* [1976] W.A.R. 175 (despite the W.A. statute's wording "conducing to the happening of the event which caused the damage"; the "event" is the injury, not the accident).
8. *Heeney v. Best* (1979) 108 D.L.R. (3d) 366 (C.A.).

1. COMMON LAW

The common law treated contributory negligence as a complete defence, defeating the plaintiff's recovery entirely. Less drastic would have been the rule of equal division of loss under admiralty law[9] or apportionment in accordance with the parties' share of responsibility favoured by the modern civil law.[10]

One looks in vain for any persuasive doctrinal justification of this "stalemate solution". In truth, it does not appear to have occurred to anyone in the original case of *Butterfield v. Forrester*,[11] or for long thereafter, that there was any alternative. This assumption would have been reinforced by the prevailing predilection of the common law for assigning occurrences to a single responsible cause:[12] the complete defeat of the plaintiff could be explained on the ground that in a practical sense he was "the author of his own wrong"[13] and hence the only effective cause of his injury.

This causal theory, however, was only a sham. It is, of course, beyond all argument that a plaintiff's negligence will not be counted against him unless it was at least *a* cause of his injury.[14] But this truism does not help to explain why it should bar recovery if it was a cause. We have long become familiar with the idea that one's liability is not precluded merely because some other legally responsible cause also contributed to the harm. If that is so when a third person's negligence concurs with the defendant's, why should it be any different when instead it is the plaintiff's? Indeed, if in a collision between two negligent motorists an innocent third person is injured, the fact that the defendants could not sue each other because of their contributory negligence had no bearing whatever on the plaintiff's claim against either of them.[15] Yet their negligence cannot very well be at once a cause vis-à-vis a third person but no cause vis-à-vis each other.

If the causal explanation of the defence was thus hypocritical, its functional operation at least was easier to perceive. Like voluntary assumption of risk and the common employment rule, it subsidised the growth of industrial and business enterprise by lightening the burden of compensation losses for accidents inevitably associated with a rapidly expanding economy and the faster and greater volume of transport.[16] These economic developments were accompanied by an individualistic philosophy which stipulated a high degree of self-reliance: the law, barely required to aid those who could not protect themselves, could well be indifferent to others who could help themselves but failed to do so. Besides,

9. Franck, *Collisions at Sea*, 12 L.Q.R. 260 (1896); Scott, 13 L.Q.R. 17 (1897); Huger, 13 Corn. L.Q. 531 (1927).
10. Honoré, XI Int. Encycl. Comp. L. ch. 7 §144-188.
11. (1809) 11 East 60; 103 E.R. 926.
12. See above, p. 220.
13. E.g. *Butterfield v. Forrester* (1809) 11 East 60 at 61; 103 E.R. 926 at 927; *Bridge v. Grand Junction Rly* (1838) 3 M. & W. 244 at 248; 150 E.R. 1134 at 1135. The defence could thus be raised under the general issue in an action for negligence (though not in trespass). The causal theory however was not consistently applied, for the burden of proof was always on the defendant except to this day in a few American States.
14. See below, p. 279.
15. *Grant v. Sun Shipping Co.* [1948] A.C. 549 at 563-564.
16. Malone, *Formative Period of Contributory Negligence*, 41 Ill. L. Rev. 151 (1946).

did the rule not serve the cause of accident prevention by encouraging utmost circumspection on everyone's part?[17] If to the modern mind the sanction of withholding all redress seems rather disproportionate and punitive,[18] it must be remembered that "19th century morality was a severe thing. It demanded absolutes. Either a defendant was responsible or he was not. Compromises were not to be endured."[19]

As these uncharitable postulates were falling into discredit, growing dissatisfaction with the operation of the defence stimulated certain judicial palliatives, the most notorious of which was the so-called "last opportunity" rule.

Last opportunity

The frequent inequality in the parties' fault was bound to subject the common law solution to the severest stress. Theoretically, even a slight lapse barred the plaintiff from all recovery, however gross the defendant's fault in comparison. After first condoning surreptitious apportionment by juries in such cases,[20] the courts eventually sanctioned an exception to the stalemate rule which came to be known as the "last opportunity" or (in Canada and the United States) the "last clear chance" doctrine. It permitted *full* recovery to a plaintiff notwithstanding his own negligence if the defendant had the last opportunity of avoiding the accident but negligently failed to avail himself of it. In the parent case of *Davies v. Mann*,[21] for example, the owner of a donkey which he had left in plain view hobbled in the road, recovered from a defendant who ran down the animal with his wagon.

This exception however suffered from the same flaw as the rule it qualified. Committed to the all-or-nothing solution, the law threw the whole blame—this time—on the defendant, willing to overlook completely the plaintiff's share of responsibility for the accident. Not surprisingly, the result was again explained in the abracadabra of causation, that the defendant's later negligence "snapped the chain of causation" between the plaintiff's fault and the resulting injury so that the defendant's was alone "in any real sense the effective cause of the accident". This pretence was exposed above all by the fact that a last opportunity available to one of two *co-defendants* never prevented the negligence of the other from being a proximate cause of injury to a third party.[22] All the same, the rule came to be so deeply embedded in the common law tradition that it was widely accepted as an incontestable truism, rather than frankly recognised as merely a device for circumventing the common law refusal to countenance a theory of comparative fault. This unfortunate usage contained the seeds

17. The rule serves accident prevention as well as does apportionment, but is administratively cheaper. However, it fails generally to allocate responsibility to the best cost avoider. See Schwartz, *Contributory and Comparative Negligence: A Reappraisal*, 87 Yale L.J. 697 (1978).
18. Lord Halsbury placed it squarely on the penal maxim "in pari delicto potior est conditio defendentis" (*Wakelin v. L.S.W. Rly* (1886) 12 App. Cas. 41 at 45).
19. Green, *Judge and Jury* (1930) 122.
20. *Raisin v. Mitchell* (1839) 9 C. & P. 613; 173 E.R. 979; *Smith v. Dobson* (1841) 3 Man. & G. 59; 133 E.R. 1057.
21. (1842) 10 M. & W. 546; 152 E.R. 588.
22. *Edwards v. Joyce* [1954] V.L.R. 216 at 220.

of future trouble, once apportionment legislation had dispensed with the need for this stratagem.

Over the century of its sway, the last opportunity doctrine developed into a plastic instrument for allocating the loss to either plaintiff or defendant in accordance with the court's view of whose was the disproportionately greater share of responsibility. With "actual" came to be equated "unconscious" last opportunity, that is, one that a defendant would have had but for his negligent inattention;[23] even "constructive" last opportunity, that is, one that he never actually had at all because his earlier negligence disabled him from taking effective countermeasures when the need arose (for example, starting a trip with defective brakes).[24] The resulting casuistry tended to make the task of appellate review a veritable farce and eventually prompted a retreat.[25]

Reform would most probably have come earlier but for two factors. Settlements tended to discount the odds, on the one hand, of the plaintiff being defeated because of contributory negligence and, on the other, of the defendant being held liable in full; this resulted in apportionment, though admittedly not based on the parties' respective shares of responsibility. Secondly, juries tended to mitigate the harshness of the law by frequently apportioning behind the accommodating screen of a general verdict which gave little scope for appellate review.[26] The disappearance of juries in England accordingly added a spur to reform, just as the survival of jury trial in New South Wales[27] and the United States[28] accounted to some extent for its long delay. Overall, however, the law remained capricious, unpredictable and often unfair in operation.

2. APPORTIONMENT

Apportionment of damages in accordance with the parties' degree of fault was first introduced into the English maritime law in 1911 pursuant to the Brussels Convention, in lieu of the old rule of equal division.[29] In its application to land, it was pioneered in Canada;[30] but it was the English

23. First sanctioned in *Radley v. L. & N.W. Rly* (1876) 1 App. Cas. 754.
24. *B.C. Electrical Rly v. Loach* [1916] 1 A.C. 719. See MacIntyre, *Rationale of Last Clear Chance*, 18 Can. B. Rev. 665 at 682-687 (1940).
25. *Alford v. Magee* (1952) 85 C.L.R. 437 at 460-461.
26. E.g. *Williams v. Comm. Road Transport* (1933) 50 C.L.R. 258.
27. The reform of 1965 belatedly came more that 15 years after all other Australian States.
28. In the U.S. "comparative negligence" has now been widely adopted since the defence lobby shifted from opposition to declared neutrality in the late 60s: Fleming, *Comparative Negligence At Last*, 64 Cal. L. Rev. 239 (1976).
29. *Maritime Conventions Act* 1911 s. 1. In Australia, collisions *inside* territorial waters are governed by *State* legislation to the same effect: *Supreme Court Act* 1958 (Vic.) s. 64; *Supreme Court Act* 1935 (S.A.) s. 111; *Supreme Court Civil Procedures Act* 1932 (Tas.) s. 11. In N.S.W., W.A. and Qld, the apportionment statutes apply to *all* claims for negligent damage. Cf. *Stein v. The Kathy K* [1976] 2 S.C.R. 802.

    Collisions *outside* territorial waters or in territorial waters of a territory or between ships engaged in interstate or foreign trade are governed by the *Navigation Act* 1912 (Cth) ss 2, 259-263. This legislation is in force throughout the British Commonwealth. *Shipping and Seamen Amendment Act* 1912 (N.Z.) s. 21.
30. Some Provinces eventually adopted the English version; others retained their own. See Cheifetz, *Apportionment of Fault in Tort* (1981); Klar, *Studies in Canadian Tort Law* (1977) ch. 5. A Uniform Act was promulgated in 1981.

model, passed in 1945,[31] which was eventually adopted throughout Australia and New Zealand.[32] It provides:

> "where any person suffers damage as the result partly of his own fault and partly of the fault of any other person or persons, a claim in respect of that damage shall not be defeated by reason of the fault of the person suffering the damage, but the damages recoverable[33] in respect thereof shall be reduced to such extent as the court thinks just and equitable having regard to the claimant's share in the responsibility of the damage."

Mode of apportionment

Our legislation confers a general mandate to apportion, not specifically limited (like most American statutes) to cases where the plaintiff's fault was "not greater than" (or worse still: "not as great as") the defendant's.[34] A claimant may recover a proportion of his loss whether he was 5 per cent or 95 per cent to blame.[35]

Damages "shall be reduced to such extent as the court thinks just and equitable having regard to the claimant's share in the responsibility for the damage". According to one view, this formula calls for an assessment of the plaintiff's responsibility alone, according to another for a comparison between the plaintiff's and the defendant's. Only the former, it is argued, can make sense if the defendant's liability is strict,[36] and is preferable if the plaintiff's negligence did not contribute to the accident itself but only to his injury as in drunk driver and seat belt cases.[37] But the almost universal practice is to compare the parties' responsibilities.[38] Accordingly, if responsibility for a collision is attributed to A and B in the proportion of 75:25, A will recover from B 25 per cent and B from A 75 per cent of their respective losses.[39] But while the recoverable fraction of

31. *Law Reform (Contributory Negligence) Act* 1945. The Act extends to Scotland and has been copied in N. Ireland. Its classical analysis is by Williams, *Joint Torts*.
32. N.S.W.: *Law Reform (Miscellaneous Provisions) Act* 1965; Vic.: *Wrongs Act* 1958 s. 26; Qld.: *Law Reform (Tortfeasors' Contribution, Contributory Negligence and Division of Chattels) Act* 1952; S.A.: *Wrongs Act* 1936 s. 27a; W.A.: *Law Reform (Contributory Negligence and Tortfeasors' Contribution) Act* 1947 s. 4; Tas.: *Tortfeasors and Contributory Negligence Act* 1954 s. 4; A.C.T. and N.T.: *Law Reform (Miscellaneous Provisions) Act* Pt 5 (1955 and 1956 respectively); N.Z.: *Contributory Negligence Act* 1947. The W.A. statute is somewhat differently worded: see below, n. 42.
33. Interpreted as synonymous with "sustained" so as to require reduction *before* applying statutory limits on liability (e.g. a railway's) or on the court's jurisdiction: *Marks v. Victorian Rlys* [1955] V.L.R. 1; *Unsworth v. Comm. Rlys* (1958) 101 C.L.R. 73; *Civil Liabilities Act* 1961 (Eire) s. 41. Same with regard to deducting workers' compensation, where it tends to prejudice plaintiffs: *Bassanese v. Freightbases* (1982) 29 S.A.S.R. 300 (F.C.); contra, *Workers' Compensation Act* (Vic.) s. 65(2) (since 1981).
34. The first formula, but not the second, allows recovery in the common case of a 50:50 apportionment. However, it raises the problem of set-off: see below, n. 40.
35. See *Cumming v. Murphy* [1967] V.R. 865; *Hodkinson v. Wallwork* [1955] 1 W.L.R. 1195. English judges rarely find in excess of 50 per cent: Glenn, *Hard Bargaining* 121 (1987).
36. Payne, 18 Mod. L. Rev. 344 (1955); see below, p. 275.
37. Gravells, *Three Heads of Contributory Negligence*, 93 L.Q.R. 581 (1977).
38. *Barisic v. Devenport* [1978] 2 N.S.W.L.R. 111 (passim).
39. Thus while it is not absolutely necessary that apportionment be first expressed in terms of a fraction, the amounts awarded must reflect shares of responsibility for the accident aggregating neither more nor less than 100%. It would therefore be improper in a case like the foregoing to award A more than 25% of his loss, if B is awarded 75%: *Black v. McCabe* [1964] N.I. 1.

their loss is thus dependent on their individual share of responsibility, the net amount is determined by the size of their loss. Thus it may happen that, though B's responsibility was only 25 per cent, he may have to pay A a far larger sum than he could himself claim from the latter.[40]

Although some thought has been given to the formulation of factors which should properly influence apportionment, it seems to be generally regarded as undesirable to perplex juries with detailed instructions and so abridge their discretion in determining, on the basis of common sense and experience, what is "just and equitable" in accordance with the statutory formula.[41] However, certain patterns have emerged which help to standardise awards to some extent.

The prescribed criterion under the English (and Australian) legislation is the claimant's "responsibility of the damage".[42] Paramount is the element of fault, provided only such fault be taken into account as contributed to the injury. Hence culpability should be measured by the degree of departure from the standard of conduct exacted by law rather than by *moral* blameworthiness.[43] In the case of intoxication, whether as driver or pedestrian, this directive has led to a split of opinion. On one view, it should not matter whether the negligent act was due to insobriety any more than to stupidity or bad eyesight: what matters alone is that he drove too fast or stepped off the kerb without looking. On another, and the better view, however, intoxication is relevant to the extent that it caused the negligent act because of its bearing not on moral blameworthiness but on the extent of the actor's departure from the standard of reasonable care.[44] Thus comparison is now openly invited between degrees of fault which may range from trivial inadvertence to the grossest recklessness.[45] Deliberate disregard of safety rules, for example, must be judged more severely than

40. E.g. if A's loss was $500 and B's $100, A could claim $125 but B only $75. This aspect prompted the American formulas (above) which would deny A all recovery.
    A second alternative is to set off one against the other (as required in British Columbia), so that A would recover $50 and B nil. This is certainly imperative if one is insolvent, but otherwise tends only to help insurers and impair loss distribution. With set-off A and B must absorb $550 between them; without, only $400. Our practice does not seem to require set-off: e.g. *Burke v. Coveney* (1968) 89 W.N. (Pt 1) (N.S.W.) 46 at 51; *Earl v. Morris* [1950] N.Z.L.R. 33 at 41; Canada: *Linden* 475; (P.E.I.) *Contributory Negligence Act* s. 9 (added in 1959); *Civil Liabilities Act* 1961 (Eire) s. 36(5); Williams, *Joint Torts* §122. The (American) *Uniform Comparative Fault Act* §6 contains a sophisticated formula to deal with underinsurance by only one party.
41. *Winter v. Bennett* [1956] V.L.R. 612 at 626. The duty to apportion must be performed even in cases of doubt, when the practice will invariably be to reduce the award by 50%: *Bird v. Ward* [1954] V.L.R. 20. Some juries display a finesse verging on eccentricity, e.g. deductions of 6% and 52% in *Baxter v. Halliday* [1959] N.Z.L.R. 961 and *Joll v. Watson* [1953] N.Z.L.R. 788.
42. Except in W.A. ("negligence"). In most Canadian provinces, in Eire and S. Africa it is "fault", following the *Maritime Conventions Act*. The English-Australian formula is the same as that for contribution between tortfeasors: see above, p. 261.
43. *Pennington v. Norris* (1956) 96 C.L.R. 10 at 16; *Karamalis v. Rlys Com.* (1977) 15 A.L.R. 629 at 633 (non-causal negligence irrelevant). In *Westood v. P.O.* [1974] A.C. 1 plaintiff's disobedience may have been morally reprehensible but without risk to his safety. Yet was it not a "fault" (trespass) within the definition section: see below, p. 281?
44. See *Kilminster v. Rule* (1982) 32 S.A.S.R. 39 (F.C.); *Amend v. Bell* 570 P. 2d 138 (F.C.) (Wash. 1977). A form of reversed punitive damages *against* the plaintiff?
45. In the case of a child, allowance is due for his lesser capacity to take care of himself: see below, p. 286.

merely imperfect reaction to a crisis: a driver who deliberately cuts a corner as compared with one who fails to react promptly to an emergency.[46]

Besides fault, causal responsibility is also frequently cited as relevant for comparison.[47] The parties' misconduct must of course have been causal, but in what sense can one be more causal than another?[48] What it must mean is that weight be given to the comparative gravity of the risk. In situations, for instance, where even slight negligence is fraught with exceptional peril to others, the main blame must fall on him who created that danger or brought to the accident the dangerous subject matter, since he was in a sense master of the situation. Suppose, for example, that in the celebrated *Donkey Case*[49] the plaintiff had left a barrel of gunpowder in the road instead of a donkey. Far from being totally excused, should he not actually bear a much larger share of responsibility for a resulting explosion than someone who collided with it because he drove too fast or kept an inadequate lookout?[50] Similarly the danger presented by stationary vehicles on the road at night or in fog without warning lights is so great that it just cannot be taken lightly any more or even excused, as it was so often in the past at common law on the ground that the owner's negligence was merely passive instead of dynamic or that the oncoming motorist had the last opportunity of avoiding the accident.[51]

The danger factor also typically differentiates the respective responsibilities of plaintiff and defendant. While the latter ex hypothesi created a danger for someone else, the former—in most cases other than motor collisions—fell short only of self-care.[52] This explains why, in claims by injured pedestrians, a heavier share of responsibility usually falls on the motorist although the degree of carelessness by each may have been equal.[53]

Finally, it must be remembered that while the defendant's apportioned share will typically be absorbed by liability insurance, the plaintiff must bear his own share of the loss. That the fault principle thus continues to operate only against plaintiffs is widely felt to be harsh, if not unfair, and no doubt helps in practice towards a more lenient view of their share of responsibility: just as in the past, when contributory negligence was still a complete defence, it tempted to acquit them entirely.[54]

46. *The Miraflores* [1967] 1 A.C. 826; *Jennings v. Maumill* (1956) 30 A.L.J. 100 (H.C).
47. First canvassed in relation to contribution: see above, p. 264. See *Davies v. Swan Motor* [1949] 2 K.B. 291 at 326 per Lord Denning L.J.; *Stapley v. Gypsum Mines* [1953] A.C. 663 at 682 (which cause contributed "more immediately" to the accident?), trenchantly criticised by Williams, 17 Mod. L. Rev. 66. Comparative: Honoré, XI Int. Encycl. Comp. L. ch. 7 §175.
48. "Causation itself is difficult enough; degrees of causation would really be a nightmare" (Chapman, 64 L.Q.R. 26 at 27 (1948)).
49. *Davies v. Mann* (1842) 10 M. & W. 546; 152 E.R. 588.
50. Redmond, *Limits to the Defence of Contributory Negligence*, 28 A.L.J. 3 at 6 (1954); also *Fault and Apportionment Acts*, 31 A.L.J. 520 (1957).
51. *March v. Stramare* (1991) 171 C.L.R. 506 (30%); *Harvey v. Road Haulage* [1952] 1 K.B. 120 (50%); *Bruce v. McIntyre* [1955] S.C.R. 251 (50%).
52. Even if the plaintiff's conduct was also fraught with risk to others, that would be reflected in his liability for any harm he thereby caused; otherwise should it not be deemed irrelevant? Cf. above, n. 43.
53. *Pennington v. Norris* (1956) 96 C.L.R. 10; *Karamalis v. Rlys Comm.* (1977) 15 A.L.R. 629 (railway crossing); *Evers v. Bennett* (1982) 31 S.A.S.R. 228 (F.C.).
54. Hence the trend in some countries (e.g. Sweden) even *officially* to restrict the defence to plaintiffs' gross negligence or recklessness.

How should one apportion in cases where the defendant's liability arises, not from negligence, but from breach of statutory duty or some rule of strict liability? If fault (in the literal sense) were the sole test, there would not only be lacking a common standard of comparison, but the slightest degree of contributory negligence should defeat the plaintiff's claim entirely. Such a conclusion would clearly subvert the legal policy behind the imposition of liability without fault and would nullify its function of loss distribution. This undesirable result will be avoided if due attention is given to the statutory criterion being responsibility, not fault.[55] Some have cited this situation as a principal reason for applying "causation" as a relevant criterion; others will find a source of "responsibility" in the rationale for strict liability. Moreover, the overriding mandate to allocate responsibility in accordance with what is "just and equitable" always provides an open authority to import such other dominant considerations of contemporary policy as the desirability to exploit the loss distributing capacity of a defendant, whilst at the same time disciplining the individual plaintiff.[56]

Multiple defendants

A complicating factor arises where apportionment is required not between two, but between three or more parties. Suppose that responsibility is allocated to P for 30 per cent, to D1 for 20 per cent and D2 for 50 per cent. Will P be entitled to judgments in solidum against both D1 and D2 for 70 per cent of his damage or only to judgments against each corresponding to his individual share of responsibility? It is commonplace that where P is faultless, he is entitled to judgment against each and all defendants in solidum; he may collect from them in any proportion he wishes and leave it to them to straighten out inter se by claiming contribution or indemnity.[57]

The same solution also applies where P is partially at fault: first, his own share of responsibility will be assessed against the totality of the tortious conduct of the others; only thereafter will the shares of the defendants inter se be assessed for purposes of contribution.[58]

It follows that as a corollary of "joint and several" liability P would become entitled to judgment for 70 per cent against both D1 and D2. If D2 is insolvent, D1 then has to bear D2's share. This may be as unfair to D1 as it would be to P to treat his claim against D1 and D2 as "several" only, that is to say for 20 and 50 per cent respectively. The more equitable solution would be to distribute D2's share in proportion to their own

55. On the contrary, the absoluteness of the duty should weigh heavily against the defendant. Cf. *Civil Liabilities Act* 1961 (Eire) s. 43 which, given its premise of "fault", consistently directs that where one or the other's liability is strict, he may be completely relieved: see *O'Sullivan v. Dwyer* [1971] I.R. 275.
56. See Parsons, *Negligence and Contributory Negligence*, 1 Melb. U.L. Rev. 163 at 182 ff. (1957).
57. See above, p. 257.
58. *Fitzgerald v. Lane* [1989] A.C. 328; *Barisic v. Devenport* [1978] 2 N.S.W.L.R. 111; *Campbell v. Calgary Power* (1988) 46 C.C.L.T. 229; 104 L.Q.R. 6 (1988). Under the *Maritime Conventions Act* 1911 P's fault is assessed separately against each defendant, liability being "several" only: *The Miraflores* [1967] A.C. 826.

responsibilities.[59] This can be accomplished by a "secondary judgment", on the basis of what is "just and equitable" in case of supervening insolvency. But only the Irish Act has so far adopted this solution.[60]

A related problem arises when not all the tortfeasors are before the court. In cases uncomplicated by the plaintiff's contributory negligence, it has been held that contribution between, say, D1 and D2 must proceed without regard to the possible complicity of someone else (D3).[61] To do otherwise would presume a decision as to D3's responsibility without having him before the court; besides, the risk of D3's share remaining uncollectable will be borne proportionally between D1 and D2.[62] If P himself bore equal responsibility with D1 and D2, their shares are also best determined without reference to the possible complicity of others.[63] That way, the risk of not being able to collect from such others will at least be borne equally between the three.

Judge and jury

If the case is tried with a jury, the task of apportionment falls to it, not the judge. But as a restraint upon their notorious generosity to plaintiffs, juries are required to make a separate finding, first, of the total damages which would have been recoverable if the claimant had not been at fault, and, secondly, of the extent to which those damages should be reduced. To discourage appeals and leave the issue, as far as practicable, unencumbered by technicality and legal dogma, appellate courts are slow to interfere with apportionments just as in the kindred case of contribution between co-tortfeasors,[64] unless the trial judge or jury obviously proceeded on a misunderstanding of the evidence or clearly put a wrong value upon parts of it.[65]

The judicial discretion in awarding costs is not abridged by the power to apportion damages. In particular, reduction of the plaintiff's claim is no reason for either depriving him of his costs altogether or, as required by some Canadian statutes, diminishing them in the same proportion.[66]

59. Cf. above, p. 264.
60. *Civil Liabilities Act* 1961 s. 38, follg Williams, *Joint Torts* §102-104. Also recommended by American *Uniform Comparative Fault Act* §2(d). Samuels J.A. in *Barisic* thought it required legislation.
61. *Maxfield v. Llewellyn* [1961] 1 W.L.R. 1119 (C.A.); *Civil Liabilities Act* 1961 (Eire) s. 25; Williams, *Joint Torts* §47.
62. *Inglis v. Southshore* (1979) 104 D.L.R. (3d) 507 at 518; Williams, *Joint Torts* §109-111, where the possible alternatives are thoroughly examined. The same rule should apply where D3 had settled with P, at any rate when (as under our law) D3 does not thereby gain immunity from contribution.
63. *Vail v. Formato* (1989) 10 M.V.R. 12; Williams, *Joint Torts* §110; contra, *Barisic v. Devenport* at 122-123.
64. Especially when made by a jury: *Podrebersek v. A.I. & S.* (1985) 59 A.L.J.R. 492.
65. E.g. *Watt v. Bretag* (1982) 56 A.L.J.R. 760 (from 85:15 to 50:50 to 60:40).
66. *Howitt v. Alexander* 1948 S.C. 154; *Jason v. Hobbs* [1953] V.L.R. 397; *Devine v. Greeves* [1957] Tas. S.R. 27. But often the same proportion is adopted in practice, e.g. *Burke v. Coveney* (1968) 89 W.N. (Pt 1) (N.S.W.) 46 at 50.

In case of successful claim and counterclaim, various solutions have been tried: no order as to costs, cost to each party on his claim, to the winner on the eventual balance, in inverse proportion to their degree of responsibility and certain refinements thereof: see Williams, *Joint Torts* §136-137; Boberg, 79 S. Af. L.J. 141 (1962).

3. LIMITS ON APPORTIONMENT

As already observed, the statutes do not specifically fetter the discretion to apportion in the light of either party's relative share of responsibility. Even a very great disparity does not preclude apportionment as such, though it may conceivably reach a point where for all practical purposes 100 per cent of the blame may fairly be attributed to one of the parties with the result that he recovers nothing for his own loss and must pay for the whole of the other's.[67]

Apportionment may however be peremptorily excluded for other reasons. By the plaintiff's voluntary assumption of risk? Or the defendant's "last opportunity"? The first will occupy a separate chapter; hence we may immediately address the second.

Last opportunity

The sole function of the doctrine of last opportunity, as we saw, was to obviate the harshness of the common law stalemate rule by sanctioning full recovery against *defendants* whose fault was disproportionately gross. No significance then attached to the *plaintiff's* last opportunity, since contributory negligence without more barred him in any event. But once the stalemate rule was abolished, "last opportunity" demanded consideration in its application to both parties alike.[68]

The English statute deliberately refrained from resolving the problem,[69] and so did the Australian versions, except the Western Australian which abrogated the last opportunity doctrine *in the case of the plaintiff*. Elsewhere a few statutes have abolished it entirely,[70] but otherwise the problem was left to the courts: diverse conclusions have been drawn.

At one extreme stands the proposition that the last opportunity doctrine remained intact. Two arguments are advanced. The first is that apportionment is only authorised where damage is suffered "as the result" of the fault of both plaintiff and defendant, thereby excluding cases where the negligence of either was, according to that doctrine, legally irrelevant. "All the legislature intended to do was to alter the legal consequences of the negligence of both parties causing or contributing to the damage,"[71] but it built on the old rules which determine whether the conduct in question "caused" the loss. The second argument is that, since "fault" is defined as "negligence, breach of statutory duty or other act or omission which gives rise to a liability in tort or would, apart from this Act, *give rise to the defence of contributory negligence*", apportionment is not authorised in cases where, formerly, the defence of contributory negligence would have been excluded by the defendant's last opportunity.[72]

67. E.g. below, p. 278.
68. As in *March v. Stramare* (1991) 171 C.L.R. 506, an exact reverse of the *Donkey Case* where the "dynamic" party suffered the damage by running into a stationary vehicle.
69. See Law Revision Committee's Report 16 (1939). In Canada, five jurisdictions have adopted an optional section of the *Uniform Act* which acknowledges the survival of the rule.
70. E.g. Eire (1961), British Columbia (1978), S. Africa (1956).
71. *Davies v. Swan Motor Co.* [1949] 2 K.B. 291 at 310 per Bucknill L.J.
72. The argument is exhaustively examined by Keeler, *Alford v. Magee and the Apportionment Legislation*, 41 A.L.J. 148 (1967).

Opposing this is the view that "last opportunity" was implicitly abrogated by apportionment legislation. The doctrine, though sometimes couched in the cabalistic terminology of causation, was merely an escape hatch from the stalemate rule, and once the latter was abolished the former disappeared with it. So much for the argument based on causation. Nor does the definition section help, because the same interpretation applied to the defendant's negligence would virtually rule out all apportionment and thus stultify the whole legislation.[73] All that the definition seeks to do is to identify the kind of conduct which could *in appropriate circumstances* (but would not necessarily *always*) raise the defence at common law.

The first view has attracted little support except at one time in Canada.[74] The English[75] courts have on the whole sought to live down the old tradition of explaining "last opportunity" as a causal doctrine by sidestepping it with the argument that:

> "The practical effect of the Act is wider than its legal effect. Previously, . . . the courts in practice sought to select from a number of competing causes, which was *the* cause—the effective and predominant cause—of the damage and to reject the rest. Now the courts have regard to all the causes and apportion the damages accordingly."[76]

The Australian High Court has also disavowed the old doctrine. Already prior to the legislation it had dissociated itself from its pseudo-causal explanation and preferred to regard it candidly as merely a device for mitigating the harshness of the statement rule.[77] Subsequent pronouncements appear to treat the doctrine as extinct, on the view that its raison d'être lapsed with the introduction of the power to apportion.[78] This conclusion frees the law from the technicalities and transparent fictions of old and thereby eliminates the principal cause of unnecessary appeals. Besides, in cases of extreme disparity of fault it is still possible to throw the whole blame on one party alone, but that can be accomplished in the exercise of the statutory discretion to do what is "just and equitable" without resorting to any artificial doctrine like "last opportunity". Clearly the tendency will, and for admonitory reasons should, be not to ignore entirely even proportionately very slight fault: as revealed from time to time by awards of 90 per cent damages to a plaintiff who almost certainly before the legislation would have recovered in full.[79]

73. If "defence of contributory negligence" covered only cases where a pre-Act plaintiff was *effectively* barred (excluding those where his contributory negligence would not have defeated him because of the defendant's last opportunity), then, by parity of reasoning, negligence which gives rise to a liability in tort would exclude all defendants who before the Act would have escaped "liability" because of the plaintiff's contributory negligence. See *Winter v. Bennett* [1956] V.L.R. 612 at 622-644; *Evans v. Parberry* (1969) 92 W.N. (N.S.W.) 146.
74. Canadian law is examined in detail by Caswell, *Avoiding Last Clear Chance*, 69 Can. B. Rev. 129 (1990).
75. *Davies v. Swan Motor Co.* [1949] 2 K.B. 291; *Harvey v. Road Haulage* [1952] 1 K.B. 120; *Chisman v. Electromation* (1969) 6 K.I.R. 456 (Edmund Davies L.J. at 459: "I personally now decline to play any part in administering the kiss of life to the mummy").
76. *Davies v. Swan Motor Co.* [1949] 2 K.B. 291 at 322 per Denning L.J; *Rouse v. Squires* [1973] Q.B. 889 at 896-898.
77. *Alford v. Magee* (1952) 85 C.L.R. 437 at 451.
78. *March v. Stramare* (1991) 171 C.L.R. 506; Windeyer J. in *Teubner v. Humble* (1963) 108 C.L.R. 491 at 502; *Evans v. Parberry* (1969) 92 W.N. (N.S.W.) 146.
79. E.g. *Elms v. Comm. Rlys* [1965] Qd R. 471.

Causal irrelevance

The spurious causal theory of "last opportunity" just discussed must be distinguished from genuine lack of causality. Thus the plaintiff's own negligence will not prejudice him at all, any more than it would a defendant,[80] unless it was causally relevant to his injury in the sense that "but for it" he would not have been hurt. For example, driving without tail lights cannot be a cause of a head-on collision even at night.[81]

In this connection, it is important to recall that a causal relation must exist not just between the injury and the relevant act or omission, but specifically between the injury and that aspect of the conduct which is wrongful.[82] Thus according to the prevailing view, a plaintiff is not prejudiced merely because he "just happened" to be engaged in an unlawful (or careless) activity, such as driving without a licence or parking in a prohibited area.[83] To say in such a case that he would not have been involved in a collision had he obeyed the law is not enough, unless his disobedience increased the risk of a collision in accordance with *general* causal phenomena; if he would have been hurt just the same had he possessed a licence or parking been permitted, his violation of the law is not "to the point" and must be excluded from all consideration.

An alternative approach is to ask whether the plaintiff's injury was "within the risk" that made his conduct negligent. If the accident is wholly unrelated to the purposes of the rule he has violated, his default will not be counted against him.[84] This principle is neatly illustrated by two cases, one American and the other Australian. In the first,[85] a workman went on an unguarded end of a slippery platform in disobedience of instructions and was there injured by a collapsing wall. Yet, despite his carelessness, he recovered because the risk to which he had unreasonably exposed himself was a fall from the platform, not injury from falling bricks. In the second case,[86] the plaintiff accepted a lift as pillion rider on a motorcycle although aware that the lights were defective. A collision occurred with an oncoming car, because the driver of the cycle was riding on the wrong side of the road and failed to keep a proper look-out. In a claim against his host, it was held that the risk to which the plaintiff had unreasonably exposed himself was a collision arising from absence of headlights, not the driver's failure to avoid an approaching vehicle which was plainly visible.

It would, however, be a mistake to assess the scope of the apparent risk engendered by the plaintiff's conduct with overdue refinement, especially since apportionment. Thus just as in dealing with the extent of a *defendant's* liability,[87] the test is whether the plaintiff should reasonably have foreseen the general class of accident rather than the precise

80. See above, p. 193.
81. See *Fitzgerald v. Penn* (1954) 91 C.L.R. 268 esp. at 276-277. Generally: *March v. Stramare* (1991) 171 C.L.R. 506.
82. See above, p. 194.
83. See also above, p. 216.
84. *Rest. 2d* §468; *Civil Liabilities Act* 1961 (Eire) s. 34(2).
85. *Smithwick v. Hall & Upson Co.* 59 Conn. 261; 21 A. 924 (1890).
86. *Gent-Diver v. Neville* [1953] Q.S.R. 1; likewise *Marshall v. Batchelor* (1949) 51 W.A.L.R. 68.
87. See above, pp. 208ff. In particular, the defendant may have to anticipate the negligence of others, like the plaintiff: *March v. Stramare* (1991) 171 C.L.R. 506.

circumstances of the actual event.[88] Moreover, many forms of conduct are rightly regarded as deficient because of their generally dangerous character, and do not admit of nice distinctions according to their tendency to create only particular hazards.[89] For example, in *Jones v. Livox Quarries*,[90] a workman was standing on the back of a traxcavator when a dumper crashed into it from behind and injured him. An express prohibition had been issued against unauthorised riding on these vehicles to obviate the obvious danger of falling off or becoming trapped in some part of the machine, "but those were not the only risks to which [the plaintiff] had subjected himself. He had put himself in the dangerous position which, in fact, exposed him to the particular danger which came upon him . . . If he unreasonably, or improperly, exposed himself to this particular risk . . . he ought [not] to be allowed to say that it was not a cause operating to produce the damage, even though one may think that the prohibition against riding on the vehicle was not made with that particular risk in mind."[91] The court considered the instant case clearly distinguishable from one where a man negligently sits on an unsafe wall and the driver of a car, failing to keep a proper look-out, runs into the wall and knocks it down, or where a person is hit by a shotgun while riding on a towbar in a dangerous position. In such cases the plaintiff's fault would be inoperative on the ground either that there is no causal connection with the harm (it would have happened just the same if he had stood in front of the wall or been sitting inside the vehicle[92]) or that the accident was outside the scope of the risk to which he had unreasonably exposed himself.

In accordance with the foregoing principle, a particular plaintiff's negligence may be found to have been contributory to only part of the damage, but not to all.[93] Thus a moped rider with extensive head injuries aggravated by his negligent failure to wear a crash helmet, suffered a reduction only with respect to such additional injury.[94] Similarly, failure to use an available seat belt is relevant only if, and to the extent that, the injury would have been significantly less serious if it had been worn. Accordingly, apportionment may be applied only to that extent of the injury which could have been avoided.[95] The leading English case proposed a reduction in general of 25 per cent of such additional injury, but

88. *Hanly v. Berlin* [1975] Qd R. 52 (protruding elbow: 10%). *Rest. 2d* §468, comment *c* suggests that there is a difference here between negligence and contributory negligence, attributable to the more restrictive judicial attitude to the latter. Although the effect of taking a more expansive view of a plaintiff's, as opposed to a defendant's, negligence is to limit recovery, this is no longer too punitive since apportionment.
89. Cf. *Rest 2d* §468, comment *b*.
90. [1952] 2 Q.B. 608 (C.A.).
91. Ibid. at 614. Lord Denning's concurring opinion, rejecting the risk approach in favour of the *Polemis* rationale, must now be discounted.
92. See the instructive analysis of *McLaughlin v. Long* [1927] 2 D.L.R. 186 by Williams, *Joint Torts* 264.
93. Applied to separate injuries suffered in same accident, e.g. personal injury and damage to car: *Azzopardi v. Bois* [1968] V.R. 183 at 188; *The Calliope* [1970] P. 172.
94. *O'Connell v. Jackson* [1972] 1 Q.B. 270 (C.A.) (but expressed as 15% of the whole injury).
95. Ibid.; *Coe v. Kernovske* (1990) 10 M.V.R. 563 (Qld F.C.). The *Motor Accidents Act* 1988 (N.S.W.) s. 74 seems to mandate reduction regardless. Comparative: Wayand, 30 I.C.L.Q. 165 (1981).

of only 15 per cent where it would have occurred but been less severe.[96] Such a predetermined deduction is justified where, as here, the negligent conduct is readily identifiable, repetitive and generally uniform.[97]

Tort and contract

Even at common law contributory negligence was not a defence to all torts. Thus it did not apply to intended injury as distinct from unintended consequences of wilful wrongdoing.[98] Here the policy of repressing flagrant misconduct clearly outweighed any competing social benefit.

On the other hand, contributory negligence was not confined as a defence to actionable negligence in the strict sense of breach of a duty of care. Indeed, it emerged prior to the full development of that tort in a case of nuisance.[99] There is every reason in policy for (and none against) its relevance to any tort claim for negligent injury, whether that claim be formulated as actionable negligence or as an independent cause of action, like trespass[100] or perhaps even conversion.[101] It even qualifies strict liability, sometimes under the specific name of contributory negligence (for example breach of statutory duty),[102] more often under some other label like "act of plaintiff" as in relation to extra-hazardous substances,[103] cattle-trespass[104] and dangerous animals.[105]

Under the standard legislation, apportionment is now authorised whenever (1) the defendant's fault consists in "negligence, breach of duty or other act or omission which gives rise to liability in tort", and (2) the plaintiff's fault "would, apart from the Act, give rise to the defence of

96. *Froom v. Butcher* [1976] Q.B. 286 (C.A.). Also *Wrongs Act* 1936 (S.A.) s. 35a(1)(i) (at least 15%). But *Hallowell v. Nominal Defendant* [1983] Qd R. 266 rejected any rule of thumb.
97. Cf. Holmes (below, p. 311).
98. *Quinn v. Leathem* [1901] A.C. 495 at 537; *Venning v. Chin* (1974) 10 S.A.S.R. 299 at 315. *Sindle v. N.Y. Transit* 307 N.E. 2d 245 (N.Y. 1973) held it a defence that plaintiff sought to escape from confinement of moving bus by negligently jumping off. Deceit: see below, p. 636.
99. *Butterfield v. Forrester* (1809) 11 East 60; 103 E.R. 926; similar Australian cases are *Easton v. Kooistra* [1956] Tas. S.R. 1; *Tree v. Crenin* (1913) 15 W.A.L.R. 47. As a defence to nuisance see further below, p. 442.
100. *Venning v. Chin* (1974) 10 S.A.S.R. 299 at 317-322 (negligent driving on highway); cf. *Bell Canada v. Cope* (1980) 119 D.L.R. (3d) 254 ("fault"). Moreover, the suggestion that a modern plaintiff might avoid the defence by pleading his claim in trespass runs counter to the better view that even if negligent trespass is not defunct, he must meet all the requirements of tortious negligence: see above, pp. 20-22.
101. *Helson v. McKenzies* [1950] N.Z.L.R. 878; *Lumsden v. London Bank* [1971] 1 Ll. R. 114 (cheque); revd: *Torts (Interference with Goods) Act* 1977 (Eng.) s. 11; *Civil Liabilities Act* 1961 (Eire) s. 34(2); Goldring, 11 Melb. U.L. Rev. 91 (1977). Contra, principally for lack of precedent: *Australian Guarantee v. State Bank of Victoria* [1989] V.R. 617; *Day v. Bank of N.S.W.* (1978) 18 S.A.S.R. 163 (F.C.); *Wilton v. Commonwealth Bank* [1973] 2 N.S.W.L.R. 644.
102. Rather incongruously, this is true even when the very purpose of the statutory prescription is to safeguard the protected class against its own inexperience or lack of circumspection, as when a retailer sells a gun or ammunition to a child (*Wasney v. Jurazsky* [1933] 1 W.W.R. 155) or an employer is in breach of an industrial safety statute: see below, p. 517. The result has become more acceptable since apportionment.
103. See below, p. 346.
104. See below, p. 357.
105. See below, p. 363.

contributory negligence''.[106] The first requirement evidently qualifies all tort claims, including those of strict liability[107] and (except in New South Wales)[108] breach of statutory duty.[109] On the other hand, battery remains disqualified under the second leg.[110]

Differing views prevail regarding breach of contract, due partly to unresolved ambiguities in the above-mentioned definition of ''fault'', partly to a lack of consensus as to what would be a desirable rule.[111] The principal arguments against inclusion are that contributory negligence was not a defence at common law and that not even ''negligent'' breaches of contract are included in the definition of ''fault'' which, it is argued, must ''give rise to a liability in tort''. Opposing views are influenced by the modern tendency to treat some breaches of a contractual duty of reasonable care as actionable alternatively in contract or in tort,[112] and seek to avoid different results according to the choice of pleading. A growing consensus differentiates between claims solely contractual and claims concurrent in contract and tort.[113] To the former, contributory negligence is not a defence, any more under the statute than at common law, even for breach of an undertaking to exercise reasonable care, let alone for a negligent breach of an absolute contractual obligation, such as a warranty of fitness incidental to sale or hire[114] or a promise to lend a contractor a ladder.[115] Contract law sometimes helps itself on its own terms, as by ingeniously concluding that the plaintiff's fault deprived the defendant's breach of

106. See above, p. 277. It is possible but implausible to read the definition so that a plaintiff's fault would also qualify under (1). The F.C. in *Venning v. Chin* (1974) 10 S.A.S.R 299 divided on this issue.

107. *Southgate v. Commonwealth* (1987) 13 N.S.W.L.R. 188 (ground damage by aircraft). But see below, n. 118 with regard to the second requirement. Because in W.A. apportionment is limited to claims founded on ''negligence'' (defined to include breach of statutory duty), contributory negligence remains a complete defence to nuisance: *Przetak v. Metropolitan Transport* [1961] W.A.R. 2. Canadian statutes do not define ''fault'' or ''fault or negligence''; re strict liability see *McNeill v. Frankenfield* (1963) 44 D.L.R. (2d) 132.

108. In 1945 contributory negligence was entirely abrogated as a defence to claims for personal injuries based on breach of statutory duty: *Statutory Duties (Contributory Negligence) Act* 1945. *All* claims for breach of statute were specifically excluded from the 1965 apportionment statute (s. 7) with the (probably unintended) result that property damage claims are still absolutely barred.

109. For the mode of apportioning in cases of statutory negligence see above, p. 275.

110. *Horkin v. N. Melbourne Club* [1983] V.R. 153; Hudson, 4 Leg. Stud. 322 (1984). Some dissent: see below, n. 118.

111. See Swanton, *Contributory Negligence as a Defence to Actions for Breach of Contract*, 55 A.L.J. 278 (1981); Palmer & Davies, *Contributory Negligence and Breach of Contract—English and Australian Attitudes Compared*, 29 I.C.L.Q. 15 (1980). Only the *Civil Liabilities Act* 1961 (Eire) s. 2 expressly defines ''wrong'' as including breach of contract.

112. See above, p. 187.

113. The Law Com. (Working Paper No. 114) provisionally recommends extending the defence to all contract claims, whether based on strict liability or negligence.

114. *Lambert v. Lewis* [1982] A.C. 225.

115. As in *Quinn v. Burch Bros* [1966] 2 Q.B. 370 (affd on the different ground that defendant's breach did not cause the injury). Accord: *Maritrans v. Comet Shipping* [1985] 1 W.L.R. 1270; *Belous v. Willetts* [1970] V.R. 45; *James v. Duncan* [1970] V.R. 705; *Read v. Nerey* [1979] V.R. 47; *Tenant Radiant Heat v. Warrington* [1988] 1 E.G.L.R. 41 (converse situation where P's fault consists solely in breach of contract). Contra: *Doiron v. Caisse Pub.* (1985) 17 D.L.R. (4d) 660 (N.B.C.A.); *Ribic v. Weinstein* (1982) 140 D.L.R. (3d) 259 asserts a common law basis for apportioning contract claims.

causality or by relying on the plaintiff's duty to mitigate the loss.[116] On the other hand, if the defendant's conduct "gives rise to a liability in tort", the possibility that it also entails a concurrent liability in contract does not preclude application of the Act so that damages may be reduced.[117]

The statutory formula is also ambiguous on the question of whether it authorises apportionment only in cases where contributory negligence was a defence before the Act or whether there is room for a developing common law which would now allow a reduction of damages in cases where formerly a complete denial seemed too punitive. The uncertain response in dealing with battery[118] and strict liability[119] may reflect this puzzle.

4. CONDUCT CONSTITUTING CONTRIBUTORY NEGLIGENCE

In theory, a plaintiff is required to conform to the same standard of care as a defendant, with due allowance for the fact that here the enquiry is directed to what is reasonable for his own safety rather than the safety of others.[120] The reasonableness of his conduct is judged by the same process of balancing the importance of the interest he is seeking to advance against the gravity of the risk to himself.[121] A shopper in a self-service store is not required to keep his eyes on the floor,[122] nor is a policeman in pursuit of a felon.[123] So, when confronted with a dilemma, the plaintiff may reasonably choose to incur a slight risk for the sake of avoiding a greater inconvenience (not necessarily even a physical danger), like someone accidentally locked into a public toilet attempting to climb out[124] or a person aboard a train, surprised by its premature departure, deciding to jump off rather than be carried to the next stop 100 kilometres away.[125] Indeed, sometimes the social value of what the plaintiff is doing is so highly esteemed that he may even encounter a known and substantial risk without

116. *Quinn v. Burch Bros* (above); *Lambert v. Lewis* (above); *Tenant Radiant Heat v. Warrington* [1988] 1 E.G.L.R. 41 (unorthodox apportionment).
117. *Forsikrings Vesta v. Butcher* [1989] A.C. 852; *Bains Harding Constr. v. McCredie* (1988) 13 N.S.W.L.R. 437; *Mouat v. Clark Boyce* [1992] N.Z.L.R. 559 (C.A.). Contra: *Arthur Young v. W.A. Chip & Pulp* [1989] W.A. 100 (F.C.), based on different wording of W.A. statute. Query, where contract not coextensive with tort, as in *Vacwell Engineering v. B.D.H.* [1971] 1 Q.B. 88 (implied condition of fitness).
118. Contributory negligence was rejected in *Harkin v. N. Melbourne Club* [1983] 1 V.R. 153 (after thorough review), but admitted in *Hoebergen v. Koppens* [1974] 2 N.Z.L.R. 597 (see [1975] N.Z.L.J. 262); *Murphy v. Culhane* [1977] Q.B. 94 at 99. See Hudson, 4 Leg. Stud. 322 (1984). Provocation: see above, p. 84.
119. Contributory negligence was admitted in *Southgate v. Commonwealth* (1987) 13 N.S.W.L.R. 188 (ground damage by aircraft), but not in *Higgins v. Inglis* [1978] 1 N.S.W.L.R. 649 (scienter). Apportionment applies to (strict) products liability under *Consumer Protection Act* 1987 (U.K.) s. 6.
120. See *Rest. 2d* §466, comment *f*.
121. *Porter Co. v. Irving Oil* [1954] 3 D.L.R. 295 at 313-314.
122. *Suttons v. Goldsworthy* [1969] S.A.S.R. 282; *Diederichs v. Metropolitan Stores* (1956) 6 D.L.R. (2d) 751. He is expected to look up, not down.
123. *Bittner v. Tait-Gibson* (1964) 44 D.L.R. (2d) 113; also *Hambley v. Shepley* (1967) 63 D.L.R. (2d) 94 (road block); *Lewis v. Todd* [1980] 2 S.C.R. 694 (accident site).
124. Cf. *Sayers v. Harlow U.D.C.* [1958] 1 W.L.R. 623. Also *Clayards v. Dethick* (1848) 12 Q.B. 439; 116 E.R. 932 (braving obstruction of sole exit).
125. *Caterson v. Comr Rlys* (1973) 128 C.L.R. 99.

prejudice, like a rescuer who cannot be charged with contributory negligence any more than with voluntary assumption of risk unless he is downright foolhardy.[126]

Ordinarily, it is true, we may proceed on the assumption that other people will act with care and in accordance with accepted canons of propriety, but prudence demands as much from a potential plaintiff as from a defendant that he take guard as soon as he has reason to suspect that assumption to be ill-founded.[127] Moreover, it is unreasonable—where there is no necessity for it—to cut things so fine as to allow no margin of safety for the mistakes or thoughtlessness of others.[128] This counsel of wisdom is of singular relevance to motorists. On the other hand, a person's conduct in the face of sudden emergency cannot be judged from the standpoint of what would have been reasonable in the light of hind-knowledge and in a calmer atmosphere conducive to a nicer evaluation of all alternatives.[129] A certain latitude is allowed when "in the agony of the moment" he seeks to extricate himself from an emergency not created by his own antecedent negligence.[130] The degree of judgment and presence of mind expected of the plaintiff is what would have been reasonable in such a situation, and he will not be adjudged guilty of negligence merely because, as it turns out, he unwittingly took the wrong course. Thus when in the classical case of *Jones v. Boyce*,[131] a passenger decided to jump from a coach out of control, he recovered although it appeared that had he stayed on he would have escaped all injury. This principle is not, according to the better opinion, confined to situations of personal danger but applies equally where property is imperilled.[132]

It is perhaps questionable whether, under apportionment, courts will continue quite the same indulgence. The "agony of the moment" has frequently been invoked in the past to enable a plaintiff to escape from the stalemate rule, although his conduct did not in every respect attain the standard of reasonable prudence. As in connection with last opportunity, it was unfair to penalise the victim of another's much more reprehensible conduct by an out-and-out denial of redress on account merely of a momentary lapse in self-protection,[133] but where the courts have power to apportion the need for it has largely disappeared. The question is simply whether in all the circumstances the plaintiff has acted reasonably.[134]

126. See above, p. 172.
127. See above, p. 121.
128. *Municipal Tramways v. Ashby* [1951] S.A.S.R. 61 at 64.
129. " 'Errors of judgment', however, would not count against him, if they resulted 'from the excitement and confusion of the moment'. The reason that was exacted of him was not the reason of the morrow. It was reason fitted and proportioned to the time and the event" (*Wagner v. Intern. R.R.* 232 N.Y. 176 at 177 per Cardozo J. (1921)).
130. Inapplicable when plaintiff's negligence has contributed to the emergency: *Municipal Tramways v. Ashby* [1951] S.A.S.R. 61.
131. (1816) 1 Stark 493; 171 E.R. 540. Accord: *Ansell v. Arnold* [1963] S.A.S.R. 355 (avoiding collision); *Workers Compensation v. Schmidt* (1977) 80 D.L.R. (3d) 696 (dousing flames with cleaning fluid).
132. *Wilson v. United Counties Bank* [1920] A.C. 102 at 105; contra, *The Paludina* [1927] A.C. 16 at 28.
133. Where the emergency was created by the defendant, the situation bears a close analogy to "last opportunity" in the sense of involving an evaluation of comparative negligence. But the principle also applies where the emergency was due to other forces: see *Municipal Tramways v. Ashby* [1951] S.A.S.R. 61.
134. See *Antonon v. Leane* (1989) 53 S.A.S.R. 60 (F.C.).

The same observation applies to yet another judicial device of tempering the winds to the shorn lamb. Courts have frequently connived at jury verdicts exonerating plaintiffs, which on any objective assessment of the evidence could not have been sustained but for the elusive distinction between mere heedlessness or error of judgment on the one hand, and culpable neglect on the other.[135] In addition, there is a general inclination by juries to give more weight to the individual characteristics of plaintiffs than of defendants, and thus apply a subjective standard to contributory negligence.[136] This dual standard is but a reflection of general tendencies in modern tort law. Strict adherence to an external standard for a defendant's negligence promotes compensation of accident victims, especially where he is a suitable channel for loss distribution, as in the case of motorists and entrepreneurs; by the same token, a relaxed standard for contributory negligence tends to cut down a defence that would otherwise prejudice recovery. In view of the notorious compassion of juries for plaintiffs in face of defendants known or suspected to carry insurance, and the sparse exercise by appellate courts of their power to interfere with verdicts, the *actual* standard of care for plaintiffs is without much doubt often appreciably lower than that for defendants. Indeed, there are even judicial pronouncements favouring a dual standard as a matter of law.[137] Here again, however, it is worth noting that apportionment has removed the strong pull for excusing a plaintiff entirely,[138] though not of course for taking a sympathetic view of his share of responsibility.[139]

Children

That the plaintiff is a child or subject to some mental or physical handicap may have a bearing on the standard of care demanded from either party. So far as the defendant is concerned, he is of course ordinarily free to act on the assumption that others will take normal precautions for their own safety and that he need not adjust his own conduct in deference to *extra*ordinary disabilities or shortcomings of substandard members of the community, unless he knows or ought to anticipate their presence within the range of his own activities.[140] Thus when within the vicinity of children,

135. *Williams v. Comm. Road Transport* (1933) 50 C.L.R. 258 at 266-267; *Allen v. Redding* (1934) 50 C.L.R. 476 at 482.
136. Revealing is *Black v. McCabe* [1964] N.I. 1, where the jury reduced both claim and counterclaim for damage arising out of the same collision by 30% and 25% respectively. This meant that, as plaintiff, one of the parties was only 30% to blame, but as defendant 75%. A new trial was ordered by a divided court.
137. E.g. *McHale v. Watson* (1966) 115 C.L.R. 199 at 224. Menzies J. (dissenting) would have confined the accredited child standard to plaintiffs only. *Mochen v. State* 352 N.Y.S. 2d 290 (1974) approved a dual standard for the mentally deficient; cf. *Rest. 2d* §464, comment *g*. Also Parsons, *Negligence and Contributory Negligence*, 1 Melb. U.L. Rev. 163 (1957). Calabresi's *Ideals, Beliefs and Attitudes* (1985) ch. 2 links it to a societal commitment favouring the "disadvantaged".
138. See *Laszczyk v. N.C.B.* [1954] 1 W.L.R. 1426 (5% deducted).
139. The proportion of cases involving contributory negligence in 1973 ranged from 13% in S.A., 15-16% in N.S.W. and Victoria, to 23% in Queensland. Median reduction of damages ranged from 30% in Queensland to 50% in N.S.W. (*Compensation and Rehabilitation in Australia* (1974) 52-53). In N.Z. 14% of claimants in 1970 suffered a median reduction of 25% (27 Stan. L. Rev. at 669).
140. See above, p. 219. Illustrated in relation to children by *Cotton v. Comm. Road Transport* (1942) 43 S.R. (N.S.W.) 66 at 68-69; *Wells v. Cosgrove Motor* [1941] S.A.S.R. 191 at 194; *Griffiths v. Doolan* [1959] Qd R. 304.

and all the more when driving past a school or playground, he must reduce his speed to allow for the prevalent risk of youngsters dashing into traffic.

Only if the defendant has been found remiss in this respect and thus in breach of duty, does it become relevant to consider the plaintiff's own responsibility for the accident. The handicapped are of course by no means absolved from taking such reasonable care of themselves as their own capacity permits. Singularly lenient as the law has admittedly been with children and "very ready to find remedies for their injuries",[141] yet this indulgence cannot be carried to the point of acquitting them altogether from a duty of self-protection. There is no arbitrary minimum age for civil, as there is for criminal, responsibility.[142] Each case is handled individually, having regard to the particular child's capacity to cope with the relevant risk involved; and unless the child is so young as to be clearly incapable, the question is one for the jury.[143]

The appropriate standard, most widely accredited, is that of "children of like age, intelligence and experience".[144] This formula makes allowance even for the varied rate of development in children's intelligence and learning. In contrast, a somewhat stricter view seeks to objectify the standard to that of "normal children of like age", independent of the degree of intelligence, emotional stability and education of the particular child.[145] Few cases have necessitated a choice between these alternatives.[146]

Apparently the child standard applies, at least in theory, until the age of majority. Whether it is proper for adult activities like driving may well be doubted, especially since apportionment.[147]

Formerly, the child standard was relevant only to the question of whether there was negligence at all; today it bears also on apportioning damages.[148]

141. *Latham v. Johnson* [1913] 1 K.B. 398 at 413 per Hamilton L.J.
142. *Cotton v. Comm. Road Transport*; *Farrall v. Stokes* (1954) 54 S.R. (N.S.W.) 294. Except perhaps in case of violation of a penal safety statute when the child must at least be responsible by criminal standards: *Acadia Coal v. MacNeil* [1927] S.C.R. 497.
143. As regards traffic risks, at age five the expected capacity is in practice close to zero: *Beasley v. Marshall* (1977) 17 S.A.S.R. 456 at 459, but 5 years 10 months was sufficient in *Wilkins v. Allaby* (1988) 43 C.C.L.T. 101 (C.A.). *Pearson* §1077 recommended a 12-year minimum for traffic accidents. Zelling J. in *Wiech v. Amato* (1973) 6 S.A.S.R. 442 made a strong plea for making more allowance for small children's lack of spatio-temporal perception (Piaget). Other risks: *Yachuk v. Oliver Blais* [1949] A.C. 386 (nine-year-old not expected to be familiar with petrol); *Bye v. Bates* (1989) 51 S.A.S.R. 67 (6 years old: 12.5% for playing with electric appliance).
144. This is the orthodox formula in the U.S. (*Rest. 2d* §464(a); 32 A.L.R. 4d 56) and Canada: *McEllistrum v. Etches* [1956] S.C.R. 787 at 793; *Wade v. C.N.R.* [1978] 1 S.C.R. 1064 at 1074-6; *Finbow v. Domino* (1957) 11 D.L.R. (2d) 493 excused an eight-year-old, mentally aged three; quoted with approval in *McHale v. Watson* (1966) 115 C.L.R. 199.
145. Espoused by Kitto J. in *McHale v. Watson* (1966) 115 C.L.R. 199 at 214 and Salmon L.J. in *Gough v. Thorne* [1966] 1 W.L.R. 1387 at 1391; cf. *Mye v. Peters* (1967) 68 S.R. (N.S.W.) 298 at 304.
146. E.g. *Andrews v. Armitt (No. 2)* (1971) 2 S.A.S.R. 273.
147. In *Broadhurst v. Millman* [1976] V.R. 208 the child standard was applied to a 15½-year-old bicyclist; in *Ralph v. Henderson* [1968] N.Z.L.R. 759 to a 16½-year-old who operated a machine dangerous only to himself. American law increasingly applies the adult standard: *Rest. 2d* §283A, comment *c*; *Prosser & Keeton* 181.
148. E.g. *Guerin v. Rossiter* (1984) 37 S.A.S.R. 312.

Statutory violation

Just as a defendant's statutory breach may be held to confer a civil remedy on someone thereby injured, in addition to any penal sanction expressly enacted,[149] a plaintiff's own disobedience may by the same token be counted against him as contributory negligence per se. This, of course, would not be proper unless, in the first instance, the particular statute had the object of preventing accidents (for example industrial safety statutes)[150] rather than to maintain public order or raise revenue, like a prohibition against driving an unregistered or uninsured car or driving without a licence.[151] In addition, the injury must have been of a kind which it was the purpose of the statute to obviate—it must fall within the contemplated risk. Hence, if a cyclist were injured by falling masonry from an adjacent building, it would be no answer that he was illegally riding on the footpath, since that prohibition is designed to protect pedestrians from cyclists, not cyclists from falling masonry.

But according to what is probably the dominant view, once it is found that the policy of the statute was to compel obedience from the plaintiff in order to safeguard him against the very kind of injury he sustained, his unexcused violation thereof constitutes contributory negligence per se.[152] The Australian High Court[153] once suggested that the statute must in addition evince a positive intention to deprive the offender of his civil remedy—mirror image of a defendant's liability for statutory violation—but this requirement has been largely ignored in practice and in any event lost its urgency since apportionment.

5. IMPUTED CONTRIBUTORY NEGLIGENCE

In some situations the innocent victim of a concurrent tort, instead of being able to pursue both tortfeasors, may have the negligence of one imputed to him (because of a special relation between them) so as to impair his recovery against the other just as if he had been guilty of contributory negligence himself. This doctrine of identification is difficult to harmonise with the philosophy of individualism which shrinks from holding an innocent person responsible for the fault of another. Like the parent defence of contributory negligence, it was a stratagem of the early 19th century to ease the load of vulnerable tortfeasors.

Master and servant

The modern tendency has been to confine the incidence of identification to those relations alone where one person is held responsible for another's fault, whether he be sued or suing. This has been conveniently described as

149. See above, pp. 124ff.
150. Where public policy is sufficiently and better served by apportioning than defeating the claim: *N.C.B. v. England* [1954] A.C. 403 at 419, 422, 424, 428.
151. See below, p. 130 for an extended discussion of the effect of illegality.
152. E.g. *Canning v. R.* [1924] N.Z.L.R. 118.
153. *Henwood v. Municipal Tramways* (1938) 60 C.L.R. 438; also *Crotty v. Woolworths* (1942) 43 S.R. (N.S.W.) 133.

the "both ways" test:[154] the plaintiff is identified with another if, but only if, that other's negligence would be imputed to him, were he a defendant. Identification is thus coextensive with vicarious liability.[155]

Historically, vicarious liability developed first and identification followed as a deduction from it. It has little to commend it (apart, perhaps, from providing an incentive to the master to discipline his servant), because only a misguided sense of symmetry would regard it as "an extraordinary result to make the master liable for damage done by his servant to another vehicle and yet to allow him to recover in full for damage done to his own".[156] Vicarious liability is based primarily on the economic policy of assuring effective redress for tortious harm by allowing recourse against the employer who profits from his servant's activity and is best able to absorb the loss. There is no corresponding reason for protecting a culpable tortfeasor to the prejudice of his victim, and it is doubtful if the courts have ever squarely faced the question of why a master should bear all risks of his servant's activity, including the risk of harm to himself as well as the risk of harm to strangers.[157]

Under the regime of apportionment, a master is of course no longer completely debarred, but his damages are merely reduced in proportion to his servant's share of responsibility for the injury to his person or property.[158]

Car owner and driver

Next to master and servant, the relation of car owner and driver furnishes the most important instance of identification in modern law. True, bailment as such is no longer considered sufficient to justify imputing the bailee's negligence to his bailor as plaintiff, since it is not after all imputed to him as defendant (the "both ways" test).[159] In the case of motor vehicles, however, overriding concern for the compensation of traffic victims has prompted several modern developments which impose liability on the owner for the conduct of the driver in order to make the former's insurance available to plaintiffs.

One expression of this trend is the flat enactment of vicarious liability under several Australian statutes which deem "the driver (whether with or without the authority of the owner) . . . to be the agent of the owner acting

154. Gregory, *Vicarious Responsibility and Contributory Negligence*, 41 Yale L.J. 831 (1932).
155. *Chaplin v. Hawes* (1828) 3 C. & P. 554; 172 E.R. 543; *Pennell v. O'Callaghan* [1954] V.L.R. 320; *Unsworth v. Comm. Rlys* (1958) 101 C.L.R. 73.
156. Williams, *Joint Torts* 433. Besides, identification has never been pushed to the length of precluding the master from suing the servant himself: see above, p. 265.
157. MacIntyre, *Rationale of Imputed Negligence*, 5 U. Tor. L.J. 368 at 373 (1954). American courts increasingly reject the "both ways" test with respect to automobile "consent" statutes: see below, n. 62. *Weber v. Stokely-Van Camp* 144 N.W. 2d 540 (Minn. 1966) became the first to extend this trend to an ordinary master-servant relation (as against other motorists!): see *Prosser & Keeton* 526; Cheifetz, *Apportionment of Fault in Tort* (1981) 216 advocates the same rule for Canada.
158. Although the standard legislation refers only to cases "where any person suffers damage as the result partly of his *own* fault", it has been interpreted to include the fault of any person for whose act the plaintiff is responsible: *T.T.C. v. R.* [1949] S.C.R. 510; *Jay v. Veevers* [1946] 1 All E.R. 646. Specifically in S.A. (s. 27a(2); *Perrotta v. Cavallo* [1971] S.A.S.R. 163); W.A. (s. 3); Tas. (s. 4(7)) and A.C.T. (s. 14(2)).
159. *France v. Parkinson* [1954] 1 W.L.R. 581; *Fletcher v. Thomas* [1931] 3 D.L.R. 142.

within the scope of his authority''.[160] This type of legislation is also common in North America,[161] except that the Australian generally limits itself expressly to "proceedings *against* the owner" and therefore does not impinge on claims *by* him for personal injury or damage to the car due to the combined negligence of the driver and a third party.

Another instance of vicarious liability is to treat the owner as responsible for the driver when he was either in the car himself or had entrusted it for a purpose at least partially his own.[162] By thus stretching the conventional ambit of vicarious liability, this modern rule plainly reveals its underlying purpose of seeking to reach the owner's insurance. Without qualm, however, it has been applied against the owner not only as defendant but also as plaintiff.[163] His claim against the third party for damage to the car or even personal injuries is thus liable to reduction, though not (of course) his claim against his own driver.[164]

Passenger and carrier

In an early case,[165] a passenger in a bus was identified with his own driver so as to debar him from recovery against the negligent driver of another vehicle. The reasoning unrealistically emphasised that the plaintiff, by selecting his own means of conveyance, had control over his driver, but the more probable reason behind the decision was a feeling that it would be unfair to burden one person with all the consequences of the dual fault. The conclusion may thus have been partially prompted by a desire to escape from the harshness of the rule against contribution among concurrent tortfeasors, which has since been abolished. The decision was overruled in 1888[166] so that, in the absence of genuine contributory negligence on his own part[167] or some other special reason for holding him responsible for the driver (like being the owner of the car[168]), a passenger is no longer prejudiced in proceeding against the third party.[169]

Domestic relations

At one time, a child injured in an accident was identified with, and his right of action barred by, the contributing negligence of the person in charge of him at the time.[170] This barbarous rule[171] which visited the sins of fathers upon their offspring could obviously not be supported by

160. See below, p. 388.
161. See above.
162. See below, p. 385.
163. *Pennell v. O'Callaghan* [1954] V.L.R. 320; *Manawatu County v. Rowe* [1956] N.Z.L.R. 78; *Milkovits v. Federal Press* (1972) 20 F.L.R. 311 (by statute: see above, n. 158).
164. E.g. *Perrotta v. Cavallo* [1971] S.A.S.R. 163. Thus he might well collect in full if his insurance policy covers the risk.
165. *Thorogood v. Bryan* (1849) 8 C.B. 115; 137 E.R. 452.
166. *The Bernina* (1888) 13 App. Cas. 1; *Little v. Hackett* 116 U.S. 366 (1886).
167. E.g. if he rides with a drunken driver (as in *Ins. Comm. v. Joyce* (1948) 77 C.L.R. 39) or in an unlighted vehicle: as in *Bourke v. Jessop (No. 3)* [1935] N.Z.L.R. 246.
168. See above, n. 160.
169. See e.g. *Blight v. Warman* [1964] S.A.S.R. 163.
170. *Waite v. N.E. Rly* (1858) 1 E.B. & E. 719; 120 E.R. 679.
171. *Prosser & Keeton* 531.

reasoning based on "selection", but was attributed to the allegedly incomplete legal personality of a child in the care of an adult member of the family.[172] No doubt, the court was influenced by the thought that the negligent parent might ultimately reap the benefit of the verdict, ignoring the fact that the child would recover in his own right and be legally entitled to the damages.

After the identification of passenger and driver had been exploded, it became increasingly difficult to maintain it in this situation, because "how much less ought an infant to be bound by the negligence of a person in whose care and control he is, without any volition or choice on his part, and over whose acts he has no power to control?"[173] It was last asserted in 1909[174] and finally abrogated by an English decision of 1933.[175]

A married woman's separate legal personality has long been taken for granted. But prior to the Married Women's Property Acts the husband was a necessary party to any proceedings by her[176] and, as a corollary, his own negligence barred all recovery against the tortfeasor. With the disappearance of this procedural requirement, spouses are no longer (any more than other members of the same family) in any way identified with each other for purposes of contributory negligence.[177]

Imputed negligence in domestic relations is also encountered in connection with claims for loss of services[178] and wrongful death,[179] but these are more conveniently considered elsewhere.

172. See *Russell v. Jorgenson* (1909) 9 S.R. (N.S.W.) 164 at 167: "The child is not an independent personality but is bound to obey the directions of the person in whose charge he is." But is the conclusion drawn from it "fair and logical"? (ibid. at 169).
173. *Russell v. Jorgenson* (1909) 9 S.R (N.S.W.) 164 at 166-167 per Simpson A.-C.J. (dissenting).
174. Ibid. at 164.
175. *Oliver v. Birmingham Omnibus Co.* [1933] 1 K.B. 35; *Kaplan v. Canada Safeway* (1968) 68 D.L.R. (2d) 627. But the parent's own claim for medical expenses may be impaired: see below. Sometimes also an occupier or carrier may assume that infants are accompanied and supervised by careful parents: see below, p. 682.
176. See below, p. 679.
177. Except perhaps in community property States (western U.S.).
178. See below, p. 662.
179. See below, p. 667.

13

VOLUNTARY ASSUMPTION OF RISK

"Voluntary assumption of risk" as a defence to negligence corresponds to the plea of "consent" in actions for intended harm. Both are expressions of the same philosophy of individualism, that no wrong is done to one who consents: volenti non fit injuria. The plaintiff, by agreeing to assume the risk himself, absolves the defendant from all responsibility for it.[1] The latter's duty of care is thus suspended.[2]

Obviously this defence bears much resemblance to contributory negligence. Most often, indeed, the two defences overlap: viz. whenever knowingly to assume a risk is also negligent, for example riding in a car with a drunk driver. But, like intersecting circles, some cases support one defence without the other; thus to assume the risk may in some circumstances be perfectly reasonable or (per contra) the risk, though unreasonable, may not be fully appreciated and assumed.

As long as either defence defeated the plaintiff entirely, precise demarcation served only academic interest, but the introduction of apportionment for contributory negligence has posed a serious problem concerning the future role of voluntary assumption of risk as a complete defence.[3] It seems rather odd that a plaintiff who is himself negligent might now fare better than one who is not, for example that an intoxicated passenger should stand a better chance against a drunk driver than a passenger who is sober. The judicial response to this dilemma has been to impose ever stricter requirements for the defence of volenti to the point where it is now but rarely successful.[4]

Presumably the reason for not formally drawing the defence within the net of apportionment (or what would amount to the same, flatly abolishing it) is the feeling that people should remain free to forgo their legal rights, at least under conditions of free and informed choice. Such a waiver contemplates, of course, a complete shifting of the legal risk, absolving the defendant from *all*—not just an apportioned share of—responsibility for resulting injury.

1. While it would be bizarre to say that the plaintiff agrees to the defendant being as careless as he likes, he *does* agree not to hold the defendant responsible even for an accident caused by the latter's negligence.
2. Volenti is a waiver of duty, in contrast to contributory negligence which is a plea of confession and avoidance to an admitted breach of duty: *Thomas v. Quartermaine* (1887) 18 Q.B.D. 685 at 697-698. It has therefore been argued (e.g. James, 78 Yale L.J. 185 (1969)) that one could (*and should*) do without the defence eo nomine by employing instead the "duty" concept. Sed cui bono? Is it not safer to confront a known than a disguised devil? See also below, p. 303.
3. Typically apportionment statutes stand mute. Exceptional is the *Civil Liabilities Act* 1961 (Eire) s. 34(1)(b) which limits volenti to cases where "the plaintiff before the act complained of agreed to waive his legal rights." In the U.S. the trend has been to abrogate the defence, either legislatively or judicially, wherever it is in competition with a regime of apportionment ("comparative negligence"): *Prosser & Keeton* 495-498.
4. I.e. in cases other than of *express* waiver.

The central element of the defence, around which the tides of shifting social policy have eddied, is the supposition that the risk was *voluntarily assumed.* How real must be the proof? By giving it short shrift, the 19th century moulded the defence into an effective shield for industry and business. Because of this ruthless past, the defence continues to be widely viewed with suspicion and distaste. Much however has been done to bring it into line with a more realistic contemporary view of human and social relations.

1. EXPRESS TERMS

Frequently a person is prepared to establish a relation with others only on terms expressly defined by him. Thus in offering his services to clients, permitting entry to his premises or giving someone a ride in his car, he may stipulate conditions which modify in his favour the usual allocation of risks. Ordinarily, these terms will become binding on the offeree on his accepting that relationship with express or implied agreement to these terms. To the extent that they purport to relieve the defendant from responsibility, the plaintiff thereby assumes the risk for himself.

Such a reallocation of risks may be assumed to express what the parties believe to be in their best interest and to serve the most efficient allocation of resources. In many situations, their choice will be influenced by who will be in the better position to control the risk or to insure against it at least cost;[5] for example, property insurance is usually more economical than liability insurance, and a low charge for services argues against assumption of large potential losses.[6] These assumptions, however, presuppose roughly equal access to information and equal bargaining power, as mostly between commercial parties. But under modern conditions of monopoly services and highly integrated trade practices the only choice for the "little man" is typically to "take or leave" the standard terms offered to him. These adhesion contracts often contain exemption clauses limiting or even disclaiming the liability that would otherwise rest on the defendant as a matter of law and sound risk allocation.

Protection against unreasonable and oppressive exemption or indemnity clauses has eventually come both from the legislature and the courts. Frontal attack, according to the British view, is proper only for Parliament. Exemption clauses have thus been variously outlawed in the case of carriers,[7] even private vehicles covered by compulsory third party insurance,[8] the sale or supply of goods to consumers,[9] industrial safety

5. *Photo Products v. Securicor* [1980] A.C. 827 at 851 per Lord Diplock.
6. E.g. security services in *Ailsa Craig Fisheries v. Malvern Fishing Co.* [1983] 1 W.L.R. 964 (H.L.); *Photo Productions v. Securicor*; *Davis v. Pearce Parking* (1954) 91 C.L.R. 642 at 652 (parking garage).
7. E.g. in England limitations on liability of carriers of passengers are banned by the *Road Traffic Act* 1960 s. 115 (public service vehicles) and the Passenger Charges Scheme 1954, para. 32 (railways), while conditions for the carriage of goods must be "just and reasonable" (*Railways and Canal Traffic Act* 1854 s. 7). See Kahn-Freund, *Law of Inland Transport* (4th ed. 1965) esp. ch. 9. N.S.W. and Tas. have voided all limitations on liability for public motor vehicles (*Motor Vehicles (Third Party Insurance) Act* 1942 (N.S.W.) s. 19(2); *Traffic Act* (Tas.) s. 23(3); N.Z. for all carriers (*Carriers Act* 1948).
8. See below, n. 48.
9. See below, p. 479.

legislation,[10] landlord and tenant.[11] An English Act of 1977 finally generalised this trend by nullifying all contract terms or notices which exclude or restrict liability for death or personal injury resulting from negligence as well as such terms with respect to other loss or damage unless they satisfy the test of reasonableness.[12]

But our courts, unlike American courts,[13] have resigned themselves to the task of "construction" alone. For a time, the English Court of Appeal under Lord Denning promoted a more interventionist policy, but this has now been repudiated by the House of Lords against the background of the legislative reform of 1977.[14] The judicial bias against disclaimers may now express itself only in the following, more modest ways: first, in a most pronounced reluctance to find that adequate notice has been given to the party to be bound.[15] The disclaimer may be on a ticket issued by a carrier or parking garage, it may be in an invoice or on a sticker fixed to the dashboard of a car;[16] it may be contractual or non-contractual (like a notice board at the entrance of premises).[17] Sometimes the notice is found to have come too late, after the contract between the parties had already been entered into,[18] or everything reasonable had not been done to bring the disclaimer to the plaintiff's attention. In the absence of an explanation, the plaintiff is entitled to assume that a printed document contains nothing unusual, unreasonable or oppressive.[19] Also, any written disclaimer yields to a prior inconsistent oral representation.[20] On the other hand, if the plaintiff signs the form, at least some cases have held him bound in the absence of fraud or misrepresentation, whether he knew the terms or not.[21]

Secondly, the terms if otherwise binding are construed strictly against the proponent, especially when he had a bargaining advantage, as generally over consumers. Ordinarily in order to exclude liability for negligence, the stipulation must either specifically refer to it or be couched in language that cannot conceivably be construed as referring to some other head of liability (like warranty) alone, such as an exemption for damage *howsoever*

10. E.g. *Factories Act* 1962 (N.S.W.) s. 149; and of course workers' compensation.
11. E.g. *Defective Premises Act* (Eng.) 1972 s. 6(3).
12. *Unfair Contract Terms Act* 1977 (limited to "business activities"). Guidelines for reasonableness are contained in Sched. 2. See *Smith v. Bush* [1980] 1 A.C. 831 (mortgage valuation); Coote, 41 Mod. L. Rev. 312 (1978); Sealy, 37 Cam. L.J. 15 (1978). The *Contracts Review Act* 1980 (N.S.W.) authorises relief against harsh, oppressive, unconscionable and unjust contracts: see Peden, *Unjust Contracts* (1982); Jackson, 65 A.L.J. 507 (1991).
13. Intervening where the public interest is engaged: Fleming, "Exemption Clauses", in *Law in the United States in Social and Technical Revolution* (1974) 105. Comparative: Eörsi, *Validity of Clauses Excluding or Limiting Liability*, 23 Am. J. Comp. L. 215 (1975).
14. *Photo Productions v. Securicor* [1980] A.C. 827.
15. E.g. *M'Cutcheon v. MacBrayne* 1964 S.C. (H.L.) 28; [1964] 1 W.L.R. 125; *Olley v. Marlborough Court* [1949] 1 K.B. 532; *Causer v. Browne* [1952] V.L.R. 1.
16. "Passenger travels at own risk" or "Passenger not insured" (*Birch v. Thomas* [1972] 1 W.L.R. 294 (C.A.) (full comprehension not required)). Binding on minor of 16: *Buckpitt v. Oates* [1968] 1 All E.R. 1145.
17. *Ashdown v. Williams* [1957] 1 Q.B. 409 (C.A.); see below, p. 454.
18. E.g. *Thornton v. Shoe Lane Parking* [1971] 2 Q.B. 163 (C.A.).
19. E.g. *Jacques v. Lloyd D. George* [1968] 1 W.L.R. 625 at 630 per Lord Denning.
20. *Mendelssohn v. Normand* [1970] 1 Q.B. 177 (C.A.).
21. *L'Estrange v. Graucob* [1934] 2 K.B. 394; *Curtis v. Chemical Cleaning Co.* [1951] 1 K.B. 805. Not so modern Can. cases: *Crocker v. Sundance Resorts* [1988] 1 S.C.R. 1186.

caused.[22] In Australia, the rule applies with equal stringency to limitations as to exclusions,[23] but in England "strained constructions" have latterly been discouraged on the ground (?) that there is a lesser probability that the plaintiff would not have agreed to it.[24] There is least justification for such shifts where courts have been empowered to address directly whether a term is "fair and reasonable". Moreover, it should be remembered that these are mere guidelines or aids to construction and not to be read like words in a statute.[25]

Third party beneficiaries

The question of whether third parties may invoke the benefit of exemption clauses has received no consistent or straightforward reply. Not infrequently services, like transporting passengers or goods, are being contracted for on terms contemplating vicarious performance by servants or other agents and limiting liability for injury or loss. There used to be impressive authority for permitting the latter to invoke such a limitation in defence to a tort claim, especially in the case of bailments when it was realistic to suppose that the (sub)bailee had accepted custody of the goods only on terms of the head contract.[26] But this doctrine of "vicarious immunity" was eventually repudiated as incompatible with the contractual "privity" requirement even when the clause expressly purported to extend the benefit to them.[27] This position may however no longer be tenable in jurisdictions[28] which have abolished or weakened the privity rule.

In any event, several points may be raised against this conclusion. First, the privity doctrine had previously been understood only to deny third parties the right to sue for a contractual benefit, not to prevent them from using it as a shield to a tort claim. Secondly, that limitations of liability need not be contractual at all is exemplified by decisions holding that suitably displayed notices may effectively exclude liability to persons entering an occupier's land[29] and perhaps even minors.[30] Exemption clauses in contracts appear therefore to have been singled out for exceptional treatment. Thirdly, it runs counter to the general rule that servants and agents are entitled to the same immunities and duty limitations as their principal (for example vis-à-vis trespassers),[31] thereby engrafting an

22. *Canada Steamship Lines v. R.* [1952] A.C. 192; *Smith v. S. Wales Switchgear* [1978] 1 W.L.R. 165 (H.L.). Equally applicable to indemnity clauses: *A.M.F. v. Magnet* [1968] 1 W.L.R. 1028 at 1055-8.
23. *Darling Futures v. Delco* (1986) 161 C.L.R. 500 at 510.
24. *George Mitchell v. Finney Lock Seeds* [1983] 2 A.C. 803.
25. See Swanton, *Exclusion of Liability for Negligence*, 15 U.Q.L.J. 183 (1988).
26. See Coote, *Exception Clauses* (1964) ch. 9; Yates, *Exclusion Clauses* (2nd ed. 1982) ch. 5.
27. *Scruttons v. Midland Silicones* [1962] A.C. 446; *Canadian G.E. v. Pickford* [1971] S.C.R. 41.
28. *Property Law Act* 1974 (Qld) s. 55; *Property Law Act* 1969 (W.A.) s. 11; *Contracts Privity Act* 1982 (N.Z.); semble, *Trident Gen. Insurance v. McNeice Bros* (1988) 165 C.L.R. 107 (Mason C.J. and Wilson J.).
29. See below, p. 454.
30. See below, n. 80.
31. In cases of *statutory* limitations, commonly enacted in favour of carriers, the question is perhaps in the last resort one of construction. It was on this basis that a divided C.A. in N.Z. held a carrier's *negligent* servant not entitled to the £20 limit per package: *Campbell v. Russell* [1962] N.Z.L.R. 407. The decision was promptly reversed by amendments in 1962 of the *Carriers Act*, the *Government Railways Act*, and

anomalous exception for *contractual* limitations. Finally, though the traditional hostility against exemption clauses has been frequently invoked as an auxiliary reason for excluding third parties, the rule in fact makes no discrimination between situations of suspected overreaching or unfairness and others. In some of the personal injury cases where ticket holders were permitted to bypass the carrier's exemption clause by suing his culpable servant (bus driver or crew member) instead, it may have seemed justified by the desire to extricate the plaintiff from an unfair adhesion contract.[32] But in other cases of purely commercial background, the rule defeats business purposes and sound cost allocation.[33]

Perhaps in recognition of these criticisms, and with the avowed object of closing the gap between English and American law in the important area of ocean transport, the Privy Council more recently sounded a retreat by opening the benefit of exemption ("Himalaya") clauses in charterparties to stevedores, intermediate carriers etc. who were specifically included, if it can be inferred that the carrier, in addition to contracting on his own behalf, was also contracting as agent for the stevedore etc.[34] This agency doctrine has since been invoked also in other situations.[35]

An alternative route to the same result has been to say that when a plaintiff has expressly assumed the risk of a third party's negligence, it would not be "just and reasonable" to entitle him to a tort duty from the latter. This has precluded a building owner from holding a subcontractor liable;[36] and a bailor suing the bailee's employees even in the absence of a Himalaya clause.[37]

Burdening third parties

In the converse situation, would an exemption clause under which a defendant supplied goods or services provide a shield against a non-contracting party? Ordinarily it would no doubt seem unfair and contrary to the goal of consumer protection to defeat a person's legal claim by a stipulation to which he did not expressly or at least impliedly consent.

31. *Continued*
the *Sea Carriage of Goods Act*. There is a similar amendment in article 25A of the Warsaw Convention and art. 4 bis, r. 2 of the Hague-Visby Rules (Brussels Protocol 1968, enacted in Britain by *Carriage of Goods by Sea Act* 1971).
32. *Cosgrove v. Horsfall* (1945) 62 T.L.R. 140 (C.A.); *Adler v. Dickson* [1955] 1 Q.B. 158 (C.A.); *Gore v. Van der Lann* [1967] 2 Q.B. 31 (Odgers, *Strange Case of Mrs Gore*, 86 L.Q.R. 69 (1970)); Tedeschi, 55 A.L.J. 876 (1981).
33. A striking example, *Cooper v. Jeakins* [1967] 2 Q.B. 1 (like *Philip Morris v. Transport Comm.* [1975] Tas. S.R. 128) is criticised by Weir [1965] Cam. L.J. 186.
34. *N.Z. Shipping v. Satterthwaite (The Eurymedon)* [1975] A.C. 154 (P.C.); *Port Jackson Stevedoring v. Salmond* [1981] 1 W.L.R. 138; 144 C.L.R. 300 (P.C.); also *ITO v. Miida Electronics* [1986] 1 S.C.R. 752. See Clarke, *Reception of the Eurymedon in Australia, Canada and New Zealand*, 29 I.C.L.Q. 132 (1980). "Himalaya clause" takes its name from *Adler v. Dickson* [1955] 1 Q.B. 158.
35. *Life Savers v. Frigmobile* [1983] 1 N.S.W.L.R. 431 (C.A.) (land transport); *Dyck v. Man. Snowmobile Assoc.* (1981) 17 C.C.L.T. 225 (race); cf. *Greenwood Plaza v. Beattie* [1980] 2 S.C.R. 228 (lease).
36. *Southern Water v. Carey* [1985] 2 All E.R. 1077, relying on dicta by Lord Roskill in *Junior Books v. Veitchi* [1983] 1 A.C. 520 at 546 which had misinterpreted *Hedley Byrne* (where the clause was in the subcontract). See above, p. 185.
37. *London Drugs v. Kuehne* (1990) 70 D.L.R. (4th) 51 (B.C.C.A.), distg *Greenwood Plaza v. Beattie* [1980] 2 S.C.R. 228. See Blum, 70 Can. B. Rev. 156 (1991).

Hence consumers will not as a rule be prejudiced by exemption clauses stipulated by manufacturers of defective products.

Exculpatory clauses by subcontractors have fared better. For example, an owner who entrusts his goods for transport or repair may be bound by the conditions under which a sub-bailee is alone prepared to assume possession. If the goods have been lost as a result of theft, the owner's claim would be barred by a suitable exemption clause, perhaps even regardless of whether he expressly or impliedly consented to a sub-bailment containing such a clause.[38] This can be put on the ground that since the owner can only establish his claim by relying on the bailment (otherwise the defendant would have been under no responsibility to guard against theft), he cannot both approbate and reprobate it.

As previously noted,[39] subcontractors have also been able to defeat claims by third parties like the building owner for property damage no less than for pure economic loss on the basis of an exemption clause in their contract with the head-contractor. The rationale was that it was not "just and reasonable" to impose on the defendant a tort duty unqualified by the terms on which he undertook the job.[40] Its application must obviously be limited to network contracts such as in construction projects, where the plaintiff is not an outsider.

2. IMPLIED ASSUMPTION OF RISK

Even more radical has been the transformation of the defence in situations where there is no express agreement to modify the ordinary duty relation between the parties. Nineteenth century theory had readily endorsed the proposition that one who encountered a known danger tacitly assumed the risk of an accident, content to absolve anyone responsible for it even if he turned out to be negligent. "Volenti" was interpreted as if it were synonymous with "scienti non fit injuria". This approach was most ruthlessly invoked in employment cases so as to debar injured workers on the barest finding that they continued in their job after becoming cognisant that the working conditions were hazardous. But with the growing strength of industry and changing social ideas, this draconic doctrine began to yield, culminating in the drastic reformulation of the defence in the great case of *Smith v. Baker*.[41] It was there laid down that voluntary assumption of risk cannot be imputed to a plaintiff merely because he encountered a known hazard and thereby consented to the risk of being hurt; in order to disqualify him from all redress, he must be shown to have consented to run

38. *Johnson, Matthey v. Constantine* [1976] 2 Ll. Rep. 215 at 222; *Morris v. Martin* [1966] 1 Q.B. 716 at 729 (Lord Denning: consenting to sub-bailment); *Singer v. Tees & Hartlepool Port* [1988] 2 Ll. R. 164; contra, *Philip Morris v. Transport Comm.* [1975] Tas. S.R. 135. More problematical would be a loss due to negligent handling of the goods: Palmer, *Bailment* (2nd ed. 1991) 1631ff.; *Schiffahrt v. Chelsea Maritime* [1982] Q.B. 481 at 486 (bill of lading: Diamond, *Hague-Visby Rules* [1978] Lloyd's Maritime L.Q. 225 at 248).
39. See above, p. 185.
40. While prior cases were undoubtedly influenced by the claim being for purely economic loss, *Norwich City v. Harvey* [1989] 1 W.L.R. 828 (C.A.) applied it (sub silentio) to property damage.
41. [1891] A.C. 325.

that risk at his own expense so that he, and not the negligent defendant, should bear the loss in the event of an accident.[42] In other words, the defence was henceforth available only in those rare cases where it can be genuinely predicated that the injured person assumed not merely the *physical* but also the *legal* risk of injury.[43] Even more important, this stricter test has been given teeth by progressively raising the standard of evidence required to support the conclusion that it has been met.

As a result, the defence virtually disappeared from what had formerly been its most conspicuous sphere, that of work accidents.[44] But although this dramatic change was largely influenced by the need to protect employees from bargaining away their rights under economic pressure, the new approach has not been confined to master-servant cases. The absence of true bargaining equality between worker and employer increases the difficulty of establishing that the risk was *voluntarily* assumed, but it is as true in other contexts that the defence cannot succeed any more unless the evidence supports a genuine inference that the plaintiff consented not merely to the risk of injury, but also to the lack of reasonable care which may produce that risk.[45]

This tendency has become more pronounced since the introduction of apportionment. Formerly it mattered nothing whether a plaintiff was defeated on the ground of volenti or contributory negligence. Now, however, the distinction has become critical, since apportionment does not apply to volenti. In the United States it has become the practice to merge *unreasonable* assumption of risk into contributory negligence, leaving reasonable assumption of risk to be taken care of by a denial of duty. Somewhat similarly, in New South Wales the defence has been abolished for motor accident cases in favour of reducing damages "as is just and equitable on the presumption that the injured or deceased person was negligent in failing to take care of his or her own safety".[46] Failing that, courts have seen all the more reason for taking an ever more restrictive view of the defence in order to avoid the distasteful consequence of defeating the plaintiff entirely instead of merely reducing his award. In the result, the defence is nowadays but rarely invoked with success.

The central problem, to which divergent answers continue to be given, is what justifies the conclusion that a particular risk has been *assumed.*[47] At one extreme are statements demanding an "agreement" or even "bargain" between the parties whereby one assents to waive his right of recourse against the other in return for an expected favour, like being given

42. *Kelly v. Farrans* [1954] N.I. 41 at 45. But a jury need not be specifically asked if the plaintiff assumed the risk "without expecting the defendant to compensate her [his wife] if she were injured" (*Sara v. G.I.O.* (1969) 89 W.N. (Pt 1) (N.S.W.) 203 (C.A.)).
43. The distinction was thus first formulated by Williams, *Joint Torts* 308.
44. See below, p. 512.
45. *Wooldridge v. Sumner* [1963] 2 Q.B. 43 at 69.
46. *Motor Accidents Act* 1988 s. 76. Presumably reduction is authorised even for reasonable assumption of risk (*pre*sumption, not *as*sumption). The *Personal Injuries Damages Bill* 1991 proposes extension to all torts. The defence was also abrogated for passengers of motor vehicles by the *Road Traffic Act* 1972 (U.K.); applied to a drunken spree in *Pitts v. Hunt* [1991] 1 Q.B. 24 (but not pre-empting defence of illegality). *Contracts* to avoid liability are nullified by *Motor Vehicles Acts* of Qld (s. 6(1)); S.A. (s. 133); W.A. (s. 26); A.C.T. (s. 41)—all in train with compulsory insurance.
47. Morison, *'Volens' Principle*, 1 Syd. L. Rev. 77 (1953).

a free ride.[48] But this requirement is both psychologically unrealistic and incompatible with a course of decisions which have found plaintiffs volentes on the basis of far less positive conduct. Particularly troubling in this respect are situations in which the question of assumption of risk arises in advance of the defendant's conduct, instead of the defendant's negligence preceding the plaintiff's confrontation of it. Such are cases dealing with a passenger's rights against a drunk or incompetent driver, nowadays the principal testing ground of the defence.

Drunk drivers

From a policy point of view, many good reasons militate against the defence in this situation. In the first place, there is no longer any doubt that contributory negligence may be invoked against a passenger who was or should have been aware of his host's condition, and that the plea cannot be defeated either on the ground that the driver had the last opportunity or that the passenger did nothing to contribute to the accident.[49] Secondly, contributory negligence by merely reducing, instead of extinguishing, recovery serves as a deterrent for *both* parties, the driver as well as the passenger. By not letting the former escape scot-free, the law of torts is thus doing its share to combat drunk driving by prompting his insurance company to discipline him by exercising its contractual or statutory[50] right of indemnity and increasing his future premiums. Nor is it unjust to permit the passenger some recovery, for his fault is usually much the lesser,[51] and there is no sense whatever in discriminating against one who was aware of his driver's impaired condition rather than so intoxicated himself as to be beyond realising it (in which case assumption of risk would fail for want of full comprehension of it).[52]

We have already noted some legislation abrogating the defence generally for motor accidents.[53] South Australia has done so specifically in cases of drunk or drugged drivers, instead presuming the passenger's contributory negligence.[54] Elsewhere, the judicial response has not been entirely uniform beyond a common desire to keep the defence within narrow bounds. Of critical importance is the degree of the driver's intoxication. When does it reach the point that accepting a ride with knowledge of his condition implies assumption of the legal risk of any future negligence? Clearly when the driver is so drunk as to be incapable of driving safely,[55]

48. Most explicit is Williams (*Joint Torts* 308) who drafted the Eire statute (see above, n. 3): "agreed to waive". This must be actually communicated: *O'Hanlon v. Electrical Supply* [1969] I.R. 75. Jaffey ([1985] Cam. L.J. 87) goes so far as to argue that such agreement, absent consideration, cannot be made *after* the tortious conduct has occurred.
49. See above, p. 268.
50. Compulsory insurance legislation, while outlawing any attempt to exclude coverage for a drunk driver, uniformly permits the insurer an indemnity from him.
51. *Owens v. Brimmell* [1977] Q.B. 859 (20%); *Spicer v. Coppins* (1991) 56 S.A.S.R. 175 (25%); *Morton v. Knight* [1990] 2 Qd R. 419. In the U.S. intoxication is often linked with recklessness as the sole basis of liability to guest passengers.
52. *Duncan v. Bell* [1967] Qd R. 425 (where the plaintiff's fault was the worse for having contributed to the defendant's drunkenness).
53. See above, n. 47.
54. *Wrongs Act* 1936 s. 35a(4).
55. As in *Morris v. Murray* [1991] 2 W.L.R. 195 (C.A.) (drunk air pilot); *Walker v. Watson* [1974] 2 N.Z.L.R. 175 and probably in *Miller v. Decker* [1957] S.C.R. 624. Not otherwise: *Sloan v. Kirby* (1979) 20 S.A.S.R. 263.

or when he has warned the passenger that he will be driving in a dangerous manner.[56] Unexpressed reservations by the passenger would not then avail him to defeat the conclusion that he was both sciens and volens. Nor should it make any difference that such knowledge came to him only after commencement of the trip, so long as he had a practical opportunity to get out. To postulate that the conditions of the trip are irrevocably fixed at the outset and that no subsequent change in the driver's condition can thereafter "release" him from the duty originally undertaken,[57] is to confuse the situation with false contractual notions, alien to a tort context and the true nature of the defence.

More debatable is the case of the driver who has been drinking without being quite incapable of driving safely. Is the mere risk of his being perhaps occasionally negligent sufficient? The weight of authority leans to the contrary. For it would otherwise mean that knowledge of a mere propensity, based on past acts of negligence, could be construed (not merely as contributory negligence, but) as actual *assumption* of the risk of future negligence.[58] Moreover, it is incompatible with decisions that merely participating in a dangerous activity, such as competitive sports,[59] cross-over water skiing[60] or hot-rodding on a country road,[61] does not involve assumption of the risk of acts of negligence like cutting-in, failure to warn of obstacles, etc. In contrast, an older line of Australian cases tended to a more expansive view of the accepted risk in the case of drinking drivers: mere knowledge that the driver's fitness and sense of circumspection has been reduced by drink being treated as making the passenger volens as to all possible future acts of negligence by such a driver.[62] That approach gives an unnecessarily broad berth to the defence, especially since apportionment. It is contrary to English[63] and Canadian[64] authority, and also appears now to be on the retreat in Australia.[65]

Understandably, assumption of risk has more readily been inferred against plaintiffs who actively incited the defendant's negligent conduct, like racing a police car,[66] embarking on a premeditated binge[67] or, in an industrial case, where two miners agreed on a dangerous method of exploding a charge in deliberate defiance of safety rules.[68] In these cases,

56. As apparently in *Dann v. Hamilton* [1939] 1 K.B. 509 (but the passenger nonetheless recovered).
57. As by Rand and Kellock JJ. in *Car & General Ins. v. Seymour* [1956] S.C.R. 322, but not in subsequent opinions. Adopted in *Crossan v. Gillis* (1979) 96 D.L.R. (3d) 611, it has the support of *Dann v. Hamilton* [1939] 1 K.B. 509 and Williams, *Joint Torts* ch. 12.
58. Driver's addiction to speeding not sufficient: *Perry v. G.I.O.* (1955) 73 W.N. (N.S.W.) 1; *Davies v. Jones* (1957) (noted 34 N.Z.L.J. 95 (1958)).
59. *Condon v. Basi* [1985] 1 W.L.R. 866.
60. *Rootes v. Shelton* (1967) 116 C.L.R. 383.
61. *Bondarenko v. Sommers* (1968) 69 S.R. (N.S.W.) 269 (C.A.).
62. *Ins. Comr v. Joyce* (1948) 77 C.L.R. 39 (but note Dixon J.'s dissent); *Roggenkamp v. Bennett* (1950) 80 C.L.R. 292; *Sara v. G.I.O.* (1969) 89 W.N. (Pt 1) (N.S.W.) 203 (C.A.).
63. *Morris v. Murray* [1991] 2 W.L.R. 195 (C.A.). *Dann v. Hamilton* [1939] 1 K.B. 509, which seemed to exclude the defence altogether, is now discredited.
64. *Dube v. Labar* [1986] 1 S.C.R. 649; *Lehnert v. Stein* [1963] S.C.R. 38.
65. Specifically abolished in S.A. (*Wrongs Act Amendment Act* 1986); and see *Sloan v. Kirby* (1979) 20 S.A.S.R. 263; *O'Shea v. Permanent Trustee* [1971] Qd R. 1 (F.C.).
66. *Cheney v. Steinke* (1980) 13 C.C.L.T. 50.
67. *Miller v. Decker* [1957] S.C.R. 624.
68. *I.C.I. v. Shatwell* [1965] A.C. 656: see below, p. 519.

the defence of volenti merges with the notion of "joint illegal enterprise" which has figured also as an independent ground for denying relief.[69]

In contrast, a more sympathetic attitude has been shown towards instructors of learner drivers, sometimes explicitly on the ground that their social utility bears no comparison with complicity in drunk driving.[70]

Restricted risks

The preceding discussion already emphasised that the risk assumed need not necessarily extend to the whole range of negligent acts or omissions open to the defendant. A plaintiff may assume one risk but not another. Thus by accepting a ride on a motorcycle with faulty lights, a pillion rider may lose his right to complain of an accident due to the absence of lights, such as running into a stationary object, but not of the driver's unrelated negligence in colliding with an oncoming car that should have been perfectly visible to him.[71]

For the same reason, participation in a sport involves assumption of the risks inherent therein, but not necessarily the risk of avoidable negligence. An alternative way of expressing this is to say that the defendant's duty of care is conditioned by the enterprise. Not every infringement of the rules of the game necessarily spells negligence, but serious and dangerous foul play would.[72]

Comprehension of risk

Assumption of risk presupposes at the very least knowledge of it; one cannot be volens without being sciens. Indeed, the plaintiff must not only have been aware of the condition spelling danger, but also have fully appreciated the risk inherent therein.[73] The increasing stringency with which this requirement is being applied has probably contributed as much as anything to the contemporary eclipse of the defence.

Accordingly, unless there is a clear appreciation of the hazard, the plaintiff's persistence in the face of impending danger can at most amount to contributory negligence. Nor is there room for any doctrine of "constructive" comprehension of the risk. A passenger, for instance, himself too intoxicated to appreciate the risk of being at the mercy of a drunk driver, can in no event be taken to have accepted the risk nor be

69. See *Pitts v. Hunt* [1991] Q.B. 24. See below, p. 306.
70. *Chang v. Chang* [1973] 1 N.S.W.L.R. 708 (C.A.) (risk of student's failure to apply brakes not assumed; revd on contributory negligence: (1983) 48 A.L.J.R. 362); *Nettleship v. Weston* [1971] 2 Q.B. 691 (C.A.), not folld in *Cook v. Cook* (1986) 162 C.L.R. 376: see below, n. 100.
71. *Gent-Diver v. Neville* [1953] Qd S.R. 1 (aliter, if that vehicle was also proceeding without lights as in *Bourke v. Jessop (No. 3)* [1935] N.Z.L.R. 246); also *Ranieri v. Ranieri* (1973) 7 S.A.S.R. 418; *Marshall v. Batchelor* (1949) 51 W.A.L.R. 68; *Kent v. Scattini* [1961] W.A.R. 74. An analogous solution pertains to contributory negligence: see above, p. 279.
72. *Rootes v. Shelton* (1967) 111 C.L.R. 383 (water skiing); *Condon v. Basi* [1985] 1 W.L.R. 866 (C.A.: soccer); *Turcotte v. Fell* (N.Y. 1986) 502 N.E. 2d 964 (jockey).
73. Like the trespasser on railway lines in *Titchener v. Brits Rlys* [1983] 1 W.L.R. 1247. *Smith v. Austin Lifts* [1959] 1 W.L.R. 100 (H.L.) insists on a subjective standard, so that miscalculation exonerates.

estopped from denying it, however guilty he may be of contributory negligence.[74]

On the other hand, it would be going too far to insist that one can never assume the risk of future acts of negligence (as contrasted with an existing risky condition, like a structural defect) for lack of full knowledge of the nature and extent of the risk involved.[75] For to say the least, that risk may already be inherent in the defendant's present condition, as when he is so drunk or overtired as to be quite incapable of driving safely. Nonetheless, it is true—and another welcome corrective against lightly indulging the defence—that it can rarely, if ever, apply where the risk arises from lack of circumspection, which must usually be incalculable, as compared with something like lack of skill which can be a "known quantity".[76]

In certain situations, knowledge of the risk alone disqualifies a plaintiff, regardless of whether he voluntarily consented to absolve the defendant from legal responsibility. This occurs whenever the duty owed to him is discharged by full disclosure of the peril. For example, it was once the rule that an occupier of dangerous premises was not answerable to visitors who had either been warned or independently gained knowledge of the danger. Ordinarily, however, one may not with impunity expose others to unreasonable risks merely by acquainting them of their existence. There is no magic in giving a warning. If the injured person knew of the peril, it is a question of fact in each case whether it was such that no sensible person would have incurred it; and if it was not, the fact that he knowingly encountered it does not entitle the defendant to be acquitted from all responsibility.[77]

In other cases, the duty has been so formulated that it may be adequately discharged without even informing the plaintiff of the danger. For instance, the rule that spectators of sporting events cannot complain of inherent hazards, like a cricket ball or hockey puck flying into the crowd, is best explained as resting on an initial absence of duty on the part of the promoter as regards risks which any ordinary spectator would take for granted.[78] If the defendant's immunity rested on assumption of risk properly so-called, it would be difficult to explain why a six-year-old boy should be defeated in such a case,[79] as he could hardly be deemed to have a full comprehension of the risk involved; but "in considering liability under an implied term in this contract it would not be right to introduce a wider term because one of the parties is a youth".[80]

74. *Dixon v. King* [1975] 2 N.Z.L.R. 357; *Ins. Comr v. Joyce* (1948) 77 C.L.R. 39 at 60 per Dixon J. A lesser standard in some English passenger cases may be per incuriam: cf. *Scanlon v. Am. Cigarette Co.*[1987] V.R. 289.
75. Asquith J. in *Dann v. Hamilton* [1939] 1 K.B. 509 seemed to go that far, in an opinion that was as extravagant in result as it was vulnerable in reasoning.
76. *Walker v. Turton-Sainsbury* [1952] S.A.S.R. 159 at 163.
77. *Billings (A.C.) v. Riden* [1958] A.C. 240 at 252-253.
78. *Wooldridge v. Sumner* [1963] 2 Q.B. 43 (C.A.); *Wilks v. Cheltenham Cycle Club* [1971] 1 W.L.R. 668; Luntz, *Compensation for Injuries Due to Sport*, 54 A.L.J. 588 (1980).
79. It has been held for example, that a ten-year-old boy cannot be taken to have consented to the risk of a fellow employee's negligence so as to bring him within the, then still extant, defence of common employment: *Holdman v. Hamlyn* [1943] K.B. 664.
80. *Murray v. Harringay Arena* [1951] 2 K.B. 529 at 536; *Wooldridge v. Sumner* [1963] 2 Q.B. 43 at 70.

Voluntary

The defence relates only to risks incidental to a relationship of free association between the parties: the defendant must have the right to confront the plaintiff with the dilemma: "take it or leave it".[81] Hence, it is peculiar to consensual relations alone, such as that between occupier and visitor or host driver and passenger; indeed, according to an extreme modern view,[82] it is strictly speaking inapplicable to all non-contractual relations where the duty of care is based solely on the Atkinian formula of responsibility.

Whether the situation is one in which the defendant is permitted to exact such a waiver obviously involves a value judgment in which social policy becomes the controlling factor. The most striking illustration of the dependence of the judicial estimate of "free volition" upon current social ideas is to be found in the approach to the master and servant problem.[83] During the greater part of the 19th century, under the influence of laissez-faire ideology, courts took the view that an employee who encountered a manifest danger could not shift the legal risk of injury to his master. Pharisaically, they propounded that "this is a country of free labour. We have no such things as travaux forcés. The servant is no less powerful than the master; and certainly he is quite as able to enforce the contract, and to defend his rights".[84] It was a case of the free fox in a free hen house. But as already indicated, this attitude later yielded to a more realistic recognition of the fact that it was the servant's "poverty, not his will" that consented.[85] The modern view is that "for the purpose of this rule, if it be a rule, a man cannot be said to be truly 'willing' unless he is in a position to choose freely, and freedom of choice predicates, not only full knowledge of the circumstances on which the exercise of choice is conditioned, so that he may be able to choose wisely, but the absence from his mind of any feeling of constraint so that nothing shall interfere with the freedom of his will."[86] Hence, the worker's dilemma of having to choose between loss of employment and loss of his right of action prima facie deprives any encountering by him of the risks of employment of its voluntary character. It will not suffice that he obeyed an order even under protest; he must have agreed that what risk there was should lie on him, for example by accepting "danger money".[87] This viewpoint now prevails whenever an employee encounters danger in the performance of his duties—as much in claims against third parties[88] as against his own employer.

Another poignant illustration of judicial reallocation of risks is found in the rescue cases. The older common law, committed to the austere

81. *Harper, James & Gray* §21.3. Cf. *Ins. Comr v. Joyce* (1948) 77 C.L.R. 39 at 57-58 per Dixon J.
82. *Wooldridge v. Sumner* [1963] 2 Q.B. 43 at 69 per Diplock L.J.
83. See further below, p. 512.
84. *Crichton v. Keir* (1863) 1 Macph. 407 at 410-411; cited by Gow, *Defence of Volenti Non Fit Injuria*, 61 Jur. Rev. 37 at 38-39 (1949).
85. *Thrussell v. Handyside* (1888) 20 Q.B.D. 359 at 364 per Hawkins J.
86. *Bowater v. Rowley Regis Corp.* [1944] K.B. 476 at 479 per Scott L.J.; *Standfield v. Uhr* [1964] Qd R. 66.
87. [1944] K.B. 476 at 481 per Goddard L.J.
88. *Burnett v. British Waterways* [1972] 1 W.L.R. 1329 (despite having read disclaimer sign on dock to which he had been sent).

philosophy "every man for himself", considered that to help someone else in an emergency was an extravagance which the Samaritan indulged at his own risk and expense.[89] But today, a more generous attitude towards altruistic behaviour has displaced the earlier exaggerated emphasis on individualism; and "the doctrine of assumption of risk [no longer applies] where the plaintiff has, under an exigency caused by the defendant's wrongful misconduct, consciously and deliberately faced a risk, even of death, to rescue another from imminent danger of personal injury or death, whether the person endangered is one to whom he owes a duty of protection, as a member of his family, or is a mere stranger."[90] Nor is a fireman or policeman volens when confronting danger in the line of duty.[91]

Again, statutes imposing an obligation of care for the safety of a particular class of persons may be intended to protect them against their own inability to protect themselves, and it would be flying in the face of the underlying legislative policy to permit a member of the protected class to bargain away his right of relying on the defendant's compliance with the statutory prescription. Thus, a worker is not permitted to assume the risks of accidents which the legislature has sought to prevent by compelling employers to fence dangerous machinery and places.[92]

On the other hand, our permissive society allows individuals a free choice to engage in even highly dangerous activities, from scuba- to sky-diving. "If they insist upon taking abnormal and completely unnecessary risks, they cannot complain of the consequences inherent in the very risk that makes the activity challenging and attractive."[93]

Volenti and the duty of care

With the defence of volenti thus in retreat, can its fortunes be restored by presenting it in the guise of diminished "duty"? The doctrinal kinship between the two concepts has already been noted: for, if the plaintiff has indeed voluntarily assumed the risk, a common explanation is to say that he has thereby absolved the defendant from the ordinary duty of care due to him. In short, the defendant owes him no duty, or only a duty of lesser care.

In Australia a practice emerged of pleading "no duty" (or "no breach of duty") as a distinct alternative defence to volenti in actions against

89. E.g. *Stevens v. McKenzie* (1899) 25 V.L.R. 115; *Evenden v. Manning S.* (1929) 30 S.R. (N.S.W.) 52.
90. *Haynes v. Harwood* [1935] 1 K.B. 146 at 157 per Greer L.J.; *Baker v. Hopkins* [1959] 1 W.L.R. 966. Even if the rescue is foolhardy, it would be ascribed to contributory negligence rather than volenti.
91. Firemen: *Ogwo v. Taylor* [1988] A.C. 431; police: *A.-G. v. Keller* (1978) 86 D.L.R. (3d) 426.
92. *Wheeler v. New Merton Mills* [1933] 2 K.B. 669 (C.A.); *I.C.I. v. Shatwell* [1965] A.C. 656 (at least where the breach was due to the employer's own fault or that of a more senior co-employee). Though it remains an open question, one should not be capable of waiving such a statutory exception *expressly* any more than impliedly: *Hawkes Bay v. McLeod* [1972] N.Z.L.R. 289 at 303.
93. *Murphy v. Steeplechase Amusement* 166 N.E. 173 ("the flopper") (N.Y. 1929). Aliter when, to the organisers' knowledge, a participant is unable to cope, as in *Crocker v. Sundance Resorts* [1988] 1 S.C.R. 1186 (intoxicated competitor in tube racing).

intoxicated or incompetent drivers.[94] Inspired by, and endowed with the immense aura of authority, of Chief Justice Dixon,[95] the idea behind it was this: If a person asks a blacksmith to repair his watch, he cannot complain if the blacksmith damages it through lack of skill—the customer accepts a lower standard of performance than that required from an expert watchmaker. Similarly, one who accepts a lift from an obviously incompetent driver: in case of an accident caused by the driver's lack of proficiency, there is "no breach of duty" because the ordinary standard has been attenuated by the special relationship in which the plaintiff has joined the defendant. In extreme cases, the duty may become so modified as to disappear altogether;[96] the plea of "no breach of duty" may then be formulated flatly as "no duty".

The insidious thrust of this argument lies in its potential for resuscitating ideas painfully excoriated from the defence of volenti. Most important, it tends to equate knowledge with acceptance of the risk, as in the contention that knowingly to get into a car with an incompetent driver establishes without more a relation with a proportionately reduced expectation (and duty) of care.[97] Judicial endorsements of this approach in the past lose at least some of their force in the light of the fact that they preceded apportionment for contributory negligence. Now however it matters a great deal whether apportionment is to be circumvented, and plaintiffs defeated entirely, by diluting "acceptance of the risk" under a new label.

This has led to a split of authority with respect to learner drivers. The English Court of Appeal would have none of the whole idea by holding that (except perhaps in case of an actual bargain) a driver's duty to his passengers does not vary according to their individual knowledge of his competence, and that therefore an amateur driving instructor was entitled from his pupil to the ordinary standard of a competent driver just like everybody else inside and outside the car, and did not have to content himself merely with the learner trying as best she could.[98] Two reasons were given: the first, unconvincing, that varying standards of care would produce "unpredictability, uncertainty and, indeed, impossibility of arriving at fair and consistent decisions";[99] the second, that it would turn the flank of apportionment. Knowledge by the passenger may go to show contributory negligence and thus reduce his damages, but does not take away the duty of care nor diminish the standard of care demanded from all drivers alike.

The High Court of Australia, on the other hand, refused to budge from its previous position that a driver's known incompetence and inexperience controlled his relationship with the passenger and that the duty thus

94. See Blackburn, *Volenti Non Fit Injuria and the Duty of Care*, 24 A.L.J. 351 (1951); Sykes, *Drunken Motorist and the Guest Passenger*, 24 A.L.J. 444 (1951). The principal cases were *Ins. Comr v. Joyce* (1948) 77 C.L.R. 39 and *Roggenkamp v. Bennett* (1950) 80 C.L.R. 292.
95. *Ins. Comr v. Joyce* (1948) 77 C.L.R. 39.
96. "In the case of the drunken driver, all standards of care are ignored" (Latham C.J. in *Ins. Comr v. Joyce* (1948) 77 C.L.R. 39 at 46).
97. Thus Burt C.J. in *Jeffries v. Fisher* [1985] W.A.R. 250.
98. *Nettleship v. Weston* [1971] 2 Q.B. 691 (C.A.: volenti was negatived because the plaintiff had specifically assured himself that there was insurance cover; it succeeded in *Cook v. Cook* (see below, n. 100).
99. Ibid. at 383 per Megaw L.J.

modified defined the degree of care to be expected. It was "for the legislature, and not the courts, to decide whether considerations of social policy make it desirable that the traditional standards of the law of negligence shall be abandoned in favour of a system of liability without fault."[100] In the case in question, however, the learner driver's misconduct had been so egregious as still to qualify as actionable carelessness.

Joint illegality

The notion of a modified or suspended duty of care, with overtones of assumption of risk, has lately also been invoked in dealing with the problem of joint participation in an illegal enterprise.[101]

Generally speaking, the mere fact that the plaintiff happened to be engaged in something unlawful at the time of his injury is no disqualification in tort.[102] The victim of a motor accident may be a child playing truant from school, an employee absent from work in breach of contract, a burglar on his way to a professional engagement, or someone driving without a licence[103] or an unregistered[104] or uninsured[105] car: none of this has any bearing on his rights against a negligent driver.[106] It is neither causally relevant in the accepted sense, since it did not in any significant way increase the risk of his injury,[107] nor is the need to deter unlawful conduct nowadays considered so urgent that it is better public policy to make the offender in effect an outlaw by depriving him of tortious redress.[108]

100. *Cook v. Cook* (1986) 162 C.L.R. 376 at 395-396. Criticised: Todd, 105 L.Q.R. 24 (1989); *Radford v. Ward* (1990) A.T.R. 81-046 (Vic. F.C.). Generally: Kidner, 11 Leg. St. 1 (1991).
101. See Ford, 11 Melb. U.L. Rev. 32, 164 (1977); Swanton, 9 Syd. L. Rev. 304 (1981); Weinreb, 26 U. Tor. L.J. 28 (1976); Fridman, 18 McG. L.J. 275 (1972).
102. "It shall not be a defence in an action of tort *merely* to show that the plaintiff is in breach of the civil or criminal law" (*Civil Liabilities Act* 1961 (Eire) s. 57). This is declaratory of the common law. Of course, if it increases the risk of injury, it could be contributory negligence: *Hackshaw v. Shaw* (1984) 155 C.L.R. 614; *P.T.C. v. Perry* (1977) 137 C.L.R. 107 at 147.
103. See above, p. 130.
104. *Vancouver v. Burchill* [1932] 4 D.L.R. 200 (nor can he be treated as a trespasser on the defendant city's highway).
105. *Andrews v. Nominal Defendant* (1965) 66 S.R. (N.S.W.) 85 (F.C.), a case which is the stronger because the defendant would not have been liable at all but for the plaintiff's permitting the car to be driven without insurance.
106. *Henwood v. Municipal Tramways* (1938) 60 C.L.R. 438 at 446; *Westwood v. P.O.* [1974] A.C. 1 at 7 (trespasser).
107. True, he might otherwise well have been elsewhere, but what matters is that he would have been injured just the same if he had been there on a lawful errand. See above, p. 216.
108. The maxim "ex turpi causa non oritur actio" is nowadays handled with caution. According to a widely held view, its sole legitimate function is to deny a plaintiff legal aid for accomplishing an illegal object, like enforcing a contract; at most to preclude him from relying on an illegal transaction necessary to establish his claim. Neither is generally applicable to negligence claims. The maxim's bite is least where the illegality is not even associated with the accident but only with damages: public policy would rarely oppose recovery of lost earnings merely because they would have been made in a tainted employment: *Mills v. Baitis* [1968] V.R. 583 (trade in prohibited area); *Le Bagge v. Buses* [1958] N.Z.L.R. 630 (Sunday driving); contra: *Brownbill v. Kenworth Sales* (1982) 39 A.L.R. 191 (excessive loads); *Burns v. Edman* [1970] 2 Q.B. 541 (professional criminal). See *Luntz* 260-263.

Is there any reason in logic or policy for a different result where the plaintiff is involved in a joint illegal enterprise with the defendant? The plaintiff does not appear more culpable than if he had acted alone, and offering immunity to the defendant would as likely encourage as deter the enterprise. In some situations recovery might conceivably be barred by genuine assumption of risk (for example a drag race) or by specific statutory policy.[109] But not so long ago the High Court of Australia countenanced the extreme view of denying a remedy against the joint participant for every accident occurring in furtherance or in the course of committing a serious offence, even such as could have happened on a lawful occasion like an ordinary traffic collision in a stolen car.[110]

Since then the court retreated to the more moderate position that a denial of relief must be related not to the illegal character of the enterprise but to the hazards inherent in its execution. A plaintiff would fail only if the appropriate standard of care cannot be determined without reference to the illegal nature of the activity.[111] Thus in the school example of one burglar blowing up his accomplice in cracking a safe, the courts will not—it is said— engage in the invidious inquiry of determining the care that might be appropriate for such an occasion.[112] Similarly, in the case of speeding in a stolen car in order to race or escape the police;[113] even on a joy ride in a stolen car after excessive consumption of alcohol.[114] Not so, however, when the appropriate standard of care is unaffected by the illegal nature of the enterprise, as in the case of an ordinary outing by two unlicensed drivers[115] perhaps even driving a stolen car in the ordinary manner days after the theft.[116] Or the careless operation of a hoist which was prohibited for carrying workers, when the duty to apply the brakes would be the same whether goods or a man were hoisted.[117]

There has been reluctance to draw and express the dividing line according to the nature of the joint offence. In particular, a "public conscience" test is now disfavoured as being linked to factors of an emotional nature and leading to a "graph of illegalities" according to moral turpitude.[118] Still, the policy of the law has been stressed repeatedly in dealing with vehicular

109. Murphy J. in *Jackson v. Harrison* (1978) 138 C.L.R. 438 at 466 would confine disqualification to these rare instances. Illegality is a distinct defence from volenti; that the latter is barred (e.g. by statute for passengers) does not bar the former: *Pitts v. Hunt* [1991] 1 Q.B. 24.
110. *Smith v. Jenkins* (1970) 119 C.L.R. 397 (most pointedly Barwick C.J. who dissented in *Jackson*).
111. *Jackson v. Harrison* (1978) 138 C.L.R. 438; *Gala v. Preston* (1991) 172 C.L.R. 243; *Pitts v. Hunt* (per Balcombe L.J.; contra, Beldam L.J.: duty not diminished).
112. *N.C.B. v. England* [1954] A.C. 403 at 428-429 per Lord Asquith; *Ashmore v. Dawson* [1973] 1 W.L.R. 828 (overloaded truck overturned); *O'Connor v. McDonnell* [1972] Ir. Jur. 98 (night poacher shooting accomplice); also Scrutton L.J.'s example of the smuggler who lowers contraband by a defective rope and drops it on his companion: *Hillen v. I.C.I.* [1934] 1 K.B. 455-467.
113. *Bondarenko v. Sommers* (1968) 69 S.R. (N.S.W.) 269; *Ashton v. Turner* [1981] Q.B. 137.
114. *Gala v. Preston* (1991) 172 C.L.R. 243; *Pitts v. Hunt* [1981] 1 Q.B. 24 (C.A.).
115. *Jackson v. Harrison* (1978) 138 C.L.R. 438.
116. *Jackson v. Harrison* at 460, per Jacob J.
117. *Progress & Properties v. Craft* (1976) 135 C.L.R. 651.
118. *Pitts v. Hunt* at 564 per Dillon L.J. In reality the victim falls charge to social welfare rather than the motoring public.

offences, as indicative that the denial of a civil remedy would enhance the effectiveness of criminal penalties as a deterrent.[119] But here, as in the context of volenti,[120] Australian judges have preferred to find the key in the duty relationship between the joint offenders, though this explanation does not offer much guidance as to when the character of the enterprise does or does not make it impossible for courts to determine the appropriate standard of care.[121] Only actual decisions reveal their sense of policy in particular cases. "Illegality" should not become an easy substitute, any more than the related "no duty" plea, for the now disfavoured defence of volenti.

119. Ibid. (Beldam L.J.); Brennan J. in *Gala* at 271-272.
120. Esp. *Cook v. Cook* (above, n. 100).
121. E.g. how to distinguish between using the hoist in *Progress & Properties* and Scrutton L.J.'s example of the smuggler who lowers contraband by a defective rope and drops it on his companion? Toohey J. in *Gala* at 288.

14

PROCEDURE AND PROOF

1. FUNCTIONS OF JUDGE AND JURY

The allocation of functions between judge and jury is vital to an understanding of negligence litigation. The distinction between questions of "law" and "fact" is commonly used to indicate their respective tasks; but if ever meaningful, it long ceased to be truly descriptive of the complex modern position. Today, the terms "law" and "fact", as used in this context, are merely shorthand expressions for the functions of judge and jury, but do not assist in ascertaining what they are. The allocation of these functions is not determined by any a priori meaning of these terms, but is the result of historical growth and legal policy.[1]

In truth, the jury's function is twofold, partaking in the determination of legal consequences no less than of facts. For, aside from its traditional task of weighing the evidence as to facts alleged to give rise to liability or defences, the jury participates in a significant measure in settling the legal consequences flowing from the facts thus found. For instance, it falls within their province to translate the metaphysical standard of the reasonable and prudent person into a concrete standard applicable to the particular case before them and, in that light, to decide whether the defendant failed to conform. This process involves not a determination of fact, but the formulation of a value judgment or norm which is qualitatively of almost equal significance to the enunciation of a rule of law by the court. The only difference between them is that the jury's evaluation is decisive alone in the particular case before it, whereas the judge's pronouncement of principle is endowed with generality and precedential potential.

Control over jury

The courts have perfected a number of techniques to maintain control over the handling of the various issues by the jury. The judge is the dominant partner, and it is he who decides to what extent, if at all, the jury may participate in the judging process. Specifically, he rules in the first instance whether the defendant is under any obligation at all to observe care for the benefit of the plaintiff. The duty issue furnishes an opportunity to prevent the plaintiff from getting to the jury, if on broad grounds of policy it is deemed unwise to protect the plaintiff's interest against negligent interference of the kind charged against the defendant.[2] In this manner,

1. Thayer, *Law and Fact in Jury Trials*, 4 Harv. L. Rev. 147 (1890).
2. The duty question may be raised on demurrer (or modern procedural equivalents like application to strike out as disclosing no cause of action under R.S.C. (Eng.) Ord. 18, r. 19), i.e. on the assumption that the facts alleged by the plaintiff are true: e.g. *Donoghue v. Stevenson* [1932] A.C. 562.

paramount considerations of social policy will be safeguarded against the impact of the recognised jury tendency to let compassion for the particular plaintiff divert attention from the general effect which their decision will have on the future pattern of legal protection.

Next it is for the court to lay down the general standard of care required by law for the protection of persons in the plaintiff's position. This will ordinarily take the form of an incantation of the traditional formula of the reasonable and prudent man. In a few situations, however, the legal standard of reasonable conduct has been defined with greater precision. For example, at common law the care an occupier must observe for the safety of persons who have come upon his land used to be precisely formulated in accordance with a fine gradation of standards corresponding to the degree of benefit which he derives from their visit—ranging from business visitors (invitees) down to trespassers.[3] Again, the standard may have been fixed by the legislature prescribing specific safety precautions, non-compliance with which constitutes negligence per se. In such cases, the jury's function is reduced to the mechanical role of determining merely whether the precaution has been taken.[4]

Besides declaring the general standard of care prescribed by law, the judge will give binding directions on other principles of substantive law, such as the formula for determining whether or not the damage is too remote, what is the effect of contributory negligence and how to assess, and perhaps apportion, damages. Indeed, in the light of all these considerations, he may form the opinion that, upon the facts in evidence, there is no issue fit to go to the jury at all.

The degree of control exercisable by the judge in withholding the case from the jury reflects a delicate balance of powers. It is for him to decide whether there is a prima facie case, that is, sufficient evidence which, if believed, would support (though by no means necessarily compel) a conclusion in favour of the party on whom the onus of proof with respect to the particular issue is placed by law. If there is not, he will non-suit the plaintiff or direct a verdict for the defendant whenever the onus lies on the plaintiff,[5] or direct a verdict for the plaintiff whenever the onus is on the defendant.[6] For this purpose, he must consider not only the proof of

2. *Continued*
But the jury is not necessarily excluded from participation on the duty issue. Once the court rules that there is a duty relation bounded by the foreseeable range of danger, it is a question of "fact" whether there was such a foreseeable risk of injury to *this* plaintiff: see e.g. *King v. Phillips* [1953] 1 Q.B. 429. In such cases, the negligence and duty issue left to the jury are in fact telescoped into one inquiry. The importance of the duty issue as a question of "law" lies in the fact that duty is not invariably measured by the scope of the foreseeable risk.
3. Below ch. 22.
4. See above, p. 124.
5. The difference between these motions is explored by Windeyer J. in *Jones v. Dunkel* (1959) 101 C.L.R. 298 at 323 ff.; Fisher, *Non-suits* [1970] N.Z.L.J. 232. Judgment notwithstanding verdict may require parties' leave: *Prestinenzi v. Steel Tank* [1981] V.R. 421.
6. Under British (though not American) practice, the court cannot direct a verdict in favour of the party on whom the onus of proof lies. This is subject to one important exception, which stealthily entered modern practice in jurisdictions not applying apportionment of loss, so as to allow a directed verdict for the *defendant*, if the only reasonable inference

"primary" facts, but also such reasonable inferences as may be drawn therefrom; yet he is not entitled to weigh or balance conflicting evidence, however strongly it may preponderate on one side, provided there is some evidence to support a prima facie case. Occasionally, it is no doubt difficult to distinguish between a case where there is no evidence upon which a jury could reasonably find for the plaintiff and one where there is some evidence for the plaintiff but greatly preponderating for the defendant; yet the distinction must be observed so as not to trench upon the legitimate province of the jury. It must also be remembered that it is not for the court to go into the question whether the plaintiff's evidence should be believed or not. Once a plaintiff has adduced evidence which, standing on its own, would support a verdict, no amount of contradictory evidence will justify the withdrawal of the case from the jury,[7] even if the judge is of the opinion that a verdict for the plaintiff would be set aside as against the weight of evidence.

Jury verdicts are also difficult to attack on appeal. The only recognised ground is that the verdict was perverse in the sense that the jury must have either disregarded the evidence or failed to understand it.[8] It could hardly be otherwise since the generality of the verdict precludes any segregation of their findings of "primary facts" and no reasons are given for their "ultimate findings" concerning negligence, etc. Appeals from findings of fact by a judge sitting alone present a very different aspect. The judge supports his decision with a reasoned judgment concerning both aspects, which is available for appellate scrutiny. Appeal courts therefore may, and do, exercise a much wider power of review. Although not free from controversy, the dominant view appears now to be that while the judge's conclusions are entitled to respect, an appellate court is free to draw its own inferences from the primary facts found by the judge, because it is in as good a position to do so as he.[9]

Appraisal of the jury's role

The value of this infusion of the popular element into the administration of law is a highly controverted question. Against the much vaunted advantages of bringing the assumed common sense wisdom of the layman to bear on the problem of evaluating conduct,[10] it has been contended that the "featureless generality" of a jury verdict ought to be gradually

6. *Continued* from the plaintiff's own case is that he was guilty of contributory negligence and the relevant facts are not genuinely in dispute: *Williams v. Smith* (1960) 103 C.L.R. 539; Tilley, *Directed Verdicts of Contributory Negligence*, 51 L.Q.R. 500 (1935).
7. *Dublin Rly v. Slattery* (1878) 3 App. Cas. 1155 at 1168. This was a strong case because all their Lordships were unanimous that the verdict for the plaintiff was against the weight of evidence, and yet refused to enter a verdict for the defendant. See also *Metropolitan Rly v. Jackson* (1877) 3 App. Cas. 193 at 207; *De Gioia v. Darling Island Stevedoring Co.* (1941) 42 S.R. (N.S.W.) 1; *Hocking v. Bell* (1947) 75 C.L.R. 125 at 131-132 (P.C.).
8. See e.g. *Mitchell v. Wachter* [1961] V.R. 537 (a rarer case of a *defendant's* verdict being set aside).
9. *Warren v. Coombes* (1979) 142 C.L.R. 531; *Commonwealth v. Introvigne* (1982) 150 C.L.R. 258 (even against *concurrent* findings of trial and intermediate appeal court). See Goodhart, *Appeals on Questions of Fact*, 55 L.Q.R. 402 (1955).
10. See e.g. Evatt, *Jury System in Australia*, 10 A.L.J. (Supp.) 49 (1937); Chalmers, *Trial by Jury in Civil Cases*, 7 L.Q.R. 15 (1891).

superseded by fixed and uniform standards enunciated by the court so that people should the better know in advance what they are expected to do in any given situation. To leave the question of negligence in every case, without rudder or compass, to the jury is a confession of the courts' inability to state a very large part of the law which they require the defendant to know and asserts by implication that nothing can be learned from experience.[11] This attitude has from time to time led to judicial attempts to prescribe precise rules of conduct for relatively informal situations, such as the canon that anyone driving in the dark must be able to pull up within the limits of his vision.[12] But this and similar experiments have foundered,[13] because experience has demonstrated the futility of forcing infinitely variable fact situations into a Procrustean mould of inflexible legal precepts.[14] The more widely held belief is that relative lack of uniformity is not too high a price for an individualised administration of justice, in a sphere of legal control which is concerned less with the regulatory function of fashioning patterns of human conduct in advance than with the adjustment of losses that have occurred without adversion to legal consequences. Indeed where trial is without jury, as it is in most jurisdictions nowadays, the distinction between questions of law and fact gets blurred and all rulings by the judge are apt to have precedential force attributed to them. This would harden the arteries of the law and condemn the precedent system to "die from a surfeit of authorities".[15]

Much stronger is the case for uniformity in the calculation of damages. Justice, it is widely felt, postulates equality in its awards to the injured as much as in its punishment of the guilty. Besides, it fosters settlements when there is less room for controversy and no chance to win an outsize verdict. Such a desirable pattern of regularity, however, can only be achieved by professional judges, for current practice does not permit so much as even mention to the jury of awards in comparable cases.[16] All that can be done to control their awards is to upset them when they are unreasonably large or small (that is when they transgress the judicially conceived range of tolerance) and order a reassessment by another jury or, as in some jurisdictions under statutory authority, by a judge.[17] The idea, so familiar in criminal trials, of leaving the issue of guilt to the jury but sentencing to

11. Holmes, *Common Law* (1881) 111-112, also 123-124 (advocating that in repetitive situations a jury verdict once taken should be accepted as precedent for the future).
12. This "rule" in *Baker v. Longhurst* [1933] 2 K.B. 461 was repudiated in *Tidy v. Battman* [1934] 1 K.B. 319; *Lee Transport v. Watson* (1940) 64 C.L.R. 1; *Stewart v. Hancock* [1940] N.Z.L.R. 424 (P.C.).
13. E.g. the rule laid down by Holmes J. that all drivers approaching a level crossing without clear vision along the tracks must reconnoitre on foot: rejected in *Pokora v. Wabash Rly* 292 U.S. 98 (1934).
14. Contrast repetitive and generally uniform situations like non-use of seat belts: above, p. 280.
15. *Qualcast v. Haynes* [1959] A.C. 743 at 758.
16. See above, p. 236. The proposal for trial judges to indicate an acceptable range was rejected in *Howes v. Crosby* (1984) 6 D.L.R. (4th) 698 (Ont. C.A.) but recommended by Ont. L.R.C. (1987). U.S. counsel are widely permitted to mention the ad damnum clause (damages claimed); aliter: *Gray v. Alanco* (1967) 61 D.L.R. (2d) 652 (Ont. C.A.); *Sawyer v. O'Brien* [1970] V.R. 333 disagreeing with *Buchanan v. Byrne* [1970] V.R. 330.
17. Even a second verdict is not sacrosanct (*Harding v. Willman* (1964) 82 W.N. (Pt 1) (N.S.W.) 205; *Simmonds v. Hillsdon* [1965] N.S.W.R. 837), though less vulnerable: *Watson v. Burley* (1962) 108 C.L.R. 635.

the judge, has not hitherto been emulated in civil cases, though it would provide a procedure for enlisting the advantages of a jury trial on the issue of liability without prejudice to a regular, judicially sponsored, tariff of awards. As it is, the overriding importance attached to the latter goal, especially in England, has militated strongly against jury trial, which is in consequence rarely allowed whenever the mode of trial is within judicial discretion.[18]

Another complaint is the juries' propensity to let their judgment be deflected by sentiment and prejudice. Instinctive compassion with the plaintiff and a corresponding bias against defendants, especially if credited with liability insurance[19] or "deep pockets", notoriously dominate jury evaluations. Less so perhaps in motor accident cases, with awareness by a near-universal motoring public of the adverse effect of large verdicts on insurance premiums. In Australia compulsory insurance has progressively led to the disappearance of jury trial in running-down actions.[19a] But in other areas of tort litigation, including industrial accidents,[19b] the jury system survives behind the protective screen of tradition, vested professional interests and the pressure of organised labour, despite its manifest administrative disadvantages of slowing down the process of adjudication and offering a lesser incentive to settlements, at any rate in the absence of effective pre-trial procedure.[20] Exceptional in this regard are South Australia[21] and the Capital Territory[22] where, as in England and most of the British Commonwealth,[23] the civil jury has virtually disappeared.

Our estimate of the value of jury participation in the judgment process is, in the last resort, dependent on the degree of confidence reposed in the existing body of legal rules. The general verdict of the jury is a convenient cloak for ignoring "expressed" doctrines of law which no longer correspond with prevailing notions of what the law ought to be on any given

18. See above, p. 236, n. 104.
19. Disclosure of insurance may even justify a retrial: see *Gowar v. Hales* [1928] 1 K.B. 191 (in England the problem has gone with the demise of jury trial). In Australia a severe view still seems to be taken of disclosures in jury cases, even where insurance is compulsory: see *A.M.P. v. Dixon* [1982] V.R. 833 at 835. Canada: *Bowhey v. Theakston* [1951] S.C.R. 679; and generally Castles, *Juries and Compulsory Insurance Legislation*, 31 A.L.J. 638 (1958). U.S.: Green, *Blindfolding the Jury*, 33 Tex. L. Rev. 157 (1954) and Annot. 4 A.L.R. 2d 761 (1949). For joinder of insurance company by a defendant claiming indemnity see *Liverpool Ins. v. Waianiwa Transport* [1965] N.Z.L.R. 262 at 731.
19a. In N.S.W. the practice is to deny jury trial, in contrast to industrial accident cases: Crawford, *Australian Courts of Law* (2nd ed. 1988). In Victoria claims under the *Transport Accidents Act* 1986 (see below, p. 404) are handled by administrative tribunals; residuary common law claims can be tried by jury at the request of either party.
19b. In Victoria common law claims are now confined to non-economic loss: see above, p. 240.
20. N.S.W.: *Supreme Court Act* 1970 s. 86; Residuary discretion: s. 89; *Pambula District Hospital v. Herriman* (1988) 14 N.S.W.L.R. 387 (C.A.) (medical). Vic.: R.S.C., O. 36; *County Court Act* 1958 s. 67; Qld: R.S.C., O. 39; W.A.: R.S.C., O. 36, r. II; Tas.: R.S.C., O. 38, r. 6.
21. *Juries Act* 1927 s. 5 (except only if it appears to the court that a question may or will arise whether any party has been guilty of an indictable offence).
22. *Australian Capital Territory Supreme Court Act* 1933 s. 14 (Cth).
23. See Smith & Bailey, *Modern English Legal System* (1984) 534-540; Devlin, *Trial by Jury* (8th Hamlyn Lecture) ch. 6. In Canada, the civil jury is still important only in Ontario and B.C.: Royal Commission Civil Rights (Ont. Report I, 1968) vol. 2, 859-860.

point. It has been shrewdly observed that "hard cases tried with a jury do not make bad law, for they make no law at all, as far as the findings of the jury are concerned. The principle is kept intact while the jury do justice in the particular case by not applying it."[24] There is a great deal of scepticism as to how far juries heed the detailed instructions by the judge, even assuming they are capable of comprehending the exposition of complex legal principles.[25] Thus, the harsh operation of the stalemate rule of contributory negligence used often to be averted by compromise verdicts of juries long before the official introduction of apportionment.[26] Any rule of substantive law or procedure which expands the jury's sphere tends to enlarge liability and, conversely, any rule which restricts it tends to abridge liability. Particularly in periods of transition, the jury becomes a safety valve for keeping the administration of the law in accord with changing views of the community until the courts or legislature are persuaded to adjust the formal legal rules themselves. Hence, those who advocate replacing the present system of fault liability by a regime of social insurance for industrial and road accidents are inclined to see in the jury a suitable instrument for hastening the process of transition.[27] By the same token, others who believe in maintaining the purity of our legal lore welcome the transfer of jury functions to judges who are more reliable guardians of the existing fabric of the law.

2. BURDEN OF PROOF

Allocation of the burden of proof is a function of substantive law, not evidence, and determined by considerations of policy, fairness and probability.[28]

The role of legal policy is by no means exhausted in prescribing the various elements that go to make up the cause of action; it also has a large voice in allocating these elements to one or the other litigant. For by setting up a procedural handicap, a particular cause of action may be to some extent discouraged, as by imposing on a plaintiff in an action for malicious prosecution the burden of proving absence of reasonable and probable cause.[29] Conversely, the law may deliberately seek to assist recovery by shifting the burden to the defendant, as in contributory negligence and perhaps still in actions of trespass.[30]

Fairness, in turn, might suggest that if evidence relating to a particular element is apt to be within the control of one party, his should also be the burden of proving it. Finally, the factor of probability promotes a minimum of inaccurate results.

24. Chalmers, *Trial by Jury in Civil Cases*, 7 L.Q.R. 15 at 21 (1891).
25. For the American experience see Farley, *Instructions to Juries—their Role in the Judicial Process*, 42 Yale L.J. 194 (1931). A similar scepticism pervades Frank's *Law and the Modern Mind* (1949) (ch. 16) and *Courts on Trial* (ch. 8). Much more sanguine was Haines J., "Future of Civil Jury" in *Studies in Canadian Tort Law* (1968) ch. 2.
26. See above, p. 271.
27. 2 *Harper, James & Gray* §15.5; Derham, *Some Notes on the Role of Juries*, 36 A.L.J. 59 (1963).
28. See generally, Stone, *Burden of Proof and the Judicial Process*, 60 L.Q.R. 262 (1944); Cleary, *Presuming and Pleading*, 12 Stan. L. Rev. 55 (1959).
29. See below, p. 618.
30. See above, p. 22.

Bailees furnish a good illustration of the interplay of all three of these factors. The burden of proof that the law places on them, whether as carriers or warehousemen, that loss or damage to the goods was *not* due to their negligence[31] is supported by their superior knowledge of what happened, by the probability that they were responsible and by the need to remove the "moral hazard" of carelessness or dishonesty.[32]

Ordinarily, however, in negligence litigation the plaintiff carries the burden of proof with respect to all facts in issue—that the defendant owed him a duty of care, that he broke that duty by careless conduct, that such breach was a legally sufficient cause of injury as well as the extent[33] of that injury, that is, all elements of the cause of action save the defences of contributory negligence and voluntary assumption of risk. Although it was once fashionable to speak of a "defence" of inevitable accident, stemming perhaps from the earlier practice of trespass,[34] it is—if still occasionally pleaded today—nothing more than a denial of negligence (with particulars of how, in the defendant's view, the accident occurred)[35] without shifting to him the legal burden of proof, still less suggesting that something more than ordinary care was needed to clear himself.[36]

Whoever carries the legal burden of proof on a particular issue need not, it is true, meet the criminal standard of proof beyond all reasonable doubt. In all civil proceedings, even when the fact in issue amounts to the commission of a crime, like fraud or assault, he need only tilt the "balance of probability".[37] This requires more than a mere mechanical comparison of probabilities independently of any belief in its reality; the tribunal must feel an actual persuasion based on a preponderance of probability.[38] Thus a merely mathematical or statistical probability of barely 51 per cent is not sufficient because it carries no conviction that the case falls within the 51

31. Applicable regardless of the form of the bailor's action—detinue, case or assumpsit—and apparently as much to a gratuitous bailment as to one for reward: *Hobbs v. Petersham Transport* (1971) 124 C.L.R. 220; *Port Swettenham v. Wu* [1979] A.C. 580 (P.C.). *Nat. Trust Co. v. Wong Aviation* [1969] S.C.R. 481 held the presumption inapplicable when the bailee and the chattel had perished.
32. *Common* carriers are, for the same reasons, virtual insurers: *Coggs v. Bernard* (1703) 2 Ld Raym. 909 at 918; 92 E.R. 107 at 112. Other instances of reversal of proof: liability under the Warsaw Convention for accidents on international flights (below), for unseaworthiness under the Hague Rules (*Sea Carriage of Goods Act* 1924 (Cth) art. 4, r. 1 or automobile injuries to pedestrians under Canadian statutes: *Winnipeg Electric Co. v. Geel* [1932] A.C. 690—the "pedestrian section").
33. *Vandeloo v. Waltons* [1976] V.R. 77 (F.C.) Mitigation: above, p. 254.
34. See above, pp. 20-22.
35. Usually suggesting a catastrophic or purely fortuitous cause, like a sudden mechanical breakdown in a traffic accident.
36. E.g. *Jokel v. Jokel* [1963] S.R. (N.S.W.) 230. See Pape, *Burden of Proof of Inevitable Accident in Actions for Negligence*, 38 A.L.J. 395 (1965). The contrary view seems to persist in Canada: *Dobbs v. Mayer* (1985) 32 C.C.L.T. 191 (Ont.).
37. *Reifek v. McElroy* (1965) 112 C.L.R. 517. This is mitigated by allowing, however, that "the degree of satisfaction for which the civil standard of proof calls may vary according to the gravity of the fact to be proved" (at 521).
38. *Briginshaw v. Briginshaw* (1938) 60 C.L.R. 336 at 360-362. But the standard may be satisfied by drawing inferences from proven facts (e.g. position of vehicles after collision), as distinct from mere general considerations as to likelihood of negligence ("conjecture or surmise"): *T.N.T. v. Brooks* (1979) 53 A.L.J.R. 267, suggesting a more relaxed standard than in the past. See also Eggleston, *Probabilities and Proof*, 4 Melb. U.L. Rev. 180 (1963); Ligertwood, *Uncertainty of Proof*, 10 Melb. U.L. Rev. 367 (1976).

rather than the 49.[39] But suppose a car crash in which its three occupants are incinerated beyond recognition. Should failure to identify the driver preclude recovery by everyone or should the 2:1 odds on each being a passenger suffice in claims against the owner of the car?

Causation

Proof of causality often poses acute difficulty for plaintiffs. Especially in the case of culpable *omission*, it becomes harder to show that "but for it" the injury would have been avoided. As a compromise, the burden might well have been shifted to the defendant, once his negligence had been established, to disprove its causal relevance.[40] The case for modification becomes even stronger when the defendant's very negligence created the proof-uncertainty, for example a hospital's delay in supplying life-saving aid or a captain's refusal to turn the ship around and look for a man overboard.[41] Equally troubling are cases of alternative causation implicating multiple defendants. But, as already noted,[42] British courts have refused to bend the rules; instead of openly modifying the allocation of proof, they might rather assist plaintiffs by applying in practice a lower standard of proof.[43]

3. RES IPSA LOQUITUR

In some circumstances, the mere fact that an accident has occurred raises an inference of negligence against the defendant. A plaintiff is never obliged to prove his case by direct evidence. Circumstantial evidence is just as probative, if from proof of certain facts other facts may reasonably be inferred. Res ipsa loquitur is no more than a convenient label to describe situations where, notwithstanding the plaintiff's inability to establish the exact cause of the accident, the fact of the accident by itself is sufficient in the absence of an explanation to justify the conclusion that most probably the defendant was negligent and that his negligence caused the injury. The maxim contains nothing exceptional; it is based on common sense, since it is a matter of ordinary observation and experience in life that sometimes a thing tells its own story. Unfortunately, the use of a Latin phrase to describe this simple notion has become a source of confusion by giving the

39. It only tells us that out of 100 cases, 51 are of one kind rather than another: it tells nothing about any one case out of the 100. See Tribe, *Trial by Mathematics: Precision and Ritual in the Legal Process*, 84 Harv. L. Rev. 1329 at 1374 (1971). Empirical studies in the U.S. tend to confirm that judges and juries place the preponderance standard between 55-75%, compared with "beyond all reasonable doubt" between 80-100%: Simon, *Trial Lawyers Guide* (1969) 103; Simon & Mahan, 5 Law & Soc. Rev. 319 (1971). An English study found about the same conviction rate under civil and criminal instructions: Cornish, *Juries and the Rules of Evidence*, [1973] Crim. L. Rev. 208. See also Eggleston, *Evidence, Proof and Probability* (1978).
40. Contrast this with reversing the onus of proving negligence, once causality has been established. The latter disposition used, of course, to prevail under the old law of trespass (above, p. 22) and is today a general principle of Socialist legislation: Fleming, *Role of Negligence in Modern Tort Law*, 53 Va. L. Rev. 815 at 830 (1967).
41. The onus was so reversed by American courts in *Haft v. Lone Palm Hotel* 478 P. 2d 465 (Cal. 1970) and *Gardner v. National Bulk Carriers* 310 F. 2d 284 (4 Cir. 1962).
42. Above, p. 199.
43. As in *Farrell v. Snell* [1990] 2 S.C.R. 311.

impression that it represents a special rule of substantive law instead of being only an aid in the evaluation of evidence, an application merely of "the general method of inferring one or more facts in issue from circumstances proved in evidence".[44]

It is impossible to catalogue res ipsa loquitur cases: every accident is in some respects singular and proof of facts by facts incapable of reduction to a formula. Nonetheless, it is feasible to indicate in general terms the conditions which must subsist to call the maxim into operation. Clearly, the occurrence must bespeak negligence and that negligence be the defendant's; it must be such as to raise two inferences: (1) that the accident was caused by a breach by somebody of a duty of care to the plaintiff, and (2) that the defendant was that somebody.[45]

Inference of negligence

In the first place, then, the accident must have been of a kind which does not ordinarily happen without negligence. Experience suggests that a stone is not imbedded in a bun,[46] a crane does not collapse[47] or a barrel of flour drop from a warehouse[48] or a bale from a passing lorry,[49] except on the supposition that someone's negligence is the most likely explanation. Here as elsewhere in civil proceedings, proof is concerned with a balance of probabilities, not speculation as to mere possibilities. It is both necessary and sufficient that the odds are decidely in favour of the defendant's negligence.[50] Courts should not, however, postulate too strong a balance of probabilities lest its aid be withheld when it is most needed.[51] Especially where, as in Australia, the effect of the maxim is merely to help the plaintiff past a non-suit and not to absolve him from the ultimate burden of persuading the trier of facts that, more probably than not, the defendant was to blame, it is often fairer to demand that the accident should at the outset call for an explanation from a defendant who is in a better position to tell the true story than to compel the plaintiff to disprove every conceivable hypothesis on pain of failing at the threshold.

Over the years, the general trend has undoubtedly become more sympathetic to plaintiffs. Concomitant with the rise in safety standards and expanding knowledge of the mechanical devices of our age, less hesitation is felt in concluding that the miscarriage of a familiar activity is so unusual that it is most probably the result of some fault on the part of whoever is responsible for its safe performance. Accordingly, when a vehicle veers out of control into the opposite traffic lane or on to the footpath, the most

44. *Davis v. Bunn* (1936) 56 C.L.R. 246 at 268 per Evatt J. Thus it is not necessary to plead the maxim. as distinct from the facts supporting the inference: *Bennett v. Chemical Constructions* [1971] 1 W.L.R. 1571 (C.A.).
45. *Mahon v. Osborne* [1939] 2 K.B. 14 at 21.
46. *Chaproniere v. Mason* (1905) 21 T.L.R. 633.
47. *Swan v. Salisbury Constructions* [1966] 1 W.L.R. 204 (P.C.).
48. *Byrne v. Boadle* (1863) 2 H. & C. 722; 159 E.R. 299; *Fitzpatrick v. Cooper* (1935) 54 C.L.R. 200; *Lander v. Australian Glass Manufacturers* [1962] S.R. (N.S.W.) 152.
49. *Bellizia v. Meares* [1971] V.R. 641.
50. *Langham v. Wellingborough School* (1932) 101 L.J.K.B. 513 at 518. A mere statistical preponderance of even 60% would therefore not necessarily be sufficient: *Daniels v. Heskin* [1954] I.R. 73 at 79; see above, p. 314.
51. A pessimum exemplum is *Mummery v. Irvings* (1956) 96 C.L.R. 99.

likely explanation is some failure by the driver in operation or maintenance.[52] The accident may admittedly be consistent with causes that do not imply negligence, such as a fainting spell,[53] sudden mechanical failure,[54] an unexpectedly treacherous condition of the road[55] or an attempt to avoid hitting a jay-walker;[56] but such "unavoidable" causes are sufficiently unusual (and, in any event, more easily provable by the defendant) that they may be justly discounted as improbable.[57] Even proof that the accident was due to a skid is ordinarily insufficient to displace this inference, since it is still more consistent with negligence than some innocent cause.[58] Likewise, the impressive safety record of modern aviation lends increasing support to the generally accepted view that a crash under most conditions suggests negligence against the operator, in face of the ever lessening likelihood that unaccountable weather conditions or latent defects in design or construction of the aircraft were solely responsible.[59] Even in medical negligence actions, earlier doubts about invoking the doctrine have been dispelled, at the very least when the sensible layman is in as good a position as the expert to draw his own conclusion, as in cases of swabs or surgical instruments left in a patient's body or injury sustained outside the area of medical treatment;[60] indeed, the typical inequality in knowing what happened as between the (often anaesthetised) patient and surgeon adds a special incentive for inducing the latter to explain.

On the other hand, many an accident is singular in the sense of not representing a model of similar or identical occurrences which permit a generalisation as to responsibility. The conventional stress that the accident be "unusual" assumes a basis of experience for concluding that "ordinarily" it would not have happened *without negligence*: merely that

52. *Davis v. Bunn* (1936) 56 C.L.R. 246; *G.I.O. v. Fredrichberg* (1968) 118 C.L.R. 403; *McGowan v. Stott* (1930) 143 L.T. 216. Aliter, in motorcycle "scramble": *Wilks v. Cheltenham Cycle Club* [1971] 1 W.L.R. 668.
53. See *Gootson v. R.* [1948] 4 D.L.R. 33.
54. See *Nominal Defendant v. Haslbauer* (1967) 117 C.L.R. 448; *Heywood v. A.-G.* [1956] N.Z.L.R. 668. In Australia, such failure has been held insufficient to raise *by itself* an inference of negligence: *Piening v. Wanless* (1968) 117 C.L.R. 498. But in case of latent defects, *Henderson v. Jenkins* [1970] A.C. 282 placed the evidentiary burden on defendant to establish his care in maintenance.
55. See *Lomax v. Reed* [1952] S.A.S.R. 225.
56. See *Turner v. Comm. Road Transport* (1951) 51 S.R. (N.S.W.) 145; *O'Hara v. S.M.T. Co.* 1941 S.C. 363.
57. So the derailment of a train, even more a collision between trains, raises an inference of negligence despite the possibility that it was due (as in *Latch v. Rumner Rly* (1858) 27 L.J. Ex. 155) to sabotage.
58. *Laurie v. Raglan Building Co.* [1942] 1 K.B. 152; *Richley v. Faull* [1965] 1 W.L.R. 1454; *Knott v. Royal Exchange Assoc.* [1955] S.A.S.R. 33; *Wells v. Smith* [1955] S.A.S.R. 58.
59. *Fosbroke-Hobbes v. Airwork* [1937] 1 All E.R. 108; *Zerka v. Lau-Goma Airways* (1960) 23 D.L.R. (2d) 145; McNair, *Law of Air* (3rd ed.) 79; U.S.: 25 A.L.R. 4th 1237 (1983). In Australia the problem has been rendered largely academic by statutory strict liability: see below, p. 331.
60. *Holt v. Nesbitt* [1951] 4 D.L.R. 478 (affd [1953] 1 D.L.R. 671); *Crits v. Sylvester* (1956) 1 D.L.R. 2d 502; *Mahon v. Osborne* [1939] 2 K.B. 14; *MacDonald v. Pottinger* [1953] N.Z.L.R. 196; Dudley, *Safety in the Operating Theatre* (1976). But Canadian, in contrast to American, courts have applied res ipsa also to the treatment area: e.g. *Wilcox v. Cavan* [1975] 2 S.C.R. 663; *Holmes v. Hospital Bd* (1977) 81 D.L.R. 3d 67; *Saunders v. Leeds H.A.* [1985] C.L.Y. 2320.

it was rare is not a qualification, because it may only mean that common knowledge and experience are lacking to account for its probable cause.[61]

Sometimes, a plaintiff will be well advised to introduce evidence of past experience or technical expertise to supplement the range of common knowledge regarding the particular happening and thereby raise an uninformed guess to the level of a persuasive hypothesis.[62] Res ipsa loquitur, though serving a function not unrelated to the doctrine of judicial notice in permitting shortcuts to proof, yet differs from the latter in dealing not with proof of elementary data, but with inferences that may be rationally drawn from proven facts. If a "common sense" notion, it need not be artificially restricted to the realm of matters in which judge and jury are capable of forming an opinion solely on the basis of their own inexpert knowledge. Hence there is no reason why, in medical negligence actions, expert testimony may not properly lay the foundation for a permissible inference that the patient's injury could have been avoided by due care in diagnosis or treatment.[63]

Defendant's responsibility

No less important a requirement is that the res must not only bespeak negligence, but pin it on the defendant. Negligence in the air will never do. It is not enough that the accident spell negligence on the part of someone or other without linking it specifically to the person charged. Thus, if several contractors were engaged in the construction of a building, its collapse does not without more evidence point to the negligence of any particular one of them.[64] A broken draining tube left in a patient's bladder does not implicate the surgeon when post-operative treatment involved its periodical replacement by personnel of an independent hospital.[65] For the same reason the maxim is often inapplicable to cases of complicated surgery by a team, for even if an inference of negligence is permissible, it frequently fails to single out any of the participants.[66] Of course, where one person is in law responsible for the acts of others, like an employer for his servants or a hospital for its staff, this difficulty disappears.[67] For the same reason, in an action against a manufacturer, it is not necessary for the plaintiff to point either to the exact stage in the production process where the defect was introduced or to the particular person who was culpable, because the manufacturer is responsible for the final product in the condition in which it leaves the factory.[68]

61. E.g. *Hughston v. Jost* [1943] 1 D.L.R. 402 (pentothal leaking into surrounding tissue).
62. *Franklin v. Victorian Rly* (1959) 101 C.L.R. 197 at 204; *Mummery v. Irvings* (1956) 96 C.L.R. 99 at 117; *Interlake Mills v. Salmon* [1949] 1 D.L.R. 207.
63. *Cassidy v. M.O.H.* [1951] 2 K.B. 343; *Roe v. M.O.H.* [1954] 2 Q.B. 66; *Watson v. Davidson* [1966] N.Z.L.R. 853; *Kapur v. Marshall* (1978) 85 D.L.R. (3d) 566 at 574. For supplementing expert testimony regarding the unclear aetiology of a pathological condition see also *Tubemakers v. Fernandez* (1976) 50 A.L.J.R. 720.
64. *Carruthers v. Macgregor* 1927 S.C. 816.
65. *Morris v. Winsbury-White* [1937] 4 All E.R. 494.
66. *MacDonald v. Pottinger* [1953] N.Z.L.R. 196; *Roe v. M.O.H.* [1954] 1 W.L.R. 128 (affd on another ground: [1954] 2 Q.B. 66).
67. Though no claim could be maintained against any individual employee or staff member: see *Interlake Tissue Mills v. Salmon* [1949] 1 D.L.R. 207.
68. *Grant v. Australian Knitting Mills* [1936] A.C. 85, 101; (1935) 54 C.L.R. 49 at 62; see below, p. 486.

The necessity of linking the accident with the defendant accounts for the conventional postulate that he must have been in "exclusive control" of the instrumentality or "thing" which caused the injury. If such can be established, it eliminates or minimises, of course, the likelihood of someone else's responsibility. But rigid insistence on such a requirement would be needlessly restrictive, because an accident may well implicate an individual who was not literally on the scene at the time. Thus, after some earlier doubts,[69] the maxim is now regularly invoked in actions against manufacturers of harmful products which have caused injury long after release to the public: control during the process of manufacture is sufficient, at any rate if there is no evidence that the article had been tampered with after leaving the defendant and the plaintiff himself has been eliminated as a likely cause of the harm.[70] This relaxation is sometimes expressed by saying that the requisite control need only relate to the time of the hypothetical negligent act rather than to the time when the "accident" or "injury" occurred. Yet it would surely be at once more accurate and less confusing to abandon all reference to "control" and postulate simply that the apparent cause of the accident must be such that the defendant would most probably be responsible for any negligence connected therewith.[71]

Much will, of course, depend on the details of the evidence. Strongest in this regard are cases of botulism in tinned food or of foreign objects, like ground glass or a dead mouse, in sealed containers.[72] Rather weaker, though now regarded as sufficient, are exploding bottles for which excessive pressure or defective glass usually provide a more likely explanation than subsequent mishandling.[73] Again, a passenger's fall from a moving train points more clearly to the railway's negligence if he falls through the door of an empty compartment shortly after departure[74] than from the corridor of an express after a lengthy run.[75] Least conclusive is a fall from an *open* train—which is, if anything, more consistent with his own carelessness or that of a fellow passenger or sheer accident than with negligence in the operation of the train, even if it lurched or jolted somewhat when he lost his balance.[76]

Vehicle collisions call for similar discrimination. There is obviously a world of difference between one car crashing into another that is stationary and a collision between fast-moving vehicles in heavy traffic. The first clearly calls for an explanation,[77] and so may a rear end collision or even

69. *Donoghue v. Stevenson* [1932] A.C. 562 at 622-633 per Lord Macmillan. This was an obiter dictum because the case was argued on demurrer.
70. See *Fletcher v. Toppers Drinks* [1981] 2 N.S.W.L.R. 911; *Kilgannon v. Sharpe Bros* (1986) 4 N.S.W.L.R 600 (exploding bottles).
71. *Moore v. R. Fox* [1956] 1 Q.B. 596 at 611 (C.A.); *Lloyde v. W. Midlands Gas* [1971] 1 W.L.R. 749 (C.A.); *Godfrey's v. Ryles* [1962] S.A.S.R. 33 at 42; *Tatavyn v. Co-op* (1975) 65 D.L.R. (3d) 99 (plane with dual controls). Cf. *Kouris v. Prospector's Motel* (1977) 19 A.L.R. 343.
72. *Zeppa v. Coca-Cola* [1955] 5 D.L.R. 187; *Arendale v. Canada Bread* [1941] 2 D.L.R. 41; *Shandloff v. City Dairy* [1936] 4 D.L.R. 712.
73. *Fletcher v. Toppers Drinks* [1981] 2 N.S.W.L.R. 911. See also *Yelland v. National Cafe* [1955] 5 D.L.R. 560; *Godfrey's v. Ryles* [1962] S.A.S.R. 33 (fire in kerosene fridge).
74. *Gee v. Metropolitan Rly* (1873) L.R. 8 Q.B. 161.
75. *Easson v. L. & N.E. Rly* [1944] K.B. 421.
76. *Franklin v. Victorian Rly* (1959) 101 C.L.R. 197.
77. *Nominal Defendant v. Haslbauer* (1967) 117 C.L.R. 448.

a head-on collision on the wrong side of the road.[78] Otherwise, however, the maxim has generally been excluded on the ground that, since every driver has to adapt his conduct to that of others, there is lacking that degree of exclusive control which would warrant an inference of negligence against one or the other or both.[79] But, as already noted, a more liberal attitude has been gaining ground in some recent English decisions which allowed an inference against both drivers involved in head-on collisions near the centre of the road, in view of the strong probability of dual fault.[80] So far, however, there has been no inclination to extend this ruling to collisions at intersections.

Evidently, then, the requirement that the accident speak of the defendant's negligence does not necessarily exclude the maxim merely because more than one human force was active on the scene. The plaintiff may either be able to eliminate the likely complicity of the others or the accident may point to the negligence of all of them. Not even the plaintiff's own participation in the events leading to the accident is necessarily fatal, as when a chair collapses on sitting down or a blind comes off its brackets upon being pulled.[81] All that is required in such cases is that the odds exclude an inference of the plaintiff's, rather than the defendant's, responsibility. Indeed, under the regime of apportionment of loss, a plaintiff can now avail himself of the maxim despite an inference of *contributory* negligence, provided the accident also implicates the defendant.[82] In such cases, as we have seen, damages are usually divided equally.[83]

Cause unknown to plaintiff

The principal function of the maxim is to prevent injustice which would result, if a plaintiff were invariably compelled to prove the precise cause of the accident and the defendant's responsibility for it, even when the facts bearing on these matters are at the outset unknown to him and often within

78. *Cream v. Smith* [1961] S.A.S.R. 349; *Richley v. Faull* [1965] 1 W.L.R. 1454.
79. See *Wing v. L.G.O. Co.* [1909] 2 K.B. 652 at 664 (contrast collision between trains belonging to same company: *Skinner v. L.B. & S.C. Rly* (1850) 5 Ex. 787). This decision offers no support for the widely accepted modern American rule (*Capital Transit Co. v. Jackson*, 149 F. 2d 839 (D.C. Cir. 1945)) that a passenger may invoke the maxim against his own (public) carrier. That rule rests in turn largely on the premise that "the highest measure of care" is due to a passenger. It is doubtful if English law postulates an equally high standard—at least as a matter of black-letter rule rather than as an apt description of what is demanded in practice: cf. 4 Halsbury (4th ed.) 174; *Kauffman v. Toronto Transit Comm.* [1960] S.C.R. 251 at 255: "care required is of a very high degree".
80. *Baker v. Market Harborough* [1953] 1 W.L.R. 1472 (C.A.); *Leaman v. Rea* [1954] 4 D.L.R. 423. In these situations, there is of course a *strong* inference that both drivers were at fault for being too close to the centre line: *Bagnall v. Schmidt* (1980) 25 S.A.S.R. 93. Inapplicable to other collisions (*West v. G.I.O.* (1981) 35 A.L.R. 437), still less to non-contemporaneous links: *Kilgannon v. Sharpe Bros* (1986) 4 N.S.W.L.R. 600 (exploding bottle).
81. *Griffith Hospital v. Hayes* (1962) 108 C.L.R. 50.
82. *Turk v. Prange Co.* 119 N.W. 2d 365 (Wis. 1963). Besides, it should not be overlooked that the burden of proving contributory negligence is on the defendant, while res ipsa is concerned only with the plaintiff's establishing a prima facie case against the defendant, without negativing all or any possible defences. His concern is only with establishing the defendant's negligence as *a*, not necessarily *the sole*, responsible cause.
83. See above, p. 273, n. 41.

the knowledge of the defendant. But though the parties' relative access to evidence is an influential factor, it is not controlling. Thus, the fact that the defendant is as much at a loss to explain the accident or himself died in it,[84] does not preclude an adverse inference against him, if the odds otherwise point to his negligence. Conversely, a plaintiff's ignorance or lack of information is too exiguous unless the accident itself raises an incriminating inference against the defendant.

Yet courts are not insensitive to the litigants' comparative ability to shed light on what happened, and in various ways exert pressure to enable a plaintiff to get at facts known only to his adversary. Apart from discovery and other pre-trial procedures, it is established practice in cases where the facts are peculiarly within the defendant's knowledge, to allow rather slight evidence of negligence to support a verdict and demand that the jury's attention be directed to the defendant's refusal to testify.[85] Beyond that, res ipsa loquitur itself has occasionally been invoked, even at the cost of distorting its evidentiary basis, in order to advance a distinct policy objective. This tendency has been most prominent in medical negligence actions as a counterweight to the notorious aversion of professionals to testify against each other and because a patient is under a singular disadvantage in knowing what happened to him while under anaesthetic.[86] It also accounts for the increasing leniency in situations involving products liability[87] and multiple defendants.[88] In this manner, the maxim is in effect used as a straddle between fault and strict liability.[89]

It is often said that res ipsa loquitur applies only where the "exact" or "ultimate" cause of the accident remains unexplained. This means no more than that once a particular act or omission by the defendant has been established as a cause of the harm, there is no longer any need for an inference as to causal responsibility and the question resolves itself simply into whether the cause thus established connotes negligence. Thus, when an omnibus careered into a ditch by reason of a tyre-burst which was eventually traced to a previous impact fracture, the question ceased to be one where the facts spoke for themselves and fell to be decided on the narrower basis whether the defendant's system of maintenance was at fault.[90] On the other hand, there is no justification whatever for depriving a plaintiff of the benefit of a general inference of negligence against the defendant merely because he pleaded and unsuccessfully sought to substantiate specific allegations. It is senseless to put a plaintiff to an election between different methods of proof; and provided his pleadings so

84. E.g. *Knott v. Royal Exchange Assoc.* [1955] S.A.S.R. 33 at 40.
85. *Hampton Court v. Crooks* (1957) 97 C.L.R. 367 at 371; *Jones v. Dunkel* (1959) 101 C.L.R. 298; *Nuhic v. R. & R. Excavations* [1972] 1 N.S.W.L.R. 204; *Nada v. Knight* (1990) A.T.R. 81-032 (W.A.).
86. E.g. *Nesbitt v. Holt* [1951] 4 D.L.R. 478 at 481. The classical illustration is *Ybarra v. Spangard* 154 P. 2d 687 (Cal. 1944) where it was invoked against all members of a surgical team some of whom were clearly innocent.
87. See below, p. 485.
88. See *Roe v. M.O.H.* [1954] 2 Q.B. 66 at 82; also above, p. 199.
89. See Wright, "Res Ipsa Loquitur", *Lectures of the Law Society of Upper Canada* (1955) 115-118, reprint. *Studies in Canadian Tort Law* (1968) ch. 3; Jaffe, *Res Ipsa Loquitur Vindicated*, 1 Buff. L. Rev. 1 (1951).
90. *Barkay v. S. Wales Transport* [1950] A.C. 185; also *Britannia Laundry v. Thornycroft* (1925) 95 L.J.K.B. 237; *Mummery v. Irvings* (1956) 96 C.L.R. 99 at 121-122.

allow[91] and the facts elicited at the trial do not preclude it,[92] he may fall back on circumstantial evidence in support of a general allegation of negligence.[93]

Procedural effect

There has been much controversy concerning the precise procedural advantage that a plaintiff gains from the maxim. Most pointedly the question is when, if ever, the jury may, despite the accident speaking of the defendant's negligence, refuse to heed this voice of experience and actually return a verdict *for* him? That issue may well seem of less practical than academic interest, because cases will be rare when a plaintiff, having once reached the jury, loses his verdict, unless his opponent presents an overwhelming case.

Not least of the difficulties besetting inquiry into the functional operation of the maxim are several semantic snares. In the first place, all too many pronouncements are less than precise about the exact procedural posture with which they purport to be concerned. Often this is so because the particular issue to which they are directed—for example whether a verdict is against the weight of evidence—does not demand any finer discrimination, or because certain distinctions critical enough in jury trials—like that between what would warrant and what compel a verdict—have lost much of their edge when trial is before a judge alone who can afford to be just as nonchalant about the distinction between "fact" and "law" as an appellate court in reviewing his findings.[94] Yet it is singularly important to identify the precise procedural context of any particular judicial ruling and be circumspect in not attributing to it a wider bearing than that context clearly justifies.

A second source of obfuscation is the use of concepts—like burden of proof, presumptions of law and fact—which, though long part of the standard legal vocabulary, still fail to command anything like uniformly accepted meanings. The seeds of all these perplexities were already apparent in the landmark case of *Byrne v. Boadle*,[95] where Pollock C.B. spoke of a "presumption" arising from the fall of a barrel out of the window. Actually all that was at issue was whether this amounted to sufficient evidence—a prima facie case—fit to go to the jury, not with what weight a jury ought to attach to the adverse inference (presumption?) raised by it.

For the sake of clarification, it may therefore be helpful to say something about the use of these concepts and their role in the course of a trial. As already explained,[96] in negligence litigation the "legal" or "ultimate"

91. See *Esso Petroleum v. Southport Corp.* [1956] A.C. 218; *Heywood v. A.-G.* [1956] N.Z.L.R. 668 at 684.
92. As in *Mummery v. Irvings* (1956) 96 C.L.R. 99 where the mere fact of being hit by a flying piece of wood as he entered the workshop would have supported the maxim, but proof that it shot out from a circular saw was held to destroy it in the absence of evidence as to such operations.
93. *Anchor Products v. Hedges* (1966) 115 C.L.R. 493; *Voice v. Union S.S. Co.* [1953] N.Z.L.R. 176; *Neal v. Eaton Co.* [1933] 3 D.L.R. 306.
94. Where even "questions of fact", including the whole record of evidence, are open to review: see above, p. 310.
95. See above, n. 48.
96. See above, p. 314.

burden of proving all facts in issue (save in respect of the twin defences) ordinarily lies on the plaintiff and remains with him throughout the trial in the sense that he must eventually, in order to gain a verdict, persuade the trier of fact that on all the evidence the balance of probability preponderates in his favour. In order to discharge that burden, he will seek to prove relevant facts from which the ultimate fact in issue (for example the defendant's negligence or his causal responsibility) can be deduced; and for this purpose he may avail himself of circumstantial no less than direct evidence, such for example that the instrumentality which caused the injury was under the defendant's exclusive control. Thus he might succeed in establishing a prima facie case, that is sufficient evidence from which the fact in issue may (not *must*) be inferred. Once he has crossed the threshold of being no longer vulnerable to a non-suit, the defendant faces the risk of the jury returning a verdict against him ("risk of non-persuasion"), as they are entitled to do unless he dispels the plaintiff's case. Accordingly, as the trial proceeds, the balance may now tilt to and fro so that, at any given point, one or the other party faces the risk of a probably, but not necessarily, adverse verdict until eventually the trier of fact will have to conclude whether the balance preponderates in favour of the plaintiff.

Certain fact patterns are treated by law as not merely sufficient to support a given conclusion, but as compelling it. From the former (variously designated as "inferences", "presumptions of fact" or "permissive presumptions") the conclusion *may* be drawn, from the latter (identified as "presumptions", "presumptions of law" or "compelling presumptions") it *must* be drawn. The first merely affects the "burden of going forward with the evidence", the trier of fact not being obliged to heed it even if it is so strong that an inconsistent verdict would be set aside as unreasonable. The latter, however, goes so far as to shift the legal burden of proof so that, in the absence of evidence sufficient to rebut it on a balance of probability, a verdict must be directed.[97] A familiar example of the former is that one who drives someone else's car does so as his agent,[98] of the latter that a child born in wedlock is legitimate.

Where exactly does res ipsa loquitur fit into this complex conceptual framework? According to the predominant, and correct, view[99] the maxim raises only a "permissive presumption", exemplifying merely "the general principle of inferring a fact in issue from circumstantial evidence where the circumstances are meagre but significant".[100] Indeed, what justification could there possibly be for attributing greater weight to circumstantial than to direct evidence, seeing that it has never been suggested that the legal burden of proof shifts to the defendant once the plaintiff has established a prima facie case by direct evidence? The maxim is based merely on an estimate of logical probability in a particular case, not on any overriding

97. *Fitzpatrick v. Cooper* (1935) 54 C.L.R. 200 at 219 per Dixon J. See also Denning, *Presumptions and Burdens*, 61 L.Q.R. 379 (1945); Cross, *Evidence* ch. 6.

98. See below, p. 387.

99. Australia: *Nominal Defendant v. Haslbauer* (1967) 117 C.L.R. 448; *G.I.O. v. Fredrichberg* (1968) 118 C.L.R. 403. N.Z.: *Hawke's Bay Motor v. Russell* [1972] N.Z.L.R. 542. Can.: *United Motors Service v. Hutson* [1937] S.C.R. 294; *Temple v. Terrace Co.* (1966) 57 D.L.R. (2d) 631; Schiff, *A Res Ipsa Loquitur Nutshell*, 26 U. Tor. L.J. 451 (1976); *Linden* ch. 5. Eng.: *Ng v. Lee Chuen Tat* [1988] R.T.R. 298. U.S.: *Prosser & Keeton* §39.

100. *Davis v. Bunn* (1936) 56 C.L.R. 246 at 271-272 per Evatt J.

legal policy that controls the initial allocation of the burden of proof or, by means of mandatory presumptions, its reallocation regardless of the probabilities of the particular case in hand.

Accordingly, if the accident remains wholly unexplained[101] or is open to two hypotheses, one consistent, the other inconsistent with the defendant's negligence, and both are evenly poised, the plaintiff has not discharged the onus incumbent on him of proving the issue on a preponderating balance. For example, if a truck suddenly swerves across the road, this would without more explanation raise an inference of negligence against the driver. Yet the plaintiff would fail, if the trier of fact at the end of the case deems it no less probable that the accident was caused by an unexpected break of the steering arm than by culpable maintenance of the wheel assembly (the wreck being consistent with either explanation), leaving unanswered whether the fracture was a consequence or cause of the wheel coming off.[102]

In procedural terms,[103] the maxim certainly enables the plaintiff to establish a prima facie case sufficient to survive a non-suit despite the paucity of his evidence.[104] Beyond that, however, the jury is in control. It will of course be wise for the defendant to seek, by evidence or argument or both, if not to establish, at least to suggest an explanation of the accident consistent with the absence of negligence on his part or, failing that, to prove that he took all reasonable precautions and was therefore not negligent. But the sanction is a probably adverse verdict from the jury, not a verdict directed by the judge. The inference to be drawn from what is known of the accident goes to the weight of the evidence and is therefore, as always, a matter for the jury: it may find against the defendant,[105] but is not compelled to do so. If an exception to this is allowed at all, it can only be in the rare case of a defendant being able to tell the story but choosing not to do so, for it may then perhaps be permissible to draw upon the combined weight of the maxim and the censurable demeanour of the defendant[106] to justify ruling against him as a matter of law.

Otherwise, however, the only means of controlling a jury is to order a new trial on the ground that the verdict is against the weight of evidence. Often, of course, the verdict will have gone for the plaintiff; and although he will almost always be allowed to hold it, there is no categorical rule against a new trial being ordered.[107] On the other hand, if verdicts for a defendant are indeed rare in res ipsa cases, they are also more vulnerable to being set aside. For instance, when a bus struck an awning stretched over the sidewalk and the driver admitted swerving into it, it was held unreasonable to find for the defendant without actually accepting his

101. Like the fire in *Kouris v. Prospector's Motel* (1976) 14 S.A.S.R. 407.
102. See *Davis v. Bunn* (1936) 56 C.L.R. 246.
103. The best explanation remains Evatt J.'s epitome of eight rules in *Davis v. Bunn* (1936) 56 C.L.R. 246 at 267-268.
104. This was all that was at issue in the seminal decision of *Byrne v. Boadle* (1863) 2 H. & C. 722; 159 E.R. 299.
105. And should be so instructed: *Bellizia v. Meares* [1971] V.R. 641.
106. See above, n. 85.
107. *Davis v. Bunn* (1936) 56 C.L.R. 246 was not such an instance because the new trial was ordered on the ground of misdirection as to the burden of proof and imperfect explanation of the evidence.

explanation that he did so in order to avoid hitting a child.[108] Yet, since the plaintiff is not relieved of the legal burden of proof, the defendant may not only have no verdict directed against him, but may well hold a verdict that has actually gone in his favour. Even in so telling a case as that of a car swerving over to the wrong side of the road into oncoming traffic[109] or of a bag of plaster falling from a skip on a building site,[110] a defendant's verdict has been allowed to stand because the jury might well, after all, have felt unconvinced of his negligence.

In contrast, for a time English courts gave a stronger effect to the maxim than that of a merely permissive inference of fact: in order to exculpate himself, the defendant had to rebut the presumption of negligence by proving either that the accident was due to a cause which does not connote negligence on his part or, if he can point to no specific cause, that he took all reasonable care.[111] Such statements seem to be due to a tendency to exalt particular inferences from given facts to the status of propositions of law.[112] Since the virtual disappearance of civil juries in England, the temptation has been strong to blur what, on the one hand, would *justify* and, on the other, *compel* a verdict for the plaintiff, since it is no longer so important to distinguish between questions of law and fact when both issues are decided by the trial judge himself. Hence it was easy to mistake for a principle of law what was merely intended to be the view of the court as to what the defendant in a particular case had to do, if he wished to protect himself by way of rebutting evidence against a probably adverse verdict. A return to orthodoxy was eventually sounded by the Privy Council proclaiming, presumably for England also, that the plaintiff's legal burden of proof remains unaffected in res ipsa situations.[113]

The obvious effect of increasing the procedural disadvantages of defendants is that res ipsa loquitur becomes, to that extent, a more effective device for imposing strict liability under the pretence of administering rules of negligence.[114] In some instances, the brocard has no doubt been deployed as an instrument of policy to impose liability without any real concern for a demonstration of negligence. This has been particularly evident in actions against manufacturers of defective merchandise, which were brought under the regime of res ipsa only after first moderating the "exclusive control" requirement. Today, the maxim is impervious even to evidence of a "foolproof" process of production—rightly, because the very fact that the source of danger has been introduced at some stage shows that

108. *Turner v. Comm. Road Transport* (1951) 51 S.R. (N.S.W.) 145, as explained in *Mummery v. Irvings* (1956) 96 C.L.R. 99 at 120. Similarly *Green v. Rawlings* [1963] W.A.R. 46 (verdict for driver not justified in absence of positive belief in his story that passenger grabbed the steering wheel). The explanation must be based on evidence as in *Ng v. Lee Chuen Tat* [1988] R.T.R. 298, not pure imagination.
109. *G.I.O. v. Fredrichberg* (1968) 118 C.L.R. 403.
110. *Fitzpatrick v. Cooper* (1935) 54 C.L.R. 200.
111. *Moore v. Fox* [1956] 1 Q.B. 596 (C.A.); and see Atiyah, *Res Ipsa Loquitur in England and Australia*, 35 Mod. L. Rev. 337 (1972).
112. *Easson v. L.N.E. Rly* [1944] K.B. 421 per du Parcq L.J.
113. *Ng v. Lee Chuen Tat* [1988] R.T.R. 298 (Hongkong).
114. The significance of the maxim in diluting the fault requirement is stressed by Ehrenzweig, *Negligence without Fault* (1951).

someone or something must have gone wrong. In the result, the outcome may become indistinguishable from strict products liability.[115]

115. E.g. *Zeppa v. Coca-Cola* [1955] 5 D.L.R. 187; *Martin v. Thorn Industries* [1978] W.A.R. 10. Significantly, in the American landmark case of *Escola v. Coca-Cola* 150 P. 2d 436 (Cal. 1944), Traynor J. first propounded outright strict liability for defective products in preference to the majority's invocation of res ipsa.

15

STRICT LIABILITY

Introduction

We have seen that the early common law, preoccupied with breaches of the peace, displayed little concern about the moral responsibility or "fault" of the wrongdoer. Damages were offered primarily to deflect the aggrieved individual from resorting to private vengeance,[1] and it mattered nothing whether he was the outraged victim of flagrant aggression or of mere accidental injury, so long as his misfortune was traceable to the defendant. To all appearances, primitive law imposed liability for causation rather than fault. In times when life was both brutish and short, this may have been due not so much to a conscious refusal to link legal sanctions with moral blame as to an unwillingness or inability to conceive the *unintentional* infliction of harm.[2] With progressive sophistication this primitive assumption slowly yielded to a gradual differentiation between degrees of moral responsibility for legal purposes. Not until the 19th century, however, was there any marked progress toward subjecting civil liability to the general test of fault.

Once established, the fault theory struck deep roots. It stimulated the growth of negligence as an independent basis of liability until it eventully became the principal touchstone for the adjustment of losses in the modern law of torts, permeating such old-fashioned concepts as trespass[3] and nuisance,[4] and not even shrinking from rationalising vicarious liability as a liability for fault.[5] "No liability without fault" became the banner of an individualistic society set on commercial exploitation and self-help. Such fragmentary areas of the law, in which the strict liability of earlier precedent managed to resist the pressure for reorientation, like responsibility for the escape of fire and animals, were thought of as vestigial anomalies of an uncivilised past when individual freedom was less esteemed than in the new era of laissez faire.

Inevitably, the impetus of this movement began to subside as the principal reason for repressing strict liability lost its force with the growing strength of industry and its ability to distribute the cost of tort losses by insurance and higher prices. Public opinion became—because it could afford to be—more social minded. Society is today much more concerned with salvage and preservation than with acquisition and creation.[6]

1. Holmes, *Common Law* (1981) 2ff.
2. Pollock & Maitland, *History of English Law* (1968) ii, 472-473; Ehrenzweig, *Psychoanalysis of Negligence*, 47 Nw. U.L. Rev. 855 (1953).
3. See above, pp. 18-24.
4. See below, p. 427.
5. E.g. Denning L.J. in *Broom v. Morgan* [1953] 1 Q.B. 597 at 608 (vicarious liability); Du Parcq L.J. in *Read v. Lyons* [1945] K.B. 216 at 249 (dangerous animals: "presumed negligence"); *Blackstone* iii, 211 and Street, *Foundations* (1906) i, 52 (cattle-trespass).
6. Harper, 10 Ind. L.J. 494 at 500 (1935).

Therefore, increasing consideration is being given to the compensatory aspect of tort law and to the social value of shifting accident losses by widely distributing their cost among those who benefit from the accident producing activity. It is realised that the result of letting accident losses lie where they fall is not only to impoverish the victim but ultimately to throw the loss on the community as a whole, which must in the last resort foot the bill of rehabilitation and income maintenance through taxation. In effect, society and the victim, by paying the bill, subsidise the activity that produced the loss. Yet it is difficult to see why a subsidy or exemption from payment of a normal cost should be offered to any particular section of the community; and it seems better public policy, in the framework of our existing social and economic system, to devise legal rules that will require each to bear the burden of its own costs. This tendency has been inevitably reflected in a gradual return to strict liability, but unlike their early common law forerunners, these new intrusions of "liability without fault" are justified by considerations of social and economic expediency of our own age.

Rationale of strict liability

Many activities, now more than ever, exact a high toll of life, limb and property. Faced with this situation, society may adopt any one of three possible courses. It may proscribe the activity altogether, as by a statute declaring it illegal or a court enjoining it as a nuisance. Alternatively, it may choose to incur the danger of the enterprise for the sake of its social utility, but forbid it to be carried on except under specified conditions or in a prescribed manner: hence the proliferation of safety statutes enforced by licensing,[7] inspection, criminal penalties and the doctrine of negligence per se. Or it may decide to tolerate the activity on condition that it pay its way regardless of whether it is carried out carelessly or not. This last is the solution of strict liability. The defendant is held liable not for any *particular* fault occurring in the course of the operation, but for the inevitable consequences of a dangerous activity which could be stigmatised as negligent on account of its foreseeably harmful potentialities, were it not for the fact that its generally beneficial character requires us to tolerate it in the public interest.

In one sense, strict liability is but another aspect of negligence, both being based on responsibility for the creation of an abnormal risk.[8] Negligence, however, has been concerned primarily with an improper manner of doing things which are safe (and therefore reasonable) enough when properly carried out, and not with activities which remain dangerous despite all reasonable precaution.[9] The explanation for this lies in the dilemma that if

7. Notable newcomers are the various Radioactive Substances Acts (as in Britain (1960), N.S.W. (1957), N.Z. (1949), and statutes dealing with aerial spraying: see below, n. 26).
8. Prosser, *Selected Topics on the Law of Torts* (1954) ch. 3.
9. The general assumption being that negligence is negatived if all reasonable (let alone, all *possible*) precautions were taken. This is perfectly serviceable in dealing with commonplace, but not with extra-hazardous activities (as illustrated by *A.I. & S. v. Krstevski* (1973) 128 C.L.R. 666 which held that even an extreme risk of frightful consequences in working a blast furnace does not connote negligence unless precautions could and should have been taken to obviate it, presumably short of abandoning the operation). See Fleming, *Role of Negligence in Modern Tort Law*, 53 Va. L. Rev. 815 (1967).

such an activity were branded as negligent on account of its irreducible risk, it would be tantamount to condemning it as unlawful. Some activities, no doubt, deserve that fate either because the object they serve is not sufficiently beneficial or because it can be attained in a safer manner. Other activities, however, may have to be tolerated despite their irreducible risk, like drilling for oil and gas, testing rockets, flying high speed aircraft and driving motor vehicles. These should not be penalised as reprehensible by labelling them negligent although the risk they entail may not be avoidable (at least statistically) despite all possible precaution. If all the same they should pay their way, it must be on some principle other than negligence. That principle is strict liability.

The hallmark of strict liability is therefore that it is imposed on lawful, not reprehensible activities. The activities that qualify are those entailing extraordinary risk to others, either in the seriousness or frequency of the harm threatened. Permission to conduct such an activity is in effect made conditional[10] on its absorbing the cost of the accidents it causes, as an integral part of its overhead.

The prevailing opposition to strict liability is linked to the view that the essence of tort law is corrective justice, that is, to impose an obligation to repair only on a wrongdoer. Strict liability is more compatible with an economic policy of internalising the cost of accidents to an activity best able to reduce accidents (the "cheapest cost avoider"), but it substitutes an instrumentalist goal of tort law in which the reason for imposing liability is not for what a defendant has done wrongfully but for advancing the goal of economic efficiency. The continuing vitality of corrective justice in tort theory explains why common law (though not all statutory) applications of strict liability have been linked to the few situations of creating "abnormal risks", which, as just explained, can be reconciled more easily with traditional concepts of fault.

In accordance with general principles of causality,[11] this exceptional liability should apply only to harm within the scope of the abnormal risk which provided the reason for strict liability: it therefore would not apply to a trespassing cow biting rather than bumping into a neighbour,[12] or to a bomb rolling over someone's foot instead of exploding. Not so clear is whether strict liability should include the risk of abnormal conduct by victims: workers' compensation usually excludes only intentionally self-inflicted injury, but the tendency has been to allow defences at common law like voluntary assumption of risk, contributory negligence or "act of plaintiff".

Moreover, strict liability is as yet unorganised and fragmentary in application. For one thing, our courts have openly endorsed it only in cases where the non-negligent creation of serious risk arises from an *abnormal*

10. See Keeton, *Conditional Fault in the Law of Torts*, 72 Harv. L. Rev. 401 (1958), linking strict liability with the "incomplete privilege" of *Vincent v. Lake Erie Transportation Co.*: see above, p. 97.
11. See above, p. 194. See *Rest. 2d* §519, comment *e*. Thus some problems of "remoteness" are transposed into the definition of the exceptional risk. It is an open question whether liability is otherwise limited to foreseeable risks: *British Celanese v. Hunt* [1969] 1 W.L.R. 959 at 964; *The Wagon Mound No. 2* [1967] 1 A.C. 617 (P.C.) spoke only to liability for fault. U.S.: *Prosser & Keeton* 560; Harper, 30 Mich. L. Rev. 1001 (1932).
12. See below, p. 356.

activity.[13] This explains the exclusion of motoring (no less than of domestic plumbing), and is probably based on the view that if the risky activity is fairly common, the incidence of harm and of responsibility are so evenly matched that nothing would be gained by imposing strict liability. But advanced thought would reject so crude a balance sheet. Just as a major "public benefit" flowing from a hazardous activity (like nuclear power stations and other public utilities) is no longer a good reason for leaving it unburdened but rather reinforces the wisdom of distributing the loss among its beneficiaries, so the very fact that it is widespread and exposes the community to a *typical* hazard may furnish a sufficient reason for tolerating it only on condition that it pay its own passage. This is particularly germane to such common hazards as motoring and flying.

American law has been somewhat bolder. After an at first cool reception, strict liability is now generally applied to "abnormally dangerous" activities, that is, those with inherent risks that cannot be eliminated by the exercise of reasonable care.[14] An even clearer perspective guided the Pearson Commission in its recommendation to impose strict liability on controllers of things or operations in each of two categories—first, those which by their unusually dangerous nature require the closest supervision, like flammable chemicals; and secondly, those which pose a risk of serious and extensive casualties, like public bridges, stadiums and large buildings.[15] Especially the second category and the additional proposal of strict liability for vaccine damage and medical research volunteers[16] clearly reject the plea for exemption of publicly beneficial projects.[17]

Work and road accidents

Legislation has already introduced strict liability in a few distinct spheres. The most prominent is workers' compensation, which in Australia still follows the original British pattern of making the employer absolutely liable to pay compensation to employees suffering work injuries. In most other countries, this pseudo-tort model of strict liability, backed by compulsory liability insurance, has long been replaced by an independent insurance plan on the lines of, or integrated into, a system of social security.[18] So also with respect to road accidents, early no-fault schemes adopted the pattern of strict liability with compulsory liability insurance,[19] but modern reforms have favoured plans based on first party insurance or a centralised social security model.[20] But whatever their precise form, the significant impact of these statutory reforms is that the two statistically most numerous types of accident are already, or about to come, under a system of no-fault

13. This is true both of liability for dangerous animals and under *Rylands v. Fletcher*: see below, ch. 16. Cf. *Rest 2d* §520 (activity must not be "in common usage").
14. *Rest. 2d* §519. See *Prosser & Keeton* ch. 13; *Harper, James & Gray* ch. xiv.
15. Ch. 31. Rather than leaving it to the common law process, §1656 recommends a listing of included activities by means of statutory regulation. The second criterion was first suggested by Strahl ("spectacular" rather than "abnormal"): *Tort Liability and Insurance*, 3 Scand. Stud. L. 213 (1959).
16. Respectively ch. 24 and para. 1341.
17. Para. 1653 also recommends abolition of the defence of statutory authority.
18. See below, p. 519.
19. E.g. the German statute of 1909. See Tunc, XI Int. Encycl. Comp. L. ch. 14 §10-44.
20. See below, p. 522.

compensation which either replaces or complements the traditional tort remedy for negligence. Both will be considered later in greater detail.

A related development has overtaken aircraft accidents which may be conveniently discussed at this point.

Aviation

Britain,[21] several Australian States[22] and New Zealand[23] have subjected owners of aircraft to strict liability for all ground damage to person or property during flight, take-off and landing; and pursuant to the Rome Convention this has been extended by Commonwealth legislation to foreign aircraft and Australian aircraft on international flights.[24] The legislation affords protection not only against aircraft crashes, but also against sonic booms[25] and anything ejected from aircraft, including drift from aerial spray upon neighbouring land.[26] Its rationale is based on fairness, considering the inequality between the parties where one is wholly at the mercy of the other, has not voluntarily exposed himself to the risk,[27] and does not benefit, unlike the other, from the activity.

Rather different considerations underlie the imposition in Australia of strict liability for personal injury or death to passengers and damage to their luggage.[28] Passengers are voluntary participants in the venture and arguably should be given the option of deciding themselves whether to incur the extra cost of insurance. Private insurance is readily available at airports (though at very high overhead costs) and the travelling public is well informed concerning the risks. Instead, the imposition of strict liability on the carrier amounts to compulsory insurance for passengers, since the extra expense will be passed on to them in the price of their ticket. This "benefit" was conceived as the quid pro quo for limiting a carrier's liability to

21. *Civil Aviation Act* 1982 s. 76(2).
22. Damage by Aircraft Acts of N.S.W. (1952, s. 2: comment 1 Syd. L. Rev. 229 (1954)); W.A. (1964, s. 5): Tas. (1963, s. 4); and the *Wrongs Act* 1958 (Vic.) s. 31. See Richardson's *Aviation Law in Australia*, 1 Fed. L. Rev. 242 (1965), a useful complement to the standard English treatises on air law by McNair (3rd ed. 1964) and Shawcross *Air Law* (3rd ed. 1966).
23. *Civil Aviation Act* 1964 s. 23.
24. *Civil Aviation (Damage by Aircraft) Act* 1958 (subject to a ceiling of approx. $A30,000). Neither Britain, New Zealand nor the U.S. have hitherto ratified the Rome Convention (1952).
25. See *Laird v. Nelms* 406 U.S. 797 (1972); *Southgate v. Commonwealth* (1987) 13 N.S.W.L.R. 188 (low-flying helicopter startling horse with rider). Low overflights interfering with the operation of a chicken farm should qualify, but would loss of home comforts?
26. *Weedair (N.Z.) v. Walker* [1961] N.Z.L.R. 153. Some States now have additional regulatory legislation for aerial spraying, requiring licensing of pilots, liability insurance ($30,000), notice of damage to the Director of Agriculture and the proclamation of hazard areas: *Aerial Spraying Control Act* of N.S.W. (1969) unproclaimed, Vic. (1966), W.A. (1966); *Agricultural Chemicals Control Act* 1966 of W.A.
27. American authority leans towards that conclusion even apart from statute (like the *Uniform Aeronautics Act* §4, 5, in force in nine States), though most of the cases deal with stunt flying or crop spraying which can be classified as abnormally dangerous: *Rest. 2d* §520A.
28. *Civil Aviation (Carriers' Liability) Act* 1959 (Cth), Pt IV. Extended to interstate flights by uniform legislation: N.S.W. (1967), Vic. (1961), Qld (1964), S.A. (1962), W.A. (1961), Tas. (1963). See Edwards, *Liability of Air Carriers*, 56 A.L.J. 108 (1982).

$100,000, on the model of the Warsaw Convention.[29] In the upshot, passengers are thus automatically insured for a minimum amount, but may voluntarily increase their cover by private insurance. All this, of course, is a long way from the rationale of common law liability for abnormally dangerous activities, but it is symptomatic of a complementary trend towards strict liability based on consumer protection and loss distribution.

While rail transport exacts few casualties and the common law is generally considered adequate, an International Convention imposes strict liability for injury to passengers on international journeys by analogy to the domestic law of many countries. Britain is a party of that Convention,[30] and has been urged to extend the same rule also to domestic journeys.[31]

Products liability

Throughout the preceding chapters on negligence liability, special attention has already been given to the creeping erosion of fault and its replacement by a stricter liability especially in areas where the defendant is recognised as a good loss distributor. In recent years this tendency has made the most spectacular progress throughout the highly developed Western world with respect to products liability. Defective products account for the largest number of injuries besides accidents at work and on the road. The consumer is singularly dependent on the manufacturer for safety, ill-equipped to make an informed choice whether to incur the risks of the product and handicapped in proving fault. The manufacturer, on the other hand, is a convenient conduit for spreading the accident cost among the consumers of the product who, in reality, thus buy compulsory insurance for themselves. In economic terms, the accident cost is internalised in the cost of the product and may even encourage extra safety procedures.

This theorem underlies the American adoption of strict products liability in the last 30 years and inspired the current reform mandated in the European Community and proposed in other countries, including Australia.[32]

The future

Proposals to add other candidates to this growing list of no-fault compensation have been flourishing in recent years, including victims of drug and vaccine, medical and sporting accidents, research volunteers and victims of crime.[33] Common features are that negligence is perceived as peculiarly deficient in one or more respects in dealing with the particular

29. Applicable to international flights. Cth: *Civil Aviation (Carriers' Liability) Act* 1959, Pts II and III; N.Z.: *Carriage by Air Act* 1962. The Convention was made applicable also to domestic flights in Britain (see McNair, *Law of Air* (1964) 23 and app. 5) and N.Z. (*Carriage by Air Act* 1967, Pt 2). The monetary ceiling is $A15,000 as between signatories of the Hague Protocol, otherwise half that sum. Flights from and to the U.S. are now, under the Montreal Agreement, subject to liability up to $75,000. The Montreal Protocol No. 3 would substitute 100,000 I.M.F. special drawing rights (about $A150,000). See Miller, *Liability in International Air Travel* (1977).
30. *Carriage by Railway Act* 1972.
31. *Pearson* ch. 21. Prussia adopted strict liability as early as 1838.
32. See below, ch. 23.
33. See above, p. 35.

type of accident, that the victims are especially appealing to popular compassion and that financing is relatively painless. This trend would portend a spreading mosaic of negligence and no-fault, perhaps an eventual replacement of all fault-based tort liability by a comprehensive compensation system for all accidents, as has already occurred in New Zealand.[34]

34. See below, p. 405.

16

THE PRINCIPLE OF RYLANDS v. FLETCHER

The modern doctrine of strict liability for the escape of dangerous substances had its genesis in 1866, in the leading case of *Rylands v. Fletcher.*[1] The defendant mill owners decided to construct a water reservoir on their land for the purpose of supplying water to their factory. On the chosen site was a disused shaft of an abandoned mine, but owing to the negligence of the engineers, a firm of independent contractors who had been entrusted with the work, this fact was not discovered until the water broke into the shaft and flooded the plaintiff's adjoining mine through communicating passages. An arbitrator found that the defendants themselves had been ignorant of the existence of the old shaft and exonerated them for personal negligence. Nonetheless, they were held liable for the damage on the principle enunicated by Blackburn J., that a "person who for his own purposes brings on his lands and collects and keeps there anything likely to do mischief if it escapes, must keep it in at his peril, and, if he does not do so, is prima facie answerable for all the damage which is the natural consequence of its escape".[2]

The case did not precisely fit into any of the rules of tort liability recognised at the time. It was not trespass because the damage by flooding was not a direct and immediate consequence of the defendant's activity.[3] Nor was it an actionable nuisance because, apart from there being only an isolated escape and not a continuous or recurring invasion,[4] it was not contemplated for another decade that the employer of an independent contractor might in some circumstances become liable for a nuisance created in the course of the job.[5] Yet for all that, Blackburn J. seemed less conscious of propounding a novel principle than a mere generalisation of accepted rules. He could point to the analogies of cattle-trespass, nuisance by escaping fumes and an early precedent relating to the flow of filth from a privy;[6] and on one view, these instances of strict liability "wandered about, unhoused and unshepherded, except for a casual attention, in the pathless fields of jurisprudence, until they were met . . . by the mastermind of Mr Justice Blackburn who guided them into the safe fold where they have since rested. In a sentence epochal in its consequences this judge co-ordinated them all in their true category."[7] On the other hand, the

1. (1866) L.R. 1 Ex. 265, affd (1868) L.R. 3 H.L. 330.
2. (1866) L.R. 1 Ex. 265 at 279-280.
3. *Fletcher v. Rylands* (1865) 3 H. & C. 774 at 792; 159 E.R. 737 at 744 per Martin B.; *Read v. Lyons* [1947] A.C. 156 at 166. Conversely, an intentional release of a projectile falls to trespass, not *Rylands*: *Rigby v. Chief Constable* [1985] 1 W.L.R. 1242 at 1255.
4. It is probably no longer true that nuisance cannot be founded on isolated escapes: see below, p. 420. Conversely, *Rylands v. Fletcher* cases often involve conditions of some duration.
5. *Bower v. Peate* (1876) 1 Q.B.D. 321. See below, p. 391.
6. *Tenant v. Goldwin* (1703) 2 Ld Raym. 1089; 92 E.R. 222.
7. Wigmore, 7 Harv. L. Rev. 441 at 454 (1894).

decision was far more than a mere summary of the theory underlying these specific torts. Behind the screen of analogies drawn from existing precedents, it created new law by extending the incidence of strict liability to the general category of all inherently dangerous substances and making the occupier from whose land they escape responsible, even if he had used the utmost care and diligence in devising means for preventing their escape. Though it was arguable that the decision itself, as distinct from the reasoning, was linked to the finding of negligence by the contractors, subsequent interpretation has emphasised that a defendant cannot avail himself of the absence of all negligence on his part or of those over whom he has any measure of control.[8] He is charged with keeping them at his peril and excused only for an escape caused by an act of God or the unexpectable and malicious intervention of strangers.

Viewed against the background of the predominant fault theory, the decision seemed startling indeed. This is attested by the unfavourable reception it first encountered in American courts which reacted even more strongly to the facts of the case than to the legal principle.[9] It was difficult to accept the idea that the construction of a water reservoir was an outlandish activity fraught with exceptional risk rather than a commonplace, indeed indispensable undertaking, clearly justified on any cost/benefit scale.[10] But there is no evidence to support the suggestion[11] that the court deliberately espoused the cause of the dominant class of landed gentry against the interests of developing industry;[12] rather, its effect was to protect one industry (mining) against another (milling) because the latter was obviously a far better loss avoider. Whatever the true explanation of the reasons behind the decision, it found additional favour in more recent times among the proponents of "enterprise liability". Anyone, they contend, whose activity entails exceptional peril to others notwithstanding all reasonable safety precautions should fairly treat typical harm resulting from it as a cost item ("internalised"), which can be absorbed in pricing and passed on to the consumer, spread so thin that no one will be seriously hurt by it.[13] Even if the activity is not a business venture, the defendant should not prosecute it for his own purposes, unless he is willing to pay the price.[14] Besides, the cost of liability can be controlled by liability insurance.

Yet, despite this modern rationalisation and the general trend towards stricter liability, the rule in *Rylands v. Fletcher* has not evoked enthusiastic judicial response. Indeed, from its inception, it was subjected to a process of constriction which has greatly impaired its potential as a catalyst for a

8. *Dunn v. Birmingham Canal Co.* (1872) L.R. 7 Q.B. 244 at 259.
9. Paradoxically, this inauspicious start later changed to much more enthusiastic support than in the Commonwealth. See *Rest. 2d* §519; Prosser, *Selected Topics* (1953) ch. 3; Gregory, *Trespass to Negligence to Absolute Liability* 37 Va. L. Rev. 359 (1951).
10. But see Simpson, *Legal Liability for Bursting Reservoirs: The Historical Context of Rylands v. Fletcher*, 13 J. Leg. Stud. 209 (1984) who documents the impact of several contemporary dam disasters, but also the judicial ambivalence of how to deal with them.
11. This economic interpretation was advanced by Bohlen in his classical study, *Rule in Rylands v. Fletcher* 59 U. Pa. L. Rev. 298 (1911), reprinted in his *Studies* ch. 7.
12. Molly, 9 U. Chic. L. Rev. 266 (1942).
13. The Calabresi version of this theorem (above, p. 11) by contrast looks for optimal deterrence of accidents by higher prices and lessening consumer demand.
14. See Sharp, *Aristotle, Justice and Enterprise Liability*, 34 U. Tor. Fac. L. Rev. (1976).

broader and more systematic pattern of loss distribution pertaining to accidents caused by dangerous operations. Many of the exceptions engrafted on the rule show a steady re-encroachment of the "fault" dogma and, in the aggregate, have constricted it to such an extent that its sphere of operation has become rather unpredictable.

Natural use of land

Mr Justice Blackburn's broad formulation, though gaining the express approval of the House of Lords, was at the outset substantially qualified by Lord Cairns' suggestion that it applied only to damage from a non-natural user of land.[15] In illustration he cited two mining cases, in one of which the defendant's normal operations resulted in flooding a neighbouring mine through mere gravitation,[16] while in the other seepage was caused by pumping water to a higher level.[17] The first was a "natural user" of mining land, the second was not: which explained why the defendant was exonerated in the former but not in the latter case. Yet for long it remained unclear whether this exemption was intended only for *natural* accumulations of water and the like, released by a "natural user" of the land in question,[18] or extended also to artificial accumulations for the purpose of "ordinary" or "natural" use—whether, in other words, "natural" referred to the introduction of the dangerous substance or to the use which caused the escape.[19] This ambiguity inspired a good deal of confusion until in *Rickards v. Lothian*,[20] the Privy Council authoritatively adopted the second meaning and thereby withdrew a wide range of activities from the ambit of strict liability.

Much of the earlier criticism of the distinction[21] has been discounted by dispelling the impression that non-natural was synonymous with "artificial"[22] or that natural meant "primitive".[23] For it is now settled that "there must be some *special* use bringing with it *increased* danger to others, . . . not merely the ordinary use of the land or such a use as is proper for the general benefit of the community."[24] In applying this qualification, the courts have looked not only to the thing or activity in

15. (1868) L.R. 3 H.L. 330 at 338-339. Non-natural user being an essential element of liability, the burden of proving it rests on the plaintiff: *Pett v. Sims Paving Co.* [1928] V.L.R. 247 at 255.
16. *Smith v. Kenrick* (1849) 7 C.B. 515; 137 E.R. 205. See also *Rouse v. Gravelworks* [1940] 1 K.B. 489.
17. *Baird v. Williamson* (1863) 15 C.B. (N.S.) 376; 143 E.R. 831.
18. If in no manner interfered with, the escape of things "naturally on the land", like gravitating rain water, would not ordinarily involve the occupier in any responsibility whatever: see below, p. 432.
19. See Newark, *Non-Natural User and Rylands v. Fletcher*, 24 Mod. L. Rev. 557 (1961).
20. [1913] A.C. 263; 16 C.L.R. 387.
21. In *Brown v. Collins* (1873) 53 N.H. 442 at 448, a celebrated decision by Doe C.J., it was described as merely emphasising that *Rylands v. Fletcher* imposes "a penalty upon efforts . . . to rise above a condition of barbarism". Also modern critics have not been at a loss to point to "anomalous" results, e.g. the inclusion of cattle-trespass: *Leakey v. National Trust* [1980] Q.B. 485 at 521.
22. Note, e.g., the application of strict liability to the roof of a dwelling-house dislodged in a storm, in *Lamb v. Phillips* (1911) 11 S.R. (N.S.W.) 109 where the question of "natural user" was not even mooted. See now *Wilkins v. Leighton* [1932] 2 Ch. 106.
23. *Read v. Lyons* [1947] A.C. 156 at 187.
24. *Rickards v. Lothian* [1913] A.C. 263 at 280; 16 C.L.R. 387 at 400-401 (P.C.).

isolation, but also to the place and manner in which it is maintained and its relation to its surroundings. Time, place and circumstances, not excluding purpose, are material.[25] The distinction between natural and non-natural use is both relative and capable of adjustment to the changing patterns of social existence.[26] Thus, whatever the merit of the seminal decision that the storage of water in a reservoir for industrial purposes created an exceptional danger in the particular locality,[27] the accumulation of water for irrigation is a proper method of using land in an ordinary manner, at least in a proclaimed irrigation district.[28] In contrast, aerial spraying of weedkiller next to sensitive crops on neighbouring land presents too great a danger from drift to qualify as "normal", however accepted the general practice of applying herbicide.[29] So also does "fill" for home construction on a ravine.[30]

"Natural" has long ceased to be linked, if it ever was, to uses of land appropriate to an agricultural community; today it is applied to most residential, recreational and even many industrial uses. Thus it is a natural use to collect water in a cistern or ordinary supply pipes in a home[31] as well as on commercial premises.[32] So also a gas and electricity supply, whether in dwelling-houses[33] or commercial premises,[34] provided it is not carried in bulk.[35] Nor does strict liability attach to the lighting of fires for cooking food,[36] heating a room from a fireplace[37] or building from an oil burning furnace,[38] operating a steam boiler in a ship[39] or in a flour mill,[40] a ship bunkering oil in port,[41] playing cricket[42] or golf[43] and even to the firing of hunting rifles.[44] The above-mentioned discrimination against use

25. *Torette House v. Berkman* (1940) 62 C.L.R. 637 at 655.
26. *Read v. Lyons* [1947] A.C. 156 at 176; and see Stallybrass, *Dangerous Things and Non-Natural User*, 3 Cam. L.J. 376 (1929). In this, and other respects, it bears some resemblance to the "reasonable use" concept in nuisance: below, ch. 21.
27. *Rylands v. Fletcher* (1866) L.R. 1 Ex. 265, affd (1868) L.R. 3 H.L. 330.
28. *Bayliss v. Lea* [1962] S.R. (N.S.W.) 521. For tin mining? (*Hiap Lee v. Weng Lok* [1974] 2 Mal. L.J. 1 (P.C.).)
29. *Mihalchuk v. Ratke* (1966) 57 D.L.R. (2d) 269; *Cruise v. Niessen* [1977] 2 W.W.R. 481; *Langan v. Valicopters* 567 P. 2d 218 (Wash. 1977); *Metson v. DeWolfe* (1980) 117 D.L.R. (3d) 278 (manuring). Left open in *A.-G. v. Geothermal* [1987] 2 N.Z.L.R. 348 (C.A.).
30. *Chu v. N. Vancouver* (1982) 139 D.L.R. (3d) 201.
31. *Rickards v. Lothian* [1913] A.C. 263. Somewhat inconsistently, sewage from a privy apparently still attracts strict liability: *Smeaton v. Ilford Corp.* [1954] Ch. 450 at 471; Kadirmagar, 37 Conv. 325 (1973).
32. *Torette House v. Berkman* (1940) 62 C.L.R. 637; *Kara v. Rhodes* [1966] V.R. 77. Even a sprinkler system: *Peters v. Prince of Wales Theatre* [1943] K.B. 73.
33. *Miller v. Addie* 1934 S.C. 150; *Bloom v. Creed* [1937] 3 D.L.R. 709.
34. *Collingwood v. Home & Colonial Stores* [1936] 3 All E.R. 200.
35. Ibid. (electricity); *Northwestern Utilities v. London Guarantee* [1936] A.C. 108 (gas); *Western Engraving v. Film Laboratories* [1936] 1 All E.R. 106 (water).
36. *Hazelwood v. Webber* (1934) 52 C.L.R. 268: see below, p. 351.
37. *Sochacki v. Sas* [1947] 1 All E.R. 344: see below, p. 351.
38. *Nikka Overseas Agency v. Canada Trust. Co.* (1961) 31 D.L.R. (2d) 368.
39. *Howard v. Furness Houlder Lines* [1936] 2 All E.R. 781.
40. *Wise Bros v. Comm. Rlys* (1947) 75 C.L.R. 59.
41. *The Wagon Mound (No. 2)* [1963] S.R. (N.S.W.) 948; *Eastern Asia Navigation Co. v. Fremantle Harbour Trust* (1951) 83 C.L.R. 353 at 388, 396.
42. *Bolton v. Stone* [1951] A.C. 850 at 867.
43. *Matheson v. Northcote College* [1975] 2 N.Z.L.R. 106.
44. *Dahlberg v. Naydiuk* (1969) 10 D.L.R. (3d) 319. But calling for "consummate caution" (*Potter v. Faulkner* (1861) 1 B. & S. 800 at 805; 121 E.R. 911 at 912).

or storage in bulk, while primarily reflecting the excessive danger, also promotes a sound distinction between utilities and private users based on their relative capacity for absorbing the loss.

The distinction between natural and non-natural use has served the function principally of lending the rule in *Rylands v. Fletcher* a desirable degree of flexibility by enabling the courts to infuse notions of social and economic needs prevailing at a given time and place.[45] Admittedly, it is not always handled intelligibly (or intelligently) under the screen of treating it as a question of fact; and by countenancing the notion of "reasonable user" tends to confuse strict liability with negligence. We must not lose sight of the fact that if "natural user" is given too wide a berth, it will quickly dismantle most of strict liability. Thus we should beware of the proposal[46] that approval of a particular use by a planning authority automatically qualify it as "natural" regardless of the risk it poses to the community, or occasional suggestions to exempt all activities redounding to the "general benefit of the community", such as nationalised industries[47] or even the manufacture of munitions in time of war.[48] Not only is there no warrant in principle for prejudicing private rights by the facile plea of overriding public welfare,[49] at least in the absence of statutory authorisation; indeed, many are the decisions which have attached strict liability to enterprises engaged in community services, such as public utilities.[50]

Dangerous things

As originally (and perhaps rather carelessly) formulated, the rule of strict liability purported to apply to "anything likely to do mischief if it escapes". There are, alas, few objects which do not in *some* circumstances present a risk of harm *if* they escape. According to one summation,[51] therefore, the only objects to qualify are those that are both likely to escape and, in doing so, entail exceptional peril to others. Yet the category of "*Rylands v. Fletcher* objects" has never become narrowed to that of "inherently dangerous" things which, as we shall see later,[52] has attracted a very

45. Bohlen, *Studies* 349-351. The question is one of law: *Hazelwood v. Webber* (1934) 52 C.L.R. 268 at 278, 281.
46. Williams, *Non-natural User of Land* [1973] Cam. L.J. 310, accepted in *Tock v. St John's* [1989] 2 S.C.R. 1181.
47. *Dunne v. N.W. Gas Bd* [1964] 2 Q.B. 806 at 832 (did the defendant collect and distribute gas "for its own purposes" (Blackburn's phrase)?).
48. Thus Lords Simon and Macmillan in *Read v. Lyons* [1947] A.C. 156 at 169-170, 173-174.
49. Far from justifying an exemption, it supplies an added reason for spreading the cost which not only should, but easily can be shared by the larger community through taxation or pricing: e.g. the redoubtable individualist, Bramwell B. in *Brand v. Hammersmith Rly* (1867) L.R. 2 Q.B. 223 at 230; and the civilised French doctrine of "*La Fleurette*" (egalité devant les charges publiques).
50. *Smeaton v. Ilford Corp.* [1954] Ch. 450 at 468-471; *Porter v. Bell* [1955] 1 D.L.R. 62 (blasting on defence project); *Handcraft Co. v. Comm. Rlys* (1959) 77 W.N. (N.S.W.) 84 (burning off along railway track); *Gertsen v. Metro. Toronto* (1973) 41 D.L.R. (3d) 646 (gas generated by garbage fill); *Gas Act* 1965 (U.K.) s. 14 (underground gas storage). Wrongheadedly, public authorities acting pursuant to statutory powers are usually exempt from strict liability, by the defence of statutory authority: see below, p. 347.
51. Stallybrass, *Dangerous Things and Non-Natural User of Land*, 3 Cam. L.J. 376 at 382-385 (1929).
52. See below, p. 490.

stringent duty of care, though not of strict liability. In truth, the task of confining the strict liability of *Rylands v. Fletcher* to extra-hazardous conditions (out of control) has fallen to the criterion of non-natural user rather than to any distinction based on the quality of a "thing" looked at in isolation without reference to its quantity or environment.

Thus the reason why motor cars,[53] even defective motor cars,[54] do not entail strict liability is not because of any doubt that they are "likely to do mischief if they escape", but because their use is normal nowadays rather than excessive. By the same token, one would look in vain at the long list of included objects for a clue as to why strict liability *was* imposed. They range from water,[55] electricity,[56] gas,[57] oil,[58] fire,[59] explosives[60] and acid smuts[61] to poisonous trees[62] and apparently even flagpoles,[63] chimney stacks[64] and the roof of a house.[65] Liability has even been imposed for vibrations, although not tangible at all;[66] and in at least one case for human beings, when the owner of a disused brickfield was made responsible for the unhygienic habits of caravan dwellers whom he had licensed to camp there at a weekly rent.[67] There need not even have been a *miscarriage* in the sense of something gone awry: sonic booms would surely qualify, although they are an inevitable accompaniment of supersonic flying.[68] The harm done must, however, result from a risk which called for the imposition of strict liability: a falling stack of dynamite that knocks over the plaintiff without exploding is a matter for negligence, not strict liability.[69]

53. The early inclination to attach strict liability (nuisance) to motor vehicles merely because they might skid was defeated in *Wing v. L.G.O. Co.* [1909] 2 K.B. 652. See Spencer, *Motor Cars and Rylands v. Fletcher* [1983] Cam. L.J. 65.
54. *Phillips v. Britannia Hygienic Laundry* [1923] 1 K.B. 539 esp. at 550-555 (defective axle). The closest we have come to strict liability is to reverse the onus of proof and require the defendant to establish that he was not negligent in relation to a latent defect: *Henderson v. Jenkins* [1970] A.C. 282.
55. Whether in reservoirs or drains: *Simpson v. A.-G.* [1959] N.Z.L.R. 546.
56. *National Telephone v. Baker* [1893] 2 Ch. 186; *Eastern & S. African Telegraph v. Cape Town Tramways* [1902] A.C. 381.
57. *Batcheller v. Tunbridge Wells Gas Co.* (1901) 84 L.T. 765.
58. *Smith v. Gt W. Rly* (1926) 135 L.T. 112. Pollution by tankers attracts strict liability under the *Merchant Shipping (Oil Pollution) Act* 1971 (U.K.).
59. See below, ch. 17.
60. *Rainham Chemical v. Belvedere Guano* [1921] 2 A.C. 465; *Porter v. Bell* [1955] 1 D.L.R. 62; *Jackson v. Drury Constructions* (1974) 49 D.L.R. (3d) 183.
61. *Halsey v. Esso Petroleum* [1961] 1 W.L.R. 683.
62. *Crowhurst v. Amersham Bd* (1878) 4 Ex. D. 5; *Ponting v. Noakes* [1894] 2 Q.B. 281.
63. *Shiffman v. Order of St John* [1936] 1 All E.R. 557.
64. *Nichols v. Marsland* (1875) L.R. 10 Ex. 255 at 259-260.
65. *Lamb v. Phillips* (1911) 11 S.R. (N.S.W.) 109.
66. *Hoare v. McAlpine* [1923] 1 Ch. 167; *Western Silver Fox v. Ross & Cromarty C.C.* [1940] S.L.T. 144; questioned in *Barrette v. Franki Pile* [1955] O.R. 413 and *Phillips v. Western Californian Standard* (1960) 31 W.W.R. 331 on the spurious grounds, propagated by Pollock (39 L.Q.R. 145 (1923)), that they are not inherently dangerous, cannot be said to escape or to have been brought on the land.
67. *A.-G. v. Corke* [1933] Ch. 89; criticised in *Matheson v. Northcote College* [1975] 2 N.Z.L.R. 106 at 117-118; 49 L.Q.R. 158 (1933). See also *Smith v. Scott* [1973] Ch. 314 (landlord not liable for objectionable tenants because not "in control"). Infected persons prematurely discharged from hospital did not qualify in *Evans v. Liverpool Corp.* [1906] 1 K.B. 160.
68. For statutory liability see above, p. 331.
69. See above, p. 329. This, rather than foreseeability or directness, serves as a test of remoteness: see below, p. 343.

Occasionally, the distinction between natural and non-natural user has been confused with that between dangerous and non-dangerous things.[70] The two questions, though functionally related in that both make room for judicial discretion in applying or withholding strict liability, are otherwise distinct. Water, gas, electricity and many other *Rylands v. Fletcher* objects are perfectly usual, and in order to attract the rule there must be both an extraordinary use of the land and the subject must in the circumstances be classifiable as dangerous.

Escape

The severest brake on the rule was applied when the House of Lords in *Read v. Lyons*[71] insisted that there must be an escape of the dangerous substance from land under the control of the defendant to a place outside. The plaintiff was employed by the Ministry of Supply during war as an inspector of munitions in the defendants' factory. Whilst there on duty, she was injured by an explosion but failed to recover, because she was unable to establish negligence and recourse to strict liability was precluded for want of an "escape". The decision has been applauded by some as a reminder that *Rylands v. Fletcher* is but a branch of the wider principle of nuisance,[72] which regulates the mutual duties of neighbouring occupiers and leaves to the law of negligence the responsibilities of an occupier to persons who suffer injury *on* his premises. It has been deplored by other critics for widening the unfortunate distinction between the protection according to persons injured *outside* and those just *inside* the dangerous premises. The escape need not, however, be upon the plaintiff's land, as when some material drifted into a power station and interrupted the electricity supply to a nearby factory.[73]

There is at least one[74] exception to the strict requirement of "escape" from land in occupation of the defendant. For it is clearly established as offering no defence to public utilities and to others who, under licence, introduce a dangerous substance (like gas) into mains on or under the highway from whence it escapes, by leak or explosion, unto neighbouring premises.[75] Other decisions have also imposed strict liability for bringing dangerous things on the highway, such as locomotive engines emitting sparks and setting fire to adjacent land.[76] Moreover, it is doubtful whether the rule in fact postulates occupation by the defendant of the land from which the escape occurs, so long as he introduced the dangerous substance

70. See the citations by Stallybrass, 3 Cam. L.J. 376 at 395-396 (1929).
71. [1947] A.C. 156.
72. Differing from it only by allowing recovery for an isolated escape: Newark, *Boundaries of Nuisance*, 65 L.Q.R. 480 at 488 (1949).
73. *British Celanese v. Hunt* [1969] 1 W.L.R. 959.
74. In Britain, atomic reactor operators are now strictly liable for ionising radiations causing personal injury or property damage, whether sustained *on* or *off* the reactor site: *Nuclear Installations Act* 1965 s. 7. See Street & Frame, *Law Relating to Nuclear Energy* (1966) ch. 4. U.S.: *Price-Anderson Act* 1957-1966 ("extraordinary nuclear occurrences").
75. *Midwood v. Manchester* [1905] 2 K.B. 597. This was accepted in *Benning v. Wong* (1969) 122 C.L.R. 249.
76. *Powell v. Fall* (1880) 5 Q.B.D. 597; *Mansel v. Webb* (1918) 88 L.J.K.B. 323; also *Rigby v. Chief Constable* [1985] 1 W.L.R. 1242 at 1254. Indeed, why should we not follow *Siegler v. Kuhlman* 502 P. 2d 1181 (Wash. 1972), which held a large petrol truck that overturned and burned to strict liability to another motorist?

and had control of it at the relevant time.[77] After all, there is no such requirement for nuisance,[78] which *Read v. Lyons* itself regarded as the wider genus.

The most damaging effect of the decision in *Read v. Lyons* is that it prematurely stunted the development of a general theory of strict liability for ultra-hazardous activities.[79] Prior to 1944, several strands of authority seemed to hold out promise that a law of dangerous operations was in the making. Thus, the duty of an owner of dangerous animals is not merely to keep them *in* his peril, but to keep them at his peril,[80] and since that principle was a major historical source of the rule in *Rylands v. Fletcher*, it would have been easy to extend the analogy. In addition, several decisions imposed liability on employers of independent contractors for damage caused in the performance of dangerous operations,[81] and these could be interpreted as another instance of strict liability for ultra-hazardous activities.[82] Again, liability for inherently dangerous chattels is strict in all but name, since the standard of care is so stringent as to amount "practically to a guarantee of safety".[83] But the invitation to unify these elements into a coherent principle was emphatically rejected. Scott L.J. specifically condemned as not being in conformity with English law[84] the rule of the American *Restatement*, that "one who carries on an ultra-hazardous activity is liable to another whose person, land or chattels the actor should recognise as likely to be harmed by the unpreventable miscarriage of the activity for harm resulting thereto from that which makes the activity ultra-hazardous, although the utmost care is exercised to prevent the harm."[85]

Type and extent of injury

Lord Macmillan in *Read v. Lyons* pushed his antipathy against *Rylands v. Fletcher* to the length of even questioning whether it could ever support a claim for personal injuries.[86] The doubt was certainly novel, indeed

77. *Rainham Chemical Works v. Belvedere Fish Guano* [1921] 2 A.C. 465 at 479; *Gertsen v. Metro. Toronto* (1973) 41 D.L.R. (3d) 646. But *The Wagon Mound (No. 2)* [1963] S.R. (N.S.W.) 948 held the rule inapplicable to escape of oil from a *ship* in harbour.
78. See below, p. 427.
79. The negative attitude displayed in *Read v. Lyons* [1947] A.C. 156 may have been a judicial reaction to the rapid increase of social welfare legislation; the courts taking the view that it is not their function, but that of Parliament, to augment the range of legal protection: Tylor, *Restriction of Strict Liability*, 10 Mod. L. Rev. 396 at 402 (1947); Friedmann, *Social Insurance and the Principles of Tort Liability*, 63 Harv. L. Rev. 241 (1949).
80. *Read v. Lyons* [1947] A.C. 156 at 182. But cf. *Rands v. McNeil* [1955] 1 Q.B. 253: see below, p. 358.
81. *Brooke v. Bool* [1928] 2 K.B. 578; *Honeywill v. Larkin Bros* [1934] 1 K.B. 191; *The Pass of Ballater* [1942] P. 112; see below, p. 391.
82. See the classification in Winfield, *Textbook of the Law of Torts* (5th ed., 1950) ch. 23, abandoned by his editors in later editions.
83. *Adelaide Chemical v. Carlyle* (1940) 64 C.L.R. 514 at 522 per Starke J. See below, p. 491.
84. [1945] K.B. 216 at 255 ff. His strictures are the more difficult to understand as, on his own admission, the same conclusion would have been reached on the facts of the case by following the *Rest. 2d*.
85. §519, subject to certain exceptions enumerated in §520-524. *Rest. 2d* substituted "abnormally dangerous" for "ultra-hazardous".
86. [1947] A.C. 156 at 173.

inconsistent with several precedents.[87] Moreover, its precise scope was far from clear. If the analogy of nuisance, from which it indubitably derived, provides any guidance, it would not so much justify withholding redress for personal injuries as limit recovery to persons who claim for personal injury or property damage in title of their occupation of land. But that would widen the unfortunate distinction in nuisance, itself lately questioned, between the protection for an occupier, on the one hand, and his family and licensees, on the other.[88] It might even preclude recovery by persons injured on the highway by an explosion from adjoining premises, unless the same rule were adopted which permits recovery for personal injuries suffered by reason of a *public* nuisance.[89]

The question whether the rule in *Rylands v. Fletcher* extends to personal injuries is, therefore, bound up with the related inquiry as to what nature of interest the plaintiff must have in the land on which he sustains the damage. Prior to Lord Macmillan's dictum in *Read v. Lyons*, the necessity of ownership or occupation or use of land by the plaintiff had not been broached. Indeed, once having held that strict liability attached to the escape of gas from an electric cable under the roadway to an adjacent house,[90] the courts extended it for the benefit of a co-licensee whose electricity cables were damaged by a broken water main under the same road bed.[91] Progressively the rule has since been applied to a car damaged while parked in the street,[92] to a holiday maker in Hyde Park struck by a collapsing flag pole,[93] and to a licensee of a fairground stand hit by a dislodged chair from a roundabout.[94] None of these cases lent countenance to the suggestion that standing to sue was limited as narrowly as private or public nuisance.

Nor has Lord Macmillan's suggested exclusion of all personal injury made any headway either in England[95] or elsewhere.[96] Besides lacking historical support, it would have foisted on our law the irrational distinction of testing liability for, say, explosives by whether the defendant happened to hit a casual passer-by in the street, his neighbour, or an adjoining conservatory. This would not have made much sense, even for the sake of adding another road block to strict liability.

However, purely economic loss (not resulting from damage to one's property or person) is not recoverable any more readily than in the case of negligence.[97] Thus Blackburn J. himself belittled the idea that workmen thrown out of work by the accident might have recovered their wages,[98]

87. *Miles v. Forest Rock Granite* (1918) 34 T.L.R. 500 (C.A.); *Shiffman v. Order of St John* [1936] 1 All E.R. 557; *Hale v. Jennings Bros* [1938] 1 All E.R. 579.
88. See below, p. 426. Cattle-trespass: see below, p. 355.
89. See below, p. 412.
90. *Midwood v. Manchester* [1905] 2 K.B. 597 (C.A.).
91. *Charing Cross Electricity v. Hydraulic Power Co.* [1914] 3 K.B. 772.
92. *Halsey v. Esso Petroleum* [1961] 1 W.L.R. 683.
93. *Shiffman v. Order of St John* [1936] 1 All E.R. 557 (just conceivably qualifying as an "occupier").
94. *Hale v. Jennings Bros* [1938] 1 All E.R. 579.
95. *Perry v. Kendrick's Transport* [1956] 1 W.L.R. 85 at 92 per Parker L.J. (not open to C.A.).
96. Australia: *Benning v. Wong* (1969) 122 C.L.R. 249 at 274, 277, 317. Canada: disregarded in *Aldridge v. Van Patter* [1952] 4 D.L.R. 93.
97. For negligence: see above, p. 177.
98. *Cattle v. Stockton Waterworks* (1875) L.R. 10 Q.B. 453 at 457.

and more recently auctioneers failed in a claim for the loss they suffered from the closing of a cattle market in consequence of an outbreak of foot and mouth disease due to a virus escaping from an experimental station.[99]

It is still an open question whether liability is limited to foreseeable consequences as under negligence and nuisance.[100] Several limitations on liability under different labels serve the same function as "remoteness", such as the defences (below) of Act of God and act of stranger. Moreover, as already noted,[101] the harm must fall within the risk which provided the reason for strict liability.

Defences

In the course of interpreting the rule in *Rylands v. Fletcher*, several specific exceptions or defences have been developed, in an endeavour to link it more closely to the pervasive concept of fault liability. This process has stopped only just short of actually admitting absence of negligence as an excuse. "Consent" and "default of the plaintiff" are merely versions of voluntary assumptions of risk and contributory negligence under a different name, while "act of a stranger" and "act of God" almost complete the circle of returning to negligence liability.[102] The aggregate effect of these exceptions makes it doubtful whether there is much left of the rationale of strict liability as originally contemplated in 1866.[103]

Consent of plaintiff

A plaintiff who has expressly or by implication consented to the presence of the source of danger forfeits the benefit of strict liability and is remitted to proof of negligence.[104] This principle has been most frequently invoked in cases where a lower tenant in a multiple dwelling suffers damage as the result of water seepage from an upper floor. Although sometimes explained on the ground of "common benefit", the preferred rationale seems to be that by accepting the premises with knowledge of the installation, the lower tenant consented to the risk of a non-negligent escape.[105] Its appeal is greatest when the claim is directed against the landlord[106] because of the familiar notion that a tenant takes the premises from him as they are and can complain, if at all, only of negligent injury emanating from outside the demised premises.[107] If the trouble was caused by a domestic water supply, strict liability is nowadays in any event excluded on the overriding ground of "natural user".[108]

99. *Weller v. Foot & Mouth Disease Research Institute* [1966] 1 Q.B. 569.
100. *Wagon Mound (No. 2)* [1967] 1 A.C. 617 at 639.
101. See above, p. 329.
102. These defences have an intriguing parallel in the French defences under *Civil Code* art. 1384.
103. Cf. *St Anne's Well Brewery v. Roberts* (1928) 44 T.L.R. 703 at 705.
104. *Carstairs v. Taylor* (1871) L.R. 6 Ex. 217 (water tank); *Pattison v. P.E. Conservation* (1984) 23 D.L.R. (4th) 201 (Ont.).
105. *Peters v. Prince of Wales Theatre* [1943] K.B. 73. See Samuels, *Escape of Water in Buildings*, 31 Conv. 247 (1967).
106. E.g. *British Office Supplies v. Masonic Institute* [1957] N.Z.L.R. 512; *Kiddle v. City Business* [1942] 1 K.B. 269.
107. See above, p. 471. Only a covenant may furnish additional protection.
108. See above, p. 336.

The "consent or benefit" defence retains its force, however, with regard to industrial water in bulk. It explains why the defence is not apparently available where the installation was set up after the commencement of the plaintiff's tenancy,[109] or in an action by an adjoining occupier[110] who has in no way assented to the risk, though deriving material benefit from the defendant's undertaking, as where a consumer of gas suffers damage to his house by an explosion from pipes under the control of the suppliers beneath an adjacent road.[111]

Even when denied the benefit of strict liability, the plaintiff may still succeed on proof of negligence. He obviously does not consent to a defective or dangerous water supply[112] nor to a flood caused by negligently forgetting to turn off the tap[113] or blocking up a drain with tea leaves.[114] Even if the escape was due to the act of a stranger, the defendant would be excused only if not himself remiss in guarding against it.[115]

Default of plaintiff

In *Rylands v. Fletcher* itself, it was suggested that the rule was excluded where the escape occurred owing to the plaintiff's own default.[116] This defence defeated a mine owner who, indifferent to the danger of flooding if he proceeded to work his mine under the defendant's canal, brought down the water upon himself.[117] So, by analogy to nuisance, there is no cause of complaint, at least in the absence of negligence, where the damage would not have occurred but for the abnormal sensitivity of the plaintiff's property or the use to which it is put. Thus, an action for disturbing the operation of a submarine cable by escaping electricity from a tramway system failed on the ground that one cannot increase the liability of neighbours by applying one's own property to special uses, whether for business or pleasure.[118] This argument, however, would not defeat the owner of an old building whose structural condition made it specially vulnerable to collapse from vibrations, because it would be unfair to expect him to render it proof against damage by others, not having put his property to any special or hypersensitive use.[119]

If the plaintiff's fault is not the sole cause of the "escape" but consists, for example, in failing to discover or avoid the danger, it would amount merely to contributory negligence and at most reduce his damages. Indeed

109. *Peters v. Prince of Wales Theatre* [1943] K.B. 73 at 79.
110. It is immaterial for this purpose that the plaintiff occupied adjacent, instead of subjacent, premises owned by a common landlord: *Kiddle v. City Business* [1942] 1 K.B. 269.
111. *Northwestern Utilities v. London Guarantee* [1936] A.C. 108. Cf. *Thomas v. Lewis* [1937] 1 All E.R. 137.
112. *Prosser v. Levy* [1955] 1 W.L.R. 1224.
113. *Ruddiman v. Smith* (1889) 60 L.T. 708.
114. *Abelson v. Brockman* (1890) 54 J.P. 119.
115. See below, p. 346.
116. (1866) L.R. 1 Ex. 265 at 279 per Blackburn J.
117. *Dunn v. Birmingham Canal Co.* (1872) L.R. 7 Q.B. 244. But cf. *Miles v. Forest Rock Granite Co.* (1918) 34 T.L.R. 500.
118. *Eastern & S. African Telegraph v. Cape Town Tramways* [1902] A.C. 381. Does that mean that there is a corresponding requirement of "natural user" by the *plaintiff*, as was thought in *Western Silver Fox v. Ross & Cromarty C.C.* [1940] S.L.T. 144 at 147?
119. *Hoare v. McAlpine* [1923] 1 Ch. 167.

there is some authority for excluding the defence altogether,[120] presumably on the ground that a plaintiff's negligence can be opposed only to a defendant's negligence, not to strict liability. But the risk created by one can be balanced against that of the other, and there is no obvious policy reason for abandoning here this incentive to accident prevention.

Act of God

Though recognised from the outset as a defence,[121] act of God has rarely been invoked with success. One of the few cases was *Nichols v. Marsland*,[122] where some artificial lakes had been created by damming up a natural stream. Owing to an extraordinary rainstorm of unprecedented violence, the artificial banks burst and the rush of escaping floodwater carried away some bridges. The defendant was excused after the jury had found that he could not reasonably have anticipated such an extraordinary act of nature. In a subsequent case[123] however, the correctness of this finding was challenged and, while the principle itself has stood immune from criticism, its scope is destined to be narrow.

Act of God is a term as destitute of theological meaning[124] as it is inept for legal purposes. It signifies the operation of natural forces, free from human intervention, rather than phenomena which, in common belief, are sometimes attributed to a positive intervention of deity. While it certainly includes such processes of nature as severe gales, snowstorms and cloudbursts, it may also encompass trivial occurrences like the gnawing of a rat.[125] A more appropriate term would have been vis major, were it not for the fact that this includes also malicious acts of a stranger which have been traditionally treated as a separate exception.[126]

An act of God provides no excuse, unless it is so unexpected that no reasonable human foresight could be presumed to anticipate its occurrence.[127] Sometimes it has been regarded as sufficient that it would not reasonably have been anticipated,[128] but nowadays the severer test is usually applied whether or not human foresight and prudence can be credited with reasonably recognising its *possibility*.[129] There must have been "an irresistible and unsearchable Providence nullifying all human effort".[130] It therefore seems to differ from "inevitable" accident[131] both

120. E.g. *Martins v. Hotel Mayfair* [1976] 2 N.S.W.L.R. 15 at 27. In the U.S. since apportionment, the defence is increasingly allowed against strict liability for defective products, notwithstanding *Rest. 2d* §402A comment *n*, §524; *Prosser & Keeton* §102.
121. (1866) L.R. 1 Ex. 265 at 280 per Blackburn J. It is not a defence in the U.S.: *Rest. 2d* §522.
122. (1876) 2 Ex D. 1. In *Carstairs v. Taylor* (1871) L.R. 6 Ex. 217 vis major provided one of several grounds for dismissing the action.
123. *Greenock Corp. v. Caledonian Rly* [1917] A.C. 556.
124. *The Mostyn* [1928] A.C. 57 at 93 per Lord Phillimore.
125. *Carstairs v. Taylor* (1871) L.R. 6 Ex. 217.
126. Cf. *Rickards v. Lothian* [1913] A.C. 263 at 278.
127. Thus, an ordinary whirlwind or tropical downpour, even of rather exceptional duration and intensity, cannot be set up as a defence in Australia: *Cottrell v. Allen* (1882) 16 S.A.L.R. 122; *Lamb v. Phillips* (1911) 11 S.R. (N.S.W.) 109; *Comm. Rlys v. Stewart* (1936) 56 C.L.R. 520; and cf. *Kingborough Corp. v. Bratt* [1957] Tas. S.R. 173.
128. This was the test applied in *Nichols v. Marsland* (1876) 2 Ex. D. 1.
129. *Greenock Corp. v. Caledonian Rly* [1917] A.C. 556.
130. *The Mostyn* [1928] A.C. 57 at 105 per Lord Blanesburgh. Likewise *Nugent v. Smith* (1876) 1 C.P.D. 423 at 441.
131. See above, p. 314.

in degree of unexpectability[132] and the exclusion of events having a causal link with human activity.

Act of stranger

Liability is excluded if the escape was due to the deliberate act of a stranger which could not reasonably have been anticipated. Though mentioned in the original case itself,[133] this defence is particularly difficult to reconcile with the rationale of strict liability, because it limits the duty of protection to reasonably foreseeable human interventions and equates it for this purpose with the duty of care postulated by the law of negligence. An insurer cannot plead that the accident insured against was caused by the voluntary act of a third person, because this forms an integral part of the risk. Likewise, the rule in *Rylands v. Fletcher* should consistently have exacted responsibility for all dangers inherent in the situation created by the defendant, including the risk that others may act stupidly or even maliciously.[134] The defence, however, is now well established, another example of the judicial retreat from the logic of strict liability. Thus, in an early case where it was applied to relieve a defendant from liability for the overflow of his reservoir caused by a third person emptying his own into the defendant's, the court propounded: "The matters complained of took place through no default or breach of duty of the defendants, but were caused by a stranger over whom and at a spot where they had no control."[135] This, clearly, is reasoning in terms of fault and negligent causation, not of strict liability.

The stranger's must have been "a conscious act of volition",[136] deliberate or intentional, not negligent; the owner being bound to guard against the negligence of third parties. It has been accepted as an excuse where the waste pipe of a lavatory basin was maliciously blocked up[137] and where mischievous children threw a lighted match into a petrol tank.[138] The onus is on the defendant to prove affirmatively that the escape was due to the activities of a stranger against which no reasonable precautions would have been of any use.[139] The ordinary negligence test seems to apply in determining whether, and what, measures of protection against outside interference should appropriately be taken,[140] but the high degree of risk inherent in the dangerous instrumentality may demand the most exacting standard of vigilance so as, for example, to require from a gas company a system of effective supervision to guard against interference with its mains by construction work carried out in their vicinity.[141]

132. Cf. *Comm. Rlys v. Stewart* (1936) 56 C.L.R. 520 at 528-529, 536-537.
133. *Rylands v. Fletcher* (1866) L.R. 1 Ex. 265.
134. Goodhart, *The Third Man*, 4 Cur. Leg. Prob., 178 at 183 (1951), and 72 L.Q.R. 184 (1956). Notably in the analogous case of dangerous animals, this defence is probably not recognised: see below, p. 363. *Rest. 2d* §522 exempts only deliberate mischief.
135. *Box v. Jubb* (1879) 4 Ex. D. 76 at 79.
136. *Dominion Gas Co. v. Collins* [1909] A.C. 640 at 647.
137. *Rickards v. Lothian* [1913] A.C. 263.
138. *Perry v. Kendricks Transport* [1956] 1 W.L.R. 85.
139. *Prosser v. Levy* [1955] 1 W.L.R. 1224.
140. Ibid.; also *Shiffman v. Order of St John* [1936] 1 All E.R. 557 at 561.
141. *Northwestern Utilities v. London Guarantee* [1936] A.C. 108; *Shell-Max v. Belfast Corp.* [1952] N.I. 72; *Lewis v. N. Vancouver* (1963) 40 D.L.R. (2d) 182 (water reservoir).

The category of strangers clearly includes trespassers and others who, without actually entering the defendant's premises, commit an act that causes the escape.[142] Besides, the occupier is liable not only for the defaults of his servants acting in the course of employment[143] but also of independent contractors engaged to perform work on his behalf,[144] even of invitees (like the customer who fooled about on a chair-o-plane in a fairground).[145] Should it be the same where the licensee brings the dangerous "thing" on the land for his own purposes rather than the licensor's? This would impose on the landowner a potential burden wholly disproportionate to the benefit he would derive from the licensed use; the risk potential of the licensee's activities being best known and insured by the latter. Hence gas or water leaks from pipes embedded on city or private property should be the sole responsibility of the utility.[146]

Statutory authority

Strict liability has also in large measure been withdrawn from undertakings carried out under statutory authority, like railways and public utilities supplying water, gas and electricity in bulk. Statutory authorisation has been interpreted as not only legalising the enterprise itself and thereby removing the spectre of having it enjoined as a nuisance, but also of conferring immunity for any harmful consequences which occur, without negligence, in its normal operation.[147] Thus protection is not confined only to cases were the harm suffered is a *necessary* incident of the activity expressly authorised, as where a railway empowered to run steam locomotives causes sparks or vibrations;[148] it has been extended also to cases of drains overflowing,[149] gas mains bursting[150] or electricity wires becoming dislodged.[151] This rule not only seems to be based on the fallacious assumption that there must be something unlawful about an activity to justify strict liability; it is also wrong in policy by excusing a public enterprise from internalising its own costs.[152]

The statutory immunity is lost if the grantee fails in his duty of care to avoid all unnecessary harm. He must observe the strictest safety standards, proportioned to the high degree of risk involved with respect to the

142. As in *Box v. Jubb* (1879) 4 Ex. D. 76.
143. But a servant may be a trespasser, as in *Stevens v. Woodward* (1881) 6 Q.B.D. 318 where he used a private lavatory and omitted to turn off the tap.
144. *Rylands v. Fletcher* (1866) L.R. 1 Ex. 265; *Schubert v. Sterling Trusts* [1943] 4 D.L.R. 584 (cyanide gas used by fumigator); see below, p. 391.
145. *Hale v. Jennings Bros* [1938] 1 All E.R. 579.
146. *Fenn v. Peterborough* (1979) 104 D.L.R. (3d) 174 (Ont. C.A.). Cf. *Burchett v. Comm. Rlys* [1958] S.R. (N.S.W.) 366 (involuntary licence); *Smith v. Scott* [1973] Ch. 314 (landlord not liable because not "in control").
147. The rule is much the same as for nuisance: see below, p. 439.
148. *C.P.R. v. Roy* [1902] A.C. 220; *Sermon v. Comm. Rlys* (1907) 5 C.L.R. 239. But it is under a duty of care to remove anything on its own property which increases fire hazard, such as dry grass, and to install efficient spark arresters: *Scott v. W.A. Rlys* (1957) 58 W.A.L.R. 87; *Dennis v. Victorian Rlys* (1903) 28 V.L.R. 576.
149. *Tock v. St John's Metro* [1989] 2 S.C.R. 1181.
150. *Benning v. Wong* (1969) 122 C.L.R. 249; *Dunne v. N.W. Gas Bd* [1964] 2 Q.B. 806 (C.A.).
151. *Thompson v. Bankstown Corp.* (1953) 87 C.L.R. 619.
152. Hence some modern statutes have corrected the error: e.g. *Reservoirs (Safety Provisions) Act* 1930 (U.K.); *Gas Act* 1965 (U.K.).

construction, management and possible improvement of the plant; and, to this end, is expected to avail himself of all accessible scientific aid, including independent experts.[153] There is a division of opinion, however, as to the burden of proof. According to one school, statutory authority is a defence only provided the requisite care is exercised, and this is for the defendant to establish affirmatively,[154] just as in nuisance.[155] On the other hand, a sharply divided High Court of Australia held that statutory authority completely eliminated strict liability and relegated the claimant to proof of negligence.[156]

153. *Manchester Corp. v. Farnworth* [1930] A.C. 171.

154. *Northwestern Utilities v. London Guarantee* [1936] A.C. 108 at 119, 121 per Lord Wright; consistently in Canada: e.g. *Porter v. Bell* [1955] 1 D.L.R. 62; *Turpin v. Halifax-Dartmouth* (1959) 21 D.L.R. (2d) 623.

155. See below, p. 440. Considering that *Rylands v. Fletcher* is a form of nuisance, the distinction cannot really be justified by saying, as in *Edwards v. Blue Mts C.C.* (1961) 78 W.N. (N.S.W.) 864, that the first focuses on the accumulation, the second on its consequences.

156. *Benning v. Wong* (1969) 122 C.L.R. 249. Not a word of explanation was offered whether this was fair in terms of access to evidence or compatible with the policy underlying the authorising statute. If the railway cases put the plaintiff to proof of negligence (e.g. *Rly Comm. v. Riggs* (1951) 84 C.L.R. 586), was it not because the *Fires Prevention Act* (see below, p. 349) so requires rather than just because the defendants operated under statutory authority?

17

FIRE

The law governing liability for escaping fire has undergone many changes during its long history.[1] Although the use of fire has always been recognised as a necessary adjunct to civilised existence, the measure of legal protection against its destructive potentialities has been differently assessed at progressive stages of societal development. On the one hand, improved standards of building construction and fire control have fostered a gradual relaxation of the standard of liability; fire insurance would have contributed even more towards this trend but for the fact that its prevalence in the city is not matched in the countryside.[2] On the other hand, the arid Australian climate accounts for a continuing acute sensitivity to the risk of fire and corresponding support of stricter liability as an added incentive to fire prevention.

The early common law provided a special action of trespass on the case against occupiers for "negligently using fire and allowing its escape[3] contrary to the general custom of the realm".[4] Whilst probably never absolute,[5] liability was so stringent that a defendant could acquit himself only by showing that the escape was due either to the act of a stranger or an act of God.[6] It was further presumed until the contrary was proved that the fire had been lit by him or someone for whom he was responsible.[7] The averment of negligence seems to have been mere surplusage.

The first modification was introduced by legislation, commenced in 1707 and culminating in the *Fires Prevention Act* 1775, which excused "any person in whose house, chamber, stable, barn or other building, or on whose estate any fire shall accidentally begin". The effect of this ill-drawn

1. See Ogus, *Vagaries in Liability For the Escape of Fire* [1969] Cam. L.J. 104.
2. Fire insurance offers a more efficient method of absorbing fire losses than tort liability (and liability insurance). This argues against subrogation for fire insurers and against all tort liability except for gross misconduct. Cf. Ogus [1969] Cam. L.J. 104. The problem of the uninsured victim can be resolved by leaving tort liability intact but giving the defendant a set-off for the plaintiff's fire insurance, if any, (as the Canadian *Railway Act* does; see below, n. 21), i.e. subrogating the defendant to the insurance rather than the insurer to the plaintiff.
3. From premises, not from a chattel like a fire originating in a car and damaging a public garage: *Mayfair v. Pears* [1987] 1 N.Z.L.R. 459 (C.A.).
4. The action is first heard of in *Beaulieu v. Finglam* (1401) Y.B. 2 H. IV, 18, pl. 6. Virtually nothing is known of the alternative remedies of tresspass vi et armis and the ordinary action on the case.
5. Winfield, *Myth of Absolute Liability*, 42 L.Q.R. 37 at 46-50 (1926) or *Select Essays*, 25-28; contra, Wigmore, *Responsibility for Tortious Acts: Its History*, 7 Harv. L. Rev. 315 at 448-449 (1894).
6. *Turberville v. Stampe* (1697) 1 Ld Raym. 264; 91 E.R. 1072.
7. *Becquet v. MacCarthy* (1831) 2 B. & Ad. 951 at 958; 109 E.R. 1396 at 1399.

enactment which is in force throughout Australasia[8] except in New South Wales[9] and Queensland,[10] has been a matter of some debate. Contrary to the opinion of Blackstone,[11] it was held not to excuse an occupier who was negligent with respect to the origin[12] or spread[13] of fire, although it was now for the plaintiff to show that the fire was not "accidental".[14] Moreover, for long the statute was construed as inapplicable to fires intentionally lit although non-negligent at inception and spreading without fault from the defendant's land.[15] On this view, the ancient strict liability remained intact unless the fire originated in lightning or spontaneous combustion. The favour accorded to this exceedingly narrow interpretation by some Australian courts[16] was undoubtedly influenced by their anxiety to provide maximum legal protection to landowners in face of the high danger of bushfires during summer months. Some support, however, also exists for the more liberal construction which would excuse an occupier unless either the origin or the escape of fire was due to his own negligence or that of some person for whom he can fairly be deemed responsible.[17] The dispute is of little practical significance today, because later judicial developments have further undercut the statute.

Rylands v. Fletcher

The impact of *Rylands v. Fletcher* was profound. Not only was fire itself readily treated as a *Rylands v. Fletcher* object,[18] but the position was eventually reached that the Act of 1774 afforded no defence to a *Rylands v. Fletcher* fire, however "accidental" and non-negligent.[19] Moreover, the new principle of strict liability came to be applied not only to escaping fires that had first been brought on the land (for example igniting rubbish), but also to all other things likely to catch fire and kept under conditions involving a substantial risk of spreading to neighbours, for example flammable material in a congested storage yard catching fire in an unknown

8. Vic.: *Supreme Court Act* 1958 s. 68; in other States and N.Z. by reception of English law: (S.A.) *Young v. Tilley* [1913] S.A.L.R. 87; (W.A.) *Hargrave v. Goldman* (1963) 110 C.L.R. 40 at 58; (N.Z.) *Gwynne v. Wilson* [1941] N.Z.L.R. 1 at 2.
9. *Imperial Acts Application Act* 1969 s. 8(1); *Hazelwood v. Webber* (1934) 52 C.L.R. 268.
10. *Imperial Acts Application Act* 1984. Aliter prior thereto: *Abel Lemon v. Baylin* (1985) 60 A.L.J.R. 190 (P.C.).
11. Comm. i, 431.
12. *Filliter v. Phippard* (1874) 11 Q.B. 347.
13. *Musgrove v. Pandelis* [1919] 2 K.B. 43; *Goldman v. Hargrave* [1967] 1 A.C. 645 (P.C.).
14. *How v. Jones* [1953] S.A.S.R. 82; *McAuliffe v. Hubbell* [1931] 1 D.L.R. 835; *Mason v. Levy Auto Parts* [1967] 2 Q.B. 530.
15. *Filliter v. Phippard* (1847) 11 Q.B. 347.
16. Particularly in S.A.: see *Young v. Tilley* [1913] S.A.L.R. 87 at 99. Similarly, in W.A. the statute was simply ignored in cases of fires intentionally kindled: *Craig v. Parker* (1906) 8 W.A.L.R. 161; *Prout v. Stacey* (1922) 25 W.A.L.R. 20; *Baker v. Durack* (1924) 27 W.A.L.R. 32, affd 35 C.L.R. 595. These decisions proceeded on the basis of *Rylands v. Fletcher* which seems to have been treated as identical with the common law action for the escape of fire.
17. *Eastern Asia Navigation Co. v. Fremantle Harbour* (1951) 83 C.L.R. 353 at 392-393; and see *Gwynne v. Wilson* [1941] N.Z.L.R. 1; Sutton, 34 N.Z.L.J. 87 (1958).
18. *Jones v. Festiniog Rly* (1868) L.R. 3 Q.B. 733; *Cottrell v. Allen* (1882) 16 S.A.L.R. 122; and decisions cited above, n. 16.
19. *Musgrove v. Pandelis* [1919] 2 K.B. 43; *Mulholland v. Baker* [1939] 3 All E.R. 253.

manner.[20] In the latter case neither was the fire itself brought on the land nor did the flammable object itself escape.

For a time it used to be thought that every fire intentionally lit, being a thing likely to do mischief if it escaped, entailed strict liability. Eventually however, the limitations engrafted on *Rylands v. Fletcher* also came to be applied to fires. One obvious example is the use of fire incidental to an enterprise carried on under statutory authority. Hence railways are liable only for negligence.[21] Another is the use of fire as an accepted incident of some ordinary purpose to which land is reasonably applied by the occupier.[22] Thus, while burning off in the Australian midsummer under arid conditions has been repeatedly condemned as non-natural user because of its exceptional and unjustifiable risk,[23] the lighting of fires for domestic cooking[24] or warming a room,[25] the keeping of a boiler in a flour mill for industrial purposes[26] and the use of a modern tractor for cutting a fire break even in drought conditions[27] have been held to constitute an ordinary and natural user. Aside from the purpose for which the fire is used, its reasonableness in the circumstances is also a material factor. For instance, a domestic fire for cooking food or supplying warmth assumes the use of a fireplace, a stove or some container adapted to prevent its escape; and the lighting of a fire in a suburban allotment within close proximity to a paling fence, even for the purpose of burning garden rubbish, is unreasonable and attracts strict liability.[28] In the result, this test is therefore barely distinguishable from ordinary negligence since it makes liability in effect contingent on whether the fire created an unreasonable risk of damage at the time and place.

Another encroachment of negligence is observable on the question of when an occupier is responsible for a fire started by someone else. "Act of stranger", like "act of God", was early admitted as a defence, but

20. *Mason v. Levy Auto Parts* [1967] 2 Q.B. 530; *Oceanview v. Clarry M. O'Byrne* [1989] 1 N.Z.L.R. 574.
21. See above, p. 347, n. 148. Not uncommonly statutes limit damages even for negligence: e.g. *Government Railways Act* 1912 (N.S.W.) s. 145; *Field v. State Rail* [1985] 2 N.S.W.L.R. 231; *Railway Act* (Can.) s. 338.
22. It was not until after *Rickards v. Lothian* [1913] A.C. 263 that the "natural user" exception was properly understood. "Natural user" now qualifies strict liability, whether under *Rylands v. Fletcher* or under the old common law action for the escape of fire (in so far as it has survived e.g. in N.S.W. where the 1774 Act has not been enacted): *Wise Bros v. Comm. Rlys* (1947) 75 C.L.R. 59.
23. *Hazelwood v. Webber* (1934) 52 C.L.R. 268; *Handcraft Co. v. Comm. Rlys* (1959) 77 W.N. (N.S.W.) 84; *N.Z. Forest Products v. O'Sullivan* [1974] 2 N.Z.L.R. 80. But not necessarily so, e.g. after rain: *Smith v. Badenoch* [1970] S.A.S.R. 9; *Triplett v. Cleaver* [1973] W.A.R. 173. U.S.: *Koos v. Roth* 652 P. 2d 1255 (Ore. 1982).
24. *Whinfield v. Lands Purchase Bd* (1914) 18 C.L.R. 606; *Bugge v. Brown* (1919) 26 C.L.R. 110 at 115; *Collins v. Commonwealth* (1945) 62 W.N. (N.S.W.) 245.
25. *Sochacki v. Sas* [1947] 1 All E.R. 344. Is the burning of sulphur for fumigation a natural user? Cf. *Kellett v. Cowen* [1906] Q.S.R. 116.

    A higher liability may subsist by reason of a special relationship between the parties, e.g. innkeeper and guest: *Nott v. Machurcan* (1903) 20 W.N. (N.S.W.) 135 (otherwise in States which have adopted the 1774 statute: *Williams v. Owen* [1955] 1 W.L.R. 1293 at 1298).
26. *Wise Bros v. Comm. Rlys* (1947) 75 C.L.R. 59.
27. *Mackenzie v. Sloss* [1959] N.Z.L.R. 533; *Pett v. Sims Paving* [1928] V.L.R. 247 (bitumen-melter); *Tolmer v. Darling* [1943] S.A.S.R. 81 (car fitted with gas producer).
28. *McCarty v. Leeming* [1937] S.A.S.R. 432. Accord, *Burnie Port v. General Jones* (1991) A.T.R. 81-128 (welding in vicinity of flammable material).

according to one line of authority a "stranger" must be a person over whom the occupier has no power of control.[29] Some modern cases, however, have included licensees who, in lighting a fire or allowing it to escape, acted contrary to what the occupier could have expected them to do.[30]

Negligence

Failing *Rylands v. Fletcher*, a plaintiff is remitted to proving negligence.[31] Negligence can take many forms: it may consist in the manner or place of lighting a fire (for example close to highly inflammable materials[32]) or in failing to watch it and prevent its getting out of control,[33] or in just creating a situation conducive to spontaneous combustion.[34] Again, it is now beyond question that an occupier is also in duty bound to contain a fire on his land, even if he was in no way responsible for its being there, like one lit by a trespasser or by lightning.[35] The destructive force of fire, once out of hand, is so devastating that no less could be demanded or tolerated.

Finally, a defendant is liable (whether under negligence or *Rylands v. Fletcher*) not only for actual destruction caused by the fire but also for such consequential losses as any expense reasonably incurred in attempts to save the property.[36]

29. *Holderness v. Goslin* [1975] N.Z.L.R. 46; affd on other grounds: 749. Illustrations of liability for contractors, licensees, etc.: *McInnes v. Wardle* (1931) 45 C.L.R. 548; *Casley-Smith v. Evans* (1989) A.T.R. 80-227; *Boulcott Golf Club v. Englebrecht* [1945] N.Z.L.R. 566; *Balfour v. Barty-King* [1957] 1 Q.B. 496.
30. *Eriksen v. Clifton* [1963] N.Z.L.R. 705; *Emanuel v. G.L.C.* [1971] 2 All E.R. 835 at 839 per Lord Denning.
31. In many cases, though less frequently asserted, there may also be liability for nuisance: e.g *Edwards v. Blue Mts C.C.* (1961) 78 W.N. (N.S.W.) 864 (rubbish tip).
32. *Mulholland v. Baker* [1939] 3 All E.R. 253; *Pickin v. Hesk* [1954] 4 D.L.R. 90.
33. *Bugge v. Brown* (1919) 26 C.L.R. 110; *Wise Bros v. Comm. Rlys* (1947) 75 C.L.R. 59.
34. *Vaughan v. Menlove* (1837) 3 Bing. N.C. 468; 132 E.R. 490.
35. *Goldman v. Hargrave* [1967] 1 A.C. 645; 115 C.L.R. 458 (P.C.); see below, p. 429.
36. *N.Z. Forest Products v. O'Sullivan* [1974] 2 N.Z.L.R. 80.

18

ANIMALS

In predominantly agricultural communities, like England during the formative period of the common law, damage by animals is a familiar mischief against which legal intervention is required at a very early date. Many primitive systems of law entertained the anthropomorphic notion that the animal, or even an inanimate thing,[1] was itself guilty. Later this thing-liability was exchanged for personal liability by the owner, originally with the option of surrendering the animal ("noxal surrender"). From this background of strict liability[2] emerged the two ancient principles governing a keeper of animals: he is bound at his peril to keep his cattle from trespassing and to prevent harm from animals of whose dangerous tendencies he has actual or presumed knowledge. These rules preceded the emergence of the general principle of liability for negligence and have been criticised as no longer either necessary or suitable today. They were accordingly abolished in New South Wales, South Australia and the Australian Capital Territory.[3] On the other hand, while reform is undoubtedly desirable to correct some anomalies, it is still widely felt that despite their primitive origin, these ancient instances of strict liability are not altogether incompatible with modern views of policy.[4] For, notwithstanding the usefulness of animals, their propensity for harm may well justify imposing on the owner a duty to protect the community, at his peril, against the typical risks involved in keeping them for his own benefit. Both the cattle-trespass rule and liability for dangerous animals are but instances of the wider principle of strict liability which, as we have seen, attaches to the control of all exceptionally dangerous things. They may, therefore, be linked to the rule in *Rylands v. Fletcher* for which they provided two of its principal historical sources.

In addition to these rules dealing with damage done by animals, consideration must also be given to any residuary liability under general principles of tort law, like negligence and nuisance. It is, of course, possible to be guilty of actionable negligence in the control of animals as of motor cars or other inanimate objects; and a plaintiff may find that, although recovery is precluded under the special rules, he may yet establish liability under the general. Of late, negligence has assumed greater importance in this branch of law, and several special rules have grown up which require

1. Cf. the forfeiture to the Crown, as a "deodand", the railway engine which had killed a man in *R. v. Eastern Counties Rly* (1842) 10 M. & W. 58; 152 E.R. 380. See *Deodands Abolition Act* (N.S.W.) 1849.
2. See Williams, *Animals* (1939) ch. 15. This is the classical treatise to which repeated reference is made in this chapter.
3. *Animals Act* 1977 (N.S.W.); *Wrongs Act* (S.A.) s. 17a (since 1983); *Civil Liabilities (Animals) Act* 1984 (A.C.T.). *Animals Law Reform Act* 1989 (N.Z.) s. 4 abolished the scienter rules.
4. This view of the English Law Commission is reflected in the codification of modern English law by the *Animals Act* 1971. See North, *Modern Law of Animals* (1972).

detailed attention. The subject will, therefore, be broached by considering in turn (1) cattle-trespass, (2) liability for dangerous animals, and (3) ordinary liability for negligence.

1. CATTLE-TRESPASS

Cattle-trespass is one of the most ancient causes of action known to the common law, being well established in the 14th century, if not before.[5] Whether livestock was intentionally driven or merely suffered to stray into neighbouring land, the defendant was treated as if he had committed the invasion directly, and the remedy accordingly lay in trespass rather than case.[6] Liability was strict and, unlike other forms of trespass,[7] escaped any infusion of fault. Although a progenitor of *Rylands v. Fletcher*, cattle-trespass retained its separate identity and resisted such refinements as "abnormal user", being no less controlling in predominantly grazing than in mixed farming areas or towns. In Australia, however, the rule is being viewed with increasing disfavour and has been abolished in several jurisdictions.[8]

One important exception to this stringent liability has been allowed for cattle lawfully on the highway and escaping thence unto adjoining land; this is regarded a normal hazard incident to its peculiar location, for which no redress is available to the occupier in the absence of negligence.[9] Applicable to town and country roads alike, it defeated the claim of an ironmonger into whose shop an ox strayed and there disported himself for close on an hour before being finally got out.[10] Liability devolves, however, for negligence in failing to take precautions against animals getting out of control on the highway, as when a pony attached to a milk van was left unattended in the street and bolted into a shop.[11]

Travellers on the highway cannot invoke the trespass rule and are driven to proof of negligence even as regards livestock that stray from adjoining land.[12] Yet an escape from private land across the highway and thence into adjacent property apparently engenders the strict liability of trespass.[13] This involves the anomaly that the travelling public must accept the risk of such strays, while abutting landowners need not; and that an owner of stock trespassing from the highway is liable only for negligence if he put them on the road, yet strictly liable if they strayed thither to start with. None of this makes a great deal of sense.

5. Williams, *Animals* ch. 8.
6. But there is this technical difference between the two situations: if the cattle strayed without his knowledge and against his will, the action is for cattle-trespass; whereas if he drove his cattle unto another's land or permitted them to remain there for an unreasonable time after becoming aware of their escape, the trespass is his own: *Hunt v. Shanks* [1918] S.A.L.R. 254.
7. See above, pp. 18-24.
8. See above, n. 3.
9. *Goodwyn v. Cheveley* (1859) 28 L.J. Ex. 298; *Bourchier v. Mitchell* (1891) 17 V.L.R. 27; *Rayner v. Shearing* [1926] S.A.S.R. 313.
10. *Tillett v. Ward* (1882) 10 Q.B.D. 17.
11. *Gayler & Pope v. Davies* [1924] 2 K.B. 75.
12. *Cox v. Burbidge* (1863) 13 C.B. (N.S.) 430; 143 E.R. 171. Even liability for negligence used to be circumscribed: see below, p. 365.
13. *D'Agruima v. Seymour* (1951) 69 W.N. (N.S.W.) 15.

The action is predicated on trespass to *land*. A licensee on it is therefore disqualified because neither can he complain of trespass to the land nor is a technical trespass to his person or chattel sufficient. Thus if a mare in an agistment paddock is savaged either by a trespassing bull or by another agisted horse, her owner might sue for negligence, but not for cattle-trespass.[14]

"Cattle" is a comprehensive category, synonymous with the old term "avers" and including not only oxen, horses, donkeys, sheep, goats, and pigs but also fowls, ducks, geese and possibly tame deer.[15] Dogs[16] and cats,[17] however, are excluded. This immunity has been justified on a variety of grounds, ranging from the implausible argument that they are not larcenable at common law because there is no property in them,[18] to the more convincing reasons that it is undesirable, if not impossible, to keep them under the same restraint as cattle and that their propensity for damage during transient incursions is negligible compared with that of bigger and heavier animals like cows and horses.[19] But an adjacent occupier who is pestered by his neighbour's dog or cat is not entirely bereft of remedy: a master of hounds may be liable for his own trespass "by hounds" if he either intended or negligently failed to prevent them from trespassing;[20] and if the occupier's property is threatened with destruction, he may at least resort to self-help and ward off the attack by means appropriate to the occasion.[21] Finally, dogs of mischievous propensity expose their keeper to a different rule of strict liability.[22]

Liability rests on the possessor of the straying animal, usually the adjoining occupier. But not on the owner as such, like one who has transfered possession to an agistor.[23]

Damage

Originally, cattle-trespass supported only claims for damage to the surface of the land and depasturing of crops,[24] but gradually the range of protection widened and came to include injury to the plaintiff's livestock from infection,[25] physical attack[26] or misbreeding as when a trespassing

14. *Matheson v. Stuckey* [1921] V.L.R. 637; *Manton v. Brocklebank* [1923] 2 K.B. 212; *Edwards v. Rawlins* [1924] N.Z.L.R. 333. The agistor also may be liable for negligence, as in *Smith v. Cook* (1875) 1 Q.B.D. 79; *Sanderson v. Dunn* (1911) 32 A.L.T. (Supp.) 14.
15. See Williams, *Animals* (1939) ch. 9.
16. Curiously enough, although more or less accepted for hundreds of years, there is singularly little authority. But though denied as late as 1880 in Victoria, it is now beyond challenge: *Tallents v. Bell* [1944] 2 All E.R. 474; and see Williams, *Animals* 137-146.
17. *Buckle v. Holmes* [1926] 2 K.B. 125.
18. *Mason v. Keeling* (1700) 12 Mod. 332 at 335; 88 E.R. 1359 at 1361.
19. *Cox v. Burbidge* (1863) 13 C.B. (N.S.) 430 at 440-441; 143 E.R. 171 at 174; *Buckle v. Holmes* [1926] 2 K.B. 125 at 128-129.
20. *League against Cruel Sports v. Scott* [1986] Q.B. 240.
21. See above, p. 87.
22. See below, p. 357.
23. See the English Act s. 4(2).
24. At least the agistment value may be recoverable: *Yakamia Dairy v. Wood* [1976] W.A.R. 57.
25. *Theyer v. Purnell* [1918] 2 K.B. 333.
26. *Lee v. Riley* (1865) 18 C.B. (N.S.) 722; 144 E.R. 629; *Ellis v. Loftus Iron Co.* (1874) L.R. 10 C.P. 10; *Doyle v. Vance* (1880) 6 V.L.R. (L.) 87.

"scrub" bull served a thoroughbred heifer[27] or just trespassed on land on which stud cows were grazing, with the result that their owner could no longer guarantee that none were in calf to the bull.[28] More recently the action has been applied also to the derailment of a train[29] and even bodily injury to an occupier who collided with a trespassing animal in the dark.[30]

The last-mentioned extension projected the related question of whether liability extends beyond damage natural to the species of the trespassing animal. According to one view, the action should be available even to an occupier[31] who is savaged,[32] but another would limit it to personal injuries due to bumping or other non-vicious collisions.[33] Undoubtedly, it is more consonant with the nature of the action to confine redress to the normal consequences typical of the risks involved in the trespass,[34] rather than extend its range to situations already adequately covered by the rules of liability for *dangerous* animals. This, after all, is the gist of what is often expressed in more conventional language by saying that liability does not extend beyond *foreseeable* damage, having regard both to the natural propensity of the animal and other circumstances of the accident.

Defences

Few defences have received a great deal of attention in modern times; most are identical with those under *Rylands v. Fletcher*.

First, a claim may be met with the plea that the damage was due to the plaintiff's own default, like his failure to maintain an adequate fence when under a duty to do so.[35] But in the absence of a covenant or prescriptive right between adjoining occupiers, neither is obliged to fence "out" rather than "in".[36] Only scattered legislation bars a landowner without an "adequate fence" from recovery.[37]

27. *McLean v. Brett* (1919) 49 D.L.R. 162; *Cousins v. Greaves* (1920) 54 D.L.R. 650.
28. *Halstead v. Mathieson* [1919] V.L.R. 362.
29. *Cooper v. Rly Executive* [1953] 1 W.L.R. 223.
30. *Wormald v. Cole* [1954] 1 Q.B. 614. The *Animals Act* 1971 (Eng.) s. 4 limits liability to property damage: North, *Animals* (1972) ch. 3.
31. According to the prevailing view, only the occupier can complain of trespass: *Wormald v. Cole* [1954] 1 Q.B. 614 at 631; Williams, *Animals* (1939) 175. This would invidiously exclude his licensees, employees and family members and relegate them to negligence; contra: *Waugh v. Montgomery* (1882) 8 V.L.R. (L.) 290 (daughter); *Bradley v. Wallaces* [1913] 3 K.B. 629 (semble, employee). The *Animals Act* 1971 (Eng.), by imposing liability on "straying" instead of "trespassing", has abolished this requirement: North, *Animals* (1972) 94-95.
32. *Wormald v. Cole* [1954] 1 Q.B. 614 at 625 per Lord Goddard C.J.; and cf. ibid. at 633 per Hodson L.J.
33. *Mark v. Barkla* [1935] N.Z.L.R. 347; *Cox v. Burbidge* (1863) 13 C.B. (N.S.) 430 at 436-437; 143 E.R. 171 at 173; and see *Wormald v. Cole* [1954] 1 Q.B. 614 at 620.
34. But this would include a trespassing horse kicking a plaintiff who is attempting to drive it off: *Waugh v. Montgomery* (1882) 8 V.L.R. (L.) 290; *Rest. 2d* §504; 49 A.L.R. 4d 710 (1986).
35. *Singleton v. Williamson* (1861) 7 H. & N. 410; 158 E.R. 533; *Crow v. Wood* [1971] 1 Q.B. 77 (C.A.).
36. See *Jones v. Price* [1965] 2 Q.B. 618 (C.A.); *Bruce v. Spencer* [1985] 1 Qd R. 396. Moreover, a covenant by the defendant would only avail a plaintiff privy to it: *Park v. Jobson* [1945] 1 All E.R. 222.
37. *Impounding Act* 1955 (N.Z.) s. 26; see *McKenzie v. Risk* [1974] 2 N.Z.L.R. 214. Only for crop damage: *Cattle-Trespass, Fencing and Impounding Act* 1882-1957 (W.A.) s. 22; see

Secondly, there is some authority for saying that a defendant is excused if the escape or trespass was due to the act of a third party for whom he is not responsible, as when a stranger negligently leaves a gate open[38] or actually drives the other's cattle unto the plaintiff's land.[39] It would perhaps be anomalous if this defence, clearly established under *Rylands v. Fletcher*, were not also applicable here, although there is no reason in policy why responsibility should not encompass the risk of malicious or negligent intervention of strangers.[40] It clearly does, at all events if the defendant was aware of it or could have guarded against it, as when the owner of an intervening plot failed in his duty to fence so as to keep the defendant's cattle out, but the latter was cognisant of this neglect and had taken no steps in the matter for many years.[41]

Thirdly, act of God is probably a defence just as under *Rylands v. Fletcher*, if for example an extraordinary gale were to blow down a gate or a flash of lightning strike such terror into cattle that they stampeded through a fence.[42]

2. DANGEROUS ANIMALS

Strict liability for damage by dangerous animals, though of ancient origin,[43] received its modern formulation in 1846 when, in *May v. Burdett*,[44] the plaintiff recovered for a bite by the defendant's monkey without proof of negligence. Anyone who keeps a mischievous animal does so at his peril, being responsible for the harm it may do in indulging its dangerous instincts, provided he knows or is presumed to know its vicious disposition. This rule is not so much a vestigial relic of archaic doctrine as an illustration of the strict liability which modern law places on those who expose the community to exceptional risks. There is nothing unlawful in keeping a pet tiger or a vicious bull; but society exacts for it a strict responsibility to ensure that they do not get out of control or else to compensate the victim regardless of fault. While tolerating the keeping of dangerous animals for reason of their usefulness and social acceptance, the law imposes strict liability as the price for that permission.[45] This principle is akin to *Rylands v. Fletcher* but differs in two significant respects. In the first place, liability for dangerous animals postulates knowledge, express or

37. *Continued*
Kratochvil v. Dall (1955) 57 W.A.L.R. 55. Otherwise, fencing legislation in Australia does not seem to prejudice claims for cattle-trespass: see *Rutherford v. Hayward* (1877) 3 V.L.R. (L.) 19.
38. *M'Gibbon v. M'Curry* (1909) 43 Ir. L.T.R. 132. But should the defendant not have taken precautions to guard against this eventuality? Here there was a public right of way.
39. *Smith v. Stone* (1647) Style 65; 82 E.R. 533; contra: *Topladye v. Stalye* (1649) Style 165 at 166; 82 E.R. 615; *Hunt v. Shanks* [1918] S.A.L.R. 254 at 262.
40. Cf. above, p. 346.
41. *Sutcliffe v. Holmes* [1947] 1 K.B. 147.
42. Williams, *Animals* 184-185.
43. It has been traced as far back as 1387, as an action on the case: Williams, *Animals* 278.
44. (1846) 9 Q.B. 101; 115 E.R. 1213.
45. Even when the animal is being kept for a purpose beneficial to the community, as in a zoo, rather than for private luxury or for a public entertainment run for private profit, as in a circus. Some American courts have weakened in this respect: see *Rest. 2d* §517; *Prosser & Keeton* 567-568.

imputed, of their vicious propensity (hence its name: scienter liability), whereas under the other rule it is immaterial whether the defendant appreciated the potentiality of danger. In this aspect, therefore, it straddles negligence and strict liability.[46] Secondly, the animal need not have "escaped" to adjoining land nor even been at large.[47]

The complexity of this branch of law, about to be explored, persuaded the Goddard Committee in 1953 to recommend the complete abolition of scienter liability, believing that negligence law would take sufficient account of the special risks posed by dangerous animals. New South Wales, South Australia, the Australian Capital Territory and New Zealand have adopted this reform,[48] whle England eventually followed the more modest course of merely modifying the existing law.[49]

Dangerous animals

Dangerous animals are divided into two classes: (1) animals ferae naturae, like bears and lions, which by reason of their species are normally dangerous, although individuals may be more or less tame; and (2) animals mansuetae naturae, like cows and dogs, which as a kind are ordinarily harmless, though individuals may harbour a vicious or dangerous disposition.[50] Animals of the first category are never regarded as safe, and liability attaches for the harm they may do without proof that the particular animal is savage. The law rigidly ignores the world of difference between a wild elephant in the jungle and his trained brother in the circus.[51] But as regards the second class, it must be shown that the *particular* animal was dangerous and that the defendant knew, or had reason to know, it. There is also this other difference that the very risk inherent in animals ferae naturae is that, in perpetrating harm, they are coming true to nature and are acting in accordance with the instinct of their species, whereas liability for a dangerous animal mansuetae naturae is based on the belief that it has acted contrary to the nature of its kind. Responsibility is accordingly limited to these particular hazards.

The test for classifying a species appears to be its special danger to mankind.[52] This may well seem anomalous because, despite this emphasis

46. German and French law (Louisiana: *Holland v. Buckley* 305 So. 2d 113 (1974)) do not recognise even that limitation.
47. E.g. *Christian v. Johannesson* [1956] N.Z.L.R. 644 and *McNeill v. Frankenfield* (1963) 44 D.L.R. (2d) 132 (on running leads). *Rands v. McNeil* [1955] 1 Q.B. 253 (C.A.) however postulated escape from control (farmhands gored by bulls inside their boxes), not followed in *Higgins v. Inglis* (1978) 1 N.S.W.L.R. 649 (C.A.) and abandoned by the *Animals Act* 1971 (Eng.) s. 2; North, *Animals* (1972) 70, 74.
48. *Animals Act* 1977 (N.S.W.); *Wrongs Act* (S.A.) s. 17a (since 1983); *Civil Liabilities (Animals) Act* 1984 (A.C.T.); *Animals Law Reform Act* 1989 (N.Z.).
49. *Animals Act* 1971, following the Law Commissior No. 13 (1967).
50. These Latin phrases are hallowed by traditional usage but apt to mislead. The relevant distinction is not between "wild" and "domestic" or "tame" (appropriate to questions of property in animals), but between "dangerous" and "harmless". Rabbits and pigeons may be "wild", but are classified as "harmless". For this reason, the language of *Rest. 2d* §506 is objectionable in adopting the dichotomy of "wild" and "domestic", in literal translation of the Latin terms.
51. *Behrens v. Mills Circus* [1957] 2 Q.B. 1.
52. *Buckle v. Holmes* [1926] 2 K.B. 125 at 129; *McQuaker v. Goddard* [1940] 1 K.B. 687 at 695. The *Animals Act* 1971 (Eng.) s. 6 postulates propensity for "severe" damage: North, *Animals* (1972) 34-43.

on the risk of personal injury, there is no reason to believe that liability would not extend also to property damage perpetrated by a member of that class.[53] Besides, there are some animals, like rabbits in Australia, which though harmless to human beings, are notoriously destructive. Yet these are necessarily excluded from the compass of strict liability, so long as danger to property is not recognised as an alternative criterion.[54] Hitherto only bears,[55] zebras,[56] elephants,[57] chimpanzees[58] and dingoes[59] have been branded as dangerous, camels being acquitted both in Australia[60] and England.[61] If the animal is not indigenous here, consideration has been given to its status in the countries in which it is commonly found, but there is no reason for treating as conclusive the mere fact that the species, like camels, is no longer anywhere in a wild state; for, though reduced to the service of mankind, it may still retain sufficient traces of savagery.[62] Classification of a particular species is a question of law for the court, to be decided either on the basis of judicial notice or expert evidence,[63] and once made is not, subject to the ordinary rules of precedent, open to reconsideration.[64]

Scienter

When an animal of harmless species betrays its own kind by perpetrating damage, its keeper will not be held to strict liability unless actually aware of its dangerous disposition. This proof[65] is known technically as "the scienter" which derives from the old style declaration, charging the defendant with *knowingly* keeping a dangerous animal.[66] The requisite knowledge must relate to the particular propensity that caused the damage: if a horse bites a man, it is not sufficient that it was known to bite other horses.[67]

53. Although there is no English or Australian decision on damage to property, the matter is hardly in doubt.
54. As it is now in England see above, n. 52.
55. *Besozzi v. Harris* (1858) 1 F. & F. 92; 175 E.R. 640; *Andrew v. Kilgour* (1910) 19 Man. L.R. 545 (indigenous raccoon).
56. *Marlor v. Ball* (1900) 16 T.L.R. 239.
57. *Filburn v. People's Palace* (1890) 25 Q.B.D. 258; *Behrens v. Mills Circus* [1957] 2 Q.B. 1.
58. *James v. Wellington City* [1972] N.Z.L.R. 70, 978. Possibly not all species of monkey should be treated alike (cf. the 12 in. grass monkey in *Brook v. Cook* (1961) 105 Sol. J. 684). In *May v. Burdett* (1846) 9 Q.B. 101; 115 E.R. 1213 the owner had scienter.
59. *Fischer v. Stuart* (1979) 25 A.L.R. 336 (N.T.).
60. *Nada Shah v. Sleeman* (1917) 19 W.A.L.R. 119.
61. *McQuaker v. Goddard* [1940] 1 K.B. 687.
62. The inclination in *McQuaker v. Goddard* to equate "domesticated" with "harmless" (in company with *Rest. 2d* §506) is criticised by Williams, *Camel Case*, 56 L.Q.R. 354 (1940), but was retained by the *Animals Act* 1971 (Eng.) ("commonly domesticated in the British Isles"). Also, wild animals are "assumed" (presumed) to be dangerous: *McQuaker v. Goddard* [1940] 1 K.B. 687 at 695.
63. *McQuaker v. Goddard* [1940] 1 K.B. 687 at 700-701.
64. *Heath's Garage v. Hodges* [1916] 2 K.B. 370 at 383.
65. But very slight evidence has been held sufficient to go to a jury, the matter being peculiarly within the defendant's knowledge: *Cruttendon v. Brenock* [1949] V.L.R. 366 at 368; *Newsam v. Ladd* [1972-1973] Arg. L.R. 1372 (A.C.T.); but cf. *Eather v. Jones* (1975) 49 A.L.J.R. 254. *Dowler v. Bravender* (1968) 67 D.L.R. (2d) 734 at 738 actually placed onus of disproof on defendant.
66. The same declaration was used in relation to animals ferae naturae, but the requisite knowledge was conclusively presumed.
67. *Glanville v. Sutton* [1928] 1 K.B. 571.

In proving scienter, it is not necessary that the animal had actually done the particular kind of harm on a previous occasion; it is sufficient if, to the defendant's knowledge, it had manifested a trait to do that kind of harm, as where a dog habitually rushed out of its kennel and strained on its chain to bite passing strangers.[68] Hence, the popular saw that "every dog has one free bite" is not literally accurate.

Knowledge may be imputed to the defendant. If acquired by someone to whom he delegated full custody and control of the animal, it is imputed as a matter of law;[69] in other cases it may be inferred that knowledge gained by a third party (for example, whilst having control of premises on which the dog was kept) had been communicated to him.[70] In neither situation need he be the owner's servant or a member of his family.[71]

With respect to dogs, statutes in many jurisdictions[72] dispense with scienter, that is, the need to show a previous mischievous propensity in the dog, or the owner's knowledge thereof, or that the injury was attributable to neglect on the part of the owner.[73] In most instances the owner's[74] strict liability applies to *any* injury[75] and has been liberally construed to cover not only bites and other hostile acts but also collisions with motorists and the like.[76]

Scope of liability

Strict liability is not germane to an animal of harmless species, unless it is prone to be "vicious, mischievous or fierce". Admittedly, it is not a conclusive answer that the animal was merely indulging a propensity not abnormal to its species, since otherwise an owner could too readily disclaim responsibility for all manner of aggressive mischief, despite his awareness of such dangerous traits as a bull "seeing red",[77] a ram given to butting,[78]

68. *Worth v. Gilling* (1866) L.R. 2 C.P. 1; *Barnes v. Lucille* (1907) 96 L.T. 680.
69. *Scott v. Edington* (1888) 14 V.L.R. 41 (servant); *Baldwin v. Casella* (1872) L.R. 7 Ex. 325 (servant).
70. *Applebee v. Percy* (1974) L.R. 9 C.P. 647 (servant); *Gladman v. Johnson* (1867) 36 L.J.C.P. 153 (wife). It is not enough that only servant A knows, while servant B has custody (*Maclean v. Forestry Comm.* 1970 S.L.T. 265), nor if a servant keeps a dog as a private pet: *Knott v. L.C.C.* [1934] 1 K.B. 126.
71. *Cruttendon v. Brenock* [1949] V.L.R. 366 (friend).
72. In Australia all except Qld. See *Dog Acts* of N.S.W. (1966 ss. 20-22B), Vic. (1970 s. 22), S.A. (1979 s. 52), W.A. (1976 s. 46), Tas. (*Law of Animals Act* 1962 s. 15), A.C.T. (1975 s. 40), N.T. (1980 s. 68), *Dog Control and Hydatids Act* 1982 (N.Z.) s. 61, *Law Reform (Miscellaneous Provisions) Act* (N.Z.) s. 32, Eng. (1906, 1928).
73. *Knowlson v. Solomon* [1969] N.Z.L.R. 686 held this additional negligence presumption to be rebuttable. Note also the Canadian trend of dispensing only with proof of knowledge, but not of vicious propensity (but see *Lupu v. Rabinovitch* (1975) 60 D.L.R. (3d) 641), or to reverse merely the onus of proof; deplored by Gibson, 42 Can. B. Rev. 141 (1964).
74. Under the most recent Acts, also the possessor's.
75. None of the Australian Acts are now limited, as is the English, to "injury done to horses, cattle or poultry". Vic.: "any person or any horse".
76. *Martignoni v. Harris* [1971] 2 N.S.W.L.R. 102 (C.A.); *Twentieth Century v. Howes* [1974] 1 N.S.W.L.R. 244 (C.A.); *Simpson v. Bannerman* (1932) 47 C.L.R. 378; *Irving v. Slevin* (1982) 30 S.A.S.R. 66. But in N.S.W. (1977) and W.A. (1983) strict liability is no longer applicable to dogs straying unto highway. Contributory negligence (in N.S.W. expressly), volenti and trespass are recognised defences.
77. *Hudson v. Roberts* (1851) 6 Ex. 697; 155 E.R. 724. Bulls are actually colour-blind.
78. *Jackson v. Smithson* (1846) 15 M. & W. 563; 153 E.R. 973.

or a bitch with pups to snap,[79] a hunting dog destroying pheasants,[80] dogs defending their territory[81] or worrying sheep,[82] and even a mare kicking a horse.[83] Yet the behaviour must be offensive or hostile to man or beast: a mere propensity to perpetrate occasional damage because of playfulness or some other non-aggressive characteristic, especially when it is shared by the rest of its species—such as an inclination of horses to shy,[84] of unbroken fillies to be high spirited,[85] of cats and dogs to chase each other[86] or run across traffic[87]—is not sufficient for strict liability, whatever its demands on the exercise of reasonable care.

Not unrelated is the question of whether strict liability runs to any injury a dangerous animal happens to cause or only to harm attributable to its vicious propensity. At least with respect to animals mansuetae naturae, the second solution is generally favoured since it is felt unreasonable to hold the owner of a biting dog responsible for everything that it may do, such as accidentally knocking down a child or covering a pedigree bitch.[88] Opinion is more sharply divided regarding animals ferae naturae. American courts have taken the view that, here too, responsibility should be confined to such consequences as lie within the special risk warranting strict liability, and accordingly withheld relief when a horse bolted at the mere sight of a circus elephant in a street.[89] In contrast, an English court has adopted the more stringent position that liability is not limited to savage acts but applies equally where a scared elephant runs after a barking dog or someone suffers a heart attack on seeing an escaped tiger, however amiable, on top of his bed.[90] Yet liability in the last-mentioned cases could well be reconciled with a general refusal to push responsibility beyond the special risks involved in the keeping of dangerous animals, since in both the beast was really out of control and caused harm broadly within the foreseeable risks of the situation.

The scienter action is available regardless of whether the victim was injured on his own land, on the highway[91] or even while lawfully on the

79. *Barnes v. Lucille* (1907) 96 L.T. 680.
80. *Read v. Edwards* (1864) 17 C.B. (N.S.) 245; 144 E.R. 99; and perhaps even rabbits: semble *Tallents v. Bell* [1964] 2 All E.R. 474.
81. *Curtis v. Betts* [1990] 1 W.L.R. 459 (C.A.).
82. The classical application of the scienter rule.
83. *Manton v. Brocklebank* [1923] 2 K.B. 212 where it was assumed that there would have been liability if scienter had been proved, notwithstanding that the animal had not acted "contrary to horse nature".
84. *Cutler v. United Dairies* [1933] 2 K.B. 297 at 302-303.
85. *Fitzgerald v. Cooke Bourne* [1964] 1 Q.B. 249.
86. Semble, *Clinton v. Lyons* [1912] 3 K.B. 198 at 211.
87. *Martignoni v. Harris* [1971] 2 N.S.W.L.R. 102 (C.A.) (passim).
88. *Behrens v. Mills Circus* [1957] 2 Q.B. 1 at 17; *Glanville v. Sutton* [1928] 1 K.B. 571 (known propensity to bite other horses not sufficient for biting a man).
89. *Scribner v. Kelley* 38 Barb. 14 (N.Y. 1862); *Bostock-Ferari v. Brocksmith* 73 N.E. 281 (Ind. 1905).
90. *Behrens v. Mills Circus* [1957] 2 Q.B. 1. Cf. *Brook v. Cook* (1961) 105 Sol. J. 684.
91. Although a person injured in a highway accident is otherwise bound to prove negligence, this requirement does not seem to apply to scienter actions (see e.g. *Scott v. Edington* (1888) 14 V.L.R. 41; *Hudson v. Roberts* (1851) 6 Ex. 697; 155 E.R. 724) or under the Dog Acts: *Grimwood v. Campbell* [1955] S.A.S.R. 313; *Wallis v. Dawkins* (1881) 15 S.A.L.R. 132.

defendant's premises.[92] Hence liability may well be measured by a higher standard than that ordinarily controlling the particular relationship between the parties.

Responsibility devolves not on the owner as such[93] but on the "keeper", that is whoever harbours and controls the animal, like a trainer who kept in his stables someone else's horse that he knew to be accustomed to bite,[94] or an occupier who took care of a vicious dog left on the premises by a previous tenant.[95] But the mere fact that an occupier has tolerated an animal, which he neither possesses nor owns, to stay on his land is not sufficient.[96] Thus a father was acquitted for injury by a dog owned and fed by his daughter of responsible age,[97] and a school when a pet dog kept by the caretaker mauled a charlady.[98] Nor would it seem that a keeper's liability attaches to wild animals indigenous to a national park, like grizzlies in Canada and the United States.[99] While the special statutory liability for dogs, already noted, rests expressly on the owner, it remains unclear whether owners out of possession are liable at common law. On the basis that strict liability is non-delegable, it has been held that an owner cannot escape by delegating custody to a servant or even to an independent contractor, like an auctioneer.[100]

Defences

The range of defences is exceedingly limited. Indeed, no excuse seems to be admitted except the plaintiff's own responsibility in exposing himself to injury.

It is well settled, for example, that the defendant may take advantage of the victim having brought the injury upon himself through his own fault, as by stroking a zebra that is improperly secured[101] or actually teasing an animal,[102] though not by merely walking close to it unless in unreasonable disregard of obvious danger.[103] Authority is unclear on whether contributory negligence ever constituted a defence such as would now reduce damages.[104] Voluntary assumption of risk remains a complete

92. So also under Dog Acts: *Postuma v. Campbell* (1984) 37 S.A.S.R. 321 (F.C.). Alternatively, though, he may proceed against the defendant for breach of an occupier's duty: see *Clinton v. Lyons* [1912] 3 K.B. 198. But if the plaintiff is a trespasser, he cannot ordinarily complain if bitten by a dog, and the scienter rule is only available to him in so far as it does not exceed the degree of protection which an occupier owes a trespasser: see below, p. 464. The *Animals Act* 1977 (N.S.W.) s. 7 extended this rule to all visitors.
93. Aliter, the *Animals Act* 1971 (Eng.) s. 6(3)(a).
94. *Walker v. Hall* (1876) 40 J.P. 456.
95. *M'Kone v. Wood* (1831) 5 C. & P. 1; 172 E.R. 850. Contrast *Smith v. Gt E. Rly* (1866) L.R. 2 C.P. 4.
96. But he may be liable for breach of his duty as occupier.
97. *North v. Wood* [1914] 1 K.B. 629. Contrast the "family dog" in *Stanford v. Robertson* [1946] 3 W.W.R. 767.
98. *Knott v. L.C.C.* [1934] 1 K.B. 126.
99. In *Sturdy v. R.* (1974) 47 D.L.R. (3d) 71 claim was made only for negligence.
100. *Higgins v. Inglis* [1978] 1 N.S.W.L.R. 649 at 653.
101. *Marlor v. Ball* (1900) 16 T.L.R. 239.
102. *Filburn v. People's Palace* (1890) 25 Q.B.D. 258 at 260; also *Sycamore v. Ley* (1932) 147 L.T. 342; *Lee v. Walkers* (1939) 162 L.T. 89.
103. *Besozzi v. Harris* (1858) 1 F. & F. 92; 175 E.R. 640; *Wyatt v. Rosherville Gardens* (1886) 2 T.L.R. 282; *McNeill v. Frankenfield* (1963) 44 D.L.R. (2d) 132.
104. *Higgins v. Inglis* [1978] 1 N.S.W.L.R. 649 (C.A.) found no such authority despite textbooks and the clear policy preference reflected in the *Animals Act* 1972 (Eng.) s. 10.

defence, though nowadays rarely applicable except to zookeepers, veterinarians and the like[105] or trespassers with knowledge of a vicious guard dog.[106] But trespassers cannot in any event avail themselves of strict liability for dangerous animals[107] and are relegated to the minimal standard of care demanded from occupiers;[108] ordinarily it is regarded as perfectly reasonable to employ guard dogs even for the specific purpose of protecting person or property,[109] let alone to depasture a bull in a paddock.[110] On the other hand, a passer-by in the street who unwittingly places his hand upon the fence does not thereby lose the protection to which users of the highway are entitled from an adjacent landowner who knowingly keeps a vicious dog.[111]

By analogy to *Rylands v. Fletcher*, "act of a stranger" might be considered a possible defence, but the authorities are conflicting. The House of Lords once excused the owner of a fierce dog let off its chain by a trespasser,[112] but more recent decisions have squarely taken the view that the wrongful act of a third party furnishes no defence; though it is perhaps not without significance that the culprit in the one case was actually a servant entrusted with looking after the savage dog[113] and in the other a licensee whose own pet merely provoked the defendant's circus elephant to pursuit into a midget's booth.[114] Despite some criticism, this conclusion, however stringent, appears to proceed on the unexceptionable premise that a stranger's intervention should be deemed within the risk created by the possession of dangerous animals. It finds additional support in the consideration that the owner is better placed to protect himself by insurance than the fortuitous victim of the animal's aggression.[115]

It is doubtful whether act of God is a defence;[116] in any event the narrow scope given to that plea under *Rylands v. Fletcher*[117] robs the problem of practical significance.

3. NEGLIGENCE

Notwithstanding some occasional confusion in the past, it is now well settled that the cattle-trespass and scienter rules do not abridge other

105. *James v. Wellington City* [1972] N.Z.L.R. 978 (C.A.); *Rands v. McNeil* [1955] 1 Q.B. 253 at 257 per Denning L.J. The *Animals Act* 1971 (Eng.) s. 6(5) excludes the defence (s. 5(2)) against persons employed as animal keepers.
106. *Cummings v. Granger* [1977] Q.B. 397.
107. *Pearson v. Coleman* [1948] 2 K.B. 359 at 371. Dog Acts: *Trethowan v. Capron* [1961] V.R. 460; *Chittenden v. Hale* [1933] N.Z.L.R. 836. Cf. *Animals Act* 1971 (Eng.) s. 5.
108. See below.
109. See above, p. 89.
110. Cf. *Lowery v. Walker* [1911] A.C. 10.
111. *Simpson v. Bannerman* (1932) 47 C.L.R. 378.
112. *Fleeming v. Orr* (1855) 2 Macq. 14. Though a Scottish appeal, Lord Cranworth specifically disclaimed any difference between the two systems.
113. *Baker v. Snell* [1908] 2 K.B. 825.
114. *Behrens v. Mills Circus* [1957] 2 Q.B. 1.
115. Goodhart, *The Third Man*, 4 Cur. Leg. Prob. 184 (1951). In England the defence disappeared in any event with the *Animals Act* 1971.
116. *Nichols v. Marsland* (1875) L.R. 10 Ex. 225 at 260. In England this defence was omitted from the *Animals Act* 1972.
117. See above, p. 345.

general principles of tort liability like nuisance or negligence. Thus a public nuisance may be committed by permitting cattle to obstruct road traffic.[118] Likewise, the ordinary duty of care requires that an animal, like anything else under one's control, does not become a source of harm to others. It matters nothing whether the defendant causes a collision by negligently driving his car or galloping a horse;[119] whether he trips a pedestrian by throwing a lasso or allowing his dog on a long leash to entangle him;[120] whether he causes fright to breeding mink with bulldozer or bulldog.[121]

What is more, the negligence principle plays a role not only in cases, such as the preceding, of collisions or other accidental injury caused by animals;[122] modern decisions have applied it equally to vicious or hostile aggression by animals, as a complement to scienter liability or, as in some States[123] now, the sole basis of liability. In a modern case which placed this beyond doubt,[124] an infant was savaged by a pack of terrier puppies suddenly dashing across from next door. The dogs had not previously misbehaved, but had frequently raided the adjoining premises on scavenging expeditions. Although knowledge of vicious propensity on the part of any one dog could not be imputed to the owner, he was nevertheless held responsible for his negligence in allowing the dogs to escape. As an experienced breeder he should have known their propensity, when in a pack, to attack moving persons or objects; and though aware of their habit to dash next door, had neither kept them in a compound nor even maintained a fence.

What differentiates animals from inanimate objects is their capacity for spontaneous action; but though well known, this does not by itself present a sufficient risk to make the owner liable for every mischief the animal happens to perpetrate while free of constraint. There must be a special risk of injury to others, as in the preceding case on account of the breed's pack behaviour. Moreover, the very accident that occurred must have been foreseeable: not necessarily (any more than in other contexts) the precise happening, but broadly the same kind. For example, it was sufficient to foresee that the toddler next door might get hurt from being bowled over and scratched rather than from actually being bitten all over his body. On the other hand, while it is foreseeable that a spirited horse breaking away might knock a passer-by,[125] it would not be if it celebrated its freedom by biting him.[126]

118. *S.G.I.C. v. Trigwell* (1979) 142 C.L.R. 617 at 638.
119. See e.g. *Southall v. Jones* (1879) 5 V.L.R. (L.) 402; *Barrett v. Hardie* [1924] N.Z.L.R. 228; *James v. Fullerton* 77 F.L.R. 321 (N.T. 1983) (inadequate instruction of camel rider on safari).
120. *Pitcher v. Martin* [1937] 3 All E.R. 918.
121. *Kokolsky v. Caine Furs Farms* (1961) 31 D.L.R. (2d) 556.
122. But violations of leash laws and the like have not been generally construed as negligence per se: *Heath's Garage v. Hodges* [1916] 2 K.B. 370; *Spanton v. Laviolette* (1977) 83 D.L.R. (3d) 740.
123. See above, n. 3.
124. *Draper v. Hodder* [1972] 2 Q.B. 556 (C.A.). Followed: *Galea v. Gillingham* [1987] 2 Qd R. 365 (F.C.) emphasising actual or imputed knowledge of propensity for injury, not necessarily the precise way it worked out.
125. *Tucker v. Hennessy* [1918] V.L.R. 56.
126. *Aldham v. United Dairies* [1940] 1 K.B. 507 at 511. Aliter, if attached to a van, it becomes restive and bites a passer-by: ibid.

Cattle on highways

Under an anomalous English common law rule, an owner or occupier of land owed no duty to users of an adjoining highway to maintain fencing or otherwise prevent his animals from straying into the road. This rule stemmed from a time before the inclosure movement two centuries ago had reshaped the face of the English countryside and before the advent of fast motor traffic belied the assumption that straying livestock presented no undue threat to the travelling public. Yet as late as 1946, in a singular pique of antiquarianism, the House of Lords declined to reappraise this rule in the light of the radical change in environmental conditions.[127] Today, its effect is to subsidise farmers at the expense of the motoring public, in circumstances in which the risk to the latter is quite disproportionate to the burden on the former.

The rule was judicially disowned in Canada,[128] but notwithstanding its statutory repeal in England, was followed by the High Court of Australia in the belief that the decision was essentially political and best left to the legislature.[129] The rule has since been repealed in all jurisdictions except the Northern Territory.[130]

127. *Searle v. Wallbank* [1947] A.C. 341.
128. *Fleming v. Atkinson* [1959] S.C.R. 513; 18 D.L.R. (2d) 81.
129. *S.G.I.C. v. Trigwell* (1979) 142 C.L.R. 617 (a powerful dissent by Murphy J.; and trenchantly criticised by Atkinson, 9 Syd. L. Rev. 541 (1982)).
130. Following the *Animals Act* 1971 (Eng.); *Animals Act* (N.S.W.) 1977; *Wrongs Act* (Vic.) Pt IV (since 1985); *Wrongs Act* (S.A.) s. 17a (since 1983); *Highways Liability for Straying Animals Act* 1983 (W.A.) (cap of $500,000); *Law of Animals Amendment Act* 1985 (Tas.); *Civil Liabilities (Animals) Act* 1984 (A.C.T.); *Animals Law Reform Act* 1989 (N.Z.) s. 5. Some of these contain guidelines on negligence. See Clarke, 34 Int. & Comp. L.Q. 786 (1985).

19

VICARIOUS LIABILITY

1. RATIONALE

We speak of vicarious liability[1] when the law holds one person responsible for the misconduct of another, although he is himself free from personal blameworthiness or fault. It is therefore an instance of strict (no-fault) liability. Vicarious liability is a familiar feature of most systems of primitive law, and early English law was no exception. A notorious example is the erstwhile liability of a husband for the torts of his wife.[2] The responsibility placed upon the head of the household for the conduct of his familia was also the genesis of the master's liability for the torts of his servants, which, despite a varied history reflecting considerable vacillations of judicial outlook,[3] has remained the principal instance of vicarious liability in modern law.

The early medieval idea of holding a master responsible for all his servant's wrongs gave way, with the disintegration of the feudal system, to the principle that his liability be limited to the particular acts he had ordered or afterwards ratified. As long as this command theory prevailed, the master's liability could, with some semblance to reality, be justified by reference to that hard worked maxim, "qui facit per alium facit per se". But the expansion of commerce and industry, which set in towards the end of the 17th century, necessitated an adjustment of this narrow rule. The change from home industry to ever larger units of production vitiated the assumption that a master could exercise a close control over his servants, and the increasing hazards arising from modern industry necessitated a wider range of responsibility than that previously countenanced. After some experiment with the theory of implied command, the basis of the modern principle of liability for all torts committed by the servant "in the course of his employment" was finally laid in the earlier part of the 19th century.[4] This formula represented a compromise between two conflicting policies: on the one hand, the social interest in furnishing an innocent tort

1. A term which Pollock claimed to have coined: Holmes-Pollock Letters i, 233. But it falsely suggests that the master is liable "in place of" the servant.
2. See below, p. 679.
3. The history is traced by *Holdsworth* viii, 472 ff; Holmes, *Agency*, 4 Harv. L. Rev. 345 (1891); 5 Harv. L. Rev. 1 (1891); Wigmore, *Responsibility for Tortious Acts: Its History*, 7 Harv. L. Rev. 315 at 383 (1894).
4. The change was reflected in the pleading rules. For a time, the master could be sued in trespass if the servant's wrong was trespass—which was rational enough as long as the command theory prevailed. Later, *case* became the proper action: *M'Manus v. Crickett* (1800) 1 East 106; 102 E.R. 43; *McCorquodale v. Shell Oil* (1932) 33 S.R. (N.S.W.) 151. Nowadays, there is no vicarious liability for trespass unless the defendant "ordered the trespass or any act comprising it or any act necessarily leading by a physical necessity to it" (*Stoneman v. Lyons* (1975) 133 C.L.R. 550 at 562).

victim with recourse against a financially responsible defendant and, on the other, a hesitation to foist any undue burden on business enterprise.

Despite the frequent invocation of such tired tags as "respondeat superior" or "qui facit per alium facit per se",[5] the modern doctrine of vicarious liability cannot parade as a deduction from legalistic premises, but should be frankly recognised as having its basis in a combination of policy considerations.[6] Most important of these is the belief that a person who employs others to advance his own economic interest should in fairness be placed under a corresponding liability for losses incurred in the course of the enterprise; that the master is a more promising source of recompense than his servant who is apt to be a man of straw;[7] and that the rule promotes wide distribution of tort losses, the employer being a most suitable channel for passing them on through liability insurance and higher prices.[8] The principle gains additional support for its admonitory value in accident prevention. In the first place, deterrent pressures are most effectively brought to bear on larger units like employers who are in a strategic position to reduce accidents by efficient organisation and supervision of their staff. Secondly, the fact that employees are, as a rule, not worth suing because they are rarely financially responsible,[9] removes from them the spectre of tort liability as a discouragement of wrongful conduct. By holding the master liable, the law furnishes an incentive to discipline servants guilty of wrongdoing, if necessary by insisting on an indemnity or contribution.[10]

The master's vicarious liability does not displace the servant's personal liability to the tort victim. But this conclusion is neither self-evident nor beyond all objection. For one thing, ordinarily it is positively desirable that the master absorb the cost as a matter of sound resource allocation rather than that he be considered merely as guaranteeing the servant's primary responsibility to pay for the damage. For another, to hold the servant liable will either tend to overtax his financial resources (especially under modern conditions when these have become increasingly unequal to his capacity for causing great loss) or require double insurance, covering both him and his employer against the same risk. For these reasons, there is now a growing momentum in many countries for "channelling" liability to the employer

5. "The former merely states the rule baldly in two words, and the latter merely gives a fictional explanation of it" (*Staveley Iron Co. v. Jones* [1956] A.C. 627 at 643 per Lord Reid).
6. The most valuable policy discussions are found in Atiyah's comprehensive monograph on *Vicarious Liability* (1967) ch. 2; Laski, *Basis of Vicarious Liability*, 26 Yale L.J. 105 (1916); Douglas, *Vicarious Liability*, 38 Yale L.J. 584 (1929); Flannigan, *Enterprise Control*, 37 U. Tor. L.J. 25 (1987).
7. See e.g. Willes J. in *Limpus v. London Omnibus Co.* (1862) 1 H. & C. 526 at 539; 158 E.R. 993 at 998. Christened the "deepest pocket" principle by Baty (*Vicarious Liability* (1916) 154), who roundly condemned the modern law as a gigantic error.
8. See *Hamilton v. Farmers'* [1953] 3 D.L.R. 382 at 393 per MacDonald J. Cases where the employer's "risk-bearing capacity" is not superior to the victim's are statistically too insignificant to throw doubt on that policy.
9. Also because employees are more apt to strike the jury's sympathy, it is usually in the employer's rather than the plaintiff's interest to joint the employee as defendant: see *Standen v. Varley* (1956) 73 W.N. (N.S.W.) 587. Occasionally, however, the employee may be the only available target, e.g. if he acted outside the course of employment or the employer has a personal defence.
10. See above, p. 265.

alone; the employee being freed altogether from claims by third parties and liable at most to his employer for a limited contribution when this is justified on disciplinary grounds.[11] This mostly corresponds also with *practices* elsewhere. Moreover, in Australia subrogation against employees under general liability policies has now been formally abolished[12] and in New South Wales, South Australia and the Northern Territory employees also become entitled to indemnity from their employer[13]—all except in cases of "serious and wilful misconduct".

Vicarious liability and the duty of care

According to the generally accepted modern view, the master's liability is genuinely vicarious and not based on any "constructive" fault of his own. The earlier—untraversable—fiction that the master was sued for his own negligence in selecting and employing careless servants has long been discarded. His liability is not based on breach of any personal duty that he owed, but on his servant's *tort* being imputed to him.[14] That this is the true nature of vicarious liability has not been seriously doubted in modern times, despite an occasional unorthodoxy in dealing with certain exceptional situations.[15]

The hallmark of vicarious liability, then, is that it is based neither on any conduct by the defendant himself nor even on breach of his own duty. Personal liability, in contrast, is always linked to breach of one's own duty. Certain forms of it, however, bear a marked resemblance to vicarious liability: viz. where the breach is committed not by what the defendant, but by what somebody else has done. There are several such situations: first, whenever one person orders another to commit a tort, say an assault, he is liable just as if he had committed it himself, and it matters nothing whether it is perpetrated through the instrumentality of a servant, an "agent", or a fierce dog. Here, truly, "qui facit per alium facit per se".[16] Secondly, some tort duties are formulated so as to encompass responsibility for the conduct not only of oneself, but also of certain other people varying in

11. This is so not only in most Socialist countries, but also in Germany, Sweden and even in the U.S. where federal employees are no longer since 1988 personally liable.
12. *Insurance Contracts Act* 1984 (Cth) s. 66. Excluding motor insurance: s. 9. See *Boral Resources v. Pyke* (1989) 93 A.L.R. 89.
13. *Employees Liability Act* 1991 (N.S.W.); *Wrongs Act* (S.A.) s. 27C; *Law Reform (Miscellaneous Provisions) Act* (N.T.) s. 22A.
14. But this identification, though sufficient to impute the servant's wrong also to the master qua plaintiff (see above, p. 287), does not make them "privies in interest" so as to create an issue estoppel: *Ramsay v. Pigram* (1968) 118 C.L.R. 271.
15. Two such problems have loomed largest: How to explain (1) the non-liability of a master to a hitchhiker to whom his servant has given an unauthorised lift (see below, p. 381); and (2) the vicarious liability of a master for a "tort" for which the servant is himself immune, e.g. *Broom v. Morgan* [1953] 1 Q.B. 597 (marital); *Harvey v. O'Dell* [1958] 2 Q.B. 78 (statute-barred); *Dyer v. Munday* [1895] 1 Q.B. 742 (criminal conviction); *Co-op. Ins. v. Kearney* [1965] S.C.R. 106 (Ont. guest statute); *Law Reform (Vicarious Liability) Act* 1983 (N.S.W.) s. 10(2). Generally, Williams, *Vicarious Liability: Tort of the Master or of the Servant*, 72 L.Q.R. 522 (1956).
16. *Brooke v. Bool* [1928] 2 K.B. 578; Holmes, *Collected Papers*, 52ff. The personal nature of the liabilty is emphasised by the fact that, under the old forms of action, one who had commanded another to commit an assault could himself be sued in trespass, whereas a master's liability for the tort of his servant committed without express authorisation lay in case: see above, n. 4.

range.[17] A common carrier, for example, is liable for loss of the goods (saving certain exceptions) even if caused by strangers;[18] a shipowner for unseaworthiness even if the defect was due to faulty workmanship by an independent supplier or repairer.[19] Most of these are duties of absolute obligation, but some are mere duties of reasonable care. For example, the responsibility of schools to their pupils[20] and of hospitals to their patients[21] is no longer limited to vicarious liability for servants, but is complemented by a "non-delegable, personal" duty to assure that reasonable care is taken for their safety. The growing instances of liability for independent contractors are based on the same concept, reflecting a more exacting standard of responsibility in view either of exceptional risks or special claims to exceptional protection.

2. MASTER AND SERVANT RELATIONSHIP

Vicarious liability is incident only to a relationship of controlled employment, traditionally described as that of "master and servant". Where this is absent, but one person engages another to accomplish a specified result, the relationship is that of principal and independent contractor. In such a case, the work, although done at the employer's request and for his benefit, is considered an independent function of the person who undertakes it, and does not ordinarily involve the principal in responsibility for harm caused in the performance of the task.[22]

Agents

Some difficulty arises from the several meanings attached to the term "agent".[23] It is frequently used either in the sense of a comprehensive category encompassing the two species of servant and independent contractor or to describe servants, properly so-called, whose employment is casual rather than more or less continuous.[24]

At other times, the term "agent" crops up to designate someone through whose instrumentality the defendant has committed a tort of his own, as when he has authorised an "agent" to commit a tort or ratified it afterwards.[25] It also includes situations "where the function entrusted is that of representing the person who requests its performance in a

17. See Barak, *Mixed and Vicarious Liability*, 29 Mod. L. Rev. 160 (1966) who rightly draws attention to the shifting nature of some heads of liability, from personal to vicarious. A prominent example of contemporary ambiguity is the liability of a car owner, discussed below, p. 386.
18. See Palmer, *Bailment* (2nd ed. 1991) 975.
19. *Riverstone Meat Co. v. Lancashire Shipping Co.* [1961] A.C. 807.
20. *Commonwealth v. Introvigne* (1982) 150 C.L.R. 258.
21. See below, p. 373.
22. See below, p. 388.
23. See 1 Syd. L. Rev. 242 (1954); Brooke-Smith, 70 L.Q.R. 253 (1954). On the liability of a firm for the torts of a partner see *Hamlyn v. Houston* [1903] 1 K.B. 81; *Meekins v. Henson* [1964] 1 Q.B. 472; of a parent company for a subsidiary see Muchlinski, *The Bhopal Case*, 50 Mod. L. Rev. 545 at 568-573 (1987).
24. Under common law pleading, the declaration in cases of vicarious liability alleges that the defendant acted "by himself, his servants, and agents".
25. *Hewitt v. Bonvin* [1940] 1 K.B. 188 at 191; also 69 L.Q.R. 414 (1953).

transaction with others, so that the very service to be performed consists in standing in his place and assuming to act in his right and not in an independent capacity''.[26] On this basis, an insurance agent was held to have made his principal answerable for defaming a competing company in the course of soliciting proposals, because ''he was authorised to speak, and in fact spoke, with the voice of the defendant.''[27] Whereas in the ordinary case an independent contractor carries out his work not as a representative but as principal, here the agent acts in a genuinely representative capacity for a principal who is accordingly treated as if he were conducting the transaction in person. The liability is therefore personal, not vicarious—a true instance of ''qui facit per alium facit per se''.

Control test

The conventional test of distinguishing a servant from an independent contractor or—what amounts to the same thing—a contract of service from a contract for services,[28] is that the employee is a servant if he is ''subject to the command of the master as to the manner in which he shall do his work'',[29] while ''an independent contractor undertakes to produce a given result but is not, in the actual execution of the work, under the order or control of the person for whom he does it.''[30] An employee is a servant if his superior is in a position to tell him not only *what* to do, but *how* to do it.[31] This test is the product of economic conditions in which the employer had the competence to instruct the labourer in the techniques of performing his work. In a preponderantly agricultural and primitive industrial society the master was usually at least his servant's equal in knowledge and experience, and the control test postulates this combination of managerial and technical functions in the person of the employer. But the technological developments since the late 19th century and the corresponding changes in the structure of modern business, combined with the trend of professionals entering full-time salaried employment instead of private practice, have belied this assumption, and it is found increasingly difficult to apply the control test as a meaningful working rule to many modern situations.[32] More often than not, the skilled craftsman or professional worker is engaged for the very reason that he possesses the ''know-how'' which his employer lacks. Industrial relations have changed to the point where even a crane driver's assertion ''I take no orders from anybody'' is regarded as the normal attitude of a skilled man who knows his job and will carry it out in his way.[33]

The policy underlying vicarious liability would have been jeopardised by a literal adherence to the control test, and the courts have not hesitated to

26. *Colonial Life Assurance v. Producers Assurance Co.* (1931) 46 C.L.R. 41 at 48 per Dixon J.
27. Ibid. at 47 per Gavan Duffy C.J. and Starke J. Here the ''agent'' was not a servant because he operated on his own account. Contrast the position of the ''superintendent'' in the very similar case of *Citizens' Life Assurance Co. v. Brown* [1904] A.C. 423.
28. This terminology stems from the Workers' Compensation Acts.
29. *Yewens v. Noakes* (1880) 6 Q.B.D. 530 at 532 per Bramwell L.J.
30. *Queensland Stations v. F.C.T.* (1945) 70 C.L.R. 539 at 545 per Latham C.J.
31. *Humberstone v. Northern Timber Mills* (1949) 79 C.L.R. 389 at 404.
32. Kahn-Freund, 14 Mod. L. Rev. 504 (1951).
33. *Mersey Docks v. Coggins* [1947] A.C. 1 at 20 per Lord Simonds.

hold the employer answerable "even though the work which the servant is employed to do is of a skilful or technical character, as to the method of performing which the employer himself is ignorant".[34] This transformation has necessarily involved an adjustment of the control test, which is reflected less in verbal formulation than in its application. In the first place, it is no longer asked whether any actual supervision was in fact exercised or indeed possible, but whether ultimate authority over the person in the performance of his work resided in the employer so that he was subject to the latter's orders and directions.[35] Secondly, the approach has become more flexible. The search for the seat of control must take into account a variety of factors, such as the power of dismissal, whether the employee has to furnish his own equipment, to select his own subordinates, or even delegate the work, whether the work customarily involves subordination to detailed orders and how the parties themselves viewed their relation (for example, was tax withheld?).[36] Indeed, it has been said to be a mistake to treat as decisive even an explicit reservation of control over the manner in which the work is performed, if that consideration is outweighed by other circumstantial factors.[37] A road haulier who provides his own truck may be an independent contractor even if he works almost exclusively for one customer;[38] while a radio artist engaged to participate in a particular play has been held to be a servant despite his receiving a fee rather than a salary, because he was subject to extensive directions by the producer.[39] The employment of a servant may be limited to a single occasion or extend over a long period; it may even be gratuitous. It applies alike to a manual labourer, a ship's captain,[40] a schoolteacher,[41] a circus acrobat,[42] a fireman,[43] and a son occasionally requested to drive his invalid parent in the latter's car.[44] The continued use of the word

34. *Gold v. Essex C.C.* [1942] 2 K.B. 293 at 305 per MacKinnon L.J.; *A.-G. v. Perpetual Trustee Co.* (1952) 85 C.L.R. 237 at 251-252 per Dixon J.
35. *Humberstone v. Northern Timber Mills* (1949) 79 C.L.R. 389 at 404, per Dixon J. Cf. *Zuijs v. Wirth Bros* (1955) 93 C.L.R. 561 at 571: "The duties to be performed may depend so much on professional skill or knowledge . . . or the necessity of the employee acting on his own responsibility may be so evident, that little room for direction or command in detail may exist. But that is not the point. What matters is lawful authority to command so far as there is scope for it."
36. See *Rest. Agency*, §220(2).
37. *Queensland Stations v. F.C.T.* (1945) 70 C.L.R. 539 at 552 per Dixon J., where a drover was held an independent contractor.
38. *Humberstone v. Northern Timber Mills* (1949) 79 C.L.R. 389 (owner-driver paid on a weight-mileage basis); *Stevens v. Brodribb* (1986) 160 C.L.R. 16 (logger paid on piece rate); *Wright v. A.-G.* (1954) 94 C.L.R. 406 (owner-driver paid on hourly rate, adjusted by mileage allowance: independent contractor).
39. *F.C.T. v. Thompson* (1944) 69 C.L.R. 227.
40. *Parker v. Commonwealth* (1965) 112 C.L.R. 295; *A.-G. v. Perpetual Trustee Co.* (1952) 85 C.L.R. 237 at 252, 283. For a compulsory pilot vicarious liability attaches to the ship, but (incongruously) not to his employer: *Oceanic Crest v. Pilbara* (1986) 160 C.L.R. 626.
41. *Ramsay v. Larsen* (1964) 111 C.L.R. 16 (negligence); *Ryan v. Filkes* [1938] 3 All E.R. 517 (battery). Vicarious liability is complemented by a "personal" duty of the school to assure pupils' safety: *Commonwealth v. Introvigne* (1982) 150 C.L.R. 258.
42. *Zuijs v. Wirth Bros* (1955) 93 C.L.R. 561; *Whittaker v. Minister of Pensions* [1967] 1 Q.B. 156.
43. *Kilboy v. S.E. Fire Committee* 1952 S.C. 280; *Fire Comm. v. Ardouin* (1961) 109 C.L.R. 105 at 126.
44. *Smith v. Moss* [1940] 1 K.B. 424. A mere request to render a casual, gratuitous service other than drive a car (insurance!) has rarely been considered sufficient; exceptional is *Moynihan v. Moynihan* [1975] I.R. 192 (carrying a teapot).

"servant" is perhaps unfortunate, because it carries a colloquial connotation obviously far narrower than its legal meaning, and this may supply the reason why, in its stead, the term "contract of service" is now often preferred.

The classification here involved has parallels in several other areas of law, like workers' compensation,[45] social security,[46] taxation,[47] and industrial safety.[48] But the tendency to use precedents interchangeably[49] calls for caution, because the same policy may not be involved in another context. Thus devices like "labour-only" sub-contracting chosen for fiscal convenience[50] should not obscure the crucial issue in vicarious liability of whether the employer ought not, all the same, to bear the accident risk of such persons as much as of workers hired on conventional terms.

Organisation test

Under the pressure of novel situations, courts have become increasingly aware of the strain on the traditional formulation[51] and looked for alternative tests. Some of these do little more than restate the question rather than help with answers, like "Was he in business on his own account?"[52] or "Was his a contract of service within the meaning which an ordinary person would give to the words?"[53]

Rather more useful is the "organisation" or "enterprise control" test.[54] Was the would-be servant part of his employer's organisation? Was his work subject to co-ordinational control as to the "where" and "when" rather than the "how"? As Lord Denning put it:

> "It is often easy to recognise a contract of service when you see it, but difficult to say wherein the difference lies. A ship's master, a chauffeur, and a reporter on the staff of a newspaper are all employed under a contract of service; but a ship's pilot, a taxi-man, and a newspaper contributor are employed under a contract for services. One feature which seems to run through the instances is that, under a contract of service, a man is employed as part of the business, and his

45. E.g. *Zuijs v. Wirth Bros* (1955) 93 C.L.R. 561 (circus acrobat employed under a "contract of service").
46. E.g. *Australian Mutual Provident Society v. Allan* (1978) 52 A.L.J.R. 407 (P.C.): representative not a "worker" under *Long Service Leave Act* 1987 (S.A.); *Market Investigations v. Minister of Social Security* [1969] 2 Q.B. 173 (part-time field researcher: an "employed person").
47. E.g. *Queensland Stations v. F.C.T.* (1945) 70 C.L.R. 539 (drover's pay was not "wages" subject to payroll tax).
48. E.g. *Howell v. Noojee Sawmilling* [1974] V.R. 243 (did the defendant own an "employer's duty of care", as detailed below, ch. 24). Some safety statutes cover also independent contractors: e.g. *Industrial Safety Health and Welfare Act* (S.A.) s. 3(d).
49. E.g. Kahn, *Who is a Servant?* 53 A.L.J. 832 (1979).
50. See Clark, *Industrial Law and the Labour-Only Sub-Contract*, 30 Mod. L. Rev. 6 (1967); 31 Mod. L. Rev. 450 (1968); also Drake, *Wage Slave or Entrepreneur*, 31 Mod. L. Rev. 408 (1968); McKendrick, 53 Mod. L. Rev. 770 (1990).
51. *Cassidy v. M.O.H.* [1951] 2 K.B. 343 per Somervell L.J., passim; *Humberstone v. Northern Timber Mills* (1949) 79 C.L.R. 389 at 404 per Dixon J.
52. *Market Investigations v. Minister of Social Security* [1969] 2 Q.B. 173.
53. *Simmons v. Health Laundry* [1910] 1 K.B. 543 at 553; *Cassidy v. M.O.H.* [1951] 2 K.B. 343 at 353.
54. See *Bauman v. Hulton Press* [1952] 2 All E.R. 1121 at 1124; *Co-op. v. Kearney* [1965] S.C.R. 106 (insurance agent); Flannigan, *Enterprise Control*, 37 U. Tor. L.J. 25 (1987).

work is done as an integral part of the business; whereas, under a contract for services, his work, although done for the business, is not integrated into it but is only accessory to it.''[55]

The transformation is best illustrated by the "hospital cases". Less than 50 years ago, it was accepted that a hospital was responsible to its patients only for the exercise of due care in the selection of its staff, but not for the negligence of its doctors and nurses in matters of professional skill and competence.[56] A distinction prevailed between responsibility for the performance by the staff of ministerial or administrative tasks, on the one hand, and professional duties on the other, corresponding to the hospital's degree of "control". This vestigial[57] immunity progressively eroded as it came to be realised that the charitable nature of hospitals was not really a sufficient reason for withholding redress from injured patients and that, in any event, publicly financed hospitals did not need the protection once thought desirable in the interest of privately supported charities.[58] Thus hospitals became successively liable vicariously for the negligence of their nurses,[59] resident medical officers,[60] radiographers,[61] even part-time anaesthetists[62] though not for purely "honoraries".[63] The uncontrollability for such professionals in the performance of their tasks no longer precludes recovery, so long as they are subordinated to the hospital organisation. Indeed, according to a view which has gained increasing support,[64] the distinction between servants and independent contractors becomes irrelevant whenever a hospital offers a complete range of medical treatment to the patient and thereby assumes a non-delegable, personal duty to ensure that he receive careful treatment at the hands of such staff as it provides, including visiting specialists and other independent consultants.[65] In short, the patient need no longer prove precisely where within the organisation the fault originated.[66] This in recognition of the changing function of hospitals from one offering merely facilities for the

55. *Stevenson v. Macdonald* [1952] 1 T.L.R. 101 at 111; also *Whittaker v. Minister of Pensions* [1967] 1 Q.B. 156 at 167; *Bank voor Handel v. Slatford* [1953] 1 Q.B. 248 at 295; *Roe v. M.O.H.* [1954] 2 Q.B. 66 at 91; *Macdonald v. Glasgow Hospital* 1954 S.C. 453. But cf. *Stevens v. Brodribb* (1986) 160 C.L.R. 16 at 27-28 per Mason J.
56. *Hillyer v. St Bart's Hospital* [1909] 2 K.B. 820.
57. For a brief period in the mid-19th century English law dallied openly with a comprehensive doctrine of charitable immunity, destined eventually to play a much longer role in the U.S.
58. Denning L.J. attributed the change to the nationalisation of hospitals in Britain: *Cassidy v. M.O.H.* [1951] 2 K.B. 343 at 361.
59. *Sisters of St Joseph v. Fleming* [1938] 2 D.L.R. 417; *Henson v. Perth Hospital* (1939) 41 W.A.L.R. 15. Nor does a nurse assisting a surgeon become his servant pro hoc vice: *Morris v. Winsbury-White* [1937] 4 All E.R. 494.
60. *Collins v. Herts. C.C.* [1947] K.B. 598; *Cassidy v. M.O.H.* [1951] 2 K.B. 343.
61. *Gold v. Essex C.C.* [1942] 2 K.B. 293.
62. *Roe v. M.O.H.* [1954] 2 Q.B. 66; *Toronto Hospital v. Aynsley* [1972] S.C.R. 435.
63. *Ellis v. Wallsend Hosp.* (1989) 17 N.S.W.L.R. 553 (C.A.) distg *Albrighton v. R.P.A. Hospital* [1980] 2 N.S.W.L.R. 542 (C.A.).
64. Originating in Lord Greene's judgment in *Gold* [1942] 2 K.B. 293, it was elaborated by Denning L.J.; reinforced in England by *National Health Service Act* 1946 s. 3.
65. Cf. *Ybarra v. Spangard* 154 P. 2d 687 (Cal. 1944), shifting proof of exculpation to all members of surgical team.
66. As it did in *Albrighton v. R.P.A. Hosp.* (see above, n. 63); *Yepremain v. Scarborough Hosp.* (1980) 110 D.L.R. (3d) 513 (Ont. C.A.); but not in *Ellis v. Wallsend Hosp.* (see above, n. 63) where patient had selected private surgeon.

use of a physician and his patient to one actually providing medical treatment.

This shift from vicarious to personal liability of the organiser has also been applied to a school with respect to the supervision of pupils,[67] and could conceivably be extended to other situations in quest for "deep pockets".[68]

Public servants

Since the abrogation of the Crown's immunity from suit,[69] the state is liable much like any private person for its torts, including those committed by its servants in the course of their employment. Vicarious liability is generally imputed on the same principles as in the case of private employment,[70] except for acts committed in the execution of an "independent" function vested in the officer personally by the common law or statute, like arrests[71] and other peace keeping acts[72] by a police constable. In the past this immunity has also been applied, in retrospect with undue zeal,[73] to certain discretionary acts by a collector of customs,[74] a tax commissioner,[75] a ship's pilot[76] and even a legal aid officer.[77] The whole immunity is open to serious criticism.[78] In origin it was linked to the long discredited theory that vicarious liability rested on the master having expressly or impliedly authorised the servant's tort. (Here the servant's authority derived from independent grant.) Nor can it be justified by reference to the principle that governments must be free to exercise certain functions on a policy level free from individual claims for compensation,[79] for the rule does not make such a distinction.[80] On the contrary, vicarious liability may serve the cause of deterrence and could often offer the only

67. *Commonwealth v. Introvigne* (1982) 150 C.L.R. 258.
68. *Kondis v. State Transport* (1984) 154 C.L.R. 672 at 690 (construction project?).
69. See Whitmore & Aronson, *Public Torts and Contracts* (1982) ch. 1; McNairn, *Governmental Immunity in Australia and Canada* (1977) ch. 3; Hogg, *Liability of the Crown* (1971) ch. 4.
70. *Groves v. Commonwealth* (1982) 150 C.L.R. 113 (military).
71. *Enever v. R.* (1906) 3 C.L.R. 969; *Fisher v. Oldham Corp.* [1930] 2 K.B. 364; *A.-G. v. Perpetual Trustee Co.* (1952) 85 C.L.R. 237 at 249-252, 283-284, 303-304; [1955] A.C. 457 at 478-480.
72. *Griffiths v. Haines* [1984] 3 N.S.W.L.R. 653; *Irvin v. Whitrod* [1978] Qd R. 271 (mistaken shooting in a stake-out); *Schulze v. R.* (1974) 47 D.L.R. (3d) 131 (failure to free kidnap victim). Aliter, a gaoler's duty to control prisoners: *Thorne v. W.A.* [1964] W.A.R. 147.
73. *A.-G. v. Perpetual Trustee Co.* (1952) 85 C.L.R. 237 at 284 per Fullagar J.
74. *Baume v. Commonwealth* (1906) 4 C.L.R. 97, dist. in *Oriental Ford v. Commonwealth* (N.S.W. 1983) 50 A.L.R. 452.
75. *Carpenter's Investment v. Commonwealth* (1952) 69 W.N. (N.S.W.) 175.
76. See above, n. 40.
77. *Field v. Nott* (1939) 62 C.L.R. 660.
78. Goode, *Imposition of Vicarious Liability to the Torts of Police Officers: Considerations of Policy*, 10 M.U.L.R. 47 (1975); Sawer, *Crown Liability in Tort and the Exercise of Discretions*, 5 Res Jud. 1 (1951).
79. See above, p. 156. Indeed there is more to be said for the converse proposition, viz. that an official's immunity should not necessarily exclude liability by the government itself to make compensation. Thus the S.A. (s. 51(a)) and N.S.W. (s. 6A) *Police Regulation Acts* exempt police officers for bona fide acts but not the Crown.
80. In rare cases it may even apply to private employers, e.g. *Jobling v. Blacktown C.* [1969] 1 N.S.W.R. 129 (C.A.) (manager of swimming pool).

means of redress because of the difficulty of identifying the individual culprit. The immunity at least regarding police officers has been abrogated in Britain, New Zealand and several Australian jurisdictions.[81]

Borrowed servants

An employer frequently agrees to make the services of his employee available to a third party. If in the course of performing the stipulated work, the employee injures someone, the general employer retains responsibility, unless *he* can establish that the effect of the transfer was to constitute his employee pro hac vice the servant of the hirer. In the course of the last 50 years, this burden has become increasingly heavy so that it can be discharged only in quite exceptional circumstances.[82] The principal reason for this bias may well be that the general employer, unlike the hirer, has selected the servant for the task and thereby makes himself responsible for the manner in which the work is carried out.[83] Besides, in the typical case of the general employer being in the business of lending out operating equipment and personnel, the cost of accidents can be quite economically absorbed in his own charges and rather more conveniently insured against because of his broader accident experience with this particular kind of risk.[84]

According to received doctrine, responsibility is here also identified with control. Since in most cases control is divided between lender and borrower, the most obvious conclusion would perhaps have been to impose joint responsibility.[85] Instead, the assumption prevails that control and liability must, as a rule, be allocated exclusively to one or the other. The test, we are told, is to ask "Who exercised control not only over the task to be performed but also over the method of performing it?" The ultimate question is not what specific orders, or whether any specific orders, were given but who is entitled to give the orders as to how the work should be done.[86] "Unless there be that authority, the workman is not serving the hirer, but merely serving the interests of the hirer."[87]

Although each case must be decided in the light of its own particular facts, the following have been consistently stressed in deciding the question

81. *Police Act* 1964 (U.K.) s. 48; *Crown Procedures Act* 1950 (N.Z.) s. 6; *Australian Federal Police Act* 1979 (Cth) s. 64B; *Law Reform (Vicarious Liabilities) Act* 1983 (N.S.W.); *Police Act* 1937 (Qld) s. 69B; *Police Regulations Act* (S.A.) s. 51a; *Police Administration Act* 1990 (N.T.) s. 163.
82. *Mersey Docks v. Coggins* [1947] A.C. 1 at 10.
83. Ibid. at 18-19.
84. Either way, the borrower will thus bear the actual cost and pass it to his customers. Moreover, though a specific contract term that the employee shall become the hirer's servant cannot of itself divest the general employer of his vicarious liability, it may entitle him to an indemnity from the hirer: *Spalding v. Tarmac Engineering* [1967] 1 W.L.R. 1508 (H.L.); *Thompson v. Lohan* [1987] 1 W.L.R. 649 (not subject to *Unfair Contract Terms Act* 1977); *S.G.I.O. v. Brisbane Stevedoring* (1969) 123 C.L.R. 228.
85. In the U.S., this is done in Pa. and California. Advocated by Hall, 12 U. Qld L.J. 73 (1981). But under traditional doctrine, "one cannot serve two masters at the same time" (*Oceanic Crest v. Pilbara* (1986) 160 C.L.R. 626).
86. *Mersey Docks v. Coggins* [1947] A.C. 1 at 17; *McDonald v. Commonwealth* (1945) 46 S.R. (N.S.W.) 129 at 132.
87. [1947] A.C. 1 at 21 per Lord Uthwatt.

of control: who is paymaster, who can dismiss, how long does the alternative service last, what machinery is employed,[88] was the servant skilled?[89] Under the modern spectrum of risk allocation, it would be as important to ask—Who could have better controlled the avoidance (and recurrence) of such an accident and whose insurance was more obviously calculated to cover this risk?[90] For instance, if the man is part of a self-contained squad seconded with its own foreman, he clearly remains within the organisational structure of his general employer.[91] Where a man driving a mechanical device, such as a crane, is lent, a transfer of responsibility is rarely inferred, because ordinarily it is not contemplated that the hirer shall tell the man how to handle the machine, and in any event the driver remains responsible for its safekeeping.[92] To this, as already noted, should be added that ordinarily the lender (and his insurer) is better able to calculate crane risks. The leading case is *Mersey Docks v. Coggins*[93] where the appellants, as part of their business, hired out the use of a crane, together with its operator, to the respondent stevedores for the purpose of loading a particular ship. The hirers were entitled to tell the driver where to go, what parcels to lift and where to take them, but it was held that they were not liable for his negligence, because they had no authority to tell him how to handle the crane in doing his work. This may be contrasted with another case[94] where an employer had agreed to let on hire to a government department a lorry and driver for general purposes, and the employee pursuant to orders from the works foreman undertook a job in the course of which he injured another worker. Here it was held that the hirers had assumed responsibility, because the permanent employer knew neither the general nature of the work to be done nor its location, and the employee was in fact used for any purposes that arose incidental to the work which the foreman was carrying out.

3. COURSE OF EMPLOYMENT

The employer's vicarious responsibility, unlike the husband's of yore,[95] does not necessarily cover all 24 hours of the day: it only extends to incidents "in the course of the servant's employment". Thus not even travel

88. Ibid. at 17 per Lord Porter.
89. A transfer takes place more easily when an unskilled man is lent to help with labouring work: *Denham v. Midland Employers* [1955] 2 Q.B. 437 at 444.
90. See note, *Borrowed Servants and the Theory of Enterprise Liability*, 76 Yale L.J. 807 (1967).
91. *Brogan v. Smith* 1965 S.L.T. 175; *Karuppan v. Port of Singapore* [1978] 1 W.L.R. 189 at 193 (P.C.).
92. *Mersey Docks v. Coggins* [1947] A.C. 1 at 17 per Lord Porter. The case is weaker where a driver is assigned *without* a vehicle, as in *McKee v. Dumas* (1976) 70 D.L.R. (3d) 70. In *Barisic v. Devenport* [1978] 2 N.S.W.L.R. 111 the borrower incurred joint liability for his negligent system of work.
93. [1947] A.C. 1; also *Jones v. Tivoli Collieries* [1966] Qd R. 140; *Lindsay v. Union S.S. Co.* [1960] N.Z.L.R. 486.
94. *MacDonald v. Commonwealth* (1945) 46 S.R. (N.S.W.) 129; also *Horne v. R.* [1947] N.Z.L.R. 538.
95. See below, p. 679.

to and from work is ordinarily any of the master's concern,[96] although it is now generally covered by workers' compensation.

Indeed, vicarious liability does not even attach for every wrong done by the servant while on the job for payroll purposes. The employer will of course be liable for acts which he has himself authorised or ratified, but as we have seen[97] no principle of vicarious liability is involved or needed in such cases. Besides, rarely would a master have actually employed or directed his servant to be negligent or commit some other tort. Vicarious liability is much broader than that, and extends to a servant's incidental wrongdoing, providing it falls within the "course of his employment". That phrase, like its variants "scope" or "sphere of employment", is the formula employed to indicate the outward limits of responsibility for the unauthorised wrongdoing of a servant, and represents the judicial compromise between the "social necessity" of making a master answerable for injury occasioned by servants entrusted with the power of acting in his business and the sense that it would be unjust, and indeed undesirable, to make him responsible for every act the servant chooses to do.[98] "The course of employment" is an expansive concept which provides ample scope for policy decisions and, despite the vast volume of case law, has failed to acquire a high degree of precision. No statistical measurement is possible, and precedents are helpful only when they present a suggestive uniformity on parallel facts.

In general terms, the "course of employment" is said to encompass such unauthorised acts by the servant as can be regarded wrongful and unauthorised *modes* of performing an authorised task. The precise terms of the authority conferred on him is not the test but rather the function, the operation, the class of act to be done—whatever be the instructions as to the time, the place or the manner of doing it.[99] At least as regards negligent injury, the employer's liability does not rest even on any notion of ostensible authority; indeed even an express prohibition, whether the law's or the employer's, does not necessarily take the act outside the course of employment. But the limit is exceeded when, instead of acting in furtherance of the assigned task, the servant indulges in an unrelated and independent venture of his own, that is "when he so acts as to be in effect a stranger in relation to his employer with respect to the act which he has committed".[100] Thus a decision by firemen in furtherance of an industrial dispute to delay the arrival at a fire engine until the property was

96. *Commonwealth v. Cocks* (1966) 115 C.L.R. 413; *Harrison v. British Rlys* [1981] 3 All E.R. 679. But driving or being driven in his master's vehicle on such a trip, at least when obliged to do so, has been held to raise liability: *Vandyke v. Fender* [1970] 2 Q.B. 292 (C.A.); *Nottingham v. Aldridge* [1971] 2 Q.B. 739 at 752; see below, p. 387. So has travel "in the employer's time", e.g. on outside jobs, as in *Smith v. Stages* [1989] A.C. 928; *Greenwood v. Commonwealth* [1975] V.R. 859.

97. See above, p. 369.

98. See *Bugge v. Brown* (1919) 26 C.L.R. 110 at 117-118 per Isaacs J. In exceptional cases, an employer is by statute liable for the acts of his servants and agents whether they occur in the course of employment or not: see e.g. *Sea-Carriage of Goods Act* 1924 (Cth) Schedule, art. IV s. 2.

99. *Bugge v. Brown* (1919) 26 C.L.R. 110 at 132 per Higgins J.

100. Ibid. at 118 per Isaacs J.: a much-cited statement both in Australia and Canada. Yet there is much cogency in the criticism that "the phrase is not perhaps of the happiest; it carries the crutch of fiction to sustain it" (Laski, 26 Yale L.J. 105 at 120 (1916)).

substantially destroyed was viewed as a complete repudiation of an essential obligation of their employment rather than merely as a wrongful manner of fighting fires.[101] Often it is a question of degree. If I employ a man to do navvying, I am not responsible if he takes it upon himself to drive away a truck. A bus conductor may perhaps still be acting within the course of his employment if he merely turns the bus around at the terminal during the driver's delayed absence,[102] but he certainly ventures beyond it by careering around the streets.[103] A fork lift operator who backs away a diesel lorry that is blocking his access to a warehouse[104] must be distinguished from one who drives off with it merely in order to test his ability to manage it.

Perhaps inevitably, the familiar notion of foreseeability can here be seen once more lurking in the background, as undoubtedly one of the many relevant factors is the question of whether the unauthorised act was a normal or expected incident of the employment. But one must not confuse the relevance of foreseeability in this sense with its usual function on a negligence issue. We are not here concerned with attributing fault to the master for failing to provide against foreseeable harm (for example in consequence of employing an incompetent servant), but with the measure of risks that may fairly be regarded as typical of the enterprise in question. The inquiry is directed not at foreseeability of risks from specific conduct, but at foreseeability of the broad risks incident to a whole enterprise.[105]

Prohibited conduct

This approach provides a guide through the maze of decisions dealing with the effect of disobedience to orders. Prohibitions of certain acts are relevant in ascertaining the work which the servant is employed to do, but are of no avail once the acts done are found to be within the scope of employment.[106] What is critical, therefore, is whether the order transgressed actually limited the sphere of employment or merely regulated his conduct within that sphere. For the first, the prohibition must be such that its violation makes the servant's conduct so distinctly remote and disconnected with his employment as to put him for the nonce in the position of a stranger.[107] Such was the case when a bus conductor took it upon himself during the momentary absence of the driver to move the bus himself contrary to express prohibition, albeit in the purported interest of his employer.[108] This must be contrasted with the carpenter who had

101. *General Engineering v. Kingston and St. Andrew Corp.* [1989] 1 W.L.R. 69 (P.C.).
102. Contra: *Iqbal v. London Transport Executive* (1973) 16 K.I.R. 329 (C.A.) (prohibited).
103. *Beard v. London G.O. Co.* [1900] 2 Q.B. 530, as explained in *Kay v. I.T.W.* [1968] 1 Q.B. 140 (C.A.).
104. *Kay v. I.T.W.* [1968] 1 Q.B. 140 (C.A.). The less precise the defined scope of employee's duties, the more likely that his deviation will be regarded as a mere mode of performing his authorised tasks: *L.C.C. v. Cattermoles* [1953] 1 W.L.R. 997; *Mulholland v. Reid* 1958 S.C. 290.
105. But see Morris, *Enterprise Liability and the Actuarial Process—The Insignificance of Foresight*, 70 Yale L.J. 554 (1961).
106. Otherwise it would be easy to issue secret orders countermanding the original instructions, and for the master thus at once to benefit himself and to keep on the right side of the law.
107. *Bugge v. Brown* (1919) 26 C.L.R. 110 at 119 per Isaacs J.
108. *Iqbal v. London Transport Executive* (1973) 16 K.I.R. 329 (C.A.). Contrast *L.C.C. v. Cattermoles* [1953] 1 W.L.R. 997 (C.A.).

permission to use his own car on outside jobs, provided only it was covered by insurance. Ignoring this condition, he took his uninsured car on an errand and negligently injured the plaintiff. His employers were held liable because the prohibition was not against the use of private transport in connection with their business but against the use of uninsured vehicles, being designed for no other purpose than to transfer from the master to an insurance company the obligation of compensating accident victims.[109] If the servant had been absolutely forbidden to drive his car in the course of employment, it might, per contra, have been maintained that he was employed to do carpentry work and not to drive a car. So in another case,[110] a rouseabout employed to cut thistles in a distant paddock was supplied with raw meat for his midday meal. His employer was averse to the man taking a large frying pan with him and therefore instructed him to cook it at a certain house which was a considerable distance from the place of work. In order to save time, the man constructed his own gridiron and lit a fire in an old chimney near where he was working. The fire negligently got out of control and spread to neighbouring property. The employer was held liable, because he had authorised the cooking on his land and his specific directions related only to the exact spot where this was to be done. A material, but not conclusive, factor was that the act purported to serve the interest of the employer and not to indulge a personal whim.

Thus, a prohibition relating merely to manner, time or place does not ordinarily exclude from the sphere of employment an act committed in violation of it. Thus a driver's disobedience in allowing someone else to take the wheel has been consistently so construed, no doubt with an eye to his employer's insurance.[111] Indeed, vicarious liability has been imposed even when the employer specifically prohibited the very tortious act in question,[112] as distinct merely from the general activity in the course of which the tort was committed. So, in one instance,[113] a bus driver pulled across the road in front of a rival bus, overturning it, in defiance of an explicit prohibition against racing with or obstructing another omnibus. His employers were held liable on the ground that the unlawful conduct was merely an unauthorised, and indeed forbidden, manner of doing which he was employed to do, that is drive a bus. The servant was on his master's business at the time of the accident and was not engaged on something entirely inconsistent with the discharge of his duty. This decision finds a parallel in an Australian case,[114] where an assurance company was held liable for a slander uttered by its agent to prospective customers concerning a rival company, despite an explicit prohibition in the contract of employment against the use of language reflecting on the character or conduct of any person or institution. A majority of the High Court took

109. *C.P.R. v. Lockhart* [1942] A.C. 591 (P.C.). Reversed in W.A. by *Motor Vehicle (Third Party) Insurance Act* 1943 s. 22(2).
110. *Bugge v. Brown* (1919) 26 C.L.R. 110.
111. The employee's responsibility often stems from allowing the vehicle to be driven negligently in his presence, e.g. *Black Range Tin v. Shoobert* [1973] W.A.R. 131 (F.C.); *Ilkiw v. Samuels* [1963] 1 W.L.R. 991 (C.A.); see below, p. 385.
112. It goes without saying that an employer cannot gain protection by a *general* instruction against the commission of torts.
113. *Limpus v. London General Omnibus Co.* (1862) 1 H. & C. 526; 158 E.R. 993.
114. *Colonial Mutual Life Assurance v. Producers Co.* (1931) 46 C.L.R. 41.

the view that, the agent being employed to solicit proposals, it was incidental thereto for him to use appropriate means to persuade prospective customers. The undertaking contained in the contract was not a limitation of his authority, but related to the manner of its exercise.

Frolic and detour

In an oft-repeated phrase, Parke B. once enunciated that a servant steps outside the scope of his employment when "going on a frolic of his own".[115] This is not to suggest that a master will get off merely because the servant, though on his master's business, was temporarily pursuing a personal end. The question is whether the activity was reasonably incidental to the performance of his authorised duties or involved so substantial a departure that the servant must, pro hac vice, be regarded as a stranger vis-à-vis his master. The former was the case when a lorry driver struck a match to light a cigarette whilst transferring petrol to an underground tank, thereby causing an explosion.[116] Smoking is admittedly for the employee's own comfort and not for his employer's benefit, but it is a habit which, at least in the absence of an express prohibition, must regrettably be regarded as a normal or typical incident during the performance of most kinds of work. But where, by contrast, a miner during a break ventured upon a forbidden part of the premises in order to smoke and there lit a match in defiance of orders and penal regulations, his employer was excused because such conduct could not fairly be treated as merely a forbidden mode of performing an authorised task.[117]

Again, to take the case of a driver who temporarily deviates from his route on personal business and during the detour negligently causes injury: if his private errand were alone decisive, he would in logic leave the scope of his employment as soon as he started his detour and not re-enter until he returned to his original route. But the law recognises that the employer cannot entirely dissociate himself from the trip until it ends in the home garage; hence it embarks on the uneasy task of striking a pragmatic compromise, having regard to the space, time and purpose of the deviation. So in one case,[118] a truck driver, on a long distance run, turned off the main road in order to get a drink at a hotel, and on the way negligently collided with a motorcycle. He was held to be still within the course of employment because divergence from the most direct route is not necessarily forbidden, particularly when made to obtain refreshment. Even if the employee acted in defiance of orders, it may be open in such a case to find that the detour was still incidental to his employment.[119] On the other hand, a driver who had been sent to deliver wine and collect empty bottles, and on the return trip obliged a friend by driving off in another

115. *Joel v. Morison* (1834) 6 C. & P. 501 at 503; 172 E.R. 1338. See Smith, *Frolic and Detour*, 23 Col. L. Rev. 444 at 716 (1923).
116. *Century Ins. v. N.I. Road Transport* [1942] A.C. 509.
117. *Kirby v. N.C.B.* 1958 S.C. 514.
118. *Chaplin v. Dunstan* [1938] S.A.S.R. 245; also *Angus v. Glasgow Corp.* [1977] S.L.T. 206. The contrary decision in *Crook v. Derbyshire Stone* [1956] 1 W.L.R. 432 is insupportable.
119. *Whatman v. Pearson* (1868) L.R. 3 C.P. 422. A fortiori, where the detour was not for his own purposes but to please passengers whom he was employed to transport: *Williams v. Hemphill* 1966 S.C. (H.L.) 31.

direction, was held to have started on an entirely new journey.[120] It was not merely a roundabout way of getting home: "every step he drove was away from his duty."[121]

A chauffeur who takes his employer's car without authority[122] for a joyride is obviously bent "on a frolic of his own". Hence if he collided with a cyclist, his employer would not be responsible. Yet if the car also suffered damage, and happened to have been entrusted to the employer for hire or repair, he would be answerable to the bailor.[123] How can the servant be acting, at one and the same time, both outside and inside the course of employment? The standard way of explaining this paradox[124] is that the master's duty is different: in the second case we are concerned not with vicarious or imputed liability, but with his personal duty as bailee which is so stringent that he cannot escape even by proving that the car was damaged by a servant outside the scope of his employment, if—though only if[125]—the servant had been actually entrusted with its custody. An alternative explanation[126] points to a difference in the duties of the servant: his duty to the cyclist sprang from his driving along the road, but his duty to the bailor from having custody of his car. Unlike the former, the latter occurred in the course of his employment, precisely because that custody was entrusted to him by his employer. This approach entails, however, the vexing conclusion that a servant may, for purposes of truly vicarious liability, be at once within the course of employment qua one person, but not qua another.

No less perplexing has proved the stock situation of a servant driver giving a lift to a stranger despite an express prohibition and injuring him in a collision en route his master's business. In this context, vicarious liability has been repeatedly rejected on the specious ground that, qua the passenger, the servant was as much on a frolic as if he had been driving for his amusement.[127] Although it seems to be well recognised that a servant remains in the course of employment unless the activity pursued for his private ends involves a clear deviation from the master's business, it is here suggested that a servant may assume a dual personality and that anything connected with his unauthorised object, although not competing with his

120. *Storey v. Ashton* (1869) L.R. 4 Q.B. 476. Similarly, *Johnson v. Pritchard* (1887) 8 L.R. (N.S.W.) 6; *Hall v. Halifax Transfer Co.* (1959) 18 D.L.R. (2d) 115.
121. *Storey v. Ashton* (1869) L.R. 4 Q.B. 476 at 480 per Mellor J. Nor does he "re-enter" his employment as soon as he turns homewards: *Hilton v. Burton* [1961] 1 W.L.R. 705; *Rest. Agency* §237, discussed in *Feldman v. Mall* 1945 A.D. 733 (S. Africa).
122. Equally, if his master permits him to use the car entirely for his (the servant's) purposes: see below, p. 386.
123. *Aitchison v. Page Motors* (1935) 52 T.L.R. 137; *Central Motors v. Cessnock Garage* 1925 S.C. 796; *Bamert v. Parks* (1964) 50 D.L.R. (2d) 313.
124. E.g. Lord Denning in *Morris v. Martin* [1966] 1 Q.B. 716 at 725.
125. *Sanderson v. Collins* [1904] 1 K.B. 628; *Spencer, Clark v. Goodwill Motors* [1939] N.Z.L.R. 493.
126. Jolowicz, [1965] Cam. L.J. 200.
127. *Twine v. Bean's Express* (1946) 62 T.L.R. 458; *Conway v. George Wimpey* [1951] 2 K.B. 266; *Rest. Agency 2d* §242; contra: *Hamilton v. Farmers'* [1953] 3 D.L.R. 382. An alternative explanation (now weaker than ever: *Rose v. Plenty* [1976] 1 W.L.R. 141 (C.A.)) has been that the defendant's liability must be measured by his own duty, not his servant's, and that the passenger must on that basis be treated as a trespasser; yet to others injured in the same accident, the master would be liable although he owed no duty. Cf. *Joss v. Snowball* (1969) 72 S.R. (N.S.W.) 218.

master's business, falls outside the scope of the latter's responsibility. This may be supportable where the servant's negligence is inseparable from his private venture,[128] but in the present situation the injury is caused by doing the very thing he was employed to do, that is drive the van along its proper course. In any event, the rule was held inapplicable where the prohibited passenger assisted the driver in the master's business: a boy who helped a milk roundsman distribute bottles from his float.[129]

Intentional wrongdoing

Vicarious liability may attach not only for a servant's negligence, but also for his intentional or wilful wrongdoing. Yet the fear of imposing too onerous a burden on employers, combined with a hesitation to make one person responsible for another's misconduct involving a taint of moral delinquency, has here led to a noticeably narrower definition of responsibility. This is reflected in a decided preference for the test of "real or ostensible authority" rather than "course of employment" which holds undisputed sway in cases of mere negligence.[130] Despite general protestations that vicarious liability does not rest on any notion of ostensible authority,[131] that concept continues to play a role in cushioning the employer against liability for the wilful wrongdoing of servants in situations where it is felt that "the course of employment" test would push responsibility too far.

To start with, there is the inhibiting fact that compared with negligence, a wilful tort can less frequently be viewed as merely a mode of performing an authorised duty.[132] Understandably, however, vicarious liability is readily invoked when the servant's conduct was prompted by a desire to further the interests of his employer and was reasonably incidental to his allotted duties.[133] This has been found for example when a porter ejected a passenger in the erroneous belief that he was on the wrong train,[134] when a store manager forcibly repossessed hire-purchase goods,[135] and employees protecting their master's property from depredation resorted to unlawful force[136] or wrongly accused a suspect of larceny.[137] Similarly, defamatory statements have been held within the course of employment, if incidental to an ordinary business communication in a matter of concern to

128. As when a boy, on his way to deliver a message, snatches a paper from a news-stand and while making his escape in a hurry knocks down the plaintiff: Newark, 17 Mod. L. Rev. 102 at 114-116 (1954).
129. *Ross v. Plenty* [1976] 1 W.L.R. 141 (C.A.).
130. Paton, *Liability of a Master*, 1 Res Jud. 85 (1936). Swanton discerns a more liberal trend in the offing: 16 U.W.A.L. Rev. 1 (1985).
131. But an old doctrine, that vicarious liability for trespass had to be based on specific command, is now obsolete: *Commonwealth v. Connell* (1986) 5 N.S.W.L.R. 218 at 223.
132. Isaccs J. in *Bugge v. Brown* (1919) 26 C.L.R. 110 at 116.
133. *Hayward v. Georges* [1966] V.R. 202.
134. *Bayley v. Manchester Rly* (1873) L.R. 8 C.P. 148.
135. *Dyer v. Munday* [1895] 1 Q.B. 742.
136. *Poland v. John Parr* [1927] 1 K.B. 236 where the servant was off duty at the time. Cf. *Deatons v. Flew* (1949) 79 C.L.R. 370 at 386.
137. *Bonette v. Woolworths* (1937) 37 S.R. (N.S.W.) 142. Aliter, with respect to placing the supposed offender into custody: *Abrahams v. Deakin* [1891] 1 Q.B. 516; *Hanson v. Waller* [1901] 1 Q.B. 390.

the employer,[138] or arising from the mistaken manner in which the actual authority committed to him was exercised by the employee.[139]

In cases such as these, the servant was guilty merely of an error of judgment or excessive zeal in exercising an authority devolved on him by the employer. A much narrower view, however, has prevailed with reference to other acts of aggression committed in the course of employment, especially when the victim is not a fellow employee but a customer or other stranger. One might have thought that what is called for is a distinction between work-related and personal incidents. Clearly, vicarious liability should not stretch to an employee beating up his wife's lover though it be on the working site and during working hours; nor to arson committed by a security guard on customers' premises.[140] On the other hand, quarrels in a shop over paying the bill or in a bar with a rumbustious patron might well have been considered characteristic incidents of the employment.[141] Yet the tendency has been to regard these as matters personal to the employee,[142] and to hold the master responsible only if the servant acted in pursuance of his authorised duties, for example of keeping order. Thus when a dance hall guard first assaulted a customer in the mistaken belief of being attacked by him and later gratuitously struck him again outside, well after the fracas had ended, the employer was held responsible for the first but not the second assault: the guard was authorised to evict rowdies, but not to take revenge.[143] Similarly, when a barmaid threw a bottle at an insulting customer, this was held to be a spontaneous act of retributive justice or personal resentment not connected with or incidental in any manner with her authorised work.[144] Dixon J. even doubted whether it would have made any difference if she had acted in self-protection because "from its nature self-defence is hardly a thing done by a servant on behalf of his master."[145]

At one time it was widely considered that a master could not be held responsible for his servant's fraud or other dishonest conduct perpetrated

138. *Riddick v. Thames Bd Mills* [1977] Q.B. 881 (even malicious).
139. *Colonial Mutual Life Assurance v. Producers* (1931) 46 C.L.R. 41; *Sheppard Publishing Co. v. Press Publishing Co.* (1905) 10 O.L.R. 243 (trade libel).
140. *Plains Engineering v. Barnes Security* (1987) 43 C.C.L.T. 129. Cf. *Mary M. v. Los Angeles* 814 P. 2d 1341 (Cal. 1991): city liable for police officer's rape of woman under arrest.
141. See *Bushey v. U.S.* 398 F. 2d. 167 (2 Cir. 1968) (comment 82 Harv. L. Rev. 1568) where a drunken sailor's opening of dry dock water valves was held sufficiently "characteristic".
142. *Deatons v. Flew* (1949) 79 C.L.R. 370; *Fontin v. Katapodis* (1962) 108 C.L.R. 177; *Keppel Bus Co. v. Ahmad* [1974] 1 W.L.R. 1082 (P.C.); critically discussed by Rose, *Liability for an Employee's Assaults*, 40 Mod. L. Rev. 420 (1977). In workers' compensation claims, a much more liberal view is taken of what may constitute an "accident arising out of or in the course of employment" (e.g. *S. Maitland Rlys v. James* (1943) 67 C.L.R. 496).
143. *Daniels v. Whetstone Entertainments* [1962] 2 Lloyd's Rep. 1 (C.A.).
144. *Deatons v. Flew* (1949) 79 C.L.R. 370; *Auckland Club v. Rennie* [1976] 1 N.Z.L.R. 278.
145. Ibid. at 381. If the plaintiff is a customer (like the innocent bystander in *Pettersson v. Royal Oak Hotel* [1948] N.Z.L.R. 136), his host also owes him an original duty of protection against attack from his own staff no less than from strangers (above): and cf. below *re* fellow employees. In the U.S. this duty is absolute in the case of public carriers and includes protection even against mere insults: *Prosser & Keeton* 57-58.

solely for his own benefit.[146] But in *Lloyd v. Grace Smith*[147] the House of Lords reversed this trend and held a firm of solicitors liable for the misappropriation of mortgage moneys by their managing clerk, who had induced one of their clients to transfer the mortgage to him by fraudulently misrepresenting the nature of the transaction. Some writers have attributed to this decision the far-reaching proposition that whenever a servant does dishonestly what he is engaged to do honestly, the master must answer for the fraud, even if the servant acted solely to benefit himself.[148] But so broad a principle has not been generally accepted by the courts, and the trend of authority is opposed to holding an employer liable in these cases, unless the act fell within the scope of the servant's "real or ostensible authority".[149] In order to attract vicarious liability, the servant's dishonesty must consist of "acts to which the ostensible performance of his master's work gives occasion or which are committed under cover of the authority the servant is held out as possessing or of the position in which he is placed as a representative of his master.[150] It is pre-eminently in this context that the courts have forsaken the "course of employment" test and reduced the employer's responsibility by invoking the agency doctrine of actual or ostensible authority, borrowed from the law of contract. Thus, it has been repeatedly held that a company is not liable for the fraudulent issue or forgery of share certificates by its secretary on the ground that the officer lacked, and was not held out as having, authority to perform any but purely ministerial acts in relation to the certification of transfers, such as the issue of certificates signed by the directors and in relation to shares which have been duly lodged.[151] Despite the fact that the dishonesty of the servant occurred in the very matter he was employed to do honestly, the employer was excused.

So a master to whom goods have been conveyed as bailee for reward is answerable for their conversion, if a servant of his to whom they have been entrusted for storing or carriage betrays that confidence by stealing them[152]—just as if the latter had been merely negligent in allowing someone else to steal them.[153] But the culpable servant must be one to whom the duty of custody was deputed by his employer, not just any servant whose employment simply presented him with an opportunity to steal them: to entail vicarious liability, the tort must have been committed "in the course of doing that class of acts which the employer had put the servant in his place to do."[154] This also provides the clue to the distinction between a stevedore stealing cargo and stealing a fixture on the ship: his

146. See Willes J. in *Barwick v. English Joint Stock Bank* (1867) L.R. 2 Ex. 259.
147. [1912] A.C. 716. Applied in *Uxbridge Building Society v. Pickard* [1939] 2 K.B. 248; *Briess v. Woolley* [1954] A.C. 333; *R. v. Levy Bros* (1961) 26 D.L.R. (2d) 760.
148. E.g. *Salmond & Heuston* 441.
149. See *Kooragang Investments v. Richardson* [1982] A.C. 462 (P.C.).
150. *Deatons v. Flew* (1949) 79 C.L.R. 370 at 381 per Dixon J.
151. *George Whitechurch v. Cavanagh* [1902] A.C. 117 (approved in *Lloyd*); *Kleinwort v. Automatic Machine Corp.* (1934) 50 T.L.R. 244; *Slingsby v. District Bank* [1931] 2 K.B. 588, affd [1932] 1 K.B. 544.
152. *Morris v. Martin* [1966] 1 Q.B. 716; *United Africa Co. v. Saka Owoade* [1955] A.C. 130 (P.C.). Extended to employer who contracted to provide security: *Photo Productions v. Securicor* [1980] A.C. 827 at 846, 852; *Jonson & Jonson v. C.P. Security* [1985] I.R. 362.
153. *Abraham v. Bullock* (1902) 86 L.T 796.
154. *Morris v. Martin* [1966] 1 Q.B. 716 at 737 per Diplock L.J.

employment affords an opportunity for either theft, but only the first constitutes a dishonest manner of discharging his task of handling cargo.[155]

4. CAR OWNERS

The alarming carnage of motor traffic has been responsible for various legal expedients designed to provide more effective ways of compensating its casualties. Although as we have seen negligence remains generally the lynchpin of tort recovery,[156] several extensions of vicarious liability at least enable the accident victim to reach beyond the careless driver and fasten responsibility upon the owner of the car, even if the latter is personally free from blame.[157] This development is the outcome of deliberate judicial policy, prompted by the fact that the driver is frequently a man of straw in contrast to the owner who is more likely to be insured or otherwise capable of absorbing the loss. It is the first, if only a modest, step towards a no-fault regime for road fatalities.

According to conventional theory, an owner may incur liability for an accident caused by someone else negligently driving his car in one of two possible ways: *vicariously*, if the driver was his servant or agent (for example a chauffeur), or *personally* when remiss in such respect as entrusting the car to someone of questionable competence.[158] It was a step well beyond either one when the owner came to be flatly responsible for anyone he allowed to drive the car with himself in it, if only as a passenger asleep in the back seat. This was put simply on the ground that if he retained the right to control the manner of driving (and this he is presumed to do in the absence of compelling evidence that he purposively abandoned it),[159] he fell under a corresponding duty to do so.[160] But although his explanation is suggestive of personal liability, in function it is akin to vicarious liability, since it attaches without more ado once the driver is found to have been negligent.

Even though absent at the time of the accident, an owner may yet incur responsibility for a driver who is not his servant when he requests or allows the car to be driven at least partially for his own purposes. In the case which has taken this doctrine farthest,[161] the defendant had arranged for a friend to take his car from London to Monte Carlo where he was to join him and his wife for a touring holiday in Switzerland. The friend was allowed to

155. *Leesh River Tea Co. v. British India S.N. Co.* [1967] 2 Q.B. 250 (C.A.).
156. See above, p. 19.
157. But being—as it were—only a guarantor for purposes of financial responsibility, the owner is entitled to indemnity from the driver: *Richardson v. O'Neill* [1959] N.Z.L.R. 540; *McFee v. Joss* [1925] 2 D.L.R. 1059.
158. See above, p. 153.
159. As in *Chowdhary v. Gillot* [1947] 2 All E.R. 541 (owner delivered car for servicing, and was then driven to railway station as courtesy service); *Ansin v. Evans* [1982] 1 N.Z.L.R. 184.
160. *Samson v. Aitchison* [1912] A.C. 844; *Trust Co. v. De Silva* [1956] 1 W.L.R. 376 (P.C.); *Soblusky v. Egan* (1960) 103 C.L.R. 215. The driver may be a prospective purchaser, friend, or fellow employee of a servant entrusted with the car (*Ilkiw v. Samuels* [1963] 1 W.L.R. 991) or joint owner: *Pennell v. O'Callaghan* [1954] V.L.R. 320.
161. *Ormrod v. Crosville Motor* [1953] 1 W.L.R. 1120 (C.A.).

make a personal detour in France but collided with a bus while still in England, for which the owner was held liable.

This extension of vicarious liability has occasionally been rationalised by labelling the driver the owner's "agent",[162] yet what is authorised here is not the agent's tortious act, but at most his acting on the principal's behalf. An alternative rationale which now appears to enjoy the highest support[163] is that the owner "delegated the task or duty" of driving on his behalf, but this would be true also of independent contractors whose fault is not imputed unless the delegated task is rated inherently dangerous.[164] However, the critical difference between the two cases is that in the first, the *mandator* furnishes his car, while an independent contractor (such as a hire car driver) would furnish his own.[165] That so much hinges on who owns the car is at least one significant pointer in the direction of insurance.

Doctrinal niceties apart, the judicial trend (enthusiastically promoted by Lord Denning) was steadily to increase the liability of the car owner by demanding less and less in the way of an "interest or concern" of his in the purpose of the particular trip. However, this trend has since been reversed by the House of Lords on the ground that it was impinging on the function of the legislature. In the now leading case of *Launchbury v. Morgans*,[166] the family car happened to be owned by the wife, but her husband used it regularly to drive to and from work. On the particular evening at the end of a pub crawl, he asked a friend to drive him home, as he had promised his wife he would do whenever he had had too much to drink. A fatal accident occurred for which the other passengers sought to make the wife liable. Unlike the Court of Appeal, the House of Lords regarded her interest in the "delegation" as insufficient. Clearly, the pub crawl was in no sense a purpose of hers, but did she not have an interest in the substitute driving the car as a means of protecting her husband in whose safety she had a vital stake? Evidently, that interest was not direct enough to qualify the drive as being for her purpose.[167] With this decision disappeared all chance of following the American and Canadian trail of imposing liability

162. Ibid. at 1122 per Singleton L.J.; but see Lord Wilberforce in *Launchbury v. Morgans* [1973] A.C. 127 at 135. Exceptionally, a driver has even been found to be the "agent" of *passengers*, all having joined as equal members of a party and contributed to the expenses: *Scarsbrook v. Mason* [1961] 3 All E.R. 767 (stolen car); *G.T.R. v. Dixon* (1920) 51 D.L.R. 576 (hired car); cf. the American doctrine of "joint enterprise" (*Prosser & Keeton* §72).
163. *Launchbury v. Morgans* [1973] A.C. 127.
164. See below, p. 391.
165. Judicial formulations typically speak of the owner of a chattel who "delegates the task". Thus even if the doctrine is not peculiar to cars, it appears to be confined to owners who confide the use of their property to others. There is no hint that the doctrine might also apply where the "agent" supplied the chattel or where no chattel is involved at all: cf. *Gramak v. O'Connor* (1973) 41 D.L.R. (3d) 14 where "agent" worked on the car in owner's presence. There is a dearth of cases exploring vicarious liability for family members doing errands for each other (outside the car context). Even if insurance does not explain the liability imposed on car owners, it does explain why in other situations claims are not being pursued.
166. [1973] A.C. 127.
167. Thus it will not do that the owner's purpose is served at the unilateral initiative of the borrower, as when a son driving his father's car remembers to pick up the latter's suit from the cleaners: Lord Dilhorne; ibid. at 139.

whenever the car is being used for a family purpose, still less whenever it is being driven simply with the owner's permission.[168]

Thus the purpose of each individual trip must be scrutinised: for example, a husband will be responsible for his wife's driving the family car when fetching him from the station,[169] but not when out on family shopping,[170] let alone on an errand solely her own.[171] This still leaves some leeway in deciding whether a particular journey is sufficiently for the owner's purposes. Thus it seems once more to be an open question whether use of an employer's car for the purpose of transporting oneself or a fellow employee to work will qualify.[172] Even more doubtful is an Australian decision which was content with the mere fact that the entrustment itself was profitable to the owner, as when a salesman was permitted the free use of the company's car "after hours": an arrangement which saved his employers the cost of garaging it and enabled him to start his round each morning from his home.[173]

Also relevant in the present context is the procedural device of treating car ownership as prima facie evidence, fit to go to the jury, that the driver was the owner's servant or agent acting in the course of employment or (for the purpose of the extended doctrine of agency just canvassed) at least partially for the owner's purposes.[174] This so-called presumption, applicable to private and commercial vehicles alike, does not however go so far as to change the legal burden of proof. It raises only an inference,[175] but one that the owner must seek to dispel if anxious to escape an almost certainly adverse verdict.

Compulsory insurance

In none of the preceding cases would there have been occasion to test the car owner's responsibility if his insurance policy had covered the driver's liability in addition to his own. As it was, some of the cases preceded compulsory insurance; in others the insurance covered only the owner or not the loss in question, for example because the victim was a passenger, the driver had no licence or the claim was only for property damage.

168. Lord Denning was prepared to take the first, even the second step in *Launchbury v. Morgans* [1971] 2 Q.B. 245 at 255. Several Canadian provinces have legislated for both contingencies: see *Doctrine of the "Family Car": A Study in Contrasts*, 8 Tex. Tech. L. Rev. 323 (1976); U.S.: *Prosser & Keeton* §73.
169. Ibid. at 255.
170. *Norwood v. Navan* [1981] R.T.R. 457 (C.A.): otherwise one would have to look into her shopping basket.
171. As in *Milkovits v. Federal Press* (1972) 20 F.L.R. 311 (son); *Rambarran v. Gurrucharran* [1970] 1 W.L.R. 556 (P.C.) (son); *Manawatu County v. Rowe* [1956] N.Z.L.R. 78 (wife).
172. So held in *Vandyke v. Fender* [1970] 2 Q.B. 292 (C.A.) where, however, the driver was required to carry his fellow employee. Cf. *Nottingham v. Aldridge* [1971] 2 Q.B. 739 at 752 where the servant drove his own car and the master was exonerated.
173. *Comino v. Lynch* [1959] Q.W.N. 49 (note that, the damage being to property, neither the *statutory* vicarious liability (see below, n. 177) nor the compulsory third party insurance were of avail to the plaintiff). Contra: *Morse v. Hicks* [1955] 3 D.L.R. 265. Aliter, if employer lends car to employee for an evening's entertainment: *Britt v. Galmoye* (1928) 44 T.L.R. 294.
174. *Jennings v. Hannan* (1969) 71 S.R. (N.S.W.) 226 (C.A.); *Manawatu County v. Rowe* [1956] N.Z.L.R. 78 (C.A.); *Barnard v. Sully* (1931) 47 T.L.R. 557.
175. *Rambarran v. Gurrucharran* [1970] 1 W.L.R. 556 (P.C.).

Accordingly, the problem can be largely solved by closing these gaps in the insurance scheme. As regards personal injury, this has been largely accomplished and accounts for the dearth of case law in this area.[176]

However, not content even with this seemingly foolproof scheme, some of the statutes have sought to reinforce it by legally identifying the owner with the driver of the car.[177] Thus in New South Wales

> "for the purposes of any proceedings against the owner of a motor vehicle . . . for the recovery of damages for liability in respect of the death or injury to a person caused by the fault of the driver . . . , the driver of the vehicle (whether with or without the authority of the owner) shall be taken to be the agent of the owner acting within the scope of the agent's authority in relation to the vehicle."[178]

A unique feature of the Australian legislation, in contrast to the Canadian[179] and American, is that the owner must bear responsibility not only for those who drive with his permission, express or implied, but for all drivers whatsoever, even thieves.[180]

The link between the statutory vicarious liability and compulsory insurance is emphasised by the fact that the former, just like the latter, covers only personal injury or death, not property damage or other economic loss. Nor does it apply to claims other than *against* owners.[181]

5. INDEPENDENT CONTRACTORS

As a general rule, the employment of an independent contractor does not entail responsibility for wrongs committed by him, or his employees, in the course of work for which he was engaged. This important qualification of vicarious liability, established in the early 19th century,[182] is most commonly explained on the ground that, as the employer lacks detailed control over the manner in which the work is done, it is the contractor himself who is best able to prevent the risks incidental to it and absorb such losses as occur. While there may sometimes be far greater spot control over the details of work of a contractor as compared with a servant,[183] it is nonetheless felt that, in the stock situations where work is turned over to

176. Australian legislation requires insurance cover for cars regardless of who drives (see below, p. 398). In England an owner who allows an uninsured person to drive is liable for breach of statutory duty: *Monk v. Warby* [1935] 1 K.B. 75 (see above, p. 189); see Weir, *Casebook on Tort* 274 (6th ed. 1988).
177. N.S.W.: *Motor Accidents Act* 1988 s. 53; Qld: *Motor Vehicle Insurance Act* 1936 s. 3(2); Tas.: *Traffic Act* 1925 s. 63(2); see *Cordwell v. Horton* [1964] Tas. S.R. 268; A.C.T.: *Motor Traffic Act* 1936 s. 31U; N.T.: *Motor Vehicle Act* 1949 s. 62; Cth: *Commonwealth Motor Vehicle (Liability) Act* 1959 s. 5.
178. The owner may however claim indemnity from unauthorised drivers.
179. British Columbia, Ontario and Nova Scotia. E.g. *Meulemeesters v. Smith* (1982) 38 O.R. (2d) 735. Moreover, some of these create only a rebuttable presumption.
180. *Marsh v. Absolum* [1940] N.Z.L.R. 448.
181. Only s. 3(2) of the Qld statute is at all ambiguous; it applies "for the purposes of . . . every claim for accidental bodily injury . . . to any person". Cf. above, p. 288.
182. *Laugher v. Pointer* (1826) 5 B. & C. 547; 108 E.R. 204; *Quarman v. Burnett* (1840) 6 M. & W. 499.
183. Compare a taxi driver with an interstate truck driver.

another who is in that line of business, like a taxi driver,[184] painter or builder, the risk of accident is incidental to the contractor's enterprise rather than his employer's. Though the latter benefits from the work, his contribution to the accident cost is more conveniently exacted by inclusion in the price of the services than by imposing vicarious liability, since in all save marginal cases the contractor, unlike a servant, is better equipped to carry insurance and distribute the losses.[185] Thus, the dual factors of accident prevention and efficient loss distribution support alike the exclusive responsibility of independent contractors and the vicarious liability for servants.

Yet for reasons far from clear there has been a trend, both here and in the United States, to encroach upon this principle to a point where it may now fairly be regarded as "primarily important only as a preamble to the catalogue of its exceptions".[186]

Negligence of employer

In the first place, the employer may incur liability for *personal* negligence in connection with the employment itself; for instance, if he carelessly entrusts the work to someone incompetent;[187] or if he, unlike the contractor, knows that there is a risk of harm unless special precautions are taken and fails to give instructions accordingly; or if he either authorises the commission of an unlawful act or employs a contractor to do something which necessarily involves violation of another's rights.[188] In all these cases, of course, the employer's liability rests on his own default, not the contractor's.

But there is no duty to supervise the contractor's work and therefore no liability to third parties, even if he exercised supervision and should have realised that the work was defective and dangerous, as in the case of a head- and sub-contractor on a construction project.[189] Only actual knowledge will trigger responsibility.[190]

Non-delegable duties

More controversial has been the wisdom of placing the employer, in an increasing range of situations, under responsibility for harm caused by a contractor in the performance of the work.[191] This disguised form of

184. But see *Rogers v. Night Riders* [1983] R.T.R. 324 (C.A.), a dubious decision, criticised by *Weir* 265.
185. See Williams, *Liability for Independent Contractors* [1956] Cam. L.J. 180.
186. *Pacific Fire Ins. v. Kenny Boiler Co.* 277 N.W. 266 at 288 (Minn. 1937).
187. Does this include a financially irresponsible contractor, as was held in *Becker v. Interstate Properties* 569 F. 2d 1203 (1977)?
188. See *Torette House v. Berkman* (1940) 62 C.L.R. 637 at 645; *The Pass of Ballater* [1942] P. 112 at 118.
189. *D. & F. Estates v. Church Comrs.* [1989] A.C. 177, disapproving *Mount Albert B.C. v. Johnson* [1978] 2 N.Z.L.R. 234. Aliter, *Casley-Smith v. Evans* (1989) A.T.R. 80-227 (fire on rubbish tip).
190. Ibid.
191. Divergent views obtain whether this includes injury to servants of that contractor (or another contractor engaged on the same job) or only outsiders. Negative is *Witham v. Bright S.* [1959] V.R. 790; affirmative, *Anderson v. Brady & Ross* 1964 S.L.T. (N.) 11; *Woolen v. Aerojet* 369 P. 2d 708 (Cal. 1962).

vicarious liability is imposed wherever the defendant is said to be under a "non-delegable" duty, in the sense that he cannot acquit himself by exercising reasonable care in entrusting the work to a reputable contractor but must actually assure that it is done—and done carefully.[192] From a practical standpoint, its most perplexing feature is the apparent absence of any coherent theory to explain when, and why, a particular duty should be so classified; and it has been questioned whether the resulting uncertainty and complexity of the law is matched by any corresponding advantages.[193] Now that a contractor's liability to third parties is no longer in doubt[194] and the employer would in any event be entitled to an indemnity,[195] what he is in effect called upon to do is to guarantee the contractor's ability to meet the claim. This is apt to bear harshly on individuals who, like many a home owner, are both uninsured and unable to pass on the cost. Australian courts have lately become more sensitive to their plight and reluctant to follow English and American precedents unreservedly.[196]

The list of cases where this vicarious liability, under the fictitious guise of non-delegable duties, has been found is long and diverse. Understandably, it includes all instances of strict liability, such as those relating to extra-hazardous substances[197] and fire,[198] providing lateral support for adjacent land,[199] and the near-strict duty to maintain premises abutting the highway in sound repair[200] and of bailees to guard property in their keep.[201] The very reason for importing strict liability betokens a special concern to ensure safety or else compensation. But it has been extended also to situations where the duty (as ordinarily formulated) is merely to use reasonable care, thereby converting it into the higher duty to assure that care is taken. Examples are the obligation of employers to provide a safe system of work[202] and to comply with statutory safety standards;[203] of hospitals to care for their patients,[204] though no longer of occupiers to their visitors[205] or of developers to home purchasers[206] or of manufacturers to the ultimate consumer or user of his products.[207] Apparently included also are cases where damage results from undertakings which, but for statutory authority, would be unlawful, as where a

192. See Chapman, *Liability for the Negligence of Independent Contractors*, 50 L.Q.R. 71 (1934); *Wilsons & Clyde Coal Co. v. English* [1938] A.C. 57 at 83-84 per Lord Wright. Williams [1956] Cam. L.J. 180 has rightly stigmatised the notion of "non-delegable duty" as a "logical fraud".
193. Williams, [1956] Cam. L.J. 180.
194. See below, p. 474.
195. See above, p. 265.
196. *Stoneman v. Lyons* (1975) 133 C.L.R. 550; *Torette House v. Berkman* (1940) 62 C.L.R. 637.
197. See above, p. 347.
198. See above, p. 352.
199. *Dalton v. Angus* (1881) 6 App. Cas. 740.
200. *Tarry v. Ashton* (1876) 1 Q.B.D. 314.
201. *Brit. Road Services v. Crutchley* [1968] 1 All E.R. 811 (C.A.).
202. E.g. *Kondis v. State Transport* (1984) 154 C.L.R. 672; contrast: *Stevens v. Brodribb* (1986) 160 C.L.R. 16.
203. *Groves v. Wimborne* [1898] 2 Q.B. 402 at 410.
204. See above, p. 373.
205. See below, p. 460.
206. *D. & F. Estates v. Church Comrs.* [1989] A.C. 177.
207. *Peake v. Steriline Mfg* (1988) A.T.R. 80-154 (component part).

contractor carelessly left some timber lying in a field after making trial bores on behalf of a government authority.[208] The most homogeneous group seems to consist of cases where the work involves a high risk in the absence of special precautions, so that—perhaps for the sake of additional risk prevention—the employer should be encouraged to ensure its proper performance by whomever he employs to get it done. Another common thread has been discerned in the existence of a "special protective relationship" as in the case of employers, schools and hospitals;[209] but that does not explain other instances nor why such a relation should demand this rather than some other form of increased responsibility, such as a higher degree of care or outright strict liability.

Extra-hazardous activities

It will be recalled that from its very origin, *Rylands v. Fletcher* imposed vicarious liability for independent contractors. Subsequently this was extended to all projected work involving high risk calling for special precautions.[210] In the leading case it was invoked against defendants who employed a contractor to take flashlight photographs of a cinema interior, because the use of magnesium powder was thought to create a peculiar risk of explosion and fire.[211] Likewise, where the use of implements or substances dangerous in themselves, like blowtorches or explosives, was obviously[212] incidental to the work to be performed.[213] The principle has not found favour in Australia, being criticised for the elusive nature of the category and for being incompatible with the prevailing negligence standard of liability.[214]

Nuisance

Prior to 1876 it seems to have been doubted whether liability could attach for a nuisance created by an independent contractor, unless it arose incidental to activities covered by the principle in *Rylands v. Fletcher.*[215] But in *Bower v. Peate* an action succeeded against a defendant whose contractor, engaged to pull down a house, caused damage to adjacent premises owing to the inadequacy of provisional support; and Cockburn C.J. ventured the oft-repeated generalisation that responsibility

208. *Darling v. A.-G.* [1950] 2 All E.R. 793. See also *Hardaker v. Idle D.C.* [1896] 1 Q.B. 335 at 351; *Holliday v. National Telephone* [1899] 2 Q.B. 392 at 398 (decisions which could be based on the extra-hazardous nature of the work).
209. *Kondis v. State Transport* (1984) 154 C.L.R. 672 at 687. See above, p. 373.
210. "Intrinsically dangerous" work (*Martin v. Sunlight Mining* (1896) 17 L.R. (N.S.W.) 364 at 367) or "acts which, in their very nature, involve special danger to others": *Honeywill v. Larkin Bros* [1934] 1 K.B. 191 at 197.
211. *Honeywill v. Larkin Bros* [1934] 1 K.B. 191. Also *A.-G. v. Geothermal Produce* [1987] 2 N.Z.L.R. 348 (C.A.): spraying toxic herbicide.
212. If the method employed is usual, he cannot excuse himself by pleading ignorance of its special danger: *Savage v. Wilby* [1954] S.C.R. 376; *Balfour v. Barty-King* [1957] 1 Q.B. 496.
213. *The Pass of Ballater* [1942] P. 112 at 117; *Firestone Co. v. Stoochinoff* (1964) 47 W.W.R. 102 (blowtorch); *Aga Heat v. Brockville Hotel* [1945] 1 D.L.R. 689; *St John v. Donald* [1926] 2 D.L.R. 185 (storing dynamite); *Holinaty v. Hawkins* (1965) 52 D.L.R. (2d) 289 (blasting); *Bennett v. Imperial Oil* (1961) 28 D.L.R. (2d) 55 (leaking underground petrol tank).
214. *Stevens v. Brodribb* (1986) 60 C.L.R. 16. But the problem would not be solved, as suggested, by applying a higher standard of care to dangerous activities.
215. See above, p. 334.

devolves on anyone who "orders a work to be executed from which, in the natural course of things, injurious consequences to his neighbour must be expected to arise, unless means are adopted by which such consequences may be prevented".[216]

Despite the far-reaching tenor of this proposition,[217] the weight of authority, at least in Australia, has clearly confined it to work which "of its very nature involves a risk of damage", such as bulldozing at the top of a steep slope[218] or perhaps exceptional building operations fraught with obvious danger of nuisance from noise or dust.[219] If the job is such that it is only negligence in the manner of conducting the operation, as distinct from the character of the operation itself, which will probably cause damage to others, the principal cannot be held to answer.[220] Thus vicarious liability was denied when a plumber negligently tampered with a stopcock, flooding adjacent premises,[221] and even (contrary to *Bower v. Peate* itself) when a building contractor caused a subsidence next door.[222]

Public thoroughfares

Responsibility has also been cast on those who employ contractors to carry out work in the highway or other places to which there is a public right of access, like railway platforms.[223] In these situations it seems to be assumed that because of its location, the work is fraught with exceptional risk to others and that the safety of the public is so important that he who has the work done should be answerable. In the leading case,[224] a telephone company laying cables along a street engaged a plumber to solder tubes through which the wires were passed. He negligently used a defective benzoline lamp which exploded and scattered molten solder over a passing pedestrian. For this the company was held liable. The principle is not confined to the use of dangerous implements, and has been applied where the contractor was negligent in felling a tree,[225] filling a trench,[226] leaving a heap of soil unprotected[227] or a coalhole open on a railway platform.[228] Yet it does not evidently apply to an operation off the highway, however proximate thereto, even when it results in injury thereon, as when a tree being felled in a front garden falls across the street.[229]

216. (1876) 1 Q.B.D. 321 at 326-327; invoked in *Dalton v. Angus* (1881) 6 App. Cas. 740; *Harris v. Carnegie's* [1917] V.L.R. 95; *Randall's v. Tanner* (1969) 4 D.L.R. (3d) 652.
217. See e.g. *Spicer v. Smee* [1946] 1 All E.R. 489 where it was interpreted to mean that whenever "danger is likely to arise unless work is properly done, there is a duty to see that it is properly done". Taken literally, this would swallow the non-liability rule completely.
218. *Watson v. Cowen* [1959] Tas. S.R. 194.
219. *Matania v. National Bank* [1936] 2 All E.R. 633.
220. *Torette House v. Berkman* (1940) 62 C.L.R. 637 at 648. Cf. *Rest.* §835.
221. *Torette House v. Berkman* (1940) 62 C.L.R. 637.
222. *Stoneman v. Lyons* (1975) 133 C.L.R. 550.
223. *Pickard v. Smith* (1861) 10 C.B. (N.S.) 470; 142 E.R. 535.
224. *Holliday v. National Telephone* [1899] 2 Q.B. 392.
225. *Witham v. Bright S.* [1959] V.R. 790.
226. *Gray v. Pullen* (1864) 5 B. & S. 970; 122 E.R. 1091; *Hardaker v. Idle D.C.* [1896] 1 Q.B. 335.
227. *Penny v. Wimbledon U.D.C.* [1899] 2 Q.B. 72.
228. *Pickard v. Smith* (1861) 10 C.B. (N.S.) 470; 142 E.R. 535.
229. *Salsbury v. Woodland* [1970] 1 Q.B. 324 (C.A.).

Collateral negligence

We have already noted that a non-delegable duty includes responsibility not only for the delegate's failure to perform the duty (for example to carry out a repair), but also negligence in the course of performing it (for example injuring a bystander). But it does not extend to "casual" or "collateral" acts of negligence. This limitation provides the most important distinction between a principal's liability for the acts of an independent contractor and the genuinely vicarious liability of a "master" because the latter is accountable for any wrongdoing of his servant, however incidental to the main job, so long as it falls within the course of employment.[230] Suppose a contractor is instructed to carry out dangerous work on the highway and negligently knocks down a pedestrian while bringing up machinery for the job; his employer would not be liable, because the negligence is collateral to the work itself. In the same circumstances, though, a master would clearly have to pay.

The distinction between "casual" negligence and misconduct for which a principal is held responsible has tended to be rather elusive, especially in those marginal cases which have been reported. Standard judicial definitions of "collateral" as "negligence other than the imperfect or improper performance of the work which the contractor is employed to do"[231] or "negligence in the manner of conducting the operation as distinct from the character of the operation itself"[232] are of little assistance in the solution of concrete problems. There are few decisions in which a defendant has successfully escaped responsibility on this ground,[233] but some may help to illustrate the distinction. The negligent dropping of a tool from a sill by workmen putting casements into windows is collateral to the employment,[234] but leaving an unlighted and unguarded heap of soil, as distinct from a pickaxe, in the course of road making is not.[235] That "it is not always easy to steer a definite course between one side and the other"[236] is attested by American cases which held that dropping a paint bucket out of a window while painting inside a house is collateral, but dropping it whilst painting a sign over a pavement is not.[237]

The difficulty of reconciling some of these decisions is self-evident. This is due not only to the fact that a determination of whether an act is a minor incident or operative detail of the work is highly subjective, but also to a tendency in more modern cases increasingly to minimise the scope of this limitation. There is accordingly much force in the suggestion[238] that a

230. *Cassidy v. M.O.H.* [1951] 2 K.B. 343 at 364.
231. *Hardaker v. Idle D.C.* [1896] 1 Q.B. 335 at 352 per Rigby L.J.
232. *Torette House v. Berkman* (1940) 62 C.L.R. 637 at 648 per Latham C.J.
233. *Padbury v. Holliday* (1912) 28 T.L.R. 494 is the only English case. *Reedie v. L.N.W. Rly* (1849) 4 Ex. 244; 154 E.R. 1201 and *Overton v. Freeman* (1852) 11 C.B. 867; 138 E.R. 717, cited by Chapman (50 L.Q.R. 71 at 80), were based on other grounds. The first intimation of the doctrine is found no earlier than in *Hole v. Sittingbourne Rly* (1861) 6 H. & N. 488; 158 E.R. 201.
234. *Padbury v. Holliday* (1912) 28 T.L.R. 494.
235. *Penny v. Wimbledon U.D.C.* [1899] 2 Q.B. 73; *McLellan v. N.Z. Roads* [1927] N.Z.L.R. 172.
236. *Darling v. A.-G.* [1950] 2 All E.R. 793 at 796 per Morris J.
237. See *Prosser & Keeton* 515-516.
238. *Prosser & Keeton* 516; Baker, *Independent Contractors*, 27 A.L.J. 546 at 549 (1954).

more appropriate criterion would be the dissociation of the act in question from any inherent risk created by the work itself. Negligence would thus be deemed collateral only if the performance of the work contracted for did not involve any recognisable risk of such harm to the plaintiff, such as an abnormal departure from the usual methods.[239] This suggested reformulation does not conflict with any of the more modern English decisions.[240]

239. Adoption of "a usual and ordinary method" is sufficient to saddle the principal with liability: *McInnes v. Wardle* (1931) 45 C.L.R. 548 at 550; and see *St John v. Donald* [1926] 2 D.L.R. 185 at 194.

240. Except *Padbury v. Holliday* (1912) 28 T.L.R. 494, which has remained isolated.

20

PRIVATE AND SOCIAL INSURANCE

1. INSURANCE

Private insurance has become by far the most prominent source of compensating accident losses in our time. Its relationship to tort liability varies with the type of insurance. Third party (or liability) insurance stands behind the tortfeasor and is triggered by his *liability* for the loss he has caused to someone else; in contrast, first party insurance (for example fire insurance) indemnifies the insured for his own loss without any reference to the tort system. The latter therefore affords compensation on a no-fault basis; the effect of the former in diluting the fault system is more subtle but nonetheless pervasive, as we have discovered throughout this text.

I. First Party Insurance

A first party insurer promises to pay the insured a certain sum of money in a particular event or to make good a specified loss. The former is called "sum insurance", the latter "loss or indemnity insurance". Examples of the first are life and personal accident insurance; examples of the second are insurance against fire or damage to one's own car from collision or upset. The most important consequence of this distinction for the tort context is that indemnity, unlike sum, insurance confers on the insurer a right of subrogation against tortfeasors.[1]

Subrogation

An indemnity insurer has an equitable right, whether specified in the insurance contract or not, to pursue the insured's rights in the latter's name against any defendant whose tort caused the insured loss, to the extent that the insurer has indemnified the insured for it.[2] Alternatively, if the tortfeasor has already compensated the insured, the insurer may claim repayment from the latter for the insurance benefits he had previously received.[3]

1. Generally: Sutton, *Insurance Law in Australia and New Zealand* (1980) ch. 16; Derham, *Subrogation in Insurance Law* (1985); Hasson, 5 Oxf. J. Leg. St. 416 (1985).
2. The insurer as subrogee must sue in the insured's name (*London Assurance v. Sainsbury* (1783) 3 Doug. K.B. 245; 99 E.R. 636) unless he has taken an assignment: *King v. Victoria Insurance* [1896] A.C. 250 (P.C.); *Compania Colombiana v. Pacific Steam Navigation* [1965] 1 Q.B. 101.
3. *Castellain v. Preston* (1883) 11 Q.B.D. 380; *Kenny v. Brierty* [1982] V.R. 339 at 346. The insurer cannot prevent the insured from pursuing the tortfeasor, though it be contrary to a knock for knock agreement: *Morley v. Moore* [1936] 2 K.B. 359; *Bourne v. Stanbridge* [1965] 1 W.L.R. 189. But abrogation is not defeated by a settlement between the insured and the tortfeasor aware of payments made by the insurer: *Morganite Fibres v. Sola* (1987) 11 N.S.W.L.R. 189.

In either event, the tort victim is prevented from recovering more than a simple indemnity for his loss from both sources.[4]

The primary purpose of subrogation is to vindicate the principle that the assured shall be no more than indemnified for his actual loss, a safeguard against insurance degenerating into a wager[5] and the "moral hazard" of tempting the insured to bring about the insured event. It has also been justified as an adjunct of the assumed aim of tort law to deter the guilty when the victim, having been compensated by the insurance, might not otherwise have considered it worthwhile to pursue the tortfeasor. But under modern conditions when the latter would most often be himself covered by liability insurance (since otherwise he would rarely be worth suing), subrogation is in reality exercised not against the individual defendant so as to have a residual deterrent effect, but against another insurer. The considerable legal and administrative costs of subrogation recoveries raise additional scepticism concerning the value of subrogation, especially in cases of motor car collisions when the same people pay for both collision and liability insurance so that subrogation merely adds gratuitously to the cost of premiums. This explains the widespread practice of "knock for knock" agreements whereby motor insurers agree in advance to pay their own clients on a first party basis without any recourse by way of subrogation.[6]

Subrogation, being a right independent of agreement, may be exercised not only without the insured's consent but against his very wishes. Such is likely to be the case when the loss has been caused by the tort of the insured's own employee[7] or a close member of his family whom the insured would not have thought of suing himself. To spare resentment or embarrassment, Australia has followed the example of some other countries in denying subrogation in these cases.[8]

In contrast to indemnity insurance, "sum" insurance (when a fixed sum is payable on a specified event) does not confer a right of subrogation. "Whole" life (endowment) insurance represents a form of savings to which the beneficiary is and should be entitled regardless of any other available compensation: he may thus bargain (and pay) for "double recovery".[9] "Term" life insurance and accident insurance have been traditionally treated in the same manner, in view of their common feature that the sum payable in the insured event is fixed arbitrarily in advance without reference to the actual proven loss. However, not all forms of insurance against personal injury or death are sum insurance; for example, workers' compensation, which is principally based on indemnifying injured workers for their medical expenses and loss of earnings, has been traditionally

4. But the subrogee cannot claim until the subrogor has been *fully* indemnified: *Ledingham v. Ontario Hospital Comm.* [1975] 1 S.C.R. 332.
5. It thus bears kinship to the requirement of insurable interest in life insurance.
6. See *Hobbs v. Marlowe* [1978] A.C. 16; 41 Mod. L. Rev. 201 (1978). In Canada a multilateral agreement allocates proportional loss by reference to a chart depending on angle of collision: Brown & Menezes, *Insurance Law in Canada* (1982), app. F.
7. *Lister v. Romford Ice Co.* [1957] A.C. 555.
8. *Insurance Contract Act* 1984 (Cth) ss 65, 66; Fleming, XI Int. Encycl. Comp. L. ch. 11, p. 65.
9. See above, p. 244.

invested with a statutory right of subrogation;[10] also modern accident or disability policies providing indemnity rather than predetermined amounts for medical expenses or loss of earnings are therefore entitled to subrogation.[11]

Impact on tort liability

First party insurance has in the past played a more important role in case of property damage than personal injury.[12] Especially with high market penetration, like fire and homeowner insurance, there may be every reason to regard it as a better source of compensation than tort liability, being not only more convenient to the victim but also much more cost efficient. This insight may have an increasing effect on future legal development.[13]

On the other hand, victims of personal injury are far less likely to carry first party insurance and must therefore rely to a much greater extent on tort liability as a source of compensation. Admittedly, motor car policies nowadays frequently offer options for medical costs and scheduled injury benefits, but these are far from ubiquitous and provide proportionately little help to the more seriously injured.[14] As we shall see,[15] the contemporary reform movement seeks to make such benefits available to all accident, or at least road accident, victims either complementary to or in lieu of tort liability.

II. Third Party Insurance

During this century, third party or liability insurance has become well nigh ubiquitous. It has a dual protective purpose: for the insured tortfeasor[16] it affords protection against the potentially catastrophic effects of an adverse judgment;[17] for the victim it assures that his right to recover will not become a dead letter because the defendant happens to lack the assets to meet his legal obligations. The first explains why business and even private individuals with a stake as modest as the equity in their home cannot afford to run the risk of ruinous liability without such cover. As for the second,

10. See below.
11. *Glynn v. Scottish Union Ins.* (1963) 40 D.L.R. (2d) 929 (Ont. C.A.); *Gibson v. Sun Life* (Ont. 1984) 6 D.L.R. (4th) 746; Kimball & Davis, *Extension of Insurance Subrogation*, 60 Mich. L. Rev. 841 (1962); XI Int. Encycl. Comp. L. ch. 11, pp. 17-21.
12. See generally Dinsdale, *History of Accident Insurance in Great Britain* (1954).
13. By encouraging subrogation or scaling down tort liability. Thus *Mason v. Sainsbury* (1782) 3 Doug. K.B. 61; 99 E.R. 538, the fons et origo of subrogation, was nullified by the *Metropolitan Police Compensation Act* 1886, abrogating all claims for riot damage by plaintiffs who are insured; accord: *Interstate Fire v. Milwaukee* 173 N.W. 2d 187 (Wis. 1970). For fire damage see above, p. 249.
14. Conard et al., *Automobile Accident Costs and Payments* (1964); Bombaugh, *Department of Transportation Automobile Insurance Study*, 71 Col. L. Rev. 207 (1971).
15. See below, p. 400.
16. This includes, besides the named insured, any other person to whom the policy was expressed to extend: *Insurance Contracts Act* 1984 (Cth) s. 48; *Trident Gen. Insurance v. McNiece* (1988) 165 C.L.R. 107.
17. Hence policies must not be construed to render such protection illusory. E.g. the common condition that the insured "take all reasonable precautions to prevent injury" requires only that he not act *recklessly*, i.e. without caring whether the known danger can be averted or not: *Body Corp. v. Albion Ins.* [1982] V.R. 699; *Fraser v. Furman* [1967] 1 W.L.R. 989 at 905.

effective compensation for the tort victim has in some instances[18] become of such paramount public concern that insurance has been made compulsory and acquired other features of social insurance. In multi-party ventures such as construction projects it is efficient for one global insurance policy to cover all participants so as in effect to "channel" liability. In Australia this is aided by a statute which confers insurance cover on third parties, such as subcontractors, specified in the contract though not parties to it.[18a]

Our principal focus will here be on compulsory insurance against motor car liability.

Motor car insurance

Compulsory liability insurance for the owner and driver of motor vehicles was pioneered in 1928 in New Zealand. Adopted in Britain in 1930, it later spread throughout Australia between 1935 and 1944. Since then, the system has been progressively improved by plugging gaps in the coverage and refining its administration.[19]

The duty to insure is imposed on the car owner as a prerequisite to its annual registration. Unlike in the United States, the policy must cover the liability of the owner and of the driver[20] whether he drives with or without the owner's consent.[21] The liability covered is for personal injury or death[22] "caused by or arising out of the use"[23] of his motor vehicle. Until fairly recently some of the statutes excluded compulsory coverage to non-paying passengers,[24] and until the abolition of marital immunity[25] there was consequently no coverage for interspousal accidents. Generally, the insurance must cover the total amount of the defendant's liability, unlike the varying and often very low limits in Canada and the United States.

In marked departure from convention are provisions regarding imperfect policies. Contrary to the general rule still applicable to non-compulsory

18. Apart from motor vehicle insurance, the principal instances of compulsory third party insurance are against employer's common law liability and workers' compensation: see below, p. 504. For products liability insurance, which is voluntary, see below, p. 495. Generally: Derrington & Ashton, *Liability Insurance* (1990).
18a. *Insurance Contracts Act* 1984 (Cth) s. 48. Also *Trident Ins. v. McNiece Bros.* (1988) 165 C.L.R. 107.
19. Castles, *Compulsory Automobile Liability Insurance in Australia*, 6 Am. J. Comp. L. 257 (1957); Parsons, *Death and Injury on the Roads*, 3 Annual L. Rev. 201 (1955); *Third Party Insurance in Australia* (1973) which contains a reprint of the statutes: N.S.W.: *Motor Accidents Act* 1988; Vic.: *Motor Car Act* 1958; Qld: *Motor Vehicle Insurance Act* 1936; S.A.: *Motor Vehicle Act* 1959; W.A.: *Motor Vehicle (Third Party Insurance) Act* 1943; Tas.: *Motor Accidents (Liability and Compensation) Act* 1973; A.C.T.: *Motor Traffic Act* 1936; N.T.: *Motor Vehicle Act* 1949.
20. The insurance thus "channels" liability into a single compensation pool.
21. See above, p. 388.
22. Cover for property damage is voluntary, but not in the U.K. since 1987 (pursuant to the E.E.C. Directive).
23. The problem is reminiscent of "remoteness" in tort and is approached broadly: e.g. *Fawcett v. B.H.P.* (1960) 104 C.L.R. 80; *G.I.O. v. Green* (1966) 114 C.L.R. 437; *Harvey Trinder v. G.I.O.* (1966) 144 C.L.R. 449.
24. Tas. (s. 64) retains a low monetary limit. Such exclusions are more frequent in non-compulsory insurance policies.
25. See below, p. 680.

liability insurance,[26] compensation of the victim cannot be defeated by the fact that the policy was obtained by a material misstatement or non-disclosure, or that the insured has broken a term, condition or warranty of the policy, committed a breach of the Insurance Act[27] or committed a crime by intentionally injuring the victim.[28] In case of the insured's bankruptcy, the plaintiff is now also protected against competing claims of the bankrupt's general creditors.[29] Finally, protection extends even to the victims of uninsured and unidentified vehicles who may as a rule[30] enforce their claim against the "Nominal Defendant" or "The Trust".[31]

In most European countries the tort plaintiff has been given a "direct action" against the insurer.[32] This is permitted only exceptionally in Australia[33] and most other common law countries, seemingly under the fanciful impression that the disclosure of insurance might have prejudicial effect on litigation, especially before juries. Even so, the insurer has a right to take over the conduct of proceedings and to settle or defend the claim against the insured.[34] Besides, in most jurisdictions a direct claim against the insurer lies whenever the insured is dead[35] or cannot be served with process. Also, a judgment once recovered against the tortfeasor can be enforced directly against his insurer.[36]

Compulsory third party insurance is strictly regulated and supervised. Private insurers must be licensed and maximum premiums are prescribed officially. In Australia the decided trend has been towards concentration of the market: in New South Wales the Government Insurance Office (G.I.O.) has a virtual monopoly, in Victoria the market is practically shared by two

26. E.g. *Australian Motor Insurers v. Goss* [1983] V.R. 725 (no disclosure of prior collision).
27. E.g. N.S.W.: s. 15(3); Qld: s. 4A(2). But in many such cases, the insurer has a right of reimbursement from the owner (e.g. *Insurance Act* s. 15(4)).
28. *Gardner v. Moore* [1984] A.C. 548; *Lamb v. Cotogno* (1987) 164 C.L.R. 1 (even exemplary damages). Non-compulsory insurance provides no cover against deliberate (heinous) crime, like threatening someone with a loaded gun: see above, p. 35. This result is explained as a deterrent against wickedness, which may be a good reason for denying the claim of the culprit but not of his victim. However, the rule no longer disqualifies claims arising out of negligence (even gross: *Hardy v. Motor Ins. Bureau* [1964] 2 Q.B. 745) or even wilful misconduct not plainly anti-social, like breach of a traffic regulation: *Fire & All Risks Ins. v. Powell* [1966] V.R. 513 (F.C.), even though breach of the regulation caused the precise accident sought to be avoided.
29. *Bankruptcy Act* 1966 (Cth) s. 84(1A): all liability policies. But cf. *Bradley v. Eagle Star Insurance* [1989] A.C. 957.
30. Occasionally a claimant falls victim also to poor statutory drafting: e.g. *Nominal Defendant v. Taylor* (1982) 41 A.L.R. 244 (H.C.).
31. The latter has a right of recourse against the owner or driver: e.g. (N.S.W.) s. 32; (Vic.) s. 50. England: the anomalous Motor Insurance Bureau: see Williams, *Motor Insurance Bureau* (4th ed. 1983); Lewis, *Insurers' Agreements Not to Enforce Strict Legal Rights*, 48 Mod. L. Rev. 275 (1985).
32. XI Int. Encycl. Comp. L. ch. 11, pp. 55-58.
33. E.g. *Motor Vehicles (Third Party Insurance) Act* 1942 (N.S.W.) s. 14.
34. The insured is not, however, precluded from independent representation, e.g. in case of a conflict of interest or with respect to property damage: *Wong Hing Wah v. Lopresti* (1965) 82 W.N. (Pt 1) (N.S.W.) 452.
35. E.g. *Insurance Contracts Act* 1984 (Cth) s. 51. Several states give an alternative right of action against his estate. See Britt, *Third Party Insurance in Australia* (1973) 28-36.
36. E.g. N.S.W.: s. 25; Vic.: s. 47; S.A.: s. 112. In N.S.W., exceptionally, a lien attaches against insurance moneys as soon as the claim arises, enforceable with judicial leave: see *Oswald v. Bailey* (1987) 11 N.S.W.L.R. 715 (insurer joined as co-defendant).

insurers,[37] and in Tasmania and Western Australia there is a single statutory authority.[38]

Since third party liability insurance is an instance of indemnity insurance, it entails a right of subrogation which enables an insurer to claim contribution or indemnity from other defendants, such as the driver of a second car. This does not, however, include the driver of the insured vehicle,[39] since under our legislation the policy must cover the driver as well as the owner. If more than one policy covers the risk, as when the insured carries both an employer's and a motor vehicle policy, the insurers have a right to pro rata contribution in accordance with equitable principles.[40]

Motor car insurance suffered a serious crisis in Australia in the mid-80s as revenues fell increasingly short of the cost of meeting claims and expenses.[41] The principal cause was its deviation from market principles, which was reflected in many ways. As already explained, legislation has transformed this type of insurance with provisions reflecting a social insurance philosophy, often insouciant of "moral hazards" like the compulsory cover for passengers, including members of the owner's family, and cover for any driver of the insured vehicle, without effecting premiums. To this was added the practice in general of flat-rating premiums without regard to age, sex or driving record of the owner or, indeed, anyone else driving the car; compounded by government policy of keeping premiums down for political advantage. This combination of factors first drove private insurance from the market and eventually prompted more radical legislative intervention. Some jurisdictions adopted no-fault plans, either completely abolishing or sharply curtailing negligence actions; others imposed severe restrictions on common law damages. These reforms will be considered presently.

2. MOTOR ACCIDENT PLANS

Compulsory liability insurance ensured that the victim of negligent driving would not go empty-handed because the defendant lacked the financial resources to meet his obligations. It thus helped to make the system work, but did not change the system itself. The tort system's defects however are fundamental and urgent.

We need not here retrace the arguments for concluding that negligence long ago forfeited its claim as the guardian of individual responsibility or as a significant promoter of accident prevention.[42] Especially in the case

37. State Motor and the R.A.C.V.
38. Tas.: s. 14; W.A.: s. 6.
39. As it did in *Lister v. Romford Ice Co.* [1957] A.C. 555 under the English legislation.
40. *Albion Ins. v. G.I.O.* (1969) 121 C.L.R. 342; *Commercial & General Ins. v. G.I.O.* (1973) 129 C.L.R. 374; *Comm. Union Assurance v. Hayden* [1977] Q.B. 804 (C.A.).
41. See Keeler, *The Crises of Liability Insurance*, 1 Ins. L.J. 182. Other countries also suffered insurance "crises" from a combination of expanding liability and cyclical market factors. See Priest, *The Current Insurance Crisis and Modern Tort Law*, 96 Yale L.J. 1521 (1987); Fleming, *The Insurance Crisis*, 24 U.B.C.L. Rev. 1 (1990).
42. Above, p. 8ff. Brown's *Deterrence in Tort and No-Fault: The N.Z. Experience*, 73 Col. L. Rev. 976 (1985) suggests at any rate that no-fault has not increased accidents.

of motor accidents, compulsory liability insurance revealed a greater social concern with compensating the injured than with retaining tort liability as a means of influencing human conduct. The motorist's fear of injuring himself or losing his driving licence or suffering other punishment is far more potent.

Even more negative are the inefficiencies and costs of the tort system. In the first place, too many victims are either not compensated at all or only inadequately. It has been estimated that in Australia 40 per cent of road casualties have no tort rights whatever,[43] that contributory negligence affects at least 15 per cent and that their damages are reduced by an average of 40 per cent.[44] Further reductions result from the ability of the defence in many cases to discount settlement offers sharply by the uncertainties of the "forensic lottery".[45] Next is the delay in compensating those who are entitled. Barely half are paid within the first year, and even after five years 5-10 per cent are still waiting.[46] Apart from the financial privation, the accompanying anxiety frequently has a disastrous effect on rehabilitation. Finally, there is the exorbitant cost of the system due to inherent factors such as the expense involved in the process of sifting the evidence for clues of liability and the expense of adversary proceedings.[47] Legal costs incurred by insurers alone, including amounts paid to successful claimants, reach 25 per cent of net payment to the latter.[48] To this must be added uncompensated plaintiff's costs, the administrative overhead of liability insurance[49] and the price paid by the public for supporting the judicial system and its clogged courts. Even granted that these figures are substantially lower than the American (swollen by high contingent fees and commissions),[50] they cannot bear comparison with the less than 8 per cent of premiums under the New Zealand accident compensation scheme.[51]

43. *Compensation and Rehabilitation in Australia*, Report of the National Committee of Inquiry (1974) §127 (hereinafter cited *Compensation*). The U.K. estimate is 75% (*Pearson* §994). This group comprises the victims of no-fault accidents as well as drivers of single car accidents (the latter: 20%). Over 3,500 persons are killed and almost 100,000 require medical treatment annually: *Commonwealth Yearbook* ("road accidents").
44. Ibid. §130-131.
45. See Phillips & Hawkins, *Some Economic Aspects of the Settlement Process*, 39 Mod. L. Rev. 487 (1976); generally: Ison, *Forensic Lottery* (1967). Settlements are believed to be less than half of average verdicts because of discounts for the contingencies of losing the case entirely or partially and for the risk averseness promoted by the rule that loser pays winner's legal fees. See Genn, *Hard Bargaining* (1987).
46. *Compensation* §113 (accord for U.K.: *Pearson* §992). As a palliative, the *Administration of Justice Act* 1969 (Eng.) s. 20 authorised pre-trial awards of interim payments, e.g. where liability is admitted.
47. In 1979-1980 $674.5 mill. was collected in premiums: Luntz, 55 L.I.J. 745 at 748 (1981).
48. Ibid. §153-156.
49. The enviable record by the N.S.W. G.I.O. of 3% is quite unrepresentative because of its virtual monopoly: *Compensation* §159. The ratio of management expenses and commissions by private insurers to workers' compensation premiums is around 20%: ibid. §220.
50. Fees of plaintiffs' attorneys had a median of 32.5%. Only 44c out of every premium dollar was used to compensate victims: general overhead accounted for 33c and claims administration for 23c: Volpe, *Motor Vehicle Crash Losses* (DOT 1971) 49-52.
51. In Australia, Troy & Butlin (*Cost of Collisions*, 1971) and in the U.K. *Pearson* §993 estimated a 45% cost ratio; the *Woodhouse Report* (1967) in N.Z. and the *British Columbia* report estimated 40%. In the U.S. it is even worse—55%, of which 25% accounts for legal expenses.

In summary, these data furnish a formidable bill of indictment against the present adversary system as a model for coping with the toll of the road.[52] Its inadequacy for the industrial injuries of a mass society led a century ago to the introduction of workers' compensation. Today, the same insight is being extended to motor accidents and even beyond.[53]

Mixed systems

Three different solutions, increasingly radical, have been proposed and found acceptance in different common law jurisdictions.[54] The least extreme is to offer to casualties of road traffic limited first party benefits on a no-fault basis, without in any way curtailing their right to common law damages against negligent defendants. An intermediate solution is to abolish the tort remedy for less severe injuries, the most radical makes first party compensation exclusive.

The first of these reforms has attracted the widest support, primarily because it least threatens the legal profession's stake in the tort process. Indeed, to the extent that it affords some monetary first aid to victims, it may arm them to better withstand the blandishments of an inadequate settlement offer and undertake the risk of a law suit. It therefore results in higher premiums and explains the relatively low benefits offered. While it mops up minor injuries—the overwhelming majority of all claims[55]—it paradoxically stops short of providing benefits precisely where they are most needed, viz. for the severer injuries which have a progressively lesser prospect of being adequately met from existing sources.[56]

These "add-on" plans, as they are called in the United States, were pioneered in Canada[57] and are currently in force in eight American States.[58] They provided the model for the first two Australian schemes, in Victoria[59] (since superseded by more drastic reform described below) and Tasmania.[60]

52. Motor vehicle injuries amount to about 10% (work injuries to 20%) of all injuries (Britain: 290,000; Australia: 95,000 p.a.) In Australia (1979) 5 persons were killed, 125 injured per 10,000 vehicles.
53. See Atiyah, *Accidents.* For a sceptical counter attack see Blum & Kalven, *Public Law Perspectives on a Private Law Problem—Auto Compensation Plans* (1965); countered by Calabresi, *Fault, Accidents and the Wonderful World of Blum and Kalven*, 75 Yale L.J. 216 (1965); and again Blum & Kalven, *Empty Cabinet of Dr Calabresi*, 34 U. Chi. L. Rev. 239 (1967).
54. The Continental model of strict liability with compulsory insurance has made no headway in the common law world. For this and other plans see Tunc, XI Int. Encycl. Comp. L. ch. 14 (Traffic Accident Compensation: Law and Proposals) and Symposium (Tunc ed.) *Pour une Loi sur les Accidents de la Circulation* (1981).
55. Statistics in Victoria available in 1972 indicated that 53% of all claims were finalised for $200 or less, 77% for $1,000 or less, and 94% for $5,000 or less.
56. See Blum & Kalven, *Ceilings, Costs and Compulsion in Auto Compensation* [1973] Utah L. Rev. 341.
57. The first by a long stretch was Sask. (1946), later followed by Ontario (1969), British Columbia (1970) and other Provinces. See Brown, *No-Fault Automobile Insurance in Canada* (1988), *Linden* ch. 17. The Osborne Report (1988) recommended retention for Ontario: see Klar, 68 Can. B. Rev. 301 (1989).
58. See U.S. Department of Transportation, *Compensating Auto Accident Victims: A Follow-Up Report on No-Fault Auto Insurance Experiences* (1985).
59. *Motor Accidents Act* 1973.
60. *Motor Accidents (Liabilities and Compensation) Act* 1973. The L.R.C. (No. 52) in 1988 recommended either a "pure" system or substantial modification of common law damages.

A crucial feature of the American plan, and a key to their political acceptance, is their avoidance of bureaucracy. Operating in a competitive insurance market, they prescribe first party coverage for the occupants of the car and pedestrians struck by it. They simply make compulsory an insurance cover that was and is otherwise available on a voluntary basis. Their Australian counterparts are centralised in a single insurance authority, private insurance companies having over time mostly abandoned the field as unprofitable. In contrast, the Pearson Commission in Britain recommended linking compensation for road accidents to the existing social security system by furnishing the same preferential benefits as for industrial injuries (the successor of workers' compensation).[61] These benefits would compare very favourably in amount and duration with those previously considered, and would be financed by a tax on petrol. They raise, however, the issue of "horizontal equity" (why should road victims fare better than other accident victims under social security?) and the wisdom of retaining tort claims as a back-up remedy (for the well-to-do). The social security model rather than private insurance was chosen because of its substantially lower overhead costs.

Limiting tort

The high cost of common law compensation, reflected in Australia by steep deficits in insurance funds,[62] has been countered by two strategies.[63] One was to limit the quantum of non-pecuniary damages, as in New South Wales and South Australia.[64] Alternatively, some mixed system-jurisdictions have imposed "thresholds" below which tort recourse is abolished as a trade-off for no-fault benefits.

The latter device was pioneered in the United States.[65] The overhead cost of tort compensation is distressingly high in the case of minor injuries which make up about 95 per cent of the total toll.[66] Moreover, in these cases awards for pain and suffering are least needed, especially since a large proportion of the casualties receive multiple compensation from different sources.[67] By allowing tort claims only above a certain threshold, insurance premiums can be substantially reduced to offset the extra cost of first party benefits for all automobile casualties. This type of plan was therefore welcomed most of all by a segment of the insurance industry concerned with the spiralling cost of liability insurance and its adverse effect on premiums and profitability. Its attraction was that it left their own role intact and did not involve, as the Australian and some Canadian plans do,[68] the creation of a governmental compensation authority.

61. Report I ch. 18. See Trindade, *A No-Fault Scheme for Road Accident Victims in the U.K.*, 96 L.Q.R. 580 (1980).
62. The result of inadequate flat rates set by State governments.
63. For a survey see Malkin, *Unequal Treatment of Personal Injuries*, 17 M.U.L.R. 685 (1990).
64. See above, p. 240.
65. The inspiration of this model was the Keeton-O'Connell plan, *Basic Protection of the Traffic Victim* (1965).
66. See above, n. 14.
67. Ibid.
68. In Australia private insurers had mostly withdrawn from this unprofitable line of business when rates were being fixed by government on political, not insurance, principles.

The effectiveness and success of the various plans are conditioned by the interplay between two variables: the level of no-fault benefits and the threshold which a victim must cross before qualifying for a tort claim.[69] Benefits vary greatly, ranging from $2,000 in Massachusetts to $50,000 work loss and unlimited medical expenses in Michigan and New Jersey. Only personal injury or death are covered. Thresholds are commonly expressed either in absolute monetary terms (for example $500 medical costs or $5,000 non-economic detriment) or in combination with such descriptive tests as "death, significant permanent injury, serious permanent disfigurement or more than six months of complete inability to work". In order to provide adequate benefits at no greater cost than under the previous common law regime, these thresholds have to eliminate all but the small minority of severe injuries for which tort claims are retained.

In 1986 this model was adopted in Victoria[70] for transport accidents (car, rail or tram). Common law rights to sue are restricted to cases of "serious injury" (at least 30 per cent impairment), and for pain and suffering have a threshold of $20,000 and ceiling of $200,000, for pecuniary damages a threshold of $20,000 and ceiling of $450,000. Damages for death are limited to $500,000. So severe are these restrictions that only 1 per cent of awards made in 1984-1985 were thought to qualify under the new scheme.[71] No-fault benefits cover medical costs, weekly payments of up to 80 per cent pre-accident earnings (maximum $430) and lump sum impairment benefits on a scale of $40,500.

Pure no-fault

Unlike the preceding "mixed" systems, "pure" systems of compensation replace the common law remedy completely. This is the model of workers' compensation in many countries, including the United States, Canada and most of Western Europe, where compensation is the exclusive remedy against an employer for industrial injuries.[72]

It has also made some headway in relation to traffic accidents, but so far more often in recommendation than adoption. It was enacted in Quebec (1974) and Israel (1976), and once envisaged in Victoria and New South Wales. Its first convert in Australia was, and remains, the Northern Territory which in 1979 abolished all tort claims for motor vehicle accidents, substituting no-fault benefits up to 85 per cent pre-accident earnings, medical and rehabilitation expenses up to $50,000 and lump sum payments for permanent impairment on the workers' compensation model to a maximum of $50,000 (for death $55,000).[73]

This model differs in several important respects from the strict liability model of European countries.[74] The latter, being a modification of tort liability, offers no protection to drivers in one-car accidents and is tied to

69. See DOT study (above, n. 50) and Fleming, *The American Tort Process* 169-174 (1988).
70. *Transport Accident Act* 1986. Tort abolished: s. 93. See Malkin, 16 M.U.L.R. 254 (1988). So also it was in Ontario in 1990.
71. Keeler, unpub. ms. p. 115.
72. See below, p. 504.
73. *Motor Accidents (Compensation) Act* 1979.
74. See above, n. 54.

third party insurance; the former covers, besides others, all occupants of a car and is based on first party insurance, usually administered by a central fund.

3. COMPREHENSIVE ACCIDENT COMPENSATION

New Zealand

Following the famous Woodhouse Report,[75] New Zealand launched in 1974 a comprehensive system of exclusive compensation, replacing tort recovery not only for traffic and industrial accidents but for all "personal injury by accident", including certain industrial diseases and criminal injuries.[76] The decision to embrace all accidents was based as much on the difficulty of justifying special treatment for road casualties as on the practical problems of demarcation and the manageable extra costs of covering the residue.

The guiding principle of the scheme is to replace financial loss rather than the social welfare philosophy of assuring a minimally adequate living standard. Accordingly benefits are not flat but earnings-related and fixed at a level which the public could fairly accept in exchange for their common law rights. The standard is 80 per cent of pre-accident earnings, payable in weekly instalments up to N.Z. $1,179 in 1992.[77] There is a waiting period of one week, during which the employer is responsible for work-related accidents.

Lump sums also used to be payable for permanent incapacity up to $17,000 and up to $10,000 for loss of "amenities or capacity for enjoying life, including loss from disfigurement" and for "pain and suffering, including nervous shock and neurosis". Both evoked memories of common law damages, the one for loss of faculty, the other for pain and suffering. But these awards imposed too heavy a financial and administrative burden on the system and were abolished in 1992. Instead an "independence allowance" is now available for claimants with a disability of at least 10 per cent.

Coverage

Although coverage of all "personal injury by accident" (*piba*) appears very inclusive, it has not been spared problems of demarcation.[78] A thoroughgoing reform in 1992 made a new start of clarifying and narrowing the definition. It consists of two elements, accident and personal injury.

75. *Compensation for Personal Injury in New Zealand* (1967).
76. Now *Accident Rehabilitation and Compensation Act* 1992. See *Todd* ch. 2; Palmer, *Compensation for Incapacity* (1979); Blair, *Accident Compensation in New Zealand* (2nd ed. 1983). These books antedate the 1992 reform.
77. Benefits are not indexed but raised periodically by Order in Council. Less than 1% received maximum. In case of death, dependants also receive earnings-related compensation and a small lump sum: Miller, *Fatal Claims under the A.C.A. 1972* [1979] N.Z.L.J. 173.
78. See *Todd* ch. 2 (Vennell). The Corporation must make ordinarily the initial determination of coverage in order to avoid a victim falling between two stools: *L. v. M.* [1979] 2 N.Z.L.R. 519 (C.A.). From determinations on this and other questions appeal lies to the District Court. Decisions are reported in N.Z.A.R.

The legacy of workers' compensation has been retained in construing "accident" in the popular sense of an unlooked-for mishap or untoward event, unexpected and undesigned by the victim.[79] Intentional acts like battery and rape are covered, being an "accident" to the victim;[80] and so is pregnancy, like actual bodily harm, arising from a criminal act. Personal injury narrowly includes "mental or nervous shock" as the outcome of any act in relation to the claimant or of any criminal act against him. Injury to third persons is not covered.

The most troublesome problem has been around the inclusion of "medical misadventure", now defined as "personal injury from medical error or medical mishap". Medical error covers medical negligence as interpreted at common law, but the scheme is expressly not intended to ensure the success of medical treatment. Medical mishap is determined on the basis of rarity (more than 1 per cent) or severity of outcome (hospitalisation of more than 14 days or incapacity for more than 28 days).[81] The selection of such objective criteria may in the future mitigate the difficulties encountered under prior versions of the Act,[82] in particular in drawing a line between iatrogenic causes and "disease, infection, or the ageing process". Occupational disease qualifies under certain conditions when arising out of the course of employment.[83] Also resolving prior uncertainties, the Act now specifically provides that medical misadventure does not include failures of diagnosis or to provide treatment or to obtain informed consent (omissions), unless such failure is negligent. A formerly much criticised feature was the failure to provide deterrence to health care providers; this has now been corrected by exacting contributions from them to the fund and by experience rating and no-claim bonuses.

Finance

The financing of the scheme reveals a tension between the philosophies of social welfare and resource allocation. Dominated primarily by the desire to capture the same funds available to the old system and to avoid general taxation, the original proposal of raising a flat levy from employers of 1 per cent of all wages was abandoned in favour of establishing two separate funds. The Motor Vehicle Fund is fed by levies on motor vehicles and covers the whole population; the Earners' Fund derives from levies on employees (paid by their employer) and the self-employed at differential

79. Thus there need not be some causative event which was unexpected or undesigned; the accident may consist in the suffering of the injury: *A.C.C. v. E* [1992] 2 N.Z.L.R. 426 (C.A.) (psychiatric breakdown during demanding management course); *A.C.C. v. Mitchell* [1992] 2 N.Z.L.R. 436 (C.A.) (crib death). The current reform bill would negative both decisions by defining accident as "a specific event external to the human body" and requiring that any mental disorder be the outcome of physical injuries to the claimant. See Tobin, [1992] N.Z.L.J. 44.
80. *G. v. Auckland Hospital* [1976] 1 N.Z.L.R. 638 (rape: now s. 105B). Provided they result in "personal injury": see Bullock [1982] 1 N.Z.L.J. 26. This does not preclude exemplary damages: *A v M* [1991] 3 N.Z.L.R. 228 ($20,000 for marital rape). *Re Chase* [1989] 1 N.Z.L.R. 325 declined to issue a declaration or nominal damages as a marker of police misconduct.
81. Section 5.
82. For which see Vennell, *Medical Misfortune in a No-Fault Society* (mimeo, 1989).
83. Section 7.

rates according to occupational risks, and covers only these segments of the population.[84] As already mentioned, experience rating has now been introduced as a deterrent and means to achieve some measure of internalising costs in place of the original philosophy of regarding compensation as a community responsibility.[85]

At the heart of the scheme is the complete elimination of tort recovery for those covered by its benefits.[86] Though now that coverage has been somewhat reduced by the recent reform of 1992, resort to tort law has correspondingly become more available. In particular, exemplary damages have survived, not being "damages arising directly or indirectly" out of *piba*, inasmuch as they focus on the defendant's conduct, not the plaintiff's injury (as do aggravated damages).[87] The substantial savings resulting from reduction of administrative costs[88] and channelling funds away from minor claims permit the considerable expansion of benefits for hitherto uncompensated major injuries, without noticeably increasing the total previous cost of workers' compensation and third party insurance for motor vehicles.[89] To the same end, the administration is taken out of the hands of private insurance companies and vested in an Accident Compensation Corporation, which uses the Post Office for collecting premiums. Appeals from the Corporation lie to an Appeal Authority and thence (with leave) to the High Court.

Australia

A plan based on similar principles was recommended also for Australia in 1974,[90] but its enactment failed with the fall of the Whitlam government. It differed, however, from its prototype in two crucial respects. First, it sought to cover the whole population not only for personal injury from all accidents and congenital disability (included because of the difficulty of distinguishing between them in the newborn) but eventually also for sickness to ensure equality of treatment. This would have more than doubled the cost. Secondly, it was recommended to finance the scheme by a flat 2 per cent tax on the wages paid by employers (and earnings of the self-employed) and a 10 cent excise tax on petrol. The former would have been less than the average present cost of employers' liability

84. Non-earners are now entitled to the lump sum benefits for non economic losses in all types of accident. The extra cost is met by a subvention from general revenue.
85. Prior to the 1992 reform the absence of all incentive to accident reduction was much criticised. See generally Trebilcock, *Incentive Issues in the Design of "No-Fault" Compensation Systems*, 39 U. Tor. L.J. 19 (1989).
86. Section 13.
87. *Donselaar v. Donselaar* [1982] 1 N.Z.L.R.
88. Administration costs amounted to 7% of income, compared with 30% under old workers' compensation and 40-50% under third party motor insurance.
89. In 1989 the levy on motor vehicles was $100, much lower than third party insurance in Australia. The Earners' Scheme contributions cost 1.2% of G.D.P., about the same as under the old workers' compensation but providing 24 hour cover. In Australia comprehensive third party motor insurance cost 1.7% of G.D.P.
90. *Compensation*. Its chairman, Woodhouse J., had been the author of the Woodhouse Report in N.Z.: and its Principal Assistant, Geoffrey Palmer, played a leading role in the N.Z. Government White Paper Commentary on the Woodhouse Report (1969). See Luntz, *Compensation and Rehabilitation* (1975); Palmer, *Compensation for Incapacity* (1979) Pt III, Keeler, 4 Adel. L. Rev. 121 (1975).

premiums but, as under the Beveridge Plan which inspired the modern British industrial injury scheme,[91] a flat rate would have subsidised abnormally hazardous and inefficient industries[92] and introduced a large measure of externalities. This standpoint and the embracing scope of the scheme disposed of the otherwise critical issue of whether medical plans (or Medibank) should become "primary" funds rather than shift medical costs to the insurance scheme.[93] Clearly, the philosophy of the Australian plan was that industry and road traffic are integral and inseparable features of modern life, and that their accident cost should be borne on the broadest base corresponding to their pervasive public benefit and involvement.

For the time being, however, the prospect for such a fundamental reform remains dim.

91. See below, p. 522.
92. Merit ratings were expressly rejected, but penalty ratings left to further statistical study. See also below, p. 523.
93. The predominant American view is that motoring should bear its own costs and that no-fault plans should accordingly be primary. Hence medical benefits are not deducted but generally repayable by the victim. This is also the current Canadian position, though not under the proposed *Variplan*.

21

NUISANCE

1. INTRODUCTION: PUBLIC AND PRIVATE NUISANCE

Few words in the legal vocabulary are bedevilled with so much obscurity and confusion as "nuisance".[1] Once tolerably precise and well understood, the concept has eventually become so amorphous as well nigh to defy rational exposition. Much of the difficulty and complexity surrounding the subject stems from the fact that the term "nuisance" is today applied as a label for an exceedingly wide range of legal situations, many of which have little in common with one another. Far from susceptible of exact definition, it has become a catch-all for a multitude of ill-assorted sins, linking offensive smells, crowing roosters, obstructions of rights of way, defective cellar flaps, street queues, lotteries, houses of ill-fame[2] and a host of other rag-ends of the law.

Because of the large variety of situations encompassed by the term, the crucial point is easily missed that nuisance is a field of tort liability rather than any particular type of tortious conduct. Its unifying element resides in the general kind of harm caused, not in any particular kind of conduct causing it. Aside from the complications arising from its association with "public" nuisance, it refers to invasions of an occupier's interest in the beneficial use and enjoyment of land. This branch of law is, therefore, primarily concerned with conflict over competing uses of land. It defines obligations of neighbourliness. It thereby performs a complementary function, though a minor one, to modern-day development controls in correcting external diseconomies in land use.

This role has been somewhat obscured by the fact that nuisance has come to cover not only non-physical damage, harmful to one's use and enjoyment of land, such as air pollution or noise, but also physical damage, like vibrations, discharge of water causing structural damage next door, even bodily injury. The rise of negligence as an independent basis of liability inevitably posed the problem of its relation to the older tort, but its resolution has largely gone by default. Gradually, though, it modifed nuisance law in two respects: it infused, as we shall see,[3] notions of fault which were originally foreign to nuisance. More important from the present standpoint, it has been imperceptibly displacing nuisance as the appropriate basis of liability for physical harm, especially in cases of isolated (as distinct

1. Erle C.J. once said that the answer to the question, What is a nuisance? "is immersed in undefined uncertainty" (*Brand v. Hammersmith Rly* (1867) L.R. 2 Q.B. 223 at 247). See generally Buckley, *Law of Nuisance* (1981).
2. See 31 C.C.L.T. 40 (1985) on reluctance to grant injunctions in aid of criminal law.
3. See below, p. 427.

from continuing) occurrences: today these situations are mostly either treated exclusively in terms of the general duty of care or talk of nuisance is at most added as mere surplusage.[4] Even so, the problem of overlap sows confusion and, if only for the sake of protecting nuisance against infection from negligence in the core area of non-physical harm, it might be better now to exclude all physical harm from the province of nuisance.[5]

Another perplexing feature is that the word "nuisance" is commonly used in several distinct senses.[6] It is sometimes used in a factual sense to describe a human activity or physical condition which is harmful or annoying, as when it is said that a rubbish heap or pressure drilling is a nuisance.[7] At other times, it denotes the harm caused by such an activity or condition, emphasis being less on the cause than on the type of harm resulting from it. This usage is preferable because, as already indicated, the distinguishing aspect of nuisance, as compared with other heads of liability like negligence, is that it looks to the harmful result rather than to the kind of conduct causing it. In either of the abovementioned senses, the term does not connote legal liability, and the question remains whether the particular "nuisance" is actionable. Often, however, it is used to signify both the fact situation and the legal liability arising therefrom, as when a court holds that the defendant has been guilty of maintaining a "nuisance", meaning conduct involving liability. A marked disadvantage of this usage is that it encourages the deplorable tendency to assume that, once a given situation can be factually described as a nuisance, there is nothing more to be said.[8] This ignores the necessity, which is present here as elsewhere in the law of torts, to inquire by what type of conduct—intentional, negligent or unavoidable—the harm has been occasioned. The mere tagging of a problem with the label of nuisance does not provide an easy shortcut to the allocation of responsibility.

History

Another complicating feature is the association of "public" nuisance with this branch of private law. In origin, the essence of nuisance was simply an interference with the beneficial use of another's land, be it with the exercise of so-called natural rights incidental to occupation of land or the enjoyment of servitudes, like rights of way or fisheries. It emerged with the assize of nuisance, which dates back to the early 13th century, and was designed as a remedy complementary to the assize of novel disseisin.[9] To oust the occupier from possession was a disseisin, to disturb him in a manner falling short of dispossession was either trespass or nuisance,

4. E.g. *British Celanese v. Hunt* [1969] 1 W.L.R. 959; *Smith v. Littlewoods* [1987] A.C. 241 (even omission to guard against trespassers!).
5. Gearty, *The Place of Private Nuisance in a Modern Law of Torts* [1989] Cam. L.J. 214.
6. *Rest. 2d*, vol. 4, p. 84.
7. An extreme illustration is the use of the word "nuisance" to describe a condition which is only a potential source of harm, e.g. a rotten tree *before* its collapse: thus note the loose language by Lord Atkin in *Sedleigh-Denfield v. O'Callaghan* [1940] A.C. 880, with which contrast the careful phraseology of Dixon J. in *Torette House v. Berkman* (1940) 62 C.L.R. 637 at 657-659.
8. See e.g., *Ware v. Garston Haulage Co.* [1944] K.B. 30.
9. For a survey of the various older remedies for nuisance see Winfield, *Nuisance as a Tort*, 4 Cam. L.J. 189-191 (1931).

depending on whether the offensive conduct took place on or off the plaintiff's land. Early in the 15th century, the assize was superseded by an action on the case for nuisance which had the advantage of simpler process and of not requiring the litigants to be freeholders; though, unlike its forerunner, it offered no relief by way of compulsory abatement, but only damages.[10]

Quite distinct from this civil remedy securing the free use and enjoyment of land, the name "public" nuisance came to be attached contemporaneously to a variegated assortment of petty offences whose common element was obstruction, inconvenience or damage to the public in the exercise of rights common to all Her Majesty's subjects.[11] The earliest cases involved purprestures (encroachments upon the royal domain or the public's right of way along the highway or navigable waters),[12] but by the middle of the 13th century this notion began to be extended until it gradually covered a multitude of transgressions, such as keeping a brothel, interfering with a market, emitting noxious smoke or fouling water. The sole link between these offences and private nuisances was inconvenience and annoyance, and that being the literary meaning of "nocumentum" or "nuisance", it is readily understandable how the term came to be applied to this class of petty crimes before it had acquired its more precise modern connotation of interference with the beneficial use of land. Redress for public nuisance, by abatement or indictment at the instance of the appropriate governmental authority, remained exclusively criminal until the first half of the 16th century, when the courts first countenanced a private action for damages against the offender in cases where the plaintiff suffered a "greater hurt or incovenience than everyman had".[13]

Public and private nuisance

An element of incongruity thus entered the law as a private action became available under the accommodating label of nuisance for two entirely different things. *Private* nuisance traditionally was, and still is confined to invasions of the interest in the use and enjoyment of land, although occasionally an occupier may recover for incidental injury sustained by him in the exercise of an interest in land, such as for illness caused by noxious gases from an adjoining factory. A *public* nuisance, in contrast, consisting in an interference with a public or common right, such as an obstruction of the highway, can confer a cause of action on a private individual, although no rights or privileges in land of his have been invaded at all. What is more, it came to cover not only inconvenience but also personal injury. These situations, typically street accidents, are barely distinguishable from the kind found in ordinary personal injury litigation, and their association with the concept of nuisance has been doubly unfortunate. It has blurred

10. For this reason, equity acquired a wide jurisdiction in this field at the behest of plaintiffs seeking injunctive relief rather than damages.
11. Stephen's *Digest of Criminal Law* (1950) art. 255. Actually, prejudice to a substantial section of the public—the neighbourhood—is sufficient. It is a question of degree whether it has become "so widespread in its range or so indiscriminate in its effect" to qualify as a public nuisance: *A.-G. v. P.Y.A. Quarries* [1957] 2 Q.B. 169; *A.-G. v. Haney Speedways* (1963) 39 D.L.R. (2d) 48 (7 families).
12. E.g. *Tate & Lyle v. G.L.C.* [1983] 2 A.C. 509 (access to jetty).
13. Fitzherbert J. in *Anonymous* (1535) Y.B. 27 H.VIII, f. 27. Mich., pl. 10.

the boundaries of nuisance[14] by injecting the notion that the action is available as an alternative to negligence for personal injuries,[15] and it has saddled the law with a series of capricious distinctions which are difficult to justify on any rational basis.

For example, in cases where a person is hit by falling masonry, there is one rule for the benefit of passers-by in the street and another for those injured just within the boundary. In the first instance, the occupier's liability sounds in nuisance and is, for all intents and purposes, strict; in the second, it is based on negligence and the measure of his duty of care used to be dependent on the status of the particular entrant. There is the further refinement, that the plaintiff may still be regarded as a user of the highway, if he is hurt whilst accidentally diverging from it and stepping on adjacent land.[16] Yet it is difficult to understand why a person who is walking along the road and slips into an excavation at the side, should be entitled to recover, but fail if he sustains the same accident in endeavouring to get on the road[17] or leaving it with a view to reaching an adjoining shop.[18]

Little would be lost if public nuisance as a tort were to disappear.[19] In most situations, as we shall see, liability is based on fault much as under negligence.[20] And in so far as it offers protection against purely economic loss, it may well be asked what justification there could be for divergent policies between nuisance and negligence.[21]

Particular damage

In order to complain of public nuisance, a private claimant must be prepared to show that he incurred some "particular" or "special" loss over and above the ordinary inconvenience or annoyance suffered by the public at large. This limitation has been traditionally explained on the ground that, unless his injury is in some way distinguishable from that sustained by other members of the public, redress for the wrong to the community is more appropriately left to the Attorney-General as its public representative,[22] because the wrongdoer would otherwise run the risk of being punished "a hundred times for the same cause".[23] Although firmly entrenched, this rationale would not strike everybody as particularly convincing. The mere fact that a great number of people have cause to complain is not otherwise

14. See *Jacobs v. L.C.C.* [1950] A.C. 361 at 374-375.
15. This development is traced by Newark, *Boundaries of Nuisance*, 65 L.Q.R. 480 (1949); Spencer, *Public Nuisance—A Critical Examination* [1989] Camb. L.J. 55.
16. *Barnes v. Ward* (1850) 19 L.J.C.P. 195; *Hardcastle v. S. Yorkshire Rly* (1859) 4 H. & N. 67; 157 E.R. 761.
17. *Howard v. Walker* [1947] K.B. 860.
18. *Jacobs v. L.C.C.* [1950] A.C. 361.
19. Spencer, above, n. 15.
20. See below, p. 427.
21. *Ball v. Consolidated Rutile* [1991] 1 Qd R. 524 at 546-547.
22. 4 *Blackstone* 166; *Walsh v. Ervin* [1952] V.L.R. 361 at 368. Often the A.-G.'s is a relator action at the behest of a private party or local authority. Cf. the rule that a private citizen who suffers "special damage peculiar to himself" (better: "has a special interest in the subject matter") may enforce performance of a public duty: *Onus v. Alcoa* (1981) 149 C.L.R. 27 at 71; *Lonrho v. Shell (No. 2)* [1982] A.C. 173 at 185 (above).
23. This was the reason given by Baldwin C.J. in 1535 for disallowing *all* actions by private litigants, but his extreme view was not accepted by Fitzherbert J. and later courts on proof of "particular" damage.

recognised as a disqualification from bringing suit; indeed, if the complainants could establish their standing to sue for *private* nuisance, it would not matter how many there were who shared the same plight.[24] Besides, the requirement ill befits our renewed consciousness for safeguarding the environment and the desirability of encouraging private initiative against polluters.[25]

If the rule were directed only against claims for mere general inconvenience, for example from obstruction of a street or waterway encountered by all users, it would be both tolerable and more defensible. And so indeed it seems to have become, even if declarations of principle remain equivocal.[26] According to one view, the plaintiff's injury must have been different not merely in degree, but in kind, from that shared by the general public. In its most extreme form, this has defeated the claims even of commercial fishermen for loss of their livelihood against polluters of public waters, on the ground that their fishing rights were no different from that of the general public and that their peculiar economic interest did not help.[27] The more liberal approach is to allow recovery so long as the plaintiff's injury and inconvenience was appreciably more substantial, more direct and immediate without necessarily differing in its nature. This would include all personal injury and actual pecuniary loss[28] even from mere delay and inconvenience, provided it was "particular" to him, that is, exceeded in degree what was suffered by others.

The compass in which this debate assumes material significance is relatively narrow, because most claims are today concerned with personal injury or tangible property damage, which by any standard meets the appropriate requirement. The most controversial cases are those involving delay and trouble caused by road obstructions. No doubt, a plaintiff may recover if he has thereby been put to expense. In an old case,[29] additional "labour and pains" he was forced to take with his cattle and servants was deemed sufficient, and it was stressed that the requirement of particular damage "ought not to be taken too largely". In another,[30] a bargeman

24. A nuisance may be at once public and private. This applies to noxious emissions as much as to street obstructions: e.g. *Walsh v. Ervin* [1952] V.L.R. 361; *Rose v. Groves* (1843) 5 Man. & G. 613; 134 E.R. 705 (contiguous landowner's access barred).
25. Representative (or class) actions are also ruled out because the very requirement of "particular" damage for private action precludes the existence of any community of interest. See generally Alston, *Representative Class Actions in Environmental Litigation*, 9 Melb. U. L. Rev. 307 (1973).
26. See Kodilinye, *Public Nuisance and Particular Damage in Modern Law*, 6 Leg. Stud. 182 (1986).
27. *Ball v. Consolidated Rutile* [1991] 1 Qd R. 524; *Hickey v. Electricity Reduction* (1970) 21 D.L.R. (3d) 368. See Estey, *Public Nuisance and Standing to Sue*, 10 Osg. H.L.J. 563 (1972); McLaren, *Common Law Nuisance Action and the Environmental Battle*, 10 Osg. H.L.J. 505 (1972) who concludes after a comprehensive review of the Canadian position that public nuisance offers a lesser weapon to the conservationist than private nuisance. There is more residual support for this view in America: see Prosser, 52 Va. L. Rev. 997 (1966); but see the expanded "standing to sue" for abatement in *Rest. 2d* §821C (2), explained by Bryson & Macbeath, *Public Nuisance, the Restatement (Second) and Environmental Law*, 2 Ecol. L.Q. 241 (1972).
28. Including "purely" economic loss (standing alone).
29. *Hart v. Basset* (1681) T. Jones 156; 84 E.R. 1194.
30. *Rose v. Miles* (1815) 4 M. & S. 101; 105 E.R. 773; accord: *Blagrave v. Bristol Waterworks* (1856) 1 H. & N. 369; 156 E.R. 1245; *Boyd v. G.N. Rly* [1895] 2 I.R. 555 (doctor held up at level crossing for 20 minutes).

succeeded against a defendant who had wrongfully moored his boat across a navigable river and forced him to unload his cargo and transport it overland; and it would seem to make no difference if, instead of taking his barges up to the obstruction, he had never commenced upon the voyage in the knowledge that the obstruction was there and would not be removed.[31]

There is a clear modern tendency to reject the elusive distinction between difference in kind and in degree, and to allow recovery if the obstruction causes more than mere infringement of a theoretical right which the plaintiff shares with everyone else. Thus while an ordinary traveller cannot complain of mere delay or being forced to detour,[32] a farmer who is deprived of his ordinary route to and from his property,[33] let alone a frontager whose view or light is impeded by an unlawful obstruction,[34] suffers sufficient prejudice peculiar to himself to qualify, even if it is impossible to infer actual pecuniary loss. Much of the confusion is due to the unfortunate use of the word "special" instead of "particular" in describing the appropriate requirement of damage.[35] In negligence actions and the like, "special" damage nowadays means pecuniary loss actually incurred up to the date of trial, which must be "specially" pleaded and proven in contrast to "general" damages for pain and suffering.[36] In the present context, however, "delay and inconvenience of a substantial character, direct and not merely consequential,[37] so long as not merely similar in nature and extent to that in fact suffered by the rest of the public, may amount to sufficient damage, particular to the individual plaintiff, notwithstanding that in another sense it is 'general' and not 'special' damage to him."[38]

Occasionally, a claim is dismissed on the ground that the particular damage is "too remote", as for loss of a horse which broke away when its owner dismounted to remove an obstruction.[39] On the other hand, loss of prospective customers diverted from the plaintiff's commercial premises by a street obstruction has been fairly consistently treated as recoverable, as much under the modern "foresight" as under the older "directness" test of remoteness.[40]

31. *Blundy Clark & Co. v. L.N.E. Rly* [1931] 2 K.B. 334 at 362.
32. *Winterbottom v. Derby* (1867) L.R. 2 Ex. 316.
33. *Walsh v. Ervin* [1952] V.L.R. 361; *Lynch v. Mudgee S.C.* (1981) 46 L.G.R.A. 204.
34. *Owen v. O'Connor* [1963] S.R. (N.S.W.) 1051 (encroaching building); *Campbell v. Paddington Corp.* [1911] 1 K.B. 869 (grandstand); *Benjamin v Storr* (1874) L.R. 9 C.P. 400 (long-standing horses and wagons); *Tate & Lyle v. G.L.C.* [1983] 2 A.C. 509 (ferry terminal silting water passage).
35. "It is not necessary to prove special damage in this action. It is sufficient to prove particular damage" (*Rose v. Groves* (1843) 5 Man. & G. 613 at 616; 134 E.R. 705 at 706).
36. See above, p. 229.
37. This phrase is misleading: "direct" came into use as a synonym for "particular or special"; nor is it the criterion for remoteness in nuisance: see below, p. 443.
38. *Walsh v. Ervin* [1952] V.L.R. 361 at 369 per Sholl J.; also *Vanderpant v. Mayfair Hotel* [1930] 1 Ch. 138 at 154.
39. *Harvey v. Arnaud S.* (1879) 5 V.L.R. (L.) 312. Cf. *Ball v. Consolidated Rutile* [1991] 1 Qd R. 524 (unforseeable economic damage).
40. *Smith v. Warringah S.* (1961) 79 W.N. (N.S.W.) 436; *Amalgamated Theatres v. Luney* [1962] N.Z.L.R. 226; *Blundy Clark & Co. v. L.N.E. Rly* [1931] 2 K.B. 334 at 362 (contra: 372); *Harper v. Haden* [1933] Ch. 298 at 306-307. The "queue" cases: see below, p. 416.

Unreasonableness

In the field of public as of private nuisance,[41] the interference must be both substantial and unreasonable. For, overriding all else is the "law of give and take". People, for example, who use the public streets must "have reasonable regard to the convenience and comfort of others, and must not themselves expect a degree of convenience and comfort only obtainable by disregarding that of other people. They must expect to be obstructed occasionally. It is the price they pay for the privilege of obstructing others."[42] Thus, it is by no means necessarily an actionable nuisance for a broken-down and unlit vehicle to be temporarily left on the road, unless it be abandoned for an unreasonable time or in circumstances implying negligence on the part of the driver.[43] Nor is temporary scaffolding over a pavement or even its partial enclosure for building purposes, provided the inconvenience is unavoidable in the light of its purpose and not unduly prolonged.[44] "Interruptions [of traffic] arise at every moment of the day. Carts and wagons stop at the doors of shops and warehouses for the purpose of loading and unloading goods. Coal-shoots [sic] are opened on the public footways for the purpose of letting in necessary supplies of fuel. So, for the purpose of building, rebuilding or repairing houses abutting on the public way in populous places, hoardings are frequently erected inclosing a part of the way. Houses must be built and repaired; and hoarding is necessary in such cases to shield persons passing from danger from falling substances."[45]

In a manner reminiscent of the familiar calculus of negligence, here too the task is to weigh the utility of the defendant's activity against the inconvenience caused to others. Thus it is one thing to lay a hosepipe across a lane for sheer amusement, but quite another for the purpose of augmenting one's domestic water supply in a drought.[46] No less important a consideration, besides the gravity of inconvenience or risk created, is whether it could not have been lessened or avoided by recourse to different methods.[47]

The criterion of reasonableness is also illustrated by the measure of tolerance allowed for attracting crowds who impede access to adjacent businesses. If allured by a bait set out for the specific purpose of bringing a crowd together, such as an arresting window display,[48] not to speak of a

41. Private nuisance: see below, p. 420.
42. *Harper v. Haden* [1933] Ch. 298 at 320 per Romer L.J.
43. *Maitland v. Raisbeck* [1944] K.B. 689; *Parish v. Judd* [1960] 1 W.L.R. 867; *Jones v. Shafer* [1948] S.C.R. 166; *Dymond v. Pearce* [1972] 1 Q.B. 496 (C.A.) left open the question whether in ordinary highway accidents caused by obstruction a plaintiff could still be better off in nuisance than negligence. Negative are *Everitt v. Martin* [1953] N.Z.L.R. 298; *Abbott v. Kasza* (1976) 71 D.L.R. (3d) 581 at 591. Besides, the obstruction must, temporarily or permanently, "remove the whole or part of the highway from public use altogether" (*S.G.I.C. v. Trigwell* (1979) 142 C.L.R. 617 at 628 (2 sheep not sufficient)).
44. *Harper v. Haden* [1933] Ch. 298; *Amalgamated Theatres v. Luney* [1962] N.Z.L.R. 226.
45. *Herring v. Metropolitan Bd of Works* (1865) 19 C.B. (N.S.) 510 at 525; 144 E.R. 886 at 892 per Byles J.
46. *Trevett v. Lee* [1955] 1 W.L.R. 113.
47. *Almeroth v. Chivers* [1948] 1 All E.R. 53.
48. *Wagstaff v. Edison Bell Co.* (1893) 10 T.L.R. 80; but contrast the case of the beautiful Miss Very, related in *R. v. Carlile* (1834) 6 C. & P. 636 at 646a; 172 E.R. 1397 at 1402.

tendentious exhibition unrelated to the legitimate pursuit of his business,[49] the shopkeeper will be liable for any nuisance arising from the congestion. So also for picketing which intimidates intending customers.[50] Not, however, if he carries on trade in suitable premises and a large number of customers collect on the pavement waiting to gain admittance,[51] unless he fails to adopt reasonable means within his control to prevent the congestion or adopts an unusual method of conducting business, like selling ice-cream from a window of his shop instead of inside.[52] Proprietors of cinemas are likewise liable for the formation of substantial and long-lasting queues,[53] at any rate if they can be avoided by an earlier opening of doors.[54]

2. PRIVATE NUISANCE

The gist of private nuisance is interference with an occupier's interest in the beneficial use of his land.[55] The action is thus complementary to trespass which protects his related interest in exclusive possession. The distinction is that between the old actions of trespass and case, traditionally illustrated by contrasting the pointing of a waterhose unto neighbouring land and constructing a rainspout from which the water eventually flows upon it.[56] The former invasion is trespass, being a "direct" infringement of the plaintiff's possession; the latter is nuisance, because the injury is treated as merely "consequential". The harms against which protection is afforded by either action usually differ somewhat in character, in that trespass applies only to physical intrusions by tangible objects, be they persons or things,[57] whereas nuisance extends also to invasions by noise, smell, vibrations, and even high frequency interference with television screens.[58] Again, trespass postulates that the defendant's conduct consist in a physical act done directly *unto* the plaintiff's land; whereas a nuisance must (at least

49. *R. v. Carlile* (1834) 6 C. & P. 636; 172 E.R. 1397 (libellous effigy). But a business without permit is not "unlawful trade" sufficient to constitute any minor congestion a nuisance: *Grand Central v. Tivoli* [1969] V.R. 62.
50. *Animal Liberation v. Gasser* [1991] 1 V.R. 51 (App. Div.).
51. *Silservice v. Supreme Bread* (1949) 50 S.R. (N.S.W.) 127; *Dwyer v. Mansfield* [1946] K.B. 437.
52. *Fabbri v. Morris* [1947] 1 All E.R. 315.
53. *Lyons v. Gulliver* [1914] 1 Ch. 631; *Barver v. Penley* [1893] 2 Ch. 447.
54. 62 L.Q.R. 321 (1946); and cf. *Fabbri v. Morris* [1947] 1 All E.R. 315. It has been suggested that they are liable in any event on the ground that the entertainment business aims at collecting crowds and should therefore ensure that this process does not cause injury to neighbours: *Silservice v. Supreme Bread* (1949) 50 S.R. (N.S.W.) 127 at 129.
55. Including incorporeal hereditaments, i.e. easements and profits à prendre.
56. *Reynolds v. Clarke* (1725) 2 Ld Raym. 1399; 92 E.R. 410; and see a modern illustration in *Southport Corp. v. Esso* [1954] 2 Q.B. 182 at 195-197; [1956] A.C. 218 at 244 (oil drifting ashore). Also above, p. 40.
57. E.g. cricket ball hit for a six: *Miller v. Jackson* [1977] Q.B. 966 at 978 (C.A.). Although difficult to justify in the light of modern science, the distinction seems to be between visible, tangible matter—alone capable of trespassory entry—and other matter or forces. Vibrations (*Phillips v. California* (1960) 31 W.W.R. 331) and light (*Bank of N.Z. v. Greenwood* [1984] N.Z.L.R. 525) are thus non-trespassory, and so are apparently microscopic pollutants (contra, exploding the whole distinction: *Martin v. Reynolds* 342 P. 2d 790 (Ore. 1959)).
58. *Nor-Video v. Ontario Hydro* (1978) 84 D.L.R. (3d) 221.

according to the traditional view) be caused by something taking place outside the land affected.[59] The distinction, however elusive and unattractive to the modern mind, is still attended with practical significance: for the one, there is liability without actual harm, for the other damage is essential; every trespassory intrusion is tortious unless privileged, while a nuisance is never actionable unless it is unreasonable.

The interest in the beneficial use of land protected by the action of nuisance is a broad and comprehensive notion. It includes not only the occupier's claim to the actual use of the soil for residential, agricultural, commercial or industrial purposes, but equally the pleasure, comfort and enjoyment which a person normally derives from occupancy of land, not excluding recreational amenities like television reception.[60] Accordingly, harmful interference may be manifold: it may consist in physical damage to land, buildings, and chattels thereon, through vibrations, flooding, fire, and the like; in disturbing the comfort, health, and convenience of the occupant by offensive smell, noise, smoke, dust, by reasonable fear for one's safety or health,[61] or by only affronting the susceptibility of (reasonable) neighbours by a house of prostitution or a sex shop close to a residential area.[62] Thus, certain sophisticated interests of personality which, standing alone, receive only limited protection by our law, are more amply vindicated if asserted in title of the free use and enjoyment of land, where such factors as personal taste and sensibilities are accorded fuller protection.[63]

Not all amenities, however, commonly associated with beneficial use of land, are vindicated by the law of private nuisance: not aesthetic values, like an unobstructed[64] or pleasing[65] view from one's home, or against an isolation hospital moving in next door;[66] nor such privacy values as

59. *Clearlite v. Auckland C.C.* [1976] 2 N.Z.L.R. 729 dispensed with the requirement against a non-negligent contractor.
60. *Nor-Video v. Ontario Hydro* (1978) 84 D.L.R. (3d) 221, rejecting a dictum in *Bridlington Relay v. Yorkshire Electricity Bd* [1965] Ch. 436 at 447.
61. *Newman v. Conair* (1972) 33 D.L.R. (3d) 474 (aerial spraying); *Evans v. Finn* (1904) 4 S.R. (N.S.W.) 297 (adjacent rifle range). Doubts have been raised concerning personal injury: M. Davies, 20 Univ. W.A.L. Rev. 129 (1990). But it is clearly covered by *public* nuisance (above, n. 12) and it would be odd to differentiate between fear of, and actual, personal injury. It has been assumed in many cases, e.g. *Benning v. Wong* (1969) 122 C.L.R. 249 at 318 (cf. *Rylands v. Fletcher*); *Malone v. Laskey* [1907] 2 K.B. 141; though the practice is to sue in negligence.
62. *Thompson-Schwab v. Costaki* [1956] 1 W.L.R. 335; *Laros v. Florinplace* [1981] 1 All E.R. 659. But the refusal to recognise aesthetic nuisance, based as it is on the alleged subjectivity of the criterion, has been questioned: Smith & Fernandez, 15 Harv. Environ. L. Rev. 53 (1991).
63. But see below, p. 421.
64. *William Aldred's Case* (1611) 9 Co. Rep. 57b at 58b; 77 E.R. 816 at 820; *St Pierre v. Ontario* [1987] 1 S.C.R. 906 (highway). Unless parasitic to an independent tort: *Campbell v. Paddington Corp.* [1911] 1 K.B. 869 (road obstruction); *Craig v. E. Coast C.C.* [1986] 1 N.Z.L.R. 99 (deprivation of right to object to planning exception).
65. Cf. *Coventry C.C. v. Cartwright* [1975] 1 W.L.R. 845 (rubbish tip).
66. *Shuttleworth v. Vancouver Hospital* [1927] 2 D.L.R. 573, refusing an injunction against an isolation hospital on the ground that neither the sight of human suffering nor the imaginary fear of infection was sufficient, both being founded on sentiment. Even the depreciation in value of the plaintiff's land made no difference, since it did not flow from a legal wrong, but a mere sentiment of danger. Not that a hospital can never constitute a nuisance: e.g. *Metropolitan Asylum v. Hill* (1881) 6 App. Cas. 193. See further below, ch. 26 (right of privacy).

freedom from being spied upon from a vantage point;[67] not even an absolute right to light[68] or lateral support for one's buildings.[69] These can ripen into enforceable rights (if at all) only through grant or prescription, and are better left to books on real property.

Unreasonable interference

To constitute a legal nuisance, the annoyance or discomfort must be substantial and unreasonable. "Life in organised society and especially in populous communities involves an unavoidable clash of individual interests. Practically all human activities, unless carried on in a wilderness, interfere to some extent with others or involve some risk of interference, and these interferences range from trifling annoyances to serious harms. It is an obvious truth that each individual in a community must put up with a certain amount of annoyance, inconvenience and interference, and must take a certain amount of risk in order that all may get on together. The very existence of organised society depends on the principle of 'give and take, live and let live',[70] so that the law of torts does not attempt to impose liability or shift the loss in every case where one person's conduct has some detrimental effect on another. Liability is imposed only in those cases where the harm or risk to one is greater than he ought to be required to bear under the circumstances."[71]

The paramount problem in the law of nuisance is therefore to strike a tolerable balance between conflicting claims of neighbours, each invoking the privilege to exploit the resources and enjoy the amenities of his property without undue subordination to the reciprocal interests of the other. Often the conflict is between residential land use and industrial development, for which differing social and economic values have found no easy resolution. The eventual compromise of the latter 19th century was to seek reconciliation in the notion of "reasonable use".[72] Legal intervention is warranted only when an excessive use of property causes inconvenience beyond what other occupiers in the vicinity can be expected to bear, having regard to the prevailing standard of comfort of the time and place. Reasonableness in this context is a two-sided affair. It is viewed not only from the standpoint of the defendant's convenience, but must also take into account the interest of the surrounding occupiers. It is not enough to ask: is the defendant using his property in what would be a reasonable manner if he had no neighbour? The question is, is he using it reasonably, having regard to the fact that he has a neighbour?

In striking this balance, a number of factors are given weight in accordance with traditional values relating to private property rights. Little,

67. *Victoria Park Racing Co. v. Taylor* (1937) 58 C.L.R. 479.
68. Most Australian jurisdictions are opposed to prescriptive acquisition of "ancient lights", including solar access rights.
69. See below, p. 425.
70. See *Bamford v. Turnley* (1862) 3 B. & S. 66 at 83-84; 122 E.R. 27 at 32-33 per Bramwell B.
71. *Rest.* §822, comment *j*. Thus the maxim "sic utere tuo ut alienum non laedas", popular among plaintiffs, is quite misleading: *Sedleigh-Denfield v. O'Callaghan* [1940] A.C. 880 at 903.
72. See McLaren, *Nuisance Law and the Industrial Revolution*, 3 Oxf. J. Leg. Stud. 155 (1983) for the irresolution of 19th century judges and the reasons for the limited role of tort law in that period.

if any, attention is paid directly to utilitarian criteria like cost or resource efficiency or to larger considerations of zoning or social welfare, which are thought to belong to the province of legislation and planning.[73]

Gravity of harm

Most cases of nuisance turn on the gravity of the harm to the complainant. This, in turn, depends both on its character and duration. The interference may amount to no more than a "trifling inconvenience"[74] or it may cause a complete interruption of the use of land. It may be momentary, temporary, recurrent or continuous. In order to be an actionable nuisance, there must be an inconvenience materially interfering with the ordinary comfort physically of human existence, not merely according to elegant and dainty habits of living but according to plain and sober notions among our people.[75] There is a vast difference between noxious vapours from the stacks of alkali works[76] and an occasional whiff of unpleasant smoke from a household incinerator[77] or domestic chimney,[78] between the shrill and relentless noise of circular saws,[79] a speedway track[80] or jet engines[81] and the sounds coming from a nursery,[82] music room[83] or even residential accommodation used by students in a proper manner.[84] No one can claim the law's assistance "to cut a swath of silence around him" and object to the singing of a religious congregation at reasonable hours;[85] but the blare of Salvation Army bands from early morning to late at night on Sundays[86] or the persistent and early ringing of church bells[87] may well exceed the bounds of tolerance.

The gravity of the harm depends not only on the extent, but also the kind of injury. It may consist, on the one hand, in physical discomfort and inconvenience or, on the other, in actual damage to property or injury to health. While both may be equally serious, there is this practical difference between them, that it is appreciably easier to show substantial harm in the latter case, where the injury is more readily observed and measured and the

73. See Ogus & Richardson, *Economics and the Environment: A Study of Private Nuisance* [1977] Cam. L.J. 284. But see below.
74. Mellor J.'s memorable instruction in *Tipping v. St Helens Smelting* (1863) 4 B. & S. 608 at 610; 122 E.R. 588 at 589.
75. *Walter v. Selfe* (1851) 4 De G. & Sm. 315 at 322; 64 E.R. 849 at 851; *Don Brass Foundry v. Stead* (1948) 48 S.R. (N.S.W.) 482 at 486-487; *Haddon v. Lynch* [1911] V.L.R. 230 at 231; *Ruthning v. Ferguson* [1930] Q.S.R. 325 at 326.
76. *Harkness v. Woodhead* [1950] S.A.S.R. 54 (hide and tallow factory).
77. *Don Brass Foundry v. Stead* (1948) 48 S.R. (N.S.W.) 482 at 487.
78. *Pittar v. Alvarez* (1916) 16 S.R. (N.S.W.) 618; and see *West v. Nicholas* (1915) 17 W.A.L.R. 49 (backyard privy).
79. *Spencer v. Silva* [1942] S.A.S.R. 213; *Dunstan v. King* [1948] V.L.R. 269; also *Farley & Lewers v. A.-G.* (1962) 80 W.N. (N.S.W.) 1693.
80. *Bloodworth v. Cormack* [1949] N.Z.L.R. 1058; *A.-G. v. Haney Speedways* (1963) 39 D.L.R. (2d) 48. Cf. *Kidman v. Page* [1959] Qd R. 53 (noisy trucks).
81. See above, p. 47.
82. *Moy v. Stoop* (1909) 25 T.L.R. 262 (day nursery); aliter, the crying of habitually neglected children.
83. *Gaunt v. Fynney* (1872) L.R. 8 Ch. App. 8 at 12.
84. *Clarey v. Women's College* [1953] Arg. L.R. 850 (H.C.).
85. *McKenzie v. Powley* [1916] S.A.L.R. 1.
86. Ibid.
87. *Haddon v. Lynch* [1911] V.L.R. 5, appealed [1911] V.R. 230.

damages are more easily ascertained.[88] Indeed, according to some dicta[89] "sensible material damage" precludes all balancing and can never be justified by competing values, especially location. The distinction reflects the trend, previously noted, of treating material harm on the basis of Atkinian negligence rather than nuisance. It could perhaps be reconciled by saying that, in cases of physical damage, the gravity of the harm is regarded as great though its extent be relatively small, while in cases of mere personal discomfort, the gravity of the harm is generally treated as slight unless the invasion is substantial and continuing.[90]

The oft-repeated statement that the injury must be "of a substantial character, not fleeting or evanescent"[91] is to be understood in the light of the foregoing remarks. The temporary nature of the harm is only one, but by no means a conclusive, factor in deciding whether the injury is too trivial to qualify as nuisance. Undoubtedly in many cases, continuance or recurrence are necessary to cause substantial harm, and the courts are particularly reluctant to grant an injunction where the nuisance is only temporary or occasional. But if the claim is for damages, the duration of the interference must be weighed together with all other relevant factors. Especially in cases of physical injury, the fact that the occurrence was momentary and unlikely to recur is ordinarily irrelevant. This is illustrated by the many decisions in favour of plaintiffs injured by falling masonry or other projections,[92] and applies equally to property damage, such as the destruction of goods through a single explosion of accumulated gas.[93] Many such cases of isolated occurrences have been dealt with on the basis of negligence rather than nuisance.[94]

The character of the neighbourhood has an important bearing on the standard of comfort to which the plaintiff is entitled. Certain districts, by reason of random growth or conscious planning,[95] have come to be devoted primarily to industrial, others to residential or agricultural purposes. The more exclusively an area is given to one type of enterprise, the more likely that a different activity is unsuited to it. Social friction is, therefore, most effectively minimised by compelling newcomers to accommodate themselves to the prevailing conditions of the

88. *McKenzie v. Powley* [1916] S.A.L.R. 1.
89. *Halsey v. Esso* [1961] 1 W.L.R. 683 at 690, overplaying a dictum in *St Helens Smelting v. Tipping* (1865) 11 H.L.C. 642 at 650 (identifying material damage with property value). *Salmond & Heuston* 52 accepts this distinction, but *Winfield & Jolowicz* 327 is sceptical.
90. *Rest. 2d* §827, comments *c, d*.
91. *Benjamin v Storr* (1874) L.R. 9 C.P. 400 at 407 per Brett J.
92. See below, pp. 427-439.
93. *Midwood v. Manchester* [1905] 2 K.B. 597; *Brit. Celanese v. Hunt* [1969] 1 W.L.R. 959. It is sometimes thought that the rule in *Rylands v. Fletcher* was devised to afford redress for single "escapes" (e.g. *A.-G. v. P.Y.A. Quarries* [1957] 2 Q.B. 169 at 192), but the better reason why nuisance was inapplicable in that case is that the condition had been created by an independent contractor, and at the time it was still doubtful whether his employer could be held liable in such circumstances: see above, p. 391. The origin of the idea that nuisance must be continuous or recurring apparently lay in the assize of nuisance, the object of which was abatement. This led the courts to regard nuisance as a condition capable of abatement after it was known to be injurious, but the modern trend is away from this requirement.
94. Above, pp. 409-410.
95. Note legislation which, in aiding such development, deliberately channels certain industries into segregated areas: cf. *Harkness v. Woodhead* [1950] S.A.S.R. 54 at 56.

neighbourhood. One who makes his home in an industrial area which is inevitably noisy and smoky cannot expect the same standards of immunity from pollution as a person living in a residential district,[96] although even he must not be subjected to an unreasonable increase in the amount of discomfort.[97] Likewise, an industrialist setting up a factory must select a site suitable for such a project. This often poses for him a difficult problem, which sometimes can be resolved only by securing statutory authority.[98] Unaided by legisation, the courts have faced this task of "judicial zoning"[99] by rightly giving more weight to the demands of a stable, as distinct from a changing society. The most delicate problems of adjustment arise where the locality is in a stage of transformation. Once its character is fixed, it is relatively easy to determine the appropriate standard of comfort, to state the difference between Toorak and Fitzroy, between Vaucluse and Woolloomooloo.[100]

Abnormal sensitivity

The standard of deciding whether a particular use of land exposes others to an unreasonable interference is objective, in the sense that it has regard to the reactions of normal persons in the particular locality, not to the idiosyncrasies of the particular plaintiff. The law does not indulge mere delicacy or fastidiousness.[101] Thus, it has never been doubted that the question whether smoke, dust or offensive odours cause a sufficient personal discomfort depends upon their effect on a normal person of ordinary habits and sensibilities.[102]

The same principle applies also where the uses to which the plaintiff puts his land are abnormally sensitive, because it would be unfair to allow him thus unilaterally to enlarge his own rights at the expense of another's;[103] if he desires larger protection, he must negotiate for it. In the leading case,[104]

96. But if the discomfort is so unreasonable as to amount to a nuisance, liability cannot be avoided by the plea that the plaintiff "came to the nuisance" (*Bliss v. Hall* (1838) 4 Bing. N.C. 183; 132 E.R. 758; and below, p. 442).
97. *Rushmer v. Polsue* [1906] 1 Ch. 234; [1907] A.C. 121; *Don Brass Foundry v. Stead* (1948) 48 S.R. (N.S.W.) 482 at 486-487, 491; *Halsey v. Esso* [1961] 1 W.L.R. 683. During the industrialisation of the 19th century the locality standard allowed industry to exact a heavy toll in health and well-being in adjoining working class neighbourhoods. See Brenner, *Nuisance Law and the Industrial Revolution*, 3 J. Leg. Stud. 403 (1974), focusing on *St Helens Smelting v. Tipping* (1865) 11 H.L.C 642.
98. Even then there is liability for any avoidable nuisance: *Manchester Corp. v. Farnworth* [1930] A.C. 171; and below, p. 439.
99. The phrase is *Prosser's* (4th ed. 1971) 600.
100. "What would be a nuisance in *Belgrave Square* would not necessarily be so in *Bermondsey*" (*Sturges v. Bridgman* (1879) 11 Ch. D. 852 at 865).
101. *Don Brass Foundry v. Stead* (1948) 48 S.R. (N.S.W.) 482 at 486. "Lex non favet delicatorum votis" (*William Aldred's Case* (1611) 9 Co. Rep. 57b; 77 E.R. 816). See also *Shuttleworth v. Vancouver Hospital* ([1927] 2 D.L.R. 573: mere "sentiment" not protected).
102. "This branch of law pays no regard to the special needs of invalids" (*Bloodworth v. Cormack* [1949] N.Z.L.R. 1058 at 1064). Older people, more sensitive to noise: *Spencer v. Silva* [1942] S.A.S.R. 213 at 219.
103. But he is protected against spite (*Hollywood Silver Fox Farm v. Emmett*) [1936] 1 All E.R. 825) and, apparently, a defendant's failure to adopt such reasonable precautions as would have made it possible to avoid the damage without appreciable prejudice to his own interests.
104. *Robinson v. Kilvert* (1889) 41 Ch. D. 88.

the defendant carried on a business of manufacturng paper boxes which required hot and dry air. He accordingly heated his premises, which raised the temperature on the plaintiff's floor above, thereby diminishing the value of paper of special quality warehoused there. The action was dismissed because there would have been no damage but for the plaintiff's "exceptionally delicate trade". So was a claim for electrical interference with the transmission of messages in a submarine cable,[105] though not interference with an ordinary television channel.[106] Most instructive is the American case[107] of an open air cinema which vainly sought an injunction against the casting of light onto its screen from floodlights of an adjacent night racetrack. Without deciding that the shedding of light upon another's property could under no circumstances become a nuisance, it was held that the abnormally sensitive use to which the plaintiff had put his land did not warrant protection at the expense of an enterprise of equal social utility which would not have interfered with the ordinary use of property in the area. Despite the public interest in encouraging solar energy, claims for uninterrupted solar access would founder, among other reasons because such use would be ultra-sensitive and impose an unwarranted restriction on the use of neighbouring land.[108]

Utility of defendant's conduct

Some weight is also due to the purpose or motive of the defendant's activity.[109] For instance, construction work often causes substantial inconvenience, but this and other temporary operations of a common and (by present day standards) not abnormal nature must be tolerated so long as all reasonable precautions are taken to minimise disturbance.[110] Hence there may be no liability, "even though the noise and dust and consequent annoyance be such as would constitute a nuisance if the same, instead of being created for the purpose of demolition of the house, had been created in sheer wantonness, or in execution of work for a purpose involving a permanent continuance of the noise and dust. For the law, in judging what constitutes a nuisance, does take into consideration both the object and the duration of that which is said to constitute a nuisance.[111]

Likewise, *some* consideration will be given to the fact that the offensive enterprise is essential and unavoidable in the particular locality, like a coal mine, quarry, or some public utility or service such as early morning milk delivery.[112] This argument, however, must not be pushed too far. In particular, it should be remembered that we are here concerned with reciprocal rights and duties of *private* individuals, and a defendant cannot

105. *E. & S. African Telegraph v. Cape Town Tramways* [1902] A.C. 381.
106. *Nor-Video v. Ontario Hydro* (1978) 84 D.L.R. (3d) 221; contra: *Bridlington Relay v. Yorkshire Electricity Bd* [1965] Ch. 436 (at any rate when requiring a higher standard of interference-free reception than a domestic aerial).
107. *Amphitheatres v. Portland Meadows* 198 P. 2d 847; 5 A.L.R. 2d 690 (Ore. 1948); *Rest. 2d* §821 F; accord; *Noyes v. H. & E. Mortgage Corp.* [1932] 3 D.L.R. 143.
108. Contra (isolated): *Prah v. Maretti* 321 N.W. 2d 182 (Wis. 1982).
109. *Rest. 2d* §828.
110. *Andreae v. Selfridge* [1938] Ch. 1.
111. *Harrison v. Southwark Water Co.* [1891] 2 Ch. 409 at 414 per Vaughan Williams J.
112. Cf. *Munro v. Southern Dairies* [1955] V.L.R. 332 at 337; *Painter v. Reed* [1930] S.A.S.R. 295 at 303-304.

simply justify his infliction of great harm upon the plaintiff by urging that a great benefit to the public at large has accrued from his conduct.[113] "If the public be interested, let the public as such bear the loss"[114]—a result that can be accomplished either by holding the defendant liable in the first place and letting him charge the expense to the benefiting public as a cost item of his services or alternatively by conferring statutory authorisation on the enterprise, coupled (hopefully) with provision for compensating persons injuriously affected, so that the cost is shared equally by the community at large.[115]

On the other hand, if the defendant's conduct is wholly devoid of social utility, as where his sole purpose is to cause annoyance or harm, his interference may be treated as unreasonable although otherwise short of objectionable:[116] he would have committed what civilians call an "abuse of right".[117] Thus, in one case, a defendant was held liable for hammering and beating trays against a party wall with the malicious object of interrupting his neighbour's music teaching, although the noise would not ordinarily have been sufficient to warrant an injunction.[118] In another, damages were awarded against a man who spitefully fired off guns in close proximity to his neighbour's breeding pens in order to frighten his silver foxes and cause them to miscarry.[119] Contrast this with a defendant who, driven to exasperation by the constant commotion of a flock of homing pigeons over his premises, let off firecrackers in order to scare them away. These retaliatory measures were held justifiable because, far from being motivated by spite, they were taken under stress from an existing nuisance in the hope of alleviating the annoyance.[120]

"Spite fences" present a peculiar problem, as the grant of an injunction might enable the successful plaintiff eventually to acquire a prescriptive easement of light or air,[121] and thereby prejudice the defendant in later building for a legitmate purpose. This objection, however, could perhaps be met by making relief conditional on an undertaking to stop the prescriptive period from running.[122]

113. *Schenck v. R.* (1981) 131 D.L.R. (3d) 310 (salting road for de-icing); *Shelfer v. London Electric Co.* [1895] 1 Ch. 287 at 316; *Munro v. Southern Dairies* [1955] V.L.R. 332 at 337; under *Rylands v. Fletcher*: see above, p. 347. Nor is it a defence that the plaintiff was an employee who actually derived his livelihood from the noxious enterprise, as when he resides close to a mine: *Kent v. Dominion Steel* (1964) 49 D.L.R. (2d) 241.
114. Bohlen, *Studies* 429.
115. The latter method is most familiar in case of acquisition of property for public purposes (eminent domain), as under the Commonwealth Constitution, s. 51(xxxi).
116. *Rest. 2d* §829. The cases are reviewed in *Pratt v. Young* (1952) 69 W.N. (N.S.W.) 214.
117. See Gutteridge, *Abuse of Rights*, 5 Cam. L.J. 22 (1933); Bolgar, *Abuse of Rights in France, Germany and Switzerland*, 35 La. L. Rev. 1015 (1975).
118. *Christie v. Davey* [1893] 1 Ch. 316.
119. *Hollywood Silver Fox Farm v. Emmett* [1936] 1 All E.R. 825.
120. *Frazer v. Booth* (1949) 50 S.R. (N.S.W.) 113.
121. This argument has no point in Australia (nor now in England since the *Rights of Light Act* 1959) where such easements can no longer be acquired by prescription.
122. Williams, 7 Cam. L.J. 111, 128 (1939). The prevailing American opinion treats spite fences as an actionable nuisance: *Racich v. Mastrovich* 273 N.W. 660 (S.D. 1937); but there are English dicta to the contrary: *Capital & Counties Bank v. Henty* (1882) 7 App. Cas. 741 at 766; *Allen v. Flood* [1898] A.C. 1 at 46. A similar problem arises in connection with removal of lateral support.

The relevance of malice is not incompatible with the famous decision in *Mayor of Bradford v. Pickles*[123] where the House of Lords refused to intervene against a landowner who, in annoyance over the refusal of a municipal authority to purchase his plot in connection with a water supply scheme, intercepted underground water percolating in undefined channels through his land from a high to a low level area owned by the corporation. This decision stands merely for the proposition that, where two persons have a common privilege to appropriate something, he who comes first is entitled to take it, whatever his motive in doing so. Indeed, differing views prevail as to whether causing a subsidence to neighbouring property by abstracting water may not be actionable as negligence or nuisance.[124]

Unreasonable use and negligence

Although the standard of reasonableness is the touchstone for the adjustment of competing interests in nuisance, it differs in several respects from the central notion of reasonable care in negligence. In the first place, "unreasonable risk" in negligence involves the idea of foreseeable harm to which a reasonable man would not expose others, while unreasonableness in nuisance relates primarily to the character and extent of the harm caused rather than that threatened. Secondly, we shall see that the "duty" not to expose one's neighbours to a nuisance is not necessarily discharged by exercising reasonable care or even all possible care.[125] In that sense, therefore, liability is strict. At the same time, evidence that the defendant has taken all possible precaution to avoid harm is not immaterial, because it has a bearing on whether he subjected the plaintiff to an unreasonable interference,[126] and is decisive in those cases where the offensive activity is carried on under statutory authority.[127] Moreover, while carelessness is not a requisite, fault (as we shall see) is. Thirdly, the law of nuisance allows a defendant the privilege to make use of his property within reasonable bounds though aware that he may thereby cause his neighbours some annoyance and inconvenience; whereas in negligence, given a duty to protect others from a certain kind of injury, the actor will be liable if he ought reasonably to have foreseen it as a likely consequence of his conduct. But just as in trespass, so in nuisance it is up to the *defendant* to exculpate himself, once a prima facie infringement has been established, for example, by proving that his own use was "natural" and not unreasonable.[128]

All the same, the modern law of negligence has affected nuisance in several respects. Already noted has been the tendency to measure liability for physical damage by the standards of negligence rather than nuisance.

123. [1895] A.C. 587.
124. *Stephens v. Anglian Water A.* [1987] 1 W.L.R. 1381 (C.A.) gave a negative answer on the ground that what was not actionable when malicious could not be when merely negligent. Contra: *National Capit. Comm. v. Pugliese* (1977) 79 D.L.R. (3d) 592 (C.A.). See 104 L.Q.R. 183 (1988).
125. See below, p. 427.
126. *Daily Telegraph v. Stuart* (1928) 28 S.R. (N.S.W.) 291; *West v. Nicholas* (1915) 17 W.A.L.R. 49 at 54.
127. *Manchester Corp. v. Farnworth* [1930] A.C. 171.
128. *Kraemers v. A.-G. for Tasmania* [1966] Tas. S.R. 113 (F.C.).

The intrusion of fault as a basis of liability for nuisance will be traced in the next section. Beyond that lies the unresolved question of whether the law of nuisance exclusively defines neighbourly relations or may be supplemented by liability for tortious negligence. English courts have resisted the intrusion of the Atkinian duty of care,[129] but several Commonwealth decisions are more sympathetic. The problem of abstracting water at the risk of causing subsidence next door has already been noted.[130] Another facet is the withdrawal of lateral support by excavation. According to traditional property law, lateral support of land in its natural condition is a so-called natural right incident to ownership and its withdrawal entails strict liability for nuisance;[131] in contrast, a right to extra support for buildings has to be acquired by grant or (as in England) by prescription.[132] Does this authorise excavations without any regard to the risk of causing an adjoining building to collapse in ruins? In England, such a bizarre suggestion has been defended as implicit in the right to prevent one's neighbour from acquiring a right to support by prescription.[133] But in New Zealand (and wherever else prescriptive acquisition has disappeared[134]), this rationale is inoperative; accordingly its Court of Appeal[135] felt free to hold that the owner of a building, although not entitled to an *absolute* right of lateral support (as he is with respect to the land in its natural condition), can insist on excavations next door being carried out with reasonable care to avoid subsidence. Any other conclusion would really be intolerable in closely built urban conditions.

Another illustration of the ameliorative intrusion of the negligence doctrine comes from Canadian courts which have repeatedly required that road building and other construction work be conducted with reasonable care so as not to frighten mink during the whelping season.[136] How can this be reconciled with the nuisance policy previously noted, that one cannot by adapting one's own property to a special extra-sensitive use force others to curtail their legitimate activities? The adjustment is admittedly delicate. The risk of destroying a neighbour's extra-sensitive use of property becomes unreasonable (and therefore negligent) only when it is avoidable without substantially inhibiting one's own activity: a mere temporary suspension of blasting during the brief whelping season is not too much to ask; a permanent denial of flood lights, as in the case of the night racetrack,[137] would be.

129. *Stephens v. Anglian Water A.*; *Smith v. Scott* [1973] Ch. 314.
130. See above, n. 124.
131. *Dalton v. Angus* (1881) 6 App. Cas. 740 at 791; *Blewman v. Wilkinson* [1979] 2 N.Z.L.R. 208 (C.A.: but not *strictly* liable for subsidence after severance).
132. *Dalton v. Angus* (1881) 6 App. Cas. 740 at 792.
133. Ibid., esp. Fry J. at 775.
134. See below, n. 289.
135. *Bognuda v. Upton & Shearer* [1972] N.Z.L.R. 741; sympathetic: *Stoneman v. Lyons* (1975) 133 C.L.R. 550 at 566-567 per Stephen J. Less so: *Kebewar P/L v. Harkin* (1987) 9 N.S.W.L.R. 738. Anyway, the anomoly does not apply to a third party like the neighbour's engineer: *Pantalone v. Alaouie* (1989) 18 N.S.W.L.R. 119 (C.A.)
136. *Grandel v. Mason* [1953] 1 S.C.R. 459; *MacGibbon v. Robinson* [1953] 2 D.L.R. 689, as explained in *Rattray v. Daniels* (1959) 17 D.L.R. (2d) 134.
137. See above, n. 107.

Title to sue

The right to complain of private nuisance, as of trespass, belongs exclusively to the actual possessor of the land affected. A reversioner cannot sue, unless the nuisance permanently impaired the usability of the land and thereby damaged his proprietary interest. Thus he may complain of a building obstructing his ancient lights[138] or of vibrations causing structural damage to his house,[139] because the injury would be "such as will continue indefinitely unless something is done to remove it",[140] but he has no remedy for noise, smoke or other invasions of a temporary nature, even if it drives his tenants away or reduces the letting value of the property.[141]

Possessors of land include not only owners of estates in fee simple, but also tenants for a term in actual possession.[142] Indeed, even a wrongful possessor can maintain an action for nuisance, since the defence of jus tertii is excluded;[143] it would be strange if it were otherwise, because even in conversion which, unlike nuisance, necessarily involves a reflection on the plaintiff's title, actual possession is protected against all but the rightful owner. This rule certainly applies to interferences with "natural rights" incident to land, such as withdrawing lateral support[144] or by smoke, noise and the like. It has also been extended to profits à prendre, such as pollution of a privately owned fishery,[145] but doubts still persist as to interference with easements.[146]

A licensee without possession, such as a lodger, cannot maintain an action for nuisance.[147] This disqualification has been applied even against a tenant's wife and family residing with him, thereby denying them protection against many forms of discomfort[148] and, in case of personal injury, the benefit of the potentially stricter liability for nuisance compared with negligence.[149] This senseless discrimination can be avoided by recognising that they have a "right of occupation" just like the official tenant.[150]

138. *Shadwell v. Hutchinson* (1831) M. & M. 350; 173 E.R. 1185.
139. *Meux's Brewery v. London Electric Co.* [1895] 1 Ch. 287; *Colwell v. St Pancras B.C.* [1904] 1 Ch. 707.
140. *Jones v. Llanrwst U.D.C.* [1911] 1 Ch. 393 at 404; *McCarty v. N. Sydney* (1918) 18 S.R. (N.S.W.) 210.
141. *Simpson v. Savage* (1856) 1 C.B. (N.S.) 347; 140 E.R. 143; *Cooper v. Crabtree* (1882) 20 Ch. D. 589.
142. In case of a continuing nuisance, like encroaching roots, a tenant can recover for *his* loss (e.g. cost of repair) even regarding damage that occurred before he took possession, since otherwise nobody might recover: *Masters v. Brent L.B.C.* [1978] Q.B. 841.
143. *Paxhaven Holdings v. A.-G.* [1974] 2 N.Z.L.R. 185.
144. *Newcastle Corp. v. Wolstanton* [1947] Ch. 92.
145. *Nicholls v. Ely Beet Sugar Factory* [1931] 2 Ch. 84; *Fitzgerald v. Firbank* [1897] 2 Ch. 96.
146. *Keegan v. Young* [1963] N.Z.L.R. 720 held a de facto easement protected against strangers. See *Salmond* (13th ed.) 209.
147. *Vaughan v. Halifax-Dartmouth Bridge Comm.* (1961) 29 D.L.R. (2d) 523. But see *Vaughan v. Benalla S.* (1891) 17 V.L.R. 129 (contra, semble, *Moreland Timber v. Reid* [1946] V.L.R. 237). But that the plaintiff is only a permissive occupant does not necessarily debar him if he is in fact in sole occupation: see *Ruhan v. Water Conservation Comm.* (1920) 20 S.R. (N.S.W.) 439.
148. *Oldham v. Lawson (No. 1)* [1976] V.R. 654.
149. *Malone v. Laskey* [1907] 2 K.B. 141.
150. *Devon Lumber v. MacNeill* (1987) 45 D.L.R. (3d) 300 (C.A.); U.S.: *Prosser & Keeton* 621-622.

3. BASIS OF LIABILITY

Liability for nuisance may be based either on something the defendant has done or has omitted to do when under a duty to take affirmative action. From its medieval origin stems an aura of strict liability, but the pervasive fault doctrine no more by-passed the law of nuisance during the 19th century than it did trespass. Thus although there is a regrettably lingering disposition to assume that once a condition has been labelled a nuisance there is nothing more to be said about liability, the law long ago compelled us to a more discriminating analysis. True, it is apparently for the defendant to exculpate himself (in contrast to negligence);[151] but in most situations there is no longer any liability without some measure of fault, while in others more exacting standards have prevailed in response to modern policy demands for public safety. In all cases, it is imperative to avoid confusing nuisance, descriptive of the nature of the harm sustained, with the type of conduct that will warrant liability.

Creating a nuisance

The defendant may have created the nuisance himself. Must he then have been the occupier of the land from which it emanated because nuisance is generally identified with the reciprocal duties of *neighbours*? This traditional view has been questioned,[152] both for creating unnecessary anomalies and because it is already ignored in the case of licensees[153] and persons causing a public nuisance on the highway. In any event, liability continues so long as the offensive condition remains regardless of his ability to abate it and stop the harm.[154] Thus, an occupier who erects a building which obstructs a neighbour's ancient lights cannot evade responsibility by selling or leasing it;[155] in the words of an ancient opinion, "if a wrongdoer conveys his wrong over to another, whereby he puts it out of his power to redress it, he ought to answer for it."[156]

Is this liability strict or does it nowadays depend on proof of the fault element that the actor at least knew or should reasonably have known that his doing was fraught with danger?[157] Until quite recently the view was not

151. *Radstock Co-op. v. Norton-Radstock U.D.C.* [1968] CH. 605 (C.A.); *Southport Corp. v. Esso* [1954] 2 Q.B. 182 at 197 per Denning L.J. (public nuisance).
152. *Clearlite v. Auckland C.C.* [1976] 2 N.Z.L.R. 729; criticised by Chambers, 1978 N.Z.L.J. 172. See also *Kraemers v. A.-G.* [1966] Tas. S.R. 113.
153. *Fennell v. Robson Excavations* [1977] 2 N.S.W.L.R. 486 (C.A.) where the precedents are lined up.
154. In this respect, liability of the creator of a nuisance differs from that of an occupier on whose land a nuisance subsists or develops without his active participation, because the latter's liability is contingent on occupation and ceases with it, though perhaps not excluding a duty to warn the incoming purchaser of any dangers actually known to him, now that the latter's responsibility does not commence until he has had a reasonable opportunity to discover them himself: see below, p. 429, and see *Rest. 2d* §373.
155. *Thompson v. Gibson* (1841) 7 M. & W. 456; 151 E.R. 845; also *Fennell v. Robson Excavations* [1977] 2 N.S.W.L.R. 486 (C.A.) and *Byrne v. Judd* (1908) 27 N.Z.L.R. 1106 (excavation causing later subsidence). The transferee may recover for repairing prior injury caused by a continuing nuisance: *Masters v. Brent L.B.C.* [1978] 2 All E.R. 664.
156. *Roswell v. Prior* (1701) 12 Mod. 635 at 639; 88 E.R. 1570 at 1572.
157. In general support of the view here expressed is Eckelaar, *Nuisance and Strict Liability*, 8 Ir. Jur. 191 (1973).

uncommonly voiced that this kind of knowledge, though necessary for culpable omissions somehow continued to be irrelevant for misfeasance. But most of the dicta to this effect actually antedated the modern reorientation already mentioned,[158] others were merely concerned with repudiating the notion that taking all reasonable precautions provided a conclusive defence.[159] The question was in effect settled by the decision to be noted presently,[160] that liability for nuisance is limited, just like negligence, to foreseeable consequences alone. It would seem to follow that one cannot be liable for nuisance at all unless and until some injury is foreseeable.[161]

Any contrary position, moreover, would have competed invidiously with the principle of *Rylands v. Fletcher*, by drawing within the orbit of strict liability all manner of perfectly ''normal'' activities, fraught with no more than the common level of risks. The only serious bid for exceptional treatment seems to be on behalf of certain rights appurtenant to land, like the right of natural support. These property rights, though traditionally protected by actions for nuisance, are outside the ordinary regime of nuisance at least in being treated as absolute (like the protection afforded by trespass against intrusions) rather than qualified by considerations of reciprocal reasonableness. It may just be therefore that they are also entitled to absolute protection against defendants who had no reason to anticipate an infringement, as when excavations cause a wholly unexpectable weakening of lateral support next door.[162]

Omissions

Merely being in occupation of land from which the nuisance emanates is no longer sufficient for liability. Despite earlier traces of a more rigorous standard, today an occupier is not an insurer.[163] The keynote of his responsibility, redolent of negligence, has become knowledge or means of knowledge.

158. E.g. *Bell v. Twentyman* (1841) 1 Q.B. 766; 113 E.R. 1324; *Reinhardt v. Mentasi* (1889) 42 Ch. D. 685, a decision so embarrassing to Kekewich J. that he confessed a dementi in *A.-G. v. Cole* [1901] 1 Ch. 205 at 206.

159. See above, p. 424. Nor are injunction cases informative since, unlike damages for the past, they would prohibit future conduct, necessarily implying knowledge.

160. *The Wagon Mound (No. 2)* [1967] 1 A.C. 617 (P.C.); see below, p. 443. Cf. Dias, *Trouble on Oiled Waters; Problems of the Wagon Mound (No. 2)* [1967] Cam. L.J. 62.

161. *Home Brewery v. Davis* [1987] Q.B. 339 at 351 (damming water); *Kraemers v. A.-G. for Tasmania* [1966] Tas. S.R. 113 at 156. (This decision is the more noteworthy because the trial judge (on remand) felt compelled by the intervening *Wagon Mound* to disregard the contrary mandate of the F.C. In consequence, no damages were awarded for seepage of water (caused by removal of gravel) until the defendant became aware of it and failed to abate); *Wall v. Morrissey* [1969] I.R. 10. Cases on obstruction of the highway (by parked vehicles, etc.) look in the same direction: see above, n. 43. Contra: *Clearlite v. Auckland C.C.* [1976] 2 N.Z.L.R. 729 (7 N.Z.U.L. Rev. 364).

162. *Humphries v. Brogden* (1850) 12 Q.B. 739; 116 E.R. 1048; *Mascioli v. Betteridge-Smith* (1965) 49 D.L.R. (2d) 133.

163. *Sedleigh-Denfield v. O'Callaghan* [1940] A.C. 880 at 897. See Friedmann, *Incidence of Liability in Nuisance*, 59 L.Q.R. 63 (1943).

Thus, whether the potential nuisance already burdened the land when he commenced occupation[164] or was created thereafter by an intruder[165] or an act of nature like a tree set afire by lightning,[166] responsibility devolves on him but not until he knows or by exercising reasonable care should have known of its existence and realised the hazard. This requirement was not satisfied when seepage was traced to a broken drainpipe next door of which the occupier could not reasonably be expected to know[167] or where he had no reason to realise that a high branch protruding into the road from one of his trees constituted a hazard to passing trucks piled 16 feet high.[168]

Alternatively expressed in the esoteric idiom of nuisance, the occupier is liable only for "continuing" or "adopting" a nuisance. He " 'continues' a nuisance, if with knowledge or presumed knowledge of its existence he fails to take reasonable means to bring it to an end, though with ample time to do so; he 'adopts' it if he makes any use of the erection, building, bank or artificial contrivance which constitues the nuisance".[169] This was settled in *Sedleigh-Denfield v. O'Callaghan*[170] where a local authority, without permission of the defendants as occupiers, laid a pipeline in a ditch on their land for the purpose of carrying off rainwater. They placed a grating on it so incompetently that it became blocked and the water flooded adjacent premises. The occupiers were held responsible because, in the interval of three years since the unathorised construction, they were deemed to have acquired knowledge of the dangerous condition, and were therefore liable for "continuing the nuisance". They knew through their servant, who was in charge of cleaning the ditch, of the existence of the pipe and its unguarded opening and ought to have recognised the risk of flooding. In addition, they had also "adopted the nuisance" by using the conduit for the purpose of getting rid of water from their own property without taking proper steps to make it safe.

The duty to abate applies nowadays no less to private than to public nuisance.[171] It demands reasonably prompt and effective action to terminate the offensive condition[172] and cannot be evaded by leaving the premises without a caretaker to cope with untoward events, like a window shattered by enemy action which three days later fell upon a passer-by.[173] On the other hand, allowance is made for the particular circumstances of the defendant. Besides the nature of the locality, the gravity of the danger and the difficulty of removing it, this may include the defendant's

164. *Torette House v. Berkman* (1940) 62 C.L.R. 637 at 657-659; *Sedleigh-Denfield v. O'Callaghan* [1940] A.C. 880 at 897-898; *Morgan v. Khyatt* [1962] N.Z.L.R. 791; *Richmond v. Scantelbury* [1991] 2 V.R. 38 (roots).
165. *Sedleigh-Denfield v. O'Callaghan* [1940] A.C. 880.
166. *Goldman v. Hargrave* [1967] 1 A.C. 645; 115 C.L.R. 458 (P.C.).
167. *Montana Hotels v. Fasson* (1986) 69 A.L.R. 258 (P.C.).
168. *British Road Services v. Slater* [1964] 1 W.L.R. 498.
169. *Sedleigh-Denfield v. O'Callaghan* [1940] A.C. 880 at 894 per Viscount Maugham.
170. [1940] A.C. 880; *Proprietors v. Cowell* (1991) A.T.R. 81-083 and *Proprietors of Strata Plan v. Cowell* (1989) 24 N.S.W.L.R. 478 (roots).
171. *Sedleigh-Denfield v. O'Callaghan* [1940] A.C. 880; *Cartwright v. McLaine* (1979) 143 C.L.R. 549.
172. See *Crown Diamond Paint v. Acadia Realty* [1952] 2 S.C.R. 161.
173. *Leanse v. Lord Egerton* [1943] K.B. 323. Cf. *Barker v. Herbert* [1911] 2 K.B. 633.

resources[174] and any practical restraints on his capacity to use them, such as a local government's humane concerns in relocating gypsies.[175]

The basis of liability for non-repair of artificial structures remains somewhat unsettled by the ruling of the English Court of Appeal in *Wringe v. Cohen*[176] that an occupier (or owner who has undertaken the duty to repair) of premises adjoining the highway (?) is answerable whether or not he knew or ought to have known of the danger arising from lack of repair, unless the condition was created by the act of a trespasser or by a secret and unobservable operation of nature, such as a subsidence under or near the foundation of the premises. This standard is stricter than that later formulated in *Sedleigh-Denfield v. O'Callaghan* where, as we have just seen, liability for non-feasance was put on the broad footing of knowledge or means of knowledge, without hint of any distinction between cases of non-repair and nuisances created by trespassers or predecessors in title. The pronouncement is also weakened by the fact that it was unnecessarily wide, because the disrepair of the gable, which fell upon an adjoining shop, was within the imputable knowledge of the defendants, more than two years having elapsed between the last inspection and the accident. The equipment of buildings with cornices, clocks, lamps and the like is a normal user of land and, since they are for that reason exempt from the exceptionally stringent liability of *Rylands v. Fletcher*,[177] it seems hardly justifiable to reach a different solution via nuisance. Moreover, in cases dealing with trees, it has since been affirmed by the highest authority that an occupier discharges his responsibility by exercising reasonable care to detect decay in accordance with the standards of good estate management;[178] and a tree planted by human hand is as much an artificial structure as a gable or a lamp fixed to a wall. In brief, *Wringe v. Cohen* is out of accord with current authority.[179]

Responsibility for misconduct of others

An occupier may also incur responsibility for a nuisance created by third persons. Besides being vicariously liable for his servants and, as already noted,[180] in some circumstances for independent contractors, his ability to control whom to admit and on what terms entails a corresponding responsibility for any nuisance created by a licensee as a probable consequence of the permission granted to him. Thus he may become answerable for allowing gypsies to camp on his land and creating a noisome and insanitary condition[181] or for permitting someone to operate a kiln for the manufacture of bricks causing noxious smoke.[182]

174. *Goldman v. Hargrave* [1967] 1 A.C. 645 (P.C.).
175. *Page Motors v. Epsom B.C.* (1981) 80 L.G.R. 337 (C.A.) (one year's delay).
176. [1940] 1 K.B. 229.
177. See above, ch. 16.
178. *Caminer v. N. Investment Trust* [1951] A.C. 88.
179. It was pointedly cold-shouldered in *Montana Hotels v. Fasson* (1986) 69 A.L.R. 258 (P.C.).
180. See above, p. 391. But if the contractor assumes actual occupation (e.g., of a building site), the owner ceases to be liable at least if he had neither knowledge nor means of knowledge that a nuisance was likely to be committed: *Gourock Ropework v. Greenock Corp.* 1966 S.L.T. 125.
181. *A.-G. v. Stone* (1895) 12 T.L.R. 76; *Page Motors v. Epsom & Ewell B.C.* (1981) 80 L.G.R. 337 (C.A.) (trespassing gypsies).
182. *White v. Jameson* (1874) L.R. 18 Eq. 303.

Indeed, the offensive conduct need not even have taken place on his own land: liability may be his for attracting an unreasonable concourse of people outside it and thereby causing an obstruction,[183] or for any specific misbehavour by them "if the experience of mankind must lead anyone to expect the result".[184] Thus organisers of fairs, races and other public entertainment have been repeatedly held liable for "creating" a nuisance by attracting bad elements who misbehave outside, as by trespassing on adjacent property, using profane language or urinating in the street.[185] Otherwise, however, an occupier is neither responsible for, nor under any duty to abate, a dangerous condition created by a visitor outside his premises, like oil spilt by a prospective customer on the footpath in front of his cycle shop.[186]

Natural conditions

As a concession to landowners in rural areas, the older common law inclined to exempt occupiers from any duty to remedy conditions of natural origin, whatever their potential peril to neighbours. It was prepared to excuse the spread of prickly pear,[187] the seeding of thistles over adjoining paddocks[188] and apparently even rocks falling due to the natural process of weathering.[189] Paramount undoubtedly was the fear that a duty of inspection and abatement would be unduly onerous and disproportionate to the harm usually threatened.

Progressively, however, the immunity has now been eroded to the point of extinction. In the first place, it never gained a foothold in relation to injuries *on*, as distinct from *off*, the land in question.[190] Next to be excluded were falling trees, especially in urban locations, where the peril was apt to be unduly great compared with the effort required to eliminate it.[191] Finally, the immunity was eradicated altogether.[192] Some allowance must still be made for the burden of abating natural conditions, but only in the context of determining what measures reasonable care requires in the circumstances. As already mentioned, this could include the particular defendant's resources. It may be too much to ask from a smallholder that he expend a large sum of money to extinguish a burning rubbish tip,[193] but

183. See above, p. 416.
184. *R. v. Moore* (1832) 3 B. & Ad. 184 at 188; 110 E.R. 68 at 70 (public nuisance).
185. *Bostock v. N. Staffordshire Rly* (1852) 5 De G. & Sm. 584; 64 E.R. 1253; *Walker v. Brewster* (1867) L.R. 5 Eq. 25; *Bellamy v. Wells* (1890) 63 L.T. 635; *Newell v. Izzard* [1944] 3 D.L.R. 118; *Matheson v. Northcote College* [1975] 2 N.Z.L.R. 106.
186. *McGowan v. Masterson* [1953] I.R. 101. But distinguish his liability for dangers created by himself on the footpath, like the piece of fat outside the butcher shop that either flew out or adhered to a customer's shoe in *Dollman v. Hillman* [1941] 1 All E.R. 355.
187. *Sparke v. Osborne* (1908) 7 C.L.R 51 (strict liability denied). More practicable is the statutory control scheme under the *Prickly-Pear Act* 1924 (N.S.W.) s. 9; *Vermin and Noxious Weeds Act* 1958 (Vic.) s. 13; *Weeds Act* 1956 (W.A.).
188. *Giles v. Walker* (1890) 24 Q.B.D. 656.
189. *Pontardawe R.D.C. v. Moore-Gwyn* [1929] 1 Ch. 656.
190. See *Drive-Yourself Ltd v. Burnside* [1959] S.R. (N.S.W.) 390.
191. *Davey v. Harrow Corp.* [1958] 1 Q.B. 60.
192. *Goldman v. Hargrave* [1967] 1 A.C. 645; 115 C.L.R. 458 (P.C.) (tree set afire by lightning); *French v. Auckland C.C.* [1974] 1 N.Z.L.R. 340 (seeding thistles); *Leakey v. National Trust* [1980] Q.B. 485 (C.A.: earth slide). The exception for "natural user" to the strict liability of *Rylands v. Fletcher* remains unaffected.
193. Cf. *Job Edwards v. Birmingham Navigations* [1924] 1 K.B. 341 (£1,000).

not that he pour water on fire in a tree struck by lightning.[194] Sometimes it may even be sufficient to allow the plaintiff himself to abate the nuisance, perhaps sharing expenses.[195]

Water

It is still unclear whether the preceding reform will also affect liability for water, which in the past tended in many respects to go its own way. The older cases certainly recognised an immunity for damage by water that was naturally on the land and whose flow had not been interfered with, such for example as the natural and gradual silting up of a river[196] or the collection of rainwater in a gravel pit.[197] But doubts have been raised concerning their authority in the future.[198] In any event, there is undoubted liability when the occupier impedes the natural absorption or drainage of surface water by structures such as houses, concrete driveways, or drains.[199]

In the past it has often been assumed that there is no liability for gravitation of natural surface water, even if concentrated by the upper owner by means of check banks or drainage, provided it is but a natural incident of farming or mining land and the methods employed were not unusual.[200] However that may be, as a counterweight the so-called "common law" (as distinct from the "civil law") rule permits the lower owner in rural as well as urban areas to put up barriers and pen back such surface water,[201] provided he uses reasonable care and skill and does no more than is reasonably necessary to protect his own land.[202]

Landlord and tenant

It used to be that responsibility for disrepair rested primarily on the tenant as occupier; the landlord being amenable only in exceptional circumstances, as when the premises were in ruinous condition at the time of letting and he was either aware of the defect or could have ascertained

194. *Goldmand v. Hargrave* [1967] 1 A.C. 645.
195. *Leakey v. National Trust* [1980] Q.B. 485 at 526-527.
196. *Neath R.D.C. v. Williams* [1951] 1 K.B. 489; *Loring v. Brightwood* (1974) 44 D.L.R. (3d) 161.
197. *Rouse v. Gravelworks* [1940] 1 K.B. 489.
198. *Leakey v. National Trust* [1980] Q.B. 485 at 522.
199. *Bennetts v. Honroth* [1959] S.A.S.R. 170; *Simpson v. A.-G.* [1959] N.Z.L.R. 546; *Berry v. Trinidad Leaseholds* [1953] 4 D.L.R. 504; *Slater v. Worthington Stores* [1941] 3 All E.R. 28; *Hurdman v. N.E. Rly* (1878) 3 C.P.D. 168.
200. *Smith v. Kenrick* (1849) 7 C.B. 515; 137 E.R. 205; *Rouse v. Gravelworks* [1940] 1 K.B. 489; *Drainage of Land Act* 1975 (Vic.) s. 7 ("reasonable manner").
201. As also extraordinary flood waters of a river, known as the "common enemy" (*Gerrard v. Crowe*) [1921] 1 A.C. 395; *Maxey Drainage Bd v. Gt N. Rly* (1912) 106 L.T. 429); but he may not obstruct running water in a natural stream or flood channel: *Menzies v. Breadalbane* (1828) 3 Bli. (N.S.) 414; 4 E.R. 1387; *Grant Pastoral Co. v. Thorpe's* (1953) 54 S.R. (N.S.W.) 129, affd 92 C.L.R. 317.
202. *Gartner v. Kidman* (1962) 108 C.L.R 12; *Scott v. Edwards* [1934] S.C.R. 332; *Home Brewery v. Davis* [1987] Q.B. 339; cf. *Elston v. Dore* (1982) 149 C.L.R. 480. Despite being opposed to the natural law of gravity, it has perhaps a slight edge in encouraging land improvement. N.Z. is committed to the "civil law" rule in deference to rather inconclusive dicta in *Gibbons v. Lenfestey* (1915) 84 L.J.P.C. 158; *Bailey v. Vile* [1930] N.Z.L.R. 829; *Davis v. Lethbridge* [1976] 1 N.Z.L.R. 689. See generally Derham, *Interference with Surface Waters*, 74 L.Q.R. 361 (1958); Brookfield, *Surface Waters*, 1 N.Z.U.L. Rev. 440 (1965).

it in the exercise of reasonable care.[203] In that event, the landlord would have been "in control" at the crucial time, and should not have been allowed to "pass the buck" either by just letting the premises or even by taking a repairing covenant from the tenant.[204]

Gradually, the landlord's responsibility was extended to disrepair arising even after commencement of the tenancy. This development turned on an expanding notion of "control". The starting point was the simple case where the landlord is in *actual* control of the relevant area, and he rather than the tenant would therefore bear responsibility: for example when a cornice or chimney falls off the outside of a building, only the interior of which is let to tenants.[205] The next, and bolder, step was to *impute* control, first from any express covenant to do repairs,[206] then from a mere reservation of a right to enter and do repairs,[207] and eventually from the mere fact that the law implied such a right incident to an ordinary weekly tenancy.[208] By a parallel development, the standard of liability became more exacting, progressing from an earlier requirement of knowledge[209] through means of knowledge[210] to a virtual insistence on safety; so that a landlord is now held responsible regardless of whether he knew or ought to have known of the disrepair, provided only it was not due to the act of a trespasser or to a secret and unobservable operation of nature.[211] This reallocation of responsibility, prompted largely by a desire for ampler safeguards to the public using city streets,[212] evidently rests on the conviction that landlords are in a stronger position than their tenants to adopt adequate safety measures and, in any event, better able to carry the burden of compensation and distribute the cost by insurance.[213] The suggestion,[214] that the fiction of "control" be wholly abandoned and landlords held responsible even when the duty of repair was expressly assumed by the tenant, could perhaps be justified as the culmination of this policy.

203. *Todd v. Flight* (1860) 9 C.B. (N.S.) 377; 142 E.R. 148; *Gandy v. Jubber* (1865) 9 B. & S. 15; *Cull v. Green* (1924) 27 W.A.L.R. 62; *Rest. 2d* §379. In these cases, liability was based on his actual knowledge, but later decisions equated imputed knowledge: *Spicer v. Smee* [1946] 1 All E.R. 489; *St Anne's Well Brewery v. Roberts* (1928) 44 T.L.R. 703 at 707-708; and *Wintrup v. Mitchell* (1895) 15 N.Z.L.R. 232 (liability continues until end of lease despite transfer of reversion).

Continuance of a weekly or yearly tenancy does not amount to a reletting at the beginning of each new period for the purpose of this rule: *Sykes v. Connolly* (1895) 11 W.N. (N.S.W.) 145; *Bowen v. Anderson* [1894] 1 Q.B. 164.

204. *Brew Bros v. Snax* [1970] 1 Q.B. 612 (C.A.).

205. E.g. *Hagen v. Goldfarb* (1961) 28 D.L.R. (2d) 746; *Cunard v. Antifyre* [1933] 1 K.B. 551 (negligence).

206. *Payne v. Rogers* (1794) 2 H.Bl. 350; 126 E.R. 590; *Wringe v. Cohen* [1940] 1 K.B. 229.

207. *Heap v. Ind Coope* [1940] 2 K.B. 476; *Wilchick v. Marks* [1934] 2 K.B. 56.

208. *Mint v. Good* [1951] 1 K.B. 517; *Defective Premises Act* 1972 (Eng.) s. 4.

209. See above, n. 203; and cf. *Wilchick v. Marks* [1934] 2 K.B. 56 (landlord liable on proof of knowledge).

210. *St Anne's Well Brewery v. Roberts* (1928) 44 T.L.R. 703.

211. *Wringe v. Cohen* [1940] 1 K.B. 229: criticised above, p. 430.

212. Yet it seems to apply equally to adjoining occupiers, since the courts have in recent years disclaimed any distinction in this regard between public and private nuisance: *Spicer v. Smee* [1946] 1 All E.R. 489.

213. *Mint v. Good* [1951] 1 K.B. 517 at 528 per Denning L.J.

214. Ibid.

The enhanced liability of the landlord has not entailed a lessening of responsibility for the tenant. This serves as an incentive for the tenant to make periodical inspections and promptly inform the landlord if repair is necessary. Indeed he remains liable even if the landlord has covenanted to repair; for, just as in the converse case of a tenant's covenant,[215] it does not affect third parties[216] even though it may allocate the burden of repair or abating the nuisance as between the two.[217]

Passing from cases of disrepair, the owner is not responsible for any nuisance *created* by his tenant, unless he let the premises to him for a purpose calculated to cause a nuisance, like using a hall for noisy parties.[218] In the traditional formula, the nuisance must have been either expressly authorised or certain to result from the purposes for which the property is being let. Nothing less than at least a high degree of probability ("virtual certainty") that the tenants would misbehave will suffice;[219] nor will the landlord's mere failure to intercede and terminate the tenancy after becoming aware of the nuisance.[220]

Beyond that, a landlord cannot be held to account. Thus, a purchaser or devisee of the reversion incurs no responsibility for a nuisance which he did not create, in respect of which he is under no express or implied obligation to repair and which he is unable to abate.[221]

Public authorities

Claims for nuisance often pose the critical problem of adjusting the rights of the individual in relation to administrative authorities charged with statutory powers and duties to maintain public works. At one time, courts were excessively sensitive to the fear that an unmodified application of tort liability would unduly impede local authorities in the discharge of their functions and impose an intolerable strain on their limited resources. This attitude fostered substantial immunities, yielding only lately to a more discriminating approach and mounting reaction against subordinating private rights to public powers, unless there is a warrant of statutory immunity or common law remedies would needlessly hamper the discharge of administrative functions.[222]

215. See above, n. 204.
216. It is "res inter alios acta" (*St Anne's Well Brewery v. Roberts* (1928) 44 T.L.R. 703).
217. In the absence of a controlling covenant, there may be contribution for the nuisance liability, as in *Brew Bros v. Snax* [1970] 1 Q.B. 612 (50:50).
218. *De Jager v. Paynham* (1984) 36 S.A.S.R. 498 (F.C.) ("special danger"); *Harris v. James* (1876) 45 L.J.Q.B. 545; *Jenkins v. Jackson* (1888) 40 Ch. D. 71; *Sampson v. Hodson-Pressinger* [1981] 3 All E.R. 710 (landlord acquired property with knowledge of the nuisance).
219. *Smith v. Scott* [1973] Ch. 314. Nor is there any "duty of care" (ibid.).
220. *Rich v. Basterfield* (1847) 4 C.B. 783 at 804-805; 136 E.R. 715 at 723-724 (the decision itself, as distinct from the statement of principle, cannot be supported: see *Harris v. James* (1876) 45 L.J.Q.B. 545 at 546 where it is described as involving a "desperate refinement"); and see *British Office Supplies v. Masonic Institute* [1957] N.Z.L.R. 512; *Malzy v. Eichholz* [1916] 2 K.B. 308 (covenants).
221. *Williamson v. Friend* (1901) 1 S.R. (N.S.W.) (Eq.) 133; *Wintrup v. Mitchell* (1895) 15 N.Z.L.R. 232.
222. See *Pride of Derby v. British Celanese* [1953] Ch. 149 and Sawer, *Non-Feasance Revisited*, 18 Mod. L. Rev. 541 (1955).

Although public authorities enjoy no immunity as such from ordinary tort liability,[223] a protective screen has long remained in the vestigial "non-feasance" rule that mere failure to provide a service or benefit pursuant to statutory authority would ordinarily confer no private cause of action on persons who thereby suffer loss. This has customarily been attributed either to a question-begging policy against construing positive duties imposed on a public body as intended for the benefit of citizens as individuals[224] or to a supposedly critical distinction between the non-exercise of statutory *powers* and *duties* (however, lately displaced by the more functional distinction between decisions in the area of policy (or discretion) and of operation[225]). Hitherto at any rate, no claim for damages has been held to lie to enforce the construction of a road or sewer, nor any relief merely because a work actually carried out fails to be more ameliorative in its operation, as where a more efficient drain would have carried off additional water.[226] If, on the other hand, an undertaking causes positive injury, as by dangerously increasing or lowering[227] the voltage of electricity, or by causing an overflow from a drain due to negligent construction or inadequate maintenance, the person damnified may pursue his ordinary remedies for negligence or nuisance.[228] This, however, remains subject to two exceptions, vestiges of a once wider immunity. First, drainage authorities are not accountable for pollutions caused by inadequacy of existing sewers inherited from predecessors or due to an increased load resulting from uncontrolled growth of the surrounding area.[229] These deficiencies continue to be regarded as pure non-feasance (the only alternative being the provision of a new or larger system), in contrast to damage caused by failures of maintenance, reduction in the capacity of drains and the like.[230] More far reaching and anomalous is the immunity which has survived to shield road authorities from liability for accidents caused by their failure to maintain highways in proper repair.

Highway authorities

This immunity, created by a series of English decisions during the last century[231] and applied in Australia despite a very different history of highway authorities,[232] negates both a general duty to repair (sounding in nuisance) and any specific obligation to exercise care in control and

223. *Mersey Docks T. v. Gibbs* (1866) L.R. 1 H.L. 93.
224. See above, p. 126ff.
225. See above, p. 156.
226. See *E. Suffolk Catchment Bd v. Kent* [1941] A.C. 74 (above); *Campisi v. Water Comm.* (1936) 36 S.R. (N.S.W.) 631 at 639.
227. *Birch v. W. County District* (1969) 119 C.L.R. 652.
228. Subject to the rule, to be noted presently, that activities carried on under statutory authority do not ordinarily attract liability in the absence of negligence: see *Madell v. Metropolitan Water Bd* (1935) 36 S.R. (N.S.W.) 68 and below, p. 439.
229. *Glossop v. Heston L.B.* (1879) 12 Ch. D. 102; *Robinson v. Workington Corp.* [1897] 1 Q.B. 619; *Smeaton v. Ilford Corp.* [1954] Ch. 450; *Essendon Corp. v. McSweeney* (1914) 17 C.L.R. 524.
230. *Campisi v. Water Conservation Comm.* (1936) 26 S.R. (N.S.W.) 631; *Pride of Derby v. British Celanese* [1953] Ch. 149; *Willoughby C. v. Halstead* (1916) 22 C.L.R. 352; *Hawthorn Corp v. Kannuluik* [1906] A.C. 105.
231. Its development in five phases is traced by Fullager J. in *Gorringe v. Transport Comm.* (1950) 80 C.L.R. 357 at 373-379.
232. See *Buckle v. Bayswater Road Bd* (1936) 57 C.L.R. 259 at 268-269.

management even with respect to known dangers (negligence).[233] It is, moreover, reinforced by the judicial construction that even a statutory duty to repair does not subject a road authority to liability, unless the legislature has clearly conveyed a contrary intent either expressly or by necessary implication.[234]

The immunity originated in recognition that the financial resources of local communities were notoriously inadequate for the proper execution of their functions, coupled with a fear that they would be exposed to a "multitude of actions", with no available fund for satisfying adverse judgments.[235] This reasoning has lost much of its force since central governments have, in the main, assumed financial responsibility for road construction and maintenance; and the inadequacy of revenues provides, in any event, but a paltry justification for denying redress to a victim of negligence merely in order to spare the community at large from a slightly higher impost of rates or taxes. This incongruous doctrine, long discarded in most parts of Canada,[236] finally met its legislative doom in England in 1961,[237] but the voice of reform has not yet been heeded in Australia.[238] The distaste felt for it in modern times by commentators and judges alike[239] is, however, in some measure reflected by successive and persisting judicial efforts to contain its scope, if at the cost of some rather fine spun distinctions.

In the first place, the immunity can be claimed only for non-feasance, not for accidents caused by misfeasance. The inherent ambiguity of this distinction has introduced a large element of unpredictability and become a foil for eviscerating the principal rule. True, merely because the local authority has done something to the road does not necessarily make the case one of misfeasance. The execution of superficial repairs, for example, does not attract liability, unless it increased the risk of accidents.[240] To be charged with misfeasance, the authority must have been an active agent[241] in creating or adding to an unnecessary danger in the highway, as by making

233. Decisive were *Cowley v. Newmarket L.B.* [1892] A.C. 345 in the House of Lords; *Pictou v. Geldert* [1893] A.C. 524 and *Sydney v. Bourke* [1895] A.C. 433 in the P.C. The immunity extends beyond dangers on the trafficable roadway to, e.g., a decayed tree between footpath and kerb; *Bretherton v. Hornsby S.* [1963] S.R. (N.S.W.) 334 (F.C.).

234. *Young v. Davis* (1863) 2 H. & C. 197; 159 E.R. 82 and the decisions cited in the preceding note. But mandamus may lie: *R. v. Clare C.C.* [1904] 2 I.R. 569.

235. *Russell v. Men of Devon* (1788) 2 T.R. 667; 100 E.R. 359; *M'Kinnon v. Penson* (1854) 9 Ex. 609 at 612-614; 156 E.R. 260 at 261-262.

236. Except in the Maritimes and British Columbia.

237. *Highways (Miscellaneous Provisions) Act* 1961. Adopted in Eire by *Civil Liabilities Act* 1961 s. 60 (not yet in operation). By shifting the burden of excuse to the defendant, the statute actually imposes a liability stricter than negligence: see *Griffiths v. Liverpool Corp.* [1967] 1 Q.B. 374.

238. Abolition was recommended in N.S.W. (1987), S.A. (1974), W.A. (1981) and N.Z. (1973).

239. Friedmann, *Liability of Highway Authorities*, 5 Res Jud. 21 (1951); *Guilfoyle v. Port of London* [1932] 1 K.B. 336 at 346; *Pride of Derby v. British Celanese* [1953] Ch. 149 at 188.

240. *Gorringe v. Transport Comm.* (1950) 80 C.L.R. 357; *Florence v. Marrickville C.* [1960] S.R. (N.S.W.) 562; *Kirk v. Culcairn S.* (1964) 64 S.R. (N.S.W.) 281; *Burton v. W. Suffolk C.C.* [1960] 2 Q.B. 72; *Quinn v. Minister of Commerce* [1954] N.I. 131.

241. Hence, not liable for a predecessor's misfeasance: *Baxter v. Stockton Corp.* [1959] 1 Q.B. 441.

an excavation without filling it in,[242] creating an obstruction,[243] raising the surface so as to weaken a retaining wall,[244] constructing a road that ends abruptly in an unguarded ravine,[245] repairing a road so as to give a false appearance of safety,[246] or removing all but one of a line of trees so as to convert into a trap what was once a self-evident margin of the road.[247] The improper nature of the original act or intervention of the road authority must always be the foundation of the complaint against it. If the design or execution of the work was faulty or negligent, it is no answer that the dangerous condition did not emerge immediately, so long as it was a proximate consequence;[248] but if originally safe by the prevailing standards of the time and place, no subsequent deterioration of the road surface or its use by heavier vehicles[249] will call for affirmative steps to put it right. For instance, no liability was held to devolve for a slab on a footpath which a tree root had gradually, over ten years, dangerously raised an inch, once the original construction was adjudged proper notwithstanding the irreducible risk presented by the adjacent trees.[250]

More far reaching in this respect is the responsibility for any so-called "artificial structure" placed in the highway, for this includes an obligation of care not to let it, as distinct from the road itself, fall into a dangerous state of disrepair.[251] On this basis, liability has been imposed for a defective brick drain constructed in a road,[252] a dangerous grid for draining surface water into a sewer,[253] for a broken pipe drain laid by the side of the road,[254] and for an open space around a tree planted on a footpath.[255] It has never been clearly defined what "artificial structures", found in association with the highway, are for this purpose distinguishable from the highway itself. In one case, a swing bridge was included,[256] and obviously so are seats, lamp posts, pillar boxes, direction signs and sand

242. *Sydney v. Bourke* [1895] A.C. 433 at 441.
243. *Fisher v. Ruislip-Northwood U.D.C.* [1945] K.B. 584; *Morris v. Luton Corp.* [1946] K.B. 114; *Meurs v. Taieri C.* [1954] N.Z.L.R. 1081. The duty is not lessened by the fact that the purpose of the fence was to reduce danger from disrepair of the highway: *Stoddard v. Ashburton C.* [1926] N.Z.L.R. 399.
244. Cf. *A.-G. v. Todmorden B.C.* [1937] 4 All E.R. 588 and *Woollahra C. v. Moody* (1913) 16 C.L.R. 353.
245. *McClelland v. Manchester Corp.* [1912] 1 K.B. 118.
246. *Hill v. Comr. Main Roads* (1989) A.T.R. 80-260 (N.S.W.C.A.); *Huon v. Driessen* (1991) A.T.R. 81-093; *McDonogh v. Commonwealth* (1987) 73 A.L.R. 148 (Fed. C.A.).
247. *Grafton City v. Riley Dodds* [1956] S.R. (N.S.W.) 53.
248. *Woollahra C. v. Moody* (1913) 16 C.L.R. 353; *Taylor v. Main Roads Comm.* (1945) 46 S.R. (N.S.W.) 117; *Hocking v. A.-G.* [1963] N.Z.L.R. 513 (culvert, though soundly built, was foreseeably inadequate in time of flood); *Desmond v. Mt Isa* [1991] 2 Qd R. 482.
249. *McDonogh v. Commonwealth* (1985) 61 A.C.T.R. 22 (revd on other grounds).
250. *Hellyer v. Commonwealth* [1964] Arg. L.R. 1026; 5 F.L.R. 459.
251. This theorem derives from the controversial decision in *Bathurst v. Macpherson* (1879) 4 App. Cas. 256, regarding which it has been said that, by constructing a drain in the road and failing to keep this "artificial structure" in repair, the defendants "were as much liable for a misfeasance as if they had by their direct act made a hole in the road" (*Pictou v. Geldert* [1893] A.C. 524 at 531).
252. *Bathurst v. Macpherson* (1879) 4 App. Cas. 256.
253. *White v. Hindley L. Bd* (1875) L.R. 10 Q.B. 219.
254. On this ground, McTiernan J. decided in plaintiff's favour in *Buckle v. Bayswater Road Bd* (1936) 57 C.L.R. 259 at 298.
255. *Donaldson v. Sydney* (1924) 24 S.R. (N.S.W.) 408.
256. *Guilfoyle v. Port of London* [1932] 1 K.B. 336.

bins,[257] but ordinary bridges,[258] culverts,[259] footpaths[260] and any other place over which there is a public right of passage and which forms part of the road surface seem to be treated as part of the highway proper.[261] No liability attaches, however, if the accident is caused, not by any defect in the artificial structure itself, but by disrepair of the highway whereby the structure becomes a source of danger, as where a sewer cover gradually protrudes above the road through wearing away of the surface.[262]

It is still an open question whether the "artificial structure" rule is a distinct and independent exception to the immunity or merely represents the germ of an idea that later crystallised into the "source of authority" test, which will be noted presently. Although invoked on a few occasions, it lacks modern endorsement by English courts and has been lately questioned, if not actually repudiated, by the High Court of Australia.[263] In so far as it rests on a forced extension of the misfeasance category,[264] its theoretical standing is undoubtedly vulnerable, but it may perhaps be defended as a deserving device for further narrowing the non-feasance immunity.

Most disruptive of all, however, has proved the "source of authority" test, which excludes from the immunity's ambit the maintenance of all structures by a highway authority upon or under the road pursuant to a statutory authority other than that strictly relating to the construction and repair of highways. Quite clearly, a public authority which puts up a construction, such as a drain, whether in a road or elsewhere, and fails to keep it in repair is subject to precisely the same liability as anyone else for negligence or nuisance.[265] That it happens to be at the same time a highway authority makes no difference, because its liability in these several capacities is quite distinct. As the combination of numerous functions in the hands of the same authority has become so prominent a feature of modern

257. *Drake v. Bedfordshire C.C.* [1944] 1 All E.R. 633 at 638.
258. *Pictou v. Geldert* [1893] A.C. 524.
259. *Gorringe v. Transport Comm.* (1950) 80 C.L.R. 357 at 362, 279; *Hocking v. A.-G.* [1963] N.Z.L.R. 513.
260. *Gascoyne v. Wellington Corp.* [1942] N.Z.L.R. 562.
261. *Gorringe v. Transport Comm.* (1950) 80 C.L.R. 357 at 379; *Buckle v. Bayswater Road Bd* (1936) 57 C.L.R. 259 at 286. McTiernan J. defined the category as including any "structure which is appurtenant or subservient to a road but not a component part of the road fabric. . . . It should not be applied to a road or a section or a layer of road or its foundation made of artificial materials or of both artificial and natural materials" (ibid. at 300).
262. *Thompson v. Brighton* [1894] 1 Q.B. 332. Contrast *Dublin Tramways v. Fitzgerald* [1903] A.C. 99, holding tramway liable by reason of its statutory obligation to keep both rails and adjoining road surface in repair. Accord: *S.A. Rly Comm. v. Barnes* (1927) 40 C.L.R. 179.
263. In *Buckle v. Bayswater Road Bd* (1936) 57 C.L.R. 259 it was rejected outright by Dixon J. and seemingly by Latham C.J. But since McTiernan J. supported it, and Dixon J. was forced into dissent on the facts, the ratio decidendi is obscure: 63 L.Q.R. 461 at 466-467 (1947). In *Gorringe v. Transport Comm.* (1950) 80 C.L.R. 357 Latham C.J. and Dixon J. ignored it, but Fullager J. seemed to regard it as still accepted doctrine (at 379). It was likewise accepted in *Grafton City v. Riley Dodds* [1956] S.R. (N.S.W.) 53 at 60 ff. and defended by Sawer, 12 A.L.J. 231 (1938).
264. So viewed, it could not be invoked unless the highway authority itself brought the structure there (rather than merely own or maintain it) or did something to create the danger: *Bretherton v. Hornsby S.* [1963] S.R. (N.S.W.) 334 (self-sown tree); *Grafton City v. Riley Dodds* [1956] S.R. (N.S.W.) 53 at 62-63.
265. *Essendon Corp v. McSweeney* (1914) 17 C.L.R. 524; *Willoughby C. v. Halstead* (1916) 22 C.L.R. 352.

administrative organisation, the "separate function" theorem can, not infrequently, be exploited to side-step the immunity. For instance, the cutting of a trench in a highway for drainage work has been attributed to the sanitary function,[266] the laying of a drain pipe beside the road to the agricultural function,[267] and the fixing of traffic studs to the function of the defendants as a traffic, not a road, authority.[268] Other cases pose vexing problems of demarcation. Thus, if the cause of the accident is a defective drain, it may be necessary to ascertain whether it was put there to serve a purpose arising out of a highway function, as for example to carry off surface water or drain seepage and protect the road base, or was primarily intended for draining surrounding agricultural land.[269]

It remains to note that the immunity is confined to highway authorities proper, and does not avail dock[270] or railway companies[271] charged with the maintenance of roads, such as approaches to bridges under their control. The distinction has been justified on the ground that the non-feasance rule was originally designed as a shield for the local inhabitants of a parish or county and that only genuine successors of their public road maintenance functions can claim its benefit in modern times,[272] not private organisations carrying on business for profit.[273] The exemption does not even appear to cover contractors acting for a highway authority.[274]

4. DEFENCES

In conclusion, the defendant may invoke certain defences to justify, or at least mitigate, his responsibility for a nuisance.

Statutory authority

The nuisance-causing activity may have been carried out under statutory authority. Such statutes differ greatly: some require, others merely empower the undertaking; some authorise it in a specific location, others leave the *where* and *how* to discretion; some provide for compensation, others do not address injurious effects. From statutory authorisation it is easier to infer an intent that in the public interest the activity has to be tolerated (therefore cannot be enjoined) rather than that persons injuriously

266. *Newsome v. Darton U.D.C.* [1938] 3 All E.R. 93; *Shoreditch v. Bull* (1904) 90 L.T. 210.
267. *Buckle v. Bayswater Road Bd* (1936) 57 C.L.R. 259. Latham C.J. and Dixon J. agreed on this principle but differed on its application to the facts.
268. *Skilton v. Epson & Ewell U.D.C.* [1937] 1 K.B. 112.
269. This caused the difference of opinion between Latham C.J. and Dixon J. in *Buckle's* case (1936) 57 C.L.R. 259. The former held that the drain was primarily agricultural and, therefore, joined McTiernan J. in deciding for the plaintiff; while Dixon J. regarded the agricultural purpose as "quite incidental" and consequently dissented.
270. *Guilfoyle v. Port of London* [1932] 1 K.B. 336.
271. *Swain v. S. Rly* [1939] 2 K.B. 560.
272. But probably including central governments: *McDonogh v. Commonwealth* (1985) 61 A.C.T.R. 22; (1987) 73 A.L.R. 148.
273. *Swain v. S. Ry* [1939] 2 K.B. 336 at 575; and cf. *A.-G. v. St Ives R.D.C.* [1960] 1 Q.B. 312. See the critical comment by Friedmann, 5 Res Jud. 21 at 28 (1951).
274. *Drake v. Bedfordshire C.C.* [1944] K.B. 620; but cf. *Quinn v. Minister of Commerce* [1954] N.I. 131.

affected should also lose all right to compensation. In a free society it is better policy to distribute the cost among the beneficiaries of the activity than to demand private sacrifices.[275]

The basic rule, as generally formulated, is that if the nuisance is an "inevitable" consequence of the authorised undertaking, and was not negligently carried out, it is implicitly legalised and not actionable.[276] Thus villagers near a new oil refinery, sited as authorised by statute, could not complain either of the effect of its location on the neighbourhood or of irreducible air pollution;[277] nor could residents adjoining a railway complain of vibrations from passing trains[278] or the noise of cattle traffic in the station yard.[279] On the other hand, where the grantee has a choice as to area and method, he must seek to exercise it without interfering with private rights.[280] For example, a general power to provide hospitals did not authorise the provision of a fever hospital in a populous place where it was a nuisance to neighbours.[281]

The burden of proving that the nuisance was inevitable lies on the defendant.[282] The question whether the undertaking could have been implemented without committing a nuisance calls for a practical judgment: "The criterion of inevitability is not what is theoretically possible but what is possible, according to the state of scientific knowledge at the time, having also in view a certain common sense appreciation which cannot be rigidly defined, of practical feasibility in view of situation and of expense."[283] This test, though redolent of the negligence calculus and occasionally equated with it, is more stringent: the focus is on the feasability of avoiding injury, and the utility of the defendant's enterprise receives short shrift as does the expense of adopting alternative methods. It has nonetheless been criticised as unrealistic, seeing that most of these accidents are the result, not of misconduct but of inevitable compromises between thrift and efficiency on the one hand and safety on the other: why, in this dilemma, should a sacrifice be demanded from the few for the sake of the larger public?[284] Courts have been, and should be, slow to subordinate private rights in the neighbourhood to the financial advantage of consumers of the offending facility.[285] All the same, they have not been insensitive to the need for some latitude especially when the injury is not substantial.[286]

275. The Law Reform Commission of B.C. (1977) recommended that statutory authority should no longer be a defence to claims for compensation, as distinct from injunction, for nuisance or *Rylands v. Fletcher*; also Lord Denning in *Allen v. Gulf Oil* [1980] Q.B. 156 at 168.
276. *Hammersmith Rly v. Brand* (1869) L.R. 4 H.L. 171. See also above, p. 347.
277. *Allen v. Gulf Oil* [1981] A.C. 1001.
278. *Hammersmith Rly v. Brand* (1869) L.R. 4 H.L. 171.
279. *London, Brighton Rly v. Truman* (1885) 11 App. Cas. 45.
280. Assuming that a safer alternative is possible. *Tock v. St John's* [1989] 2 S.C.R. 1181, on the other hand, would in no circumstances permit the defence when the authority is framed in discretionary terms. Criticised: Hogg, 69 Can. B. Rev. 589 (1990).
281. *Metropolitan Asylum District v. Hill* (1881) 6 App. Cas. 193.
282. *Manchester Corp. v. Farnworth* [1930] A.C. 171; *Edwards v. Blue Mts C.C.* (1961) 78 W.N. (N.S.W.) 864. Aliter, under *Rylands v. Fletcher*.
283. *Manchester Corp. v. Farnworth* [1930] A.C. 171 at 183.
284. See Kneebone, 10 U. Adel. L. Rev. 472 (1986).
285. Cf. *Allen v. Gulf Oil* [1982] A.C. 1001 at 1015 ("regardless of expense").
286. *Tock v. St John's* [1989] 2 S.C.R. 1181 at 1200 (La Forest J.).

While the absence of a compensation clause points to the retention of a nuisance remedy,[287] its presence tells against it. For in addition to thus assuring compensation either way, the first could suggest that the legislator did not contemplate injurious effects while the second specifically provided for them. Moreover, if there is a compensation clause, courts will be doubly reluctant to interfere with any broad discretion entrusted to an administrative authority as and when it is deemed necessary and expedient to exercise the statutory powers. A catchment board, for instance, charged with flood control should not be lightly deterred by the prospect of an injunction every time they dredge a river and deposit the soil on one or the other bank even if the effect is to obstruct a flood channel and thereby increase the risk of flooding adjacent properties.[288]

Prescription

The privilege to commit a private nuisance may be acquired by prescription, if it would qualify as an easement and could as such have been acquired in the particular jurisdiction by prescription.[289] After 20 years' user, the nuisance is retrospectively legalised as if it had been authorised by a grant from the owner of the servient land. Thus, one may acquire a right to discharge rainwater from eaves to adjoining land,[290] pollute a watercourse[291] or emit smoke though a flue in a party wall.[292] It is doubtful, however, whether a prescriptive right can be acquired to commit a nuisance by smell, noise, or smoke, since it is essential that there be certainty and uniformity for measuring the user by which the extent of the right is to be ascertained.[293] For a similar reason, it has been held that the defence does not apply to encroaching branches or roots, in view of the perpetual change in the quantity of the inconvenience suffered.[294] In any event, a prescriptive right cannot be set up where, during the period of user, the nuisance was not actionable or preventable by the plaintiff, for example, because the defendant's activity was secret[295] or because, as in *Sturges v. Bridgman*,[296] the operation of heavy machinery did not cause serious inconvenience and was not therefore actionable until a neighbouring doctor built a consulting room at the bottom of his garden.

No *public* nuisance can be legalised by prescription,[297] "for it cannot have a lawful beginning by licence or otherwise, being an offence against the common law".[298]

287. *Metropolitan Asylum District v. Hill* (1881) 6 App. Cas. 193 at 203.
288. *Marriage v. E. Norfolk Catchment Bd* [1950] 1 K.B. 284 (C.A.); *N. Vancouver v. McKenzie Barge Ways* [1965] S.C.R. 377.
289. As in England, but not under the Torrens system in N.Z. and most Australian States. See Bradbrook & Neave, *Easements and Restrictive Covenants in Australia* (1981) 178.
290. *Harvey v. Walters* (1873) L.R. 8 C.P. 162.
291. *Hulley v. Silversprings Bleaching Co.* [1922] 2 Ch. 268.
292. *Jones v. Pritchard* [1908] 1 Ch. 630.
293. *Hulley v. Silversprings Bleaching Co.* [1922] 2 Ch. 268 at 281.
294. *Lemmon v. Webb* [1894] 3 Ch. 1; [1895] A.C. 1.
295. *Liverpool Corp. v. Coghill* [1918] 1 Ch. 307.
296. (1879) 11 Ch. D. 852. Also *Miller v. Jackson* [1977] Q.B. 966 (C.A.).
297. *R. v. Cross* (1812) 3 Camp. 224; 170 E.R. 1362; *Mott v. Shoolbred* (1875) L.R. 20 Eq. 22.
298. *Dewell v. Sanders* (1618) Cro. Jac. 490 at 491; 79 E.R. 419.

Contributory negligence

Some writers baldly assert that contributory negligence never affords a defence to an action for nuisance,[299] while others with equal assurance maintain the opposite.[300] Neither of these views is correct, because both fail to take into account the dual function which the concept of nuisance plays in modern law and which in this context, as elsewhere, causes confusion.[301]

In one of its aspects, the law of nuisance seeks to adjust competing uses of land, and here contributory negligence does not play a significant part. Although in most of these cases the defendant is charged with intentional conduct, they rarely involve a deliberate desire to inflict injury, and the exclusion of the defence of contributory negligence cannot therefore be properly attributed to the same policy which has ruled out the plea as an answer to wilful and intentional wrongs.[302] The sounder reason is that the defendant's activity is treated as of a kind which he pursues at the risk of having to compensate his neighbours for any resulting nuisance. Besides, these cases seldom present an act or omission by the plaintiff comparable to contributory negligence in the ordinary accident case. They include the following:

(1) "Coming to a nuisance". It seems to have been supposed at one time that a person who chose to acquire property with knowledge that it was exposed to a nuisance, was precluded from complaining of it on the ground of volenti non fit injuria or contributory negligence, but this view has long been exploded.[303] In the absence of a prescriptive right, a purchaser or lessee is entitled to the reasonable use and enjoyment of his land to the same extent as any other occupier, since a defendant would otherwise be able, by his wrongful conduct, to diminish the value of neighbouring land without compensation. So much for land already subject to nuisance. Less obvious is allowing a newcomer to object to a use that before his arrival had not constitued a nuisance to *anyone*, as when a residential developer moves into an area adjoining a stock yard or cricket pitch.[304] But even in such cases it may be against economic efficiency and the public interest to freeze the character of the area for ever by a prior use.[305] (2) Use by the plaintiff of his own land in a manner that foreseeably increases his exposure to nuisance is no defence, except where such use introduces an element of "abnormal sensitiveness", as previously explained.[306] He need not keep his windows permanently closed in order to keep out the stench from a nearby factory or stay indoors to avoid being hit by golf balls from adjoining links.[307]

299. Winfield, 4 Cam. L.J. 189 at 200 (1931). There is no such statement in his *Textbook*.
300. Williams, *Joint Torts*, 203-205.
301. See James, *Contributory Negligence*, 62 Yale L.J. 691 at 715-721 (1953).
302. See above, p. 281.
303. *Bliss v. Hall* (1838) 4 Bing. N.C. 183; 132 E.R. 758; *Sturges v. Bridgman* (1879) 11 Ch. D. 852; *Khyatt v. Morgan* [1961] N.Z.L.R. 1020.
304. *Miller v. Jackson* [1977] Q.B. 966.
305. *Sturges v. Bridgman* (1879) 11 Ch. D. 852 at 865. But while this could justify an injunction against a pig farmer to protect a later residential development, might it not be conditioned by awarding him the cost of relocation, as in *Spur Ind. v. Del Webb* 494 P. 2d 700 (Ariz. 1972)? See Wittman, *First Come, First Served: An Ecomonic Analysis of "Coming to the Nuisance"*, 9 J. Leg. Stud. 557 (1980).
306. See above, p. 421.
307. *Lester-Travers v. City of Frankston* [1970] V.R. 2.

(3) Again, creation of a similar nuisance by the plaintiff provides no answer,[308] nor, probably, does (4) Failure to take reasonable steps to avert or minimise the consequences of a nuisance, at any rate when it would involve burdensome affirmative action or expenditure of money in rearranging the premises.[309]

Nuisance has, however, also intruded into the field of ordinary accident litigation, particularly in regard to personal injury suffered as the result of a public nuisance on the highway. These cases frequently involve conduct by the plaintiff constituting typical contributory negligence, such as failure to avoid apparent danger. In this context it has long been settled that a careless plaintiff cannot improve his position by claiming for nuisance rather than negligence.[310] Indeed, the earliest articulate recognition of the defence of contributory negligence occurred in an action for nuisance by a plaintiff who had inattentively collided with a pole stretched across the highway.[311] Today, of course, his claim would be merely reduced rather than defeated entirely.[312]

5. REMEDIES

Three private law remedies are available for nuisance: a common law action for damages, equitable relief by injunction with or without damages, and abatement without recourse to legal process.

Damages

Anyone injured by a nuisance may claim damages, either alone or together with injunctive relief. Common law damages can be awarded only for past losses, without prejudicing the plaintiff's right to recover later for additional loss de die in diem (from day to day); unlike equity which (as we shall see) may in exceptional cases force a final settlement for past and future loss on the plaintiff and thus allow the defendant to buy him out.

The loss must, of course, not be too remote. Resolving all prior doubts, the Privy Council in *The Wagon Mound (No. 2)*,[313] a case of public nuisance,[314] held that this depended, as in negligence, on whether the injury was reasonably foreseeable rather than, as was once thought, on whether it was merely "direct". Admittedly, negligence in the narrow sense is not always essential to liability. It will be recalled that in *The Wagon Mound* the defendants had been found negligent with respect to the spillage

308. *Colchester Corp. v. Brooke* (1845) 7 Q.B. 339; 115 E.R. 518.
309. Cf. *Miller v. Jackson* [1977] Q.B. 966 (no obligation to live behind shutters or stay out of garden during cricket games).
310. *Boyle v. Mornington S.* (1883) 9 V.L.R. (L.) 265; *McMeekin v. Maryborough C.* [1947] Q.S.R. 192; *Cull v. Green* (1924) 27 W.A.L.R. 62.
311. *Butterfield v. Forrester* (1809) 11 East 60; 103 E.R. 926.
312. Unless, as in *Dymond v. Pearce* [1972] 1 Q.B. 496, the plaintiff was wholly responsible for the collision.
313. [1967] 1 A.C. 617.
314. Applied to private nuisance in *Hiap Lee v. Weng Lok* [1974] 2 Mal. L.J. 1 (P.C.); *Fennell v. Robson* [1977] 2 N.S.W.L.R. 486 (C.A.); *Richmond v. Scantelbury* [1991] 2 V.R. 38; *Clearlite v. Auckland C.C.* [1976] 2 N.Z.L.R. 729 (C.A.).

of oil[315] and it would have been Pickwickian to determine their liability for the subsequent fire by a different test in nuisance than in negligence. But the court went further and prescribed the same rule of remoteness for all cases of nuisance regardless of whether fault or negligence happened to be a necessary element of liability. Another important step was thus taken in consolidating the fault element in the modern law of nuisance and assimilating nuisance with the pervasive theory of negligence.

But not all rules bearing on the extent of liability have thus become freely interchangeable. The law of nuisance has traditionally protected a much wider range of interests than negligence, and must therefore reject many of the limitations on the kind of injury recoverable for negligence, whether they be expressed in terms of "no duty", "remoteness" or otherwise. Thus in contrast to the strict requirement of material injury in negligence, substantial interference with comfort, convenience and other sensibilities is sufficient for nuisance.[316] Where the nuisance was committed in contumelious disregard of plaintiff's rights, aggravated or exemplary damages also lie.[317] Again, in contrast to negligence,[318] damages have been consistently awarded for purely economic losses, including loss of commercial profits.[319] This can result in odd distinctions: a road repairer who paralyses an adjoining hotel by negligently cutting a connecting electric cable will not be liable,[320] but one who does so through vibrations, noise and dust will be.[321] Thus when a house en route a royal procession was obstructed, the owner recovered for loss of contracts with prospective viewers.[322]

Despite the emphasis in nuisance on the plaintiff's right in land, there is no justification for limiting his recovery to damage only to his land and its enjoyment: damages may also be awarded for damage or loss of his chattels[323] and, as already noted, for personal injury.[324]

Damage is of the gist of nuisance, except where to insist on it would unfairly expose a plaintiff to the risk of a prescriptive right ripening against him by continued user. Such is the case with interference with servitudes[325] and encroachments, like a cornice projecting from a building[326]—when accordingly at least nominal damages are in order even in the absence of proven damages.

315. See above, p. 210.
316. Damages should not exceed the customary scale for loss of amenities in personal injury: *Bone v. Seale* [1975] 1 W.L.R. 797 (C.A.); *Oldham v. Lawson (No. 1)* [1976] V.R. 654 at 658-659.
317. *Guppys v. Brookling* (1984) 269 E.G. 942. Left open in *Oldham v. Lawson (No. 1)* [1976] V.R. 654 at 658.
318. See above, p. 177.
319. Criticised by *Cane* 175. *Louisiana v. M/V Testbank* 752 F. 2d 1019 (1985) specifically denied pollution claim, whether based on nuisance or negligence.
320. See above, p. 181.
321. *Campbell v. Paddington Corp.* [1911] 1 K.B. 869 (public nuisance).
322. E.g. *Clearlite v. Auckland C.C.* [1976] 2 N.Z.L.R. 729; *Huggard v. Power Comm.* (1970) 5 N.B.R. (2d) 758; *Grosvenor Hotel v. Hamilton* [1894] 2 Q.B. 836.
323. *Howard Electric v. Mooney* [1974] 2 N.Z.L.R. 762; *British Celanese v. Hunt* [1969] 1 W.L.R. 959.
324. See above, p. 409.
325. *Nicholls v. Ely Beet Sugar Factory* [1936] Ch. 343.
326. *Fay v. Prentice* (1845) 1 C.B. 828; 135 E.R. 769.

Injunction

Equity has played an important role in the development and application of nuisance law through the use of injunctions.[327] In general, the ordinary principles of injunctive relief apply. Hence it must appear that damages would not afford an adequate remedy, but this requirement is easily satisfied, particularly when there is likely to be a repetition of the wrong.[328] But where the nuisance is not a continuing one or the defendant does not claim a right to persist, injunction is conditional on proof of substantial injury. If the interference is trivial[329] or only temporary,[330] the plaintiff will generally be relegated to damages. Again, injunction being discretionary,[331] personal factors such as the plaintiff's dilatoriness or the triviality of his injury may militate against it.

On the other hand, considerations of economic efficiency[332] have not been encouraged. An injunction may issue although it would have been much cheaper for the plaintiff than for the defendant to prevent the annoyance.[333] Likewise, in contrast to the American trend,[334] the greater economic or social value of the offending enterprise is not considered relevant,[335] in the belief that individual property rights should be only subordinated to the public weal by statutory authority; moreover, in as much as the public interest is apt to be identified with purely commercial considerations, it would tend to subordinate residential, recreational and "environmental" concerns. All the same, this attitude pinpoints a major respect in which the common law of nuisance cannot in the long run function adequately as the sole method of environmental control under modern conditions: the rigidity of its criteria and remedies precludes any finer balancing between public and private interests (or other efficiency considerations) and makes no allowance either for the limited financial resources of many defendants (for example sewerage works becoming inadequate due to population explosion)[336] or the disproportionately greater economic benefit to the general community.

327. Abatement was the remedy for the assize of nuisance which suffered however from several disadvantages to plaintiffs, who usually preferred the action on the case and had to resort to equity for injunction.
328. *Beswicke v. Alner* [1926] V.L.R. 72; *Madden v. Coy* [1944] V.L.R. 88; *Clowes v. Staffordshire Waterworks* (1872) L.R. 8 Ch. App. 125.
329. *A.-G. v. Sheffield Gas Co.* (1853) 3 De G., M. & G. 304; 43 E.R. 119.
330. *Swaine v. Gt N. Rly* (1864) 4 De G., J. & Sm. 211; 46 E.R. 899.
331. The trend has been away from formalised rules: see *Fishenden v. Higgs* (1935) 153 L.T. 128.
332. Efficient resource allocation (Pareto optimality) is discussed in Coase's classical article, *Problem of Social Cost*, 3 J. Law & Econ. 1 (1960). With special focus on the nuisance problem, see Calabresi & Melamed, *Property Rules, Liability Rules and Inalienability*, 85 Harv. L. Rev. 1089 (1972); Ogus & Richardson, *Economics and Environment: A Study of Private Nuisance* [1977] Cam. L.J. 284.
333. But in *Bank of N.Z. v. Greenwood* [1984] 1 N.Z.L.R. 525 damages for sun glare were assessed on basis of cheaper cost of blinds for plaintiff than forcing structural alterations on defendant.
334. *Boomer v. Atl. Cement* 257 N.E. 2d 870 (N.Y. 1970).
335. *Kennaway v. Thompson* [1981] Q.B. 88 (C.A.), disavowing Lord Denning's contrary view in *Miller v. Jackson* [1977] Q.B. 966; the only concession being usually to suspend the injunction so as to permit gradual abatement: e.g. *Pride of Derby v. British Celanese* [1953] Ch. 149. See Tromans, *Nuisance—Prevention or Payment* [1982] Cam. L.J. 89.
336. As in *Pride of Derby v. British Celanese* [1953] Ch. 149.

A special feature of equitable jurisdiction is that even a prospective nuisance may be enjoined, where obviously a common law action for damages would be premature. Such quia timet injunctions, however, are issued only if there is strong probability that the nuisance will in fact arise[337] and that the damage, if it materialises, will be irreparable.[338] Moreover, by statute (*Lord Cairns Act*),[339] the court may now also award damages in lieu of injunction for prospective injury.[340] Previously, the only choices open to the court were to grant an injunction or to remit the plaintiff to his common law remedy of damages de die in diem until the nuisance was abated.[341] To this has now been added the third alternative of tolerating the continuance of a nuisance on payment of compensation once and for all. This in effect amounts to a judicial power of expropriation and is administered very cautiously so as not to become an instrument for legalising the commission of a tort by any defendant able and willing to pay for it.[342] The English, in contrast to modern American, practice also purports to exclude entirely the public interest from consideration, thereby tempting courts to avoid issuing an injunction by denying liability altogether.

Sometimes, instead of granting an injunction, the court may content itself with a mere declaration that the defendant is not entitled to commit the act complained of,[343] or refuse an injunction upon an undertaking by the defendant to remedy the offensive condition.[344]

Abatement

The privilege of abating a nuisance by self-help is of ancient origin[345] and co-existed with the early assize of nuisance, which provided a method of compelling abatement by common law process before this function was assumed by courts of equity issuing mandatory injunctions. Abatement, like most other forms of extra-judicial redress, has fallen out of favour with the progressive assertion of legal control through the judicial process, and is today much more closely harnessed than of yore. In many respects it resembles the privilege of forcibly resisting trespassory invasion of land,[346]

337. *A.-G. v. Manchester Corp.* [1893] 2 Ch. 87. When it is sometimes said that the damage must be imminent, this merely means that the claim must not be premature in the sense that nothing other than an injunction would avoid the threatened damage: *Hooper v. Rogers* [1975] Ch. 43 (C.A.); *Grasso v. Lore* [1980] V.R. 163 (F.C.).
338. *Fletcher v. Bealy* (1885) 28 Ch. D. 688.
339. Originally enacted in 1858, now *Supreme Court Act* 1981 s. 50. N.S.W.: *Supreme Court Act* 1970 s. 68; Vic.: *Supreme Court Act* 1958 s. 62(3); Qld: see *Barbagallo v. Catelan* [1986] 1 Qd R. 245; S.A.: *Supreme Court Act* 1935 s. 30; W.A.: *Supreme Court Act* 1935 s. 25(10); Tas.: *Supreme Court Act* 1932 s. 11(13), but qualified by subs. (b).
340. *Leeds Industrial Co-op. v. Slack* [1924] A.C. 851. See Jolowicz, *Damages in Equity—A Study of Lord Cairns Act* [1975] Cam. L.J. 224.
341. E.g. *Hole v. Chard Union* [1894] 1 Ch. 293.
342. See Tromans, *Nuisance—Prevention or Payment* [1982] Cam.L.J. 87. In many cases, what is at stake is not the plaintiff's willingness to sell out but his price. Equitable damages in effect impose a court-determined price, while an injunction would leave the parties to private bargaining: see *York Bros v. Main Roads Comm.* [1983] 1 N.S.W.L.R. 391 at 402.
343. *Batcheller v. Tunbridge Wells Gas Co.* (1901) 84 L.T. 765.
344. *Field v. S.A. Soccer Assoc.* [1953] S.A.S.R. 224; but note *Munroe v. Southern Dairies* [1955] V.L.R. 332 at 338.
345. Already mentioned by Bracton: see *Holdsworth* iii, 279.
346. See above, p. 86.

and still finds some justification in the fact that many minor annoyances, such as encroaching branches and roots, are more expediently removed by self-help and that on other occasions security of life and property requires a speedy remedy without time to call on the culprit or resort to law.[347]

The privilege of abatement is not confined to cases where the offending condition can be removed from the land of the party aggrieved, but also justifies entry upon the land of the other[348] and the use of reasonable force to accomplish the purpose. But care must be taken not to inflict unnecessary damage[349] and, where there are two ways of abating a nuisance, the less detrimental must be adopted unless it would injure an innocent third party or the public.[350] It seems that there is no privilege of entry and abatement unless a mandatory injunction would have issued, because otherwise one might attain an end by self-redress which would be denied to him if he had recourse to judicial process. Thus, when the damage involved in terminating a nuisance is wholly disproportionate to the threatened harm, like pulling down a house which causes only negligible obstruction to an ancient light, the privilege may not be exercised.[351] Sometimes, however, abatement is permissible although there would lie no remedy in damages. For example, the threat of imminent danger justifies instant action even if no harm has yet occurred,[352] and it appears that a neighbour may sever encroaching roots or branches, despite there being no liability for such a nuisance in the absence of actual damage.[353]

For some time now, there has been a strong tendency to deprecate self-help and to insist increasingly on notice as a prerequisite.[354] None is necessary if abatement does not involve entry on the other's land, such as lopping off overhanging branches,[355] in cases of emergency in order to protect life or property,[356] and seemingly where the land belongs to the original creator of the nuisance.[357] Beyond this, however, modern judicial opinion appears to insist on notice. It is certainly required where the nuisance was created not by the present occupier, but by his predecessor in title,[358] in all cases (excepting emergency) where the nuisance has arisen from omission,[359] and where the abatement involves demolition of an inhabited house.[360]

347. *Lonsdale v. Nelson* (1823) 2 B. & C. 302 at 311; 107 E.R. 396 at 399.
348. *Jones v. Williams* (1843) 11 M. & W. 176; 152 E.R. 764; *R. v. Hampden S.* (1886) 8 A.L.T. 74.
349. *Roberts v. Rose* (1865) L.R. 1 Ex. 82; 4 H. & C. 103.
350. *Lagan Navigation Co. v. Lambeg Bleaching Co.* [1927] A.C. 226 at 245.
351. Cf. *Lane v. Capsey* [1891] 3 Ch. 411 at 416 where the question was left open.
352. *Penruddock's Case* (1598) 5 Co. Rep. 100b; 77 E.R. 210; but see *Morrice v. Baker* (1616) 3 Bulst. 196; 81 E.R. 165.
353. *Lemmon v. Webb* [1894] 3 Ch. 1; [1895] A.C. 1.
354. Contrast *Jones v. Williams* (1843) 11 M. & W. 176; 152 E.R. 764 with *Lagan Navigation Co. v. Lambeg Bleaching Co.* [1927] A.C. 226.
355. *Lemmon v. Webb* [1894] 3 Ch. 1; [1895] A.C. 1. But the branches must be returned to avoid liability for conversion: *Mills v. Brooker* [1919] 1 K.B. 555.
356. *Jones v. Williams* (1843) 11 M. & W. 176 at 182; 152 E.R. 764 at 766.
357. Ibid. at 181; 765.
358. *Traian v. Ware* [1957] V.R. 200.
359. There is some authority for doubting whether abatement is ever available where the nuisance arises from a mere omission, except in the case of overhanging boughs: *Lonsdale v. Nelson* (1832) 2 B. & C. 302 at 311; 107 E.R. 396 at 399; *Campbell Davys v. Lloyd* [1901] 2 Ch. 518.
360. *Davies v. Williams* (1851) 16 Q.B. 546; 177 E.R. 988; *Jones v. Jones* (1862) 1 H. & C. 1; 158 E.R. 777.

Abatement is open only to those who may complain of the offending condition as a nuisance. In the case of private nuisance, that means the occupier and, perhaps, anyone acting on his behalf and by his authority. If the nuisance is public, a private individual cannot abate it unless it does him some particular injury over and above that suffered by the rest of the public. A traveller on the highway is permitted to remove an obstruction, but must not interfere with it beyond what is necessary to exercise his right of passage and cannot justify damage, if by avoiding it he might have passed on with reasonable convenience.[361]

Abatement is a privilege, not a duty.[362] An ancient ruling has it that it "destroys any right of action in respect of the nuisance".[363] But as now interpreted, it means no more than that the act of abatement has the effect of removing the nuisance so that the claimant is not entitled to future damages. He may, however, recover damages for past injury.[364] And although some dicta assume that the cost of removing the nuisance is also irrecoverable, it has been held that this does not preclude reimbursement for the cost of mitigating future damage.[365]

361. *Dimes v. Petley* (1850) 15 Q.B. 276; 117 E.R. 462; *Alexander v. Sydney Corp.* (1861) 1 S.C.R. (N.S.W.) (Appendix) 26: 2 Legge 1451.

362. It is not a *duty*, so that failure to abate (as distinct from failure to mitigate damage) does not prejudice a claim to damages (*Morgan v. Khyatt* [1962] N.Z.L.R. 791 at 796) or injunction: *Lawlor v. Johnston* [1905] V.L.R. 714.

363. *Lagan Navigation Co. v. Lambeg Bleaching Co.* [1927] A.C. 226 at 244 per Lord Atkinson; *Baten's Case* (1610) 9 Co. Rep. 53b; 77 E.R. 810.

364. *Halsbury*, 4th ed., vol. 31, p. 126.

365. *Proprietors v. Cowell* (1991) A.T.R. 81-083 and *Proprietors of Strata Plan v. Cowell* (1989) 24 N.S.W.L.R. 478 (roots); *Richmond v. Scantelbury* [1991] 2 V.R. 38 at 48 (roots); *N.Z. Forest Products v. O'Sullivan* [1974] 2 N.Z.L.R. 80 at 83 (fighting encroaching fire).

22

DANGEROUS PREMISES

1. INTRODUCTION

Injury *on*[1] dangerous premises was governed by a well-defined pattern of responsibility long before liability for negligence became generalised in *Donoghue v. Stevenson.*[2] Its distinguishing feature was that, in lieu of the general standard of care, it imposed on the occupier different duties dependent on the class of visitor—invitee, licensee, trespasser—with varying specific standards of care attached to each class. For example, the duty to an invitee demanded that the occupier prevent unusual dangers of which he knew or ought to know; that to a licensee that he warn only of concealed dangers of which he knew. In its heyday no less than seven classes with distinct standards could be counted.[3]

Eventually this increasingly complex system for categories encountered mounting unfavourable comparison with the otherwise prevailing generalised duty of reasonable care. For one thing, the apparent advantages of clear, judicially defined standards of care were in the course of time sacrificed to the tendency to manipulate them in the light of changing notions of social responsibility.[4] For another, the criterion for distinguishing the different classes of entrants according to the material benefit accruing to the occupier lost its appeal to a less commercially oriented age. Both resulted in often capricious distinctions and growing legal uncertainty, besides gratuitously encouraging appeals on what were really questions of fact dressed up as questions of law. Judicial disaffection encouraged circumvention of the occupancy duties by allowing concurrent resort to the Atkinian duty of care on the basis of any element other than mere occupancy, such as an act of commission. Thus undermined and brought into disrepute, the traditional system was ripe for reform.

Reform came earliest by statute in jurisdictions like England which no longer entertained trial by jury. Others were more reluctant to give up the greater measure of judicial control ensured by the occupancy rules, but eventually also succumbed. In some jurisdictions, finally, the old regime was dismantled by judicial decision. Such was the case not only in America but also in Australia. After more than two decades of whittling away, and finally freed from persistent obstruction by the Privy Council, the High

1. Injury caused by dangerous premises to persons outside is governed by nuisance: see above, ch. 21.
2. See Marsh, *History and Comparative Law of Invitees, Licensees and Trespassers*, 69 L.Q.R. 182, 359 (1953).
3. *Vale v. Whiddon* (1949) 60 S.R. (N.S.W.) 90 at 105-107 (Herron J.).
4. For example, by diluting the requirement of a licensor's knowledge from "actually knew" to "had reason to know", barely distinguishable from "ought to know", the hallmark of an invitor.

Court in *Australian Safeway Stores v. Zaluzna*[5] pronounced the end of the "so-called special duties resting on an occupier of land with respect to persons entering as [invitees], licensees or trespassers".

Though the recent reforms sought to sweep away the old distinctions and simplify the law, the older precedents may still provide a point of reference until overtaken by new experience. The Occupiers' Liability Acts (hereinafter the Acts) which, originating in England,[6] have been adopted, mostly with only minor modifications, in several jurisdictions in Australia,[7] Canada[8] and New Zealand,[9] give more detailed directions than the decision in *Zaluzna* which simply proclaimed the new general principle. Undoubtedly, however, even where not applicable proprio vigore, the Acts will provide a useful model for shaping the new law. Besides, they purported merely to embody "a new principle of the *common law*".[10]

2. OCCUPIERS' DUTY

Occupation

The duties of present concern are exclusively incident to occupation.[11] Responsibility is based on control, not ownership, as corollary of the power to admit and exclude. Hence the visitor must ordinarily look to the tenant, not the landlord.[12] Persons other than occupiers who are responsible for a dangerous condition on the premises, like vendors or lessors, contractors or architects, are subject to their own rules which will be dealt with separately hereafter.[13]

Not that possession need be exclusive. A licensee may qualify as well as a tenant,[14] and so may the grantee of a mere right of way or anyone with a right to invite people over someone else's land.[15] Building contractors may share occupation of the site with the owner.[16] There may be shared occupation of a wharf managed by several shipowners,[17] of a hall hired out for a dance,[18] or part of the premises run by a concessionaire,[19] or of

5. (1987) 162 C.L.R. 479 at 487.
6. *Occupiers' Liability Act* 1957. Any reference hereafter to "the Act" is to this statute.
7. *Wrongs Act* (Vic.) s. 14A-14D (since 1982); *Wrongs Act* (S.A.) s. 17b-17e (since 1987); *Occupiers' Liability Act* 1985 (W.A.). Also L.R.C. Reports in N.S.W. (1969), A.C.T. (1987) and Tas. (1988). See Handford, *Occupiers' Liability Reform in Western Australia—and Elsewhere*, 17 W.A.L. Rev. 182 (1987).
8. B.C. (1957), Alberta (1973), Ontario (1980). See *Linden* 611-626.
9. *Occupiers' Liability Act* 1962.
10. Hutton, *Mechanics of Law Reform*, 24 Mod. L. Rev. 18 at 28, cited by *Salmond & Heuston* 298.
11. The Acts retain the common law allocation on whom the duties rest: s. 1(2) Eng.; s. 4(2) W.A. Cf. *Schiller v. Mulgrave S.C.* (1972) 129 C.L.R. 116 (scenic reserve).
12. *Lane v. Cox* [1897] 1 Q.B. 415; *Cavalier v. Pope* [1906] A.C. 428.
13. See below, pp. 459ff.
14. *Humphries v. Dreamland (Margate)* (1930) 100 L.J.K.B. 137; *Napier v. Ryan* [1954] N.Z.L.R. 1234; *McDonald v. Goderich* [1949] 3 D.L.R. 788.
15. *Kevan v. Comm. Rlys* [1973] 1 N.S.W.L.R. 710.
16. *A.M.F. v. Magnet* [1968] 1 W.L.R. 1078; *Ferguson v. Welsh* [1987] 1 W.L.R. 1553 (H.L.); *Canberra Formwork v. C. & C.* (1982) 41 A.C.T.R. 1.
17. *Burton v. Melbourne Harbour* [1954] V.L.R. 353 at 357.
18. *Voli v. Inglewood Shire* (1963) 110 C.L.R. 74.
19. *Fisher v. C.H.T. (No. 2)* [1966] 2 Q.B. 75 (C.A.).

an upstairs apartment occupied by a caretaker.[20] One may even be responsible for safe access to one's premises over an area under someone else's control, like a footpath or forecourt fronting a shop.[21]

True, the occupancy duties were originally formulated with reference to landed property, and have frequently been explained as originating in a desire to shield landowners from the onerous obligations of a general duty of care, in recognition of the economic importance and social value attached to the free use and exploitation of land. However, the same have osmotically come to be applied also to accidents on defective chattels—structures on land, such as ladders or scaffolding,[22] and even movables like vessels[23] and vehicles (at least when stationary).[24]

Type of injury

The occupancy duties govern property damage no less than personal injury; nor need such damage occur in connection with personal injury.[25] Indeed, they have been applied even to a trespassing horse[26] and to a car brought on the premises with the occupier's permission by someone other than the owner.[27] It has been argued that since the owner in such cases is not an entrant (and the duty is obviously not owed to a horse or a car), the occupier's is not a duty qua occupier.[28] The Western Australian statute, adopting the latter view, applies only to "any property brought on to the premises by, and remaining on the premises in the possession and control of, that person".[29] But the point is unlikely to be of practical significance.

I. Lawful Visitors

The primary thrust of the new "general" or "common" duty of care was to replace the "special" duties to the two classes of lawful visitors, invitees and licensees.[30] The former were entrants in whose visit the occupier had a material interest, typified by customers in stores and contractors performing work on the premises; the latter were visitors from whom the occupier derived no material advantage, such as peddlars and (surprisingly) social guests. A third group, those who entered as of right rather than with the owner's consent, were subsumed under one or the other of the two classes: users of facilities open to the public, such as public parks or

20. *Wheat v. Lacon* [1966] A.C. 552. But their duties may well differ: the licensor being responsible only for design and structural condition, the licensee also for a hole in the rug.
21. *Switzer v. Becker* (1976) 75 D.L.R. (3d) 649.
22. *Woodman v. Richardson* [1937] 3 All E.R. 866; *Pratt v. Richards* [1951] 2 K.B. 208.
23. *Swinton v. China M.S.N.* (1951) 83 C.L.R. 553; *Woods v. Duncan* [1946] A.C. 401.
24. Vic.: s. 14A(b); S.A.: s. 17b; W.A.: *Wanless v. Piening* (1967) 68 S.R. (N.S.W.) 249; (1968) 117 C.L.R. 498 at 512; *Meth v. Moore* (1982) 44 A.L.R. 409 rejecting the occupancy rules in relation to moving vehicles.
25. Including consequential economic loss, provided it is not too remote: *A.M.F. v. Magnet* [1968] 1 W.L.R. 1028 at 1050-1.
26. *Transport Comm. v. Barton* (1933) 49 C.L.R. 114.
27. *Drive-Yourself v. Burnside* [1959] S.R. (N.S.W.) 390 (C.A.).
28. By Herron J. in *Drive-Yourself v. Burnside*. In *Tutton v. Walter* [1986] Q.B. 61 the court rejected the defence that bees poisoned by chemical spray on the defendant's rape field were to be treated as trespassers.
29. Section 4(1)(b).
30. Section 1(2) of the Acts provides that the new rules shall apply to the same persons as "would at common law be treated as an occupier and as his invitees and licensees".

libraries, were treated as licensees notwithstanding the fact that public funds were expended precisely for the purpose of their use; while those who entered private premises for a purpose authorised by law, like firemen or policemen, were mostly classified as invitees. The downgrading of social guests and users of public facilities were prime causes of the dissatisfaction which propelled the introduction of a "common duty" to all lawful visitors.

The English Act also includes the formerly distinct category of visitors entering under contract[31], such as the paying public in theatres, stadiums, or railway stations who used to enjoy a specially privileged position. Australian statutes, however, preserve higher[32] duties of care,[33] and the High Court has adopted the same view as a matter of the new common law.[34]

The duty towards lawful visitors calls for "such care as in all the circumstances of the case is reasonable to see that the visitor will be reasonably safe in using the premises for the purpose for which he is permitted or invited to be there".[35] The Australian Acts explain in more detail that consideration be given to (1) the gravity and the likelihood of the probable injury, (2) the circumstances of the entry onto the premises, (3) the nature of the premises, (4) the knowledge which the occupier of the premises has or ought to have of the likelihood of persons or property being on the premises, (5) the age of the person entering the premises, (6) the ability of the person entering the premises to appreciate the danger, and (7) the burden on the occupier of eliminating the danger or protecting the person entering the premises from the danger as compared to the risk of the danger to the person.[36]

Knowledge of danger

The old law attached special significance to knowledge of the dangerous condition by either occupier or visitor. Knowledge by the occupier was essential to his liability to licensees, but to invitees his duty was to warn of dangers of which he knew *or* should have known—in other words, a duty to inspect. This categorical distinction has now disappeared and liability will depend on what in all the circumstances of each case reasonable care demanded for the safety of the particular entrant. This change will most of all benefit social guests who, as archetypal licensees, were denied the benefit of the higher duty; if nothing else, today's prevalence of home insurance no longer justifies this distinction between commercial and residential premises.

The visitor's knowledge of the danger used to preclude all recovery: the duty to licensees never extended to other than "concealed" dangers, while that to invitees was limited to "unusual" dangers and, according to a much

31. Section 5. Excluded are contracts for paid transport in any vehicle, vessel or aircraft. Some statutes expressly preserve higher duties of care: e.g. S.A.: s. 17c(5); W.A.: s. 8(1).
32. The duty was higher than that due to invitees, e.g., in including liability for the fault of independent contractors and not categorically excluding liability for dangers known to the entrant.
33. S.A.: s. 5(4); W.A.: s. 8(1).
34. See below, p. 461.
35. Section 2(1) of the Act.
36. Vic.: s. 14(B)(4); S.A.: s. 17c(1); W.A.: s. 5(4).

criticised decision of the House of Lords[37] which precipitated the legislative reform in England, was also negated by the invitee's knowledge of it.

These technical distinctions have now been absorbed by the over-arching, generalised test of reasonable care appropriate to the circumstances of the individual case. The obviousness of the danger is simply one of the factors relevant in assessing the probability and magnitude of the risk by which the occupier's care falls to be determined. If, for example, the danger is simple, not hidden, and an easy manner of avoiding it is readily apparent, knowledge of its existence would be sufficient.[38] So also, the giving of notice or warning will usually suffice to discharge the ooccupier's duty if, but only if, "in all the circumstances it was enough to enable the visitor to be reasonably safe."[39] But in other situations where (by reason of infancy, the nature of the danger or the absence of any practical way for the plaintiff to avoid it) the only protection would be to remove it altogether or take some other positive precaution such as fencing off or spreading ashes over an icy entrance, it remains open to the trier of fact to conclude that the visitor's knowledge did not discharge the occupier, relevant though it may be to an issue of contributory negligence.

In any event, only such knowledge by the visitor could discharge the occupier's duty as would have enabled him to avert or avoid the peril. He must have not only knowledge of the defect, but also full appreciation of the nature and extent of the risk presented by it, sufficient to allow him "to estimate with reasonable approximation the full extent of the danger he is invited to incur so as to decide whether he will embark on it at all".[40] If though aware of the danger he mistakenly or foolishly underestimates it, this may constitute contributory negligence, but does not necessarily defeat his claim entirely.[41]

Assumption of risk: Contributory negligence

The English Act specifically provides, what would in any event be understood, that "the common duty of care does not impose on an occupier any obligation to a visitor in respect of risks willingly accepted as his by the visitor (the question whether a risk was so accepted to be decided on the same principles as in other cases in which one person owes a duty of care to another)."[42] As previously noted, modern law does not favour the defence: in particular it does not equate knowledge with assumption of the risk and prefers to collapse the defence into contributory negligence both

37. *London Graving Dock v. Horton* [1951] A.C. 737.
38. As in *Phillis v. Daly* (1988) 15 N.S.W.L.R. 65 (C.A.) (protrusion on log); *Story v. Prince George* (1979) 99 D.L.R. (3d) 464 (icy patch in parking lot).
39. Section 2(4)(a) of the English Act. *Roles v. Nathan* [1963] 1 W.L.R. 1117 (chimneysweep warned of fumes).
40. *Bond v. S.A. Rly* (1923) 33 C.L.R. 273 at 389; *Letang v. Ottawa Rly* [1926] A.C. 725; *Edmonds v. Commonwealth* [1961] S.R. (N.S.W.) 527.
41. See *Smith v. Austin Lifts* [1959] 1 W.L.R. 100 (H.L.). By the same token, the danger must have been consciously present to his mind when encountering it, not merely on some prior occasion: *Comm. Rlys v. Anderson* (1961) 105 C.L.R. 42.
42. Section 2(5); and see *Waldick v. Malcolm* [1991] 2 S.C.R. 456. W.A. (s. 5(2)) adopted the Ontario version which withholds the defence in case of intentional or reckless conduct by the occupier.

for the sake of allowing some apportioned recovery to the plaintiff and deterring a negligent defendant.[43] But in some situations such as those involving sporting events, spectators continue to be debarred either because they are volenti or—a better explanation—because the organisers are not shown to have been negligent in the provision of screening.[44]

American law denies firemen a remedy against a householder who negligently started the fire on the ground that they are paid to face the perils of fighting fires, that most fires are started negligently and that injuries are sufficiently taken care of by special employment provisions for medical care and disability. Only special perils, like explosive materials stored in a garage, can generate liability. Similar reasoning has been applied to the police.[45] British courts, however, have refused to follow this "firemen's rule": for the defence to succeed, there must be a voluntary assumption of a specific risk, not just a willingness to encounter the general risks of employment.[46] On the other hand, the occupier may rely on a fireman "in the exercise of his calling [to] appreciate and guard against any special risks ordinarily incident to it".[47]

Express assumption of risk has fared better. In the leading case, a large notice had warned persons crossing railway lines that they were entering at their own risk and had no claim for negligent injury. An employee of a nearby firm on her way to work was struck as the result of negligent shunting, but failed to recover because the occupier was free to attach conditions to its licence, including restriction or exclusion of any liability for negligence.[48] The Act specifically qualifies the occupier's duty "in so far as he is free to and does extend, restrict, modify or exclude his duty to any visitor or visitors by agreement or otherwise".[49]

Can third parties be bound by a *contractual* restriction or exclusion, for example, one purporting to bind the contractor's employees or guests? An older case held that they could when a contract for the hire of an aircraft excluded the occupier's liability to the hirer and his passengers.[50] This for the reason that the owner's obligation could not be increased by the fact that the person with whom he made his contract chose to bring others along (though this was obviously contemplated). It was for the host to acquaint his guests with the exclusion of liability. This questionable ruling has been reversed by several of the Acts.[51] However, exclusion by notice, at the entrance of the premises or otherwise, probably remains unaffected: the explicit affirmation of the defence of voluntary assumption of risk implies that the purpose of the statute was only to prevent entrants being deprived of their rights without their knowledge.

43. *Waldick v. Malcolm* [1991] 2 S.C.R. 456. See above, p. 297.
44. See above, p. 301.
45. E.g. *Walters v. Sloan* 571 P. 609 (Cal. 1977).
46. *Ogwo v. Taylor* [1988] A.C. 431.
47. Section 2(3)(b) of the Act.
48. *Ashdown v. Williams* [1957] 1 K.B. 409 (C.A.). Aliter, if in course of employment: *Burnett v. British Waterways* [1972] 1 W.L.R. 1329.
49. Section 2(1). In England the *Unfair Contract Terms Act* 1977 withdrew the right of business occupiers to exempt themselves from liability to persons paying for admission.
50. *Fosbroke-Hobbes v. Airwork* [1937] 1 All E.R. 108.
51. England: s. 3(1) which also confers on them the benefit of additional obligations under such a contract. S.A.: s. 17c(4); W.A.: s. 7.

Contributory negligence is a defence, just as under the prior regime, resulting in apportionment of loss.[52]

Supermarkets

Responding to strong community expectations of safety in public malls, supermarkets and the like, has been a tendency to demand a very high standard of safety precautions, in effect straddling negligence and strict liability. In the traditional view, when a shopper slips and falls on a spilt substance, the burden is on him to prove that the defendant's inadequate maintenance and supervision of the area caused his injury. But courts have become increasingly sensitive to the plaintiff's difficulty of proving the cause issue of how long the substance has been lying around. The English are apparently prepared to reverse the onus of proof;[53] Australian courts, precluded by precedent from following this line, have sometimes, though not always, reached the same result by postulating that reasonable care in the circumstances required a system of constant inspection and cleaning-up. The public nature of the premises, the defendant's interest in encouraging the greatest number of people to come there, the likelihood of spillage and the general expectation of safety precautions anchor this high standard of care.[54] The spillage of foodstuffs at or near food centres calls for special vigilance. Where, in contrast, the risk of injury is slight and fewer people use the area, reasonable care may require no more than inspection at regular intervals, when a plaintiff would not be relieved from proving the time interval between spillage and accident.[55]

Occupancy and activity duties

Often overlooked is that the occupancy duties from the first countenanced a responsibility, however circumscribed, to protect entrants from risks on the premises whatever their origin, not merely those created by the occupier himself. Most often the cause of complaint was not that the defendant engaged in some activity on the premises, involving acts of commission fraught with unreasonable risk, but rather that he failed to take positive steps to protect the visitor from structural defects. In such cases, the question is whether the occupier must respond to an affirmative duty to make safe or warn, and we have already seen that the common law, imbued with the dominant values of an individualistic society, was generally cool to the plea that anyone should be obliged to exert himself on behalf of another, at least in the absence of some corresponding benefit. This factor goes far to explain the erstwhile reluctance to expose occupiers to the

52. Vic.: s. 14D; W.A.: s. 10. Otherwise by virtue of apportionment legislation: e.g. *Macginley v. B.R.B.* [1983] 1 W.L.R. 1427 at 1434.
53. *Ward v. Tesco Stores* [1976] 1 W.L.R. 810 (C.A.) based on a diluted res ipsa loquitur. Followed in *Brown v. Target Australia* (1984) 37 S.A.S.R. 145 (F.C.).
54. *Shoeys v. Allan* (1991) A.T.R. 81-104; *Drakos v. Woolworths* (1991) A.T.R. 81-135; *Brady v. Girvan Bros* (1988) 7 N.S.W.L.R. 241 (C.A.), approving the outcome, though not the reasoning, of *Ward v. Tesco Stores* and *Brown v. Target Australia*.
55. *Griffin v. Coles Myer* (1991) A.T.R. 81-109 (food on floor of variety store), explaining *Hampton Court v. Crooks* (1957) 97 C.L.R. 367 and *Dulhunty v. J. B. Young* (1975) 50 A.L.J.R. 150.

discipline of a general duty of care, and accounts in large measure for the esoteric classification of plaintiffs by reference to what advantage their visit would confer on the occupier. However, it unduly belittles the competing factors, now increasingly heeded, that the occupier is in a peculiarly strategic position to prevent accidents and that others depend upon his co-operation for their effective protection.[56] Far from supporting any claim to immunity, as they once did, occupation and control have at long last come to be recognised as a positive source of responsibility.

Under the old law, as already mentioned, the special duties of occupiers were later complemented by a general duty of care for activities on, as distinct from the condition of, the premises. Thus if the occupier engaged in a positive activity, like knocking down a wall, felling a tree or running a train,[57] he had to conduct himself just like everybody else so as to avoid unreasonable risks to those whom he knew or had reason to believe to be on his land and likely to be endangered. This approach somewhat broadened, as was intended, the protection of permissive entrants and eventually even of trespassers, but introduced a new element of uncertainty as the category came to be expanded to all dynamic, as disinct from static, dangers. Indeed it was just such a definitional problem in *Zaluzna v. Australian Safeway Stores*[58] (rain-soaked floor of a supermarket) that prompted the High Court to abandon the whole complex of concurrent "special" and "general" duties in favour of a simplified general or common duty of care.

Not all the Acts made such a clean sweep of the past. Closest comes the English Act which purports to "regulate the duty which an occupier of premises owes to his visitors in respect of dangers due to the state of the premises *or* to things done or omitted to be done on them".[59] The Victorian Act adds "in relation to the state of the premises",[60] while South Australia confines liability to injury "attributable to the dangerous state or condition of the premises".[61] But since the standards are in practice the same, the problem is at best only of academic interest.

Duty to control others

The occupier's power to admit or exclude also places him under duty of care to control such entrants for the safety of others. In a leading case, the manageress of a tearoom who permitted a tea urn to be carried by picnickers through a crowd of customers was held liable when the urn was accidently dropped, scalding the plaintiff.[62] Places of entertainment must

56. See Lücke, *Towards a General Theory of Negligence and Occupiers' Liability*, 2 M.U.L.R. 472 (1960).
57. *Comm. Rlys v. McDermott* [1967] 1 A.C. 169 (level crossing); *Public Transport Comm. v. Perry* (1977) 137 C.L.R. 107 (see below, p. 467).
58. (1987) 162 C.L.R. 479.
59. Section 1(1). Even so, a majority of commentators contend that activities are excluded: e.g., *Winfield & Jolowicz* 207; *Clerk & Lindsell* para. 12-03 report the English practice ignoring the Act. Contra: *Salmond & Heuston* 244.
60. Section 14B(3).
61. Section 17C(1).
62. *Glasgow Corp. v. Muir* [1943] A.C. 448.

protect customers from each other;[63] just as commercial establishments like parking garages must guard users from robbers and rapists.[64]

Management's responsibility for accidents to patrons of sporting events or theatrical performances has been examined in a number of cases. In *Cox v. Coulson*[65] the defendant charged admission to his theatre in which a travelling company was performing when a spectator was injured by a cartridge fired from a pistol during a scene of the play. The court repudiated the suggestion of any general warranty on the part of the occupier that all persons connected with the performance would observe reasonable care not to expose the audience to unreasonable risks; he was responsible only for personal negligence in failing to exercise reasonable care in supervising incidents in a play which were intrinsically dangerous unless carefully performed, like scenes involving the use of firearms. Hence there is no liability for such "casual" acts of negligence as a chorus girl kicking the heel of her shoe into the stalls[66] or for the carelessness of concessionaires in the conduct of an ordinary show.[67]

Moreover, the organiser is not responsible at all for dangers inherent in the particular spectacle which any ordinary spectator can foresee[68]—risks like being hit by a cricket ball or coming into collision with a fielder over the boundary in an attempt to stop a four,[69] being struck by an ice hockey puck[70] or golf ball,[71] or by an aeroplane at a flying exhibition or a car at a race.[72] Some of these hazards, it is true, may require from him obvious precautions or safety devices in accordance with prevailing standards of what is expected. So, where a performer on a tightrope negligently dropped a chair into the audience, the proprietor of the hall was held responsible for omitting to install a safety net;[73] and with respect to motor races and the like, it is always a question of fact whether the barrier is a reasonably adequate safeguard for spectators.[74]

Children

The English Act directs that "the circumstances relevant for the present purposes include the degree of care, and want of care, which would

63. Ibid.; *Chordas v. Bryant* (1989) 91 A.L.R. 149; *Hislop v. Mooney* [1968] 1 N.S.W.R. 559; see above, p. 152.
64. *Allison v. Rank City Wall* (1984) 6 D.L.R. (4th) 144. But a duty to protect an invitee's belongings was denied in *Tinsley v. Dudley* [1951] 2 K.B. 18.
65. [1916] 2 K.B. 177.
66. Cf. *Frazer-Wallas v. Waters* [1939] 4 All E.R. 609.
67. *Sheehan v. Dreamland (Margate)* (1923) 40 T.L.R. 155. Cf. *Humphreys v. Dreamland (Margate)* (1931) 100 L.J.K.B. 137.
68. This is better explained as a qualification of the occupier's duty than as an application of the defence of volenti: see above, p. 297.
69. *Hall v. Brooklands Club* [1933] 1 K.B. 205 at 209.
70. *Murray v. Harringay Arena* [1951] 2 K.B. 529; *Payne v. Maple Leaf Gardens* [1949] 1 D.L.R. 369 (Ont. C.A.).
71. *Potter v. Carlisle Golf Club* [1939] N.I. 114 (C.A.); *Ellison v. Rogers* (1967) 67 D.L.R. (2d) 21.
72. *Hall v. Brooklands Club* [1933] 1 K.B. 205; *Moloughney v. Wellington Racing Club* [1935] N.Z.L.R. 800 (horse race).
73. *Welsh v. Canterbury & Paragon* (1984) 10 T.L.R. 478.
74. The plaintiff failed in *Hall v. Brooklands Club* [1933] 1 K.B. 205, but succeeded in *Australian Racing Club v. Metcalf* (1961) 106 C.L.R. 117, *Green v. Perry* (1955) 94 C.L.R. 606 and *Chatwood v. National Speedways* [1929] Q.S.R. 29.

ordinarily be looked for in such a visitor, so that (for example) in proper cases—(a) an occupier must be prepared for children to be less careful than adults, and (b) an occupier may expect that a person, in the exercise of his calling, will appreciate and guard against any special risks ordinarily incident to it, so far as the occupier leaves him free to do so."[75]

Experience under the old law had taught that the standard of safety due to children must be applied with due regard to the physical powers and mental faculties which the occupier knew or should have known the child to possess. Youngsters obviously cannot be judged by adult standards and are usually incapable of contributory negligence. Commonplace features of a building or land may be a danger to a little child: it may see much but apprehend little; it is usually impervious to warning.[76] Is then the occupier "practically bound to see that the wandering child is as safe as in a nursery"? Not only would this impose an intolerable burden, but it could lead to the disappearance of amenities which many local authorities and private persons voluntarily provide for the entertainment of children. Moreover, it might be thought socially unfortunate if parents of very young children were allowed to evade their own responsibilities by shifting the obligation of looking after them to strangers.

The preferred approach has been to "compromise between the robustness which would make children take the world as they found it and the tenderness which would give them nurseries wherever they go. On this view, the [occupier] is not entitled to assume that all children will, unless they are allured, behave like adults; but he is entitled to assume that normally little children will in fact be accompanied by a responsible adult and to discharge his duty of warning accordingly."[77] To every rule there are, of course, exceptions. He may have to take into account the social habits of the neighbourhood and, if he knows or ought to anticipate that children of tender years go to play unaccompanied, he may also have to take steps to protect them. The general responsibility for the safety, however, must rest with the parents whose duty it is to ensure that their offspring do not wander about by themselves or, at least, to satisfy themselves that the places to which they resort unaccompanied are safe for them to go.[78]

It had long been recognised that an occupier must not expose children, even trespassing children, to danger from alluring traps. Now, as before, he is duty bound not merely not to dig pitfalls for them, but not to lead them into temptation. In order to constitute a trap in this sense, it was said, the object or condition must combine the properties of temptation and retribution; it must be fascinating and fatal.[79] Being attractive to children is not sufficient unless it also harbours an element of insidious danger. This quality can be present because the object is actually in motion or liable to be easily set in motion, or poisonous or deleterious to eat or handle, or explosive, or so defective as to be inherently dangerous.[80] But it is by no

75. Section 2(3).
76. *Phipps v. Rochester Corp.* [1955] 1 Q.B. 450 at 458 (licensee).
77. Ibid. at 469-470.
78. Ibid. at 472.
79. *Latham v. Johnson* [1913] 1 K.B. 398 at 416 (Hamilton L.J.).
80. *Donovan v. Union Cartage* [1933] 2 K.B. 71 at 74. Examples: *Chapman v. Amos* (1957) 18 D.L.R. (2d) 140 (poison in tin); *Cooke v. Midlands Rly* [1909] A.C. 229 (turntable); *Gough v. N.C.B.* [1954] 1 Q.B. 191 (moving trucks).

means confined to mechanical devices, having also been found in poisonous berries in a botanical garden,[81] a defective wall,[82] and a bank on a rubbish tip covered with broken glass.[83] On the other hand, mindful of the fact that a child can get into mischief and hurt himself with anything, the following incidents have been attributed to a mere ordinary danger which was or should have been present to the mind of any youngster fit to be let even temporarily out of his parents' sight: getting his finger caught in a closing door,[84] falling into natural or artificial water[85] or an open hole in broad daylight,[86] or off a sound and stationary vehicle,[87] a heap of stones,[88] a wall,[89] a well-constructed playground chute,[90] or tobogganing on a blanket down a vertical bluff.[91]

Parental co-operation is even more to be expected on behalf of an accompanied child. In one such case an infant of just under four, accompanying his mother into a city store, injured his fingers by putting them into a space between the moving treads of an escalator. A notice prohibited children from riding unless accompanied by an adult; this was clearly insufficient to warn against the particular danger, but was such a warning required? The High Court thought not, because the defendant was entitled to assume that the accompanying adult herself would observe reasonable care to safeguard the child against inherent hazards on the escalator.[92] Not that the presence of an adult will relieve an occupier from responsibility for all situations that are dangerous to a child, though not to an adult: for example, for an actually defective condition or one which is abnormal in the sense that an accompanying adult, let alone the child, would not usually expect to find it in such a place.[93]

Contractors

Homeowners who engage an independent contractor to work on their premises may expect him to appreciate and guard against any special risk ordinarily incident to the job, to satisfy himself as to the safety of the working site and to decide how he will perform his tasks. For example, a window cleaner has normally no cause to complain about any injury attributable to the insecurity of some part of the exterior of the premises which he uses as a foot or handhold for the purpose of cleaning the outside

81. *Glasgow Corp. v. Taylor* [1922] 1 A.C. 44; also *Ramsay v. Appel* (1972) 46 A.L.J.R. 510 (slaked lime).
82. *Boyd v. Glasgow Iron & Steel* 1923 S.C. 758.
83. *Williams v. Cardiff Corp.* [1950] 1 K.B. 514.
84. *Gwynne v. Dominion Stores* (1963) 43 D.L.R. (2d) 290.
85. *Sproat v. Prestwick Magistrates* 1955 S.C. 271.
86. *Perry v. Thomas Wrigley* [1955] 1 W.L.R. 1164.
87. *Donovan v. Union Cartage* [1933] 2 K.B. 71. Contrast *Lynch v. Nurdin* (1841) 1 Q.B. 29; 113 E.R. 1041 (horse and cart liable to move).
88. *Latham v. Johnson* [1913] 1 K.B. 398.
89. *Liddle v. Yorkshire C.C.* [1934] 2 K.B. 101.
90. *Dyer v. Ilfracombe U.D.C.* [1956] 1 W.L.R. 218; aliter, the *defective* chute in *Bates v. Stone Parish* [1954] 3 All E.R. 38.
91. *Simkiss v. Rhondda B.C.* (1983) 81 L.G.R. 460 (C.A.).
92. *David Jones v. Stone* (1970) 123 C.L.R. 185.
93. Ibid. at 204 per Walsh J. An example might be *Swan v. C.P.R.* (1959) 19 D.L.R. (2d) 51 (falling through ramp railing).

of the windows,[94] in contrast to some peril he encounters outside the working area properly so-called, like a dangerous staircase inside the house that he is using to get to the first floor windows.[95] Even less would an occupier be responsible to an employee of a contractor for an unsafe manner of work adopted by the employer.[96] Not that a contractor's negligence will always completely negate the occupier's responsibility, as when the latter fails to warn of an unusual danger of his own making and not discoverable by a skilled worker.[97]

Liability for independent contractors

Since the occupier's obligation is only to exercise reasonable care, not to ensure that reasonable care is taken, it may be fulfilled by delegating construction, maintenance and repair jobs to an independent contractor.[98] He may entrust to a reputable expert the performance of tasks calling for special knowledge and experience which he himself lacks, such as repair of electrical wiring or maintenance of lifts, and he will not be responsible for defects in the contractor's work, provided he has used reasonable care in selecting him and in supervising as well as inspecting his work after completion.[99] Whether in the last-mentioned respect he is entitled to rely on his own lay judgment or should in turn employ an expert must depend on the nature of the job: simple rewiring he can inspect himself, but building construction may call for a supervising architect.[100]

Another line of authority, however, places the occupier under a "non-delegable" duty, at least with respect to non-technical jobs that he could have performed himself, like cleaning stairs[101] or clearing walkways.[102] The suggested distinction is difficult to justify otherwise than as a unprincipled compromise between two quite opposed lines of thought[103] and was expressly disavowed by the English Act.[104]

94. *Christmas v. General Cleaning Contractors* [1952] 1 K.B. 141; *Bates v. Parker* [1953] 2 Q.B. 231. Also *Wright v. Commonwealth* [1958] V.R. 318 (crane capsizing on landfill); *Roles v. Nathan* [1963] 1 W.L.R. 1117 (chimneysweep overcome by fumes).
95. *Bates v. Parker* [1953] 2 Q.B. 231 at 236.
96. *Ferguson v. Welsh* [1987] 1 W.L.R. 1553 (H.L.).
97. *Papatonakis v. Telecom* (1985) 156 C.L.R. 7 (linesman injured by tampered cable); *Bates v. Parker* [1953] 2 Q.B. 231 at 240-241 (failure to warn of changed condition).
98. Indeed, it may be negligent for him to undertake them himself: see *Haseldine v. Daw* [1941] 2 K.B. 343 at 356; *Wells v. Cooper* [1958] 2 Q.B. 256.
99. Most of the cases imposing liability, like *Woodward v. Hastings Corp.* [1945] K.B. 174, *Bloomstein v. Rly Executive* [1952] 2 All E.R. 418 and *Voli v. Inglewood S.* (1963) 110 C.L.R. 74 can be explained as properly resting on failure to detect defective work rather than vicarious liability for the work itself.
100. Contrast *Green v. Fibreglass* [1958] 2 Q.B. 245 with *A.M.F. v. Magnet* [1968] 1 W.L.R. 1028.
101. *Vial v. Housing Comm.* [1976] 1 N.S.W.L.R. 388 (C.A.).
102. *Woodward v. Hasting Corp.* [1945] K.B. 174 (snow); *Bloomstein v. Rly Executive* [1952] 2 All E.R. 418 (protruding bolt).
103. The root of the trouble is the doubtful authority and rationale of *Thomson v. Cremin* [1956] 1 W.L.R. 103 (H.L.).
104. Section 2(4)(b).

II. Contractual Entrants

Persons entering under a contract with the occupier constituted a separate category under the old common law. As already explained,[105] the English Act subsumed such entrants under lawful visitors, entitled to the common duty of care. Not so the Australian statutes which preserved higher standards of care by virtue of contract or other rule of law.[106] *Zaluzna* did not pass on the question whether contractual entrants were included in the reform expressly extended to invitees, licensees and trespassers, but the High Court has since come down in favour of their survival.[107] Two arguments support this conclusion: First, the duty to contractual entrants was in several respects higher than the ordinary duty of care and, as expressed in the Australian Acts, the purpose of the reform was to increase, not lessen, the level of protection for visitors.[108] Secondly, the duty was concurrently contractual as well as tortious; and it was not intended to modify contractual obligations.

Contractual duties

When someone enters another's premises pursuant to a contract which expressly sets out the nature and extent of the occupier's obligations in relation to its safety, the contractual standard prevails, whether it is more or less onerous to the occupier or advantageous to the visitor than that which would otherwise apply under the general law. Usually, however, the contract is silent on the matter; in which event, according to conventional theory, the law will imply such terms as appear reasonable and appropriate in all the circumstances. No single or universal norm obtains. In some situations a well settled standard has been evolved: for example, the letting on hire of vehicles and vessels imports an absolute warranty of reasonable fitness for their intended purpose, whereas carriers of passengers are held, oddly enough, only to the less exacting standard of reasonable care and do not warrant the soundness of their vehicles or otherwise guarantee the safety of their passengers.[109]

In other situations, the occupier's responsibility has not been formulated with uniform consistency.[110] At one time, the courts favoured an actual warranty of safety: while the occupier was not treated as an outright insurer, the only excuse seems to have been act of God or malicious acts of third parties.[111] No doubt, a prevalent assumption that the obligation was contractual rather than tortious helped to sponsor warranty as the basis of liability. Later, however, the occupier's obligation was subsumed under the

105. See above, p. 452.
106. Vic.: s. 14B ("or any contract"); S.A.: s. 17c(5) ("higher standard of care by contract"); W.A.: s. 8 ("higher standard of care by any enactment or rule of law").
107. *Calin v. Greater Union* (1991) 100 A.L.R. 746.
108. See Swanton, *Occupier's Liability Towards Contractual Entrants*, 15 Monash L. Rev. 69 (1989); Kirby P. in *Morawski v. State Rail* (1988) 14 N.S.W.L.R. 374 at 378-379.
109. *Redhead v. Midland Rly* (1869) L.R. 4 Q.B. 379. In contrast, a *common* carrier of goods and passengers' luggage is virtually an insurer: see above, p. 314.
110. The appropriate standard is for the court, and not the jury: *Hall v. Brooklands Club* [1933] 1 K.B. 205 at 213, 222; *Metcalf v. Australian Racing Club* (1961) 78 W.N. (N.S.W.) 1158 at 1163.
111. See *Watson v. George* (1953) 89 C.L.R. 409 at 421-422.

concept of negligence.[112] Today, an occupier who admits a person for reward for a mutually contemplated purpose must ensure (but no more than) that the premises are as safe for that purpose as reasonable care and skill on the part of anyone can make them.[113] This duty is primarily in tort, even if it is permissible to plead alternatively in contract. For that matter, although the plaintiff must have entered "under" a contract, he need not apparently have been the one to contract with the occupier: the shadow cast by privity of contract has been dispelled from this area of tort. Thus, at any rate with respect to premises for hire to the public, it does not matter who made the arrangement under which the plaintiff gained admission.[114] Also, according to the better view, contributory negligence is now a matter for apportionment, since the claim is or at least can be pleaded in tort.[115]

Contrasted with common duty

In several respects, the duty to contractual entrants is higher than to other lawful visitors. In the first place, liability attaches not only for personal negligence by the occupier or his servants, but also in respect of dangers created by independent contractors employed in connection with the construction, alteration or repair of the premises. In the leading case of *Francis v. Cockrell*,[116] a ticketholder was hurt when a grandstand collapsed owing to poor workmanship by the contractor who had put it up. Still, the proprietor was held responsible although entirely free from personal negligence. Secondly, there is authority for saying that responsibility attaches even for defects negligently created before the defendant commenced occupation. It might perhaps seem unfair to burden an occupier with liability for the acts of persons over whom he had no control (unless the defect were reasonably discoverable),[117] but more compelling was the argument that the plaintiff had been induced to rely on the safety of the premises and that, from this point of view, the right to recover should not depend on the fortuitous date on which the defect originated.

In other respects, the standard of safety is virtually identical with the duty to other lawful visitors. It is now unquestioned that "liability depends on a breach by somebody at some stage of a common law duty to use reasonable care,"[118] and usually the issue will resolve itself practically into

112. Although it is still common to speak of an "implied warranty" to use reasonable care, this is confusing because "there is a clear distinction between a warranty that a thing is so and an obligation to take reasonable care to make it so" (*Liebigs v. Mersey Docks Bd* [1918] 2 K.B. 381 at 396).
113. *Maclenan v. Segar* [1917] 2 K.B. 325 at 332-333; *Watson v. George* (1953) 89 C.L.R. 409.
114. *Voli v. Inglewood S.* (1963) 110 C.L.R. 74 at 93. Under the English Act (s. 3) contractual terms are binding on strangers only if they impose a more onerous obligation on the occupier.
115. *Sole v. Hallt* [1973] Q.B. 574 (under the Act). The tenor of *Voli* and *Sayers v. Harlow U.D.C.* [1958] 1 W.L.R. 623 suggests that it should not matter how the plaintiff pleads. *Smith v. Buckley* [1965] Tas. S.R. 210 assumed that apportionment applies also to contract claims. Cf. above, p. 282.
116. (1890) L.R. 5 Q.B. 501; likewise *Voli v. Inglewood S.* (1963) 110 C.L.R. 74 (negligent architect).
117. *Francis v. Cockrell* (1870) L.R. 5 W.B. 501 at 507.
118. *Watson v. George* (1953) 89 C.L.R. 409 at 424-425.

the question of whether the defendant has been guilty of negligence in connection with the source of danger. The earlier formulation of the rule, in terms of warranty, might well have implied that the burden of excuse was on the defendant, but modern law insists on the plaintiff carrying the burden of proof, as in other cases of negligence.[119] Moreover, the occupier's obligation to render the premises as safe "as reasonable care and skill on the part of *anyone* can make them" is not broken merely because an expert would have discovered the defect, provided he himself fulfilled the requirement of reasonable inspection and could not, in the circumstances, have been expected to employ an expert for the purpose. So in one case[120] a paying guest in a lodging house died from carbon monoxide fumes emitted from a bath-heater which had gradually deteriorated over 20 years. The defect could have been readily discovered by an expert, but there was nothing to cause the occupier to believe that the heater required attention. The defendant was exonerated, since it could not be said that it would or should have occurred to an ordinary person that the heater required periodical testing.

The duty also requires exercise of reasonable care by the occupier to control the conduct of persons likely to endanger others on the premises. This aspect has been examined in a number of cases dealing with accidents to patrons of sporting events and other entertainment, and has already been explained.[121]

The trend of assimilating the position of contractual visitors with that of invitees was further advanced by the suggestion that the high responsibility formulated in *Francis v. Cockrell* applies only where the use of the premises is the main purpose of the contract, like renting a hotel bedroom, but that where it is merely incidental to some other purposes the occupier meets his obligation by taking reasonable care to see that the premises are in all respects reasonably safe for such a purpose. This lower standard has been invoked in cases where a member of a physical training class slipped on a highly polished floor,[122] a train passenger injured his foot on the station platform,[123] and a hotel guest slipped on the cobble stones of the drive as distinct from the interior of the hotel.[124] But these English decisions, stemming from a policy to lighten the burden of railways and other public authorities, have been spurned in Australia. The higher standard applies to anyone who enters premises to which the general public is denied entry but which he enters under a contract for consideration: once past the barrier he is in a privileged position as much in a lavatory as on any part of the platform and, of course, on the train.[125] On the other hand, a customer in a restaurant pays not for admission but for his meal and is not therefore a person entering by dint of contract.[126]

119. *Watson v. George* (1953) 89 C.L.R. 409.
120. Ibid.
121. See above, p. 457.
122. *Gilmore v. L.C.C.* [1938] 4 All E.R. 311.
123. *Protheroe v. Rly Executive* [1951] 1 K.B. 376.
124. *Bell v. Travco Hotels* [1953] 1 Q.B. 473; *Beaudry v. Fort C. Hotel* (1971) 24 D.L.R. (3d) 80 preferred the higher standard.
125. *Morawski v. State Rail* (1988) 14 N.S.W.L.R. 374 (C.A.).
126. *Calvert v. Stollznow* [1982] 1 N.S.W.L.R. 175 (C.A.).

The contractual duty of occupiers "applies alike to premises and to vehicles. It matters not whether the subject be a race stand, a theatre, or an inn; whether it be a taxi cab, an omnibus or a railway carriage."[127] It extends to any land or structure which a person has been invited to use under a contract for valuable consideration and in some circumstances even though it is not under the actual control of the defendant. Thus, a shipping company is responsible to its passengers not only for the safety of its own vessel, but also of the access provided for their embarkation or landing; and it is no answer that the plank, gangway or pontoon supplied for the purpose is under somebody else's control, because it is nonetheless part of the method of transport covered by the contract of carriage.[128]

III. Trespassers

During its formative period the common law gave unstinted support to landowners in their claim to indisturbed possession and exploitation of their domain, free from any concern for the safety of intruders. But since this immunity originated, vast changes have occurred both in the climate of social responsibility and in the uses to which land is being put. The advent of railways, of power transmission lines and machinery introduced hazards of injury and death beyond all contemplation in the rural conditions preceding the industrial revolution. These, in turn, pose peculiar temptation and risk to children, especially in the poorer neighbourhoods, who lack both adequate parental supervision and, often, safe playgrounds. On the other hand, not only are trespassers unwanted "neighbours" who force themselves upon the occupier, but the burden of protective measures may also well exceed his capacity.

To strike a fair balance in this complex situation almost seemed to overtax the ingenuity of the common law. The pace of legal adjustment was in this instance painfully slow and, until quite recently, wholly inadequate. A major reason for this paralysis was the endemic distrust of juries and a preference for clear-cut draconian rules even at the cost of flexibility and humanitarianism. Yet even this stern philosophy, repeatedly reiterated by conservative majorities in the House of Lords and Privy Council, was often circumvented or flouted by lower courts. To its great credit, the High Court of Australia became in later years the persistent standard bearer of reform.[129] In a growing number of jurisdictions, including England, statutes eventually had to overcome the excessive judicial caution.[130]

Trespasser defined

The trouble starts with the over-inclusive definition of a trespasser, which covers any person who happens to enter someone else's land without consent or privilege. This category, it is therefore well to apprehend at the outset for the sake of disciplining emotional bias, is wide enough to brand

127. *Maclean v. Segar* [1917] 2 K.B. 325 at 333 per McCardie J.
128. *Timbrell v. Waterhouse* (1885) 6 L.R. (N.S.W.) 77; *John v. Bacon* (1870) L.R. 5 C.P. 437.
129. Especially in the trilogy of *Thompson v. Bankstown Corp.* (1953) 87 C.L.R. 619; *Rich v. Comm. Rly* (1959) 101 C.L.R. 135 and *Comm. Rlys v. Cardy* (1960) 104 C.L.R. 274.
130. See below, p. 468.

so motley a lot as a poacher and burglar, a toddler too young to know better as well as a respected stockbroker who has lost his way or is taking a shortcut across vacant land to the station. To treat all these alike would indeed be to emulate Procrustes.

The most time-honoured way of improving the lot of a deserving plaintiff was to raise his status to that of licensee by inferring an assent to his presence. The occupier may of course give his consent expressly or by so conducting himself as to imply it.[131] The test of consent is objective. On the one hand, one may be a trespasser without being conscious of it, as when under a mistake that the property is his or that he has the owner's permission.[132] On the other hand, the occupier's frame of mind is not decisive if it is belied by his actions: any conduct amounts to permission which gives others reason to believe that they may freely enter. Thus in the absence of a prohibiting notice, any member of the public entering a driveway or path to an ordinary residence for a legitimate purpose is a lawful visitor.[133]

Consent may be inferred from acquiescence in persistent instrusions.[134] Mere knowledge, however, does not constitute a licence. There must, at the least, be knowledge coupled with a failure to object. The occupier must take steps to show that he resents and will try to prevent the invasion, but he need not resort to every possible device to keep intruders out.[135] Factors to be taken into account are how available and practical are the means at his disposal. A railway, for example, is under no obligation to keep constant watch against trespassers on its lines lest they become licensees, because the burden would be wholly unreasonable. In the past, well-meaning courts have frequently been astute to "infer", or more realistically, to "impute" consent, particularly in favour of children, in situations where any implication of acquiescence involved a manifest strain on language.[136]

A licence may of course be circumscribed. Thus, a person entering as a lawful visitor may subsequently become a trespasser by either making an improper use of the premises, venturing into an unauthorised area or overstaying his welcome. "When you invite a person into your house to use the staircase you do not invite him to slide down the bannisters."[137] This has often proved a pitfall to invitees in search of a toilet in places of public entertainment who enter doors marked "Private", only to be precipitated down unlighted steps into the basement.[138] The modern trend is to insist

131. No less is he bound by an employee's consent within his authority: *Hillen v. I.C.I.* [1936] A.C. 65; *Mountney v. Smith* (1904) 1 C.L.R. 146.
132. *Conway v. George Wimpey* [1951] 2 K.B. 266 at 273. Conversely, one may apparently be a licensee without actually knowing that the occupier has extended an implied invitation: *Cardy v. Comm. Rlys* [1959] S.R. (N.S.W.) 230; *Rest. 2d* §330, comment *f.*
133. *Halliday v. Nevill* (1984) 155 C.L.R. 1; *Dunster v. Abbott* [1954] 1 W.L.R. 58; *Christian v. Johannesson* [1956] N.Z.L.R. 664 ("Keep Out" sign ineffective if neither seen nor reasonably capable of being seen).
134. As in *Gough v. N.C.B.* [1954] 1 Q.B. 191 (C.A.).
135. *Edwards v. Rly Executive* [1952] A.C. 737.
136. This led in the U.S. to a separate rule for child trespassers (*Rest. 2d* §339), to which the new rule in *Herrington* bears strong resemblance (without, however, being exactly limited to children).
137. *The Carlgarth* [1927] P. 93 at 110 per Scrutton L.J.; *Hillen v. I.C.I.* [1936] A.C. 65; *Pettiet v. Sydney C.C.* (1936) 36 S.R. (N.S.W.) 125.
138. But see *Pearson v. Coleman Bros* [1948] 2 K.B. 359 (little girl straying from circus to zoo in search of toilet, and there mauled by lion, held licensee).

that an occupier wishing to limit the invitation, in terms of area or time, does so clearly.[139]

In one case, a passenger collapsed on a railway platform and fell upon the track. Admittedly, she would not have been *liable* for trespass because her action was involuntary; but that could decide her status as *plaintiff* only if the "trespasser rule" was aimed against unlawful (rather than merely unconsented) presence in the locus quo. A majority of the High Court preferred to hold that at least a person who was invited to be close to the lines did not forfeit her right to reasonable care from an oncoming train upon falling on the lines involuntarily, especially when such accidents happened quite a lot.[140]

The precise location of the accident, not policy-oriented considerations, determine the status of the plaintiff; thereby sometimes saving him from the fate of being a "trespasser".[141] That he would not have met with the accident but for an act of trespass does not seem to matter, so long as he actually happened to be on neutral ground at the crucial moment. Examples: a boy who stole detonators from the defendant's land but was injured elsewhere;[142] another who was hit by a falling box when about to jump aboard a moving lorry;[143] and a swimmer who came ashore on private land but in diving off a platform was electrocuted by a falling wire while *then* above public waters.[144]

Duty of common humanity

Once classified as a trespasser, the plaintiff got but short shrift from the older law. Its sheet anchor was the rule propounded in 1929 by the House of Lords in *Addie v. Dumbreck* that the occupier was liable only for "some act done with reckless disregard of [his] presence".[145] He was under no duty at all until becoming aware of the trespasser, and then only to abstain from intentionally or recklessly injuring him.

The naive expectation that this would settle the law once and for all in a clear and definitive manner was destined to disappointment by persistent and partially successful attempts to undermine this immunity with exceptions. That in turn stimulated a crescendo of appeals and contributed to its eventual downfall. One of these inroads was the popular device of classifying the victim as a licensee rather than as a trespasser by fictitiously inferring consent to his presence, often from little more than mere knowledge of intrusions. Most frequently invoked in favour of infants, it

139. *Stone v. Taffe* [1974] 1 W.L.R. 1575 at 1580 (C.A.).
140. *Public Transport Comm. v. Perry* (1977) 137 C.L.R. 107.
141. It may however also work against him, e.g. inadvertent deviation from the road: see *Hardcastle v. S. Yorkshire Rly* (1859) 4 H. & N. 67; 157 E.R. 761; contra: *Rest. 2d* §367.
142. *Purtill v. Athlone U.D.C.* [1968] I.R. 205 (but entitled to recover also as trespasser). The trespasser, as distinct from the foreseeability, element is of course clearly irrelevant where third parties are injured by the explosion: *McCarthy v. Wellington Corp.* [1966] N.Z.L.R. 481; *McVeigh v. N.C.B.* 1970 S.L.T. 3 at 12.
143. *Farrugia v. Gt W. Rly* [1947] 2 All E.R. 565.
144. *Hynes v. N.Y. Central Rly* 131 N.E. 898; 17 A.L.R. 803 (N.Y. 1921). Similarly, *Albion v. Cochrane* (1969) 4 D.L.R. (3d) 667.
145. [1929] A.C. 358 at 364.

and its special version in the doctrine of "allurement" sufficed in practice to convert many a temptation into an invitation.[146]

Another device, persistently supported by the High Court of Australia, was to discover an "overriding duty" which could define the relationship in terms of Atkinian neighbourliness rather than occupier and trespasser. This was found, for example, in cases of activities, or dynamic as distinct from static conditions,[147] where the occupier brought something lethal or highly dangerous on his land, like high voltage poles sited on or near public places,[148] and in the many cases of children injured on defective or improperly secured vehicles or other attractive objects on, or structures abutting, the highway.[149]

Eventually, the House of Lords relented by adopting a new general standard, not that of the reasonable man but of his cousin, the "humane man with financial and other limitations".[150] This was intended to signify an intermediate position between the former standard of recklessness, now viewed as too undemanding, and the Atkinian standard of neighbourly care, still coyly avoided as too radical. The distinguishing feature from the duty owed to lawful visitors was primarily that the burden for the occupier must here be given extra weight.

First as to the likelihood of trespass: it still remained the law that an occupier was under no duty to fence his land or otherwise prevent trespassing. The old law raised a duty only to trespassers whose intrusion was at least highly probable. This requirement was now relaxed on the ground that there was no logical or pragmatic basis for stopping there, once the threshold from knowledge to foreseeability had been crossed. Hence, although the "occupier may neglect a bare possibility that trespassers may come to a particular place on his land, he is bound at least to give consideration to the matter when he knows facts which show a substantial chance that they may come there."[151] It was in this connection especially that the character of the intruder would become a material factor. "A wandering child or a straying adult stands in a different position from a poacher or a burglar."[152]

146. "While it is very plain that temptation is not invitation, it may be held that knowingly to establish and expose, unfenced, to children of an age when they follow a bait as mechanically as a fish, something that is certain to attract them, has the legal effect of an invitation to them although not to an adult" (Holmes J. in *United Zinc v. Britt* (1921) 258 U.S. 268 at 275).

147. *Hackshaw v. Shaw* (1984) 155 C.L.R. 614 (firing shotgun to disable car involved in theft, negligently hitting passenger); *Videan v. B.T.C.* [1963] 2 Q.B. 650 (C.A.).

148. *Thompson v. Bankstown Corp.* (1953) 87 C.L.R. 619 (pole on highway, trailing wire touched by boy on bicycle); *Munnings v. Hydro-Electric Comm.* (1971) 125 C.L.R. 1 (11-year-old climbed pole on vacant land, touching non-defective installation; insufficient obstacle to climbing).

149. *Lynch v. Nurdin* (1841) 1 Q.B. 29; 113 E.R. 1041, and its progeny.

150. *Herrington v. British Rlys* [1972] A.C. 877; followed by P.C. in *Southern Portland Cement v. Cooper* [1974] A.C. 623. Adopted in *Veinot v. Kerr-Addison Mines* [1975] 2 S.C.R. 311.

151. *Pannet v. McGuiness* [1972] 2 Q.B. 599 at 607 per Lord Denning. Knowledge need not be positive; it may be of facts from which an inference can reasonably be drawn (*Rest. 2d* §12: "has reason to know"): *Harris v. Birkenhead* [1976] 1 W.L.R. 279 (C.A.).

152. Ibid. at 607.

Secondly, what must the occupier do to lessen the peril? Certainly he is under no duty to make his land safe to be trespassed upon; ordinarily at most a warning is required. However, as in the case of allurements under the old law, child trespassers may well be entitled to more effective safeguards, even so much as standing watch over a bonfire that was attracting little children despite repeated warnings-off.[153] No hard and fast rules can apparently be laid down; and it has been allowed that while the occupier may not be required to incur any great expense with respect to dangers that he did not himself create, he may have to do more in other cases. Ordinarily he could not be expected to be hampered in his own pursuits, at least if lesser measures would alert the trespasser. Moreover, what "common humanity" demanded from him must be adapted to his financial and other resources. An impecunious occupier with little assistance at hand might be excused where large organisations like railways, public utilities or public authorities, have to perform. Thus rather than saying that trespassers must take the land as they find it, one might say that they must take the occupier as they find him.

Common duty of care

Freed from the tutelage of the Privy Council, the High Court of Australia in *Zaluzna v. Australian Safeway Stores*[154] swept away the prevarications of the past and prescribed the general standard of care for trespassers as well as lawful visitors. Reference to common humanity, however, may still be "appropriate in describing the reasonable care which shall be exercised by the reasonable man when it is reasonably foreseeable that acts or omissions are likely to injure a trespasser who has forced a relationship of proximity upon him".[155]

In England statutory reform belatedly came in 1984, though in somewhat guarded terms. The duty to persons other than lawful visitors is owed only if (1) the occupier is aware of the danger or has reasonable grounds to believe that it exists; (2) he knows or has reasonable grounds to believe that the other is in, or may come into, the vicinity of the danger; and (3) the risk is one against which, in all the circumstances of the case, he may reasonably be expected to offer the other some protection.[156] Equally cautious is the South Australian Act which denies a duty of care unless the presence of trespassers and their exposure to danger was reasonably foreseeable, and the nature and extent of the danger was such that measures which were not in fact taken should have been taken for their protection.[157]

The two other Australian statutes, like the Scottish Act of 1960, from the start applied the common duty of care to all entrants, including trespassers. But among the factors to be considered in applying the standard, of peculiar relevance to trespassers, are "the circumstances of the entry into the premises, the knowledge which the occupier of premises has or ought to have of the likelihood of persons or property being on the premises and the burden on the occupier of eliminating the danger or protecting the person

153. Ibid.
154. (1987) 162 C.L.R. 479.
155. *Hackshaw v. Shaw* (1984) 155 C.L.R. 614 at 662 (Deane J.).
156. *Occupiers' Liability Act* 1984 s. 1(3).
157. *Wrongs Act* s. 17c(6).

entering the premises compared to the risk of the danger to the person''.[158] These statutory formulas express reservations which are certain to be given weight also under *Zaluzna*. Illustrative is a House of Lords decision on the claim of a 15-year-old girl who was struck by a train when crossing the tracks after climbing through a gap in the fence. The plaintiff had been fully cognisant of the risk and was debarred either because the defendants did not owe to *her* a duty to maintain the fence in a better condition, whatever might have been their responsibility to little children[159] or persons inadvertently straying on the lines, or because she had voluntarily assumed the risk.[160]

The Western Australian and Ontario statutes withhold protection altogether from persons who are on the premises with the intention of committing, or in the commission of, an offence punishable by imprisonment. These are treated as having willingly assumed the risk and are entitled to complain only if intentionally or recklessly injured.[161] In New Zealand and a few other jurisdictions statutes still exclude all trespassers from the ''common duty'' of care; indeed, in Alberta the duty was expressly retrenched to the old common law standard of ''intent or recklessness'' except in favour of children.[162]

3. LESSORS AND VENDORS

Responsibility for the safety of premises at common law goes with occupation, not ownership. A lessor or vendor, by parting with control, may accordingly shift that responsibility to the incoming tenant or purchaser and acquit himself for subsequent mishaps, even those due to hazards existing at the time of transfer.[163] As pithily stated by Erle C.J. in 1863, ''fraud apart, there is no law against letting a tumbledown house.''[164] This immunity long remained singularly stubborn to the civilised demand of the modern age for a general duty of care. At last, however, reform is now under way, some of it judicial, some legislative.

Lessors

Upon a lease of land, the tenant must, in general, take the demised premises as he finds them, for better or worse. In the absence of an express covenant, the rule is ''caveat lessee''.[165] No warranties of fitness

158. Vic.: s. 14B(4); W.A.: s. 5(4).
159. As in *Herrington v. British Rlys* [1972] A.C. 877.
160. *McGinlay v. British Rlys* [1983] 1 W.L.R. 1427.
161. *Occupiers' Liability Act* 1985 (W.A.) s. 5(2); *Occupiers' Liability Act* 1980 (Ont.) s. 4(2).
162. Section 12. (The duty to children is defined in terms of *Rest. 2d* §339). The Ontario Statute applies the traditional trespasser standard to persons whose entry is prohibited under the *Trespass to Property Act*, as it also does to snowmobiles in response to *Veinot v. Kerr-Addison Mines* [1975] 2 S.C.R. 311. Thus, in Canada only the B.C. statute does not specifically discriminate against trespassers.
163. Lease implies exclusive possession. Letting a hall for a meeting (of tobacco growers in Texas, Qld) did not create a tenancy, even though the hirers had the right to control admission: *Voli v. Inglewood S.* (1963) 110 C.L.R. 74 at 91.
164. *Robbins v. Jones* (1863) 15 C.B. (N.S.) 221 at 240.
165. *Cheater v. Cater* [1918] 1 K.B. 247 at 255, 256.

(habitability), such as attach to the sale and hire of chattels, are implied in his favour,[166] except in the case of a furnished letting[167] and under legislation, here and there, dealing with low rent housing.[168] Nor, contract apart, is the landlord under any duty of care to protect his tenant and others from dangers on the premises, not even if they existed at the commencement of the lease.[169] This is unobjectionable enough where the defect is obvious or discoverable by reasonable inspection, because the landlord is entitled to assume that the tenant will familiarise himself with the premises, if not prior to taking the lease, at least upon going into possession,[170] and thereafter it is the tenant's responsibility rather than the landlord's to make repairs or take other suitable precautions for his own safety and that of others.

Rather different considerations arise where the danger is latent. If known to the landlord, his failure to warn might well have been treated as active wrongdoing, tantamount to leading the lessee and those using the premises by his permission into a trap. In similar circumstances, no less had ever been demanded from a bare licensor, whose failure to warn of concealed dangers actually known to him was very early on deemed the equivalent of fraud. Landlords, however, have hitherto escaped a similar reappraisal, despite their original identification with licensors through the common denominator of liability for fraud and fraud alone. Thus, active concealment apart, no duty to warn seems in fact required; and although perhaps still open to challenge, the past assumption has been to regard knowledge as immaterial.[171]

More progress has been made where the landlord is himself responsible for creating the dangerous condition, whether by designing, building, or repairing. First with respect to repairs during the tenancy,[172] later even for structural conditions at its commencement,[173] he is at long last responsible just like any third party contractor. Here his responsibility derives not from being a landlord, but from having actively engendered the risk: he is blamed for misfeasance rather than non-feasance. The immunity avails, if at all, only "bare landlords".

166. *Hart v. Windsor* (1843) 12 M. & W. 68; 152 E.R. 1114; *Sleafer v. Lambeth B.C.* [1960] 1 Q.B. 43 (C.A.).
167. *Smith v. Marrable* (1943) 11 M. & W. 5; 152 E.R. 693; *Wilson v. Finch Hatton* (1877) 2 Ex. D. 336. The distinction has been defended on the ground that there is a lesser opportunity for prior inspection and that the tenant obviously took the lease for habitation (rather than, perhaps, for storage). A third reason sometimes professed, viz. that the contract is mixed, is the more tenuous because it matters nothing whether the defect stemmed from the condition of the furniture or the premises. See West, *Implied Obligations of a Landlord as to Condition of Premises at the Time of Letting*, 25 Convey. 184 (1961); North, *Liability of Landlord for Dangerous Premises*, 29 Convey. 207 (1965).
168. E.g. the *Landlord and Tenant Act* (Eng.) s. 8(1).
169. *Cavalier v. Pope* [1906] A.C. 428. In the U.S. the rule no longer applies to premises let for public use: *Rest. 2d* §359.
170. This may explain why a licensee (and according to a dictum in *Voli v. Inglewood S.* (1963) 110 C.L.R. 74 at 91, even an entrant under a lease of a public hall for a short period) remains by contrast entitled to a high duty of care.
171. *Sleafer v. Lambeth B.C.* [1960] 1 Q.B. 43 (C.A.). *Rest. 2d* §358 requires a duty to warn against known dangers, as also recommended by Law Com. No. 40, but not embodied in *Defective Premises Act* 1972.
172. *Billings v. Riden* [1958] A.C. 240 at 253, 264.
173. *Rimmer v. Liverpool C.C.* [1985] Q.B. 1 (C.A.). Nor was the tenant debarred by his knowledge, since he was not "really and truly free to act on it" (glass wall panel).

Covenants to repair

A landlord who defaults on a covenant to repair is responsible to his tenant not only for any financial detriment, but also for consequential personal injury and tangible property damage.[174] He must, however, have had actual notice of the defect and thereafter omitted to rectify it with reasonable dispatch.[175] This principle applies whether the covenant is expressed in the lease or imposed by law as it now increasingly is under modern housing legislation.[176]

At common law, however, resort to such covenants was seriously impaired by the anachronistic corollary that a contractual duty to repair, whether express or implied, is owed to the tenant alone and does not avail his family or visitors who are injured on the demised premises.[177] This pusillanimous view rests on the spurious reasoning that a contractual duty cannot confer rights upon strangers who are not privy to the obligation, nor put the landlord in control of the premises so as to make him liable as occupier.[178] The rule has now been reversed in many jurisdictions by the Occupiers' Liability Acts.[179] Moreover, a recent decision in South Australia deemed it no longer compatible with the modern view of social responsibility since *Donoghue v. Stevenson*: the obligation undertaken by the landlord created a relationship of dependency and reliance which availed not only the tenant but also his family and visitors likely to be endangered by his unreasonable failure to heed a call for repair.[180]

Dangers from outside

A landlord cannot invoke his immunity against persons who meet with an accident on premises retained in his own occupation, such as common stairs and other conveniences for the use of tenants and their visitors. But what is the position where, as the result of such a dangerous condition, someone is injured on the portion of the premises demised? On this question the authorities are in conflict. It is settled that a tenant assumes the risk of static dangers existing at the commencement of the lease and therefore cannot complain, for example, if his horse is poisoned by a yew tree which overhangs the boundary fence from a neighbouring plot retained by the landlord.[181] But this understandable proposition was later extended to an entirely different situation where a labourer, in the employment of the tenant, was killed by a falling branch from a decayed tree which stood on the lessor's adjoining land.[182] This startling conclusion seems wrong on a

174. *Summers v. Salford Corp.* [1943] A.C. 283 (under housing legislation; now *Landlord and Tenant Act* 1985 ss 8, 11).
175. *O'Brien v. Robinson* [1973] A.C. 912. Aliter, if the landlord has covenanted to repair premises in his own possession: *Melles v. Holme* [1918] 2 K.B. 100.
176. E.g. *Residential Tenancies Acts* of N.S.W. (1987 s. 25); Vic. (1980 s. 97); S.A. (1978 s. 46); N.Z. (1986 s. 45); *Landlord and Tenant Act* 1972 (Eng.) s. 11. See Gray, *Elements of Land Law* 916-925, 949-950 (1987).
177. *Cavalier v. Pope* [1906] A.C. 428.
178. Ibid. at 431, 433.
179. S.A.: s. 17d(b); W.A.: s. 9; N.Z.: s. 8; A.C.T.: *Law Reform (Miscellaneous Provisions) Act* s. 29. England: now *Defective Premises Act* 1972 s. 4.
180. *Parker v. South Australian Housing Trust* (1986) 41 S.A.S.R. 493 (F.C.).
181. *Cheater v. Cater* [1918] 1 K.B. 247.
182. *Shirvell v. Hackwood Estates* [1938] 2 K.B. 577 (C.A.).

double count: first, because it is one thing for a tenant to take his land subject to the inconvenience and detriment of an overhanging branch, but quite another to impute to him acceptance of the risk that the branch will fall owing to the landlord's negligence. Secondly, if the landlord's assumed immunity rests on the tenant's contractual acceptance of the risk, why should this affect his labourers? If a stranger cannot claim the benefit of the lessee's covenant, neither should he in all fairness be prejudiced by it.[183]

In other cases, a sounder approach has prevailed. Thus, when a piece of guttering fell from the roof of a block of flats through the skylight of a kitchen and injured the wife of a subtenant, the landlords were held liable on the ground that, being in control of the roof, they owed a duty of care to prevent it from becoming a danger to adjoining property or persons lawfully thereon, and it was immaterial by whom and where the injury was sustained.[184] This decision has been followed in cases where the tenant's premises were damaged by water flowing from a blocked gutter in the landlord's possession[185] and where a tenant's daughter was injured in the yard by a brick falling from a defective chimney.[186] The better opinion, therefore, seems to be that the landlord's immunity has been carried far enough by precluding relief against dangerous static conditions subsisting at the commencement of the tenancy; it cannot legitimately be carried to the point of imputing to the tenant and his visitors acceptance of the risk of projections falling on the demised premises, all the more where the danger did not exist or was not apparent at the date of the lease.[187]

Vendors

The position of a vendor of land is rather similar to that of a lessor. By parting with title and possession, his control ceases and he is thereby, in general, released from further responsibility for the condition of the premises. Purchasers of homes and other buildings customarily arrange their own survey, and it is arguable that it would unnecesarily duplicate costs if vendors were put under obligation to *discover* defects. However, the time is ripe for requiring a duty to warn of known defects.[188]

Vendor-*builders*, however, do not enjoy such a privileged position. In the first place, for defects which they have themselves created prior to sale, the old immunity has now been laid to rest.[189] It had become indefensible

183. See Hamson, 2 Mod. L. Rev. 215 (1938); Goodhart, 54 L.Q.R. 459 (1938). Since the majority of the court found that there was no negligence, its statements on the point of law should be rejected as obiter dicta: *Taylor v. Liverpool Corp.* [1939] 3 All E.R. 329 at 338.
184. *Cunard v. Antifyre* [1933] 1 K.B. 551. It is doubtful whether the conclusion would have been different had the defendant been the landlord instead of the head-landlord of the plaintiffs.
185. *Bishop v. London Properties* (1933) 102 L.J.K.B. 257; *Cockburn v. Smith* [1924] 2 K.B. 119; *Victor Weston v. Kenny* [1954] I.R. 191.
186. *Taylor v. Liverpool Corp.* [1939] 3 All E.R. 329.
187. In *Shirvell v. Hackwood Estates* [1938] 2 K.B. 577 (C.A.) there was evidence that the risk of the branch falling had not increased since the commencement of the tenancy.
188. *McGrath v. MacLean* (1979) 95 D.L.R. (3d) 144 (Ont. C.A.); *Rest. 2d* §353; recommended by English Law Commission (No. 40 §54). Concealment may be fraud.
189. *Anns v. Merton L.B.C.* [1978] A.C. 728 at 759; *Batty v. Metropolitan Property* [1978] Q.B. 554 (C.A.).

since *Donoghue v. Stevenson* to impose a duty of care on manufacturers of goods but to exempt manufacturers of buildings after disposal; it appeared outright capricious once building contractors employed by an owner had become responsible for negligence in the construction. Their liability, however, as we shall see, does not extend to damage to the defective structure itself, only to personal injury and damage to "other" property.[190]

Secondly, there is a residuary and increasing sphere of warranties. The common law imposes, on the sale of an *unfinished* house by a builder who agrees to complete it, the standard implied warranty by builders that the work will be done in a workmanlike manner, with proper materials and so that the dwelling when completed will be fit for habitation.[191] Unfortunately, the efficacy of this warranty is limited in two ways: first, warranties (express[192] or implied) afford no protection to anyone other than the purchaser himself;[193] and secondly, no similar warranty applies to the sale of completed houses.[194] The given reason for this distinction is that the purchaser of an uncompleted house has no opportunity to inspect the completed structure for defects; ignoring the fact that in practice the ordinary home purchaser would tend to rely on the builder's workmanship in both cases alike. Mindful of the great need for consumer protection, American courts are increasingly extending the warranty of habitability to the sale of all houses,[195] completed as well as uncompleted. In England, a similar obligation has been imposed by statute not only on vendor-builders, but on all persons "taking on work for or in connection with the provision of a dwelling".[196]

4. BUILDING CONSTRUCTION

As already noted, the peculiar duties of occupiers do not define the responsibility of others for the dangerous condition of premises. Not so long ago, contractors and builders were treated with exceptional leniency on

190. See below, p. 474.
191. This covers also part of the building already finished at the time of sale: *Perry v. Sharon Developments* [1937] 4 All E.R. 390 (C.A.); *Hancock v. Brazier* [1966] 1 W.L.R. 1317 (C.A.); *Streeter v. McLennan* [1959] Qd R. 136; *Croft v. Prendergast* [1949] 2 D.L.R. 708 (C.A.). But no such warranty is implied where there is an express contract as to the way in which the building is to be completed and the specifications have been exactly complied with: *Lynch v. Thorne* [1956] 1 W.L.R. 303.
192. Express warranties by vendors are also vulnerable to the doctrine that they "merge in the conveyance". Providentially, building contracts are exempt: *Lawrence v. Cassel* [1930] 2 K.B. 83 (C.A.); *Hancock v. Brazier* [1966] 1 W.L.R. 1317 (C.A.).
193. See *Otto v. Bolton* [1936] 2 K.B. 46 where the daughter recovered when the ceiling caved in, but not her mother.
194. *Hoskins v. Woodham* [1938] 1 All E.R. 692; *Fraser-Reid v. Droumtsekas* [1980] 1 S.C.R. 720. In special circumstances warranties concerning defects may be implied, e.g. *Gabolinscy v. Hamilton* [1975] 1 N.Z.L.R. 150.
195. Many decisions extend the warranty to subpurchasers, some even to used homes: see Mallor, 20 Am. Bus. L.J. 361 (1982).
196. *Defective Premises Act* 1972 s. 1 (in favour of anyone who acquires an interest, legal or equitable, in the premises). In practice, the Act covers only repairs and renovations, new houses falling under the voluntary N.H.B.C. scheme: see Holyoak & Allen, *Civil Liability for Defective Premises* (1982) 92.

the footing that duties of care in relation to dangers on land could be founded on occupancy or contract alone, but today, far from enjoying whatever limited indulgence may still be accorded to an occupier, they stand fully exposed to the bracing demands of the Atkinian general duty of care even after acceptance of their work.[197] Thus, a gas company was made to answer for a faulty installation causing an explosion,[198] a building contractor for insufficiently guarding passers-by while the work was in progress,[199] and an architect for the defective design of a collapsed stage.[200] A developer or contractor, however, is not responsible for the faults of his independent contractors, such as subcontractors on a building project.[201]

Damage to defective structure

So much for personal injury and damage to *other* tangible property. But what if the damage is only to the defective structure itself? In the controversial case of *Anns v. Merton L.B.C.*[202] the cost of repairing defective foundations, imminently dangerous to health and safety, was held recoverable by labelling it "damage to property", and some later cases went so far as to include damages for diminution in value—clearly economic loss.[203] At its extreme, a building owner recovered from a subcontractor (with whom he had no privity) the cost of replacing defective flooring which was not dangerous at all but merely shoddy.[204]

This legal adventure was emphatically repudiated by the House of Lords in *D. & F. Estates v. Church Comrs*[205] in an avowed return to the traditional demarcation between the realms of tort and contract. Here defective plaster had fallen from ceiling and walls of an apartment, but the owners were denied recovery from the builder even for the cost of repairing the damage, let alone for additional threatened damage. Tort liability was limited to actual physical damage such as damage to furniture; it did not cover even the imminent risk of such damage because that would be merely economic loss (for which any remedy lay solely in contract) once the danger was recognised in time and averted. Thus even the intermediate view[206] was repudiated, that the cost of averting physical injury should be as much within the purview of tort as the cost of repairing injury that had eventuated: tort did not countenance "preventive damages".[207] Nor

197. *Billings v. Riden* [1958] A.C. 240. Nor can they aver against third parties that they complied with their contract with the developer: *Voli v. Inglewood S.* (1963) 110 C.L.R. 74 at 85 (architect); *Bowen v. Paramount Builders* [1977] 1 N.Z.L.R. 394 at 407.
198. *Dominion Natural Gas v. Collins* [1909] A.C. 640.
199. *Kimber v. Gas, Light & Coke* [1918] 1 K.B. 439.
200. *Voli v. Inglewood S.* [1963] 110 C.L.R. 74.
201. *D. & F. Estates v. Church Comrs* [1989] A.C. 177, not follg *Mount Albert B.C. v. Johnson* [1979] 2 N.Z.L.R. 234 (C.A.).
202. [1978] A.C. 728.
203. E.g. *Bowen v. Paramount Builders* [1977] 1 N.Z.L.R. 394 (C.A.).
204. *Junior Books v. Veitchi Co.* [1983] 1 A.C. 520; see above, p. 184.
205. [1989] A.C. 177; affd in *Dept of Environment v. Bates* [1991] A.C. 449; follg *Murphy v. Brentwood D.C.* [1991] A.C. 398. Critical: Cane, 52 Mod. L. Rev. 200 (1989). *Opat v. Nat. Mutual Life* [1992] 1 V.R. 283 reveals the uncertainty in Australia regarding the likely reception.
206. Laskin J. in *Rivtow Marine v. Washington Iron Works* [1974] S.C.R. 1189 at 1221-2 (diss.).
207. Forgetful of the practice in nuisance: see above, p. 446.

obviously did it matter that there had been an accident; relevant alone was the nature of the loss, and loss to the defective product—land or chattel—was excluded.[208] To this there is no exception even for "complex structures": if a component part damages the larger unit, like an electrical fitting setting the whole house on fire, the manufacturer of the fitting may be liable in tort for what, to him, is damage to "other" property, but not the building contractor.[209] A sole survivor from an earlier, more positive attitude towards economic loss was apparently the responsibility for negligent advice,[210] notwithstanding the brittle distinction between words and acts and the incongruity of demanding more from surveyors and other information professionals than from builders.

The decision not only ran counter to earlier "binding" precedents, with unconvincing efforts to distinguish them, but—more importantly—failed to justify the line it drew between the province of contract and tort. For whether the claim is described as for "damage to property" or "economic loss", it treats physical damage to the defective thing itself, actual or threatened, a priori as a mere defect of quality, exclusively within the purview of contract. There being no contract between the parties, how—it is asked—is the court to determine the appropriate standard of quality? The answer, surely, is that this has not presented an insuperable obstacle in other situations, such as those involving services or representations. Besides, there is no reason why the contractual standard should not be binding on third parties in these circumstances.[211] The dominant reason for caution in imposing liability for economic loss is the fear of unlimited liability; yet here liability would be limited both in regard to person and amount. In sum, would not a more principled line of demarcation be that between defects affecting safety and those merely lessening the value of the premises or things?

Anns had imposed liability not only on builders but also on local authorities for defective foundations resulting from negligent failure to comply with their own bylaws regarding building safety. This conclusion was readily accepted in Canada[212] and New Zealand,[213] but challenged in Australia for imposing an affirmative duty of intervention without any corresponding reliance or control and pretending that the loss was not economic but damage to property.[214] Yet perpetuating the artificial distinction between misrepresentation and other conduct causing economic

208. So also the builders' standard insurance policy covers only damage to *other* property. Insurers are unwilling to guarantee the quality of builders' work, unlike one-off accidents. Is insurance wagging the tail of liability?

209. *Murphy v. Brentwood D.C.* [1991] A.C. 398 at 470, 497.

210. Lord Keith in *Murphy* at 466 explained away *Pirelli v. Oscar Faber* [1983] 2 A.C. 1 and *Junior Books v. Veitchi Co.* [1983] 1 A.C. 520 on this ground.

211. See above, p. 185.

212. *Kamloops v. Nielsen* [1984] 2 S.C.R. 2; *Rothfield v. Manolakis* [1989] 2 S.C.R. 1259; *University of Regina v. Pettick* (1991) 77 D.L.R. (4th) 615 (roof fabricator).

213. The N.Z.C.A. on the basis of broader objectives (not merely "health and safety") has allowed recovery even for non-dangerous defects such as deformed weatherboards and obstructed view, thereby further obscuring the distinction between property damage and economic loss: *Brown v. Heathcote C.C.* [1986] N.Z.L.R. 76, affd [1987] N.Z.L.R. 720 (P.C.) but reserving this question; *Stieller v. Porirua C.C.* [1986] N.Z.L.R. 84; *Craig v. E. Coast Bays C.C.*, ibid. 99. See *Todd* 175-184.

214. *Sutherland S.C. v. Heyman* (1985) 157 C.L.R. 424.

loss, this ruling did not question earlier and later decisions to the effect that reliance on a misleading *certificate* that the bylaws had been complied with could indeed create a duty to purchasers of defective structures.[215] Eventually, the House of Lords, having earlier rejected the claim against builders, found no principled argument for demanding more from local authorities, and accordingly took the exceptional step in *Murphy v. Brentwood D.C.*[216] of expressly overruling *Anns*.

Jerry-building is a perennial problem which *Anns* sought to address. In England legislation now offers some protection to purchasers and tenants of *dwellings* either by an insurance-backed warranty or by a duty of care on builders and developers to ensure habitability.[217] This leaves only commercial buildings unprotected in England; elsewhere, however, residential as well as commercial owners still have to fend for themselves.[218] Compulsory insurance would be the best solution for the biggest asset most home owners ever have. It would solve the problem of insolvent contractors and place the cost on the purchaser, the beneficiary, rather than on the local authority, the ratepayers.[219] But pressure on contractors to "clean up their act" should not be sacrificed by abandoning tort liability (and subrogation) against them, as the English decisions have now decreed. Deterrence, as much as compensation, remains an objective of a principled system of tort law.

Other economic losses

Economic losses unrelated to physical damage (or the threat of it) are ordinarily not recoverable by non-contracting parties. In building construction, for example, the participating parties typically enter into relations in the context of a contractual network which does not necessarily contemplate complementary obligations in tort. Thus even nominated subcontractors will not be liable for economic loss sustained by the employer of the head-contractor, despite the latter's reliance and the foreseeability of the loss.[220] Nor are engineers or architects employed by the owner answerable to contractors for extra costs of construction due to faults in design, supervision or certification.[221]

215. *Shaddock v. Parramatta C.* (1981) 150 C.L.R. 225 (but see now *Local Gvt Act* ss 317AE-317AF, added in 1983); *Pisano v. Fairfield C.* (1991) A.T.R. 81-126 (N.S.W.C.A.).
216. [1991] 1 A.C. 398. See Duncan Wallace, 107 L.Q.R. 228 (1991); Grubb & Mullis, 55 Convey. 225 (1991). Critical: Cooke, *An Impossible Distinction*, 107 L.Q.R. 46 (1991). It remained open if liability was also foreclosed for physical injury.
217. *Defective Premises Act* 1972, s. 1. The warranty protects successive owners but is subject to ungenerous limitation periods. Some Australian statutes exact similar warranties from builders of houses in favour of purchasers and their successors in title: *Defective Houses Act* 1976 (S.A.); *Builders' Registration and Home Owners' Protection Act* 1979 (Qld).
218. See e.g. Smillie, [1990] N.Z.L.J. 310.
219. E.g. *Builders' Registration and Home Owners' Protection Act* 1979 (Qld). But with subrogation against culpable builders.
220. *Greater Nottingham Co-op v. Cementation* [1989] Q.B. 71 (C.A.); *Simaan v. Pilkington (No. 2)* [1988] Q.B. 758 (C.A.): defective material supplied to subcontractor. *Junior Books* is overruled.
221. *Pacific Associates v. Baxter* [1990] 1 Q.B. 993 (C.A.). For over-certification the owner has his contract remedy against the engineer; for under-certification the contractor's remedy is against the owner, not the engineer.

23

PRODUCTS LIABILITY

Liability for defective products ("products liability") is shared by contract and tort law.[1] Until recently this combination offered greater protection to the buyer against the retail seller than to the ultimate consumer against the manufacturer. Against his seller the buyer could invoke warranties, *guaranteeing* the quality of his purchase; against the manufacturer, however, tort liability was for long denied altogether and thereafter limited to negligence only. Contemporary demands for stronger consumer protection have now promoted a new model of strict tort liability for injury from defective products. Originating in the United States, it has since been adopted in the European Community and is spreading to other countries, including Australia. Thus products liability is at last attaining coherence.

1. WARRANTIES

The liability of distributors to their immediate transferees depends on the naturc of their relationship and terms of agreement. As between buyer and seller of goods it is largely controlled by certain implied warranties which, during the 19th century at the crest of imaginative judicial reform, progressively replaced an earlier individualistic philosophy epitomised in the maxim "caveat emptor". By attaching "implied" warranties to the contract, reflecting the parties' presumed intent, the seller in effect became an insurer of his goods with respect to their quality and fitness. The two principal warranties now have statutory force under the Sale of Goods Acts:[2] (1) where the buyer, expressly or by implication, makes known to the seller the particular purpose for which they are required (so as to show that the buyer relies on the seller's skill and judgment) and the goods are of a description which it is in the course of the seller's business to supply, there is an implied warranty that the goods shall be reasonably fit for such purpose, except where the sale is of a specified article under its patent or other trade name; and (2) where goods are bought by description from a seller who deals in goods of that description, there is an implied warranty of merchantable quality, provided that if the buyer has examined the goods

1. See the comprehensive studies of *Products Liability*, in Australia by Cavanagh & Phegan (1983), in England by Miller & Lovell (1977), in Canada by Waddams (1974).
2. Reproducing the English *Sale of Goods Act* 1893 (now 1979), s. 14; N.S.W. (1923 s. 19), Vic. (1958 s. 19), Qld (1896 s. 17), S.A. (1895 s. 14), W.A. (1895 s. 14), Tas. (1896 s. 19), A.C.T. (1954 s. 19), N.T. (1972 s. 15), N.Z. (1908 s. 16). These warranties were somewhat expanded by the English *Supply of Goods (Implied Terms) Act* 1973 and *Sale of Goods Act* 1979, followed by the *Consumer Protection and Trade Practices Act* 1974 (Cth) ss 66-72, *Goods (Sales and Leases) Act* 1981 (Vic.), *Consumer Transactions Act* 1972 (S.A.) s. 8 (consumer sales only). Generally: Sutton, *Sales and Consumer Law* (1983) chs 9-10.

there is no warranty as regards defects which such examination ought to have revealed.

Although originating in the desire to protect the commercial buyer against financial loss in marketing the goods,[3] warranties attained added and, for present purposes, momentous significance as their reach expanded to property damage[4] and eventually to personal injury.[5] Thereby a mercantile concept became a device for consumer protection, the more remarkable for ensuring strict liability long before the courts were ready to endorse so much as a tort duty sounding in negligence. For these warranties, notwithstanding their ancestral link with deceit, withstood the corroding influence of the fault doctrine,[6] and survived into modern law as absolute guarantees even against latent and undiscoverable defects[7] or against contributory negligence.[8]

The "logic" of this development, however, was never pursued to the point of jettisoning the privity requirement which continues to deny the benefit of warranties to all but the immediate purchaser. Warranties do not run with the goods,[9] nor is there any "vertical" privity between the manufacturer and the ultimate retail purchaser, let alone with persons outside the chain of commercial distribution ("the bystander"). And only exceptionally may the purchaser himself recover for an injury suffered by a third party, as in the case of an injury[10] or death[11] to his wife or child[12] (action for loss of services) or when he purchased as agent[13] or expressly for the benefit[14] of another.

Less constrictive a corollary of the privity requirement is that it compels the consumer to look to the retailer rather than the manufacturer for

3. Hence the name *merchantable* (i.e. saleable) quality. See also *Sale of Goods Act* 1979 (Eng.) s. 53(3) which contemplates only commercial loss in prescribing the measure of damages for breach of warranty.
4. *Smith v. Green* (1875) 1 C.P.D. 92; *Randall v. Newson* (1877) 2 Q.B.D. 102.
5. *Wren v. Holt* [1903] 1 K.B. 610 (arsenic in beer); *Preist v. Last* [1903] 2 K.B. 148 (bursting hotwater bottle); *David Jones v. Willis* (1934) 52 C.L.R. 110 (shoe); *Grant v. Australian Knitting Mills* [1936] A.C. 85; 54 C.L.R. 49 (dermatitis from underpants); *Andrews v. Hopkinson* [1957] 1 Q.B. 299 (car).
6. Some (non-sales) warranties were reduced to mere warranties of due care, e.g. carriers of passengers: *Readhead v. Midland Rly* (1869) L.R. 4 Q.B. 379.
7. *Hill v. Ashington Piggeries* [1972] A.C. 441 at 498. The standard is codified in s. 14(6) of the English Act: *Aswan Engin. v. Lupdine* [1987] 1 W.L.R. 1 (C.A.) For unknowable risks and (practically) undiscoverable defects see below, n. 93.
8. Plaintiff's misconduct might, however, be such as to put the injury outside reasonable contemplation and thus too remote, e.g. by use with actual knowledge of the defect: see *Lambert v. Lewis* [1982] A.C. 225.
9. As they do e.g. under Que. *Civil Code: G.M. v. Kravitz* [1979] 1 S.C.R. 790 (consumer buyer recovers purchase price from *manufacturer*); comment, 25 McG. L.J. 335 (1980).
10. *Preist v. Last* [1903] 2 K.B. 148 (C.A.). He is of course denied such recovery if the wife herself was the buyer, but in that event she may sue in her own right. Thus, the court will accede to either the husband's or the wife's claim.
11. *Jackson v. Watson* [1909] 2 K.B. 193 (husband's claim includes damages for wife's death). Cf. *Woolworths v. Crotty* (1942) 66 C.L.R. 603 (son's death confers fatal accident claim on mother: see below, p. 664).
12. *Square v. Model Farm Dairies* [1939] 2 K.B. 365.
13. E.g. *Lockett v. Charles* [1938] 4 All E.R. 170.
14. Cf. *Jackson v. Horizon Holidays* [1975] 1 W.L.R. 1468 (C.A.) where a father recovered for the inconvenience, disappointment etc. of his wife and children over a spoiled holiday.

recovery. This seemingly capricious allocation of responsibility is in practice redressed by means of successive indemnities which ordinarily (that is in the absence of a missing link in the chain of distribution,[15] of exemption clauses, jurisdictional obstacles,[16] or time bars) allow the loss to be shifted to its ultimately responsible source;[17] besides offering the consumer the advantage of a readily identified target and thus relieving him of the burden of tracing, perhaps even chasing abroad, the retailer's far off sources of supply.

By far the most serious handicap for consumers in the past has been the law's tolerance of exemption clauses in form contracts whereby the buyer could unwittingly sign away his protection under the statutory warranties. The courts, however strict in their construction of these clauses,[18] in the end proved no match to the drafting ingenuity of sellers, so that eventually legislation had to come to the rescue. Contracting-out was first severely restricted in the case of hire-purchase, on the view that the instalment buyer was in greater need of protection than the cash buyer because he had generally more at stake and was less able to look after himself.[19] Eventually the same indulgence was extended to all other *consumer* sales in England[20] and Australia.[21]

Express warranties

Express warranties have followed much the same rut as implied warranties. In particular, the privity requirement precludes recourse by anyone not privy to the contract of sale.[22] Only in a few cases has it been possible to evade this restriction and hold manufacturers directly liable to the retail purchaser by artificially construing their representations as the basis of a "collateral contract" with him.[23] This tactic however is ordinarily not available against advertising to the general public, supposedly because such representations are not intended as promissory.[24] For English law, in contrast to American, has insisted (with admittedly lessening severity in application) that express warranties must be promissory and intended to be contractual as distinct from mere representations

15. As in *Lambert v. Lewis* [1982] A.C. 225 at 259-267 (claim by retailer v. manufacturer, wholesaler not identified).
16. Only lately has it become easier to gain "extended" jurisdiction under Ord. XI over foreign manufacturers: *Distillers v. Thompson* [1971] A.C. 458 (P.C.).
17. See *Kasler v. Slavouski* [1928] 1 K.B. 78 (involving no less than four successive indemnities of the retailer's liability to his purchaser).
18. See also above, p. 293.
19. See below, n. 28.
20. *Supply of Goods (Implied Terms) Act* 1973; *Unfair Contract Terms Act* 1977 (applicable to sale, hire purchase and other contracts passing possession or ownership of goods; for non-consumers the terms must be "reasonable").
21. *Trade Practices Act* 1974 (Cth) s. 68; *Commercial Transactions (Miscellaneous Provisions) Act* 1974 (N.S.W.); *Goods Act* (Vic.) s. 97; *Consumer Transactions Act* 1972 (S.A.) s. 10. Can.: Waddams, *Products Liability* (1974) 161-171.
22. Not so American law: *Rest. 2d* §402B.
23. *Shanklin Pier v. Detel Products* [1951] 2 K.B. 854; *Wells v. Buckland Sand* [1965] 2 Q.B. 170; *Jones v. Grais* (1961) 78 W.N. (N.S.W.) 955. All involved economic loss. More venturous Canadian cases are discussed by Clarke, *Product Liability Actions in Australia: Is the Collateral Contract Remedy an Option?* 5 Qd U.T.L.J. 111 (1989).
24. *Lambert v. Lewis* [1982] A.C. 225 at 262 (C.A.); contra: *Murray v. Sperry Rand* (1979) 96 D.L.R. (3d) 113; *Leitz v. Sask. Drug* (1980) 112 D.L.R. (3d) 106.

inducing the contract.[25] In the result, much sales talk reasonably relied upon by trusting buyers has proved a broken reed. In England, South Australia and the Australian Capital Territory at least such misrepresentations, if negligent, have now been declared by statute actionable in damages; elsewhere doubts remain as to the common law position.[26] More important, in Australia the federal *Trade Practices Act* 1974 (Cth) has now made manufacturers liable to the ultimate consumer for breach of express warranty in connection with the promotion of their products.[27]

Quasi-sales

The strict liability incident to the sale of goods has had an osmotic effect on related transactions. An obvious extension was to instalment sales, whether by hire-purchase or otherwise.[28] So also contracts of simple hire (like car or equipment leasing)[29] and contracts for work and materials[30] ordinarily import a warranty, analogous to sale, that the article or material supplied is of good quality and reasonably fit for its agreed or contemplated use. Thus a contractor or repairer in effect guarantees the quality of anything he installs (though concerning his own services no more than reasonable care is required[31] unless he has actually warranted his work[32]). So does a hairdresser with respect to a hair dye[33] and a veterinarian with respect to cattle serum.[34] The reason is that the customer should be no worse off than if he had procured the material himself from the supplier, and the contractor would normally demand indemnity from the supplier so that the cost can eventually be passed on to the responsible manufacturer. Exclusion of these implied terms is generally subject to the same restrictions as in the case of sales.

Extension beyond privity

Privity of contract remained a recalcitrant obstacle to the extension of warranties between buyer and manufacturer. A first step in extending protection for consumer injuries was to replace privity of contract with

25. See below, p. 651.
26. See below, p. 481.
27. Section 76G; also ss 53, 82 (false representations in connection with supply and promotion of goods or services). Also *Fair Trading Act* 1985 (Vic.) s. 12.
28. *Trade Practices Act* 1974 (Cth) ss 4, 66-74. Warranties are also contained in the various State Hire-Purchase Acts. The Cth statute s. 73 imposes the obligations exclusively on the dealer; others impose it on the seller (financier): e.g. *Consumer Transactions Act* 1972 (S.A.) s. 13.
29. *Derbyshire Building Co. v. Becker* (1962) 107 C.L.R. 633.
30. *Young & Marten v. McManus* [1969] 1 A.C. 454; *Reg. Glass v. Rivers* (1968) 120 C.L.R. 516; *Laminated v. Woodworkers* [1962] S.C.R. 160; *Trade Practices Act* 1974 (Cth) s. 74; *Goods Act* (Vic.) Pt IV; *Supply of Goods and Services Act* 1982 (Eng.) s. 4(4) and (5).
31. See statutes cited above, n. 30.
32. As in *Schreiber Roofing v. Steel Co.* (1964) 48 D.L.R. (2d) 212 (Ont. C.A.).
33. *Samuels v. Davis* [1943] K.B. 526 (C.A.). But customer must disclose allergy: *Ingham v. Emes* [1955] 2 Q.B. 366 (C.A.).
34. *Dodd v. Wilson* [1946] 2 All E.R. 691. Not so blood transfused by hospital: *E v. Australian Red Cross* (1991) 105 A.L.R. 53 (F.C.).

privity of title to include the relation between manufacturer and the retail *buyer*. Following pioneering statutes in South Australia and the Australian Capital Territory,[35] the Australian national *Trade Practices Act*[36] imposed the familiar express and implied sales warranties[37] on manufacturing corporations[38] in favour of the consumer to whom defective "goods of a kind ordinarily acquired for personal, domestic or household use or consumption" are supplied and, in the case of unmerchantable quality, to anyone deriving title through him. Other users and "innocent bystanders" remain outside the pale and had to await the introduction of strict *tort* liability by the more recent reform discussed in s. 3 below. But unlike the last-mentioned, damages are not limited to personal injury and (other) property loss, but include economic loss, such as the depreciated value of, or damage to, the defective product itself.[39] The warranties cannot be excluded, and time does not run until the consumer first became, or ought reasonably to have become, aware of the defect.

2. NEGLIGENCE

Warranty for long offered the only avenue of redress for those injured by defective products. Its limitations became the more frustrating with the transformation in the system of producing and marketing of goods in the course of the last 150 years. The developing mass market entailed an almost universal dependence on wholesalers and retailers for efficient distribution of products. The intervention of these middlemen severed privity between manufacturer and consumer and thereby impaired the effectiveness of warranties. By availing himself of modern advertising methods, the manufacturer was able to "produce the psychological effect of representation without incurring its penalties".[40]

Yet until well within the 20th century the law of torts turned a deaf ear to pleas for extending the responsibility of suppliers to persons other than their immediate transferees. The theoretical obstacle was another version of the privity rule which derived from *Winterbottom v. Wright*,[41] enunciated in 1842. It was there held that one who had let a mail coach to the plaintiff's employer with an undertaking to keep it in repair was not liable to the coachman who was injured by reason of a defective axle. Narrowly construed, the decision went no further than the axiom that A cannot found a claim against B for a breach of contract, subsisting between B and C, to which he (A) is not a party; but it was interpreted in the wider sense that

35. Respectively, *Manufacturers Warranty Act* 1974 and *Law Reform (Manufacturers Warranties) Act* 1977. Both extend *all* warranties to the purchaser and anyone deriving title through him, and complement the federal *Trade Practices Act*.
36. *Trade Practices Act* s. 74 (Pt V, Div. 2A). See Gregg & Tzovaras, 10 Fed. L. Rev. 398 (1979). Actions exclusively in State courts: *Zavavinos v. Dairy Farmers* (1983) 59 A.L.R. 603.
37. Somewhat more qualified, e.g. when the defect is attributable to someone else's act or default or to a cause independent of human control.
38. Because passed pursuant to the "corporations" power. But see also s. 6(2)(c) for additional interstate coverage.
39. Section 82. But no exemplary damages: *Musca v. Asle Corp.* (1988) 80 A.L.R. 251 at 262.
40. *Foote v. Wilson* 178 P. 430 (Kan. 1919).
41. (1842) 10 M. & W. 109; 152 E.R. 402.

conduct which constitutes a breach of a contractual obligation to C could not concurrently furnish a cause of action for breach of a *tort* duty to A. This fallacy supported the conclusion that the manufacturer of a defective article owed a duty to those alone who were in contractual privity with him. Apart from the non-sequitur, it ignored the critical distinction between non-feasance and misfeasance: in *Winterbottom* the lessor was charged merely with an omission, and a duty to act could be founded on contract alone; whereas the manufacturer would have actively created the risk in breach of a tort duty not to injure consumers. But behind the explanation that otherwise there was "no point at which such an action would stop", there lay in all probability the conviction that it was in the best interest of the community to foster the growth of industry by arbitrarily limiting the liability of manufacturers to their immediate transferees.

Gradually, exceptions were engrafted which paved the way to its ultimate reversal.[42] Apart from cases where the supplier had knowingly made a false representation of safety[43] or, aware of the defect, had failed to give warning,[44] the most disruptive force was a duty of care appertaining to articles which fell into the ambiguous and ever expanding category of "inherently dangerous" things.[45] This formula was at best a transparent device for whittling away the immunity before the time had arrived for its outright rejection; it was arbitrary in operation and misconceived in principle because the crux of the matter was whether the article was dangerous when carelessly, not when carefully, made.

Following the momentous opinion in 1916 by Cardozo J. of New York in *MacPherson v. Buick Motor Co.*,[46] the House of Lords in 1932 eventually closed this lengthy chapter of equivocation by adopting, in *Donoghue v. Stevenson*,[47] the general principle of liability for articles dangerous when negligently made. The plaintiff alleged injury as the result of consuming ginger beer from an opaque bottle ordered by a friend at a local café, which contained the decomposed remains of a snail. By a narrow majority it was held that these facts, if proved, disclosed a cause of action against the maker of the beverage. The guiding principle was formulated by Lord Atkin in these terms: "A manufacturer of products which he sells in such a form as to show that he intends them to reach the ultimate consumer in the form in which they left him with no reasonable possibility of intermediate examination, and with the knowledge that the absence of reasonable care in the preparation or putting up of the products will result in an injury to the consumer's life or property, owes a duty to the consumer to take that reasonable care."[48] The wider rationale was that one who brings himself into a relation with others through an activity which foreseeably exposes them to danger if proper care is not observed, must

42. This process of erosion is dramatically described by Levi, *Introduction to Legal Reasoning* (1950) 6-19.
43. *Langridge v. Levy* (1837) 2 M. & W. 519; 150 E.R. 863.
44. *Heaven v. Pender* (1883) 11 Q.B.D. 503 at 517.
45. See e.g. *Faulkner v. Wischer* [1918] V.L.R. 513. The test was first propounded in *Longmeid v. Holliday* (1851) 6 Ex. 761; 155 E.R. 752.
46. 217 N.Y. 382; 111 N.E. 1050.
47. [1932] A.C. 562. More light on the dramatis personae: Rodger, *Mrs Donoghue and Alfenus Varus*, 41 Cur. L. Prob. 1 (1988); McBryde, *The Story of the "Snail in the Bottle" Case*, in *The Paisley Papers* 25 (1991).
48. [1932] A.C. 562 at 599.

exercise reasonable care to safeguard them from physical injury. The relation arises from conduct and creates a duty notwithstanding the absence of a contractual tie between the parties.[49]

Plaintiffs and products

From the outset, the new mandate was implemented with little hesitation and increasing liberality. Responsibility not being tied to privity runs even beyond the ultimate consumer or user[50] to "innocent bystanders", in short, to everyone within the foreseeable range of the product's harmful effects. In the case of a defective car this may include, besides the driver and passenger, other road users[51] and even repairmen[52]—all alike within "the vicinity of its probable use".[53]

Responsibility, far from being limited to food and drink,[54] was progressively applied to such varied commodities as cosmetics,[55] underwear,[56] motor cars,[57] lifts,[58] and eventually even to houses.[59] It covers all products, natural or processed, which are not reasonably safe to the life, health or property of others. Excluded only are products whose sole risk is economic loss (like a carpet with a disfiguring flaw): these fall to the province of warranty, express or implied, but not of tort.[60]

Defects

Danger from products may stem from negligence in the process of manufacture, design or marketing. The first category, production defects (bench errors) are least problematical. By definition, the flawed product does not conform to the manufacturer's own design specifications and is usually an isolated deviant. The proper standard of product safety is not therefore in controversy and the extent of potential liability is limited. Whether the fault be managerial or vicarious, realistically it is attributable to inadequate quality control. Both on grounds of social responsibility and economic efficiency, the cost of such failure should be borne by (internalised to) the product.

Design defects present greater problems of proof and policy. Since the design itself is challenged, the standard of reasonable safety to which it

49. See above, p. 139.
50. As in *Barnett v. Packer* [1940] 3 All E.R. 575 (ultimate purchaser); *Donoghue v. Stevenson* [1932] A.C. 562 (lady friend); *Adelaide Chemical Co. v. Carlyle* (1940) 64 C.L.R. 514 and *Mason v. Williams* [1955] 1 W.L.R. 549 (his employee); *Power v. Bedford Motor Co.* [1959] I.R. 391 (subsequent owner of repaired car).
51. *Stennett v. Hancock* [1939] 2 All E.R. 578; *Marschler v. Masser's Garage* (1956) 2 D.L.R. (2d) 484.
52. *Hobbs Manufacturing v. Shields* [1962] S.C.R. 716; *Daley v. Gypsy Caravan* [1966] 2 N.S.W.R. 22.
53. The formulation is that of *Rest.* §395.
54. Supply of noxious drinking water: *Read v. Croydon Corp.* [1938] 4 All E.R. 631; *Barnes v. Irwell Valley* [1939] 1 K.B. 21.
55. *Watson v. Buckley* [1940] 1 All E.R. 174.
56. *Grant v. Australian Knitting Mills* [1936] A.C. 85; 54 C.L.R. 49.
57. *Herschtal v. Stewart & Ardern* [1940] 1 K.B. 155.
58. *Haseldine v. Daw* [1941] 2 K.B. 343.
59. See above, p. 473.
60. See below, p. 495.

should conform is not a "given" (unless laid down by statute)[61] but must be determined by balancing the risk of harm against the cost of reducing or preventing it by an alternative design. This presents little difficulty where the design is self-defeating, like a collapsing crane,[62] malfunctioning carburettor or exploding drain solvent.[63] In other cases, a safer design, such as provision of a guard on a lawnmower, might have reduced or negated the risk.[64] Much more complex are cases where the particular design did not cause the accident but at most failed to protect against its consequences, for example in complaints that a car was not crashworthy, that is, did not offer sufficient protection in a collision caused by the driver's or a third party's negligence.[65] In principle, that should be no obstacle, since it is well established that negligence may consist in failing to avoid aggravation of injuries, as by omitting to wear a seatbelt.[66] Typically the design is the outcome of a conscious choice, often made by the manufacturer on the basis of relative cost so as to accommodate consumer preferences or even the public interest (for example light cars offer less collision protection but are cheaper and save petrol). Some caution in reviewing such managerial decisions is appropriate because the judicial system is ill-equipped to cope with such "polycentric" issues.[67] Moreover, an adverse decision condemns the whole production line and therefore has far greater cost implications.[68]

Lastly, there may be negligence in marketing the product, exemplified by wrong labelling[69] or failure to warn of dangerous qualities.[70] Many products, however carefully made, entail irreducible risks, like medical drugs with harmful side effects or cosmetics harmful only to allergic users.[71] Because their potential benefit outweighs those risks, their distribution cannot be condemned as negligent, but suitable warnings can

61. In Britain regulations under the *Consumer Protection Act* 1961 lay down safety requirements for an increasing range of goods. Violation is actionable against any seller in the chain of supply and imports strict liability.
62. *Rivtow Marine v. Washington Iron Works* [1974] S.C.R. 1189.
63. E.g. *Lambert v. Lewis* [1982] A.C. 225 (trailer coupling); *Adelaide Chemical Co. v. Carlyle* (1940) 64 C.L.R. 514 (unsuitable container); *Nicholson v. J. Deere* (1986) 34 D.L.R. (4th) 542 (lawnmower: warning insufficient where safer alternative available). But to what extent should a product be proof against wear and tear? *Bull v. Rover Mowers* [1984] 2 Qd R. 489 took a very lenient view.
64. *Shepherd v. S. J. Banks* (1987) 45 S.A.S.R. 437.
65. E.g. *Gallant v. Beitz* (1983) 148 D.L.R. (3d) 522.
66. See above, p. 268.
67. These difficulties are magnified where the basis of liability is strict rather than negligence because the focus is then solely on the product rather than also on the producer. See Henderson, 73 Col. L. Rev. 1531 (1973). American experience suggests that, in any event, only a negligence standard can really be applied in determining design safety.
68. E.g. *Wyngrove's Curator v. Scottish Omnibuses* [1966] S.C. (H.L.) 47 (600 buses carrying 200,000 passengers each year without such accident).
69. E.g. *Kubach v. Hollands* [1937] 3 All E.R. 907.
70. See *Vacwell Engineering v. B.D.H. Chemicals* [1971] 1 Q.B. 88 (explosion on contact with water); *Cuckow v. Polyester* (1970) 19 F.L.R. 122 (smoke of insulating material); *Murphy v. Alt. Propane* (1979) 103 D.L.R. (3d) 545 (failure to odourise gas); *O'Dwyer v. Leo Buring* [1966] W.A.R. 67 (exploding cork); *Distillers v. Thompson* [1971] A.C. 458 (hence defendant's act which created the cause of complaint was failure to warn in N.S.W. where Thalidomide was marketed). For warnings and other precautions in handling "inherently dangerous" things see below, p. 490; for breach of contract: see Macleod, *Instructions as to Use of Consumer Goods*, 97 L.Q.R. 550 (1981).
71. *Devilez v. Boots* (1962) 106 Sol. J. 552.

either render them safe or at least give the user an informed choice whether to run the risk. In the case of a prescription drug, it should be sufficient to warn the physician who exercises his professional judgment whether to prescribe it or not and on whose judgment, rather than on the drug manufacturer, the patient relies.[72] Exceptional perhaps are IUDs and oral contraceptives, the choice of which is primarily dictated by the patient and in which the intermediacy of the physician plays a secondary role.[73] In general, warnings are cheap and offer an easy alternative to more costly design changes; but for that very reason, the duty to warn, being lightly invoked, has explosive potential for products liability.[74] Mere suspicion of the risk has been said to be sufficient to trigger the duty.[75]

A duty to warn can of course be demanded only when the risk is known or should have been known. But it may arise not only when the product is first put on the market, but also as soon as dangerous qualities become (or should become) known thereafter. In that event, the manufacturer must either cease production or henceforth attach a warning;[76] indeed, he may have to warn or recall items already marketed.[77]

The product must be reasonably safe not only for its intended but for its foreseeable use. Thus motor vehicles must give reasonable protection against rear-end collisions; and warning is required against leaving a toxic product within reach of little children or against accidentally spilling it over sensitive parts of the body.[77a]

Proof

The standard of responsibility demanded from manufacturers quickly assumed some characteristics of strict liability through the operation of the procedural device of res ipsa loquitur. Less than four years after *Donoghue v. Stevenson*, the Privy Council rejected the contention that the maxim was inapplicable merely because the manufacturer relinquishes control on releasing the article upon the market and intermediaries handle it before it reaches the consumer.[78] Control during the process of manufacture was

72. The "learned intermediary" rule is generally accepted in the U.S. by analogy to "intermediate examination" (below, p. 488). See *Buchan v. Ortho* (1986) 25 D.L.R. (4th) 658 (Ont. C.A.). Cf. *Wright v. Dunlop Rubber* (1972) 13 K.I.R. 255 (sufficiency of warning to employer). Criticised: Ferguson, 12 Oxf. J.L. St. 59 (1992); Peppin, 70 Can. B. Rev. 473 (1991).
73. *Buchan*. U.S. is divided: see *Humes v. Clinton* 792 P. 2d 1032 (Ky. 1990).
74. As American experience bears out.
75. *Wright v. Dunlop Rubber* (above at 271). A much more lenient standard was postulated in *Thompson v. Johnson & Johnson* (1991) 2 V.R. 449 (tampons).
76. *Wright v. Dunlop Rubber Co.* at 272.
77. *Thompson v. Johnson & Johnson* (tampons); *Rivtow Marine v. Washington Iron Works* [1974] S.C.R. 1189; *Trade Practices Act* 1974 (Cth) s. 65F. Such a continuing duty has a parallel also in the law of misrepresentation (below, p. 147) and is assisted by the fact that the cause of action in tort (unlike warranty) is incomplete until injury. This point in time determines the *when* (*Watson v. Fram Concrete* 1960 S.C. (H.L.) 92), though not necessarily the *where* for purposes of jurisdiction or choice of law: *Distillers v. Thompson* [1971] A.C. 458 (P.C.); *Moran v. Pyle National* [1975] 1 S.C.R. 393; Fridman, *Where is a Tort Committed*, 24 U. Tor. L.J. 247 (1974).
77a. *Derilez v. Boots Pure Drug Co.* (1962) 106 Sol. Jo. 552.
78. *Grant v. Australian Knitting Mills* [1936] A.C. 85, strikingly rev. (1933) 50 C.L.R. 387 at 409.

sufficient, once the plaintiff has eliminated himself and other extraneous forces as likely causes of the injury. The maxim has been applied to toxic underwear,[79] an exploding light bulb,[80] a stone in a bun[81] and fire in a television set.[82] The inference raised in these cases is twofold: it suggests either the manufacturer's negligence in using an improper system of work or the carelessness of his employees[83] in failing to carry out the system properly. The crucial point is that the plaintiff "is not required to lay his finger on the exact person in all the chain who was responsible, or to specify what he did wrong,"[84] and, in order to exculpate himself, the defendant must disprove *both* hypotheses—in particular, that his employees were not negligent—a daunting task.[85]

The practical result of thus shifting the onus of proof is to make the manufacturer virtually an insurer against manufacturing defects,[86] thereby complementing the strict liability to which he is already exposed—if indirectly—through the operation of successive warranties reaching down the chain of distribution to the ultimate purchaser of his products. Its impact on the manufacturing industry, however, was rather modest because, far from demanding higher standards of performance, it merely spread the mantle of protection for the benefit of these casualties to whom the shibboleth of privity or exemption clauses (in fine print) capriciously deny redress for breach of warranty.

But all this is still a far cry from assuring compensation for every accident caused by a defective product. In the first place, a manufacturer is only responsible for the condition in which he released the article and not for flaws subsequently introduced in the process of marketing and use. This truism, as valid for strict liability as for negligence, defeats any recourse to res ipsa loquitur unless the plaintiff is able to eliminate the likelihood of other responsible causes. Hence, although the possibility of intermediate tampering or deterioration no longer categorically relieves a manufacturer and only goes to the question of proof, in practice it is much easier to disprove in the case of food and other products in sealed containers than articles more vulnerable to interference in the course of distribution.

In the case of exploding bottles, for example, the probability must be that the defect is attributable to the bottler (excessive carbonation or defective bottle) rather than to subsequent handling by the carrier, retailer or consumer.[87] In regard to articles for use rather than consumption, there

79. Ibid.
80. *Martin v. Thorn Industries* [1978] W.A.R. 10.
81. *Chaproniere v. Mason* (1905) 21 T.L.R. 633; *Tarling v. Nobel* [1966] Arg. L.R. 189 (bone in chicken sandwich); *Zeppa v. Coca-Cola* [1955] 5 D.L.R. 187 (glass in soft drink).
82. *MacLachlan v. Frank's Rental* (1979) 10 C.C.L.T. 306.
83. Vicarious liability is of course a sufficient ground, which is not disproved by adequate supervision: *Martin v. Thorn Industries* [1978] W.A.R. 10.
84. *Grant v. Australian Knitting Mills* [1936] A.C. 85 at 101 per Lord Wright.
85. In *Grant v. Australian Knitting Mills* it did not help defendant that over 5-year period when 5 mill. garments were sold no complaint had been received. In practice the standard may be as high as applied in *Smedleys v. Bread* [1974] A.C. 839, construing "unavoidable" as unpreventable.
86. "The care necessary approximates to and almost becomes an absolute liability" (*Shandloff v. City Dairy* [1936] 4 D.L.R. 712 at 719).
87. See *Kilgannon v. Sharpe Bros* (1986) 4 N.S.W.L.R. 600; *Fletcher v. Toppers Drinks* [1981] 2 N.S.W.L.R. 911.

remains the problem of the defect being due to wear and tear, inadequate maintenance or faulty repairs; and the more protracted the use, the more formidable the array of hypotheses, prone to stifle any claim against the manufacturer to extinction.[88] Finally, even if the flaw can be shown to have existed when the product left the defendant's factory, res ipsa loquitur may yet prove a broken reed either because the defect is traced to a component part procured from a subcontractor—and what slender authority there is disclaims any vicarious liability by the manufacturer of a finished product for the negligence of the maker of the component part[89]—or because conjecture as to the cause of the accident remains equally balanced between two components, for only one of which the defendant would be responsible.[90] The increasing complexity of modern machinery, combined with spreading reliance on outside supply for specialised parts, gives growing prominence to these difficulties of proof which are often magnified, especially in the case of motor cars, by the likelihood that the accident destroyed much of the evidence.[91]

There remains one other important difference between negligence (even aided by res ipsa loquitur) and warranty or strict liability. In determining the requisite standard of safety, negligence does not demand more than what reasonable care should have assured. A significant contributon to accident prevention is made by statutory safety standards, violation of which, moreover, an injured plaintiff may invoke as breach of statutory duty.[92] But negligence law does not demand protection against risks which the highest standard of quality control could not have eliminated. Excluded therefore are defects which are (practically) undiscoverable, like serum hepatitis in blood plasma; even more, risks which remained unknown despite all proper precautions, as possibly with new drugs.[93] Unlike extravagant extensions of the American law of strict liability,[94] the appropriate standard regarding knowledge of the risk and feasibility of precautions is determined by the "state of existing art", not imputed hindsight.[95]

Mass disasters resulting from harmful products often pose additional problems of proof, causation being particularly troublesome in case of pharmaceuticals and chemicals. The plaintiff may be unable to establish on a balance of probabilities which of several manufacturers of a generic

88. E.g. *Evans v. Triplex Glass* [1936] 1 All E.R. 283 (fragmented windscreen); *Phillips v. Chrysler Corp.* (1962) 32 D.L.R. (2d) 347 (intervening repairs); *Phillips v. Ford Motor Co.* (1971) 18 D.L.R. (3d) 641 (repairer); *Hart v. Bell Telephone* (1979) 10 C.C.L.T. 335 (TV used by eight lessees in 1½ years).
89. See below, p. 492.
90. See above, p. 199.
91. See *Phillips v. Chrysler Corp.* (1962) 32 D.L.R. (2d) 347.
92. Some modern Consumer Protection Acts expressly confer a cause of action for breach of safety regulations: e.g. *Consumer Protection Act* of N.S.W. (1969 ss 38, 39G) and Eng. (1961 s. 2); *Consumer Affairs Act* of Vic. (1972 s. 61) and W.A. (1971 s. 23T). See also *Trade Practices Act* 1974 (Cth) s. 82.
93. On serum hepatitis see Kessel, *Transfused Blood, Serum Hepatitis and the Coase Theorem*, 17 J. Law & Econ. 265 (1974); on "development risks" Teff, *Products Liability in the Pharmaceutical Industry*, 20 McG. L.J. 102 (1974).
94. E.g. *Beshada v. Johns-Manville* 447 A. 2d 539 (N.J. 1982) (mesothelioma, 1930s). See Henderson, *Coping with the Time Dimension*, 69 Cal. L. Rev. 919 (1981).
95. E.g. *Footner v. B.H. Smelters* (1983) 33 S.A.S.R. 58 (mesothelioma, 1944-1952).

product was the one that caused his injury or that his injury was due to the defendant's product or emission rather than to one of natural origin in the environment.[96] Some American courts have relaxed the traditional standard of proof by either shifting the burden to defendants once shown to have been negligent, by relaxing the conditions of joint liability for acting in concert, or by reducing the defendants' liability to their probabilistic share of the disaster.[97] The high expense of separate individual actions also tends to impede access to justice; class actions are not generally possible under prevailing rules of procedure.[98]

Intermediate examination

Lord Atkin's original insistence that the manufacturer must have sold his products "in such a form as to show that he intends them to reach the ultimate consumer in the form in which they left him" gave some semblance of support to the argument that responsibility did not attach unless the defective article was put out in a sealed container. This restrictive interpretation was soon rejected. In *Grant v. Australian Knitting Mills*,[99] underpants which contained a noxious chemical and caused dermatitis were in fact wrapped in paper packets but opened by the retailer prior to sale. The manufacturer was nevertheless held liable because the previous judicial emphasis on "control" was merely intended to draw attention to "the essential factor that the consumer must use the article exactly as it left the maker, that is in all its material features, and use it as it was intended to be used. In that sense, the maker may be said to control the thing until it is used."[100] The possibility of intermediate tampering with the article, therefore, goes only to burden of proof, not to the existence of duty.

A further and related limitation, suggested in Lord Atkin's original formulation, was that responsibility was excluded by a "reasonable possibility of intermediate examination".[101] Progressive interpretation, however, has dispelled the view that a mere opportunity for inspecting the product after the defendant has parted with it is sufficient to excuse him.[102] Indeed, with the decay of older causal theories of "last opportunity" and "last wrongdoer", a defendant cannot any longer even claim exemption merely because an intermediary was under a duty of inspection and was negligent in either failing to carry it out or in doing it improperly.[103] Rather, the dual fault in such cases gives rise to concurrent liability, enabling the victim to have recourse against both.

96. See *Sindell v. Abbott Laboratories* 607 P. 2d 924 (Cal. 1980). See above, p. 200.
97. Ibid.
98. *G.M. of Canada v. Naken* [1983] 1 S.C.R. 72; generally, Ontario Law Reform Commission, *Report on Class Actions* (1982). Even American courts are reluctant to certify a class action in mass products cases: see Fleming, *Process* ch. 7.
99. [1936] A.C. 85.
100. Ibid. at 104. Hence, that the article was intended to be mixed or likely to be used in conjunction with some other substance does not necessarily exclude liability: *Grant v. Cooper* [1940] N.Z.L.R. 947; *Willis v. F.M.C.* (1976) 68 D.L.R. (3d) 127.
101. *Donoghue v. Stevenson* [1932] A.C. 562 at 599.
102. *Herschtal v. Stewart & Ardern* [1940] 1 K.B. 155; *Haseldine v. Daw* [1941] 2 K.B. 343 at 375-377.
103. See *Grant v. Sun Shipping* [1948] A.C. 549 at 563-564; *Miller v. Electricity Bd* 1958 S.C. (H.L.) 20; *Power v. Bedford Motor Co.* [1959] I.R. 391.

If "possibility" of intermediate examination will not excuse, would "probability"? The answer is—only if the defendant was justified in regarding the expected test as sufficient to defuse the danger prior to use and thus provide a safeguard to persons who might otherwise be harmed. A vague warning, for example, that the repair carried out on a car was only "temporary", might not be enough to alert an ordinary customer.[104] Nor would the mere fact of a governmental certification.[105] On the other hand, a hair dye manufacturer may well be entitled to rely on professional hairdressers heeding instructions specially addressed to them before applying the product to customers.[106] All the more is it a defence that some person, duty bound to deal with such a situation, acquired actual knowledge of the defect; as when a foreman, after being himself hurt by a defective tool, failed to either withdraw it from circulation or report the incident.[107]

In short, the ordinary rules of remoteness are no less applicable here than in other areas of negligence, that is, subject to the broad and increasingly liberal test of foreseeability. Thus not even the unauthorised removal by an independent deliveryman of a grounding prong from a refrigerator could preclude the manufacturer from being liable to a user for an electric shock caused by defective wiring.[108] A safety feature cannot exempt a manufacturer from his duty to provide a non-defective product, when it is not foolproof and its removal is foreseeable. It was just like leaving a loaded gun around whose safety catch is later released by a meddler: no new force is added, rather a dormant force is unchained.

Contributory negligence—misuse

Much the same applies to inspections by the ultimate consumer himself. Since apportionment, however, a distinction must now be drawn between mere contributory negligence by the plaintiff and the negation of all duty by the defendant: for the first (unlike the second) will now only reduce the claim instead of defeating it entirely. The tendency has become not to acquit the defendant of all responsibility, unless the victim had been aware of the defect with full appreciation of the attendant risk[109] or unless, at the very least, he could reasonably have been expected to make his own inspection sufficient to alert him to the danger and confront it with safety.[110] A repairer, for example, called in to deal with the precise cause of the danger cannot recover, because he can be expected to look out for himself.[111] Otherwise, however, his failure to guard himself will only be treated as contributory negligence, as when an electrician failed to "ground" a

104. *Jull v. Wilson* [1968] N.Z.L.R. 88.
105. *Willis v. F.M.C.* (1976) 68 D.L.R. (3d) 127.
106. *Holmes v. Ashford* [1950] 2 All E.R. 76; *Kubach v. Hollands* [1937] 3 All E.R. 907.
107. *Taylor v. Rover Co.* [1966] 1 W.L.R. 1491.
108. *Smith v. Inglis* (1978) 83 D.L.R. (3d) 215.
109. As in *Farr v. Butters* [1932] 2 K.B. 606. Unless apparently, it could reasonably be assumed that the plaintiff despite his knowledge might still reasonably incur the risk, no practical alternative being open: *Denny v. Supplies & Transport* [1950] 2 K.B. 374.
110. See *Jull v. Wilson* [1968] N.Z.L.R. 88, modifying *Cathcart v. Hull* [1963] N.Z.L.R. 333. Some of the older cases are now tainted with obsolescence.
111. *Daley v. Gypsy Caravan* [1966] 2 N.S.W.R. 22 (C.A.).

machine in the process of installation and was electrocuted owing to faulty wiring in a sealed switchbox.[112]

In this connection, no categorical distinction can be drawn between latent and patent dangers. The user, especially an employee at work, may have no practical alternative to encountering a known risk, for example in adjusting an unguarded machine while it is in operation. In that case, the manufacturer can be said to have induced him to incur the risk and cannot avoid responsibility by pleading that the operator assumed it with open eyes.[113]

A manufacturer or other supplier of chattels bears responsibility only for dangers they pose in the contemplated use. If rendered dangerous only because handled in an improper or otherwise unforeseeable manner, they are simply not "defective" in any relevant sense. For example, a ladder does not have to be capable of supporting the weight of two men using it as a horizontal platform between uprights.[114] Nor need covers or guards on a machine be designed so as to be irremovable.[115] But the usual stress in this context on "contemplated" or "intended" use is only a synonym for, and not meant to abridge, responsibility for dangers arising from any "reasonably foreseeable use". A misuse from the manufacturer's point of view may be a possible use or mode of operation that should have been foreseen and guarded against. Or if the environment in which the product will probably be used poses a substantial risk of misuse, such as infants tampering with poisonous furniture polish, reasonable care may well call for a warning label or other special precaution.[116]

Inherently dangerous chattels

The category of things "dangerous in themselves" or, as they are sometimes called, "inherently dangerous" long used to hold a special place in our law of negligence. The danger is said to be inherent when it derives from the nature of the chattel itself, as opposed to hazards associated with a defectively made product that is otherwise harmless—the difference, in a nutshell, between poison, which is fraught with constant and invariable peril, and ginger beer which is ordinarily innocuous in the absence of some extraneous, hazard-creating factor.[117]

The only *legitimate* function which this distinction serves is to focus attention on the fact that, whereas liability for a defectively made article is

112. *Hobbs Manufacturing Co. v. Shields* [1962] S.C.R. 716; *Smith v. Inglis* (1978) 83 D.L.R. (3d) 215.
113. *Suosaari v. Steinhardt* [1989] 2 Qd R. 477 (F.C.).
114. *Campbell v. O'Donnell* [1967] I.R. 226; also *Poole v. Crittal Metal Windows* [1964] N.Z.L.R. 522 (C.A.). But see *Hill v. Crowe* [1978] 1 All E.R. 812 (stood on box).
115. *Dallaire v. P.-E. Martell* [1989] 2 S.C.R. 419.
116. *Spruill v. Boyle-Midway* 308 F. 2d 79 (4 Cir. 1962).
117. Examples of items within the category are loaded guns (*Burfitt v. Kille* [1939] 2 K.B. 743), detonators (*McCarthy v. Wellington City* [1966] N.Z.L.R. 481), sulphuric acid (*Adelaide Chemical Co. v. Carlyle* (1940) 64 C.L.R. 514), mustard gas (*Swinton v. China M.S.N.* (1951) 83 C.L.R. 553), and an explosive fluid (*Anglo-Celtic S. Co. v. Elliott* (1926) 42 T.L.R. 297; *Ayoub v. Beaupré* 1964 S.C.R. 448); outside it are bow and arrows (*Ricketts v. Erith B.C.* [1943] 2 All E.R. 629), a catapult (*Smith v. Leurs* (1945) 70 C.L.R. 256 at 259), a long-spouted can (*Wray v. Essex C.C.* [1936] 3 All E.R. 97), a locked sedan with a dog inside it (*Fardon v. Harcourt-Rivington* (1932) 48 T.L.R. 215), and a domestic steam boiler: *Ball v. L.C.C.* [1949] 2 K.B. 159.

primarily based on negligence in causing the defect,[118] the hazard peculiar to inherently dangerous commodities stems from failure to give notice of the danger. In other words, the negligence, if any, is associated with the distributive rather than the manufacturing process. Unfortunately, this aspect was obscured when the category of things dangerous per se emerged in mid 19th century[119] as a ploy for narrowing the immunity afforded by the privity rule to manufacturers of negligently *defective* products. Henceforth, a duty of care was demanded for the manufacture of dangerous things, though not yet of products ordinarily harmless unless negligently made. *Donoghue v. Stevenson* eventually dispensed with this devious use of the category, though an analogous function in limiting the liability of contractors and landlords for negligent installations actually survived for another 25 years.[120] Its only remaining significance in this respect is a reminder that, though no longer a determinant of duty, inherently dangerous things may yet call for more in the way of fulfilling that duty, commensurate with their aggravated risk.[121]

Thus the degree of requisite diligence has been variously described as amounting "practically to a guarantee of safety",[122] to an "insurance against risk", postulating the observance of "consummate care".[123] A warning would not be sufficient unless it is given to a competent person and adequate to acquaint him fully with the dangerous properties of the substance so that he can himself adopt suitable precautions to prevent it from becoming a source of injury to himself and others.[124]

But however strict, liability is not completely unqualified and requires some showing of fault, however slight.[125] Some substances, like explosives and poison, can never be made entirely safe and protected against every conceivable interference by extraneous elements. In such cases, the duty ought to be regarded as discharged if the custodian selects a method of storing which, so far as humanly possible, eliminates the danger of explosion and reduces to a minimum the possibility that persons unacquainted with its dangerous character could gain access to it. Yet how exacting the standard in practice is dramatically illustrated by a New

118. In exceptional cases it may also be based on failure to detect a defect by reasonable inspection.
119. *Longmeid v. Holliday* (1851) 6 Ex. 761; 155 E.R. 752.
120. *Billings (A.C.) v. Riden* [1958] A.C. 240.
121. *Donoghue v. Stevenson* [1932] A.C. 562 at 596; *Todman v. Victa* [1982] V.R. 849; *Beckett v. Newalls* [1953] 1 W.L.R. 8 at 15; *Rae v. Eaton Co.* (1961) 28 D.L.R. (2d) 522.
122. *Donoghue v. Stevenson* [1932] A.C. 562 at 612 per Lord Macmillan. This has been repeatedly endorsed, e.g. *Ayoub v. Beaupré* [1964] S.C.R. 448 at 451; *Holinaty v. Hawkins* (1965) 52 D.L.R. (2d) 289.
123. *Adelaide Chemical Co. v. Carlyle* (1940) 64 C.L.R. 514 at 522-523 per Starke J.
124. Cf. *Norton v. Streets Ice Cream* (1968) 120 C.L.R. 635 ("highly inflammable" sufficient) with *Lambert v. Lastoplex* [1972] S.C.R. 569 (insufficient). Also *Streets Ice Cream v. Australia Asbestos* [1967] 1 N.S.W.R. 50; *Ward v. Hopkins* [1959] 3 All E.R. 225 at 239; *Ruegger v. Shell Oil* (1963) 41 D.L.R. (2d) 183 (2-4D). Products for the retail market should carry prominent warning on their labels, but if for specialist use only, like hair dye supplied to hairdressers, it is sufficient to warn the latter alone and rely on them to take the directed precautions: *Holmes v. Ashford* [1950] 2 All E.R. 76.
125. *Hercules Textile Mills v. Textile Engineers* [1955] V.L.R. 310 at 313. *Ives v. Clare Bros* (1970) 15 D.L.R. (3d) 529 suggests a rebuttable presumption of negligence. The dangerous nature of the article, if not notorious, must have been known to the defendant: *Imperial Furniture v. Automatic Fire Sprinklers* [1967] 1 N.S.W.R. 29.

Zealand decision[126] which declined to excuse a defendant for storing detonators in a metal box on a high shelf in a dark corner of a disused house on an isolated farm, when a labourer who took shelter there from the rain on his way to work cleaned out the detonator in ignorance of its nature and was killed by an explosion.

Nor is the duty in cases such as these owed only to persons who unwittingly pick up the explosive or perhaps those who are injured in the immediate vicinity. It has been held to be foreseeable, for example, that teenagers might break into an insufficiently secured safe in an open quarry containing detonators and, unaware of the risk, give them to another child who inadvertently sets off an explosion after having taken them home.[127]

Responsibility for taking precautions rests not only on the manufacturer but on everyone alike who transfers a dangerous thing to another or has custody or control over it. Here, at any rate, it is irrelevant that the defendant is only a gratuitous bailor, donor[128] or mere distributor who has not himself increased the hazard inherent in the object beyond creating an opportunity where it might cause harm to others, as when a shopkeeper sold a dangerous toy pistol to a child of 12 who injured a companion with blank ammunition.[129] Moreover, when work is set on foot involving the use of inherently dangerous implements by an independent contractor, his employer is held to vicarious liability for harm resulting from its negligent use.[130]

Manufacturers and other suppliers

The responsibility laid upon manufacturers by *Donoghue v. Stevenson* has been progressively extended to makers of component parts integrated into a final product by someone else,[131] to repairers,[132] erectors,[133] assemblers,[134] even to building contractors who render[135] a chattel, house or structure[136] dangerous. Beyond that, reasonable care demands from those handling or distributing goods some measure of inspection to detect defects in the creation of which they may not have had a hand at all. The maker of a beverage, for instance, owes a duty to inspect the bottles he uses,[137] even if this need not be nearly as exacting as the tests for flaws

126. *Marcroft v. Inger* [1936] N.Z.L.R. 121. But a trespasser was disqualified in *Clayton v. Victoria* [1968] V.R. 562 (sulphuric acid in school laboratory).
127. *McCarthy v. Wellington City* [1966] N.Z.L.R. 481 (C.A.); *Holian v. United Grain* (Man. 1980) 112 D.L.R. (3d) 611.
128. See *Ball v. L.C.C.* [1949] 2 K.B. 159.
129. *Burfitt v. Kille* [1939] 2 K.B. 743.
130. See above, p. 391.
131. *Evans v. Triplex Glass* [1936] 1 All E.R. 283 at 286 (windscreen).
132. *Haseldine v. Daw* [1941] 2 K.B. 343; *Jull v. Wilson* [1968] N.Z.L.R. 88; *Godfrey's v. Ryles* [1962] S.A.S.R. 33. But the repairer may well have been justified in relying on an intermediate examination.
133. *Brown v. Cottrill* (1934) 51 T.L.R. 21.
134. *Stennett v. Hancock* [1939] 2 All E.R. 578; *Howard v. Furness Houlder* [1936] 2 All E.R. 781; *Malfroot v. Noxal* (1935) 51 T.L.R. 551.
135. Even complete failure to repair, as distinct from negligent execution of repair may be a source of tort liability, at least when there is an implied representation that it has been carried out and the article rendered harmless.
136. See above, p. 473.
137. *Hart v. Dominion Stores* (1968) 67 D.L.R. (2d) 675; *Adelaide Chemical Co. v. Carlyle* 64 C.L.R. 514 (unsuitable container).

required from the bottle manufacturer, since to demand more would be needlessly wasteful and often impracticable. Similarly, people who loan out equipment[138] must carry on a reasonable system of maintenance and inspection to minimise the risk of injury to likely users, such as dock workers operating a rented truck[139] or using slings furnished by stevedores for the purpose of their common task of unloading a ship.[140]

Nor are manufacturers of composite products like motor cars absolved from all responsibility for component parts or other fabrication of subcontractors. Their duty of reasonable care is not necessarily exhausted in the selection of specialists who are competent. Car manufacturers, for example, were held remiss in not addressing their engineering skill to the design of a carburettor obtained from a large-scale supplier.[141] More commonly, however, a less exacting standard has been posed, so that if nothing looked amiss to the naked eye, no more probing tests with special equipment were required.[142] So far at least there has been no disposition[143] to adopt the growing American doctrine of making manufacturers of completed products responsible for negligence by anyone in the production process, outsiders no less than their own employees, in token of the consumer reliance on the brand name of the final product sedulously fostered by advertising.[144] Nor is an electricity supplier connecting up a new circuit under any duty to check that the particular unit to be hooked up is safe and properly installed. Earthing a washing machine, for instance, is the job of the electrical contractor who installed it and on whose competence the electricity supplier may rely, at least in the absence of suspicious circumstances.[145] To ask more from him would increase costs with no commensurate benefit of added safety.

Distributors

Retail dealers and other distributors are not altogether exempt from responsibility for defective products manufactured by others. Besides being strictly liable for breach of warranty to their own customers, they also owe an independent duty of care to them and to third parties.

Their duty, in the first place, is to warn of dangers of which they know or should know.[146] This includes a duty to inspect merchandise but one far less demanding than the quality control of manufacturers.[147] None would

138. *White v. John Warwick* [1953] 1 W.L.R. 1285; *Godfrey's v. Ryles* [1962] S.A.S.R. 33.
139. *Sullivan v. Gallagher* 1959 S.C. 243.
140. *Oliver v. Saddler* [1929] A.C. 584.
141. *Winward v. T.V.R. Engineering* [1986] B.T.L.C. 366 (C.A.) imposed on a small firm a duty even to conduct its own engineering review of a Ford design.
142. *Taylor v. Rover Co.* [1966] 1 W.L.R. 1491 (hardening chisels).
143. *Peake v. Steriline Mfg* (1988) A.T.R. 80-154 (regretfully). Contrary (semble) *Farro v. Nutone* (1990) 68 D.L.R. (4th) 268 (Ont. C.A.).
144. E.g. *Boeing v. Brown* 291 F. 2d 310 (9 Cir. 1961); *Rest. 2d* §400. Indeed, "channelling" liability from the component manufacturer to the final assembler makes more insurance sense. See *Goldberg v. Kollsman Instruments* 191 N.E. 2d 81 (N.Y. 1963) (defective altimeter).
145. *Sellars v. Best* [1954] 1 W.L.R. 913.
146. *Rest. 2d* §402 postulates liability only for dangers which they know or "have reason to know". Cf. *Clarke v. Army & Navy* [1903] 1 K.B. 155.
147. Still less than of employers: *Cross v. T.N.T. Management* (1987) 46 S.A.S.R. 105 (importer).

be exacted where it is impossible to test the goods without destroying the condition in which the maker intended them to reach the consumer.[148] Even if the commodity is not packed in a sealed container, the retailer would not be bound to subject it to elaborate tests, since the maker is usually better equipped to do so. He should not, however, be excused from measures which a qualified dealer in that class of merchandise could expediently adopt for the better protection of the consumer. A car dealer would not be inordinately burdened by having to test the brakes and steering,[149] or a department store by ensuring that there is no nail protruding from the inner sole of a shoe offered to a customer.[150] His responsibility is all the greater if he makes any representation that the article is safe.[151] A dealer has a duty to warn even if he becomes aware of the defect only after the sale.[152]

Dealers are of course liable also for creating risks themselves. Their negligence may arise from their manner of handling the product, as when a chemist supplies a doctor with belladonna instead of dandelion extract[153] or a grocer stores tinned food in such a manner that it perishes.[154] It may also consist in selling a chattel to a purchaser whom the dealer knows to be incompetent to handle it safely (like entrusting a gun or a car to a child)[155] or to be bent on using it for a dangerous purpose (like selling a light tyre for a heavy truck).[156]

Even a non-commercial seller, like the private owner of a used car, is under a duty to warn at least if aware of any very real danger of driving it without further examination.[157] It is questionable whether this duty extends also to risks that only an inspection would have revealed.

Donors

In the traditional view, a donor or gratuitous bailor of a chattel is treated just like a licensor of old: indeed, it was he who originally set the pattern for the familiar formula colloquially epitomised in the axiom "one must not look a gift horse in the mouth"—that a gratuitous transferor or licensor need do no more than warn of defects actually known to him,[158] besides abstaining from creating sources of danger by active negligence, like

148. *Gordon v. M'Hardy* (1903) 6 Fraser 210 (tinned salmon); *Rae v. Eaton Co.* (1961) 28 D.L.R. (2d) 522 (aerosol can).
149. See *Andrews v. Hopkinson* [1957] 1 Q.B. 229 (defect in steering of secondhand car detectable by jacking up the car and pulling on ball pin).
150. *Santise v. Martins* 17 N.Y.S. 2d 741 (1940) (store held liable).
151. *Watson v. Buckley* [1940] 1 All E.R. 174; *Pack v. Warner County* (1964) 44 D.L.R. (2d) 215.
152. *Rivtow v. Washington Iron Works* [1974] S.C.R. 1189.
153. *Thomas v. Winchester* 6 N.Y. 397 (1852); cited with approval in *Donoghue v. Stevenson* [1932] A.C. 562 at 617.
154. *Gordon v. M'Hardy* (1903) 6 Fraser 210 at 212.
155. See *Burfitt v. Kille* [1939] 2 K.B. 743 (selling pistol to 12-year-old); *Good-Wear v. D. & B. Holdings* (1979) 8 C.C.L.T. 87 (selling with knowledge that buyer would misuse).
156. *Good-Wear Treaders v. D. & B. Holdings* (1979) 98 D.L.R. (3d) 59 (warning insufficient).
157. *Hurley v. Dyke* [1979] R.T.R. 265 at 290, 303 (H.L.).
158. *Gautret v. Egerton* (1867) L.R. 2 C.P. 371; *Coughlin v. Gillison* [1899] 1 Q.B. 145; *Oliver v. Saddler* [1929] A.C. 584 at 596.

manufacturing a defective product and then giving it away as an advertising sample.[159] But as already noted, the modern attitude has become distinctly unsympathetic to continuing discrimination against gratuitous relations.[160] Accordingly, there is quite sufficient latitude for nowadays allowing a donee the same claim to neighbourly consideration of care (including an affirmative duty to inspect the article for discoverable defects) as is due to anybody else.[161]

Economic loss

The purpose of this branch of law being the promotion of safety, its concern is primarily with physical injury.[162] The range of protection has however been progressively extended beyond bodily injuries at least to all forms of property damage. Thus liability may now attach to a product whose *sole* foreseeable risk is damage to property, as in the case of mislabelled herbicide, noxious dog food or sheep dip.[163] Nor is it necessary that the product actually cause the damage; it is sufficient that it failed in its function to protect against damage, for example fungicides or alarm systems.[164] In this respect, at any rate, it is no answer to a tort claim that the product was merely "ineffective".

More controversial is damage to the article itself.[165] It was once thought that such damage could be classified as "damage to property",[166] but this has now been emphatically rejected: such loss is to be treated as "purely economic".[167]

One possible line of distinction might have been between dangerous products and products that are merely qualitatively substandard (shoddy), such as leaky roof tiles[168] or a big game rifle that failed during a tiger shoot.[169] The former are closer to the central concern of torts with safety, while the latter merely suggest that the purchaser made a bad bargain for

159. *Hawkins v. Coulsdon U.D.C.* [1954] 1 Q.B. 319 at 333; *Levi v. Colgate-Palmolive* (1941) 41 S.R. (N.S.W.) 48 (passim); *Pease v. Sinclair Refining* 104 F. 2d 183 (1939).
160. E.g. Lord Devlin in *Hedley Byrne v. Heller* [1964] A.C. 465 at 526-527.
161. *Griffiths v. Arch Engineering* [1968] 3 All E.R. 217 at 220; *Hawkins v. Coulsdon U.D.C.* [1954] 1 Q.B. 319 at 333; Marsh, *Liability of the Gratuitous Transferor: A Comparative Study*, 66 L.Q.R. 39 (1950). Cf. *Fraser v. Jenkins* [1968] N.Z.L.R. 816 (no liability to one who appreciated risk); *Pivovaroff v. Chernabaeff* (1978) 21 S.A.S.R. 1 at 32-33.
162. Including indemnity claims in respect of liability for personal injury: e.g. by employer (*Suosaari v. Steinhardt* (1989) A.T.R. 80-268) or distributor against manufacturer (*Lambert v. Lewis* [1982] A.C. 225 at 278 (Lord Diplock)); contra: C.A. at 257-67; *Southern Water v. Carey* [1985] 2 All E.R. 1077 at 1092.
163. *Grant v. Cooper* [1940] N.Z.L.R. 947; *Siemens v. Pfizer* (1988) 49 D.L.R. (4th) 481. Or the contents of leaking pails, in *Aswan Engineering v. Lupdine* [1989] 1 W.L.R. 1?
164. See *Nunes Diamonds v. D.E.P.* [1972] S.C.R. 769.
165. See Feldthusen, *Economic Negligence* ch. 4; Cane, 95 L.Q.R. 117 (1979); Schwenzer, 9 Tel Aviv Stud. L. 127 (1989) (comparative). Product liability insurance policies usually exclude such coverage as being a "commercial risk": see Heppel, *Products Liability Insurance* (1967) ch. 3.
166. *Anns v. Merton L.B.C.* [1978] A.C. 728; above, p. 474.
167. *D. & F. Estates v. Church Commrs* [1989] A.C. 177; *Murphy v. Brentwood U.D.C.* [1991] A.C. 398. Cf. *Merlin v. British Nuclear Fuels* [1990] 2 Q.B. 557 ("damage to property" means physical damage, not pure economic loss to property rights, like lessened value due to contamination).
168. *Young & Marten v. McManus Child* [1969] 1 A.C. 454 at 469.
169. *Thomas v. Olin Mathieson* 255 C.A. 2d 806 (Cal. 1967).

which his remedy lies exclusively in contract. This approach would permit at least reimbursement of expenses incurred in repairing the dangerous product for the sake of averting future injury, though not necessarily damages for loss of profits.[170] Nor would this portend unlimited liability ("floodgates"). But the view which ultimately prevailed was to focus exclusively on the type of injury and to remit all economic loss to contract. Accordingly, if the defect in a potentially dangerous article is discovered before any damage has been caused, the product is no longer considered dangerous but only defective in quality: the buyer may be entitled to the benefit of a relevant warranty of quality from his immediate supplier but not to a remedy in tort against the remote manufacturer.[171]

Several reasons appear to have been persuasive: the traditional demarcation between contract and tort, that this criterion is easier to apply than others, that in the absence of actual injury public policy is not sufficiently engaged to justify tort intervention and that it would be unfair to deprive the defendant of defences such as contractual limitations on liability.[172] On the other hand, in the case of an accident it may lead to rather fine distinctions between different types of loss, as in the case of an oxygen pump which failed and destroyed a tankful of lobsters. The fish merchant recovered from the manufacturer the value of the fish and "financial loss suffered in consequence of that physical damage", like the cost of boiling salvaged lobsters; not however for the loss of profits on intended sales.[173]

Another incongruity would arise if the producer of a defective component part were to be treated differently from the assembler of the completed product. Suppose a defective switch supplied by the former causes a fire and complete destruction of an appliance. That this could be treated as damage to *other* property, has been denied as regards the liability of the assembler, but not of the component manufacturer.[174] Yet the nature of the plaintiff's loss is the same in both cases, and the would-be policy of confining him to his contractual remedy, if any, is equally pertinent.

3. STRICT LIABILITY

The recent period has witnessed a strong move for adopting strict liability for product injuries, originating in the United States and now the law of Europe in the E.E.C. It is also about to be adopted in Australia.[175]

170. Thus Laskin J. in *Rivtow Marine v. Washington Iron Works* [1974] S.C.R. 1189. (The majority did however allow recovery for lost profits during repair of the defective crane on the basis of failure to warn.) This represents the views of most American cases, at any rate for threatened personal injury.
171. Accord: *Consumer Protection Act* 1987 s. 5(2), giving effect to the E.E.C. Directive (below, p. 501); *East River S.S. v. Transamerica* 476 U.S. 858 (1986) (malfunctioning turbines affecting performance, not safety).
172. See above, p. 474.
173. *Muirhead v. I.T.S.* [1986] Q.B. 507 (C.A.).
174. *Murphy v. Brentwood U.D.C.* [1991] A.C. 398 at 478. See above, p. 475.
175. For incorporation in the *Trade Practices Act* 1974 (Cth) as Pt VA. The Bill was introduced on 19 December 1991.

Traditionally, as we have seen,[176] strict liability has been associated exclusively with abnormally dangerous things and activities, but the marketing of products generally does not fit that description. Its rationale is different.

Both fairness for the consumer and accident deterrence combine in placing responsibility for defective products squarely on the manufacturer. Through marketing techniques manufacturers seek to create implicit consumer reliance on product safety. Consumers are ill equipped to make their own assessment of a product's safety, while the manufacturer is in a strategic position to control quality of production and design. The cost of accidents should be "internalised" to the enterprise that is the best cost-avoider; and in so far as that cost is passed on by the producer to the customer, it may not only reflect itself in competitive pricing but the cost will be spread among all consumers of the product. The price of the product will in effect include the cost of insurance[177] for injury from defective products.

The negligence regime only imperfectly achieves these objectives. The injured consumer is in a singularly disadvantageous position in carrying the burden of proof. To the extent that this has been mitigated by shifting the burden (res ipsa loquitur), the law already approaches strict liability and might just as well embrace it openly. Strict liability already controls the relation between buyer and seller; to extend it between manufacturer and ultimate consumer will only permit a direct action where formerly the same result could mostly be achieved by successive claims up the ladder of vertical privity. Negligence law by offering escape hatches is both unfair to the consumer and does not exert optimal pressure on producers to make the most effective investment in safety.

Indeed, the aforementioned sellers' warranties served as a bridge from contract to strict liability in tort. American courts simply discarded the privity requirement.[178] The Australian *Trade Practices Act* originally extended warranties, more modestly, (only) to the ultimate purchaser, thereby replacing privity of contract by privity of title (warranties run "with the goods") and leaving only non-buyers (bystanders) beyond the pale.[179] The proposed amendment would complete the transformation to pure tort by extending protection to any person injured by the defective product.

Defectiveness

Strict liability is focused not, like negligence, on the conduct of the producer, but on the quality of the product. Not every accident caused by a product entails liability; only one caused by a defective product.

American courts have long been wrestling with a criterion for defectiveness.[180] The British *Consumer Protection Act* 1987, mandated by

176. See above, ch. 15.
177. For the role of insurance see A.L.R.C., *Product Liability Research Paper No. 2* (1989) ch. 5.
178. Prosser, *The Assault Upon the Citadel*, 69 Yale L.J. 1099 (1960) and *The Fall of the Citadel*, 50 Minn. L. Rev. 791 (1966).
179. See above, p. 481.
180. See *Prosser & Keeton* 99; *Harper, James & Gray* §28.32A; Fleming, *Of Dangerous and Defective Products*, 9 Tel Aviv Stud. L. 11 (1989).

the *E.E.C. Directive* of 1985, stipulates that "there is a defect in a product if the safety of the product is not such as persons generally are entitled to expect;" taking into account, inter alia, the manner in which the product was marketed and its expected use.[181] This, the consumer expectation test, derives from the law of warranties, slightly adjusted by substituting the expectation of "persons generally" for purchaser so as to take account of casualties outside the line of commercial distribution.

Defectiveness is easy to determine in relation to manufacturing defects, which are deviants from the standard set by the manufacturer himself. Although foolproof quality control may in practice be unattainable and not even economically optimal, the risk must be shouldered by the manufacturer and cannot be escaped by pleading that inevitable and unpredictable flaws are expectable nor that the extra cost of super-controls would be unjustifiable. Here liability is truly strict.

The appropriate standard presents greater difficulty in relation to design defects and failure to warn. Easy enough are malfunctioning products such as collapsing jacks or sticking carburettors. The difficulty centres on cases where the particular design was consciously adopted in preference over competing alternatives. To vet the designer's choice may involve the judicial process in unfamiliar, even unjusticiable, inquiry, exacerbated by the fact that an adverse conclusion will condemn a whole production line rather than merely a single item. How safe is safe enough? The roof of a car overturned in a collision might not have collapsed if the steel had been stronger and the car had been equipped with a roll bar. But such added safety would have been at the cost of consumer appeal and fuel economy. It would be different if an alternative design or additional safety device were readily available at small cost.

Some American courts invoke a risk/utility test complementary, or as an alternative, to consumer expectation, which suffers from a tendency to validate jury decisions based on emotion rather than even-handed reasoning. The risk/utility test calls for a weighing of "the likelihood that the product would cause the plaintiff's harm or similar harms, and the seriousness of those harms, against the burden on the manufacturer to design a product that would have prevented those harms, and the adverse effect that alternative design would have on the usefulness of the product. Examples of evidence that is especially probative in making this evaluation include: (a) any warnings and instructions provided with the product; (b) the technological and practical feasibility of a product designed and manufactured so as to have prevented claimant's harm while substantially serving the likely user's expected needs; (c) the effect of any proposed alternative design on the usefulness of the product; (d) the comparative costs of producing the product as designed or as alternatively designed; and (e) the new and additional harms that might have resulted if the product had been so alternatively designed."[182] This test, by focusing on alternative design, gives specificity to the determination of defectiveness. Essentially the familiar test for negligence, it reveals the inescapable fault element

181. Section 3(1). Clause 75 of the Australian Bill is similar.
182. The (U.S.) model *Uniform Product Liability Act* §104(B).

linked to human behaviour despite the pretence of strict liability focused only on the product.[183]

Exempt are generically "unavoidably dangerous" products, such as alcoholic beverages, butter, drugs and even asbestos. These contain irreducible risks but are entitled to tolerance on account of their countervailing utility. They cannot be charged with design defect because they cannot be made safer, though suitable warnings should accompany their distribution.

The potential harshness of strict liability is further mitigated by the so-called development risks defence. The defendant may show that "the state of scientific and technical knowledge at the relevant time was not such as to enable the existence of the defect to be discovered."[184] This defence limits liability to foreseeable risks as determined not by imputed hind knowledge, but by knowledge prevailing when the product was put into circulation.[185] It thus embodies what is also known as the "state of the art" defence, covering not only unforeseeable risks but also undiscoverable defects, such as blood plasma infected with serum hepatitis. This wide-ranging exclusion, of special significance to the pharmaceutical industry, has been criticised as a betrayal of the compensation objective and of the claim that the liability is not conduct based, but is defended on the ground that otherwise the marketing of novel products would be inhibited and because insurance would be unavailable. In the upshot, the fault standard has largely survived in relation to defective design and failure to warn cases, except that the burden of proof is reversed.[186]

Finally, failure to warn of the risks may make a product defective. Especially unavoidably dangerous products, like drugs with dangerous side effects, and other products which cannot be made safer but are sufficiently beneficial to escape interdiction (for example, asbestos) must be accompanied by suitable warnings. So must products injurious only to an irreducible minority of exceptionally allergic users. The duty to warn is not measured by hindsight; it depends on knowledgeability of the risk at the time the product is marketed.

Defences

The consumer expectation test might also have excluded liability for patent dangers, but just as under negligence it does not automatically bar the plaintiff. If the latter with full knowledge of the defect continues to use

183. The difference is that strict liability purports to evaluate the product, not the conduct (design process) of the producer. California hardens liability by reversing the onus of proof.

184. Section 4(e). See Newdick, *Risk, Uncertainty and Knowledge in the Development Risk Defence*, 20 Anglo-American L. Rev. 309 (1991). The British version, currently being challenged by the E.E.C. Commission and not followed in the Australian Bill (cl. 75AH), is even more forgiving. It speaks of knowledge "such that a producer of products of the same description as the product in question *might be expected* to have discovered the defect".

185. Reinforced by art. 6(2) of the Directive, s. 3(2) of the British Act and cl. 75AC(3) of the Australian Bill (defect not to be inferred from the sole fact that a better product is subsequently marketed).

186. See Newdick, *The Future of Negligence in Product Liability*, 103 L.Q.R. 288 (1987).

the product, he will be taken to have voluntarily assumed the risk.[187] Short of that, however, contributory fault will merely reduce damages.[188] Such will be the case where he fails to appreciate the risk or where he negligently uses the product, like the driver who after losing control of his car was ejected due to a faulty door latch.[189]

Misuse of the product will provide a complete defence if entirely unforeseeable and thus not contributing to make the product defective, such as using a knife as a toothpick or pouring perfume over a lighted candle. The Act specifically directs that, in determining "defect", account must be taken of "what might reasonably be expected to be done with or in relation to the product".[190] The product must be proof, however, against foreseeable misuse so as, for example, to require warning against drugs or toxic household substances being left accessible to little children. Alterations of the product like dismantling of guards or other safety features would also preclude liability, because the defect would then not have existed at the time it left the manufacturer.[191]

In these examples remoteness of damage is pre-empted by the threshold question of the defectiveness of the product, just as it is not foreseeability but the scope of the abnormal risk which delimits the strict liability under *Rylands v. Fletcher*.[192]

Producers

American law imposes strict liability on all commercial sellers of a product: the manufacturer, middlemen and retailers. This stems from its origin in sellers' warranties and is defended on the ground that the consumer should be free to select from whom to claim, leaving the ultimate allocation of the loss to the potential defendants. The British statute, following the E.E.C. Directive, confines liability to the producer, anyone who has held himself out as such and any importer. Other suppliers are exempt, unless they fail to identify on request anyone of the previously mentioned class.[193]

Products comprise "any goods and electricity", including component parts.[194] Presumably, however, not information contained in publications, however hardbound.[195] Nor pure services: a designer is not liable, unlike a producer of a defectively designed product. Misleading or inadequate warnings may make an accompanying product defective,[196] but defective

187. *Murphy v. Brentwood D.C.* [1991] 1 A.C. 398 at 464.
188. While the theoretical difficulty of relating contributory *negligence* to strict liability ("apples and oranges") has been expressly resolved by the Directive (art. 8) and the British statute (s. 6(4)), the practical difficulty of assessing relative shares remains. Cf. above, p. 275.
189. *Daly v. G.M.* 575 P. 2d 1162 (Cal. 1978).
190. Section 3(2)(b); cl. 75AC(2)(e).
191. Section 4(1)(d); cl. 75AH(a).
192. See above, p. 329.
193. Section 2; *Trade Practices Act*, s. 74A; Australian Bill cl. 75AG.
194. Section 1(2) of the British Act. The E.E.C. Directive arts 2, 15(1)(a) excludes optionally primary agricultural products and game. Cf. s. 2(4) of the British Act.
195. Cf. *Winter v. Putnam's* 938 F. 2d 1033 (1991). Nor is there even a duty of care: below, p. 645.
196. Section 3(2)(a) of the British Act.

software instructions, addressed to the computer, not the user, are not "goods".[197] What is the reason for drawing this distinction between goods and services, seeing that the rationale for the former—consumer protection—seems to apply equally to the latter? The distinction is doctrinally difficult to justify, seeing that the human element, albeit masked, is as much involved in the creation of products as in services and that the accident-preventive rationale necessarily targets human behaviour.[198] The reasons are accidental and pragmatic. Foremost is the provenance of warranties attached to the sale of goods, from which the seminal American tort liability derived. More fundamental may be the fact that professional services are excluded because their product is furnished for one client at a time so that the cost of liability cannot be spread as widely as over a whole line of tangible products; also that they typically cause economic loss (which is excluded in any event) rather than physical injury. All the same, a new draft Directive of the E.E.C. proposes to extend strict liability to "defective services" rendered in the course of professional activities or by way of public service.[199]

Damages

The only loss for which protection is countenanced is personal injury (or death) and damage to other goods ("of a kind ordinarily acquired for personal, domestic or household use");[200] not damage to or loss of the defective product itself.[201] This provision, excluding purely economic loss, resolves an otherwise agitated question.[202] Personal injury presumably includes psychic injury from shock. American case law has applied the same conditions on recovery as in negligence cases, for example excluding claims by unrelated bystanders but allowing one by a purchaser of a rabid skunk who had to submit to a painful rabies injection.[203] The policy behind these shock rules does not seem to be affected by the basis of liability, whether negligent or strict.

The E.E.C. Directive contains an optional provision, not enlisted by the British Act or the Australian Bill, limiting damages to 70 mill. ECU in contemplation of serial injuries stemming, for example, from pharmaceutical products.

In both respects, as also in its development risks defence, the legislation is sensitive to the problem of insurability.

A controversial provision of the Australian Bill directs that "if on the evidence (whether direct or circumstantial) and in all the circumstances of

197. Stapleton, *Software, Information and the Concept of Product*, 9 Tel Aviv U. Stud. L. 147 (1989). Cf. Whittaker, *Product Liability and Intellectual Products*, 105 L.Q.R. 125 (1989).
198. Stapleton, *Problems with the New Product Liability*, in *Essays for Atiyah* (1991) ch. 11.
199. Reprinted in 2 Prod. Liab. L.J. 214 (1991).
200. Clause 75AD(2) of the Australian Bill.
201. Section 5. Specifically excluded also is the liability of manufacturers of a component part which damages the assembled product: cf. above, p. 496. The Australian *Trade Practices Act* covers any "loss or damage".
202. See above, p. 495.
203. Respectively *Kennedy v. McKesson* 448 N.E. 2d 1332 (N.Y. 1983) and *Sease v. Taylor's Pets* 704 P. 2d 514 (Or. 1985).

the case, it is reasonable to infer that loss was caused by a defect in goods, then the inference must be made.''[204] This appears to be a somewhat modified version of the original proposal frankly to reverse the onus of proof.

The Australian Bill provides a three year period of limitation from the time the claimant became, or ought to have become, aware of both the damage and the identity of the producer. Claims are further subject to a long stop of 20 years for personal injury (ten for property damage) from the date upon which the product was put on the market.[205]

204. Clause 75AJ.
205. Clause 75AN. Cf. ss 5(5) and (6), and s. 6(6) of the English Act.

24

EMPLOYERS

The relation between "master and servant" is contractual but, in the absence of specific terms in the contract of employment, the law attaches to it certain tort[1] obligations on the part of the master for the servant's safety.[2] The standard of that responsibility has changed a great deal in response to evolving social attitudes to the problem of industrial relations.

After the eclipse of the paternalistic economy by the industrial revolution, the courts created a pattern of industrial law in the first half of the 19th century which inevitably reflected the postulates of contemporary individualism. Its basis was the optimistic belief that a free interplay of economic forces would enure to the welfare of society, for the sake of which it was prepared to ignore both the inequality in bargaining between management and employee and the measure of economic compulsion which left the latter no realistic choice between acceptance of the conditions of work offered to him and starvation or equally hazardous employment elsewhere. With a view to encouraging and subsidising burgeoning capitalistic enterprise, the standard of protection conceded to employees was the minimum employers were regarded as capable of affording in the light of the unexacting standards of the time. By means of reading fictitiously implied terms into the contract of employment, the courts denied redress for injury from inherent dangers of the work, besides excusing the master from vicarious liability for the negligence of fellow servants (doctrine of common employment). The employee was regarded as voluntarily assuming these risks, incident to the free bargaining position which was imputed to employee and employer alike. In consequence, the vast bulk of industrial accidents remained uncompensated.

Moderating influences began to stir in the last quarter of the 19th century, in response to growing scepticism regarding the underlying assumptions of laissez-faire liberalism.[3] Largely under the influence of legislation, in particular the *Employers' Liability Act* of 1880, the courts began to adjust legal theory to changing public opinion. This judicial reorientation, in company with the introduction of workers' compensation and, more lately, the legislative abrogation of the doctrine of common employment, has resulted in a virtual rewriting of the legal regime for work

1. *Davie v. New Merton Mills* [1959] A.C. 604 at 642. A plaintiff may alternatively frame his claim in contract: *Mathews v. Kuwait Bechtel Corp.* [1959] 2 Q.B. 57; *Wright v. T.N.T.* (1988) 85 A.L.R. 442 (N.S.W. C.A.).
2. Specialist works on this topic are: in Australia (esp. N.S.W.) Glass, McHugh & Douglass, *Liability of Employers* (2nd ed. 1979); in England, Munkman, *Employers' Liability At Common Law* (11th ed. 1990).
3. See Woodard, *Reality and Social Reform: Transition from Laissez-Faire to Welfare State*, 72 Yale L.J. 286 (1962); Bartrip & Burman, *Wounded Soldiers of Industry* (1983); Tucker, *Law of Employers' Liability in Ontario 1861-1900*, 22 Osg. H.L.J. 213 (1984).

injuries and furnishes a classic illustration of the interaction between public opinion, legislative policy and judicial doctrine.

In many countries the tort remedy against employers (and fellow employees) was abolished right from the start in exchange for workers' compensation.[4] Not so in Britain or Australia. One of the reasons for its retention was a naive belief in the deterrent potential of tort claims,[5] which is neither documented nor rendered credible by the prevalence of liability insurance[6] and the widespread opposition to penalty rating for poor safety records.[7] In recent years there have been second thoughts in Australia. The Northern Territory abolished the common law action entirely[8] (as had originally New South Wales); the Commonwealth, New South Wales, Victoria and South Australia abolished damages for pecuniary loss.[9]

1. COMMON LAW DUTIES

Today it is well settled that an employer,[10] besides being vicariously liable for the casual negligence of his servants towards one another,[11] also owes an overriding managerial responsibility to safeguard them from unreasonable risks of personal injury[12] in regard to the fundamental conditions of employment—the safety of plant, premises and method of work.[13] The relevant standard of care exacted from employers is high[14] and over many years tended to increasing stringency. In Britain it has been observed that when an employee is injured at work, there is now a near presumption—in fact—that the employer is, or ought to be, liable.[15] In

4. See Fleming, *Work Injuries*, XV Int. Encycl. Comp. L. ch. 9.
5. Voiced even by *Pearson* §909.
6. Insurance against common law liability is increasingly mandatory: Workers Compensation Acts: N.S.W. (s. 18), Qld (s. 8), Tas. (s. 34); England, *Employers' Liability (Compulsory Insurance) Act* 1969. See *A.M.P. v. Miltenburg* (1982) 39 A.L.R. 557 (P.C.).
7. See below.
8. *Work Health Act* 1986 s. 52. As did N.S.W. temporarily in 1987-1989.
9. *Compensation (Commonwealth Government Employees) Act* 1988 ss 44-45; *Workers Compensation Act* 1987 (N.S.W.) Pt 5 (except in cases of serious injury); for its effect on third party claims see *Leonard v. Smith* (1992) A.T.R. 81-155; *Accident Compensation Act* 1985 (Vic.) s. 135; *Workers Rehabilitation and Compensation Act* 1986 (S.A.) s. 54 (completely against fellow workers). The Cth, N.S.W. and Vic. Acts also capped non-pecuniary damages to $110,000, $180,000 and $155,000 respectively.
10. Employment is defined as with respect to vicarious liability: see above, p. 376. Thus it does not apply to certain activities of the police: *Griffiths v. Haines* (1984) 3 N.S.W.L.R. 653. But a company director can be an employer (*Nicol v. Allyacht Spars* (1987) 163 C.L.R. 611) or "worker" (*Lee v. Lee's Air Farming* [1961] A.C. 12 (P.C.)).
11. Since the abolition of the doctrine of common employment: see below, p. 515.
12. Not economic loss: *Reid v. Rush & Tompkins* [1990] 1 W.L.R. 212 (C.A.) (no duty to provide accident insurance).
13. *Wilsons & Clyde Coal Co. v. English* [1938] A.C. 57; *Smith v. Baker* [1891] A.C. 325.
14. The phrase "high standard" (as used e.g. by Lord Porter in *Winter v. Cardiff R.D.C.* [1950] 1 All E.R. 819 at 822) is here used in a merely descriptive sense of the legal standard of reasonable care; juries should not be so charged, at least without cautioning them against misunderstanding: *Daniell v. Velekou* [1955] N.Z.L.R. 645 (C.A.); See below, p. 509.
15. See Rideout, *Principles of Labour Law* (2nd ed. 1978) 342. *Pearson* §922 recommended against any *formal* reversal of the burden of proof.

Australia the High Court long sought to oppose this trend but has now become more forgiving. Concededly, in comparison with decisions only 20 or 30 years ago, the standard has risen substantially in response not only to technological improvements but more yet to "changing ideas of justice and increasing concern with safety in the community".[16] This adaptability is aided by the fact that the question what reasonable care demands from an employer is one of fact and the decision, whether by judge or jury, is without precedential effect.[17] As a descriptive statement it may not therefore be far off the mark to say that the standard "has moved close to the border of strict liability", even if the official position remains that the employer's obligation is to exercise reasonable care, not to warrant safety. Few industrial jobs are altogether free from risk; in particular, there is a sphere in which it is legitimate to leave to a skilled worker the decision whether any difficulty he may encounter calls for managerial assistance, for it would be a mistake to treat the relation between him and his employer as equivalent to that of imbecile child and nurse.[18] Despite the strong temptation, especially for juries, to tilt the scales heavily against management on account of its superior loss bearing capacity, it should perhaps not be forgotten that social insurance against work injuries is the function of workers' compensation, whilst the task of common law liability is merely to complement the former by administering a deterrent lash to those employers who, through indifference, ignorance or inexperience, fail to ensure the elimination of risks which reasonable prudence demands.

The employer's common law duty of managerial care appeared to assume a significant element of strict liability as the result of the decision that it could not be discharged by delegating its performance to a subordinate, however expert.[19] If, for example, a plant manager failed in his entrusted task of maintaining a safe system of work, the employer's responsibility was henceforth treated as based on breach of his own duty of care and not on breach of a duty by the servant or agent.[20] Though this refinement was primarily designed to sidestep the doctrine of common employment, it also gave colour to the view that the employer's responsibility extended even to the negligence of manufacturers of tools and machinery on whom he relied for furnishing safe plant and appliances.[21] But the tide turned when the pressure for so unorthodox a solution lessened with the abolition of the fellow-servant rule and the concurrent extension of manufacturers' and suppliers' liability beyond the narrow radius of contractual privity. Accordingly, the employer's managerial responsibility again contracted to the default of those alone to whom he had, properly speaking, delegated the performance of his duties, such as a superior employee[22] or even a third party[23] charged with maintaining a safe system of work or an independent

16. *Bankstown Foundry v. Braistina* (1986) 160 C.L.R. 301 at 309. Cf. *Mihaljevic v. Longyear* [1985] 3 N.S.W.L.R. 1 at 9, 18.
17. *Qualcast v. Haynes* [1959] A.C. 743 at 758, also 759.
18. *Smith v. Austin Lifts* [1959] 1 W.L.R. 100 at 105 per Simonds.
19. *Wilsons & Clyde Coal Co. v. English* [1938] A.C. 57.
20. "It is the obligation which is personal to him, and not the performance" ([1938] A.C. 57 at 81 per Lord Wright).
21. *Donnelly v. Glasgow Corp.* 1953 S.C. 107.
22. *Wilsons & Clyde Coal Co. v. English* [1938] A.C. 57.
23. *McDermid v. Nash* [1987] A.C. 906 (inexperienced worker).

contractor employed to make repairs or handle machinery.[24] But except by statute (as now in England[25]), he is not answerable for the negligence of a manufacturer of plant or tools, so long as he or his agent entrusted with the task was careful in dealing with a seller of repute and made a reasonable inspection for discoverable defects.[26]

The master's general responsibility for the safety of his employees finds its principal illustration in the following specific obligations:

1. Competent staff: The employer is required to observe reasonable care in the selection of competent fellow employees and in the provision of an adequate staff so that the work can be carried out in reasonable safety. The obligation is continuous in the sense that if the employer becomes aware that an employee is incompetent or otherwise likely to prove a source of danger to his fellows,[27] it behoves him to take remedial action. Since the abolition of the defence of common employment this obligation has lost much of its former importance, now that in most cases the employer will be vicariously answerable for the specific misconduct of fellow servants.

2. Safe place of work: The employer is under a duty of care to ensure that the premises where his employees are required to work are reasonably safe. In probably no respect more than this, has the level of managerial responsibility risen so significantly over the years. Long since abandoned is the mid 19th century view, categorically demanding ignorance of the danger in the servant and knowledge in the master.[28] Far from being treated like a mere licensee (under the old law), a servant's position became in several respects more favourable even than an invitee's: for neither is the employer's duty limited to unusual dangers[29] nor is it necessarily discharged by giving warning of the hazard.[30] For knowledge actually to disqualify the employee, it must either have been such as to enable him efficiently to carry out work without least risk to himself or, per contra, the risk must have been so great that no sensible person would in any circumstances have incurred it; otherwise, the fact that he voluntarily and knowingly encountered it is relevant only to the question of contributory negligence, when recovery will now be merely reduced, but no longer defeated.[31]

But however high, the duty is not one of insurance; it demands no more than the provision and maintenance of work premises in as safe a condition

24. *Kondis v. State Transport* (1984) 154 C.L.R. 672 at 279 per Mason J.; *Sumner v. Henderson* [1964] 1 Q.B. 450 (revd on other grounds [1963] 1 W.L.R. 823); *Marshment v. Borgstrom* [1942] S.C.R. 374.
25. *Employers' Liability (Defective Equipment) Act* 1969. See Lang, *Employers' Liability (Defective Equipment) Act—Lion or Mouse?* 47 Mod. L. Rev. 48 (1984); *Coltman v. Bibby Tankers* [1988] A.C. 276.
26. *Davie v. New Merton Mills* [1959] A.C. 604; *Sullivan v. Gallagher* 1959 S.C. 243; and see Goodhart, *Master's Liability for Defective Tools*, 74 L.Q.R. 397 (1958).
27. *Hudson v. Ridge Manufacturing Co.* [1957] 2 Q.B. 348 (horseplay); *Antoniak v. Commonwealth* (1962) 4 F.L.R. 454 (vicious attack). There would have been no vicarious liability for isolated acts of such misbehaviour.
28. E.g. *Griffiths v. London Docks* (1884) 13 Q.B.D. 259.
29. E.g. *General Cleaning Contractors v. Christmas* [1953] A.C. 180 (system of work).
30. *London Graving Dock v. Horton* [1951] A.C. 737 at 746; *Smith v. Austin Lifts* [1959] 1 W.L.R. 100 at 118.
31. *Minto v. Great N. Transport* [1959] N.Z.L.R. 749.

as reasonable care by a prudent employer can make them. For example, if danger is presented by some unprecedented situation, like a bomb among scrap metal, it must at least come to managerial attention.[32] So also when a factory was flooded in an exceptional storm and the floor became slippery by an admixture of oil, the management was excused for taking the view that the risk was not sufficiently great to justify a complete shut-down, after all other practicable safety measures had been taken.[33]

Responsibility extends not only to the actual working site but to any area the servant uses in connection with or in furtherance of his employment, such as necessary access from the street;[34] exceptionally even to off-the-job premises as when accommodation is furnished for hospital employees or fettlers.[35] It was once thought that no duty devolved on the master with respect to premises outside his control,[36] but the view has prevailed that he cannot renounce all responsibility for the safety of outside jobs.[37] Much depends on the nature of the premises in question and the efficacy of alternatives available. Thus there is a substantial difference between the hatches of a ship which are notoriously dangerous for stevedores,[38] and a respectable private residence to which a plumber is sent to mend a leak.[39] Also, in some instances an employer is justified in relying on the occupier or the employee himself taking the necessary precautions, while in others a thorough safety inspection would be a necessary preliminary to sending in an employee.

3. Proper plant and appliances: The preceding duty is but one aspect of the wider obligation to observe reasonable care in the provision and maintenance of proper plant and appliances.[40] True, as we have already seen, an employer neither *warrants* the safety of tools nor incurs responsibility as such for negligence on the part of anyone concerned with their manufacture and supply.[41] He does however owe a duty of *care* to procure suitable tools from a reputable source, inspect them for fitness and thereafter maintain a proper system of continuing supervision and inspection.[42]

32. *O'Reilly v. National Rail & Tramway Appliances* [1966] 1 All E.R. 499.
33. *Latimer v. A.E.C.* [1953] A.C. 643.
34. *A.C.I. Metal v. Boczulik* (1964) 110 C.L.R. 372 (even when over somebody else's land); *Ashdown v. Williams* [1957] 1 Q.B. 409 (C.A.).
35. *Key v. Comm. Rlys* (1941) 64 C.L.R. 619; *Milligan v. Hooker* (1966) 85 W.N. (Pt 1) (N.S.W.) 160 (C.A.); *McCormick v. Ballarat Hospital* [1967] V.R. 498.
36. *Cilia v. James* [1954] 1 W.L.R. 721.
37. *Wilson v. Tyneside Window Cleaning* [1958] 2 Q.B. 110; *Sinclair v. Arnott* (1963) 64 S.R. (N.S.W.) 88.
38. E.g. *O'Connor v. Port Waratah* (1975) 13 S.A.L.R. 119.
39. *Wilson* [1958] 2 Q.B. 110 at 121; *Mace v. Green* [1959] 1 Q.B. 14.
40. Hence, Lord Wright spoke of the "threefold duty" in *Wilsons & Clyde Coal Co. v. English* [1938] A.C. 57 at 84-85.
    The instant duty applies not only to tools and industrial equipment, but also to items like a car supplied to a commercial traveller (*Wingrove v. Sheehy* (1961) 35 A.L.J.R. 313) or a dress to a film extra: *Naismith v. London Film* [1939] 1 All E.R. 794.
41. See above, p. 505. In contrast, however irrational, an independent contractor may claim the benefit of such an implied warranty with respect to equipment supplied to him by his "employer" pursuant to contract: *Derbyshire Building Co. v. Becker* (1962) 107 C.L.R. 633; *Southland Harbour v. Vella* [1974] 1 N.Z.L.R. 526 (C.A.).
42. Even with respect to latent defects, the evidential burden rests on the employer to establish his care in maintenance: *Pearce v. Round Oak Steel* [1969] 1 W.L.R. 595 (C.A.). But if liable in any one of these respects, he may well have a right to full indemnity from the supplier based on the latter's breach of warranty, express or implied: *Sims v. Foster Wheeler* [1966] 1 W.L.R. 769 (C.A.).

4. Safe system of work: Although of relatively modern formulation,[43] one of the most important facets of the employer's duty is to establish and enforce a safe system of work. Managerial control over organisation exacts a corresponding responsibility for such matters as the co-ordination of activities, layout of equipment, method of using machines and carrying out particular processes, safety instruction of personnel,[44] provision of safety devices and encouragement of their use; in addition to the residual task of planning and supervising the general conditions under which the work is carried out. The duty is continuous, demanding vigilance and attention to the need for modification and improvement; and extends to the organisation of isolated tasks no less than of permanent systems. Since the demise of the common employment doctrine, it has become less important to distinguish between managerial failure to enforce a safe system of work and a casual failure by a co-employee,[45] but it may still occasionally be relevant, as where the culpable worker is himself injured or is an independent contractor.[46]

There is an element of risk in the performance of even the most simple industrial operations, but an employer is not expected to ensure that his system of work is in fact accident-proof. He need only guard against unreasonable or (in the much favoured phrase) "unnecessary"[47] risks, having regard alike to the likelihood of danger, gravity of injury and means for avoiding it.[48] Moreover, at least in theory, the burden of proof rests on the plaintiff to prove the availability of a safer system, notwithstanding that the employer would (and should) know much more about that.[49] The standard of awareness demanded from the employer regarding the technological and scientific "state of art" only requires that he "keep reasonably abreast of [developing knowledge] and not be too slow to apply it".[50] With respect to industry practices, it used to be fashionable to call upon Lord Dunedin's apothegm that when an employer is charged with a fault of omission, there must be proof either that he failed to adopt a precaution in common practice or that it would be "folly" not to adopt it.[51] But valuable though this warning may be against a facile finding that a precaution is necessary in the absence of general usage,[52] the touchstone

43. Little was heard of such a claim prior to *Wilsons'* case [1938] A.C. 57, but there is now a formidable mass of case law.
44. Including screening of employees exposed to harmful substances: *Wright v. Dunlop Rubber* (1972) 13 K.I.R. 255.
45. See *Katsilis v. B.H.P.* (1977) 52 A.L.J.R. 189.
46. As in *Kondis v. State Transport* (1984) 154 C.L.R. 672.
47. *Smith v. Baker* [1891] A.C. 325 at 362 per Lord Herschell.
48. *Hamilton v. Nuroof* (1956) 96 C.L.R. 18; *Retsas v. Commonwealth* (1975) 50 A.L.J.R. 104.
49. *Neill v. N.S.W. Fresh Food* (1963) 108 C.L.R. 362; *Kingshott v. Goodyear* (1987) 8 N.S.W.L.R. 707 (C.A.).
50. *Stokes v. G.K.N.* [1968] 1 W.L.R. 1776 at 1783.
51. *Morton v. Dixon* 1909 S.C. 807 at 809.
52. See *Great Western Gold Mines v. Downey* (1956) 31 A.L.J. 470; *Bressington v. Comm. Rlys* (1947) 75 C.L.R. 339; *Daniell v. Velekou* [1955] N.Z.L.R. 645; *Drummond v. British Building Cleaners* [1954] 1 W.L.R. 501. The strength of such evidence varies with each case, but is not necessarily sufficient either to warrant a non-suit or preclude a plaintiff's verdict: *Morris v. West Hartlepool Navigation Co.* [1956] A.C. 552; *Cavanagh v. Ulster Weaving* [1960] A.C. 145.

of the common law is not "folly" but failure of reasonable care.[53] A distinction has been seen between a recognised practice followed without mishap and one which in the light of common sense or increased knowledge is clearly bad. Between these extremes there is a type of risk which is regarded at any time (though not necessarily later) as an inescapable feature of industry. For these the employer is not liable either, although subsequent changes in knowledge may transfer them into the last category.[54]

An employer cannot disclaim responsibility for devising a safe method of work merely because his workers are experienced and might, if they were in the position of master, be able to lay down such a system themselves. Workers are not in the position of employers. Their duties are not performed in the calm atmosphere of a boardroom with the advice of experts; they have to make their own decisions in places of danger and in circumstances in which such dangers are frequently obscured.[55] Accident prevention, a vital factor in productive efficiency, is at least as much the responsibility of management as of the individual worker. Where a practice of ignoring an obvious danger has grown up, it is not reasonable to expect the worker to take the initiative in devising precautions, as used to be thought. It is the duty of the employer to devise a suitable system, warn him of unexpected risks and instruct him how best to secure himself against injury.[56] Although an experienced worker can generally be expected to exercise his own judgment on how to carry out routine tasks, superior instructions may negative his discretion and expose him to unnecessary risk.[57] And in the provision of safeguards, the employer must allow for the fact that inadvertence and inattention are common features of everyday work. Now that contributory negligence is no longer a complete defence, an employer cannot avoid planning even against culpable carelessness by his employees.[58] This is particularly pertinent where the employee's job exposes him constantly to the risk of injury unless there is unremitting care on his part; in contrast to casual or isolated tasks of a simple character which do not involve any real hazard if ordinary care is used.[59]

Besides prescribing a safe system, the employer must also enforce it, even against employee resistance.[60] For example, admonition and pressure, even on skilled employees, for using safety equipment may be called for; but if this be so where the dangers are insidious, as in the case of silicosis[61] or dermatitis,[62] no similar obligation exists when they are patent and the decision can reasonably be left to the individual worker whether to use it

53. *Hamilton v. Nuroof* (1956) 96 C.L.R. at 26; *Cavanagh v. Ulster Weaving* [1960] A.C. 145 at 165-166; *Paris v. Stepney B.C.* [1951] A.C. 367 at 382.
54. *Thompson v. Smiths Shiprepairers* [1984] Q.B. 405 at 415-416.
55. *General Cleaning Contractors v. Christmas* [1953] A.C. 180 at 190; *Watson v. Telecom* (1985) 40 S.A.S.R. 221.
56. *Wilson v. Tyneside Window Cleaning* [1958] 2 Q.B. 110; *Raimondo v. South Australia* (1979) 23 A.L.R. 513; *Electric Power v. Cuiuli* (1961) 104 C.L.R. 177 (elementary job).
57. *Perkovic v. McDonnell* (1989) 45 S.A.S.R. 544 (F.C.).
58. *McLean v. Tedman* (1984) 155 C.L.R. 306.
59. *Smith v. B.H.P.* (1957) 31 A.L.J. 664 at 666; *Jellie v. Commonwealth* [1959] V.R. 72.
60. *McLean v. Tedman* (1984) 155 C.L.R. 306.
61. *Crookall v. Vickers-Armstrong* [1955] 1 W.L.R. 659.
62. *Clifford v. Challen* [1951] 1 K.B. 495.

or not.[63] In this as in other respects, no categorical rules are warranted because every case depends on its own peculiar facts, having regard to the nature of the risk, the worker's appreciation of it and the gravity of possible injury. However strong the temptation to seek uniformity of standards by converting decisions on particular questions of fact into peremptory propositions of law, this tendency[64] must be resisted as it unduly curbs the decision-making role of juries (or trial judges in their stead) and reduces that measure of flexibility which still seems desirable in applying common law, as distinct from statutory, standards of liability.[65]

Finally, what due care requires may vary according to the particular employee's degree of experience or susceptibility to injury. Although an employer need not take active steps to acquaint himself with any special weakness or predisposition to injury,[66] he must take special precautions once he has, or had the means to, become aware of it, for example that the particular employee is half blind,[67] an untrained foreigner,[68] or suffering from an allergy.[69] Responsibility might even attach for exposing an employee with a known psychological problem to exceptionally stressful working conditions causing a lasting psychoneurosis.[69a]

2. STATUTORY DUTIES

Dominating the industrial field nowadays is a vast volume of statutory regulations[70] imposing detailed duties upon employers for the protection of their workers, such as Factory Acts requiring the fencing of dangerous machinery. These statutes have been construed to confer a claim for damages on any employee injured as the result of his employer's failure to comply even if, as is usual, the statute provides only a penal sanction for its enforcement.[71] Not infrequently these statutory duties are couched in absolute terms demanding compliance even if it would render the work in

63. *Qualcast v. Haynes* [1959] A.C. 743 (spats in iron foundry); *McWilliams v. Sir W. Arrol* [1962] 1 W.L.R. 295 (H.L.) (safety belt). Nor is an employer bound to dismiss an employee who is willing to continue in a job that exposes him to a known but irreducible risk— "their relationship is not that between schoolmaster and pupil" (*Withers v. Perry Chain* [1961] 1 W.L.R. 1314 (dermatitis); *Foufoulas v. Strang* (1970) 123 C.L.R. 168).
64. Which is the more pronounced in jurisdictions, like England, where juries have practically disappeared.
65. *Qualcast v. Haynes* [1959] A.C. 743.
66. *Blackman v. Commonwealth* (1978) 20 A.C.T.R. 33 (back injury).
67. *Paris v. Stepney B.C.* [1951] A.C. 367; see above, p. 116.
68. *Hawkins v. Ross* [1970] 1 All E.R. 180.
69. *Silvestro v. Verbon* [1973] 2 N.S.W.L.R. 513 (C.A.) (spray paint); *Qualcast v. Haynes* [1959] A.C. 743 at 753.

69a. Cf. *Gillespie v. Commonwealth* (1991) 104 A.C.T.R. 1 (F.C.).

70. Often subordinate legislation: see *Jacob v. Utah Constructions* (1966) 116 C.L.R. 200; *Darling Island Stevedoring Co. v. Long* (1957) 97 C.L.R. 36.
71. The fons et origo is *Groves v. Wimborne* [1898] 2 Q.B. 402, which held the defence of common employment inapplicable and thus in turn increased the popularity of the action. A forerunner of sorts was the fines occasionally awarded to victims: Howells, *Priestley v. Fowler and the Factory Acts*, 26 Mod. L. Rev. 366 (1963). A vigorous proponent of statutory standards as an accident preventive device is Williams, *Accidents and Ill-Health at Work* (1960).

question commercially impracticable or mechanically impossible.[72] Failure to conform to the legislative safety standard is negligence per se,[73] and if the statutory command is peremptory rather than demanding merely all reasonable care, liability is in effect strict and independent of fault in the conventional sense.[74]

Most commonly such regulations prescribe specific precautions to be taken for particular industrial operations, like the use of specified scaffolding for work above minimum heights, of guards around moving machinery or duck boards for work on glass roofs. Regulations of this type in effect merely spell out precisely and beyond argument what the general duty of reasonable care would in any event require. More drastic by far in promoting strict liability are regulations, increasingly common, which prescribe that certain equipment be of sound construction, suitable material and adequate strength. These in effect import a warranty of fitness, covering even latent defects,[75] and thereby far transcend the common law duty of employers.[76] Although this has in other areas, as we have already seen,[77] militated conclusively against attaching civil sanctions, no similar scruples have prevailed in the industrial context. This striking difference in judicial attitude, which has indeed for all practical purposes—at least in Britain—made the whole doctrine of statutory negligence an almost exclusive preserve of industrial accident law, is of course in no small measure due to a desire to make up for the lower level of workers' compensation.

The high incidence of employees' actions for breach of statutory duty provides a telling index of the wide extent to which the administration of modern industrial accident law has become emancipated from notions of conventional fault. But judicial attitudes have not been wholly consistent.

72. *Summers v. Frost* [1955] A.C. 740; *Galashiels Gas v. O'Donnell* [1949] A.C. 275; *Hamilton v. N.C.B.* [1960] A.C. 633. Quite common, however, is the statutory modifier "so far as is practicable" or even "reasonably practicable", the onus usually being on defendants, who "start as insurers and have by evidence to divest themselves of that status" (*Edwards v. N.C.B.* [1949] 1 K.B. 704 at 710; also *Nimmo v. Cowan* [1968] A.C. 107; *Kingshott v. Goodyear* (1987) 8 N.S.W.L.R. 707 (C.A.)). Moreover, the same modifier may be imposed by judicial fiat, as courts have brought much subtlety to this task of what is politely called "statutory construction". Thus the duty to "securely fence" is unqualified, yet "to take such steps as may be necessary for keeping . . . secure" has been held to impose in effect only a duty of the highest care: *Brown v. N.C.B.* [1962] A.C. 574; *Marshall v. Gotham* [1954] A.C. 360. But the proposal by the Monckton Committee on Alternative Remedies (1946. Cmd. 6860) to introduce it as a *general* qualifier was defeated in the Commons in 1948.

73. See above, p. 124.

74. E.g. the risk may have been too negligible for common law negligence, as in *Boyle v. Kodak* [1969] 1 W.L.R. 661 (H.L.). But "reasonable foreseeability of risk" may still be relevant for such subsidiary questions as whether part of a machine is "dangerous" so as to require fencing: see e.g. *Burns v. Terry* [1951] 1 K.B. 454; *Irwin v. White* [1964] 1 All E.R. 545 at 550 (H.L.); *Tinto v. Stewarts & Lloyds* 1962 S.L.T. 314 (is foothold secure against unexpectable explosion?). But so long as the kind of accident was within the foreseeable risk (e.g. getting caught in a machine), it matters nothing that the precise way in which it happened was unforeseeable: *Millard v. Serck Tubes* [1969] 1 W.L.R. 211 (C.A.). Cf. above, p. 212.

75. *Doherty v. Wallboard Mills* [1968] I.R. 277; *Sonka v. N.C.B.* 1965 S.L.T. (N.) 64.

76. See above, p. 134.

77. Ibid.

For despite the courts' crucial role in the creation of this species of liability, they have not been beyond occasionally impeding its own logic. One such fetter was the belated admission of the defence of contributory negligence, even if its effect has in practice been largely countered in one way or another.[78] Another example is the Australian High Court's refusal, in the teeth of much contrary authority, to attach *vicarious* liability for breach of a statutory duty.[79] The resulting distinction between breach of statutory and common law duty seems as difficult to justify on grounds of policy as by reference to the conventional basis of vicarious liability.[80] It has been reversed in New South Wales.[81] A third incongruity was the refusal to impose on the defendant the burden of proving that his violation was not causal. Still, in practice at least an *inference* of causality is easily drawn when the accident is one which the statutory duty was designed to prevent.[82]

3. DEFENCES

For long, the employer's obligations were, in effect, substantially qualified by the "unholy trinity" of common law defences—voluntary assumption of risk, common employment and contributory negligence. These were at one time given the widest scope in order to ease the employer's financial burden and, where applicable, deprived the injured worker of all right to compensation. The profound reallocation of responsibility for industrial accidents during this century could not have been accomplished if the progressive rise in the standard of employers' obligations had not been matched by a simultaneous reduction in the importance of these defences. As the result of the combined effect of legislative and judicial initiative, one of these has been abolished altogether, another condemned to virtual atrophy and the third deprived of its lethal sting.

I. Assumption of Risk

> "Assumption of risk is a judicially created rule which was developed in response to the general impulse of common law courts . . . to insulate the employer as much as possible from bearing the 'human overhead' which is an inevitable part of business. The general purpose behind this development in the common law seems to have been to give maximum freedom to expand industry. The assumption of risk doctrine for example was attributed by this court to 'a rule of public policy, inasmuch as an opposite doctrine would not only subject

78. See below, p. 515.
79. *Darling Island Stevedoring Co. v. Long* (1957) 97 C.L.R. 36. Many English decisions have tacitly proceeded on a contrary assumption, but the question is still considered open: *I.C.I. v. Shatwell* [1965] A.C. 656 at 688-689.
80. See e.g. *Mines and Quarries Act* 1954 (U.K.) s. 159 (for the removal of doubts).
81. *Law Reform (Vicarious Liability) Act* 1983 s. 7.
82. *Quigley v. Commonwealth* (1981) 55 A.L.J.R. 579 at 584; see above, p. 195.

employers to unreasonable and often ruinous responsibilities, thereby embarrassing all branches of business', but would also encourage carelessness on the part of the employee."[83]

The doctrine, as applied until the last decade of the 19th century, meant that a worker who knew of the risk but continued in his job was deemed to have absolved his employer from all liability for resulting injury. For example, when a labourer working in a dark railway tunnel was knocked down by a passing train, his knowledge of the danger disqualified him from recovering against the company for their negligence in not providing a guard for the purpose of warning the men of approaching trains. Admittedly, "the workman who depends on his employment for the bread of himself and his family is tempted to incur risks to which, as a matter of humanity, he ought not to be exposed. But looking at the matter in a legal point of view, if a man, for the sake of the employment, takes it or continues in it with knowledge of its risks, he must trust himself to keep clear of injury."[84] The notion of assumption of risk, thus interpreted, rested in the context of our industrial society upon pure fiction;[85] and, after some misgivings expressed in 1887,[86] the defence was put on its modern foundation four years later, in the great case of *Smith v. Baker*.[87] It was there laid down that the plea cannot be sustained unless the plaintiff, with full knowledge of the risk, had expressly or by implication agreed to waive his right to redress for any injury he might sustain therefrom—thus assuming not only the physical, but also the legal, risk of harm. This was coupled with a realistic appraisal of the economic and psychological compulsion which ordinarily prevents a worker from being able to choose freely between acceptance and rejection of a risk. So it came at last to be recognised that the defence had little, if any, part to play in the context of employment which rarely provides a genuine opportunity for that freedom of choice upon which it is predicated.[88]

The fact that notwithstanding protests, the plaintiff continued with his work, no longer justifies but rather destroys any inference that he voluntarily assumed (not merely encountered) the risks of his employment.[89] Nor is it any more material that the hazard emanated from a machine he was using himself rather than from something over which he had no control. In *Smith v. Baker*,[90] the plaintiff was a quarry worker who was hit by a stone dropped from a crane which other workers were in the habit of negligently operating overhead. Although he knew of the danger and had remonstrated with the crane driver, recovery was sustained. Here the danger arose in another "department" of the works which the

83. *Tiller v. Atlantic Coast Line Rly* 318 U.S. 54 at 58-59 (1943).
84. *Woodley v. Metropolitan Rly* (1877) 2 Ex. D. 384 at 389 per Cockburn C.J.
85. *Tiller v. Atlantic Coast Line Rly* 318 U.S. 54 at 69 per Frankfurter J. (1943).
86. *Thomas v. Quartermaine* (1887) 18 Q.B.D. 685.
87. [1891] A.C. 325.
88. *Hewertson v. Courtaulds* [1957] S.R. (N.S.W.) 398; *Cianciarulo v. H.P. Products* [1959] V.R. 170.
89. *Yarmouth v. France* (1887) 19 Q.B.D. 647; *Bowater v. Rowley Regis Corp.* [1944] K.B. 476.
90. [1891] A.C. 325.

plaintiff could not control by any action of his own, but the same principle has been applied in later cases to situations where he suffered harm through defective machinery or equipment which he was obliged to handle himself in his work.[91]

The distance which legal theory has travelled since then has been immense, and judicial expressions of the social policy underlying earlier applications of the defence are now only of historical interest. The plea in employment cases has been almost totally eclipsed by the contemporary view to regard industrial accidents as part of the cost of enterprise which ought more fairly to be borne by management.[92] And even if it is still possible in an exceptional case for a worker unequivocally to absolve his employer from providing a safe system of work, perhaps in consideration of a higher wage—a question that is still open—it is at all events clearly against legal policy to permit an employer to contract out of any duty laid on him by a safety statute.[93]

As previously emphasised, the defence of voluntary assumption of risk presupposes that the employer has prima facie violated a duty of care owed to his employee. Industrial conditions abound with hazards that no amount of care by the employer can avoid, but to say that the worker assumes these risks is only a longhand way of asserting that the common law basis of liability is fault, not insurance.[94] Where, for example, the risk is necessarily involved in the very nature of the work, as in the case of a steeplejack or zoo keeper,[95] recovery fails not because he impliedly agreed to assume it, but because his employer is not responsible for risks which reasonable care could not remove or lessen. A warning, however, should be sounded lest the notion of assumption of risk, which as a formal defence has practically disappeared from industrial accidents, should stealthily re-enter in the different guise of lowered standards of care from employers, for example by postulating only a duty to warn employees unaware of the risk. Such tendency has been staunchly resisted in England,[96] though until recently less fervently in Australia.[97]

91. *Bowater v. Rowley Regis Corp.* [1944] K.B. 476; *Dewell v. Hackshalls* (1956) 74 W.N. (N.S.W.) 191 (employees entrusted with unruly horse).
92. In N.S.W. absorbed in the defence of contributory negligence: *Workers' Compensation Act* 1987 s. 151O.
93. *Wheeler v. New Merton Mills* [1933] 2 K.B. 669 (C.A.). But *I.C.I. v. Shatwell* [1965] A.C. 656 allowed the defence in answer to a claim against the employer based *solely* on his *vicarious* liability for the statutory violation of a fellow servant (not being the superior of the plaintiff nor one whose orders he was bound to obey)—i.e. in cases of joint and flagrant disobedience of a safety rule by fellow servants, when the pull of policy is plainly the opposite way.
94. Note the careful analysis by Frankfurter J. in *Tiller v. Atlantic Coast Line Rly* 318 U.S. 54 at 68 ff. (1943).
95. *James v. Wellington City* [1972] N.Z.L.R. 70 (chimpanzee).
96. See e.g. *General Cleaning Contractors v. Christmas* [1953] A.C. 180; *Smith v. Austin Lifts* [1959] 1 W.L.R. 100 (H.L.); *Bill v. Short Bros* [1963] N.I. 1 (H.L.). *Withers v. Perry Chain Co.* [1961] 1 W.L.R. 1314, far from being an exception, only goes to emphasise that an employee is still free to decide for himself whether to run risks (peculiar to himself, e.g. propensity to dermatitis) of which he is aware and which no practical precaution by the employer can eliminate.
97. *Quigley v. Commonwealth* (1981) 55 A.L.J.R. 579 at 584 per Murphy J. See now *Turner v. South Australia* (1982) 42 A.L.R. 669.

II. Common Employment

The most common nefarious judicial ploy for reducing the charges on industry was the so-called doctrine of common employment which relieved employers from vicarious liability for accidents caused by the negligence of a fellow servant.[98] Whatever its original justification when industry was vulnerable and the worker enured to hardship, it gradually fell into disrepute under the influence of changing social ideas and economic growth. Progressively whittled down by legislation and judicial doctrine, it was at long last finally abrogated by statute.[99]

The effect of that reform has been profound because it added, in substance, a new branch to the liability of employers. Managerial responsibility, formerly limited to the fundamental conditions of employment, was now reinforced by liability for negligence even in routine operations so that it no longer matters for most purposes, whether a particular accident is attributable to negligence falling within the master's personal province of duty or to a "casual" default by a fellow servant.[100] The master will be liable for both, even if there remains the technical distinction that his responsibility for the former is personal, for the latter vicarious.

III. Contributory Negligence

A worker is of course bound to exercise reasonable care for his own safety. At one time, this requirement was very rigorously applied so as to deprive him of all relief against a negligent employer, even if only a slight and casual lapse on his part contributed to the accident. This position has been vitally transformed in recent years.

Most profound was the change wrought by the introduction of apportionment,[101] as the penalty for contributory negligence ceased to be disproportionate to the victim's fault and some, at least, of the loss could henceforth be shifted to the culpable employer who would be better able to absorb it. In furtherance of this policy, the courts have on the whole emphasised the heavy managerial responsibility of employers[102] and discouraged attempts to evade apportionment by the devious practice of either exonerating employers from all causal responsibility on account of

98. Originating in *Priestley v. Fowler* (1837) 3 M. & W. 1; 150 E.R. 1030; and endorsed by the Lords in *Bartonshill Coal Co. v. Reid* (1858) 3 Macq. 266. Its rise and fall is set into its proper social context by Friedman & Ladinsky, *Social Change and the Law of Industrial Accidents*, 67 Col. L. Rev. 50 (1967). It is also notable as the first reported claim by an employee against his own employer.

99. *Workers Compensation Act* 1987 (N.S.W.) s. 151; *Wrongs Act* 1945 (Vic.) s. 24A; *Law Reform Act* 1951 (Qld); *Employers' Liability Act* 1943 (Tas.); *Law Reform (Miscellaneous Provisions) Act* 1955 (A.C.T.) s. 21; and *Law Reform (Miscellaneous Provisions) Act* (N.T.) s. 22.

100. The duty which fellow workers owe each other is defined in *Quinn v. Hill* [1957] V.R. 439 at 446. The doctrine of common employment, despite its pretended basis in assumption of risk, never was applied to preclude claims against the culpable fellow servant himself. Nor was, or is, there any legal obstacle to the common employer (if held vicariously liable) seeking from him an indemnity: *Lees v. Dunkerley Bros* [1911] A.C. 5.

101. See above, p. 271.

102. E.g. *Wingfield v. Ellerman's Line* [1960] 2 Lloyd's Rep. 16 at 23 per Devlin J.

the worker's misconduct[103] or simply postulating a lowered standard of care from defendants. Thus knowledge of the dangerous condition will disqualify an employee in only the most exceptional circumstances;[104] since it has come to be generally recognised that the employer's common law duty to protect his employees from reasonably foreseeable dangers may require safeguards against their own foreseeable carelessness;[105] whilst, a fortiori, duties of absolute obligation under factory legislation demand strictest compliance for the sake, not only of "the careful, the vigilant and the conscientious workman but [also] the careless, the indolent, the inadvertent, the weary and even perhaps in some cases the disobedient".[106]

In step with the rising standard of care demanded from employers has been a trend to take a more charitable view of the mistakes and slips of employees. For instance, a worker is today entitled to assume that his employer's system of work will provide reasonable protection, and he is not required to stop his work and imagine possible risks unless they become obvious to him.[107] All the more are learners entitled to rely on adequate instruction and supervision.[108] Again, the conditions of industrial employment are given due weight in determining whether an occasional lapse is sufficiently heinous to attract the quality of contributory negligence, and a generous view is taken in drawing the line where "mere thoughtlessness or inadvertence or forgetfulness ceases and where negligence begins".[109] Admittedly, apportionment has weakened the incentive to continue quite the same measure of indulgence;[110] but a worker is still, if no longer wholly, at least *largely* excused for inattention to his personal safety when absorbed in his work or taking a risk in the interest of his employer or taking it for granted that dangers have been eliminated by those charged with that responsibility.[111]

103. The most significant milestone was *Stapley v. Gypsum Mines* [1953] A.C. 663. Yet very gross misconduct by a worker, like deliberately courting danger in known disregard of safety regulations, is sporadically still treated as if it were the sole cause of the accident: *Norris v. Moss* [1954] 1 W.L.R. 346 ("inexcusably careless", "fantastically wrong"); *Rushton v. Turner* [1960] 1 W.L.R. 96 ("crazy"); *Sherman v. Nymboida Collieries* [1962] S.R. (N.S.W.) 757 at 770 ("wholly unreasonable"); (1963) 109 C.L.R. 580. This "proximate cause" rationale must of course be distinguished from a genuine issue of whether the defendant's breach was a cause-in-fact, in the sense that "but for it" the accident would not have happened: see above, p. 194.
104. See above, p. 509.
105. *Mt Isa v. Bates* (1972) 46 A.L.J.R. 408 (foreseeable non-use of goggles); *Baker v. Hopkins* [1959] 1 W.L.R. 966 (disobedience); *O'Hanlon v. Electric Bd* [1969] I.R. 75.
106. *Carr v. Mercantile Produce* [1949] 2 K.B. 601 at 608; *Quintas v. National Smelting* [1960] 1 W.L.R. 217 at 222 ("some degree of recklessness"); *Summers v. Frost* [1955] A.C. 740. Note also that a machine is "dangerous" and therefore requires fencing if it imperils persons "guilty of inadvertence, inattention, carelessness or folly" (*Dunlop Rubber Co. v. Buckley* (1952) 87 C.L.R. 313 at 324.)
107. *Carlyle v. Comm. Rlys* [1954] 54 S.R. (N.S.W.) 238 at 241, 249; *Westwood v. P.O.* [1974] A.C. 1 at 17. Obedience to specific orders virtually excludes contributory negligence: *Prestinenzi v. Steel Tank* [1981] V.R. 421.
108. *Shepherd v. S. J. Banks* (1987) 45 S.A.S.R. 437; *Commr Rlys v. Halley* (1978) 20 A.L.R. 409 (H.C.).
109. *Caswell v. Powell Duffryn Collieries* [1940] A.C. 152 at 176; also below, n. 116. Cf. *Sungravure v. Meani* (1964) 110 C.L.R. 24.
110. E.g. *Hicks v. B.T.C.* [1958] 1 W.L.R. 493.
111. *Knight v. Laurie* [1961] W.A.R. 129 at 133; *Machray v. Stewarts & Lloyds* [1965] 1 W.L.R. 602; Fagelson, 42 Mod. L. Rev. 646 (1979). Murphy J. in *Comm. Rlys v. Ruprecht* (1979) 142 C.L.R. 563 at 577 advocated that only exposure with full appreciation of the danger could amount to contributory negligence.

Illustrative of the forgiving mood is a decision absolving a garbage collector who was hit by a car while running across a road carrying a humper on his shoulder (his employer being held in breach for failing to adopt a safer system). The following factors were deemed significant: (1) the prevailing conditions of poor light which diminished the man's ability to pick out the vehicle and locate its speed and position accurately; (2) performance of his task necessarily involved preoccupation with the matter in hand; (3) the carrying of the humper on his right shoulder, which (4) restricted very considerably his vision and (5) he was expected to run across the road and keep up with the truck.[112] A single dissent stressed that the man's task was not repetitive nor so engrossing or difficult as to cause him to be either preoccupied or confused.

Breach of statutory duty

The effect of contributory negligence on breach of statutory duty has had a chequered career. On first principle, it might indeed seem bizarre that anyone should forfeit his right to redress when the very contingency of his carelessness was the principal reason why the defendant was put under statutory duty to safeguard him against its consequences: to allow that would be tantamount to stultifying the statute. Accordingly, the view prevailed in Australia of excusing mere contributory negligence, as distinct from severer misconduct,[113] until the House of Lords readmitted the defence on the specious ground that it was an ineluctable corollary of the concept of causation.[114] The High Court of Australia at that time considered itself bound.[115]

As a counterweight, however, a very lenient view came to be taken, both in England and Australia, of what conduct to stigmatise as contributory negligence.[116] The standard of care must be adapted to the conditions of industrial employment and due regard paid to the circumstances "under which men work in a factory or mine, to the long hours and the fatigue, to the slackening of attention which naturally arises from constant repetition of the same operation, to the noise and confusion in which men work, to his preoccupation in what he is actually doing at the cost perhaps of some inattention to his own safety."[117] While this admonition was appropriate also to actions for common law negligence, in practice an even more lenient standard came to prevail in claims for breach of statute. But since the introduction of apportionment made it possible to rebuke a plaintiff without altogether depriving him of the statutory protection, a dual standard is officially deprecated.[118] Nowadays, "mere carelessness,

112. *McLean v. Tedman* (1984) 155 C.L.R. 306 at 315-316.
113. *Bourke v. Butterfield* (1926) 38 C.L.R. 354.
114. *Caswell v. Powell Duffryn Collieries* [1940] A.C. 152.
115. *Piro v. Foster* (1943) 68 C.L.R. 313. N.S.W. abrogated the decision in the *Statutory Duties (Contributory Negligence) Act* 1945, which however no longer applies to claims against employers: *Workers Compensation Act* 1987 s. 151N. Not so limited is the *Law Reform (Miscellaneous Provisions) Act* (A.C.T.) s. 20A.
116. *Caswell v. Powell Duffryn Collieries* [1940] A.C. 152 at 178; *Davies v. Adelaide Chemical Co.* (1946) 74 C.L.R. 541 at 545.
117. *Caswell v. Powell Duffryn Collieries* [1940] A.C. 152 at 178 per Lord Wright.
118. While peculiarly appropriate to cases of "unsafe system", this admonition also applies to vicarious liability for casual negligence of fellow employees: *Comm. Rlys v. Ruprecht* (1979) 142 C.L.R. 563.

inadvertence or lack of judgment" do not as a matter of law entitle a plaintiff to complete excuse, though on the facts it may often be found not to amount to contributory negligence.[119] In any event, ample allowance will be made in apportioning responsibility so as not to eviscerate the statutory provision.[120]

The lower standard of care thus postulated for plaintiffs opens the door to the intriguing prospect that one and the same act may have different consequences according to whether the careless worker sues the employer or the latter is charged with vicarious liability by a third party, including another employee. If, for example, two fellow servants are injured by carelessness on the part of both, each may sue the employer founding on the negligence of the other, but neither might be held guilty of contributory negligence if their conduct could, for that purpose alone, be condoned as an excusable lapse.[121] This is probably the most striking example of the dual standard which has emerged from the contemporary policy of maximising loss distribution in the sphere of industrial accidents.

Complete defence

In a few situations, despite the power to apportion, it is still considered proper to bar recovery entirely. One such situation occurs where the employer is put in breach of duty[122] solely by the injured employee himself. Commonly, a statutory duty imposed on the employer (for example, to keep guards properly adjusted or a ladder firmly secured) cannot be performed by him except through the very employee whose own disobedience causes himself to get hurt. For the latter then to say to the employer "You are liable to me for my own wrongdoing" is neither good morals nor good law.[123]

But in order to entitle the employer to this defence, he must clear himself of all responsibility for the accident. The plaintiff must, quite literally, be the *sole* author of his own plight, as when an experienced asbestos sheeter was specifically told not to work on asbestos roofs without using boards and knew that it was prohibited by regulation, that boards were available and that the particular roof was unsafe.[124] The statutory duty to *use* boards could only be vicariously discharged through the plaintiff himself, and it was his disobedience alone that brought the employer into a technical (vicarious) breach. In contrast, the defence is not available in the many

119. *Kakouris v. Gibbs Burge* [1970] V.R. 502 (F.C.); *Hawkins v. Ian Ross* [1970] 1 All E.R. 180 at 188. Cf. *Rigter v. Taylor Constructions* (1974) 9 S.A.S.R. 282 at 288 ("the defence is construed more strictly").
120. *McGuiness v. Key Markets* (1972) 13 K.I.R. 249 at 253 (C.A.); *Mullard v. Ben Line* [1970] 1 W.L.R. 1414 (C.A.).
121. *Staveley Iron v. Jones* [1956] A.C. 627 at 642, 648.
122. Although mostly applied in cases of statutory violation, the defence is equally available against a worker to whom his employer has delegated performance of his common law duty to ensure a safe system of work: *Witham v. S. Bright* [1959] V.R. 790; *Richardson v. Stephenson Clarke* [1969] 1 W.L.R. 1695.
123. *Boyle v. Kodak* [1969] 1 W.L.R. 661 at 673 per Lord Diplock.
124. *Ginty v. Belmont Building Supplies* [1959] 1 All E.R. 414. Accord: *Shedlezki v. Bronte Bakery* (1970) 72 S.R. (N.S.W.) 378 (C.A.) (employee was sole manager and owner of his own company).

cases involving some independent fault by the employer, be it in managerial responsibility, like failure to give instructions or supervision where necessary,[125] or in vicarious responsibility for another servant.[126] Thus hedged, the defence does not offer undue encouragement for bypassing the statutory policy of apportionment.

A related problem, due to the added effect of the abolition of the common employment doctrine, arises where two fellow servants agree to engage in a joint enterprise fraught with danger to themselves, such as failing to secure the roof of a mine or not taking cover when testing an explosive. If they do so in conscious flouting of safety rules and with due appreciation of the risk, it would be serving neither the cause of accident prevention nor fairness to permit either one to sue his common employer, founding on the negligence of the other; for, to say the least, it would be odd if *one* careless and disobedient servant who injured himself could not recover from his master, yet *two* such servants acting jointly could. It has accordingly been held that one can neither sue the common employer nor apparently the fellow culprit.[127] This conclusion it has been found convenient to explain on the ground of voluntary assumption of risk (volenti);[128] alternatively it might have been based on joint illegal enterprise which, as previously noted,[129] could debar one participant from suing others for the sake of deterrence.

4. WORKERS' COMPENSATION

The overwhelming proportion of claims for industrial accidents is today met under workers' compensation rather than by recourse to the traditional concepts of tort liability.[130]

By the end of the 19th century, the common law pattern of liability, linked to fault and heavily tilted against recovery, was no longer considered a tolerable method of dealing with the social problem created by the vast volume of industrial injuries. The erstwhile assumption that industry could not afford to shoulder the cost of its accidents, had given way to the modern view that the welfare of its workers should be its first charge and that the cost of injury be debited to the expenses of production. The conditions of industrial employment exacted an inevitable toll in human suffering, and the fault principle, whatever its merit in other fields of tort liability, was no longer sound in its application to an area where injuries were so widespread as to be an inevitable incident of industrial activity.

125. *Boyle v. Kodak* [1969] 1 W.L.R. 661 (H.L.): failure to instruct need not amount to common law negligence.
126. *Nicol v. Allyacht Spars* (1987) 163 C.L.R. 611; *Ross v. Portland Cement* [1964] 1 W.L.R. 768 (H.L.); *McMath v. Rimmer Bros* [1962] 1 W.L.R. 1 (C.A.).
127. *I.C.I. v. Shatwell* [1965] A.C. 656; *Hugh v. N.C.B.* 1972 S.L.T. (N.) 56. See Atiyah, 43 Can. B. Rev. 609 (1965); Dias, [1966] Cam.L.J. 75.
128. Ibid.
129. See above, p. 305.
130. 500,000 claims Australia-wide more than half in N.S.W. (1980-1981). In the U.K. 10.5% of work injuries receive tort damages (*Pearson* §24); Australia would be much the same.

In response to these pressures, Workmen's Compensation Acts[131] introduced a pioneer system of social insurance, designed to protect the worker and his family against financial ruin in the wake of work injuries.[132] Its most important feature is that entitlement to benefits is a matter of right, and not dependent on proof of fault in the employer and absence of culpable neglect in the employee.[133] This dispenses with the protracted litigation necessitated by the common law conditions of recovery, and ensures compensation for loss or reduction in earning capacity—for the sake of society as much as for the welfare of the immediate recipients. As previously explained,[134] the cost of the system[135] is borne by industry and passed to the consumer in the price of the product. Although the resulting "internalisation" has been claimed as a potential spur to accident reduction, other deterrents are in practice much more important, especially work disruption, demoralisation, adverse publicity and public safety inspection.

Benefits

The tremendous load of the scheme compels a high degree of standardisation of benefits.[136] Moreover, the benefits are not designed to provide anything like full compensation for all injurious consequences of a work accident expressible in monetary terms. Thus, unlike the general tort measure of damages, compensation is calculated without reference to pain and suffering, the overriding criterion being loss or reduction in earning capacity.[137] The usual award is for a weekly subsistence allowance, linked to pre-accident earnings but limited both in amount and duration.[138] In

131. The English Act of 1897, inspired by Bismarck's historical measure of 1884, was in turn speedily adopted throughout Australia. Thereafter however, legislation has deviated in many particulars from the English model which was itself replaced by National Insurance in 1946: see below, p. 523. The current Acts are cited above, n. 9. See Sykes & Yerbury, *Labour Law in Australia* (1980) vol. 1, ch. 13, 14. A comprehensive study is Wilson & Levy, *Workmen's Compensation* (1939) 2 vols. The leading English text is by Willis, *Workmen's Compensation Acts* (37th ed. 1945), for N.S.W. by Boulter, *Workers' Compensation Practice in New South Wales* (1966).
132. Under the original formulation, the claimant had to prove "injury *by accident* arising out of *and* in the course of employment". This postulated a strict causal connection between injury and employment and precluded recovery in most cases of disease, but gradually certain industrial diseases were specifically included. Coverage was also significantly extended by replacing "and" by "or" and even eliminating "by accident". See Luntz, *Workmen's Compensation and a Victorian Amendment of 1965*, 40 A.L.J. 179 (1966). "Journey injuries" from and to work are now also included. But neither development has occurred in England: Ogus & Berendt, *Law of Social Security* (1978) 276-293.
133. Only serious and wilful misconduct bars recovery, and not even then if the worker suffered death or serious and permanent disablement: see e.g. *Murray v. Moppett* [1958] S.R. (N.S.W.) 59.
134. See above, p. 9.
135. $775 mill. in premiums for employers' liability insurance in 1979-1980.
136. See *Workers' Compensation Legislation in Australia 1980* (Dept of Social Security) Table 2.
137. Except in N.S.W. since 1987 (s. 67: proportionate to $43,700). To the extent that benefits fall below actual losses, the cost of accidents is subsidised by ("externalised" to) the worker or society in general: Egner, *Personal Injury Awards and Workmen's Compensation*, 18 U.W. Ont. L. Rev. 269 (1979).
138. A useful tabulation of benefits is found in *Compensation and Rehabilitation in Australia* (1974) 76-84; also *Pearson* III 158-161. Benefits are either indexed or updated by amendment.

the case of death, dependants are entitled to lump sums which in some States are fixed by the relevant statute, and in others are calculated by reference to the earnings of the deceased during the preceding three or four years. In case of disablement, additional to medical expenses, lump sums are also payable for specified permanent injuries, like loss of limbs, in accordance with a scale, and therefore commonly referred to as "schedule injuries" or "Table of Maims"; since payable independently of lost earnings, they resemble common law damages for loss of faculty. Between 20 and 30 per cent of all payments go towards medical and hospital expenses, but even these are not uniformly without "caps".

Claim administration

With a view to expediting and de-legalising procedure, several Australian States[139] have entrusted the administration of workers' compensation, including the settlement of contested claims, to special tribunals, variously called workers' compensation "commissions", "boards" or "industrial courts", some of which include lay representatives of working class organisations and of employers' or insurance interests.[140] In other States, the adjudication of disputes falls either to industrial magistrates,[141] arbitrators specifically appointed by the parties,[142] or to the ordinary courts of law.[143] A common requirement is that disputes be settled in accordance with equity and good conscience and without regard to strict rules of evidence or precedent, but the almost uniform practice of legal representation has had the result that the "trial" tends to follow accustomed legal techniques even in the "special tribunal" States, while the continued tendency to resort to precedent is attested by the existence of at least one series of reports of compensation cases.[144]

Unhappily, the participation of private insurance companies contributes significantly to the very high cost of administration.[145] These and other inefficiencies, including the neglect of rehabilitation, provide a strong argument for replacing the existing set-up with a centralised system of compensation, as in Britain, New Zealand and now in Victoria.[146]

Alternative remedies

Varying solutions have been adopted in different countries for correlating workers' compensation with tort recovery and other sources of accident compensation. One of the most widespread—prevailing in the United

139. N.S.W., S.A., W.A. and N.T.
140. As in Victoria and W.A., but not in N.S.W.
141. Queensland.
142. A.C.T.
143. Tasmania.
144. See Sawer, "Industrial Law" in Paton (ed.), *The British Commonwealth—Australia*, 293-294.
145. Management expenses and commissions alone account for at least 20% of premiums. The cost of delivering $1 in benefits is 50c. See *Compensation and Rehabilitation in Australia* (1974) 86-87. The Canadian record is much better, because the schemes are carried by State funds: Ison, *Workers' Compensation in Canada* (1983).
146. *Accident Compensation Act* 1985, which established a Compensation Commission.

States, Canada, Germany and France—was to abolish the employer's and co-employees' tort liability except for intended injury and other very serious transgressions.[147] The British model, on the other hand, left the common law remedy intact, partly for its imagined effect on accident prevention, partly because it was felt unfair to deprive a victim of negligence of his own claim to damages, especially as compensation benefits in Britain were always meagre. It survived there into the modern system of National Insurance for industrial injuries.[148] As already noted, recent Australian legislation has progressively abandoned this tradition by also severely restricting or totally abolishing tort claims against employers and fellow employees.

Co-existence of workers' compensation and tort liability in turn raised the problem of overlapping benefits. For long, the solution was to put the claimant to his election. This entailed several unsatisfactory features. First, it tempted him to renounce the benefits of compensation for the prospect of larger recovery at common law. If the gamble did not succeed, the very evils which workers' compensation was intended to avoid at once reappeared; in any event the notorious congestion of court lists delayed the plaintiff's alleviation from financial plight until his case was finally brought to a successful conclusion. Secondly, endless litigation and numerous legislative amendments bear witness to the difficulty of devising a satisfactory formula for what constituted an irrevocable exercise of option. Most of these objections have at last been met by following in varying measures the erstwhile New Zealand model of permitting the worker to exercise both rights cumulatively, subject to deducting from any subsequent damages the value of compensation benefits already received.[149]

If the accident was caused by the negligence of a third party, the plaintiff may pursue his tort remedy against him, notwithstanding legislation restricting his right to sue his employer or co-employees. His damages will, however, be reduced by any compensation benefits paid; the employer may in turn claim from the third party.[150]

Social insurance in Britain

In Great Britain, in train with the fundamental post-war reorganisation of social security inspired by the Beveridge Report of 1942, workers' compensation was (as from 1948) replaced by a system of benefits for

147. Fleming, *Work Injuries*, XV Int. Encycl. Comp. L. ch. 9.
148. This controversial recommendation of the Monckton Committee on Alternative Remedies (1946) §74 was reaffirmed by *Pearson* §913. In the U.K. 10.5% of work injuries receive tort compensation (*Pearson* §24).
149. See Sykes & Yerbury, *Labour Law in Australia* (1980) 310-332; *Fox v. Wood* (1981) 148 C.L.R. 438; *Batchelor v. Burke* (1981) 55 A.L.J.R. 494.
150. *Commonwealth Employees' Rehabilitation and Compensation Act* 1988 s. 50; *Workers Compensation Act* 1987 (N.S.W.) s. 150; *Accident Compensation Act* 1985 (Vic.) s. 138; *Workers Rehabilitation and Compensation Act* 1986 (S.A.) s. 54; the Workers' Compensation Acts (Qld Schedule s. 24), W.A. (s. 93), Tas. (s. 9), A.C.T. (s. 12). On the question, dependent on statutory language, whether the employer's "indemnity" may exceed the employee's entitlement to damages, see *Xpolitis v. Sutton* (1977) 51 A.L.J.R. 509. In the U.S. it is universally derivative. Canadian provinces still insist on election.

industrial injuries within a unified social insurance scheme.[151] Although as a matter of first impression a good case could have been made for undifferentiated benefits whatever the cause of disability,[152] the view prevailed that industrial injuries deserved a higher level of benefits, if only because this discrimination had become an established fact of life in the past half century. However, this "industrial preference" has been allowed gradually to erode and is now significant only as regards long-term disability benefits. In accordance with the prevailing social welfare dogma, benefits were related to need, including family responsibility, rather than earnings. Since then, however, the mood has been to return to earnings-related benefits and contributions. "Injury benefits" for incapacity to work, not exceeding six months, are payable at a flat rate, with an earnings-related supplement since 1966. Thereafter sufferers of long-term injury become entitled to "disablement benefit" for "loss of faculty", the degree being assessed by reference to a tariff; the benefit is in the form of a pension of an amount legislatively prescribed from time to time. Being based on an abstract loss (functional disability) rather than loss of earnings, it resembles common law awards for "loss of faculty". As an accommodation to the totally disabled for their loss of earnings, an unemployability supplement is payable on a flat rate, increased by family allowances. In totality, the benefits can well equal pre-accident earnings and may in the end be more beneficial than common law damages, especially for workers injured early in life and with large families.[153]

New also is that the cost is no longer an exclusive charge on industry; contributions are exacted also from employees as part of their general social security contributions, earnings-related up to a certain maximum but at a flat percentage.[154] By opting for a contribution rate independent of the accident experience of the particular industry, let alone of any particular unit within that industry, all opportunity was abandoned of using the rating structure as a catalyst for added safety by rewarding the diligent and penalising the indifferent.[155] Indeed, as a matter of deliberate policy, dangerous industries like mining, which are almost always credited with significant national importance, were considered entitled to this disguised subsidy.

151. Now, *Social Security Act* 1975 ch. 4. See Atiyah, *Accidents* ch. 15; Ogus & Barendt, *Law of Social Security* (3rd ed. 1988) ch. 8.

152. The disproportionate cost of line-drawing between different entitlements is emphasised by Lewis, *Tort and Social Security: The Importance Attached to the Cause of Disability*, 43 Mod. L. Rev. 514 (1980). Total administration cost is 13%.

153. *Pearson* §182. The total annual cost (1976: 600,000 new cases) was £250 mill.; cf. £70 mill. in tort for 90,000 (*Pearson* §772).

154. Ogus & Barendt, op. cit., ch. 2. Employees contribute 6.5%, employers 12% of earnings.

155. However, there is now renewed interest in exploring differentials: Phillips, *Economic Deterrence and Prevention of Industrial Accidents*, 5 Ind. L.J. 148 (1976).

25

DEFAMATION

1. INTRODUCTION

The law of defamation seeks to protect individual reputation. Its central problem is how to reconcile this purpose with the competing demands of free speech. Both interests are highly valued in our society, the one as perhaps the most dearly prized attribute of civilised man, the other the very foundation of a democratic community. This antithesis is particularly acute when the matter at issue is one of public or general interest. Not surprisingly, the balance has shifted over the years, generally in favour of freer flow of information and criticism. But in contrast to the United States which is constitutionally committed to "freedom of speech [and] of the press", libel actions still play a prominent role in our own public affairs as a regular arsenal of political combat.[1]

The complex web of checks and balances which characterises the contemporary law of defamation can be explained in part as the law's—however inadequate—attempt to come to terms with this difficult dilemma. But it also bears the scars of old and long-forgotten battles. The upshot is a patchwork of rules, many of which had their origin in false starts and later attempts to correct previous errors.[2] Over the last century, legislation periodically contributed its share to this ongoing but frustrating process of reform.[3] In most jurisdictions, the current law is therefore a mosaic of statute and common law. Its complexities are enhanced by the variations, often considerable, in State legislation. Since the media, especially radio and television, nowadays reach a national audience, the argument for a uniform Australian codification is irrefutable. After a failed start by the Commonwealth to enact a national law,[4] New South Wales, Victoria and Queensland finally joined to adopt "uniform" defamation laws in 1992. This will ease the lot of interstate media running the gauntlet of differing laws of each jurisdiction.[5]

1. See Newcity, *The Sociology of Defamation in Australia and the U.S.*, 26 Tex. Internl. L.J. 1 (1991); Fleming, *Libel and Constitutional Free Speech*, *Essays for Atiyah* 333 (1991).
2. See e.g. Weiler, *Defamation, Enterprise Liability and Freedom of Speech*, 17 U. Tor. L.J. 278 (1967). The leading English text is *Gatley on Libel and Slander* (8th ed. 1981).
3. In post-war Britain, there have been two systematic inquiries: the Porter (1948) and the Faulks Committees (1975); in Australia the A.L.R.C. (1979) and the N.S.W.L.R.C. (1971); in N.Z. the Committee on Defamation (1977).
4. Based on an initiative by the A.L.R.C.'s *Unfair Publication* (1979).
5. Conflict rules require application of the law of each State of publication: *A.B.C. v. Waterhouse* (1991) A.T.R. 81-147, where Samuels J.A. compared the American "single publications rule" and considered reform measures.

Codes

An earlier codification movement was largely inspired by Sir Samuel Griffith who, as Chief Justice of Queensland, was responsible for the relevant legislation in 1889 and 1899.[6] This codification provides a complete repository of the principles of actionable defamation,[7] so that common law decisions are relevant only to explain ambiguity or to furnish a guide to the application of analogous principles enacted in the Code itself. Although intended primarily as an enactment declaratory of the common law, it introduced several material changes into the contemporary law of defamation, and later judicial development of the common law has widened this gap.

The Queensland model was successively adopted by Tasmania (1895),[8] Western Australia (1902),[9] and for a time in New South Wales (1958-1974).[10] Elsewhere, the law is a mosaic of common law overlaid by, far from uniform, statutory modifications.[11]

2. CAUSE OF ACTION

I. What is Defamatory

A defamatory statement may be defined as one which tends to lower a person in the estimation of his fellows by making them think the less of him. Frequently, it takes the form of an imputation calculated to bring the plaintiff "into hatred, contempt or ridicule",[12] whether by direct statement, irony, caricature or any other means; but it is not necessary that the words have the tendency to excite feelings of disapprobation, provided they cause him to be shunned and avoided.[13] To say of a man that he is

6. The Defamation Law 1889 originally dealt both with civil and criminal proceedings, but the *Criminal Code* 1899 (modelled on Fitzjames Stephen's) repealed the greater part of the earlier statute and is now the sole source of the criminal law. The former enacts that "it is unlawful to publish defamatory matter unless such publication is protected, or justified, or excused by law" (s. 8), and "the unlawful publication of defamatory matter is an actionable wrong" (s. 9). The Code contains the definition of "defamatory matter" (s. 370) and the conditions under which its publication is "excused".
7. But it has been argued that the Codes are exclusive only as to defences with which they deal: Sykes, 1 U. Qld L.J. (No. 3) 19 at 24-27.
8. Now: *Defamation Act* 1957.
9. Now: *Criminal Code* 1913 ch. 35. This statute has only limited application to civil claims, viz. ss 354 (fair reports), 355 (fair comment), 356 (truth), specifically declared "lawful", but not s. 357 which declares qualified privilege a "lawful excuse" (*W.A. Newspaper v. Bridge* (1979) 141 C.L.R. 535).
10. This yielded a formidable harvest of case law, of continuing value in the remaining Code States as well as a trenchant and exhaustive critique in the N.S.W.L.R.C. (Report 11, 1971). Replaced by a new codification, *Defamation Act* 1974.
11. Vic.: *Wrongs Act* 1958; S.A.: *Wrongs Act* 1936; A.C.T.: *Defamation Act* 1901; N.T.: *Defamation Act* 1938. Many of these provisions derive from 19th century English statutes: *Lord Campbell's Act* 1843, *Law of Libel Amendment Act* 1888, *Slander of Women Act* 1891.
12. Parke's B. definition in *Parmiter v. Coupland* (1840) 6 M. & W. 105 at 108; 151 E.R. 340 at 341.
13. In the Codes, "defamatory matter" is defined as "any imputation concerning any person, or any member of his family, whether living or dead, by which the reputation of that person is likely to be injured, or by which he is likely to be injured in his profession or trade, or by which other persons are likely to be induced to shun or avoid or ridicule or despise him" (Qld: s. 366; W.A.: s. 346; Tas.: s. 5; see below, p. 528).

insane[14] or of a woman that she has been raped[15] does not arouse sentiments of animosity but rather sympathy and pity in the minds of decent people. Yet such assertions are defamatory because, without suggesting discreditable conduct, they impute to the plaintiff a condition calculated to diminish the respect and confidence in which he is held. A person's standing in the community, taking people as they are with their prejudices and conventional standards, is just as likely to be impaired by an attribution of misfortune as of contemptible conduct. In this matter, it is to shut one's eye to realities to indulge in nice distinctions.[16]

Defamation is not limited to aspersions upon an individual's private character—his reputation for honour, honesty or integrity—but embraces also disparagements of his reputation in trade, business, profession or office.[17] Thus it may be defamatory to attribute authorship of an inferior book to a prestigious writer[18] or to accuse a doctor,[19] architect[20] or official of incompetence[21] or even a politician of having lost the confidence of his party.[22]

The question of what standard to apply in determining whether a statement is defamatory has not been answered uniformly.[23] The criterion commanding the widest verbal support seems to be the reaction aroused in citizens of "fair average intelligence"[24] or "ordinary decent folk in the community, taken in general".[25] This test is not identical with "reasonable", still less with "ideal". Thus it was held defamatory to impute to a lady that she had been raped;[26] so also, depending on time and place, to call someone a German,[27] a Communist,[28] a Jew,[29] a

14. *Morgan v. Lingen* (1863) 3 L.T. 800.
15. *Youssoupoff v. M-G-M* (1934) 50 T.L.R. 581.
16. Ibid. at 587 per Slesser L.J.
17. But if tainted with illegality, like unlicensed practice of medicine or bookmaking, plaintiff must fall back on injury to his private reputation: *Smith's Newspaper v. Becker* (1932) 47 C.L.R. 279; *Wilkinson v. Sporting Life* (1933) 49 C.L.R. 365; *Kings Cross Whisper v. Ray* (1970) 72 S.R. (N.S.W.) 339 (C.A.); *Macintosh v. Truth (N.Z.)* [1962] N.Z.L.R. 137.
18. *Ridge v. English Illustrated Magazine* (1913) 29 T.L.R. 592. Similarly, to publish a mutilated edition of an author's work: *Lee v. Gibbings* (1892) 67 L.T. 263. Cf. *Moore v. News of the World* [1972] 1 Q.B. 441 (false attribution additionally actionable under *Copyright Act* 1956 s. 43).
19. *Jools v. Mirror Newspaper* (1984) 57 A.L.R. 1; *Drummond-Jackson v. B.M.A.* [1970] 1 W.L.R. 688 (C.A.).
20. *Andrews v. Fairfax* [1980] 2 N.S.W.L.R. 225 ("building looks like a sieve").
21. *Pratten v. Labour Daily* [1926] V.L.R. 115; *Potts v. Moran* (1976) 16 S.A.S.R. 284. Contra: *Boyd v. Mirror Newspaper* [1980] 2 N.S.W.L.R. 449 (rugby player "fat and cumbersome").
22. *Fairfax v. Punch* (1980) 31 A.L.R. 624.
23. See also below, p. 530 (interpretation).
24. *Slatyer v. Daily Telegraph* (1908) 6 C.L.R. 1 at 7 per Griffith C.J.
25. *Gardiner v. Fairfax* (1942) 42 S.R. (N.S.W.) 171 at 172 per Jordan C.J. So "meaning" in general is that of "ordinary sensible" persons (see below, p. 530).
26. *Youssoupoff v. M-G-M* (1934) 50 T.L.R. 581.
27. *Slazengers Ltd v. Gibbs* (1916) 33 T.L.R. 35.
28. See *Cross v. Denley* (1952) 52 S.R. (N.S.W.) 112; *Braddock v. Bevins* [1948] 1 All E.R. 450; *Brannigan v. Seafarers' Union* (1963) 42 D.L.R. (2d) 249.
29. *Camrose v. Action Press* (1937) unreported.

Jew-hater,[30] a scab[31] or a homosexual.[32] The increasing diversity of beliefs and attitudes in modern (Australian) society precludes an appeal to a single standard of "right-thinking" people[33] and suggests as sufficient that the allegation was calculated to stir up adverse feelings among a substantial and respectable group of the community, without them being shared in other quarters.[34] Thus to call a doctor an abortionist would be defamatory in the estimation of all "right to life" advocates, without so much as a suggestion that she was an *unlawful* abortionist.[35]

On the other hand, it is not sufficient that the words are regarded as prejudicial by only a small minority whose standards are so anti-social that it would not be proper for courts to recognise them. This reservation has been used to support the questionable conclusion that it is never defamatory to accuse someone of giving information to the police even if the community's attitude to the particular type of informer is one of contempt—on the specious ground that to hold it defamatory would be condoning the alleged offence, like the keeping of gambling machines.[36] Under the standard of the "right-thinking" man, the question becomes, not what most people in fact think of informers, but what they *should* think. This is not only inconsistent with the ordinary practice of deferring to actual community attitudes however prejudiced, but confuses the courts' duty to enforce all crimes alike with the accepted purpose of the law of defamation to protect individuals against (false) allegations calculated to lower them in the esteem of their fellows.

Defamation can be conveyed in any number of styles. What matters is the tendency of the utterance, not its form. Ridicule, for example, is a familiar weapon for attacking reputation, as by juxtaposing the plaintiff's portrait with that of a gorilla in a magazine article[37] or by publishing a photo of him in what appears to be an obscene posture.[38] On the other hand, if the expression is so extravagant that it cannot be regarded as going to character[39] or is made as a harmless joke and so understood, its defamatory barb may thereby disappear, as when one smilingly greets another with the words, "How are you, you old horse thief?"

30. *De Stempel v. Dunkels* [1938] 1 All E.R. 238; *Templeton v. Jones* [1984] 1 N.Z.L.R. 448.
31. *Murphy v. Plasterers Society* [1949] S.A.S.R. 98; *Ellis v. Grant* (1970) 91 W.N. (N.S.W.) 920 (particulars ordered because of multiple meanings).
32. *R. v. Bishop* [1975] Q.B. 274 at 281.
33. A test endorsed by Lord Atkin in *Sim v. Stretch* (1936) 52 T.L.R. 669 at 671. The A.L.R.C. (1982) defended it for its protection of innocent publishers so long as liability is not based on fault.
34. *Hepburn v. TCN* [1983] 2 N.S.W.L.R. 682 (C.A.).
35. Ibid. at 694 per Glass J.A.
36. *Rest. 2d* §559, comment *e* respects "substantial and respectable" minority views but would agree with *Byrne v. Deane* [1937] 1 K.B. 818 and *Mawe v. Pigot* (1869) 4 Ir. R.C.L. 54 which refused to condone anti-social views like contempt for police informers. The cases are criticised by Fricke, *Criterion of Defamation*, 32 A.L.J. 7 (1959).
37. *Zbyszko v. New York American* 239 N.Y.S. 411 (1930).
38. *Burton v. Crowell Publishing Co.* 82 F. 2d 154 (2d Cir. 1936); *Ettingshausen v. Aust. Consol. Press* (1991) 23 N.S.W.L.R. 443.
39. *Gwynne & Small v. Wairarapa* [1972] N.Z.L.R. 586 (protest marchers likened to "Hitler's puppets").

It is often said that mere vulgar abuse or insulting name-calling does not qualify as defamation. This must be understood in the sense that vituperative epithets are frequently insulting to pride rather than disparaging reputation. If intended as mere abuse and so understood by the hearer, such remarks are not actionable at common law,[40] unless accompanied by physical aggression amounting to assault or calculated to cause and in fact resulting in physical injury, such as nervous shock.[41] Much, of course, depends on the manner and surrounding circumstances in which the words are spoken.[42] The same remark may be slander or insult according to whether it is made with due deliberation or bawled out at the height of a violent quarrel. Hence there is less occasion for drawing the distinction in cases of written, as distinct from spoken, words because they usually convey the impression of calculated reflection and are more easily understood as discrediting rather than just insulting.[43]

Not all falsehoods calculated to injure are defamatory: defamation is confined only to those striking at character or reputation. The dividing line is sometimes delicate, and (subject to the usual judicial control) is for the jury to decide. A disparaging remark concerning the quality of merchandise may or may not import a reflection on the plaintiff's conduct of his business; to say that *all* his goods are shoddy undoubtedly would; not so, however, that one particular article was defective.[44] So, to say that someone is seriously ill is not defamatory in the absence of an innuendo that he is malingering.[45] The distinction is important because non-defamatory falsehood is not actionable at common law unless made with intent to injure and actual damage be proved,[46] whereas liability for defamation attaches irrespective of fault and mostly regardless of whether actual injury be shown. In the result, it is easier to sue for a falsehood that imputes to the plaintiff some peccadillo than for one alleging that he has ceased to carry on business[47] or ascribing to a parliamentary candidate political beliefs he does not profess. The Codes, however, treat the last-mentioned falsehoods as defamatory by including "imputations concerning any person by which he is likely to be injured in his *profession or trade*".[48]

Who may be defamed

Any living person may be defamed, but no action lies for defamation of the dead, however distressing to relatives and friends: neither do they have a derivative cause of action for defamation nor a direct claim for injury to

40. *Mundey v. Askin* [1982] 2 N.S.W.L.R. 369 ("vermin"); *Hoebergen v. Koppens* [1974] 2 N.Z.L.R. 597 at 601 ("Dutch bastard").
41. As in *Wilkinson v. Downton* [1897] 2 Q.B. 57; see above, p. 32.
42. See *Penfold v. Westcote* (1806) 2 B. & P. (N.R.) 335; 127 E.R. 656.
43. The point was not even taken in *Theaker v. Richardson* [1962] 1 W.L.R. 151.
44. See *Drummond-Jackson v. B.M.A.* [1970] 1 W.L.R. 688 (C.A.) (attack on dentist's technique may be defamatory); *South Hetton Coal v. N.E. News* [1894] 1 Q.B. 133 at 139.
45. *Grappelli v. Block* [1981] 1 W.L.R. 822.
46. *Ratcliffe v. Evans* [1982] 2 Q.B. 524; see below, p. 710.
47. *Dawson v. Mirror Newspaper* [1979] 1 N.S.W.L.R. 16.
48. See above, n. 13. This expansive construction, probably unintended by the draftsman, was established in *Hall-Gibbs v. Dun* (1910) 12 C.L.R. 84; reaffirmed in *Sungravure v. M.E. Airlines* (1975) 134 C.L.R. 1. Also recommended by A.L.R.C. 78; and see the *T.P.A.* (below, pp. 651, 713).

their feelings. Indeed, reputation is regarded as so "personal" an attribute that an action for defamation does not survive for the benefit of the plaintiff's estate.[49] While biographers and historians deserve some latitude, support has been gaining for allowing close relatives to obtain at least a declaration of falsity and injunction (but no damages) for the first few years after death.[50] A residual, though now virtually obsolete, safeguard against gross abuse remains in criminal prosecutions for libel of the dead.[51] A defamatory statement primarily directed against a dead person may, of course, involve a slur on the living, as by impugning a person's parentage by calling his dead mother a whore.[52]

Corporations may vindicate attacks upon their reputation in civil actions no less than criminal prosecutions.[53] Notwithstanding earlier doubts stemming from unrealistic notions concerning their artificial status, a corporation may have a character for stability, soundness and fair dealing, as essential to its commercial success as it is vulnerable to attack, quite like the business reputation of a natural person. A trading company may accordingly complain of any defamation calculated to damage its business interests or goodwill, such as false imputations of insolvency, mismanagement or improper, unfair and dishonest conduct of its affairs.[54] Even a local government body,[55] professional association[56] or trade union[57] may vindicate its "governing" or "professional" reputation. Appropriately, damages are due only for injury to its trade or business reputation;[58] indeed, it has been suggested that they be confined to proven special damage, that is, actual identifiable financial loss, or at least to allegations likely to cause such loss.[59]

A corporation may accordingly now complain of libels affecting not only property, but also its institutional reputation, though it obviously cannot recover damages for hurt feelings. True, the libel must have been directed against itself rather than against its individual officers. But a corporation itself can be guilty of misconduct *through* its officers, and such an imputation may qualify as a libel actionable in its own right. Thus a municipal corporation successfully sued for an attack on its governing

49. See below, p. 677.
50. A.L.R.C. 54-56; *Faulks* 114-116 and N.Z. Committee. See Symmons, *New Remedies against Libellers of the Dead*, 18 U.W. Ont. L. Rev. 521 (1980).
51. *R. v. Critchley* (1734) 4 T.R. 129n. Abolished in N.S.W. (1974 s. 50).
52. The Code definition of "defamatory matter" (see above, n. 13) makes special allowance for that situation, but does not seem to enlarge it beyond the common law: *Livingstone-Thomas v. Assoc. Newspapers* (1969) 90 W.N. (Pt 1) (N.S.W.) 223 at 235.
53. *R. v. Macnamara* (1893) 14 L.R. (N.S.W.) 515.
54. *S. Hetton Coal v. N.E. News* [1894] 1 Q.B. 133; *Barnes v. Sharpe* (1910) 11 C.L.R. 462.
55. *Bognor Regis U.D.C. v. Campion* [1972] 2 Q.B. 169, excoriated for its suppression of political speech by Weir [1972A] Cam. L.J. 238.
56. *Sask. College of Physicians v. C.C.F. Publishers* (1965) 51 D.L.R. (2d) 442.
57. *National Union v. Gillian* [1946] K.B. 81 (nullified by English legislation: *Electrical Union v. Times Newspaper* [1980] Q.B. 585); *Pulp & Paper Workers v. International Brotherhood* (1973) 37 C.L.R. (3d) 687 ("Communist Front organisation").
58. *A.B.C. v. Comalco* (1986) 68 A.L.R. 259: no damages for "reputation as such", as approved by Mahoney J.A. in *Andrews v. Fairfax* [1980] 2 N.S.W.L.R. 225.
59. *Faulks* ch. 13, inspired by Weir, see above, n. **000**. Contra: *Mount Cook Group v. Johnstone Motors* [1990] 2 N.Z.L.R. 488.

body[60] and a trade union for being accused of deliberately rigging a ballot of its members.[61]

II. Interpretation

Frequently words are ambiguous or capable of being understood in several senses, defamatory in one but not another. What meaning is to be attached to them: that intended by the author? that understood by the addressee? or some tertium quid?

The first (intended meaning) was long ago disqualified: one may be liable though innocent of any intention to defame.[62] The second (comprehended meaning) seems most compatible with the purpose of damages being to compensate for actual injury, provided only that to understand the words in a defamatory sense was not unreasonable. In some respects, indeed, this test is important. The words, for example, must have been published to someone capable of understanding them in a defamatory sense, not in a foreign language he could not comprehend.[63] So also, if the words are not defamatory on their face but only with the aid of additional information, they must have been published to someone with that information.[64] Otherwise, however, the strange dogma prevails that the words must be understood in their "natural and ordinary" meaning, in defiance of the plain semantic truth that it is futile to look for any single meaning as being the "right" meaning. Thus, testimony as to how the words were actually understood is irrelevant, perhaps even inadmissible.[65]

At one time bent on discouraging actions for slander, courts insisted that oral words be interpreted in their most favourable sense and that the plaintiff negative any innocent meaning they might bear.[66] Thus it would not have been actionable to say of a man that he married his aunt, for she could conceivably have been his uncle's widow. But this artificially restrictive approach has long been abandoned under the influence of the more liberal rules of libel, and all expressions however published now fall to be scrutinised for any damaging meaning that would be put on them by "ordinary sensible men [or women]"[67] who strike the golden mean of being neither unusually suspicious nor unusually naive.[68] "The ordinary reasonable reader does not, we are told, live in an ivory tower. He can, and does, read between the lines, in the light of his general knowledge and experience of worldly affairs. He is a layman, not a lawyer, and his capacity for implication is much greater than that of a lawyer. Especially in

60. *Bognor Regis U.D.C. v. Campion* [1972] 2 Q.B. 169.
61. *Willis v. Brooks* [1947] 1 All E.R. 191: and see *National Union v. Gillian* [1946] K.B. 81.
62. See below, p. 539.
63. See below, p. 536.
64. Ibid.
65. *Toomey v. Fairfax* (1985) 1 N.S.W.L.R. 291 (on the spurious ground that it would encroach on the jury function). Cf. Diplock L.J.'s scornful comments in *Slim v. Daily Telegraph* [1986] 1 Q.B. 157 at 177ff. Yet allowance is made for the fact that words may have a secondary "ordinary" meaning: see below, p. 532.
66. Known as the "mitior sensus" rule, it disappeared under Holt C.J. in the early 18th century. Extravagant examples are *Holt v. Astgrigg* (1607) Cro. Jac. 184; 79 E.R. 161; *Foster v. Browning* (1625) Cro. Jac. 688; 79 E.R. 596.
67. *Lewis v. Daily Telegraph* [1964] A.C. 234 at 286 per Lord Devlin.
68. Ibid. at 259 per Lord Reid.

newspaper cases, he is understandably prone to engage in a certain amount of loose thinking. On the other hand, the reader of a book would read it with more care than he would a newspaper. But in both cases, there is also a very wide degree of latitude given to the capacity of the matter complained of to convey particular imputations where the words are imprecise, ambiguous, loose, fanciful or unusual."[69]

For example, different interpretations can be placed upon the common statement that a person has been charged with crime. It might or might not carry the additional imputation that reasonable grounds exist for suspecting that he committed the offence, or the even more damaging imputation that the charge is well founded.[70] The same goes for an announcement that the plaintiff has ceased to be an employee or agent of the declarant.[71] As Lord Devlin warned, "a man who wants to talk at large about smoke may have to pick his words very carefully if he wants to exclude the suggestion that there is also a fire. . . . Loose talk about suspicion can very easily convey the impression that it is a suspicion that is well founded."[72]

Meaning cannot be discovered without regard to the context of the expression. However disparaging at first blush, it may reveal its complete innocence if explained in the light of the circumstances attending its publication. Particularly, the meaning of oral words can never be divorced from the speaker's gesture, tone of voice and facial expression. "One recalls the instance of the lady who in a West End drawing-room accused a noble lord of being a thief, but when one is told that she said, with a smile, 'Lord X, you are a thief, you have stolen my heart' one recognises that to call a person a thief is not necessarily actionable."[73] Nor must a particular statement be taken out of context. The sting may be drawn by what follows immediately afterwards—"the bane and the antidote must be taken together", as when a libel was repeated in the report of a verdict the plaintiff obtained against the libeller.[74] But as we shall see, mere contradiction or expressions of doubt do not ordinarily justify repetition by others.[75]

Innuendo

Conversely, an apparently innocent statement may well hide a defamatory barb. Such a secondary meaning may be derived either from the words themselves by "reading between the lines", as it were, or with the aid only of additional, extrinsic information. An assertion, for example that a Labor candidate is endorsed by the Communist Party is fairly, and without more, open to the insinuation that he is a fellow traveller or

69. *Farquhar v. Bottom* [1980] 2 N.S.W.L.R. 380 at 386 per Hunt J., distilling a series of descriptions from prior case law.
70. *Sergi v. A.B.C.* [1983] 2 N.S.W.L.R. 669 at 676. Upon its precise meaning will depend how it can be justified: see below, p. 555.
71. E.g. *Munro v. Coyne* [1990] W.A.R. 333 (F.C.).
72. *Lewis v. Daily Telegraph* [1964] A.C. 234 at 285. E.g. *Hayward v. Thompson* [1982] Q.B. 47 (C.A.). See also *Morris v. Sanders* [1954] 1 W.L.R. 67 (employees "dismissed"); *Baker v. Australian & N.Z. Bank* [1958] N.Z.L.R. 907 (cheque returned "present again"); *Church of Scientology v. Anderson* [1980] W.A.R. 71 ("evading taxes").
73. *Broome v. Agar* (1928) 138 L.T. 698 at 702 per Sankey L.J.
74. *Chalmers v. Payne* (1835) 2 Cr. M. & R. 156; 150 E.R. 67.
75. See below, p. 555.

communist sympathiser, just as a report that the police are investigating a certain individual may be understood to imply that there is reason to suspect him of crime. By contrast, a newspaper notice mistakenly announcing that the plaintiff has given birth to twins is wholly innocuous, howsoever read, until it appears aliunde that she was married only four weeks before;[76] an erroneous identification of a woman as "Mrs X" looks utterly harmless in the absence of an explanation that X is really married to someone else;[77] and displaying the model of the plaintiff in a waxwork exhibition assumes a distinctly derogatory connotation only in the light of the additional fact that the figure was juxtaposed to three criminals and immediately adjoining the "Chamber of Horrors".[78]

To lawyer and layman alike, all types of secondary meaning have come to be known as "innuendos", for in order to be on the safe side the practice developed early of pleading an innuendo whenever the defamation was not absolutely explicit in the sense of being necessarily inherent in the peccant expression.[79] Somewhat perplexingly, however, a "true" innuendo (in the technical sense of a separate cause of action, with distinct verdict) is now confined to those derogatory implications alone which require the aid of extrinsic evidence.[80] On the other hand, our courts have not, like some American courts,[81] discriminated against such libels by making them actionable only, like slander, on proof of special damage. Once qualifying as defamatory, whether on their face or aliunde, they are treated as libel for all purposes.

Judge and jury

Ever since Fox's *Libel Act* 1792 it has been looked upon as a staunch safeguard of democratic liberty that the issue of "libel or no libel" be within the exclusive province of the jury.[82] Indeed, so entrenched is this principle that the widespread scepticism regarding jury participation in civil litigation has not cast the slightest shadow on their function in defamation cases and, with but isolated exceptions,[83] trial by jury in actions for libel

76. *Morrison v. Ritchie* (1902) 4 F. 645; *Bell v. N. Constitution* [1943] N.I. 108.
77. *Cassidy v. Daily Mirror* [1929] 2 K.B. 331; *Hough v. London Express* [1940] 2 K.B. 507. For innuendo of identification see also below, p. 539.
78. *Monson v. Tussauds* [1894] 1 Q.B. 671.
79. Indeed, "popular" or "false" innuendos must still be pleaded or particulars will be ordered when words are capable of multiple meanings: *D.D.S.A. v. Times Newspapers* [1973] Q.B. 21; *Australian Consolidated Press v. Rogers* [1971] 1 N.S.W.L.R. 682; *James v. N.Z. Tablet* [1976] 2 N.Z.L.R. 545. *Prichard v. Krantz* (1984) 37 S.A.S.R. 379 held plaintiff bound by the meanings so alleged.
80. *Lewis v. Daily Telegraph* [1964] A.C. 234; *Barclay v. Cox* [1968] V.R. 664; *Bowles v. Truth (N.Z.)* [1965] N.Z.L.R. 768. The "separate cause of action" theorem was criticised by the Faulks (§104) and N.S.W. (§50) Committees and rejected for Qld in *Composite Buyers v. Clarke* [1988] 2 Qd R. 602 (F.C.).
81. Known as libel per quod, this departure was probably in origin due to muddled thinking (confusing per se with ex facie), but owes its vogue to the belief that libels not defamatory on their face are ordinarily innocuous and that an innocent publisher deserves sympathy. Since fault is now required in all cases, the latter argument has been undermined: see *Rest. 2d* §569.
82. The Act applied in terms only to criminal cases but its principle was extended to civil claims.
83. S.A. and the A.C.T.

and slander has remained a matter of right in Australasia, as it has in England.[84]

But the exercise of this function is, as always, subject to judicial control. For not unless the court is first satisfied that the words are reasonably capable of bearing the defamatory meaning ascribed to them by the plaintiff, would the jury be allowed to pass upon whether, in their opinion, they so bear it.

The discharge of this preliminary function calls for the exercise of restraint, lest the jury be ousted from a task entrusted to it on high constitutional grounds. In the past there was, it is true, a tendency to give perhaps undue weight to a possible innocent meaning.[85] Today, however, as already noted, the courts will only reject those "meanings which can only emerge as the product of some strained or forced or utterly unreasonable interpretation".[86] If judges should exercise sparingly the power of withdrawing a case from the jury, appellate courts are all the more reluctant to interfere with verdicts except in the most egregious cases.[87] This is so especially in actions for slander. Where the allegation is in writing, the court on appeal may well be in as good a position to determine the issue as was the jury, but not in oral defamation where so much depends on the defendant's behaviour attending the publication.[88] Thus when a mistress orally accused her chauffeur of "joyriding" in her car and of being a "rotter", a verdict in her favour was allowed to stand.[89] In brief, it is only when the words are necessarily defamatory[90] or palpably innocent[91] that a court is justified in setting aside a contrary finding.

III. Reference to the Plaintiff

A defamatory statement is not actionable unless published "of and concerning" the plaintiff. True, he need not be specifically mentioned or identified, nor need there be so much as a "peg or pointer",[92] so long as the tenor reasonably implicates him. For instance to say that A (a married man) is a bachelor[93] or a cuckold[94] may defame his wife. But to allege that

84. See *Rothermere v. Times Newspaper* [1973] 1 W.L.R. 448 (C.A.).
85. E.g. *Capital Bank v. Henty* (1882) 7 App. Cas. 741 ("the principles were never better formulated nor perhaps ever worse applied": *Slim v. Daily Telegraph* [1968] 2 Q.B. 157, 187).
86. *Jones v. Skelton* [1963] 1 W.L.R. 1362 at 1370 (P.C.).
87. *Cairns v. Fairfax* [1983] 2 N.S.W.L.R. 708 (upholding defence verdict).
88. *Lang v. Willis* (1934) 52 C.L.R. 637 at 670.
89. *Broome v. Agar* (1928) 44 T.L.R. 339.
90. *Gwynne & Small v. Wairarapa Times Age* [1972] N.Z.L.R. 586.
91. *Somers v. Fairfax* (1879) 2 S.C.R. (N.S.) (N.S.W.) 140 at 144.
92. *Morgan v. Odhams Press* [1971] 1 W.L.R. 1239 (H.L.). Still less is there any shelter behind pseudonyms (*J'Anson v. Stuart* (1787) 1 T.R. 748) or the familiar blurb that the "characters and incidents in this book are fictional and have no reference to any person living or dead" (*Corrigan v. Bobbs-Merrill Co.* 126 N.E. 260; 10 A.L.R. 662 (N.Y. 1920)).
93. See *Cassidy v. Daily Mirror* [1929] 2 K.B. 331; *Hough v. London Express* [1940] 2 K.B. 507.
94. *World Hosts v. Mirror Newspaper* [1976] 1 N.S.W.L.R. 712 at 727 (affd 141 C.L.R. 632) where "reflective imputation" is fully discussed. But vice versa? *Krahe v. TCN* (1986) 4 N.S.W.L.R. 536.

A's father became a psychiatric patient does not injure A's reputation, however it may injure his filial feelings.[95]

The test for identification is the same as for defamatory meaning: *not* "Did the defendant intend to aim at the plaintiff",[96] but "would a *sensible* reader reasonably identify the plaintiff as the person defamed?"[97] Here also the standard of reasonableness is not high: the ordinary reader of a newspaper article, especially of the sensational variety, is not expected to read "with cautious and critical analytical care",[98] he may read "casually and not expecting a high degree of accuracy"[99] and indulge "in a certain amount of loose thinking"[100] and even "rather far-fetched inferences".[101] Evidence of witnesses that they believed the defamation to refer to the plaintiff is certainly admissible, even necessary when identification depends on special knowledge of the plaintiff, but it is of course not conclusive. The recent trend reveals an increasing latitude not only in the relevant standard but also in passing the issue to the jury. Thus it was deemed sufficient to link the plaintiff with a kidnapping gang merely because he had been seen with the victim about that time,[102] and to link another plaintiff with a large scale wheat theft because she was engaged in the wheat business in the area and had a criminal record of dishonesty.[103] Since liability is not dependent on fault,[104] this liberality imposes a correspondingly greater burden on publishers.

Because the plaintiff's cause of action must arise at the time of the defendant's publication, his being named in a subsequent publication is not ordinarily admissible, because it would be unfair to hold the defendant responsible for somebody else's subsequent action in fingering the plaintiff. Thus an announcement by the plaintiff's ex-agents that his concert had been cancelled because he was seriously ill was not rendered actionable by a later newspaper announcement that he was to appear elsewhere, although it suggested that he had been lying.[105] It would be different if the later publication had been the defendant's, as where the first was defamatory on its face and the second identified the plaintiff as the person referred to[106] or where the first invited the reader to ascertain the plaintiff's identity in a forthcoming TV programme.[107]

95. *Livingstone-Thomas v. Assoc. Newspapers* (1969) 90 W.N. (Pt 1) (N.S.W.) 233 (C.A.). The odd Code definition of defamatory matter ("concerning any person, *or any member of his family*": see above, n. 13) is not credited with any difference.
96. See below, p. 539.
97. *Morgan v. Odhams Press* [1971] 1 W.L.R. 1239 (H.L.). If words in their natural meaning do not identify plaintiff, "true" innuendo is required: *Vadic v. Ballarat News* [1981] V.R. 213.
98. *Morgan v. Odhams Press* [1971] 1 W.L.R. 1239 at 1254 per Lord Morris.
99. Ibid. at 1270 per Lord Pearson.
100. Ibid. at 1245 per Lord Reid.
101. Ibid. at 1244 per Lord Reid.
102. *Morgan v. Odhams Press* [1971] 1 W.L.R. 1239 (H.L.), described as a "thin case" (at 1250).
103. *Steele v. Mirror Newspaper* [1974] 2 N.S.W.L.R. 348 (C.A.).
104. See below, p. 539.
105. *Grapelli v. Block* [1971] 1 W.L.R. 822.
106. *Hayward v. Thompson* [1982] Q.B. 47; *Ware v. Associated Newspapers* (1969) 90 W.N. (N.S.W.) 180 at 184-185.
107. *Baltinos v. Foreign Language Publ.* (1986) 6 N.S.W.L.R. 85.

Group defamation

The problem of identification becomes singularly acute in cases of group defamation. The common law set its face against civil sanctions for vilification, not of individuals, but of a whole class of persons distinguishable by race, colour, creed or calling, in part because of concern over multiplicity of claims,[108] in part for fear of unduly inhibiting political discussion and criticism.[109] In the last resort, the criminal law of seditious libel provides a residual, though no longer favoured, weapon for combating the most odious of this kind of demagoguery.[110] At any rate, so far as civil claims are concerned, the plaintiff is up against the requirement that the words were published "of and concerning" him, and "the reason why a libel published of a large or indeterminate number of persons described by some general name generally fails to be actionable is the difficulty of establishing that the plaintiff was, in fact, included in the defamatory statement, for the habit of making unfounded generalisations is ingrained in ill-educated or vulgar minds, or the words are occasionally intended to be a facetious exaggeration".[111]

But this difficulty the plaintiff may yet overcome by proving himself to be specifically identified, either because the group is so small that the accusation can reasonably be understood to refer to any one of its members, or because the circumstances of publication permit the conclusion that it was he who was aimed at from amongst the group.[112] Most relevant, though not necessarily decisive, are of course the size of the class, the generality of the charge and its extravagance. Thus while it would clearly not be actionable to say that "all lawyers are thieves",[113] a charge levelled against a group of seven Roman Catholic clergymen was held to point an accusing finger at every one of them,[114] and an allegation of cruelty "in some of the Irish factories" capable of supporting a jury verdict that it referred specifically to the plaintiff's.[115] But as always it is for the judge to rule initially whether the offending words can be considered capable of referring to the plaintiff as an individual, and the practice in this instance has not erred on the side of liberality. For example, if the defendant indulged in some unfounded generalisation, conveying imputations of disgraceful conduct to a group, but there is nothing to point to any individual member, the mere fact that the mind of some of the plaintiff's

108. But why not a (class) action for an injunction?
109. A limited remedy by way of declaration, injunction (Manitoba *Defamation Act* s. 19) or right of reply might mitigate those concerns, as recommended by A.L.R.C. §102, Faulks §423 and N.Z. Commission §442.
110. See Riesman, *Democracy and Defamation: Control of Group Libel*, 42 Col. L. Rev. 727, 1085 (1952) who argues that prohibition is less effective than correction, and often self-defeating in creating martyrs. In the U.S., the remedy is now of questionable constitutional validity, despite *Beauharnais v. Illinois* 343 U.S. 250 (1950): see Arkes [1974] Sup. Ct Rev. 281.
111. *Knupffer v. London Express* [1944] A.C. 116 at 122 per Lord Atkin.
112. E.g. if to an article, vilifying all city taxi drivers, there is appended a photo of the plaintiff's cab. Also perhaps if the defendant intended to aim at the plaintiff: *Lloyd v. David Syme* [1986] A.C. 350 at 364 (the "West Indies").
113. *Eastwood v. Holmes* (1858) 1 F. & F. 347 at 349; 175 E.R. 758 at 759.
114. *Browne v. Thomson* 1912 S.C. 359.
115. *Le Fanu v. Malcolmson* (1848) 1 H.L.C. 637; 9 E.R. 910; also *Godhard v. Inglis* (1902) 2 C.L.R. 78.

friends turned to him on reading it is quite immaterial and insufficient to get him to the jury.[116]

Even if only one (but unidentified) member of a small group is attacked, all may be under suspicion and thus defamed.[117] So also if the imputation is against "some" or "most" of a small group.[118] All the more, where two persons are accused in the alternative.[119]

IV. Publication

The essence of tortious defamation lies in the communication of the disparaging statement to someone other than the person defamed. For unlike the criminal law,[120] the civil law was concerned not so much with insult as with injury to reputation, the esteem in which one is held by others. This requirement is known by the name of "publication".[121] It is not necessary that the communication be made public, in the sense of being addressed to a large audience. "Utterance" to a single individual is enough, provided he is someone other than the plaintiff himself. Dictation to a secretary[122] or the handling of a telegraphic message in the course of transmission[123] are sufficient. Publication may be to any third party, even to a servant of a company defamed,[124] except that the common law exempted communications between spouses.[125] This exception originally rested on the threadbare fiction of identity between husband and wife, but is better explained as an absolute privilege in recognition of the confidential nature of the conjugal relation.[126]

The publication must have been made to a person capable of understanding the defamatory meaning; not, for example, in a foreign language which the reader or listener is unable to understand, nor on a postcard when none but a "privileged" addressee could know that it contains a reference to the plaintiff.[127] If the allegation is ex facie defamatory and refers by name to the person defamed or, without mentioning him by name, describes him in such a way that the man in the

116. *Knupffer v. London Express* [1944] A.C. 116; *Dowding v. Ockerby* [1962] W.A.R. 110.
117. *Pryke v. Advertiser* (1984) 37 S.A.S.R. 175 (one out of four); *Forrington v. Leigh* (*The Times*, 10 Dec. 1987) (C.A.). But see *McCormick v. Fairfax* (1989) 16 N.S.W.L.R. 485.
118. *Rest. 2d* §564A, comment *c*; *Bjelke-Petersen v. Warburton* [1987] 2 Qd R. 465 (F.C.) ("some"); *Neiman-Marcus v. Lait* 13 F.R.D. 311 (S.D.N.Y. 1952) ("most of the sales staff are fairies").
119. *Albrecht v. Burkholder* (1889) 18 O.R. 287; contra: *Chomley v. Watson* [1907] V.L.R. 502.
120. *R. v. Adams* (1888) 22 Q.B.D. 66. But some modern statutes (e.g. in N.S.W., N.Z.) have adopted the requisite of publication.
121. For proof see *Gaskin v. Retail Credit* [1965] S.C.R. 297.
122. *Riddick v. Thames Bd Mills* [1977] Q.B. 881 at 898-899. But such publication may enjoy incidental privilege: see below, p. 576.
123. *Tobin v. City Bank* (1878) 1 S.C.R. (N.S.) (N.S.W.) 267; *Williams v. Freer* (1874) L.R. 9 C.P. 393.
124. *Traztand v. G.I.O.* [1984] 2 N.S.W.L.R. 598.
125. *Wennhak v. Morgan* (1888) 20 Q.B.D. 635. Aliter, publication to the *plaintiff's* spouse: *Wenman v. Ash* (1853) 13 C.B. 836; 138 E.R. 1432; *Howard v. Howard* (1885) 2 W.N. (N.S.W.) 5.
126. See below, p. 563.
127. *Sandgrove v. Hole* [1901] 2 K.B. 1.

street would know to whom it referred,[128] it is unnecessary to prove that the person to whom it was published had any knowledge of the plaintiff or that the allegation led him to think the less of him. But if it is not ex facie defamatory or does not clearly identify the person alleged to be defamed, and the defamatory character which is attributed to the imputation or the identity of the person defamed would be apparent only to persons who had knowledge of special circumstances, it is necessary in proof of publication to establish that it was communicated to someone with such knowledge.[129] In *Cross v. Denley*[130] the defendants, trading under the name of "Denley Print", printed leaflets attacking a motion picture on familiar communist lines and placed at the foot "Express Print, Auburn". They handed the pamphlets to an emissary of the "Peace Movement", and a quantity of them was subsequently showered into an audience at the picture theatre where the film was being shown. On the following day, a newspaper published an item reporting the incident and drew attention to the imprint. The plaintiff's registered trade name was "X-press Printery, Auburn", and some of his customers reading the report formed the conclusion that he was a communist sympathiser. He failed, however, to recover because, relying solely on the publication at the theatre, he was unable to produce a witness who possessed the special knowledge of being able to identify him with the person referred to in the pamphlet. But it need not apparently be shown that anyone possessing such special knowledge actually understood the imputation in the sense alleged, provided reasonable persons who knew of the special circumstances might so understand it.[131] Moreover, it is quite immaterial that the person to whom the communication was made did not give credence to the allegation.[132]

Every participant in the publication incurs liability, regardless of the precise degree of his involvement. Included is not only everyone concerned in the actual distribution or dissemination, but also those who composed the libel, such as press agencies, advertisers or even freelancers employed to prepare the script.[133] So are, besides the newspaper proprietor, the printer[134] and all involved in its circulation; though as we shall see hereafter, the standard of liability has been relaxed in favour of mere mechanical distributors.[135] Beyond that, a person may incur liability not only for his own acts of publication, but also when others foreseeably

128. Thus, if the description is such as to identify him clearly to reasonably informed people, e.g. by referring to the plaintiff as "the Prime Minister of Australia", it is not necessary to call a witness to attest that he had read the defamatory matter and knew who the Prime Minister was.
129. *Consolidated Trust v. Browne* (1948) 49 S.R. (N.S.W.) 86; *Kruse v. Lindner* (1978) 19 A.L.R. 85 (Fed. C.A.); *Fullam v. Newcastle Chronicle* [1977] 1 W.L.R. 651. Aliter in Code States where imputation need not be disparaging: *Mirror Newspaper v. World Hosts* (1979) 53 A.L.R. 243.
130. (1952) 52 S.R. (N.S.W.) 112.
131. *Hough v. London Express* [1940] 2 K.B. 507 at 515.
132. *Morgan v. Odhams Press* [1971] 1 W.L.R. 1239 at 1246, 1252 (H.L.). But it may affect damages: *Bekker v. Wrack* [1937] N.Z.L.R. 549.
133. *Webb v. Bloch* (1928) 41 C.L.R. 331 at 362-366. Advertiser and newspaper are *joint* tortfeasors, unlike press agency and independent newspaper: *Eyre v. N.Z.P.A.* [1968] N.Z.L.R. 736.
134. *Eglantine Inn v. Smith* [1948] N.I. 28 at 33.
135. See below, p. 541.

publish or republish his defamatory utterances.[136] And although, generally speaking, a plaintiff cannot complain who has himself assented to or acquiesced in the publication,[137] let alone happened to be the one who gave currency to the libel, it is otherwise if he foreseeably published it in performance of a duty, like the union secretary who passed on a member's requisition for an executive meeting containing libels on himself,[138] or in justifiable self-defence, like the 14-year-old who sought his older brother's advice after receiving a letter accusing him of theft.[139]

Exceptionally, one may even become responsible for a libel by failing to take affirmative steps to prevent its publication by someone else, as when the manager of a club omitted to remove a defamatory notice pinned to a board by a member.[140] By knowingly permitting a libel to remain after reasonable opportunity to remove it, the person in control of the premises becomes liable as for its republication, if the inference is drawn that he has made himself responsible for its continued presence[141]—at all events unless its obliteration or removal would involve a great deal of trouble and expense.

Multiple publication

Every single copy of a book or newspaper is treated as a separate publication furnishing its own cause of action. Thus although the edition may originally have appeared ages ago, any copy procured within the period of limitation even for the sole purpose of suing thereon, will qualify.[142] So also in the case of television or radio broadcasting, every reception can be sued for separately so that a plaintiff can select the law most favourable to him in an interstate transmission.[143] However, damages may be assessed for the entire issue wherever published;[144] and in order to discourage multiple ligitation, some statutes now prohibit more than one action in respect of a multiple publication without leave of the court[145] and allow evidence in mitigation of any previous recovery of damages.[146]

136. See below, p. 552.
137. *Chapman v. Ellesmere* [1932] 2 K.B. 431 (stewards' decisions to be published in "Racing Calendar"); *Kirk v. Reed* [1968] N.Z.L.R. 801 (consent to being photographed did not imply consent to publication of photo); and see below, p. 568.
138. *Collerton v. MacLean* [1962] N.Z.L.R. 1045. Also *Jones v. Amalg. T.V. Services* (1991) 23 N.S.W.L.R. 364.
139. *Hedgpeth v. Coleman* 111 S.E. 517 (N.C. 1922). Aliter in case of a middle-aged woman: *Hills v. O'Bryan* [1949] 2 D.L.R. 716.
140. *Byrne v. Deane* [1937] 1 K.B. 818.
141. Ibid. at 838; *Urbanchich v. Drummoyne M.C.* (1988) A.T.R. 81-127.
142. *Duke of Brunswick v. Harmer* (1849) 14 Q.B. 185; 117 E.R. 75.
143. E.g. *Gorton v. A.B.C.* (1973) 22 F.L.R. 181 (A.C.T.); *Allsopp v. Incorporated Newsagencies* (1975) 26 F.L.R. 238 (newspaper).
144. *Toomey v. Mirror Newspaper* (1985) 1 N.S.W.L.R. 173.
145. E.g. *Defamation Act* 1974 (N.S.W.) s. 9(3); recommended by Faulks 80 and A.L.R.C. 59. It is also ordinarily vexatious to prosecute more than one action simultaneously in different jurisdictions: *Maple v. David Syme* [1975] 1 N.S.W.L.R. 97. Judicial power to consolidate actions was conferred by the (Eng.) *Law of Libel Amendment Act* 1888, since adopted in most Australian jurisdictions.
146. See below, n. 667.

V. The Fault Element

Reputation is so stringently protected that liability for publishing defamatory statements attaches without any showing of fault. Liability does not depend on the intention of the defamer, but on the fact of defamation.[147] This has not always been so. At one time, the plaintiff was put to proof that the defendant was inspired by malice[148] but, as memory of the ecclesiastical and Star Chamber heritage faded, the pleading of malice gradually withered into a meaningless formality. In 1825, it was finally settled that absence of ill-will against the person defamed and honest belief in the truth of the allegation did not excuse.[149] Malice remains of importance today only for the purpose of defeating the defences of qualified privilege and fair comment, or as a reason for awarding exemplary damages.

The law of defamation does not even look to the meaning intended by the writer or speaker, but to the meaning attached by a reasonable reader or listener.[150] "A person charged with libel cannot defend himself by showing that he intended in his own breast not to defame, or that he intended not to defame the plaintiff, if in fact he did both."[151] In consequence, a publisher may be held liable for a statement, harmless on its face, which by reason of extrinsic facts unknown to him unhappily turns out to be defamatory. In *Cassidy v. Daily Mirror*[152] a newspaper published a photograph with the caption: "Mr Corrigan, the racehorse owner, and Miss 'X' whose engagement has been announced." Corrigan himself had supplied this information to the photographer and authorised its publication. Unknown to the publisher, however, Corrigan was lawfully married to the plaintiff, who complained that the item was libellous of her because it suggested that she was an immoral woman who had illicitly cohabited with a man who was not her husband. Armed with evidence that acquaintances had understood the words in the suggested sense, she recovered substantial damages.

Not only is the intention of the writer immaterial in considering whether the meaning of his statement is defamatory, but it is equally irrelevant that he did not mean to refer to the plaintiff at all. If the identification used is not specific but could refer to one of several individuals, the writer takes the risk that it will be understood as referring to someone other than the person he had in mind. "The question is not who was aimed at, but who was hit." Thus there is a risk that a person named can be reasonably

147. *Cassidy v. Daily Mirror* [1920] 2 K.B. 331 at 354. "If the publication was libellous the defendant took the risk. As was said of such matters by Lord Mansfield, 'Whatever a man publishes, he publishes at his peril' " (*Peck v. Tribune Co.* 214 U.S. 185 at 189 per Holmes J. (1909)). The statement by Lord Mansfield is found in *R. v. Woodfall* (1774) Lofft 776 at 781; 98 E.R. 914 at 916.

148. Holdsworth, *Defamation in the 16th and 17th Centuries*, 41 L.Q.R. 13 at 24-26 (1925).

149. *Bromage v. Prosser* (1825) 4 B. & C. 247; 107 E.R. 1051.

150. A compromise formulation, best avoided, is to ask: Was the defendant reasonably *perceived* as having intended to defame the plaintiff?

151. *Lee v. Wilson* (1934) 51 C.L.R. 276 at 278 (Dixon J.). Somewhat incongruously, evidence that the defendant intended to defame the plaintiff is relevant and admissible: *Lloyd v. David Syme* [1986] A.C. 350 at 364 (P.C.); *Lee v. Wilson* (1934) 51 C.L.R. 276 at 288-289; criticised in *Baltinos v. Foreign Language Publ.* (1986) 6 N.S.W.L.R. 85.

152. [1929] 2 K.B. 331 (C.A.); foll. *Hough v. London Express* [1940] 2 K.B. 507.

identified with someone else, as when a newspaper published a report of a police inquiry, containing allegations of bribery against a ''Detective Lee''. The reference was intended for a Constable Lee of the Motor Registration Branch, but was understood by some persons to relate to each of two Detectives Lee who were attached to the C.I.B. Since the allegations were reasonably capable or referring to them, both succeeded in their actions.[153] By more detailed identification liability could have been avoided.

In the leading case of *Hulton v. Jones*[154] this rule was applied to fiction. The defendants published a libellous narrative, intended to refer to a fictitious person, one Artemus Jones. The plaintiff who answered to this unlikely name was allowed to recover, because the description was capable of being reasonably understood to refer to him and was actually so read by several acquaintances. Obviously, fiction must not become a shield for character assassination, but the law's concern is with defamatory lies masquerading as truth, not with defamatory tales purported to be fiction. By ignoring the writer's intent and indulging a latitudinal standard of identification, creative literature is unnecessarily victimised.[155]

Nor, all the more, can liability be avoided for accidental typographical or similar errors which have the effect of conveying a meaning, or referring to a person, other than intended, for example the mistaken substitution of ''coloured'' for ''cultured gentlemen'',[156] a reference to a firm under the heading ''First Meetings under the Bankruptcy Act'' instead of under ''Dissolutions of Partnership'',[157] or the erroneous insertion of the plaintiff's photograph in an advertisement for whiskey.[158]

Innocent publication

The justification for this stringent liability is presumably that it is more equitable to protect the innocent defamed rather than the innocent defamer (who, after all chose to publish); another is that the publication, not the composition of the libel, is the actionable wrong, making the state of mind of the publisher, not the writer, relevant. On the other hand, since one does not as a rule *act* at one's peril, why should the law demand that one publish at one's peril, especially when what one says is not defamatory on its face? Does reputation deserve a higher level of protection than personal safety?

The rule has come to be widely viewed as an unwarranted restriction on freedom of expression in a democratic society. In the United States it was indeed eventually held in violation of the constitutional guarantee of freedom of speech and of the press in its application to matters of public concern, and replaced by a minimal requirement of proven fault.[159] Actually there is little evidence that it has imposed too onerous a burden

153. *Lee v. Wilson* (1934) 51 C.L.R. 276; *Newstead v. London Express* [1940] 1 K.B. 377.
154. [1910] A.C. 20.
155. Other defences become untenable: as fiction, the matter is obviously false. Worse still, being known to be false, punitive damages may be in order. This declension has caused concern in the U.S.: e.g. 42 Md. L. Rev. 387 (1983).
156. *Upton v. Times-Democrat* (1900) 104 La. 141.
157. *Shepheard v. Whitaker* (1875) L.R. 10 C.P. 502.
158. *Peck v. Tribune Co.* 214 U.S. 185 (1909). The portrait was that of a female teetotaller.
159. *Gertz v. Welsh* 418 U.S. 323 (1974); *Rest. 2d* §§558, 580A and 580B.

on the publishing industry.[160] In most instances the publisher's error is avoidable with care, either by diligent checking of the proofs or by identifying the person aimed at in such a manner as to exclude the possibility of the description fitting anyone else.[161] It should also be remembered that an action for defamation is the sole means available to plaintiffs desirous of clearing their reputation.

An alternative solution was the English statutory reform of 1952, since widely adopted in Australia and in New Zealand,[162] exonerating an innocent defamer who has made an offer of amends by means of publishing a suitable correction and sufficient apology. "Innocent publication", however, is defined rather narrowly to comprise only two situations: (1) where the publisher did not intend to publish the words of and concerning the plaintiff and did not know of circumstances by virtue of which they might be understood to refer to him; and (2) where the words are not defamatory on the face of them and the publisher did not know of circumstances by virtue of which they might be understood to be defamatory of that person, and where in either case the publisher exercised all reasonable care in relation to the publication. It does not cover the more common case of a plainly defamatory libel which the publisher reasonably but erroneously believed to be true.[163] Because this test is too strict and the procedure too cumbersome,[164] the defence has been practically a dead letter.

Strict liability has also been modified in the following other respects:

Distributors

Liability for unintentional defamation, not preventable by the exercise of due care, devolves only on primary participants in the publication, such as the writer, newspaper company or its owner.[165] Persons who are not concerned with the production but play the more subordinate role of mere distributors, like newsagents,[166] booksellers,[167] libraries[168] and, it is

160. Juries are averse to awarding large sums of money in these actions: in *Newstead v. London Express* [1940] 1 K.B. 377, plaintiff recovered one farthing; in *Lee v. Wilson* (1934) 51 C.L.R. 276, £50. Damages and legal costs are in any event tax-exempt: *Herald v. F.C.T.* (1932) 48 C.L.R. 113. The A.L.R.C. recommended against any change.
161. In *Lee v. Wilson* (1934) 51 C.L.R. 276, the reporter had originally taken down the evidence correctly in shorthand, but transcribed it carelessly by altering "First Constable" to "Detective" Lee—"possibly because the statement then appeared more sensational"(!): Starke J. at 286.
162. Respectively the Defamation Acts of England (1952 s. 4), (N.S.W.) (1974 ss 36-45; *Mirror Newspaper v. Fitzpatrick* [1984] 1 N.S.W.L.R. 643); Tas. (1957 s. 17), N.Z. (1954 s. 6). Proposed also by Vic. and Qld.
163. It is doubtful whether it covers even cases like *Upton v. Times-Democrat* and *Peck v. Tribune Co.*. In *Bell v. N. Constitution* [1943] N.I. 108 failure to authenticate a birth notice communicated by telephone was stigmatised as "gross negligence". Moreover, in England and Tasmania it does not avail the innocent publisher of someone else's malicious libel. (Criticised by Faulks as contrary to *Egger v. Chelmsford* [1965] 1 Q.B. 248).
164. See *Goldsmith v. Sperrings* [1977] 1 W.L.R. 478 at 486-488 per Lord Denning.
165. *Levien v. Fox* (1890) 11 L.R. (N.S.W.) 414.
166. *Emmens v. Pottle* (1885) 16 Q.B.D. 354. The A.L.R.C. recommended extension to wholesalers (§187).
167. *Bottomley v. Woolworth* (1932) 48 T.L.R. 521 (American magazines).
168. *Martin v. British Museum* (1894) 10 T.L.R. 338.

suggested, printers under modern technological conditions,[169] are treated more sympathetically. According to the most accepted view, these escape responsibility on proof that they neither knew nor had reason to know or suspect that they were handling defamatory material.[170] Even this reduced responsibility has been criticised as too onerous. For apart from uncertainty as to precisely what precautions are required to negative negligence, the defendant is in a quandary once a claim of libel is made. More reasonable would be to require distributors to yield only to an injunction.[171]

The debate over whether to treat radio defamation as libel or slander[172] has a parallel in the controversy concerning the basis of liability of broadcasting stations for defamatory utterances by persons other than employees using the station's facilities.[173] On the one hand, it is argued[174] that the radio is indistinguishable from the press in its capacity to injure reputation, its financial resources and the fact that, at any rate so far as commercial stations are concerned, broadcasting is a business for profit. To exonerate the radio station where the newspaper would be liable is to favour one medium of mass communication in its competitive struggle with the other.[175] Moreover, the facilities offered by a broadcasting station to the defamer involve a more active co-operation than the more or less mechanical part played by telephone and telegraph companies, which have been held to be mere secondary participants in the publication.[176] On the other side, it is emphasised that radio defamation presents problems to which rules of liability applicable to kindred wrongs cannot be easily adapted. Radio programmes are not controllable in the same way as printed matter prior to release, and extemporaneous interpolations are virtually unpreventable, unless stations take the precaution—as they now usually do—of broadcasting only recorded productions.[177] Influenced by a general bias against strict liability, it is urged that radio defamation should be

169. Unlike the A.L.R.C. (§188), *Faulks* recommended extending the defence of innocent dissemination to printers (82-84) and qualified privilege to translators (84-85).

170. *Vizetelly v. Mudie's Library* [1900] 2 Q.B. 170 (circulating library liable for negligence, because it overlooked publisher's circular requesting return of the offending book).
Under the Codes, a seller of literature is not liable unless he knows that defamatory matter is contained therein or (in the case of periodicals) that defamatory matter was habitually or frequently published therein: Qld: ss 385-386; W.A.: ss 365-366; Tas.: s. 26; but only the last applies to civil actions. Also, an employer is not liable for a sale by his servant, unless he authorised it knowing that it contained defamatory matter or (in the case of periodicals) that defamatory matter was habitually or frequently published therein: Qld: s. 387; W.A.: s. 367; Tas.: s. 27. This section applies to civil as well as criminal liability; quaere, W.A.: 2 Annual L. Rev. 43, 47-48 (1951).

171. Recommended by A.L.R.C. §186.

172. See below, p. 547.

173. *Rest. 2d* offers no decided view: §577, caveat, comment *g*. The station is, of course, liable for its own announcer.

174. Finlay, *Defamation by Radio*, 19 Can. B. Rev. 353 at 362-371 (1941); Eldredge, *Modern Tort Problems* (1941) 53-67; and see the powerful dissent by Wachenfeld J. in *Kelly v. Hoffman* 61 A. 2d 143; 54 A.L.R. 2d 951 (N.J. 1948).

175. *Sorensen v. Wood* 243 N.W. 82; 82 A.L.R. 1098 (Neb. 1932).

176. See Smith, *Liability of a Telegraph Company for Transmitting a Defamatory Message*, 20 Col. L. Rev. 30, 369 (1920).

177. Arguably the price of "live" broadcasts should include potential liability for "unpreventable" defamation. Liability is undisputed when the station fails to vet a videotape or, in a broadcast interview, invites a defamatory answer: *McRae v. S.A. Telecasters* (1976) 14 S.A.S.R. 162 (also as publisher regardless).

recognised as a new tort based on fault.[178] In the United States, a legislative pattern has developed, reflecting the effectiveness of the industry's lobby rather than any detached principle, of at once classifying radio defamation as slander and relieving stations from liability for defamatory statements by persons other than their employees or agents, provided only they exercised due care to prevent broadcasting of such statements.[179]

Unintentional publication

Another modification of strict liability is the requirement that the publication itself must have been either intended or negligent. There is no liability for intentionally defamatory matter published accidentally, unlike accidentally defamatory matter published intentionally. This perplexing result is the outcome of the one-sided emphasis on the publication rather than the composition of the libel. Functionally, the distinction has little merit because fault would rather point the other way and the victim in either case stands in equal need of vindication.

The unintentional publisher escapes responsibility only if he can clear himself of negligence. Hence, while it is not ordinarily actionable to send a libellous letter directly to the person defamed, the writer will incur liability if he should reasonably have anticipated that it might well be opened by someone else, like the addressee's husband[180] or secretarial staff,[181] or even that the addressee himself, in duty bound, would have to pass it on to others.[182] So, one who imputes a discreditable action to another's face must observe care that it is not overheard by strangers.[183] It is negligent to communicate defamatory matter on a postcard, and publication will be presumed if the postcard is circulated in such a manner as to make it probable that it would be read by third persons.[184] Nor is it an excuse that the communication was addressed to the wrong person in the mistaken belief that he was privileged to receive it.[185] But it is not necessary to anticipate unlikely contingencies, such as that an inquisitive butler would illicitly open his employer's mail, even if the letter is unsealed,[186] or that a sealed letter properly addressed to a son would be opened by his father.[187]

178. *Summit Hotel v. N.B.C.* 8 A. 2d 302; 124 A.L.R. 968 (Pa. 1939); *Kelly v. Hoffman* 61 A. 2d 143; 5 A.L.R. 2d 951 (N.J. 1948).
179. Remmers, *Recent Legislative Trends in Defamation by Radio*, 64 Harv. L. Rev. 727 (1951).
180. *Theaker v. Richardson* [1962] 1 W.L.R. 151.
181. *Pullman v. Hill* [1891] 1 Q.B. 524; *Gomersall v. Davies* (1898) 14 T.L.R. 430.
182. *Collerton v. MacLean* [1962] N.Z.L.R. 1045 (union secretary).
183. See *White v. Stone* [1939] 2 K.B. 827; *Robb v. Morrison* (1920) 20 S.R. (N.S.W.) 163. To exonerate himself, the defendant must prove that he neither knew nor had reason to expect a stranger to be within earshot.
184. *Sadgrove v. Hole* [1901] 2 K.B. 1. The burden of disproving publication is then thrust on the defendant. It may be discharged, e.g., by showing that the writing was not intelligible to persons without knowledge of special circumstances leading to an identification of the plaintiff: ibid.
185. *Hebditch v. MacIlwaine* [1894] 2 Q.B. 54.
186. *Huth v. Huth* [1915] 3 K.B. 32. Or that a trespasser would gain entrance and read a defamatory notice stuck on a wall: *Neame v. Yellow Cabs* [1930] S.A.S.R. 267.
187. *Powell v. Gelston* [1916] 2 K.B. 615.

Apology

A specific concession to the press is found in the statutory provision that, in an action for libel contained in a public newspaper or periodical, the defendant may plead that it was inserted without actual malice or gross negligence and that at the earliest opportunity he inserted or offered to publish a full apology.[188] But this defence must be accompanied by a payment of money into court by way of amends, and is now virtually obsolete.

VI. Damage: Libel and Slander

Actual injury, whether material or to reputation, is not an essential element of actionable libel. Libel originated as a crime in the Star Chamber where to insist on actual injury would have hampered the "law and order" purpose of the Tudor jurisdiction. The rule survived into the modern law of civil liability (exceptional for non-trespassory torts) primarily because proof of such damage is notoriously difficult and to require it would deprive most plaintiffs of any remedy for vindicating their reputation. It has not however passed without criticism. In the United States concern for freedom of speech ultimately prompted a constitutional requirement for proof of "actual injury", including besides material loss, injury to reputation, anxiety or illness.[189] In Commonwealth countries, however, contemporary criticism has focused on controlling damages rather than on abandoning the rule that libel is actionable per se.[190]

In contrast to libel, the common law did however require proof of material injury for slander. This distinction—broadly that between written and spoken defamation—calls for a digression into legal history.[191]

History of slander

Slander is the offspring of the common law courts which in the earlier part of the 16th century began to allow an action on the case for defamation, in competition with the ecclesiastical tribunals which had till then dominated the field. At first jurisdiction was claimed only over imputations of offences triable at common law, and such slanders were held actionable without proof of damage; eventually it extended over all defamatory allegations causing "temporal" damage.[192]

Contemporaneously, the foundations of the modern law of *libel* were being laid by the Star Chamber which, in addition to punishing the crime of political libel with a view to suppressing seditious publications that had gained in prevalence since the appearance of the printing press, also

188. See below, p. 599.
189. *Gertz v. Welsh* 418 U.S. 323 (1974). Limited to matters of public concern: *Dunn & Bradstreet v. Greenmoss* 472 U.S. 749 (1985).
190. A.L.R.C. §84.
191. *Holdsworth* viii, 333-378; Plucknett, *Concise History of Common Law* (5th ed. 1956) 483-502; Veeder, "History of the Law of Defamation" in *Anglo American Essays in Legal History* (1907-1909) iii, 446; Donnelly, *History of Defamation* [1949] Wis. L. Rev. 99; Helmholz, *Seldon Society* vol. 101 (1985).
192. The first such case seems to have been *Davis v. Gardiner* (1593) 4 Co. Rep. 16b; 67 E.R. 897.

attended to non-political libels in order to furnish a legal substitute for the prohibited duel. But although much concerned with defamatory writings, the Star Chamber still treated words as libels, while conversely in the common law courts written imputations were actionable as slander. The distinction was as yet primarily one of courts. After the fall of the Star Chamber, the relation between these hitherto separate bodies of law assumed its modern profile. Libel came to be fully recognised as a civil wrong and, probably owing to its former association with the criminal law, became actionable without proof of special damage. Thus the insult in defamation emerged as a more prominent element and the previous common law emphasis on pecuniary loss in slander was not translated into the new tort. Also, by a haphazard rather than systematic process, the line of demarcation between libel and slander came to be drawn according to the modern distinction between written and oral defamation.[193]

It has been claimed that libel endures longer than slander, that more significance is attached to the written than the spoken word by the recipient, that libel conveys the impression of deliberate calculation to injure reputation while slander is usually born of sudden irritability. In addition to these psychological arguments, emphasis has also been laid on the allegedly disparate area of dissemination, libel usually contained in newspapers or other printed matter being propagated farther than oral statements addressed to a small circle of listeners. Undoubtedly, the common law requirement of special damage for slander discourages some trivial litigation, but at the cost of striking at the deserving and unmeritorious litigant alike. The criterion which makes success or defeat in an action depend on the mere form of publication ignores the fact that there is no necessary correlation between it and the policy underlying the vindication of reputation. If a distinction is to be observed at all, it should be on the broader basis of the potentiality for harm inherent in the particular circumstances of each publication rather than the prevailing arbitrary and inflexible rule of thumb.

In 1843, a distinguished Select Committee of the House of Lords concluded that the distinctions between libel and slander, and between slander actionable per se and other oral defamation, did "not rest on any solid foundation", but their recommendation to assimilate slander to libel lapsed and was not renewed in England until 1975.[194] It was, however, taken up in Australia and, following its early adoption by New South Wales in 1847,[195] has since been enacted in several other jurisdictions[196] (leaving only Victoria, and South and Western Australia[197] to the common law), though subject to a residuary disqualification of trivial defamation which will be examined later.[198] A uniform "defamation action" has been

193. *King v. Lake* (1670) Hardres 470; 145 E.R. 552 is usually credited as decisive, but see Kaye, *Libel and Slander—Two Torts or One*, 91 L.Q.R. 524 (1975). It was finally settled in *Thorley v. Kerry* (1812) 4 Taunt. 355; 128 E.R. 367.
194. *Faulks* ch. 2.
195. 11 Vic. No. 13; now *Defamation Act* 1974 s. 8. The Act was repealed in Victoria in 1854.
196. Vic.: Defamation Bill 1991; Qld: Defamation Law 1889 s. 6; Tas.: *Defamation Act* 1957 s. 9; A.C.T.: *Defamation Act* 1901 s. 3; N.T.: *Defamation Act* 1938 s. 2.
197. The Victorian Defamation Bill 1991 proposes joining the majority. The assimilation in W.A. (*Criminal Code* 1913 ss 348-349) does not seem to extend to civil proceedings: *Mitchell v. A.B.C.* (1958) 60 W.A.L.R. 38.
198. See below, p. 552.

recommended by law reform bodies in England and Australia,[199] following recent reforms in New Zealand[200] and several Canadian Provinces.[201]

Criterion of distinction

What is the key for classifying a particular publication as either libel or slander? At the time when the distinction originated it was conceived simply as that between written and oral communications, but later libel came to be pragmatically extended to pictures,[202] statues[203] and even conduct fraught with defamatory significance, such as hanging the plaintiff in effigy[204] or placing a lighted lamp in front of his residence to indicate a brothel.[205] The underlying theory of these decisions would point to libel as a communication addressed to the sense of sight and, perhaps, of touch as in the case of a blind person reading braille, while slander is conveyed to the ear. This rationalisation, though generally accepted, does not fit all the cases, because sign language of a deaf mute seems to be only slander,[206] and in *Forrester v. Tyrrell*[207] it was held that the reading aloud of a defamatory script to an audience is libel.

The last-mentioned decision of the English Court of Appeal has assumed a central position in the controversy over the criterion of distinction between libel and slander. Its authority is not impressive. It is inadequately reported and seems to rest solely on *John Lamb's Case*,[208] which contains a series of resolutions by the Star Chamber as to acts it would punish as criminal libels. In view of its source, this pronouncement can hardly be accepted as an authoritative declaration of the common law. On the one hand, there is a long-standing tradition to regard the distinction between libel and slander as dependent on the mode of publication alone, the cause of action in defamation being the publication.[209] This points to all defamatory matter, even written, being slander so long as it is communicated by word of mouth. According to another school, however, visibility is not the only test of libel, a more important one being

199. Faulks §91; A.L.R.C. §76.
200. *Defamation Act* 1954 s. 4.
201. Alberta, Manitoba, New Brunswick and Prince Edward Island.
202. *Du Bost v. Beresford* (1810) 2 Camp. 511; 179 E.R. 1235.
203. *Monson v. Tussauds* [1894] 1 Q.B. 671.
204. *Eyre v. Garlick* (1878) 42 J.P. 68.
205. *Jefferies v. Duncombe* (1809) 11 East 226; 103 E.R. 991. Cf. *Robertson v. Keith* 1936 S.C. 29 where setting a watch of six policemen around plaintiff's residence was treated as defamatory.
206. *Gutsole v. Mathers* (1836) 1 M. & W. 495 at 501; 150 E.R. 530 at 532. Yet a charivari, consisting in firing guns, ringing bells and shouting, was thought to be libel in *Varner v. Morton* (1919) 46 D.L.R. 597 on the ground that publication by means other than speech should be treated as libel.
207. (1893) 9 T.L.R. 257.
208. (1610) 9 Co. Rep. 59b; 77 E.R. 822.
209. *Meldrum v. A.B.C.* [1932] V.L.R. 425 at 435, 438 per Mann and McArthur JJ.; *Hebditch v. MacIlwaine* [1894] 2 Q.B. 54 at 58. In *Osborn v. Boulter* [1930] 2 K.B. 226 at 231, 237 Scrutton and Slesser L.JJ. thought that if a letter after dictation to a typist is read out again aloud, it is still slander, but Greer L.J. (at 236) regarded dictation to a typist as libel. The discussion was obiter, because the occasion was privileged. After transcription by stenographer, publication was held to be libel in *Ostrowe v. Lee* 175 N.E. 505 (N.Y. 1931).

permanence, as distinct from transience, of form.[210] By this token, it is only slander to utter defamatory words with intent that they be recorded, but the record when made and published is libel and he whose voice is recorded is probably liable for that libel on the principle of agency.[211] The undisclosed reasoning in *Forrester v. Tyrrell* may have been that, because of its permanent form, the document was a potential libel and anyone who released its potentialities of harm by publication was liable. If you know of a libel, you must keep it to yourself and, if you give it currency, you do so at your peril. To read it aloud is to give circulation to the permanent defamation.[212] According to an intermediate view, the test lies in the apprehension of the person to whom the publication is made. If the hearer understands only that the defamatory matter is spoken, it is slander; but if he understands that the speaker is communicating to him defamatory matter embodied in permanent form, it is libel because it is much the same as if the listener had read it himself. Significance is attached to the fact that in *Forrester v. Tyrrell* the audience knew that the statement was read, not spoken.[213]

Radio defamation

The invention of new methods of communication has intensified these difficulties by emphasising the conflict between the two factors of visibility and permanence which in the more primitive era of the 17th century were inseparable from the concept of libel. A motion picture is libel, and so is the accompanying sound—apparently on the ground that it is ancillary to what is conveyed on the screen and identifies what is seen.[214] This reasoning could also be conveniently applied to television.[215]

More intractable, however, is the problem of radio defamation on which widely differing views have been expressed. These range from the most conservative approach of classifying all defamatory broadcasting as slander because it reaches the ear rather than the eye,[216] to a middle view which holds it to be libel if read from a script,[217] at least when this is known to the listener;[218] and culminating in the more radical proposal to treat all broadcast defamation as libel on the ground that the advent of radio demands a reappraisal similar to that which occurred with the invention of

210. Accordingly, the English and Commonwealth Acts (below) declared radio defamation to be in "permanent form".
211. Landon in *Pollock* 176. The classification of a recording was inconclusively canvassed in *Chicken v. Ham*: Herbert, *Uncommon Law* (1935) 71.
212. Barry, 23 A.L.J. 203 at 209 (1949).
213. *Meldrum v. A.B.C.* [1932] V.L.R. 425 at 429, 443 per Cussen A.C.J. and Lowe J. This interpretation was rejected in *Hartmann v. Winchell* 296 N.Y. 296; 171 A.L.R. 759 (1947).
214. *Youssoupoff v. M-G-M* (1934) 50 T.L.R. 581.
215. In New York, it has been held to be libel because of its wide dissemination: *Shor v. Billingsley* 158 N.Y.S. 2d 476 (1957); contra: *Remington v. Bentley* 88 F. Supp. 166 (S.D.N.Y. 1949) (both ad lib remarks).
216. Mann and McArthur JJ. in *Meldrum v. A.B.C.* [1932] V.L.R. 425; *Mitchell v. A.B.C.* (1958) 60 W.A.L.R. 38.
217. Porter Committee (1948) 13.
218. Lowe and Cussen JJ. in *Meldrum v. A.B.C.* [1932] V.L.R. 425. See also Lowe, 23 A.L.J. at 221 (1949).

the printing press.[219] According to this last view, neither visibility nor intransience should be regarded as more than manifestations of the real crux of libel which consists in its immense potentiality for harm. The large area of dissemination, facility of repetition and the tendency to enhance credibility of the allegation in the minds of the public are factors which operate to the same degree in the case of radio as of the press and argue for the adoption of the more stringent safeguards provided by the law of libel. Besides, there appears little reason for favouring broadcasting stations as against newspapers in their competitive struggle as the principal media of modern mass communication. This approach has now received statutory sanction in England,[220] Australia,[221] and several Canadian Provinces.[222]

Slander actionable per se

We have seen that when the common law at the beginning of the 16th century entered the field of defamation, it originally allowed an action on the case without proof of special damage in cases of slander imputing temporal crime.[223] It was merely a tactical manoeuvre during the later stage of more active competition with the ecclesiastical courts that prompted the initially cautious approach of confining further jurisdictional claims to cases of slander causing "temporal", as distinct from "spiritual", loss. Unfortunately, after the supremacy of the common law had been established and the way was clear to place the law of defamation on a coherent basis, the courts yielded to the fear of excessive litigation and retained the requirement of special damage as a counterfoil. All the same, during this formative period, they added further categories to the list of slanders actionable per se and thereby widened the division between the two kinds of oral defamation. Although the exact origin of these new exceptions is shrouded in some doubt, they were cases which then seem to have been peculiarly calculated to cause serious injury to reputation. Modern courts have disclaimed the power of creating further additions,[224] but at least one significant category has been added by statute. In the following four cases, slander is now actionable without proof of special damage:

1. Crime. Words imputing the commission of a crime[225] are the oldest category of slander actionable per se. The original test was whether the offence charged was punishable in the common law or ecclesiastical courts, and this explains why allegations of gross immorality were not included, as unchastity and similar transgressions were only cognisable by the spiritual

219. *Rest. 2d* §568A; Finlay, *Defamation by Radio*, 19 Can. B. Rev. 353 (1941); Barry, *Radio, Television and the Law of Defamation*, 23 A.L.J. 203 (1949).
220. *Defamation Act* 1952 s. 1. The *Theatres Act* 1968 (Eng.) added public plays.
221. *Broadcasting and Television Act* (Cth) s. 124 ("deemed to be publication in a permanent form"); *Wainer v. Rippon* [1980] V.R. 129 (but transient affecting eye (skywriting) or permanent affecting ear (tapes)?). Constitutionally: Miller, 4 U. Tas. L. Rev. 70 (1971); Hayes, 2 A.C.L. Rev. 218 (1971).
222. Ontario, British Columbia, New Brunswick.
223. This was an exception to the general rule that damage is the gist of case, in distinction from trespass. A likely explanation is given by Plucknett, *Concise History of Common Law* (5th ed. 1956) 463.
224. "The common law in this field is fixed and rigid" (Porter Committee 12; and see *Jones v. Jones* [1916] 2 A.C. 481 at 500).
225. Imputing guilt, not merely suspicion: *Simmons v. Mitchell* (1880) 6 App. Cas. 156.

tribunals.[226] A narrow construction has been put on expressions alleging reprehensible conduct and, unless the words clearly point to the commission of a crime recognised by law, special damage must be proved.[227] The exact offence however need not be specified; a general charge of criminality is sufficient.[228] Although in origin the basic notion was that the plaintiff was put in jeopardy of criminal prosecution,[229] this has in more recent times been replaced by a stronger emphasis on the social ostracism involved, thus including imputations that the plaintiff has been convicted and punished.[230]

In search of an acceptable criterion to distinguish between crimes involving moral turpitude and venial offences, the courts have postulated that the crime be punishable with imprisonment,[231] though not necessarily indictable.[232] If it entails at most preventive arrest,[233] a fine or disciplinary action short of imprisonment,[234] it is not sufficient. Though the words impute a criminal offence, it may be shown that they were just scurrilous abuse, having regard to the context and the occasion, in which case the plaintiff has to prove special damage.[235]

2. Loathsome Disease. The imputation of contagious disease, included because of its likely social ostracism, is for that reason confined to the most loathsome varieties, such as leprosy and syphilis. There is no modern decision applying it to other than venereal disease. Nor is it sufficient that the plaintiff was alleged merely to have had the disease in the past.[236]

3. Trade or Profession. Allegations of unfitness for a profession, trade or office are obviously calculated to cause temporal loss. For this reason, slandering someone[237] in the way of his trade or profession is actionable per se. At first, the rule seems to have been confined to plaintiffs professing a definite calling in accordance with the old medieval notions of status,[238] but it may now be invoked by anyone in any occupation, however lowly.[239] In other respects, however, a narrower construction has prevailed, undoubtedly influenced by a desire to discourage actions for slander. For example, an irrational distinction has been introduced between

226. *Holdsworth* viii, 348.
227. *Lemon v. Simmons* (1888) 57 L.J.Q.B. 260 (accused of "robbing" his wife, no proof that the spouses lived apart). Cf. *Barnes v. Sharpe* (1910) 11 C.L.R. 462 at 474.
228. *Curtis v. Curtis* (1834) 10 Bing. 477; 131 E.R. 980 ("You have committed an act for which I can transport you"); *Webb v. Beavan* (1883) 11 Q.B.D. 609.
229. *Heming v. Power* (1842) 10 M. & W. 564 at 569; 152 E.R. 595 at 597.
230. *Gray v. Jones* [1939] 1 All E.R. 798 ("You are a convicted person").
231. Hence, it is doubtful if a corporation can rely on this category of slander. The question was left open in *D. & L. Caterers v. D'Ajou* [1945] K.B. 364.
232. *Webb v. Beavan* (1883) 11 Q.B.D. 609. This also disposed of an earlier test of whether the crime entailed "infamous" or "villainous" punishment, i.e. such as disqualified a convict from giving evidence in legal proceedings.
233. *Hellwig v. Mitchell* [1910] 1 K.B. 609 (breach of peace).
234. *Gray v. Chilman (No. 2)* [1935] S.A.S.R. 359 (special constable accused of general inattention to duty).
235. *Hodgson v. Bulpit* (1880) 6 V.L.R. (L.) 440.
236. *Smith's Case* (1604) Noy 151; 74 E.R. 1112; *Halls v. Mitchell* [1927] 1 D.L.R. 163. Is there any inconsistency with the later decision in *Gray v. Jones* [1939] 1 All E.R. 798?
237. This includes a corporation: *D. & L. Caterers v. D'Ajou* [1945] K.B. 364.
238. *Holdsworth* viii, 349.
239. E.g. *Taylor v. Hamilton* [1927] S.A.S.R. 314 (wharf labourer). But fire watching in wartime is a duty, not an office: *Cleghorn v. Sadler* [1945] K.B. 325.

gainful occupations on the one hand and offices of credit or honour on the other.[240] For, as regards the latter, a charge of unfitness (unlike actual misconduct or "malversation") is not actionable per se,[241] unless it would furnish a ground for deprivation.[242] Moreover, since the purpose of the category is to protect a person in his employment or office, it is not sufficient that the words refer to him in relation thereto, but he must still be holding that office when the slander was published.[243]

The most serious qualification is that the defamatory charge must not only have been calculated to harm the plaintiff in his occupation, but must also have been directed against him in relation to such occupation or office:[244] the slander must have been spoken of him "in the way of his calling".[245] Hence to accuse a headmaster of adultery with a cleaner on the school premises is not actionable per se,[246] but to impute to a teacher impropriety with a pupil may be.[247] Members of the legal profession have been frequently prejudiced by this rule. In one case, a solicitor was accused of defrauding his creditors and having been "horsewhipped off the course at Doncaster";[248] in another, of being a "pimp" whose references were worthless because he wrote whatever suited his clients best;[249] and, in a third, an American attorney was called "a bum in a gin mill":[250] but none was able to recover. By the same token it has been held that to call a wharf labourer a "dirty scab" was not a reflection on him in his occupation, but related to his union membership which was only collaterally connected with his employment.[251] The injustice of this refinement has been the subject of much adverse criticism, sufficient to prompt its statutory abrogation in England.[252]

4. Unchastity. A slanderous accusation of unchastity was not actionable per se at common law, because immoral conduct fell within the sphere of the spiritual courts. The plaintiff was put to proof of special damage, even if the words were intended to injure her in any trade in which she was engaged. In certain cases, it is true, she might have taken advantage of the preceding exception if the imputation reflected directly on her conduct in business but, as was once pithily stated, "chastity was not part of [her] duty as a publican. . . . To have imputed to the plaintiff that she kept a disorderly house would have been very different from charging her with adulterous intercourse."[253] This "barbarous rule"[254] was removed in

240. This distinction was accepted without enthusiasm in *Alexander v. Jenkins* [1892] 1 Q.B. 797; and see *Livingston v. McCartin* [1907] V.L.R. 48.
241. *Alexander v. Jenkins* [1892] 1 Q.B. 797.
242. *Booth v. Arnold* [1895] 1 Q.B. 571.
243. *Bull v. Vazquez* [1947] 1 All E.R. 334.
244. Unless apparently the slander was published with the object of causing the plaintiff's employer to dismiss him: *De Stempel v. Dunkels* [1938] 1 All E.R. 238.
245. *Chomley v. Watson* [1907] V.L.R. 502; *Ronald v. Harper* (1910) 11 C.L.R. 63.
246. *Jones v. Jones* [1916] 2 A.C. 481. Similarly, an imputation of drunkenness (not habitual drunkenness) to a schoolmaster: *Brandrick v. Johnson* (1875) 1 V.L.R. (L.) 306.
247. *Thompson v. Bridges* 273 S.W. 529 (Ky 1925).
248. *Doyley v. Roberts* (1837) 3 Bing. N.C. 835; 132 E.R. 632.
249. *Hopwood v. Muirson* [1945] K.B. 313.
250. *Weidberg v. La Guardia* 10 N.Y.S. 2d 445 (1939).
251. *Taylor v. Hamilton* [1927] S.A.S.R. 314.
252. *Defamation Act* 1952 s. 2.
253. *Albrecht v. Patterson* (1886) 12 V.L.R. 597 at 602-603.
254. *Lynch v. Knight* (1861) 9 H.L.C. 577 at 594 per Lord Brougham.

England by the *Slander of Women Act* 1891 and analogous legislation in Australia.[255] Evidently, the statutory protection was thought to be needed only by women.[256]

Special damage

All other instances of slander, however insulting and outrageous, are actionable only on proof of special damage. Moreover, unlike libel and the limited class of slanders per se, mere loss of reputation does not entitle to relief; as a further safeguard against "trivial" litigation, the common law insisted on proof of material or "pecuniary" loss. Thus mere deprivation of the society of friends is insufficient[257] unless accompanied by loss of hospitality.[258] An occasional dinner has material value, but not so mere social intercourse with one's fellows. Even physical illness brought on by anguish and humiliation was once reckoned insufficient,[259] but it is not clear whether this was because mental distress was then considered beyond all tortious redress or because the injury, not being "pecuniary", could not qualify as special damage; the question is therefore clearly open to review.[260] Also, notwithstanding an isolated decision in Victoria to the contrary,[261] it would seem that once the requisite foundation of special damage has been laid, general parasitic damages for loss of reputation are recoverable for the slander just as in all other cases of defamation.[262] There is no justification for pushing the policy of discouraging actions for slander beyond the point where the potentiality for mischief has been demonstrated by proof of actual damage.[263]

The special damage on which the plaintiff relies must not be too "remote".[264] "To make the words actionable by reason of special damage, the consequences must be such as, taking human nature as it is, with its infirmities, and having regard to the relationship of the parties concerned, might fairly and reasonably have been anticipated and feared would follow from the speaking the words."[265] Though this formula seems to replicate the test of remoteness familiar in negligence, it has been applied in singularly narrow fashion in this context, but the few decisions are old and must be treated with reserve. Recovery, for example, was once

255. Vic.: *Wrongs Act* 1958 s. 8; S.A.: *Wrongs Act* 1936 s. 5; N.T.: *Defamation Act* s. 4.
256. *Kerr v. Kennedy* [1942] 1 K.B. 409 (lesbianism). In Newfoundland, the relevant statute protects "any person", apparently regardless of sex.
257. *Allsop v. Allsop* (1860) 5 H. & N. 534; 157 E.R. 1292.
258. *Moore v. Meagher* (1807) 1 Taunt. 39; 127 E.R. 745; *Davies & Wife v. Solomon* (1871) L.R. 7 Q.B. 112; *Albrecht v. Patterson* (1886) 12 V.L.R. 597.
259. *Allsop v. Allsop* (1860) 5 H. & N. 534; 157 E.R. 1292.
260. Cf. *Rigby v. Mirror Newspaper* (1963) 64 S.R. (N.S.W.) 34; *Brook v. Flinders Univ.* (1988) 47 S.A.S.R. 119 at 130.
261. *Albrecht v. Patterson* (1886) 12 V.L.R. 821.
262. Cf. the position in actions for seduction where the father may recover for the insult to family honour, once the actionable quality has been established by proof of loss of services.
263. *Salmond* (17th ed. 1977) 191; *Prosser & Keeton* 794; contra: Gatley, *Libel and Slander* (8th ed. 1981) §1460.
264. Initially, of course, causal relationship between the slander and the damage must be established; a case where the plaintiff was unable to do so is *Taylor v. Hamilton* [1927] S.A.S.R. 314.
265. *Lynch v. Knight* (1861) 9 H.L.C. 577 at 600; 11 E.R. 854 at 863 per Lord Wensleydale.

denied to a wife whose husband expelled her from the matrimonial home in consequence of a slanderous reflection on her morals, on the ground that since the imputation did not charge her with adultery but only laxity of manners prior to her marriage, the husband's response was more drastic—apparently even by Victorian standards—than "could have been expected in the ordinary course of events".[266] Similarly, a barman falsely accused of leaving his lodgings without paying rent failed to recover on account of his consequent dismissal by his employer, because the defendant could not fairly have contemplated anything more than a severe remonstrance.[267] On the other hand, losing the gratuitous services of his sons was held to be a sufficient foundation for special damage resulting from an accusation of incest.[268] A slandered candidate's defeat at the polls, however, would almost certainly be dismissed as too speculative.

At one time, a good deal of countenance was given to the "last wrongdoer" doctrine in insulating defendants from responsibility for libel or slander. It was argued that if A defamed B, and C in consequence did something injurious to B which was also wrongful, like dismissing him from a subsisting contract of employment, A was not liable for the harm because it was not "the legal and natural consequence of the words spoken".[269] B might have recourse against C for breach of contract, but not against A for the defamation, since one could not be held for the unlawful act of another. This grudging approach has long fallen into disfavour in the law of defamation[270] as elsewhere,[271] the issue now being resolved quite genuinely by what was foreseeable in the circumstances. Much the same has been the fate of the older, artificial rule which used to treat all voluntary re-publication by a third person as "too remote".[272] Nowadays, the originator will be liable for any foreseeable re-publication, not only one specifically authorised, like a politician who utters a slander at a press conference that is subsequently published as a libel.[273]

Triviality

Even those Australian jurisdictions which dispensed altogether with the requirement of special damage for slander deemed it advisable to retain a limited safeguard against frivolous actions for oral defamation. To this end, it was made a defence (in all cases other than that of words intended to be read) that the publication was made on an occasion and under circumstances when the person defamed was not likely to be injured

266. *Lynch v. Knight*. But loss, even postponement, of marriage has been held sufficient: *Bordeaux v. Jobs* (1913) 14 D.L.R. 451 (man); *Speight v. Gosnay* (1891) 60 L.J.Q.B. 231 (woman).
267. *Speake v. Hughes* [1904] 1 K.B. 138.
268. *Byrne v. Potter* (1873) 7 S.A.L.R. 52.
269. *Vicars v. Wilcocks* (1806) 8 East 1; 103 E.R. 244.
270. *Lynch v. Knight*; cf. *Longdon-Griffiths v. Smith* [1950] 2 All E.R. 662 at 678.
271. See above, p. 220.
272. *Ward v. Weeks* (1830) 7 Bing. 211; 131 E.R. 81 (loss of customer from repeated slander did not qualify as special damage).
273. *Sims v. Wran* [1984] 1 N.S.W.L.R. 317; *Slipper v. B.B.C.* [1991] 1 Q.B. 283 (C.A.) (review republishing libel).

thereby.[274] This safeguard against trivial claims has been extended in New South Wales to libel as well as slander.[275]

Unlike an earlier version,[276] the defence is excluded by likelihood of any "injury", not just "injury to character". Serious mental distress might thus be sufficient, now that it qualifies for "parasitic" damages in all actionable defamation.[277] Nor need actual injury be shown; likelihood is sufficient; however "no", not "less" injury must have been likely.

Not all circumstances but "circumstances of the publication" may be taken into account. Thus the narrow construction prevailed of excluding the plaintiff's bad reputation, in contrast to evidence that, prior to the publication, the recipients already knew the allegation.[278] The defence is peculiarly applicable to publications of limited extent, as in a jocular statement to a few people in a private home, who know the plaintiff too well to take it seriously. Generally relevant factors are the nature of the defamatory matter, and the manner in which, the persons to whom and the place where it is published.[279] The defence is not categorically excluded from publications to a wider audience or the media. For example, when Lang, the popular Labor leader, made an offensive speech in a public election meeting, Rich (and Evatt) JJ. held the jury entitled to find for him "with their knowledge of local elections and policies and their understanding of the manner in which speeches at elections are received by bystanders. . . . They might take one view of words spoken at a vestry meeting or a meeting of directors, and another where it is in the heat of a family squabble or a quarrel in a shearing shed or a taproom or bar."[280]

3. JUSTIFICATION: TRUTH

At common law, truth is a complete answer to a civil action for defamation and the only defence known by the name of "justification".[281] Actionable defamation consists in a *false* statement impairing another's reputation. "The law will not permit a man to recover damages in respect of an injury to a character which he either does not, or *ought not*, to possess."[282] This is an expression of policy rather than a corollary of the principle that the gist of the civil action is compensation for damage suffered, for the latter

274. Qld: Defamation Law 1889 s. 20; W.A.: *Criminal Code* 1913 s. 362 (probably inapplicable to civil proceedings); Tas.: *Defamation Act* 1957 s. 9. The A.C.T. recognises a similar, though not identical, defence under the *Defamation Act* 1901 s. 4, which differs in making it optional for the jury to apply the defence, in excluding it when the words impute an indictable offence, and in restricting the likelihood of injury to "character".
275. *Defamation Act* 1974 (N.S.W.) s. 13; Defamation Bill 1991 (Qld); also recommended by A.L.R.C. (§191).
276. In force in N.S.W. until 1958, and still in the A.C.T.: see above, n. 274.
277. See below, p. 595.
278. *King v. McKenzie* (1991) 24 N.S.W.L.R. 305.
279. *Morosi v. Mirror Newspaper* [1977] 2 N.S.W.L.R. 749 at 800.
280. *Lang v. Willis* (1934) 52 C.L.R. 637 at 651. Aliter, Starke and Dixon JJ.
281. Faulks §129 recommended renaming the defence "truth".
282. *M'Pherson v. Daniels* (1829) 10 B. & C. 263 at 272; 109 E.R. 448 at 451 per Littledale J. Nor is there any duty of care not to injure the plaintiff's reputation by truthful statements: *Bell Booth Group v. A.-G.* [1989] 3 N.Z.L.R. 148 (C.A.).

leaves open whether the law protects security of an existing or only of a deserved reputation. In contrast, the criminal law of libel, as formulated by the Star Chamber with the object of preventing breaches of the peace, directed its attention to the insult offered, and it was therefore no defence to a prosecution either that publication was to the person defamed or that the allegations were true. For, "as the woman said, she would never grieve to have been told of her red nose if she had not one indeed."[283] This was epitomised in the saying, attributed to Lord Mansfield: "The greater the truth, the greater the libel."

Truth is a matter of defence or, alternatively expressed, the falsity of defamation is presumed until dispelled by the defendant.[284] Casting the burden on him rather than the plaintiff has the effect, if not the purpose, of inhibiting defamatory speech.[285] For in practice it acts not only as a serious deterrent against dissemination of falsehoods but, in view of the difficulties of adducing legal proof of truth in all particulars or unwillingness to reveal confidential sources of information, constitutes also a powerful brake on public debate and the flow of information by underscoring the wisdom of caution and self-censorship.[286]

What is justification

Justification must be as broad as the defamatory imputation itself.[287] The defendant must prove the truth of all material statements contained in the libel; there must be a substantial justification of the whole. A charge that the plaintiff is a habitual liar can only be justified by proof that on repeated occasions he made false statements without an honest belief in their truth.[288] An allegation that the plaintiff was convicted of a crime cannot be proved true by showing that he was convicted, though the conviction was quashed.[289] Yet it is sufficient that the statement is true in substance. Justification need not conform to the exact letter of the accusation, provided the gist of it is proved to be correct: it must "meet the sting" of the libel. Erroneous details which do not aggravate the defamatory allegation may be ignored. Thus to say of someone that he has been convicted of travelling in a train without a ticket and fined £9 and three weeks' imprisonment in default may be justified by establishing that

283. Quoted by Windeyer, *Truth of a Libel*, 8 A.L.J. 319 at 322 (1935).

284. See *Beevis v. Dawson* [1957] 1 Q.B. 195. It must also be specially pleaded for (although not really a defence by way of confession and avoidance because it denies an essential element of the cause of action) the "general issue" admits the falsity of the facts: Bullen & Leake, *Precedents of Pleading* (3rd ed. 1867) 700; *Leersnyder v. Truth (N.Z.)* [1963] N.Z.L.R. 129.

In N.S.W. there is no presumption either way, because truth is not by itself a defence: *Singleton v. Ffrench* (1986) 5 N.S.W.L.R. 425 (C.A.).

285. Other justifications are the presumption of innocence which places the burden on the accuser, and the inequity of requiring (in most instances) proof of a negative. Yet the plaintiff must prove falsity in misrepresentation.

286. Faulks §141 was for that reason opposed to any change. On the contrary, in the U.S. the burden of proof for speech on matters of public concern lies on the plaintiff: *Philadelphia Newspaper v. Hepps* 475 U.S. 767 (1986).

287. *Crowley v. Glissan (No. 2)* (1905) 2 C.L.R. 744 at 767.

288. See *Penton v. Calwell* (1945) 70 C.L.R. 219.

289. *Howden v. Truth Ltd* (1937) 58 C.L.R. 416. See also below, n. 298.

he was sentenced to two weeks' imprisonment in default.[290] But if the defamation consists of several distinct allegations, all must be justified seriatim and if the defendant fails in regard to any of them, the plaintiff will be entitled to a verdict and costs, although the unproved charge could have caused no appreciable damage in view of the truth of the rest. Hence, where the plaintiff was described as a blackmailer, liar, and swindling share pusher and was alleged to have entered the country illegally, the defendant was held liable in the amount of £50 because he was unable to prove the last, and relatively least infamous, of the charges.[291] On the other hand, if several allegations have a common sting (a question of degree), it is sufficient to justify the sting, for example promiscuity in case of several separate episodes.[292] Also with a view to encouraging a less literal interpretation, several Australian jurisdictions and New Zealand have adopted the English reform that the defence of justification shall not fail if the untrue elements do not materially injure the plaintiff's reputation, having regard to the truth of the remaining charges.[293]

Repetition of a libel cannot be justified merely by proving that it was a true report of what was said by someone else: otherwise too glib an excuse would be at hand for perpetuating and spreading calumnies under the facile guise of cautioning that "it is rumoured" or "I was told".[294] Not even expressions of doubt or disbelief furnish excuse,[295] though the unqualified refutation of a libel may draw its sting.[296] The press has to bear the brunt of this rule, mitigated only by qualified privilege for good faith reporting in a narrow range of situations. A more general defence, advocated in Australia, would protect a defendant who published, without adoption or influence, a statement attributed to a person other than his employee or agent, where it was reasonable to publish it, and subject to a right of reply.[297]

With respect to such common news items as that a prosecution has been launched against the plaintiff or that the police are inquiring into his affairs, the threshold question must be whether it was reasonably capable of being understood as nothing but a factual report that a charge was made

290. *Alexander v. N.E. Rly* (1865) 6 B. & S. 340; 122 E.R. 1221; *Sutherland v. Stopes* [1925] A.C. 47 at 79-80.
291. *Alexander v. N.E. Rly* (1865) 6 B. & S. 340; 122 E.R. 1221; *Sutherland v. Stopes* [1925] A.C. 47 at 79-80.
292. *Khashoggi v. I.P.C. Magazines* [1986] 1 W.L.R. 1412 (C.A.); *Polly Peck v. Trelford* [1986] Q.B. 1000 (C.A.).
293. Respectively, the Defamation Acts of England (1952 s. 5), N.S.W. (1974 s. 16), Tas. (1957 s. 8), and proposed in Vic. and Qld; N.Z. (1954 s. 7) also *Libel and Slander Act* 1958 (Ont.) s. 23. The wording has been improved in the N.S.W. Act ("contextual truth"; see *Hepburn v. TCN* [1984] 1 N.S.W.L.R. 386; *Pioneer International v. Knox* (1991) 22 N.S.W.L.R. 266); elsewhere the reform applies only to "*actions* involving several distinct defamatory charges", so that it can be evaded by suing only for those libels that cannot be justified.
294. *Truth (N.Z.) v. Holloway* [1960] 1 W.L.R. 997: [1961] N.Z.L.R. 22 (P.C.); *Wake v. Fairfax* [1973] 1 N.S.W.L.R. 43; *Douglas v. Tucker* [1952] 1 S.C.R. 275. That someone else was the first defamer does not even mitigate damages, though it may help to disprove malice: see below, p. 598. See also below, n. 518.
295. *Savige v. News Ltd* [1932] S.A.S.R. 240.
296. *Sergi v. A.B.C.* [1983] 2 N.S.W.L.R. 669 (jury question whether the "antidote destroyed its bane").
297. A.L.R.C. §165ff.

(and implying at worst that there were grounds for suspicion) or of actually suggesting guilt. The former may be justified for all practical purposes by simply establishing the accuracy of the report, but the latter demands nothing less than proof of guilt in order to meet the sinister slant implanted into the story.[298] This important distinction at once allows sufficient latitude for fearless reporting of "straight news", while exacting a toll from the less responsible press for the luxury of pregnant headlines and sensational embellishments.

If a defendant seeks to justify all the defamatory matters, and these consist partly of statements of fact and partly of comment, he must under that plea prove not only the truth of the facts but also the comment.[299] Not that he would assume the higher burden of seeking to justify comment as being true, unless the defence of fair comment were precluded, for example because the comment was inspired by malice. But how can statements of *opinion* ever be proved true?[300] Literally this is of course impossible, but the defendant apparently acquits himself by establishing that the comment is "accurate, that is actually justified by, in the sense of being implicit in, the facts which are stated and proved to be true".[301] In other words, the facts must warrant the imputation, and they do not, unless the jury agrees with the defendant that it is a conclusion which *ought* to be drawn from those facts.[302]

Because of the procedural and substantive difficulties of establishing the defence of justification, most defendants prefer to rely on qualified privilege instead; though by shifting the focus from truth to malice, the action can no longer lead to an unequivocal vindication of the plaintiff.

Public benefit

To admit truth alone as a complete defence is open to the objection that it condones embarrassing exposures of purely private matters, lacking any countervailing public interest. As early as 1849 a distinguished Select Committee of the House of Lords therefore recommended that in both civil and criminal proceedings truth should be a defence if, but only if, the publication was for the public benefit. This proposal was embodied in Lord Campbell's Libel Act 1843 for criminal but not civil proceedings.[303]

298. *Lewis v. Daily Telegraph* [1964] A.C. 234; *Hayward v. Thompson* [1982] Q.B. 47; *Mirror Newspaper v. Harrison* (1982) 149 C.L.R. 293; *Sergi v. A.B.C.* [1983] 2 N.S.W.L.R. 669 at 676-679. Indeed, at common law, a conviction was not even admissible in evidence (being treated as a mere opinion of guilt): *Goody v. Odhams Press* [1967] 1 Q.B. 333; contra: *Jorgensen v. News Media* [1969] N.Z.L.R. 961 (C.A.). Statutes have made certain convictions conclusive: *Civil Evidence Act* 1968 (Eng.) s. 13; *Defamation Act* 1974 (N.S.W.) s. 55; *Evidence Act* 1977 (Qld) s. 79; *Evidence Act* (S.A.) s. 34a; *Evidence Act* 1971 (A.C.T.) s. 78; *Evidence Act (No. 2)* 1980 (N.Z.) s. 24.

299. *Walker v. Hodgson* [1909] 1 K.B. 239 at 253; *Sutherland v. Stopes* [1925] A.C. 47 at 62-63, 73-75, 95; *Truth (N.Z.) v. Avery* [1959] N.Z.L.R. 274. See below, p. 593.

300. See *Goldsbrough v. Fairfax* (1934) 34 S.R. (N.S.W.) 524 at 546-547; *Gardiner v. Fairfax* (1942) 42 S.R. (N.S.W.) 171 at 179.

301. See *Goldsbrough v. Fairfax* (1934) 34 S.R. (N.S.W.) 524 at 530 per Jordan C.J.

302. *Hunt v. Star Newspaper* [1908] 2 K.B. 309 at 320.

303. The *Rehabilitation of Offenders Act* 1974 (Eng.) s. 8 abolished the defence of truth for malicious disclosures of "spent convictions" (sentences under two and a half years).

In New South Wales the Committee's recommendation was fully adopted in 1847, presumably in order to assist the social integration of former convicts. This test still applies in Queensland, Tasmania and the Australian Capital Territory,[304] while in its parent state "public benefit" was replaced by "public interest", a somewhat wider and more familiar concept from the defence of fair comment, which is decided by the judge rather than the jury.[305] The remaining common law jurisdictions, however, have remained so opposed to the proposed adoption of this model that it became the stumbling block to a uniform defamation law for Australia.

The protection sought by the formula is really for privacy rather than reputation, and needed as much for non-defamatory as for defamatory allegations. But in the absence of an independent action for invasion of privacy against unjustifiable public disclosure of private facts, it has served at least as a second best.[306] More directly targeted at privacy is the current proposal in New South Wales, Victoria and Queensland that truth become a complete defence except with respect to imputations concerning the plaintiff's private affairs.[307]

4. ABSOLUTE PRIVILEGE

In certain situations, the law allows one to speak and write without restraint, even at the expense of another's good name and character. These are called privileged occasions. Privilege attaches not to content, but to occasion or form.[308] What a Member of Parliament says on the floor of the House is privileged, but repetition of the same words outside is not; a fair and accurate report of court proceeding enjoys immunity, but the same information cast in another form can lay no claim to special protection.

Privilege is admitted in title of a variety of individual and social interests which are deemed of sufficient importance to displace the countervailing claim to protection of reputation.[309] The interest may be valued so highly that policy requires the writer or speaker to be completely immune regardless of his motive in giving currency to the defamation. More frequently, however, the interest is of lesser weight in the scale of social values, and prevails over the plaintiff's only if the defendant was using the occasion to further the interest which the law regards as worthy of protection. In such cases, the privilege is not *absolute* but *qualified*, in the sense that it is forfeited by abuse.

304. Qld: *Criminal Code* 1899 s. 376; Tas.: *Defamation Act* 1957 s. 15; A.C.T.: *Defamation Act* 1901 s. 6. The common law remains unaffected in Victoria, S.A. and W.A. (because s. 5 neutralises s. 356 of the *Criminal Code*: *W.A. Newspaper v. Bridge* (1979) 141 C.L.R. 535 at 549.
305. *Defamation Act* 1974 (N.S.W.) s. 15.
306. A.L.R.C. preferred the privacy alternative: §125. See below, p. 607.
307. In which case, unless the defence establishes in turn an occasion of qualified privilege.
308. *Dingle v. Assoc. Newspapers* [1961] 2 Q.B. 162 at 188. Nor does privilege belong to the speaker, although it is frequently referred to as an attribute of the person who avails himself of the defence: see *Minter v. Priest* [1930] A.C. 558 at 571-572.
309. The protection given to defamation is not coincident with, though to some extent overlaps, the protection given in many cases against the disclosure in evidence of documents and oral communications: *Gibbons v. Duffell* (1932) 47 C.L.R. 520 at 529; *Minter v. Priest* [1930] A.C. 558 at 571, 579-580.

Because of its drastic effect in foreclosing all opportunity for vindicating a traduced reputation, absolute immunity is but rarely granted, and only as an aid to the efficient functioning of our governmental institutions: legislative, executive and judicial. Although prevailing even in the teeth of malice and abuse, it is of course not accorded for the sake of shielding mischief-makers who have no claim whatever to the law's sympathy. Rather, so far-reaching an immunity can be justified only to protect certain highly placed persons from the harassment of having to meet unjustified charges of malice or abuse (before somewhat unpredictable juries) and to remove the dampening effect such a spectre would inevitably have on the fearless discharge of their official functions. It should be, and with rare exceptions is, matched by a high sense of responsibility in those who are its beneficiaries, like judges and Ministers of State, or by other effective safeguards against flagrant abuse, as in the case of judicial control over the conduct of witnesses.

Absolute privilege is accordingly limited to the following occasions:

Parliamentary proceedings

A wide area of privilege is devoted to the protection of political institutions. Thus, absolute immunity attaches to anything "said or done" by Members of Parliament in the exercise of their duties in the course of proceedings of either House, because it is felt that fear of liability might induce caution destructive of the frankness that the public has a right to expect. This privilege was established in the course of the constitutional struggle between the Executive and Parliament and was confirmed by the Bill of Rights.[310] It covers not only verbal but equally written speech, such as a document tabled in the House and its ancillary preparation.[311] Also parliamentary speeches broadcast over the radio;[312] but primarily in order to ensure protection for radio stations, it has been specifically enacted that "no action or proceeding . . . shall lie against any person for broadcasting or rebroadcasting any portion of the proceedings of either House of Parliament."[313] But repetition outside Parliament of statements made inside are not generally believed to be covered.[314] Several of the States have also conferred absolute immunity on petitions to Parliament.[315]

310. (1689) art. 9; *Parliamentary Privileges Act* 1987 (Cth) s. 16; *Criminal Code* (Qld) s. 371(1); *Criminal Code* (W.A.) s. 351(1); *Defamation Act* 1957 (Tas.) s. 10(1). For Parliamentary sanctions see Leopold, *Freedom of Speech in Parliament: Its Misuse and Proposals for Reform*, 1961 P.L. 30.
311. *Holding v. Jennings* [1979] V.R. 289 (dictation to typist etc.). Canadian dicta which would include some communications by M.P.s outside Parliament were not accepted in *A.B.C. v. Chatterton* (1986) 46 S.A.S.R. 1 at 19.
312. The view expressed by Davis, *Parliamentary Broadcasting and the Law of Defamation*, 7 U. Tor. L.J. 385 (1948) that, statute apart, an M.P. enjoys at most qualified privilege in respect of broadcasts is untenable: see *Irwin v. Ashurst* 124 A.L.R. 997 (Ore. 1938) (broadcast of judicial proceedings absolutely privileged). Such a conclusion would seriously impede the freedom of speech inseparably bound up with our conception of parliamentary democracy. Nor is it supportable by the decisions cited which establish merely that *re-publication* of a parliamentary speech outside the House is not entitled to absolute privilege. N.Z. has no provision similar to our 1946 Act, but the broadcasting service enjoys Crown immunity unabridged with respect to defamation.
313. *Parliamentary Proceedings Broadcasting Act* 1946 s. 15.
314. See *A.B.C. v. Chatterton* (1986) 46 S.A.S.R. 1 (F.C.); *Beitzel v. Crabb* [1992] 2 V.R. 121; *Stopforth v. Goyer* (1979) 97 D.L.R. (3d) 369 (qualified privilege).
315. Qld: s. 371(2); W.A.: s. 351(2); Tas.: s. 10(2).

At common law, only qualified privilege attaches to fair and accurate reports of parliamentary proceedings.[316] An Act of Parliament authorising publication of any matter would, of course, impliedly give absolute protection to those acting upon it, but publication of reports or papers by order of either House alone does not carry similar immunity at common law.[317] However, statute has conferred absolute privilege upon the publication by authority of either House of reports, papers, votes or proceedings, by persons so authorised or their servants.[318] The same protection has been accorded in England[319] and all Australian States[320] (except Tasmania[321]) to their re-publication in full. Qualified[322] privilege attaches to publication of extracts from or abstracts of papers so ordered to be published, but the legislation varies in certain particulars. Some States have adopted the English formula of throwing the onus on the defendant to establish that the publication was made bona fide and without malice,[323] but others have retained the common law allocation of proof.[324]

Judicial proceedings

Freedom of speech without fear of consequences is considered indispensable for the proper and effective administration of justice. All concerned in judicial proceedings, therefore—from judge and jury to solicitor and counsel, parties and witnesses—enjoy absolute protection for what they say,[325] conceded "with the knowledge that courts of justice are presided over by those who from their high character are not likely to abuse the privilege, and who have the power and ought to have the will to check any abuse of it by those who appear before them."[326]

The privilege has been extended beyond courts of justice to other tribunals with "similar attributes". The line of demarcation, however, is less than precise if only because it ultimately depends on the cumulative effect of numerous characteristics rather than on any single element.[327]

316. See below, p. 581.
317. *Stockdale v. Hansard* (1839) 9 A. & E. 1; 112 E.R. 1112.
318. *Parliamentary Papers Act* 1908-1946 (Cth) s. 4; *Parliamentary Papers (Supplementary Provisions) Act* 1975 (N.S.W.); *Constitution Act Amendment Act* 1975 (Vic.) ss 73-74; Defamation Law 1889 (Qld) s. 40; *Criminal Code* Qld s. 371(3); S.A.: *Wrongs Act* 1936 s. 12(1); W.A.: *Papers of Parliament Act* 1891 s. 1; *Criminal Code* s. 351(3); Tas.: *Defamation Act* 1957 s. 10(3), 29; N.Z.: *Defamation Act* 1954 s. 18. The model is the *Parliamentary Papers Act* 1840 (Eng.) s. 2.
319. *Parliamentary Papers Act* 1840 s. 2.
320. N.S.W.: s. 17; Vic.: s. 65; Qld: s. 41; S.A.: s. 12(2); W.A.: s. 2; A.C.T.: s. 5(c); N.Z.: s. 19.
321. Where the privilege is only qualified: *Defamation Act* 1957 s. 13(1)(b). The matter is not covered by Commonwealth legislation.
322. In Queensland alone the privilege is absolute: Defamation Law 1889 s. 41.
323. Vic.: s. 65; S.A.: s. 12(3); W.A.: s. 3; N.Z.: s. 20. Model is the *Parliamentary Papers Act* 1840 (Eng.) s. 3.
324. N.S.W.: ss 25, 26; Tas.: *Defamation Act* 1957 ss 13, 19.
325. *Cabassi v. Vila* (1940) 64 C.L.R. 130; *Love v. Robbins* (1990) 2 W.A.R. 510; *Marrinan v. Vibart* [1963] 1 Q.B. 528; Codes of Qld (s. 372), W.A. (s. 352), Tas. (s. 11).
326. *Royal Aquarium v. Parkinson* [1892] 1 Q.B. 431 at 451 per Lopes L.J.; *Clyne v. N.S.W. Bar Assoc.* (1960) 104 C.L.R. 186 at 200.
327. Nor are constitutional decisions on the exercise of the "judicial power" helpful. See deSmith, *Judicial Review of Administrative Action* (4th ed. 1980) ch. 2 (esp. 80-89).

Each case, it has been suggested,[328] must be considered in the light of four criteria: first, under what authority the tribunal acts—it *must* be "recognised by law", though not necessarily set up by legislation,[329] in contrast to purely domestic tribunals. Secondly, the nature of the question into which the tribunal is to inquire—whether (like ordinary courts of law) it is an issue "inter partes". Thirdly, the procedure adopted by it in carrying out the inquiry, including such matters as its power to summon witnesses and compel testimony under oath, the prestige of the presiding officer. Finally, the legal consequences of the conclusion reached by the tribunal as a result of the inquiry. Courts of law render, of course, immediately binding decisions, but here it is sufficient if the report of the tribunal, though in form advisory to a superior authority, has in practice a major influence on the final decision that is binding and authoritative.[330] However, a merely preliminary investigation, the report of which could only be remitted to a prosecuting authority, would not qualify.[331] In conceding the privilege to a board of inquiry into police malpractice appointed by the Victorian government, it was considered important that the tribunal was expected to make a fearless investigation of such serious allegations, that its personnel would be peculiarly vulnerable to actions for defamation in performing their function of examining witnesses for credibility etc., and that the procedure, atmosphere and personnel were those of courts of law.[332] The same conclusion has been reached regarding a military court of inquiry,[333] proceedings by a justice of the peace for the reception of a lunatic,[334] hearings by a local authority on a town planning scheme,[335] disciplinary proceedings by the Law Society,[336] Benchers of an Inn of Court[337] or an ecclesiastical commission,[338] and appeals to the Public Service Board in New Zealand;[339] in contrast to hearings of applications for liquor or dancing licences,[340] and a creditors' meeting before an official assignee.[341]

328. *Trapp v. Mackie* [1979] 1 W.L.R. 377 at 379 per Lord Diplock.
329. E.g. *Lincoln v. Daniels* [1962] 1 Q.B. 237.
330. As in *Trapp v. Mackie* [1979] 1 W.L.R. 377 (statutory court of inquiry into dismissal of school teacher, reporting to Secretary of State); *Dawkins v. Lord Rokeby* (1873) L.R. 8 Q.B. 255 (military court of inquiry). But unlike the E.E.C. Commission procedure in *Hasselblad v. Orbinson* [1985] Q.B. 475 (C.A.).
331. *O'Connor v. Waldron* [1935] A.C. 76 (P.C.) (investigation under Canada anti-trust act).
332. *Bretherton v. Kaye* [1971] V.R. 111: since confirmed by *Evidence Act* s. 21A (see *Tampion v. Anderson* [1973] V.R. 321). A Royal Commission might not qualify, being more investigatory than judicial: *Douglass v. Lewis* (1982) 30 S.A.S.R. 50, apart from statutes like the *Royal Commissions Acts* of Cth (1902 s. 7), N.S.W. (1923 s. 6), W.A. (1968 s. 32); also the Codes of Qld (ss 372-373), W.A. (ss 352-353), Tas. (ss 12-13).
333. *Dawkins v. Lord Rokeby* (1873) L.R. 8 Q.B. 255; *Bamford v. Clarke* (1876) 14 S.C.R. (N.S.W.) 303.
334. *Hodson v. Pare* [1899] 1 Q.B. 455. A fortiori, petty sessions: *Law v. Llewellyn* [1906] 1 K.B. 487 (magistrate); *Munster v. Lamb* (1883) 11 Q.B.D. 588 (solicitor appearing for the defence).
335. *Atkins v. Mays* [1974] 2 N.Z.L.R. 459.
336. *Addis v. Crocker* [1961] 1 Q.B. 11. See also *Keenan v. Auckland Harbour Bd* [1946] N.Z.L.R. 97.
337. *Lincoln v. Daniels* [1962] 1 Q.B. 237; *Marrinan v. Vibart* [1963] 1 Q.B. 528.
338. *Barratt v. Kearns* [1905] 1 K.B. 504.
339. *Thompson v. Turbott* [1962] N.Z.L.R. 298.
340. *Royal Aquarium v. Parkinson* [1892] 1 Q.B. 431; *Attwood v. Chapman* [1914] 3 K.B. 275.
341. *Searl v. Lyons* (1908) 27 N.Z.L.R. 524.

The privilege is not confined to statements made in court, but extends to all preparatory steps taken with a view to judicial proceedings.[342] It includes any communication by a prospective witness to the parties or their legal advisers,[343] complaints addressed to the proper authority for initiating disciplinary proceedings against a lawyer[344] and a report by an official receiver to the court.[345] But the statement or document must be directly concerned with actual or contemplated proceedings; not just remotely so, like a factual report containing allegations which merely might provide a ground for future prosecution.[346]

The privilege attaches to any utterance reasonably related to the subject of the judicial inquiry, but "relevance" is liberally interpreted: a statement may qualify which, if false, would not justify a prosecution for perjury.[347] A witness is not required to guess at his risk whether the testimony may be safely given.

Solicitor and client

Professional communications between solicitor and client on matters fairly referable to their confidential relationship are privileged, though it is not certain whether the protection is absolute or qualified.[348] The English Court of Appeal once chose the former, apparently on the view that the immunity was just an aspect of "judicial" privilege,[349] but the House of Lords has reserved the question for future consideration.[350] On principle, the lesser privilege would appear sufficient to safeguard effective communication between legal adviser and client, at any rate if it does not relate to actual or intended litigation, like the drafting of wills or conveyancing. The privilege, whatever its status, is not defeated even by the fact that eventually the solicitor does not accept a retainer.[351] But the defamatory remark must have been relevant to the discussion between the parties in their relationship of solicitor and client, not irrelevant gossip idly interjected in a professional interview, such as "Have you heard that Jones has run off with Mrs Brown?"[352]

342. So it would be an abuse of process to permit a defamatory document first disclosed on discovery to found subsequent action for defamation: *Riddick v. Thames Bd Mills* [1977] Q.B. 881 (C.A.).
343. *Watson v. M'Ewan* [1905] A.C. 480; *Ronald v. Harper* [1913] V.L.R. 311; *Thompson v. Turbott* [1962] N.Z.L.R. 298; *Hasselblad v. Orbinson* [1985] Q.B. 475 (C.A.).
344. *Lilley v. Roney* (1892) 61 L.J.Q.B. 727 (Law Society); *Lincoln v. Daniels* [1962] 1 Q.B. 237 (privilege lost because complaint wrongly addressed to Bar Council instead of Benchers of Inn).
345. *Bottomley v. Brougham* [1908] 1 K.B. 584.
346. *Szalatnay-Stacho v. Fink* [1947] K.B. 1.
347. *Seaman v. Netherclift* (1876) 2 C.P.D. 53 at 60; also *Munster v. Lamb* (1883) 11 Q.B.D. at 588.
348. The Codes made no specific reference to it, but the situation falls clearly within the section of qualified privilege: Qld: s. 377; W.A.: s. 357; Tas.: s. 16.
349. *More v. Weaver* [1928] 2 K.B. 520.
350. *Minter v. Priest* [1930] A.C. 558. The question of liability for defamation cannot arise unless the communication has first been admitted in evidence. If privilege from disclosure has not been waived, cadit quaestio. The latter privilege, however, is that of the client, not the solicitor: see *Minter v. Priest* [1930] A.C. 558.
351. *Minter v. Priest* [1930] A.C. 558.
352. *More v. Weaver* [1928] 2 K.B. 520 at 525.

High executive communications

With the object of securing the free and fearless discharge of high public duty, complete protection has also been extended to the executive department of government.[353] Its limits, however, are as yet less clearly defined.

Absolute immunity does not attach to official communications by all public servants or persons implementing statutory duties, but is confined to "high officers of State". It undoubtedly covers communications between Ministers and the Crown, or among Ministers themselves.[354] In *Isaacs v. Cook*,[355] it was applied to a report by the High Commissioner of Australia in the United Kingdom to the Prime Minister of Australia, but in a later case[356] the High Court was divided on its application to the annual report furnished by the Commissioner of Taxation to the Federal Treasurer for presentation to Parliament. On one view, it stood on a higher plane than the report in *Isaacs v. Cook* because it was essential that the defendant should not be deterred by fear of litigation from reporting freely, pursuant to a statutory duty, on breaches and evasions of the *Income Tax Act*,[357] besides which the report when printed by order of Parliament would also be privileged.[358] But on another view, the Commissioner's functions were not of a sufficiently "high level" and the subject matter too indirectly related to the safety and security of the community to merit absolute protection.[359]

Besides the speaker being a "high" official, are there any additional limits on the *kind* of communication? When it is said that the speaker must be performing an "act of state", is more implied than that his status be elevated and that he was acting in his official capacity? With the expansion of government, the communication may clearly relate to commercial matters, no less than to a more traditional area of governmental concern like foreign affairs or public order.[360] Nor would it be compatible with its rationale if the privilege did not cover communications to "appropriate subordinates".[361]

On the other hand, the privilege would seem to be clearly confined to "internal" communications which present less of a menace to private reputation because their range of dissemination is relatively narrow and the recipient is usually in a better position to evaluate its accuracy and suppress it if found to be mischievous. In salutary contrast to American law,[362]

353. The A.L.R.C. §136 recommended at most qualified privilege, like the Codes.
354. *Chatterton v. Secretary of State* [1895] 2 Q.B. 189.
355. *Isaacs v. Cook* [1925] 2 K.B. 391.
356. *Jackson v. Magrath* (1947) 75 C.L.R. 293.
357. Starke and Williams JJ.
358. See below, p. 582.
359. Latham C.J., and Rich J. (dissenting on a ground not material for the present purpose). Dixon and McTiernan JJ. found it unnecessary to express an opinion, because there was no evidence of malice.
360. *Peerless Bakery v. Watts* [1955] N.Z.L.R. 339 (bread supply); *Isaacs v. Cook* [1925] 2 K.B. 391 (fruit export).
361. *Peerless Bakery v. Watts* [1955] N.Z.L.R. 339 (Minister's order to Wheat Board official).
362. *Barr v. Mateo* 360 U.S. 564 (1959) (5-4), dropped the barrier both in regard to the official's rank and the occasion, so long as the communication falls within his official function.

press releases are excluded: however desirable that government policy be explained to the public, it is not so *necessary* to the proper functioning of government as to demand a complete sacrifice of private reputation.[363]

Army, police and foreign governments

In England, it has been held that a report by a commanding officer of a regiment to the Adjutant-General is entitled to complete immunity.[364] With respect to statements made in the course of naval and military duty, the public interest in permitting free exchange of confidential opinions between officers discharging responsible duties is perhaps reinforced by the necessity of maintaining discipline and unquestioning submission to superior authority. The existence of an absolute privilege in this situation, however, is still an open question, particularly in so far as its claim involves the doubtful proposition that matters of military discipline are not cognisable by civil courts.[365] At any rate, the High Court has refused to extend it to a report by a police inspector to the Metropolitan Superintendent, because "the discipline of the Force can survive an investigation of the motives by which he is activated in detracting from the character of a subordinate."[366]

The privilege does not ordinarily extend to communications by foreign officials, except perhaps in unprecedented circumstances, as when a foreign government has been granted asylum as an ally during war.[367] The basis of the domestic privilege is public interest, whereas the protection of representatives of foreign governments is more appropriately founded on diplomatic immunity.[368]

Marital communications

Communications between husband and wife enjoy absolute immunity at common law.[369] This salutary rule used to be attributed to want of any "publication" in the technical sense, husband and wife being regarded as one in the eye of the law. But this was a threadbare fiction and difficult in any event to reconcile with the rule that a defamatory statement made to one spouse concerning the other is actionable.[370] More consonant with modern ideas is to ascribe the conjugal immunity frankly to an absolute privilege in recognition of the confidential relationship between spouses so as to avoid "results disastrous to social life".[371]

It has been maintained that in the Code States the privilege disappeared as a result of the statutory definition of publication "to any person other

363. They do however enjoy qualified privilege under widespread statutes: see below, p. 584.
364. *Dawkins v. Lord Paulet* (1869) L.R. 5 Q.B. 94.
365. *Gibbons v. Duffell* (1932) 47 C.L.R. at 520, 526-527, 531, 534.
366. Ibid. at 528; cf. *Merricks v. Nott-Bower* [1965] 1 Q.B. 57. Nor is there any longer a categorical Crown privilege to withhold such a report from evidence: *Conway v. Rimmer* [1968] A.C. 910.
367. *Szalatnay-Stacho v. Fink* [1947] K.B. 1; cf. *Richards v. Naum* [1967] 1 Q.B. 620.
368. Cf. *Wright v. Cantrell* (1943) 44 S.R. (N.S.W.) 45.
369. *Wennhak v. Morgan* (1888) 20 Q.B.D. 635.
370. *Wenman v. Ash* (1853) 13 C.B. 836; 138 E.R. 1432.
371. *Wennhak v. Morgan* (1888) 20 Q.B.D. 635 at 639. See *Prosser & Keeton* 824, *Rest. 2d* §592.

than the person defamed''.[372] But despite an isolated ruling to this effect,[373] the statutory formula does not appear sufficiently explicit to justify so drastic and undesirable a conclusion.[374]

5. QUALIFIED PRIVILEGE

The publication of defamatory statements is in some circumstances protected by qualified privilege, in recognition of certain necessities of social intercourse. Unlike absolute immunity, freedom of expression is here safeguarded only on condition that the publication is made to serve the legitimate purpose of the privileged occasion and not some ulterior motive, foreign to the interest for the protection of which the privilege is accorded. Qualified privilege may defeat the law's protection of reputation in title of a wide variety of competing interests. The most comprehensive formula to describe these situations is that the occasion must be one ''where the person who makes [the] communication has an interest or a duty, legal, social or moral, to make it to the person to whom it is made, and the person to whom it is so made has a corresponding interest or duty to receive it''.[375]

The occasions qualifying for privilege can never be catalogued and rendered exact. New arrangements of business and habits of life may project patterns which, though different from well settled instances of privilege, could nonetheless fall within the flexible definition referred to. The legal concepts employed for determining the incidence of privilege, like ''interest'' and ''duty'', are sufficiently flexible to permit courts to individualise decisions somewhat reminiscent of negligence litigation, though here the judge's control is much greater than the jury's. It is for the judge alone to determine as a matter of law upon undisputed facts, or if the facts are disputed, upon facts as found by the jury, whether an occasion is privileged.[376] If answered in favour of the defendant, it is then open to the plaintiff to prove that the defendant abused the privilege, an issue for the jury.[377]

There are no rigid categories of qualified privilege, and in many cases the defence may succeed on more than one specific ground. But, for the sake of convenience, the subject can be summarised under the following headings:

Performance of a duty

A statement made in the discharge of some public or private duty, whether legal or moral, is conditionally privileged, provided it is

372. Qld: *Criminal Code* 1899 s. 369; W.A.: *Criminal Code* 1913 s. 349 (quaere whether applicable to civil proceedings: Brett, 2 Annual L. Rev. 43, 48); Tas.: *Defamation Act* 1957 s. 7.
373. *Tanner v. Miles* [1912] Q.W.N. 7.
374. If the controlling reason for the common law exemption is the fictitious identity of spouses (and it was probably so regarded by the draftsman), there is nothing in the Codes to endow husband and wife with separate and individual legal personality in order to compel the conclusion reached in *Tanner v. Miles*.
375. *Adam v. Ward* [1917] A.C. 309 at 334 per Lord Atkinson.
376. *Guise v. Kouvelis* (1947) 74 C.L.R. 102 at 116; *Defamation Act* 1974 (N.S.W.) s. 23.
377. This division of functions applies equally under the Codes: *Telegraph Newspaper v. Bedford* (1934) 50 C.L.R. 632.

communicated to one who has a reciprocal interest in receiving it.[378] It was once thought sufficient that the recipient had a legitimate interest in the information even in the absence of any corresponding obligation in the publisher to impart it to him.[379] But the scope of the privilege was considerably narrowed in *Watt v. Longsdon*[380] which held that a stranger was not privileged to make disclosures to a wife reflecting on the morals and integrity of her husband. Notwithstanding the legitimate concern of spouses in each other's conduct, the law did not recognise a social obligation in a stranger to interfere, particularly when the information emanated from a doubtful source and no effort was made to seek corroboration. Moreover, the privilege fails if the recipient actually lacks the required interest though the defendant honestly and reasonably believes he has it.[381] Both rules are widely felt to be unduly restrictive: their statutory reversal in New South Wales[382] has been recommended for national adoption.[383]

Whether there is a moral or social duty to convey the information must be determined by reference to the standard of values entertained by persons of ordinary intelligence and moral principle in the community.[384] "Moral duty" does not imply that anyone who failed to make the communication would necessarily be regarded by his fellows as open to censure, but rather that it was made on an occasion when one who desired to do his duty to his neighbour would reasonably believe that he ought to make it.[385] Occasionally, the duty to give information may be public in character, such as to give information of suspected crime to the police.[386] In the leading case,[387] certain charges had been preferred by a Member of Parliament against a high ranking officer. The Army Council instituted an investigation and later made a pronouncement which, in the course of exonerating him, incidentally passed defamatory strictures upon his accuser. The Council authorised its publication in the press, but was held entitled to claim privilege on the ground that the statement had been made in discharge of a public obligation. Moreover, having regard to the fact that the accusation had been made in Parliament, publication of the refutation in the press was not unduly wide to be considered abusive.

The law acknowledges more readily a duty to speak if the statement is made in answer to a specific inquiry rather than volunteered. One of the most common instances of privilege is that of a former employer giving the character of a discharged servant at the request of someone proposing to engage him.[388] Similar protection is accorded to a report requested by an

378. *Toogood v. Spyring* (1834) 1 C.M. & R. 181 at 193; 149 E.R. 1044 at 1049 per Parke B.
379. Reflecting the Code privilege (4) and (5), see below, p. 574.
380. [1930] 1 K.B. 130.
381. See below, p. 571.
382. *Defamation Act* 1974 ss 21, 22. Also the Codes: see below, p. 574.
383. A.L.R.C. §142.
384. *Stuart v. Bell* [1891] 2 Q.B. 341 at 350; *Watt v. Longsdon* [1930] 1 K.B. 130 at 153.
385. *Howe v. Lees* (1910) 11 C.L.R. 361 at 369.
386. *Tipene v. Apperley* [1981] N.Z. Recent Law 110.
387. *Adam v. Ward* [1917] A.C. 309. See also *Musgrave v. Commonwealth* (1937) 57 C.L.R. 514; *Dunford v. News Media* [1971] N.Z.L.R. 961.
388. *Toogood v. Spyring* (1834) 1 C.M. & R. 181 at 193; 149 E.R. 1044 at 1049. Nor is there a duty of care, sounding in negligence: see above, p. 140.

employer from one employee on another,[389] to an accusation against a third party in reply to a police inquiry,[390] or to a requested report from one businessman on the financial standing of a prospective customer.[391]

Some uncertainty remains regarding the position of commercial credit agencies and trade protection societies which supply information concerning the financial credit of others at the request of trade subscribers. In *Macintosh v. Dun*[392] the Privy Council denied protection to an organisation conducted as a pure business venture, on the ground that it was not in the public interest to protect communications made from motives of self-interest by persons who trade for profit in the character of other people. The defendants' *contractual* duty to supply the information desired by customers could not by itself create a *social* duty recognised by law for the welfare of the general public. The decision has been generally criticised as insensitive to legitimate business needs, especially in our modern credit economy. It was promptly nullified by legislation in New South Wales,[393] (now also in Queensland and South Australia),[394] and appears to be at odds with the Codes.[395] Moreover, later decisions both in Australia[396] and England[397] re-established the privilege for persons and organisations who are themselves interested in trade and maintain a trade protection service for their own common advantage. For example, in *Howe v. Lees*,[398] stock and station agents who carried on business in the Bendigo sale yards formed an association under the rules of which a member was obliged, under penalty, to report to the secretary any purchaser who did not settle his accounts within four days after sale. An honest but mistaken report regarding the plaintiff was held privileged.[399]

A duty to speak may arise even when information was not solicited. Certain relations, like that of employer and employee[400] or father and child,[401] justify volunteered statements by one or the other relevant to their duties and interests. A parent may warn his daughter against the character of her suitor, but unsolicited interference in family affairs by outsiders is not regarded as legitimate, save in very exceptional circumstances.[402] In general it is true to say that, while more in the way of good reason to speak is required from a volunteer, the absence of a request

389. *Riddick v. Thames Bd Mills* [1977] Q.B. 881 (but for such intra-mural communications the common employer is not absolutely privileged as urged by Lord Denning ("no publication")).
390. *Kine v. Sewell* (1838) 3 M. & W. 297; 150 E.R. 1157.
391. *Robshaw v. Smith* (1878) 38 L.T. 423.
392. [1908] A.C. 390; 6 C.L.R. 303.
393. *Defamation Act* 1909 s. 6 (conditional, however, on absence of negligence). Now *Defamation Act* 1974 s. 22(3); *Kaiser v. G. Laurens* [1982] 1 N.S.W.L.R. 294.
394. *Invasion of Privacy Act* 1971 s. 23 and *Fair Credit Reports Act* 1974 s. 10 respectively.
395. Subsection (4); see below. Reform was also recommended by *Faulks* §§233-237 and A.L.R.C. §148.
396. *Howe v. Lees* (1910) 11 C.L.R. 361.
397. *London Assoc. for Protection of Trade v. Greenlands* [1916] 2 A.C. 15.
398. (1910) 11 C.L.R. 361.
399. The distinction thus drawn was doubted by Lord Parker in *Greenlands* [1916] 2 A.C. 15 at 42, and Scrutton L.J. in *Watt v. Longsdon* [1930] 1 K.B. 130 at 148.
400. *Cooke v. Wildes* (1855) 5 E. & B. 328; 119 E.R. 504.
401. *Todd v. Hawkins* (1837) 8 C. & P. 88; 173 E.R. 411.
402. *Watt v. Longsdon* [1930] 1 K.B. 130.

is merely one of the factors to be considered in determining whether the occasion warranted the defendant's conduct.

Protection of an interest

By analogy to self-defence against physical aggression,[403] qualified privilege attaches to statements made for the protection of the publisher's own legitimate interests. Thus statements in self-defence are protected, if made by a person in reply to attacks upon his own character or conduct, or in protection of an employer against attacks on him, or in protection of his own proprietary interests or those of his employer against attacks upon such interests. For example, a newspaper editor may defend himself not only against attacks upon him as a person and journalist, but may also defend the reputation of the company and newspaper because of his personal interest in the enterprise.[404] So a daughter is entitled to vindicate her father's memory, because her filial interest makes it proper for her to give an answer to any slurs cast upon him.[405]

Some latitude is granted for the reply.[406] If in defence to an attack by A, B defames C, he will be protected, so long as the reflection on C is reasonably incidental to the refutation.[407] But just as in case of physical attack, the permissible scope of self-defence is exceeded if the reply becomes a counterattack with accusations unrelated or "insufficiently related" to the original attack.[408] The privilege is a shield, not a sword.

No privilege attaches unless the communication is made to a person with a corresponding interest or duty to receive it. Whether such reciprocity either of interest or duty exists must vary with the facts of each case, but it seems clear that where the defamatory matter is published in self-defence or in protection of an interest or by way of vindication against an attack, the concept of corresponding duty or interest in the recipient is liberally interpreted.[409] The proper test is: "Would the great mass of Australians of ordinary intelligence and moral principle have recognised that the occasion or exigency warranted the communication?"[410] In *Mowlds v. Fergusson*,[411] for example, a police inspector, in reply to serious criticism levelled against him by a Royal Commissioner in relation to a matter involving the plaintiff's conduct, furnished a report at the Premier's request which contained defamatory allegations concerning the plaintiff. He showed it to his former superior who had since retired from the service. This communication was held to be privileged, because the latter had a moral

403. *Norton v. Hoare (No. 1)* (1913) 17 C.L.R. 310 at 318, 322.
404. *Penton v. Calwell* (1945) 70 C.L.R. 219; *Norton v. Hoare (No. 1)* (1913) 17 C.L.R. 310. But he may not claim privilege for a reply to an attack on newspapers generally.
405. *Bowen-Rowlands v. Argus Press* (1926), cited by Dixon J. in *Loveday v. Sun Newspaper* (1938) 59 C.L.R. 503 at 519-520.
406. But no riposte is permitted to the original defamer: *Kennett v. Farmer* [1988] V.R. 991.
407. *Loveday v. Sun Newspaper* (1938) 59 C.L.R. 503 at 520; and see *Mowlds v. Fergusson* (1940) 64 C.L.R. 206.
408. *News Media v. Finlay* [1970] N.Z.L.R. 1089 (C.A.) (a case of tit-for-tat); *Douglas v. Tucker* [1952] 1 D.L.R. 657.
409. "The law has not restricted the right . . . within any narrow limits" (*Adam v. Ward* [1917] A.C. 309 at 329 per Lord Dunedin).
410. *Mowlds v. Fergusson* (1940) 64 C.L.R. 206 at 220 per Williams J.
411. Ibid.

concern in knowing the consequences of his own past administration and an interest to hear his former subordinate's answer to the comments made upon him. Besides, he was a person to whom the defendant might legitimately look for support in his process of vindication.[412] In certain cases, a person may even resort to the public press. If attacked in public, he is free to place his case before the body whose judgment the attacking party has sought to affect, and this may comprise the entire public, for example where he is seeking to repel an attack made on him in Parliament[413] or the plaintiff has himself chosen the press for the purpose of giving publicity to his own animadversions against the defendant.[414]

Statements invited by plaintiff

Resembling retorts to an attack are communications procured at the complainant's own request or contrivance. By instigating the defamatory publication himself, a plaintiff stands to forfeit his claim to protection either on the ground of consent or, more often, by conferring on the defendant a qualified privilege to reply.[415] He will be deemed to have consented if he feeds false information to a newspaper,[416] sets afloat compromising rumours about himself,[417] or deliberately entraps the defendant into making or repeating a defamatory allegation for the sole purpose of suing thereon.[418] But merely initiating a public discussion about oneself is not an invitation to defame;[419] even a challenge "Publish if you dare" implies not consent, but defiance.[420]

If, in contrast, the defamatory reply is made to a legitimate inquiry by the plaintiff or his agents anxious to obtain information or trace a rumour to its source, it becomes decisive whether the calumny originated with the defendant. For if it did, he may not with impunity repeat,[421] as distinct

412. Ibid. at 215 per Dixon J.; adopting *Rest.* §594, comment *g*.
413. *Penton v. Calwell* (1945) 70 C.L.R. 219; *Adam v. Ward* [1917] A.C. 309.
414. *Loveday v. Sun Newspaper* (1938) 59 C.L.R. 503. The newspaper enjoys a corresponding "derivative" privilege: see below, p. 577.
415. The distinction between consent and privilege is shadowy, and neither courts nor writers have contributed much to its clarification: see *Loveday v. Sun Newspaper* (1938) 59 C.L.R. 503 at 523-525. The Codes make no specific provision for a defence of "consent", but allow a qualified privilege where "the publication is made in good faith on the invitation or challenge of the person defamed": see below, p. 574.
416. As Mr Corrigan did in *Cassidy v. Daily Mirror* [1925] 2 K.B. 331.
417. As illustrated by the film "A Touch of Larceny" where a naval officer engineered his disappearance in suspicious circumstances, hoping to be branded as a traitor and thereafter rehabilitate his fortunes by suing for libel.
418. *Jones v. Brooks* (1974) 45 D.L.R. (3d) 413; *King v. Waring* (1803) 5 Esp. 13 at 15; 170 E.R. 721 at 722; *Weatherston v. Hawkins* (1786) 1 T.R. 110; 99 E.R. 1001. *Rudd v. Cameron* (1912) 26 O.L.R. 154 treats this situation as one of privilege; the defendant lost on proof of malice. Note also that it is not prejudicial for one libelled in a newspaper to buy a copy to prove publication, because purchase is free to all: *Brunswick v. Harmer* (1849) 14 Q.B. 185; 117 E.R. 75.
419. *Loveday v. Sun Newspaper* (1938) 59 C.L.R. 503 at 513-514; *Church of Scientology v. Anderson* [1980] W.A.R. 71 (radio talk-back session).
420. *Orr v. Isles* (1965) 83 W.N. (Pt 1) (N.S.W.) 303 at 325. Just as one does not consent to a battery by resisting a threat and daring the other to hit him.
421. *Smith v. Mathews* (1931) 1 M. & Rob. 151; 174 E.R. 52; *Griffiths v. Lewis* (1945) 7 Q.B. 61; 115 E.R. 411.

from merely acknowledge,[422] his former allegation; otherwise, however, he is conditionally privileged to answer the inquiry.[423]

Common interest

A communication on a subject in which the defendant and the recipient share a common legitimate interest is privileged. Although "interest" is not used in any technical sense, it has been narrowly construed to include only "real and direct personal, trade, business or social concern[s]",[424] "such as would assist in the making of an important decision or determining of a particular course of action".[425] It must be something more than mere curiosity in the private affairs of other people. For this reason, the law has stoutly refused to recognise any community of interest between a newspaper and the general body of its readers which could justify the communication to them of imputations against another person.[426] Even the common link between members of a national minority group does not supply a sufficient mutual interest to permit one of them to broadcast calumnies against another among the group as a whole.[427] Exceptionally, however, the use of a newspaper as a communication is permissible, provided the paper is really only an enlarged circular[428] restricted to the particular group which shares a legitimate common interest with the publisher.[429]

Mutuality of interest is often encountered when there is also a moral, sometimes even a legal, duty to make the communication to the other person. Usually the common interest is pecuniary, arising from association between the parties for business purposes, as in the case of discussion of company affairs among shareholders[430] or intra-mural reports about an employee.[431] Again, a mutual interest arises from professional association like a trade union[432] or in respect of statements made to a disciplinary body and the communication of its findings to an appellate domestic tribunal.[433] The relationship of landlord and tenant justifies complaints by one to the other concerning the conduct of other tenants, lodgers or persons employed on the premises,[434] while democracy demands protection for communications between electors, as well as between candidates and

422. *Freeman v. Poppe* (1905) 25 N.Z.L.R. 529; *Griffiths v. Lewis* (1845) 7 Q.B. 61 at 65; 115 E.R. 441.
423. *Taylor v. Hawkins* (1851) 16 Q.B. 308; 117 E.R. 897; *Ryan v. Newman* (1882) 3 L.R. (N.S.W.) 309; but cf. *Andrews v. Ginn (No. 2)* [1933] N.Z.L.R. 1073.
424. *Telegraph Newspaper v. Bedford* (1934) 50 C.L.R. 632 at 662 per Evatt J.
425. *Austin v. Mirror Newspaper* [1986] A.C. 299 at 311.
426. *Telegraph Newspaper v. Bedford* (1934) 50 C.L.R. 632; *Antonovich v. W.A. Newspaper* [1960] W.A.R. 176; *Smith's Newspaper v. Becker* (1932) 47 C.L.R. 279 at 304.
427. *Andreyevich v. Kosovich* (1947) 47 S.R. (N.S.W.) 357.
428. *Morosi v. Mirror Newspaper* [1977] 2 N.S.W.L.R. 749 at 779.
429. *Chapman v. Ellesmere* [1932] 2 K.B. 431 (racing calendar); *Andreyevich v. Kosovich* (1947) 47 S.R. (N.S.W.) 357 at 365 (Croatian language); *Wells v. Wellington* [1952] N.Z.L.R. 312 (trade union).
430. *Telegraph Newspaper v. Bedford* (1934) 50 C.L.R. 632 at 658.
431. *Riddick v. Thames Bd Mills* [1977] Q.B. 881 (C.A.); *Anderson v. Ginn (No. 2)* [1933] N.Z.L.R. 1073; *Sun Life Assurance v. Dalrymple* [1965] S.C.R. 302.
432. *Duane v. Granrott* [1982] V.R. 767 (F.C.).
433. *Thompson v. Amos* (1949) 23 A.L.J. 98 (H.C.); *Allbutt v. General Council of Medical Education* (1889) 23 Q.B.D. 400.
434. *Toogood v. Spyring* (1834) 1 C.M. & R. 181; 149 E.R. 1044.

electors, regarding any matter which may properly affect their choice at the ballot.[435]

No privilege arises if the exigency of the occasion does not warrant the protection of the common interest by the means employed. In *Guise v. Kouvelis*,[436] a committeeman interfered in a dispute between members of a club who were playing cards in a room containing some 50 other persons some of whom were non-members. He charged the plaintiff with being a crook in a loud voice audible to most of those present. It was held that the interests of the defendant and the members did not justify a public accusation, because he could have simply told the plaintiff, without making any defamatory allegation, that he would report him to the committee. Any such communication would, of course, have been privileged.

It must also be reiterated that an interest solely on the part of the recipient will not qualify under this head or any other: there must additionally be either a corresponding interest or a duty on the part of the publisher. This salient common law principle has only been modified in New South Wales[437] and the Code States where it is sufficient that the recipient had an interest or apparent interest in having information on the subject and the publisher's conduct was reasonable in the circumstances.

Public interest

A defamatory publication has no claim to privilege merely because it deals with a matter of public interest.[438] True, all privilege is based on the publication being "in the public interest". But from this does not follow that publication of all matters of public interest is in *the* public interest. In contrast to American law,[439] our own has steadfastly declined to sacrifice individual reputation to recurrent demands[440] by the media for privileged dissemination of so-called "news".[441] There is no defence of "fair information on a matter of public interest";[442] otherwise there would have

435. *Braddock v. Bevins* [1948] 1 K.B. 580 (address distributed to electors). But the privilege is narrow; it cannot be claimed for publication in a general newspaper (*Jones v. Bennett* [1969] S.C.R. 277; *Templeton v. Jones* [1984] 1 N.Z.L.R. 448) nor perhaps for speeches to a large undifferentiated audience: *Lang v. Willis* (1934) 52 C.L.R. 637 at 667, 672. It was virtually abolished in England by *Defamation Act* 1952 s. 10.

436. (1947) 74 C.L.R. 102.

437. *Defamation Act* 1974 s. 22. Corresponding in substance with (5) of the Code privileges: see below, p. 574.

438. *Truth (N.Z.) v. Holloway* [1960] 1 W.L.R. 997 (P.C.); *Brooks v. Muldoon* [1973] 1 N.Z.L.R. 1; *Banks v. Globe & Mail* [1961] S.C.R. 474; *A.B.C. v. Comalco* (1986) 68 A.L.R. 259; *Morosi v. Mirror Newspaper* [1977] 2 N.S.W.L.R. 749 (C.A.).

439. See below, p. 586.

440. E.g. (U.K.) Press Council, *Reforming the Law of Defamation* (1973). *Faulks* §§211-215 was unpersuaded.

441. Nor are newspaper sources of information sacrosanct. There is no privilege of refusal to testify (*McGuinness v. A.-G.* (1940) 63 C.L.R. 73; *A.-G. v. Mulholland* [1963] 2 Q.B. 477), though most jurisdictions recognise a discretionary "newspaper rule" of excusing media from disclosing their sources in pre-trial interrogatories or discovery of documents: *Fairfax v. Cojuangco* (1988) 165 C.L.R. 346; aliter, *Broadcasting Corp. v. A. Harvey* [1980] 1 N.Z.L.R. 163 (C.A.) (matter of course). See Walker, 14 N.S.W. L. Rev. 302. The *Contempt of Court Act* 1981 (Eng.) s. 10 and widespread "shield laws" in the U.S. offer protection against disclosure.

442. *Blackshaw v. Lord* [1984] Q.B. 1 (C.A.) (even for information emanating from the government except under statutory privilege: see below, p. 572).

been no need for the special defence of fair comment which, as we shall see,[443] is limited to *comment* on true facts. For false *factual* information to the general public, even on matters of public concern, there is no qualified privilege unless there was a duty to impart such information, and this the common law has in general denied to the media and others except in very special circumstances, such as for replies to public attacks,[444] correction of previously published information,[445] or a public warning against a suspected terrorist or contaminated food.[446] Moreover, even if some members of the public have a legitimate interest in receiving the information, the publication would often be excessive to the extent that it reaches others who are not qualified.[447]

Does this not unduly cramp the public's "right to know"? First, it must be remembered that there is no stopping the publication of accurate news. Moreover, as just mentioned, there is a defence of fair comment on matters of public interest, provided the comment is based on true facts. The controversial area is therefore confined strictly to false defamatory statements of fact, and comment thereon, on matters of public interest. The question boils down to whether the free flow of information is (not) unduly stifled by imposing the risk of good faith factual error (or inability to prove truth) on the press and letting the fear of large damages chill investigative reporting. As we shall see, legislation in Australia[448] and Canada[449] has to some extent addressed this concern.[450]

It is well recognised, however, that complaints and the like addressed to the proper authorities concerning a matter of general interest are privileged. Thus every citizen may inform the police of suspected crimes,[451] or address to his Member of Parliament any grievance concerning a public official.[452] But he takes the risk that the person actually has a corresponding duty or interest to receive it. A mistaken belief, however reasonable, that the recipient is the proper authority for dealing with the complaint furnishes no excuse.[453] This harsh rule has been repealed in several jurisdictions.[454]

443. See below, p. 585.
444. See above, p. 567.
445. *Dunford v. News Media* [1971] N.Z.L.R. 961.
446. *Camporese v. Parton* (1983) 150 D.L.R. (3d) 208 (B.C.); *Blackshaw v. Lord*.
447. Aliter, newspapers addressed only to a narrow "special interest" group: see above, p. 570.
448. See below, pp. 572-575.
449. No general damages if retracted: see Fleming, *Retraction and Reply: Alternative Remedies for Defamation*, 12 U.B.C.L. Rev. 15 (1978). Also recommended in N.Z. (§237).
450. Faulks §214(b) remained opposed. A.L.R.C. §146 preferred a defence for "attributed statements".
451. Since the tort of malicious prosecution (a special form of defamation) provides additional protection in requiring lack of probable cause (plus malice) (see below, p. 616), this should apply here also.
452. *R. v. Rule* [1973] 2 K.B. 375. The M.P. may likewise be privileged in passing it on and replying: *Beach v. Freeson* [1972] 1 Q.B. 14; *Moran v. Chapman (No. 2)* [1935] V.L.R. 13.
453. *Hebditch v. MacIlwaine* [1894] 2 Q.B. 54; *Beach v. Freeson* [1972] 1 Q.B. 14.
454. Under the Codes see (2) and (5) below. Under the *Defamation Act* 1974 (N.S.W.) s. 21 the mistaken character of the recipient in all cases of qualified privilege is excused by reasonable belief of the defendant. The common law rule seems to confuse mistaken belief in the existence of a privilege with whether the recipient has the correct qualifications. *Rest. 2d* §595 applies reasonable belief to both.

This kind of privilege is therefore strictly controlled and in no circumstances justifies publication of such matters to the general public through the medium of the press. Moreover, it matters nothing that the libel relates to a subject on which the plaintiff has himself invited public discussion because, so far as the defence of volenti non fit injuria is concerned, he cannot fairly be held to have invited thereby publication of defamatory statements concerning himself.[455]

Informational privilege

New South Wales in 1974, after abandoning the Code regime (noted below), created an additional statutory privilege to protect the informational role of the media and others. It arises where "(a) the recipient has an interest or apparent interest in having information on some subject; (b) the matter is published to the recipient in the course of giving him information on that subject; and (c) the conduct of the publisher in publishing the matter is reasonable in the circumstances."[456]

"Interest" is here construed in the broadest popular sense. At common law, it will be recalled, it is confined to "an interest material to the affairs of the recipient of the information such as would assist in the making of an important decision or determining of a particular course of action".[457] Here, however, it includes information of any matter of genuine interest to readers of a general newspaper, such as comment on the manoeuvres of a national politician[458] or the training regime of a Rugby League team.[459]

The principal accent is on reasonableness in the belief that only a careful and honest publication deserves protection. The standard has been interpreted rather strictly so that few defences have been successful. It clearly requires more than belief in the truth (although it has been questioned whether such belief is necessary for reporting statements by third parties). Relevant matters, it has been said, include the manner and extent of publication, the extent of inquiries made, the degree of care exercised and any knowledge that a misleading impression was likely to be conveyed.[460] The courts have been particularly insistent on care in verification.[461] Failure to mention the plaintiff's denial of the allegations against him may be prejudicial;[462] and disclosure of informants has been compelled even prior to trial, thus considerably diminishing the attractiveness of the defence.[463] But a lesser standard of investigative care has—rightly—been demanded for stories about the public conduct of

455. *Loveday v. Sun Newspaper* (1938) 59 C.L.R. 503 at 514, 525. But cf. subs. 6 of the Codes: see below, p. 574.
456. *Defamation Act* 1974 s. 22.
457. *Austin v. Mirror Newspaper* [1986] A.C. 299 at 311 (P.C.); see above, p. 567.
458. *Calwell v. Ipec* (1975) 135 C.L.R. 321.
459. *Austin v. Mirror Newspaper* [1984] A.C. 299.
460. *Morgan v. Fairfax* (1989) per Mathews J., unrep.; cited Discussion Paper on Reform of Defamation Law No. 1 (A.-G.s of N.S.W., Qld and Vic.), p. 40 (revd on other ground: (1991) 23 N.S.W.L.R. 374).
461. Criticised by Henskens, 6 Aust. B. Rev. 267 (1990). Guidelines are suggested by the L.R.C. Report, para. 105.
462. *Wright v. A.B.C.* [1977] 1 N.S.W.L.R. 697 (C.A.).
463. *Fairfax v. Cojuangco* (1988) 165 C.L.R. 346.

politicians[464] than for imputations of sexual impropriety of private persons.[465]

In case of a newspaper article, if written by a staff journalist, the latter's reasonableness is in issue; if written by an independent author, the reasonableness must be that of the paper's staff who decided to publish it. Though reasonableness is a question of fact, the ultimate question falls to be determined by the judge, subject to the jury deciding any disputed issues of fact on which the resolution of the ultimate question may depend. For example, whether the defendant honestly believed his criticism is a primary fact which must be left to the jury before the judge can decide if a negative answer precludes a finding that he acted reasonably in the circumstances.[466]

Current bills in New South Wales, Victoria and Queensland are introducing yet another version of "public interest" privilege. This uniform legislation proposes a qualified privilege for publications relating to a matter of public interest, made in good faith and after appropriate inquiries. A relevant factor in deciding good faith will be whether the defendant was willing to publish a reply on request, and in deciding that it was published after appropriate inquiries whether the plaintiff was given an opportunity to confirm or deny the truth. If the defence is made out, but the judge holds the statement to have been false, he may order the defendant to publish a reply approved by him.[467]

Privilege under the Codes

Although intended to be primarily declaratory of the common law, the statutory enumeration of privileged publications in the Queensland Code, as subsequently adopted in Western Australia (but held inapplicable to civil claims),[468] Tasmania, and for a brief interval in New South Wales, has in effect created a marked divergence between the law of qualified privilege in those States and the rest of Australia. This is largely the result of considerable modifications of the common law since the codification was first enacted. In particular the draftsman failed to anticipate the contraction of common law privilege by the modern insistence on the requirement of reciprocity of duty and interest between the communicants. Generally, under the Codes, a unilateral interest or duty either on the part of the informant or the recipient is sufficient.[469]

Qualified "protection" arises[470]

> "if the publication is made in good faith by a person
> (1) having over another any lawful authority in the course of a censure passed by him on the conduct of that other in matters to which such lawful authority relates;

464. *Caldwell v. Ipec* (1975) 135 C.L.R. 321.
465. *Morosi v. Mirror Newspapers* [1977] 2 N.S.W.L.R. 749.
466. *Morgan v. J. Fairfax* (1990) 20 N.S.W.L.R. 511 (C.A.). It is not necessarily preclusive in case of a telecast: *Barbaro v. Amalg. T.V.* (1990) 20 N.S.W.L.R. 493 (C.A.).
467. Defamation Bills 1991.
468. *W.A. Newspaper v. Bridge* (1979) 141 C.L.R. 535; see above, n. 9.
469. *Musgrave v. Cth* (1937) 57 C.L.R. 514 at 548.
470. Qld: s. 377; W.A.: s. 357; Tas.: s. 16.

(2) for the purpose of seeking remedy or redress for some private or public wrong or grievance, from a person who has, or whom the person making the publication believes on reasonable grounds to have, authority over the person defamed with respect to the subject matter of such wrong or grievance;

(3) for the protection of the interests of the person making the publication, or of some other person or for the public good;

(4) in answer to an inquiry made of the person making the publication, relating to some subject as to which the person by whom or on whose behalf the inquiry is made has, or is believed on reasonable grounds by the person making the publication to have, an interest in knowing the truth;

(5) for the purpose of giving information to the person to whom it is made with respect to some subject as to which that person has or is believed, on reasonable grounds, by the person making the publication to have, such an interest in knowing the truth as to make his conduct in making the publication reasonable under the circumstances;

(6) on the invitation or challenge of the person defamed;

(7) in order to answer or refute some other defamatory matter published by the person defamed concerning the person making publication or some other person;

(8) in the course of, or for the purposes of, the discussion of some subject of public interest, the public discussion of which is for the public benefit, and if, so far as the defamatory matter consists of comment, the comment is fair."

Of these only the first and second heads accurately represent the common law, the remainder exceeding it in greater or lesser measure. Thus the third goes beyond the common law in sanctioning a publication made for the protection of the interests of some person other than the defendant without stipulating a corresponding duty in the recipient to protect the interests mentioned. Moreover, the ambit of the protection "for the public good" in (3) remains unclear. For long it was read down to conform to recognised principles of the common law, by holding that it was merely intended to bring within the statutory protection any instance of qualified privilege recognised at common law but not specifically covered by any other enumerated heads.[471] Lately however, a more expansive view has emerged, protecting media discussion of the public attitudes of politicians, such as their party loyalty, as distinct from their private character (and, of course, private communications). In effect it correlates "public interest" in such information with the "public good" that this interest should not be stultified.[472]

The fourth and fifth heads, which protect requested and volunteered information conveyed to a person who has a legitimate interest in receiving it, omit the requirement of reciprocal duty on the part of the informant. His belief required under the fifth head is not in the truth of the information

471. *Telegraph Newspaper v. Bedford* (1934) 50 C.L.R. 632 at 653; *Musgrave v. Cth* (1937) 57 C.L.R. 514.

472. *Calwell v. Ipec* (1975) 135 C.L.R. 321 at 336 per Jacobs and Mason JJ.

(though that may bear on his good faith) but in the recipient's interest in knowing the truth. It calls for evidence that the defendant, a newspaper publisher for instance, at least exercised its mind at the managerial level in relation to the matter. Finally, whether the publication is reasonable under the circumstances is a question of "degree, public policy, propriety, and moral rights and duties", which in the first and last resort is for the judge to determine subject only to the jury's decision on disputed questions of fact.[473]

The sixth category partly coincides with the defence of consent,[474] but may conceivably be wide enough to protect statements actionable at common law.[475] The seventh head is virtually declaratory, except that the common law does not universally recognise an interest or duty in one person to refute an attack on another.[476] The last instance of privilege is entirely without precedent. It is reminiscent of the common law defence of fair comment but differs from it in two vital particulars, by protecting false statements of fact as well as fair comment based thereon.[477]

Criticism

No feature of the Code has attracted so much adverse criticism as its treatment of qualified privilege. Its weaknesses were exposed by incessant litigation in New South Wales to the point of prompting the total repeal of the Code in 1974 after only 15 years of operation.[478]

Among its many flaws are ambiguities of scope due to the missing requirement of reciprocity and the use of unfamiliar criteria like "public good", cheek by jowl with "public interest" and "public benefit". Even more perturbing has been the discovery of endless complications in the division of functions between judge and jury. Although the existence of a privileged occasion remains a matter for the court, as at common law,[479] several subsidiary issues (for example "public benefit" and relevance) are expressly allotted to the jury.[480] In other instances, judge and jury appear both to have a voice in passing upon the same issue, as when the purpose of the publication, its relevance and the area of communication bear alike on the existence of a privileged occasion as well as on good faith. All this results in needless procedural traps and in increased unpredictability.

Abuse of Privilege

Qualified privilege is a conditional defence. It affords immunity to those alone who use the privileged occasion for the purpose which the law deems of sufficient social importance to defeat the countervailing claim to

473. *Pervan v. N. Queensland Newspaper* (1991) A.T.R. 81-119. See above, p. 572 for the same formula under s. 22 of the N.S.W. Act.
474. See *Cookson v. Harewood* [1932] 2 K.B. 478n.; and above, p. 568.
475. See *Loveday v. Sun Newspaper* (1938) 59 C.L.R. 503, but note Dixon J.'s view which approximates more closely the position taken by the Codes.
476. At common law, there must exist a special relationship between the person attacked and the defendant to justify the latter's retaliation: see above, p. 567.
477. *Pervan v. N. Queensland Newspaper*; *Rigby v. Assoc. Newspapers* (1966) 68 S.R. (N.S.W.) 414 at 425; *Anderson v. Nationwide News* (1972) S.R. (N.S.W.) 313 at 319.
478. *Defamation Act* 1974 s. 4.
479. *Justin v. Assoc. Newspapers* (1966) 86 W.N. (Pt 1) (N.S.W.) 17 (C.A.).
480. Qld: s. 379; W.A.: s. 359; Tas.: s. 20.

protection of reputation. In other words, the immunity is forfeited by an abuse of the occasion, and there must be no improper motive on the part of the publisher.[481] These limitations are a striking illustration of what Continental jurists call the doctrine of "abuse of rights".[482]

Excessive communication

Some reference has already been made to the rule that the privilege is lost if the method of its exercise exceeds the reasonable needs of the occasion.[483] Thus it is not ordinarily permissible to resort to the press for communicating privileged information. It is true that a person attacked in public may legitimately vindicate himself before the same wide audience which has become aware of the charges made against him,[484] but in general the individual or group who have an interest in receiving the information is more limited. The method of publication must never exceed what is reasonably appropriate for protecting the particular interest which the defendant is entitled to assert. If, for example, the occasion is privileged on account of a common interest, the selected medium of communication must be such as will reasonably ensure that the statement is not circulated beyond those who share that interest.[485] This rule has been somewhat relaxed in New South Wales where, in case of "multiple publications", privilege is no longer forfeited by an excessive publication to unqualified recipients, if the extent of the publication was reasonable.[486]

The inclusion of material outside the ambit of the privilege and therefore itself unprotected does not as such destroy the privilege covering the rest;[487] however, it may suggest an improper purpose for the whole.

Immunity covers all incidents of communication conforming with the reasonable and usual course of business or necessary for the effective exercise of the privilege. Nowadays dictation of a letter to a typist[488] or telegraphic communication,[489] if appropriate, is protected to the same extent as the publication to the addressee. According to the generally accepted view, this is a derivative privilege ancillary to that covering the resulting message, though attaching immediately and therefore unimpaired

481. Under the Codes, qualified protection is conditioned by "good faith" (but need not be specially pleaded by the defendant: *Motel Holdings v. The Bulletin* [1963] S.R. (N.S.W.) 208). A publication is made in good faith "if the matter published is relevant to the matters the existence of which may excuse the publication in good faith of defamatory matter; if the manner and extent of the publication does not exceed what is reasonably sufficient for the occasion; and if the person by whom it is made is not actuated by ill-will to the person defamed, or by any other improper motive, and does not believe the defamatory matter to be untrue" (Qld: s. 377; W.A.: s. 357; Tas.: s. 16(2)). The burden of proving these negatives is on the plaintiff: Qld: s. 378; W.A.: s. 358; Tas.: s. 19.
482. See Gutteridge, *Abuse of Rights*, 5 Cam. L.J. 22 (1933).
483. See above, pp. 565, 570.
484. *Penton v. Calwell* (1945) 70 C.L.R. 219; *Adam v. Ward* [1917] A.C. 309.
485. Contrast *Chapman v. Ellesmere* [1932] 2 K.B. 431 with *Cookson v. Harewood* [1932] 2 K.B. 478n.
486. *Defamation Act* 1974 s. 20(3).
487. *Dunford v. News Media* [1971] N.Z.L.R. 961; also *Defamation Act* 1974 (N.S.W.) s. 20(2).
488. *Osborn v. Boulter* [1930] 2 K.B. 226; *Holding v. Jennings* [1979] V.R. 289 (absolute privilege).
489. *Edmundson v. Birch* [1907] 1 K.B. 371.

by the fact that the message is eventually not sent at all or lost.[490] More neatly disposing of these complications would be Lord Denning's view that the privilege is original, based on a common interest between the typist and her boss in the writing of the letter, and not dependent at all on the person to whom it is intended to be sent.[491]

Lord Denning's view would also be helpful where the defamatory letter is addressed to the plaintiff himself and therefore could not technically qualify as a "publication" for a derivative privilege to attach. But the more commonly accepted explanation is that qualified privilege covers all "fairly warranted" communications between parties to a dispute, including ancillary incidents of transmission.[492] So also where the defendant makes a defamatory accusation to the plaintiff himself in the presence of a disinterested witness: since it is in the plaintiff's interest to know what accusation is being brought against him, the confrontation constitutes a privileged occasion, and it does not matter that it would not in any event have been actionable because lacking the element of publication. Once this reasoning is accepted,[493] it is easy to conclude that the presence of a disinterested witness, as a reasonable precaution, does not defeat the privilege.[494]

In cases where a secretary or other agent thus participates in a privileged communication, the latter is also protected, since a privilege would be of no value if the means for exercising it were not also protected. Such a derivative privilege may occasionally even be available to the press, for example when a person publicly attacked is justified in replying through a newspaper.[495] This, however, must be clearly distinguished from the more usual situation of a newspaper speaking for itself, when it must stand or fall on an independent privilege of its own.

Improper purpose

The privilege will be lost if the defamatory statement is published for an improper purpose. This is commonly expressed by saying that the publication must not have been "malicious". But the indiscriminate use of the term "malice" in this context is apt to mislead, because the immunity is defeated not only by spite or a desire to inflict harm for its own sake, but by the misuse of the privileged occasion for some other purpose than that for which it was given by law, such as to cover up a previous misstatement,

490. *Bryanston Finance v. de Vries* [1975] Q.B. 703 (C.A.).
491. Ibid. Alternatively, why not treat dictation to an employee as "no publication" analogous to conjugal communications?
492. Ibid. at 745 per Lawton L.J.; *Osborn v. Boulter* [1930] 2 K.B. 226 (C.A.).
493. Thus Goodhart, *Defamatory Statements and Privileged Occasions*, 56 L.Q.R. 262 (1940); contra: *White v. Stone* [1939] 2 K.B. 827.
494. *Toogood v. Spyring* (1834) 1 Cr. M. & R. 181; 149 E.R. 1044 (although this case contains the classical exposition of qualified privilege by Parke B., reciprocity of interest was not then as strictly demanded as it is today); *Taylor v. Hawkins* (1851) 16 Q.B. 308; 117 E.R. 897. Aliter, when an unwanted stranger is negligently permitted to eavesdrop, as in *White v. Stone* [1939] 2 K.B. 827; *McNichol v. Grandy* [1931] S.C.R. 696; or when a shopkeeper publicly accuses a stranger of shoplifting: *Bonette v. Woolworths* (1937) 37 S.R. (N.S.W.) 142.
495. *Loveday v. Sun Newspaper* (1938) 59 C.L.R. 503; *Adam v. Ward* [1917] A.C. 309 at 320 (secretary). For the effect of malice see below, p. 580.

to discredit a particular religious or political doctrine avowed by the plaintiff, to compound a felony rather than pursue an honest inquiry into suspected crime,[496] or to deliberately distort and sensationalise a news story in order to heighten its reader appeal.[497]

Evidence that the defamatory statement was published for a purpose foreign to the privileged occasion may be extrinsic or intrinsic. Extrinsic evidence may be supplied by facts existing before, at, or after the time when it was made.[498] The existence of personal animosity may be one such fact, though only if it supports an inference that the determining motive for the publication was spite and not a sense of duty or the promotion of a legitimate interest.[499] Evidence must make it probable that the defendant not only harboured a desire to serve some ulterior purpose, but also that it influenced him to make the defamatory statement. If antagonism were of itself sufficient to defeat privilege, the defence would be of little value besides involving the startling consequence that, where the defendant has been himself abused by the plaintiff, the grosser the attack the easier it would be to prove malice.[500] The jury should not be permitted to speculate on abuse of privilege at all, unless there is sufficient evidence which definitely, and as a matter of common sense, points to the inference that an improper motive existed and that it induced the publication of the libel. It is not sufficient that the evidence gives ground merely for speculation or conjecture.[501] There is a danger that the protection of privilege becomes illusory, unless stringent judicial control is maintained over the permissible function of the jury in these cases.

The contents of the defamatory statement itself may furnish intrinsic evidence of an improper motive, for example the extravagance of the allegation or the language in which it is expressed. But here again, "no nice scales"[502] should be used in weighing the defendant's expressions for traces of malice. Particularly when a person has been attacked abusively, the terms of his reply must be measured with some latitude: "it would be singular if an attacked person could defend himself only if he abated the

496. *Hooper v. Truscott* (1836) 2 Bing. N.C. 457; 132 E.R. 179; *Collerton v. MacLean* [1962] N.Z.L.R. 1045.

497. Cf. *Broadway Approvals v. Odhams Press (No. 2)* [1965] 1 W.L.R. 805.

498. See *Mowlds v. Fergusson* (1939) 40 S.R. (N.S.W.) 311, particularly at 328-330, 332, for the evaluation of evidence relating to the defendant's state of mind prior to or after the publication.

499. Note the contrast between cases where the defendant is under a duty by reason of his position to report on the plaintiff, e.g. because he is his supervisor and cases where there is no duty to express any opinion about the other except by virtue of some moral or social obligation. If the existence of strained relations automatically attached the stigma of malice, the supervisor would not dare furnish any report at all. In such a case, there must be clear evidence that it was ill-will, not genuine belief, which prompted the adverse criticism: *Oldfield v. Keogh* (1941) 41 S.R. (N.S.W.) 206.

500. *Horrocks v. Lowe* [1975] A.C. 135 at 151; *Sinclair v. Bjelke-Petersen* [1984] 1 Qd R. 484 (F.C.). Still less is the defendant's refusal to apologise evidence of malice (*Loveday v. Sun Newspaper* (1938) 59 C.L.R. 503 at 513), except refusal to publish an explanation under certain statutory privileges for reports: see below, n. 523.

501. *Davies v. Kott* [1979] 2 S.C.R. 686; *Oldfield v. Keogh* (1941) 41 S.R. (N.S.W.) 206; *Godfrey v. Henderson* (1944) 44 S.R. (N.S.W.) 447.

502. *Adam v. Ward* [1917] A.C. 309 at 330 per Lord Dunedin; *Calwell v. Ipec* [1975] 135 C.L.R. 321; *Pinniger v. Fairfax* (1979) 53 A.L.J.R. 691.

spirit of his reply to a degree that satisfied the aggressor."[503] Indeed, it has been recently said that where the only evidence relied on is the content of the defamatory matter itself or the steps taken by the defendant to verify its accuracy, there is only one exception to the requirement that the plaintiff must show affirmatively that the defendant did not believe it to be true. The exception relates to irrelevant matter: not that the mere introduction of objectively irrelevant matter destroys the privilege; it must support the inference that the defendant either did not believe it to be true or realised that it had nothing to do with the particular duty or interest on which the privilege was based, but nevertheless seized the opportunity to drag in irrelevant matter to vent his spite or for some other improper motive. But again, such an inference should not be drawn lightly.[504]

Finally, and most importantly, want of genuine belief in the truth of the statement puts the publisher beyond the pale of privilege because, save in exceptional circumstances,[505] one who knowingly asserts a falsehood must be using the privileged occasion for a dishonest and improper purpose.[506] By analogy to deceit,[507] reckless indifference as to whether the aspersion is true or false is equated with lack of belief in its truth. But otherwise recklessness, for example in the sense of gross and unreasoning prejudice, is not sufficient if the defendant nevertheless believed the accusation to be true.[508] Still less is mere want of reasonable grounds: carelessness is not malice.

If the publication is made, not in the course of exercising a privilege but to furnish the other party with a causc of action upon which he is challenged to sue, the defence might well have been regarded as forfeited on the ground that the object of the publication was unrelated to the interest which is entitled to protection.[509] Also it could be argued that as the defendant has invited the plaintiff to sue upon the statement, he should not be allowed to rely on any other defence than justification in order to test the truth of the defamatory assertion. It has been held, however, that such a challenge is no more than an invitation to take proceedings following the normal course.[510]

503. *Muller v. Hatton* [1952] Q.S.R. 150 at 182 per Stanley J.
504. *Horrocks v. Lowe* [1975] A.C. 135 at 150-151.
505. E.g. urgent warning to public of suspected poison (*Blackshaw v. Lord* [1984] Q.B. 1 at 27); also perhaps where defendant affords a forum to rival speakers and believes in *their* bona fide belief in the truth: *A.B.C. v. Comalco* (1986) 68 A.L.R. 259 at 294-296.
506. *Clarke v. Molyneux* (1877) 3 Q.B.D. 237 at 247. Indeed, the A.L.R.C. §148 recommended that "malice" be replaced (here as well as for "comment") by the simple requirement of belief in truth, genuine opinion or reasonable conduct.
507. See below, p. 633.
508. *Horrocks v. Lowe* [1975] A.C. 135.
509. Cf. *Strang v. Russell* (1905) 24 N.Z.L.R. 916 where it was held that although A may have leave to enter B's property, yet if he in fact enters not in pursuance thereof but in the exercise of presumed legal right adverse to B's claim as owner and with the intention of contesting B's right as alleged owner, he cannot set up leave and licence in an action for such entry as a trespass.
510. *Penton v. Calwell* (1945) 70 C.L.R. 219. "Such a challenge [is but] an invitation to the adversary to substitute for methods of unregulated and desultory combat a duel to be fought in legal form with every weapon which the law allows and involving no promise that if it is accepted the challenger will fire in the air" (Rich J. at 248).

Imputed malice

Notwithstanding some earlier authority to the contrary,[511] the malice of any one participant in the defamatory publication cannot be imputed to another, himself innocent, so as to defeat his claim to qualified privilege[512] or warrant an award of aggravated or exemplary damages against him.[513] The only apparent exception arises in ordinary cases of respondeat superior, when the malice of an employee or agent who had a hand in the libel is imputed to his principal.[514] On the other hand, in cases of joint publication, as by trustees or partners, the malice of one in no way prejudices the independent privilege of the others.[515] Not even subordinates, like secretaries or printers, who have in a sense only a derivative privilege, are at the mercy of their superiors. There may be some theoretical force in the argument that they depend on the privilege of their superiors and, when that is gone, there is nothing left to shield them. Still, the view eventually prevailed that such a principle of "respondeat *inferior*" would be altogether too harsh and could be avoided by treating as wholly independent the questions whether, in the first place, the occasion was privileged and, secondly, whether any individual's defence was defeated by malice.[516] Accordingly, even if *all* his principals are disqualified, an innocent agent would still be entitled to acquittal.

6. PRIVILEGED REPORTS

As already noted, ordinarily it is not a defence that one merely reported, rather than asserted of one's own authority, something defamatory said by somebody else[517] even if it is a matter of public interest.[518] However, an important exception is allowed for fair and accurate[519] reports of certain official proceedings that are considered deserving of qualified or even absolute privilege because of the public interest in full information on the

511. *Smith v. Streatfeild* [1913] 3 K.B. 764 (printer); *Adam v. Ward* [1917] A.C. 309 at 320, 331, 340 (secretary).
512. *Egger v. Chelmsford (Viscount)* [1965] 1 Q.B. 248 (C.A.); *Sun Life Assurance v. Dalrymple* [1965] S.C.R. 302.
513. *Egger* [1965] 1 Q.B. 248 at 265; *Dougherty v. Chandler* (1946) 46 S.R. (N.S.W.) 370.
514. *Webb v. Bloch* (1928) 41 C.L.R. 331 (solicitor employed by committee to draft circular); *Riddick v. Thames Bd Mills* [1977] Q.B. 881 at 907-910. But the primary publisher is not prejudiced by malice of a mere distributing agent: *Hay v. Australian Institute* (1906) 3 C.L.R. 1002; *Longdon-Griffiths v. Smith* [1951] 1 K.B. 295 at 303.
515. *Longdon-Griffiths v. Smith* [1951] 1 K.B. 295; *Meekins v. Henson* [1964] 1 Q.B. 472.
516. *Egger v. Chelmsford* [1965] 1 Q.B. 248.
517. See above, p. 555. If not protected by privilege, the report must be "justified", i.e. it must be shown that what is reported is not only an accurate account of the proceedings but that any allegation made in the proceedings and reported was itself true (and for the public benefit): *McCauley v. Fairfax* (1933) 34 S.R. (N.S.W.) 339. In contrast, a privileged report need not be accurate in the latter sense: *Burnett & Hallamshire Fuel v. Sheffield Telegraph* [1960] 1 W.L.R. 502.
518. But the A.L.R.C. (88-97) recommended a privilege for "attributed statements" on topics of public interest, for the sake of less inhibited media coverage of current affairs.
519. Both at common law and under the English-style legislation the privilege adheres to "fair and accurate" reports. The Codes postulate only "fair" but this implies substantial accuracy: *Anderson v. Nationwide News* (1970) 72 S.R. (N.S.W.) 313 (C.A.).

administration of public affairs. Which of these so qualify depends both on the status of the body in question and the public concern in the matter reported. From these points of view, courts and legislature stand in a class apart, both being treated as conclusively engaging the public interest in fullest publicity. In contrast, public meetings have not generally been credited with the same peremptory importance, because they lack the same safeguards against abuse and irresponsibility, and not all deal with matters of genuine civic concern. Accordingly, in this residuary field there is no blanket protection for any whole class, but each instance may and must qualify individually in support of the conclusion that publicity outweighs in social importance any incidental injury to individual reputation. The value which democratic communities increasingly attach to public interest and involvement in the processes of government is amply reflected in the considerable expansion of the range of privileged reports by modern statutes.

Indeed, this whole area of law is now largely statutory, although the common law has not disclaimed its capacity for creating new precedents.[520] But despite its basic underlying unity, there is a "bewildering"[521] variety among the various jurisdictions.[522] In several, the privilege has been upgraded from qualified to absolute; while many, especially of the new statutory, privileges are contingent on compliance with a reasonable request for retraction or reply.[523] Unlike the common law, statutory versions originally confined the privilege to newspapers, but most have now extended it to all media.[524] At all events, the privilege covers only the report as such.[525] Any defamatory comment thereon must consequently seek excuse either on the ground of fair comment or truth (and public benefit).[526]

Parliamentary proceedings

As already mentioned, Members of Parliament enjoy absolute immunity from civil and criminal liability for anything said in the course of parliamentary proceedings. This protection, however, does not extend to re-publication by Members of their speeches outside the House, even when

520. *Perera v. Peiris* [1949] A.C. 1 (where a newspaper extract from an official report of a Commission of Inquiry in Ceylon was held privileged—admittedly under Roman-Dutch law, which was however treated as in this respect identical with the common law).
521. A.L.R.C. §154. See Table 4 (82-84).
522. This strongly argues for national legislation: ibid.
523. Under English legislation (commencing in 1881 re reports of public meetings, now applicable to *all* reports listed in Sched., Pt II of the 1952 Act) qualified privilege is conditional on the defendant's publishing a reasonable explanation or contradiction, if demanded by the plaintiff. Folld: Vic. (s. 5), S.A. (s. 7), N.Z. (s. 17); A.L.R.C. §178. Certain reports however (listed in Sched. I) are "free" (e.g. judicial proceedings of foreign courts. Reason: it would be impolitic to offer a forum for retrial). Under the Codes, failure to publish a reply is merely evidence of malice: Qld (s. 374), W.A. (s. 354), Tas. (s. 13).
524. The Codes confer protection on all publications of fair reports "made in good faith for the information of the public" (Qld: s. 374; W.A.: s. 354: Tas.: s. 13; also *Defamation Act* (N.S.W.) s. 26; *Wrongs Act* (S.A.) ss 6, 7).
525. The *Defamation Act* 1974 (N.S.W.) s. 24 includes extracts and summaries.
526. See *Thompson v. Truth Ltd* (1932) 34 S.R. (N.S.W.) 21 at 25 (P.C.).

made in order to correct a false version which had previously appeared in the same newspaper.[527]

However by 1866 it was finally clarified that fair and accurate reports of parliamentary proceedings were at last entitled to qualified privilege just like those of judicial proceedings.[528] The report must be fair in the sense of not being tendentious, slanted or distorted; but it need not be a precis of the whole debate, and can be selective, like the familiar "parliamentary sketch" in modern journalism.[529] Indeed, the privilege is not confined to the press or even the printed word, but may be claimed just as well for a verbal report over the dinner table. The report itself must also be substantially accurate, although of course the speech that is being reported may well be riddled with falsehood.

Judicial proceedings

Fair and accurate reports of public judicial proceedings, whether published in a newspaper or otherwise, receive qualified privilege at common law. The privilege extends to all courts of justice, irrespective of status, but is coextensive only with the right of public admission. Since its rationale is the public benefit to be derived from the fullest publicity of what goes on in court, it is unconcerned when the proceedings themselves are not considered suitable for general admission.[530] Nor is there any privilege if the court has prohibited publication[531] or, apparently, for reports of decisions of domestic tribunals.[532] Moreover, it has also, though more questionably, been denied for pleadings, affidavits and other documents filed but not brought up in open court.[533]

For that matter, neither do reports of foreign legal proceedings qualify for any blanket protection because, besides some being open to abuse for propaganda and many lacking the common law safeguard against rigorous exclusion of all irrelevant evidence, they cannot invoke in comparable measure the standard arguments which support the public interest in publicity of domestic proceedings, viz. that it assists in keeping judicial administration under public scrutiny, in educating the public about the ways of the law, in supplying information about matters inevitably of some public interest and, perhaps incidentally, in combating spurious rumours. The only possible cogent claim to privilege is therefore that the particular matter sub judice in the foreign court happens to be of substantial enough

527. *R. v. Lord Abingdon* (1794) 1 Esp. 226; 170 E.R. 337; *R. v. Creevey* (1813) 1 M. & S. 273; 105 E.R. 102.

528. *Wason v. Walter* (1868) L.R. 4 Q.B. 73; cf. *Givens v. Syme* [1971] V.L.R. 418. In most jurisdictions the privilege is now statutory and applies to *all* Australian Parliaments: N.S.W.: *Defamation Act* 1974 Div. 5; Vic.: *Wrongs Act* 1979; Qld: *Criminal Code* s. 374(1); W.A.: *Criminal Code* s. 354(i); Tas.: *Defamation Act* 1957 s. 13; A.C.T.: *Defamation Act* 1909 s. 5(a, b), s. 5A; N.T.: *Defamation Act* s. 6; N.Z.: *Defamation Act* 1954 s. 17.

529. *Cook v. Alexander* [1974] Q.B. 279 (C.A.); *Jones v. Fairfax* (1986) 4 N.S.W.L.R. 466.

530. *Kimber v. Press Assoc.* [1893] 1 Q.B. 65.

531. Being also in contempt of court.

532. *Chapman v. Ellesmere* [1932] 2 K.B. 431 at 475.

533. *Gazette Printing Co. v. Shallow* (1909) 41 S.C.R. 339; *Mack v. North Hill News* (1964) 44 D.L.R. (2d) 147; *Gobbart v. W.A. Newspaper* [1968] W.A.R. 113. Doubted in *Little v. Law Institute of Victoria* [1990] V.R. 257 at 288.

concern to our own public, as in the Sydney report of a New York trial of Australians accused of smuggling heroin from Australia into the United States.[534]

The protection covers "what pertains to the processes of law rather than what occurs in the place where it is being administered; more specifically, to what is said in the presence of a judicial tribunal then in session, in the course of proceedings before it for consideration or determination, by those who have some right, duty, or privilege to attend or appear, or to take part therein and be heard, provided that what is said is in some way related to such proceedings. . . . The protection does not extend to a mere interrupter or by-stander, even if occurring in court, and while the proceedings are in progress; but it does cover the matters first mentioned, even though the action or application or process is misconceived or irregularly brought on, or outside the jurisdiction of the court."[535]

The report need not be in full, because otherwise the protection would be virtually illusory. A condensed summary of the proceedings or judgment is sufficient, provided the omissions do not prevent it from giving a fair account. The report must not be garbled or coloured, and headlines must give a fair idea of what follows. And above all else, it must be substantially accurate: a fair report must have its facts right, just as (we shall see)[536] a fair comment must be based on true facts.[537] Subject to the usual controls, the question of fairness is for the jury.[538]

In Australia, the common law privilege has been widely reinforced by statute. Some States, following the English model,[539] have raised it to absolute privilege;[540] others have been content with qualified privilege.[541] As a rule, the report must be contemporaneous.[542]

534. *Thompson v. Consolidated Press* (1968) 89 N.W. (Pt 1) (N.S.W.) 121, following *Webb v. Times Publications* [1960] 2 Q.B. 535 (critical comment by Payne, 24 Mod. L. Rev. 178; and *Privilege to Republish Defamation*, 64 Col. L. Rev. 1002). The *Defamation Act* 1952 (Eng.), specifically limited absolute privilege to reports of U.K. courts, but contemporaneously conferred qualified privilege re Commonwealth courts. Australian legislation (see below, nn. 540, 541) following the original English pattern has refrained from such express geographical distinctions. In N.Z. the qualified privilege re non-N.Z. courts is conditional also on compliance with request for retraction.
535. *Hughes v. W.A. Newspapers* (1940) 43 W.A.L.R. 12 at 13-14 per Dwyer J.
536. See below.
537. *Thom v. Assoc. Newspapers* (1964) 64 S.R. (N.S.W.) 376; *Jones v. Fairfax* (1986) 4 N.S.W.L.R. 466.
538. *Leslie v. Mirror Newspaper* (1971) 125 C.L.R. 332; *Kingshott v. Assoc. Newspapers* [1991] 1 Q.B. 88 (C.A.).
539. *Law of Libel Act* 1888 s. 3 ("contemporaneous" newspaper reports). Although ambiguous and probably not so designed, it has been construed as absolute: *McCarey v. Assoc. Newspapers* [1964] 1 W.L.R. 855 (revd on other grounds: [1965] 2 Q.B. 86).
540. Vic.: *Wrongs Act* 1958 s. 4 (not confined to newspapers); W.A.: *Newspaper Libel Act* 1888 s. 6 ("registered" newspaper only); otherwise only qualified privilege under *Criminal Code* s. 354(iii): *Gobbart v. W.A. Newspapers* [1968] W.A.R. 113; S.A.: *Wrongs Act* 1936 s. 6 (identical with English provision: see above, n. 539); N.T.: s. 5.
541. N.S.W.: *Defamation Act* 1974 s. 24; Vic.: *Wrongs Act* 1979 (other Australian courts); Qld: *Criminal Code* s. 374(3); Tas.: *Defamation Act* 1957 s. 13(1)(c). For W.A. see above, n. 9; A.C.T.: *Defamation Act* 1909 s. 5(d) (newspaper only); N.T.: *Defamation Act* s. 5; N.Z.: *Defamation Act* 1954 s. 17.
542. See *Bunker v. James* (1980) 26 S.A.S.R. 286; *Whear v. N.T. News* (1981) 8 N.T.R. 13.

Miscellaneous

In several Australian States qualified privilege has been specifically conferred on fair and accurate reports of public inquiries, such as a royal commission,[543] and on extracts from or abstracts of any such proceedings or the official report.[544]

Similarly privileged are notices or reports issued by a government office or department, or any of its officers, and published with their consent.[545] In view of the modern practice of "press hand-outs", it has become necessary to distinguish between statements of a genuinely official nature formally issued for the information of the public and information painfully extracted by journalists from a public relations officer,[546] or mere political propaganda supplied by such an official on behalf of a Minister.[547] The notice or report need not originally have been released in the form of writing; a broadcast announcement by a Minister accompanied by a request to the press to give it publicity is sufficient; but whether the report be oral or written, the protection only covers the actual words in the form in which they were used. There must be no omissions or additions, and it is fatal to rearrange the announcement in order to make it more arresting from a journalistic point of view.[548]

Reports of public meetings enjoy no protection at common law, because the balance of public benefit was not, during the formative period of privilege in the mid-19th century, considered sufficiently important.[549] But it is now increasingly felt that interest in public affairs should be stimulated to the extent of conferring qualified privilege on such reports, provided they deal with matters of public concern. This has been done throughout Australia,[550] except in Victoria and the Australian Capital Territory.[551] Additionally, privilege attaches to reports of proceedings of local authorities, boards, trustees or other persons duly constituted by statute for

543. *Bailey v. Truth Ltd* (1938) 60 C.L.R. 700 at 708.
544. N.S.W.: *Defamation Act* 1974 Sched. 2 para. 2(6); Vic.: *Wrongs (Defamation) Act* 1981; Qld: *Criminal Code* s. 374(4); W.A.: s. 354(4); Tas.: *Defamation Act* 1957 s. 13(1)(d); N.T.: *Defamation Act* 1938 s. 6. Newspaper only: *Wrongs Act* (S.A.) s. 7t; A.C.T. *Defamation Act* 1909 s. 5(f) (newspaper only) and *Defamation Act* 1928 s. 2; cf. *Law of Libel Amendment Act* 1888 (Eng.). The *Defamation Act* (N.Z.) s. 17 is modelled on the current *Defamation Act* 1952 (Eng.) s. 7.
545. S.A.: *Wrongs Act* 1936 s. 7; A.C.T.: *Defamation Act* 1909 s. 5(1)(g) and N.T.: s. 6; Criminal Codes of Qld: s. 374(5); W.A.: s. 354(v); Tas.: s. 13(a)(f). Copies or fair and accurate reports of such government statements are privileged in N.Z. and England: see *Boston v. Bagshaw* [1966] 1 W.L.R. 1126 (C.A.).
546. As in *Blackshaw v. Lord* [1984] Q.B. 1 (C.A.).
547. *Forster v. Watson* (1944) 44 S.R. (N.S.W.) 399 at 403.
548. *Campbell v. Assoc. Newspapers* (1948) 48 S.R. (N.S.W.) 301.
549. *Davison v. Duncan* (1857) 7 E. & B. 229; 119 E.R. 1233; *Gannon v. White* (1886) 12 V.L.R. 29.
550. Following the model of the English *Law of Libel Amendment Act* 1888 s. 4, N.S.W.: Sched. 2 para. 2(7); S.A.: s. 8(a); N.T.: s. 6; and the Codes of Qld (s. 374(1)), W.A. (s. 354(vii)), Tas. (s. 13(i)(h)). In W.A. there is, additionally, *absolute* privilege for newspaper reports of State or municipal ceremonials and political, municipal or public meetings: *Newspaper Libel Act* 1888 s. 6.
551. See *McCauley v. Fairfax* (1933) 34 S.R. (N.S.W.) 339.

the discharge of public functions.[552] Most of the statutory privileges, as already mentioned,[553] are liable to defeat if the defendant fails to publish a reasonable reply by the plaintiff.

Abuse

Privileged reports must be "fair and accurate". They do not, of course, have to be verbatim or complete, but they must be neutral and balanced. Thus the report of an incriminating statement by one witness would not be fair if exculpatory evidence by another is suppressed.

Malice destroys the privilege. But since the privilege is recognised for the sake of the public, not the media, it is none too obvious why the motive for the publication should be relevant.[554] Hence statutes have upgraded various reports from qualified to absolute privilege. While personal animosity or indirect motives like blackmail will be rare, a more serious problem concerns a reporter's doubts as to the accuracy of what he is reporting.[555] To insist on the reporter's belief in the accuracy would withdraw valuable information from the public, which should be free to make its own assessment as to the credibility of what is reported and its source. Here the case for protecting the media is even stronger than for "letters to the editor".[556]

7. FAIR COMMENT

Fair comment on matters of public interest is deemed of such surpassing social importance in a democratic community as to outweigh the competing claim to unqualified protection of individual reputation. "In the case of criticism in matters of art, whether music, painting, literature or drama, where the private character of a person criticised is not involved, the freer the criticism is, the better it will be for the aesthetic welfare of the public."[557] Likewise, untrammelled discussion of public affairs and of those participating in them is a basic safeguard against irresponsible political power. The unfettered preservation of the right of fair comment

552. Vic.: *Wrongs Act* 1958 s. 5; S.A.: *Wrongs Act* 1936 s. 7(b); A.C.T.: s. 5(h) (newspaper only); N.T. s. 6; N.S.W.: Sched. 2 para. 2(7); Qld: s. 374(b); W.A.: s. 354(vi); Tas.: s. 13(l)(g); N.T.: s. 6. In S.A. and Vic., it applies only to the first mentioned category, and then only if the public and newspaper reporters are admitted. The meaning of a body "duly constituted under the provisions of any statute for the discharge of public functions" is discussed in *Tisdall v. Hutton* [1944] Tas. S.R. 1.
S.A. also confers privilege on reports of meetings of shareholders: s. 7(d); and N.S.W. on reports of appeal proceedings before the A.J.C.: s. 14(1)(i).
553. See above, n. 523.
554. A similar criticism has been raised against the injection of malice into the defence of fair comment: see below, p. 591.
555. Gatley, *Libel and Slander* (7th ed. 1974) 344, n. 44 denies its relevance "for otherwise proceedings leading to an acquittal could not be reported". *Rest. 2d* §611 eliminated malice, and a constitutionally backed privilege of neutral reportage, superseding doubts or antagonism, has been developing in the U.S.: *Edwards v. National Audubon Society* 556 F. 2d 113 (2d Cir. 1977).
556. See below, p. 592.
557. *Lyon v. Daily Telegraph* [1943] K.B. 746 at 752 per Scott L.J.

is, therefore, one of the foundations supporting our standards of personal liberty.

In the United States, the constitutional protection of free speech has been construed to require an absolute privilege for opinion, in the belief that actionable defamation must be false and that there is no such thing as a false opinion.[558] Our law has been less permissive, the privilege being limited only to *fair* comment on matters of *public* interest.

Comment and statements of fact

For the defence to be available,[559] it must be indicated with reasonable clarity by the words themselves, taking them in their context and the circumstances in which they were published, that they purport to be comment and not statements of fact. The latter, however fair, are not protected by this defence: if defamatory, they must either be proved true or be privileged; and, as already observed, our law does not esteem freedom of speech and of the press even in matters of public concern sufficiently high to clothe false statements of fact with qualified privilege, let alone elevate it to a constitutional guarantee as in the United States.[560] Comment alone may claim indulgence, in its primary sense of "something which is or can reasonably be inferred to be a deduction, inference, conclusion, criticism, judgment, remark or observation", as distinct from a "direct statement concerning or description of a subject of public interest".[561]

Distinguishing between fact and comment is often elusive. Much depends upon the context of the impugned expression. If it purports to be a criticism of a published work or public performance, it is prima facie comment, however dogmatically expressed.[562] If the facts are set out and an opinion is then expressed upon, or an inference drawn from, then the statement is comment. On the other hand, bare inferences or allegations without reference to the facts on which they are based will generally be treated as statements of fact. "To say that a man's conduct was dishonourable is not comment, it is a statement of fact. To say that he did certain specific things and that his conduct was dishonourable is a statement of fact coupled with a comment."[563] But if the expression is ambiguous, the writer or speaker runs the risk that it will not be understood as comment, and that he will be called upon to justify. In particular, the defence of fair comment will rarely[564] protect defamatory newspaper headlines, because it is difficult to achieve the sensational effect desired by modern journalism and at the same time maintain a clear separation of facts from defamatory expressions of

558. *Gertz v. Welsh* 418 U.S. 323 at 339 (1974); *Milkovich v. Lorain Journal* (1990) 110 S. Ct. 2695; *Rest. 2d* §566.
559. The defence is now statutory in N.S.W. (ss 29-35), N.T. (s. 6A) and the Code States (Qld.: s. 375; W.A.: s. 355; Tas.: s. 14).
560. *New York Times v. Sullivan* 376 U.S. 254 (1964) (criticism of public officials); *Curtis Publishing Co. v. Butts* 388 U.S. 130 (1967) (public figure); though since *Gertz v. Welsh* 418 U.S. 323 (1974) not just any matter of general or public concern.
561. *Clarke v. Norton* [1910] V.L.R. 494 at 499 per Cussen J.
562. *Whitford v. Clarke* [1939] S.A.S.R. 434.
563. *Myerson v. Smith's Weekly* (1923) 24 S.R. (N.S.W.) 20 at 26 per Ferguson J.; *Barltrop v. C.B.C.* (1978) 86 D.L.R. (3d) 61.
564. Such a rare instance was *Kemsley v. Foot* [1952] A.C. 345 ("lower than Kemsley").

opinion.[565] The test is not what the defendant meant, but what the ordinary unprejudiced reader would take it to mean:[566] the law of defamation being concerned not with intended, but ordinary, meaning, that is, the meaning that would be attached to the utterance by the ordinary hearer or reader.[567] It is for the jury to decide what is fact and what comment, unless there can be only one answer.[568]

The defence, it is sometimes said, cannot succeed unless the opinion stated is based on facts actually presented, or in fact present, to the minds of the readers or listeners, so that they may be in a position to judge whether it is such as might be fairly formed on the facts.[569] The sting of the allegation is, of course, largely minimised if the reader is given an opportunity to form his own judgment on whether the suggested inference is supported by the facts proffered.[570] Taken literally, however, such a stringent requirement would make the freedom of the critic illusory. It is impracticable to confine criticism of a literary work to passages actually set out in the review, nor can it be genuinely assumed that a published work is "present to the mind" of all readers of the criticism, since the whole object of the comment may be to advise whether the particular work is worthy of their consideration.[571]

The law has accommodated itself to this difficulty and, rather than insist on a requirement which could only "result in absurdity",[572] recognises that the facts necessary to justify comment may be implied from the terms of the impugned utterance. "The inquiry ceases to be—Can the defendant point to definite assertions of fact in the alleged libel upon which the comment is made? and becomes—Is there subject matter indicated with sufficient clarity to justify comment being made?"[573] Thus comment may be understood to refer to facts which are notorious, such as the conduct of politicians.[574] And in the case of criticism of literary or artistic work, the public have at least the opportunity of ascertaining for themselves the subject matter on which the comment is founded. The reader need not be able to see exactly the grounds of the comment, provided the subject which, ex hypothesi, is of public importance is sufficiently indicated.[575] In *Kemsley v. Foot*,[576] an article criticising the conduct of the Beaverbrook

565. *Smith's Newspaper v. Becker* (1932) 47 C.L.R. 279 at 303-304. Here, in contrast to *Dakhyl v. Labouchere* [1908] 2 K.B. 325n. calling the plaintiff a "quack" was held to be a statement of fact, not comment. In the one case, the expression was contained in a headline, but in the other was preceded by an assertion that the plaintiff was associated with a certain institute alleged to be carrying out a system of medical imposture and the article then concluded: "*In other words*, he is a quack of the rankest species."
566. *Clarke v. Norton* [1910] V.L.R. 494 at 501 per Cussen J.
567. Cf. Williams, *Language and the Law—IV*, 61 L.Q.R. 392ff. (1945). See also above, p. 530.
568. *O'Shaughnessy v. Mirror Newspapers* (1970) 125 C.L.R. 166; *Jones v. Skelton* [1963] 1 W.L.R. 1362 (P.C.); *London Artists v. Littler* [1969] 2 Q.B. 375 (C.A.).
569. *Goldsbrough v. Fairfax* (1934) 34 S.R. (N.S.W.) 524 at 530-531.
570. *Hunt v. Star Newspaper* [1908] 2 K.B. 309 at 319.
571. *Gardiner v. Fairfax* (1942) 42 (S.R.) (N.S.W.) 171 at 179-180.
572. Ibid. at 180.
573. *Kemsley v. Foot* [1952] A.C. 345 at 357 per Lord Porter.
574. *Bjelke-Petersen v. Burns* [1988] 2 Qd R. 129 ("corruption", "hands in the till").
575. *Kemsley v. Foot* [1952] A.C. 345; but cf. *Telnikoff v. Matusevitch* [1991] 3 W.L.R. 952 (H.L.).
576. [1952] A.C. 345.

Press described it as "lower than Kemsley". Though no details were contained to substantiate the charge against Lord Kemsley, it was held that there was a sufficient substratum of fact indicated in the libel to warrant the allegation being treated as comment. The subject matter implied was that the plaintiff was in control of newspapers and that the conduct of the publishers was in question. The defendant could say: "We have pointed to your Press. It is widely read. Your readers will, and the public generally can, know at what our criticism is directed. It is not bare comment."[577]

Basis of true facts

Comment cannot be fair if based on facts which are distorted or invented.[578] There must be a sufficient basis of true fact to warrant the comment.[579] Hence truth is material in this context, not to *justify* such allegations of *fact* as are defamatory (that being the function of the distinct defence of justification), but as one step in establishing that the comment itself is fair.[580] At common law, all the facts set out in the alleged libel had to be proved for this purpose, and failure to justify one, however unimportant, defeated the defence of fair comment,[581] but by statute some jurisdictions are now content if the facts are substantially true and the comment is fair, having regard to those facts that have been proven.[582]

Is the requirement (as commonly enunciated) that the comment be based on *true* facts exhaustive or is it only a convenient shorthand statement for the proposition that the underlying facts must be *justified or defended*? The question comes to the fore in two situations. First, some jurisdictions insist that in order to justify a statement, it must not only be proved true, but its publication must have been for the public benefit.[583] Does it follow that this dual requirement must also be satisfied, not only in order to justify those facts which are defamatory, but also to lay the basis for the distinct defence of fair comment? Although theory might favour the strict view that the person making the comment must do so without thereby committing an actionable wrong, the more liberal view seems eventually to have triumphed on the ground that the dual requirement does not address itself to the defence of fair comment at all and that otherwise that defence would be unduly hampered.[584]

577. Ibid. at 357 per Lord Porter.
578. *Sutherland v. Stopes* [1925] A.C. 47 at 62-63; *Thompson v. Truth Ltd* (1932) 34 S.R. (N.S.W.) 21, 25; *Antonovich v. W.A. Newspaper* [1960] W.A.R. 176 at 180.
579. *London Artists v. Littler* [1969] 2 Q.B. 375 (C.A.).
580. Under the Codes, this is implied in the requirement that the comment be "fair" (undefined): *Bjelke-Petersen v. Burns*; *Porter v. Mercury Newspaper* [1964] Tas. S.R. 279 at 283-286.
581. *Kemsley v. Foot* [1952] A.C. 345 at 357-358; *Gooch v. N.Z. Financial Times* [1933] N.Z.L.R. 257. Aliter, where the relevant facts are found, not in the libel itself, but in the particulars delivered to support the defence: *Kemsley v. Foot* [1952] A.C. 345.
582. The *Defamation Act* of England (s. 6); N.S.W. (s. 30(3)(6)); Tas. (s. 14); N.Z. (s. 8); Ontario *Libel and Slander Act* 1958 (s. 24). See *Truth (N.Z.) v. Avery* [1959] N.Z.L.R. 274; *Broadway Approvals v. Odhams Press* [1964] 2 Q.B. 683.
583. See above, p. 556.
584. N.S.W.: s. 30(2), adopting *Orr v. Isles* (1965) 83 W.N. (Pt 1) (N.S.W.) 303 (F.C.); *Hill v. Comben* (1991) A.T.R. 81-108 (Qld).

The second question is whether fair comment may be based alternatively on facts (though defamatory and false) the publication of which is privileged. Suppose a newspaper reports that in the course of judicial proceedings an accusation of crime was levied against the plaintiff. Must the paper in commenting on his alleged conduct prove the plaintiff's guilt or may it rest on establishing that the report was fair and accurate? Here, too, the lenient view seems to have prevailed, supported this time by the argument that public policy cannot be opposed to comment on a subject matter which is itself privileged and the disclosure of which is therefore in the public interest.[585] There is some scattered support in a few Australian cases for the intermediate position that fair comment is permissible on the privileged report having been made, but not on the facts therein disclosed. A newspaper might thus comment on the fact that a Royal Commission has passed derogatory reflections on a police officer, without being liable for repetition of libel, but it would be answerable for comment proceeding on the basis that he had committed the conduct attributed to him unless it can justify those allegations.[586]

Public interest

The comment must have been on a matter of public interest.[587] Such matters fall into two broad categories. First, those in which the public in general has a legitimate interest: for example, national and local government,[588] public services and institutions; secondly, matters submitted to public attention and criticism: for example, works of authors and artists displayed in public, theatrical performances and productions at places of public entertainment.[589] On these any member of the public is entitled to express himself freely, whether by way of praise or blame; and the critic himself is as much exposed to comment for his criticism as the author or producer criticised.[590] Moreover, "people who fill public positions must not be too thin-skinned in reference to comments made upon them. It must often happen that observations are made upon public men which they know to be undeserved and unjust. Yet they must bear with them, as a matter of public policy. Freedom to criticise is the best security for the proper discharge of public duties."[591]

585. *Mangena v. Wright* [1909] 2 K.B. 958; *Jones v. Skelton* [1963] 1 W.L.R. 1362 at 1372-4 (P.C.); *Brent Walker v. Time Out* [1991] 2 W.L.R. 772 (C.A.); *Defamation Act* 1974 (N.S.W.) s. 30, adopting *Orr v. Isles* (1965) 83 W.N. (Pt 1) (N.S.W.) 303.
586. *Comalco v. A.B.C.* (1985) 64 A.C.T.R. 1 (must purport publication on privileged occasion); *Grech v. Odhams Press* [1958] 2 Q.B. 275 at 285; Dixon J. in *Bailey v. Truth Ltd* (1938) 60 C.L.R. 700 at 721-724 where it was not necessary to decide the point. McTiernan J. adopted the same premise but applied it with a different result which carries no persuasion (at 729-731). Latham C.J. and Starke J. did not commit themselves.
587. A question of law: specifically (N.S.W.) s. 12. The Codes prescribe: court and public proceedings, public conduct or public figures, literary and artistic works, public entertainment, sports, communications to the public (emanating from plaintiff: *Bjelke-Petersen v. Burns* [1988] 2 Qd R. 129). Qld: s. 375; W.A.: s. 355; Tas.: s. 14; also N.T.: s. 6A.
588. *Slim v. Daily Telegraph* [1968] 2 Q.B. 157 (C.A.).
589. *London Artists v. Littler* [1969] 2 Q.B. 375 (C.A.).
590. *Turner v. M-G-M* [1950] 1 All E.R. 449 (H.L.).
591. *Whitford v. Clarke* [1939] S.A.S.R. 434 at 439 per Napier J.

The critic must, however, confine himself to the subject of public interest. The mere fact of being a politician is not enough to make his private life a matter of public interest,[592] nor may an artist be denounced for his private morals or manner unrelated to his works.[593] Since this qualification principally serves to protect the plaintiff's interest in privacy, it would become largely unnecessary with the recognition of an independent cause of action for invasion of privacy.[594]

In the United States "public figures" enjoy even less protection. For, under the First Amendment's guarantee of "freedom of speech or of the press", public figures[595] must establish, with reference to factual allegation as much as comment, that the defendant acted with "actual malice", that is, "knowing that what he was saying was false or in reckless disregard of the truth".[596] Public officials have less reason to complain because they sought the public limelight and have superior access to the media for vindication compared to ordinary members of the public. But this approach has not met with enthusiasm from law makers in Australia or England who all too frequently seek out the courts to refight lost political battles.[597]

Attack on character

But a long time ago[598] Cockburn C.J. went farther in postulating categorically that a person's moral character was never a permissible subject of adverse comment, even if he occupied a position which made his character a matter of public interest—for fear that public affairs would not be conducted by men of honour if the law were to sanction attacks on them, destructive of their character and made without foundation. "A writer in a public paper may comment on the conduct of public men in the strongest terms, but if he imputes dishonesty, he must be prepared to justify. . . . It seems to me that a line must be drawn between hostile criticism on a man's public conduct and the motives by which that conduct may be supposed to be influenced, and that you have no right to impute to a man in his conduct as a citizen—even though it be open to ridicule or disapprobation—base, sordid, dishonest, and wicked motives unless there is so much ground for the imputation that a jury shall be of opinion, not only that you may have honestly entertained some mistaken belief upon the subject, but that your belief is well founded and not without cause."[599]

It is open to serious doubt whether this Victorian period piece should survive into the more robust atmosphere of our present public life. Nothing

592. *Mutch v. Sleeman* (1928) 29 S.R. (N.S.W.) 125 at 137 (M.P. called a wife-beater).
593. *Gardiner v. Fairfax* (1942) 42 S.R. (N.S.W.) 171 at 174.
594. A.L.R.C. §131.
595. Defined as an individual who "may achieve such pervasive fame or notoriety as to become a public figure in all contexts" or an individual "who voluntarily injects himself or is drawn into a particular controversy and thereby becomes a public figure for a limited range of issues".
596. *Gertz v. Welsh* 418 U.S. 323 (1974).
597. A.L.R.C. Report 11, App. F.; *Faulks* §617.
598. *Campbell v. Spottiswoode* (1863) 3 B. & S. 769; 122 E.R. 288.
599. As reported in 32 L.J.Q.B. at 199.

has been heard of it for a long time; it was expressly repealed in New South Wales[600] and implicitly in the Code States.[601]

Fairness

The comment must be fair in order to qualify for protection: it must express a view which an honest-minded person might hold on the facts on which the comment was made. But it need not be reasonable—far from it: it may be exaggerated, obstinate or prejudiced, provided it is honestly held. "The basis of our public life is that the crank, the enthusiast may say what he honestly thinks just as much as the reasonable man or woman who sits on a jury, and it would be a sad day for freedom of speech . . . if a jury were to apply the test of whether it agrees with the comment."[602] "A critic is entitled to dip his pen in gall for the purpose of legitimate criticism, and no one need be mealy-mouthed in denouncing what he regards as twaddle, daub or discord. English literature would be the poorer if Macaulay had not been stirred to wrath by the verses of Mr Robert Montgomery."[603] No doubt, it was unfortunate that the term "fair", with its connotation of reasonableness and moderation, ever gained currency in this context. The modern New South Wales statute has accordingly discarded the term, requiring merely that the comment represent the defendant's opinion.[604]

Malice

At one time, fair comment was considered a branch of "privilege", but eventually the view prevailed that it constitutes a defence sui generis.[605] Thus it is now settled that the defence is forfeited even in the absence of malice, if the comment exceeds the limits of fairness.[606] In *Thomas v. Bradbury*,[607] however, the Court of Appeal partially reverted to the older view by holding that comment which is prima facie fair may lose its protection by proof of malice. This conclusion is hard to justify, since fairness would seem to have reference to the criticism, not the state of mind of the critic. Against this, however, it has been urged that if there is malice, the mind of the writer would not be that of a critic[608] and that, from a policy point of view, while it is undoubtedly in the public interest that public

600. S. 30(4). Also recommended by A.L.R.C. (§131), *Faulks* (1975) and N.Z. (1977).
601. Which authorise comment on the character of a person so far as his character appears in his public conduct, a book he has published or work of art he has exhibited or public entertainment which he has conducted or in which he has participated, provided the comment is fair: Qld: s. 375; W.A.: s. 355; Tas.: s. 14; N.T.: s. 6A.
602. Diplock J.'s summing-up to the jury in *Silkin v. Beaverbrook Newspapers* [1958] 1 W.L.R. 743 at 747. See also *Turner v. M-G-M* [1950] 1 All E.R. 449 at 462 (H.L.).
603. *Gardiner v. Fairfax* (1942) 42 S.R. (N.S.W.) 171 at 174 per Jordan C.J.
604. Section 32; *Lloyd v. David Syme* [1986] A.C. 350 (P.C.). Also A.L.R.C. §129, Faulks §152.
605. *Merivale v. Carson* (1887) 20 Q.B.D. 275. The term "privilege" is here used in the technical sense assigned to it in the law of defamation. In Hohfeldian terminology, fair comment is, of course, also a privilege, and the analytical argument relied on to show that it is sui generis is probably based on faulty reasoning.
606. *Merivale v. Carson* (1887) 20 Q.B.D. 275.
607. [1906] 2 K.B. 627; followed, though not without reluctance, in *Falcke v. Herald Ltd* [1925] V.L.R. 56. N.T.: "privilege" (s. 6A) is absolute: *Cawley v. A.C.P.* [1981] 1 N.S.W.L.R. at 233-234.
608. *Merivale v. Carson* (1887) 20 Q.B.D. 275 at 281-282 per Lord Esher.

matters should be open to comment, it is not in the public interest to allow dishonest comment or comment warped by spite.[609]

Although the principle is frequently expressed as if malice conclusively destroys the plea of fairness, the only point decided in *Thomas v. Bradbury*, and the better opinion, is merely that evidence of malice is admissible: "It is, of course, possible for a person to have a spite against another and yet to bring a perfectly dispassionate judgment to bear upon his literary merits; but, given the existence of malice, it must be for the jury to say whether it has warped his judgment. Comment *distorted* by malice cannot . . . be fair on the part of the person who makes it."[610] To establish malice, it must be shown that the comment was designed to serve some purpose other than that of expressing the commentator's real opinion, for example, that of satisfying a private grudge. But while mere hostility or ill will is not by itself sufficient for malice, neither is honest belief in the truth a conclusive reply.[611] The difficulty of applying this nuanced formula prompted the reform in New South Wales (now also recommended in England) of dropping "malice" and requiring merely that the comment represent the defendant's opinion.[612]

While it is clear that no comment can be fair unless it expresses the defendant's honest opinion, it remains disputed whether this requirement goes to the question of fairness or malice. The answer will affect the burden of proof. On one view,[613] it is sufficient for the defendant to establish that the statement was comment rather than factual and that it was objectively fair, i.e., that it is one which an honest-minded person could make. But just as with other types of malice, lack of subjective honesty (which would defeat the defence) falls to proof by the plaintiff. The opposing view holds subjective honesty to be an essential ingredient in the defence of fair comment, for proof by the defendant.[614]

Differing views persist regarding the publisher of someone else's comment. A commonly held position was to identify the publisher with the writer. Thus if the writer had a good defence, it also availed the publisher; while, conversely, if the writer had none, neither did the publisher.[615] Both propositions have been challenged: the second, after a recent decision on qualified privilege held that a writer's malice is not imputable to the publisher unless he was his employee or agent under ordinary principles of vicarious liability.[616] This for the reason that the defence attaches to the individual publisher, not to the comment.

A less desirable corollary would be to deny the publisher the defence, as the Supreme Court of Canada did in relation to a letter on the

609. *Falcke v. Herald Ltd* [1925] V.L.R. 56 at 72.
610. [1906] 2 K.B. 627 at 642 per Collins M.R.; *Cawley v. Australian Consolidated Press* [1981] 1 N.S.W.L.R. 225. Also under the Codes.
611. *Renouf v. Federal Capital Press* (1977) 16 A.C.T.R. 35.
612. *Defamation Act* 1974 s. 32; A.L.R.C. §130 ("genuine opinion"); *Faulks* 40-41.
613. *Telnikoff v. Matusevitch* [1991] 3 W.L.R. 952 (H.L.); *Hawke v. Tamworth Newspaper* [1983] 1 N.S.W.L.R. 699; criticised Heery, 59 A.L.J. 371 (1985).
614. *Cherneskey v. Armadale* [1979] 1 S.C.R. 1067 (narrow majority).
615. Gatley §730.
616. *McLeod v. Jones* [1977] 1 N.Z.L.R. 441; *Egger v. Chelmsford (Viscount)* [1965] 1 Q.B. 249 at 265 per Lord Denning whose view was preferred by *Faulks* (ch. 8) to that of Davis L.J.; Kidd, 10 U. Qld L.J. 223 (1978).

correspondence page of a newspaper,[617] unless the comment expressed his own honest opinion not merely in the writer's integrity, but also in the substance of the comment. But to require the editor to share the view of all correspondents would seriously erode the role of the press as a "sounding board for the free flow of new and different ideas". The decision was accordingly widely repealed in Canada;[618] and the New South Wales Act specifically provides a defence for publishing a stranger's comment in good faith for public information or the advancement of education.[619]

Pleading

Under modern practice the defence of fair comment,[620] like privilege,[621] must be specially pleaded. For long this used to be done in the form of the "rolled-up" plea: "In so far as they consist of allegations of fact the said words are true in substance and in fact, and in so far as they consist of expressions of opinion they are fair comments made in good faith and without malice upon the said facts which are a matter of public interest." This plea has met with frequent criticism because its name and wording alike are apt to mislead. It is not a composite plea of justification and fair comment, rolled up in one, but raises only the defence of fair comment. Comment, in order to be fair, must be based on true facts, and the averment of truth—quoad facts—is intended solely to lay the necessary foundation for it. Its pleading advantages disappeared when particulars of the substratum of facts came to be ordered as of course. The plea is now obsolete.[622] Justification may be pleaded separately in the same action, both with respect to facts as well as comment; and if the defendant fails under that plea, he may still save himself under the defence of fair comment.

8. REMEDIES

As already pointed out, the law of defamation has evolved around the remedy of damages. This has left a fateful imprint on much of substantive law, besides forcing all persons desirous of vindicating their reputation in public into pursuing a form of redress not precisely adjusted to their needs. At present, however, the law offers no other means for wringing a retraction from a defamer.[623] The latter, it is true, may mitigate his

617. *Cherneskey v. Armadale* [1979] 1 S.C.R. 1067.
618. Ont., N.B., Alta., Man. See above, n. 615.
619. Section 34. See *Hawke v. Tamworth Newspaper* [1983] 1 N.S.W.L.R. 699. This would be applicable also to panel discussions (cf. *A.B.C. v. Comalco* (1986) 68 A.L.R. 259). U.S.: *Immuno A.G. v. Moor-Jankowski* 567 N.E. 2d 1270 (N.Y. 1991).
620. Under the old system of pleading, the practice developed of raising this defence under the general issue, perhaps because it was for long assumed that fair comment was a branch of privilege (though, alternatively, it would be raised by special plea).
621. At common law, this defence could be raised under the general issue, but must now be specially pleaded even in N.S.W. (O. 30, r. 30A; Rath, *Pleading in New South Wales* 139).
622. Faulks §176 recommended its abolition. It was struck out as inappropriate under the Codes in *Hill v. Comben* (1992) A.T.R. 81-150.
623. Many successful plaintiffs, however, are content with seeking only damages to cover their legal expenses. Settlement may be facilitated by agreeing to a statement in open court for vindication: see *Barnett v. Crozier* [1987] 1 W.L.R. 272.

damages by timely apology, and in some cases may even escape all liability by retracting.[624] But retraction cannot be forced on a recalcitrant defendant, nor has the plaintiff any right of reply in the defendant's media.[625]

I. Injunction

From many a plaintiff's point of view, prevention of defamation must seem infinitely preferable to any redress after the damage has once been done. But injunctions to enjoin threatened attacks or repetition have been only grudgingly admitted for fear of introducing controls amounting to advance censorship and because of judicial reluctance to usurp the jury function which, since Fox's *Libel Act* of 1792, has been regarded as a basic guarantee of free speech.[626] Injunction is therefore ruled out unless the plaintiff can establish that (1) a finding by the jury that the complaint is *not* defamatory would be set aside as unreasonable, (2) there is no real ground for supposing that the defendant may succeed with a defence of justification, privilege or fair comment, and (3) he is likely to recover more than just nominal damages.[627] In no event will an injunction issue if its effect is to restrain public discussion on matters of public interest. Where otherwise appropriate, though, injunctions are not confined to enjoin the publication or repetition of libels calculated to injure the plaintiff in his property interests,[628] and are also available against slander, at least slander actionable per se.[629]

II. Damages

The commitment of our law to damages as the principal remedy for defamation has been a mixed blessing. Perhaps its foremost ill is that it exacerbates the tension between the two competing interests of individual reputation and freedom of speech. For on occasions where freedom of

624. E.g. in case of unintentional defamation: see above, p. 541. Some Canadian statutes have followed the American model of limiting a retracting defendant's liability in some circumstances to actual damage: see Fleming, *Retraction and Reply: Alternative Remedies for Defamation*, 12 U.B.C.L. Rev. 15 (1978). Moreover, qualified privilege for certain reports may be contingent on an explanation by the defendant (see above, n. 523) or opportunity for the plaintiff to reply (recommended A.L.R.C. §§178-180).
But a principal recommendation of the A.L.R.C. (§258) was to authorise "corrective orders" which, in suitable cases, would substantially mitigate damages.
625. Except that in England privilege for certain reports is contingent on a right of reply: see above, n. 523. The *right* to reply is widespread in Europe (9 Int. Encycl. Comp. L. §§195-197). A reply is clothed with qualified privilege: see above, p. 567.
626. See Hayes, *Injunctions before Judgment in Cases of Defamation*, 45 A.L.J. 125, 181 (1971); Ford, *Protection of Reputation in Equity*, 6 Res. Jud. 345 (1954); Pound, *Equitable Relief against Defamation*, 29 Harv. L. Rev. 640 (1916). In the U.S. injunctions are regarded as categorically prohibited by the First Amendment guarantee of free speech.
627. *Bonnard v. Perryman* [1891] 2 Ch. 269 (C.A.); *Church of Scientology v. Reader's Digest* [1980] 1 N.S.W.L.R. 344. In *Chappell v. T.C.N.* (1988) 14 N.S.W.L.R. 153 Hunt J. held that (1) was not categorical.
628. *Monson v. Tussauds* [1894] 1 Q.B. 671.
629. *Hermann Loog v. Bean* (1884) 26 Ch. D. 306; *Crescent Sales v. British Products* [1936] V.L.R. 336.

speech is most highly valued, there was no alternative to creating an immunity (privilege) and depriving the defamed of all right to vindication. On the other hand, the spectre of heavy damages has a decidedly chilling effect on speech.[630]

The problem is aggravated by the rather free hand juries play in assessing damages, which are said to be "at large", ranging from "contemptuous" or "derisory" (reflecting on the weakness of the plaintiff's reputation)[631] to exemplary (reflecting on the defendant's outrageousness). What is more, the tolerated level of awards bears no comparison with those for personal injury: reputation and privacy seem to be considered of much greater value than life or limb, dishonour an infinitely greater injury than agonising and protracted physical suffering.[632]

Several reasons account for this seemingly odd situation. First and foremost is the libel rule that, aside from actual pecuniary damage, injury to reputation and feelings is itself compensable. Even in cases of slander, once "special damage" has been proved, the plaintiff has established his credentials for general damages.[633] What is more, injury to reputation by libel is presumed and does not have to be established by evidence.[634] Of course, the person defamed does not really get compensation for his damaged reputation as such. Rather, damages serve "as a vindication of the plaintiff to the public and as consolation to him for a wrong done. Compensation is here a solatium rather than a monetary recompense for harm measurable in money"[635]—indeed, just like damages for pain and suffering in case of personal injury. Included are his injured feelings, indignation and the psychological need for satisfaction. To the extent that the plaintiff's subjective hurt has been increased by the outrageous nature of the defendant's manner or motives, it may be reflected in "aggravated damages" (to be distinguished from "punitive damages", as will appear below).

Finally, there is the function of damages in vindicating the plaintiff's reputation. This looks to the attitude of others to the plaintiff. The gravity of the libel, the social standing of the parties and the availability of alternative remedies have a bearing on this. A small sum awarded to a public figure for a serious libel could be interpreted as trivialising the

630. This fear is also widely exploited by less scrupulous plaintiffs by means of "gag" or "stop" writs: see A.L.R.C. §§52-56; *Brych v. Herald* [1978] V.R. 727; *Goldsmith v. Sperrings* [1977] 1 W.L.R. 478.

631. E.g. *Dering v. Uris (No. 2)* [1964] 2 Q.B. 669 (1 sh.); *Pamplin v. Express Newspaper* [1988] 1 W.L.R. 116 (denying order for costs).

632. See *Coyne v. Citizen Finance* (1991) 172 C.L.R. 211 (appropriate to direct jury that such comparison is not helpful); *Sutcliffe v. Pressdram* [1991] 1 Q.B. 153 (C.A.). Opinion on the suitability of juries on the issue of damages, as distinct from liability, is sharply divided. The A.L.R.C. could not agree (§§288-291); Faulks recommended that juries not determine the amount but only whether damages be "substantial", "moderate", "nominal", or "contemptuous".

633. See above, p. 551.

634. This rule can be defended on the ground that harm to reputation is difficult to prove and that libel is likely to cause anguish. In contrast, the U.S. Constitution no longer permits damages for other than actual injury: *Gertz v. Welsh* 418 U.S. 323 (1974); *Dun & Bradstreet v. Greenmoss* (1985) 472 U.S. 749 (only on matters of public concern). Advocated by George Orwell in 1946. Cf. the "triviality" defence in N.S.W.: see above, p. 551.

635. *Uren v. Fairfax* (1966) 117 C.L.R. 118 at 150 per Windeyer J.

incident, and in the absence of an unequivocal apology damages are the only means of vindication.

None of these elements can be measured on any objective monetary scale. Moreover, judicial control is constrained by recognition of the constitutional role played by juries in defamation actions. Review of awards on appeal is therefore permissible only in case of gross misjudgment.[636] However, it has been suggested that the judge indicate to the jury the range of damages he considers appropriate in the particular case, so long as it is made clear that the decision is one for the jury.[637] In New South Wales and Queensland current Bills propose to transfer the responsibility of assessing damages entirely to the judge.[638]

Exemplary damages

The decision of the House of Lords in 1964, in *Rookes v. Barnard*,[639] to renounce exemplary, as distinct from aggravated, damages has had its largest impact on defamation. Henceforth it became necessary to distinguish more clearly between a defendant's contumelious conduct and its effect, if any, on the plaintiff's feelings: the former may deserve reprobation, but the latter alone compensation. One exception of peculiar relevance to defamation was retained: where the defendant sought to profit from his tort (tort must not pay!). That the libel was published in the course of a business (publishing) would not be sufficient; it must have been with guilty knowledge and the calculation that the chances of economic profit outweighed those of economic or physical cost.[640]

Australian and most other Commonwealth courts declined to follow the English example and have retained exemplary damages for defamation (and other torts),[641] mindful of the general disuse of criminal proceedings.[642] New South Wales and Queensland have by statute abolished exemplary damages for defamation in all circumstances, even in the limited exceptions countenanced in *Rookes*,[643] and the same has been recommended in England.[644] A less drastic reform would be to reserve the amount of damages, or at least of exemplary damages, for the judge rather than the jury.[645]

Aggravated damages have emerged from this reorientation as a new category in all jurisdictions. The defendant's conduct is here relevant only

636. In *Coyne* (see above, n. 632) the High Court restored a verdict of $150,000, reduced to $50,000 by the F.C. of W.A. who compared it to a recent award of $200,000 for a bad case of tetraplegia. But awards of $200,000 and $400,000 were set aside in *Fairfax v. Carson* (1991) 24 N.S.W.L.R. 259.
637. *Coyne* at 324 per Toohey J.
638. Defamation Bills 1991.
639. [1964] A.C. 1129. See above, p. 241.
640. See *Cassell v. Broome* [1972] A.C. 1136; *Riches v. News Group* [1986] Q.B. 256 (C.A.).
641. *Uren v. Fairfax* (1966) 117 C.L.R. 118; see above, p. 241.
642. Despite the rarity of prosecutions (which alone make the threat tolerable), retention has recently been recommended by the A.-G.s of N.S.W., Vic. and Qld.
643. *Defamation Act* 1974 (N.S.W.) s. 46; Defamation Bill 1991 (Qld). But aggravated damages remain and are liberally applied, largely nullifying the reform: see *Andrews v. Fairfax* [1980] 2 N.S.W.L.R. 225.
644. Faulks 94-97.
645. Recommended in N.Z. (1977).

in so far as it affects the plaintiff's feelings.[646] Damages may be aggravated by conduct in the publication[647] or thereafter as in the conduct of the defence,[648] but according to the prevailing view, it must be "unjustifiable, improper or lacking in bona fides".[649] Thus the defendant may with impunity raise any bona fide legitimate defence, including truth, even if it causes distress to the plaintiff, since the law cannot "at once permit and forbid, invite and punish".[650]

The problem of jury control is most acute in relation to awards of aggravated damages. Jury instructions are couched in general language and neither suggest figures nor cite precedents. On the one hand, the constitutional free hand given to juries in assessing damages for defamation calls for the utmost judicial restraint; on the other is the temptation for juries to infuse an unpermitted punitive element into aggravated damages. The English Court of Appeal was prepared to disallow a grossly inflated award, with a strong recommendation to trial judges to assist juries to appreciate the real value of large sums.[651]

Character evidence

In assessing damages, the law seeks to compensate the plaintiff for injury to the reputation he previously enjoyed. Though it may be shown that his reputation was not what he claimed it to be, it is irrelevant that he did not deserve it.[652] This may occasionally confer an unmerited reward upon a hypocrite who has succeeded in hiding a shameful career behind a screen of unblemished repute, but on balance it would be too unfair to expect every plaintiff to show a uniform propriety of conduct throughout his life, besides unduly lengthening trials.

Accordingly, the defence is free to lead evidence of the plaintiff's general bad repute, but not of specific discreditable conduct.[653] Not that it must actually content itself with such general evidence only as that the plaintiff's reputation was high or low, for it is permissible to elicit that "he was *known* to have had a criminal record".[654] Rumour of course, cannot claim audience in a court of law and testimony must therefore be confined to a

646. Thus a corporation cannot recover aggravated damages for loss of feelings, though it may perhaps for loss of reputation: *Andrews v. Fairfax* [1980] 2 N.S.W.L.R. 225 at 265; *Comalco v. A.B.C.* (1985) 64 A.C.T.R. 1 at 81.
647. Even failure to make inquiry may be sufficient: *Andrews v. Fairfax* [1980] 2 N.S.W.L.R. 225; but cf. *Bickel v. Fairfax* [1981] 2 N.S.W.L.R. 474 at 487.
648. *Triggell v. Pheeney* (1951) 82 C.L.R. 497 at 514; *Cassell v. Broome* [1972] A.C. 1027 at 1071. But rigorous defence does not, without more, aggravate damages: *Coyne v. Citizen Finance* (1991) 172 C.L.R. 211.
649. *Bickel v. Fairfax* [1981] 2 N.S.W.L.R. 474 at 497; *David Syme v. Mather* [1977] V.R. 516 at 530, 535 (F.C.).
650. *Herald v. McGregor* (1928) 41 C.L.R. 254 at 267.
651. *Sutcliffe v. Pressdram* [1991] 1 Q.B. 153 (£600,000, later reduced to £60,000).
652. Subject to the qualification that justification is a defence. Note also that a defendant, if unable to justify in whole, may justify in part, so as to mitigate damages: see above, p. 555.
653. *Plato Films v. Speidel* [1961] A.C. 1090. Plaintiff may lead evidence of good repute to increase damages: *Bickel v. Fairfax* [1981] 2 N.S.W.L.R. 474.
654. *Wishart v. Mirror Newspaper* [1963] S.R. (N.S.W.) 745 (F.C.). Convictions are now admissible (*Goody v. Odhams* [1967] 1 Q.B. 333) provided relevant: *Jorgensen v. N.Z. Newspapers* [1974] 2 N.Z.L.R. 45.

man's *settled* reputation.[655] Also, a character witness may be questioned as to the grounds of his belief;[656] but according to the prevailing view, he should desist from mentioning specific incidents even if sufficiently notorious to permit the inference that the plaintiff's current reputation has thereby suffered.[657] Moreover, the evidence must be relevant to the nature of the allegation made against him; it must be directed to that aspect of his character which was maligned. If the libel imputes fraud, his reputation for honesty is open to scrutiny, but not his sexual habits.[658]

This compromise has not passed without criticism. For one thing, it is "difficult to combine an aversion from rumour with an indulgence for general evidence of reputation which, unvouched, is virtually the same thing."[659] It would be fairer all around to admit evidence of particular incidents that contribute to the plaintiff's current reputation.[660] Secondly, the prohibition can be circumvented by luring the plaintiff into the witness box and cross-examining him as to credit. Nor does it preclude reduction of damages on the basis of evidence of particular incidents otherwise properly admitted, such as on a plea of justification that failed.[661] Reform has therefore been urged by several bodies.[662]

Inquiry into the "damages-worthiness" of the plaintiff is also to some extent stultified by the rule in common law jurisdictions[663] that evidence tending to justification cannot be adduced in the absence of a plea of truth. The reason for this is to acquaint the plaintiff with the defence he will have to meet, and once more to prevent furtive admission in evidence of particular facts as distinct from general reputation.[664] On the other hand, it can give the plaintiff a lever for outmanoeuvring the defendant by not relying on one of several libellous allegations: if clearly severable, the defendant cannot adduce facts in justification of that one, and may thus stand to lose the benefit of highly prejudicial evidence.[665]

Mitigation

Although, as we have seen, it is no defence even in reduction of damages that the calumny was orginally or concurrently published by others,[666] a partial modification at least allows evidence in mitigation that the plaintiff

655. Before it was put under a cloud by the instant libel. Accordingly, a previous or concurrent publication of the same libel by others, even if privileged, is no ground for mitigation (*Dingle v. Assoc. Newspapers* [1964] A.C. 371), though a defendant is of course liable only for the damage done by his own publication: *Harrison v. Pearce* (1858) 1 F. & F. 567; 175 E.R. 855.
656. *Plato Films v. Speidel* [1961] A.C. 1090 at 1138-40.
657. *Plato Films* [1961] A.C. 1090, passim.
658. Ibid. at 1140; *Morosi v. Mirror Newspapers* [1977] 2 N.S.W.L.R. 749 at 801.
659. Lord Radcliffe, ibid. at 1131.
660. Ibid.
661. *Pamplin v. Express Newspaper* [1988] 1 W.L.R. 116 (C.A.).
662. *Porter* §§146-156; Faulks §§363-372; A.L.R.C. §265.
663. In jurisdictions where justification includes a plea of "public benefit", failure to so plead does not admit falsity. Either party may therefore lead evidence on the issue as it affects damages: *Singleton v. Ffrench* (1986) 5 N.S.W.L.R. 425 (C.A.).
664. *Watt v. Watt* [1905] A.C. 115 at 118.
665. See *Plato Films v. Speidel* [1961] A.C. 1090; *S. & K. Holdings v. Throgmorton* [1972] 1 W.L.R. 1036 (C.A.).
666. *Dingle v. Assoc. Newspapers* [1964] A.C. 371; and see above, p. 555, and n. 655.

has already recovered, or brought actions for, damages or received or agreed to receive compensation in respect of a libel to the same effect as that sued upon.[667] With the same object of at once alleviating the lot of defendants and preventing a plaintiff from recovering several times over for the same elements of damage common to each libel, most jurisdictions encourage consolidation of actions brought in respect to the same or substantially the same libel and consequential apportionment of damages between the several defendants.[668]

Turning to apology: In any action for defamation the defendant may, provided he gives notice in writing at the time of delivering his defence,[669] give evidence in mitigation that he made or offered an apology before commencement of the action or at the earliest opportunity thereafter if he had none before.[670] A retraction is relevant for the purpose of showing that the plaintiff has sustained less damage to his reputation than he claims and tends to negative malice. Of course, it must be unequivocal and unconditional. To say that a man has manners not fit for a pig and then to correct it by saying that his manners *are* fit for a pig, is an aggravation, not a retraction.[671] Nor does a newspaper make amends for a defamatory attack on a politician by offering him the opportunity of replying in kind[672] or by merely reporting other people's exculpations instead of frankly putting its own authority and regrets behind the required vindication.[673]

With a view to expediting litigation, a ''fast track'' option has been proposed for New South Wales, Victoria and Queensland:[674] contemplating early application in interlocutory procccdings for a court-recommended correction of the libel, followed by later optional proceedings for appropriately reduced damages.

Apology may even furnish a complete defence. In actions for libel contained in a newspaper or periodical,[675] the defendant may in several jurisdictions plead that it was inserted without actual malice and without gross negligence[676] and that, before commencement of the action or at the

667. N.S.W.: s. 48; Vic.: s. 12; Qld: s. 24; S.A.: s. 11; Tas.: s. 25; A.C.T.: s. 7; N.T.: s. 10; N.Z.: s. 13. The defence is limited to newspapers in Vic., S.A., Qld, and Tas. These enactments reproduce in substance the *Law of Libel Act* 1888 (Eng.) s. 6 (extended to all libel and slander in 1952). See *Lewis v. Daily Telegraph* [1964] A.C. 234; *Uren v. Fairfax* (1966) 117 C.L.R. 118 at 154. It is most doubtful whether such a defendant is liable to contribution, not being ordinarily liable ''in respect of the same damage''; but see Williams, *Joint Torts* §36.
668. Qld: s. 23; S.A.: s. 13; Tas.: s. 24; A.C.T.: s. 10; N.T.: s. 11; N.Z.: s. 11. These enactments reproduce the *Law of Libel Act* 1888 (Eng.) s. 5. Also *Isaacs v. Fairfax* [1980] 2 N.S.W.L.R. 651.
669. Not *in* his defence. Matters in mitigation of damages cannot be pleaded: *Wilson v. Dun's Gazette* [1912] V.L.R. 342.
670. N.S.W.: S. Ct Rules; Vic.: s. 6; Qld: s. 21; S.A.: s. 9; W.A.: 10 Vic. No. 8; Tas.: s. 22; A.C.T.: s. 5; N.T.: s. 8; N.Z.: s. 12. These enactments reproduce the *Libel Act* 1843 (Eng.) s. 1.
671. *Winfield & Jolowicz* 297.
672. *McRae v. S.A. Telecasters* (1976) 14 S.A.S.R. 162 at 167.
673. *Dingle v. Assoc. Newspapers* [1964] A.C. 371 at 400.
674. Discussion Paper No. 2 on Reform of Defamation (1991).
675. Extended to broadcasting in Ontario: *Libel and Slander Act* 1960 s. 9.
676. See *Bell v. N. Constitution* [1943] N.I. 108: *Levin v. Fox* (1890) 11 L.R. (N.S.W.) 414.

earliest opportunity afterwards, he inserted in a newspaper or periodical a full apology, or if the periodical is ordinarily published at intervals exceeding one week, had offered to publish such apology in any newspaper or periodical selected by the plaintiff.[677] The defence must be accompanied by a payment of money into court by way of amends. Its purpose was, and is, to save the press needless court costs and to discourage litigation for inadvertent libels published in the haste of meeting deadlines.[678] But in this function it has long been displaced by the more convenient procedure, open to all defendants, of paying money into court with or without admission of liability.

Tasmania[679] and the Australian Capital Territory[680] offer a useful deterrent against frivolous actions for defamation by depriving a plaintiff of his costs if he recovers a verdict of less than $4.

677. Vic.: s. 7; Qld: s. 22; S.A.: s. 10; W.A.: see above, n. 670; Tas.: s. 23; A.C.T.: s. 8; N.T.: s. 9. These enactments reproduce the *Libel Act* 1843 (Eng.) s. 2.
678. But so as not to deprive a plaintiff of his public vindication, he may nevertheless make a statement in open court: *Eyre v. Nationwide News* (1968) 13 F.L.R. 180.
679. *Defamation Act* 1957 s. 30.
680. *Defamation Act* 1901 s. 9: "unless the judge in a case of libel certifies that the words charged as defamatory were published without reasonable grounds or excuse".

26

RIGHT OF PRIVACY

No simple answer can be given to the question to what extent contemporary law affords protection for what is often compendiously called the "right of privacy". In its broadest sense, the interest involved is that of "being left alone", of sheltering one's private life from the degrading effect of intrusion or exposure to public view.[1] Demand for legal protection of this interest appears only in a relatively advanced culture, with increasing refinement in the social and aesthetic values of the community. It becomes more insistent as the intensity of modern life renders desirable some retreat from the world and as personal modesty, dignity and self-respect are increasingly exposed to practices which overstep the bounds of propriety.

Interests of personality have received progressive protection as the common law expanded its frontiers of legal control. In very early times, the law afforded redress only for direct violations of physical security, such as physical aggression (battery) or restraint on freedom of movement (false imprisonment). Later, protection was extended to emotional security when the action for assault enjoined the putting of others in fear of such injury. The most significant modern development in this sphere was the new tort enunciated in *Wilkinson v. Downton*,[2] that is wilful conduct, whether by words or acts, calculated to inflict physical harm through emotional distress. The law of nuisance gives qualified protection to the individual against offensive noise, smell, dust, smoke and the like, in so far as it unreasonably interferes with the enjoyment and use of his land. Perhaps the closest affinity to some aspects of the right of privacy is found in the law of defamation. Though libel and slander are primarily concerned with reputation—an interest in relations with others—they incidentally also safeguard the individual's sense of honour and self-respect.[3]

Violation of privacy has not so far, at least under that name, received explicit recognition as a tort by British courts.[4] For one thing, the traditional approach has been to formulate tort liability in terms of reprehensible conduct rather than of specified interests entitled to protection. For another, our courts have been content to grope forward cautiously along the grooves of established legal concepts, like nuisance and

1. The most ambitious attempt to formulate a coherent concept of privacy is by Gavison, *Privacy and the Limits of Law*, 89 Yale L.J. 421 (1980). See also Benn, 52 A.L.J. 601, 686 (1978); Seipp, 3 Oxf. L. Leg. Stud. 325 (1983); Stoljar, 4 Leg. Stud. 67 (1984). Critical of such a compendious concept is Wacks, *Poverty of Privacy*, 96 L.Q.R. 73 (1980); *Protection of Privacy* (1980).
2. [1897] 2 Q.B. 57. See above, p. 32.
3. See above, p. 595.
4. Save for repeated nibbles in Ontario: see Irvine, 18 C.C.L.T. 37 (1982). As early as 1849, in *Prince Albert v. Strange* (1849) 2 De G. & Sm. 652; 64 E.R. 293 there are judicial references to the "right of privacy".

libel, rather than make a bold commitment to an entirely new head of liability.[5] Some of this hesitation is undoubtedly due to the fact that we are here concerned primarily with injury in the shape of mental distress, which has so frequently evoked the fear of opening the door to fanciful claims. Another factor is the difficulty of drawing a clear line between what should and should not be tolerated. The mere fact of living in the crowded society of today exposes everyone to annoying contacts with others, most of which must be borne as the price of social existence. Also, free speech and dissemination of news are important competing values, and it is only when intrusion becomes intolerably offensive by prevailing standards of taste and propriety that legal intervention would become warranted.

These difficulties, however, do not provide a convincing reason for altogether shutting out claims of this nature, since the courts have long been familiar with the delicate adjustment of similar conflicts, as in nuisance and defamation. In the United States, a famous article in 1890 by Warren and Brandeis,[6] synthesising mostly English precedents, inspired intensive judicial development of a new, independent tort of "invasion of privacy".[7] But the American experience has taught the lesson that there is no easy, embracing formula for dealing with all the different practices encountered. The proper balance to be struck between the clashing interests in these cases varies greatly and demands individualised solutions. Efforts to launch English[8] and Australian law along American lines under a broad statutory directive have not therefore made much headway, especially against the bitter opposition of the media and a reluctance to entrust the judiciary with wide powers to flesh out the right.[9] The Australian Law Reform Commission accordingly chose the alternative route of recommending a tort remedy only against certain specific abuses like commercial appropriation and publicity of private facts[10] and data misuse.[11] More legislative support has so far been given to penal rather than civil sanctions against electronic surveillance.[12]

Privacy interests may be offended by a great variety of practices which can be summarised under the following main headings:[13]

5. Winfield, *Right to Privacy*, 47 L.Q.R. 23 (1931).
6. *Right to Privacy*, 4 Harv. L. Rev. 193.
7. *Rest 2d* §652A-F; *Prosser & Keeton* ch. 20; Westin, *Privacy and Freedom* (1967); *Privacy and Economics* symposium, 12 Ga. L. Rev. 393 (1978). Modern Anglo-Australian articles draw heavily on the American experience: Neill, 25 Mod. L. Rev. 393 (1962); Dworkin, 2 U. Tas. L. Rev. 418 (1967); Storey, 47 A.L.J. 498 (1973); Swanton, 48 A.L.J. 91 (1974); Palmer, 1965 N.Z.L.J. 747; Gibson, *Studies in Canadian Tort Law* (1977) ch. 12.
8. The latest rebuff coming from the Calcutt Com. *On Privacy* (Cmd. 1102, 1990) which initiated an independent Press Complaints Commission, successor to the ineffective Press Council.
9. Unlike the "open textured" privacy statutes of B.C., Man., Sask.: Osborne, *Aspects of Privacy Law* (ed. Gibson) ch. 4 (1980).
10. See below, n. 61.
11. *Privacy and Personal Information*, Discussion Paper No. 14 (1980). The English Law Commission Working Paper No. 58 (1974) recommended a tort action for breach of confidence.
12. Like the uniform *Listening Devices Act*: N.S.W. and Vic. (1969), Qld (1971), S.A. (1972), W.A. (1978).
13. These stem from Prosser, *Privacy*, 48 Cal. L. Rev. 383 (1960) and have become familiar markers in American law. Prosser's 4th category, "putting a person in a false light", a cousin of defamation, is here omitted.

Intrusion

Perhaps the archetypal privacy interest, being "let alone", is in preventing others from the very act of intruding into one's private sphere and thereby outraging one's sense of modesty and security. Here the traditional torts of trespass and nuisance are most germane.

The "fundamental right of privacy in one's home"[14] is vindicated by the action of trespass against actual physical intrusions into the plaintiff's possession-area, such as the planting of listening devices in his home[15] or the taking of photographs after gaining unpermitted entry.[16] The outrage can be vindicated with aggravated, in Australia even with exemplary, damages.[17] Trespass, however, does not help a mere licensee, like a patient in a hospital ward;[18] nor against peeping Toms who operate outside the plaintiff's boundary.[19] Criminal statutes in some jurisdictions at last prohibit certain obnoxious activities short of trespass, like snooping,[20] illegal[21] wiretapping,[22] the use of listening and recording devices,[23] and photography by investigators without consent.[24] But for a private remedy one can only look to nuisance.

Even the law of nuisance, however, offers only very modest support. It has evinced the strongest reluctance, for example, to intercede against the privacy of one's home being violated by curious onlookers or to restrain offensive obstruction of one's view. After an earlier flirtation with a more liberal view,[25] it is now well established that there is no redress against opening new windows which command a view over neighbouring premises,[26] for building in such a manner as to obstruct another's prospect,[27] or even against aerial photography for commercial purposes.[28] A decision often cited in this respect is *Victoria Park Racing Co. v. Taylor*,[29] where the High Court of Australia declined to restrain the

14. *Morris v. Beardmore* [1981] A.C. 446 at 465 per Lord Scarman.
15. E.g. *Greig v. Greig* [1966] V.R. 376.
16. *Lincoln Hunt v. Willesee* (1986) 4 N.S.W.L.R. 457 (no implied license). For injunctions against subsequent telecasting see Handley, 62 A.L.J. 216 (1988).
17. Ibid.
18. Nor is photography a trespass to the person: *Kay v. Robertson* [1991] F.S.R. 62 (see 52 Mod. L. Rev. 802; 54 ibid. 451). Contra: *Barber v. Time* 159 S.W. 2d 291 (No. 1942).
19. *Bathurst C.C. v. Saban* (1985) 2 N.S.W.L.R. 704 (photos); cf. *Hickman v. Maisey* [1900] 1 Q.B. 752 (racing tout spying from highway).
20. E.g. *Haisman v. Smelcher* [1953] V.L.R. 625.
21. Control over wiretapping by law enforcement agencies is a separate question: see A.L.R.C., Discussion Paper No. 13, §60-160. At common law telephone tapping for crime detection is not unlawful: *Malone v. Metropolitan Police* [1979] Ch. 344, since brought into conformity with European Convention on Human Rights by *Interception of Communications Act* 1985 (U.K.).
22. *Communications (Interception) Act* 1960 (Cth): *Miller v. Miller* (1978) 22 A.L.R. 119; 3 M.U.L.R. 364; *Interception of Communications Act* 1985 (U.K.).
23. See above, n. 12. Cf. *Davis v. McArthur* (1970) 17 D.L.R. (3d) 760 (B.C. statute).
24. *Private Investigators and Security Guards Act* 1974 (N.Z.) s. 52.
25. *Cherrington v. Abney* (1709) 2 Vern. 646; 23 E.R. 1022; and see *Chandler v. Thompson* (1811) 3 Camp. 80; 170 E.R. 1312.
26. *Johnson v. Wyatt* (1863) 2 De G.J. & S. 18 at 27; 46 E.R. 281 at 284; *Tapling v. Jones* (1865) 11 H.L.C. 290 at 305, 311; 11 E.R. 1344 at 1350, 1352.
27. *William Aldred's Case* (1611) 9 Co. Rep. 57b at 58b; 77 E.R. 816 at 820.
28. *Bernstein v. Skyviews* [1978] Q.B. 479.
29. (1937) 58 C.L.R. 479.

broadcasting of races from a high platform which had been constructed with the object of gaining an unimpeded view of the plaintiff's racecourse. Although in this particular instance the defendant's activity had neither interfered, nor been intended to interfere, with the enjoyment of the plaintiff's land and its effect had been merely to make his business less profitable by providing competitive entertainment,[30] there are unnecessarily categorical dicta in support of an unqualified right to overlook another's premises, regardless of motivation or purpose, and repudiating the existence of any "general right of privacy".[31]

On the other hand, we have seen that conduct devoid of any social utility, solely directed to causing annoyance, may constitute an unreasonable interference, although the same activity pursued for a legitimate purpose would not have been actionable.[32] Besides, it is not a requisite for liability in nuisance that the offending conduct produces a palpable effect upon the plaintiff's land, since systematic telephoning,[33] "watching and besetting",[34] or surveillance,[35] calculated to interfere with the ordinary comfort of human existence or the ordinary enjoyment of the premises beset, have been held actionable wrongs. Thus there is considerable authority which could support redress against overlooking or spying on the premises of others for the sole purpose of causing annoyance and emotional distress in circumstances like the *Balham Case*[36] where, by an elaborate arrangement of large mirrors, neighbours succeeded in observing all that went on in the surgery of a nearby dentist. It would be a deplorable reflection on the expansive capacity of the common law if courts were unwilling to restrain such intolerable espionage designed solely to satisfy degraded curiosity at the expense of others. Ruthless exploitation of television and other frightful electronic devices, like long range microphones, may well "force the courts to recognise that protection against the complete exposure of the doing of the individual may be a right indispensable to the enjoyment of life".[37]

Clearly, no liability is warranted unless the intrusion is substantial and of a kind that a reasonable person of normal sensitivity would regard as offensive and intolerable. Merely knocking at another's door or telephoning on one or two occasions is not actionable, even when designed to cause annoyance; but if the calls are repeated with persistence, and in the midst of night, so as to interfere unreasonably with comfort or sleep, liability will ensue.[38]

30. This aspect is stressed by Latham C.J. ibid. at 493. In an identical American case recovery was allowed for intentional appropriation of the plaintiff's economic interests: *Pittsburgh Athletic Club v. K.Q.V. Broadcasting Co.* 24 F. Supp. 490 (1938); and see below, p. 719. In Australia, the practice (as regards television) is now prohibited by the *Broadcasting and Television Act* 1956 (Cth) s. 115. Cf. *Television Act* 1954 (U.K.) s. 391.
31. (1937) 58 C.L.R. 479 at 496 (Latham C.J.).
32. See above, p. 432.
33. *Stoakes v. Brydges* [1958] Q.W.N. 5; *Motherwell v. Motherwell* (1976) 73 D.L.R. (3d) 62 (not letters).
34. Even peaceful picketing substantially impeding access: *Hubbard v. Pitt* [1976] Q.B. 142; *Re Van der Lubbe* (1949) 49 S.R. (N.S.W.) 309.
35. *Bernstein v. Skyviews* [1978] Q.B. 479 at 489 (aerial).
36. The case is mentioned in Kenny's *Cases on Torts* (4th ed. 1926) 367; and discussed by Winfield, 47 L.Q.R. 24 at 27 (1931).
37. *Victoria Park Racing Co. v. Taylor* (1937) 58 C.L.R. 479 at 505 per Rich J.
38. *Stoakes v. Brydges* [1958] Q.W.N. 5; *Alma v. Nakir* [1966] 2 N.S.W.R. 396.

Concern about the inadequacy of existing sanctions is reflected in recommendations by law reform commissions in England and Australia to introduce a tort remedy against illegal surveillance.[39]

Appropriation of personality

The unauthorised use of a person's name or picture in aid of advertising or other commercial purposes presented the first American test for protecting "privacy".[40] This practice has no true free speech implications and presents a strong case for legal intervention. Yet our common law offers little encouragement.[41] Occasionally, protection is afforded through the rather plastic category of defamation. For example, in *Tolley v. Fry*,[42] chocolate manufacturers issued an advertisement in the form of a caricature of the plaintiff, a prominent amateur golfer, with a packet of their chocolate protruding from his pocket. The advertisement was published without his consent, and damages were awarded on the ground that the publication was defamatory, as it carried the innuendo that the plaintiff has prostituted his status as an amateur for commercial gain and thereby made himself liable to exclusion from membership of reputable clubs. The decision is difficult to support on any conventional theory of defamation, because it seems to have been assumed as sufficient that the representation was calculated to injure the plaintiff by jeopardising his status as an amateur golfer. All discussion centred on the potentiality of harm to his "name", but it was not explained how his imputed association with the advertising could be construed as tending to lower him in the estimation of his fellow men. Would it have been legally harmless to enlist a great scientist or industrialist in like manner in the service of chocolate?[43] The decision has potentially far-reaching implications and could be stretched to serve as the basis for restraining the unauthorised use of *anyone's* name or picture for commercial use under the guise of protecting reputation.[44]

There is also precedent for invoking the equitable jurisdiction to enjoin the misuse of another's name, if there is some evidence of prejudice to his economic interests.[45] Indeed, false claims of sponsorship have even been

39. The Younger Committee §565; A.L.R.C., Discussion Paper No. 13, §173.
40. In N.Y. an adverse decision in 1902 was promptly followed by a *Privacy Act* which enjoined using "for advertising purposes, or for purposes of trade, the name, portrait or picture of any living person without first obtaining his consent". This has since formed the nucleus of a judicially developed right of privacy. See now Treece, *Commercial Exploitation of Names*, 51 Tex. L. Rev. 637 (1973).
41. See Frazer, *Appropriation of Personality*, 99 L.Q.R. 280 (1983); Pannam 40 A.L.J. 4 (1966); Irvine, *Aspects of Privacy* (1980) ch. 7.
42. [1931] A.C. 333.
43. See Lord Blanesburgh's dissent, ibid. at 347; and the jury verdict in *Dockrell v. Dougall* (1899) 80 L.T. 556 (not libellous to attribute to a doctor sponsorship of patent medicine he actually regarded as "disastrous"). There is no difficulty where the appropriation of plaintiff's name is accompanied by humiliating comment, as in *Mazatti v. Acme Products* [1930] 4 D.L.R. 601.
44. Other (unreported) cases illustrating a liberal use of defamation concepts in combating commercial appropriation of personality are *Honeysett v. News Chronicle* (*The Times*, 14 May 1935), *Plumb v. Jeyes*' (15 Apr. 1937), *Hood v. W. H. Smith* (5 Nov. 1937), *Griffith v. Bondor* (11 Dec. 1935), *Funston v. Pearson* (12 Mar. 1955).
45. *Dixon v. Holden* (1869) L.R. 7 Eq. 488; *Routh v. Webster* (1847) 10 Beav. 561; 50 E.R. 698. The first involved an unfounded claim that plaintiff was the partner of a bankrupt firm, the second (in a prospectus) that he was associated with the company's management.

enjoined as "passing-off", as when a professional dancing couple were portrayed on a record cover.[46] But in those cases, protection is not really afforded to any privacy interest, that is, against humiliation and embarrassment, but rather against interference with economic values, often enough interference with nothing else than the plaintiff's claim to exploit for himself the publicity value of his personality. In sum, what is at stake is a right not so much of privacy as of publicity—which is more appropriately left to another context.[47]

If the courts are too timid, legislation must intervene. The Australian Law Reform Commission considered the case for protection against unauthorised appropriation of name, identity and reputation as "irresistible".[48]

Disclosure of private facts

The most troublesome issue in the whole field of privacy is protection against unwanted publicity, in view of the competing claim of the public's "right to know". Clearly, *public* facts however embarrassing to the individual may be aired in public, provided they are true.[49] Even a plaintiff who has become an involuntary object of public attention, like a victim of crime or accident, cannot ordinarily complain of the attendant publicity;[50] nor is there any remedy against unwanted photography in public and its subsequent publication.[51]

The matter stands differently with respect to disclosure of private facts, for here the public's claim to know is not a legitmate interest in news and information relevant to public affairs but only idle curiosity or hunger for gossip. An early, celebrated case looked promising. In *Prince Albert v. Strange*,[52] an injunction was granted against lithographic copies of drawings and etchings which the royal couple had made for their own amusement. Though its ostensible basis was to protect a property right in literary and artistic compositions, it has been forcibly argued[53] that it was in reality an interest of personality—the claim to inviolate privacy—that was vindicated, since the plaintiff was concerned, not with the commercial aspect of securing the profits of publication, but with maintaining his emotional tranquillity in knowing that he could prevent any publication

46. *Henderson v. Radio Corp.* [1960] S.R. (N.S.W.) 576.
47. See below, p.719.
48. *Unfair Publication* (1979) 248-250.
49. But if false and defamatory, an action will lie, even if the matter is of public interest: see above, p. 571.
50. Some states prohibit media identification of rape victims (e.g. *Sexual Offences Act* 1976 (U.K.)). Held unconstitutional in *Cox Broadcasting v. Cohn* (1975) 420 U.S. 469.
51. *Bathurst C.C. v. Saban* (1985) 2 N.S.W.L.R. 704. Unless perhaps the photo is offensive: at 708; or is used in connection with advertising when his interest is to protect his right of publicity rather than privacy: see below, p. 719: passing-off. Cf. *Rest. 2d* §652E.
52. (1849) 2 De G. & Sm. 652; 64 E.R. 295; 1 Mac. & G. 25.
53. By Warren & Brandeis, in their pioneering article in 4 Harv. L. Rev. 193. As much can be said of *Gee v. Pritchard* (1818) 2 Swans. 402; 36 E.R. 670 (commercialisation of correspondence: see Pound, *Equitable Relief against Defamation*, 29 Harv. L. Rev. 640 at 642 (1916)); *Thurston v. Charles* (1905) 21 T.L.R. 659 (substantial damages for conversion of letter), and *Williams v. Settle* [1960] 1 W.L.R. 1072 (exemplary damages for mental suffering to plaintiff and his wife caused by infringement of copyright in photograph).

whatever. Are we then entitled to infer judicial interposition not only against piracy of intellectual products but also against the exploitation of a person's name, physiognomy and past? In some cases, such jurisdiction has been asserted based on breach of an implied contract or of trust or confidence, as when a photographer was restrained from exhibiting a customer's photograph without consent[54] and an ex-husband from disclosing confidential information imparted to him by his wife during their marriage concerning her private life.[55] In another case, a wife's physician was held liable for giving the husband a report on her mental condition, which was later disclosed in domestic proceedings and caused her shock.[56] But this judicial device affords no assistance against offensive publicity of private facts obtained otherwise than under conditions of confidentiality.[57]

Most resented and hurtful is the practice of the media of raking up disreputable incidents from the depths of an individual's past, often with the intentional devastating effect on his dignity, even health.[58] But although such portrayals are almost always defamatory, the defence of truth would defeat any action for libel at common law. We have seen, however, that in several Australian jurisdictions the publication, besides being true, must also have been "for the public benefit" or "in the public interest".[59] A new initiative is now in the offing. Current Bills in New South Wales, Victoria and Queensland will create in effect two distinct causes of action: defamation and defamatory invasion of privacy. Truth alone would be a defence to the first; not to defamation concerning the plaintiff's private affairs, such as his health, private behaviour, home life or personal or family relationships, unless the matter was relevant to a topic of public interest.[60] This formula would in substance enact an earlier recommendation by the Australian Law Reform Commission for uniform legislation[61] which had foundered on the opposition of the remaining States.

Data misuse may result from collection as well as disclosure of private facts. False information, stored or disseminated, is usually beyond the reach of actionable defamation because of privilege between the bank and

54. *Pollard v. Photographic Co.* (1888) 40 Ch. D. 345. Cf. *Kirk v. Reed* [1968] N.Z.L.R. 801 (defamation to publish jocular photo intended only for private use).
55. *Argyll v. Argyll* [1967] Ch. 302 (breach of *implied* obligation of confidence); *Stephens v. Avery* [1988] Ch. 449 (not limited to spousal pillow-talk; disclosing lesbian relation). On limits see *Malone v. Metropolitan Police* [1979] Ch. 344 at 375ff. Most cases of breach of confidence, however, involve betrayal of "know-how" to the plaintiff's *economic* loss. See Gurry, *Breach of Confidence* (1984). The cause of action is thought to be equitable, but English and N.Z. courts have lately consistently awarded tort damages.
56. *Furniss v. Fitchett* [1958] N.Z.L.R. 396. The case proceeded on a theory of negligence rather than breach of confidence. See Rodgers-Magnet, *Disclosures of Confidential Medical Information*, in *Issues in Tort Law* (1982) 265. U.S.: 48 A.L.R. 4th 668 (1986).
57. Exceptional was injunction in a wardship case prohibiting disclosure of identity and whereabouts of a child and ex-convict mother: *Re X* [1984] 1 W.L.R. 1422.
58. In *Tucker v. News Media* [1986] 2 N.Z.L.R. 716 intentional infliction of mental disturbance (see above, p. 31) was considered a possible remedy in a particularly distressing case of a patient awaiting heart transplant.
59. See above, p. 556.
60. See above, p. 557.
61. *Unfair Publication* (1979) para. 124, 236-240.

the recipient.[62] However, some measure of protection to the individual, compatible with the useful flow of credit information, has been found in legislation compelling disclosure by credit reporting agencies of adverse information to the person affected and providing means for its correction.[63] But protection is needed also against misuse of *accurate* private information. For example, the *Privacy Act* 1988 (Cth) prescribes standards governing the use of, and access to, personal information by Commonwealth departments and agencies, and provides for complaints to the Privacy Commissioner.

62. See above, p. 567.
63. *Credit Reporting Act* 1978 (Vic.) (damages for knowingly false information); *Invasion of Privacy Act* 1971 (Qld), Pt 3; *Fair Credit Reports Act* (S.A.); *Consumer Credit Act* 1974 (Eng.) s. 158; inspired by the *Consumer Credit Protection Act* 1968 (U.S.A.). Can. Model Act: Gibson, *Aspect of Privacy Law* (1980) ch. 5.

27

ABUSE OF LEGAL PROCEDURE

1. MALICIOUS PROSECUTION

The tort of malicious prosecution is dominated by the problem of balancing two countervailing interests of high social importance: safeguarding the individual from being harassed by unjustifiable litigation and encouraging citizens to aid in law enforcement. On one side, it needs no emphasis that the launching of scandalous charges is apt to expose the accused to serious injury, involving his honour and self-respect as well as his reputation and credit in the community. Malicious prosecution, therefore, bears close resemblance to defamation, both being infringements of essentially the same complex of interests on the part of the plaintiff.[1] On the other side, however, is the competing interest of society in the efficient enforcement of the criminal law, which requires that private persons who co-operate in bringing would-be offenders to justice, no less than prosecutors,[2] should be adequately protected against the prejudice which is likely to ensue from termination of the prosecution in favour of the accused. Moreover, there exist other sanctions against misconducting informants.[3] So much weight has been attached to this consideration that the action for malicious prosecution is held on tighter rein than any other in the law of torts.[4] Incidentally, it may also explain why this action was never absorbed into the law of defamation.[5] For, though we have seen that the stringent liability of defamation is tempered by privileges when the importance of encouraging free speech outweighs the competing value of vindicating those unjustly defamed,[6] it was probably felt that this would be an insufficient safeguard for the social interests here at stake. Thus, malicious prosecution has remained a distinct cause of action which in several particulars, notably in the allocation of the burden of proof and the functions between judge and jury, affords greater protection to private persons who initiate criminal proceedings than is accorded by conditional privileges to publish defamation.

1. Exceptionally, the action will vindicate pecuniary interests alone, as in *Coleman v. Buckingham's* [1963] S.R. (N.S.W.) 171.
2. See below, n. 39.
3. Making false statements to the police and perjury are crimes, defamation is a tort.
4. Other subsidiary policies are: (1) discouraging any challenge to the integrity of the law's administration, and (2) the desirability of letting the disposal of the principal litigation settle all collateral matters: Green, *Judge and Jury* (1930) 338-339.
5. Its antecedents predate those of libel and slander. For a historical conspectus see Winfield, *History of Conspiracy* (1921) 118-130: *Holdsworth* viii, 385-391.
6. For privileges to publish defamatory matter as part of and in the course of judicial proceedings, see *Fenn v. Paul* (1932) 32 S.R. (N.S.W.) 315-316 and above, p. 559.

The elements of the cause of action for malicious prosecution are:

(1) Institution of criminal proceedings by the defendant.

(2) Termination of proceedings in favour of the plaintiff, if from their nature they were capable of so terminating.

(3) Absence of reasonable and probable cause.

(4) Malice, or a primary purpose other than that of carrying the law into effect.

Actionable proceedings

The insistent judicial concern for stringent control over actions for malicious prosecution fostered a series of limitations in the course of its long and varied history. Foremost, and earliest, was the requirement that the proceedings must have either tended to involve the accused in scandal, or exposed him to the jeopardy of imprisonment or other corporeal punishment, or actually caused pecuniary loss.[7] Though interpreted with increasing leniency in latter years,[8] this formula still imposes a severe and arbitrary brake.

Thus the first of the three qualifying grounds, scandal, was long confined solely to charges which would have been actionable as slander per se in accordance with the prevailing, and originally most rigorous, test applied to oral defamation, only to be eventually replaced by the present criterion whether the charge was "necessarily and naturally" defamatory.[9] Reminiscent of a technique once favoured to discourage actions for slander and quite the converse of the question of law involved in modern actions for defamation,[10] it requires the court to satisfy itself that no circumstances are conceivable in which a person may be prosecuted for the offence and yet escape with an unsullied reputation. Moreover, relevant alone is the scandalous tendency of the charge itself, regardless of the evidence which is or might be adduced to support it. Accordingly, failure to pay a tram fare has been held sufficient to qualify as an inescapable slur on the "fair fame" of the accused, because it carried an imputation that he was a common cheat;[11] but not so an omission to comply with a *Public Health Act* notice requiring a landlord to cleanse his rooms,[12] since it did not necessarily convey a discreditable reflection any more than riding a bicycle without a rear light, keeping a pig in an improper place, allowing a dog to wander about unmuzzled, or pulling a communication cord in a train without reasonable and sufficient cause.[13]

The second qualifying ground originally contemplated actual loss of liberty, such as arrest on mesne process, but was later relaxed to cover the

7. *Savile v. Roberts* (1698) 1 Ld Raym. 374; 91 E.R. 1147.
8. See the instructive historical account by Diplock J. in *Berry v. B.T.C.* [1961] 1 Q.B. 149.
9. *Wiffen v. Bailey & Romford U.C.* [1915] 1 K.B. 600 (C.A.).
10. See above, p. 530.
11. *Rayson v. S. London Tramways Co.* [1893] 2 Q.B. 304, as explained in *Wiffen v. Bailey & Romford U.C.* [1915] 1 K.B. 600.
12. *Wiffen v. Bailey & Romford U.C.* [1915] 1 K.B. 600.
13. *Berry v. B.T.C.* [1961] 1 Q.B. 149 (revd on another ground [1962] 1 Q.B. 306).

mere risk of it. Yet imprisonment must have been the immediate consequence of a conviction, not just a contingent risk such as follows from non-payment of a fine or debt[14]—a test which accords significantly with that for determining whether slander will lie without proof of special damage when words impute the commission of a crime.[15] In any event, the third head of damage—actual pecuniary loss—became for all practical purposes dominant when legal costs by a successful *criminal* defendant were held to qualify, even if the court trying the offence gave him an allowance towards the cost of his defence.[16]

Extending the action to wrongful *civil* proceedings has encountered anything but enthusiastic response. Admittedly, there is nothing in the history of the action[17] nor any pronouncement of binding authority to suggest that the action is confined to criminal proceedings. Yet in practice this came close to being the case in consequence of so interpreting the conventional requirements of legally recognised damage. First of all, it has been peremptorily denied that commencing civil proceedings could possibly expose the person sued to scandal, save bankruptcy[18] and winding-up petitions[19] which stand in singular need for a deterrent against the abusive practice of extorting the payment of debts by means of proceedings aimed at wrecking credit.[20] The distinction was justified on the specious ground that, whereas in bankruptcy proceedings and criminal prosecutions injury to credit is done before the accused has a chance to dispel the false imputation, in an ordinary civil action it is not the bringing of the suit that does the harm but the publicity of the proceedings, and the fair fame of a person improperly maligned is supposedly cleared in open court by a determination in his favour. In the one, it is said, the poison comes before the antidote and mischief may be wrought before it can be undone; in the other poison and the antidote are presented simultaneously.[21] Though this would not be true if the charge is only refuted on appeal, it may have been linked to 19th century procedure which minimised the chance of publicity prior to the hearing. Hence the Victorian Supreme Court, on appeal, recently found itself free to hold that this assumption no longer applied under modern conditions such as public access to pleadings and wide dissemination of publicity by the media. It accordingly held that a malicious injunction restraining a solicitor from practising could qualify as scandalous as well as causing pecuniary damage to his professional

14. *Houghton v. Oakley* (1900) 21 L.R. (N.S.W.) 26; *Wiffen v. Bailey & Romford U.C.* [1915] 1 K.B. 600.
15. See above, p. 148.
16. *Berry v. B.T.C.* [1962] 1 Q.B. 306 (C.A.). Unless a sum was awarded which, in the court's view, represented all the costs allowable on taxation, as was perhaps the case in *Barnett v. Eccles Corp.* [1900] 2 Q.B. 423 and *Wiffen v. Bailey & Romford U.C.* [1915] 1 K.B. 600.
17. Winfield, *Abuse* 199, 202.
18. *Johnson v. Emerson* (1871) L.R. 6 Ex. 329. But for reasons which will appear presently, it is doubtful whether the malicious institution of bankruptcy proceedings against a non-trader is actionable in the absence of "special" damage.
19. *Quartz Hill Gold Mining Co. v. Eyre* (1883) 11 Q.B.D. 674 (C.A.); *Q.I.W. Retailers v. Felview* [1989] 2 Qd R. 245.
20. *Quartz Hill Gold Mining Co. v. Eyre* at 693 per Bowen L.J.
21. *Wiffen v. Bailey & Romford U.C.* [1915] 1 K.B. 600 at 607, 613.

practice.[22] However, unreimbursed legal costs incurred by a successful defendant still do not qualify. For unless the civil court lacked all power to award costs, like a small debts court in some jurisdictions,[23] the pusillanimous view prevails that if the person wrongly sued was not awarded costs, he either did not ask for them, had not incurred any or did not deserve them; and if he got his costs, any difference between them and his actual expenses must be ignored because of the fanciful doctrine that the difference between party and party costs and solicitor and client costs is not recognised as legal damage.[24] Otherwise, it is said, every successful plaintiff might bring a second action against the same defendant to recover costs not awarded to him on taxation.[25] In the United States, there is no similar basis for such a pretence since attorney's fees are not usually allowed; in consequence the majority of courts entertain actions for malicious prosecution of civil proceedings.[26]

Institution of proceedings

To incur liability, the defendant must play an active role in the conduct of the proceedings, as by "instigating" or setting them in motion. This requirement brings into play some subtle distinctions. Thus, in cases of arrest, it is important to recall the difference between false imprisonment and malicious prosecution which, as already explained,[27] hinges on the intervention of independent legal authority. False imprisonment, being trespass, involves a direct interference with the plaintiff's person, whilst malicious prosecution is consistent with the defendant proceeding under colour of proper legal process. Hence, if a warrant has been obtained from a court or magistrate, there is no basis for false imprisonment, and the plaintiff must assume the heavier burden of proving malice and absence of reasonable and probable cause.

The defendant must have been "actively instrumental" in setting the law in motion.[28] Merely supplying information, however incriminating, to the police on which they eventually decide to prosecute is not the equivalent of launching a prosecution; the critical decision not being his, "the stone set rolling [is] a stone of suspicion only."[29] These days one should hesitate to credit an informant with having overcome the scepticism of a police trained to test the reliability of complaints. On the other hand, an informant may be regarded as a prosecutor if his information virtually compels the police to prosecute, even more where he deliberately deceives the police by

22. *Little v. Law Institute of Victoria* [1990] V.R. 257. See also *N.Z. Social Credit League v. O'Brien* [1984] 1 N.Z.L.R. 84 at 88-89, 98. But see *Fenn v. Paul* (1932) 32 S.R. (N.S.W.) 315 (co-respondent); *Jones v. Foreman* [1917] N.Z.L.R. 798 (bastardy); *Barker v. Sands* (1890) 16 V.L.R. 719 and *Cross v. Commercial Agency* (1899) 18 N.Z.L.R. 153 (debt).
23. *Coleman v. Buckingham's* [1963] S.R. (N.S.W.) 171 (F.C.).
24. *Quartz Hill Gold Mining Co. v. Eyre* (1883) 11 Q.B.D. 674; *Houghton v. Oakley* (1900) 21 L.R. (N.S.W.) 26.
25. *Berry v. B.T.C.* [1962] 1 Q.B. 306 at 322-323.
26. *Prosser & Keeton* §120: *Rest.* ch. 30, and comment at 462.
27. See above, p. 30.
28. *Danby v. Beardsley* (1880) 43 L.T. 603 per Lopes J.
29. *Danby v. Beardsley* (1880) 43 L.T. 603 per Lindley J.; *Maine v. Townsend* (1883) 4 L.R. (N.S.W.) 1.

supplying false information without which they would not have proceeded.[30]

It used to be thought that the requisite stage of prosecution would not have been reached unless the magistrate actually issued a summons or warrant for arrest, or the grand jury returned a true bill.[31] Modern decisions have preferred the more liberal test whether the proceedings have reached a point prejudicial to the reputation of the plaintiff, deeming it sufficient that the magistrate inquired into the merits in open court though eventually dismissing the complaint,[32] or even that the prosecutor himself withdrew the charge but not before the magistrate had taken it under actual advisement.[33] For much the same reason, it is no answer that the court in issuing a warrant acted without jurisdiction, because the injury to reputation is not effaced by the consoling assurance that, technically, there was no prosecution at all.[33a]

A defendant may be liable not only for initiating, but also for adopting or continuing proceedings. Thus a prosecution, commenced under a bona fide belief in the guilt of the accused, may become actionable, if at a later stage the prosecutor acquires positive knowledge of his innocence, yet perseveres bent on procuring a conviction.[34] But no civil action whatever lies for bearing false witness, as distinct from maliciously maintaining proceedings: the advancement of public justice is thought to be best served by not fettering testimony, aside from the criminal sanction for perjury.[35] On the other hand, liability may devolve on someone who is not, strictly, a party to the proceedings at all, like a solicitor who on behalf of his client applies for a bench warrant to arrest an absent witness[36] or a person who supplies counsel to conduct the prosecution in the name of the Crown and undertakes to meet all legal costs.[37]

Differing views obtain on the liability of *public* prosecutors. Only absolute immunity, it is claimed, will secure prosecutorial independence and stem unmeritorious claims.[38] To others, the existing stringent safeguards (absence of reasonable and probable cause, and malice) seem sufficient to control misuse and to draw a salient distinction between abuse of governmental power (for which the public deserves redress) and mere errors of judgment or discretion.[39]

30. *Commercial Union Assurance v. Lamont* [1989] 3 N.Z.L.R. 187 (C.A.); Kodilinye, *Setting in Motion Malicious Prosecutions: The Commonwealth Experience*, 36 Int. & Comp. L.Q. 157 (1987).
31. *Gregory v. Derby* (1839) 8 C. & P. 749 at 750; 173 E.R. 701 at 702; and see *Rest.* §653, comment *a*; §654, comment *b*.
32. *Mohamed v. Bannerjee* [1947] A.C. 322 (P.C.). Semble, aliter if he dismissed for want of jurisdiction: at 331.
33. *Casey v. Automobiles Renault* [1965] S.C.R. 607.
33a. *Arnold v. Johnson* (1876) 14 S.C.R. (N.S.W.) 429; *Prosser & Keeton* 871.
34. *Fitzjohn v. Mackinder* (1861) 9 C.B. (N.S.) 505 at 531; 142 E.R. 199 at 208; *Coleman v. Buckingham's* [1963] S.R. (N.S.W.) 171 (F.C.).
35. *Cabassi v. Vila* (1940) 64 C.L.R. 130; *Hargreaves v. Bretherton* [1959] 1 Q.B. 45; *Marrinan v. Vibart* [1963] 1 Q.B. 528; *Evans v. London Hospital* [1981] 1 W.L.R. 184. *Wrongs Act* (S.A.) s. 36 in 1983 enacted civil liability for perjury.
36. *Dunshea v. Ryan* (1901) 1 S.R. (N.S.W.) 163; *Johnson v. Emerson* (1871) L.R. 6 Ex. 329.
37. *Commonwealth Life Assurance v. Brain* (1935) 53 C.L.R. 343.
38. *Love v. Robbins* (1990) 2 W.A.R. 510 (F.C.); *Imbler v. Pachtman* 424 U.S. 409 (1976).
39. *Nelles v. Ontario* [1989] 2 S.C.R. 170; *Riches v. D.P.P.* [1973] 1 W.L.R. 1019 at 1026.

Favourable termination

It is for the plaintiff to establish that the prosecution against him ended in his favour. Several reasons have been advanced for this requirement.[40] One is that if the proceedings terminated adversely to him, a reopening of the issue of his guilt would permit a collateral attack on the conviction and countenance the previous judgment "blowed off by a side-wind".[41] Another is that a conviction of the accused is sufficient to show that there was reasonable and probable cause for the prosecution.[42] It has also been suggested that the plaintiff's innocence is a fundamental element of his cause of action and that the termination of proceedings is evidence of that innocence or guilt.[43] Whichever of these explanations be the most convincing,[44] it is a settled rule that conviction is a peremptory bar, even if the plaintiff could show that he is innocent and that the conviction was procured through chicanery.[45] This applies alike to a determination by a magistrate that the offence was proven, though followed by a dismissal of the information under the first offender's rule, since the proceedings clearly terminated unfavourably to the accused.[46] It is, moreover, immaterial that the adverse judgment cannot be attacked by way of appeal, like an order requiring a person to enter into a recognisance to be of good behaviour.[47]

On the other hand, if the proceedings terminated in favour of the plaintiff, it matters naught how this came about. The crux is not so much whether he has been proved innocent as that he has not been convicted. This, of course, accords with the presumption of his innocence until found guilty according to law. Thus he is not required to show an acquittal on the merits; it may as well have been based on some defect in the indictment[48] or on his conviction being quashed on appeal for some irregularity of procedure.[49] It is not even necessary that the proceedings had advanced to a stage where a further prosecution was precluded on the ground of double jeopardy,[50] so long—it would seem—as they have terminated in such a manner that they cannot be revived without starting afresh. This explains why it has been held to be enough that a magistrate refused to commit the accused for trial,[51] a grand jury declined to find a true bill,[52] or (its

40. It was not settled until 1713: Winfield, *Abuse* 181-183.
41. *Vanderbergh v. Blake* (1661) Hardr. 194; 145 E.R. 447 per Hale C.J.
42. *Mellor v. Baddeley* (1834) 2 C. & M. 675; 149 E.R. 932.
43. *Davis v. Gell* (1924) 35 C.L.R. 275; contra: *Commonwealth Life Assurance v. Smith* (1938) 59 C.L.R. 527.
44. Note the caution that these reasons "do not affect the nature and application of the rule itself and . . . are not principles having any independent and further operation in imposing some additional condition as a necessary element to the cause of action" (*Commonwealth Life Assurance v. Smith* (1938) 59 C.L.R. 527).
45. *Basébé v. Matthews* (1867) L.R. 2 C.P. 684; *Bouvy v. Count de Courte* (1901) 20 N.Z.L.R. 312. Cf. *Stimac v. Nicol* [1942] V.L.R. 66; *Kennedy v. Tomlinson* (1959) 20 D.L.R. (2d) 273 (false imprisonment).
46. *Cameron v. James* [1945] V.L.R. 113.
47. *Everett v. Ribbands* [1952] 2 Q.B. 198.
48. *Wicks v. Fentham* (1791) 4 T.R. 247; 100 E.R. 1000. Even acquittal on only one part of the indictment is enough: *Boaler v. Holder* (1887) 3 T.L.R. 546.
49. *Herniman v. Smith* [1938] A.C. 305.
50. *Commonwealth Life Assurance v. Smith* (1938) 59 C.L.R. 527 at 538.
51. *Balbhaddar Singh v. Badri Sah* (P.C. No. 66 of 1924), discussed in (1938) 59 C.L.R. at 535-536.
52. *Barnes v. Constantine* (1605) Yelv. 46; 80 E.R. 33; *Morgan v. Hughes* (1788) 2 T.R. 225 at 232; 100 E.R. 123.

counterpart in New South Wales) the Attorney-General refused to file an indictment.[53] Even the mere discontinuance of a prosecution[54] or the entry of a nolle prosequi after an indictment had once been filed may now, despite some earlier doubts, be regarded as in every way sufficient.[55] In none of these cases is it permissible for either party to reopen the question of innocence or guilt: it is neither incumbent on the plaintiff to establish his innocence, nor may the defendant set out to prove that the accused was in fact guilty of the crime charged against him.[56]

A split of opinion, however, persists concerning the effect of a compromise.[57] On the one hand, it is argued that all that is required is a termination of proceedings which falls short of establishing the guilt of the accused.[58] But there is also much cogency in the contrary view that, having voluntarily consented to an inconclusive termination, it does not lie in his mouth to assert that the proceedings have ended in his favour—and this is what he must show, no more and no less, in accordance with the conventional formula.[59]

One important relaxation of the requirement has been allowed. For although it applies to all proceedings, whether criminal or otherwise,[60] which involve a judicial determination inter partes, it is dispensed with where it is impossible that the proceedings could have terminated in the plaintiff's favour, since otherwise the aggrieved party would be altogether precluded from redress.[61] Hence the concluding words of the formula, requiring proof of favourable termination, *if the proceedings were capable of so terminating.* This applies in particular to various forms of legal process which may issue ex parte such as search warrants,[62] writs of capias to arrest defendants suspected of intention to abscond,[63] and writs of execution.[64]

53. *Commonwealth Life Assurance v. Smith* (1938) 59 C.L.R. 527.
54. *Watkins v. Lee* (1839) 5 M. & W. 270; 151 E.R. 115; *Machattie v. Lee* (1861) 10 L.R. (N.S.W.) (L.) 182; *Johns v. Hansen* (1900) 19 N.Z.L.R. 319; *Romegialli v. Marceau* (1963) 42 D.L.R. (2d) 481.
55. *Mann v. Jacombe* (1960) 78 W.N. (N.S.W.) 635. The majority decision in *Davis v. Gell* (1924) 35 C.L.R. 275 that a nolle prosequi, whilst not an absolute bar, required the plaintiff to prove his innocence, may be safely discounted in the light of *Commonwealth Life Assurance v. Smith* (1938) 59 C.L.R. 527 which rejected this compromise for the analogous case of an A.-G.'s refusal to file an indictment. See Donovan, 12 A.L.J. 457 (1939).
56. But though a defendant cannot controvert the favourable termination of the criminal proceedings as a separate issue, he may perhaps do so in order to disprove the plaintiff's contention that the prior proceedings lacked reasonable and probable cause: see *Earnshaw v. Loy (No. 1)* [1959] V.R. 248. In the U.S., the plaintiff's guilt is a bar to recovery, analogous to the defence of truth in defamation, and it is always open to the defendant to establish such guilt by a mere preponderance of evidence as distinguished from the heavier burden of proof beyond reasonable doubt required in criminal proceedings: *Rest. 2d* §657.
57. This problem cannot arise in connection with criminal prosecutions in the strict sense, and for this reason there is little authority on it.
58. *Craig v. Hasell* (1843) 4 Q.B. 481; 114 E.R. 980.
59. *Baxter v. Gordon Ironsides* (1907) 13 O.L.R. 598; *Rest.* §660, comment *c*.
60. E.g. bankruptcy: *Metropolitan Bank v. Pooley* (1885) 10 App. Cas. 210.
61. *Varawa v. Howard Smith* (1911) 13 C.L.R. 35 at 52.
62. *Wyatt v. White* (1860) 5 H. & N. 371; 157 E.R. 1226; *Fitzalan v. Nicholson* (1896) 13 W.N. (N.S.W.) 51.
63. *Delancey v. Dale* (1959) 20 D.L.R. (2d) 12; *Varawa v. Howard Smith* (1911) 13 C.L.R. 35 at 47-53 per Griffith C.J.; contra, at 90 per Isaacs J.
64. *Smith v. Cotton* (1926) 27 S.R. (N.S.W.) 41; *Gilding v. Eyre* (1861) 10 C.B. (N.S.) 592; 142 E.R. 584.

Reasonable cause

Malicious prosecution postulates two fault requirements: the proceedings complained of must have been instituted without reasonable and probable cause *and* for an improper purpose. Both must be satisfied because the prosecution of persons reasonably and honestly suspected of crime is considered of greater social importance than disapproval of unworthy motives.

Reasonable and probable[65] cause has been defined as "an honest belief in the guilt of the accused based upon a full conviction, founded on reasonable grounds, of the existence of a state of circumstances which, assuming them to be true, would reasonably lead any ordinary prudent and cautious man, placed in the position of the accuser, to the conclusion that the person charged was probably guilty of the crime imputed."[66] This formula bears some resemblance to that of reasonable care in negligence, but differs from it in two important respects. For not only, as we shall presently see, is this question entrusted to the judge instead of the jury, but it contains both an objective and a subjective element. It is not enough that a discreet and reasonable person would have believed in the guilt of the accused, unless the defendant himself honestly shared it. There must be both actual and reasonable belief.[67]

At first blush, it may seem odd that the prosecutor's belief should be material so long as malice, standing alone, is not deemed sufficiently reprehensible to forfeit his protection. But even if the law in its erstwhile anxiety to encourage the initiative of private prosecutors had to compromise its ideals by recognising that their motives would often be tarnished, it was not—at least on second thoughts—prepared to go to the "monstrous"[68] length of condoning a combination of improper motive *and* dishonesty. In any event, unshakable certainty in the guilt of the accused is not demanded, since a fair minded person may well feel justified in bringing a suspect to justice without, in his own mind, prejudging the issue. It is sufficient, if he believes that the probability of guilt is such that upon general grounds of justice a charge is warranted.[69] In other words, he may have probable cause for initiating a prosecution, although lacking a conviction of guilt beyond reasonable doubt such as a jury must entertain to justify a verdict of guilty.[70]

The prosecutor's belief must be based on facts known to him at the time when he initiated the proceedings, not on evidence coming to light thereafter.[71] A prosecution instituted without it cannot be retrospectively

65. There is no distinction between these adjectives, their conjunction being a heritage from old-pleading redundancies: Winfield, *Abuse* 192.
66. *Hicks v. Faulkner* (1878) 8 Q.B.D. 167 at 171 per Hawkins J.
67. *Haddrick v. Heslop* (1848) 12 Q.B. 267; 116 E.R. 869; *Commonwealth Life Assurance v. Brain* (1935) 53 C.L.R. 343.
68. *Broad v. Ham* (1839) 5 Bing. N.C. 722 at 727; 132 E.R. 1278 at 1280 per Erskine J.
69. *Sharp v. Biggs* (1932) 48 C.L.R. 81 at 106; also *Glinski v. McIver* [1962] A.C. 726 at 758, 767; *Abbott v. Refuge Assurance Co.* [1962] 1 Q.B. 432 at 454, 462; *Tempest v. Snowden* [1952] 1 K.B. 130 at 140.
70. *Rest. 2d* §662, comment *c*.
71. *Delegal v. Highley* (1837) 3 Bing. N.C. 950; 132 E.R. 732; *Turner v. Ambler* (1847) 10 Q.B. 252; 116 E.R. 98.

justified, except by guilt in fact as evidenced by conviction. For the same reason, one who continues a prosecution after gaining knowledge that it is groundless may lose his protection, unless he at least makes a disclosure to the court of the facts he has discovered.[72]

However honest the defendant's subjective belief in the guilt of the accused, it must be based on evidence that persons of reasonably sound judgment would regard as sufficient for launching a prosecution. Only limited guidance can be furnished on this score, since we lack precise and universal criteria by which to measure the degree of caution and prudence that a reasonable person should observe in the evaluation of infinitely variable incriminating data.[73] This much however is clear, that he should take reasonable steps to inform himself of the true state of the case instead of acting upon mere imagination and surmise,[74] consider the matter in the light of such evidence alone as he reasonably believes to be sufficient to sustain a conviction,[75] and, in all but the plainest cases, lay the facts fully and fairly before counsel of standing and receive his advice that a prosecution is justified.[76] He need not, however, go to the length of verifying seemingly reliable information or invariably ask the accused himself for an explanation, because this might lead to the fabrication or disappearance of evidence.[77] Advice of counsel provides a valuable, but not always impenetrable, shield.[78] For one thing, in difficult and complex cases it might be prudent to seek more than one legal opinion; for another, all facts must have been fairly and squarely placed before him, including such information as that the police declined to prosecute or that other advisers counselled against proceeding with the matter.[79]

It is sometimes suggested that a mistake of law can never be considered evidence of absence of reasonable cause,[80] but this is too sweeping. Undoubtedly, an action is not maintainable where the prosecution failed on account of some highly technical or doubtful legal point,[81] but ultimately the question must always be whether the defendant had reasonable grounds for believing the plaintiff guilty, and this requires some consideration on the part of the accuser of the legal elements of the crime, including obvious

72. *Tims v. John Lewis* [1951] 2 K.B. 459 at 472-474 (revd on other grounds: [1952] A.C. 676); *Rest. 2d* §662, comment *f*.
73. Although for the judge, it is nevertheless an issue of fact, and therefore precedents are rarely controlling: *Herniman v. Smith* [1938] A.C. 305 at 317.
74. *Mitchell v. John Heine* (1938) 38 S.R. (N.S.W.) 466 at 469.
75. *Meering v. Grahame White Aviation Co.* (1919) 122 L.T. 44 at 56.
76. *Abbott v. Refuge Assurance Co.* [1962] 1 Q.B. 432 at 454.
77. *Herniman v. Smith* [1938] A.C. 305 at 319. But if the accused gives a reasonable explanation, an inquiry into its truth should ordinarily precede further action: *Jenner v. Harbison* (1879) 5 V.L.R. (L.) 111.
78. *Glinski v. McIver* [1962] A.C. 726 at 745, 759.
79. *Abbott v. Refuge Assurance Co.* [1962] 1 Q.B. 432. The defence failed in *Mackenzie v. Hyam* (1908) 8 S.R. (N.S.W.) 587 and *Hewlett v. Crutchley* (1813) 5 Taunt. 277; 128 E.R. 696 because the advice was plainly incompetent; in *Assheton v. Merrett* [1928] S.A.S.R. 11 because it was not even professional (policemen); and in *Stevenson v. Banbury* (1878) 12 S.A.L.R. 43 because the defendant had withheld information and failed to make adequate preliminary inquiries as to the facts.
80. *Johnson v. Emerson* (1871) L.R. 6 Ex. 329 at 365.
81. *Barry v. Tully* (1888) 9 L.R. (N.S.W.) 476; *Bardwell v. Galvin* (1867) 6 S.C.R. (N.S.W.) 91; *Phillips v. Naylor* (1859) 4 H. & N. 565; 157 E.R. 962.

defences open to the accused.[82] Moreover, just as an acquittal is insufficient proof of absence of reasonable cause,[83] so the fact that the accused was convicted at first instance and only acquitted on appeal does not conclusively establish its presence, because the original conviction might have been procured by improper means or on evidence of which the defendant was not aware when laying the charge.[84]

In general, the defendant must have had reasonable cause for the whole of the prosecution, not merely part of it. Hence, where an indictment contained several assignments of perjury or theft, proof that some of them lacked reasonable cause warrants a verdict for the plaintiff.[85] There is much to be said, however, for the suggestion that ultimately the question is one of degree.[86] If on a charge of theft of $10 reasonable cause is shown as regards $9, it may well be that the prosecutor is entitled to succeed, since he was in substance justified in making the charge,[87] whereas the contrary must apply if it were $1.

The jealousy with which the law views the action for malicious prosecution is most clearly revealed by the hedging devices with which it has been surrounded in order to protect private citizens who discharge their public duty of prosecuting those reasonably suspected of crime. Chief among these fetters is the allocation of the burden of proof and the division of functions between judge and jury, on the issue of reasonable and probable cause.

Burden of proof

Perhaps the most serious impediment was to place the burden of proving absence of reasonable and probable cause on the plaintiff, since his is thereby the notoriously difficult task of establishing a negative.[88] Moreover, he has been held to a very high standard of proof to avoid a non-suit or directed verdict.[89]

Thus in order to establish the prosecutor's disbelief in his guilt, the plaintiff must give evidence from which an inference may be drawn as to what the defendant's belief actually was. It is not enough merely to adduce reasons for non-belief, without showing that they were in fact operative.[90] The requisite evidence may be supplied, for example, by proving that the defendant had before him facts pointing so overwhelmingly to the plaintiff's innocence that no reasonable person could have believed in his guilt, but it is not sufficient merely that he had information, some of which pointed to guilt and some to innocence.

82. *Crowley v. Glissan (No. 2)* (1905) 2 C.L.R. 744. Also the accused must at least have been charged with a crime known to law: *Mackenzie v. Hyam* (1908) 8 S.R. (N.S.W.) 587.
83. *Rest. 2d* §667(2).
84. See *Herniman v. Smith* [1938] A.C. 305; but note the more cautious view of *Rest. 2d* §667(1).
85. *Leibo v. Buckman* [1952] 2 All E.R. 1057; *Dent v. Standard Life Assurance* (1904) 4 S.R. (N.S.W.) 560; *Birchmeier v. Rockdale* (1934) 51 W.N. (N.S.W.) 201.
86. *Leibo v. Buckman* [1952] 2 All E.R. 1057 at 1071.
87. Cf. *Sutton v. Johnstone* (1785-6) 1 T.R. 493 at 510; 99 E.R. 1215.
88. *Abrath v. N. E. Rly* (1883) 11 Q.B.D. 440; (1886) 11 App. Cas. 247; *Cox v. English, Scottish & Australian Bank* [1905] A.C. 168.
89. An excellent statement on the burden of proof is found in the judgment by Jordan C.J. in *Mitchell v. John Heine* (1938) 38 S.R. (N.S.W.) 466 at 469-471.
90. *Crowley v. Glissan (No. 2)* (1905) 2 C.L.R. 744; *Trebeck v. Croudace* [1918] 1 K.B. 158.

Judge and jury

The second impediment is the anomalous[91] rule that the existence of reasonable and probable cause is for the judge and not the jury.[92] Experience over many centuries has taught the lesson that in this action juries must be kept on a tight rein,[93] and as early as 1599 it was regarded as unsafe to send the general issue to the "lay gents",[94] who are too easily swayed by the feeling that, merely because an innocent man has been subjected to prosecution, he deserves recompense.[95] Not that the jury is entirely excluded from participation, because they will have to decide all preliminary questions of fact on which the existence of reasonable cause depends. Yet it is at this point that most of the difficulties in malicious prosecution cases arise, because of the very substantial danger that unless strictly controlled, the submission of questions to the jury becomes a loophole through which the issue of reasonable cause slips out of the hands of the judge to whom it has been confided as a guardian of vital public policies.

If there are any disputed facts sufficiently relevant to make it necessary that they be ascertained in order to enable the judge to pass on the ultimate question of reasonable cause, any necessary questions should be put to the jury. Thus, they may be asked: "What were the facts on which the prosecutor acted?", "Did he lack available information pointing to his innocence?" On the other hand, questions like whether the defendant took reasonable care to inform himself of the true state of facts, or whether the accuser's belief in the existence of facts on which he acted was reasonable, or whether the facts so believed amount to reasonable cause for believing the accused to be guilty, are for the judge alone.[96]

The greatest caution is required where the honesty of the accuser's belief is being challenged. We have seen that absence of genuine belief in the guilt of the accused conclusively establishes want also of reasonable cause; unfortunately, a further source of complication was added by allocating this issue to the jury, undoubtedly because of its deceptive resemblance to the question of malice. Trial and appellate courts have been constantly vexed by this requirement, because experience has taught that a jury inflamed by its own finding of malice will all too readily proceed to a finding also of want of honest belief. To obviate this danger and its concomitant threat to the court's control over the issue of reasonable cause, it has become settled that the jury should not be consulted at all in the absence of genuinely contested evidence as to the defendant's belief, such

91. Recall that the analogous issue of "reasonable conduct" in negligence is pre-eminently a jury issue.
92. *Panton v. Williams* (1841) 2 Q.B. 169; *Lister v. Perryman* (1870) L.R. 4 H.L. 521.
93. *Leibo v. Buckman* [1952] 2 All E.R. 1057 at 1062. Note, however, the paradoxical importance attached to jury participation in actions for malicious prosecution, e.g. in England among the few actions in which the plaintiff may demand a jury as of right: *Administration of Justice (Miscellaneous Provisions) Act* 1933 s. 6.
94. *Pain v. Rochester & Whitfield* (1602) Cro. Eliz. 871; 78 E.R. 1096.
95. *Leibo v. Buckman* [1952] 2 All E.R. 1057 at 1062-3.
96. *Herniman v. Smith* [1938] A.C. 305 at 316-317; *Mitchell v. J. Heine* (1938) 38 S.R. (N.S.W.) 466 at 470-471.

as statements revealing doubt or disbelief[97] or compromising conduct like the concealment of material evidence, as distinct from anything that could merely be inferred from the strength or weakness of his case for prosecuting.[98] Moreover, the question for the jury should be precisely formulated and contain no reference whatever to reasonable cause. It should be either: "Did the defendant honestly believe in the plaintiff's guilt?" or "Did he honestly believe in the charges he was preferring?" The rolled-up question "Did he honestly believe that there were reasonable grounds for the prosecution?" is an improper invitation to the jury to pass on the whole issue of reasonable cause.[99]

As regards the general course of conducting a trial, the court has in effect two alternatives open to it.[100] The choice, though within its unfettered discretion, has an important bearing on the allocation of functions between judge and jury, and herewith on the outcome of litigation. The judge may leave the jury to find a general verdict, having instructed them on what constitutes reasonable cause and to apply their findings on disputed facts accordingly. Alternatively, he may ask the jury specific questions, reserving to himself the power of entering judgment upon their findings. The second course is much preferable, because it ensures greater judicial control and denies the jury an opportunity to disregard instructions and find an unwarranted verdict for the plaintiff which may be difficult to impeach thereafter.

Malice

No prosecution, however devoid of reasonable cause, exposes the accuser to liability, unless he was also animated by malice.[101] For, many an honest prosecutor might be deterred from doing his public duty by fear of risking liability, if it were sufficient merely to question the soundness of his judgment. On the other hand, no policy could justify shielding a person who instigates groundless proceedings, lacking both reasonable cause *and* proper motive.[102]

"Malice" has proved a slippery word in the law of torts, and should long have been replaced, in this context just as in defamation, by "improper purpose". At the root of it is the notion that the only proper purpose for the institution of criminal proceedings is to bring an offender to justice and thereby aid in the enforcement of the law, and that a prosecutor who is primarily animated by a different aim steps outside the pale, if the proceedings also happen to be destitute of reasonable cause. "Malice" has, therefore, a wider meaning than spite, ill-will or a spirit of vengeance, and includes any other improper purpose, such as to gain a private collateral advantage. Indignation or anger aroused by the imagined crime is, of

97. *Haddrick v. Heslop* (1848) 12 Q.B. 267; 116 E.R. 869.
98. *Glinski v. McIver* [1962] A.C. 726; *Dallison v. Caffery* [1965] 1 Q.B. 348.
99. *Tempest v. Snowden* [1952] 1 K.B. 130.
100. *Abrath v. N. E. Rly* (1883) 11 Q.B.D. 440 at 458-459; *Brain v. Commonwealth Life Assurance* (1934) 35 S.R. (N.S.W.) 36 at 42; *Earnshaw v. Loy (No. 1)* [1959] V.R. 248. See also Green, *Judge and Jury* (1930) 341-347.
101. This also negatives any duty of care: *Business Computers v. Company Registrar* [1988] Ch. 229 (winding-up petition misaddressed).
102. See *Brown v. Hawkes* [1891] 2 Q.B. 718 at 723.

course, not sufficient because, far from being a wrong or devious motive, it is one on which the law relies to secure the prosecution of offenders.[103] Nor is it reprehensible that the prosecution was launched in order to pave the way to a civil action[104] in conformity with the requirement that a felon must first be prosecuted.[105] On the other hand, the paramount purpose of securing the ends of justice is incompatible with lack of honest belief in the guilt of the accused, which is thus at once conclusive of the improper purpose of the proceedings and want of reasonable cause. Other examples of an improper purpose are prosecutions instigated with a view to extorting money, closing the plaintiff's mouth in another legal proceeding[106] or punishing him for having given evidence against the police on a previous occasion,[107] blocking a meeting of shareholders,[108] and recovering a debt or property in situations where recourse should properly be had to civil instead of criminal process.[109] In one borderline case,[110] a son procured the arrest of his mentally disordered mother on a charge of being a person deemed to be insane wandering at large. Although he lacked reasonable cause, since he knew this was untrue, he was held entitled to a verdict, as he honestly believed that the course he took was for the protection of his mother and her property rather than motivated by a desire to gain some indirect personal advantage.

The burden of proving malice lies on the plaintiff, and may be discharged by showing either what the motive was and that it was improper, or that the circumstances were such that the prosecution can only be accounted for by imputing some wrong and indirect motive to the prosecutor.[111] Occasionally it has been somewhat loosely said that absence of reasonable cause is evidence of malice, but that malice is never evidence of want of reasonable cause. Neither proposition is universally correct. Proof of a particular fact may supply evidence on both counts, such as lack of honest belief in the guilt of the accused or evidence that the prosecution was set on foot in the complete absence of, or upon ludicrously and obviously insufficient, information. On the other hand, evidence that the prosecutor was animated primarily by a desire to injure the plaintiff would not furnish even a prima facie case of absence of reasonable cause; and conversely evidence that the defendant had too hastily formed a belief in the guilt of the plaintiff on unreasonably insufficient grounds, does not ordinarily suffice to warrant an inference of malice.[112]

The question of malice falls to the jury,[113] unlike that of reasonable cause which, as we have seen, is retained by the court. To this there are two

103. *Brown v. Hawkes* [1891] 2 Q.B. 718 at 722.
104. *Abbott v. Refuge Assurance Co.* [1962] 1 Q.B. 432.
105. See above, p. 35.
106. *Haddrick v. Heslop* (1848) 12 Q.B. 267; 116 E.R. 869.
107. *Glinski v. McIver* [1962] A.C. 726.
108. *Commonwealth Life Assurance v. Brain* (1935) 53 C.L.R. 343 at 387.
109. *Rest. 2d* §668, comment *g*. Cf. *Assheton v. Merrett* [1928] S.A.S.R. 11 at 15.
110. *Rapley v. Rapley* (1930) 30 S.R. (N.S.W.) 94; folld in *Williams v. Webb* (1961) 27 D.L.R. (2d) 465.
111. *Brown v. Hawkes* [1891] 2 Q.B. 718 at 722. See the observations on this statement in *Trobridge v. Hardy* (1955) 94 C.L.R. 147 at 163-165, 174.
112. *Mitchell v. J. Heine* (1938) 38 S.R. (N.S.W.) 466 at 474.
113. *Mitchell v. Jenkins* (1833) 5 B. & Ad. 588; 110 E.R. 908; *Longden v. Weigall* (1877) 3 V.L.R. (L.) 266.

qualifications. First, the question whether any particular purpose is improper is a matter of law, because the appropriate criterion is what the law disapproves, not what may be displeasing to the jury.[114] Secondly, unless there is sufficient evidence to establish a prima facie case, the court will non-suit the plaintiff and thus prevent him from getting to the jury at all.[115]

Damages

We have seen that a claim for malicious prosecution must be founded on actual injury.[116] This must consist either in injury to reputation, presumed wherever the plaintiff was accused of a crime involving scandalous reflection on his fair name; or injury to the person, as when he was imprisoned or put in jeopardy of it; or damage to his pecuniary interests, such as being put to expense in defending himself against the charge. But once this stringent requirement is satisfied, damages are at large, just as in defamation,[117] and may take account of injury to the plaintiff's repute and credit as well as any mental distress inseparable from a serious criminal accusation, incidental arrest or detention. Indeed, once the plaintiff has successfully negotiated the difficult hurdles set by law in this action, juries are not discouraged from responding with a liberal verdict, since the assessment of damages provides a good opportunity for registering the condemnation, shared by judges and laymen alike, of flagrant abuses of legal process.[118]

In addition, the plaintiff may recover for any "special" damage proximately caused, like the legal costs incurred in repelling the charge levelled against him—a significant item, in view of the fact that, under our criminal procedure, the cost even of a successful defence must be borne largely, if not completely, by the accused—unless he can indemnify himself in a successful claim for malicious prosecution.

2. ABUSE OF PROCESS

Apart from malicious prosecution, there are certain other abuses of legal procedure, like malicious arrest on mesne process[119] and malicious execution[120] which resemble the parent action too much to warrant separate treatment. Quite distinct, however, are cases where a legal process, not itself devoid of foundation, has been perverted for some extraneous purpose, such as extortion or oppression. Here an action will lie at the suit

114. *Salmond & Heuston* 395.
115. E.g. *Reed v. Hales* (1872) 11 S.C.R. (N.S.W.) 317.
116. See above, p. 610.
117. Whether this applies also to claims based solely on pecuniary loss is unclear: *Coleman v. Buckingham's* [1963] S.R. (N.S.W.) 171 at 182.
118. Green, *Judge and Jury* (1930) 349.
119. E.g. *Roy v. Prior* [1971] A.C. 470; *Varawa v. Howard Smith* (1911) 13 C.L.R. 35; *Delancey v. Dale* (1959) 20 D.L.R. (2d) 12.
120. See *Clissold v. Cratchley* [1910] 2 K.B. 244.

of the injured party for what has come to be called "abuse of process"—probably the clearest illustration in our law of what civilians call an "abuse of right".[121]

In the leading case which established this tort,[122] the mortgagee of a vessel procured the issue of a writ of capias to arrest the owner pursuant to an action for recovery of the money lent. The sole purpose of the execution of the writ however was to obtain the ship's register, which was outside the scope of the capias. Yielding to the duress, the plaintiff gave up the register and was thereby prevented from making several profitable voyages. He was allowed to recover for this loss, without proof that the proceedings were destitute of reasonable and probable cause or had terminated in his favour.

Unlike malicious prosecution, the gist of this tort lies not in the wrongful procurement of legal process[123] or the wrongful launching of criminal proceedings, but in the misuse of process, no matter how properly obtained, for any purpose other than that which it was designed to serve.[124] It involves the notion that the proceedings were "merely a stalking-horse to coerce the defendant in some way entirely outside the ambit of the legal claim upon which the court is asked to adjudicate."[125] It is therefore immaterial whether the suit thus commenced was founded on reasonable cause or even terminated in favour of the instigator: the improper purpose is the gravamen of liability.

In addition to the improper purpose, there must be some overt act or threat, distinct from the proceedings themselves, in furtherance of that purpose, such as in the abovementioned case the extortion accompanying the capias. Were it otherwise, any legal process could be challenged on account of its "hidden agenda".[126] Thus, again in the seminal case, the fact that the mortgagee's underlying action falsely alleged that the debt was due would not have been sufficient. It is not a tort merely to present a dishonest claim or defence, because such would not have a purpose other than that for which it was designed, that is for promoting, however dishonestly, one's cause before the court.[127] Even proceedings constituting a contempt of court do not arm the plaintiff with a cause of action in tort.[128]

Of course, not every collateral advantage sought by a litigant becomes improper merely because it is beyond the court's power to grant it. Actions

121. See above, p. 423.
122. *Grainger v. Hill* (1838) 4 Bing. N.C. 212; 132 E.R. 769; explained by Priestley J.A. in *Spautz v. Gibbs* (1990) 21 N.S.W.L.R. 230 at 270-280.
123. Thus it is no surrogate for an action for malicious institution of a civil action: see *Metall & Rohstoff v. Donaldson* [1990] 1 Q.B. 391 at 570-572.
124. *Rest.* §682; *Prosser & Keeton* §121.
125. *Varawa v. Howard Smith* (1911) 13 C.L.R. 35 at 91 per Isaacs J.
126. *Hanrahan v. Ainsworth* (1990) 22 N.S.W.L.R. 73 at 107-123 per Clarke J.A.; *Cholkan v. Brinker* (1990) 1 C.C.L.T. (2d) 291; Irvine, 47 C.C.L.T. 217. This seems sometimes to have been overlooked: e.g. *Speed Seal v. Paddington* [1985] 1 W.L.R. 1327; *Q.I.W. v. Felview* [1989] 2 Qd R. 245. Nor does an improper or collateral purpose by itself justify dismissal of the action as an abuse of process: *Rajski v. Bainton* (1990) 22 N.S.W.L.R. 125 (C.A.); *Goldsmith v. Sperrings* [1977] 1 W.L.R. 478 (C.A.).
127. *Metall & Rohstoff v. Donaldson* [1990] 1 Q.B. 391 (C.A.).
128. *Chapman v. Honig* [1963] 2 Q.B. 502 (C.A.).

are commonly settled on terms that a court could not impose, for example an apology for libel, specific performance of certain contracts. In order to be improper the ulterior advantage must be one not reasonably related to the subject matter of the litigation and but for which the defendant would not have commenced the proceedings.

The specific limitations on damages in actions for malicious prosecution most probably do not apply to abusive process, in particular the refusal to recognise that an ordinary civil action can touch the "fame" of the plaintiff. On the other hand, "extra" legal costs (beyond those taxed) are not allowed here any more than there because of the general policy against double adjudication.[129]

3. MAINTENANCE AND CHAMPERTY

The promotion or support of contentious legal proceedings by a stranger who has no direct concern in them, is a wrong actionable at the suit of the other party, in the absence of justifying circumstances. This tort, known as maintenance, stems from a time when officious interference in litigation was a widespread evil, practised by powerful royal officials and nobles to oppress their vulnerable neighbours.[130] But after the Tudors had crushed the baronage and purged the judiciary, the prevalence of maintenance as an "engine of oppression"[131] rapidly diminished, and later cases reveal it rather as a deplorable mode of paying off a score against an adversary.[132] Its survival in modern law, though in greatly attenuated form, must be attributed to a persisting, if perhaps exaggerated, fear that it is still needed as a safeguard against blackmail and speculation in lawsuits prone to increase litigation. This policy against maintenance is, on the whole, amply safeguarded by the availability of penal sanctions[133] and by the continued refusal to recognise assignment of causes of action in tort.[134] Accordingly, the modern tendency has been to discourage the civil action almost to the point of extinction; in England and Victoria it has been abolished entirely.[135]

129. *D. K. Investments v. S.W.S. Investments* (1984) 59 B.C.L.R. 333 (damages at large); *Q.I.W. v. Felview* excluded "extra" legal costs.
130. For the history see Winfield, *History of Conspiracy* (1921) ch. 6.
131. *Blackstone*, 4 Comm. 135.
132. Winfield, 35 L.Q.R. 233 (1919).
133. Such criminal proceedings, however, are in fact very rare indeed.
134. At least "personal torts" (*Trendtex v. Credit Suisse* [1980] Q.B. 629 at 656, 670; [1982] A.C. 679 at 702). Permitted are also assignments of damages to be recovered by the person injured (*Glegg v. Bromley* [1912] 3 K.B. 474) or assignment to his insurer in lieu of subrogation of the assured's rights against the tortfeasor: *King v. Victoria Ins.* [1896] A.C. 250 (P.C.); *Compania Colombiana v. Pacific Steam Navigation Co.* [1965] 1 Q.B. 101. Moreover, tort claims by a bankrupt pass to his trustee, if they involve damage to a property interest as distinct from injury to his person, reputation or feelings: see *Wilson v. United Counties Bank* [1920] A.C. 102. In the U.S. non-assignability, where still surviving, applies only to personal injury claims: 40 A.L.R. 3d 500 (1971).
135. *Criminal Law Act* 1967 (Eng.); *Wrongs Act* (Vic.) s. 32 (since 1969). Both include champerty, but leave such assignments unenforceable.

Maintenance differs in many respects from malicious prosecution. It applies only to litigation actually pending,[136] it may be devoid of malice,[137] and it is immaterial whether there was reasonable and probable cause.[138] Indeed, it is equally unlawful whether the party maintained is eventually successful or not, because the evil consists in the very act of officious intermeddling with litigation rather than in supporting an unfounded claim or defence.[139] It also matters nothing whether the assistance is given to a plaintiff or defendant, the grievance to the other party being the same in either case.[140] Lastly, maintenance can be committed only in relation to civil proceedings; the promotion of criminal prosecutions is not actionable except under the stringent conditions of malicious prosecution.[141]

Usually maintenance consists in financial assistance, such as giving or lending money, bearing the whole or part of the cost of the action or saving a litigant expenses that he might otherwise incur. An aggravated form of maintenance, known as *champerty*,[142] consists in unlawfully maintaining a suit in consideration of a bargain to receive, by way of reward, part of anything that may be gained as a result of the proceedings, or some other profit. This has attracted special condemnation because of the imagined temptation for the champertous maintainer to suppress or manufacture evidence or even suborn witnesses for his own special gain. In these respects solicitors occupy a special position in that it is their business to assist clients in litigation. Thus in Australia contingency fees are by no means unlawful: a solicitor may conduct a case on the basis that he will be paid if he wins but not if he loses, provided he believes the case has merit;[143] though he may not, unlike American attorneys,[144] stipulate for fees apportioned to the damages recovered.

Damage

The severest brake was applied in *Neville v. London Express*,[145] which settled that maintenance was not actionable without proof of actual loss, purportedly on the ground that no private injury could ensue from support of a just action or defence owing to the absurdities that would otherwise result. Yet this is difficult to reconcile with the second ruling in the same case, admittedly reached by a differently constituted majority, that the success of the person maintained is not per se a bar to recovery. The first

136. *Flight v. Leman* (1843) 4 Q.B. 883; 114 E.R. 1130. See, however, *Bradlaugh v. Newdegate* (1883) 11 Q.B.D. 1 at 9.
137. *Bradlaugh v. Newdegate* (1883) 11 Q.B.D. 1.
138. *Schultz v. Ocean Accident Co.* (1923) 23 S.R. (N.S.W.) 153 at 167-168.
139. *Neville v. London Express* [1919] A.C. 368. But see below.
140. *Neville v. London Express* [1919] A.C. 368 at 395, 428; *British Cash Conveyors v. Lamson* [1908] 1 K.B. 1006 at 1021.
141. *Grant v. Thompson* (1895) 72 L.T. 264.
142. Derived from campi partitio (division of the field).
143. *Clyne v. N.S.W. Bar Association* (1960) 104 C.L.R. 186; *Sheehan v. Sheehan* (1991) F.L.C. 92-221; *Courts and Legal Services Act* 1990 (Eng.) s. 58. See also *Contingency Fees* (Discussion Paper No. 3) (Senate Committee on Legal and Constitutional Affairs, 1991).
144. See Fleming, *Process* ch. 6.
145. [1919] A.C. 368. See also *Southern Cross Assurance v. Shareholders Assoc.* [1935] S.A.S.R. 480.

represents a fairly decisive break from the medieval spirit of action, which was dominated by the conviction that any interference with private litigation was a public wrong to be deterred at all costs,[146] whereas the second reflects a hesitation to acknowledge openly that changed social conditions have called for drastic reform. In effect, of course, this conflict of attitudes is resolved in favour of the modern approach, because it is difficult to conceive situations in which an unsuccessful litigant can recover, in view of his inability to prove special damage. Suppose A sues B for an alleged debt and C unlawfully maintains B's defence. A loses his original action and now sues C for maintenance. What special damage can he prove? Not the debt claimed from B, because it was never legally due, nor the costs payable to B, for they followed the event in the original action; nor his own costs, as they were incurred in advancing an unfounded legal claim. He might point to extra costs incurred by reason of C's intervention, perhaps being prompted to engage counsel, but this claim appears also to be precluded on the broad ground that expenses incurred in endeavouring to put forward futile legal claims or to evade legal obligations cannot be considered legally recognisable damage.[147]

Where, in contrast, the plaintiff was successful in the original proceeding, a surer basis is laid for an action against the person guilty of maintaining the other party. He may clearly recover such costs as have been actually awarded to him in the maintained action,[148] most probably even a complete indemnity, beyond those taxed as "party and party" costs. Against it is the analogy of actions for malicious prosecution;[149] for it is the argument that here the claim is made against a third party without involving double adjudication.[150]

Privileges

No clearer illustration of the extent by which the old law of maintenance has been modified to accord with modern notions of public policy can be found than in the vastly extended range of situations in which interference with litigation may now be justified. At one time, notions of propriety were so strict that even the assignment of a chose in action or the giving of testimony without being subpoenaed were regarded as obnoxious, but this ancient lore is now largely obsolete. Today few litigants bring or defend suits on their own; most are championed either by insurers or trade unions. These practices have become perfectly acceptable, especially when the latter are prepared to pay the cost of the other side in case they lose.[151] The law has adjusted itself to this reality.

146. The dissent proceeded on the basis that maintenance being illegal, nominal damage ought to be awarded by analogy to trespass and libel. Winfield favoured this view: *Abuse* 81-88; contra: *Holdsworth* viii, 400-402.
147. *Neville v. London Express* [1919] A.C. 368 at 380; Winfield, 35 L.Q.R. 233 at 237-238 (1919). For a suggestion of two instances where an unsuccessful litigant might satisfy the requirement of special damage, see *Weld-Blundell v. Stephens* [1920] A.C. 956 at 968-970.
148. An action for maintenance will be his only means of recovering costs where the party maintained is insolvent, as in *Cotterell v. Jones* (1851) 11 C.B. 713; 138 E.R. 655.
149. *Schultz v. Ocean Accident Corp.* (1923) 23 S.R. (N.S.W.) 153 at 165-167. See above, p. 612.
150. *Q.I.W. Retailers v. Felview* [1989] 2 Qd R. 245.
151. *Hill v. Archbold* [1968] 1 Q.B. 686 at 695 per Lord Denning M.R.

One broad ground of privilege covers relations of common interest between the maintainer and the maintained. Thus persons engaged in a particular trade or profession or linked by some proprietary or other legitimate common bond may lawfully associate themselves with a view to protecting, if necessary by litigation, the interests of each in the common field at the expense of all.[152] For example, it is perfectly proper for manufacturers to combine in defending an infringement action by a patentee against one of their number,[153] for a mutual protection society of fishery owners to support proceedings by some of its members against a factory accused of polluting a river,[154] or for a trade union to assist an employee in a claim for wages[155] or one of their own officials who has been libelled in relation to his duties.[156] Likewise, insurance and indemnity contracts may provide a sufficient business interest. Thus, there is no objection to a manufacturer securing business from customers of a rival on terms that he would indemnify them in respect of any liability arising from a transfer of their custom,[157] or to a workers' compensation insurer investigating proceedings by an injured worker against a third party tortfeasor.[158]

Even a prima facie champertous agreement may be valid if the maintainer has a sufficient "interest in the thing at variance". Thus, in one case, a bargain was upheld whereby the lessee of a coal mine undertook to support proceedings by the owner against a trespasser who had removed a large amount of coal from the seam prior to the lease, in consideration of receiving 92 per cent of the damages recovered. Justification was found in the fact that, while the lessee could have claimed to be relieved of the lease on the ground that one third of it had been worked out, it was in the mutual interest of both parties to maintain the lease and divide the damages in such a way that the owner would receive compensation for his loss of royalties and the lessee for the coal which should have been, but was no longer, under the land.[159]

Closely related to common interest are such other, rather old-fashioned grounds of justification as kinship,[160] the relation of landlord and tenant, master and servant[161] and courtesy.[162] The category of exceptions, however, is not closed; indeed, on one view, the overriding question is always whether the defendant was prompted by a desire to advance the cause of justice rather than to intermeddle for some collateral reason. The most familiar illustration is when he acted from motives of charity, as by assisting an indigent or, indeed, anyone who would have been unable to go

152. See *Trendtex v. Credit Suisse* [1980] Q.B. 629 (C.A.) (affd [1982] A.C. 679).
153. Cf. *Plating Co. v. Farquharson* (1881) 17 Ch. D. 49.
154. *Martell v. Consett Iron Co.* [1955] Ch. 363.
155. *Greig v. National Union of Shop Assistants* (1906) 22 T.L.R. 274 at 275.
156. *Hill v. Archbold* [1968] 1 Q.B. 686 (C.A.).
157. *British Cash Conveyors v. Lamson Service* [1908] 1 K.B. 1006.
158. *Schultz v. Ocean Accident Corp.* (1923) 23 S.R. (N.S.W.) 153.
159. *Re Bulli Coal Mining Co.* (1897) 18 L.R. (N.S.W.) (Eq.) 146; affd [1899] A.C. 351.
160. *Hayes v. Levinson* (1890) 16 V.L.R. 305 at 308; but it does not justify champerty: *Hutley v. Hutley* (1873) L.R. 8 Q.B. 112.
161. *Hill v. Archbold* [1968] 1 Q.B. 686 (C.A.).
162. See *Bradlaugh v. Newdegate* (1883) 11 Q.B.D. 1 at 11; Winfield, *Abuse* 28-44.

to law.[163] It is sufficient that he entertained a bona fide belief in the litigant's inability to sustain the financial burden, nor is he put to inquiry whether there is reasonable ground for the litigation, since charity need not necessarily be discreet.[164] The privilege, however, must not be abused; it is defeated by any improper motive, as when a pauper was used merely as a pawn in order to advance the defendant's own private interests.[165] Similarly, supposed charitable motives cannot excuse champerty because charity, though it may be indiscreet, must not and, indeed, cannot be mercenary.[166]

163. *Brew v. Whitlock* [1967] V.R. 449 (infirm person whose assets were controlled by Public Trustee).
164. *Harris v. Brisco* (1886) 17 Q.B.D. 504; *Stevens v. Keogh* (1946) 72 C.L.R. 1.
165. *Pechell v. Watson* (1841) 8 M. & W. 691; 151 E.R. 1217.
166. *Cole v. Booker* (1913) 29 T.L.R. 295.

28

MISREPRESENTATION

We have repeatedly had occasion to notice that misrepresentation may be a mode of committing various torts, without there being any call to treat it as a separate or independent basis of liability. Thus, a battery may be committed by gaining consent to physical contact through misrepresenting its true character,[1] intentional infliction of nervous shock may be procured by telling a lie,[2] or a conversion committed by obtaining possession of goods through fraud. Besides, many forms of negligent misconduct involve misrepresentations, even if this aspect is frequently obscured and submerged amidst other attendant factors.[3] For example, the liability of manufacturers and occupiers is, in essence, based on a false assurance as to the safety of their products or premises, even though the duties in question are rarely defined by reference to the fact of implied misrepresentation as such. In these familiar situations, involving the creation of unreasonable risks of physical injury, scant importance is attached to the particular form of the defendant's conduct, and no need is usually felt for treating misrepresentation as a separate basis of liability.[4]

In addition, however, primarily in the context of claims for pecuniary loss, specialised rules for actionable misrepresentation developed, including the entirely distinct action for deceit, followed much later by an action for negligent words and the strict liability for express warranties. These will now be discussed in turn.

1. DECEIT

Deceit, as an independent and general cause of action in tort, is of relatively novel origin, although traces of it are encountered as early as the 13th century when a writ of that name became available against misuse of legal procedure for the purpose of swindling others.[5] Later this remedy expanded and played a modest part in developing the incipient law of contract, principally in connection with false warranties.[6] Its scope, however, remained confined to direct transactions between the parties until in 1789, in *Pasley v. Freeman*,[7] it was freed from this link with contractual relations and held to lie whenever one person, by a knowingly false statement, intentionally induced another to act upon it to his detriment. There, the plaintiff had made an inquiry from the defendant

1. See above, p. 80.
2. *Wilkinson v. Downton* [1897] 2 Q.B. 57.
3. See above, p. 173.
4. *Prosser & Keeton* 725-726.
5. See Winfield, *History of Conspiracy* (1921) ch. 2.
6. *Holdsworth* iii, 428ff.
7. (1789) 3 T.R. 51; 100 E.R. 450.

concerning the financial standing of a merchant with whom he was negotiating for the sale of 16 bags of cochineal and received the assurance that he could safely extend credit, although the defendant well knew the party to be insolvent. Despite the want of any contractual bargain with the plaintiff, the defendant was held to answer for the loss in an action for deceit. At about the same time, the remedy for breach of warranty was absorbed by the action of assumpsit and henceforth regarded as purely contractual.[8] Thereafter, the two theories of misrepresentation began to diverge and are now quite distinct. The tort action for deceit requires proof of fraudulent intent, while breach of contractual warranty became independent of any intention to mislead or other fault. Nevertheless, the close association of deceit with bargaining transactions has inevitably coloured the elements of the action, which largely reflect the ethical and moral standards of the market place as they relate to permissible methods of obtaining contractual or other economic benefits and of inflicting pecuniary loss through reliance on false statements. Not that the action is inapplicable to personal injuries or harm to tangible property,[9] but such instances are rare, and the typical cases in which the action is enlisted involve pecuniary loss.

Nature of misrepresentation

Misrepresentations are usually conveyed by words, oral or written, but may consist of any other form of conduct creating a misleading impression.[10] Actions often speak louder than words: hence it is fraud to obtain goods on credit in a university town by disguising oneself as an undergraduate,[11] or actively to conceal a defect in merchandise, as by floating a ship in order to hide her rotten keel.[12]

Ordinarily, mere silence or passive failure to disclose the truth are not actionable, however deceptive in fact.[13] This rule no doubt reflects generally accepted ethics for parties dealing at arm's length; even if its tolerance has sometimes been put to the severest stress as when a seller of typhoid-infected pigs successfully insisted that his failure to disclose the disease was neither fraud nor reason for disregarding an express disclaimer of all warranties.[14] Several qualifications are in any event recognised. In the first place, a half-truth may just as much be a false representation as

8. *Stuart v. Wilkins* (1778) 1 Doug. 18; 99 E.R. 15.
9. *Langridge v. Levy* (1837) 2 M. & W. 519; 150 E.R. 863; 4 M. & W. 337; 150 E.R. 1459; *Burrows v. Rhodes* [1899] 1 Q.B. 816; *Nicholls v. Taylor* [1939] V.L.R. 119.
10. *Ward v. Hobbs* (1878) 4 App. Cas. 13 at 22, 26; *Bodger v. Nicholls* (1873) 28 L.T. 441 at 445; *Garnaut v. Rowse* (1941) 43 W.A.L.R. 29 (bigamous marriage); and cf. *Legh v. Legh* (1930) 143 L.T. 151.
11. *R. v. Barnard* (1837) 7 C. & P. 784; 173 E.R. 342.
12. *Schneider v. Heath* (1813) 3 Camp. 506; 170 E.R. 1462; also *Abel v. McDonald* (1964) 45 D.L.R. (2d) 198 (baulking inspection by subterfuge).
13. *Peek v. Gurney* (1873) L.R. 6 H.L. 377 at 392, 403; *Scott Fell v. Lloyd* (1906) 4 C.L.R. 572; (1907) 7 S.R. (N.S.W.) 512.
14. *Ward v. Hobbs* (1878) 4 App. Cas. 13 (sale "with all faults"); but there might now be liability for negligence: *Hurley v. Dyke* [1979] R.T.R. 265 at 290, 303. It is permissible (though no longer since the *Misrepresentation Acts* 1967 (Eng.) and 1971 (S.A.)) to contract out of liability for negligent misrepresentation, but not fraud (which would be contrary to public policy): *Boyd v. Glasgow Rly* 1915 S.C. (H.L.) 20 at 35-36; *Commercial Banking Co. v. Brown* (1972) 126 C.L.R. 337.

a complete lie:[15] for example, setting out favourable passages of a report without the qualifications.[16] Secondly, one who makes a false statement honestly believing it to be true but later discovers that it was false,[17] or one who makes a true statement which later events falsify,[18] must correct it at any time before the deal is actually closed.[19] Finally, a duty of disclosure is demanded when the parties stand in some fiduciary relation to each other, like principal and agent[20] or trustee and beneficiary or where a special need for public protection has been recognised by legislation, as under company law which now requires directors to include specified information in a prospectus.[21] Another should be incident to intimate personal relations, such as a duty to disclose veneral disease or AIDS.[22]

Beyond that, however, the law has faltered. Even yet it does not seem to insist on a duty of disclosure merely because the parties' position is unequal, as when one is aware of the other's misapprehension regarding material facts of which he has sole knowledge and unique access.[23] The harshness of this view is somewhat mitigated by the dominant role that implied warranties have come to play in ensuring consumer protection. In any event it is confined to bargaining transactions: duties to warn against risks of physical injury are of course commonplace.

It is commonly postulated that only misrepresentations of past or present *fact* are actionable as deceit. This is contrasted with statements of future intent or promise, breach of which is not actionable either as a tort or on any other basis than contract.[24] Yet every promise contains an implied statement of fact, that is, of a present intent as to the future. What is really meant is that, if I make a promise with every intention of fulfilling it, I cannot be held liable for deceit,[25] should I subsequently become unable or

15. *Tapp v. Lee* (1803) 3 Bos. & Pul. 367; 127 E.R. 200; *Curtis v. Chemical Cleaning Co.* [1951] 1 K.B. 805; *Link v. Schaible* (1961) 27 D.L.R. (2d) 461.
16. *Arkwright v. Newbold* (1881) 17 Ch. D. 301 at 317-318; *Awaroa v. Commercial Securities* [1976] 1 N.Z.L.R. 19 at 32.
17. *Robertson & Moffat v. Belson* [1905] V.L.R. 555; *Brownlie v. Campbell* (1880) 5 App. Cas. 925 at 950; *Dalgety & Co. v. Australian Mutual Provident Society* [1908] V.L.R. 481 at 506; and see *Holmes v. Jones* (1907) 4 C.L.R. 1692.
18. *Jones v. Dumbrell* [1981] V.R. 199; *With v. O'Flanagan* [1936] Ch. 575 at 584.
19. Yet conversely, "if false when made but true when acted upon, there is no misrepresentation" (*Briess v. Woolley* [1954] A.C. 333 at 353; *Ship v. Crosskill* (1870) L.R. 10 Eq. 73).
20. Bribery of an agent is treated as a "fraud" on the principal, for which both the giver and receiver are held as joint tortfeasors: *Mahesan v. Malaysia Housing* [1979] A.C. 374 (P.C.). See Tettenborn, 95 L.Q.R. 68; Needham, ibid. 536.
21. Australian *Companies Act* 1981 (Cth) s. 98; *Companies Act* 1955 (N.Z.) s. 48. Non-compliance confers a right to damages against responsible directors: *Re South of England Natural Gas Co.* [1911] 1 Ch. 573; *Commonwealth Homes v. Smith* (1937) 59 C.L.R. 443 at 460. The point was left open in *Nash v. Lynde* [1929] A.C. 158.
22. Repeatedly recognised in the U.S. See above, p. 81.
23. See *Lietzke v. Morgan* (1973) 5 S.A.S.R. 88 (F.C.) (no duty to disclose to trade customers that one is operating under scheme of arrangement). Aliter if he contributed to the misapprehension, as in *Bristow v. Moffat-Virtue* [1962] Qd S.R. 377. *Rest. 2d* §551(2)(e) requires disclosure of "facts *basic* to the transaction, if he knows that the other is about to enter into it under a mistake as to such facts, and the other, because of the relationship between them, the customs of the trade, or other objective circumstances, would reasonably expect a disclosure of such facts".
24. *Jorden v. Money* (1854) 5 H.L.C. 185; 10 E.R. 868; *Combe v. Combe* [1951] 2 K.B. 215.
25. But it can qualify as a misleading statement under the *Trade Practices Act* 1974 (Cth) s. 51A (deeming it to be made without reasonable grounds unless disproved).

unwilling to do so. The reason for this, however, is not that my promise is not a statement of fact, but rather that I believed the statement of my present intention to be true when I made it. So, if I never entertained an intention of fulfilling my promise, I commit a fraud by falsifying my present intention, as when I pass a cheque, knowing that it is not covered and not intending to honour it.[26] As Bowen L.J. once said in a celebrated passage, "the state of a man's mind is as much a fact as the state of his digestion. It is true that it is very difficult to prove what the state of a man's mind at a particular time is, but if it can be ascertained it is as much a fact as anything else."[27] Hence, company directors were held liable for falsely professing in a prospectus that the money raised by an issue of debentures would be used for expanding activities, when in truth they were set upon using it for paying off pressing debts.[28]

Not only statements of intention but also statements of opinion, known to be false, may be actionable as deceit, because "the existence of the opinion in the person stating it is a question of fact."[29] It is true that where the facts are equally well known to both parties, a false opinion expressed thereon by one does not give a cause for complaint to the other. The real explanation for this, however, is not that a statement of opinion is not a statement of fact about the condition of one's mind, but that parties, bargaining at arm's length, are assumed to be competent to draw their own conclusions. It follows that if the facts are not known to both alike, a statement of opinion by one who knows the facts best is often treated as a material representation, for he might be held to imply that he knows facts which justify his opinion.[30] The individualistic attitude of the common law to bargaining transactions has, in general, encouraged distrust of others in the market place and the discounting of sales talk as unworthy of justifiable reliance. "There are some kinds of talk which no sensible man takes seriously, and if he does he suffers from his credulity. If we were all scrupulously honest, it would not be so; but, as it is, neither party usually believes what the seller says about his own opinions and each knows it."[31] This warning is particularly pertinent to exaggerated commendation of their wares commonly made by sellers, which must be dismissed as mere "puffs" unworthy of credence by reasonable buyers. Increasingly,[32] however, the tendency has been to raise the ethical standards of bargaining, and, with the possible exception of misstatements by the vendor of the lowest price which he is prepared to take or by the purchaser of the highest he will give, neither party is any longer excused for false representations as to material facts peculiarly within his knowledge, even if they relate to such matters as the

26. See *Re Shackleton* (1875) L.R. 10 Ch. App. 446 at 449-450; *Re Eastgate* [1905] 1 K.B. 465 at 467; *Gardiner v. Suttons* (1983) 48 A.L.R. 142 (T.P.A.); also *Legal Effect of Promises Made with Intent Not to Perform*, 38 Col. L. Rev. 1461 (1938).
27. *Edgington v. Fitzmaurice* (1885) 29 Ch. D. 459 at 483.
28. Ibid. See also T.P.A. s. 51A(1).
29. *Bisset v. Wilkinson* [1927] A.C. 177 at 182. See also *Fitzpatrick v. Michel* (1928) 28 S.R. (N.S.W.) 285.
30. *Brown v. Raphael* [1958] Ch. 636; *Ballard v. Gaskill* [1954] 4 D.L.R. 427.
31. *Vulcan Metals v. Simmons Manufacturing Co.* (1918) 248 F. 853 at 856 per Learned Hand J.
32. Especially under the *Trade Practices Act* s. 52: e.g. *Given v. Prior* (1979) 24 A.L.R. 442 ("wonderful place to live" held to be actionably misleading).

value of the property[33] or the price which he has given[34] or been offered for it.[35]

Likewise, there is no good reason for doubting that deliberate misstatements of law are sufficient to support an action for deceit,[36] at any rate where the parties are not on an equal footing with respect to knowledge of the law or general intelligence and education.[37] The argument that all men know the law and therefore cannot be misled about it is a threadbare fiction which was never intended to shield swindlers.

Scienter

Not until the great case of *Derry v. Peek*[38] in 1889 was it finally settled by the House of Lords that deceit would lie only for knowingly false representations. Directors of a tramway company had issued a prospectus claiming that they were empowered by statute to use steam-powered cars. Actually, the authorisation was conditional on governmental consent which the directors honestly believed would be given as a matter of course. It was, however, withheld, and in consequence the company went into liquidation. The plaintiff who had become a shareholder on the faith of the prospectus instituted an action against the directors for deceit and succeeded in persuading the Court of Appeal that negligence was sufficient to support liability. But this decision was reversed on the ground that a false statement, honestly believed to be true, could not qualify as fraud, even if made carelessly and without reasonable grounds. Earlier precedents which had given some countenance to the importation of "equitable fraud" were repudiated as based on a mistaken view of the effect of the *Judicature Act*. Though courts of equity might grant their own appropriate relief, like rescission, in cases falling short of wilfully false representation, the meaning of "deceit" in a common law action for *damages* could not be stretched beyond actual fraud. In an oft-quoted passage, Lord Herschell insisted on proof "that a false representation has been made (1) knowingly, or (2) without belief in its truth, or (3) recklessly, careless whether it be true or false".[39] In short, the representor must have lacked an honest belief in the truth of his statement.[40] Carelessness is not equivalent to dishonesty.[41] Even recklessness in the sense of gross negligence will not suffice, unless the defendant is consciously indifferent to the truth[42] and thus lacks an honest

33. *Haygarth v. Wearing* (1871) L.R. 12 Eq. 320 at 327-328.
34. *Clarke v. Dickson* (1859) 6 C.B. (N.S.) 453; 141 E.R. 533.
35. *Nicholas v. Thompson* [1924] V.L.R. 554.
36. *Public Trustee v. Taylor* [1978] V.R. 289; *Oudaille v. Lawson* [1922] N.Z.L.R. 259. Reservations expressed in some older cases should in any event have less weight in cases of fraudulent than innocent misrepresentations.
37. *Rest. 2d* §545. See also Keeton, *Fraud—Misrepresentations of Law*, 15 Tex. L. Rev. 409 (1937).
38. (1889) 14 App. Cas. 337.
39. Ibid. at 374.
40. But *motive* is immaterial, so that one may be liable who meant no harm: *Polhill v. Walter* (1832) 3 B. & Ad. 114; 110 E.R. 43.
41. Note that the word "careless" (in the third alternative) means "not caring" rather than "without due care".
42. The equivalence of "indifferent" and "reckless" was approved in *Lamb v. Johnson* (1914) 15 S.R. (N.S.W.) 65 at 74-75.

belief. Of course, there may be "such an absence of reasonable ground for his belief as, in spite of his assertion, to carry conviction to the mind that he had not really the belief which he alleges".[43] So, where the representor deliberately shuts his eyes to the facts, purposely abstains from investigation, or consciously lacks sufficient information to support an assertion couched in positive and unqualified form,[44] the conclusion is open that his belief is not really honest.

But though negligence, however gross, would not support a charge of fraud, it might still be actionable in some circumstances as breach of an independent duty of care. In fact, it took another 75 years before this was finally resolved. The conditions of liability are treated separately below.[45]

If the statement is ambiguous, the meaning to be attached (in claims for fraud) is that which was actually intended by the defendant rather than what it would convey to the ordinary mind.[46] In other words, the law will look to its intended, and not its ordinary or comprehended, meaning.[47] This follows from the requirement that the defendant must have had a guilty state of mind. "Unless he is conscious that it will be understood in a different manner from which he is honestly though blunderingly using it, he is not fraudulent. An honest blunder in the use of language is not dishonest."[48] On the other hand, if he purposely expressed himself equivocally in order to convey a misleading impression, and is so understood, he will not be heard to protest that such a meaning was not "natural" or "ordinary".

Principal and agent

The requirement of proving a guilty mind in the defendant cannot be satisfied by "combining an innocent principal and agent so as to produce dishonesty. . . . You cannot add an innocent state of mind to an innocent state of mind and get as a result a dishonest state of mind."[49] Admittedly, a principal, besides being vicariously responsible for his agent's *deceitful* practices in the course of employment,[50] will also incur personal liability if he actually authorises his agent to make a statement which he knows to be

43. *Derry v. Peek* (1889) 14 App. Cas. 337 at 369. The gravity of the issue calls for the clearest persuasion, but only on a balance of probability, i.e. the civil standard of proof: *Rejfek v. McElroy* (1965) 112 C.L.R. 517.
44. E.g. *Van den Esschert v. Chappell* [1960] W.A.R. 114; *Snarski v. Barbarich* [1969] W.A.R. 46.
45. See below, p. 640.
46. *Akerhielm v. De Mare* [1959] A.C. 789 ("subscribed in Denmark" intended to cover "subscribed in Kenya for services in Denmark"); *McGrath Motors v. Applebee* (1964) 37 A.L.J.R. 363 ("new" car intended to mean "not secondhand" rather than "not old"); *Sargent v. Campbell* [1972-1973] Arg. L.R. 708.
47. See Williams, *Language and the Law—IV*, 61 L.Q.R. 384 at 392 (1945); Devlin, 53 L.Q.R. 344 at 360-361 (1937).
48. *Angus v. Clifford* [1891] 2 Ch. 449 at 472 per Bowen L.J.
49. *Armstrong v. Strain* [1951] 1 T.L.R. 856 at 872 per Devlin J.
50. In such cases, the innocent principal is liable even where the agent's false statement reaches the plaintiff through the principal himself (*Pearson v. Dublin Corp.* [1907] A.C. 351, as explained in *Anglo-Scottish Beet Sugar Corp. v. Spalding U.D.C.* [1937] 2 K.B. 607), or through another innocent agent (*London County Properties v. Berkeley Property Co.* [1936] 2 All E.R. 1039, as explained in *Spalding*); *Armstrong v. Strain* [1952] 1 K.B. 232 at 243, 248; *Stratford B. v. Ashman* [1960] N.Z.L.R. 503 at 520-521.

false, even though the agent does not;[51] or if he purposely employs an agent, ignorant of the truth, in order that such agent might innocently make a false statement believing it to be true, and thereby deceive the other party of the transaction.[52] But, in the absence of such express authorisation or active concealment, the mere fact that he knows of facts which falsify his innocent agent's representation does not provide a sufficient link to charge him with deceit, at any rate if he has no reason to believe that the agent would make the peccant statement.[53] Conscious knowledge of falsity by the representor, as an essential of liability, simply is not present in the case of an innocent division of ingredients between two persons, even if they stand to each other in the relation of principal and agent. Hence, when in the course of negotiating the sale of a bungalow the owner's agents innocently made false representations concerning its condition, the purchaser failed to pin liability on the vendor who, though aware of structural defects, had neither authorised the statements nor known that they were being made nor deliberately kept his agents in ignorance with any intention of misleading the plaintiff.[54]

A composite liability for negligence was, however, imposed on an organisation for the acts of several servants, none of whom individually could be proved culpable.[55] The defendant firm's buyer made a misrepresentation in reliance on information supplied to him by their accountant based on inadequate data. The latter was not liable because he was not negligent in passing it on. Yet their firm was held responsible, not vicariously, but presumably for breach of its personal duty of care.

Intended reliance

A fraudulent misrepresentation is not actionable unless made with the intent that the plaintiff should act upon it as he in fact did. That reliance was foreseeable may just be sufficient for negligence,[56] but for deceit reliance must have been intended.[57] So if A sells certain shares to B in C's presence and makes a fraudulent claim affecting their value, he is not liable if C purchases some from a third person on his own account and suffers loss, unless A intended to influence both B and C.[58] But representation need not have been made directly to the plaintiff, provided he was intended to rely upon it. It can be made to one, to be passed to another.[59] Nor need

51. *Ludgater v. Love* (1881) 44 L.T. 694. If the agent shares the guilty knowledge, both are liable as joint tortfeasors.
52. *Cornfoot v. Fowke* (1840) 6 M. & W. 358 at 370, 374; 151 E.R. 450.
53. *Armstrong v. Strain* [1952] 1 K.B. 232 (C.A.); *Stratford B. v. Ashman* [1960] N.Z.L.R. 503 (C.A.); *Awaroa v. Commercial Securities* [1976] 1 N.Z.L.R. 19.
54. *Armstrong v. Strain* [1951] 1 T.L.R. 856.
55. *Anderson v. Rhodes* [1967] 2 All E.R. 850; comment 31 Mod. L. Rev. 322 (1968).
56. See below, p. 645.
57. Cf. *Rest. 2d* §531 ("persons or class of persons whom he intends or has reason to expect to act in reliance").
58. *Rest. 2d* §531, ill. 1, 2. Cf. *Pilmore v. Hood* (1838) 5 Bing. N.C. 97; 132 E.R. 1042.
59. *Langridge v. Levy* (1837) 2 M. & W. 519; 150 E.R. 863; 4 M. & W. 337; 150 E.R. 1459 (to co-purchasers); *Leslie Leithead v. Barber* (1965) 65 S.R. (N.S.W.) 172 (to promoter of company). But representations do not run with the property sold; they cannot be invoked by subsequent buyers: *Gross v. Lewis Hillman* [1970] Ch. 445 (C.A.); contra: *Woodward v. Dietrich* 548 A. 2d 301 (Pa. 1988), invoking *Rest. 2d* §531.

the plaintiff have been aimed at as a specifically identified individual, as when a city bank furnished a false credit report on a wool buyer at the request of a bank from a country district which must have been intended for a wool grower.[60] But if addressed to a limited class, no outsider can sue upon it. Thus, in the leading case of *Peek v. Gurney*,[61] it was held that a company prospectus was addressed only to members of the public invited to take up shares from the company itself, and did not avail an investor who purchased on the market from another shareholder. Like the analogous limitation on liability for negligence,[62] it serves as a reminder of the law's pervasive concern lest liability for misrepresentation entail an excessive burden out of all proportion to the fault involved.

Besides being intended to rely on the misrepresentation, the plaintiff must have actually done so.[63] A mere attempt to deceive is not actionable.[64] Hence, if the representee did not allow the falsehood to affect his judgment, as where he either knew the statement to be false or regarded it as so unimportant that he would have acted in the same way without it,[65] he cannot complain even if he acted in the way intended and suffered harm in consequence. At the same time, a defendant cannot excuse himself by proving that his misrepresentation was not the *sole* inducing cause, because it might have been precisely what tipped the scales, as in the case of the plaintiff who had taken up debentures, partly by reason of a falsehood contained in the prospectus, partly in the mistaken belief that they created a charge on the company's property.[66] Nor is it a defence that the plaintiff was negligent or foolish in relying on the misrepresentation or had an opportunity for verifying it.[67] Whilst actual knowledge of the untruth is a bar to recovery, the mere availability of means of knowledge is not sufficient.[68] Thus company directors were held responsible to a shareholder, although the deceitful prospectus stated that certain documents were open to inspection at the company's offices and the fraud would have been discovered if they had been checked.[69] Indeed, a cheat may not escape even by cautioning his victim to verify all representations himself, for this might be but a ruse to promote his fraud.[70]

To complain of deceit, the plaintiff must have acted himself to his detriment in reliance thereon; if it merely induced *others* to act to his prejudice, his only recourse will be for injurious falsehood, a wrong more limited in scope which will be considered later.[71] Such, for example, is the

60. *Commercial Banking Co. v. Brown* (1972) 126 C.L.R. 337.
61. (1873) L.R. 6 H.L. 377. Aliter, if the prospectus was intended to influence dealings on the stock exchange: *Andrews v. Mockford* [1896] 1 Q.B. 372.
62. See below, p. 645.
63. *Holmes v. Jones* (1907) 4 C.L.R. 1692. Burden of proof is on plaintiff: *Gould v. Vaggelas* (1985) 157 C.L.R. 215.
64. *Horsfall v. Thomas* (1862) 1 H. & C. 90 at 99; 158 E.R. 813 at 817.
65. *Macleay v. Tait* [1906] A.C. 24; *Wilcher v. Steain* (1961) 79 W.N. (N.S.W.) 141.
66. *Edgington v. Fitzmaurice* (1885) 29 Ch. D. 459; *Barton v. Armstrong* [1976] A.C. 104 at 118 (P.C.); *Leighton v. Hurley* [1984] 2 Qd R. 534 (F.C.).
67. Contributory negligence was not a defence at common law nor is it under apportionment: *United Services Funds v. Richardson* (1988) 48 D.L.R. (4th) 98; see above, p. 281.
68. *Nocton v. Ashburton* [1914] A.C. 932 at 962; *Wilkinson v. Detmold* (1890) 16 V.L.R. 439.
69. *Central Rly v. Kisch* (1867) L.R. 2 H.L. 99.
70. *Pearson v. Dublin Corp.* [1907] A.C. 351 at 360.
71. See below, p. 709.

case if an architect were to misrepresent that the work had not been completed so that money due to the builder is withheld.[72]

Damages

Damage is of the gist of actionable deceit, the remedy being an offspring of the old form of action on the case.

One of the most common types of fraud is to inveigle a purchaser into a disadvantageous bargain in the belief that the article is of greater value than it actually is. There are two conceivable standards for measuring his damages. One would give him the benefit of what he was promised, that is, the difference between the actual value and the value it would have had if the representation had been true. The other would merely put him in the position he would have been in had the misrepresentation not been made, that is the difference between the purchase price and the value of the article at the time of sale. The one purports to give him the "benefit of the bargain", the other to compensate him merely for his "out of pocket" loss. The first clearly applies to breach of warranty, but for deceit British[73] (in contrast to American[74]) authority favours the second rule on the ground that the purpose of tort damages is to compensate the plaintiff for a loss actually sustained rather than to give him the benefit of a contract bargain, though this may actually allow a cheat to escape scot-free and even profit from his fraud. The distinction may be illustrated by the following example: suppose a purchaser were persuaded to pay $500 for a car worth $600 by a false representation which (if true) would have made it worth $700. For fraud he would recover nothing, since he suffered no loss in paying $500 for a $600 car; but for breach of warranty he would be entitled to all of $100, for the question would be, not what he has lost, but how much more he would have had if the car had been as warranted.[75]

An apparent exception exists where the lost benefit is referable to an opportunity foregone by reason of reliance on the misrepresentation, as where the plaintiff could and would have entered into a different contract. Here the measure of damages in tort resembles the expectation element of contract damages, but requires proof of reliance.[76]

Ordinarily, the value of the article must be assessed as of the time of purchase.[77] But if it depreciates thereafter due to an inherent flaw that only comes to light later, such loss may simply reflect the lower real value it had all along. In applying this distinction to shares in a company promoted for a speculative venture, the question will be: "Was it because the enterprise was misconceived and hopeless from the beginning or was it

72. *Larkins v. Chelmer Holdings* [1965] Qd R. 68.
73. Established in Australia since *Holmes v. Jones* (1907) 4 C.L.R. 1692 (e.g. *Szucs v. Wise Bros* (1959) 78 W.N. (N.S.W.) 184); also *N.Z. Refrigeration Co. v. Scott* [1969] N.Z.L.R. 30; *McConnell v. Wright* [1903] 1 Ch. 546. While rejected in Aust. and N.Z., Can. courts are prepared to presume that the price paid equalled the value *as represented* (not actual) and allow the difference: *Hepting v. Schaaf* [1964] S.C.R. 100. See McLauchlan, 6 Otago L. Rev. 370 (1987) for comprehensive analysis of case law.
74. *Prosser & Keeton* 767; *Rest. 2d* §549; aliter §552B (negligence).
75. The difference is clearly illustrated by *Ellul v. Oakes* (1972) 3 S.A.S.R. 377.
76. See below, p. 650.
77. *Potts v. Miller* (1940) 64 C.L.R. 282.

owing to misfortunes or difficulties not reasonably to be expected?"[78] Similarly if the property appreciates in the meantime, only increase due to an intrinsic cause will reduce recovery.[79] Inflationary increases must be disregarded on all account as reflecting merely changes in price, not value.

On the other hand, losses due to accidental or extrinsic causes are disregarded. Thus, if a man buys a racehorse misrepresented to have won some great race, and it later catches some disease and dies, the purchaser cannot recover its total value, but only the difference between the price he paid and the value of the horse at the time he bought it.[80] This might suggest that the loss must result from (be related to) the misrepresentation rather than the contract. But authority, scant though it is, suggests the contrary. Thus when a car had ten previous owners instead of only two as represented, the plaintiff recovered although the lesser value was due to the *first* owner being unbeknownst to the plaintiff a rental agency.[81] This conclusion is defensible on the ground that the complaint is having been induced to enter the contract and that any, at least direct, loss flowing from that event should be recoverable.[82]

Another substantial modifier is the modern rule to allow consequential damages, in recognition of the fact that otherwise the plaintiff would often not be adequately compensated by a tortfeasor guilty of egregious wrong. Such loss, however, must be "direct", not necessarily foreseeable as for negligent misrepresentation.[83] For example, when on the sale of a hairdressing salon the defendant falsely represented that he would not be personally working at his other salon in the neighbourhood, the buyer recovered for loss of profits incurred while attempting to sell the property. But her damages were assessed on the basis not of what the defendant had previously earned (which would have been appropriate if he had warranted that customers would continue to patronise the establishment), but of the profits which she might have made in another business bought for the same price.[84] Similarly recoverable are expenses reasonably incurred in looking for alternative employment, even bank interest on loans assumed for financing the transaction.[85] So a buyer of a diseased cow successfully claimed for other livestock that had become infected,[86] and the purchaser of a second-hand car for personal injuries and damage to the vehicle when it capsized owing to a bursting tyre which had been fraudulently represented

78. *Potts v. Miller* (1940) 64 C.L.R. 282 at 299 per Dixon J.
79. Ibid.
80. *Twycross v. Grant* (1877) 2 C.P.D. 469, 544. See McLauchlan, 6 Otago L. Rev. 370 at 410-419 (1987) but cf. *Rest. 2d* §548A.
81. *Capital Motors v. Beecham* [1975] 1 N.Z.L.R. 576 at 581.
82. Cf. *Carson Ent. v. Boughton* [1991] 3 S.C.R. 534 (not liable for subsequent act of third party).
83. *Doyle v. Olby* [1969] 2 Q.B. 158 (C.A.) ("it does not lie in the mouth of the fraudulent person to say that they could not have been foreseeable" (at 167)); *Royscot Trust v. Rogerson* [1991] 3 W.L.R. 57 (C.A.).
84. *East v. Maurer* [1991] 1 W.L.R. 461 (C.A.). Also *Gould v. Vaggelas* (1985) 157 C.L.R. 215.
85. *Archer v. Brown* [1985] Q.B. 401.
86. *Mullett v. Mason* (1866) L.R. 1 C.P. 559.

as new.[87] Aggravated damages for injured feelings can also be awarded,[88] even exemplary damages to discourage the deceiver making a profit from his wrong.[89]

Representations as to credit

A not uncommon type of fraud consists in misrepresenting a third person's credit. Yet here the tort action was liable to be exploited for the purpose of circumventing the *Statute of Frauds* which requires guarantees to be in writing. Precluded from suing on a verbal promise guaranteeing the debt of another, the plaintiff might instead frame his claim in deceit, alleging that the defendant had made a false representation, express or implied, as to the debtor's credit. To discourage this practice, the courts at first resorted to the device of urging juries not to act on the oral testimony of a single witness, but later the legislature intervened[90] and enjoined any action being "brought whereby to charge any person upon or by reason of any representation or assurance made or given concerning or relating to the character, conduct, credit, ability, trade or dealings of any person, to the intent or purpose that such other person may obtain credit, money or goods [upon[91]], unless such representation or assurance be made in writing signed by the party to be charged herewith."

A narrow construction has been placed upon this section so as to limit the generality of its language to the type of situation with which it was originally designed to deal. Thus, it has been read down to apply to actions based on *fraudulent* misrepresentations, but not negligence[92] or breach of contract.[93] Besides, it is confined to misrepresentations concerning credit-worthiness, and of no avail to a defendant who has misled the plaintiff into buying another's business by orally misrepresenting its value or prospects.[94]

In one respect, the requirement of the section is stricter than the *Statute of Frauds*, for the signature of the defendant's agent will not suffice. A company therefore cannot be held liable except on the signature of a high official representing its "mind and will", not merely (for example) the branch manager of a bank.[95]

87. *Nicholls v. Taylor* [1939] V.L.R. 119.
88. Ibid. (as in contract); *Mafo v. Adams* [1970] 1 Q.B. 548 (physical inconvenience); *Clemance v. Hollis* [1987] 2 N.Z.L.R. 471 (inconvenience and distress).
89. *Musca v. Astle Corp.* (1988) 80 A.L.R. 251 (but not under F.T.P.A.); *Archer v. Brown* (to prevent deceiver making profit).
90. *Statute of Frauds Amendment Act* 1828 (commonly known as *Lord Tenterden's Act*). N.S.W.: *Usury, Bills of Lading and Written Memoranda Act* 1902 s. 10; Vic.: *Instruments Act* 1958 s. 128; Tas.: *Mercantile Law Act* 1935 s. 11; S.A., W.A. and N.Z.: by reception; Qld: repealed in 1972.
91. The word in brackets does not make sense. It has been suggested that the word "credit" was accidentally transposed and should follow "upon" or that "upon" should be placed before "credit". Alternatively, "upon" may have been inserted in mistake for "thereupon", and it is so rendered in the Victorian and Queensland transcriptions. The word is omitted altogether in the Tasmanian statute.
92. *M.L.C. v. Evatt* (1968) 122 C.L.R. 556; *Anderson v. Rhodes* [1967] 2 All E.R. 850.
93. *Banbury v. Bank of Montreal* [1918] A.C. 626.
94. *Christian v. Woods* (1885) 6 L.R. (N.S.W.) 24; *Diamanti v. Martelli* [1923] N.Z.L.R. 663.
95. *Hirst v. West Riding Banking Co.* [1901] 2 K.B. 560.

2. NEGLIGENCE

We saw how in *Derry v. Peek* the law had set its face against admitting negligent misrepresentation into the fastness of fraud.[96] No one could quarrel with this refusal to equate credulity with dishonesty. Fraud is so damaging a reflection on a person's integrity that the courts were wise not to dilute its legal import far and beyond the popular understanding. What censure the decision did incur rather concerned the implication, which soon came to be attached[97] and long enjoyed judicial favour, that the law of torts furnished no remedy whatever for non-fraudulent misrepresentations, that there was a duty of common honesty but not of care, and that no more could be demanded from professional people like surveyors, valuers or accountants than from just anyone expressing a casual opinion on a social occasion.

A claim for pecuniary loss[98] due to "innocent" (that is non-fraudulent) misrepresentation had to be founded on contract or at least on a fiduciary relationship. Both were limited in range and growth potential: the first by the doctrine of privity, the second because the lower courts kept clinging to the view that a "special duty" attached only to fiduciary relations in the conventional equity sense, like those between trustee and beneficiary, solicitor and client,[99] or banker and customer.[100]

Eventually in 1964, a decade after a classical dissent by Lord Denning deploring the prevailing judicial timidity,[101] the House of Lords, in *Hedley Byrne v. Heller*,[102] set the law upon a new course by recognising that negligent misrepresentation causing purely economic loss might well be actionable as breach of a tortious duty of care.

For reasons already explored,[103] it is widely assumed that responsibility for negligent words should be more circumscribed than for negligent acts. To consign it to the familiar, open-ended formula of "foreseeability" would have merely confirmed the forebodings of the traditionalists that it was opening a Pandora's box to admit a duty under any circumstances. A more conservative principle was required to reconcile the insistent demand for legal protection against careless information and advice with the well recognised need for safeguards against extravagant liability.

Assumption of responsibility

A duty of care arises only from what the House signified as a "special relationship". The key to it, it was said, is the speaker's assumption of responsibility. This must be understood not in a subjective sense, but with

96. See above, p. 633.
97. *Le Lievre v. Gould* [1893] 1 Q.B. 491 (C.A.); reaffd in *Candler v. Crane, Christmas & Co.* [1951] 2 K.B. 164 (C.A.).
98. Liability for *physical* injury was much more expansive: see above, p. 174.
99. *Nocton v. Ashburton* [1914] A.C. 932 (client induced to improvident release of a mortgage held entitled to an equitable indemnity—rather than damages for misinformation).
100. *Woods v. Martins Bank* [1959] 1 Q.B. 55; *Coleman v. Myers* [1977] 2 N.Z.L.R. 225 (C.A.: company directors vis-à-vis shareholders).
101. *Candler v. Crane, Christmas & Co.* [1951] 2 K.B. 164 at 195.
102. [1964] A.C. 465. See Cane, *Metes and Bounds of Hedley Byrne*, 55 A.L.J. 862 (1981).
103. See above, p. 173.

reference "to circumstances in which the law will deem the maker of the statement to have assumed responsibility".[104] In other words, the recipient must have had reasonable grounds for believing that the speaker expected to be trusted. There is a world of difference between casual statements on social or informal occasions[105] and serious communications made in circumstances warranting reliance.[106] The latter are principally encountered in the sphere of business or professional affairs, though not necessarily between persons linked by a contractual or fiduciary tie in the conventional sense. The test is much more easily satisfied when the information or advice is requested rather than volunteered: commercial advertising, for example, does not qualify.[107]

Is the duty confined only to professional advisers (like doctors,[108] solicitors,[109] stockbrokers,[110] accountants,[111] valuers,[112] or surveyors[113]) and public bodies which supply information, like a local authority answering zoning inquiries[114] or an inspector issuing a building permit?[115] Or does it extend in effect to anyone who takes it upon himself to make representations inviting justifiable reliance, especially in a business context? By the slenderest margin,[116] this issue was resolved in a conservative vein by the Privy Council in *M.L.C. v. Evatt.*[117] While a divided High Court of Australia had found no principled reason for categorically exempting non-experts who proffer information or advice, the narrower view ultimately prevailed that a "special duty" of care was demanded only from persons whose business or profession it is to provide information or advice of a kind calling for special skill and competence, or who at least give the recipient

104. *Smith v. Bush* [1989] A.C. 831 at 862 (where defendant was held liable despite express disclaimer voided by *Unfair Contract Terms Act* 1977 (Eng.)). Also Lord Roskill in *Caparo v. Dickman* [1990] 2 A.C. 605 at 627.
105. E.g. *Mohr v. Cleaver* [1986] W.A.R. 67 (F.C.); *Howard Marine v. Ogden* [1978] Q.B. 574: in both "off the cuff" though in business context; but cf. *Chaudry v. Prabhakar* [1989] 1 W.L.R. 29 (liable for advice to friend).
106. *M.L.C. v. Evatt* [1971] A.C. 793 at 806.
107. *Lambert v. Lewis* [1982] A.C. 225 at 264 (C.A.).
108. *Smith v. Auckland Hospital* [1965] N.Z.L.R. 191 (C.A.).
109. *Allied Finance v. Haddow* [1983] N.Z.L.R. 22 (seller's solicitor's assurance to buyer).
110. *Elderkin v. Merrill Lynch* (1977) 80 D.L.R. (3d) 313.
111. See below, p. 646.
112. *B.T. Australia v. Raine & Horne* [1983] 3 N.S.W.L.R. 221 (trust fund); *Arenson v. Arenson* [1977] A.C. 405 (shares); *Kendall Wilson v. Barraclough* [1986] 1 N.Z.L.R. 576 (C.A.); *Sutcliffe v. Thackrah* [1974] A.C. 727 (architect's certificate). Only judges and probably arbitrators, who decide formulated disputes, are immune from such collateral attack on their decisions.
113. *Smith v. Bush* [1990] 1 A.C. 831 (mortgage).
114. *Shaddock v. Parramatta C.C.* (1981) 150 C.L.R. 225 (but now *Environmental Planning Act* 1979 (N.S.W.) s. 149); *Minister of Housing v. Sharp* [1970] 2 Q.B. 223 (C.A.); *Rutherford v. A.-G.* [1976] 1 N.Z.L.R. 403 (government inspector's certificate of fitness for truck); distd *Moorgate v. Twitchings* [1977] A.C. 890. Cf. *Rest. 2d* §552(3).
115. *Hull v. Canterbury* [1974] 1 N.S.W.L.R. 300; *Knight v. Warringah* [1975] 2 N.S.W.L.R. 796; *Windsor Motors v. Powell River* (1969) 4 D.L.R. (3d) 155. These fall within the "operational level" of administrative action: see above, p. 156.
116. And over the dissent of Lords Reid (and Morris) whose had been the principal judgments in *Hedley Byrne*.
117. [1971] A.C. 793; 122 C.L.R. 628, revd 122 C.L.R. 556. See Lindgren, 46 A.L.J. 176 (1972); Stevens, 5 N.Z.U.L. Rev. 39 (1972).

to understand that they claim to possess such.[118] However, the mere giving of advice, even in a business context, with knowledge that the plaintiff intended to rely on it did not by itself amount to a claim by the informant that he possessed such skill and competence. In the result, no responsibility was incurred merely for supplying to an insurance policy holder, on request, a report on the affairs of a fellow subsidiary finance company. The avowed justification was hardly convincing, viz. that there is an ascertainable standard of skill appropriate only for professionals (vide the "common callings", all of them specialists, to whom the law had first attached a duty of care), and no halfway house between that and the general duty of honesty. Surely, even the standard for professionals would vary depending on what level of skill and care was professed,[119] and could therefore as well be applied to non-professionals who proffer advice justifying reliance. An unexpressed premise may well have been that professional advisers alone would be insured against this risk and capable of internalising the cost of liability among their professional customers.[120]

The *Evatt* decision has been widely deplored for reversing the liberal development of the *Hedley Byrne* principle promoted in the meantime by English and Commonwealth courts. The English Court of Appeal has declined to accept it as a binding statement of English law,[121] and most Commonwealth courts have either rejected, ignored or evaded its waning authority.[122] The High Court of Australia, no longer bound by the Privy Council, has firmly refused to apply it to public bodies supplying information within their competence, such as answering zoning inquiries; indeed, the court seemed poised either to "distinguish it away" altogether or reject it outright.[123]

Evatt did allow an exception where the representor had a financial interest in the advice.[124] The potential of this exception is still unsettled. On a narrow view, the financial stake must raise in the plaintiff a belief that the representor assumed responsibility by professing special skill or

118. The majority invoked *Rest.* §552 which ambiguously speaks of "one who in the course of his business or profession supplies information for the guidance of others in their business transactions". *Rest. 2d* §552 inserts after "profession", "or employment, or in any other transaction in which he has a pecuniary interest".
119. In *Norris v. Sibberas* [1990] V.R. 161 a distinction was drawn between statements of an estate agent in three different areas of expertise: the market, motel management and financial prospects of the deal. She was expert only in the first two.
120. Insurers have hitherto been reluctant to offer "act, error and omission" policies to applicants outside the traditional professions: Stevens, 27 Mod. L. Rev. 153 (1964). And note: "Everyone knows that all prudent professional men carry insurance, and the availability and cost of insurance must be a relevant factor when considering which of two parties should be required to bear the risk of loss" (*Smith v. Bush* [1989] 2 W.L.R. 790 at 810 per Lord Griffiths).
121. *Howard Marine v. Ogden* [1978] Q.B. 574 at 591, 600.
122. N.Z.: *Scott v. McFarlane* [1978] 1 N.Z.L.R. 553 (passim); Canada: see 13 C.C.L.T. 202-203.
123. *Shaddock v. Parramatta C.C.* (1981) 150 C.L.R. 225; contra: *Mohr v. Cleaver* [1986] W.A.R. 67. *Meakes v. A.-G.* [1983] N.Z.L.R. 308 (C.A.) applied liability to Ministers for advice on government policy to developers, disregarding the public law dimension.
124. [1971] A.C. 793 at 805, 809, citing *Anderson v. Rhodes* [1967] 2 All E.R. 850. In *Evatt*, the financial common interest within the conglomerate did not so qualify. The suggestion has its source in *Rest. 2d* §552: see above, n. 118.

knowledge,[125] while the liberal view regards the defendant's financial interest as a self-sufficient basis for a duty of care.[126]

Contractual context

In the case of representations made in the context of pre-contractual and contractual relations the additional hurdle has to be faced that a tort duty might unsettle hallowed principles of contract law.

As regards pre-contractual representations, our law had in the past assumed that negotiating parties are ordinarily at arm's length and self-reliant. Moreover, it had long been a settled principle that damages (as distinct from rescission) are not recoverable for non-fraudulent misrepresentations inducing a contract unless promissory in nature and contractual in intent.[127] Such an intent is nowadays generally found if the representor may be regarded as having accepted responsibility for his statement—a test similar to that predicated for a "special duty" of care.[128] It is therefore argued that it would be largely superfluous to extend tort liability to pre-contractual relations.[129] Most courts, however, have taken the view that the existence of pre-contractual relations does not preclude a tort duty of care.[130] Moreover, here and there legislation has reinforced this trend: either on the English model of holding the representor liable ("had the representation been made fraudulently") unless he can prove that he believed on reasonable grounds the statement to be true,[131] or (as in New Zealand[132]) by treating the representation in effect as a contractual warranty.

Recognition of a tortious culpa in contrahendo[133] might also undermine other established principles of contract law. For example, may an offeror henceforth revoke his offer with impunity if he gave a careless quotation

125. *Presser v. Caldwell E.* [1971] 2 N.S.W.L.R. 471 (commission agent's fee from seller not sufficient); *Plummer-Allinson v. Ayrey* [1976] 2 N.Z.L.R. 254.
126. *O'Leary v. Lamb* (1973) 7 S.A.S.R. 159 (with the curious implication that its rationale is false appearance of disinterestedness. Such was not present in *Foster Adv. v. Kleenberg* (1986) 27 D.L.R. (4d) 141: self-serving statement at press conference); *Day v. Ost* [1973] 2 N.Z.L.R. 385.
127. See below, p. 651.
128. In many cases liability has been found on both grounds: e.g. *Esso v. Mardon* [1976] Q.B. 801; *Sodd v. Tessis* (1977) 79 D.L.R. (3d) 632 (Ont. C.A.). Differences remain: e.g. warranty may assure accuracy rather than due care; parol evidence rule does not apply to tort.
129. E.g. McLauchlan, *Pre-contractual Negligent Misrepresentation*, 4 Otago L. Rev. 23 (1977).
130. *Esso v. Mardon* [1976] Q.B. 801 (C.A.); *Howard Marine v. Ogden* [1978] Q.B. 574 (C.A.); *Johnson v. S.A.* (1980) 26 S.A.S.R. 1 (F.C.); *Dillingham v. Downs* [1972] 2 N.S.W.L.R. 49; *Sodd v. Tessis* (1977) 79 D.L.R. (3d) 632 (Ont. C.A.); also Greig, *Misrepresentations and Sales of Goods*, 87 L.Q.R. 179 (1971). Besides, company promoters have long been under a statutory duty of care with respect to prospectuses: *Companies Act* 1981 (Cth) ss 107-108; *Companies Act* 1955 (N.Z.) s. 53. See below, n. 161.
131. *Misrepresentation Act* 1967, followed in S.A. (1971) and A.C.T. (1977). See *Royscot Trust v. Rogerson* [1991] 2 Q.B. 297 (C.A.); 45 Mod. L. Rev. 139 (1982).
132. *Contractual Remedies Act* 1979 s. 6; see McLauchlan, *Assessment of Damages for Misrepresentations Inducing Contracts*, 6 Otago L. Rev. 370 (1970). Also *Consumer Protection Act* 1971 (Man.) s. 58(8); in effect adopting the long established American doctrine (UCC 2-313; also *Rest. 2d* §552C, §552D).
133. See Kessler & Fine, 77 Harv. L. Rev. 401 (1964).

on which the offeree relied in making a forward contract with a third party?[134] Is reliance on an unaccepted offer ever reasonable? Again, must an estimate of building costs be made with reasonable care or at any rate must the contractor correct the mistake as soon as it is discovered?[135]

When a negligent representation is made *after* the formation of the contract by one party to another in the course of performance, additional opposition has been voiced on the principle "if contract, no tort". In *Nunes Diamonds v. D.E.P.*[136] a diamond merchant's safe was protected by the defendant's alarm system. After a burglary at another customer's the defendant's manager gave the negligent assurance that the system performed properly. The Supreme Court of Canada, by a narrow majority, dismissed the claim for loss in a subsequent burglary on the broad ground, among others, that liability in tort could be based only on a tort unconnected with the performance of the contract.[137] But this rationale is no longer reliable now that contract and tort claims generally are viewed as concurrent.[138] The decision must therefore rest on the alternative ground that the installation contract had expressly negatived all "conditions, warranties or representations" and that the court was opposed to tort becoming an escape hatch from inconvenient disclaimer clauses.

Exclusions

That a duty of care may be negatived by a suitable disclaimer of responsibility was itself established in *Hedley Byrne* where the request to the defendant's bank for a credit report on one of its clients opened with the assurance that it was wanted "in confidence and without responsibility". More likely, of course, are disclaimers initiated by the representor. The efficacy of a disclaimer, resting as it does not necessarily on contract but on negativing an initial assumption of responsibility in tort,[139] is all the greater for not being bounded by contractual notions of privity. It can thus operate with respect to non-contractual as well as (we have just seen) with respect to pre- and post-contractual representations.[140]

Responsibility may also be negatived implicitly; for example, where free legal advice is offered off the cuff on a social occasion,[141] or where the plaintiff, even in a business setting, is expected to consult his own lawyer.[142] Thus even in the absence of a disclaimer it is doubtful whether an inquiry from one bank to another concerning a customer's credit would ordinarily raise a legal duty of careful investigation and reply. In the first place, the trouble and expense involved would seem to be beyond all that is normally contemplated when a brief expression of opinion, rather than

134. Cf. *Holman v. Delta Timber* [1972] N.Z.L.R. 1081 (now unreliable decision denying liability).
135. *Abrams v. Ancliffe* [1978] 2 N.Z.L.R. 420; both duties affirmed.
136. [1972] S.C.R. 769.
137. As in *Nelson Lbr. v. Koch* (1980) 111 D.L.R. (3d) 140 (Sask. C.A.).
138. See above, p. 186.
139. This does not prevent application of *Unfair Contract Terms Act* 1977 (Eng.): *Smith v. Bush* [1990] 1 A.C. 831.
140. E.g. *Capital Motors v. Beecham* [1975] 1 N.Z.L.R. 576 at 580; *Carman Constructions v. C.P.R.* [1982] 1 S.C.R. 958.
141. *Fish v. Kelly* (1864) 17 C.B. (N.S.) 194; 144 E.R. 78.
142. *Dorsch v. Weyburn* (Sask. C.A. 1985) 23 D.L.R. (4th) 379.

a detailed and formal report, is sought. This suggests that even if there were a duty of care in some respects, as for example not to report on the wrong client, there is none to embark on detailed research: the amount of diligence due should depend on what responsibility has been assumed. Moreover, the dilemma confronting a banker of reconciling his desire to give a reasonably balanced reply with the duty to his customer to be discreet concerning his affairs and not betray confidential information, might conceivably support an understanding that he assumes no higher responsibility than that of being honest.[143]

Possible conflict of interest may also militate against responsibility, for example a solicitor's for information to someone dealing with his client. If the latter has his own legal adviser, reliance would rarely be justified;[144] if unrepresented especially in a conveyancing transaction, greater responsibility may be expected.[145] Similar would be the position of an accountant or banker advising a target company towards a takeover bidder.[146]

Newspapers,[147] tickertape services[148] and other media of mass communication would be exempt, because the burden of their putative liability is incompatible with any assumption on their part of responsibility for misinformation so widely disseminated and apt to affect or influence their captive public in countless ways.

Assumption of responsibility may be negatived by the public law dimension of the occasion. For example, a local authority's development plan does not contain any implicit assurance that it will be implemented without modification.[149] Nor does it seem proper to hold a Minister accountable in tort for advice on government policy to developers.[150]

Protected class

Of even greater importance in harnessing the range of responsibility are limitations on the class of persons protected. The plaintiff must qualify as one of the class to whom the defendant owed a duty of care. Information

143. *Hedley Byrne v. Heller* [1964] A.C. 465 at 505, 513. When, in contrast, a bank holds itself out to actual or potential clients as an adviser on financial affairs, it may well find itself involved in a special relation importing a duty of care: *Woods v. Martins Bank* [1959] 1 Q.B. 55; *Mutual Mortgage Corp. v. Bank of Montreal* (1965) 55 D.L.R. (2d) 164; Huxley, *Hedley Byrne and the Commonwealth Bank Manager*, 3 Oxf. J. Leg. Stud. 130 (1983).
144. *Gran Gelato v. Rachcliffe* [1992] 2 W.L.R. 867; *Allied Finance v. Haddow* [1983] N.Z.L.R. 22 (C.A.). See Dugdale [1984] N.Z.L.J. 336. Still less does the solicitor owe a duty to his client's opponent: *Business Computers v. Registrar* [1988] Ch. 229.
145. *Tracy v. Atkins* (B.C.C.A. 1980) 105 D.L.R. (3d) 632.
146. Cf. *Morgan Crucible v. Hill Samuel* [1991] Ch. 295 at 324.
147. See *Guay v. Sun Publishing Co.* [1953] 2 S.C.R. 216 (false report of husband's death inducing nervous shock); likewise *MacKown v. Illinois Publishing Co.* 6 N.E. 2d 526 (Ill. 1937) (recommendation of dandruff remedy). Contra: *Sirois v. Féd. Enseig.* (N.B. 1984) 8 D.L.R. (4th) 279.
148. *Jaillet v. Cashman* 139 N.E. 714 (N.Y. 1923). A closer case is *Dickson v. Reuter's* (1877) 3 C.P.D. 1 (telegraph message misdelivered to plaintiff). Though no action lies against the Postmaster-General, some older decisions have held the culpable official liable, because charged with a *public* duty, for misdelivery (*Hamilton v. Clancy* [1914] 2 I.R. 514; contra: *Blakeney v. Pegus* (1885) 6 L.R. (N.S.W.) 223) as well as for non-delivery: *Rowning v. Goodchild* (1773) 2 W. Bl. 906; 96 E.R. 536.
149. *San Sebastian v. Minister* (1986) 162 C.L.R. 340.
150. As held in *Meakes v. A.-G.* [1983] N.Z.L.R. 308 (C.A.). *Rowling v. Takaro Properties* [1986] 1 N.Z.L.R. 22; revd [1988] A.C. 473 (see above, p. 158) is another example of the N.Z. courts' inclination to judicial review of political action through tort litigation.

being easily and widely disseminated, liability is feared to impose a crushing burden on professions and services that live by the printed or spoken word, unless the law were to insist on restrictions upon potential claimants.[151] Differing formulas have been employed. Even the most liberal, linked in some measure to foreseeability, insist that the foreseeable class be "limited"[152] or that the defendant should have foreseen that some *one* (not otherwise identified from among the general public) might reasonably rely on the representation for the purpose of making an investment or takeover.[153] There is no suggestion, however, to accept as sufficient ("proximate") that the statement or report would foreseeably be communicated to and perhaps acted on by an unspecified number of individuals for unspecified transactions.

According to the stricter English view, the only plaintiff to qualify is one to whom information or advice is passed directly or through an intermediary and who, as the defendant knows or should know, will place reliance on it in a *particular* transaction.[154] Such clearly was the American case of the bean weigher who overweighed a lot as a result of which the purchaser overpaid; his certificate was "the end and aim of the transaction".[155] So, a valuer employed by a building society was held liable for a negligent report which was shown to and relied on by the borrower in purchasing the property.[156] In a companion case it was held sufficient even that the prospective purchaser, without actually seeing the report, inferred from the building society's willingness to close the transaction that the report was favourable.[157] That the plaintiff paid for the valuation made the relationship almost "akin to contract".[158] It is, of course, easier if the information was directly requested by the plaintiff, but it is not necessary. If the information is passed through an intermediary, the precise identity of the plaintiff need not be known to the defendant, provided he is or should be aware that it is wanted by someone in particular for a specific purpose or transaction.[159] This test expresses best the concern about liability "in an indeterminate amount to an indeterminate class"[160] by limiting the exposure of the professional to a calculable risk.

151. See above.
152. *Rest. 2d* §552(2)(a); *Haigh v. Bamford* [1977] 1 S.C.R. 466 ("actual knowledge of limited class").
153. *J.E.B. Fasteners v. Marks, Bloom* [1981] 3 All E.R. 289; *Scott v. McFarlane* [1978] 1 N.Z.L.R. 553 (C.A.).
154. *Hedley Byrne v. Heller* [1964] A.C. 465 at 486, 503, 514; *Candler v. Crane, Christmas & Co.* [1951] 2 K.B. 164 at 180-184 ("for the guidance of the very person in the very transaction in question"); *Rest. 2d* §552 ("through reliance upon it in a transaction which he knows that the recipient intends [to influence] or in a substantially similar transaction").
155. *Glanzer v. Shepard* 135 N.E. 275 (N.Y. 1922).
156. *Smith v. Bush* [1990] 1 A.C. 831.
157. *Harris v. Wyre Forest D.C.* [1990] 1 A.C. 831.
158. Ibid. at 846 (Lord Templeman).
159. E.g. in *Hedley Byrne v. Heller* [1964] A.C. 465 it was sufficient that the defendant bank knew the information to be required in connection with an advertising contract worth £100,000 (see esp. at 482).
160. *Ultramares Corp. v. Touche* 174 N.E. 441 at 444; 74 A.L.R. 1139 per Cardozo J. (N.Y. 1931).

On the other hand, the test excludes auditors and accountants from liability to unidentified members of the general public who merely happen to make an investment in reliance on a negligent audit. For this purpose it does not matter whether the plaintiff was an outsider or an existing shareholder who either bought or sold shares on the faith of an over- or under-valued audit. Statutory audits, it has been said, are addressed to shareholders as an entity, not as individuals; for the purpose of enabling them to check on management, not to make individual investment decisions.[161] What makes this conclusion "fair and reasonable" in contrast to, say, the duty of manufacturers of products?[162] Unlike the latter, the auditor is unable to spread the cost among a multitude of clients. Insurance would be prohibitively expensive to the cost of clients, while third party investors get the benefit without paying for it. Unlike the consumer, the investor is usually well placed to protect himself by making his own inquiries. More doubtful is the sacrifice of deterrence, since the potential liability to the client company provides little incentive for care in the interest of shareholders and investors.[163]

The current conservatism of English courts has denied a duty of care by auditors even towards a particular takeover aspirant to whom a negligent financial report ordered by the target company for its own information is handed on. The following aspects were said to be relevant: the purpose for which the statement was made and for which it was communicated; the relationship between the adviser, the advisee and the plaintiff; the size of any class to which the advisee belongs; the state of knowledge of the adviser and the reliance by the advisee. But notwithstanding the fact that the defendant knew the plaintiff to be a likely purchaser and that its report was shown to him, what told most against the plaintiff was that he was an experienced businessman who could be expected to make his own inquiries.[164]

On the other hand, in a different context protection has been extended even to persons who suffer injury without themselves relying on the false representation, as when a search clerk omitted the plaintiff's land charge from a conclusive certificate issued to a purchaser,[165] or a valuer misled the investment manager of a trust with resulting loss to unit holders.[166] Whether or not cases like these are governed by *Hedley Byrne*, the spectre

161. *Caparo Industries v. Dickman* [1990] 2 A.C. 653, not follg *Scott v. McFarlane* [1978] 1 N.Z.L.R. 553 (C.A.); analysed in Australian conspectus by Davies, 14(1) U.N.S.W.L. Rev. 171 (1991); Nicholson, 40 I.C.L.Q. 551 (1991). American cases are in accord, though not uniformly: *Credit Alliance Corp. v. Arthur Anderson* 483 N.E. 2d 110 (N.Y. 1985). Under *Companies Act* (Cth) misrepresentation in prospectus incurs liability to subscribers, not purchasers in the market: *Al Nakib v. Longcroft* [1990] 1 W.L.R. 1390.
162. See Siliciano, *Negligent Accounting*, 86 Mich. L. Rev. 1929 (1988); Bishop, *Negligent Misrepresentation through Economists' Eyes*, 96 L.Q.R. 360 (1980).
163. For alternative solutions see A.L.I.'s proposed *Federal Securities Code* §1708(c) ($200,000 or 2% of revenues of past fiscal year or profits from transaction) for non-wilful violations; Com. on Auditors' Responsibilities (Cohen Report) 154 (N.Y. 1978).
164. *McNaughton v. Hicks Anderson* [1991] 2 Q.B. 113 (C.A.); see also *Morgan Crucible v. Hill Samuel* [1991] Ch. 295 (C.A.); Percival, 54 Mod. L. Rev. 739. Contra: *Scott v. McFarlane* [1978] 1 N.Z.L.R. 553 (C.A.).
165. *Minister of Housing v. Sharp* [1970] 2 Q.B. 233 (C.A.).
166. *B.T. Australia v. Raine & Horne* [1983] 3 N.S.W.L.R. 221.

of incalculable liability argues against a duty to all who might foreseeably suffer economic loss.[167]

Misstatements. Non-disclosure. Contributory negligence.

Finally, the liability with which we are here concerned relates only to *negligent misstatements*. Both elements are limiting. In the first place, the speaker does not *warrant* the accuracy of his information or the soundness of his advice; his duty is only to exercise reasonable care. Secondly, the care he must take is not to *mislead*. In case of ambiguity, therefore, the meaning which controls is that which the maker knew or should have known the recipient would put on it—not necessarily either that intended by the maker or understood by the recipient.[168] Thus even a literally accurate statement may mislead.[169] Moreover, what is important is not so much whether he made adequate inquiries or kept proper accounts as whether he gave the recipient to understand that he had.[170]

By the same token care may be required not only for statements of fact or advice on an existing situation, but also for opinion or belief as to the future. A doctor may become liable for prognosis as well as diagnosis, an investment adviser for an analysis of a company's prospects as well as its past performance.[171] The distinction may, however, have a bearing on whether the defendant accepted responsibility and on whether the plaintiff reasonably relied on it.

Failure to speak up may be as misleading as a positive misstatement. A duty of care would obviously arise in the situations, already noticed,[172] where a deliberate failure to disclose information is treated as fraud, like updating earlier information since falsified.[173] Beyond that, it is found whenever one assumed responsibility (in fact or law) to supply the information and the other relied on his doing so, as where a practice had grown up for a public authority to warn inquirer about zoning proposals.[174] In the absence of reliance there will be few instances to justify such an obligation. One such to be recognised was the duty of a solicitor, custodian of a will, to inform the executor of the testator's death.

167. *Sharp* applied the foreseeability formula, but has been criticised in Australia. *B.T.* accordingly contented itself with stressing that the recipient was under a known duty to the plaintiffs.
168. *McInerny v. Lloyds Bank* [1974] 1 Ll. Rep. 246 at 254.
169. *392980 Ontario v. Welland* (1984) 6 D.L.R. (4th) 151.
170. See *Anderson v. Rhodes* [1967] 2 All E.R. 850 (esp. Jones' acquittal).
171. *M.L.C. v. Evatt* (1968) 122 C.L.R. 556 at 572; *Roots v. Oentory* [1983] 2 Qd R. 745.
172. See above, p. 630.
173. E.g. *Abrams v. Ancliffe* [1978] 2 N.Z.L.R. 420 (builder must warn client of cost escalation).
174. *Shaddock v. Parramatta C.C.* (1981) 150 C.L.R. 225. *Brown v. Heathcote C.C.* [1987] 1 N.Z.L.R. 720 (P.C.) (flood information by drainage board); *Al-Kandari v. Brown* [1988] Q.B. 655 (husband's solicitor failed to inform wife in custody proceedings that his passport had been let go); *Fletcher v. Manitoba Public Ins.* [1990] 3 S.C.R. 191 (prospective insurer failed to alert customer to available coverage). Cf. T.P.A. s. 52 (conduct may mislead when it is or should be known that purchaser is under error: *Rhone-Poulenc v. U.I.M. Services* (1986) 68 A.L.R. 77; *Elconnex v. Gerard Ind.* (1991) 105 A.L.R. 247 Not, however, under *Misrepresentation Act* 1967 (Eng.) or *Contractual Remedies Act* 1979 (N.Z.), which assume a positive misrepresentation. The N.Z. statute abrogates the commom law remedy for pre-contractual misrepresentation.

On one view, the custodianship entailed a responsibility to carry out the deceased's testamentary intentions, on another the key lay in the plaintiff's reasonable expectation to be furnished with information necessary for the exercise of his right to assume executorial functions.[175] That ordinarily reasonable expectation is not sufficient to found a duty of disclosure was affirmed by the House of Lords in holding that, even in a contract uberrimae fidei, failure by an insurer to disclose the fraud of a client's agent could support only a claim for rescission, not damages.[176] Exceptional is the narrow band of fiduciary relations, such as that between principal and agent or solicitor and client, demanding a duty of loyalty to disclose at least conflicts of interest prejudicial to the beneficiary.[177]

The negligent misstatement must also have been causal. Reliance must not only have been foreseeable but have actually occurred. This would not be the case where the plaintiff relied on some other adviser instead[178] or knew the statement to be false or would have acted no differently if he had known the true situation.[179] But the statement need not any more than in the case of fraud, have been the sole inducing cause.[180] Imprudent reliance, amounting to contributory negligence, will provide a partial defence.[181]

Damages

As in the case of deceit,[182] damages for negligent misrepresentation are restricted to reliance losses and do not include expectation losses (loss of bargain) as could a claim for breach of warranty.[183] Thus a plaintiff who had been misled into buying an insurance in the belief that it contained a certain cover in the event of injury, recovered nothing because the policy he purchased was worth (even without that cover) what he paid for it.[184] The court allowed, however, that he would have prevailed if he could have proved that he forwent an opportunity to purchase elsewhere a policy containing the extra cover.[185] Similarly, when a mistaken certificate from

175. *Hawkins v. Clayton* (1988) 164 C.L.R. 539. Comment, 105 L.Q.R. 15 (1989).
176. *Banque Keyser Ullmann v. Skandia* [1991] 2 A.C. 249. Comment, 105 L.Q.R. 191 (1989); 107 L.Q.R. 24 (1991). Statutes, like the *Companies Act* 1981 (Cth) s. 98, may found a duty to disclose certain information, sounding in damages.
177. E.g. *Day v. Meade* [1987] 2 N.Z.L.R. 443. See Finn, *Good Faith and Non-Disclosure*, in Finn (ed.), *Essays in Tort* (1989) 161-170.
178. E.g. *Norris v. Sibberas* [1990] V.R. 161 (F.C.).
179. *J.E.B. Fasteners v. Marks, Bloom* [1983] 1 All E.R. 583 (C.A.); *Siman v. Barclays Bank* 1984 (2) S. Af. L.R. 888 (A.D.). Burden of proof is on the defendant who alleges that plaintiff would have entered into the transaction though on different terms: *Rainbow Caterers v. C.N.R.* (1991) 8 C.C.L.T. (2d) 225 (S.C.C.).
180. Nor is liability precluded by a later, foreseeable negligence, as in *Thorpe Nominees v. Henderson & Lahey* [1988] 2 Qd R. 216 (solicitor's failure to insist on insurance).
181. *Kendall Wilson v. Barraclough* [1986] 1 N.Z.L.R. 576; *Yianni v. Evans* [1982] Q.B. 438 at 457; *Grand Restaurants v. Toronto* (1981) 123 D.L.R. (3d) 349 (not necessarily inconsistent with a requirement that reliance be reasonable). Rare if reliance is foreseeable.
182. See above, p. 637. Pre-contractual misrepresentation: *Royscot Trust v. Rogerson* [1991] 3 W.L.R. 57; see above, p. 643.
183. But not breach of all contracts. E.g. a surveyor ordinarily does not warrant accuracy. Hence damages are the same as in tort: *Watts v. Morrow* [1991] 1 W.L.R. 1421 (C.A.).
184. *Gates v. City Mutual Life* (1986) 160 C.L.R. 1 (under T.P.A.).
185. Ibid. at 11-13.

a local authority led a prospective purchaser to believe that the land was zoned for subdivision, his damages were assessed on the basis of its lesser value (plus conveyancing costs) but not including profits from any subdivision. These would have been recoverable only on proof that he lost an opportunity of buying another property which would have earned profits.[186] While the possibility of recovering opportunity costs moves the tort measure closer to the expectancy measure of contracts, it is not identical with it. In case of a promise by a seller that the property yielded a certain return, the promisee's recovery (in contract) will be measured by the expected gains, whereas in tort for misrepresentation it would by the (usually lesser) return of an alternative investment.[187]

Opportunity costs are thus allowed on proof of reliance. It would seem to follow that in the converse situation of a negligent advice *against* a particular transaction, profits that would have been made are also recoverable. Thus negligent advice that an additional insurance was not needed because the risk was already covered by an existing policy would entitle the plaintiff to the amount of the policy he would have taken out.[188]

Must the loss relate to the very matter misrepresented or is it sufficient simply that it would not have been incurred if the representation had not been made? Suppose a car is misrepresented as having had no more than two owners, but the reason for its lesser value than the price paid is that the *first* owner was a car rental company. The difference in value was nonetheless allowed because the purchaser would not have bought the car but for the misrepresentation.[189]

Consequential damages are also recoverable. But unlike for fraud, damages for negligent misrepresentation must be foreseeable rather than "direct".[190] However, in practice this may be a distinction without much difference.[191] Mental distress is also compensable.[192]

The statute of limitations begins to run when the loss is incurred. In cases of negligent advice by solicitors it has been held to commence when the advice was given and relied upon, no matter that the plaintiff was unaware that he had suffered loss.[193] Where the misrepresentation induces the faulty construction of a building, the same rule could analogically apply,

186. *Kyogle Shire v. Francis* (1988) 13 N.S.W.L.R. 396 (C.A.); *Rentokil v. Channon* (1990) 19 N.S.W.L.R. 417 (C.A.); *Swingcastle v. Gibson* (1991) 2 W.L.R. 1091; *Mason v. Bank of Nova Scotia* [1985] 1 S.C.R. 271 at 285.
187. But cf. *Esso v. Mardon* [1976] Q.B. 801 where Denning M.R. allowed a disappointed tenant, alike in contract or tort, damages for loss of profits by analogy to personal injury (?).
188. Cane, *Negligence, Economic Interests and the Assessment of Damages*, 10 Monash U.L. Rev. 17 (1984); *Cane* 144-148, 180-182.
189. *Capital Motors v. Beecham* [1975] 1 N.Z.L.R. 576; McLauchlan at 410-419. Semble contra: *Rest. 2d* §548A.
190. Damages for pre-contractual misrepresentation under the English *Misrepresentation Act* 1967 (see above, p. 643), deemed to be fraudulent, have been held to be the same as for deceit: *Royscot Trust v. Rogerson* [1991] 2 Q.B. 297 (C.A.); criticised: Brown & Chandler, [1992] M.C.L.Q. 40.
191. See above, p. 638.
192. *Mouat v. Clark Boyce* [1992] 2 N.Z.L.R. 559.
193. *Forster v. Outred* [1982] 1 W.L.R. 86 (C.A.). Australian case law is reviewed in *Crisp v. Blake* (1992) A.T.R. 81-158.

assuming—as we now must[194]—that the loss is characterised as economic, not physical. Thus, despite its unfairness, time would run from the date of construction, not when physical damage occurred or when the loss was reasonably discoverable.[195]

3. STRICT LIABILITY

The common law, cautious enough with liability for negligent misrepresentation, has been even more wary of strict liability for words. Here its principal concern has been with representations in a contractual context.

Contracting parties are held to their contractual representations. For example, goods must accurately meet the description under which they were sold and comply with any express warranties that were given. But this rule has not been extended to representations made in the course of bargaining, as distinct from terms incorporated into the contract itself. No claim for damages can be founded on what a seller (neither fraudulent nor negligent) says to induce the buyer into the bargain, unless "intended" as a contractual promise either as a term of the principal contract or a collateral contract.[196] In substance, if not in so many words, he must say—"I guarantee".[197] After a long period of "caveat emptor", this test is now applied more liberally and considered satisfied whenever the representor can reasonably be understood to have assumed responsibility for the accuracy of his statement. A most significant pointer would be his greater skill and knowledge, commonly found in relation to consumers.[198]

Modern consumer legislation has propelled this tendency much further. In Australia (and New Zealand) the *Trade Practices Act* 1974 (Cth), reinforced by State legislation,[199] now prohibits any corporation from engaging in conduct, in trade or commerce, that is misleading or deceptive or likely to mislead or deceive.[200] It also specifically prohibits various false representations in connection with the supply or promotion of goods.[201] The protection thereby given is much wider than that by the common law, being neither limited to false statements of fact, nor contingent on proof of fault, nor in any way limited to defendants professing "special skill" or to plaintiffs who are "consumers".[202] Its potential for consumer protection is therefore remarkable, as already borne out by its liberal

194. See above, p. 474.
195. See McKendrick, *Pirelli Re-examined*, 11 Leg. St. 326 (1991).
196. *Heilbut, Symons v. Buckleton* [1913] A.C. 30. See Greig, *Misrepresentations and Sales of Goods*, 87 L.Q.R. 179 (1971); *Treitel* 267-272. Except under the *Contractual Remedies Act* 1979 (N.Z.) s. 6: see above, p. 643.
197. *Oscar Chess v. Williams* [1957] 1 W.L.R. 370; *Blakney v. Savage* [1973] V.R. 385 (1968), affd (1970) 119 C.L.R. 435; *Kenny v. Brierty* [1982] V.R. 339; *Jones v. Grais* [1962] S.R. (N.S.W.) 410.
198. E.g. *Dick Bentley v. Smith* [1965] 1 W.L.R. 623 (C.A.) (odometer).
199. *Fair Trading Acts* of N.S.W. (1987 s. 41), Vic. (1985 s. 11), S.A. (1987 s. 56), W.A. (1987 s. 10). These apply to individuals as well.
200. Section 52; extended by s. 6 within const. powers to natural persons. See French, *Essays in Tort* (ed. Finn) ch. 8 (1989). Similarly *Trade Practices Act* 1986 (N.Z.) s. 9.
201. Section 53; *Fair Trading Act* 1985 (Vic.) s. 12.
202. *Nelson v. Concrete Constructions* (1990) 64 A.L.J.R. 293.

application in the courts. It does not, however, extend to misrepresentations in all contexts: not, for example, to one by a foreman to a worker who suffered personal injury; this was excluded because the representation lacked a trading or commercial character though it occurred in carrying on an activity in trade or commerce.[203] Besides other remedies such as injunction or rescission, damages are awarded to "any person who suffers loss or damage by [prohibited] conduct",[204] generally on the tort model.[205]

203. Ibid. See Nicholson, 40 I.C.L.Q. 551 on whether it would have helped the plaintiffs in *Caparo*.
204. Section 82.
205. *Gates v. City Mutual* (1986) 160 C.L.R. 1. But see *Frith v. Gold Coast* (1983) 47 A.L.R. 547.

29

DOMESTIC RELATIONS

A person may demand protection from the law against interference not only with his bodily security and property, but also with interests which he has in valuable relations with others, especially members of his own family. These include interests of substance vulnerable to pecuniary loss, no less than interests of personality vulnerable to emotional distress and loss of such benefits as mutual affection, society and sexual intercourse.

The law in this area used to be dominated by a concept of social relations—the commanding position of the paterfamilias—from which we are only just escaping. Law reform has made much progress, starting about a century ago and especially during the last decades, in correcting the uneven balance between husband and wife. Archaisms however still survive and the transition is yet incomplete.

Tort may impinge on the family circle in several different ways. We will discuss in turn wilful interference, like seduction of a spouse or child; negligent interference, like injuring or killing a breadwinner in an accident; and lastly, torts between members of the same family.

1. WILFUL INTERFERENCE

I. Husband and Wife

Enticement

Displacing the ancient "writ of ravishment",[1] an action on the case became available during the 18th century to support a husband's claim for loss of his wife's "company and society" consequent upon her enticement or "harbouring" by the defendant.[2] It was modelled on the venerable action of trespass per quod consortium amisit which lay in case of physical injury to the wife,[3] differing from it only in that the wife's complicity precluded the tort from being treated as trespass vi et armis.[4]

Enticement (or alienation of affections) consists, of course, in deliberately inducing a wife to leave her husband, with knowledge of her marital status and intent[5] to interfere with the spouses' mutual duty to

1. *Blackstone* iii, 139. A useful historical survey is by Brett, *Consortium and Servitium: A History and Some Proposals*, 29 A.L.J. 321, 389, 428 (1955).
2. *Winsmore v. Greenbank* (1745) Willes 577; 125 E.R. 1330.
3. See below, p. 658.
4. *Wright v. Cedzich* (1930) 43 C.L.R. 493 at 521.
5. The not uncommon substitution of the word "malicious" (e.g. *Best v. Fox* [1952] A.C. 716 at 726) is rather misleading, because it is not necessary to show that the defendant was actuated by spite against the husband.

give consortium to one another. The interloper may have employed persuasion, inducement or incitement, but it is by no means necessary that his was the stronger or overbearing personality.[6] Mere advice, however, is not actionable. In any event regard should be had to contemporary standards of proper behaviour rather than to any hyper-censorious model of the past. Indeed, it has been doubted that the action could nowadays ever be wielded as a retributive weapon within the family circle, for example against a meddlesome mother-in-law; today it seems at most available only against a lover or perhaps a stranger for enticing a spouse into a commune or the like.[7] A husband's ill-treatment of his wife does not seem to justify a stranger enticing her away and making her his mistress (as distinct from merely harbouring her).[8]

"Harbouring" consists merely in providing shelter for an errant wife.[9] That this should be an actionable tort strains our modern outlook even more than does enticement. It has, however, been rendered virtually obsolete by requiring proof (damage being essential) that the wife would otherwise have returned to her husband.[10]

True to its origin, the gist of the claim is the husband's loss of his wife's services and society. The emphasis is thus on material loss, though injury to honour and feelings swells the damages.[11] There must be an interruption of cohabitation or withholding of services; mere adultery or "alienation of affections"[12] will not suffice.

Nowadays, the action bears a distinctly archaic image. The underlying assumption of a husband's proprietary rights in his wife has become obsolete and heart balm unfashionable. Besides, the action is liable to serious abuse of blackmail and perjury.[13] Sex equality demanded one or other alternative: either to extend the right also to wives, which was long ago accomplished by English[14] and Canadian[15] courts but refused by the High Court of Australia,[16] or to abolish the action altogether, as was finally done by legislation in England,[17] Australia,[18] New Zealand,[19] and Canada.[20]

6. *Place v. Searle* [1932] 2 K.B. 497.
7. *Gottlieb v. Gleiser* [1958] 1 Q.B. 267 n.; *Hay v. Williamson* [1975] 1 N.Z.L.R. 526.
8. *Spencer v. Relph* [1969] N.Z.L.R. 713 (C.A.).
9. If the defendant is unaware of the marital situation, it is not clear whether the husband must first make demand: see *Spencer v. Relph* [1969] N.Z.L.R. 713 at 727, 734 (C.A.).
10. *Winchester v. Fleming* [1958] 1 Q.B. 259. The action for harbouring was abolished by the *Domestic Actions Act* 1975 (N.Z.)
11. Not under the *Domestic Actions Act* 1975 (N.Z.) s. 3(4).
12. *Kungl v. Schiefer* [1962] S.C.R. 443; *Hartridge v. Harvie* [1978] N.Z.L.J. 280.
13. Blackmail through collusion between husband and wife, perjury through collusion between wife and seducer.
14. *Gray v. Gee* (1923) 39 T.L.R. 429 per Darling J. (a bachelor); *Best v. Fox* [1952] A.C. 716 at 726, 729-730.
15. *Applebaum v. Gilchrist* [1946] 4 D.L.R. 383; *Wener v. Davidson* (1970) 15 D.L.R. (3d) 631. U.S.: *Rest 2d* §683, comment *d; Prosser & Keeton* 916.
16. *Wright v. Cedzich* (1930) 43 C.L.R. 493.
17. *Law Reform (Miscellaneous Provisions) Act* 1970 s. 5.
18. *Family Law Act* 1975 (Cth) s. 120; Wrongs Act 1936 (S.A.) s. 36 (since 1972).
19. *Family Proceedings Act* 1980 s. 190.
20. See *Davenport v. Miller* (1990) 70 D.L.R. (4th) 181 (incompatible with Charter).

Adultery

Even more offensive to the modern mind is a husband's claim of damages for mere adultery, since it purports to compensate him for being cuckolded without even having lost his wife. Yet this is precisely what the common law offered him in the action of criminal conversation,[21] which did not necessitate proof that he had lost his wife's society and cohabitation.[22] It was independent of proof of pecuniary loss and allowed recovery for emotional distress as such.

In England, the action for criminal conversation was abolished in 1857, but simultaneously the newly established Divorce Court received the mandate to award damages on the same principles against co-respondents in divorce or judicial separation. The same transfer of jurisdiction occurred in Australia. This removed its most objectionable feature by at least confining the claim to situations where the marriage had actually broken down. Later, damages were no longer necessarily pocketed by the petitioner but could be set aside for the benefit of the children of the marriage or even the offending spouse. In Australia the action also lost its taint of sex discrimination when it was at last extended to wives.[23] Eventually, however, it was totally abolished in England,[24] Australia,[25] New Zealand[26] and Canada.[27]

II. Parent and Child

From the outset, legal protection of the parental relationship was moulded by a one-sided concern for the parent's pecuniary interests. In the Middle Ages, a writ of trespass for the ravishment of a ward vindicated the father's or guardian's interest in the marriage of his heir—a feudal incident of considerable value.[28] The claim of a parent as such, however, received no recognition: trespass, it was said, was based upon a proprietary interest, and in a son or daughter a father had no property.[29] Eventually,[30] the courts came to sanction a more general remedy by extending to the relation of parent and child the writ which had long served to protect a master's interest in his servant;[31] tied though it was to the notion of loss of services which was somewhat incongruous, if less so than today, in its application to a child. This anomalous link between child and servant has survived into modern law.

A parent may complain of abduction or enticement of his child in violation of his right to legal custody, as when a girl of 16 was persuaded

21. This action is first encountered towards the end of the 17th century.
22. *Wilton v. Webster* (1835) 7 C. & P. 198; 173 E.R. 87 (where husband recovered although he had only become aware of his wife's indiscretion when she made a confession on her death-bed).
23. *Matrimonial Causes Act* 1950 (Cth) s. 44; also *Matrimonial Proceedings Act* 1963 (N.Z.).
24. *Law Reform (Miscellaneous Provisions) Act* 1970 s. 4.
25. *Family Law Act* 1975 (Cth) s. 120.
26. *Domestic Actions Act* 1975 s. 2.
27. See above, n. 20.
28. *Holdsworth* viii, 427-428.
29. *Barham v. Dennis* (1600) Cro. Eliz. 770; 78 E.R. 1001.
30. Probably not earlier than the 17th century: *Winfield* (8th ed. 1967) 528.
31. See below, p. 684.

to join a nunnery against her father's will.[32] In this respect, his claim to damages serves the same, or a complementary, purpose to the writ of habeas corpus or wardship proceedings. The more common function of the action, however, is to wreak retribution against one who raped[33] or seduced his daughter (her consent affording no defence), though loss of services is a condition precedent in this no less than in the former case. Technically, therefore, seduction is "an incident rather than the essence of the action"[34] and the parent is put to proof of some pecuniary loss, such as his daughter's inability to perform her household duties in consequence of illness, pregnancy or confinement.[35] But that requirement gradually came to be reduced virtually to vanishing point by courts anxious to find a peg for recovery, even on so meagre a basis as an errant daughter's delay in fetching a jug of rum for her father.[36]

And once pecuniary loss, however exiguous, has been established, the door is opened for recovery beyond actual expenditures incurred or the calculable value of the service lost during the daughter's disability.[37] "The plaintiff comes into court as a master; he goes before the jury as a father",[38] entitled to aggravated and even exemplary damages for "the mental distress caused to [him] by the dishonour of his child, and the punishment of the man who has brought such dishonour on the home".[39] But though he is suing for injury to his own rights (any damage to the daughter, whether in person, reputation or prospect being her own affair), her bad character or conduct may be averred in mitigation, since it goes to the value of her services, like that of a wife in a husband's action.[40]

Loss of services postulates a right to services. This requirement has likewise been attenuated to little more than a pretence.[41] If the child is under age a mere right to its service is deemed sufficient; though if of tender years, its inability to render domestic assistance would still preclude recovery,[42] except for necessary medical expenses.[43] If of full age, proof of actual services rendered is required, though the evidence need be but slight[44] and any de facto service, however trivial, such as making a cup of

32. *Lough v. Ward* [1945] 2 All E.R. 338.
33. *Mattouk v. Massad* [1943] A.C. 588.
34. *Brownlee v. MacMillan* [1940] A.C. 802 at 809.
35. *Murray v. Kerr* [1918] V.L.R. 409; *Brankstone v. Cooper* (1943) 43 W.A.L.R. 51.
36. *Potter v. Linden* (1867) 6 S.C.R. (N.S.W.) 351.
37. Including, apparently, the cost of maintaining a child born as the result of the seduction, even in the absence of any legal obligation of maintenance: *Flynn v. Connell* [1919] 2 I.R. 427; sed quaere?
38. *Briggs v. Evans* (1844) 27 N.C. 13 at 16, 20; cited by *Prosser & Keeton* 926 n. 54.
39. *Murray v. Kerr* [1918] V.L.R. 409 at 412 per Irvine C.J. Even mere "harbouring" (*Lough v. Ward* [1945] 2 All E.R. 338).
40. *Verry v. Watkins* (1836) 7 C. & P. 308; 173 E.R. 137. So may his own conduct in conducing to the seduction, as in *Reddie v. Scoolt* (1794) Peake 316; 170 E.R. 169 (non-suit).
41. Unless the parental right to services has been definitely suspended by the child living away from home on a permanent basis with her employer: *Hedges v. Tagg* (1872) L.R. 7 Ex. 283; *Rogers v. Bridge* (1900) 21 L.R. (N.S.W.) 328. Even then, a residual right has often qualified: *Rist v. Faux* (1863) 4 B. & S. 409; 122 E.R. 513.
42. *Hall v. Hollander* (1825) 4 B. & C. 660; 107 E.R. 1206.
43. See below, n. 66.
44. *Harper v. Luffkin* (1827) 7 B. & C. 387; 108 E.R. 767 (daughter, a married woman, separated from her husband, had returned to her father as his servant).

tea,[45] milking cows[46] or occasionally assisting in the running of the household, is sufficient. Ordinarily the proper person to complain is the father as head of the household; under the traditional law the mother's rights arose only if she was herself entitled to custody of the child or otherwise entitled to its services,[47] as on the death of the father[48] or in respect of an illegitimate child.[49] Indeed, the plaintiff need not be the natural parent at all, any person in loco parentis may sue.[50]

Some States have entirely abrogated the fiction of loss of services, by creating a conclusive statutory presumption of the relationship of master and servant and loss of service in actions for seduction by a parent or person in loco parentis.[51] This broad mandate has been read down to require at least proof of some resulting disability by the girl to perform ordinary domestic functions,[52] but may yet conceivably support a parent's claim in respect of a daughter whom he has not seen for half a lifetime, or who has a husband and a family,[53] or supports an establishment of her own.[54] Welcome though it may be for releasing the law from the pretence of fiction, it might well be questioned whether the time is not overdue for abolishing the whole action, based as it is on economic relations between parent and child and social views concerning parental honour which have long become outmoded. It is even less appropriate to enforce one parent's right of access against the other.[55] Legislation has abolished the action in several jurisdictions.[56]

Though of much deeper psychological and social importance, a child's reciprocal interest in an unimpaired family life has never been vindicated by the law granting a remedy at its behest against an interloper who disrupts the home.[57]

2. NEGLIGENT INTERFERENCE

Relational interests within the family are much more liable to suffer from conduct which, rather than being aimed at disrupting that relation as by enticing a wife, merely happens to impinge upon it unwittingly, as when a

45. *Carr v. Clarke* (1818) 2 Chit. 260.
46. *Bennett v. Allcott* (1787) 2 T.R. 166 at 168; 100 E.R. 90 at 91.
47. As in *Oakes v. Hindman* [1934] 4 D.L.R. 190.
48. If the widowed mother remarried, it is the second husband alone who may ordinarily bring the action: see *Stoner v. Skene* (1918) 44 O.L.R. 609.
49. Aliter, if the child is brought up by her natural father: *Beetham v. James* [1937] 1 K.B. 527.
50. *Peters v. Jones* [1914] 2 K.B. 781 (adoptor).
51. Vic.: *Wrongs Act* 1958 s. 14; W.A.: *Evidence Act* 1906 s. 49; Tas.: *Evidence Act* 1910 s. 228; following the N.Z. *Evidence Act* 1908 s. 22. Similar Canadian legislation is discussed in *Brownlee v. MacMillan* [1940] A.C. 802.
52. *Murray v. Kerr* [1918] V.L.R. 409; *Brankstone v. Cooper* (1941) 43 W.A.L.R. 51; *Clapp v. De la Perrelle* (1899) 17 N.Z.L.R. 413 is not necessarily inconsistent.
53. Analogous Canadian legislation is confined to seduction of an "*unmarried* female" (see *Seduction Act* 1960 (Ont.) s. 1).
54. *Brankstone v. Cooper* (1941) 43 W.A.L.R. 51.
55. *Frame v. Smith* [1987] 2 S.C.R. 790, denying all other tort remedies.
56. E.g. *Law Reform (Miscellaneous Provisions) Act* 1970 (Eng.) s. 5; *Wrongs Act* 1972 (S.A.) s. 35.
57. A sufficient justification is probably that it would in practice only furnish another cudgel for the displaced spouse to belabour the unfaithful partner.

husband incurs household and medical expenses consequent upon his wife being injured in a road collision. Such loss is an indirect and unintended secondary consequence of the defendant's tort against his primary victim, the wife. Ordinarily, as we have already seen,[58] our law is on principle opposed to claims for relational injury, fearful lest it add an excessive burden, once it is borne in mind that serious injury to most accident victims entails prejudice also for other people connected with him. Yet in the case of close relatives, the claim is exceptionally compelling.

I. Husband and Wife

The husband's action for loss of services against anyone who has wrongfully injured his wife is of ancient origin.[59] Like the action for enticement, it was originally based on the notion that the husband had a proprietary interest in his wife and her services, the impairment of which amounted to nothing less than trespass. Injury to a wife was not only a wrong to her, but also to her husband for which he might have redress quite independently of her.[60] Later, after the action had come to be laid in Case,[61] it was eventually extended beyond intentional aggressions to negligent injury, but not for loss resulting from death.[62] Today, the injury sustained by her need not even have been inflicted by direct impact so that in New South Wales, for example, it will now suffice that she suffered nervous shock upon hearing of her daughter's death in an accident.[63]

The husband's remedy was originally tied to the notion of loss of "services". Gradually, it seems to have become recognised that the value of the conjugal relationship to him consisted not only in his wife's domestic assistance and the care of children, but also in the less tangible elements of her comfort and companionship—a transformation reflected in the terminological change from "servitium" to "consortium". There remains however a difference of opinion as to the scope of its protection. According to one view, hostile to the action, consortium is indivisible; there must be a total (even if temporary) disruption of the whole, as during the wife's stay in hospital. The impairment of merely one or another of its strands, however, would not be enough, as when on her return she is only sexually disabled or incapable of fulfilling some of her household duties.[64]

Australia has rejected this narrow view and continues to support claims for "all practical domestic disadvantages suffered by a husband in consequence of his wife's impaired health or bodily condition", even if they

58. See above, p. 145.
59. *Hyde v. Seyssor* (1619) Cro. Jac. 538; 79 E.R. 462; *Guy v. Livesey* (1629) Cro. Jac. 501; 79 E.R. 428.
60. E.g. his cause of action neither abated on her death (*Mallet v. Dunn* [1949] 2 K.B. 180 at 184-185) nor was it prejudiced by any prior recovery for her own injuries: *Brockbank v. Whitehaven Rly* (1862) 7 H. & W. 834; 158 E.R. 706.
61. Trespass always was anomalous if only because special damage was of the gist of the action from its inception.
62. *Baker v. Bolton* (1808) 1 Camp. 493; 170 E.R. 1033: see below, p. 663. Nor to loss after divorce, even if caused by the accident: *Parker v. Dzundza* [1979] Qd R. 55.
63. *State Rail v. Sharp* [1981] 1 N.S.W.L.R. 240 (C.A.).
64. Thus the C.A. in *Best v. Fox* [1951] 2 K.B. 639 (the Lords were divided on this issue: [1952] A.C. 716); *Spaight v. Dundon* [1961] I.R. 201; also Forbes, *Loss of Consortium: A Restatement*, 32 A.L.J. 239 at 276 (1958).

fall short of total disruption of the consortium.[65] Recoverable in the first instance are medical expenses debited to him,[66] the cost of hospital visits and in some circumstances even loss of earnings due to attending upon her during her illness.[67] Additionally, he may recover for his wife's reduced capacity to manage household affairs[68] and render him conjugal support and assistance,[69] but such services must relate to the domestic sphere: he must claim qua husband, not qua employer or business partner.[70] Some concern has been evident that allowances should remain realistic[71] and not overlap with her own recovery.[72] High among non-pecuniary items is loss of sexual relations, which is considered "material" and deserving substantial, if modest, awards. "Mere sentiment and feelings", however, are excluded, such as distress over the wife's condition as distinct from its effect on the quality of her companionship.[73]

Wife

A corresponding bid by a wife for loss of her husband's consortium (sexual incapacity) was categorically defeated by the House of Lords in *Best v. Fox.*[74] Not only was there no precedent for such a claim, but its absence could not be readily explained by reference to the long lasting procedural disability of married women as in cases of enticement or seduction, since there would have been every inducement for the husband to participate in an action, additional to his own, against the tortfeasor. The old common law never recognised a right in a wife to the services of her husband corresponding to his; and yet it was arguable that the wife's interest in consortium had gradually gained recognition to the extent, at least, that its

65. *Toohey v. Hollier* (1955) 92 C.L.R. 618. Canada is divided, with Ontario leaning against such recovery: *Canestraro v. Larade* (1972) 28 D.L.R. (3d) 290.
66. The basis being his legal duty to supply necessary medical aid: *Best v. Fox* [1952] A.C. 716 at 733 per Lord Goddard; *Kirkham v. Boughey* [1958] 2 Q.B. 338 at 342; but see reservation expressed by Street, *Principles of Law of Damages* (1961) 224. According to *Gage v. King* [1961] 1 Q.B. 188, *Oliversen v. Mills* (1964) 50 D.L.R. (2d) 768, ordinarily a wife's medical expenses are legally incurred by her husband and he alone can claim. But this is contrary to *Lang v. Gambareri* (1968) 70 D.L.R. (2d) 464 and Scott L.J.'s conclusion in *Rees v. Hughes* [1946] K.B. 517 (C.A.) that since the Married Women's Property Acts, a husband is liable only if she pledged his credit. If, as happens in so many road accidents, he was contributorily negligent, it will be to the family's advantage if the claim can be made in her name so as to avoid reduction.
67. *Kealley v. Jones* [1979] 1 N.S.W.L.R. 723; *McNeill v. Johnstone* [1958] 1 W.L.R. 888. Not however the value of gratuitous services for her (*Johnson v. Kelemic* (1979) F.L.C. 78,487), though *she* might recover that under *Griffiths v. Kerkemeyer*: see above, p. 230, n. 52.
68. But the value of her services can alternatively be claimed by *her*, and her claim should nowadays have priority over his. See above, p. 235.
69. *Toohey v. Hollier* (1955) 92 C.L.R. 618 (£1,000); *State Rail v. Sharp* [1981] 1 N.S.W.L.R. 240 ($15,000 for loss of society and sex); *Lawrence v. Biddle* [1966] 2 Q.B. 504.
70. *Behrens v. Bertram Mills Circus* [1957] 2 Q.B. 1.
71. E.g. claims for his own greater burden of domestic services may not include gratuitous services customary in the family: *Keally v. Jones* [1979] 1 N.S.W.L.R. 723; cf. *Kovac v. Kovac* (above, p. 230, n. 52).
72. *Norman v. Sutton* (1989) A.T.R. 80-282 (N.S.W.C.A.) (prior settlement does not disqualify).
73. *Johnson v. Kelemic* (1979) F.L.C. 78,487, modifying dicta in *Keally*; *Andrewartha v. Andrewartha* (1987) 44 S.A.S.R. 1 (banco).
74. [1952] A.C. 716; *Dahm v. Harmer* [1955] S.A.S.R. 250; *Marx v. A.-G.* [1974] 1 N.Z.L.R. 164 (C.A.).

impairment might furnish the basis for parasitic damages in actions for defamation[75] or personal injuries,[76] and had come to be protected independently against enticement. But the last step in equalising the position of spouses was not taken. Since the husband's action itself was now widely considered an anachronism, there was no reason for extending it beyond the strictest requirements of precedent.[77] Indeed so peremptory is the policy that a wife did not fare any better by basing her claim instead on general negligence (no "duty").[78]

The sting of sex discrimination apparent in this decision is only slightly alleviated by the fact that, unlike a husband, a wife does not ordinarily incur expenses for medical treatment and household services as the result of the other's disablement. If exceptionally she does incur them, including the cost of visiting him in hospital, she is probably in any event entitled to recover these items in her own right, by analogy to similar claims now allowed to husbands, parents and even employers on the independent ground, apparently, that these expenses were incurred in performance of a legal duty to maintain the other.[79] Moreover, if she gave up a lucrative occupation in order to nurse him, at least *he* can recover for most of that loss, it seems.[80] All this is rather makeshift; motivated no doubt by the wish not to shortchange the conjugal exchequer while avoiding the evil of double recovery. In the upshot, however, the wife's non-pecuniary losses go completely uncompensated.

In the interest of equality, two solutions are open. One is to abolish all spousal claims for loss of consortium, as in England, several Australian jurisdictions and New Zealand.[81] The other is to confer equal rights on wives, as in Queensland and South Australia.[82] The former is preferable because it avoids overlapping of claims by spouses and because the very basis of consortium claims has become incongruous.

II. Parent and Child

Like a husband, a parent also may claim for loss to himself consequent on tortious injury to his child. This version of the action for loss of services is akin to that for enticement or seduction of a daughter, except that

75. *Lynch v. Knight* (1861) 9 H.C.L. 577; 11 E.L.R. 854.
76. E.g. husband's desertion because of her disfigurement: *Hird v. Gibson* [1974] Qd R. 14.
77. It is doubtful whether the decision would have been different if the husband had been the victim of *intentional* aggression; *Johnson v. Commonwealth* (1927) 27 S.R. (N.S.W.) 133 would probably not be followed today.
78. *Marx v. A.-G.* [1974] 1 N.Z.L.R. 164 (C.A.).
79. See above, n. 66; below, n. 83.
80. See above, p. 230, n. 52.
81. *Administration of Justice Act* 1982 (Eng.) s. 2; *Law Reform (Marital Consortium) Act* 1984 (N.S.W.); *Acts Amendment (Actions for Damages) Act* 1986 (W.A.) s. 4; *Common Law (Miscellaneous Actions) Act* 1986 (Tas.) s. 3; *Law Reform (Miscellaneous Provisions) Act* 1955 (A.C.T.) s. 32; *Married Persons (Equality of Status) Act* 1989 (N.T.); *Barlow v. Humphrey* [1990] 2 N.Z.L.R. 373; *Shkwarchuk v. Hansen* (Sask. 1984) 30 C.C.L.T. 121 (Can. Charter of Rights); also Alberta: *Woelk v. Halvorson* [1980] 2 S.C.R. 430. The American constitutional guarantee of equal protection has stimulated similar *judicial* reorientation: *Rest 2d* §693, comment *d*; *Prosser & Keeton* 931-932.
82. *Law Reform (Husband and Wife) Act* 1989 (Qld); *Wrongs Act* 1936 (S.A.) s. 33; *Law Reform (Miscellaneous Provisions) Act* 1955 (A.C.T.) (for loss of the other's ability to do housework).

recovery is here clearly confined to economic harm, like medical expenses[83] and such loss as the parent qua master sustained in being deprived of filial assistance, to the exclusion of any compensation for grief and injured feelings.[84]

The incongruous requirement of "service" has been eroded just as in the context of seduction. De facto assistance or just the mere right to it are sufficient,[85] but no claim can be maintained with respect to a child that has been emancipated;[86] nor one too young to render services,[87] except for medical expenses *necessarily* incurred.[88] In England the parent's action, like the husband's, has now been abolished by statute.[89]

The common law has never recognised a corresponding claim for pecuniary loss, let alone loss of consortium, sustained by a child as the result of wrongful injury to a parent. For the most part, such tangible economic loss as may flow from the injuries and affect the standard of living of the victim's family would be recoverable at the instance of the parent himself; but no allowance is made for the fact that "a daughter may have to give up work which she enjoys and stay at home to nurse a father who has been transformed into an irritable invalid."[90] A fortiori, emotional distress so natural especially among children of tender years also remains uncompensable. Only when injuries prove fatal, has a dependant now a statutory remedy for pecuniary loss resulting from the parent's death.[91]

III. Defences

While it is true that in an action for loss of services the husband or parent is asserting the violation of an interest of his own, it is nevertheless a condition precedent that the defendant's conduct was wrongful against the wife or child. In this regard, enticement and seduction are exceptional in conferring on him a claim although his wife or daughter, in the absence of duress, have none.[92]

83. Including the costs of recovery-assisting hospital visits, but not apparently loss of earnings by the father due to his giving up more lucrative employment in order to accompany the family to where the child is hospitalised: *Timmins v. Webb* [1964] S.A.S.R. 250; *Cook v. Wright* [1967] N.Z.L.R. 1034; *Gow v. Motor Vehicle Insurance Trust* [1967] W.A.R. 55 (mistakenly based on foreseeability instead of reasonableness of expenditure).
84. *Taylor v. Bristol Omnibus Co.* [1975] 1 W.L.R. 1054. In the U.S. the majority trend to include damages for "loss of companionship" in fatal accident cases (see below, p. 671) has rarely been extended to mere injury: *Prosser & Keeton* 934.
85. *Jones v. Brown* (1874) Peake 306; 170 E.R. 165. But the statutory modifications, noted in connection with seduction (see above, p. 657) have not been transgrafted.
86. *Pratt v. Pratt* [1975] V.R. 378 (mother giving up job to nurse adult daughter).
87. *Hall v. Hollander* (1825) 4 B. & C. 660; 107 E.R. 1206.
88. *Lloyd v. Lewis* [1963] V.R. 277; *Beckerson v. Dougherty* [1953] 2 D.L.R. 498 at 508; and above, n. 66. The claim, if advanced by parent rather than child, is neither liable to reduction for the child's contributory negligence nor vulnerable to the argument that the child was under no legal obligation to pay them: cf. *Blundell v. Musgrave* (1956) 96 C.L.R. 73 at 92.
89. *Administration of Justice Act* 1982 s. 2.
90. *Best v. Fox* [1952] A.C. 716 at 734 per Lord Morton; *Porpaczy v. Truitt* (1990) 5 C.C.L.T. (2d) 94.
91. See below, p. 665. The *Family Law Reform Act* 1978 (Ont.) extended the death benefits to injury.
92. E.g. *Rogers v. Goddard* (1682) 2 Show. K.B. 255; 89 E.R. 925 (action for battery of wife, presumably sexual intercourse, although she was a consenting party).

Does this mean that the defendant must have committed an in all respects actionable tort against the victim? Clearly, his conduct must at least have been prima facie wrongful:[93] not outside a recognised duty relation, as where the common law duty to gratuitous passengers had been modified by statute.[94] Beyond this however, authority is divided. On one view, the defendant's conduct must be culpable in law, and its quality vis-à-vis the wife or child conclusively defines also his liability to the husband or parent. The nature of the action is "derivative" and any defence like contributory negligence, open against the primary victim, is imputable to the relational claimant. This view is widely held in the United States[95] and Canada[96] and has been given statutory force in New South Wales[97] and South Australia.[98] Another school, however, entrenched in England[99] and elsewhere in Australia,[100] holds the relational claim to be genuinely independent[101] and unaffected by the victim's contributory negligence. This position has of course the merit of aiding recovery and thus helping to distribute losses, even if it happens to be at odds with the contemporary bias against relational claims and adds another anomalous distinction between non-fatal and fatal injuries (surviving dependants are identified with the person killed[102] just as a master is with his servant[103]). In terms of fairness and social policy, moreover, it does not make a great deal of sense that a defendant should be required to foot the whole of the medical bill if, but only if, his contributorily negligent victim turns out to be a married woman whose husband can providentially espouse the cause of their joint domestic budget.[104]

The plaintiff's own contributory negligence or assumption of risk will, of course, affect his right of recovery. Thus if a wife is injured in a collision as the result partly of her husband's negligent driving, rather than her own, his claim against the other motorist for her medical expenses will be reduced accordingly,[105] just like the claim of a parent whose negligence in supervision contributed to his child being run over in the street.[106]

93. *Mallett v. Dunn* [1942] 2 K.B. 180 at 185.
94. *A.-G. v. Jackson* [1946] S.C.R. 489 (servant); *Scott v. Marshall* (1965) 55 D.L.R. (2d) 58 (wife).
95. See 25 A.L.R. (4th) 118 (1983).
96. The cases are reviewed in *Trapp v. Hnatuk* (1976) 71 D.L.R. (3d) 63.
97. *Motor Accidents Act* 1988 s. 75; *Workers Compensation Act* 1987 s. 151N(5).
98. *Wrongs Act* 1936 s. 27a(9); *Meadows v. Maloney* (1972) 4 S.A.S.R. 567.
99. *Mallett v. Dunn* [1949] 2 K.B. 180.
100. *Curran v. Young* (1965) 112 C.L.R. 99.
101. So independent that the husband would never be estopped if his wife's claim had been previously dismissed.
102. See below, p. 667.
103. See above, p. 287; loss of services: see below, p. 688.
104. He cannot even claim contribution from the wife because she owed no duty to her husband with respect to her services and was thus not a co-tortfeasor who would "have been liable in respect of the same damage"; (*Lawrence v. Slatcher* [1968] V.R. 337). In South Africa contribution has been conferred by the *Apportionment of Damages Amendment Act* 1971.
105. *Gage v. King* [1961] 1 Q.B. 188.
106. *Beckerson v. Dougherty* [1953] 2 D.L.R. 498; *Cameron v. Comm. Rlys* [1964] Qd R. 480 at 494-495. But because such a negligent parent does not owe a duty of supervision to the child and is therefore not a tortfeasor, he would not be liable to contribution (as distinct from having his own claim for medical expenses reduced): see below, p. 682.

IV. Reform

The present state of the law, fashioned as it has been out of an archaic survival, is open to a number of objections. First is the debatable question whether modern law should at all entertain relational claims for other than material injury. There is good reason for compensating pecuniary loss suffered or expenses incurred by others, especially family members of the victim. This is already the case where the victim is killed rather than injured. But there is no similar widespread support for awarding damages for psychological and other non-material injury, especially when available only to a husband or parent but not to a wife or child. Secondly, limiting damages to material loss opens the possibility of vesting the claim, not in the dependant but exclusively in the victim himself. In respect of services *to* the victim this has already been accomplished.[107] Not so, however, in regard to other losses, including loss of the victim's services by others. In the case of a housewife, for example, it is much more in accordance with modern ideas to let her rather than her husband recover for loss of her services.[108] This would also have the advantage of exposing the defendant to one claimant only and so dispel the risk of overlapping claims and double liability.[109] Thirdly, the class of family dependants qualified by statute to claim for death (below, Section 3) is considerably larger than that of husband and parent who, for now obsolete reasons, are alone qualified by the common law in case of non-fatal injury. There is no justification today for such discrimination.

Reform[110] along varying lines, some extending relational claims to a wider class of family members,[111] others abolishing all,[112] is now gaining pace.

3. FATAL ACCIDENTS

I. Common Law

With singular harshness, the common law disclaimed all concern with tort losses in the wake of wrongfully inflicted death. The taunt that it was cheaper to kill than to maim really had its barb in the fact that it actually cost nothing at all; for death was not a compensable injury either to the victim himself[113] or to surviving members of his family, disappointed in their expectation of continued support. The reason for this rule is obscure. It made its first appearance in 1808 when Lord Ellenborough, in *Baker v. Bolton*,[114] categorically enunciated that "in a civil court the death of a

107. See above, p. 230.
108. See above, p. 235.
109. See e.g. *Norman v. Sulton* (1989) A.T.R. 80-282.
110. See Kutner, *Law Reform in Tort: Abolition of Liability for "Intentional" Interference with Family Relationships*, 17 W.A.L. Rev. 25 (1987) concerning Commonwealth.
111. *Family Law Reform Act* 1978 (Ont.). In 1973 the L.C. (No. 56, §159(a)) recommended claims by the victim himself for losses and expenses by others.
112. See above, n. 81.
113. Far from death conferring a cause of action on him (or rather his estate), all causes of action in tort vested in him prior thereto abated on his death: see below.
114. Camp. 493; 170 E.R. 1033.

human being could not be complained of as an injury." The claim rose from an accident caused by the negligent driving of a stage coach in which a husband and wife were passengers and the latter sustained fatal injuries. The husband recovered for his own bruises and for the loss of his wife's consortium up to the time of her death, but not for loss accruing thereafter.

The decision seems to be the result of a misreading of legal history.[115] It has been linked[116] with the archaic rule[117] that, where the tort constitutes at the same time a felony, no civil action can be maintained until the wrongdoer has been prosecuted. At one time, when every felony was punishable by death and all a felon's chattels were forfeited to the Crown upon conviction, the result may well have been that in all cases of wrongful death a civil action would in practice have been futile. But later it came to be recognised[118] that the right of action for damages was only suspended, not destroyed; and in any event, this explanation cannot account for the rule in cases where the death was not caused by felonious conduct. It has also been suggested[119] that the action of trespass never dealt with homicide, but there is no authority for this beyond the rule already referred to, that in the interest of justice a felon must first be prosecuted. In all likelihood, the principle in *Baker v. Bolton* must be ascribed to a confusion between the "merger" rule and the unrelated maxim "actio personalis moritur cum persona", which meant that any cause of action in tort vested in the deceased did not survive for the benefit of his estate. That principle has, of course, no relevance in the present context, where the plaintiff and defendant are both still alive and the action is brought for the death of a third party. We are here concerned with death creating, not extinguishing, a cause of action.

But despite its questionable antecedents and lack of authority, apart from a single nisi prius decision, the rule was accepted more than half a century later[120] over the powerful dissent of Bramwell B. and eventually endorsed by the House of Lords in 1916.[121] Significantly, this final review coincided with the first expressions of dissatisfaction with the action for loss of services itself, which the court saw no reason for extending beyond strict precedent to cases of death.

That the rule represents less than a peremptory policy of our law is however attested by allowing recovery for loss of dependency resulting from death when it is merely an item of damage in a cause of action "arising independently of the wrong causing the fatality", such as a breach of contract. Thus, a husband whose wife died from consuming a tin of poisoned salmon successfully sued the grocer for breach of implied warranty and recovered, besides medical and funeral expenses, damages for

115. *Holdsworth* iii, 333-336, 676-677. The English and American history is traced by Malone, *Genesis of Wrongful Death*, 17 Stan L. Rev. 1043 (1965).
116. *Osborne v. Gillett* (1873) L.R. 8 Ex. 88 at 96.
117. See above, p. 35.
118. *Wells v. Abrahams* (1872) L.R. 7 Q.B. 554; *Smith v. Selwyn* [1914] 3 K.B. 98.
119. *The Amerika* [1917] A.C. 38 at 56-60 per Lord Sumner.
120. *Osborne v. Gillett* (daughter) (1873) L.R. 8 Ex. 88.
121. *The Amerika* [1917] A.C. 38. Also beyond judicial review in Australia: *Swan v. Williams (Demolition)* (1987) 9 N.S.W.L.R. 172 (C.A.).

loss of her services.[122] This loophole has somewhat incongruously survived wrongful death legislation, and on occasion still helps to transcend the statutory limits of recovery, in awards such as for non-pecuniary losses or funeral expenses.[123]

II. Lord Campbell's Act

The advent of railways and the concomitant increase of fatal accidents gave the impetus to reform. By a statute of 1846, generally known as *Lord Campbell's Act*,[124] a limited measure of protection was at last accorded to the interests of dependants in the continued life of close relatives. This statutory remedy for wrongful death has been adopted throughout Australia.[125]

The Act makes it a wrong, at the suit of certain designated relatives, to cause the death of a human being "by a wrongful act, neglect or default, which is such as would (if death had not ensued) have entitled the party injured to maintain an action and recover damages in respect thereof, notwithstanding that the death was caused under circumstances amounting in law to felony".[126] Although the primary legislative object was to furnish a remedy for death caused by tort, it has been beneficently extended to fatalities resulting from such other "defaults" as breach of contract. Thus a mother recovered for the death of her son who was electrocuted by a defective light bulb purchased from the defendants. Negligence on the part of the retailers could not be established, but it was held sufficient to rely on breach of the implied warranty of fitness which would have conferred a right of action on the deceased.[127]

Beneficiaries

The relatives protected by the Act are the wife, husband, parents, grandparents, step-parents, children, grandchildren and step-children. Posthumous children are also included, but the trial is usually stayed until their birth.[128] Moreover, amending legislation has also variously qualified

122. *Jackson v. Watson* [1909] 2 K.B. 193. Its correctness was not doubted in *The Amerika*: see *Rose v. Ford* [1937] A.C. 826 at 851; *Woolworths v. Crotty* (1942) 66 C.L.R. 603 at 616.
123. E.g. in *Sellars v. Best* [1954] 1 W.L.R. 913 a husband whose wife had been electrocuted owing to faulty installation of a boiler recovered a sum for funeral expenses under the *Fatal Accidents Act* as well as £100 for loss of her consortium (non-financial), based on breach of contract. In *Jackson v. Watson* [1909] 2 K.B. 193 recovery included funeral expenses which were not then recoverable under the statute.
124. Now consolidated in *Administration of Justice Act* 1982.
125. N.S.W.: *Compensation to Relatives Act* 1897; Vic.: *Wrongs Act* 1958, Pt III; Qld: *Common Law Practice Act* 1867; S.A.: *Wrongs Act* 1936, Pt II; W.A.: *Fatal Accidents Act* 1959; Tas.: *Fatal Accidents Act* 1934; A.C.T. and N.T.: *Compensation (Fatal Injuries) Acts* of 1968 and 1974.
126. Proviso: see above, n. 117.
127. *Woolworths v. Crotty* (1976) 66 C.L.R. 603; also *Grein v. Imperial Airways* [1937] 1 K.B. 50 (C.A.). American interpertation has been the other way, except (which matters most) regarding breach of warranty which is, at least for this purpose, widely classified as tortious: *Prosser & Keeton* 946-947.
128. See *Manns v. Carlon* [1940] V.L.R. 280.

divorced spouses[129] and blood,[130] illegitimate,[131] adoptive[132] and foster relationships.[133] Not so, however, non-familial relationships. Dependency without more is generally not sufficient, except now in Victoria[134] and increasingly in cases of unmarried cohabitation.[135]

Action must be commenced within a special time limit from death, which is generally shorter than the ordinary period of limitation.[136] Not more than one action will lie, and every action, whoever brings it, is for the benefit of all the dependants whose interests have been infringed.[137] The proper party to sue is, in the first instance,[138] the executor or administrator: though not as representative of the deceased, but as fiduciary for the dependants.[139] Hence, the damages he recovers are not part of the estate liable for debts or death duty.[140] Thus as a matter of social policy, the equally vital interest of creditors in the continuing earning capacity of the deceased is wholly sacrificed to the claims of his surviving family; *their* reach being confined to such damages alone as the estate may now recover under survival legislation.[141]

Nature of action

A condition precedent to recovery is that the deceased himself would have been entitled to maintain an action against the defendant had he not died of his injuries. This requirement has been strictly construed, much to the prejudice of the dependants. It is clearly not satisfied if the deceased could have been met with the defence of voluntary assumption of risk[142] or

129. W.A.: Sched. 2; N.T.: s. 4; Eng.: s. 4 (as amended in 1982).
130. N.S.W.: s. 4; S.A.: *Wrongs Act* 1936 s. 3a; Tas.: s. 3; N.T.: s. 4.
131. W.A.: s. 3; Tas.: s. 3 as amended in 1943; A.C.T.: s. 4 ("ex-nuptial" child); N.T.: s. 4; N.Z.: s. 2. Otherwise "child" does not include an illegitimate child: *Dickinson v. N.E. Rly* (1863) 2 H. & C. 735; 159 E.R. 304, doubted in *Brule v. Plummer* [1979] 2 S.C.R. 342 at 360.
132. Qld.: see *Bairstow v. Queensland Industries* [1955] Q.S.R. 335; W.A.: Sched. 2; A.C.T.: s. 4; N.T.: s. 4.
133. N.S.W.: s. 7 (*Johnson v. Ryan* [1977] 1 N.S.W.L.R. 294; natural father "in loco parentis"); *Nash v. Comm. Rlys* [1963] S.R. (N.S.W.) 357.
134. *Wrongs (Dependants) Act* 1982. The definition of dependency does not clearly exclude employees, employers etc.
135. N.S.W.: ss 4, 7 (since 1984); S.A.: ss 3a, 20(3) ("putative spouse"); A.C.T.: s. 4(2)(h); N.T.: s. 4; *Australian Telecom v. Parsons* (1985) 59 A.L.R. 535. The process of extension has gone furthest in England (1982).
136. One year (W.A.); 30 months (Tas.); three years (Qld, S.A., A.C.T., N.T.) and six years (N.S.W., Vic.). In Tasmania, it may be extended up to six years. There are additional limitations when the wrongdoer dies.
137. Dependants whose interests have perchance been ignored ordinarily lose all recourse against the defendant, being remitted to redress from the recovering party for breach of fiduciary duty.
138. If there is no personal representative or no action is brought by him within six months of the death, all or any of the statutory beneficiaries may institute proceedings themselves: see *Erwin v. Shannon's Brick Co.* (1938) 38 S.R. (N.S.W.) 555; *Jeffrey v. Kent C.C.* [1958] 3 All E.R. 155. Also *McIntosh v. Williams* [1979] 2 N.S.W.L.R. 543 (p.r. hostile to beneficiary).
139. See *Anderson v. Liddy* (1949) 49 S.R. (N.S.W.) 320.
140. *Hall v. Wilson* [1939] 4 All E.R. 85 at 86.
141. See below, p. 676.
142. *Griffiths v. Dudley* (1882) 9 Q.B.D. 357.

contributory negligence,[143] though now the latter no longer defeats but merely reduces their award.[144] Moreover, the deceased must have been able to maintain an action at the time of his death rather than the injury, although the statute itself is silent on this matter and the relevant condition seems to be concerned rather with the quality of the defendant's conduct which caused the death.[145] Thus the deceased may defeat his family by accepting compensation from the defendant in full satisfaction of his own claim[146] or by allowing it to become barred by lapse of time[147] or by just losing an action in his own lifetime.[148] He need not, however, have satisfied every procedural requirement, such as giving notice in an action against a local authority, provided his failure to do so did not destroy his right of action. If he could have served the prescribed notice, had he survived, his dependants are not prejudiced.[149]

In postulating that the deceased must have had a right of action, is it necessary that not only his original injury but also his subsequent death was a foreseeable consequence of the defendant's tort? This seems to have been generally assumed until the contrary contention recently gained some judicial support[150] that the statutory formula, on a literal reading, requires only that the death be "caused" by an act which wrongfully injured the deceased; in other words, that the death itself need only be "caused", but not necessarily foreseeably caused, by the wrongful act. This finicky construction may assist plaintiffs over such obstacles as the death of the

143. *Senior v. Ward* (1859) 1 E. & E. 385; 120 E.R. 954. Likewise, contributory negligence by a claiming (but not a different) *dependant* affects his recovery: *Benjamin v. Currie* [1958] V.R. 259; *Dodds v. Dodds* [1978] Q.B. 543. An award may accordingly be liable to double reduction for the contributory negligence, first of the deceased, and secondly of the claimant.

144. Qld: *Law Reform (Tortfeasors' Contribution and Contributory Negligence) Act* 1952 s. 10(4); S.A.: *Wrongs Act* 1936 s. 27a(8); W.A.: *Law Reform Contributory Negligence and Tortfeasors Contribution Act* 1947 s. 4(2); Tas.: *Tortfeasors' and Contributory Negligence Act* 1954 s. 4(4); A.C.T.: *Law Reform (Miscellaneous Provisions) Act* 1968 s. 11; N.T.: *Compensation (Fatal Injuries) Act* 1974 s. 22.

Identification was abolished in N.S.W. (1965) except with respect to motor and industrial accidents (1987, 1988), Vic. (1982) and the A.C.T. (1991). In S. Africa it was replaced by contribution by the tortfeasor against the estate (*Apportionment of Damages Amendment Act* 1971), following Williams, *Joint Torts* 442-443.

145. *Harding v. Lithgow Corp.* (1937) 57 C.L.R. 186 at 195-196.

146. *Read v. Gt E. Rly* (1868) L.R. 3 Q.B. 555; *Conrod v. R.* (1914) 49 S.C.R. 577. In so far as the deceased's own recovery is based on his pre-accident life expectancy (see above, p. 233), this rule may be justified as a precaution against duplication of damages.

147. *Williams v. Mersey Docks & Harbour Bd* [1905] 1 K.B. 804; *Bergfels v. Port Stephens* [1983] 2 N.S.W.L.R. 578. Here again, the decision finds support in the policy against stale claims rather than in the inexorability of the statutory language.

148. *Noall v. Middleton* [1961] V.R. 285 at 288 (a previous successful action by the defendant resulted in a verdict negating the former's contributory negligence. This was held to create an issue estoppel barring the widow because the deceased would also have been barred.)

149. *Harding v. Lithgow Corp.* (1937) 57 C.L.R. 186; *Crawford v. Hydro-Electric Comm.* [1963] Tas. S.R. 83 (deceased retained a qualified cause of action dependent on judicial discretion for another 18 months).

150. *Haber v. Walker* [1963] V.R. 339 (F.C.); *Cuckow v. Polyester Products* (1970) 19 F.L.R. 122 at 134. Disdained by Herron C.J. in *Versic v. Conners* (1969) 90 W.N. (Pt 1) (N.S.W.) 33 at 35-36.

deceased by suicide[151] or in some other bizarre occurrence,[152] although foreseeability is now once more[153] so liberally interpreted that it has not affected the outcome of any reported decision. It also has the disadvantage of requiring a new framework of reference for determining "legal cause"[154] in lieu of the familiar calculus in other tort cases.

Aside from the preceding derivative feature, the cause of action is "new in its species, new in its equality, new in its principle".[155] The Act did not transfer any claim of the deceased to his personal representative, but created a new right protecting specifically and exclusively the interests of his family. No account is therefore taken, in assessing damages, of the personal injuries and suffering for which the deceased would have been able to recover, had he survived.[156] Provided he had *a* right of action at the time of his death which could not have been defeated by a complete[157] defence, the damages to which his dependants are entitled are assessed on an entirely independent basis. Thus if by agreement he limited, but did not extinguish the defendant's liability, his family are not precluded from recovering a larger amount.[158] Nor is their claim affected by time which may have started to run against him under some statute of limitation[159] so long as it was not altogether barred.[160] As we have seen, *their* claim is subject to its own period of limitation, with respect to which time does not run until it has vested upon his death.

The independence of the statutory right of action from any claim vested in the deceased creates some difficulty with respect to its survival on the *wrongdoer's* death. Where the latter dies *after* his victim, indisputably the cause of action against him, having vested in the relatives of the deceased, survives against his estate, under modern legislation enacting that "on the death of any person all causes of action subsisting against (or vested in) him shall survive against (or for the benefit of) his estate."[161] But where the order of deaths is reversed and the tortfeasor dies first, it cannot be predicated that a cause of action subsisted in the dependants against him at the time of his death, since the person wrongfully injured was then still alive and his relatives' rights did not crystallise until *his* death. The resulting difficulty has been overcome by relying on another provision which fictitiously treats damage accruing after the tortfeasor's death as if it had

151. *Haber v. Walker* [1963] V.R. 339 (F.C.); see above, p. 224.
152. E.g. in *Versic v. Conners* (1969) 90 W.N. (Pt 1) (N.S.W.) 33 where a collision victim, pinned under his car, was drowned by accumulating rainwater.
153. Since *The Wagon Mound (No. 2)* [1967] 1 A.C. 617.
154. Smith J. in *Haber v. Walker* [1963] V.R. 339 at 357-358 (F.C.) outlined such a framework, based essentially on Hart & Honore's "common sense" notions of causation (see above, p. 203) reinforced by decisions from workers' compensation and insurance law.
155. *The Vera Cruz* (1884) 10 App. Cas. 59 at 70-71 per Lord Blackburn.
156. *Pym v. Gt N. Rly* (1862) 2 B. & S. 759; 121 E.R. 1254.
157. With the exception of contributory negligence under apportionment legislation: see above, n. 144.
158. *Nunan v. S. Rly* [1924] 1 K.B. 223 (workmen's ticket); *Grein v. Imperial Airways* [1937] 1 K.B. 50 (air ticket).
159. *British Electricity Co. v. Gentile* [1914] A.C. 1034.
160. *Williams v. Mersey Docks & Harbour Bd* [1905] 1 K.B. 804.
161. See below, p. 677.

done so before. Dependants' rights are thus safeguarded regardless of the fortuitous sequence of deaths.[162]

Damages[163]

In no other respect more than this do damages fall short of compensating for the total loss: here, for the value of life. For one thing, the surviving family are restricted to their own loss of dependency, severely curtailed at that; for another, the estate is compensated, as we shall see, only for loss to the deceased prior to his death, with the result that what the deceased would have spent on himself in future years remains uncompensated. So does non-economic loss. The reason for this pusillanimity is partly historical, partly a matter of deliberate choice. Compensation being denied altogether at common law, the statutory modifications have been piecemeal and fragmentary. Also, the law has been content to meet only needs, not to assure restitution or provide maximum safety incentives (alas, it remains true that it is cheaper to kill than to maim).

Lord Campbell's Act has been read down to allow recovery for loss only of economic or material advantages to the survivors.[164] Damages in the nature of solatium for grief or bereavement (unless amounting to psychiatric illness),[165] for loss of consortium[166] or allowance for the gravity of the injury preceding death are rigorously excluded.[167] Dependants are protected in their interests of substance, not of personality. Even funeral and medical expenses occasioned by the fatal injury are disallowed[168] except by amendment in some States[169] and under survival legislation which uniformly ensures reimbursement to the *estate*.[170]

Compensation is due, and due only, for loss of the claimant's reasonable expectation of pecuniary benefit. This means primarily for loss of support or dependancy.[171] Unlike awards for personal injury which (at least in Australia)[172] purport to compensate for loss of a capital item—earning capacity—dependants are entitled to a sum which will secure for them an

162. *Partridge v. Chick* (1951) 84 C.L.R. 611; *Genders v. G.I.O.* (1959) 102 C.L.R. 363.
163. See esp. *Luntz* ch. 9; *Cooper-Stephenson & Saunders* ch. 9.
164. But the criterion is loss, not need: *Sheils v. Cruikshank* [1953] 1 All E.R. 874 (H.L.) (widow with independent means).
165. And qualifying as "shock" (above, p. 160), as in *Swan v. Williams (Demolition)* (1987) 9 N.S.W.L.R. 172 (C.A.); *Hinz v. Berry* [1970] 2 Q.B. 40.
166. See below, p. 671.
167. *Blake v. Midland Rly* (1852) 18 Q.B. 93; 118 E.R. 35. Today the rule is no longer so popular: see *Doody v. Federation Ins.* (1977) 16 S.A.S.R. 173. Distaste for it may account for *West v. Shephard* and *Rose v. Ford* [1937] A.C. 826 and the widescale cumulation of collateral benefits: see below, p. 672.
168. *Clark v. L.G.O.* [1960] 2 K.B. 648; also expense of attending funeral: *Thomson v. Neilly* 1973 S.L.T. (N.) 53.
169. N.S.W.: s. 3(2); S.A.: s. 20(2a); W.A.: s. 5; Tas.: s. 10(2); A.C.T.: s. 10. In N.S.W. this includes (by specific amendment) a tombstone but elsewhere decisions are conflicting: *Cunningham v. Nominal Defendant* (1970) 17 F.L.R. 61.
170. See below, p. 676. The latter claim may be more advantageous, not being subject to reduction on account of the beneficiary's contributory negligence: see *Mulholland v. McCrea* [1961] N.I. 135.
171. For some examples see *Evans v. Anderson* [1992] 1 V.R. 411; *Jacobs v. Varley* (1976) 50 A.L.J.R. 519: *Peipman v. Turner* (1960) 78 W.N. (N.S.W.) 362; *Daniels v. Jones* [1961] 1 W.L.R. 1103; Kemp & Kemp, *Quantum of Damages* (1974) vol. 2.
172. See above, p. 231.

annuity of continuous periodical payments for the period of dependancy.[173] But in other respects the personal injury model has been followed. Thus most courts now split the award into pre- and post-trial earnings and value the latter on the basis of earnings at the time of trial rather than death and without interest for the earlier period.[174]

Where the person killed was the breadwinner, the principal source of pecuniary detriment is the loss of the deceased's net earnings, present and future. The basis of calculation is, therefore, the amount of his wages or other income from which must be deducted an estimated amount of what the deceased required for his own personal and living expenses.[175] The value of the dependancy thus includes not only expected maintenance but also savings.[176]

Future earnings may be either more or less than at the time of death. Reasonable contingencies arising from promotion, on the one hand, and ill-health, unemployment, and other interruptions of earning power, on the other, must also be taken into account.[177]

Particularly troublesome are the problems of a widow's remarriage or return to gainful employment. A widow or widower's[178] remarriage is debited, whether it is merely prospective or has already taken place. The first invites an embarrassing inquiry into nubility, although to ignore it in all cases may condone blatant windfalls.[179] Some legislation concluded that the latter was the lesser evil,[180] but periodical payments would be a better solution.[181] If the marriage has already occurred, it will reduce, though not necessarily extinguish, her claim—on the general principle that hindknowledge prevails if at the time of assessing the damages, prospective loss or diminution of damage has become actual and speculation has been replaced by certainty.[182] Some statutes have also reversed this rule on the more questionable basis that it encourages non-marital cohabitation.[183]

173. Thus while only the deceased's after-tax earnings are relevant (*Lincoln v. Gravil* (1954) 94 C.L.R. 430: *Keizer v. Hanna* [1978] 2 S.C.R. 342), the discount rate for "present value" (3%) purports to allow for the tax on income from notional investment after the award: see above, p. 232.
174. This pattern was set by *Cookson v. Knowles* [1979] A.C. 556 and countenanced in *Thompson v. Faraonio* (1979) 24 A.L.R. 1 (P.C.) and *S.G.I.O. v. Biemann* (1983) 154 C.L.R. 539. *Wright v. W.A. Trustee Co.* [1987] V.R. 771, very critical, allowed interest on the whole award up to judgment on the basis that damages are to be assessed as of death.
175. In practice, one third. The remainder is attributable one third to the spouse's and one third to joint expenditures like housing and car: *Harris v. Empress Motors* [1984] 1 W.L.R. 212 at 217 (C.A.).
176. *Taylor v. O'Connor* [1971] A.C. 115 at 130 (H.L.); *Gavin v. Wilmot Breeden* [1973] 1 W.L.R. 1117.
177. *Williams v. Usher* (1956) 94 C.L.R. 450; *Nance v. B.C. Electric Rly* [1951] A.C. 601 (P.C.); *McIntosh v. Williams* [1979] 2 N.S.W.L.R. 543 (C.A.). English courts employ multipliers: *Cookson v. Knowles* [1979] A.C. 556; *Mallett v. McMonagle* [1970] A.C. 166.
178. *Hermann v. Johnston* [1972] W.A.R. 121 (F.C.).
179. *Jones v. Schiffman* (1971) 124 C.L.R. 303.
180. (Eng.) s. 3(3); (N.T.) s. 10(4).
181. See Law Commission No. 56 §249-250; *Pearson* §409-416.
182. Applied to prior death in *Williamson v. Thornycroft* [1940] 2 K.B. 658; *Richters v. Motor Tyre Service* [1972] Qd R. 9 (C.A.).
183. See above, n. 180. But cohabitation "on a bona fide domestic basis" may also reduce: *Tegel v. Madden* (1985) 2 N.S.W.L.R. 591 (C.A.).

By contrast, a widow's resumption of gainful employment, although nowadays increasingly probable as well as socially desirable, is ignored.[184] The reason given for this distinction is that her wages would not replace her husband's support, any more than would a lodger's rent.[185] In the last resort, the matter is one of judgment, not logic.[186]

In respect of the death of a wife and mother, damages can be claimed for loss, not only of outside earnings by which she contributed to the family purse, but also of her domestic services in looking after the home, husband and children.[187] The husband need no longer prove that he actually hired a housekeeper[188] or nurse,[189] since the test is not expenses incurred but loss suffered; nor does pecuniary or material loss mean monetary outlay, but merely that it must be susceptible to pecuniary valuation. Thus according to the modern view, a parent's care and guidance, i.e. personal attention in a child's upbringing, can now qualify as material loss, even if "love" still does not.[190] And so can a spouse's.[191]

The most repulsive impact of the prevailing economic calculus occurs on the death of young children, when the bereaved parents can claim only a crude child-labour standard. Apart from statutory reform here and there,[192] no allowance is made for grief or even loss of companionship,[193] the sole question being whether the parents had any reasonable (more than merely speculative) possibility of an eventual favourable balance of financial benefit.[194] Not infrequently the matter is beset with so many doubts and uncertainties that the claim is "pressed to extinction by the weight of multiplied contingencies".[195] Adverse factors are the extreme youth of the child, the risks of illness, disease, accident and death, the

184. *Carroll v. Purcell* (1961) 107 C.L.R. 73; *Dolminish v. Astill* [1979] 2 N.S.W.L.R. 368 (C.A.); *Howitt v. Heads* [1973] Q.B. 64. Implicit is that she is under no duty to mitigate by taking a job.

185. *Tegel v. Madden* [1985] 2 N.S.W.L.R. 591 (C.A.). The alternative explanation, that death revived her legal capacity to remarry, whereas she always had the capacity to resume employment, received some favour in *Carroll v. Purcell* but is incompatible with treating de facto cohabitation like remarriage.

186. *Dominish v. Astill* [1979] 2 N.S.W.L.R. 368 (C.A.).

187. *Nguyen v. Nguyen* (1989) 169 C.L.R. 245. Alternative ways to calculate that loss in case the husband gives up his employment to take over domestic tasks are considered in *Nguyen v. Nguyen* [1992] 1 Qd R. 405 (F.C.). Generally: Yale, *Valuation of Household Services*, 34 U. Tor. L.J. (1984); Quah, 24 Osg. H.L.J. 467 (1986).

188. Ibid.

189. *Hay v. Hughes* [1975] Q.B. 790 (C.A.).

190. *Spittle v. Bunney* [1988] 1 W.L.R. 847 (C.A.) ("nanny", not foster home, as base standard); *Regan v. Williamson* [1976] 1 W.L.R. 305; N.T.: s. 10(3)(e); Can.: *Vana v. Tosta* [1968] S.C.R. 71; *Family Reform Act* 1978 (Ont.) s. 60.

191. Ibid.; S.A.: s. 33; *Sloan v. Kirby* (1979) 20 S.A.S.R. 263; N.T.: s. 10(3)(d).

192. For statutory solatium to bereaved parents see below, p. 674. In England parents have been indirectly compensated through an award to the estate for the child's fictitious loss of expectation of life and loss of faculties, as in *Andrews v. Freeborough* [1967] 1 Q.B. 1: see below, p. 678.

193. American law widely regards the latter loss as compensable; as does Ontario: *Family Law Reform Act* s. 60: *Mason v. Peters* (1982) 139 D.L.R. (3d) 104 ($45,000).

194. *Barnett v. Cohen* [1921] 2 K.B. 461. The expectation need not, however, amount to an actual probability (any more than in other inquiries as to expectancy, e.g. whether a deserting wife would have returned to her husband, as in *Davies v. Taylor* [1974] A.C. 207). The odds will be reflected in the rate of discount. An alternative economic standard is advocated by Bruce, 66 Can. B. Rev. 344 (1967).

195. Ibid. at 472 per McCardie J.

expense of bringing him up before he could be expected to contribute to his parents' income, and the possibility that they might not have survived him.[196] When damages are awarded, the reasons usually are that the child had already made contributions to the home budget, that his prospects in life were good, and that there was a strong likelihood of household services (like babysitting)[197] or financial support forthcoming or continuing.[198]

The pecuniary advantage, for loss of which the statute allows compensation, must have accrued to the claimant by virtue of his familial relationship with the deceased. Accordingly, where husband and wife had been professional dancing partners and their joint earning capacity greatly exceeded that of either of them individually, his loss due to her death was disallowed because it derived from the partnership and their marriage was merely a convenient, if usual, incident of it.[199] In contrast, a more liberal view prevailed with respect to the salary paid to the wife as nominal director of a company substantially owned and run by her husband, because the arrangement was primarily designed for tax avoidance and did not reflect a business relationship.[200]

When there is more than one qualified dependant, it is permissible either to calculate each loss separately and then add up the total or first to assess a composite sum and then divide it.[201] The latter method is simpler and avoids duplication, but the former tends to be more accurate, especially when different set-offs are required on account of gains received or contributory negligence.[202]

Collateral benefits

The liberal construction originally placed on *Lord Campbell's Act* entailed the strictest balancing of gains against losses accruing from the death.[203] More lately however this policy has been reversed. Legislation has played a principal role not only in progressively reversing specific decisions which had become patently intolerable, but also in setting a new

196. Ibid. *Fenn v. Peterborough* (1976) 73 D.L.R. (3d) 177 speaks of a former Ontario rule of thumb to award $100 a year per child.
197. See *Buckland v. Guildford Gas Co.* [1949] 1 K.B. 410 (£500 for 13-year-old girl).
198. *Duckworth v. Johnson* (1860) 29 L.J. Ex. 25; *Taff Vale Rly v. Jenkins* [1913] A.C. 1.
199. *Burgess v. Florence Nightingale Hospital* [1955] 1 Q.B. 349.
200. *Malyon v. Plummer* [1964] 1 Q.B. 330 (no deduction for excess of her salary over market rates of services actually rendered); *Henry v. Perry* [1964] V.R. 174 (spouses dividing hotel profits equally, though deceased husband contributed more); and see *Taverner v. Swanbury* [1944] S.A.S.R. 194 (son assisting father for less than market rate).
201. *Raper v. Bertrand* [1967] V.R. 53 (F.C.); *Dwyer v. Wright* [1960] N.S.W.R. 406; *Eifert v. Holt's Transport* [1951] W.N. 467 (C.A.); Street, *Damages* 150-155 (severely critical of second method). In N.Z. (s. 13) courts could create a class fund, not to be apportioned, but held in trust and payments being made from time to time at the trustee's discretion according to need. This relieved the courts from speculating about contingencies like the widow's remarriage: e.g. *Public Trustee v. Fletcher Steel* [1960] N.Z.L.R. 40.
202. See *Gullifer v. Pohto* [1978] 2 N.S.W.L.R. 353 (C.A.). Such deductions must be made from each appropriate share, first on account of any pecuniary advantage and then for contributory negligence: *Darroch v. Dennis* [1954] V.L.R. 282; *Warnar v. Wright* [1956] Tas. S.R. 100; *Ylitalo v. Mt Isa Mines* [1969] Qd R. 406.
203. *Davies v. Powell Duffryn Collieries* [1942] A.C. 601. An exhaustive study of Commonwealth authority is Boberg's *Deductions from Gross Damages*, 81 S. Af. L.J. 194, 346; 82 S. Af. L.J. 96, 247, 324 (1964-1965).

general course of increased liberality.[204] The conventional starting point is that (only) benefits "resulting from" the death must be brought into account, a test which has encouraged much sterile speculation on causation and conclusions difficult to reconcile. For example, can a widow's remarriage really be more confidently regarded as "resulting from" her husband's death than the orphans' support from their new stepfather,[205] or a voluntary bounty from an employer more than a gift from fellow employees?[206] The modern tendency is more pragmatic, invoking the common sense approach of a jury and frankly favouring the plaintiff unless peremptorily precluded by precedent. Here are some principal illustrations:

Benefits accruing to the plaintiff from arrangements set up to meet the eventuality of death qualify most plausibly as "resulting from the death", such as any disposition in favour of his widow under the will of the deceased,[207] though by no means all of it since she may have gained little by merely stepping into full control of assets that had formerly been at her disposal anyway, such as the home and furniture[208] or even capital.[209] The full amount will only be deducted for true "windfalls", such as damages recovered by the estate from the tortfeasor (and devolving on the dependant), for the deceased's clothing destroyed in the accident[210] or for his pain and suffering (where recoverable at all).[211] Similarly, life and accident policies had to be brought into account, except that the benefit of the former would consist, not of the whole proceeds but only of their accelerated receipt.[212] So also, a pension from the deceased's employer, even if gratuitous, has been held deductible since not only certain but also probable benefits resulting from the death must be accounted for.[213]

204. *Hay v. Hughes* [1975] Q.B. 790 (C.A., passim). In several instances, this improved (at least temporarily) the position of plaintiffs in fatal accident compared with personal injury claims, although for most of their history the position had been reverse.

205. Both were held deductible in *Mead v. Clarke Chapman* [1956] 1 W.L.R. 76 (C.A.), but at least in England the first was expressly reversed by statute (see above, n. 180) and the second doubted in *Hay v. Hughes* [1975] Q.B. 790 at 806, 816.

206. The former was held deductible in *Baker v. Dalgleish S.S. Co.* [1922] 1 K.B. 361 (C.A.), unlike the latter: see below, n. 214.

207. *Pym v. Gt N. Rly* (1863) 4 B. & S. 396; 122 E.R. 508.

208. *Heatley v. Steel Co. of Wales* [1953] 1 W.I.R. 405 (C.A.); A.C.T.: s. 10.

209. *Flannery v. Ward* [1973] 1 N.S.W.L.R. 28; *Public Trustee v. Nickisson* (1964) 111 C.L.R. 500; *Taylor v. O'Connor* [1971] A.C. 115.

210. *Bishop v. Cunard White Star* [1950] P. 240.

211. *Davies v. Powell Duffryn Collieries* [1942] A.C. 601; *Murray v. Shuter* [1976] Q.B. 972 (C.A.); below, p. 678. Damages for loss of earnings between injury and death need not be brought into account because they would largely have been spent on his dependants anyway.

212. *Wills v. Commonwealth* (1946) 73 C.L.R. 105 at 110; *Baker v. Dalgleish* [1922] 1 K.B. 361 at 362.

213. *Baker v. Dalgleish* [1922] 1 K.B. 361 (C.A.). If the employer also happens to be the defendant, as in *Jenner v. West* [1959] 1 K.B. 544 (C.A.), the benefit is not even collateral, besides being more in the nature of an advance. Pensions as of right and contributory superannuation have been generally treated like life assurance (above, n. 212): *McPhee v. Carlsen* [1946] V.I.R. 316; *Bowskill v. Dawson* [1955] 1 Q.B. 13; contra: *Smith v. B.E.A.* [1951] 2 K.B. 893; *Public Trustee v. Wilson* [1955] S.A.S.R. 117 at 128. But pensions under government schemes like the *Social Services Act* (Cth), with a basis in social welfare rather than contract, have been held totally deductible (*Lincoln v. Gravil* (1954) 94 C.L.R. 430), though the effect is to make the widow dependent on public funds and relieve the tortfeasor at the taxpayer's expense.

On the other hand, gifts of money[214] or other assistance (like assuming the care of orphans),[215] whether from relatives or strangers (for example a disaster fund, workmates or institutional charity) are nowadays ignored: here the test of probable causation has received rough sledding[216] because to do otherwise would be odious, besides being apt to dry up the founts of compassion.[217]

As already mentioned, amending legislation has substantially modified common law rules for deduction, besides influencing judicial reform. Everywhere insurance policies must now be disregarded.[218] Several States also exempt all sums paid or payable out of any superannuation, provident or like fund, or by way of benefit from a friendly or benefit society or trade union.[219]

A growing number have also exempted certain specified pensions payable under State and Commonwealth statutes.[220] Others have exempted all gratuities[221] or the dependant's home and contents. Tasmania includes the value of the estate up to $10,000; finally, the Northern Territory and England[222] "any benefits" accruing to the deceased's estate or to any claimant. In the upshot, fatal accidents are in this respect much more generously treated than personal injuries.

Solatium

Not all jurisdictions have remained content with the settled construction against recovery for all non-economic loss. But legislative reform—in South Australia,[223] the Northern Territory,[224] and England[225]—has been

214. *Mockridge v. Watson* [1960] V.R. 405; *Papowski v. Commonwealth* [1958] S.A.S.R. 293; *Wilson v. Rutter* (1955) 73 W.N. (N.S.W.) 294; *Redpath v. Belfast & County Down Rly* [1947] N.I. 167. Aliter, *Jenner v. West* [1959] 1 W.L.R. 554 (gratuity from employer set off against his own liability).
215. *Hay v. Hughes* [1975] Q.B. 790 (C.A.).
216. Ibid.
217. In cases like *Peacock v. Amusement Equipment* [1954] 2 Q.B. 347 and *Rawlinson v. Babcock* [1967] 1 W.L.R. 481 gifts from relatives who could themselves ill-spare the outlay can thus be repaid.
218. Vic. (s. 19); Qld (s. 15c); S.A. (s. 20) and Tas. (s. 10) employ the formula "all sums paid or payable on the death of the deceased under any contract of assurance or insurance". Compulsory superannuation schemes do not qualify, whether statutory (e.g. *Superannuation Act* (Cth): *Anderson v. Cron* [1966] V.R. 588; contra *Canada Pacific v. Gill* [1973] S.C.R. 654) or otherwise: *Smith v. B.E.A.* [1951] 2 K.B. 893. Exempt are not only payments to which the deceased or his dependants were legally or equitably entitled, but also payments contractually made for their benefit, even if not directly enforceable by them: *Green v. Russell* [1959] 1 Q.B. 28; *Bowskill v. Dawson* [1955] 1 Q.B. 13.
219. N.S.W.: s. 3(3); Vic.: s. 19; W.A.: s. 10; A.C.T.: s. 5(3); N.T.: s. 10. Applicable to statutory no less than voluntary funds: *Peipman v. Turner* (1960) 78 W.N. (N.S.W.) 362.
220. N.S.W.: s. 3(3); Vic.: s. 19; Qld: s. 15c; S.A.: s. 20(2aa); W.A.: s. 5(2); Tas.: s. 10(1); A.C.T.: s. 10; N.T.: s. 10. See *Watson v. Dennis* (1968) 88 W.N. (Pt 1) N.S.W. 491 (C.A.).
221. Vic.: s. 19; Qld: s. 15c; S.A.: s. 20(2aa); A.C.T.: s. 10; also Eng. (1959) and Eire (1961).
222. Section 10(4) (N.T.); s. 4 (Eng.). This includes non-monetary benefits like better care by a stepmother: *Stanley v. Saddique* [1992] 1 Q.B. 1.
223. Section 23a-c (since 1940).
224. Section 10(f): without financial limits.
225. *Fatal Accidents Act* 1976 s. 1A(bereavement). Also under Warsaw Convention (see *Preston v. Hunting Air* [1956] 1 Q.B. 454) and in case of domestic airline facilities: *Civil Aviation (Carriers' Liability) Act* 1959 (Cth) s. 35(8).

cautious, limiting awards to spouses and parents of minors and usually setting a low monetary limit or a fixed sum;[226] the latter mode dispenses with any embarrassing inquiry into the bereavement. In South Australia, for example, the court may in the case of a deceased child, award to the surviving parents a sum not exceeding $3,000 in the aggregate, and in the case of husband or wife $4,200, as it thinks just, by way of solatium for the suffering to them by the death. This claim, unlike one for the benefit of the estate of the protected relative, is additional to any rights under *Lord Campbell's Act*. Nor can it be set off against the pecuniary loss consequent upon the death,[227] because it is awarded in title of a different interest: the one founded on the economic advantages of the marriage, the other on affection and feelings.[228]

The concept of solatium was borrowed from Scots law.[229] Primary consideration must be given to the suffering of the claimants and to the loss of pleasure derived from association with the deceased in the family circle, including the hopes and thoughts of parents upon the future of the children. The nature and circumstances of the death may also be taken into account.[230] In short, solatium should have regard to the whole situation—to the past, and to the future, as well as to the pain which will soften, if it cannot heal.[231]

III. Survival of Actions

Death may affect tort liability in two ways: it may create or extinguish it. Regarding the first—where the tortfeasor has caused the death of the person injured, we have to ask ourselves whether this confers a new cause of action on the estate or adds a new element of damages to a survival claim. (The additional question whether the death also creates a new cause of action in favour of his survivors, especially members of his family who had a stake in his continued life, we already discussed in the preceding section.) A second, and quite distinct, question is whether the death of the tortfeasor or his victim (from a conceivably unrelated cause) terminates an existing cause of action.

Common law

At common law, personal representatives could neither sue nor be sued for any tort committed against or by the deceased in his lifetime: "actio

226. S.A. and Eire (*Civil Liability Act* 1961 s. 49) chose a limit; Eng. a fixed sum, presently £3,500, Alta, $3,000 (1980).
227. E.g. like damages recovered by the *estate* for the deceased's pain and suffering, and devolving upon the dependant by succession (*Davies v. Powell Duffryn Collieries* [1942] A.C. 601)—a situation which cannot arise in Australia where such recovery is proscribed: see below, p. 678.
228. *Public Trustee v. Zoanetti* (1945) 70 C.L.R. 266. This, the reason given by Dixon J., is more convincing than Latham C.J.'s and Starke J.'s, that solatium went directly to the dependant unlike the damages in *Davies* which in the first instance swelled the estate: for widow's pensions are clearly deductible (statute apart).
229. See Veitch, *Solatium—A Debt Repaid?*, 7 Ir. Jur. (N.S.) 77 (1972).
230. *Taverner v. Swanbury* [1944] S.A.S.R. 194.
231. *Jeffries v. Commonwealth* [1946] S.A.S.R. 106 at 108 per Napier C.J.; and see *Meynell v. Zalitis* [1960] S.A.S.R. 251 (£100 in view of remarriage). The statutory maximum is not the top of a scale against which each award must be measured proportionately; the maximum is frequently awarded: in *Re Poore* (1973) 6 S.A.S.R. 308 (F.C.).

personalis moritur cum persona." Although somewhat obscure,[232] in origin this principle seems to have been linked with the criminal flavour of early tort remedies. At the dawn of the common law, the victim of a felony could seek redress against the culprit by an "appeal of felony", which was more in the nature of a private or civil than a public or criminal proceeding, though sufficiently penal to abate if the appellor or appellee died pending it. The writ of trespass which later superseded it retained this primitive connection with the criminal law, and the infection passed from trespass to tort actions generally.

To all appearances, this solution was long accepted without protest. The probable explanation is that, if the *defendant* had died, the retributive character of tortious redress made it natural to look upon his demise as having settled the score; in any event, it seems to have been common practice for testators to direct their executors to make good the wrongs which they had done or, in cases of intestacy, for the administrator to devote part of the estate to pious uses, including the reparation of injuries.[233] If it was the *plaintiff* who had died, in many cases the defendant would have been guilty of homicide, for which he would have been executed and his property forfeited to the Crown, so that nothing remained for compensation. At any rate, this explanation probably accounts for the ancillary rule that the infliction of death is not, as such, a tort against the person killed for which his estate can claim redress.[234] Progressive legislation, commencing in the 14th century, first enabled personal representatives to sue for any injury done to the personal[235] or real estate[236] of the deceased and later even to be sued in corresponding circumstances.[237] But as regards personal injuries, the non-survival rule remained in full force so that any action, not brought to a verdict before either of the parties died, abated and could not be recommenced by or against his personal representatives.

Survival legislation

Eventually reform caught up: following the English model of 1934,[238] it came to be uniformly enacted throughout Australasia[239] that, on the death

232. The history is traced by Winfield, *Death as Affecting Liability in Tort*, 29 Col. L. Rev. 239 (1929); Holdsworth iii 576ff; Goudy, *Essays in Legal History*, 215-232.
233. *Holdsworth* iii, 582-583.
234. If the felon was pardoned, as in cases of accidental homicide, the indictment lapsed but not the relatives' right to appeal him, and this gave them the power to extort compensation by licensed blackmail: see Pollock & Maitland, *History of English Law* (1968) ii, 482-485.
235. By a statute of 1330, as amended in 1351.
236. *Civil Procedure Act* 1883.
237. Ibid. Exceptionally, the common law also allowed claims for restitution of property misappropriated and added to the estate of a deceased: *Phillips v. Homfray* (1883) 24 Ch. D. 439.
238. *Law Reform (Miscellaneous Provisions) Act* 1934. Canada had acted earlier, starting with Ontario in 1886. Only the Maritimes have adopted the English model. A uniform Act was published in 1964: see Bowker, *Uniform Survival of Actions Act*, 3 Alb. L. Rev. 197 (1964).
239. N.S.W.: *Law Reform (Miscellaneous Provisions) Act* 1944; Qld: *Succession Act* 1981 s. 66; S.A.: *Survival of Actions Act* 1940; W.A.: *Law Reform (Miscellaneous Provisions) Act* 1941; Tas.: *Administrative Probate Act* s. 27; A.C.T. and N.T.: *Law Reform (Miscellaneous Provisions) Acts* 1955 and 1956, Pt II; N.Z.: *Law Reform Act* 1936 s. 3. Can: *Cooper-Stephenson & Saunders* ch. 8.

of any person, all causes of action subsisting against or vested in him shall survive against or, as the case may be, be for the benefit of his estate. Excepted as too personal are causes of action for defamation,[240] seduction, enticement of spouses, and damage claims for adultery.[241]

The quantum of damages is subject to several restrictions when claim is made on behalf of a deceased. Exemplary damages are excluded altogether, although one might have thought this more appropriate where it was the tortfeasor, not the victim, who had died.[242] In the event of the victim's death the really critical distinction is between cases where the death was caused by the tort and where it was unrelated. In the former, damages must be calculated without reference to any loss or gain to the estate consequent on the death, except that a sum in respect of funeral expenses[243] may be included. This excludes any set-off for the proceeds of an accident or life policy, but by the same token denies compensation for losses such as the cost of probate or administration.[244]

How to mesh recovery under survival and wrongful death legislation? Clearly the estate is entitled to damages incurred up to the time of death, such as medical expenses and lost earnings,[245] but what of the deceased's earnings during his "lost years"? These were held recoverable, first, by anyone who sued in his own lifetime for reduction of his life expectancy;[246] later even by his estate, if he had died as a result of the accident.[247] That, however, was apt to duplicate the damages earmarked for his dependants under *Lord Campbell's Act* (that is the surplus of what he would have earned in his lost years after allowing for his own expenses) or benefit persons succeeding to his estate who, not being qualified dependants, were deliberately excluded by *Lord Campbell's Act*. To avoid this result, legislation quickly intervened to limit the estate's recovery to loss sustained by the deceased prior to his death.[248]

240. Save in Tasmania and recommended by A.L.R.C. §107. Cf. *Defamation Act* 1974 (N.S.W.) s. 46 which remained stillborn because the 1944 Act was in the event not amended.
241. The common link appears to be injury to dignitary interests, but by identifying torts rather than the nature of the harm, some claims are invidiously excluded from the list (e.g. false imprisonment and malicious prosecution, both of which are included in Manitoba), while others are unjustifiably included (e.g. "special damages" for defamation). Besides, it would have been more sensible to distinguish, as the Canadian Uniform Act does, between the wrongdoer's death and the victim's. The first does not mitigate the plaintiff's damages at all and should accordingly be ignored. Only the latter has relevance in so far as most survival legislation (like the Australian and Canadian) sets its face against recovery for non-pecuniary loss and should be dealt with from that viewpoint alone.
242. Its purpose was to limit damages to loss to the estate and therefore covers post-*Rookes v. Barnard* aggravated damages: *Re Chase* [1989] 1 N.Z.L.R. 325 (C.A.).
243. An agent of necessity, having arranged the funeral, may recover the expenses directly from the tortfeasor: *Croskery v. Gee* [1957] N.Z.L.R. 586.
244. *Rose v. Ford* [1937] A.C. 826 at 842 per Lord Wright.
245. E.g. *Curator v. Fernandez* (1977) 28 F.L.R. 340 (N.T.), including fares for family visits during six months.
246. See above, p. 237.
247. *Gammell v. Wilson* [1982] A.C. 27; *Fitch v. Hyde-Cates* (1982) 150 C.L.R. 482.
248. Following the English, the N.S.W. and S.A. Acts apply this rule to death however caused; others correctly limit it to death caused by the defendant. (The principal Acts were amended 1982-1986.) An alternative but more drastic solution would be to repeal *Lord Campbell's Act*, as recommended by Waddams, 47 Mod. L. Rev. 437 (1984). This would avoid, besides overlap, other awkward problems of evaluating dependencies, but permit the deceased to cut off his dependants with a shilling and benefit creditors.

Finally there is the question of non-pecuniary losses, like pain and suffering, physical disfigurement or loss of expectation of life. All of these are in a sense personal to the victim and do not represent a loss to the estate, comparable to a wrecked car or his medical and funeral expenses. And although as a general proposition, recovery in a survival action is measured by loss not to the estate, but to the deceased, it is widely felt to be against sound policy to confer on the estate what would in effect be a windfall. If close relatives deserve recognition of their grief, it should be done openly by awarding a solatium[249] rather than by this stratagem. From the outset, Australian legislation therefore excluded claims for the *decedent's* non-pecuniary losses.[250] New South Wales, Victoria and the two Territories[251] do so only when the death was actually caused by the injury in question,[252] but all others[253]—with more consistency—are of general application and also extend therefore to those, admittedly rarer, instances where death supervenes from some unconnected cause.[254]

Limitation of actions

Unlike proceedings under *Lord Campbell's Act*,[255] there is no special period of limitation for actions brought *by* personal representatives under survival legislation. On the other hand, where it is the tortfeasor who has died, there is a greater urgency for disposing of outstanding claims in order to hasten distribution of the estate. As originally enacted, proceedings against his estate could accordingly not be maintained in respect of a cause of action in tort[256] surviving by virtue of this legislation, unless they were pending at the date of his death or the cause of action arose not earlier than six months before his death, and proceedings are taken not later than six months after his personal representative took out representation.[257] Most jurisdictions have since substantially liberalised these requirements by enlarging both the relevant periods from between six months and three years.[258]

Where the cause of action does not arise until damage is sustained and the wrongdoer dies before, it is expressly provided that there shall be deemed to have been subsisting against him before his death such cause of

249. See above, p. 674.
250. "Damages for pain and suffering or for any bodily or mental harm." This includes "loss of expectation of life" as well as "loss of faculties" (e.g. *Child v. Stevenson* (1973) 37 D.L.R. (3d) 429) and the value of gratuitous services: *Harper v. Phillips* [1985] W.A.R. 100. Most Canadian statutes exclude non-pecuniary loss: *Cooper-Stephenson & Saunders* 393; England abolished loss of expectation of life completely in 1982.
251. See *Jaksic v. Cossar* (1966) 85 (Pt 1) (N.S.W.) 102.
252. Because dependants would then claim under *Lord Campbell's Act*.
253. Qld, S.A., W.A., Tas., Eire: *Civil Liabilities Act* 1961 s. 7.
254. As in *Sellick v. De Young* [1955] S.A.S.R. 191.
255. See above, p. 666.
256. For classification see above, p. 186; *Chesworth v. Farrar* [1967] 1 Q.B. 407 (claim against bailee: tortious).
257. Representation can be enforced: *E. of Simpson* [1936] P. 40.
258. As regards the first condition (date prior to death), the period is still six months in Victoria and S.A., but 12 months in N.S.W., A.C.T., W.A., and Tasmania. The second, or true limitation, period is 12 months in N.S.W., A.C.T. and N.Z., and remains six months only in Victoria, (but extendable: *Martinus v. Kidd* (1982) 150 C.L.R. 648), S.A., W.A., and Tasmania. England and Queensland have discarded all special limitations.

action as would have subsisted if he had died after the damage was suffered. This proviso saves not only claims with respect to disturbance of rights of support and the like, but may also be invoked in personal injury actions, as where dependants of a person killed sue the estate of a tortfeasor who died himself as the result of the same accident but before his own victim.[259]

4. TORTS WITHIN THE FAMILY

Domestic relations figure in the law of torts, not only when an outsider infringes a relational interest of a member of the family group, but also when one member of that group injures another member or a stranger.

Here the law was for long shaped by theories based on the dominance of the husband. Reform occurred in two, widely separated stages. First, in the late Victorian era which emancipated wives in their property rights; secondly, in recent legislative changes reflecting the impact of liability insurance.

I. Husband and Wife

Liability to third parties

At common law, a married woman was just as capable of rendering herself liable in tort as any other person, though if sued her husband had to be joined "for conformity" as co-defendant. But a judgment against her was ordinarily of little value so long as she ceased to command any assets after marriage and even her separate estate, if any, was protected in equity against claims arising from her general torts. In England, the *Married Women's Property Act* of 1882 eventually stripped the husband of control over his wife's estate and introduced the regime of separation of property. Promptly adopted throughout Australasia,[260] it had the effect of investing married women with the financial resources to become answerable like any other wrongdoer, and it was consequently enacted that a married woman was henceforth capable of suing and being sued in tort in all respects as if she were a feme sole.

At common law, the husband besides being a necessary party as co-defendant in any proceedings against his wife, was also personally liable for all her torts whether committed during marriage or before. From a doctrinal point of view this form of joint liability was no doubt sufficiently explained as just a corollary of the compulsory joinder rule (co-defendant meant co-tortfeasor), but more compelling was the economic justification that, so long as the husband acquired all his wife's personal property and a judgment against her alone would therefore have been worthless, fairness demanded that he be accountable for her debts and wrongs. This rationale

259. *Partridge v. Chick* (1951) 84 C.L.R. 611: see above, p. 669.

260. The current acts are—N.S.W.: *Married Persons (Property and Torts) Act* 1901; Vic.: *Marriage Act* 1958 s. 156; Qld: *Married Women's Property Act* 1890; S.A.: *Law Property Act* 1936 s. 92 ff.; W.A.: *Married Women's Property Act* 1892; Tas.: *Married Women's Property Act* 1935; *Matrimony Property Act* 1976; *Married Persons (Equality of Status) Act* 1989 (N.T.); *Married Persons (Torts) Act* 1968 (A.C.T.). Can.: Da Costa, "Husband and Wife in the Law of Torts" in *Studies in Canadian Tort Law* (1968) ch. 16.

ceased when the Married Women's Property legislation enabled a wife to command her own financial resources. In its wake, though it proved to be protracted,[261] the husband's liability was eventually also swept away.[262]

Between spouses

Interspousal relations used to be dominated by the common law doctrine of unity, according to which the legal personality of each was merged in the other's. This fiction found expression in two rules.[263] The first precluded any claim for a tort committed by one against the other during marriage, regardless of when the claim was raised even if after divorce; the second enjoined all litigation between spouses during their marriage,for pre-nuptial no less than for post-nuptial torts.

The Married Women's Property legislation of the 1880s reaffirmed this immunity in the belief that it was necessary for the sake of family harmony.[264] This argument proved at once too little and too much: too little, because it was never credited with sufficient weight to proscribe actions between parent and child, and because the commission of most intentional wrongs is mostly proof enough that there is no domestic tranquillity left to be saved. Too much, because claims for unintended injury are not likely to be prosecuted within the family, unless the putative tortfeasor is insured—in which event he is in no real sense an adversary but only a nominal party to the litigation, and the real objection far from being its tendency to weaken the marriage bond is that the intimate relation between the parties is apt to encourage collusion against the insurer.[265]

Though long delayed by insurance opposition, reform eventually succeeded in the 1960s. At first, two Australian States[266] lifted the immunity with respect to motor accidents, which give rise to most interspousal torts (wife passenger) and are covered by compulsory insurance; most others[267] followed the English model[268] of complete abolition except for petty domestic quarrels. In the end, however, a Commonwealth statute abolished the immunity across the board.[269]

Summary settlement of disputes

Interspousal disputes with respect to property pose special problems especially concerning the matrimonial home on the breakdown of normal marital relations. Even before spouses could sue each other in tort, courts

261. Due to the pedantry in *Edwards v. Porter* [1925] A.C. 1 which necessitated renewed legislative attention, last in line being N.S.W. in 1964.
262. N.S.W. (s. 18), Vic. (s. 159), Qld (s. 3), S.A. (s. 94), W.A. (*Law Reform Act* 1941 s. 2), Tas. (s. 13), A.C.T. (*Law Reform Act* 1955 s. 9), N.Z. (s. 14).
263. For other applications, since exploded, see *Midland Bank v. Green (No. 3)* [1982] Ch. 529 (C.A.).
264. But it allowed an exception for remedies for the "protection and security of her own separate property". As construed, this permitted also claims for "all" pre-nuptial torts.
265. E.g. *Rostek v. Keegan* (1967) 85 W.N. (Pt 1) (N.S.W.) 555 (husband's insurer permitted to examine husband as hostile witness).
266. N.S.W. and W.A.
267. All except Victoria and the A.C.T.
268. *Law Reform (Husband and Wife) Act* 1962.
269. *Family Law Act* 1975 s. 119. Also N.T. (s. 4); Ont. (1978), Man. In the U.S. by judicial reform: *Prosser & Keeton* §122.

were invested with discretionary jurisdiction for the settlement of "any question between husband and wife as to the title or possession of property".[270] This did not empower the court to reallocate title[271] but allowed a welcome flexibility in reconciling conflicting claims to possession, though probably only within the basic framework of the spouses' common law right to consortium and the wife's right to be housed.[272] In Australia this legislation has since been superseded by a Commonwealth statute empowering the family court to make orders "as it thinks fit altering the interests of the parties in the property".[273]

II. Parent and Child

The common law never entertained a doctrine of unity for parent and child, nor was it to all appearances sufficiently impressed by the spectre of domestic discord and threat to parental authority to outlaw all tort litigation between them on the model of the interspousal immunity. There is ample precedent for proceedings between parent and child in matters affecting property, though actually very little (outside America) relating to personal wrongs. This is not altogether surprising, because ordinarily there would be no incentive for such claims, but the modern prevalence of indemnity insurance has raised the question to practical importance in exactly the same way as in the case of husband and wife. In the United States, accordingly, opposition to such actions nowadays seeks support in the fear of collusion rather than disharmony.[274] British courts, however, have evidently not shared these apprehensions and allowed without much argument proceedings by children in reality aimed at the parent's insurer[275] (and visa versa[276]).

This liability obviously covers torts like assault and negligent driving which would be clearly actionable between strangers. But does it also create a specifically parental duty of care to safeguard the child from injury by others? For example, for a mother to protect her daughter against a father bent on incest?[277] If so, it might be invoked not only by the child (which is unlikely), but also by third party tortfeasors (and their insurers) with a view to claiming contribution from the parent. This would tend to resuscitate the obsolete doctrine of identification[278] and shift a portion of the loss from an insured to an uninsured defendant.[279] No wonder the suggestion has met with little enthusiasm.

270. N.S.W. (s. 22), Vic. (s. 161), Qld (s. 21), S.A. (s. 105), W.A. (s. 17), Tas. (s. 8); following the Eng. Act of 1882 s. 17.
271. *Wirth v. Wirth* (1956) 98 C.L.R. 228; *Pettitt v. Pettitt* [1970] A.C. 777.
272. See *Short v. Short* [1960] 1 W.L.R. 833 (C.A.); *Pettitt v. Pettitt* [1970] A.C. 777. For common law rights see *Lynch v. Lynch* [1974] Tas. S.R. 19.
273. *Family Law Act* 1975 s. 79. See Hardingham & Neave, *Australian Family Property Law* (1984).
274. Such opposition however is now in strong retreat: *Prosser & Keeton* 904-905.
275. *Dobel v. Dobel* [1963] S.R. (N.S.W.) 758 (F.C.); *Hahn v. Conley* 126 C.L.R. 276 at 283. A fortiori brother and sister: e.g. *Kerr v. Stephen* [1930] 1 W.W.R. 896. But indemnity policies frequently exclude injury to "a relative or friend of the insured ordinarily residing with the insured" (e.g. *Clarke v. Clarke* [1964] V.R. 773 (daughter)).
276. E.g. *Chang v. Chang* [1973] 1 N.S.W.L.R. 708.
277. *D.L.H. v. G.A.F.* (1987) 43 C.C.L.T. 110 (motion to dismiss denied).
278. See above, p. 287.
279. Policies typically exclude liability to resident family members.

After widely conflicting decisions by lower courts, the High Court of Australia provided some authoritative guidance, without however clearing up all doubts.[280] There is consensus that the parents' duty to feed, clothe, maintain, educate and generally care for their child is not enforceable in tort, whatever its moral, or other legal (for example criminal) sanctions.[281] Also denied is any *general* custodial duty of care towards the child,[282] like that of a nurse or school[283] or indeed (as we shall presently see) the parental duty to third parties.[284] Parents incur liability only when they take charge of the child on a specific occasion, that is when they are present on the scene and either lead the child along or across the road,[285] or (according to a more expansive view) are at least aware of the child's peril and need for assistance.[286] If this narrow approach strikes one as difficult to reconcile with first principle, it should at least be applauded for its reluctance to intrude unduly into the sphere of family relations and for discouraging third parties from shifting the accident cost to usually uninsured parents.

Parental liability to strangers

Since a child is amenable for his torts without having his parent joined as co-defendant,[287] there never existed the same doctrinal basis for imputing liability as in the case of husband and wife. But children as defendants are rarely worth powder and shot, except in regard to adult activities like driving, with a certain background of insurance.[288] Most legal systems have therefore been quick to assist recourse against their parents. Although the common law declined the general solution of vicarious liability[289] or even that of casting the onus on the parent to disprove his presumed negligence on the model of French and German law,[290] it has been by no means insensitive to the possibilities of exploiting the superior parental capacity for absorbing certain losses by insurance and exercising discipline with a view to accident prevention.

280. *Hahn v. Conley* (1971) 126 C.L.R. 276.
281. E.g. *Rogers v. Rawlings* [1969] Qd R. 262 at 274, 277 (F.C.). American cases agree: e.g. *Goller v. White* 122 N.W. 2d 193 (Wis. 1963); *Rest 2d* §895G, comment *k*.
282. *Robertson v. Swincer* (1989) 52 S.A.S.R. 356 (F.C.); *Towart v. Adler*, ibid. 373; and other cases discussed therein.
283. See above, p. 153.
284. Contra: *Arnold v. Teno* [1979] 2 S.C.R. 287.
285. As in *McCallion v. Dodd* [1966] N.Z.L.R. 710 (C.A.).
286. This would go beyond the duty owed by strangers. In *Hahn v. Conley* (1971) 126 C.L.R. 276 the court was divided on this subsidiary question (grandfather).
287. A child defends an action by his guardian ad litem, but the latter acts in a purely representative capacity and does not incur personal liability.
288. Not ignoring the possibility that a successful litigant has anything between six years (Eng.), 12 (Qld, Tas., W.A.), 15 (Vic. and S.A.) or 20 years (N.S.W.) for suing on the judgment. Besides lack of financial resources, consider also children's attenuated standard of responsibility: see above, p. 113.
289. I.e., unless the child was in fact the parent's servant or agent acting within the course of his employment or by his direction: *Moon v. Towers* (1860) 8 C.B. (N.S.) 611 at 615; 141 E.R. 1306 at 1307; *Gray v. Fisher* [1922] S.A.S.R. 246.
290. Waller, *Visiting the Sins of Children*, 4 Melb. U. L. Rev. 17 (1963), strongly advocates adoption of the latter alternative. See also Alexander, *Tort Responsibility of Parents and Teachers* 16 U. Tor. L.J. 165 (1965). Louisiana imposes unqualified strict liability: *Turner v. Bucher* 308 So. 2d 270 (La. 1975).

The best known illustration of the first is of course the manner in which legislatures and courts have variously striven to hold the driver of a motor vehicle, including the family car driven by son or daughter, to be the owner's agent so as to provide access to the latter's insurance.[291] Secondly, a parent may, as already noted,[292] incur responsibility for failing in his *personal* duty to control the child's activities. Such liability, however, is not "strict": "Young boys, despite their mischievous tendencies, cannot be classed as wild animals."[293] The standard exacted by law is that of reasonable care and has regard to the practices and usages prevailing in the community and the common understanding of what is practicable.[294] This requires a weighing of the risks to others which the child's conduct involves against the competing need, to which courts have been much alive, of giving those growing up sufficient scope to develop a sense of personal responsibility and reasonable latitude in pursuing forms of amusement and activity not necessarily restricted to those alone that are *perfectly* safe and harmless. On the other hand, when tolerating the use of dangerous objects or activities, parents must at the very least ensure that the child receives proper instruction in using them safely and carefully, that he understands and heeds such instruction and is physically capable of following it safely.[295]

The parents' duty is by no means exhausted by attending to the mischievous ventures of their progeny; it demands vigilance also against their wholly innocent (though often no less dangerous) behaviour, such as toddlers escaping into the road and imperilling traffic.[296] The liability, being personal not vicarious, requires proof of negligence in the parent, but not at all in thc child.

In order to promote parental control, especially against vandalism and delinquency, legislation here and there also authorises juvenile courts to order the parent (or child) to pay damages to the victim.[297] But in Australia, so far only the Northern Territory has emulated the American trend of imposing statutory liability on parents for intentional damage to property by a child ordinarily resident at home, subject to a monetary limit.[298]

291. See above, p. 388.
292. See above, p. 153.
293. *Smith v. Leurs* (1945) 70 C.L.R. 256 at 260 per Starke J.
294. Ibid. at 262 per Dixon J.; *Hatfield v. Pearson* (1956) 6 D.L.R. (2d) 593; *Wrongs Act* 1936 (S.A.) s. 27d.
295. *Newton v. Edgerley* [1959] 1 W.L.R. 1031; *Ingram v. Lowe* (1974) 55 D.L.R. (3d) 292 (guns); *Ryan v. Hickson* (1974) 55 D.L.R. (3d) 196 (snowmobile).
296. See *Carmarthenshire C.C. v. Lewis* [1955] A.C. 549.
297. E.g. *Children and Young Persons Act* 1933 (Eng.) s. 55. In the U.S. generally subject to dollar limits.
298. *Law Reform (Miscellaneous Provisions) Act* s. 29A. The Wrongs (Parents' Liability) Amendment Bill 1992 (S.A.) proposes a more diluted reform.

30

ECONOMIC RELATIONS

Reluctant as we have seen the common law to be in protecting economic interests against negligence, our legal tradition has displayed no similar coyness in furnishing legal sanctions against conduct aimed at impairing advantageous relations or causing other kinds of financial loss.[1] All the same, no general theory of intentional tort has emerged.[2] The principal reason for this failure is that it would have to be balanced by a calculus of justifications, which judges in the British tradition would have rather left to the legislative role.[3] The contexts in which these conflicts arise are exceedingly varied and, especially in the industrial sphere, singularly vulnerable to conflicting ideologies and changes in social climate. Not that judges have escaped the pull of ideology, but the tension between free market enterprise and regulation is generally obscured behind studiedly neutral legalisms. On the industrial scene, the record is that of alternating passivity and over-reaction, which in England has had to be repeatedly corrected by legislation.[4] In Australia, it is hardly presumptuous to say that the law is tolerable only because tort remedies against industrial action are widely shunned in favour of arbitration and conciliation.[5]

1. LOSS OF SERVICES

The early common law protected a master's economic interests by a writ of trespass against any stranger who either abducted or so injured his servant that he thereby lost his services. This ancient remedy[6] was the product of

1. Heydon, *Economic Torts* (2nd ed. 1978); *Future of the Economic Torts* 12 U.W.A.L. Rev. 1 (1975); Cane, *Tort Law and Economic Interests* (1991).
2. Despite its advocacy by Pollock: see above, p. 34. Holmes' efforts bore fruit in the American "prima facie tort" doctrine. See Vandevelde, *A History of Prima Facie Tort*, 19 Hofstra L. Rev. 447 (1990); *Rest. 2d* §870.
3. Instead, a recent newcomer is the "genus tort" of unintentional interference with trade or business by unlawful means: below, p. 698. Unlawfulness is more abstract than a frank appeal to policy.
4. The game of "catch" between Parliament and the courts is the theme of Elias & Ewing, *Economic Torts and Labour Law* [1982] Cam. L.J. 321.
5. See Mitchell, *Liability in Tort Causing Economic Loss and its Application to Australian Industrial Disputes*, 5 Adel. L. Rev. 428 (1976). Injunction may be refused because an "industrial dispute" under the *Conciliation and Arbitration Act* 1904 (Cth): *Harry Miller v. Actors* [1970] 1 N.S.W.R. 614. Injunction against tortious picketing, after defiance of Conciliation Commissioner was granted in *Dollar Sweets v. Federated Confectioners Assoc.* [1986] V.R. 383. In S.A. tort proceedings are delayed until conciliation or arbitration has failed: *Industrial Conciliation and Arbitration Act* (1984) s. 15a. Civil remedies (against secondary boycotts) were actually reinforced in 1977 by *Trade Practices Act* (Cth) ss 45D and 45E: e.g. *Mudginberri Station v. A.M.I.E.U.* (1985) 61 A.L.R. 280; Jackson, 64 A.L.J. 266 (1990).
6. Its history is traced by Jones, *Per Quod Servitium Amisit*, 74 L.Q.R. 39 (1958).

feudal society, which conceived the relation between master and servant in terms of status rather than contract, and attributed to the master a quasi-proprietary interest in his subordinates. In truth, the action for loss of services belonged originally to the order of domestic relations and, as we have seen, protected the rights of the head of the household not only qua master, but also qua husband and parent.[7] It later passed into the capitalist era which placed economic relations, like that between employer and employee, on a contractual footing. The necessary adjustment was made by crediting the master with a proprietary interest, no longer in the servant himself, but rather in his services.[8] Although medieval cases happened to involve a trespass injury to the servant, it actually matters nothing whether the latter had been the victim of intentional aggression or merely accidental harm,[9] like an occupier's failure to warn an invitee of danger on the premises.[10] However the action never did apply to wrongful death.[11]

Nowadays, it has become fashionable to stigmatise the action as anomalous, for (in addition to its peculiar origin) it is also at odds with the contemporary aversion against recovery for economic loss sustained by one person—at any rate outside the range of domestic relations—in consequence of injury negligently inflicted on another.[12] A servant, for example, could never in the converse case of his employer being disabled, proceed against the tortfeasor for losing his job.[13]

Servants

The first move in this contemporary policy of retrenchment was to disqualify members of the armed services[14] and the police,[15] on the arbitrary ground that these were not servants in the true conventional sense. A distinction was drawn between "public officers" who, though commonly viewed as "servants" of the public, are invested with "original authority" not derived from the command of a master, and private domestic service where the master's authority is an essential and characteristic feature. We have seen that the Crown is relieved from vicarious liability for wrongs committed by public servants in the discharge of certain duties traceable to an independent legal authority, such as an arrest by a police officer on suspicion of felony;[16] and although it has been rightly emphasised that the incidence of vicarious responsibility does not necessarily depend on the same considerations as the present question, strong reliance has in fact been

7. See above, ch. 29.
8. Some writers cite as evidence of the metamorphosis the fact that the master could, after a time, sue at his option either in trespass or case, even where the injury to the servant was a trespass: see *Chamberlain v. Hazelwood* (1839) 5 M. & W. 515; 151 E.R. 218.
9. *Martinez v. Gerber* (1841) 3 Man. & G. 88; 133 E.R. 1069.
10. *Mankin v. Scala Theodrome* [1947] K.B. 257.
11. *The Amerika* [1917] A.C. 38; *Swan v. Williams (Demolition)* (1987) 9 N.S.W.L.R. 172 (C.A.).
12. See above, p. 179.
13. *Best v. Fox* [1952] A.C. 716 at 731.
14. *Commonwealth v. Quince* (1944) 68 C.L.R. 227; contra: *R. v. Buchinsky* [1983] 1 S.C.R. 481 (based partly on statute).
15. *A.-G. v. Perpetual Trustee Co.* [1955] A.C. 457; 9 C.L.R. 113 (P.C.); *Receiver for Metropolitan Police v. Croydon Corp.* [1957] 2 Q.B. 154 (C.A.).
16. See above, p. 374.

placed on that analogy.[17] In doing so, the courts chose to ignore the fact that most police activities actually fall within ordinary "command" situations,[18] and much ingenuity is required to explain on this ground the exclusion of military personnel who have been traditionally treated as servants of the Sovereign in the strictest personal sense.[19] The denial of a remedy to the Crown is also vulnerable on the score of policy, because its effect is to confer a windfall on tortfeasors (and their insurers) at the expense of the taxpayer.[20]

Emboldened by this peripheral attack, initiated in Australia and eventually accepted by the Privy Council, the English Court of Appeal promptly proceeded to enlarge the breach by restricting the action to domestic employment.[21] Contrary to the practice of the last 100 years and more,[22] it would henceforth lie only with respect to such persons as a wife, child or menial servant, who could properly be deemed as within the realm of domestic relations,[23] and would no longer avail governments, limited companies and other employers who keep no household. But this drastic judicial reform in England (since completed by total statutory abolition[24]) has not been followed in Australia,[25] New Zealand,[26] or Canada,[27] on the view that the effect of the "policeman's case" was merely to confine the action to the "domestic relationship" of master and servant, not to that of master and "domestic servant". Even if the origin of the requisite relation was in the household of the master, the concept had gradually expanded so as eventually to cover all employment relations, including company employees,[28] save that between the Crown and the holder of a public office. This moderate view has undoubtedly the support of precedent, besides avoiding the paradoxical result that the protection for an employer should stand in inverse ratio to his loss, since obviously the more responsible the employee's position, and therefore the greater the difficulty

17. *A.-G. v. Perpetual Trustee Co.* [1955] A.C. 457 at 477-480; 92 C.L.R. 113 at 118-120.
18. *A.-G. v. Perpetual Trustee Co.* (1952) 85 C.L.R. 237 at 252 per Dixon J.
19. Indeed, members of the military forces are not even servants of the Crown, but of the monarch personally: Brett, 29 A.L.J. 389 at 392-393 (1955).
20. *U.S. v. Standard Oil* 332 U.S. 301 at 317-318 (1947) per Jackson J. Scholarly reaction has been uniformly unfavourable: Cowen, 19 A.L.J. 2 (1945) and 2 Annual L. Rev. 263 (1952); Fleming, 26 A.L.J. 122 (1952); Goodhart, 71 L.Q.R. 308 (1952); Sawer, 18 Mod. L. Rev. 488 (1955).
21. *I.R.C. v. Hambrook* [1956] 2 Q.B. 641 (civil servant). Independently, this is also the position in Scots (*Reavis v. Clan Lines* 1925 S.C. 725) and South African law: *Union Government v. Ocean Accident*, 1956 (1) S. Afr. 577. Eire did not go beyond "all public servants" in *A.-G. v. Ryan's* [1965] I.R. 642.
22. E.g. *Martinez v. Gerber* (1841) 3 Man. & G. 88; 133 E.R. 1069 (traveller); *Mankin v. Scala Theodrome* [1947] K.B. 257 (artiste); *Bermann v. Occhipinti* [1954] 1 D.L.R. 560 (manager).
23. Like the daughter nursing an invalid father, in *Chapman v. McDonald* [1969] I.R. 188.
24. *Administration of Justice Act* 1982 s. 2. In the U.S. the action is virtually obsolete.
25. *Comm. Rlys v. Scott* (1959) 102 C.L.R. 392 (engine driver); *Marinovski v. Zutti* [1984] 2 N.S.W.L.R. 571 (C.A.) (company director).
26. *A.-G. v. Wilson* [1973] 2 N.Z.L.R. 238 (C.A.) (fork lift operator; leaving open its application to "superior servants").
27. *Genereux v. Peterson* (1972) 34 D.L.R. (3d) 614 (Ont. C.A.); *R. v. Buchinsky* [1983] 1 S.C.R. 481 (countenancing Provincial option).
28. Partnerships do not qualify except in S.A. (*Wrongs Act* 1936 s. 34) between spouses. Whether the injured partner can recover his lost value of the partnership remains unsettled: *Luntz* 256-60.

and cost of replacing him, the less chance his employer would have to be recompensed for losing his services.

Damages

Although the action originally sounded in trespass, damage has always been of its gist.[29] Apart from a daughter's seduction when aggravated damages for mental distress are allowed, recovery is strictly limited to the pecuniary loss actually sustained through the loss of services and any other expenditure necessarily incurred in consequence of the servant's injury.[30] Ordinarily, therefore, the master is at least entitled to compensation for the *extra* cost of obtaining and training a substitute or paying overtime rates to existing staff.[31] Beyond that some courts have allowed lost profits, as when an incorporated family business had to be prematurely sold after its principal director-employee was incapacitated,[32] or when a music hall turn, consisting of master and servant, had to be suspended in consequence of the latter's injury.[33] But according to a more conservative view, damages are limited to the actual value of the services lost, both because of the very nature of the action and because it would unduly enlarge liability contrary to the general exclusion of consequential business losses in cases of negligence.[34]

Arguably more consonant with modern ideas, as already observed, would be the use of the action to secure reimbursement for "fringe benefits" conferred on the injured employee, such as the cost of medical expenses and sick pay.[35] In its favour is that, without necessarily increasing the aggregate burden of the defendant, it would prevent him profiting from the fact that the employer footed the bill, seeing that the employee might not be entitled to recover these items himself.[36] On the other hand, there are three objections:[37] First, where such recovery has been sustained it was on the ground either that these expenses were at least prima facie evidence of the value of the services lost or constituted damage resulting from the loss of services. Yet the first explanation rests on the questionable assumption that the true measure of damages is the value of the lost services rather than the damage to the master from losing the services. And as regards the second, it may be objected that voluntary payments could not in any event

29. *Hall v. Hollander* (1825) 4 B. & C. 660; 107 E.R. 1206 (child too young to render services to father).
30. See the jury direction by Abbott C.J. in *Flemington v. Smithers* (1826) 2 C. & P. 292; 172 E.R. 131.
31. As in *Chapman v. McDonald* [1969] I.R. 188 (nursing invalid mother) and apparently in *Ure v. Humes* [1969] Q.W.N. 25.
32. *Mercantile Ins. v. Argent* (1972) 46 A.L.J.R. 342; *Marinovski v. Zutti* [1984] 2 N.S.W.L.R. 571 (C.A.). According to *Ward v. Jacques* [1976] 3 W.W.R. 400 lost profits are recoverable only in such "alter ego" cases. Alternatively, the victim could claim such losses himself; *Ashcroft v. Curtin* [1971] 1 W.L.R. 1731 (C.A.).
33. *Mankin v. Scala Theodrome* [1947] K.B. 257 (comment, 63 L.Q.R. 18).
34. *Genereux v. Peterson* (1972) 34 D.L.R. (3d) 614 (Ont. C.A.). Criticised: Irvine, 11 C.C.L.T. 241 (1980).
35. *Sydney C.C. v. Bosnich* [1968] 3 N.S.W.L.R. 725 (C.A.: payments reasonably made).
36. *Genereux v. Peterson* (1972) 34 D.L.R. (3d) 614.
37. See the comprehensive analysis of this problem and the relevant case law by Richmond J. in *A.-G. v. Wilson* [1973] 2 N.Z.L.R. 238 at 252 ff. (the C.A. disallowed the claim).

be fairly charged against the defendant[38] and that contractual make-up pay would not require the employer to expend more than if the servant had not been disabled. Only if a substitute had to be engaged or other staff paid overtime would there be a loss qualifying under the second measure of damages.

The second objection is that refunding raises a tricky problem of co-ordination with the servant's own claim lest the defendant have to pay twice. Pensions and voluntary payments, for example, would not reduce the employee's own recovery, though sick-pay and make-up pay in lieu of wages would.[39] The final objection is policy based. The ordinary, large scale employer calculates these expenses into his own cost structure as a relatively negligible item compared with similar outlay due to sickness and other causes for non-attendance.[40] If the employer is thus in reality as able as the defendant to absorb the cost, is not the argument against the futility of reimbursing social security benefits[41] almost as persuasive here?

While these arguments have prevailed in relation to claims for loss of services,[42] Australian dicta, somewhat inconsistently, support recovery for medical costs on a restitutionary theory as expenses reasonably incurred on behalf of a victim of negligence.[43]

Contributory negligence

Whether contributory negligence by the servant will be imputed to the master so as to reduce his recovery will depend, as in the analogous claim by a husband or parent,[44] on whether the action is viewed as derivative (in the United States and Canada[45]) or independent (England and Australia[46]).

2. INTERFERENCE WITH CONTRACTUAL RELATIONS

An offshoot of the preceding tort is that of intentional interference with the performance of contract. Its origin stretches back to the 14th century when, by analogy to the writ of trespass for abducting a servant, a remedy was

38. *The Amerika* [1917] A.C. 38 at 61; *Esso Petroleum v. Hall Russell* [1989] A.C. 643.
39. See above, p. 246. In none of the cases allowing the employer's claim (e.g. *Bosnich*) was there a risk of double liability.
40. Besides, by making a loan rather than a non-refundable payment, the employer can assure eventual repayment.
41. See above, p. 248.
42. *A.-G. v. Perpetual Trustee Co.* (1952) 85 C.L.R. 237 at 290-291; *Holland v. Jordin* (1985) 36 N.T.R. 1; *A.-G. v. Wilson* [1973] 2 N.S.W.L.R. 238 (C.A.).
43. *A.-G. v. Perpetual Trustee Co.* (1952) 85 C.L.R. 237; *Blundell v. Musgrave* (1956) 96 C.L.R. 73 at 97-98; *Comm. Rlys v. Scott* (1959) 102 C.L.R. 392 at 408-409. However refunding of other expenditures like sick pay on grounds of unjust enrichment has been rejected: *Receiver for Metropolitan Police v. Croydon Corp.* [1957] 2 Q.B. 154 (C.A.).
44. See above, p. 662.
45. Cf. *A.-G. v. Jackson* [1946] S.C.R. 489 (gratuitous passenger).
46. But see *Anderson v. Blazeley* [1966] Tas. S.R. 281.

devised against taking away a servant by persuasion rather than force.[47] This common law action was shortly reinforced by a statutory action based on the *Statute of Labourers*, which was passed to cope with the economic chaos in the wake of the Black Death that struck England in 1348 and produced a great scarcity of labour and rise in wages. The statute made it an offence for a labourer or servant to leave his agreed service prematurely, as well as for a stranger to receive or retain him in his service. No civil remedy was expressly given to the first master, but the courts quickly devised an action based on the statute, by which he could recover damages from the second. In the course of the next three centuries, these two actions, the one for enticing a servant, the other for retaining him after gaining knowledge of his uncompleted service, became absorbed in a general action on the case, and its link with the *Statute of Labourers* was forgotten. Gradually, the remedy was expanded beyond labourers and menial servants, but it was not until 1853 that, in the great case of *Lumley v. Gye*,[48] the basis was laid for its universal application to all manner of contractual relations.

In *Lumley v. Gye*, Miss Johanna Wagner, a well known opera star, was engaged by the plaintiff to perform for a season exclusively at the Queen's Theatre, London, of which he was the manager. Before the season opened, the defendant persuaded her to break that contract and sing for him. When sued, he defended on the ground that Miss Wagner's position as an artiste lay outside the purview of the action for enticement, which was confined to "servants" within the meaning of the *Statute of Labourers*. This argument was rejected in favour of the broader view that any malicious interference with contractual relations was an actionable wrong, no matter whether the servant had repudiated the contract before commencing its performance or only thereafter.

Since then the action has been actively promoted by the courts. Leaving behind its original link with personal service, it now applies to every kind of contractual relation, including purely commercial.[49] Viewed as an illustration of the generalisation that unjustified "violation of a legal right committed knowingly is a cause of action,"[50] it is now wide enough to include even civil rights existing independently of contract: thus it would be an actionable wrong to induce a common carrier to refuse, in breach of his common law duty, goods tendered to him for carriage.[51] More doubtful is

47. The history, and particularly its controversial relationship to the *Statute of Labourers*, is discussed by Jones, *Per Quod Servitium Amisit*, 74 L.Q.R. 39 (1958). The *Administration of Justice Act* 1982 (Eng.) s. 2 abolished the action for enticing and harbouring a servant.
48. E. & B. 216; 118 E.R. 749. Previously the plaintiff had failed to get specific performance but succeeded in getting an injunction against her singing for anyone but himself: *Lumley v. Wagner* (1852) 1 De G.M. & G. 604; 42 E.R. 687. See *Tortious Interference with Contractual Relations in the 19th Century*, 93 Harv. L. Rev. 1510 (1980).
49. E.g. *Stratford v. Lindley* [1965] A.C. 269 (hire of barges); *Torquay Hotel v. Cousins* [1969] 2 Ch. 106 (oil supply). It thereby emphasised the quasi-proprietary nature of contractual rights—an important form of wealth in the modern economy. But unlike interference with tangible property (conversion), which entails strict liability, here protection is only against knowing interference.
50. *Quinn v. Leathem* [1901] A.C. 495 at 510 per Lord Macnaghten.
51. *James v. Commonwealth* (1939) 62 C.L.R. 339 at 370; also *Cunard S.S. Co. v. Stacey* [1955] 2 Ll. Rep. 247 (C.A.) (breach of statute conferring right on shipowner); *Associated British Ports v. T.G.W.U.* [1989] 1 W.L.R. 939 (C.A.). But not breach of trust: *Metall & Rohstoff v. Donaldson* [1991] 1 Q.B. 391 (C.A.).

the role of the action for vindicating non-economic relations; it has been denied for the right of parental access in custody disputes because it would likely be exploited for spiteful litigation and is better left to matrimonial proceedings.[52]

Also, the tort though conventionally known as "procuring *breach*", has in recent years been extended to lesser forms of interference, like preventing or hindering one party from performing his contract short of breach. This has included situations not only where the breach was excused on account of a force majeure clause or the doctrine of frustration,[53] but also where performance became more difficult though not impossible[54] and where an employee, short of losing his job, suffered harassment and injury to his reputation.[55]

However in the absence of unlawful means, it is not actionable to dissuade anyone from not entering into, or renewing a contract with the plaintiff: while contractual rights are protected, mere expectancies are not.[56]

Manner of interference

The tort's major role has been in the area of trade rivalry and labour relations. In both it is apt to cramp competitive initiative severely. Accordingly, early in this century legislation in England stepped in and exempted most labour disputes.[57] In the last decade however, the tort has become revitalised; the courts contributing their share both by expanding the scope of actionable interference and by an increasingly narrow construction of the statutory immunity.[58]

The expansive promotion of the tort by English courts has brought an increasing range of activities within its fold. Liability will attach if the intervenor, with knowledge of the contract and intent to prevent or hinder its performance, either (1) persuades, induces or procures one of the contracting parties not to perform his obligations, or (2) commits some act, wrongful in itself, to prevent such performance.[59] The first is usually described as "direct", the second as "indirect" interference; the first involving immediate pressure on one of the contracting parties, while in the

52. *Frame v. Smith* [1987] 2 S.C.R. 790.
53. *Torquay Hotel v. Cousins* [1969] 2 Ch. 106; *Merkur Island Corp. v. Laughton* [1983] 2 A.C. 570 (indirect interference by unlawful means). Aliter, if the contract is legally ineffective, e.g. void for mistake (*Said v. Butt* [1920] 3 K.B. 497), infancy (*De Francesco v. Barnum* (1890) 45 Ch. D. 430), or perhaps voidable (*Greig v. Insole* [1978] 1 W.L.R. 302 at 333) or not complying with the *Statute of Frauds*: *Doust v. Godbehear* (1925) 28 W.A.L.R. 59.
54. *Dimbleby v. N.U.J.* [1984] 1 W.L.R. 67 (C.A.).
55. *MacKenzie v. MacLachlan* [1979] 1 N.Z.L.R. 670.
56. *Allen v. Flood* [1898] A.C. 1 (below, p. 698); *McKernan v. Fraser* (1931) 46 C.L.R. 343; *Midland Cold Storage v. Steer* [1972] Ch. 630 at 643-645. Contra: *Gershman v. Marketing Bd* (1976) 69 D.L.R. (3d) 114 (Man. C.A.) (renewal).
57. See below, p. 696. Can.: Burns, 58 Can. B. Rev. 103 (1980).
58. Especially *Thompson v. Deakin* [1952] Ch. 646 (C.A.); *Stratford v. Lindley* [1965] A.C. 269; *Daily Mirror v. Gardner* [1968] 2 Q.B. 762 (C.A.); *Torquay Hotel v. Cousins* [1969] 2 Ch. 106 (C.A.).
59. The plaintiff must also prove special damage, except in a quia timet action when likelihood of damage is sufficient: *Greig v. Insole* [1978] 1 W.L.R. 302 at 332.

second the intervenor acts "at one remove", so to speak, typically by procuring the withdrawal of the contractor's labour with a vew to making it impossible for him to perform his contract with the plaintiff. In the first case, it is invariably the other—innocent—party to the contract who has cause to complain, the breacher having presumably gained from his inducement. But where unlawful means have been employed to force rather than persuade him into breach, he may himself have suffered financial loss for which he is entitled to recover.[60]

Direct interference

Examples of direct intervention in the abovementioned sense occur when a union unequivocally calls out its members on strike,[61] retailers induce wholesalers to suspend their standing order from a manufacturer, or when the I.C.C. threatened to disqualify from test matches cricketers who had signed on with Packer's World Series.[62] When a businessman inveigles the employee of a competitor, it matters nothing who took the first step—whether the plaintiff's servant or the defendant, for the latter's eventual offer to employ the former with knowledge of his existing ties serves as the decisive, and sufficient, inducement to break them. Similarly, it has been held actionable, as "inconsistent dealings",[63] to accept an offer to purchase a piece of land in known violation of a restrictive convenant,[64] or a motor car in disregard of a covenant against resale,[65] which in either case contractually bound the vendor.

A distinction has been suggested between persuasion, inducement or procurement, on the one hand, and advice on the other: the former being actionable, but not the latter. Inducing a breach of contract, it is said, means to create a reason for breaking it, whereas advising a breach is merely to point out the reasons which already exist.[66] But this distinction has been criticised for confusing the question of causation with the defence of justification: the relationship between the parties (for example familial or professional) and the artfulness of the adviser may be just as effective in inducing the desired breach as the creation of new reasons for it.[67] Both imply pressure and that is enough; even though merely imparting information may not be.

60. *Dimbleby v. N.U.J.* [1984] 1 W.L.R. 67 (C.A.).
61. E.g. *S.W. Miners Federation v. Glamorgan Coal Co.* [1905] A.C. 239.
62. *Greig v. Insole* [1978] 1 W.L.R. 302.
63. Jenkins L.J.'s phrase in *Thomson v. Deakin* [1952] Ch. 646 at 694 (C.A.). However such "dealings" seem to be confined to the making of inconsistent contracts: a gift to finance an inconsistent undertaking was excused in *Batts Combe Quarry v. Ford* [1943] Ch. 51. To extend it would also require substantial modification of the requirement that the defendant must have "intended" to interfere with the plaintiff's contract: see below, p. 694.
64. *Sefton v. Tophams* [1964] 1 W.L.R. 1408 (Aintree racetrack for housing development).
65. *B.M.T.A. v. Salvadori* [1949] Ch. 556 (during post-war supply shortage).
66. *Salmond & Houston* 372; *Thomson v. Deakin* [1952] Ch. 646 at 686, 694-695, 702; *Woolley v. Dunford* (1972) 2 S.A.S.R. 243 at 290.
67. Payne, *Interference with Contract*, 7 Cur. Leg. Prob. 94 at 102-104 (1954); *Rest. 2d* §76 comment *h*, also postulates a mere causal test, modified by a privilege of honest advice in response to a request: §722. In *Camden Nominees v. Forcey* [1940] Ch. 352 at 363. Simonds J. also thought advice justifiable only when given by a person in whom the law recognises a moral duty to give it (as below, p. 695).

Apparently, holding out temptation is not always sufficient. In one Australian case[68] wholesale suppliers of petrol informed dealers that they would not sell them their own brands at a discount, so long as they continued to sell the plaintiff's petrol at a lower price than their own. The retailers were contractually bound to the plaintiff not to sell his product above a price fixed by him, and were therefore placed in the dilemma of losing all profit on the resale of the defendant's petrol or discontinuing the sale of the plaintiff's. On the evidence, the court reached the conclusion that the defendants had simply exercised their privilege to refuse to sell their own goods except on their own terms, and that they had not deliberately attempted to procure the breach of subsisting contracts with the plaintiff. Also, the retailers could have fallen into line with the defendants' price policy by terminating their contract with the plaintiff, and would then have been able to obtain the defendant's petrol at a discount.

Exceptionally, mere failure to *terminate* "inconsistent dealings" is actionable: at least with respect to retaining a servant after becoming aware that he is already bound to someone else.[69] But if the interference consists in making an inconsistent contract, knowledge attained only thereafter comes too late, even when the inconsistent contract could be rescinded with impunity.[70]

Indirect interference

Interference with contract rights may also be procured indirectly, that is by means other than direct suasion on the other contracting party. But in order to be actionable the means must have been independently unlawful.[71] It may for example, take the form of intentionally preventing that party from carrying out his contract with the plaintiff by placing him under physical restraint,[72] taking away essential tools or machinery,[73] or defrauding him.[74] So also, where a car manufacturer had agreed with a tyre company that all cars he exhibited would be fitted with tyres of its make, a competitor who secretly removed them and substituted his own was held liable, not only to the manufacturer for trespass to his goods, but also to the tyre company for unlawful interference with its contract.[75]

This list was further augmented when it was held also to be an actionable interference to prevail upon some third person to commit a wrongful act, with the intention of thereby indirectly procuring a breach of contractual

68. *Independent Oil Industries v. Shell Co.* (1937) 37 S.R. (N.S.W.) 394. Cf. *Rest. 2d* §766 comment.
69. *De Francesco v. Barnum* (1890) 63 L.T. 514. But this ancient action of knowingly harbouring a servant (without prior enticement) was dealt a virtual death blow in *Jones Bros v. Stevens* [1955] 1 Q.B. 275 by requiring the plaintiff to prove that his servant would otherwise have returned to him.
70. *Sleight v. Blight* [1969] V.R. 931.
71. *Thomson v. Deakin* [1952] Ch. 646 (C.A.). They are therefore examples of the "genus" tort of unlawful interference (below, p. 703), the breach of contract being only make-weight unlike "procuring".
72. *Thomson v. Deakin* [1952] Ch. 646 at 694, 702. Cf. *Williams v. Hursey* (1959) 103 C.L.R. 30 at 77.
73. *Thomson v. Deakin* at 702.
74. *National Phonograph Co. v. Edison Bell Co.* [1908] 1 Ch. 335.
75. *G.W.K. v. Dunlop Rubber Co.* (1926) 42 T.L.R. 376, 593.

relations between others.[76] A common illustration is a so-called "secondary boycott", such as occurs when employees of A are called out on strike to stop him supplying goods to B, the real target. Here, B has a cause of action against the instigator if the following stringent conditions are fulfilled:[77] it must be shown first, that he knew of the existence of the contract between A and B and intended to procure its breach; secondly, that he did definitely and unequivocally persuade, induce or procure A's employees to break their contract of employment with such intent; thirdly, that the employees did in fact break their contracts of employment; and fourthly, that breach of the contract between A and B ensued in *necessary*[78] consequence of the breach by the employees of their contracts of employment with A. Clear proof of causal connection between the defendant's conduct and breach of the relevant contract is required. For example, proof merely that all of A's truck drivers were called out on strike would not be enough, if for all one knows A might have hired some others or procured alternative transport.[79] Nor are general exhortations, such as "Stop supplies to B", "Refuse to handle B's goods", "Treat B as black" and the like, treated as having "induced" any legally wrongful act that follows, because the objects advocated might have been achieved by lawful means, as by giving proper notice to quit.[80]

The hallmark of indirect interference, then, is that the means employed must have been independently unlawful. Otherwise most strikes would have become unlawful and commercial competition unduly hampered. If acts lawful in themselves became actionable merely because they were intended to, and did, bring about a breach of contract between other people, it would have meant that, if A knew that B had contracted to supply C with certain goods, he could not with impunity buy up all such goods in the market so as to disable B from performing his contract with C. But that is not the law.[81]

In this respect, as in another to be noticed presently,[82] modern law has come to attach crucial significance to the use of unlawful means; justifying the generalisation that the infliction of intended economic loss (including frustration of contractual expectations) is actionable, at all events if the means employed to that end are independently unlawful. Yet in the complex factual context especially of industrial relations, this can produce capricious results in which the distinction between permissible and impermissible tactics comes to turn on fictitious and, from a practical viewpoint, even irrelevant factors.

76. This extension of the tort was established in *Thomson v. Deakin* [1952] Ch. 646 and endorsed in *Stratford v. Lindley* [1965] A.C. 269.
77. *Thomson v. Deakin* [1952] Ch. 646. See also *Trade Practices Act* 1974 (Cth) ss 45D and 45E.
78. Foreseeable is sufficient for direct interference.
79. *Thomson v. Deakin* [1952] Ch. 646 at 699. Aliter in *Stratford v. Lindley* [1965] A.C. 269 where it was practically impossible to get anyone else to return the barges; also *Woolley v. Dunford* (1972) 3 S.A.S.R. 243.
80. "A person who advocates the object without advocating the means is [not] to be taken to have advocated recourse to unlawful means" (*Thomson v. Deakin* [1952] Ch. 646 at 697-698). For the same reason, advertising and solicitation are privileged, even if they induce someone to break his contract with a competitor in favour of dealing with the advertiser.
81. Ibid. at 680, 697.
82. See below, p. 699.

A union wishing to blacklist B might effectuate their embargo either by dissuading A from supplying him (for example by threats of calling out A's men) or by instructing A's men to cease co-operation. If A is contractually bound to supply B to the union's knowledge, the first alternative is clearly tortious; but not so the second, unless the instruction to A's men and the terms of their employment are subsequently construed as independently amounting to tortiously procuring breach of *their* contract. Even if it does not so qualify, the stop notice might yet be interpreted as a method of communicating with A directly and thus amount to a *direct* (and therefore tortious) inducement.[83] Since the legal outcome is often unpredictable, the law can hardly be considered satisfactory; for it is either apt to paralyse industrual action excessively or the spectre of illegality will be ignored and thus promote disrespect for the law.

Motive and intent

Malice, in the sense of spite or ill-will, is no longer an essential element.[84] Nor is an intent to injure, not even that the defendant's conduct was aimed at the plaintiff. All that need be shown is that he acted with the necessary knowledge and intent of procuring a breach of contract.[85] Merely that the breach was a natural consequence of his conduct is not sufficient: he must have intended it. Not that he need have actually known the precise terms of it or that his object could be accomplished only through its breach. If—turning a blind eye—he went about it regardless of whether it would involve a breach, he will be treated just as if he had knowingly procured it.[86] Indifference is equated with intent. It is otherwise if he acted under a bona fide belief that he would not infringe contractual rights, for example after going to the trouble of seeking legal advice, mistaken though it may turn out to be.[87]

There is this difference, however, between direct and indirect procurement: for the latter, breach must be a *necessary* consequence;[88] for the former it need only be foreseeable.[89]

Interference with contract has thus remained an intentional tort, one that does not extend to negligent conduct by which the performance of a contract is prevented or rendered more onerous. Thus a tugmaster failed to recover his remuneration when the barge he was towing was negligently sunk;[90] and a contractor his extra cost of driving a tunnel when an adjoining waterworks allowed water to escape into the diggings.[91] The

83. Stop-notices were so interpreted in *Daily Mirror v. Gardner* [1968] 2 Q.B. 762 and by Lord Pearce in *Stratford v. Lindley* [1965] A.C. 269 (the other opinions proceeded via breach of the *employees'* contract).
84. *Quinn v. Leathem* [1901] A.C. 495 at 510.
85. *Hill v. F.N.E.C.* [1989] 1 W.L.R. 225 at 234 (Stuart-Smith L.J.).
86. *Stratford v. Lindley* [1965] A.C. 269; *Emerald Constructions v. Lowthian* [1966] 1 W.L.R. 691; *Woolley v. Dunford* (1972) 3 S.A.S.R. 243. But it cannot be assumed, without more, that the contract will be continuing: *Schindler Lifts v. Debelak* (1989) 89 A.L.R. 275.
87. *British Plastics v. Ferguson* [1940] 1 All E.R. 479; *Short v. City Bank* (1912) 15 C.L.R. 148.
88. *Stratford v. Lindley* [1965] A.C. 269 at 333 ("reasonable consequence").
89. See above, p. 691.
90. *La Société Anonyme v. Bennetts* [1911] 1 K.B. 243.
91. *Cattle v. Stockton Waterworks* (1875) L.R. 10 Q.B. 453.

master's action for loss of services is treated as anachronistic and without counterpart in an employee's claim for losing his job as the result of negligent injury to his employer.[92] Modern extensions of liability for negligent economic loss are unlikely to effect any changes in this context.[93]

Justification

While spite or an improper motive on the part of the defendant is not an essential part of the plaintiff's cause of action, his ultimate purpose may, on the other hand, be so meritorious as to require sacrifice of the plaintiff's claim to freedom from interference. But in contrast to defamation, this tort has not yet developed formalised privileges; the issue in each case being rather whether, upon consideration of the relative significance of all the factors involved, the defendant's conduct should be tolerated despite its detrimental effect on the interests of the other. For this purpose, it has been said, the most relevant are the nature of the contract, the position of the parties to it, the grounds for the breach, the means employed to procure it, the relation of the person procuring it to the contract breaker, and the object of the person procuring the breach.[94] For example, fraud or physical violence cannot be justified in any cirumstances.[95]

An impersonal or disinterested motive may afford justification, particularly where the defendant, acting under a moral duty, seeks to protect a person to whom he stands in a relation of responsibility, like a father persuading his daughter in good faith to break off an engagement to marry an undesirable suitor[96] or a physician counselling his patient to give up his employment for reasons of health, even a lawyer who advises a client (mistakenly) that he has a right to terminate a contract.[97] This conclusion could be justified either on the ground of privilege or by distinguishing, as has been suggested, between mere advice, on the one hand, and active inducement or procurement, on the other. In several cases, a privilege to protect the public interest has been recognised, as where the defendant acted for the sake of upholding public morality.[98] Illustrations are a licensing authority banning an objectionable film which the plaintiff had arranged to exhibit at another's theatre,[99] and an actors' protection society persuading a theatre proprietor to break his engagement with the manager of a troupe who paid his chorus girls so low a wage that they were driven

92. Contra: *Nicholls v. Richmond* (1983) 145 D.L.R. (3d) 362 (B.C.C.A.) (e.g. job loss resulting from negligent medical check).
93. See above, p. 177.
94. *Glamorgan Coal Co. v. S. Wales Miners Federation* [1903] 2 K.B. 545 at 574 per Romer L.J.; see Heydon, *Defence of Justification in Cases of Intentionally Caused Economic Loss*, 20 U. Tor. L.J. 139 at 161-171 (1970). American courts have been more frequently occupied with the problem of privilege than ours: *Prosser & Keeton* 982-989; Sayre, *Inducing Breach of Contract*, 36 Harv. L. Rev. 663 (1923); *Rest. 2d* §767-774.
95. But not all unlawful means necessarily disqualify: see *Re Ranger Uranium Mines* (1987) 54 N.T.R. 6 (peaceful picketing); *Latham v. Singleton* [1981] 2 N.S.W.L.R. 843 at 869.
96. *Findlay v. Blaylock* 1937 S.C. 21; *Gunn v. Barr* [1926] 1 D.L.R. 855; *Crofter Handwoven Harris Tweed v. Veitch* [1942] A.C. 435 at 442-443.
97. *Spectra Group v. Eldred Sollows* [1991] 7 C.C.L.T. (2d) 169.
98. Cf. the growing support for disclosure of "iniquity" as a defence to breach of confidence: *Initial Services v. Putterill* [1968] 1 Q.B. 396 (C.A.); *Hubbard v. Vosper* [1972] 2 Q.B. 84 (C.A.).
99. *Stott v. Gamble* [1916] 2 K.B. 504.

to supplement their earnings by prostitution.[100] Another might be the promotion of the health and safety of fellow workers.[101] The mere fact, however, that an association has undertaken a duty to its members to protect their interest and acted in pursuance thereof, does not by itself provide a justification, for otherwise a ready excuse would be at hand for almost any actionable interference promoted by collective action at the prompting of trade unions, trade associations, and other protective societies.[102]

Most profound in the context of industrial relations is the privilege created by legislation in England for the sake primarily of carving out a legitimate area for union strike action against employers: rendering immune any act in contemplation or furtherance of a trade dispute which would be actionable on the ground only that "it induces another person to break a contract or interferes or induces another person to interfere with its performance."[103]

No justification is otherwise accorded to the advancement of the defendant's own trade interest[104] or of those with whom he is associated[105] or of a common trade or business interest subsisting between the intervener and the contract breaker,[106] because there is no good reason for giving precedence to the defendant's self-interest over the legally protected claim of the plaintiff to maintain an existing contract relation unimpaired from outside interference. It is different if the defendant seeks to assert "an equal or superior right" himself, as when a mortgagee instead of exercising his power of sale made an accommodation with the mortgagor conditioned on dismissal of the latter's architect,[107] or where A had entered into two inconsistent contracts with B and C, and B insisted on his contractual rights.[108] But the breach by A of his contract with B will not justify B in procuring C to break an independent contract with A.[109] Thus, where one tenant instigated another tenant of the same landlord to withhold his rent

100. *Brimelow v. Casson* [1924] 1 Ch. 302, criticised in *Camden Nominees v. Forcey* [1940] Ch. 352 at 366.
101. *Re Ranger Uranium Mines* (1987) 54 N.T.R. 6.
102. *S.W. Miners Federation v. Glamorgan Coal Co.* [1905] A.C. 239; *Ansett v. Air Pilots* (1989) 95 A.L.R. 211 at 254; *B.W.I.U. v. O.D.C.D.* (1991) 99 A.L.R. 735. Perhaps a distinction should here be drawn between promoting and *protecting* the interest of members, e.g. to avoid retaliation from another union, as in *Pete's Towing v. N.I.U.W.* [1970] N.Z.L.R. 32.
103. *Trade Union and Labour Relations Act* 1974 s. 13, as amended in 1976. See Simpson, *Not So Golden Formula, In Contemplation and Furtherance for Trade Dispute*, 46 Mod. L. Rev. 463 (1983). For a (qualified) counterpart in S.A. see above, n. 5. The *Labour Relations Act* 1987 (N.Z.) s. 242 bars any action based on any of the economic torts in relation to lawful strikes or lockouts.
104. *De Jetley Marks v. Greenwood* [1936] 1 All E.R. 863 at 873 (avoid insolvency).
105. *Pratt v. B.M.A.* [1919] 1 K.B. 244.
106. *Camden Nominees v. Forcey* [1940] Ch. 352.
107. *Hill v. F.N.E.C.* [1989] 1 W.L.R. 225 (C.A.).
108. *Read v. Operative Stonemasons* [1902] 2 K.B. 88 at 95; *Smithies v. Operative Plasterers* [1909] 1 K.B. 310 at 337. On whether any importance attaches to the chronological order in which the inconsistent contracts were concluded: see 98 L.Q.R. at 288-290 (1982). The second agreement is not invalid, unless *both* parties knew at the time of the earlier contract: *British Homophone v. Kunz* (1935) 152 L.T. 589 at 592-593; Lauterpacht, *Contracts to Break a Contract*, 52 L.Q.R. 496 (1936).
109. *Smithies v. Operative Plasterers* [1909] 1 K.B. 310 at 341.

in order to force the latter to remedy common grievances, it was held that the landlord's breach of his own obligations was no justification.[110]

A servant or agent, acting within the scope of his employment or authority, is not liable for inducing or procuring a breach of contract by his employer, at any rate if he acts in good faith for the protection of his employer's interests.[111] Thus, where a company acting by its directors breaks a contract, the party aggrieved is confined to suing the company for breach of contract and has no remedy against the directors in tort.[112] The immunity has been justified on the technical ground that, since a master is responsible for the acts committed by his servant in the course of employment, the "extraordinary result" would otherwise ensue that the master could be held liable not only for breaking his own contract, but also for inducing himself to break it. It may be doubted whether this argument provides a convincing reason for letting off the servant, and it would be more realistic to admit that, on grounds of policy, a privilege is warranted wherever a servant or agent acts, not in capricious pursuit of self-advantage, but for the bona fide protection of his employer.

A proposal or threat to institute legal peoceedings with a view to deterring a contracting party from performing his obligations which the intervenor honestly and reasonably believes to be illegal, is not a wrongful procurement of a breach of contract, because the law always countenances resort to the courts, whether by criminal or civil processes, as the proper means for determining any assertion of right. Actionable interference with contractual relations must involve an element of impropriety or of reliance upon some power or influence independent of lawful authority. The privilege for threats to put the law in motion is not forfeited merely because it turns out that the defendant was in error in believing that performance of the contract was illegal, provided at any rate that he was acting honestly in performance of a duty to maintain or enforce the law and, perhaps, had reasonable grounds for his belief. Thus, it was held that the Commonwealth incurred no liability when one of its officers, relying on a statute subsequently declared unconstitutional, warned shipowners that they would be prosecuted for carrying a prohibited cargo for the plaintiff.[113]

Damages

This tort, like the others considered in this chapter, is not actionable without proof of damage. But recovery is not limited to specific or special damage and may, for example in case of wrongful dismissal, include compensation for the inconvenience and unhappiness caused by a change of job. Neither are damages limited to those recoverable from the contract-

110. *Camden Nominees v. Forcey* [1940] Ch. 352.
111. *Said v. Butt* [1920] 3 K.B. 497; *Rutherford v. Pool* [1953] V.L.R. 130; *Official Assignee v. Dowling* [1964] N.Z.L.R. 578; *Imperial Oil v. C. & G.* (1989) 62 D.L.R. (4th) 261.
112. *O'Brien v. Dawson* (1942) 66 C.L.R. 18; contra: *Einhorn v. Westmount Investments* (1969) 6 D.L.R. (3d) 71 and note *De Jetley Marks v. Greenwood* [1936] 1 All E.R. 863 at 872. Possible difficulties presented by the existence of cumulative remedies in contract and in tort are discussed by Starke, 7 Res. Jud. 136 at 145 (1956).
113. *James v. Commonwealth* (1939) 62 C.L.R. 339; *Willims v. Metropolitan Abattoirs* (1953) 89 C.L.R. 66; *Lovell v. McKechnie* (1989) 6 B.R. 238. A fortiori *Roman Corp. v. Hudson's Bay Co.* [1973] S.C.R. 820 where government had a right to carry out warning.

breaker; they may include the prospect of continuing employment beyond the contractual period.[114] Also, while aggravated damages are not recoverable in contract,[115] they are in tort; as are exemplary damages in many jurisdictions.[116]

3. UNLAWFUL INTERFERENCE WITH TRADE OR BUSINESS

Free competition

Not until the end of the 19th century did the view finally prevail that, in the absence of additional factors such as the use of illegal means or conspiracy, no liability accrues for intentionally inflicting economic loss, as by tempting or even procuring others not to do business with the plaintiff (short of interfering with his contract rights). At one time, there was some support for the broad proposition that "he that hinders another in his trade or livelihood is liable to an action for so hindering him",[117] but since *Allen v. Flood*[118] in 1898 it has been regarded as settled that interference with economic relations, which are merely in prospect and not yet cemented by contract, is not a tort. For the sake of ensuring some elbow-room for the aggressive pursuit of self-interest in a society dedicated to free enterprise, the law recognised a deep "chasm"[119] between interference with a subsisting contract and procuring a person not to enter or renew a contract with another. Not even the presence of an intent to injure or malice (injuring for injury's sake) was held to make any difference, on the rather glib view that just as unlawful conduct cannot be saved by good intentions, so what is lawful cannot be rendered unlawful by an improper motive. (In both respects, American law disagrees.[120]) The result was plainly influenced by a desire to reduce judicial intervention in labour disputes and the market place. Certainly, during its heyday the rule operated in a policy neutral fashion, sometimes promoting free competition, sometimes monopoly, in such diverse situations as strikes by labour against employers,[121] inter-union disputes where one faction seeks to exclude

114. See *Ansett v. Air Pilots* [1991] 1 V.R. 637.
115. *Bliss v. S. E. Thames H.A.* [1987] I.C.R. 700; *Vorvis v. Ins. Corp.* [1989] 1 S.C.R. 1085. See 106 L.Q.R. 8 (1990).
116. E.g. *Weiss v. Omnus* [1976] 1 S.C.R. 776. *Rookes v. Barnard* [1964] A.C. 1129 (above, p. 241) disallowed these in an action for intimidation, but its reach is confined to England.
117. *Keeble v. Hickeringill* (1707) 11 East. 574 n. at 575; 103 E.R. 1127 per Holt C.J. The last invocation of a general tort of intentional infliction of injury without justification was by Lord Bowen in *Mogul S.S. v. McGregor* (1889) 23 Q.B.D. 598 at 613. It survives as the "prima facie tort" doctrine in the U.S. and, limited to physical injury, was affirmed in *Wilkinson v. Downton*: above, p. 32.
118. [1898] A.C. 1 (below, n. 148): It was given statutory force in Eng. by what is now the *Trade Union and Labour Relations Act* 1974 s. 2: "for the avoidance of doubt".
119. *Allen v. Flood* [1898] A.C. 1 at 121 per Lord Herschell. The decision was close (6: 3); among all participating judges only 8 out of 21 voted for the defendant.
120. See *Prosser & Keeton* §130; Perlman, *Interference with Contract and Other Economic Expectancies*, 49 U. Chi. L. Rev. 61 (1982); *Rest. 2d* ch. 37.
121. Since manual workers are rarely employed on an hourly or daily basis, few such strikes involve inducement to break contracts of employment.

members of another from employment,[122] a union dispute with a worker,[123] consumers' boycotts,[124] and the maintenance of price-rings.[125]

In the post-war period, however, judicial activism has been revived, primarily over concern for the individual (whether dissident worker or businessman) victimised by labour unions or other powerful interests. This trend is reflected, besides the substantial extension of the tort of interference with contractual relations (already noted), by the emergent tort of intentional interference with a person's trade or business by unlawful means.

Unlawful means

Invoking scattered precedents of an older era,[126] the House of Lords in *Rookes v. Barnard*[127] in 1964 confirmed beyond all doubt as a tort, commonly known as intimidation, to coerce a person by unlawful threats into doing or abstaining from doing something that he would otherwise have every right to do, like firing a particular employee or ceasing to do business with an old customer. It is actionable at the instance of the employee or customer[128] and probably even the very person threatened;[129] the first being known as the "three party", the second as the "two party" situation. Moreover it has now become clear that intimidation is but an instance of a wider emergent tort of unlawful interference with trade or business. In effect these developments have largely outflanked *Allen v. Flood*. Our courts, unlike the American,[130] may have felt uneasy about adopting an amorphous principle of intentional interference with economic relations, which would have entailed controversial judgments about "justification";[131] instead they preferred the safer criterion of "unlawful means".

What is encompassed by unlawful means?[132] Obviously included are common law crimes, like battery or fraud,[133] and all torts.[134] Thus if A

122. *McKernan v. Fraser* (1931) 46 C.L.R. 343; *Allen v. Flood* [1898] A.C. 1; *Stratford v. Lindley* [1965] A.C. 269; *Morgan v. Fry* [1968] 2 Q.B. 710.
123. *Rookes v. Barnard* [1964] A.C. 1129 (closed shop); *Latham v. Singleton* [1981] 2 N.S.W.L.R. 843 (disobedient member).
124. *Rogers v. Rajendro Dutt* (1860) 13 Moo. P.C. 209; 15 E.R. 78.
125. *Ware & De Freville v. M.T.A.* [1921] 3 K.B. 40.
126. *Anon.* (1410) Y.B. 11 H. IV, 47 (frightening away customers from market); *Garret v. Taylor* (1621) Cro. Jac. 567; 79 E.R. 485 (scaring off customers and workmen); *Keeble v. Hickeringill* (1707) 11 East 574 n; 103 E.R. 1127 (scaring off game); *Tarleton v. M'Gawley* (1793) Peake 270; 170 E.R. 153 (scaring off customers with firearms); and cf. *Gregory v. Duke of Brunswick* (1844) 6 Man. & G. 205, 953; 134 E.R. 866, 1167 (conspiracy to hiss actor off stage).
127. [1964] A.C. 1129.
128. Ibid.
129. Ibid. at 1205-1206 (personal violence); *Huljich v. Hall* [1973] 2 N.Z.L.R. 279 (C.A.) (unlawful distress).
130. Sometimes revealingly called the "prima facie" tort doctrine: see *Rest. 2d* §870.
131. Cf. *Holmes-Pollock Letters* (2nd ed. 1961) 84.
132. Precedents have been applied interchangeably between the various torts involving "unlawfulness", i.e. intimidation, interference and unlawful conspiracy.
133. *Lonrho v. Fayed* [1990] 2 Q.B. 479.
134. E.g. *Sid Ross v. Actors Equity* (1970) 90 W.N. (Pt 7) (N.S.W.) 743 (unlawful picketing); *Huljich v. Hall* [1973] 2 N.Z.L.R. 279 (illegal distraint); *Plessey v. Wilson* [1982] I.R.L.R. 198 (trespass: sit-in).

threatens B with violence in order to cause economic loss to C, he will be liable to B for assault and to C for intimidation. Beyond that, the approach has been casuistic, without any evident rationale related to policy ends, and suffering from some inexplicable inconsistencies.

The most controversial extension was the inclusion, in *Rookes v. Barnard*, of a mere breach of contract, when the defendant threatened to strike his employer in breach of an anti-strike clause in his employment contract in order to coerce the dismissal of the plaintiff, a non-unionist fellow employee.[135] This decision has been criticised on a number of grounds. For putting an excessive brake on competitive activities especially in industrial disputes, in view of the prevalence of anti-strike clauses[136] which in Australia are commonly included in arbitration awards and entail a penalty for breach.[137] It is also inappropriate to "two party" situations because, unlike threats of violence against a contract partner, a mere threat to break the contract with him does not inject an extraneous unlawful element vis-à-vis him (as distinct from a third party) and would make every such threat also a tort of intimidation.[138]

No clear view has yet emerged regarding breaches of regulatory statutes. Against it seems to be the decision of the House of Lords in *Lonrho v. Shell*[139] that violation of the trading sanctions against Southern Rhodesia conferred no cause of action on a competitor for consequential losses. Although not involving *intentional* interference with trade or business because the conduct was not targeted against the plaintiff, the decision gave support to the traditional view that a penal statute does not authorise civil liability unless intended for the protection of a defined class of beneficiaries or having created a public right. Its bearing on the intentional tort however has been questioned and remains in doubt.[140] Also contempt of court is the subject of conflicting decisions.[141] In any event, not every incidental and trivial illegality committed in the course of an industrial dispute[141a] like holding an illegal street procession, now promises to taint the whole enterprise as tortious; for the doctrine would become intolerably oppressive

135. See above, n. 127.
136. *Coal Miners Union v. True* (1959) 33 A.L.J.R. 224 at 227, 230. See Wedderburn, *Intimidation and the Right to Strike*, 22 Mod. L. Rev. 257 (1964); Hoffman, *Rookes v. Barnard*, 81 L.Q.R. 116 (1965). In the absence of such a clause, not every strike or threat thereof would constitute a breach of contract: *Morgan v. Fry* [1968] 2 Q.B. 710 (C.A.). All depends on sufficient notice to quit. If the strike notice is too short, opinion is divided: *Cooper v. Millea* [1938] I.R. 749, holding a shorter notice fatal, was respected by Lord Denning and Davies L.J., but Russell L.J. joined Lord Devlin (*Rookes v. Barnard* [1964] A.C. 1129 at 1204) in doubting its causality. *Latham v. Singleton* [1981] 2 N.S.W.L.R. 843 sided with the former.
137. Evidently the absence of statutory defences in Australia does not affect the precedential value of the English decisions: *Sid Ross v. Actors Equity* (1970) 90 W.N. (Pt 7) (N.S.W.) 743.
138. The plaintiff is left with contractual or restitutionary (economic duress) remedies. Is actual breach unlawful interference with economic interests?: see below, p. 703.
139. [1982] A.C. 173.
140. It would be incompatible with *Daily Mirror v. Gardner* [1968] 2 Q.B. 762 (C.A.) and was not accepted in *Associated British Ports v. T.G.W.U.* [1989] 1 W.L.R. 939 (C.A.) nor (sub silentio) in *Ansett v. Air Pilots* [1991] 1 V.R. 637 (offence against *Industrial Relations Act* 1988 (Cth) s. 312).
141. *Acrow v. Rex Chainbelt* [1971] 1 W.L.R. 1676 (C.A.: Lord Denning again)—yes; *Chapman v. Honig* [1967] 1 W.L.R. 1165 (C.A.)—no.
141a. *Rookes v. Barnard* [1964] A.C. 1129 at 1218 per Lord Devlin.

if it were not restricted to situations where the threat to commit the unlawful act, or its actual commission, is not only part of the design (rather than a casual incident in its execution), but also the very intimidating factor that proved decisive in coercing submission.

It remains an open question what part, if any, justification plays in the tort of intimidation. On the one hand, it has been said that unlawful conduct can never be justified;[142] on the other hand, unless palliated, the doctrine is apt to become too oppressive especially in Australia where the political climate does not favour the British example of legislating broad-scale immunities for strike action.[143] Possible justification may be as open-ended as in relation to interference with contract. It has been suggested that at any rate a refusal to work side by side with troublemakers may well justify an otherwise illegal threat to strike.[144] On the other hand, merely believing that it served the interest of the union and its members is not sufficient.[145]

A threat to commit a *lawful* act cannot, of course, confer a cause of action any more than if it were actually carried out.[146] Evocative terms like "coercion", "intimidation", or "threats", which in common parlance carry an opprobrious connotation, are for legal purposes colourless, and extreme pressure is treated no differently from a polite warning.[147] Thus, in the leading case of *Allen v. Flood*,[148] the plaintiffs were employed to carry out woodwork on a ship. A union of ironworkers objected to their employment because they had previously done ironwork on another ship without belonging to that particular union. The defendant, a union delegate, peremptorily informed the employer that unless he discharged the plaintiffs, the ironworkers engaged on the job would be called out on strike. The employer accordingly dismissed the men as he had a legal right to do without infringing the terms of their engagement. But notwithstanding a finding by the jury that the defendant had acted maliciously, the House of Lords held that no wrongful act has been committed, since unlawful means had not been employed in procuring the plaintiff's discharge. The courts have even declined to condemn price maintenance schemes whereunder a defaulting member of a trade association is threatened with being put on a "stop-list", unless he pays a fine as determined by the association. Since there is nothing unlawful in cutting off a defaulter's supply, so long as it does not involve a breach of contract,[149] the extortion of money as the price for withholding that sanction is not treated as introducing an element

142. See above, p. 695.
143. *Rookes v. Barnard* was abrogated in England in 1965 (now the *Trade Union and Labour Relations Act* 1974 s. 13) with respect to acts "in contemplation or furtherance of a trade dispute".
144. *Morgan v. Fry* [1968] 2 Q.B. 710 at 729 per Lord Denning; *Pete's v. N.I.U.W.* [1970] N.Z.L.R. 32 ("fairness and justice"). See Heydon, *Defence of Justification* 20 U. Tor. L.J. 139 at 171-182 (1970).
145. *Latham v. Singleton* [1981] 2 N.S.W.L.R. 843 at 867 ff.; *Ansett v. Air Pilots* [1991] 1 V.R. 637 at 678.
146. *Sorrell v. Smith* [1925] A.C. 700 at 747.
147. *Hodges v. Webb* [1920] 2 Ch. 70.
148. [1898] A.C. 1.
149. *Ware & De Freville v. M.T.A.* [1921] 3 K.B. 40; approved in *Sorrell v. Smith* [1925] A.C. 700.

of illegality, because it is done in furtherance of a legitimate business interest and does not, therefore, amount to the crime of blackmail.[150]

Intended injury

The defendant's manoeuvre must have been *targeted* against the plaintiff, although its predominant purpose might well have been to advance his own interests thereby rather than to injure the plaintiff.[151] The commission of an illegal act or threat thereof does not entail liability merely because someone happened to suffer damage in consequence. An illegal strike against an employer may cause foreseeable loss to customers and suppliers but to confer a cause of action on them would have unduly restricted industrial action.[152] So also the loss must have been suffered as the result of the plaintiff's acting in the manner desired by the defendant: not like the farmer who drove her cattle into hiding to avoid the defendant's illegal threat to distrain it, which was quite the reverse of what he desired.[153]

These limitations were overlooked by the Australian High Court in a controversial decision.[154] A landowner drew water from a pool in an adjacent river under licence from an authority in whom the riverbed was vested. By taking away large quantities of gravel without (the latter's) permission, the defendant destroyed the pool, thereby causing damage to the plaintiff's crops. Without proof that the defendant so much as knew of the plaintiff's operations, let alone intended to interrupt them, the latter recovered on the spurious principle, destitute of all authority, that "independently of trespass, negligence or nuisance but by an action for damages upon the case, a person who suffers harm or loss as the inevitable consequence of the unlawful, intentional and positive acts of another is entitled to recover damages from that other."[155] This principle has found no more favour from courts than from scholars,[156] because it would countenance liability to an indeterminate class of persons only incidentally affected by unlawful action, like customers or suppliers of an employer involved in an unlawful strike. In practice it has been either flatly repudiated or evaded under the pretence that the act was not "unlawful" enough or the injury was not an "inevitable" consequence. Thus it was held

150. *Thorne v. M.T.A.* [1937] A.C. 797.

151. *Lonrho v. Fayed* [1990] 2 Q.B. 479 (C.A.), rejecting the "predominant purpose" test of the conspiracy tort (below, p. 707); *Ansett v. Air Pilots* [1991] 1 V.R. 637.

152. *Barretts & Baird v. I.P.C.S.* [1987] I.R.L.R. 3; *Van Camp Chocolates v. Aulsebrooks* [1984] 1 N.Z.L.R. 354 at 360 (distinguishing "deliberate" from "incidental"); *Can. Cement LaFarge v. B.C. Aggregate* [1983] 1 S.C.R. 452 (conspiracy directed at consumers, not supplier). But see *Lonrho v. Fayed* at 494 (per Woolf L.J.: "if the defendant has deliberately embarked on a course of conduct, the probable consequence of which on the plaintiff be appreciated . . .").

153. *Huljich v. Hall* [1973] 2 N.Z.L.R. 279 (C.A.).

154. *Beaudesert S. v. Smith* (1966) 120 C.L.R. 145 (any reconsideration by full bench: *Elston v. Dove* (1983) 57 A.L.J.R. 83 at 88).

155. *Beaudesert S. v. Smith* at 156. Note that "intentional and positive" refers to the defendant's *acts*, not its consequences.

156. Dworkin, *Intentionally Causing Economic Loss*, 2 Monash U.L. Rev. 4 (1974); but defended by Sadler, 5 A.L.J. 38 (1948). This and other generalisations are discussed by Heydon, *Future of Economic Torts*, 12 U.W.A.L. Rev. 1 at 9ff. (1975).

inapplicable to one who traded without a permit,[157] to a local authority which denied a building permit pursuant to an invalid resolution,[158] to an invalid port clearance which allowed a ship to be sailed away without the owner,[159] and against oil companies whose defiance of the oil embargo during the Rhodesian crisis caused loss to owners of a pipeline.[160]

Unlawful interference

As already mentioned, the tort of intimidation by unlawful means is now widely understood to be but an instance of the "genus" tort of unlawful interference with trade or business.[161] While this development would not be strictly incompatible with *Allen v. Flood*, its effect is largely to outflank that decision because of the ambiguity and wide scope of "unlawfulness" on the contemporary scene.

In favour of the generalisation is the logic that if the threat is unlawful, its implementation cannot be any the less so. Yet there are some difficulties. Problematic as was the very decision in *Rookes v. Barnard* to include breach of contract among unlawful means, its extension from intimidation to "unlawful interference" would convert many breaches of contract into torts. The new tort would also absorb those traditionally independent economic torts linked to unlawful means, like intimidation itself, "indirect" interference with contractual relations and unlawful conspiracy, thereby justifying its claim as the "genus" tort.

The details of the young tort still await clearer definition.[162] It does not seem to be limited to interference with an existing business or trade relationship between the plaintiff and the third party against whom the unlawful act is committed. For example, it has not been questioned that by passing-off his goods as X's, the defendant might have committed a tort not only against X but also against X's distributors.[163] "Trade or business" appears to be merely a synonym for economic interests.

Again, what would qualify as unlawful means has not yet, as we have seen,[164] attained consensus. One aspect fell for decision in a recent case where the plaintiffs sought to acquire control of another company but had been temporarily foiled by a reference to the Monopoly and Mergers Commission. The defendants allegedly got ahead of them by fraudulent submissions to the Commission about their financial background, as a result of which the plaintiffs lost their bid. The court held that such fraud, though practised on a third party which did not itself suffer injury, would

157. *Grant Central Car Park v. Tivoli* [1969] V.R. 62; *Van Camp Chocolates v. Aulsebrooks* [1984] 1 N.Z.L.R. 354 (C.A.) (trading in violation of know-how).
158. *Dunlop v. Woollahra M.C.* [1982] A.C. 158 (P.C.).
159. *Kitano v. Commonwealth* (1974) 129 C.L.R. 151.
160. *Lonrho v. Shell (No. 2)* [1982] A.C. 173.
161. Its architect was Lord Denning, abetted by Lord Diplock. See *Torquay Hotel v. Cousins* [1969] 2 Ch. 106 at 139; *Acrow v. Rex Chainbelt* [1971] 1 W.L.R. 1676 (C.A.); *Hadmor Products v. Hamilton* [1983] 1 A.C. 190 at 225; *Merkur Island v. Laughton* [1983] 2 A.C. 570 at 609.
162. See Carty, *Intentional Violation of Economic Interests*, 104 L.Q.R. 250 (1988).
163. *Van Camp Chocolates v. Aulsebrooks* [1984] 1 N.Z.L.R. 354 (C.A.). Also *Barretts & Baird v. I.P.C.S.* [1987] I.R.L.R. 3 (meat dealers who depended on certification by inspectors). Both actions failed for want of intent: above, n. 152.
164. See above, pp. 699-702.

be sufficient to confer a cause of action on the plaintiffs, but left undecided whether they had a sufficient business interest to support the tort.[165]

Another unresolved problem concerns justification. This is linked to the scope of unlawful means: the more diluted the latter concept, the greater the pressure to recognise conflicting public policy as justification.[166]

4. CONSPIRACY

In some circumstances, the added element of combination may make unlawful an act which, if done by one person alone, would not be actionable. The reason for attaching such magical significance to plurality is far from clear. According to one suggestion, "the common law may have taken the view that there is always the danger that any combination may be oppressive, and may have thought that a general rule against injurious combinations was desirable on broad grounds of policy."[167] Yet it is all too evident, at least under modern social and economic conditions, that there is no inherent magic in numbers and it is unrealistic to assume categorically that it is easier to resist the coercive power of one person than of several. The power and influence of a big corporation, a trade union or business tycoon, like Carnegie or Rockefeller, may be infinitely greater than that of a large number of smaller fry and, besides, there is something crude about an arbitrary line between one individual and two. An historical explanation is that the tort of conspiracy, though not definitely settled in its modern formulation until very recently, derived originally from the crime of conspiracy, which was developed by the Star Chamber during the 16th century in order to crush the prevalent evil of combinations to subvert legal process and exercise oppression. When, after the fall of that tribunal, the common law courts assumed its jurisdiction, a civil action for damages was framed on the pattern of the crime of conspiracy, and traces of this original link have survived in the requirement of concerted action as an essential element of the civil wrong.[168]

The tort has remained anomalous. To start with, although an offshoot of the crime, it differs from the latter in that, damage being essential, there can be no liability until the agreement is executed. "So the tort, unlike the crime, consists not of agreement but of concerted action taken pursuant to agreement."[169] Then, the action fell into steep disfavour in revulsion against the ugly manner in which the conspiracy doctrine used to be wielded by civil and criminal courts alike to stem the tide of organised labour. From this checkered past and the resulting confusion regarding its elements the action was eventually rescued, but greatly shrunk in scope. The recent extension of the tort of intentional interference by unlawful means

165. *Lonrho v. Fayed* [1990] 2 Q.B. 479 (C.A.). In *Associated British Ports v. T.G.W.U.* [1989] 1 W.L.R. 939 two judges opined that where unlawful means consisted in breach of statutory obligation, it was unnecessary that breach be actionable by the plaintiff.

166. See Heydon, *The Defence of Justification in Cases of Intentionally Caused Economic Harm*, 20 U. Tor. L.J. 139 (1970).

167. *Crofter Hand Woven Harris Tweed v. Veitch* (hereinafter referred to as the *Crofter* case) [1942] A.C. 435 at 468 per Lord Wright.

168. Ibid. at 443-444 per Simon L.C. See Winfield, *History of Conspiracy* (1921).

169. *Lonrho v. Shell* [1982] A.C. 173 at 188 per Lord Diplock.

(actionable against single individuals) discussed in the preceding section, added another reason for taking a less expansive view of the conspiracy doctrine. Thus after a long and controversial history, its role assigned in modern law is indeed tame.

Modern history

The starting point of the modern law was the *Mogul Case* in 1891, which lifted the threat of tortious conspiracy from cartels.[170] The defendants, a group of shipping companies, associated together in order to obtain a monopoly of the tea carrying trade between China and England and to keep up the rates of freight. To this end, they deliberately undercut the plaintiff, at a temporary loss to themselves, and threatened his agents with boycott, if they continued to act for him. This scheme had its desired effect of driving the plaintiff out of the market; but the House of Lords denied him a cause of action, because the combination was inspired by the lawful purpose of protecting the legitimate trade interests of its members. The defendants had done nothing more than pursue to the bitter end a war of competition waged in the interests of their own trade, and it was not the proper function of the courts to police prices at which traders could sell or hire, for the purpose of protecting or extending their business. Competition between rivals, even when carried out in combination, did not have to meet the test of "fairness", so long as it stopped short of using unlawful means, such as fraud, intimidation or interference with contractual rights.

Later the question arose whether the same formula was applicable to a secondary boycott by concerted union action aimed at enforcing the "closed shop". In *Quinn v. Leathem*[171] the defendants, five trade union officials, demanded of the plaintiff, a flesher, that he discharge certain non-union men employed by him. He refused to comply, though offering to pay all fines and back dues for his employees if they were admitted to the union. Instead of accepting this compromise, the defendants compelled a butcher who had been a regular customer of the plaintiff's to withhold further orders from him, under threat of calling out his men. The jury found that the defendants had maliciously conspired to induce the plaintiff's customer to cease dealing with him, and judgment against them was affirmed by the House of Lords. Although it seems to have been assumed that the principle of the *Mogul Case* applied as much to concerted union action as to conflicts between trade rivals, the conclusion that the defendants had not acted in pursuance of legitimate trade interests, reveals a thorough lack of understanding of the aspirations of organised labour. Whilst there may have been no conscious discrimination,[172] the decision proceeded on the naive view that, as the defendants' purpose was not immediately concerned with wages or working conditions, their refusal to accept the plaintiff's compromise could only be attributed to a desire for vengeance. Yet there was clearly no evidence of any personal vindictiveness, and their action,

170. *Mogul Steamship Co. v. McGregor Gow & Co.* [1892] A.C. 25. The formulation is usually credited to Lord Coleridge: (1888) 21 Q.B.D. 544.
171. [1901] A.C. 495. In addition to conspiracy, there was also a claim for procuring breaches of contract, with which we are not here concerned.
172. But see Stevens, *Law and Politics* (1977) 93-94; Klarman, *The Judges versus the Unions: The Development of British Labour Law, 1867-1913*, 75 Va. L. Rev. 1487 (1989).

though ruthless, was no less directly motivated by a legitimate economic object than the combination in the *Mogul Case*. It was simply not understood at the time that, from the union point of view, it might have been considered harmful to their bargaining power to convey the impression that non-unionists could always, after years of non-membership, gain the advantages of membership by simply paying fines and back dues.

The damaging effect of the decision was arrested by two developments. The first was the enactment of the still surviving immunity in England for conspiracy to injure while acting "in contemplation and furtherance of a trade dispute".[173] The second, and now more important, response was a judicial reassessment of the tort of conspiracy, starting with the important Australian decision of *McKernan v. Fraser*.[174] The case arose from a conflict between rival unions of seamen. Officials of the established union, with a view to defeating a breakaway movement, coerced a shipping company to refuse employment to the plaintiffs who had identified themselves with the dissident faction, under threat of calling out their own members. It was held that the defendants' action was inspired by a legitimate object of furthering the interests of their union, even if this involved depriving followers of the rival group of their means of livelihood, because the dominant purpose was not to indulge personal spite but rather to convince them and others of the unwisdom of disloyalty. The decision was a significant milestone in the recognition it gave to the special status which had been won by trade unions after years of industrial strife, and in ensuring that the privilege recognised in the *Mogul Case* was not confined to competitive trade rivalries between entrepreneurs[175] but applied equally to the concerted action of trade unions, whether their immediate object was to improve working conditions or to discipline disloyal members for the ultimate purpose of maintaining their bargaining strength.

This view was confirmed when the tort of conspiracy was reconsidered by the House of Lords in 1942, in the leading case of *Crofter Hand Woven Harris Tweed Co. v. Veitch*.[176] The plaintiffs were modern producers of tweed cloth in the Island of Lewis who, by using imported yarn from the mainland, were able to compete advantageously with other mill owners who continued to process spun yarn woven manually by the crofters on the island. Most of the spinners in the mills using handwoven yarn and the dockers in the island port were members of a union of which the defendants were officials. These struck a bargain with the older producers whereby, in return for a promise of a "closed shop" and increased wages, they undertook to help eliminate the competition of the modern producers. To this end, they instructed the dockers not to handle the plaintiffs' yarn or to export their finished cloth. As a result, a total embargo was imposed; but it was held that the combination was justifiable inasmuch as its aim was the improvement of industrial conditions for members of the union, by

173. See above, n. 103.
174. (1931) 46 C.L.R. 343; similarly *Morgan v. Fry* [1968] 2 Q.B. 710 (C.A.).
175. The principle of the *Mogul Case* had in the meantime been applied to economic warfare between trade associations in the newspaper distributing trade (*Sorrell v. Smith* [1925] A.C. 700), to the disciplining of members of professional organisations (*Pratt v. B.M.A.* [1919] 1 K.B. 244), and to the blacklisting of defaulting members of trade associations: *Ware & De Freville v. M.T.A.* [1921] 3 K.B. 40.
176. [1942] A.C. 435.

eliminating unregulated competition and thus helping to secure the economic stability of the island industry.

The critical issue, it was made clear, was the object and purpose of those acting in concert. If the "sole or predominant" motive was to advance an interest of their own rather than to cause injury to the plaintiff, it was not actionable.[177] In particular, malice in the sense of spite or ill-will, which had often been touted as a decisive factor, was now banished from the scene: if the defendants acted in pursuit of a legitimate object, their combination was not vitiated by glee at their adversary's expected discomfiture;[178] conversely, absence of malice was insufficient to establish that they had a just cause or excuse.

Unlawful purposes

This redefinition doomed the tort of conspiracy to negligible significance in the context of trade and employment relations. It is true that, throughout the speeches in the *Crofter* case, there are recurring references to the requirement that a lawful combination must have its object in the furtherance of "legitimate" trade or business interests. But since any economic advancement or benefit apparently suffices, it is difficult to imagine trade or business interests which would not pass muster. Besides, legitimate purposes are not limited to the furtherance of a material interest; the promotion of morality,[179] of religious interests of a parish,[180] or the lifting of a colour bar[181] may furnish justification. On the other hand, the following were canvassed as examples of unlawful combinations: agreements inspired by hostility towards the religious or political views or the race or colour of the plaintiff,[182] or to demonstrate the power of those combining to dictate policy to prove themselves master in a given situation,[183] those actuated by sheer wantonness[184] or a spirit of vengeance[185] or by purely mercenary motives unconnected with any other interest.[186] In short, the purpose of the combination must be wholly destructive by prevailing community standards. If it is constructive, or destructive only as a means to be constructive, it is justifiable.[187] A combination for the sole purpose of victimisation or punishment is actionable, but it is lawful if the real object in disciplining the plaintiff, or "teaching him a lesson", is to deter others from acting similarly in a manner which those combining honestly believe to be detrimental to their legitimate interests.[188]

177. The burden of proof lies on the plaintiff; there is no longer a "prima facie tort" doctrine.
178. Ibid. at 471 (Lord Wright).
179. Ibid. at 496.
180. Ibid. at 478.
181. *Scala Ballroom v. Ratcliffe* [1958] 1 W.L.R. 1057.
182. *Crofter* case [1942] A.C. 435 at 451.
183. Ibid. at 445.
184. Ibid. at 471. An example might be an agreement to hiss an actor off the stage out of spite: cf. *Gregory v. Duke of Brunswick* (1844) 6 Man. & G. 205, 953; 134 E.R. 866, 1178.
185. Ibid. at 493. Illustrated by *Huntley v. Thornton* [1957] 1 W.L.R. 321 where a union committee persecuted a member solely from a desire to punish him for his public opposition to them personally.
186. Ibid. at 451.
187. *Boots v. Grundy* (1900) 82 L.T. 769 at 773 per Phillimore J.
188. *McKernan v. Fraser* (1931) 46 C.L.R. 343 at 395-396; *Crofter* case [1942] A.C. 435 at 475; *Williams v. Hursey* (1959) 103 C.L.R. 30.

Usually, the motives in the minds of each participant of a combination are mixed. Hence the question whether the defendants' object was to inflict injury on the plaintiff or to further their own interests, rarely presents true alternatives. For example, almost every strike is undertaken for the purpose of both harming the adversary and advancing the standards of the unionists. Hence to ask whether they desired to protect their own interests or injure the employer, is equivalent to asking of a soldier who shoots to kill in battle, whether he does so for the purpose of defeating his enemy or of defending his country. Moreover, as the struggle draws out, actual ill-will increasingly develops. Yet, what in isolation may look like hatred, vindictiveness or spite is usually only evidence of the clash of the economic interests involved. Hence, the search must always be for the real or predominant purpose of the combination, which may lie behind the immediate intention to inflict harm.[189]

Mixed purposes

A related question arises where there is a difference in the object of the various members of the combination. In the first place, it seems clear that there need be no identity of interests between them all. "It is sufficient if all the various combining parties have their own legitimate trade or business interests to gain, even though these interests may be of differing kinds."[190] Reasonable self-interest is sufficient even if each member has his own axe to grind.[191] Thus in the *Crofter* case, there was, on one view, a combination between the union officials and the mill owners, which was not vitiated by the difference of interest between the two groups. The former were concerned to promote the advantage of the employees in the industry, the latter sought to benefit themselves by obtaining a monopoly in the milling trade on the island; both sides co-operating in a joint undertaking for the advancement of their own respective economic interests.

Secondly, if the sole object of one member of the combination is a desire for the plaintiff's ruin as an end in itself, does this convert the whole combination into an unlawful conspiracy, even though the object of the other participants is otherwise legitimate? It seems that if the others knew of and countenanced his purpose by giving assistance to his malicious acts, the whole agreement would be tainted and they would become participants in the wrong.[192] Otherwise however, none should be liable. There would be no justification for imputing the malice of A to B and C, since the essence of conspiracy is mutual consent to a common purpose and there is here no common design to gratify a private grudge which is shared by B and C with A. And just as B and C cannot be held responsible for the uncommunicated evil purpose of A, neither can A be made accountable himself because in a case of conspiracy it is not possible to adjudge that A has conspired with B, but that B did not conspire with A. Unless both are liable, neither is.[193]

189. See the masterly analysis by Evatt J. in *McKernan v. Fraser* (1931) 46 C.L.R. 343 at 402-405.
190. *Crofter* case [1942] A.C. 435 at 453.
191. Ibid.
192. Ibid. at 495; *McKernan v. Fraser* (1931) 46 C.L.R. 343 at 402.
193. *McKernan v. Fraser* (1931) 46 C.L.R. 343 at 401-409 where the whole question is thoroughly canvassed by Evatt J.; contra: *Pratt v. B.M.A.* [1919] 1 K.B. 244 at 279.

Unlawful means

So much for the "unlawful purpose" conspiracy as defined in modern cases. How has it affected the older version of conspiracy—"unlawful means" conspiracy—consisting in an agreement (and its execution) to pursue an otherwise lawful object by unlawful means? In *Lonrho v. Shell*,[194] the plaintiff's oil refinery suffered loss as the result of the defendants' criminal violation of the sanctions on Rhodesia. Its first cause of action, based on the proposition that the loss was caused by an unlawful act, failed because the statute they had violated was not intended to confer a private right. Its second cause of action, based on conspiracy to commit an unlawful act, also failed for lack of proof of an intent to injure the plaintiff. The mere fact that such injury was a consequence of the defendant's illegal conduct did not suffice; it was desirable to keep the action of conspiracy in short rein.

This left the question whether a "sole or predominant purpose" to injure was as necessary for this as for the other form of conspiracy. In conformity with previous decisions in Australia[195] and Canada,[196] the House of Lords in a later case preferred the older view that it was not.[197] Thus mere intent to injure is here sufficient, though it does not appear that "conspiracy" adds anything of substance to the conditions under which a single individual would be liable for the modern tort of interference with business by "unlawful means".[198]

5. INJURIOUS FALSEHOOD

False advertising is addressed by two torts: by injurious falsehood in this section, and by passing-off in the next.

The first originated towards the end of the 16th century in cases involving a challenge of the plaintiff's title to land and thereby prejudicing his efforts to dispose of it;[199] from this association the tort acquired the name "slander of title". Gradually, its scope expanded to cover aspersions not only on title, but also on the quality of land or goods,[200] like knowingly making false assertions that the plaintiff's products were inferior[201] or that

194. [1982] A.C. 173.
195. *Williams v. Hurley* (1959) 103 C.L.R. 30 (assaults, picketing); *Ansett v. Air Pilots* [1991] 1 V.R. 637.
196. *Cement Lafarge v. Lightweight Aggregate* [1983] 1 S.C.R. 452 (picketing). "The conduct is directed towards the plaintiff (alone or together with others) and the defendants should know in the circumstances that injury to the plaintiff is likely to and does result" (at 471-472). Consistent with *Lonrho v. Shell*?
197. *Lonrho v. Fayed* [1991] 3 W.L.R. 188.
198. The defendants can be sued as joint tortfeasors, conspiracy being mere surplusage: *Galland v. Mineral Underwriters* [1977] W.A.R. 116 (F.C.); *Ward v. Lewis* [1955] 1 W.L.R. 9 at 11 ("the agreement merges in the tort").
199. *Bliss v. Stafford* (1573) Owen 37; 74 E.R. 882; *Banister v. Banister* (1583), cited in 4 Co. Rep. 17a; 76 E.R. 899.
200. The first such case seems to have been *Kerr v. Shedden* (1831) 4 C. & P. 528; 172 E.R. 811.
201. *W. Counties Manure Co. v. Lawes Chemical Co.* (1874) L.R. 9 Ex. 218.

his house was haunted.[202] Eventually it was applied to many other lies calculated to injure a person in his trade, such as imputations that he has ceased to carry on business,[203] that members of his staff are suffering from infectious disease,[204] that he is not available for future employment[205] or that not he, but the defendant had designed a yacht.[206] Indeed, today it is broad enough to encompass any damaging falsehood which interferes with prospective advantage, even of a non-commercial nature, as when a defendant falsely and maliciously wrote a letter to the plaintiff's fiancé, claiming that she was his own wife with the result that she thereby lost her marriage.[207] Although this tort has been called by various names, such as "slander of goods or title", "trade libel" and "disparagement", the best and most inclusive description is that of "injurious falsehood", coined by Salmond.

In some respects, injurious falsehood bears a marked resemblance to defamation. Both involve a false and harmful imputation concerning the plaintiff, made not to him directly but to a third person. They differ, however, in this respect that the law of defamation protects an interest in personal reputation, while injurious falsehood protects an interest in the disposability of one's property, products or business. Hence, if a statement charges the plaintiff with discreditable conduct in his business and involves a reflection on his character, it is libel; if it disparages him merely in respect of his property, as by casting an aspersion on the nature of his business or the quality of his merchandise as such, it is injurious falsehood. Although the line of demarcation may sometimes be rather thin,[208] it is attended by significant consequences. Defamation is mostly actionable without proof of damage, falsehood is presumed, and liability is strict; whereas in an action for injurious falsehood the plaintiff must prove that he sustained actual economic loss, that the offensive statement was false and made with intent to cause injury without lawful justification. But for their different origins, this disparity between the two actions might be harder to explain. It has however been somewhat minimised in several Australian States[209] which apply the stricter liability of defamation to "any imputation concerning any person . . . by which he is likely to be injured in his profession or trade", even if his reputation is not involved, as in the case of a false allegation that the plaintiff has gone out of business.[210] Expressly excepted from this

202. *Barrett v. Associated Newspapers* (1907) 23 T.L.R. 666; *Manitoba Press v. Nagy* (1907) 39 S.C.R. 340.
203. *Ratcliffe v. Evans* [1892] 2 Q.B. 524; *Hall-Gibbs v. Dun* (1910) 12 C.L.R. 84.
204. *Riding v. Smith* (1876) 1 Ex. D. 91 at 94.
205. *Shapiro v. La Morta* (1923) 40 T.L.R. 201.
206. *Customglass Boats v. Salthouse Bros* [1976] 1 N.Z.L.R. 36.
207. Cf. *Sheperd v. Wakeman* (1662) 1 Sid. 79; 82 E.R. 892.
208. Indeed, one and the same statement may be both a personal libel and a disparaging falsehood in relation to the plaintiff's business: *Griffiths v. Benn* (1911) 27 T.L.R. 346 at 350.
209. Qld: *Criminal Code* s. 366 (quaere whether applicable to civil proceedings: above, p. 525); W.A.: *Criminal Code* s. 346 (quaere whether applicable to civil proceedings); Tas.: *Defamation Act* 1957 s. 5.
210. *Hall-Gibbs v. Dun* (1910) 12 C.L.R. 84. But it must still be an imputation "concerning the plaintiff". Disparaging a particular model of a car would not be concerning a distributor, though it might the manufacturer: *Sungrave v. M.E. Airlines* (1975) 134 C.L.R. 1 at 23.

reform is "slander of title",[211] though whether this includes other forms of injurious falsehood remains an open question.[212]

Elements of liability

Injurious falsehood, then, consists in the publication of false statements, whether oral or in writing, concerning the plaintiff or his property, calculated to induce others not to deal with him. Unlike the wrong of deceit, which is committed by making a false statement to the plaintiff himself so that he acts to his own detriment, here the falsehood must be communicated to a third person. In this respect, it resembles defamation but differs from it in that falsity is not presumed but must be affirmatively established by the plaintiff.[213] Our law, unlike that of some other countries, flatly condones truthful disparagement of competitors.[214] Moreover, the falsehood must relate to the plaintiff's goods, not the defendant's; it is not sufficient that the lie claims qualities for the defendant's own goods, whether or not they are also lacking in the plaintiff's. This is so notwithstanding that the two are in direct competition and the defendant is seeking to increase his market share by the falsehood.[215]

It is essential that the falsehood was published with "malice". But, as in other contexts in the law of torts, that "weasel word" has been a source of uncertainty and confusion. Originally, the averment of malice seems to have been only a superfluous pleading form[216] and meant nothing more than that the words were published with intent to disparage the plaintiff's title. Malice, in the ordinary legal sense of an intention to injure, crept into the cases where it was necessary to defeat a privilege raised by the defendant, the most common being where his words amounted to a claim of title in himself. Later however, malice came to be treated as a necessary element even where no question of privilege was involved; and today the dominant view seems to be that malice, in the sense of some indirect, dishonest or improper motive,[217] or at any rate an intent to injure without just cause or excuse,[218] must be proved by the plaintiff.[219] It is sufficient evidence of malice that the defendant knew the disparaging statement to be false, as where a landlord deliberately lied to inquirers and the postal authorities that his tenant was no longer "available" in order to drive him

211. Defamation Law 1889 (Qld) s. 46; *Defamation Act* (Tas.) s. 4.
212. *Hall-Gibbs v. Dun* (1910) 12 C.L.R. 84: O'Connor J. thought so (at 104), Barton J. thought not (at 98) and Griffith C.J. withheld his opinion. See Morison, *Verbal Injury*, 3 Syd. L. Rev. 4 at 11-18 (1959).
213. *Burnett v. Tak* (1882) 45 L.T. 743; *Roberts v. Gray* (1897) 13 W.N. (N.S.W.) 241.
214. Criticised by Wolff, *Unfair Competition by Truthful Disparagement*, 47 Yale L.J. 1304 (1938).
215. *Young v. Macrae* (1862) 3 B. & S. 264; 122 E.R. 100; *Cambridge U.P. v. University Tutorial Press* (1928) 45 R.P.C. 335; *American Washboard v. Saginaw Mfg Co.* 103 F. 281 (1900). Cf. *Rima Electric v. Rolls Razor* [1965] R.P.C. 4.
216. "But the clerk's drawing" (*Elborow v. Allen* (1623) Cro. Jac. 642; 79 E.R. 553). The historical evolution is traced by Newark, *Malice in Actions on the Case for Words*, 60 L.Q.R. 366 (1944).
217. *London Ferro-Concrete Co. v. Justicz* (1951) 68 R.P.C. 261 at 265; *Serville v. Constance* [1954] 1 W.L.R. 487 at 490.
218. The second formulation was preferred in *Joyce v. Motor Surveys* [1948] Ch. 252.
219. See Prosser, *Injurious Falsehood*, 59 Col. L. Rev. 425 (1959), correcting *Rest.* §625. Critical are Wood, *Disparagement of Title and Quality*, 20 Can. B. Rev. 296 (1942); and Newark, 60 L.Q.R. 366 (1944).

out of business and so destroy his will to resist a notice to quit.[220] Conversely, an honest belief in an unfounded claim is not actionable;[221] nor is mere carelessness (in contrast to recklessness or conscious indifference to truth),[222] as when a businessman negligently told a prospective customer that the plaintiff, with whom the latter had previous dealings, was still in the firm's employment and would therefore earn a commission on any order given by him.[223] But although in the absence of malice no action for damages can succeed, the plaintiff can obtain some measure of protection against unfounded assertions of title by claiming a judicial declaration as to his title to the disputed property.[224]

Special damage

Unlike libel, actual damage is of the gist of injurious falsehood even when it is reduced to writing.[225] Hence the action cannot be used merely for the purpose of vindicating one's title to or the quality of one's possessions, in a manner analogous to actions for defamation which usually serve the primary purpose of clearing reputation by the verdict of a jury. Indeed, in the absence of damage, even an injunction against repetition of the falsehood will be refused, on the stringent view that equitable relief is contingent on the commission of an actionable tort.[226] The loss, moreover, must be monetary; for injured feelings the plaintiff must look to the law of defamation.[227]

Insistence on special damage has seriously impaired the usefulness of this action, because all too often grave loss caused by the dissemination of falsehoods is beyond the reach of redress owing to the difficulties encountered in proving it strictly as special damage. Thus, the plaintiff must establish either that he was unable to dispose of the property or that it lowered the price.[228] In some cases however, where it would be practically impossible ever to satisfy the standards of strict proof, a more liberal view has eventually prevailed. Thus, where a trader's goods have been disparaged, a general loss of custom as distinct from the loss of identifiable customers, is now deemed sufficient.[229] More far reaching still has been the legislative modification in England, as yet adopted only in New Zealand,[230] dispensing altogether with proof of special damage, on the

220. *Joyce v. Motor Surveys* [1948] Ch. 252.
221. See *Loudon v. Ryder (No. 2)* [1953] Ch. 423.
222. *Clarke v. Meigher* (1917) 17 S.R. (N.S.W.) 617 at 622; *Manitoba Press v. Nagy* (1907) 39 S.C.R. 340.
223. *Balden v. Shorter* [1933] Ch. 427; accord: *Clarke v. Meigher* (1917) 17 S.R. (N.S.W.) 617. This has remained unaffected by recent extensions of negligence liability for economic loss: see above, p. 177.
224. *Loudon v. Ryder (No. 2)* [1953] Ch. 423; *Roberts v. Gray* (1897) 13 W.N. (N.S.W.) 241.
225. *Malachy v. Soper* (1836) 3 Bing. N.C. 371; 132 E.R. 453 (newspaper).
226. *White v. Mellin* [1895] A.C. 154; criticised by McCardie J. in *British Rly Traffic Co. v. C.R.C.* [1922] 2 K.B. 260 at 272-273.
227. *Fielding v. Variety Inc.* [1967] 2 Q.B. 841 (C.A.).
228. *Lachaume v. Broughton* (1903) 3 S.R. (N.S.W.) 475; *Malachy v. Soper* (1836) 3 Bing. N.C. 371; 132 E.R. 453.
229. *Ratcliffe v. Evans* [1892] 2 Q.B. 524; *George v. Blow* (1899) 20 L.R. (N.S.W.) 395. The original publisher's liability for repetition by others is determined on the same principles as in defamation: *Rest. 2d* §631.
230. Respectively the Defamation Acts of 1952 (s. 3) and 1954 (s. 5); also *Libel and Slander Act* (Ont.) s. 19(a).

familiar pattern of defamation, whenever falsehood is published in permanent form or calculated to cause pecuniary damage to the plaintiff.

In Australia the *Trade Practices Act* 1974 (Cth) now offers an alternative remedy against "misleading and deceptive conduct" by trade rivals, which unlike injurious falsehood is not dependent on proof of malice and special damage, besides offering procedural advantages.[231] It does not however apply, in the interest of free speech, to disparaging statements unconnected with the supply of goods, such as a T.V. programme airing consumer complaints.[232]

Privilege

It was early recognised that liability for injurious falsehood had to be tempered by certain privileges or become too oppressive. Thus, from its inception an immunity was admitted for bona fide claims to property, so as not to deter rival claims genuinely believed to be well founded.[233] But this privilege was only qualified and liable to defeat on proof of malice, such as that the claimant did not honestly believe in the truth of his assertion.[234] As a result of the modern trend to postulate malice as an essential element in all cases of injurious falsehood, these situations have lost the characteristics of privilege, properly so-called, and simply become illustrations of the requirement of malice as an essential ingredient of this tort.[235] Likewise, one who makes a disparaging assertion, not as a mere volunteer impertinently interfering with another's concern but impelled by a duty imposed upon him, is entitled to excuse either on the ground of privilege or because actual malice cannot be established against him.[236] Thus, where a Railway Commissioner had arranged to run special trains for a race meeting and, acting on a false but apparently authentic message, put up notices that the special trains were cancelled owing to the postponement of the races, he was excused for the resulting loss because he had the highest possible interest, if not a duty, to put up the notice, both for his own protection and for the convenience of intending passengers, if he honestly believed the message to be true.[237]

In all probability, the same absolute privileges will be recognised in actions for injurious falsehood as for defamation.[238] Thus, although there is no British or Commonwealth case law in point, it would seem that disparagements by judicial officers, litigants or witnesses in the course of judicial proceedings, by members of Parliament in the performance of their legislative functions and by high officers of State in the course of official communications, are absolutely protected.

231. Similarly, *Fair Trading Act* 1986 (N.Z.) s. 9. Its American counterpart is the *Lanham Act* of 1946 §45(a); also *Rest. Unfair Competition*, Tent. Draft No. 1 (1988).
232. Section 65A: *Advanced Hair Studio v. T.V.W.* (1987) 77 A.L.R. 615.
233. *Banister v. Banister* (1583) cited 4 Co. Rep. 17a; 79 E.R. 899.
234. *Freen v. Button* (1835) 2 Cr. M. & R. 707; 150 E.R. 299.
235. But might privilege not affect the burden of proving malice? Most dicta place the onus indiscriminately on the plaintiff, but there is slight authority for presuming malice (reversing the onus) in cases not involving privilege: *Loan Co. v. Lindsay* (1883) 4 Ont. R. 473 at 484; Prosser, 59 Col. L. Rev. 425 at 439 (1959).
236. *Pater v. Baker* (1847) 3 C.B. 831; 136 E.R. 333; *Langdon's Coach Lines v. T.T.C.* (1956) 1 D.L.R. (2d) 319.
237. *Mentone Racing Club v. Victorian Rly* (1902) 28 V.L.R. 77.
238. *Rest. 2d* §635.

A more prominent privilege relates to comparisons with competitive merchandise. General comparisons by a trader, claiming that his goods are the best or better than the plaintiff's,[239] are not actionable at all. Such trade puffing is tolerated because nobody would reasonably take it seriously. But tolerance is exceeded when a trader passes beyond mere general comparisons between his own goods and another's, and ventures into a specific disparagement of a rival product liable to be taken seriously, as by alleging that it contains a harmful ingredient or that specific tests show it to be spurious or unfit.[240]

6. UNFAIR COMPETITION: PASSING-OFF

Yet another form of misrepresentation concerning the plaintiff's business—unfair competition par excellence—is the tort of passing-off. While it is injurious falsehood for a defendant to claim that your goods are his, it is passing-off for him to claim that his goods are yours. Though traces of the tort stretch back as far as the reign of the first Elizabeth,[241] its formulation is essentially modern and its potentialities for growth not yet exhausted.[242] From its inception it has had some affinity with deceit and was for long regarded as a mere variety of it, though differing from the parent action in that it furnished redress, not to the person deceived, but to him whose mark, name or get-up was used to deceive. This link was however completely severed when the requirement of fraud disappeared as the result of equity intervention. At common law, the action was not maintainable unless an intent to deceive could be established; but as early as 1838 it was held that an injunction would issue to restrain passing-off, regardless of whether the defendant had been fraudulent or not.[243] On the same basis, courts of equity began to award compensation, either in the form of an account of profits or as damages in lieu of, or in addition to, an injunction under *Lord Cairn's Act*. After the *Judicature Act*, this conflict between law and equity was resolved in favour of the equitable practice, and it is now settled that proof of fraud is unnecessary, whether the relief asked for be an injunction or damages.[244] It is sufficient that the offensive practice was calculated or likely, rather than intended, to deceive. But for innocent passing-off at most nominal damages are appropriate.[245]

Neither actual deception nor actual resulting damage need be proved.[246] It is sufficient that the defendant's practice was likely to mislead the public *and* involved an appreciable risk of detriment to the plaintiff, whether in

239. Cf. the vendor's deceit privilege to "puff" his goods.
240. The cases are reviewed in *De Beers v. International Gen. Electric* [1975] 1 W.L.R. 972.
241. *Southern v. How* (1618) Cro. Jac. 468 at 471; 79 E.R. 400 at 402.
242. *Warnink v. Townend* [1979] A.C. 731 (passim).
243. *Millington v. Fox* (1838) 3 My. & Cr. 338; 40 E.R. 956.
244. *Spalding Bros v. Gamage* (1915) 84 L.J. Ch. 449 (H.L.).
245. *Draper v. Trist* [1939] 3 All E.R. 513 at 518, 525, 528 (C.A.).
246. The weight of authority seems to favour the propriety of at least nominal damages. An injunction—the stock relief—requires a showing of irreparable damage, present or prospective, as whenever the plaintiff's goodwill is jeopardised: see *Henderson v. Radio Corp.* [1960] S.R. (N.S.W.) 576. In Vic. damage is presumed only where goods or services of rivals are of similar kind competing in the same market: *Petersville Sleigh v. Sugarman* [1988] V.R. 426 (F.C.).

diversion of sales or impairment of his credit or commercial repute.[247] If the defendant acted with intent to defraud it will be readily assumed that he succeeded in what he set out to accomplish,[248] but failing deliberate deceit, the onus on the plaintiff to show that there was a likelihood to deceive is heavier. The test for determining whether deception was probable is the likely impression on the casual and unwary customer,[249] and it is no answer that an observant person making a careful examination would not have been misled:[250] "Thirsty folk want beer, not explanations."[251] The appropriate standard is that of the typical customer for the goods in question. For example, much more sophistication may be assumed from purchasers of vintage port than of champagne (the vast bulk of which, in England at all events, is in demand for weddings and other festive occasions by people with only the foggiest notion of its origin and thus quite vulnerable to be misled into thinking that "Spanish champagne" is the genuine article.)[252] It is also entirely sufficient that the purchasing public associates the product with a particular trade source without necessarily knowing the specific identity of the plaintiff. The deception may be achieved as much by the appearance or "get-up" of the product (for example, Haig's dimple bottle) as by verbal attribution.[253]

By freeing the tort from any requirement of actual damage and intention to injure, the law created an effective instrument of economic regulation, in response to an undoubted need for stronger legal weapons to combat commercial misrepresentations. Even so, its purpose is primarily to protect the plaintiff's proprietary interest in his goodwill rather than to champion the consumer. Thus it is irrelevant that the defendant's goods were actually cheaper or of superior quality, or that this competition (however unfair to the plaintiff) otherwise enured for the benefit of the public.[254]

In Australia the *Trade Practices Act* 1974 (Cth), since also followed in New Zealand,[255] has provided a concurrent statutory remedy against any corporation which in trade or commerce engages in "conduct that is misleading or deceptive or is likely to mislead or deceive".[256] While

247. E.g. if the defendant's product is inferior. Some occasional confusion without probable economic injury is not sufficient: *F.M.C. Engineering v. F.M.C.* [1966] V.R. 529 (F.C.).
248. *Society of Motor Manufacturers v. Motor Manufacturers* [1925] Ch. 675 at 686.
249. *Singer Manufacturing Co. v. Loog* (1882) 8 App. Cas. 15 at 18.
250. Even in case of a first instance sale to a jobber, the proper criterion is still that of the ultimate consumer: *Wotherspoon v. Currie* (1872) L.R. 5 H.L. 508; *Draper v. Trist* [1939] 3 All E.R. 513.
251. *Montgomery v. Thompson* [1891] A.C. 217 at 225 per Lord Macnaghten.
252. *Bollinger v. Costa Brava Wine (No. 2)* [1961] 1 W.L.R. 277; also *Lee Kar Choo v. Lee Lian Choon* [1967] 1 A.C. 602 (illiterates); *White Hudson v. Asian Organisation* [1964] 1 W.L.R. 1466 (non-English speaking).
253. E.g. *Reckitt v. Colman* [1990] 1 W.L.R. 491 (H.L.), in effect recognising a monopoly in plaintiff's lemon-shaped containers of juice. *Oxford Pendaflex v. Korr* [1982] 1 S.C.R. 494 was more adept, in finding that trays had become generic.
254. See the sceptical comments by Frank J. in *Standard Brands v. Smidler* 151 F. 2d 34 (2 Cir. 1945).
255. *Fair Trading Act* 1986. See Pengilley [1987] N.Z.L.J. 59; *Taylor Bros. v. Taylors Group* [1988] 2 N.Z.L.R. 1 (C.A.).
256. Section 52; also *Fair Trading Act* 1985 (Vic.) s. 12. See *Hornsby Centre v. Sydney Centre* (1978) 140 C.L.R. 216; *Taco Co. v. Taco Bell* (1982) 42 A.L.R. 177. So also the *Lanham Act* 1946 (U.S.) §43(a), but not the *Merchandise Marks Acts* (Eng.): *Bollinger v. Costa Brava Wine* [1960] Ch. 262.

intended for the protection of consumers, it quickly became a favoured remedy against trade rivals because of procedural advantages over the common law action.[257] The distinction between them—the one focused on protecting goodwill as a proprietary interest, the other on misrepresentation—plays a diminishing role in practice.

Unfair practices

The scope of the tort has been increasingly expanded to reach practices of "unfair trading"[258] far beyond the simple, old-fashioned passing-off consisting of an actual sale of goods accompanied by a misrepresentation as to their origin, calculated to mislead the purchaser and divert business from the plaintiff to the defendant. Today, any misrepresentation in the course of trade to prospective customers or consumers of his goods or services, prejudicial to the plaintiff's goodwill, constitutes an actionable wrong in the absence of any exceptional competing policy.[259] For example, it is no longer limited to the name or trademark of a product or business but encompasses other identifications, such as the "get-up"[260] or visual images in advertising campaigns,[261] including character merchandising.

The latest development has been to include even false claims by a competitor that his goods have qualities which they actually lack but the plaintiff's peculiarly have. Thus the goodwill attaching to a geographical description, like "champagne",[262] "sherry",[263] or "Scotch",[264] or to a qualitative description like "advocaat" liqueur,[265] entitle producers of the genuine article to protection against pretenders. This was an advance in two respects: in allowing members of a class to sue who claim an exclusive right to the use of the name, and in no longer requiring that the defendant's product be misrepresented as the plaintiff's. It was a misrepresentation to sell "Spanish champagne" not because it implied that it came from France but because the consumer public was led to believe that it was the genuine article.[266] Protection was thus offered both against direct loss of sale and

257. *Parkdale v. Puxu* (1982) 149 C.L.R. 191, 202. There being no need for injury, injunction is more readily available: *Taco* at 179; *Taylor* at 39. A common law claim can be joined to confer on the Federal Court "accrued jurisdiction" on "common substratum of transactions" (*Fencott v. Muller* (1983) 152 C.L.R. 570. See Donald & Heydon, 2 *Trade Practice Law* (1978) §11.3).

258. This includes not only situations where A passes off his own goods as B's but also where he passes off C's goods as B's, like a publican swapping brands of beer.

259. See *Spalding Bros v. Gamage* (1915) 84 L.J. Ch. 449; *Illustrated Newspaper v. Publicity Services* [1938] 1 Ch. 414.

260. See above.

261. *Cadbury-Schweppes v. Pub Squash* [1981] 1 W.L.R. 193 (P.C.).

262. See below, n. 266.

263. *Vine Products v. Mackenzie* [1969] R.P.C. 1.

264. *John Walker v. McGibbon* 1972 S.L.T. 128.

265. *Warnink v. Townend* [1979] A.C. 731 (H.L.) (consumers aware that "Old English Advocaat" was not a spirit drink like the Dutch original). Cf. *Rest.* §761; and *Lanham Act* 1946 §43(a), as interpretated in *L'Aiglon Apparel v. Lana Lobell* 214 F. 2d 649 (3 Cir. 1954); *Mutation Mink Breeders v. Nierenberg* 23 F.R.D. 155 (1959).

266. *Bollinger v. Costa Brava Wine Co.* [1960] Ch. 262 ("Spanish champagne"); *Comité du Vin v. Wineworth* [1991] 2 N.Z.L.R. 432 ("Australian champagne"); but *Institut v. Andres Wines* (1987) 40 D.L.R. (4th) 239 ("Canadian champagne" not deceptive).

against indirect loss from debasement or dilution[267] of the name to which the plaintiff's goodwill has attached.

This extension bodes well also for the recognition of "reverse confusion". Instead of the defendant representing that his goods are the plaintiff's, here he is representing in effect that the plaintiff's are those of the defendant. Such, for example, was the reality of a salesman displaying pictures of a competing product, pretending that they portrayed his own,[268] and a representation that test results of a competing product referred to his own,[269] although in neither case was the picture or test associated with the plaintiff. These practices, it was held, nonetheless resulted in diversion of customers who ordered the defendant's product under a false belief as to their commercial source.[270]

Actionable practices include not only selling but also leasing[271] and buying[272] merchandise under a deceptive name, knowingly supplying a conspirator with the means to pass off goods under a false trade description (like shipping whisky to South America for blending with local liquor and ultimate distribution as "Scotch"),[273] or applying a process for waving hair other than the plaintiff's branded process requested by customers.[274] Again, it is no longer necessary that the goods in question should be asserted to be of the plaintiff's manufacture; it is sufficient if there is a representation that the plaintiff has been associated with their production or distribution, as where merchandise is procured from the plaintiff's suppliers and sold with the plaintiff's mark[275] or a book is published with the name of a well known author falsely put on the title page.[276] Goodwill and reputation may also be put at risk by interfering with the plaintiff's control of his product, as by placing advertising inserts into copies of his newspaper.[277]

Nor is protection confined to "traders" in the narrow sense of businessmen engaged in the marketing of goods; it extends equally to persons who have acquired a commercial reputation in professional, artistic or literary activities.[278] This provides a link with the forthright extension

267. American decisions have interceded against "dilution" as such, as when Budweiser's beer slogan "Where there is life . . . there's Bud" was jeopardised by the promotion of insecticide under the slogan "Where there's life . . . there's bugs" (*Chemical Corp. v. Anheuser-Busch* 306 F. 2d 433 (5 Cir. 1962); Treece, 51 Tex. L. Rev. 637 (1973). Also below, n. 290.
268. *British Conservatories v. Conservatories Custom Built* [1989] R.P.C. 455 (C.A.).
269. *Plomien Fuel v. Nat. School of Salesmanship* [1943] R.P.C. 209.
270. Both would be "misleading or deceptive" practices in violation of the *T.P.A.*
271. *Caterpillar Tractor v. Caterpillar Loader* (1982) 44 A.L.R. 377.
272. *F.W. Woolworth & Co. v. Woolworths (Aust.)* (1930) 47 R.P.C. 337.
273. *John Walker v. Ost* [1970] 1 W.L.R. 917; *John Walker v. McGibbon* 1972 S.L.T. 128.
274. *Sales Affiliates v. Le Jean* [1947] 1 All E.R. 287.
275. *Vokes v. Evans* (1932) 49 R.P.C. 140.
276. *Lord Byron v. Johnston* (1816) 2 Mer. 29; 35 E.R. 851; *Samuelson v. Producers' Distributing Co.* [1932] 1 Ch. 201 (film); *Copyright Act* 1968 (Cth) s. 190; 1988 (U.K.) s. 77; *Moore v. News of the World* [1972] 1 Q.B. 441 (C.A.).
277. *Assoc. Newspapers v. Insert Media* [1991] 1 W.L.R. 571 (C.A.).
278. *Ramsay v. Nicol* [1939] V.L.R. 330; *Hines v. Winnick* [1947] Ch. 708. But it does not extend beyond appropriation of such *commercial* reputation. Thus it will not lie to restrain the imitation of the name of a private residence (*Day v. Brownrigg* (1878) 10 Ch. D. 294) or of a telegraphic address, causing inconvenience but no confusion to custom: *Street v. Union Bank of Spain* (1885) 30 Ch. D. 156.

of the remedy against false attribution of sponsorship, such as spurious claims of endorsement by a well known doctor of quack remedies[279] or the display of a sign at a garage or hotel carrying the recommendation of an automobile association.[280] Nor for that matter does modern authority confine protection only against competing goods or services.[281] To demand a "common field or activity" would be incompatible with the modern trends of diversification and franchising well-known names. That the businesses are unrelated is thus no longer a categorical defence, though it will remain relevant in determining whether, as a fact, the conduct amounted to a misrepresentation of a business connection.[282]

However, English courts have been less forthcoming than American in protecting the publicity value of celebrities. Thus a pop group failed to enjoin the sale of T-shirts bearing its name,[283] the Kojak film character failed against the marketing of Kojak lollies,[284] and a television personality against a breakfast cereal called "Uncle Mac's Puffed Wheat".[285] Even if the practice of licensing the sponsor's name or other personality attribute (character merchandising) were widely known, that would not be sufficient in the absence of an additional inference of quality control so as to suggest that the plaintiff guaranteed the quality of the defendant's product. Australian courts have been more sympathetic. In the "Sesame Street" case[286] the originators of the program succeeded in interdicting the unauthorised sale of shoddy toys of the famous "Muppett" characters on proof that by licensing they had established a business reputation in relation to toys and were therefore operating in the same field. In another case a record of ballroom dance music was enjoined at the behest of a team of exhibition dancers who were portrayed on the cover. Customers of the record would probably believe that the plaintiffs, because of their occupational link to dance music, recommended the record, even if there was not exactly a common field of activity between the parties.[287] In another case it was held sufficient that shoe distributors, in their advertising by poster and T.V., had merely invoked the image of the actor Paul Hogan in a well-known scene from Crocodile Dundee.[288]

279. *B.M.A. v. Marsh* (1931) 48 R.P.C. 565; *Henderson v. Radio Corp.* [1960] S.R. (N.S.W.) 576 at 583-584.
280. *R.A.A.S.A. v. Hancock* [1939] S.A.S.R. 60. Charities: *Dr Barnardo's Homes v. Barnardo Industries* (1949) 66 R.P.C. 103.
281. *Totalizator v. Turf News* [1967] V.R. 605. See e.g. *Ronson Ltd v. J. Ronson Ltd* [1957] V.R. 421; [1957] V.R. 731 (cigarette lighters and car polish); *Turner v. G.M.* (1929) 42 C.L.R. 352 (new and secondhand cars); *Lego Systems v. Lego* [1983] F.S.R. 155 (toy bricks and garden sprinklers); *Taylor Bros v. Taylors Group* [1988] 2 N.Z.L.R. 1 (dry cleaners and linen hire). On common territorial market see *Orkin v. Pestco* (1985) 19 D.L.R. (4th) 90 (U.S. and Ont.).
282. E.g. not in *Grenada Group v. Ford* [1973] R.P.C. 49 (broadcasting and car manufacture).
283. *Lyngstad v. Anabas Products* [1977] F.S.R. 62.
284. *Tavener Rutledge v. Trexapalm* [1977] R.P.C. 275 (though declining the "common field" requirement). See Phillips & Coleman, 101 L.Q.R. 242 (1985).
285. *McCulloch v. Lewis A. May* [1947] 2 All E.R. 845.
286. *Childrens T.V. v. Woolworths* [1981] 1 N.S.W.L.R. 273.
287. *Henderson v. Radio Corp.* [1960] S.R. (N.S.W.) 576; [1969] R.P.C. 218.
288. *Hogan v. Pacific Dunlop* (1988) 83 A.L.R. 403. See also *Shoshana v. 10th Cantanae* (1987) 79 A.L.R. 279 (T.V. personality under *T.P.A.*); Terry, 65 A.L.J. 587 (1991).

American courts have gone further and recognised a "right of publicity" as a property right as such,[289] that is an exclusive right to exploit the publicity value of one's name, likeness or other personality attributes.[290] Such a right is of course readily protectible by contract, but some Canadian courts have already joined the American trend of giving it independent protection by tort remedies.[291] Thus even in the absence of any suggestion of sponsorship or the like, the unconsented use of the plaintiff's name or image would be actionable, provided it is not merely incidental but designed specifically to promote the defendant's commercial interest.

In Australia, the common law has been reinforced by the prohibition of the *Trade Practices Act* of false representations in connection with the supply or promotion of goods or services, including representations that they "have a sponsorship, approval, performance, characteristics, accessories, uses or benefits that they do not have".[292]

Free competition

But not all harmful competition is unfair or unlawful.[293] Most important, the countervailing public interest in free competition often demands priority even at the cost of condoning practices which deserve censure as dishonest trading. As already noted,[294] "the market in which the action[s] for passing-off [and injurious falsehood] originated was no place for the mealy-mouthed; advertisements are not on affidavit; exaggerated claims by a trader about the quality of his wares are permitted as venial puffing."[295] Also permitted are claims to use one's own surname in business even at the cost of some confusion with the competitor,[296] and in the use open to all of generic and descriptive, as distinct from fanciful, terms[297] unless they have acquired a so-called secondary meaning by exclusive association with the plaintiff.[298] Thus everyone is now free to sell "shredded wheat buscuits" under that name and looking like the original, once it had become generic during the original patent term.[299] Similarly,

289. *Haelan Laboratories v. Topps Chewing Gum* 202 F. 2d 866 (2d Cir. 1953) (exclusive licence protected); see Gordon, *Right of Property in Name, Likeness Personality and History*, 55 Nw. U.L. Rev. 553 (1960). Advocated by Frazer, *Appropriation of Personality*, 99 L.Q.R. 280 (1983).
290. Such as one's voice: *Midler v. Ford Motor Co.* 849 F. 2d 460 (1988). Cf. *Sim v. Heinz Co.* [1959] 1 W.L.R. 313 (C.A.).
291. *Krouse v. Chrysler* (1973) 40 D.L.R. (3d) 15 (Ont. C.A.); *Athans v. Canadian Adventure* (1977) 80 D.L.R. (3d) 583; Howell, 2 Intellectual Prop. J. 149 (1986).
292. Section 53; *Fair Trading Act* 1985 (Vic.) s. 12.
293. *Moorgate Tobacco v. Phillip Morris* (1984) 156 C.L.R. 414 at 440ff., critical of the term "unfair competition" in so far as it suggests a wider principle than passing-off.
294. See above, p. 714.
295. *Warnink v. Townend* [1979] A.C. 731 at 742 per Lord Diplock.
296. *Jay's v. Jacobi* [1933] Ch. 411, but the same indulgence does not extend to first names or nicknames: *Biba Group v. Biba Boutique* [1980] R.P.C. 413.
297. E.g. *Office Cleaning Services v. Westminster Office Cleaning Assoc.* [1944] 2 All E.R. 269; *Cut Price Stores v. Nifty Thrifty Stores* [1967] Q.W.N. 13.
298. *Birmingham Vinegar Brewery v. Powell* [1897] A.C. 710 ("Yorkshire Relish"); *Reddaway v. Banham* [1896] A.C. 199 (camel hair belting no longer meant just any belting made from camel hair, but only the plaintiff's).
299. *Canadian Shredded Wheat Co. v. Kellogg Co.* (1938) 55 R.P.C. 125 (P.C.); *Kellogg Co. v. National Biscuit Co.* 305 U.S. 111 (1938). Trade names may also fall back into the public domain as the result of non-user, the faster the less distinctive: *Kark v. Odhams Press* [1962] 1 W.L.R. 380.

unless the "get-up" of a product has acquired secondary meaning or is protected by the patent, trademark or registered design laws, mere imitation or copying is permitted.[300] And so is merely taking advantage of a market developed by the plaintiff's advertising, since otherwise heavy investment might confer a monopoly on big firms.[301]

300. *Parkdale v. Puxu* (1982) 149 C.L.R. 191 (Brennan J.; following *Sears, Roebuck v. Stiffel* 376 U.S. 225 (1964). Gibbs C.J. and Mason J.: at least when properly labelled); *Oxford Pendaflex v. Korr* [1982] 1 S.C.R. 494. Except when secret information is obtained in breach of confidence: see above, p. 607, n. 55.

301. *Cadbury-Schweppes v. Pub Squash* [1981] 1 W.L.R. 193 at 205; *Consumers v. Seiko* [1984] 1 S.C.R. 583 (parallel importation).

INDEX